Maudsley and Burn's Land Law: Cases and Materials

Maudsley and Burn's
Land Law:
Cases and Materials

by E. H. Burn

B.C.L., M.A.
Honorary Bencher of Lincoln's Inn;
Student and Tutor in Jurisprudence of Christ Church, Oxford;
Sometime Lecturer in the Law of Land in the Inns of Court

Fifth Edition

London
Butterworths
1986

United Kingdom	Butterworth & Co (Publishers) Ltd, 88 Kingsway, LONDON WC2B 6AB and 61A North Castle Street, EDINBURGH EH2 3LJ
Australia	Butterworths Pty Ltd, SYDNEY, MELBOURNE, BRISBANE, ADELAIDE, PERTH, CANBERRA and HOBART
Canada	Butterworths. A division of Reed Inc, TORONTO and VANCOUVER
New Zealand	Butterworths of New Zealand Ltd, WELLINGTON and AUCKLAND
Singapore	Butterworth & Co (Asia) Pte Ltd, SINGAPORE
South Africa	Butterworth Publishers (Pty) Ltd, DURBAN and PRETORIA
USA	Butterworth Legal Publishers, ST PAUL, Minnesota, SEATTLE, Washington, BOSTON, Massachusetts, AUSTIN, Texas and D & S Publishers, CLEARWATER, Florida

© Butterworth & Co (Publishers) Ltd 1986
Reprinted 1989

British Library Cataloguing in Publication Data

Burn, E. H.
  Maudsley and Burn's land law: cases and materials. — 5th ed.
  1. Real property — England — Cases
  I. Title   II. Maudsley, R. H. Land Law
  344.2064'3'0264   KD828

  ISBN Hardcover 0 406 62308 2
       Softcover 0 406 62309 0

Printed and bound in Great Britain by
Mackays of Chatham PLC, Chatham, Kent

Preface

Ronald Maudsley and I wrote the first four editions of *Land Law* together. When he died in 1981, I lost a friend of long standing, and Anglo-American law one of its most devoted servants. Although our partnership has now come to an untimely end, its spirit continues. This new edition seeks to maintain the original purpose of our writing: "This book is intended to provide the most important readings in Land Law which cannot, in the nature of things, be included in text-books. It contains a selection of cases and statutes, extracts from books, articles and other materials, linked by passages of explanation — and asks some questions. It is essentially a supplement to, and not a substitute for, a text-book."

This edition incorporates the main changes which have taken place since 1980 when the last edition appeared. There has been widespread judicial activity throughout the land law, and extracts from some forty cases have been added. In particular, the House of Lords has given a literal interpretation both to the Land Charges Act 1925 and to the Land Registration Act 1925 (the two decisions are suitably juxtaposed in the Law Reports of the House of Lords for 1981); reverted to a rigid test for the distinction between a lease and a licence; and elucidated certainty of rent in the context of an option to renew a lease. The Privy Council has scrutinised the duty of a mortgagee who sells to a company in which he has an interest. The Court of Appeal, on the other hand, has developed the doctrine of constructive notice; differentiated between a right of pre-emption and an option to purchase; undermined the doctrine of overreaching of equitable interests under a trust for sale (the Appellate Committee of the House of Lords has now given leave to appeal); adopted conflicting approaches to the exercise of the court's jurisdiction under section 30 of the Law of Property Act 1925; examined the application of section 146 of the same Act to forfeiture for the breach of a positive covenant in a lease; extended the duty of a mortgagee when exercising his powers of sale; and thrice examined his right to enter into possession of the mortgaged premises. Important judgments at first instance include those on the constructive trust, limitation of actions and equitable easements — all in the context of registered land; the perpetually renewable lease; the criteria for the creation of an estoppel licence (reported three years after the judgment was given); and the limits on the automatic effect of section 78 (1) of the Law of Property Act 1925 in the area of restrictive covenants.

New legislation since the last edition has also been incorporated: for example, the Limitation Act 1980, the Housing Act 1980 (introducing the protected shorthold tenancy) and the Matrimonial Homes Act 1983. There are also brief encounters with the Companies, Insolvency and Housing Acts of 1985, and the Agricultural Holdings Act of 1986.

There has been a significant recent increase in the activity of the Law Commission. Of its twelve Reports on Land Law, seven appeared in 1985. Two of the more expansive — and expensive — were on Positive and Restrictive Covenants in 1984, and on Forfeiture of Tenancies in 1985. And of its six Working Papers, four were published in 1985, in particular the one on Trusts of Land.

All this new material and much else besides has necessitated some re-arrangement and re-writing. In order to compensate for the inevitable increase, the detailed treatment of planning law has been abandoned; it is expected that this will now form the basis of a separate book written by its originator, Keith Davies, Reader in Law in the University of Reading.

I am again most grateful to all those friends and critics who have given me their help and advice. I would particularly like to thank John Cartwright, my colleague at Christ Church, for compiling the index, reading the proofs and for making many valuable suggestions of form and substance.

Finally I wish to thank the authors and publishers for permission to reproduce material of which they own the copyright; and the staff of Butterworths for undertaking the compilation of the Tables of Cases, Statutes and Statutory Instruments, and for their ready help and expert advice at all times.

This edition purports to state the law as it was on 1 January 1986, but more recent developments have been incorporated where space permitted.

Christ Church   E. H. B.
Oxford
1 April 1986

Contents

List of Abbreviations

Statutes and Rules

AEA	Administration of Estates Act
AJA	Administration of Justice Act
CTTA	Capital Transfer Tax Act
FA	Finance Act
LCA	Land Charges Act
LLCA	Local Land Charges Act
LPA	Law of Property Act
LP(A)A	Law of Property (Amendment) Act
LRA	Land Registration Act
LRR	Land Registration Rules
MHA	Matrimonial Homes Act
P&AA	Perpetuities & Accumulations Act
SLA	Settled Land Act
TA	Trustee Act
TCPA	Town and Country Planning Act

Journals

Anglo-Am	Anglo-American Law Review
Aust LJ	Australian Law Journal
CLJ	Cambridge Law Journal
CLP	Current Legal Problems
CLY	Current Law Year Book
Conv	Conveyancer
Conv (NS)	Conveyancer (New Series)
Conv Prec	Precedents for the Conveyancer
Cornell LQ	Cornell Law Quarterly
EG	Estates Gazette
HLR	Harvard Law Review
JPL	Journal of Planning and Environment Law
LJ News	Law Journal Newspaper
LQR	Law Quarterly Review
LSG	Law Society's Gazette
LT	Law Times
Mich LR	Michigan Law Review
MLR	Modern Law Review
NILQ	Northern Ireland Legal Quarterly
NLJ	New Law Journal
OJLS	Oxford Journal of Legal Studies
SJ	Solicitor's Journal
U of WALR	University of Western Australia Law Review
Yale LJ	Yale Law Journal

Books

C & B	Cheshire and Burn, The Modern Law of Real Property (13th edn. 1982)
Dawson & Pearce	Licences Relating to the Occupation or Use of Land (1979)
Farrand	Contract and Conveyance (2nd edn. 1973; 4th edn. 1983)
Fisher and Lightwood	Law of Mortgage (9th edn. 1977)
Gale	Easements (14th edn. 1972)
H & M	Hanbury and Maudsley, Modern Equity (12th edn. 1985)
Holdsworth	A History of English Law
Jackson	Law of Easements and Profits (1978)

Maudsley	The Modern Law of Perpetuities (1979)
M & B	Maudsley and Burn, Trusts and Trustees: Cases and Materials (3rd edn. 1984)
M & W	Megarry and Wade, The Law of Real Property (5th edn. 1984)
MM	Megarry, Manual of the Law of Real Property (5th edn. 1982)
Morris & Leach	The Rule Against Perpetuities (2nd edn. 1962)
Preston & Newsom	Restrictive Covenants Affecting Freehold Land (7th edn. 1982)
Ruoff & West	Concise Land Registration Practice (3rd edn. 1982)
Ruoff & Roper	The Law and Practice of Registered Conveyancing (4th edn. 1979)
Snell	Principles of Equity (28th edn. 1982)
Waldock	The Law of Mortgages (2nd edn. 1950)
W & C	Wolstenholme and Cherry, Conveyancing Statutes (13th edn. 1972)

Table of Statutes

Page references printed in **bold** type indicate where the Act is set out in part or in full.

PAGE

PAGE

Table of Statutory Instruments

Page references printed in **bold** type indicate where a Statutory Instrument is set out in part or in full.

Table of Cases

Cases which are set out in this work are indicated by page numbers in bold type.

PAGE

E

I

Q

R

PAGE

Part One. Basic Concepts

1. Introductory Topics

I. Estates and Interests in Land

A. Introduction

i. FREEHOLD AND LEASEHOLD ESTATES

The theory of the common law is that all land is held of the King who is the supreme feudal lord. Subjects may hold directly of the King or of other

3

subjects superior to themselves. Those who hold directly of the King are tenants in chief. Intermediate holders between the King and the tenants in actual possession are mesne lords.

A holder of land is entitled to a number of legal rights in respect of his landholding, and these legal rights are "crystallised into one thing[1]". This is the tenant's "estate". To ascertain his rights, it is necessary to decide what estate he owns and to know what rights and duties the law attaches to that type of estate.

Freehold estates, i.e. the estates held by freehold tenure, are those which were in use in the feudal system. In medieval times that system was the basis of the social, military and economic structure of the state; and the holding of freehold land was itself the basis of social position, wealth and power. It was essential for the security of the state and of the social structure that the ownership of freehold estates should be protected; and it is not surprising that the land law was the first of the fields of private law to be undertaken by the King's Court[2].

The freehold estates are the fee simple, fee tail, life estate and estate pur autre vie. They are freehold because they were recognised by the feudal order, because persons holding such estates in possession were recognised as standing upon a rung in the feudal ladder, and because the remedies available in the King's Court were available to the owner of such an estate and gave a claimant specific recovery. Such estates are "real property" or "realty", and are contrasted with the term of years, a leasehold estate, whose owners were never on the feudal ladder; they could not protect themselves by the same actions as the freeholder; their estate as personal property, or "personalty", passed on intestacy with chattels. A convenient way of distinguishing between freeholds and leaseholds is to note that freeholds are always of indefinite duration, leaseholds for a fixed period or such as can be made certain. But this is just a label; it does not help to understand the basic gulf between the two, which was so obvious to the medieval lawyer.

Something will be said here of the freehold estates; leaseholds will be considered in a later chapter. But a further sub-division must be introduced here because of the treatment of estates by the 1925 legislation. This is the distinction between legal estates and equitable interests. Pursuant to the Legislature's insistence upon the legal estate being the basis of conveyancing with beneficial interests kept off the title, the 1925 legislation permits two estates only to exist as legal estates, one freehold and one leasehold, all other interests being capable of existing in equity only.

ii.   CONVEYANCING

A knowledge of the estates and interests recognised at law and in equity is necessary to an understanding of Conveyancing; that is, the practice of creating and transferring estates and interests in land. The owner of an estate may transfer it to another, as on the sale of a house, or create a series of smaller interests out of it, as on the creation of a settlement; or create other

---

[1] Hargreaves, *Introduction to Land Law* (4th edn, 1963), p. 46.
[2] Maitland, *Forms of Action at Common Law*, pp. 20 et seq.

rights which are recognised at law or in equity, but which are not estates in land, such as a licence or a restrictive covenant. Details of the practice of Conveyancing are beyond our present scope[3]; but it is material to say here that there are two quite separate and distinctive methods of conveyancing in operation in England and Wales at the present day; that relating to unregistered land and that relating to registered land. The former is the development of techniques which reach back to medieval times. The system in essence is one whereby the estate owner proves his title to land by showing from deeds and documents in his possession that he derives his title lawfully from some person or persons who have been in peaceful possession for a long period of time. In the nature of things, the title to his estate can never be proved absolutely, for there may have been an interference with the rights of the true owner many years back. However, with the assistance of the Limitation Acts[4], proof of title during the last fifteen years is, for practical purposes, sufficient; and a purchaser is now required to trace the title back to a good root of title at least fifteen years' old[5]. On completion of the purchase, the deeds are handed over to the purchaser, and he will make title in a similar manner when he decides to sell.

A much more satisfactory system of proof of title is that of registration of the title in a central registry. New countries and states commonly use such a system. The practical difficulties, however, of changing over from a system of unregistered conveyancing to one of registered conveyancing are great. The change involves the recording of all interests in land which need to be placed on the register and this is a huge undertaking. In England and Wales, a system of registration of title, introduced in 1862[6], was superseded by more comprehensive legislation in 1925[7]. It provides for registration of title following the first conveyance of land after the Act has been made applicable to the district in question; and subsequent conveyancing will be based on the title so registered. The system of registration is explained in Chapter 2.

The present decade is one of transition from unregistered to registered conveyancing, from the old to the modern. As yet, the registered system is not universally applicable, but compulsory registration of title will extend to areas comprising some 87% of the population of England and Wales by 1987[8]. It is still necessary to understand the unregistered system, and to distinguish between the doctrines applicable to the two. In the discussions which follow, the two systems will be compared wherever possible. There is no doubt where the emphasis of a present day student should be.

---

[3] On conveyancing reform, see the Second Report of the Conveyancing Committee: Conveyancing Simplifications 1985 (The Farrand Committee). The Lord Chancellor announced on 31 July 1985 that a Conveyancing standing committee was to be established by the Law Commission "to promote changes in practice and procedure necessary to create and maintain a cheap, simple and effective conveyancing system from the point of view of buyers and sellers of land." Its first objective would be to bring about within two years improvements which would be apparent to ordinary housebuyers and sellers. For a critique of the Second Report, see [1985] Conv 101 (J.E. Adams). See AJA 1985, Part II and s. 66; which introduce the new profession of licensed conveyancing.

[4] See p. 162, post.

[5] LPA 1969, s. 23, p 77, post.

[6] Land Registry Act 1862.

[7] LRA 1925, p. 94, post.

[8] Report of Chief Land Registrar for 1984–1985, para. 20.

B. Legal Estates

i. THE FEE SIMPLE ABSOLUTE IN POSSESSION[9]

Challis, *Law of Real Property* (3rd edn, 1911), p. 218

"A *fee simple* is the most extensive in *quantum*, and the most absolute in respect to the rights which it confers, of all estates known to the law. It confers, and since the beginning of legal history it always has conferred, the lawful right to exercise over, upon, and in respect to, the land, every act of ownership which can enter into the imagination, including the right to commit unlimited waste; and, for all practical purposes of ownership, it differs from the absolute dominion of a chattel, in nothing except the physical indestructibility of its subject."

The rights of a fee simple owner are, however, limited by the rights of his neighbour and by statute, in particular by the Town and Country Planning Acts[10] and the Rent Acts[11].

A fee simple may be absolute[12], determinable, subject to a condition[13] or base[14].

(a) *Definition*

LAW OF PROPERTY ACT 1925

1.   Legal estates and equitable interests. — (1) The only estates in land which are capable of subsisting or of being conveyed or created at law are —

    (*a*) An estate in fee simple absolute in possession;

    (*b*) A term of years absolute[15].

(2) The only interests or charges in or over land which are capable of subsisting or of being conveyed or created at law are —

    (*a*) An easement[16], right, or privilege in or over land for an interest equivalent to an estate in fee simple absolute in possession or a term of years absolute;

---

[9] C & B, pp. 147–161; M & W, pp. 49–53, 59–76, 123–129; MM, pp. 28–29, 33–35, 37–38, 39–44.

[10] P. 831, post.

[11] P. 377, post.

[12] A fee simple may also be (*a*) a "flying freehold", where "a man may have an inheritance in an upper chamber though the lower buildings and soil be in another": Co Litt 48b; Lincoln's Inn Act 1860 which regulates flying freeholds in New Square, Lincoln's Inn. See the claim to a "subterranean flying freehold" of a cellar in *Grigsby v Melville* [1974] 1 WLR 80 at 83, [1973] 3 All ER 455 at 458. (*b*) a "movable fee", where "the fee itself is a continuing estate, but it is an estate in land which from time to time changes its position": *Baxendale v Instow Parish Council* [1982] Ch 14 at 20, [1981] 2 All ER 620 at 625 per MEGARRY V-C (foreshore capable of being granted as it might be from time to time); *Welden v Bridgewater* (1595) Moore KB 302, Cro Eliz 421 (lot meadows, where two or more have a fee simple in a measured part of a meadow, but the precise part owned is determined by lots at specified times). See [1982] Conv 208 (R.E. Annand).

[13] P. 23, post.

[14] P. 15, post.

[15] See pp. 375 et seq., post.

[16] See pp. 561 et seq., post.

(*b*)   A rentcharge[17] in possession issuing out of or charged on land being either perpetual or for a term of years absolute;

(*c*)   A charge by way of legal mortgage[18];

(*d*)[19]   . . . and any other similar charge on land which is not created by an instrument[20];

(*e*)   Rights of entry exercisable over or in respect of a legal term of years absolute, or annexed, for any purpose, to a legal rentcharge.

(3) All other estates, interests, and charges in or over land take effect as equitable interests.

(4) The estates, interests, and charges which under this section are authorised to subsist or to be conveyed or created at law are (when subsisting or conveyed or created at law) in this Act referred to as "legal estates," and have the same incidents as legal estates subsisting at the commencement of this Act; and the owner of a legal estate is referred to as "an estate owner" and his legal estate is referred to as his estate.

(5) A legal estate may subsist concurrently with or subject to any other legal estate in the same land in like manner as it could have done before the commencement of this Act.

(6) A legal estate is not capable of subsisting or of being created in an undivided share in land[1] or of being held by an infant.

7.   Saving of certain legal estates and statutory powers. — (1) A fee simple which, by virtue of the Lands Clauses Acts, the School Sites Acts, or any similar statute[2], is liable to be divested[3], is for the purposes of this Act a fee simple absolute, and remains liable to be divested as if this Act had

---

[17] See LP (Entailed Interests) A 1932, s. 2. The Rentcharges Act 1977 is phasing out certain kinds of rentcharge: C & B, pp. 603–614; M & W, pp. 818–829; MM, pp. 390–395.

[18] See pp. 650 et seq., post.

[19] As amended by Finance Act 1963, s. 73, Sch. 14, Part VI, and Tithe Act 1936, s. 48, Sch. 9.

[20] E.g. tithe redemption annuity (which replaced tithe rentcharge in 1936. See M & W, pp. 830–834). This was itself extinguished as from 2 October 1977: FA 1977, s. 56.

[1] See p. 243 et seq., post.

[2] The main statutes are School Sites Act 1841, Literary and Scientific Institutions Act 1854, Consecration of Churchyards Act 1867 and Places of Worship Sites Act 1873. See also *Tithe Redemption Commission v Runcorn UDC* [1954] Ch 383, [1954] 1 All ER 653 (Local Government Act 1929).

[3] These Acts provide that land granted for certain public purposes shall revert to the grantor, his successors or some other person, if the purpose fails or is not carried out. In *Re Rowhook Mission Hall, Horsham* [1985] Ch 62, [1984] 3 All ER 179, NOURSE J held that the legal estate reverts automatically, as in *Re Ingleton Charity* [1956] Ch 585, [1956] 2 All ER 881, and is not held on trust, as in *Re Clayton's Deed Poll* [1980] Ch 99, [1979] 2 All ER 1133. See [1981] Conv 186 (C.J. Allen and S. Christie); (1984) 81 LSG 1851 (J.H.G. Sunnucks); (1984) 100 LQR 527 (D.E. Evans).

The Law Commission has recommended that existing rights of reverter under the School Sites Act 1841 and similar statutes should be registrable (possibly in the Land Registry); that failure to register within a three-year period should bar the revertee's claim; and that they should no longer be capable of taking effect where the grantor of land received consideration for the grant or where the land was given for use as a church or chapel: Law Commission Report on Rights of Reverter 1981 (Law Com No. 111, Cmnd 8410).

not been passed, [and a fee simple subject to a legal or equitable right of entry or re-entry is for the purposes of this Act a fee simple absolute][4].

(2) A fee simple vested in a corporation which is liable to determine by reason of the dissolution of the corporation is, for the purposes of this Act, a fee simple absolute.

205.   General definitions. — (1) (xix) "Possession" includes receipt of rents and profits or the right to receive the same, if any.

In *District Bank Ltd v Webb* [1958] 1 WLR 148, [1958] 1 All ER 126[5], the question was whether an estoppel was raised against vendors by reason of a recital that they were "seised in unencumbered fee simple in possession upon trust for sale," when the property was subject to a lease. DANCKWERTS J held that the representation was not sufficiently unambiguous to create an estoppel, and added at 150, at 127: "Secondly, the words 'in possession' are relied upon, but I do not think that 'in possession' means vacant possession. It seems to me that the meaning is 'fee simple in possession' as opposed to 'fee simple in reversion' and there again it seems to me impossible for the bank to rely upon such representation in the recital to cause the vendors to be bound by any estoppel."

(b) Creation[6]

LAW OF PROPERTY ACT 1925

60.   Abolition of technicalities in regard to conveyances and deeds. — (1) A conveyance of freehold land to any person without words of limitation, or any equivalent expression, shall pass to the grantee the fee simple or other the whole interest which the grantor had power to convey in such land, unless a contrary intention appears in the conveyance[7].

(2) A conveyance of freehold land to a corporation sole by his corporate designation without the word "successors" shall pass to the corporation the fee simple or other the whole interest which the grantor had power to convey in such land, unless a contrary intention appears in the conveyance.

(4) The foregoing provisions of this section apply only to conveyances and deeds executed after the commencement of this Act:

---

[4] The words in square brackets were added by LP (A) A 1926 Sch., and the intention of the Legislature appears to have been to include as legal estates certain holdings, common in the North of England, where a fee simple is purchased in return for a perpetual rentcharge upon the land. But the enactment is, in its terms, wider than this, and appears to include a grant to A in fee simple subject to a right of entry in the grantor on the happening of some event, such as, for example, A's marrying outside a certain religious persuasion. One would have expected a fee simple subject to such a condition to have been an equitable interest, and for such a grant to have created a settlement. Indeed SLA 1925, s. 1 (1) (ii) (*b*) provides that a grant of a fee simple . . . subject to an executory limitation over on the happening of some event shall create a settlement; it would be strange if the distinction were to depend upon the difference between an executory gift over and the right of the grantor to re-enter and terminate for breach of condition. It is tempting to suggest that the words of the amendment are wider than the Legislature intended; how they will be construed is not known. C & B, pp. 150–151; M & W, pp. 126–129; MM, pp. 86–87; [1985] Conv 311.
[5] See also *Re Morgan* (1883) 24 ChD 114 at 116.
[6] C & B, pp. 150–154; M & W, pp. 49–53; MM, pp. 33–35.
[7] A similar rule applies to devises: Wills Act 1837, s. 28.

Provided that in a deed executed after the thirty-first day of December, eighteen hundred and eighty-one[8], it is sufficient —

    (*a*) In the limitation of an estate in fee simple, to use the words "in fee simple," without the word "heirs".

205. General definitions. — (1) In this Act unless the context otherwise requires, the following expressions have the meanings hereby assigned to them respectively, that is to say:—

(ii) "Conveyance" includes a mortgage, charge, lease, assent, vesting declaration, vesting instrument, disclaimer, release and every other assurance of property or of an interest therein by any instrument, except a will. . . .

(c) *Alienability*[9]

RE BROWN
[1954] Ch 39, [1953] 2 All ER 1342 (ChD, HARMAN J)

The testator devised freehold properties in trust for his wife for life, and after her death, on his youngest son attaining 21, for all the sons then living in equal shares as tenants in common. Clause 6 of the will provided that if any son should allow his share to be vested in any person other than one of the brothers, that share should be held on discretionary trusts for the son and his wife and children. The question, on one son wishing to sell outside the family, was whether the restriction upon alienation was good.

Held. No.

HARMAN J: This is a point on which it appears that the authorities give no certain guide, and the various editors of Jarman on Wills give it up, as textbook writers, therein more fortunate than judges, are entitled to do with the bland statement that the law is uncertain.

The point is a very narrow one, and it is whether a restriction on alienation appended to an absolute devise of real estate is good or no. The instinct of any equity lawyer is, to start with, to say that all restraints on absolute interests which tend to negative the rights attached to those interests are abhorred by the law and disallowed. That is a general rule cited by Jarman (8th edn, vol. 2, p. 1477): "A power of alienation is necessarily and inseparably incidental to an estate in fee."

The view at the outset is that anything which seeks to deprive the feoffee (so to call him) of his rights is void, but there is no doubt that some degree of restriction may be put upon him . . .

As I have said, the instinct of any Chancery lawyer is to say that this is a restriction quite inconsistent with an absolute interest in real estate (or in proceeds of sale, for that matter) and that the restriction is not good. Mr Thompson[10], however, has been able to persuade me that there is a great deal to be said for the view that a restriction of this sort may be good, if it do

---

[8] The Conveyancing Act 1881 came into force on 1 January 1882.

[9] C & B, pp. 349–351; M & W, pp. 72–73; MM, p. 42; (1917) 33 LQR 11 (E. Jenks); (1917) 33 LQR 236, 342 (C. Sweet); (1954) 70 LQR 15 (R.E.M.). A life interest may be made determinable upon the happening of various events, including alienation. This is the basis of protective trusts: *Brandon v Robinson* (1811) 18 Ves 429; *Rochford v Hackman* (1852) 9 Hare 475; H & M, p. 188.

[10] Counsel for infants interested under the discretionary trusts.

not amount to a total restriction. He starts with Coke upon Littleton (11th edn., Part 1, book 3, section 360), where the translation is as follows: "Also if a feoffment be made upon this condition, that the feoffee shall not alien the land to any, this condition is void because when a man is enfeoffed of lands or tenements, he hath power to alien them to any person by the law: For if such a condition should be good, then the condition should oust him of all the power which the law gives him, which should be against reason; and therefore such a condition is void." That is to say, it is repugnant to the gift. The passage following (section 361) is in these terms: "But if the condition be such that the feoffee shall not alien to such a one, naming his name, or to any of his heirs, or of the issues of such a one, etc. or the like, which conditions do not take away all power of alienation from the feoffee, etc., then such condition is good." That merely says that you may point out a certain person (or, I suppose, persons) and prohibit alienation to him or them: quaere as to how many persons may you extend that prohibition? According to two cases to which I shall refer in a moment, you may extend it to all the world except a certain class of people; but that seems to me to be a very curious way to read the doctrine of Coke, which, after all, merely says that you may exclude A or B from the world of people to whom it is permissible to alienate.

The earliest case to which I was referred is a decision of the Court of King's Bench, where the judgment was given by Lord Ellenborough CJ, *Doe* d. *Gill v Pearson* (1805) 6 East 173. The gift in that case was of a piece of land to "my daughters . . . Ann and Hannah, their heirs and assigns for ever, as tenants in common, and not as joint tenants; *upon this special proviso and condition*, that in case my said daughters Ann and Hannah Collett, or either of them, shall have no lawful issue, that then and in such case they or she having no lawful issue as aforesaid shall then have no power to dispose of her share in the said estates so above given to them except to her sister or sisters, or to their children." The exception was confined to sisters and the children of sisters, which is a narrow enough class, although one does not know exactly how many there were in the class. There were five daughters. . . . the whole court, the Court of King's Bench, decided apparently that the condition not to alienate except to a class consisting of four sisters and their children was good.

That case was considered in *Attwater v Attwater* (1853) 18 Beav 330, where Sir John Romilly MR refused to follow the Court of King's Bench, and merely said that, notwithstanding *Doe* d. *Gill v Pearson*, he held the opposite. The limitation in *Attwater v Attwater* was: "I bequeath to *Gay Thomas Attwater*, jun., eldest son of my niece, the family estate at *Charlton, Wilts.*, to become his property on attaining the age of 25 years, with an injunction never to sell it out of the family; but, if sold at all, it must be to one of his brothers hereafter named." He had three brothers. Sir John Romilly declined to hold that condition good; in his judgment he said: "It is obvious, that if the introduction of one person's name, as the only person to whom the property may be sold, renders such a proviso valid, a restraint on alienation may be created, as complete and perfect as if no person whatever was named; inasmuch as the name of the person who alone is permitted to purchase, might be so selected, as to render it reasonably certain that he would not buy the property, and that the property could not be aliened at all. It appears to me also, that this is the true construction of the words used by the testator; it is, in truth, an injunction never to sell the hereditaments devised at all. . . . It is not, in my opinion, desirable to impose fresh fetters on the enjoyment of property, and it appears to me, that this proviso is distinctly at variance with the rules laid down by Lord Coke, and which have always been considered and treated as good law. I am of opinion, therefore, that this clause is merely inoperative."

That is a decision on a limitation exactly in pari materia to the one before me. I should feel no difficulty about following it, rather than *Doe* d. *Gill v Pearson* (1805) 6 East 173, but for the fact that in *Re Macleay* (1875) LR 20 Eq 186, the great authority of Sir George Jessel appears to be on the other side. In that case the devise was "to my brother J. on the condition that he never sells out of the family". The limitation was not, therefore, to named persons, it was "out of the family". Sir George Jessel said at 187: . . . "It has been suggested, however, that it is void as being repugnant to the quality of the estate, that is to say, that you cannot restrict the right of an owner in fee of alienating in any way in which he may think fit. If that were the law, the condition would be plainly void. But, with the exception of one authority, a case decided by my immediate predecessor, I am not aware that the law has ever been laid down in that way." Sir George Jessel then discussed the point in Coke on Littleton, *Muschamp v Bluet* (1617) J Bridg 132, *Attwater v Attwater* (1853) 18 Beav 330 and *Jacobs v Brett* (1875) LR 20 Eq 1. He decided at 189: "So that, according to the old books, Sheppard's Touchstone being to the same effect, the test is whether the condition takes away the whole power of alienation substantially: it is a question of substance, and not of mere form." . . . He came to the conclusion that the words were not sufficiently restrictive to be in substance an absolute bar. His reason was that "the family" was a larger term than "sister or sisters, or their children" and that the only restriction was to sell and not to dispose, which might include leases or mortgages. He came to the conclusion that the limitation in that case was a good one.

That decision, therefore, inclines to the view for which Mr. Thompson has argued. In *Re Rosher* (1884) 26 ChD 801, however, Pearson J felt it necessary to make an elaborate attack upon Sir George Jessel's decision in *Re Macleay* (1875) LR 20 Eq 186. Although the decision in *Re Rosher* was, as a matter of construction that the restriction was in effect an absolute one, Pearson J delivered a long judgment explaining why he could not agree that *Re Macleay* was well decided. The restriction in *Re Rosher* was that if the testator's "son, his heirs or devisees" wished to sell over a certain period, property worth £15,000 had to be offered to the testator's wife during her lifetime at a price of £3,000; and the judge held that that meant in effect that it could not be sold at all, because nobody would give away property worth £15,000 for £3,000. Although *Re Rosher*, qua its decision, is not of much help, it shows that in the view of Pearson J, *Re Macleay* was wrongly decided.

I need take the law no further. I have to choose one way or the other . . .

It is most pertinent to remember, as Mr. Armstrong[11] has also pointed out to me, that the class to whom it is permissible to alienate begins with three for any one share and that the prohibition goes on not only during the joint lives of all the brothers, but during the lives of the survivors and survivor of them, and therefore a period will be reached when there are two, and then only one, and at last no person to whom any alienation is allowed. If none it

---

[11] Counsel for the sons.

is plainly bad. If it is only one, that in substance, as in *Muschamp v Bluet*, is equivalent to none. If one be bad, are two good? It seems to me that a class of this sort, which is bound to be a diminishing class, brings it about, in substance, that this is a general prohibition on alienation. It would be an extraordinary thing if no-one could postulate of any one of these brothers that he would or would not during his lifetime be able to dispose of his own share; and that it must depend on whether he outlives two of his brothers. In my view, this is the kind of restriction which the law views, or should view, with dislike. It is exactly the same kind of condition as in *Attwater v Attwater*, and I think that I should be at liberty to follow that decision were it necessary for me to do so, but I do not think that I need follow any case in this region, because the cases are inconsistent with one another, and I am entitled to take my own view. It is pertinent that a number of persons, as in this clause, is in essence different from a class consisting, for instance, as Sir George Jessel's did in *Re Macleay*, of members of the family, which he said was a large indeterminate class of people and might, of course, increase as time went on; whereas, if alienation be restricted to three or four or five persons such as brothers, the class is bound to diminish as death takes its toll of the members. I hold therefore, that the restriction in clause 6 of the will is an attempt to fetter the natural qualities of the interest given, and is accordingly void and can be disregarded[12].

ii.   THE TERM OF YEARS ABSOLUTE[13]

LAW OF PROPERTY ACT 1925

1.   Legal estates and equitable interests. — (1) p. 6, ante.

C.   Equitable Interests

LAW OF PROPERTY ACT 1925

1.   Legal estates and equitable interests. — (3) All other estates, interests, and charges in or over land take effect as equitable interests.

(7) Every power of appointment over, or power to convey or charge land or any interest therein, whether created by a statute or other instrument or implied by law, and whether created before or after the commencement of this Act (not being a power vested in a legal mortgagee or an estate owner in right of his estate and exercisable by him or by another person in his name and on his behalf), operates only in equity.

(8) Estates, interests, and charges in or over land which are not legal estates are in this Act referred to as "equitable interests," and powers which by this Act are to operate in equity only are in this Act referred to as "equitable powers."

4.   Creation and disposition of equitable interests. — (1) Interests in land validly created or arising after the commencement of this Act, which are

---

[12] Cf. *Caldy Manor Estate Ltd v Farrell* [1974] 1 WLR 1303, [1974] 3 All ER 753. A fee simple determinable (whether on alienation or for any other reason) is settled land under SLA 1925, s. 1 (1) (ii) (c) and the land thus becomes alienable by the tenant for life (p. 275, post). Any term which would operate to restrict the tenant for life's freedom of alienation is void: SLA 1925, s. 106, p. 289, post.

[13] Chap. 8, p. 375, post.

not capable of subsisting as legal estates, shall take effect as equitable interests, and, save as otherwise expressly provided by statute, interests in land which under the Statute of Uses or otherwise could before the commencement of this Act have been created as legal interests, shall be capable of being created as equitable interests:

Provided that, after the commencement of this Act (and save as hereinafter expressly enacted), an equitable interest in land shall only be capable of being validly created in any case in which an equivalent equitable interest in property real or personal could have been validly created before such commencement[14].

i.   ENTAILED INTERESTS[15]

(a) *Creation*[16]

LAW OF PROPERTY ACT 1925

60.   Abolition of technicalities in regard to conveyances and deeds. — (4) The foregoing provisions of this section[17] apply only to conveyances and deeds executed after the commencement of this Act:

Provided that in a deed executed after the thirty-first day of December, eighteen hundred and eighty-one[18], it is sufficient —

(b) In the limitation of an estate tail, to use the words "in tail" without the words "heirs of the body"[19]; and

(c) In the limitation of an estate in tail male or in tail female, to use the words "in tail male" or "in tail female," as the case requires, without the words "heirs male of the body," or "heirs female of the body."

130.   Creation of entailed interests in real and personal property. — (1) An interest in tail or in tail male or in tail female or in tail special (in this Act referred to as "an entailed interest") may be created by way of trust in any property, real or personal[20], but only by the like expressions as those by which before the commencement of this Act a similar estate tail could have been created by deed (not being an executory instrument) in freehold land, and with the like results, including the right to bar the entail either absolutely or so as to create an interest equivalent to a base fee, and accordingly all statutory provisions relating to estates tail in real property shall apply to entailed interests in personal property.

Personal estate so entailed (not being chattels settled as heirlooms) may be invested, applied, and otherwise dealt with as if the same were capital money

---

[14] See the discussion in *National Provincial Bank Ltd v Ainsworth* [1965] AC 1175, [1965] 2 All ER 472, on the question of interests capable of existing as proprietary rights; p. 121, post.

[15] C & B, pp. 237–256; M & W, pp. 54–58, 76–92; MM, pp. 29, 36–39, 44–51.

[16] C & B, pp. 237–250; M & W, pp. 54–58; MM, pp. 36–39.

[17] See p. 8, ante.

[18] The Conveyancing Act 1881 came into force on 1 January 1882.

[19] Note that the words "heirs of the body" remain sufficient. The technical common law required that an estate tail be created by the use of the word "heirs" plus words of procreation: "heirs of the body" was the most common formula. The Conveyancing Act 1881 provided the alternative.

[20] Before 1926 an estate tail could not be created in personalty; and not, therefore, in an interest under a trust for sale.

or securities representing capital money arising under the Settled Land Act, 1925, from land settled on the like trusts.

(2) Expressions contained in an instrument coming into operation after the commencement of this Act, which, in a will, or executory instrument coming into operation before such commencement, would have created an entailed interest in freehold land[1], but would not have been effectual for that purpose in a deed not being an executory instrument, shall (save as provided by the next succeeding section) operate in equity, in regard to property real or personal, to create absolute, fee simple or other interests corresponding to those which, if the property affected had been personal estate, would have been created therein by similar expressions before the commencement of this Act[2].

(3) Where personal estate (including the proceeds of sale of land directed to be sold and chattels directed to be held as heirlooms) is, after the commencement of this Act, directed to be enjoyed or held with, or upon trusts corresponding to trusts affecting, land in which, either before or after the commencement of this Act an entailed interest has been created, and is subsisting, such direction shall be deemed sufficient to create a corresponding entailed interest in such personal estate.

(b) Rule in Shelley's Case[3]

LAW OF PROPERTY ACT 1925

131. Abolition of the rule in Shelley's case. — Where by any instrument coming into operation after the commencement of this Act an interest in any property is expressed to be given to the heir or heirs or issue or any particular heir or any class of the heirs or issue of any person in words which, but for this section would, under the rule of law known as the Rule in Shelley's case, have operated to give to that person an interest in fee simple or an entailed interest, such words shall operate in equity as words of purchase and not of limitation, and shall be construed and have effect accordingly, and in the case of an interest in any property expressed to be given to an heir or heirs or any particular heir or class of heirs, the same person or persons shall take as would in the case of freehold land have answered that description under the general law in force before the commencement of this Act.

---

[1] Before 1926 an entail could be created in a will or executory instrument without the use of the formal words required for creation of a fee tail by deed. In a will or executory instrument informal words were sufficient if the intention was clear. C & B, pp. 245–246; M & W, p. 57; MM, p. 37.

[2] For the effect of this provision, see (1938) 6 CLJ 67 (S. J. Bailey); (1947) 9 CLJ 46 (R. E. Megarry); 185 (S. J. Bailey); 190 (J. H. C. Morris); *Re Crossley's Settlement Trusts* [1955] Ch 627, [1955] 2 All ER 801; C & B, pp. 246–248; M & W, pp. 57–58; MM, pp. 37–38.

[3] C & B, pp. 248–250; M & W, pp. 50, 56, 1161–1163; MM, p. 38; Challis, *Law of Real Property* (3rd edn, 1911), pp. 152–167. The rule still applies to an instrument coming into operation before 1926: *Re Routledge* [1942] Ch 457, [1942] 2 All ER 418 (testator died in 1874); *Re Williams* [1952] Ch 828, [1952] 2 All ER 502 (testator died in 1921).

(c) Barring an Entail[4]

1. INTER VIVOS

FINES AND RECOVERIES ACT 1833

1. Meaning of certain words and expressions. — "estate" shall extend to an estate in equity as well as at law . . . ; "base fee" shall mean exclusively that estate in fee simple into which an estate tail is converted where the issue in tail are barred, but persons claiming estates by way of remainder or otherwise are not barred; . . .

15. Power, after 31st Dec. 1833, to dispose of entailed lands in fee simple or for a less estate, saving the rights of certain persons. — . . . After the thirty-first day of December one thousand eight hundred and thirty-three every actual tenant in tail, whether in possession, remainder, contingency or otherwise, shall have full power to dispose of for an estate in fee simple absolute or for any less estate the lands entailed, as against all persons claiming the lands entailed by force of any estate tail which shall be vested in or might be claimed by . . . the person making the disposition, at the time of his making the same, and also as against all persons . . . whose estates are to take effect after the determination or in defeasance of any estate tail[5]; saving always the rights of all persons in respect of estates prior to the estate tail in respect of which such disposition shall be made, and the rights of all other persons, except those against whom such disposition is by this Act authorized to be made[6].

19. Power, after 31st Dec. 1833, to enlarge base fees; saving the rights of certain persons. — . . . After the thirty-first day of December one thousand eight hundred and thirty-three, in every case in which an estate tail in any lands shall have been barred and converted into a base fee, either before or on or after that day, the person who, if such estate tail had not been barred, would have been actual tenant in tail of the same lands, shall have full power to dispose of such lands as against all persons, . . . whose estates are to take effect after the determination or in defeasance of the base fee into which the estate tail shall have been converted, so as to enlarge the base fee into a fee simple absolute; saving always the rights of all persons in respect of estates prior to the estate tail which shall have been converted into a base fee, and the rights of all other persons, except those against whom such disposition is by this Act authorized to be made[6].

---

[4] C & B, pp. 251–256; M & W, pp. 76–85, 88–89, 91–92; MM, pp. 44–47, 48–51.
[5] *Re St Albans' Will Trust* [1963] Ch 365, [1962] 2 All ER 402, where a disentailing assurance was held good under this section when executed by the heir presumptive (contingent upon the Duke dying without issue) with the consent of the protector of the settlement, on the ground that he was a "tenant in tail in contingency". But it was held in *Re Midleton's Will Trusts* [1969] 1 Ch 600, [1967] 2 All ER 834 that such a person did not have a contingent interest, but a mere expectancy.
[6] If the tenant in tail is not in possession, the interests of the remaindermen are only affected if the entail is barred with the consent of the protector of the settlement: ss. 22, 34, *infra*.

22.   The owner of the first existing estate under a settlement, prior to an estate tail under the same settlement, to be the protector of the settlement. — . . . If, at the time when there shall be a tenant in tail of lands under a settlement, there shall be subsisting in the same lands or any of them, under the same settlement, any estate for years determinable on the dropping of a life or lives, or any greater estate (not being an estate for years), prior to the estate tail, then the person who shall be the owner of the prior estate, or the first of such prior estates if more than one then subsisting under the same settlement, or who would have been so if no absolute disposition thereof had been made, (the first of such prior estates, if more than one, being for all the purposes of this Act deemed the prior estate), shall be the protector of the settlement so far as regards the lands in which such prior estate shall be subsisting, and shall for all the purposes of this Act be deemed the owner of such prior estate[7].

34.   Where there is a protector, his consent requisite to enable an actual tenant in tail to create a larger estate than a base fee. — Provided always, . . . that if at the time when any person, actual tenant in tail of lands under a settlement, but not entitled to the remainder or reversion in fee immediately expectant on the determination of his estate tail, shall be desirous of making under this Act a disposition of the lands entailed, there shall be a protector of such settlement, then and in every such case the consent of such protector shall be requisite to enable such actual tenant in tail to dispose of the lands entailed to the full extent to which he is herein-before authorized to dispose of the same; but such actual tenant in tail may, without such consent, make a disposition under this Act of the lands entailed, which shall be good against all persons who, by force of any estate tail which shall be vested in or might be claimed by, or which but for some previous act or default would have been vested in or might have been claimed by, the person making the disposition at the time of his making the same, shall claim the lands entailed.

35.   Where a base fee, and a protector, his consent requisite to the exercising of a power of disposition. — Provided always, . . . that where an estate tail shall have been converted into a base fee, in such case, so long as there shall be a protector of the settlement by which the estate tail was created, the consent of such protector shall be requisite to enable the person who would have been tenant of the estate tail if the same had not been barred to exercise, as to the lands in respect of which there shall be such protector, the power of disposition herein-before contained.

---

[7] Section 32 allowed a settlor to appoint not more than three persons to act as protector of the settlement in lieu of the person described in s. 22. This power of appointing a special protector has been abolished for settlements made after 1925: LPA 1925, 7th Sch., repealing s. 32 Fines and Recoveries Act 1833.

    If there is no protector under s. 22, the Court may be protector (s. 33); or the tenant in tail in remainder may disentail without consent: *Re Darnley's Will Trusts* [1970] 1 WLR 405, [1970] 1 All ER 319.

2. BY WILL

LAW OF PROPERTY ACT 1925

176. Power for tenant in tail in possession to dispose of property by specific devise or bequest. — (1) A tenant in tail of full age[8] shall have power to dispose by will, by means of a devise or bequest referring specifically[9] either to the property or to the instrument under which it was acquired or to entailed property generally —

  (*a*) of all property of which he is tenant in tail in possession at his death; and

  (*b*) of money (including the proceeds of property directed to be sold) subject to be invested in the purchase of property, of which if it had been so invested he would have been tenant in tail in possession at his death;

in like manner as if, after barring the entail, he had been tenant in fee-simple or absolute owner thereof for an equitable interest at his death, but, subject to and in default of any such disposition by will, such property shall devolve in the same manner as if this section had not been passed.

(2) This section applies to entailed interests authorised to be created by this Act as well as to estates tail created before the commencement of this Act, but does not extend to a tenant in tail who is by statute restrained from barring or defeating his estate tail, whether the land or property in respect whereof he is so restrained was purchased with money provided by Parliament in consideration of public services or not, or to a tenant in tail after possibility of issue extinct, and does not render any interest which is not disposed of by the will of the tenant in tail liable for his debts or other liabilities.

(3) In this section "tenant in tail" includes an owner of a base fee in possession who has power to enlarge the base fee into a fee-simple without the concurrence of any other person.

(4) This section only applies to wills executed after the commencement of this Act, or confirmed or republished by codicil executed after such commencement.

(d) Descent

LAW OF PROPERTY ACT 1925

130. Creation of entailed interests in real and personal property. — (4) In default of and subject to the execution of a disentailing assurance or the exercise of the testamentary power conferred by this Act, an entailed interest (to the extent of the property affected) shall devolve as an equitable interest, from time to time, upon the persons who would have been successively entitled thereto as the heirs of the body (either generally or of a particular class) of the tenant in tail or other person, or as tenant by the curtesy, if the entailed interest had, before the commencement of this Act, been limited in respect of freehold land governed by the general law in force immediately before such commencement, and such law had remained unaffected.

---

[8] See Family Law Reform Act 1969, s. 1, p. 288, n. 20, post.

[9] See *Acheson v Russell* [1951] Ch 67, [1950] 2 All ER 572, where the section was held to apply to a will which said: "All other my estate and interest in the family property at" K.H. It was clear from the context that entailed interests were intended to be included: (1950) 66 **LQR** 449 (R. E. Megarry).

QUESTION
Ought entailed interests to be abolished? Law Commission Working Paper
No. 94 (1985) para. 6.8; M & W, p. 1151.

ii.   LIFE INTERESTS[10]

(a) Creation

A life interest may be created by the use of any words showing an intention to
create a life interest[11]. As explained above[12], the rule now is that a conveyance
executed after 1925 passes to the grantee the whole interest which the grantor
had power to convey, unless a contrary intention appears in the conveyance.
For conveyances executed before 1926, the rule was that, in a conveyance
inter vivos[13], a life estate only was conveyed unless the correct technical
words for the conveyance of a greater estate were used[14].

The significance of the grant of a life interest is much increased since the
coming into operation of the Settled Land Act 1882, under which a tenant for
life[15] enjoys powers which extend far beyond his beneficial life interest. The
crucial question in a grant of land at the present day therefore is not whether
a claimant may enjoy the land for his life, but whether he has the powers of a
tenant for life under the Settled Land Act 1925[16].

(b) Waste[17]

A limited owner may not use land to the prejudice of those entitled in
reversion or remainder. The remedy is by action for damages or an
injunction. There are four forms of waste.

1.   PERMISSIVE

In *Woodhouse v Walker* (1880) 5 QBD 404, a devise to a tenant for life provided
that she should keep the premises in repair. She failed to do so, and after her
death the remainderman brought an action against her executor under a
statute of William IV[18] which gives an action against the executor of a
deceased person in respect of wrongs committed by the testator to another in
relation to his property. In upholding the action, LUSH J said at 406: "This
action is brought to recover out of her personal estate the expenses he has so
incurred. It is remarkable that no direct authority is to be found for a case
which must, we should suppose, have frequently occurred, and that we have
to go back to first principles in order to find a solution of the question raised.

---

[10] C & B, pp. 93, 257–265; M & W, pp. 40, 92–102; MM, pp. 51–56.
[11] See also LPA 1925, s. 149 (6), p. 20, n. 1, post, and p. 8, ante.
[12] See p. 8, ante; LPA 1925, s. 60 (1).
[13] Wills Act 1837, ss. 28, 34, reversed this rule with regard to wills.
[14] Litt 1; Co Litt 20a; Conveyancing Act 1881, s. 51; LPA 1925, s. 60 (4) and pp. 8, 13, ante.
[15] Now defined by SLA 1925, ss. 19, 20; p. 286, post.
[16] See pp. 289 et seq., post; and for the problems which arise where the court seeks to protect a
tenant for life: *Bannister v Bannister* [1948] 2 All ER 133 p. 503, post; *Binions v Evans* [1972] Ch
359, [1972] 2 All ER 70, p. 499, post; *Dodsworth v Dodsworth* (1973) 228 EG 1115, p. 548, post;
Ivory v Palmer [1975] ICR 340; *Griffiths v Williams* (1977) 248 EG 947, p. 550, post.
[17] C & B, pp. 260–265; M & W, pp. 95–102; MM, pp. 52–56; (1950) 13 Conv (NS) 278 (M. E.
Bathurst).
[18] Civil Procedure Act 1833.

Before the statutes of Marlbridge[19] (52 Hen 3) and of Gloucester (6 Edw 1, c. 5), an action for waste lay against a tenant in dower and tenant by the curtesy, but none against a tenant for life or years. The reason was, as stated by Coke in 2 Inst 300, 'for that the law created their estates and interests, therefore the law gave against them a remedy: but tenant for life or years came in by demise and lease of the owner of the land, &c., and therefore he might in his demise have provided against the doing of waste by his lessee, and if he did not, it was his negligence and default.'

Here it is plainly implied that, where the grantor in his grant provides against the doing of waste, the grantee will be liable for waste in like manner as a tenant in dower or by curtesy was liable, and this is in perfect accordance with legal principle as expressed by the maxims, 'Qui sentit commodum, sentire debet et onus et transit terra cum onere': Co Litt 231a and see per Holroyd J in *Burnett v Lynch* (1826) 5 B & C 589 at 607. The first of these maxims has a very wide application in our law. See Broom's Maxims.

The statute of Marlbridge, c. 23, extended the common law liability by ordaining that 'fermors during their term shall not make waste, sale nor exile of house, woods or men, nor of anything belonging to the tenements that they have to ferm without special licence had by writing of covenant making mention that they may do it, which if they do and thereof be convict they shall yield full damage and shall be punished by amerciament grievously.'

The term 'fermors' here, says Coke, 2 Inst 145, comprehended all who held by lease for life or lives, or for years by deed or without deed, and the words 'do or make waste' in legal understanding in this place (as well as in the statute of Gloucester) includes as well permissive waste which is 'waste by reason of omission or not doing, as for want of reparation, as waste by reason of commission, as to cut down timber trees or prostrate houses and the like: for he that suffereth a house to decay which he ought to repair doth the waste.'

The 'special licence' mentioned in the statute of Marlbridge is commonly expressed by the well-known phrase 'without impeachment of waste.'

The statute of Gloucester gives, as a more stringent remedy, a writ of waste under which the tenant was liable to forfeiture of the thing wasted and treble damages.

The right of action against a tenant for life belongs to the owner in fee of the immediate reversion.

In course of time an action on the case founded on the statute of Westminster 2, came to be substituted for the writ of waste, as being a more simple and practical remedy, and the writ of waste having fallen into disuse was ultimately abolished by 3 & 4 Wm 4, c. 27, s. 36. But the rights and liabilities of the parties remained as before, the remedy only being changed: *Bacon v Smith* (1841) 1 QB 345. It is not necessary in this case to enter into the question whether an action on the case for permissive waste can be maintained against a tenant for life or years, upon whom no express duty to repair is imposed by the instrument which creates the estate. The modern authorities, or rather the dicta upon this point, appear to be strangely in

---

[19] "I prefer Marlborough to Marlberge, to say nothing of Marlbridge which is an idiotism" (F. W. Maitland in a letter to H. A. L. Fisher 7 July 1893, quoted in *Letters of Frederick William Maitland*, ed. C. H. S. Fifoot, p. 122).

conflict with the ancient reading of the statutes[20]. See notes to *Greene v Cole* (1672) 2 Wms Saund 252.

We think it must be held, upon the principle before mentioned, that in this case the tenant for life was liable at common law, and that the plaintiff as immediate reversioner had a right of action, and probably might have obtained an injunction against her for the permitted waste, if he had made such an application in her lifetime. The right of action which at common law would have died with the person is continued by 3 & 4 Wm 4, c. 42, s. 2, against the executor."

2. VOLUNTARY

In *Dashwood v Magniac* [1891] 3 Ch 306, a testator gave to his widow an equitable life tenancy[1] in the West Wycombe estate, which was situated partly in Buckinghamshire and partly in Oxfordshire, the devise requiring her to keep the estate in repair and entitling her to fell timber (not being ornamental timber) necessary for such repairs.

The estate contained beech trees which were timber in Buckinghamshire, though not in Oxfordshire. The widow cut and sold a large number of these trees to furniture manufacturers in High Wycombe and the proceeds of the sale were treated as her income.

On the widow's death, the remainderman brought this action for (inter alia) voluntary waste. The defendants relied on a local usage which would permit a limited owner to cut beech trees (even though they were "timber") and to treat the proceeds as income; and on the fact that the testator had so treated the beech trees during his lifetime.

The Court of Appeal (LINDLEY and BOWEN LJJ, KAY LJ dissenting) affirmed CHITTY J in holding that, by reason of the local usage, the widow had not committed waste.

LINDLEY LJ said at 351: "Laying aside all custom, whether ancient or modern, this action would fail, for the tenant for life would have done nothing wrong; she cut beech in the ordinary course of good forestry, and, apart from custom, that was not waste.

As regards the beech woods in *Oxfordshire*, where beech trees are not timber, this is admitted to be true. But as regards the beech woods in *Buckinghamshire*, where beech is timber, the case is said to be different. The testator made no distinction between his estates in the one county and those in the other; he gave the rents and profits of both alike to Lady *Dashwood* for life, with power to cut timber for repairs; but yet it is contended that, although she was entitled to cut and sell beech trees in those parts of the estates which were in *Oxfordshire*, she was not entitled to do the same with beech trees on those parts of the estates which were in *Buckinghamshire*. Such a conclusion would, I think, startle the testator, and would be to defeat, and not carry out, his intentions as expressed in his will.

---

[20] KAY J held in *Re Cartwright* (1889) 41 ChD 532 that, in the absence of express provisions, a tenant for life was not liable for permissive waste. *Warren v Keen* [1954] 1 QB 15, [1953] 2 All ER 1118 contains a dictum of DENNING LJ that a weekly tenant is not liable for permissive waste.

[1] The estate was given to her for 100 years if she should so long live. After 1 January 1926, such leases, if granted at a rent or a fine, became leases for 90 years. If no rent or fine is payable, an equitable life interest is given: LPA 1925, s. 149 (6), p. 383, post.

It is contended by the Appellants that, beech being timber by custom in *Buckinghamshire*, cutting it, even in the ordinary course of good forestry, is necessarily waste and actionable.

. . . if it is said that there cannot be a custom to commit waste, the answer is that there may be a usage which renders that not waste as between persons claiming under a particular instrument framed with reference to the usage which would be waste as between other persons . . . .

The ordinary law of waste is, therefore, I think, not applicable as between the persons claiming under the will with which we have to deal. In other words the cutting of beech woods according to the usage was not waste in the contemplation of this testator; and, it not being waste, the Plaintiffs cannot claim the proceeds of their sale. . . ."

KAY LJ (dissenting) said at 371: "The custom or usage relied on in the present case is one which would entirely alter the ordinary common law of waste as applicable to this estate, and would enable the tenant for years, who is made impeachable of waste, to commit waste, notwithstanding the infirmity of her estate in that respect. It seems to me that, to produce that effect, it must be at least proved that from time immemorial such a limited owner, though impeachable of waste, has been accustomed to exercise the right so claimed.

In this case there is not the slightest evidence that any limited owner who was impeachable of waste ever attempted to exercise any such right, and the usage for the owners of the fee simple, or for limited owners who were not impeachable of waste, to manage the woods in the way which is complained of, cannot, as it seems to me, possibly justify a limited owner, who is impeachable of waste, in doing the same[2]."

3.   AMELIORATING

In *Doherty v Allman* (1878) 3 App Cas 709, a tenant for a long term of years had covenanted in the lease to "uphold, support, maintain and keep the demised premises . . . in good order, repair and condition". The premises which had been used as a corn store, and then for military purposes, fell into disrepair. The lessee decided to convert the store premises into dwelling houses, which would greatly increase their value. The question was whether he could be restrained on the grounds that he would be in breach of contract or would be committing waste.

The House of Lords (Lord CAIRNS LC, Lords O'HAGAN, BLACKBURN and GORDON) refused an injunction on either ground[3]. Lord O'HAGAN said at 724:

"Now we have, I think, established for the purposes of this decision the principles in this case by which we ought to abide. In the case of *Mollineux v Powell* (1730) 3 P Wms 268, n., which contains perhaps the clearest dictum we have upon the matter, two conditions as to the exercise of jurisdiction in

---

[2] Larch is not timber. A tenant for life does not therefore commit waste by felling a plantation of larch when ripe for felling; he is entitled to the proceeds of sale and is under no obligation to replace it at his own expense: *Re Harker's Will Trusts* [1938] Ch 323, [1938] 1 All ER 145.

[3] There is, however, technically an act of waste for which an action for damages would lie at law. But, no damage being suffered, no damages would be recoverable. See *Mancetter Developments Ltd v Garmanson Ltd* (1986) Financial Times, 22 January (tenant who, in removing trade fixtures, failed to make good holes left behind in landlord's brickwork, held liable in damages for voluntary waste); p. 93, n. 11.

cases of waste have been very clearly pointed out, and one at least of those conditions is expressly recognised afterwards in the Irish case of *Coppinger v Gubbins* (1846) 3 Jo & Lat 411. Those conditions are that the waste with which a Court of Equity, or your Lordships acting as a Court of Equity, ought to interfere, should be not ameliorating waste, nor trivial waste. It must be waste of an injurious character — it must be waste of not only an injurious character, but of a substantially injurious character, and if either the waste be really ameliorating waste — that is a proceeding which results in benefit and not in injury — the Court of Equity, and your Lordships acting as a Court of Equity, ought not to interfere to prevent it. I think that is perfectly well established. On the other hand, if the waste be so small as to be indifferent to the one party or the other — if it be, as has been said by a great authority in our law, such a thing as twelvepence worth of waste, a Court of Equity, and your Lordships acting as a Court of Equity, ought not to interfere on account of the triviality of the matter. Now, in my view of the case, those principles decide the question so far as this portion of it is concerned; for it appears to me that we have here established to the full satisfaction of your Lordships, by a series of authorities to which I shall not refer, that the waste, to be of any sort of effect with a view to an injunction, must be a waste resulting in substantial damage."

4. EQUITABLE

LAW OF PROPERTY ACT 1925

135. Equitable waste. — An equitable interest for life without impeachment of waste does not confer upon the tenant for life any right to commit waste of the description known as equitable waste, unless an intention to confer such right expressly appears by the instrument creating such equitable interest.

VANE *v* LORD BARNARD
(1716) 2 Vern 738 (Earl COWPER LC)

The Defendant on the Marriage of the Plaintiff his eldest Son with the Daughter of *Morgan Randyll*, and 10,000*l* Portion settled (*inter alia*) *Raby Castle* on himself for Life, without Impeachment of Waste Remainder to his Son for Life, and to his first and other Sons in Tail Male.

The Defendant the Lord *Barnard* having taken some Displeasure against his Son, got *two Hundred* Workmen together, and of a sudden, in a few Days, stript the Castle of the Lead, Iron, Glass, Doors, and Boards, &c. to the value of 3,000*l*.

The Court upon filing the Bill, granted an Injunction to stay Committing of Waste, in pulling down the Castle; and now, upon the Hearing of the Cause, decreed, not only the Injunction to continue, but that the Castle should be repaired, and put into the same Condition it was in, in *August* 1714, and for that Purpose a Commission was to issue to ascertain what ought to be repaired, and a Master to see it done at the Expence and Charge of the Defendant the Lord *Barnard*; and decreed the Plaintiff his Costs.

In *Turner v Wright* (1860) 2 De GF & J 234, Lord CAMPBELL LC held that an owner in fee simple subject to an executory limitation over was liable for equitable waste. He said at 243: "Equitable waste is that which a prudent man would not do in the management of his own property. This Court may interfere where a man unconscientiously exercises a legal right to the prejudice of another — and an act may in some sense be regarded as unconscientious if it be contrary to the dictates of prudence and reason, although the actor, from his peculiar frame of mind, does the act without any malicious motive. The prevention of acts amounting to equitable waste may well be considered as in furtherance of the intention of the testator, who, no doubt, wished that the property should come to the devisee over in the condition in which he, the testator, left it at his death; the first taker having had the reasonable enjoyment of it, and having managed it as a man of ordinary prudence would manage such property were it absolutely his own."

iii.　DETERMINABLE INTERESTS AND INTERESTS SUBJECT TO A CONDITION

There is a basic difference between determinable interests and interests subject to a condition. The former is a grant of something less than the interest specified; the latter is a grant of the interest subject to a liability to be cut down. To give land to trustees so long as it is used for Church purposes is a grant less than a fee simple. To give land to trustees in fee simple subject to a condition that the fee simple shall terminate if the land is not used for Church purposes is a fee simple subject to a condition. The difference is that between an eleven inch ruler and a foot ruler subject to the last inch being cut off. Whether or not a grant is one or the other is a matter of construction, and is thus reduced to a matter of words. There are many difficulties and fine distinctions, but these are unavoidable; the interests are similar, but different, and the line between the two must be drawn somewhere[4].

In *Re Bowen* [1893] 2 Ch 491, STIRLING J said at 495:
"The question which I have to decide, therefore, appears to me to reduce itself to one of the construction of the testator's will — *i.e.*, whether the testator has given the property to charity, in perpetuity, subject to an executory gift in favour of the residuary legatee, or whether he has given it for a limited period, leaving the undisposed of interest to fall into residue."

In *Re Sharp's Settlement Trusts* [1973] Ch 331 at 340, [1972] 3 All ER 151 at 156, PENNYCUICK V-C referred to: "the extremely artificial distinction between a 'determinable fee' and a 'fee simple on condition.' For explanation of these expressions see *Megarry and Wade, The Law of Real Property*, 3rd edn (1966) p. 75 et seq. and in particular the statement at p. 77:
'The question is whether the words limit the utmost time of continuance of the estate, or whether they mark an event which, if it takes place in the course

[4] For the differences between a determinable fee and a fee subject to a condition, see C & B, pp. 341–349; M & W, pp. 64–75; MM, pp. 39–43.

of that time, will defeat an estate already granted; in the first case the words take effect as a limitation, in the second as a condition. A limitation marks the bounds or compass of the estate, a condition defeats the estate before it attains its boundary.'

The distinction has been described in an Irish case as 'little short of disgraceful to our jurisprudence': see the quotation in *Megarry and Wade* at p. 78. I am bound to say that according to modern ideas this criticism appeals to me. However, the distinction is well established and must be accepted so far as it is comprehensible."

II.   Registration and Notice

A.   The Doctrine of the Bona Fide Purchaser of a Legal Estate for Value Without Notice[5]

The recognition of the use, and later of the trust[6], has given to English law a unique form of duality of ownership. The feoffees to uses (later the trustees) own a legal estate which, like other forms of legal ownership, is valid against all the world. They obtain, however, no personal benefit from their legal ownership, for they must hold the land and all the income from it for the benefit of the beneficiaries.

The interest of the beneficiaries has its origin in the willingness of the Chancellor to give relief in a situation in which the owner of the legal estate had undertaken to hold his legal estate to the use of another. The conscience of the feoffee to uses was affected and the Chancellor compelled him to observe his obligation. So long as the original parties to the arrangement remained, the position is comparatively simple; but complications arise where the legal or equitable ownership changes. A change of legal ownership raises the question whether the use is enforceable against a person other than the original feoffee; a change of equitable ownership raises the question of the form of equitable ownership which the Chancellor will recognise. In general, equity followed the law and recognised in equity estates corresponding to those which were recognised at law. But that is another story; here, we are concerned with the question of enforcement of equitable interests against persons other than the original feoffee.

The use was based upon conscience. If a feoffee to uses transferred to a purchaser with notice, the purchaser was bound as being a party to the fraud; if he had no notice, the use was "transferred" to him. A donee was bound, notice or no notice; for, without consideration being given, the original use was not changed. A use was however only binding on persons claiming through the original feoffee; and a disseisor therefore took free[7]. With the rise of the trust, however, this technicality disappeared; and an interest under a trust is now valid against all the world with the exception of

---

[5] C & B, pp. 60–66; M & W, pp. 142–153; MM, pp. 64–69; H & M, pp. 33–41; Snell, pp. 48–58; Maitland, pp. 106–116.
[6] Holdsworth, vol. 4, pp. 407–480 and Simpson, *Introduction to the History of the Land Law* (1961), pp. 163–194.
[7] Simpson, pp. 169–170.

a bona fide purchaser[8] of the legal estate for value[9] without notice actual, constructive or imputed[10].

It may be helpful to add three comments upon the application of this doctrine in modern law. First, in respect of rights and interests which are registrable as land charges under the Land Charges Act 1972[11], registration constitutes notice. Thus, a purchaser takes subject to registered land charges whether he knows about them or not; and, conversely, he takes free from unregistered (but registrable) land charges even if he knows about them[12].

Secondly, where there are successive beneficial interests in land, a settlement exists; the tenant for life has power to sell the fee simple, and the equitable interests are "overreached", that is, transferred from the land to the purchase money. Thus, the purchaser takes the land free of the equitable interests, although he knows that some exist; and, after the sale, the equitable interests exist in a fund of money whose value is equivalent to the land. A similar result is reached where land is held upon trust for sale. In other situations the doctrine may still apply. The pattern of the 1925 legislation was that all interests in land, other than the fee simple absolute in possession and the term of years absolute[13] should be either registrable or overreachable[14]. Situations have arisen to destroy the tidiness of this pattern, and in these cases the old doctrine will apply[15]. An understanding of the doctrine is essential to an appreciation of the relationship between law and equity.

---

[8] As to the meaning of "purchaser", see C & B, pp. 60, 151, n. 20; M & W, p. 143; MM, p. 64.

[9] M & W, p. 143. "It means any consideration in money, money's worth . . . or marriage. 'Money's worth' extends to all forms of non-monetary consideration in the sense used in the law of contract, but it also includes the satisfaction of an existing debt. 'Marriage', however, extends only to a future marriage: an ante-nuptial agreement . . . is deemed to have been made for value as regards both the spouses and the issue of the marriage; but a promise made in respect of a past marriage . . . is not."

[10] In the case of those interests and charges which are registrable under the LCA 1972, registration constitutes notice: LCA 1972, ss. 2, 4, pp. 30–49, post. For the meaning of imputed notice, see LPA 1925, s. 199 (1) (ii) and p. 45, n. 11, post.

The doctrine of constructive notice applies differently with personalty. A transferee cannot disregard equitable interests of which he is aware or which present themselves to his notice: *Nelson v Larholt* [1948] 1 KB 339, [1947] 2 All ER 751: but, as there are no title deeds to chattels, there is no duty to examine the title: *Joseph v Lyons* (1884) 15 QBD 280 (pledgee under no obligation to search register of bills of sale, and not bound by a bill of sale assigning after-acquired property); H & M, p. 37.

Similarly with negotiable instruments; a holder may be "in due course" without having taken steps to examine the title of the transferor: *London Joint Stock Bank v Simmons* [1892] AC 201.

[11] See pp. 30–49, post. LCA 1972 consolidates LCA 1925 (apart from local land charges) and other enactments relating to the registration of land charges. It does not make any substantive alterations.

[12] Pp. 41–49, post.

[13] LPA 1925, s. 1, p. 6, ante.

[14] See RUSSELL LJ in *Shiloh Spinners Ltd v Harding* [1972] Ch 326 at 340–341, [1971] 2 All ER 307 at 313.

[15] I.e. (1) where an interest is not registrable, e.g. restrictive covenant entered into before 1926; LCA 1972, s. 2 (5), Class D (ii); *Shiloh Spinners Ltd v Harding* [1973] AC 691, [1973] 1 All ER 90 (equitable right of re-entry on breach of covenant), p. 34, post; *E. R. Ives Investment Ltd v High* [1967] 2 QB 379, [1967] 1 All ER 504 (estoppel licence), p. 542, post; *Poster v Slough Estates Ltd* [1969] 1 Ch 495, [1968] 3 All ER 257 (right of entry to remove fixtures at end of lease).

(2) where an interest is not overreachable, e.g. *Caunce v Caunce* [1969] 1 WLR 286, [1969] 1 All ER 722; (1974) 38 Conv (NS) 226 (capital money paid to only one trustee), p. 255, post.

Thirdly, the doctrine of the purchaser for value of the legal estate without notice is relevant only to *un*registered land. The concept of the duality of ownership, legal and equitable, developed in that context. Where a totally new system of registration of *title* to and of certain *interests* in land is introduced, wholly different concepts apply. It will be seen from Chapter 2 that such a system was made available in 1925, and is spreading throughout the country. The essence of a system of registration of title is that the Register controls and that any person dealing with the land will be safe in relying on the Register. The basic division is thus between estates and interests which appear on the Register and those which do not, rather than between legal estates and equitable interests[16]. But it will be seen that some modern cases do seem to allow this old distinction to penetrate the registered land system, and cause the greatest confusion in its administration[17].

i.   THE DOCTRINE

PILCHER *v* RAWLINS
(1872) 7 Ch App 259 (Lord HATHERLEY LC, JAMES and
MELLISH LJJ)

In 1851 the trustees of Jeremiah Pilcher's settlement advanced the funds to Rawlins on the security of land including the 'Whitchurch' property, which was conveyed by Rawlins to the trustees in a deed which noticed the trusts.

In 1856 W.H. Pilcher, the surviving trustee of the settlement, reconveyed the Whitchurch property to Rawlins, who repaid only part of the loan. Rawlins, with W.H. Pilcher's connivance, mortgaged that property to Stockwell and Lamb, showing only the title deeds prior to the 1851 mortgage and thus appearing as unincumbered owner in fee simple.

Stockwell and Lamb thus received the legal estate, not under the title deeds which showed that Rawlins had a good title prior to 1851, but through the 1851 mortgage and later reconveyance also. The complete deeds thus disclosed the trusts. There was no way in which Stockwell and Lamb could have discovered the missing deeds, or learned of their contents. The question was whether the fact that the title deeds disclosed the trusts constituted constructive notice.

Held. Stockwell and Lamb took free from the trusts as bona fide purchasers of the legal estate for value without notice.

JAMES LJ: I propose simply to apply myself to the case of a purchaser for valuable consideration, without notice, obtaining, upon the occasion of his purchase, and by means of his purchase deed, some legal estate, some legal right, some legal advantage; and, according to my view of the established law

---

[16] *Williams and Glyn's Bank Ltd v Boland* [1981] AC 487 at 503, [1980] 2 All ER 408 at 412, HL, where Lord WILBERFORCE said: "The registered system is designed to free the purchaser from the hazards of notice — real or constructive . . . The only kind of notice recognised is by entry on the register."; *Parkash v Irani Finance Ltd* [1970] Ch 101 at 109, [1969] 1 All ER 930 at 933, where PLOWMAN J found a plaintiff's reliance on the doctrine "a little surprising, since one of the essential features of registration of title is to substitute a system of registration of rights for the doctrine of notice." See also CROSS J in *National Provincial Bank Ltd v Hastings Car Mart Ltd* [1964] Ch 9 at 16, [1963] 2 All ER 204 at 208; *Miles v Bull (No. 2)* [1969] 3 All ER 1585.

[17] *Barclays Bank Ltd v Taylor* [1974] Ch 137, [1973] 1 All ER 752, p. 745, post; *Peffer v Rigg* [1977] 1 WLR 285, [1978] 3 All ER 745, p. 145, post; *Lyus v Prowsa Developments Ltd* [1982] 1 WLR 1044, [1982] 2 All ER 953, p. 146, post. See also *Hodgson v Marks* [1971] Ch 892, [1971] 2 All ER 684; *Williams and Glyn's Bank Ltd v Boland*, supra, p. 121, post.

of this Court, such a purchaser's plea of a purchase for valuable consideration without notice is an absolute, unqualified, unanswerable defence, and an unanswerable plea to the jurisdiction of this Court. Such a purchaser, when he has once put in that plea, may be interrogated and tested to any extent as to the valuable consideration which he has given in order to shew the *bona fides* or *mala fides* of his purchase, and also the presence or the absence of notice; but when once he has gone through that ordeal, and has satisfied the terms of the plea of purchase for valuable consideration without notice, then, according to my judgment, this Court has no jurisdiction whatever to do anything more than to let him depart in possession of that legal estate, that legal right, that legal advantage which he has obtained, whatever it may be. In such a case a purchaser is entitled to hold that which, without breach of duty, he has had conveyed to him.

In the case of *Carter v Carter* (1857) 3 K & J 617, which was decided by the present Lord Chancellor, and which was followed by the Master of the Rolls in this case, and with which I am bound to say I am unable to agree, an exception from that rule was, under the circumstances, supposed to exist.

It is very clearly expressed in a few lines of the judgment in that case: "But here the purchaser taking the conveyance under one will, supposed by all parties to be really the last will of the testator, finds himself driven to rely upon another and a second will containing on the face of it all the trusts which the testator has created;" — and that circumstance is supposed to create the exception. To my mind there are to that supposition two short and conclusive answers — the one a matter of principle, and the other a matter of fact. My view of the principle is, that when once you have arrived at the conclusion that the purchaser is a purchaser for valuable consideration without notice, the Court has no right to ask him, and has no right to put him to contest the question, how he is going to defend himself, or what he is going to rely on. He may say, honestly and justly, "I am not going to tell you. I have got the deeds; I defend them, and you will never be able to make me produce them, and you will never be able to produce secondary evidence of them. I am not obliged to produce them at all; probably before you get half way through your action of ejectment you will find a *jus tertii* which you will not dispose of; the estate is in the hands of a legal tenant to whom I have let it, and no one can determine that tenancy without notice, and no one can give that notice but myself; I will not give that notice, and no Court has any power to compel me to give it. I have a right to rely, as every person defending his position has, on the weakness of the title of the person who is seeking to displace me." That seems to be exactly the position of such a purchaser as this. . . .

I am therefore of opinion that whatever may be the accident by which a purchaser has obtained a good legal title, and in respect of which he has paid his money and is in possession of the property, he is entitled to the benefit of that accident, just as a purchaser would be entitled to avail himself of the possession so acquired, without any reference to the rights of the persons who may be otherwise interested. . . .

The decision in the case of *Carter v Carter* (1857) 3 K & J 617, which has been so much referred to, is a decision which I have considered for some years, and I have more than once thought it right to express my views of that case. I differ in some respects in my views from those of the Lord Chancellor with regard to that case, but I say that the right of a person without notice is absolute and unqualified, when once he has made it out.

In *Wilkes v Spooner* [1911] 2 KB 473, Spooner, the lessee of two premises, No. 137 and No. 170, in High St., East Ham, assigned the lease of No. 170 to the plaintiff and covenanted, in effect, not to compete with the plaintiff's business of general butcher. Spooner then surrendered the lease of No. 137 to the landlord with a view to terminating the restrictive covenant. The landlord knew nothing of the covenant; he accepted the surrender and granted a new lease to Spooner's son, who did. The son opened a business in competition with the plaintiff, who sued to restrain this breach of the covenant. The Court of Appeal (VAUGHAN WILLIAMS, FLETCHER MOULTON and FARWELL LJJ, reversing SCRUTTON J) held that the restrictive covenant was not binding. The landlord was a bona fide purchaser for value without notice; and the covenant, once destroyed, did not revive on the passing of the land to the son. VAUGHAN WILLIAMS LJ said at 483: "I think that this appeal must be allowed. This case has been very well argued, but really, when certain conclusions of fact are arrived at, there is very little left to argue. It cannot seriously be disputed that the proposition which I quoted from Ashburner's Principles of Equity, p. 75, is good law. It is as follows: 'A purchaser for valuable consideration without notice can give a good title to a purchaser from him with notice. The only exception is that a trustee who has sold property in breach of trust, or a person who has acquired property by fraud, cannot protect himself by purchasing it from a bona fide purchaser for value without notice.' The learned author cites as authorities for that proposition the cases *Sweet v Southcote* (1786) 2 Bro CC 66, and *Re Stapleford Colliery Co, Barrow's Case* (1880) 14 ChD 432."

---

ii.   CONSTRUCTIVE NOTICE

In *Midland Bank Ltd v Farmpride Hatcheries Ltd* (1980) 260 EG 493, the bank lent money in 1971 to the company to enable it to expand its chicken hatchery business. The loan was secured by a mortgage on a "well-preserved 16th century mansion" at Mundford, in Norfolk, together with two cottages and hatcheries and other outbuildings. Under a service agreement with the company in 1968, Mr Willey had been given a licence for himself and his family to live rent free on the premises for 20 years. Mr Willey and his wife were the sole shareholders and the only directors of the company. The licence was never disclosed to nor discovered by the bank when it was negotiating the mortgage with Mr Willey, who was acting as the company's agent. The bank's negotiator, Mr Timbers, was aware that the family was living in the house.

The company defaulted on the mortgage repayment, and the bank brought an action for possession. Mr Willey claimed that his licence was binding on the bank because it had taken the mortgage with constructive notice[18]. The Court of Appeal held that the bank was entitled to possession.

---

[18] The issues of the binding effect of a licence on a third party (p. 493, post); and of the lifting of the veil of corporate personality were not raised. See (1982) 132 NLJ 68 (H. W. Wilkinson); [1982] Conv 67 (R. E. Annand); (1982) 79 LSG 464 (H. Lowless and J. Alder). On constructive notice generally, see *Northern Bank Ltd v Henry* [1981] IR 1, p. 255, n. 14, post.

SHAW LJ said at 497: "In my judgment Mr Willey set up a smoke-screen designed to hide even the possible existence of some interest in himself which could derogate from the interest of the company ostensibly conferred by the mortgage. To change the metaphor, he deliberately put Mr Timbers off the scent and the bank accepted the mortgage as a consequence. They would not have done so but for Mr Willey's subtle but positive indication that he had communicated all that had to be told which could be relevant to the bank's consideration of the company's application.

This being so, I am of the opinion that Mr Willey is estopped from setting up any facts which would go to show that he held an interest which overrides or stands in priority to their interest as mortgagees from the company[19]".

And OLIVER LJ said at 498: "Now of course, an agent who negotiates a sale or mortgage on his principal's behalf does not thereby make any representation that his principal has an indefeasible title to the property offered for sale or as security. As to that the purchaser or mortgagee must satisfy himself by making the usual enquiries before he completes. But in negotiating on his principal's behalf he does, in my judgment, at least represent that he has his principal's authority to offer the property free from any undisclosed adverse interest of his own. I would therefore be prepared to hold that the purchaser or mortgagee dealing with such an agent can reasonably assume that if the agent with whom he is dealing has himself an interest adverse to the title which he offers on his principal's behalf, he will disclose it. It was in my judgment reasonable for Mr Timbers not to make enquiry about an adverse interest of the negotiating agent which that agent's own reticence entitled him to assume did not exist and he did not, therefore, have constructive notice of it."

B. Registration of Land Charges

i.   UNREGISTERED LAND[20]

(a) Registration Constitutes Actual Notice

LAW OF PROPERTY ACT 1925

198.   Registration under the Land Charges Act, 1925, to be notice. — (1) The registration of any instrument or matter in any register kept under the Land Charges Act 1972 or any local land charges register[1] shall be deemed to constitute actual notice of such instrument or matter, and of the fact of such registration, to all persons and for all purposes connected with the land affected, as from the date of registration or other prescribed date and so long as the registration continues in force.

(2) This section operates without prejudice to the provisions of this Act respecting the making of further advances by a mortgagee[2], and applies only to instruments and matters required or authorised to be registered in any such register[3].

---

[19] Cf. in registered land, the proviso to LRA 1925, s. 70 (1) (*g*), p. 119, post.
[20] C & B, pp. 96–99, 105–107, 707–719; M & W, pp. 169–193; MM, pp. 90–111; Barnsley, *Conveyancing Law and Practice* (2nd edn, 1982), pp. 189–196, 378–408; Report of the Committee on Land Charges 1956 (Cmd 9825); [1956] CLJ 216 (H. W. R. Wade); Law Commission Report on Land Charges Affecting Unregistered Land 1969 (Law Com. No. 18, HC 125).
[1] As amended by LLCA 1975, s. 17 (2), Sch. 1.
[2] See p. 739, post.
[3] As amended by LLCA 1975, s. 17 (2), Sch. 1.

LAW OF PROPERTY ACT 1969

24.   Contracts for purchase of land affected by land charge, etc. —
(1) Where under a contract for the sale or other disposition of any estate or
interest in land the title to which is not registered under the Land
Registration Act 1925 . . . any question arises whether the purchaser had
knowledge, at the time of entering into the contract, of a registered land
charge, that question shall be determined by reference to his actual
knowledge and without regard to the provisions of section 198 of the Law of
Property Act 1925 . . .

(b) What Interests are Registrable

LAND CHARGES ACT 1972[4]

1.   The registers and the index. — (1) The registrar shall continue
to keep at the registry[5] in the prescribed manner the following registers,
namely —

    (*a*) a register of land charges;
    (*b*) a register of pending actions;
    (*c*) a register of writs and orders affecting land;
    (*d*) a register of deeds of arrangement affecting land;
    (*e*) a register of annuities[6],

and shall also continue to keep there an index whereby all entries made in
any of those registers can readily be traced.

(6) Subject to the provisions of this Act, registration may be vacated
pursuant to an order of the court[7].

---

[4] See also Land Charges Rules 1974 (S.I. 1974 No. 1286).

[5] In Plymouth, where there are some 13 million names on the computerised index, related to
some 7 million land owners: Report on H.M. Land Registry, 1983–84, para. 73. In 1975 the
Land Registry received the John Player award given by the British Computer Society. See
generally Ruoff, *Searching without Tears* (1974); H.M. Land Registry, *Computerised Land Charges
Department* (1974); (1974) 118 S J 692; 48 ALJ 593 (T. B. F. Ruoff). In 1984–85, there were 324,
186 new registrations (including priority notices) rectifications and renewals of land charges,
and 5,210,895 searches of the Register: Report on H.M. Land Registry 1984–85, para. 46.

[6] Sch. 1. No entries have been possible in this register since 1925.

[7] This is wider than the corresponding LCA 1925, s. 10 (8): *Calgary and Edmonton Land Co Ltd v
Dobinson* [1974] Ch 102 at 109, [1974] 1 All ER 484 at 490, per MEGARRY J. See also *Heywood v
BDC Properties Ltd* [1963] 1 WLR 975, [1963] 2 All ER 1063 CA; *Heywood v BDC Properties Ltd
(No 2)* [1964] 1 WLR 971, [1964] 2 All ER 702; *Georgiades v Edward Wolfe & Co Ltd* [1965] Ch
487, [1964] 3 All ER 433; *Taylor v Taylor* [1968] 1 WLR 378, [1968] 1 All ER 843; *Rawlplug Co
Ltd v Kamvale Properties Ltd* [1968] 20 P & CR 32; *Boobyer v Thornville Properties Ltd* (1968) 19 P &
CR 768; *Re Longlands Farm* [1968] 3 All ER 552; *Thomas v Rose* [1968] 1 WLR 1797, [1968] 3 All
ER 765 (all discussed in (1968) 118 New LJ 1167 (S. M. Cretney) pointing out that a charge
can be registered without any proof of its validity, the function of the Registry being purely
ministerial; but the registration of such a charge might in practice make the land unsaleable);
Hooker v Wyle [1974] 1 WLR 235, [1973] 3 All ER 707; *Jones v Morgan* (1973) 231 E G 1167; *Mens
v Wilson* (1973) 231 E G 843; *Haslemere Estates Ltd v Baker* [1982] 1 WLR 1109, [1982] 3 All ER
525; [1983] Conv 69 (J.E.M.).
    Cf. the position in registered land: LRA 1925, ss. 56 (3), 82, p. 149, post; *Rawlplug Co Ltd v
Kamvale Properties Ltd*, supra; *Calgary and Edmonton Land Co Ltd v Discount Bank (Overseas) Ltd*
[1971] 1 WLR 81, [1971] 1 All ER 551; *Clearbrook Property Holdings Ltd v Verrier* [1974] 1 WLR
243, [1973] 3 All ER 614; *Tiverton Estates Ltd v Wearwell Ltd* [1975] Ch 146 at 161, 171, [1974] 1
All ER 209 at 219, 228; *Lester v Burgess* (1973) 26 P & CR 536 (a useful analysis of the
jurisdiction by GOULDING J); *Price Bros (Somerford) Ltd v J Kelly Homes (Stoke-on-Trent) Ltd* [1975]
1 WLR 1512, [1975] 3 All ER 369; *Calgary and Edmonton Land Co Ltd v Dobinson*, supra; *Norman v
Hardy* [1974] 1 WLR 1048, [1974] 1 All ER 1170; (1974) 38 Conv (NS) 208 (F. R.

(7) In this section "index" includes any device or combination of devices serving the purpose of an index.

2. The register of land charges. — (1) If a charge on or obligation affecting land falls into one of the classes described in this section, it may be registered in the register of land charges as a land charge of that class[8].

(2) A Class A land charge is —

(*a*) a rent or annuity or principal money payable by instalments or otherwise, with or without interest, which is not a charge created by deed but is a charge upon land (other than a rate) created pursuant to the application of some person under the provisions of any Act of Parliament, for securing to any person either the money spent by him or the costs, charges and expenses incurred by him under such Act, or the money advanced by him for repaying the money spent or the costs, charges and expenses incurred by another person under the authority of an Act of Parliament[9]; or

(*b*) a rent or annuity or principal money payable as mentioned in paragraph (*a*) above which is not a charge created by deed but is a charge upon land (other than a rate) created pursuant to the application of some person under any of the enactments mentioned in Schedule 2 to this Act[10].

(3) A Class B land charge is a charge on land (not being a local land charge)[11] of any of the kinds described in paragraph (*a*) of subsection (2) above, created otherwise than pursuant to the application of any person[12].

(4) A Class C land charge is any of the following (not being a local land charge)[13], namely —

(i) a puisne mortgage[14];
(ii) a limited owner's charge[15];
(iii) a general equitable charge[16];
(iv) an estate contract[17];

and for this purpose —

(i) a puisne[18] mortgage is a legal mortgage which is not protected by a deposit of documents relating to the legal estate affected;

Crane); *Northern Developments (Holdings) Ltd v UDT Securities Ltd* [1976] 1 WLR 1230, [1977] 1 All ER 747; (1976) 41 Conv (NS) 173 (F. R. Crane); *Sowerby v Sowerby* (1982) 44 P & CR 192; *Alpenstow Ltd v Regalian Properties plc* [1985] 1 WLR 721, [1985] 2 All ER 545; *Hynes v Vaughan* (1985) 50 P & CR 444. For the liability of a solicitor in negligence for failing to ensure that a notice under Matrimonial Homes Act 1967 was cancelled, see *Holmes v Kennard & Son* (1984) 49 P & CR 202, p 260, n. 9, post.

[8] For the date of effective registration and priority notices, see LCA 1972, s. 11; (1977) 74 LSG 136 (P. Freedman).

[9] E.g. a statutory charge under the Improvement of Land Act 1864.

[10] E.g. Landlord and Tenant Act 1927, s. 12, Sch. 1, para. 7 (charge in respect of improvements to business premises).

[11] As amended by LLCA 1975, s. 19, Sch. 2.

[12] E.g. a charge on property recovered or preserved for an assisted person arising under the Legal Aid Act·1974, s. 9.

[13] As amended by LLCA 1975, s. 17 (1) (*b*).

[14] P. 737, post.

[15] P. 284, post.

[16] This does not include mortgages of equitable interests which are treated separately; p. 738, post.

[17] P. 80, post.

[18] Puisne is derived from the old French *puis* (after) *né* (born); hence a later or subsequent mortgage.

(ii) a limited owner's charge is an equitable charge acquired by a tenant for life or statutory owner under the Capital Transfer Tax Act 1984 or under any other statute by reason of the discharge by him of any capital transfer tax[19] or other liabilities and to which special priority is given by the statute;

(iii) a general equitable charge is any equitable charge which —

(*a*) is not secured by a deposit of documents relating to the legal estate affected; and

(*b*) does not arise or affect an interest arising under a trust for sale or a settlement; and

(*c*) is not a charge given by way of indemnity against rents equitably apportioned or charged exclusively on land in exoneration of other land and against the breach or non-observance of covenants or conditions; and

(*d*) is not included in any other class of land charge;

(iv) an estate contract is a contract by an estate owner or by a person entitled at the date of the contract to have a legal estate conveyed to him to convey or create a legal estate, including a contract conferring either expressly or by statutory implication a valid option to purchase[20], a right of pre-emption[1] or any other like right.

(5) A Class D land charge is any of the following (not being a local land charge)[2], namely —

(i) an Inland Revenue charge;

(ii) a restrictive covenant[3];

(iii) an equitable easement[4];

and for this purpose —

(i) an Inland Revenue charge is a charge on land, being a charge acquired by the Board under the Capital Transfer Tax Act 1984[5];

(ii) a restrictive covenant is a covenant or agreement (other than a covenant or agreement between a lessor and a lessee) restrictive of the user of land and entered into on or after 1st January 1926;

(iii) an equitable easement is an easement, right or privilege over or affecting land created or arising on or after 1st January 1926, and being merely an equitable interest.

(6) A Class E land charge is an annuity created before 1st January 1926 and not registered in the register of annuities.

(7) A Class F land charge is a charge affecting any land by virtue of the Matrimonial Homes Act 1983[6].

(8) A charge or obligation created before 1st January 1926 can only be registered as a Class B land charge or a Class C land charge if it is acquired under a conveyance made on or after that date.

---

[19] As amended by FA 1975, s. 52, Sch. 12, para. 18; CTTA 1984, s. 276, Sch. 8, para. 3 (1) (*a*). See CTTA 1984, ss. 237, 238.

[20] *Beesly v Hallwood Estates Ltd* [1960] 1 WLR 549, [1960] 2 All ER 314; *Taylors Fashions Ltd v Liverpool Victoria Trustees Co Ltd* [1982] QB 133n, [1981] 1 All ER 897, p. 514, post (option to renew, contained in lease, held registrable as option to purchase).

[1] *Pritchard v Briggs* [1980] Ch 338, [1980] 1 All ER 294, p. 86, post; (1980) 39 CLJ 35 (C. Harpum); Barnsley, *Land Options* (1978), chap. 7.

[2] As amended by LLCA 1975, s. 17 (1) (*b*).

[3] Pp. 457, 761, post.

[4] P. 577, post.

[5] As amended by FA 1975, s. 52, Sch. 12, para. 18; CTTA 1984, s. 276, Sch. 8, para. 3 (1) (*b*).

[6] As amended by MHA 1983, s. 12, Sch. 2; pp. 257–262, post.

3. Registration of land charges. — (1) A land charge shall be registered in the name of the estate owner whose estate is intended to be affected[7].

(2) A land charge registered before 1st January 1926 under any enactment replaced by the Land Charges Act 1925 in the name of a person other than the estate owner may remain so registered until it is registered in the name of the estate owner in the prescribed manner.

(3) A puisne mortgage created before 1st January 1926 may be registered as a land charge before any transfer of the mortgage is made.

Report on H.M. Land Registry for the Year 1984–1985, paras. 47–49.

47. The new registrations of land charges made during the year (excluding priority notices) were divided amongst the various classes as follows:

Class of land charge	Number of registrations	Percentage increase or decrease compared with 1983–84
A	11	*
B	3,636	+ 3.9
C(i) (puisne mortgages)	162,714	+ 7.3
C(ii) (limited owners' charges)	144	+ 33.3
C(iii) (general equitable charges)	6,186	+ 11.6
C(iv) (estate contracts)	29,403	− 1.5
D(i) (Inland Revenue charges)	272	+ 25.3
D(ii) (restrictive covenants)	73,391	+ 11.4
D(iii) (equitable easements)	1,849	+ 24.2
F (matrimonial homes)	5,873	− 11.2

* There was only one application during the previous year.

48. The number of registrations relating to bankruptcy proceedings showed no marked change. The figures are as follows:

Type of registration	Number of registrations	Percentage increase or decrease compared with 1983–84
Pending actions in bankruptcy	11,918	− 2.4
Receiving orders in bankruptcy	8,489	+ 4.4
Deeds of Arrangement	27	− 28.9

---

[7] P. 44, post. Registration against the name of a person who has contracted to purchase land is not sufficient: *Barrett v Hilton Developments Ltd* [1975] Ch 237, [1974] 3 All ER 944; (1975) 39 Conv (NS) 65 (F. R. Crane); *Property Discount Corp Ltd v Lyon Group Ltd* [1981] 1 WLR 300, [1981] 1 All ER 379. For the machinery of registration, see *Oak Co-operative Building Society v Blackburn* [1968] Ch 730, [1968] 2 All ER 117. See also [1979] Conv 249 (A. M. Prichard).

49.   The number of registrations of pending land actions and writs or orders, excluding petitions in bankruptcy and receiving orders in bankruptcy, was as follows:

Type of registration	Number of registrations	Percentage increase or decrease compared with 1983–84
Pending land actions	3,959	+ 4.3
Writs or orders	10,366	+ 18.5

In *Shiloh Spinners Ltd v Harding* [1973] AC 691, [1973] 1 All ER 90[8], the respondents were assignees of part of leasehold premises which was subject to covenants. The appellants had the right to re-enter and retake the premises in the event of breach. The respondents were aware of this all the time, and, in breach of covenant, they demolished the premises, and argued that the right of entry was void against them because it was not registered.

The House of Lords held that the right of entry was not registrable, and was enforceable against purchasers with notice. Lord WILBERFORCE said at 718, at 96:

"The right of entry, it is said, is unenforceable against the respondent, although he took with actual notice of it, because it was not registered as a charge under the Land Charges Act 1925. There is no doubt that if it was capable of registration under that Act, it is unenforceable if not registered: the appellants deny that it was so capable either (i) because it was a legal right, not an equitable right, or (ii) because, if equitable, it does not fall within any of the classes or descriptions of charges registration of which is required.

[His Lordship held that the right of entry was equitable and continued:]

So I pass, as did the Court of Appeal, to the Land Charges Act 1925. The original contention of the respondents was that the equitable right of entry was capable of registration under Class D (iii) of the Act. In the Court of Appeal an alternative contention was raised, apparently at the court's suggestion, that it might come within Class C (iv). In my opinion this is unmaintainable. Class C (iv) embraces:

'Any contract by an estate owner or by a person entitled at the date of the contract to have a legal estate conveyed to him to convey or create a legal estate, including a contract conferring either expressly or by statutory implication a valid option of purchase, a right of pre-emption or any other like right (in this Act referred to as "an estate contract").'

The only words capable of including a right of entry are 'any other like right,' but, in my opinion, no relevant likeness can be found. An option or right of pre-emption eventuates in a contract for sale at a price; this is inherent in 'purchase' and 'pre-emption'; the right of entry is penal in character and involves the revesting of the lease, in the event of default, in a

---

[8] (1973) 32 CLJ 218 (P. B. Fairest).

previous owner. There is no similarity in law or fact between these situations[9].

Class D (iii) reads:

'A charge or obligation affecting land of any of the following kinds, namely:— . . . (iii) Any easement right or privilege over or affecting land created or arising after the commencement of this Act, and being merely an equitable interest (in this Act referred to as an "equitable easement").'

The argument for inclusion in this class falls into two parts. First it is said that a right of entry falls fairly within the description, or at least that, if the words do not appear to include it, they are sufficiently open in meaning to admit it. Secondly it is said that the provisions of the Law of Property Act as to 'overreaching'[10] compel the conclusion that a right of entry must fall under some class or sub-class of the Land Charges Act, and since this is the only one whose words can admit it, they should be so interpreted as to do so. Thus the argument depends for its success upon a combination of ambiguity, or openness of Class D (iii) with compelling consideration brought about in the overreaching provisions. In my opinion it fails under both limbs: Class D (iii) cannot be interpreted so as to admit equitable rights of entry, and no conclusive, compelling, or even clear conclusions can be drawn from the overreaching provisions which can influence the interpretation of Class D (iii).

Dealing with Class D (iii), I reject at once the suggestion that any help (by way of enlarging the content of this class) can be derived either from the introductory words, for they limit themselves to the 'following kinds,' or from the words 'and being merely an equitable interest,' for these are limiting, not enlarging, words. I leave out of account the label at the end — though I should think it surprising if so expert a draftsman had attached that particular label if the class included a right of entry. To include a right of entry in the description of 'equitable easement' offends a sense both of elegance and accuracy. That leaves 'easement right or privilege over or affecting land.' If this were the only place where the expression occurred in this legislation, I should find it difficult to attribute to 'right' a meaning so different in quality from easement and privilege as to include a right of entry. The difference between a right to use or draw profit from another man's land, and a right to take his land altogether away, is one of quality, not of degree. . . . I do not further elaborate this point because a reading of their judgments leaves little doubt that the Lords Justices would themselves have read Class D (iii) as I can only read it but for the influence of the overreaching argument.

So I turn to the latter. This, in my opinion, only becomes compelling if one first accepts the conclusion that all equitable claims relating to land are either registrable under the Land Charges Act, or capable of being overreached under section 2 of the Law of Property Act; i.e., are capable by use of the appropriate mechanism of being transferred to the proceeds of sale of the land they affect. If this dilemma could be made good, then there could be an argument for forcing, within the limits of the possible, an equitable right of entry into one of the registrable classes, since it is obviously not suitable for

---

[9] But a proviso in a lease requiring a lessee, who wishes to assign, first to offer a surrender of the lease to the lessor is an estate contract: *Greene v Church Comrs for England* [1974] Ch 467, [1974] 3 All ER 609; *Bocardo SA v S and M Hotels Ltd* [1980] 1 WLR 17, [1979] 3 All ER 737.
[10] P. 205, post.

overreaching. But the dilemma cannot be made good. What may be overreached is any 'equitable interest or power affecting that estate': yet 'equitable interest' (for powers do not enter into the debate) is a word of most uncertain content. The searcher after a definition has to be satisfied with section 1 (8) 'Estates, interests, and charges in or over land which are not legal estates are in this Act referred to as "equitable interests" ' — a tautology rather than a definition. There is certainly nothing exhaustive about the expression 'equitable interests' — just as certainly it has no clear boundaries. The debate whether such rights as equity, over the centuries, has conferred against the holder of the legal estate are truly proprietary in character, or merely rights in personam, or a hybrid between the two, may have lost some of its vitality in the statutory context but the question inevitably rises to mind whether the 'curtain' or 'overreaching' provisions of the 1925 legislation extend to what are still conveniently called 'equities' or 'mere equities,' such as rights to rectification, or to set aside a conveyance. There is good authority, which I do not presume to doubt, for a sharp distinction between the two — I instance Lord Upjohn in *National Provincial Bank Ltd v Hastings Car Mart Ltd* [1965] AC 1175 at 1238, [1965] 2 All ER 472 at 488 and *Snell's Principles of Equity*, 25th edn. (1960) p. 38. I am impressed by the decision in *E R Ives Investment Ltd v High* [1967] 2 QB 379, [1967] 1 All ER 504, p. 542, post, in which the Court of Appeal held that a right by estoppel — producing an effect similar to an easement — was not registrable under Class D (iii). Lord Denning MR referred to the right as subsisting only in equity. Danckwerts LJ thought it was an equity created by estoppel or a proprietary estoppel: plainly this was not an equitable interest capable of being overreached, yet no member of the court considered that the right — so like an easement — could be brought within Class D (iii). The conclusion followed, and the court accepted it, that whether it was binding on a purchaser depended on notice. All this seems to show that there may well be rights, of an equitable character, outside the provisions as to registration and which are incapable of being overreached.

That equitable rights of entry should be among them is not in principle unacceptable. First, rights of entry, before 1925, were not considered to confer an interest in the land. They were described as bare possibilities (*Challis's Real Property*, 3rd edn. (1911), p. 76) so that it is not anomalous that equitable rights of entry should not be treated as equitable interests. Secondly, it is important that section 10 of the Land Charges Act 1925[11] should be given a plain and ordinary interpretation. It is a section which involves day to day operation by solicitors doing conveyancing work: they should be able to take decisions and advise their clients upon a straightforward interpretation of the registration classes, not upon one depending upon a sophisticated, not to say disputable, analysis of other statutes. Thirdly, the consequence of equitable rights of entry not being registrable is that they are subject to the doctrine of notice, preserved by section 199 of the Law of Property Act. This may not give complete protection, but neither is it demonstrable that it is likely to be less effective than the present system of registration against names. I am therefore of opinion that Class D (iii) should be given its plain prima facie meaning and that so read it does not comprise equitable rights of entry. It follows that non-registration does not make the appellants' right unenforceable in this case.

---

[11] Now LCA 1972, s. 2.

The consequence is that the appellants' claim to re-enter must succeed unless the respondent can and should be relieved in equity against the appellants' legal right."

Relief against forfeiture was refused[12].

(c) Effect of Registration
LAND CHARGES ACT 1972

4. Effect of land charges and protection of purchasers[13]. — (5) A land charge of Class B and a land charge of Class C (other than an estate contract) created or arising on or after 1st January 1926 shall be void as against a purchaser of the land charged with it, or of any interest in such land, unless the land charge is registered in the appropriate register before the completion of the purchase.

(6) An estate contract and a land charge of Class D created or entered into on or after 1st January 1926 shall be void against a purchaser for money or money's worth[14] (or, in the case of an Inland Revenue charge, a purchaser within the meaning of the Capital Transfer Tax Act 1984)[15] of a legal estate in the land charged with it, unless the land charge is registered in the appropriate register before the completion of the purchase.

(7) After the expiration of one year from the first conveyance occurring on or after 1st January 1926 of a land charge of Class B or Class C created before that date the person entitled to the land charge shall not be able to enforce or recover the land charge or any part of it as against a purchaser of the land charged with it, or of any interest in the land, unless the land charge is registered in the appropriate register before the completion of the purchase.

(8) A land charge of Class F shall be void as against a purchaser of the land charged with it, or of any interest in such land, unless the land charge is registered in the appropriate register before the completion of the purchase.

17. Interpretation. — (1) In this Act, unless the context otherwise requires, — "purchaser" means any person (including a mortgagee or lessee) who, for valuable consideration, takes any interest in land or in a charge on land, and "purchase" has a corresponding meaning.

MIDLAND BANK TRUST CO LTD v GREEN
[1981] AC 513, [1981] 1 All ER 153
(HL, Lords WILBERFORCE, EDMUND-DAVIES, FRASER OF TULLYBELTON, RUSSELL OF KILLOWEN and BRIDGE OF HARWICH)[16]

In 1961 a father (Walter) granted to his son (Geoffrey) a 10 year option to purchase Gravel Hill Farm, Thornton-le-Moor, Lincolnshire, of which the

---

[12] P. 452, post.
[13] Sub-ss. (1)–(4) contain provisions relating to land charges Class A.
[14] *Midland Bank Trust Co Ltd v Green* [1981] AC 513, [1981] 1 All ER 153, infra.
[15] As amended by FA 1975 s. 52; Sch. 12; CTTA 1984, s. 276, Sch. 8, para. 3 (2).
[16] The "Green Saga", which "bids fair to rival in time and money the story of *Jarndyce v Jarndyce*" (see [1980] Ch 590 at 622, [1979] 3 All ER 28 at 32, per Lord DENNING MR), continues. For the liability of the solicitor for failing to advise the son to register the option and for failing to register it, see *Midland Bank Trust Co Ltd v Hett, Stubbs and Kemp* [1978] Ch 384, [1978] 3 All ER 571; and for conspiracy between husband and wife, see *Midland Bank Trust Co Ltd v Green (No 3)* [1982] Ch 529, [1981] 3 All ER 744. For a full review of all three cases by Sir Peter OLIVER, who tried them at first instance, see *The Green Saga* (1983) Child & Co Oxford Lecture. See also [1981] CLJ 213 (C. Harpum); (1981) 97 LQR 518 (B. Green).

son was his tenant. The option was not registered under LCA 1925. In 1967 the father, wishing to deprive the son of his option, conveyed the farm, then worth about £40,000, to the mother (Evelyne) for £500. When the son discovered this, he registered the option and purported to exercise it.

The son's executors claimed that the option was binding on the mother's estate.

Held (reversing CA, and restoring OLIVER J). Option void. The mother was a "purchaser of a legal estate for money or money's worth" under LCA 1925, ss. 13 (2) and 20 (8)[17].

LORD WILBERFORCE: This option was, in legal terms, an estate contract and so a legal charge, class C, within the meaning of the Land Charges Act 1925. The correct and statutory method for protection of such an option is by means of entering it in the Register of Land Charges maintained under the Act. If so registered, the option would have been enforceable, not only (contractually) against Walter, but against any purchaser of the farm.

The option was not registered, a failure which inevitably called in question the responsibility of Geoffrey's solicitor. To anticipate, Geoffrey in fact brought proceedings against his solicitor which have been settled for a considerable sum, payable if the present appeal succeeds. . . .

[His Lordship read LCA 1925, ss. 13 (2), 20 (8) and continued:]

Thus the case appears to be a plain one. The "estate contract," which by definition (section 11) includes an option of purchase, was entered into after January 1, 1926; Evelyne took an interest (in fee simple) in the land "for valuable consideration" — so was a "purchaser": she was a purchaser for money — namely £500: the option was not registered before the completion of the purchase. It is therefore void as against her.

In my opinion this appearance is also the reality. The case is plain: the Act is clear and definite. Intended as it was to provide a simple and understandable system for the protection of title to land, it should not be read down or glossed: to do so would destroy the usefulness of the Act. Any temptation to remould the Act to meet the facts of the present case, on the supposition that it is a hard one and that justice requires it, is, for me at least, removed by the consideration that the Act itself provides a simple and effective protection for persons in Geoffrey's position — viz. — by registration.

The respondents submitted two arguments as to the interpretation of section 13 (2): the one sought to introduce into it a requirement that the purchaser should be "in good faith"; the other related to the words "in money or money's worth."

The argument as to good faith fell into three parts: first, that "good faith" was something required of a "purchaser" before 1926; secondly, that this requirement was preserved by the 1925 legislation and in particular by section 13 (2) of the Land Charges Act 1925. If these points could be made good, it would then have to be decided whether the purchaser (Evelyne) was in "good faith" on the facts of the case.

My Lords, the character in the law known as the bona fide (good faith) purchaser for value without notice was the creation of equity. In order to affect a purchaser for value of a legal estate with some equity or equitable interest, equity fastened upon his conscience and the composite expression was used to epitomise the circumstances in which equity would or rather

---

[17] Now LCA 1972, ss. 4 (6) and 17 (1).

would not do so. I think that it would generally be true to say that the words "in good faith" related to the existence of notice. Equity, in other words, required not only absence of notice, but genuine and honest absence of notice. As the law developed, this requirement became crystallised in the doctrine of constructive notice which assumed a statutory form in the Conveyancing Act 1882, section 3. But, and so far I would be willing to accompany the respondents, it would be a mistake to suppose that the requirement of good faith extended only to the matter of notice, or that when notice came to be regulated by statute, the requirement of good faith became obsolete. Equity still retained its interest in and power over the purchaser's conscience. The classic judgment of James LJ in *Pilcher v Rawlins* (1872) 7 Ch App 259 at 269, p. 26, *ante*, is clear authority that it did: good faith there is stated as a separate test which may have to be passed even though absence of notice is proved. And there are references in cases subsequent to 1882 which confirm the proposition that honesty or bona fides remained something which might be inquired into (see *Berwick & Co v Price* [1905] 1 Ch 632 at 639; *Taylor v London and County Banking Co* [1901] 2 Ch 231 at 256; *Oliver v Hinton* [1899] 2 Ch 264 at 273).

But did this requirement, or test, pass into the property legislation of 1925?

My Lords, I do not think it safe to seek the answer to this question by means of a general assertion that the property legislation of 1922–25 was not intended to alter the law, or not intended to alter it in a particular field, such as that relating to purchases of legal estates. All the Acts of 1925, and their precursors, were drafted with the utmost care, and their wording, certainly where this is apparently clear, has to be accorded firm respect. As was pointed out in *Grey v IRC* [1960] AC 1, [1959] 3 All ER 603, the Acts of 1922–4 effected massive changes in the law affecting property and the House, in consequence, was persuaded to give to a plain word ("disposition") its plain meaning, and not to narrow it by reference to its antecedents. Certainly that case should firmly discourage us from muddying clear waters. I accept that there is merit in looking at the corpus as a whole in order to produce if possible a consistent scheme. But there are limits to the possibilities of this process: for example it cannot eliminate the difference between registered and unregistered land, or the respective charges on them.

As to the requirement of "good faith" we are faced with a situation of some perplexity. The expression "good faith," appears in the Law of Property Act 1925 definition of "purchaser" ("a purchaser in good faith for valuable consideration"), section 205 (1) (xxi); in the Settled Land Act 1925, section 117 (1) (xxi) (ditto); in the Administration of Estates Act 1925, section 55 (1) (xviii) (" 'Purchaser' means a lessee, mortgagee or other person who in good faith acquires an interest in property for valuable consideration") and in the Land Registration Act 1925, section 3 (xxi) which does not however, as the other Acts do, include a reference to nominal consideration. So there is certainly some indication of an intention to carry the concept of "good faith" into much of the 1925 code. What then do we find in the Land Charges Act 1925? We were taken along a scholarly peregrination through the numerous Acts antecedent to the final codification and consolidation in 1925 — the Land Charges Registration and Searches Act 1888, the Law of Property Act 1922, particularly Schedule 7, the Law of Property (Amendment) Act 1924 as well as the Yorkshire and Middlesex Deeds Registration Acts. But I think, with genuine respect for an interesting argument, that such solution as there is of the problem under consideration must be sought in the terms of the various Acts of 1925 themselves. So far as concerns the Land Charges Act 1925, the definition of "purchaser" quoted above does not mention "good faith" at all. "Good faith" did not appear in the original Act of 1888, nor in the extension made to that Act by the Act of 1922, Schedule 7, nor in the Act of 1924, Schedule 6. It should be a secure assumption that the definition of "purchaser for value" which is found in section 4 of the Act of 1888 (. . . "person who for valuable consideration takes any interest in land") together with the limitation which is now the proviso to section 13 (2) of the Act of 1925, introduced in 1922, was intended to be carried forward into the Act of 1925. The expression "good faith" appears nowhere in the antecedents. To write the word in, from the examples of contemporaneous Acts, would be bold. It becomes impossible when it is seen that the words appear in section 3 (1) and in section 7 (1), in each case in a proviso very similar, in structure, to the relevant proviso in section 13 (2). If canons of constructions have any validity at all, they must lead to the conclusion that the omission in section 13 (2) was deliberate.

My Lords, I recognise that the inquiring mind may put the question: why should there be an omission of the requirement of good faith in this particular context? I do not think there should be much doubt about the answer. Addition of a requirement that the purchaser should be in good faith would bring with it the necessity of inquiring into the purchaser's motives and state of mind. The present case is a good example of the difficulties which would exist. If the position was simply that the purchaser had notice of the option, and decided nevertheless to buy the land, relying on the absence of notification, nobody could contend that she would be lacking in good faith. She would merely be taking advantage of a situation, which the law has provided, and the addition of a profit motive could not create an absence of good faith. But suppose, and this is the respondents' argument, the purchaser's motive is to defeat the option, does this make any difference? Any advantage to oneself seems necessarily to involve a disadvantage for another: to make the validity of the purchase depend upon which aspect of the transaction was prevalent in the purchaser's mind seems to create distinctions equally difficult to analyse in law as to establish in fact: avarice and malice may be distinct sins, but in human conduct they are liable to be intertwined. The problem becomes even more acute if one supposes a mixture of motives. Suppose — and this may not be far from the truth — that the purchaser's motives were in part to take the farm from Geoffrey, and in part to distribute it between Geoffrey and his brothers and sisters, but not at all to obtain any benefit for herself, is this acting in "good faith" or not? Should family feeling be denied a protection afforded to simple greed? To eliminate the necessity for inquiries of this kind may well have been part of the legislative intention. Certainly there is here no argument for departing —violently — from the wording of the Act.

Before leaving this part of the case, I must comment on *Re Monolithic Building Co* [1915] 1 Ch 643, which was discussed in the Court of Appeal. That was a case arising under section 93 of the Companies (Consolidation) Act 1908 which made an unregistered mortgage void against any creditor of the company. The defendant Jenkins was a managing director of the company, and clearly had notice of the first unregistered mortgage: he himself subsequently took and registered a mortgage debenture and claimed priority over the unregistered mortgage. It was held by the Court of Appeal, first that this was not a case of fraud: "it is not fraud to take advantage of legal rights, the existence of which may be taken to be known to both parties" (*per* Lord Cozens-Hardy MR, at 663), secondly that section 93 of the Act was clear in its terms, should be applied according to its plain meaning, and should not be weakened by infusion of equitable doctrines applied by the courts during the 19th century. The judgment of Lord Cozens-Hardy MR contains a valuable critique of the well known cases of *Le Neve v Le Neve* (1747) 3 Atk 646 and *Greaves v Tofield* (1880) 14 ChD 563 which, arising under the Middlesex Registry Act 1708 and other enactments, had led the judges to import equitable doctrines into cases of priority arising under those Acts, and establishes that the principles of those cases should not be applied to modern Acts of Parliament.

My Lords, I fail to see how this authority can be invoked in support of the respondents' argument, or of the judgments of the majority of the Court of Appeal. So far from supporting them, it is strongly the other way. It disposes, for the future, of the old arguments based, ultimately, upon *Le Neve v Le Neve* for reading equitable doctrines (as to notice, etc.) into modern Acts of Parliament: it makes it clear that it is not "fraud" to rely on legal rights conferred by Act of Parliament: it confirms the validity of interpreting clear enactments as to registration and priority according to their tenor.

The judgment of Phillimore LJ in *Re Monolithic Building Co* [1915] 1 Ch 643 at 669, 670 does indeed contain a passage which appears to favour application of the principle of *Le Neve v Le Neve* and to make a distinction between a transaction designed to obtain an advantage, and one designed to defeat a prior (unregistered) interest. But, as I have explained, this distinction is unreal and unworkable: this whole passage is impossible to reconcile with the views of the other members of the Court of Appeal in the case, and I respectfully consider that it is not good law.

My Lords, I can deal more shortly with the respondents' second argument. It relates to the consideration for the purchase. The argument is that the protection of section 13 (2) of the Land Charges Act 1925 does not extend to a purchaser who has provided only a nominal consideration and that £500 is nominal. A variation of this was the argument accepted by the Court of Appeal that the consideration must be "adequate" — an expression of transparent difficulty. The answer to both contentions lies in the language of the subsection. The word "purchaser," by definition (section 20 (8)), means one who provides valuable consideration — a term of art which precludes any inquiry as to adequacy. This definition is, of course, subject to the context. Section 13 (2), proviso, requires money or money's worth to be provided: the purpose of this being to exclude the consideration of marriage. There is nothing here which suggests, or admits of, the introduction of a further requirement that the money must not be nominal.

The argument for this requirement is based upon the Law of Property Act 1925 which, in section 205 (1) (xxi) defining "purchaser" provides that "valuable consideration" includes marriage but does not include a "nominal consideration in money." The Land Charges Act 1925 contains no definition of "valuable consideration," so it is said to be necessary to have resort to the Law of Property Act definition: thus "nominal consideration in money" is excluded. An indication that this is intended is said to be provided by section 199 (1) (i). I cannot accept this. The fallacy lies in supposing that the Acts —

either of them — set out to define "valuable consideration"; they do not: they define "purchaser," and they define the word differently (see the first part of the argument). "Valuable consideration" requires no definition: it is an expression denoting an advantage conferred or detriment suffered. What each Act does is, for its own purposes, to exclude some things from this general expression: the Law of Property Act includes marriage but not a nominal sum in money; the Land Charges Act excludes marriage but allows "money or money's worth." There is no coincidence between these two; no link by reference or necessary logic between them. Section 199 (1) (i) by referring to the Land Charges Act 1925, necessarily incorporates — for the purposes of this provision — the definition of "purchaser" in the latter Act, for it is only against such a "purchaser" that an instrument is void under that Act. It cannot be read as incorporating the Law of Property Act definition into the Land Charges Act. As I have pointed out the land charges legislation has contained its own definition since 1888, carried through, with the addition of the reference to "money or money's worth" into 1925. To exclude a nominal sum of money from section 13 (2) of the Land Charges Act would be to rewrite the section.

This conclusion makes it unnecessary to determine whether £500 is a nominal sum of money or not. But I must say that for my part I should have great difficulty in so holding. "Nominal consideration" and a "nominal sum" in the law appear to me, as terms of art, to refer to a sum or consideration which can be mentioned as consideration but is not necessarily paid. To equate "nominal" with "inadequate" or even "grossly inadequate" would embark the law upon inquiries which I cannot think were contemplated by Parliament.

I would allow the appeal.

(d) Registers in Existence before 1926

LAND CHARGES ACT 1972

5.   The register of pending actions. — (1) There may be registered in the register of pending actions —

(*a*) a pending land action[18];

(*b*) a petition in bankruptcy filed on or after 1st January 1926.

(7) A pending land action shall not bind a purchaser without express notice of it unless it is for the time being registered under this section.

(8) A petition in bankruptcy shall not bind a purchaser of a legal estate in good faith, for money or money's worth, unless it is for the time being registered under this section[19].

(10) The court, if it thinks fit, may, upon the determination of the proceedings, or during the pendency of the proceedings if satisfied that they are not prosecuted in good faith, make an order vacating a registration under

---

[18] Defined in LCA 1972, s. 17 (1) as "any action or proceeding in court relating to land or any interest in or charge on land." See *Calgary and Edmonton Land Co Ltd v Dobinson* [1974] Ch 102, [1974] 1 All ER 484; *Whittingham v Whittingham* [1979] Fam 9, [1978] 3 All ER 805; *Greenhi Builders Ltd v Allen* [1979] 1 WLR 156, [1978] 3 All ER 1163; *Selim Ltd v Bickenhall Engineering Ltd* [1981] 1 WLR 1318, [1981] 3 All ER 210; *Regan & Blackburn Ltd v Rogers* [1985] 1 WLR 870, [1985] 2 All ER 180; *Sowerby v Sowerby* (1982) 44 P & CR 192; *Haslemere Estates Ltd v Baker* [1982] 1 WLR 1109, [1982] 3 All ER 525; [1983] Conv 69 (J.E.M.); and generally (1986) 136 NLJ 157 (H. W. Wilkinson).

[19] As amended by Insolvency Act 1985, s. 235, Sch. 8, para. 21 (2), and Sch. 10.

this section, and direct the party on whose behalf it was made to pay all or any of the costs and expenses occasioned by the registration and by its vacation[20].

6. The register of writs and orders affecting land. — (1) There may be registered in the register of writs and orders affecting land —

(a) any writ or order affecting land issued or made by any court for the purpose of enforcing a judgment or recognisance[1];

(b) any order appointing a receiver or sequestrator of land;

(c) any bankruptcy order, whether or not the bankrupt's estate is known to include land[21].

(4) Except as provided by subsection (5) below and by section 37 (5) of the Supreme Court Act 1981[2] and section 107 (3) of the County Courts Act 1984[3] (which make special provision as to receiving orders in respect of land of judgment debtors) every such writ and order as is mentioned in subsection (1) above, and every delivery in execution or other proceeding taken pursuant to any such writ or order, or in obedience to any such writ or order, shall be void as against a purchaser of the land unless the writ or order is for the time being registered under this section.

(5) Subject to subsection (6) below, the title of a trustee in bankruptcy shall be void as against a purchaser of a legal estate in good faith for money or money's worth, unless the bankruptcy order is for the time being registered under this section[21].

(6) Where a petition in bankruptcy has been registered under section 5 above, the title of the trustee in bankruptcy shall be void as against a purchaser of a legal estate in good faith for money or money's worth claiming under a conveyance made after the date of registration, unless at the date of the conveyance either the registration of the petition is in force or a receiving order on the petition is registered under this section[21].

7. The register of deeds of arrangement affecting land. — (1) A deed of arrangement affecting land may be registered in the register of deeds of arrangement affecting land, in the name of the debtor, on the application of a trustee of the deed or a creditor assenting to or taking the benefit of the deed.

(2) Every deed of arrangement shall be void as against a purchaser of any land comprised in it or affected by it unless it is for the time being registered under this section.

8. Expiry and renewal of registrations. — A registration under section 5, section 6 or section 7 of this Act shall cease to have effect at the end of the period of five years from the date on which it is made, but may be renewed from time to time and, if so renewed, shall have effect for five years from the date of renewal.

---

[20] *Calgary and Edmonton Land Co Ltd v Discount Bank (Overseas) Ltd* [1971] 1 WLR 81, [1971] 1 All ER 551; *Norman v Hardy* [1974] 1 WLR 1048, [1974] 1 All ER 1170; *Northern Developments (Holdings) Ltd v UDT Securities Ltd* [1976] 1 WLR 1230, [1977] 1 All ER 747. Cf. LCA 1972, s. 1 (6), p. 30, ante.

[21] As amended by Insolvency Act 1985, s. 235, Sch. 8, para. 21 (3), and Sch. 10.

[1] E.g. an order charging the land of a judgment debtor with the payment of the money due: Charging Orders Act 1979, p. 271, post. See *Stockler v Fourways Estates Ltd* [1984] 1 WLR 25, [1983] 3 All ER 501 (Mareva injunction prohibiting a party from disposing of his assets held not registrable).

[2] As amended by Supreme Court Act 1981, s. 15 (2), Sch. 5.

[3] As amended by County Courts Act 1984, s. 148 (1), Sch. 2, para. 18.

(e) Registration Against Estate Owners Prior to Root of Title

Since the system of registration of land charges provides for the registration of charges against the name of the estate owner, a purchaser can only search against those persons whom he knows to have been estate owners. He will find their names from the deeds. But if the number of years between 1926, when the Register of Land Charges began, and the date of the purchase is greater than 15 years, which is the statutory period of search[4], then it is possible that persons may have been estate owners since 1925 without the purchaser knowing about them. He would then be bound by land charges registered against their names without having any way of searching against them. This hazard began in 1956, 30 years (then the statutory period of search[5]) after registration began.

When, as will be seen[6], the statutory period of search was reduced in 1969 to 15 years, the purchaser's risk greatly increased, and some protection was needed.

LAW OF PROPERTY ACT 1969

25. Compensation in certain cases for loss due to undisclosed land charges. — (1) Where a purchaser of any estate or interest in land under a disposition to which this section applies has suffered loss by reason that the estate or interest is affected by a registered land charge, then if —

(*a*) the date of completion was after the commencement of this Act; and

(*b*) on that date the purchaser had no actual knowledge of the charge; and

(*c*) the charge was registered against the name of an owner of an estate in the land who was not as owner of any such estate a party to any transaction, or concerned in any event, comprised in the relevant title;

the purchaser shall be entitled to compensation for the loss[7].

(2) For the purposes of subsection (1) (*b*) above, the question whether any person had actual knowledge of a charge shall be determined without regard to the provisions of section 198 of the Law of Property Act 1925 (under which registration under the Land Charges Act 1925 or any enactment replaced by it is deemed to constitute actual notice)[8].

(9) This section applies to the following dispositions, that is to say —

(*a*) any sale or exchange and, subject to the following provisions of this subsection, any mortgage of an estate or interest in land;

(*b*) any grant of a lease for a term of years derived out of a leasehold interest;

(*c*) any compulsory purchase, by whatever procedure, of land; and

(*d*) any conveyance of a fee simple in land under Part I of the Leasehold Reform Act 1967;

but does not apply to the grant of a term of years derived out of the freehold or the mortgage of such a term by the lessee; and references in this section to a purchaser shall be construed accordingly.

---

[4] P. 5, ante; p. 77, post.
[5] LPA 1925, s. 44 (1).
[6] LPA 1969, s. 23, p. 77, post.
[7] Payable by the Chief Land Registrar out of public funds.
[8] P. 29, ante.

(10) In this section —
"relevant title" means —

    (*a*) in relation to a disposition made under a contract, the title which the purchaser was, apart from any acceptance by him (by agreement or otherwise) of a shorter or an imperfect title, entitled to require; or

    (*b*) in relation to any other disposition[9], the title which he would have been entitled to require if the disposition had been made under a contract to which section 44 (1) of the Law of Property Act 1925[10] applied and that contract had been made on the date of completion.

(11) For the purposes of this section any knowledge acquired in the course of a transaction by a person who is acting therein as counsel, or as solicitor or other agent, for another shall be treated as the knowledge of that other.

(*f*) *Effect of Non-Registration. Actual and Constructive Notice*

LAW OF PROPERTY ACT 1925

199. Restrictions on constructive notice. — (1) A purchaser shall not be prejudicially affected by notice of —

    (i) any instrument or matter capable of registration under the provisions of the Land Charges Act, 1925, or any enactment which it replaces, which is void or not enforceable as against him under that Act or enactment, by reason of the non-registration thereof;

    (ii) any other instrument or matter or any fact or thing unless —

        (*a*) it is within his own knowledge, or would have come to his knowledge if such inquiries and inspections had been made as ought reasonably to have been made by him; or

        (*b*) in the same transaction with respect to which a question of notice to the purchaser arises, it has come to the knowledge of his counsel, as such, or of his solicitor or other agent, as such, or would have come to the knowledge of his solicitor or other agent, as such, if such inquiries and inspections had been made as ought reasonably to have been made by the solicitor or other agent[11].

In *Hollington Bros Ltd v Rhodes* [1951] 2 TLR 691, [1951] 2 All ER 578n, the plaintiffs purported to take an unsealed 7 year underlease from the defendants at a rent of £612 a year. They went into possession and paid rent, but did not register the informal lease as a land charge. The defendants then sold the legal reversion to Daymar Estates Ltd "subject to and with the benefit of such tenancies as may affect the premises". On the same day Daymar Estates Ltd served half a year's notice to quit on the plaintiffs, contending that Daymar Estates Ltd were not bound by the equitable lease but only by the legal tenancy from year to year. The plaintiffs agreed to take a new lease from Daymar Estates Ltd at a premium and an increased rent and sued the defendants for the difference between their old rent and the new payments.

---

[9] E.g. compulsory purchase or acquisition under Leasehold Reform Act 1967.
[10] P. 77, post.
[11] This re-enacts Conveyancing Act 1882, s. 3. See also *Sharpe v Foy* (1868) 4 Ch App 35 and *Re Cousins* (1886) 31 ChD 671.

HARMAN J held that there was no concluded agreement between the plaintiffs and the defendants, and so the plaintiffs failed. He then considered what the position would have been had there been a contract. He referred to the pre-1926 law and quoted FARWELL J· in *Hunt v Luck* [1901] 1 Ch 51:

"(1) A tenant's occupation is notice of all that tenant's rights, but not of his lessor's title or rights; (2) actual knowledge that the rents are paid by the tenants to some person whose receipt is inconsistent with the title of the vendor is notice of that person's rights."

HARMAN J continued at 695, at 579: "After 1925, however, by virtue of section 10 of the Land Charges Act 1925[12], this contract came within Class C (iv) as a charge on or obligation affecting land, and therefore might be registered as a land charge in the Registry of Land Charges. Accordingly, by virtue of section 13 (2)[13], this being a land charge of Class C is void 'against a purchaser of the land charged therewith, or of any interest in such land, unless the land charge is registered in the appropriate register before the completion of the purchase.' Moreover, by section 199 of the Law of Property Act 1925, a purchaser is not to be prejudicially affected by notice of any instrument or matter capable of registration under the Land Charges Act 1925, which is void against him by reason of non-registration. This land charge was not registered, and accordingly it is said that it was void against Daymar Estates, Limited, notwithstanding their notice or knowledge, and, moreover, that there was no duty lying on the plaintiffs to register the contract in order to prevent this result. This has been held to be so by Wynn Parry J in *Wright v Dean* [1948] Ch 686, [1948] 2 All ER 415 where he said that it could not be urged that there was any such duty on the plaintiff. I propose to follow that decision, although I may observe in passing that there is in section 200 (4) of the Law of Property Act 1925, a reference to 'the obligation to register a land charge in respect of . . . any estate contract.'

The defendants' answer to this point was that in fact Daymar Estates, Limited, did not contract to obtain, and did not by the assignment get, any estate in the land expressed to override the plaintiffs' rights, and that consequently they took subject to those rights which are expressly mentioned, and that the land which they purchased was in fact only an interest in the land subject to the rights of the plaintiffs in it. This argument seemed to me attractive because it appears at first glance wrong that a purchaser, who knows perfectly well of rights subject to which he is expressed to take, should be able to ignore them. It was, moreover, pointed out that *Wright v Dean* was distinguishable in this respect because there the option which was overriden by the conveyance was not mentioned in it, nor did the purchaser take expressly subject to it. It seems to me, however, that this argument cannot prevail having regard to the words in section 13 (2) of the Land Charges Act 1925 which I have quoted, coupled with the definition of 'land' in the Act. The fact is that it was the policy of the framers of the 1925 legislation to get rid of equitable rights of this sort unless registered. . . .

Finally, as under section 13 of the Land Charges Act 1925 . . . an unregistered estate contract is void, and under section 199 of the Law of Property Act 1925, the purchaser is not to be prejudicially affected by it, I do

---

[12] Now LCA 1972, s. 2, p. 31, ante.
[13] Now LCA 1972, s. 4 (6). An estate contract is void only against a purchaser for money or money's worth of the legal estate.

not see how that which is void and which is not to prejudice the purchaser can be validated by some equitable doctrine."

In *Smith v Jones* [1954] 1 WLR 1089, [1954] 2 All ER 823, the defendant Jones purchased, at an auction, a farm which the plaintiff, to Jones' knowledge, occupied as a tenant.

Disputes arose between the plaintiff and defendant as to the liability for certain repairs, and eventually the plaintiff brought this action claiming that his tenancy agreement should be rectified so as to make the defendant liable for structural repairs.

The defendant contended that, even if a case for rectification could be established against the original lessor, he, as a bona fide purchaser for value, was not bound by the equity to rectify. UPJOHN J held that there was no equity for rectification; and even if there had been, the defendant would have taken free of it. On the second point, he said at 1091, at 827:

"Lastly, Mr. Arnold for the plaintiff argued that as the plaintiff was in actual occupation as tenant, the defendant was affected with notice of all his rights and all his equities, including an equity to rectify. On the view I have formed of the facts and law as to rectification, this point does not strictly arise, but as it has been fully argued, I think that I ought to express my views thereon.

In *Barnhart v Greenshields* (1853) 9 Moo PCC 18, where the law is clearly and compendiously stated, the judgment of the Privy Council was delivered by Mr. Pemberton Leigh, afterwards Lord Kingsdown, who said at 32: 'With respect to the effect of possession merely, we take the law to be, that if there be a tenant in possession of land, a purchaser is bound by all the equities which the tenant could enforce against the vendor, and that the equity of the tenant extends not only to interests connected with his tenancy, as in *Taylor v Stibbert* (1794) 2 Ves 437, but also to interests under collateral agreements, as in *Daniels v Davison* (1809) 16 Ves 249, *Allen v Anthony* (1816) 1 Mer 282, the principle being the same in both classes of cases; namely, that the possession of the tenant is notice that he has some interest in the land, and that a purchaser having notice of that fact, is bound, according to the ordinary rule, either to inquire what that interest is, or to give effect to it, whatever it may be.'

Then a little later on he cited the language of Lord Eldon in *Allen v Anthony* at 284: 'It is so far settled as not to be disputed, that a person purchasing, where there is a tenant in possession, if he neglects to inquire into the title, must take, subject to such rights as the tenant may have.'

On the other hand, Mr. Arnold has not produced any case which goes so far as to say that an equity of rectification is an equity which is enforceable against a purchaser. In my judgment it would be extending the doctrine of notice and the obligation to make inquiry far too much if the doctrine was intended to cover an equity of rectification. Of course the purchaser is bound by the rights of the tenant in occupation — that is quite clear. He is not entitled to assume — as was argued in the earlier cases, notably, I think, *Taylor v Stibbert* — that the tenant is in possession from year to year. He must look at the agreement and he is bound by the agreement, and if, as in *Daniels v Davidson*, the tenant not only has a tenancy agreement but an option to purchase, he is also bound by that.

But, in my judgment, a purchaser is not only entitled but bound to assume, when he is looking at the agreement under which the tenant holds, that that agreement correctly states the relationship between the tenant and the landlord; and he is not bound to assume or to ask or make inquiry whether the tenant has any rights to rectify that contract.

Barnhart v Greenshields (1853) 9 Moo PCC 18 was followed in the Court of Appeal by the well-known case of *Hunt v Luck* [1902] 1 Ch 428, where the principle was again stated, but as Cozens-Hardy LJ pointed out in argument, and Vaughan Williams LJ pointed out at the beginning of his judgment, the real question for determination was the true construction of the Conveyancing Act 1882; Farwell J, who heard the case at first instance [1901] 1 Ch 45, having dealt with the matter without reference to the statutory enactment. I have no doubt that that was because he treated the Act as merely declaratory of the existing law; but it is after all a matter of construction of the Act, although I have already expressed an opinion as though the matter rested solely upon decided cases.

The relevant section which re-enacts exactly, so far as relevant, the provisions of the Conveyancing Act 1882, is to be found in s. 199 (1) of the Law of Property Act 1925 [His Lordship read sub-ss. (i) and (ii) (*a*) and continued]:

The question which I have to answer is this: What inspection and inquiries ought reasonably to have been made by the defendant of the tenant before the sale, so far as relevant to this question? I think the only relevant inquiry that he would have made would have been this: 'May I see your tenancy agreement? I want to see whether it corresponds with the copy agreement I have seen in the auction rooms.' That is the document which governed the rights of the parties.

He ought to have asked whether he had seen a correct copy, but he was under no obligation, in my view, to proceed further and say: 'Does that correctly represent your rights?' In fact, if he had asked that question, the answer honestly but erroneously given would have been 'Yes'. Still less was he bound to take the tenant step by step through the document and ask how the tenant interpreted its provisions. He could not be so bound, and it would be most unwise for any intending purchaser to do so.

In my judgment the defendant is entitled and bound to rely on the terms of the document, and the document speaks for itself. Accordingly, had I come to a contrary conclusion upon the claim for rectification, I should have found that this action was barred by the plea of bona fide purchaser of [*sic*] value without notice. In the circumstances, I must dismiss the action.''

In *McCarthy & Stone Ltd v Julian S Hodge & Co Ltd* [1971] 1 WLR 1547, [1971] 2 All ER 973, the plaintiffs, who were engaged in building work on the premises of Cityfield Properties Ltd, obtained on 17 February 1964 an option to purchase. On 14 March 1964, Cityfield Properties Ltd created an equitable mortgage by deposit of title deeds[14] with the defendant bank. On 13 April 1964, the bank registered the equitable mortgage under the Companies Act 1948, s. 95[15].

On 27 September 1965 the plaintiffs registered their option as an estate contract. On 21 June 1967, Cityfield Properties Ltd were in liquidation.

---

[14] P. 658, *post.*
[15] Now Companies Act 1985, s. 396, p. 57, *post.*

One question was whether the plaintiffs' estate contract had priority over the bank's equitable mortgage. FOSTER J held that it had. The Land Charges Act 1925, s. 13 (2) (now Land Charges Act 1972, s. 4 (6)) did not apply, because the bank was not a purchaser for value of a legal estate. The bank was only an *equitable* mortgagee, and the priority as between the plaintiffs and the bank depended on the time of creation, in accordance with the equitable principle *Qui potior est tempore, potior est jure*. The option was created before the mortgage and therefore the bank took subject to it[16].

---

ii. REGISTERED LAND

The Land Charges Act 1972 is not applicable where the title to land is registered[17]. Interests or charges which are registrable against the name of the estate owner under the Land Charges Act 1972 in the case of unregistered land must be protected in the case of registered land by the entry of a notice or caution on the register of title to the land itself.

The principles of notice work differently in the two systems. An interest or charge which is not registrable under the Land Charges Act 1972 may be enforceable under the old doctrine of notice in the case of unregistered land; but in the case of registered land, it must either be protected by an entry on the register or take effect as an overriding interest[18]. There is theoretically no room in the registered system for a residual category of third party rights whose enforceability depends on the old doctrine of notice[19].

On the other hand there is no place in the unregistered system for the safety net provision of an overriding interest under section 70 (1) (*g*) of the Land Registration Act 1925. Under that paragraph, as we shall see, the rights of every person in actual occupation are protected even if the occupant has not registered them[20]. In the case of unregistered land, however, the Draconian solution is adopted whereby the failure to register a registrable interest under the Land Charges Act 1925 renders it void against a purchaser, even though he is in bad faith or actually knows[1], and even though the holder of the right is in possession[2]. This vital difference between

---

[16] At 1555, at 980; [1972A] CLJ 34 (P. B. Fairest), where the point is made that if the plaintiffs' interest had been a land charge in a different category within Class C (e.g. a puisne mortgage), the bank would not have been bound. An unregistered puisne mortgage is void against a purchaser for value of any interest in the land. See also (1976) CLP 26 (D. J. Hayton).

[17] LCA 1972, s. 14.

[18] LRA 1925, s. 70 (1), p. 118, post. Rights such as those in p. 25, n. 15, ante may be protected by an entry under LRA 1925, ss. 49 (1) (*f*) (notice), 54 (1) (caution), or 58 (1) (restriction), pp. 135–145, post. Ruoff and Roper, pp. 699 n. 25, 724 n. 4.

[19] P. 25, ante.

[20] P. 117, post; *Williams and Glyn's Bank Ltd v Boland* [1981] AC 487, [1980] 2 All ER 408, p. 121, post.

[1] *Midland Bank Trust Co Ltd v Green* [1981] AC 513, [1981] 1 All ER 153, p. 37, ante; *Hollington Bros Ltd v Rhodes* [1951] 2 TLR 691, [1951] 2 All ER 578n, p. 45, ante. These two cases would have been decided differently in registered land. As to whether such a purchaser might be bound by a constructive trust, see (1981) 97 LQR at pp. 521–522 (B. Green); p. 145, post.

[2] The purchaser may nevertheless be bound by an unregistered registrable charge under LCA 1925 (*a*) by estoppel: *Taylors Fashions Ltd v Liverpool Victoria Trustees Co Ltd* [1982] QB 133n, [1981] 1 All ER 897, p. 514, post, (*b*) by failure to plead the non-registration when sued: *Balchin v Buckle* (1982) Times, 1 June ("One would have thought that the purchaser could waive its effect and agree to be bound by the covenant (Class D (*ii*)). If he chose, whether from incompetence of his own or his legal advisers or from gentlemanly consideration for the rights or convenience of others, to be bound by the covenant or not to raise the point that it was void, there was no reason why the court should raise the point for him" per STEPHENSON LJ).

the two systems may well have been due to an error on the part of the draftsman of the 1925 legislation.

[1982] Conv 213 (M. Friend and J. Newton), pp. 215–217

"It is as well to quote section 14 of the Law of Property Act 1925 in full: '14.   This part of this Act shall not prejudicially affect the interest of any person in possession or in actual occupation of land to which he may be entitled in right of such possession or occupation.'

The crucial words are, *This part of this Act*, for this makes it clear that it is only Part I of the Act (i.e. the first 39 sections) which are relevant. . . .

The root of the problem may be traced back to the Law of Property Act 1922[3], most of whose provisions were repealed before they ever came into force, where this particular provision originally appeared as section 33, and where it made a good deal more sense than it makes as it stands in the 1925 Act which replaced it. Part I of the Law of Property Act 1922 dealt with the "Assimilation and amendment of the law of real and personal estate." In particular, section 10 dealt with undivided shares (by reference to Schedule 3 to the Act); section 11 dealt with dispositions on trust for sale (by reference to Schedule 4); and section 14 dealt with land charges (by reference to Schedule 7). The various schedules to the 1922 Act contained provisions broadly similar to those contained in the main body of the 1925 Act. Moreover, paragraph 1 (1) (*f*) of Schedule 7 introduced a new category of land charge, namely: "(*f*) Any contract, by an estate owner or by a person entitled to have a legal estate conveyed to him, to convey a legal estate (including a contract conferring a valid option of purchase, a right of pre-emption and any other like right) entered into after the commencement of this Act . . ."

In other words, the idea behind this provision seems to have been that estate contracts (e.g. contracts to convey a legal estate, agreements for a lease, etc.) should have been registrable as land charges, but that a person who did not so protect his interest and who was in possession or actual occupation, and who was entitled to such land in right of his possession or occupation should not thereby be prejudiced. This idea seems to be an extension of the rule in *Hunt v Luck*[4]. Had section 33 of the 1922 Act found an appropriate context in the 1925 legislation many of the present problems could have been avoided. If the section had been re-enacted in the Land Charges Act 1925, the enforceability of unregistered estate contracts in registered and unregistered conveyancing would have been identical: this would also have accorded with the general scheme of the 1925 legislation, which must surely have been to ensure that there should be no differences of substantive law between registered and unregistered conveyancing. The absence of section 33 of the 1922 Act from the Land Charges Act 1925 may be regarded as merely an error in the final stages of drafting; the consequences for property law, however, were serious. One such consequence was the decision in *Hollington Bros Ltd v Rhodes*[5] to the effect that a purchaser (as

---

[3] This idea is not new. The writers wish to acknowledge the views expressed by Mr Charles Harpum of Downing College, Cambridge, and by Mr David Ibbetson in (1977) 41 Conv (NS) 415, 419, n. 31.

[4] [1901] 1 Ch 51.

[5] [1951] 2 All E.R. 578, p. 45, ante.

defined[6]) takes free from an unregistered estate contract where the title to the land is unregistered, even though the holder of the estate contract is in possession of the land.

This is clearly anomalous. There can be no doubt that the Law of Property Act 1922, s. 33 (as replaced by the Law of Property Act 1925, s. 14) was designed to have the same effect in unregistered conveyancing as the Land Registration Act 1925, s. 70 (1) (*g*) has for registered land. The Land Registration Act 1925, s. 70 (1) (*g*) refers to "the rights of every person in actual occupation of the land or in receipt of the rents and profits thereof. . . ." The Law of Property Act 1925, s. 14 refers to ". . . the interest of any person in possession or in actual occupation of land. . . ." The definition of "possession" in the Law of Property Act 1925, s. 205 (1) (xix) includes "the receipt of rents and profits"; in other words, both the Law of Property Act 1925, s. 14 and the Land Registration Act 1925, s. 70 (1) (*g*) were designed to protect the rights of those in actual or constructive possession of land. Yet as the law now stands, the protection afforded to such persons is radically different, depending on whether the title to the land is registered or not. There is no good reason, legal or historical for an arbitrary distinction of this sort; the fact that the law now requires it to be made suggests a need for legislative reform"[7].

C.   Other Registers

i.   LOCAL LAND CHARGES[8]
Registers are maintained under the Local Land Charges Act 1975 by all district councils in England and Wales, and also by London boroughs and the Common Council of the City of London[9]. Only those land charges which would not normally be disclosed by an inspection of the property or the title deeds have been made registrable. The register relates to both unregistered and registered land[10].

LAW OF PROPERTY ACT 1925

198.   Registration under the Land Charges Act, 1925, to be notice. —
p. 29 ante.

---

[6] LCA 1925, ss. 13 (2), 20 (8); and cf. LCA 1972, ss. 4 (6), 17 (1).
[7] See also M & W, pp. 186–187; MM, p. 91, which adds the point that the Lords and Commons Joint Committee had erroneously certified that the consolidation of LPA 1922 and LP(A)A 1925 into the various 1925 Acts made no change in the law.
[8] LLC Rules 1977 (SI 1977 No. 985); LLC(A) Rules 1978 (SI 1978 No. 1638); 1982 (SI 1982 No. 461); 1983 (SI 1983 No. 1591). The Act came into force on 1 August 1977 and replaces LCA 1925, s. 15 and other sections set out in LCA 1972, s. 18, Sch. 4. See Law Commission Report on Local Land Charges 1974 (Law Com No. 62 HC 71); Garner, *Local Land Charges* (9th edn 1982), which has a useful table of all local land charges arranged alphabetically and the part of the register in which each is registrable (pp. 102–110). On the computerisation of local land charges, see LLCA 1975, s. 3 (3); (1985) 82 LSG 1216, 1530. See also Aldridge, *Enquiries of Local Authorities* (1982).
[9] LLCA 1975, s. 3 (1). This includes the Inner Temple and the Middle Temple, s. 3 (4).
[10] See LRA 1925, s. 70 (1) (*i*), p. 120, post.

LOCAL LAND CHARGES ACT 1975

1.   Local land charges. — (1) A charge or other matter affecting land is a local land charge if it falls within any of the following descriptions and is not one of the matters set out in section 2 below:—

(*a*) any charge acquired either before or after the commencement of this Act by a local authority, water authority or new town development corporation under the Public Health Acts 1936 and 1937, the Public Health Act 1961 or the Highways Act 1980 (or any Act repealed by that Act)[11], or any similar charge acquired by a local authority under any other Act, whether passed before or after this Act, being a charge that is binding on successive owners of the land affected;

(*b*) any prohibition of or restriction on the use of land —

(i) imposed by a local authority on or after 1st January 1926 (including any prohibition or restriction embodied in any condition attached to a consent, approval or licence granted by a local authority on or after that date), or

(ii) enforceable by a local authority under any covenant or agreement made with them on or after that date,

being a prohibition or restriction binding on successive owners of the land affected;

(*c*) any prohibition of or restriction on the use of land —

(i) imposed by a Minister of the Crown or government department on or after the date of the commencement of this Act (including any prohibition or restriction embodied in any condition attached to a consent, approval or licence granted by such a Minister or department on or after that date), or

(ii) enforceable by such a Minister or department under any covenant or agreement made with him or them on or after that date,

being a prohibition or restriction binding on successive owners of the land affected;

(*d*) any positive obligation affecting land enforceable by a Minister of the Crown, government department or local authority under any covenant or agreement made with him or them on or after the date of the commencement of this Act and binding on successive owners of the land affected;

(*e*) any charge or other matter which is expressly made a local land charge by any statutory provision not contained in this section.

(2) For the purposes of subsection (1) (*a*) above, any sum which is recoverable from successive owners or occupiers of the land in respect of which the sum is recoverable shall be treated as a charge, whether the sum is expressed to be a charge on the land or not.

2.   Matters which are not local land charges. — The following matters are not local land charges:—

(*a*) a prohibition or restriction enforceable under a covenant or agreement made between a lessor and a lessee;

(*b*) a positive obligation enforceable under a covenant or agreement made between a lessor and a lessee;

---

[11] As amended by Highways Act 1980, s. 343 (2), Sch. 24, para. 26.

(c) a prohibition or restriction enforceable by a Minister of the Crown, government department or local authority under any covenant or agreement, being a prohibition or restriction binding on successive owners of the land affected by reason of the fact that the covenant or agreement is made for the benefit of land of the Minister, government department or local authority;

(d) a prohibition or restriction embodied in any bye-laws;

(e) a condition or limitation subject to which planning permission was granted at any time before the commencement of this Act or was or is (at any time) deemed to be granted under any statutory provision relating to town and country planning, whether by a Minister of the Crown, government department or local authority;

(f) a prohibition or restriction embodied in a scheme under the Town and Country Planning Act 1932 or any enactment repealed by that Act;

(g) a prohibition or restriction enforceable under a forestry dedication covenant entered into pursuant to section 5 of the Forestry Act 1967;

(h) a prohibition or restriction affecting the whole of any of the following areas:—

   (i) England, Wales or England and Wales;

   (ii) England, or England and Wales, with the exception of, or of any part of, Greater London;

   (iii) Greater London.

5. Registration. — (1) Subject to subsection (6) below, where the originating authority as respects a local land charge are the registering authority, it shall be their duty to register it in the appropriate local land charges register.

(2) Subject to subsection (6) below, where the originating authority as respects a local land charge are not the registering authority, it shall be the duty of the originating authority to apply to the registering authority for its registration in the appropriate local land charges register and upon any such application being made it shall be the duty of the registering authority to register the charge accordingly.

(3) The registration in a local land charges register of a local land charge, or of any matter which when registered becomes a local land charge, shall be carried out by reference to the land affected or such part of it as is situated in the area for which the register is kept.

(4) In this Act, "the originating authority", as respects a local land charge, means the Minister of the Crown, government department, local authority or other person by whom the charge is brought into existence or by whom, on its coming into existence, the charge is enforceable;[12]. . .

(5) The registration of a local land charge may be cancelled pursuant to an order of the court.

(6) Where a charge or other matter is registrable in a local land charges register and before the commencement of this Act was also registrable in a register kept under the Land Charges Act 1972, then, if before the commencement of this Act it was registered in a register kept under that Act,

---

[12] In the case of charges under the Highways Act 1980, s. 224, the originating authority is the street works authority for the street concerned.

there shall be no duty to register it, or to apply for its registration, under this Act and section 10 below shall not apply in relation to it.

10. Compensation for non-registration or defective official search certificate. — (1) Failure to register a local land charge in the appropriate local land charges register shall not affect the enforceability of the charge but where a person has purchased any land affected by a local land charge, then —

    (*a*) in a case where a material personal search[13] of the appropriate local land charges register was made in respect of the land in question before the relevant time, if at the time of the search the charge was in existence but not registered in that register; or

    (*aa*) in a case where the appropriate local land charges register is kept otherwise than in documentary form and a material personal search of that register was made in respect of the land in question before the relevant time, if the entitlement to search in that register conferred by section 8 above was not satisfied as mentioned in subsection (1A) of that section; or[14]

    (*b*) in a case where a material official search[15] of the appropriate local land charges register was made in respect of the land in question before the relevant time, if the charge was in existence at the time of the search but (whether registered or not) was not shown by the official search certificate as registered in that register,

the purchaser shall (subject to section 11 (1) below[16]) be entitled to compensation for any loss suffered by him in consequence.

(3) For the purposes of this section —

    (*a*) a person purchases land where, for valuable consideration, he acquires any interest in land or the proceeds of sale of land, and this includes cases where he acquires as lessee or mortgagee and shall be treated as including cases where an interest is conveyed or assigned at his direction to another person;

    (*b*) the relevant time —

        (i) where the acquisition of the interest in question was preceded by a contract for its acquisition, other than a qualified liability contract, is the time when that contract was made;

        (ii) in any other case, is the time when the purchaser acquired the interest in question or, if he acquired it under a disposition which took effect only when registered under the Land Registration Act 1925, the time when that disposition was made;

and for the purposes of sub-paragraph (i) above, a qualified liability contract is a contract containing a term the effect of which is to make the liability of the purchaser dependent upon, or avoidable by reference to, the outcome of a search for local land charges affecting the land to be purchased.

    (*c*) a personal search is material if, but only if —

        (i) it is made after the commencement of this Act, and

---

[13] S. 8.
[14] As added by Local Government (Miscellaneous Provisions) Act 1982, s. 34.
[15] S. 9.
[16] S. 11 (1) deals with the position of mortgagees in respect of a claim.

(ii) it is made by or on behalf of the purchaser or, before the relevant time, the purchaser or his agent has knowledge of the result of it;

(*d*) an official search is material if, but only if —

(i) it is made after the commencement of this Act, and

(ii) it is requisitioned by or on behalf of the purchaser or, before the relevant time, the purchaser or his agent has knowledge of the contents of the official search certificate.

(4) Any compensation for loss under this section shall be paid by the registering authority in whose area the land affected is situated; and where the purchaser has incurred expenditure for the purpose of obtaining compensation under this section, the amount of the compensation shall include the amount of the expenditure reasonably incurred by him for that purpose (so far as that expenditure would not otherwise fail to be treated as loss for which he is entitled to compensation under this section).

(7) In the case of an action to recover compensation under this section the cause of action shall be deemed for the purposes of the Limitation Act 1939[17] to accrue at the time when the local land charge comes to the notice of the purchaser; and for the purposes of this subsection the question when the charge came to his notice shall be determined without regard to the provisions of section 198 of the Law of Property Act 1925[18] (under which registration under certain enactments is deemed to constitute actual notice).

LOCAL LAND CHARGES RULES 1977

3. Parts of the Register. — The register shall continue to be divided into parts, for the registration of different types of charge, as follows:

Part 1, for general financial charges;[19]

Part 2, for specific financial charges;

Part 3, for planning charges;

Part 4, for charges not registrable in another part of the register ("miscellaneous charges");[20]

Part 5, for charges falling within section 8(4) of the Agriculture (Miscellaneous Provisions) Act 1941 ("fenland ways maintenance charges");

Part 6, for charges falling within section 8(4) or 52(8) of the Land Compensation Act 1973 ("land compensation charges");

Part 7, for charges falling within section 1(4) or 9 of the New Towns Act 1965 ("new towns charges");[1]

Part 8, for charges falling within section 33 of the Civil Aviation Act 1949, section 21 of the Civil Aviation Act 1968 or section 16(2) of the Civil Aviation Act 1971 ("civil aviation charges");[2]

Part 9, for charges falling within section 11(1) or 16(6) of the Opencast Coal Act 1958 ("opencast coal charges");

---

[17] P. 166, post.

[18] P. 29, ante.

[19] LLCA 1975, s. 6.

[20] This includes a variety of prohibitions of and restrictions on the user or mode of user of land or buildings, other than planning charges.

[1] Now New Towns Act 1981, ss. 1 (5), 12.

[2] Now Civil Aviation Act 1982, s. 55 (1).

Part 10, for charges falling within section 54(6) of the Town and Country Planning Act 1971 ("listed buildings charges");

Part 11, for charges falling within section 2(4) of the Rights of Light Act 1959 ("light obstruction notices");[3]

Part 12, for charges falling within section 31(4) of the Land Drainage Act 1976 ("drainage scheme charges").

ii. COMPANIES

A register is maintained by the Registrar of Companies under the Companies Act 1985 of land charges created by a company for securing money[4].

LAND CHARGES ACT 1972

3. Registration of land charges. — (7) In the case of a land charge for securing money created by a company before 1st January 1970 or so created at any time as a floating charge, registration under any of the enactments mentioned in subsection (8) below shall be sufficient in place of registration under this Act, and shall have effect as if the land charge had been registered under this Act[5].

(8) The enactments referred to in subsection (7) above are section 93 of the Companies (Consolidation) Act 1908, section 79 of the Companies Act 1929, section 95 of the Companies Act 1948 and sections 395 to 398 of the Companies Act 1985[6].

COMPANIES ACT 1985

395. Certain charges void if not registered. — (1) Subject to the provisions of this Chapter, a charge created by a company registered in England and Wales and being a charge to which this section applies is, so far as any security on the company's property or undertaking is conferred by the charge, void against the liquidator and any creditor of the company, unless the prescribed particulars of the charge together with the instrument (if any) by which the charge is created or evidenced, are delivered to or received by the registrar of companies for registration in the manner required by this Chapter within 21 days after the date of the charge's creation.

(2) Subsection (1) is without prejudice to any contract or obligation for repayment of the money secured by the charge; and when a charge becomes void under this section, the money secured by it immediately becomes payable.

---

[3] P. 639, post.

[4] Records are microfilmed and can be inspected at Crown Way, Maindy, Cardiff and Companies House, City Road, London. A limited company must also keep a register of charges at its registered office: Companies Act 1985, ss. 406–409. See generally *Buckley on the Companies Acts* (14th edn), vol 1, pp. 238–269; generally *Gore-Brown on Companies* (43rd edn) 18-11-18-39; Palmer, *Company Law* (23rd edn chap. 45). The Secretary of State for Trade and Industry has initiated an enquiry to consider reforms of the Companies Act provisions on the registration of charges: HC Deb, 17 December 1985, col. 136.

[5] *Property Discount Corpn Ltd v Lyon Group Ltd* [1981] 1 WLR 300, [1981] 1 All ER 379 (registration in companies register held sufficient, even though it was not in name of estate owner as required by LCA 1972, s. 3 (1), p. 33, ante); [1982] Conv 43 (D. M. Hare and T. Flanagan).

[6] As amended by Companies Consolidation (Consequential Provisions) Act 1985, s. 30, Sch. 2.

396. Charges which have to be registered. — (1) Section 395 applies to the following charges —

    (*a*) a charge for the purpose of securing any issue of debentures,

    (*b*) a charge on uncalled share capital of the company,

    (*c*) a charge created or evidenced by an instrument which, if executed by an individual, would require registration as a bill of sale[7],

    (*d*) a charge on land (wherever situated) or any interest in it, but not including a charge for any rent or other periodical sum issuing out of the land[8],

    (*e*) a charge on book debts of the company[9],

    (*f*) a floating charge on the company's undertaking or property[10],

    (*g*) a charge on calls made but not paid,

    (*h*) a charge on a ship· or aircraft, or any share in a ship,

    (*j*) a charge on goodwill, on a patent or a licence under a patent, on a trademark or on a copyright or a licence under a copyright.

(2) Where a negotiable instrument has been given to secure the payment of any book debts of a company, the deposit of the instrument for the purpose of securing an advance to the company is not, for purposes of section 395, to be treated as a charge on those book debts.

(3) The holding of debentures entitling the holder to a charge on land is not for purposes of this section deemed to be an interest in land.

(4) In this Chapter, "charge" includes mortgage[11].

399. Company's duty to register charges it creates. — (1) It is a company's duty to send to the registrar of companies for registration the particulars of every charge created by the company and of the issues of debentures of a series requiring registration under sections 395 to 398; but registration of any such charge may be effected on the application of any person interested in it.

iii. AGRICULTURAL CHARGES

AGRICULTURAL CREDITS ACT 1928[12]

5. Agricultural charges on farming stock and assets. — (1) It shall be lawful for a farmer as defined by this Act by instrument in writing to create in favour of a bank as so defined a charge (hereinafter referred to as an agricultural charge) on all or any of the farming stock and other agricultural

---

[7] *Borden (UK) Ltd v Scottish Timber Products Ltd* [1981] Ch 25, [1979] 3 All ER 961. Charges created by companies are exempt from registration under Bills of Sale Acts 1878 and 1882.

[8] *Re Molton Finance Ltd* [1968] Ch 325, [1967] 3 All ER 843 (equitable sub-mortgage); *Re Wallis & Simmonds (Builders) Ltd* [1974] 1 WLR 391, [1974] 1 All ER 561 (equitable charge by deposit of title deeds).

[9] *Re Peachdart Ltd* [1984] Ch 131, [1983] 3 All ER 204; *Re Welsh Irish Ferries Ltd* [1985] 3 WLR 610.

[10] *Re Bond Worth Ltd* [1980] Ch 228, [1979] 3 All ER 919.

[11] See also s. 400 which provides for the registration of charges existing on property acquired by a company: *Capital Finance Co Ltd v Stokes* [1969] 1 Ch 261, [1968] 3 All ER 625; *Burston Finance Ltd v Speirway Ltd* [1974] 1 WLR 1648, [1974] 3 All ER 735.

[12] Agricultural Credits Regulations 1928 (S.R. & O. 1928 No. 667/L 25); Agricultural Credits Fees Order 1975 (SI 1975 No. 1314). In 1983–84 there were 2,665 new registrations, 1,040 cancellations and rectifications and 7,099 searches: Report of Chief Land Registrar for 1984–85, para. 51. The register is kept at the Land Registry at Plymouth.

assets belonging to him as security for sums advanced or to be advanced to him or paid or to be paid on his behalf under any guarantee by the bank and interest, commission and charges thereon.

9. Registration of agricultural charges. — (1) Every agricultural charge shall be registered under this Act within seven clear days after the execution thereof, and, if not so registered, shall be void as against any person other than the farmer:

Provided that the High Court on proof that omission to register within such time as aforesaid was accidental or due to inadvertence may extend the time for registration on such terms as the Court thinks fit.

(2) The Land Registrar shall keep at the Land Registry a register of agricultural charges in such form and containing such particulars as may be prescribed.

(8) Registration of an agricultural charge under this section shall be deemed to constitute actual notice of the charge, and of the fact of such registration, to all persons and for all purposes connected with the property comprised in the charge, as from the date of registration or other prescribed date, and so long as the registration continues in force:

Provided that, where an agricultural charge created in favour of a bank is expressly made for securing a current account or other further advances, the bank, in relation to the making of further advances under the charge, shall not be deemed to have notice of another agricultural charge by reason only that it is so registered if it was not so registered at the time when the first-mentioned charge was created or when the last search (if any) by or on behalf of the bank was made, whichever last happened.

iv.   COMMONS AND TOWN AND VILLAGE GREENS[13]

COMMONS REGISTRATION ACT 1965

1.[14] Registration of commons and town or village greens and owner-ship of and rights over them. — (1) There shall be registered, in accordance with the provisions of this Act and subject to the exceptions mentioned therein[15], —

    (a) land in England or Wales which is common land or a town or village green;

    (b) rights of common over such land; and

    (c) persons claiming to be or found to be owners of such land or becoming the owners thereof by virtue of this Act;

---

[13] C & B, pp. 535–536; M & W, pp. 895–897; MM, p. 429. See generally Harris and Ryan, *Outline of the Law relating to Common Land and Public Access to the Countryside* (1967); Clayden, *Our Common Land* (1985); [1977] JPL 352 (R. Vane); Report of Royal Commission on Common Land, 1955–1958 (Cmnd 462); (1972) 122 NLJ 1127 (V. Chapman). Decisions of the Commons Commissioners are reported in Campbell, *Decisions of the Commons Commissioners* (1972), in Current Law and in the Annual Reports of Commons, Open Spaces and Footpaths Preservation Society. See (1973) 117 SJ 537; (1974) 118 SJ 434 (I. Campbell). The office is at Golden Cross House, Duncannon Street, London.

[14] Commons Registration (General) Regulations 1966 (SI No. 1471), as amended by SI 1968 No. 658; SI 1980 No. 1195; SI 1982 Nos. 209, 210.

[15] The Act does not apply to the New Forest, Epping Forest or to any land exempted by an order of the Secretary of State, s. 11: Commons Registration (Exempted Land) Regulations 1965 (SI 1965 No. 2001).

and no rights of common over land which is capable of being registered under this Act shall be registered under the Land Registration Acts 1925 and 1936.

(2) After the end of such period, not being less than three years from the commencement of this Act, as the Minister may by order determine[16] —

    (a) no land capable of being registered under this Act shall be deemed to be common land or a town or village green unless it is so registered; and

    (b) no rights of common shall be exercisable over any such land unless they are registered either under this Act or under the Land Registration Acts 1925 and 1936[17].

2. Registration authorities. — (1) The registration authority for the purposes of this Act shall be —

    (a) in relation to any land situated in any county, the council of that county[18]; or, if the county is a metropolitan county, the council of the metropolitan district in which the land is situated[18a]; and

    (b) in relation to any land situated in Greater London, the council of the London borough in which the land is situated . . .[18a]

3. The registers. — (1) For the purposes of registering such land as is mentioned in section 1 (1) of this Act and rights of common over and ownership of such land every registration authority shall maintain —

    (a) a register of common land; and

    (b) a register of town or village greens;

and regulations under this Act may require or authorise a registration authority to note on those registers such other information as may be prescribed.

(2) Any register maintained under this Act shall be open to inspection by the public at all reasonable times.

22. Interpretation. — (1) In this Act, unless the context otherwise requires, —

"common land" means —

    (a) land subject to rights of common (as defined in this Act) whether those rights are exercisable at all times or only during limited periods;

    (b) waste land of a manor not subject to rights of common[19];

but does not include a town or village green or any land which forms part of a highway;

"rights of common" includes cattlegates or beastgates (by whatever name known) and rights of sole or several vesture or herbage or of sole or several

---

[16] 31 July 1970. Commons Registration (Time Limits) Order 1966 (SI 1966 No. 1470), as amended by Commons Registration (Time Limits) (Amendment) Order 1970 (SI 1970 No. 383). Applications for registration had to be made before 3 January 1970. For registration where land becomes common land or a town or village green after 2 January 1970, see Commons Registration (New Land) Regulations 1969 (SI 1969 No. 1843).

[17] *Central Electricity Generating Board v Clwyd County Council* [1976] 1 WLR 151, [1976] 1 All ER 251; *Re Turnworth Down, Dorset* [1978] Ch 251, [1977] 2 All ER 105.

[18] As amended by Local Government Act 1972, s. 272 (1), Sch. 30.

[18a] As amended by LGA 1985, s. 16, Sch. 8, para. 10 (6).

[19] *Re Britford Common* [1977] 1 WLR 39, [1977] 1 All ER 532; *Re Box Hill Common* [1980] Ch 109, [1979] 1 All ER 113; *Re Yateley Common, Hampshire* [1977] 1 WLR 840, [1977] 1 All ER 505; *Re Chewton Common* [1977] 1 WLR 1242, [1977] 3 All ER 509; *Baxendale v Instow Parish Council* [1982] Ch 14, [1981] 2 All ER 620.

pasture, but does not include rights held for a term of years or from year to year;

"town or village green" means land which has been allotted by or under any Act for the exercise or recreation of the inhabitants of any locality or on which the inhabitants of any locality have a customary right[20] to indulge in lawful sports and pastimes or on which the inhabitants of any locality have indulged in such sports and pastimes as of right for not less than twenty years[1].

10. Effect of registration. — The registration under this Act of any land as common land or as a town or village green, or of any rights of common over any such land, shall be conclusive evidence of the matters registered, as at the date of registration, except where the registration is provisional only.

———————

Registration under the Act may be final or provisional. It is final if no objection was lodged before August 1972[2]; and final registration is conclusive evidence of the matters registered at the date of registration[3]. If there is any such objection, the registration is provisional, and only becomes final if it is confirmed after a hearing before a Commons Commissioner[4]. There is a right of appeal from his decision by a person aggrieved to the High Court on a point of law[5]. There are three full time and one part time Commissioners. In 1983 some 1,350 disputed registrations and 1,880 claims to ownership remained to be heard by the Commissioners[6].

After July 1970, no land capable of being registered under the Act is to be deemed to be common land unless it is so registered, and no rights of common shall be exercisable over any such land unless they are either

———————

[20] Unaccompanied local children, picnicking, fishing in a pond, collecting bullrushes and picking mushrooms; local children, accompanied by adults, playing, picking blackberries, and studying fish and plant life; local adults picnicking, taking dogs for walks, and fishing in the pond held to amount to pastimes indulged in as of right: *Re White Lane Pond, Four Dales and Clay Pits, Thorne and Stainforth, South Yorkshire (No. 1)* [1984] CLY 287; cf. *Re River Don and its Banks* [1984] CLY 284, where it was held that walking with or without dogs along the banks of the River was not indulging.

[1] *Re The Rye, High Wycombe, Bucks* [1977] 1 WLR 1316, [1977] 3 All ER 521. 20 years means 20 years immediately preceding the passing of the Act (5 August 1965); *New Windsor Corpn v Mellor* [1975] Ch 380, [1975] 3 All ER 44.

[2] Commons Registration (Objections and Maps) Regulations 1968, SI 1968 No. 989, as amended by SI 1970 No. 384; *Smith v East Sussex County Counil* (1977) 76 LGR 332.

[3] Commons Registration Act 1965, s. 10; *New Windsor Corpn v Mellor*, supra at 392, at 51, per Lord DENNING MR; *Cooke v Amey Gravel Co Ltd* [1972] 1 WLR 1310, [1972] 3 All ER 579 (provisional registration is itself no evidence of the existence of the right registered); *Corpus Christi College Oxford v Gloucestershire County Council* [1983] QB 360, [1982] 3 All ER 995 (registration conclusive even where entry on register was wrong).

[4] Ibid., ss. 4–7; Commons Commissioners Regulations 1971 (SI 1971 No. 1727); Commons Registration (Second Period References) Regulations 1973 (SI 1973 No. 815). The onus of establishing the validity of the registration is on the person making the registration; *Re Sutton Common Wimborne* [1982] 1 WLR 647, [1982] 2 All ER 376; *Re West Anstey Common* [1985] Ch 329, [1985] 1 All ER 618.

[5] Ibid., s. 18. See *Wilkes v Gee* [1973] 1 WLR 742, [1973] 2 All ER 1214; *R v Chief Commons Comr, ex p Constable* (1977) 37 P & CR 67; *Re Tillmire Common, Heslington* [1982] 2 All ER 615.

[6] House of Commons, 29 March 1983. This backlog was expected to take until at least the end of 1985 to clear.

registered under the Act or have been previously registered under the Land Registration Act 1925[7].

The Commons Registration Act "is ill-drafted and has given rise to many difficulties."[8]

QUESTIONS

1. Why is no provision made in unregistered land for the registration of equitable beneficial interests?

2. Francis David Blackburn entered into a contract to sell a house to a purchaser who registered the contract as an estate contract against the name of Frank David Blackburn, which was the name in which Francis David Blackburn carried on business as an estate agent.

   Is the registration valid:

   (a) against a mortgagee who does not search?

   (b) against a mortgagee who searches against the name of Francis David Blackburn and receives a nil certificate?

   (c) against a mortgagee who searches against the name of Francis Davis Blackburn and receives a nil certificate?

   See *Oak Co-Operative Building Society v Blackburn* [1967] Ch 1169, [1967] 2 All ER 340, reversed [1968] Ch 730, [1968] 2 All ER 117; LCA 1972, s. 10 (4); *Du Sautoy v Symes* [1967] Ch 1146, [1967] 1 All ER 25; (1968) 84 LQR 303 (PVB); *Diligent Finance Co Ltd v Alleyne* (1972) 23 P & CR 346; Ruoff, *Searching Without Tears* (1974), Chaps. 9, 10, 11. As to errors in searches in respect of registered titles, see LRA 1925, s. 83 (3), p. 150, post, and *Parkash v Irani Finance Ltd* [1970] Ch 101, [1969] 1 All ER 930.

   Of what significance would be the fact that the erroneous entry or certificate was due to the negligence of a clerk in the Land Registry?

   See *Ministry of Housing and Local Government v Sharp* [1970] 2 QB 223, [1970] 1 All ER 1009; *Coats Patons (Retail) Ltd v Birmingham Corpn* (1971) 69 LGR 356; LCA 1972, s. 10.

3. Is a decision that an equitable right or interest is registrable likely to improve or reduce its prospects of being enforceable against third parties?

   See *ER Ives Investment Ltd v High* [1967] 2 QB 379, [1967] 1 All ER 504, p. 542, post; *Shiloh Spinners Ltd v Harding* [1973] AC 691, [1973] 1 All ER 90, p. 34, ante.

4. Consider how the registration of a non-existent land charge can prejudicially affect a land owner. Should the Land Registrar be required to find a prima facie case for registration before adding a charge to the register?

   See MEGARRY J in *Thomas v Rose* [1968] 1 WLR 1797 at 1805, [1968] 3 All ER 765 at 769, and *Rawlplug Co Ltd v Kamvale Properties Ltd* (1969)

---

[7] Commons Registration Act 1965, s. 1 (2); SI 1970 No. 383; *Central Electricity Generating Board v Clwyd County Council* [1976] 1 WLR 151, [1976] 1 All ER 251 (right of common not registered by closing date held to be extinguished); *Re Turnworth Down, Dorset* [1978] Ch 251, [1977] 2 All ER 105. For the liability of a solicitor who failed to search the register, see *G and K Ladenbau (UK) Ltd v Crawley and De Reya* [1978] 1 WLR 266, [1978] 1 All ER 682.

[8] *Corpus Christi College Oxford v Gloucestershire County Council*, supra, at 370, at 1002, per Lord DENNING MR. There is to be further legislation about the management and improvement of registered common land as well as about its user by the public. The Department of the Environment issued a consultative document in 1978.

On the difficulties, see (1982) 126 SJ 405 (K. Heynes); (1982) 126 SJ 815 (G. D. Gadsden); (1982) 132 NLJ 956 (R. Annand); (1984) 81 LSG 3401 (D. Green); [1985] Conv 24 (A. Samuels) which contains a detailed bibliography.

20 P & CR 32 at 39; (1968) 118 NLJ 1167; and BRIGHTMAN J in *Jones v Morgan* (1973) 231 EG 1167; p. 30, n. 7, ante.

Consider this in the context of the Matrimonial Homes Act 1983; see MEGARRY J in *Miles v Bull* [1969] 1 QB 258 at 261, [1968] 3 All ER 632 at 634; *Wroth v Tyler* [1974] Ch 30, [1973] 1 All ER 897, p. 262, post.

5. Could/should the Land Charges Act 1925 have established a better system of registration than that of registration against the name of the estate owner? Report of the Committee on Land Charges (the Roxburgh Committee) 1956 (Cmd. 9825); Report on Land Charges Affecting Unregistered Land 1969 (Law Com. No. 18 HC 125); LPA 1969, s. 25, p. 40 ante.

6. Consider —
   (i) the moral and other difficulties which are raised by allowing a purchaser with notice to ignore an equitable interest of which he is aware;
   (ii) the legal difficulties of allowing the Register to be overridden by the doctrine of constructive notice;
   (iii) the absurdity of putting a purchaser with his eyes shut in a better position than one with his eyes open.

D. Mere Equities[9]

A mere equity (rescission for fraud, undue influence, rectification for mistake, the rights to consolidation or to reopen a foreclosure, and, perhaps, an equitable right of entry), as opposed to an equitable interest, is not binding on a bona fide purchaser of an equitable interest for value without notice.

Lord WESTBURY in *Phillips v Phillips* (1862) 4 De GF & J 208, when speaking of the occasions on which the ordinary rules of priority in point of time among claimants in equity would be disturbed by the doctrine of bona fide purchaser, said at 218:

"Thirdly, where there are circumstances that give rise to an equity as distinguished from an equitable estate — as for example, an equity to set aside a deed for fraud, or to correct it for mistake — and the purchaser under the instrument maintains the plea of purchaser for valuable consideration without notice, the court will not interfere."

III. Creation and Transfer of Estates and Interests

A. Legal Estates. Contract and Conveyance

i. CONTRACT[10]

A contract usually precedes the conveyance which in unregistered land effects the transfer of the legal estate to a purchaser; and a contract also usually precedes a transfer in registered land. In practice such contracts are generally in standard form. The Law Society's General Conditions of Sale (1984 Revision) and the National Conditions of Sale (20th edn 1981) are

---

[9] [1955] CLJ 160–161 (H. W. R. Wade); (1955) Conv (NS) 346 (F. R. Crane); H & M, pp. 875–882; Snell, p. 26; C & B, pp. 60–61; (1976) 40 Conv (NS) 209 (A. R. Everton).

[10] C & B, chap. 6; M & W, chap. 12; MM, pp. 134–147; Barnsley, *Conveyancing Law and Practice* (2nd edn, 1982), chaps. 5 and 6; Farrand, *Contract and Conveyance* (4th edn, 1983), chaps. 2 and 3.

both standard forms of contract containing a set of general conditions of sale[11]. They are usually employed with such alterations as the parties may make for the purpose of the particular transaction.

A contract for the sale or other disposition of land must comply with the general rules of the law of contract. Thus, it must be a final and complete agreement between the parties on its essential terms[12], i.e. the parties, the property, the consideration and the interest to be granted. It is usual to make a preliminary agreement "subject to contract", the effect of which is that, until a formal contract has been concluded, there is no contract and either party can withdraw from the negotiations with impunity[13].

Further, a valid contract for the sale or other disposition of land will only be enforceable by action, if there is a sufficient memorandum in writing that complies with section 40 of the Law of Property Act 1925, or, failing that, if there is a sufficient act of part performance.

(a) *Formalities*[14]

LAW OF PROPERTY ACT 1925

40. Contracts for sale, &c., of land to be in writing. — (1) No action may be brought upon any contract for the sale or other disposition of land or any interest in land, unless the agreement upon which such action is brought, or some memorandum or note thereof, is in writing, and signed by the party to be charged or by some other person thereunto by him lawfully authorised.

(2) This section applies to contracts whether made before or after the commencement of this Act and does not affect the law relating to part performance, or sales by the court.

46. Forms of contracts and conditions of sale. — The Lord Chancellor may from time to time prescribe and publish forms of contracts and conditions of sale of land, and the forms so prescribed[15] shall, subject to any modification, or any stipulation or intention to the contrary, expressed in the correspondence, apply to contracts by correspondence[16], and may, but only

---

[11] Wilkinson, *Standard Conditions of Sale of Land* (3rd edn 1982); Silverman, *Standard Conditions of Sale* (1983); Aldridge, *Guide to Law Society's Conditions of Sale* (2nd edn. 1984); *Guide to National Conditions of Sale* (1981); [1980] Conv 404 (H. W. Wilkinson); [1982] Conv 85 (IND); [1984] Conv 396. See also *Conveyancing Lawyers' Conditions of Sale* (1978); (1979) 129 NLJ 286 (H. W. Wilkinson); [1981] Conv 38.

[12] See, e.g., *Fletcher v Davies* (1980) 257 EG 1149 (flat in Inner Temple).

[13] See *Alpenstow Ltd v Regalian Properties plc* [1985] 1 WLR 721, [1985] 2 All ER 545, where this effect was displaced in "a very strong and exceptional context"; The Law Commission Report on "Subject to Contract" Agreements 1975 (Law Com No. 65, HC 119) recommended no change in the present law and practice. [1984] Conv 173, 251 (R. W. Clark), comparing English and Irish law.

[14] C & B, pp. 112–117; M & W, pp. 571–587; MM, pp. 136–141; Farrand, pp. 32–49; Cheshire and Fifoot, *Law of Contract* (10th edn, 1981), pp. 183–190; Barnsley, pp. 110–116; (1967) 31 Conv (NS) 182, 254 (H. W. Wilkinson), suggesting reform. The Law Commission is examining LPA 1925, s. 40: Annual Report 1984–1985 (Law Com No. 155 HC 247), para. 2.29. See Second Report of the Conveyancing Committee: Conveyancing Qualifications, paras. 7.4–11, 9.36, "strongly recommending" a stricter form of contract for domestic conveyancing as part of a new Sale of Land Act; Law Commission Working Paper No. 92 Formalities for Contracts of Sale etc. of Land (1985), outlining various suggestions for reform.

[15] S R & O 1925, No. 779.

[16] *Stearn v Twitchell* [1985] 1 All ER 631 (contract arising out of acceptance by single letter of oral offer to buy or sell land held not to be contract by correspondence).

by express reference thereto, be made to apply to any other cases for which the forms are made available.

(b) Subject to Contract

TIVERTON ESTATES LTD v WEARWELL LTD[17]
[1975] Ch 146, [1974] 1 All ER 209 (CA, Lord DENNING MR, STAMP and SCARMAN LJJ)

On 4 July 1973, Tiverton Estates Ltd, the registered proprietors of the lease of Empire House, Stepney, orally agreed to sell it to Wearwell Ltd for £190,000. On the same day, Wearwell Ltd's solicitors wrote to Tiverton Estates Ltd's solicitors: "We understand that you act for the vendor in respect of the proposed sale . . . to our clients . . . at £190,000 leasehold subject to contract."

On 9 July Tiverton Estates Ltd's solicitors replied: "We refer to your letter dated the 4 July, upon which we have taken our clients' instructions. We now send you draft contract for approval . . .". On 19 July, Tiverton Estates Ltd decided not to go on with the sale. Wearwell Ltd lodged a caution to prevent dealings with the lease. Tiverton Estates Ltd asked for an order that the registration of the caution be vacated. The question was whether the letter of 9 July together with the draft contract was a sufficient memorandum of the oral agreement of 4 July to satisfy section 40 of the Law of Property Act 1925.

Held. Vacation of the register ordered. There was no sufficient memorandum.

LORD DENNING MR: So I turn to the point of substance, which is this: is there any writing sufficient to satisfy the Statute of Frauds, now section 40 of the Law of Property Act 1925. . . .

During the argument before us, it became clear that there are two lines of authority to be considered. According to the one line, in order to satisfy the statute, the writing must contain, not only the terms of the contract, *but also* an express or implied recognition that a contract was actually entered into.

According to the other line, it is *not necessary* that the writing should acknowledge the *existence* of a contract. It is sufficient if the contract is by word of mouth and that the *terms* can be found set out in writing without any recognition whatsoever that any contract was ever made.

[1] *Sale of goods cases which require recognition of a contract*
This line of authority is derived from a problem which arose under section 17 of the Statute of Frauds which required a writing in the case of the sale of goods over £10. The seller would write a letter demanding payment. The purchaser would write denying liability on the ground that the goods were not up to contract and he had rejected them. . . .

It was essential that the writing should contain an admission of the existence of the contract and of all the terms of it. If it failed to do so, it was not sufficient to satisfy the statute. That is plain from the decision of this court in *Thirkell v Cambi* [1919] 2 KB 590. . . .

The requirement of writing [for contracts of sale of goods] was repealed on 4 June 1954, by the Law Reform (Enforcement of Contracts) Act 1954. But

---

[17] (1974) 38 Conv (NS) 127 (F. R. Crane). See generally *Emmet on Title* (18th edn, 1983), pp. 48, 58; Barnsley, pp. 101–108.

those cases on sale of goods are of good authority in relation to the sale of land. The words of sections 4 and 17 of the Statute of Frauds are so similar as to preclude any distinction between them. In *Re Hoyle* [1893] 1 Ch 84 at 99, Bowen LJ so treated them.

[2] *The "offer cases" requiring only the terms to be set down in writing*
This line of authority is derived from a problem which arose when one party made an offer in writing which was accepted by the other party by word of mouth or by conduct. It has always been held that the party who signed the offer was bound by it. The contract could be enforced against him, but he could not enforce it against the other. The first of this line was an obiter dictum in 1856 in *Warner v Willington* (1856) 3 Drew 523 at 532, which was approved in the next year by the Court of Common Pleas in *Smith v Neale* (1857) 2 CBNS 67 at 88 and established beyond doubt by a strong Court of Exchequer Chamber in *Reuss v Picksley* (1866) LR 1 Exch 342. In that case Willes J, giving the judgment of the court, said, at 351:
". . . The only question is, whether it is sufficient to satisfy the statute that the party charged should sign what he proposes as an agreement, and that the other party should afterwards assent without writing to the proposal? As to this it is clear, both on reasoning and authority, that the proposal so signed and assented to, does become a memorandum or note of an agreement within section 4 of the statute."
Now, I can well understand the reason why the courts established this doctrine about a written offer. Very often the offer was accepted by conduct. A good instance is where a man gives a guarantee in writing for the price of goods thereafter to be supplied to a buyer. Once the seller supplies the goods, he can sue on the guarantee. In *Reuss v Picksley*, the defendant made in writing an offer to the plaintiffs of an agency for Russia for 10 years, if the plaintiffs would bear a part of the expenses of an exhibition. The plaintiffs accepted the offer by conduct. They sent goods to the exhibition at much expense. They thus accepted a written offer. It would be most unfortunate if they could not thereafter sue upon it. It was held that they could. Seeing that the common law knew nothing of the doctrine of part performance (see *Britain v Rossiter* (1879) 11 QBD 123), these decisions — about the acceptance of a written offer — were very necessary to meet the justice of the case. They were bold decisions on the words of the statute, just as were the decisions in equity on part performance: see *Britain v Rossiter* (1879) 11 QBD 123 at 129 approved in *Maddison v Alderson* (1883) 8 App Cas 467. That is perfectly plain from a comment made by Bowen LJ on the offer cases. He said in *Re New Eberhardt Co, ex p Menzies* (1889) 43 ChD 118 at 129:
". . . We are bound by *Reuss v Picksley*, and that no doubt pushed the literal construction of the Statute of Frauds to a limit beyond which it would perhaps be not easy to go".
I would only add this. It is well settled that a written offer accepted orally or by word of mouth is a contract in writing: see *Mercantile Bank of Sydney v Taylor* [1893] AC 317 at 321 and *L'Estrange v F Graucob Ltd* [1934] 2 KB 394 at 405. So these cases come with the words of the statute as an "agreement in writing."

[3] *The "subject to contract" cases*
During the last three years the "offer cases" have been extended far beyond the limit thus set by Bowen LJ. They have been stretched so as to cover

correspondence which is expressly stated to be "subject to contract." This was done because the "offer cases" were thought to support a wide principle which was stated in these words by Buckley LJ in *Law v Jones* [1974] Ch 112 at 124, [1973] 2 All ER 437 at 444:

". . . it is not, in my judgment, necessary that the note or memorandum should acknowledge the existence of a contract. It is not the fact of agreement but the terms agreed upon that must be found recorded in writing."

In accordance with that principle, this court held that a solicitor's letter setting out terms "subject to contract" was a sufficient writing to satisfy the statute.

The court said that the words "subject to contract" are a suspensive condition which can be waived by subsequent oral agreement between the parties. They can be removed from the document by oral evidence: see *Griffiths v Young* [1970] Ch 675, [1970] 3 All ER 601, by Widgery LJ at 685, at 607, by Cross LJ at 686, at 608 and by Russell LJ at 687, at 609 and *Law v Jones*, at 126, at 445, by Buckley LJ.

This court acknowledged that a letter which denied the very existence of a contract would not satisfy the statute: see *Law v Jones*, at 125, at 445, by Buckley LJ. But it held that the words "subject to contract" were not to be treated as a denial of the contract, but only as imposing a suspensive condition, the subsequent waiver of which could be established by oral evidence: see at 128, at 447, by Orr LJ[18].

Law v Jones has sounded an alarm bell in the offices of every solicitor in the land. And no wonder. It is everyday practice for a solicitor, who is instructed in a sale of land, to start the correspondence with a letter "subject to contract" setting out the terms or enclosing a draft. He does it in the confidence that it protects his client. It means that the client is not bound by what has taken place in conversation. The reason is that, for over a hundred years, the courts have held that the effect of the words "subject to contract" is that the matter remains in negotiation until a formal contract is executed: see *Eccles v Bryant and Pollock* [1948] Ch 93, [1947] 2 All ER 865. But *Law v Jones* has taken away all protection from the client. The plaintiff can now assert an oral contract in conversation with the defendant *before* the solicitor wrote the letter and then rely on the letter as a writing to satisfy the statute, even though it was expressly "subject to contract": or, alternatively, the plaintiff can assert that *after* the solicitor wrote the letter, he met the defendant and in conversation orally agreed to waive the words "subject to contract." If this is right, it means that the client is exposed to the full blast of "frauds and perjuries" attendant on oral testimony. Even without fraud or perjury, he is exposed to honest difference of recollections leading to law suits, from which it was the very object of the statute to save him.

The decision in *Griffiths v Young* [1970] Ch 675, [1970] 3 All ER 601 can be justified on other grounds. It would appear that, after the initial oral contract, there was a new and separate oral contract on 3 May 1963, of which the letter of 3 May was a sufficient memorandum. Alternatively, the letter of 3 May was an offer in writing which was accepted by the giving of a guarantee.

---

[18] See the "explanatory observations" by BUCKLEY LJ, with which ORR LJ "entirely agreed", in *Daulia Ltd v Four Millbank Nominees Ltd* [1978] Ch 231 at 249, [1978] 2 All ER 557 at 569.

The decision in *Law v Jones* cannot be, however, justified on other grounds. Was it correctly decided? I do not think it was. Russell LJ dissented from the majority. I find his reasoning convincing. Take an imaginary case where there is said to have been an oral contract between vendor and purchaser. The vendor writes: "This is to confirm our agreement today, whereby you agreed to buy Blackacre for £10,000."

1.   The purchaser writes back: "I know we discussed the purchase of Blackacre for £10,000: but we did not come to any agreement about it." Clearly that is no sufficient memorandum.

2.   The purchaser writes back: "I agree that, in the course of negotiation, we had arrived at a figure of £10,000 for Blackacre, but the whole matter is still in the course of negotiation: we have not finally agreed." That would also be no sufficient memorandum. It cannot be distinguished from the first case.

3.   The purchaser writes back: "I know that I agreed to buy Blackacre for £10,000, but I made it clear to you that it was subject to contract, and I repeat it now. It was all subject to contract." That, too, is no sufficient memorandum. It cannot be distinguished from the second case.

I cannot myself see any difference between a writing which — (i) denies there was any contract; (ii) does not admit there was any contract; (iii) says that the parties are in negotiation; or (iv) says that there was an agreement "subject to contract", for that comes to the same thing. The reason why none of those writings satisfies the statute is because none of them contains any recognition or admission of the existence of a contract.

[4]   *Is this court bound by Law v Jones?*

In my opinion ... we are not bound to follow *Law v Jones*. The legal profession should be freed from the anxieties which beset them. It should be done at once without delay. I would, therefore, hold here and now that *Law v Jones* was wrongly decided and should be overruled. The writing here, being expressly "subject to contract," was not sufficient to satisfy the statute. There is no enforceable contract between the parties. There was no sufficient reason for entering a caution on the register. It should be vacated at once. . . .

[5]   *Other points*

Such is sufficient for the decision of this case. But I may say that there is another fatal objection to the alleged note or memorandum. It does not contain all the terms of the oral contract as sworn to by Mr. Nadir in his affidavit. The draft omits the term that: "within a short time of completion, the Tiverton company would move out, giving vacant possession of the parts of the premises occupied by his company." The draft adds a term that: "the prescribed rate of interest will be 12 per cent per annum." Those seem to me to be material terms which, being omitted from the note or memorandum, are fatal to its validity: see *Hawkins v Price* [1947] Ch 645, [1947] 1 All ER 689[19].

---

[19] See *Sherbrooke v Dipple* (1980) 41 P & CR 173; *Cohen v Nessdale Ltd* [1982] 2 All ER 97 (where the parties have started negotiations under a subject to contract formula, their later negotiations will continue to be qualified by it until they agree expressly or by necessary implication that the qualification be expunged); [1981] Conv 165; [1982] Conv 71 (M. P. Thompson).

(c) *The Doctrine of Part Performance*[20]

In the absence of a note or memorandum as required by the Law of Property
Act 1925, s. 40, equity will decree specific performance of an oral agreement
if there are acts sufficient to satisfy the equitable doctrine of part performance.

In applying this doctrine, "the defendant is really 'charged' upon the
equities resulting from the acts done in execution of the contract, and not
(within the meaning of the statute) upon the contract itself." When will this
be done? Before *Steadman v Steadman* [1976] AC 536, [1974] 2 All ER 977,
infra, the authorities indicated that the doctrine applied if "the acts in
question be such as must be referred to some contract and may be referred to
the alleged one: that they prove the existence of some contract and are
consistent with the contract alleged[2]." Thus, in *Kingswood Estate Co Ltd v
Anderson* [1963] 2 QB 169, [1962] 3 All ER 593, a widow vacated rent-
controlled premises in favour of others provided by her landlord under an
oral agreement that she would be permitted to remain there for the rest of her
life. She was able to set up the oral agreement in answer to a claim for
possession by the landlord. And in *Wakeham v Mackenzie* [1968] 1 WLR 1175,
[1968] 2 All ER 783, Mr. Ball, a widower of 72, orally agreed with Mrs.
Wakeham, a widow of 67, that if she would give up her council flat, move
into his house and look after him and the home for no wages, he would leave
his house and contents to her in his will. After he died without making
provision for her, she was able to enforce the contract. In *Maddison v Alderson*
(1883) 8 App Cas 467, where a housekeeper continued in service in a similar
situation, the House of Lords took the view that the housekeeper could not
enforce the contract because "her mere continuance in Thomas Alderson's
service . . . was not such an act as to be in itself evidence of a new contract,
much less of a contract concerning her master's land[3]."

The acts of part performance commonly involve a change of possession;
but not necessarily. In *Rawlinson v Ames* [1925] Ch 96, the landlord of a flat
made alterations to premises in accordance with the wishes of the defendant
who had orally agreed to take a lease of the flat. Specific performance was
granted. But it had been laid down that money payments could never be a
sufficient act of part performance. "Payment of money" it was said, ...
raises no equity except possibly a right to recover it back[4]."

The jurisdiction was extended in *Steadman v Steadman*.

---

[20] C & B, pp. 117–122; M & W, pp. 587–599; MM, pp. 141–146; H & M, pp. 665–672; Snell,
    pp. 582–585; Heydon, Gummow and Austin, *Cases and Materials on Equity and Trusts* (2nd edn),
    pp. 815–825.
[1] *Maddison v Alderson* (1883) 8 App Cas 467 at 475, per Lord Selborne LC.
[2] Fry, *Specific Performance* (6th edn.) p. 278, quoted by Stamp J in *Wakeham v Mackenzie* [1968] 1
    WLR 1175 at 1181, [1968] 2 All ER 783 at 787; *New Hart Builders Ltd v Brindley* [1975] Ch 342,
    [1975] 1 All ER 1007.
[3] At p. 480 per Lord Selborne LC.
[4] *Thursby v Eccles* (1900) 49 WR 281 at 282, per Bigham J, quoted by Swinfen Eady LJ in
    Chaproniere v Lambert [1917] 2 Ch 356 at 360.

STEADMAN *v* STEADMAN[5]
[1976] AC 536, [1974] 2 All ER 977 (HL, Lords REID and MORRIS OF BORTH-Y-GEST, Viscount DILHORNE, Lords SIMON OF GLAISDALE and SALMON.)

An oral compromise was made between spouses of various claims by the wife to a half share in the matrimonial home, and £194 arrears of maintenance payments. The compromise was that; (i) the wife should surrender her interest in the house for £1,500; (ii) the wife's maintenance order should be discharged; (iii) the arrears should be remitted if £100 was paid by 30 March; (iv) the maintenance order for the daughter should continue.

The husband paid the £100, and on 2 March, in proceedings before the justices, who were told of the compromise, orders were accordingly made in respect of the maintenance payments.

The husband's solicitors prepared the deed of transfer of the wife's interest in the house. She refused to sign it, and demanded £2,000 for her interest in the house or further maintenance payments. In proceedings under s. 17 of the Married Women's Property Act 1882, the question was whether or not the wife was bound by the oral compromise. She relied on s. 40 of the Law of Property Act 1925.

Held. (Lord MORRIS OF BORTH-Y-GEST dissenting). There were sufficient acts of part performance by the husband, and the compromise was enforceable.

LORD SALMON: During the last 300 years there has been a mass of authority on this topic. Unfortunately many of the cases are irreconcilable with each other and it is by no means easy to discover the true answer to the question with which we are faced, namely, what are the essential elements of part performance in relation to contracts disposing of an interest in land. One rule, however, emerges clearly; a parol contract relating to land cannot be enforced unless the acts relied on as part performance, of themselves, establish a prima facie case that they were done in the performance of a contract. Then, but only then, may parol evidence of the contract be accepted. In order to discover the significance of the alleged acts of part performance, the circumstances in which they were performed must, I think, clearly be relevant. What is perhaps not so clear is whether the acts are sufficient to constitute part performance if they establish only that they were done in the performance of some contract which might but equally well might not be a contract disposing of an interest in land. There is certainly powerful authority for the view that this is not enough but that the acts relied on must of themselves show prima facie that they were done in performance of a contract disposing of such an interest.

It is perhaps not very difficult to see the reason for this view. Acts relied on as part performance which show that a parol contract of the kind referred to in the statute was probably made and that it has been partly performed by the party who seeks to enforce it, raises a substantially stronger equity in his favour than acts which are equally consistent with the existence and part performance of a contract having nothing to do with land. The object of the statute was to prevent a dishonest person from fraudulently inventing a parol contract under which someone was supposed to have disposed of an interest

---

[5] (1974) 38 Conv (NS) 354 (F. R. Crane) 388–391; (1974) 90 LQR 433 (H. W. R. Wade); [1974] CLJ 205 (C. T. Emery).

in land to him and then bringing perjured evidence in support of his claim under the spurious contract. An act which proves that probably a contract for the disposal of an interest in land had been concluded and that the person seeking to enforce it had done his part under it goes further to obviate the mischief at which the statute was aimed than an act which shows merely the existence of some contract which may equally well have nothing to do with land.

The celebrated but perhaps somewhat Delphic passage in the speech of the Earl of Selborne LC in *Maddison v Alderson* (1883) 8 App Cas 467 at 475 which has been cited by my noble and learned friend, Viscount Dilhorne, is not inconsistent with either view. I think, however, that it is plain from other passages in the Earl of Selborne's speech that he took the view, generally held in his time, that for an act of alleged part performance to preclude a defendant from relying on the statute it must be an act "indicative of a contract concerning land". . . .

To my mind, Lord Blackburn clearly agreed with the Earl of Selborne LC that, to take a case out of the statute, the act of part performance must show the existence of a contract concerning land. Indeed, he went a good deal further. He said, at 489:

". . . there are cases that for the purpose of enforcing a specific performance of a contract for the purchase of an interest in land, a delivery of possession of the land will take the case out of the statute.". . .

I respectfully consider that Lord Blackburn went too far in limiting part performance to a change of possession but, in my opinion, all the speeches in *Maddison v Alderson* laid down that acts which prima facie establish the existence of some contract no more likely to be concerned with land than with anything else cannot be sufficient part performance for the purpose of taking a case out of the statute. This expression of opinion may have been obiter because the House concluded that no contract of any kind had been established. Nevertheless, it is a highly persuasive authority and for the reasons I have already indicated, I am not prepared to reject it.

We have certainly been referred to no reported case, and I have found none, in which an act of part performance which did not point to the existence of a contract concerning land has been held sufficient to take the case out of the statute. *Kingswood Estate Co Ltd v Anderson* [1963] 2 QB 169, [1962] 3 All ER 593 did not explode the idea accepted in *Maddison v Alderson* and a host of other cases. It exploded only the idea which had been expressed in some of the older authorities that, in order to take a case out of the statute, the act of part performance had to show not only the existence of a contract concerning land but also the very terms of the contract upon which the party seeking to enforce it relied. In the *Kingswood Estate* case a widow had for 45 years resided in premises of which she had become the statutory tenant. Her landlords were anxious to obtain possession of these premises in order to redevelop them. They acquired other premises to which they asked her to move. Having regard to the value of these premises, the Rent Acts did not apply to them, and she would, therefore, have had no security of tenure except by agreement. She entered into a parol agreement with the landlords under which she agreed to move on the terms that she would be left in possession of the new premises for the rest of her life. After she had moved, the landlords served her with a notice to quit. She set up the parol agreement. The landlords relied on the statute, arguing, unsuccessfully, that although the facts established a contract between them and the tenant relating to land, they did not take the case out of the statute because they did not show that the contract was for a life tenancy; they were equally consistent with a weekly tenancy. In his judgment, Upjohn LJ at 189 cited a passage from *Fry on Specific Performance*, 6th edn., p. 278. . . . That passage in its context does not, in my view, mean more than that if the acts of part performance relate prima facie to some contract concerning land, then parol evidence may be given to show what the terms of that contract are. I think that Upjohn LJ would have been surprised if anything which he said in that case were to be construed as throwing any doubt on the long-established principle that the only acts which can take a case out of the statute are acts which establish prima facie that they were done in part performance of a contract concerning land — especially as the point did not arise for decision since it was there necessarily conceded that the acts relied on did raise such a prima facie case. . . .[6]

It has never been held, nor, so far as I can discover, ever before the present case, suggested, that acts alleged to be in part performance of a parol contract take the contract out of the statute unless they make plain the general nature of the contract. I can find no reason for departing from that principle.

This, however, by no means concludes the appeal. Although I accept the authorities which show that acts of part performance, if they are to take a parol contract out of the statute, must be acts from which the nature of the contract can be deduced, I do not accept the line of authority which, overruling Lord Hardwicke LC in *Lacon v Mertins* (1743) 3 Atk 1 and *Hill v Allen* (1748) 1 Ves Sen 83, laid down that payment can never constitute such an act because it is impossible to deduce from payment the nature of the contract in respect of which the payment is made. It is no doubt true that often it is impossible to deduce even the existence of any contract from payment. For example, a payment by a parent to his child or a husband to his wife is in general no evidence of a contract; indeed, the presumption is to the contrary. Nevertheless the circumstances surrounding a payment may be such that the payment becomes evidence not only of the existence of the contract under which it was made but also of the nature of that contract. What the payment proves in the light of its surrounding circumstances is not a matter of law but a matter of fact. There is no rule of law which excludes evidence of the relevant circumstances surrounding the payment — save parol evidence of the contract on behalf of the person seeking to enforce the contract under which the payment is alleged to have been made.

My Lords, let us assume evidence of the following facts: A is anxious to sell an attractive house at a reasonable price of, say, £20,000. Full particulars of the house are sent to B by A's estate agents. The estate agents tell B, truthfully, that there are several people anxious to buy the house for the price asked but that owing to present economic conditions they have not yet been

---

[6] See *Re Gonin* [1979] Ch 16 at 31, [1977] 2 All ER 720 at 736, where WALTON J followed this view, that the act must be referable to some contract concerning land; [1979] Conv 402 (M. P. Thompson). In *Elsden v Pick* [1980] 1 WLR 898 at 905, [1980] 3 All ER 235 at 240, SHAW LJ said that the act relied on "must be in furtherance of the contract and not merely a recognition of its existence or of its contemplation" but need not amount to "the discharge of any primary obligation imposed by it."

able to complete the necessary financial arrangements. They are expecting to do so at any moment. The estate agent, at B's request, makes an immediate appointment for B to inspect the house and meet A. B keeps the appointment. No written contract of sale comes into existence. B's cheque in favour of A for £20,000 is specially cleared by A the day after the appointment. A then refuses to convey the house to B and there is good reason to suppose that he is unable to repay the £20,000. Can anyone doubt that this evidence, unexplained, establishes a strong prima facie case that A orally agreed with B to sell him the house for £20,000 and that B performed his part of the contract by paying A the purchase price? If B sues A for specific performance of the parol agreement and applies for an interlocutory injunction to restrain A from parting with the house pending the trial of the action, it is surely inconceivable that our law can be so defective that it would allow A to shelter behind the statute. Yet A could succeed in doing so if the authorities which hold that payment can never substitute part performance for the purpose of taking a contract out of the statute were correctly decided. In my opinion, they were not.

Suppose another set of facts. B sues A for specific performance of a parol contract for the sale of A's house to him for £X,000 and alleges that he has paid A the £X,000. B gives evidence of the payment. A pleads the statute. A would have no case to answer because there would be no evidence of any circumstances surrounding the payment to connect it with the parol agreement. Suppose, however, that B, who is unrepresented, says to the judge at the trial: "Of course I agreed with A to sell him my house for £X,000 and he has certainly paid me that sum which unfortunately, I cannot repay." A's admission would, in my view, be sufficient to connect the payment with the parol contract, establish part performance and deprive A of his defence under the statute. Once a party to a parol contract relating to land admits to any court the existence of the contract and that he has received a benefit under it which he is unable or unwilling to restore, the mischief aimed at by the statute disappears. It would be most unreasonable and unjust that, in such circumstances, he should be able to rely on the statute in order to break his word and evade performing his part under the contract. There is certainly no authority binding on this House which would enable him to do so.

In the present case, the payment of £100 by the husband to his wife who had divorced him — looked at without regard to its surrounding circumstances — would not be any evidence of any contract, let alone of a contract concerning land. If the proposition that payment in part or even in full can never be part performance is correct, which, in my view, it is not, then the circumstances surrounding the payment must be irrelevant. I think, however, that the Court of Appeal were bound to accept this proposition by the authorities referred to with approval by the Earl of Selborne in *Maddison v Alderson* (1883) 8 App Cas 467, 469. On this basis, the reasons given by Edmund Davies LJ for reluctantly dismissing the appeal appear to me to be impeccable. The proposition has, however, never yet been debated before this House. In *Maddison v Alderson* it was assumed, without argument, to be correct: in any event it was wholly unnecessary for the decision of that appeal. This House is, therefore, not bound to accept the proposition and, for my part, I am unable to do so. I believe that the analysis of the proposition which I have attempted demonstrates that the proposition is fundamentally unsound and would lead to grave injustice.

If, in the present case, the payment of the £100 is looked at in the light of its surrounding circumstances, it is, in my opinion, quite plain that that sum was paid in part performance of a parol contract concerning land. The correspondence prior to 2 March 1972 shows that the only outstanding differences between the husband and the wife were then (a) the amount which he was to pay to her for transferring to him the interest which she claimed in the former matrimonial home and (b) what was to be done about the amount of arrears of maintenance to the wife which were then outstanding.

The husband had applied for the whole of these arrears to be remitted, and for an order for the wife's maintenance to be discharged. She had agreed to the discharge of that order. It is plain that the parties had very nearly reached agreement under which the wife should accept a total of £1,250 in full discharge of both her claims. Her solicitors then wrote on 17 February 1972, "Our client feels that she cannot compromise her claims for less than £1,500." The husband's solicitors wrote on 21 February 1972, stating that he would pay the £1,500 providing it was accepted in full discharge of both claims and asking the wife's solicitors to confirm that this was finally agreed. Having had no answer to that letter, the solicitor wrote on 29 February "Perhaps we could meet you at the court to finalise the final terms of settlement and then explain them to the magistrates." The next day the wife's solicitors wrote to say that they did not propose to attend the court and that they found difficulty in advising their client that the £1,500 should cover the arrears of maintenance as well as the purchase of the wife's interest in the house.

On 2 March the husband's solicitor met the wife outside the magistrates' court. There is no suggestion that he put any pressure upon her or behaved otherwise than with complete propriety. He and the wife came into court and he told the magistrates that they had come to an agreement settling all differences between the wife and the husband as follows. 1. She was to transfer her interests in the house to the husband for £1,500. 2. The husband was to pay her £100 not later than 30 March 1972, in full discharge of the arrears of maintenance, the balance of such arrears to be remitted. 3. The order for her maintenance was to be discharged but he was to continue paying maintenance (as previously ordered) in respect of the child of the marriage. The clerk then asked the wife if she had indeed come to this agreement. She replied that she had. The magistrates made an order implementing the agreement so far as they were able to do so. They also adjourned the proceedings until 30 March with an intimation that if the husband did not then pay the £100, further proceedings might be taken against him. He did pay the wife that sum on 30 March.

It is plain from the registrar's finding that the wife admitted in open court the parol agreement which she had made. It was a composite indivisible agreement, the integral parts of which were that she was to receive £100 within one month and that she was to transfer her interest in the house for £1,500.

The wife's admission in open court plainly connected the payment of the £100 with the parol agreement relating to the disposition of an interest in land and showed that the payment was in part performance of that agreement. She has not repaid or ever offered to repay any part of the £100. This payment, in my opinion, bars the wife from relying on the statute and she is accordingly bound to perform her part of the agreement.

I had some doubt whether incurring the costs incidental to the preparation of the deed of transfer and the transmission of that deed to the wife's solicitors also constituted part performance. A deed could well be prepared and transmitted in contemplation of a concluded agreement so as to save time. This clearly could not constitute part performance. The unchallenged evidence, however, shows that the deed in fact was not prepared until after 2 March 1972, the date upon which the wife admitted before the magistrates that the parol agreement was made. According to established practice, such an agreement calls for the transferee to incur the expense of preparing the deed and forwarding it to the transferor for approval. I am, therefore, inclined to think that in the circumstances of this case the preparation and transmission of the deed of transfer also amounted to part performance of the parol agreement[7].

My Lords, for these reasons I would dismiss the appeal.

LORD MORRIS OF BORTH-Y-GEST (dissenting): Courts of equity did not set out to make the terms of an Act of Parliament virtually nugatory. What the courts did was to consider the alleged acts of part performance and to decide whether the reasonable explanation of them was that the parties must have made (or stated otherwise had made) some contract such as the contract alleged. As the whole area of the law of part performance relates to contracts "for the sale or other disposition of land or any interest in land," I would have thought that it followed that on a consideration of alleged acts of part performance it has to be decided whether their reasonable explanation is that the parties must have made some contract in relation to land such as the contract alleged. I read the speeches in *Maddison v Alderson* (1883) 8 App Cas 467 as having proceeded on that basis. Thus, in that part of his speech in which he said that it was settled that part payment of purchase price was not enough to amount to part performance, Lord Selborne said, at p. 479, that the best explanation of that was that the payment of money is an equivocal act, not (in itself) until the connection is established by parol testimony, "indicative of a contract concerning land." It is because of this that the taking of possession of land will often be considered to be an act having strong claims to be regarded as an act of part performance indicative of a contract concerning the land.

I turn then to the question whether the payment of £100 by the husband can be regarded as an act of part performance. In my view, it cannot possibly

---

[7] See *Re Windle* [1975] 1 WLR 1628, [1975] 3 All ER 987 (instructions to solicitors to prepare transfer and the payment of their costs and disbursements held sufficient acts of part performance, but payment of mortgage arrears and instalments insufficient). For other insufficient acts of part performance, see *New Hart Builders Ltd v Brindley* [1975] Ch 342, [1975] 1 All ER 1007 (submission by purchasers of application for planning permission); *Re Gonin* [1979] Ch 16, [1977] 2 All ER 720 (unmarried daughter's returning home after compassionate release from wartime service to look after ageing parents); *Daulia Ltd v Four Millbank Nominees Ltd* [1978] Ch 231, [1978] 2 All ER 557 (purchasers' tender of draft contract together with banker's draft for deposit); cf. *Cohen v Nessdale* [1981] 3 All ER 118 affirmed on other grounds [1982] 2 All ER 97 (payment of one year's ground rent would have been sufficient act, if there had been final agreement).

For sufficient acts of part performance, see *Liddell v Hopkinson* (1974) 233 EG 513 (vacation of matrimonial home by divorced wife so that husband could sell it, in return for his offer of two-thirds of proceeds of sale if she would give up her right of occupation); *Sutton v Sutton* [1984] Ch 184, [1984] 1 All ER 168 (wife's consent to divorce on terms that matrimonial home be conveyed to her).

be. The money was paid by the husband to the petty sessional court in Bromley. It was paid after that court had made the order of 2 March 1972, in the terms which I have set out. The payment into court by a husband of a sum of money to be sent by the court to his wife does not, in my view, prove that there had been some contract between them: even more emphatically it does not prove that there had been any contract concerning land. The only inference that would be drawn from the payment of £100 into court by a husband in matrimonial proceedings would be that he was in arrears in regard to some payments that he had been ordered to make. Without a connection established by parol testimony the payment of the money would not begin to suggest or to establish either the existence of a contract or of a contract in relation to land.

The other suggested acts relied upon on behalf of the husband do not, in my view, possess any greater merit. Nor, in my view, if they fail to qualify as acts of part performance do they have an accrual of merit by being linked with other suggested acts which also fail to qualify. It was submitted that the fact of mentioning the agreed terms to the magistrates and inviting them to make orders can be regarded as an act of part performance. But in agreement with Edmund Davies LJ I consider that an act of part performance, in order to be such, must be an act in relation to that term of a contract (in a case where there are other terms) which alone is required to be in writing if it is to be enforceable as satisfying section 40. In the present litigation what is being considered is whether an oral and prima facie unenforceable contract in relation to land has been made enforceable by reason of there being some act of part performance which shows that there must have been a contract in relation to land. An oral statement (or concurrence in an oral statement) that there was such an oral contract cannot, in my view, suffice.

Nor do I consider that any abandonment on the part of the husband of any attempt to ask the magistrates to remit the whole amount of the arrears of maintenance he owed to his wife can qualify as an act of part performance in relation to land. The fact that he incurred legal costs and then caused a draft conveyance to be sent to his wife's solicitors (which she ignored after receiving it — indicating to her solicitors that she was very reluctant to agree the terms) could certainly indicate a belief on his part that there had been an oral contract or it could indicate a hope or expectation that agreement would in the future be reached. Without more I do not think that an act of part performance was established.

This is most unfortunate litigation. Having regard to the findings of fact which must be accepted, I must regret that I am reaching a different conclusion from that of your Lordships. The case is a very special one, but even so I consider that the decision of the majority in the Court of Appeal involves extending the law relating to part performance in a way which I do not consider to be warranted.

I would allow the appeal.

QUESTIONS
1. In negotiations for the purchase of land, X and Y orally agree terms and further agree to exchange contracts the next day. X then orally promises Y that he will enter into a formal contract if Y attends at X's office before 10 a.m. the next day and tenders his part of the contract duly signed

together with a banker's draft for the deposit. When Y complies with the
conditions, X refuses to exchange contracts.
  (*a*) Is there a valid oral contract between X and Y?
  (*b*) If so, does LPA 1925, s. 40 apply to that contract?
  (*c*) If it does, is there a sufficient act of part performance by Y? *Daulia
        Ltd v Four Millbank Nominees Ltd* [1978] Ch 231, [1978] 2 All ER 557;
        [1978] Conv 375 (F.R. Crane); (1979) 38 CLJ 31 (C. Harpum and
        D.L. Jones).
2. Are the following sufficient acts of part performance?
  (*a*) As a result of an oral agreement with X that he will leave his house
        and contents to Y in his will, Y gives up her council flat and looks
        after X and his house for no wages. X dies without making provision
        for Y. *Kingswood Estate Co Ltd v Anderson* [1963] 2 QB 169, [1962] 3
        All ER 593; *Wakeham v Mackenzie* [1968] 1 WLR 1175, [1968] 2 All
        ER 783.
  (*b*) In a similar situation,
     (i) Y, instead of moving house, continues to keep house for X.
          Maddison v Alderson (1883) 8 App Cas 467.
     (ii) Y leaves X's house, and then, as a result of X's oral agreement,
          Y returns to X's house and to the kind of position and standing
          which Y had before. *Re Gonin* [1979] Ch 16, [1977] 2 All ER 720;
          (1977) 41 Conv (NS) 350 (F.R. Crane); (1978) 128 NLJ 449
          (J.G. Miller).
  (*c*) X orally agrees to take a lease of a flat from Y, who agrees to make,
        and does make, alterations to it in accordance with the wishes of X.
        Rawlinson v Ames [1925] Ch 96.
  (*d*) X orally agrees to transfer the matrimonial home to his wife, Y, in
        consideration of her covenanting with his mortgagees to pay to them
        the mortgage arrears and instalments. Y pays them, instructs her
        solicitors to prepare the transfer, and pays X's costs and disburse-
        ments. *Re Windle* [1975] 1 WLR 1628, [1975] 3 All ER 987.

ii.   CONVEYANCE

(*a*) *Formalities*[8]

LAW OF PROPERTY ACT 1925

51.   Lands lie in grant only. — (1) All lands and all interests therein lie in
grant and are incapable of being conveyed by livery or livery and seisin, or by
feoffment, or by bargain and sale[9]; and a conveyance of an interest in land
may operate to pass the possession or right to possession thereof, without
actual entry, but subject to all prior rights thereto.

52.   Conveyances to be by deed. — (1) All conveyances of land or of
any interest therein are void for the purpose of conveying or creating a legal
estate unless made by deed.

---

[8] C & B, pp. 371–373, 721–723; M & W, pp. 636–638, 1172; MM, pp. 150, 335–336. S. 54 (1)
  follows Statute of Frauds, s. 1; and s. 52 (1) follows Real Property Act 1845, s. 3. See Law
  Commission Working Paper No. 93 Formalities for Deeds and Escrows (1985).
[9] For these old methods of conveyancing, see M & W, pp. 1169–1172, and Holdsworth, vol. 3,
  pp. 217–246; vol. 7, pp. 356–362.

(2) This section does not apply to —

(*a*) assents by a personal representative[10];

(*b*) disclaimers made in accordance with section 91 or 161 of the Insolvency Act 1985[11], or not required to be evidenced in writing;

(*c*) surrenders by operation of law, including surrenders which may, by law, be effected without writing;

(*d*) leases or tenancies or other assurances not required by law to be made in writing;

(*e*) receipts not required by law to be under seal;

(*f*) vesting orders of the court or other competent authority;

(*g*) conveyances taking effect by operation of law[12].

54. Creation of interests in land by parol. — (1) All interests in land created by parol and not put in writing and signed by the persons so creating the same, or by their agents thereunto lawfully authorised in writing, have, notwithstanding any consideration having been given for the same, the force and effect of interests at will only.

(*b*) *Title*[13]

LAW OF PROPERTY ACT 1925

44. Statutory commencements of title. — (1) After the commencement of this Act thirty years shall be substituted for forty years as the period of commencement of title which a purchaser of land may require; nevertheless earlier title than thirty years may be required in cases similar to those in which earlier title than forty years might immediately before the commencement of this Act be required.

LAW OF PROPERTY ACT 1969

23. Reduction of statutory period of title. — Section 44 (1) of the Law of Property Act 1925 . . . shall have effect, in its application to contracts made after the commencement of this Act[14], as if it specified fifteen years instead of thirty years as the period of commencement of title which may be so required.

(*c*) *Conveyance to Self*

LAW OF PROPERTY ACT 1925

72. Conveyances by a person to himself &c. — (3) After the commencement of this Act a person may convey land to or vest land in himself.

(4)[15] Two or more persons (whether or not being trustees or personal representatives) may convey, and shall be deemed always to have been

---

[10] But assents to the vesting of a legal estate in land must be in writing, signed by the personal representative: AEA 1925, s. 36 (4); *Re King's Will Trusts* [1964] Ch 542, [1964] 1 All ER 833; *Re Edwards' Will Trusts* [1982] Ch 30, [1981] 2 All ER 941.

[11] As amended by Insolvency Act 1985, s. 235, Sch. 8, para. 4.

[12] E.g. probates and letters of administration.

[13] C & B, pp. 702–704; M & W, pp. 150–151; MM, pp. 68–69. See also Law Commission Interim Report on Root of Title to Freehold Land 1967 (Law Com. No. 9).

[14] 1 January 1970; LPA 1969, s. 31 (2).

[15] *Rye v Rye* [1962] AC 496, [1962] 1 All ER 146; p. 424, post.

capable of conveying, any property vested in them to any one or more of themselves in like manner as they could have conveyed such property to a third party . . .

(d) Savings

LAW OF PROPERTY ACT 1925

55. Savings in regard to last two sections. — Nothing in the last two foregoing sections shall —
    (*a*) invalidate dispositions by will; or
    (*b*) affect any interest validly created before the commencement of this Act; or
    (*c*) affect the right to acquire an interest in land by virtue of taking possession; or
    (*d*) affect the operation of the law relating to part performance.

(e) Precedent

PRECEDENT OF A CONVEYANCE ON SALE OF A FREEHOLD[16]

THIS CONVEYANCE made the .... day of .... [*date*] BETWEEN *AB* of .... [*address and description*] (hereinafter called "the Vendor") of the one part and *CD* of .... [*address and description*] (hereinafter called "the Purchaser") of the other part.
WHEREAS the Vendor is seised for his own sole benefit of the property hereby conveyed for a legal estate in fee simple in possession free from incumbrances and has agreed with the Purchaser for the sale thereof to him for the sum of £................ [*price*].
NOW THIS DEED WITNESSETH as follows:
    1.   In pursuance of the said agreement and in consideration of the sum of £................ paid by the Purchaser to the Vendor (the receipt whereof the Vendor hereby acknowledges) the Vendor as beneficial owner HEREBY CONVEYS unto the Purchaser ALL .... [*parcels*] TO HOLD unto the Purchaser in fee simple.
    2.   The Vendor HEREBY ACKNOWLEDGES the right of the Purchaser to the production of the documents mentioned in the Schedule hereto (the possession of which is retained by the Vendor) and to delivery of copies thereof AND HEREBY UNDERTAKES with the Purchaser for the safe custody of the same documents.
    3.   It is hereby certified that the transaction hereby effected does not form part of a larger transaction or of a series of transactions in respect of which the amount or value or the aggregate amount or value of the consideration exceeds [£30,000].
IN WITNESS whereof the said parties hereto have hereunto set their respective hands and seals the day and year first above [*or* "before"] written.

---

[16] Reproduced from Hallett's *Conveyancing Precedents* (1965), p. 192.

THE SCHEDULE

[*Here list the documents acknowledged*]
[*To be executed by the Vendor (and, if desired, the Purchaser) and attested*]

iii.   LEASES

(*a*) *Formalities*

LAW OF PROPERTY ACT 1925

54. Creation of interests in land by parol. — (2) Nothing in the foregoing provisions of this Part of this Act shall affect the creation by parol of leases taking effect in possession for a term not exceeding three years (whether or not the lessee is given power to extend the term) at the best rent which can be reasonably obtained without taking a fine[17].

52. Conveyances to be by deed. — (2) (*d*), p. 77, ante.

205. General definitions. — (1) (ii), p. 9, ante.

(*b*) *Title*

This is dealt with later[18].

(*c*) *Savings*

LAW OF PROPERTY ACT 1925

55. Savings in regard to last two sections. — p. 78, ante.

B.   Equitable Interests[19]

i.   REQUIREMENT OF WRITING

LAW OF PROPERTY ACT 1925

53. Instruments required to be in writing.[20] — (1) Subject to the provisions hereinafter contained with respect to the creation of interests in land by parol —

    (*a*) no interest in land can be created or disposed of except by writing signed by the person creating or conveying the same, or by his agent thereunto lawfully authorised in writing, or by will, or by operation of law;

    (*b*) a declaration of trust respecting any land or any interest therein must be manifested and proved by some writing signed by some person who is able to declare such trust or by his will;

    (*c*) a disposition of an equitable interest or trust subsisting at the time of the disposition, must be in writing[1] signed by the person disposing

---

[17] I.e. a premium paid on the granting of the lease and operating in reduction of the rent.
[18] See p. 457, post.
[19] C & B, pp. 723–725; M & W, pp. 477–480; MM, pp. 311–312.
[20] See generally H & M, pp. 78–90; M & B (T), pp. 38–48.
[1] This may be satisfied by joinder of documents: *Re Danish Bacon Co Ltd Staff Pension Fund Trusts* [1971] 1 WLR 248, [1971] 1 All ER 486; cf LPA 1925, s. 40 (1), p. 63, ante; *Timmins v Moreland St Property Co Ltd* [1958] Ch 110, [1957] 3 All ER 265; *Elias v George Sahely & Co (Barbados) Ltd* [1983] 1 AC 646, [1982] 3 All ER 801.

of the same, or by his agent thereunto lawfully authorised in writing or by will[2].

(2) This section does not affect the creation or operation of resulting, implied or constructive trusts[3].

ii.   SAVINGS

LAW OF PROPERTY ACT 1925

55.   Savings in regard to last two sections. — p. 78, ante.

C.   Creation and Transfer in Equity. Estate Contracts

i.   AN ESTATE CONTRACT IS A GRANT IN EQUITY

An enforceable contract to convey or create a legal estate in land is one of the categories of contract which equity will specifically enforce[4]. If that remedy is available in respect of a particular contract, equity looks on that as done which ought to be done, and treats the situation as if the land were already conveyed. Such a contract is thus effective as a conveyance in equity[5]. This differs in various ways from a conveyance at law; just as interests in equity differ from estates and interests at law. The doctrine is applicable to contracts for the sale of land, contracts to grant a lease, a mortgage, an easement or profit, indeed a contract to convey or create a legal estate in any hereditament, corporeal or incorporeal[6]. Such a contract is termed an estate contract, and is defined in, and made registrable by, the Land Charges Act 1972, s. 2 (4), Class C (iv)[7].

---

[2] *Grey v IRC* [1960] AC 1, [1959] 3 All ER 603; (1960) 76 LQR 197 (R. E. Megarry); *Oughtred v IRC* [1960] AC 206, [1959] 3 All ER 623; *Re Tyler* [1967] 1 WLR 1269, [1967] 3 All ER 389; *Vandervell v IRC* [1967] 2 AC 291 at 310–312, [1967] 1 All ER 1 at 6–8; [1966] CLJ 19 (G. H. Jones); *Re Vandervell's Trusts (No. 2)* [1974] Ch 269, [1974] 3 All ER 205; (1975) 38 MLR 557 (J. W. Harris); see generally [1979] Conv 17 (G. Battersby); (1984) 47 MLR 385 (B. Green).

[3] *Bannister v Bannister* [1948] 2 All ER 133, p. 503, post; *Hodgson v Marks* [1971] Ch 892, [1971] 2 All ER 684; *Binions v Evans* [1972] Ch 359, [1972] 2 All ER 70, p. 499, post; *Ottaway v Norman* [1972] Ch 698, [1971] 3 All ER 1325.

[4] On specific performance, see H & M, chap. 23; Snell, pp. 569–599; Spry, *Equitable Remedies* (2nd edn, 1984).

[5] C & B, pp. 66, 122–124, 711; M & W, pp. 122, 176–177, 601–607; *Lysaght v Edwards* (1876) 2 ChD 499, infra. See also *Earl of Egmont v Smith* (1877) 6 ChD 469; *Abdulla v Shah* [1959] AC 124 (vendor must not remove parts of the realty after the date of the contract); *Clarke v Ramuz* [1891] 2 QB 456 (removal of soil by trespasser); *Phillips v Lamdin* [1949] 2 KB 33, [1949] 1 All ER 770 (removal of door). The risk passes to the purchaser who should therefore insure: *Paine v Meller* (1801) 6 Ves 349; *Rayner v Preston* (1881) 18 ChD 1; LPA 1925, s. 47 (reversing the decision in *Rayner v Preston*); *Berkley v Poulett* (1976) 241 EG 911, 242 EG 39 (discussing the rights of a sub-purchaser); *Ware v Verderber* (1978) 247 EG 1081 (duty of vendor to take reasonable care of property).

[6] As to the distinction between grants of interests in real property and sales of chattels, see M & W, pp. 573–575. The distinction also arises under LPA 1925, s. 40 with regard to the necessity for evidence in writing. See also Chap. 9, post; *Wood v Manley* (1839) 11 A & E 34; *James Jones & Son Ltd v Earl of Tankerville* [1909] 2 Ch 440.

[7] See p. 31, ante.

Sir George JESSEL MR, in *Lysaght v Edwards* (1876) 2 ChD 499, said at 506:
". . . the effect of a contract for sale has been settled for more than two
centuries; certainly it was completely settled before the time of Lord
Hardwicke, who speaks of the settled doctrine of the court as to it. What is
that doctrine? It is that the moment you have a valid contract for sale the
vendor becomes in equity a trustee for the purchaser of the estate sold, and
the beneficial ownership passes to the purchaser, the vendor having a right to
the purchase-money, a charge or lien on the estate for the security of that
purchase-money, and a right to retain possession of the estate until the
purchase-money is paid, in the absence of express contract as to the time of
delivering possession."

WALSH *v* LONSDALE[8]
(1882) 21 ChD 9 (CA, Sir George JESSEL MR, COTTON and
LINDLEY LJJ)

On 29 May 1879, the defendant agreed to grant to the plaintiff a lease of a
mill for seven years at a rent which varied with the number of looms operated
by the plaintiff, and at a rate per loom which depended on whether the lessor
or lessee provided the steam power. The minimum rent payable was
calculated on the smallest number of looms which the plaintiff was contractually bound to operate, and at the lowest rate was £810. The rent was
payable in advance if demanded. The plaintiff entered and paid rent
quarterly, not in advance. He was in arrears with rent due in January, 1882,
and in March the defendant demanded a year's rent in advance. It was not
paid, and the defendant distrained. The plaintiff brought this action for
damages for illegal distress and also for specific performance of the agreement and for an interim injunction to restrain the distress.

Held. The landlord (defendant) had a right to distrain. An injunction to
restrain the distress would be granted only on payment by the plaintiff of
£810, the lowest sum that could be due for rent under the lease.

SIR GEORGE JESSEL MR: The question is one of some nicety. There is an
agreement for a lease under which possession has been given. Now since the
Judicature Act[9] the possession is held under the agreement. There are not two
estates as there were formerly, one estate at common law by reason of the
payment of the rent from year to year, and an estate in equity under the
agreement. There is only one court, and the equity rules prevail in it. The
tenant holds under an agreement for a lease. He holds, therefore, under the
same terms in equity as if a lease had been granted, it being a case in which
both parties admit that relief is capable of being given by specific perform-

---

[8] *Tottenham Hotspur Football and Athletic Co Ltd v Princegrove Publishers Ltd* [1974] 1 WLR 113,
[1974] 1 All ER 17; (1974) 90 LQR 149 (M. Albery); *Warmington v Miller* [1973] QB 877,
[1973] 2 All ER 372; *Industrial Properties (Barton Hill) Ltd v Associated Electrical Industries Ltd*
[1977] QB 580, [1977] 2 All ER 293, infra.
[9] Supreme Court of Judicature Act 1873 provided for the creation of the Supreme Court of
Judicature and for the application in all branches thereof of the rules both of law and of equity.
In s. 25 (1)–(10) rules applicable to particular points are laid down, and sub-s. (11) (now
Supreme Court Act 1981, s. 49 (1)) provides:
"Generally in all matters not herein-before particularly mentioned in which there is any
conflict or variance between the Rules of Equity and the Rules of the Common Law with
reference to the same matter, the Rules of Equity shall prevail."

ance. That being so, he cannot complain of the exercise by the landlord of the same rights as the landlord would have had if a lease had been granted. On the other hand, he is protected in the same way as if a lease had been granted; he cannot be turned out by six months' notice as a tenant from year to year. He has a right to say, "I have a lease in equity, and you can only re-enter if I have committed such a breach of covenant as would if a lease had been granted have entitled you to re-enter according to the terms of a proper proviso for re-entry." That being so, it appears to me that being a lessee in equity he cannot complain of the exercise of the right of distress merely because the actual parchment has not been signed and sealed.

In *Industrial Properties (Barton Hill) Ltd v Associated Electrical Industries Ltd* [1977] QB 580, [1977] 2 All ER 293, the Parker trustees agreed in 1959 to sell part of an industrial estate to the plaintiff company. The purchase money was paid and the contract registered as a land charge, but, in order to save stamp duty, the legal estate was never conveyed to the company. In 1966 the company, which was a mere equitable owner, entered into negotiations with the defendants for the grant of a lease, and their solicitors inadvertently stated that the plaintiffs were the freeholders. The lease contained a covenant to keep the premises in good and tenantable repair and condition and so to yield them up at the determination of the term. When the lease expired, the defendants gave up possession, leaving the premises badly out of repair. The plaintiff company brought an action for damages for breach of the covenant. The defendants argued that the plaintiff company had no legal title to the premises.

The Court of Appeal (Lord DENNING MR, ROSKILL and LAWTON LJJ) held that the defendants were liable. There was a tenancy by estoppel under which the defendants were estopped from denying the plaintiff company's title[10]. The Court of Appeal also held that the defendants were liable under the doctrine of *Walsh v Lonsdale*. Lord DENNING said at 598, at 303:

"Thus far I have considered the position at common law. But in equity there is a much shorter way to a decision. It is quite plain that, if the lease to A.E.I. was defective in point of law, nevertheless it was good in equity, and for this simple reason. There were two agreements of which specific performance would be granted. One was the agreement by the Parker trustees to convey to the plaintiff company. The other was the agreement by the plaintiff company to grant a lease to A.E.I. In respect of each of these agreements, equity looks upon that as done which ought to be done. It follows that, by combining the two agreements, the tenants, A.E.I., hold upon the same terms as if a lease had actually been granted by the Parker trustees to A.E.I. This is, of course, an extension of the doctrine of *Walsh v Lonsdale* (1882) 21 ChD 9 where there was only one agreement. But I see no reason why the doctrine should not be extended to a case like the present, where there were two agreements, each of which was such that specific performance would be granted."

---

[10] P. 418, post.

In *McManus v Cooke* (1887) 35 ChD 681, the plaintiff and defendant were owners of adjoining houses. Between them was a party wall to which were fixed the lower ends of skylights which provided light to the basements of both houses, the upper end of the skylights being fixed to the respective buildings.

The parties planned to rebuild their respective premises, and orally agreed that the wall should be rebuilt, and improved, and that each party should be entitled to make a lean-to skylight with its lower end resting on the wall.

The plaintiff built the skylight as agreed, but the defendant erected his in such a way that it obstructed the access of light to the plaintiff's skylight. The plaintiff claimed an injunction to restrain the defendant from permitting his skylight to remain in its present position.

KAY J held that the oral agreement was enforceable under the doctrine of part performance, and that the plaintiff was entitled to an easement on the terms of the agreement. He made an exhaustive analysis of the authorities and said at 697: "These authorities seem to me to establish the following propositions: (1) The doctrine of part-performance of a parol agreement, which enables proof of it to be given notwithstanding the *Statute of Frauds*, though principally applied in the case of contracts for the sale or purchase of land, or for the acquisition of an interest in land, has not been confined to those cases. (2) Probably it would be more accurate to say it applies to all cases in which a Court of Equity would entertain a suit for specific performance if the alleged contract had been in writing. (3) The most obvious case of part-performance is where the defendant is in possession of land of the plaintiff under the parol agreement. (4) The reason for the rule is that where the defendant has stood by and allowed the plaintiff to fulfil his part of the contract, it would be fraudulent to set up the statute. (5) But this reason applies wherever the defendant has obtained and is in possession of some substantial advantage under a parol agreement which, if in writing, would be such as the court would direct to be specifically performed. (6) The doctrine applies to a parol agreement for an easement, though no interest in land is intended to be acquired.

I have no doubt that the present case comes within the principle of these decisions."

In *Mason v Clarke* [1955] AC 778, [1955] 1 All ER 914, a landlord (the appellant company) granted a lease of land to a farmer (the respondent). The landlord orally agreed to grant to Mason (the appellant) the right to catch rabbits on the land for the period of one year in consideration of the payment of £100. The farmer interfered with Mason's activities and took up his rabbit snares. On the assumption that there was no evidence of a grant to Mason which would satisfy the Law of Property Act 1925, section 40, Mason could only rely upon an oral grant followed by entry upon the land, and the setting of traps. One question was whether this could be the basis of a grant.

LORD MORTON OF HENRYTON said at 798, at 923: "A profit à prendre is an interest in land, and no legal estate therein can be created or conveyed except by deed (Law of Property Act 1925, s. 52). At the time when the respondent did the acts of which complaint is made, there had been no grant by deed of the profit à prendre to Mr Mason, but prima facie he had the benefit of an oral agreement for the grant thereof, and he had entered into possession thereof in the only possible way, viz., by exercising his rights thereunder . . .

. . . I am inclined to agree that there was no sufficient memorandum until 30 December 1950, but it is unnecessary to examine the relevant documents in detail because I am quite satisfied that the acts of Mr Mason, already described, were a part performance of the oral agreement of 11 October 1950. Mr Mason set snares, took rabbits and paid helpers, and, in my view, the work done and expense incurred were exclusively referable to the oral agreement. Accordingly, at the relevant time Mr Mason had a contract, specifically enforceable against the appellant company, for the grant of a profit à prendre, and had entered into possession thereof. In these circumstances he was clearly entitled to bring an action for trespass against the respondent: see *Holford v Pritchard* (1849) 3 Exch 793 and *Fitzgerald v Firbank* [1897] 2 Ch 96."

In *Ex parte Wright* (1812) 19 Ves 255 Lord ELDON LC said at 258: "In that case [a deposit of deeds with a mortgage] the deposit is evidence of an agreement for a mortgage: and an equitable title to a mortgage is here as good as a legal title."

ii.   SPECIFIC PERFORMANCE IS DISCRETIONARY

COATSWORTH *v* JOHNSON[11]
(1886) 54 LT 520 (CA Lord ESHER MR, LINDLEY and LOPES LJJ)

The plaintiff entered into possession of the defendant's farm under an agreement to execute a lease in accordance with a draft lease which had already been signed but not sealed. This draft contained, among other covenants, a covenant by the tenant to use the land in a good and husbandlike manner, and there was a power of re-entry on breach of any of the covenants.

The plaintiff failed to cultivate the farm properly, and the defendant, before any rent was due or paid, gave notice to quit and, acting under the power of re-entry, turned the plaintiff out of possession. The plaintiff brought this action for damages for trespass, claiming protection under section 14 Conveyancing Act 1881[12].

Held. The plaintiff was not entitled to the protection of the statute.

LOPES LJ: In this case the tenant, the plaintiff, who brings this action for trespass, is in possession of the land in question under an agreement for a lease. No rent has been paid, and that agreement contains a covenant to cultivate the land according to the approved course of husbandry — the usual covenant — and it has been found by the jury that that covenant has

---

[11] *Williams v Greatrex* [1957] 1 WLR 31, [1956] 3 All ER 705; *Cornish v Brook Green Laundry Ltd* [1959] 1 QB 394, [1959] 1 All ER 373; (1959) 75 LQR 168 (R. E. M.); *Kingswood Estate Co Ltd v Anderson* [1963] 2 QB 169, [1962] 3 All ER 593; (1963) 79 LQR 19 (R. E. M.); *Warmington v Miller* [1973] QB 877 at 887, [1973] 2 All ER 372 at 377; *Bell Street Investments v Wood* (1970) 216 EG 585; *Henry Smith's Charity Trustees v Hemmings* (1982) 45 P & CR 377, 265 EG 383, CA.

On the jurisdiction of the county court to grant specific performance, see County Courts Act 1984, s. 23 (*d*); County Courts Jurisdiction Order 1981 (SI 1981 No. 1123).

[12] See now LPA 1925, s. 146, p. 434, post.

been broken. But, as I have said, no rent has been paid. If rent had been paid the position of things would have been very different. Then the plaintiff would have been a tenant from year to year on the terms of that agreement, so far as those terms are not inconsistent with a yearly tenancy. But no rent having been paid, I am clearly of opinion that the plaintiff is a tenant at will only.

But it is said in this case that he is more than a tenant at will, because the court of equity would have decreed specific performance of this agreement for a lease, and that he must be regarded as lessee for the term of years mentioned in that agreement on the ground that we must regard that as done which a court of equity would have done. No doubt that is perfectly correct. But then the point arises, would the court of equity have decreed specific performance under the particular circumstances of this case? The plaintiff, the tenant, when he went to the court of equity and asked for specific performance, would have had to admit that which has been proved here, namely, that he himself had failed to perform a material portion of the contract — in point of fact, that he had broken a portion of the agreement. I take it that, under those circumstances, it is perfectly clear that the court of equity would have refused specific performance. If that is so, he is only a tenant at will. The notice had been given; the tenancy was determined; and the landlord, the defendant, makes out the justification which he sets up in this action. It might have been that a very different and important question might have arisen under section 14 of the Conveyancing Act 1881. I do not think, however, that that arises under the circumstances of this case. It is not necessary for us to consider what the position of the tenant under the lease would have been, and I therefore do not give any opinion with regard to that section.

iii.   REGISTRATION

Estate contracts, being interests in equity only, are liable to destruction by a bona fide purchaser of the legal estate for value without notice.

Maitland, *Equity* (2nd edn) p. 158:

"An agreement for a lease is not equal to a lease. An equitable right is not equivalent to a legal right; between the contracting parties an agreement for a lease may be as good as a lease; just so between the contracting parties an agreement for the sale of land may serve as well as a completed sale and conveyance. But introduce the third party and then you will see the difference. I take a lease; my lessor then sells the land to X; notice or no notice my lease is good against X. I take a mere agreement for a lease, and the person who has agreed to grant the lease then sells and conveys to Y, who has no notice of my merely equitable right. Y is not bound to grant me a lease."

Estate contracts are registrable as land charges Class C (iv) under the Land Charges Act 1972[13].

---

[13] LCA 1972, s. 2 (4), p. 31, ante.

iv.   OPTION TO PURCHASE AND RIGHT OF PRE-EMPTION[14]

(a) *Option to Purchase*

An option to purchase is an offer to sell which "the grantor is contractually precluded from withdrawing so long as the option remains exercisable"[15]. A contract to purchase is formed when the notice exercising the option is given to the grantor. Although the option does not itself form a contract, it does create an immediate equitable interest in favour of the grantee as soon as it is granted. The grantee's right to call for a conveyance of the land is an equitable interest; as far as the grantor is concerned, "his estate or interest is taken away from him without his consent, and the right to take it away being vested in another, the covenant giving the option must give that other an interest in the land[16]".

(b) *Right of Pre-emption*

In *Kling v Keston Properties Ltd* (1983) 49 P & CR 212, the question was whether a right of pre-emption over a garage in Chelsea was enforceable by the grantee against a purchaser of the garage from the grantor. In holding that it was, VINELOTT J followed the views of the majority of the Court of Appeal in *Pritchard v Briggs* [1980] Ch 338, [1980] 1 All ER 294[17] that the right of pre-emption, although not initially an interest in land, became an equitable interest when the grantor agreed to sell the garage to the purchaser. He said at 215:[17a]

"The question whether a right of pre-emption or first refusal over land creates an equitable interest in the land capable of binding a purchaser was for many years a controversial one. It was settled so far as this court is concerned by the decision of the Court of Appeal in *Pritchard v Briggs* . In that case, the owners of a piece of land granted the defendants' predecessor in title a right of first refusal. It was granted in the form of a negative stipulation 'that so long as the [grantee] shall live and the [owners] or the survivors of them shall also be alive the [owners] will not nor will either of them sell or concur in selling all or any part of the [land] without giving to the [grantee] the option of purchasing [the land]' — at a stated price. Later the owners granted a lease to the plaintiff and the lease contained an option giving the

---

[14] C & B, pp. 124–125; M & W, pp. 571–572, 604–607; MM, pp. 78–79. See generally Barnsley, *Land Options* (1978); (1974) 38 Conv (NS) 8 (A. Prichard); [1984] CLJ 55 (S. Tromans).

[15] *Beesly v Hallwood Estates Ltd* [1960] 1 WLR 549 at 556, [1960] 2 All ER 314 at 321, per BUCKLEY J. See also *Brown v Gould* [1972] Ch 53 at 58, [1971] 2 All ER 1505 at 1509, p. 388, post. The option must be sufficiently certain in its terms; *Sudbrook Trading Estate Ltd v Eggleton* [1983] 1 AC 444, [1982] 3 All ER 1, p. 390, post.

[16] *London and South Western Rly Co v Gomm* (1882) 20 ChD 562 at 581, per JESSEL MR; *Griffith v Pelton* [1958] Ch 205 at 225; *Webb v Pollmount Ltd* [1966] Ch 584 at 597, [1966] 1 All ER 481 at 485; *Mountford v Scott* [1975] Ch 258, [1975] 1 All ER 198, CA; *George Wimpey & Co Ltd v IRC* [1974] 1 WLR 975 at 980, [1974] 2 All ER 602 at 606; affd. [1975] 1 WLR 995, [1975] 2 All ER 45; *Pritchard v Briggs* [1980] Ch 338 at 418, [1980] 1 All ER 294 at 328. For the application of the rule against perpetuities, see pp. 354–356, post.

[17] (1980) 96 LQR 488 (H. W. R. W.); [1980] Conv 433 (J. Martin). See also *Manchester Ship Canal Co v Manchester Racecourse Co* [1901] 2 Ch 37; *Murray v Two Strokes Ltd* [1973] 1 WLR 823, [1973] 3 All ER 357; (1973) 89 LQR 462 (M. J. Albery); *First National Securities Ltd v Chiltern District Council* [1975] 1 WLR 1075, [1975] 2 All ER 766; cf. *Birmingham Canal Co v Cartwright* (1879) 11 ChD 421.

[17a] The case concerned registered land. The right was not entered on the register, but was protected as an overriding interest under LRA 1925, s. 70 (1) (g); p. 117, post.

plaintiff the right to purchase the land on three months' notice after the death of the survivor of the owners, again at a fixed price. A further lease was subsequently granted and the option was repeated in it. Both the right of pre-emption and the option were registered as estate contracts under the Land Charges Act 1925. Under that Act, and under the Land Charges Act 1972 (which is a consolidating Act) the contracts registrable as estate contracts expressly include a contract conferring "a valid option or right of pre-emption or any other like right." The survivor of the owners, a Major Lockwood, in fact sold the land to the defendants, purportedly in pursuance of the right of pre-emption. After the death of Major Lockwood, the plaintiff gave notice exercising the option. Goff LJ was of the opinion that the right of pre-emption created a merely personal right and did not create an interest in land even after the conditions for its exercise had been satisfied. Accordingly the defendants could not claim priority over the plaintiff's option. In his opinion the Land Charges Act 1972, in so far as it provided for registration of a right of pre-emption as an estate contract, proceeded on a wrong view of the law[18]. However, Templeman and Stephenson LJJ took a different view of the nature and effect of a right of pre-emption. Templeman LJ explained the effect of a right of pre-emption in a passage which I should, I think, cite in full. He said at 418, at 328:

'Rights of option and rights of pre-emption share one feature in common; each prescribes circumstances in which the relationship between the owner of the property which is the subject of the right and the holder of the right will become the relationship of vendor and purchaser. In the case of an option, the evolution of the relationship of vendor and purchaser may depend on the fulfilment of certain specified conditions and will depend on the volition of the option holder. If the option applies to land, the grant of the option creates a contingent equitable interest which, if registered as an estate contract, is binding on successors in title of the grantor and takes priority from the date of its registration. In the case of a right of pre-emption, the evolution of the relationship of vendor and purchaser depends on the grantor, of his own volition, choosing to fulfil certain specified conditions and thus converting the pre-emption into an option. The grant of the right of pre-emption creates a mere spes which the grantor of the right may either frustrate by choosing not to fulfil the necessary conditions or may convert into an option and thus into equitable interest by fulfilling the conditions. An equitable interest thus created is protected by prior registration of the right of pre-emption as an estate contract but takes its priority from the date when the right of pre-emption becomes exercisable and the right is converted into an option and the equitable interest is then created. The holder of a right of pre-emption is in much the same position as a beneficiary under a will of a testator who is still alive, save that the holder of the right of pre-emption must hope for some future positive action by the grantor which will elevate his hope into an interest. It does not seem to me that the property legislation of 1925 was intended to create, or operated to create an equitable interest in land where none existed.'

---

[18] For similar provisions, see LPA 1925, s. 2 (3) (iv); s. 186; SLA 1925, ss. 58 (2), 61 (2); PAA 1964, s. 9 (2), p. 356, post. See also Housing Act 1985, s. 33.

Accordingly the plaintiff's claim succeeded, for:

'After the grant of Mr. Pritchard's option, Major Lockwood was not in a position to make an offer to Mr. and Mrs. Briggs or to grant an option to them pursuant to their right of pre-emption or at all save subject to Mr. Pritchard's option. After the registration of Mr. Pritchard's option, Mr. and Mrs. Briggs could not accept an offer or exercise an option granted by Major Lockwood pursuant to the right of pre-emption or at all save subject to Mr. Pritchard's option. In short Major Lockwood could only sell and the Briggs could only purchase subject to Mr. Pritchard's option; . . .'

Stephenson LJ said at 423, at 332:

'The 1944 conveyance — (which created the right of pre-emption) — refers to giving the option of purchasing but as a future act, not as a present right; and Mr. Scott has satisfied me that what is granted as a right of pre-emption, on the true construction of the grant, is only properly called an option when the will of the grantor turns it into an option by deciding to sell and thereby binding the grantor to offer it for sale to the grantee. That it thereby becomes an interest in land is a change in the nature of the right to which, unlike Goff LJ, I see no insuperable objection in logic or in principle. And, as I understand his opinion on this point, its consequence would be that a right of pre-emption could never be enforceable against a successor in title whether it is registered or not.

I accordingly prefer the opinion of Templeman LJ on this point."

QUESTIONS

1. It has often been said that the Judicature Act effects a fusion of procedure but not of substantive law. "But the two streams of jurisdiction, though they run in the same channel run side by side, and do not mingle their waters." Ashburner, *Principles of Equity* (2nd edn, 1933), p. 18. What light is thrown on this question by the cases considered in this section? See also (1870) 14 SJ 548; (1954) 70 LQR 326 (Lord Evershed); (1961) 24 MLR 116 (V.T.H. Delany); (1977) 93 LQR 529 (P.V. Baker); (1977) 6 Anglo-Am 119 (T.G. Watkin); H & M, pp. 22–26; Meagher, Gummow and Lehane, *Equity: Doctrines and Remedies* (2nd edn, 1984), chap 2; Pettit, *Equity and the Law of Trusts* (4th edn, 1979), pp. 6–10; *United Scientific Holdings Ltd v Burnley Borough Council* [1978] AC 904, [1977] 2 All ER 62.

2. Work out, step by step, the way in which the *Walsh v Lonsdale* litigation would have proceeded before 1875. H & M pp. 15–17.

3. Is a contract for a lease as good as a lease? p. 426, post. What is the effect of the Land Charges Act 1972 upon this?

IV.   Fixtures[19]

A.   What is Land?

Since land and chattels are treated differently by the law and since a chattel may, by being affixed to land, become part of the land, it is necessary to have

---

[19] C & B, pp. 135–141; M & W, pp. 730–738; MM, pp. 19–23. LPA 1925, s. 205 (1) (ix); SLA 1925, s. 117 (1) (ix); TA 1925, s. 68 (6); LRA 1925, s. 3 (viii); LCA 1972, s. 17 (1); Interpretation Act 1978, s. 5, Sch. 1.

a test to determine whether or not such a change has taken place. For example, a brick in a builder's yard is a chattel; once used to build a wall, it becomes part of the land; and if the wall is knocked down the bricks become chattels again. When land is sold, the conveyance includes the land but not the chattels[20]; but includes those things which were once chattels but which have become land.

The question whether a chattel remains a chattel or has become part of the land can arise in many contexts, namely, whether it passes to a purchaser[1], or sub-purchaser[2], on a sale of the land; whether it is included as part of the security on a mortgage of the land[3]; whether it is owned by the estate of a tenant for life or passes to the remainderman[4]; whether it is owned by a tenant for years or by the freeholder[5]; whether it passes on a death as realty or personalty[6]; and whether a drainpipe, placed underground in the exercise of an easement of drainage, remains the property of the party entitled to the easement[7].

A related but separate question follows[8]. There are some occasions in which the owner of a one-time chattel may remove it even though it has now

---

[20] By LPA 1925, s. 62, p. 586, post, a conveyance of land includes buildings, erections and fixtures, in the absence of a contrary intention: *HE Dibble Ltd v Moore* [1970] 2 QB 181, [1969] 3 All ER 1465 (greenhouses resting on own weight on concrete dollies held to be removable chattels).

[1] *Colgrave v Dias Santos* (1823) 2 B & C 76 (fixtures, including those which a tenant could have removed, passed on sale of freehold); *Phillips v Lamdin* [1949] 2 KB 33, [1949] 1 All ER 770 (purchaser entitled to reinstatement of Adam door removed by vendor); *Hynes v Vaughan* (1985) 50 P & CR 444 (purchaser not entitled to chrysanthemum growing frame and sprinkler system); *Dean v Andrews* (1985) Times, 25 May (purchaser not entitled to large prefabricated greenhouse bolted to concrete plinth resting by its own weight). For the effect of hire-purchase agreements, see (1963) 27 Conv (NS) 30 (A. G. Guest and J. Lever).

[2] *Berkley v Poulett* (1976) 241 EG 911, 242 EG 39. Cf. *Hamp v Bygrave* (1982) 266 EG 720, p. 92, n. 10, infra.

[3] *Holland v Hodgson* (1872) LR 7 CP 328; *Hobson v Gorringe*]1897] 1 Ch 182, (machinery affixed. The judgment of SMITH LJ contains a resumé of the cases up to that time); *Lyon & Co v London City and Midland Bank* [1903] 2 KB 135 (tip-up seats screwed to bolts fastened to floor and hired to mortgagors held to be chattels); *Vaudeville Electric Cinema Ltd v Muriset* [1923] 2 Ch 74 (similar seats owned by mortgagor held to be land); *Reynolds v Ashby & Sons* [1904] AC 466 (machines bolted to the floor held to be land); *Hulme v Brigham* [1943] KB 152, [1943] 1 All ER 204 (heavy printing machinery resting by its own weight held by BIRKETT J to be chattels).

[4] *D'Eyncourt v Gregory* (1866) LR 3 Eq 382 (ornamental statues in park, resting by their weight on plinth, held to be part of realty); *Leigh v Taylor* [1902] AC 157 (tapestries stretched over canvas and tacked thereto held to remain chattels); *Re Lord Chesterfield's Settled Estates* [1911] 1 Ch 237 (proceeds of sale of ornamental wood carvings by Grinling Gibbons treated as capital money under SLA 1882).

[5] *Culling v Tufnal* (1694) Bull NP 34; *Elwes v Maw* (1802) 3 East 38 (Dutch barn resting by own weight in hollow of brick foundations remained a chattel); *Webb v Frank Bevis Ltd* [1940] 1 All ER 247 (similarly a corrugated iron building held to floor by iron strips).

[6] *Bain v Brand* (1876) 1 App Cas 762 (machinery in colliery passed to heir and not to executor); *Re Whaley* [1908] 1 Ch 615 (pictures and tapestries in dining-room designed as a "complete specimen of Elizabethan dwelling-house" passed under devise of house and not under bequest of chattels).

[7] *Simmons v Midford* [1969] 2 Ch 415, [1969] 2 All ER 1269 (plaintiff's drainpipe under roadway held to be chattel with which neighbour claiming an easement of drainage could not interfere); cf. *Montague v Long* (1972) 24 P & CR 240 (bridge over river).

[8] The two questions are not always kept separate: *Leigh v Taylor* [1902] AC 157; cf. Lords HALSBURY and MACNAGHTEN with Lord SHAND. In the Court of Appeal, sub nom *Re De Falbe* [1901] 1 Ch 523, STIRLING LJ said: "It appears to me, therefore, both on principle and on authority that the exception from the rule extends to ornamental fixtures as well as to trade fixtures. Now, what are the objects as to which the dispute arises here? Tapestries. Photographs of some of them have been produced, and they shew that the tapestries are of an ornamental character, and, therefore, it appears to me that the exception from the rule applies."

become part of the land. A tenant for years has long been able to remove trade, ornamental and domestic fixtures, and may now, by statute, remove agricultural fixtures also[9]. A tenant for life was in the same position at common law, but has not been given the statutory right to agricultural fixtures.

BERKLEY v POULETT
(1976) 241 Estates Gazette 911, 242 Estates Gazette 39 (CA, STAMP, SCARMAN and GOFF LJJ)

The eighth Earl Poulett agreed to sell the Hinton St. George Estate to Effold Ltd, and Effold Ltd agreed, as Earl Poulett knew, to sell Lot 1, which included the mansion house, to the plaintiff. The properties were duly conveyed.

Prior to the conveyance to Effold Ltd, the Earl removed a number of treasures from the house, and sold them. Effold Ltd was unconcerned; but the plaintiff claimed that, by virtue of the sub-contract between himself and Effold Ltd, he became the owner of the treasures.

The treasures in question were —
  (i) a number of pictures which, while still in their frames, had been affixed by screws into the recesses in the panelling of the dining room:
  (ii) a white marble statue of a Greek athlete, weighing half a ton, and a sundial; each resting by its own weight on a plinth or pedestal outside the house.

The plaintiff claimed that these treasures were fixtures. The further question whether, assuming they were fixtures, the plaintiff was entitled to them by virtue of this sub-contract, is omitted here.

Held. The treasures were not fixtures.

SCARMAN LJ: As so often, the difficulty is not the formulation but the application of the law. I think there is now no need to enter into research into the case law prior to *Leigh v Taylor* [1902] AC 157. The answer today to the question whether objects which were originally chattels have become fixtures, that is to say part of the freehold, depends upon the application of two tests: (1) the method and degree of annexation; (2) the object and purpose of the annexation. The early law attached great importance to the first test. It proved harsh and unjust both to limited owners who had affixed valuable chattels of their own to settled land and to tenants for years. The second test was evolved to take care primarily of the limited owner, for example a tenant for life. In *Leigh v Taylor* the House of Lords invoked it to protect the interest of the tenant for life who had affixed large and valuable tapestries to the walls of the house for the purpose of adornment and enjoyment of them as tapestries. As I read that decision, it was held that she had not made them fixtures. "They remained chattels from first to last," said Lord Lindley at p. 164 of the report. In the law of landlord and tenant the law's protection went further: even if the chattel affixed by the tenant must be held to have become a fixture, that is to say part of the realty, a rule was evolved that it was to be treated as the property of the tenant and

---

[9] Agricultural Holdings Act 1986, s. 10.

could be removed by him if it fell into a class recognised by law as "tenant's fixtures," that is to say if it be a trade, agricultural, or an ornamental fixture. We are not concerned, on the view I take of the case, with "tenant's fixtures." The governing relationship with which this case is concerned is that of a beneficial owner of the legal estate selling the freehold to a purchaser. Such a seller can sell as much or as little of his property as he chooses. Lord Poulett excluded certain named objects from the sale, but the contract was silent as to the objects claimed by the plaintiff. I think it was conceded by the defendants — certainly I so read the contract of sale — that, if the pictures, statue, and sundial were fixtures at the time of the contract, they were included in it as part of the freehold (subject of course to a valuation if they should prove to be tenant's fixtures). The preliminary, and basic, question is therefore whether these objects were at that time fixtures.

Since *Leigh v Taylor* the question is really one of fact. The two tests were explained in that case by the Lord Chancellor (see the report at 158 and 159), who commented that not the law but our mode of life has changed over the years; that what has changed is "the degree in which certain things have seemed susceptible of being put up as mere ornaments whereas at our earlier period the mere construction rendered it impossible sometimes to sever the thing which was put up from the realty." In other words, a degree of annexation which in earlier times the law would have treated as conclusive may now prove nothing. If the purpose of the annexation be for the better enjoyment of the object itself, it may remain a chattel, notwithstanding a high degree of physical annexation. Clearly, however, it remains significant to discover the extent of physical disturbance of the building or the land involved in the removal of the object. If an object cannot be removed without serious damage to, or destruction of, some part of the realty, the case for its having become a fixture is a strong one. The relationship of the two tests to each other requires consideration. If there is no physical annexation there is no fixture. *Quicquid plantatur solo solo cedit*. Nevertheless an object, resting on the ground by its own weight alone, can be a fixture, if it be so heavy that there is no need to tie it into a foundation, and if it were put in place to improve the realty. *Prima facie*, however, an object resting on the ground by its own weight alone is not a fixture: see *Megarry and Wade*, p. 716. Conversely, an object affixed to realty but capable of being removed without much difficulty may yet be a fixture, if, for example, the purpose of its affixing be that "of creating a beautiful room as a whole" (Neville J in *Re Whaley* [1908] 1 Ch 615 at 619). And in the famous instance of *Lord Chesterfield's Settled Estates* [1911] 1 Ch 237 Grinling Gibbons carvings, which had been affixed to a suite of rooms 200 years earlier, were held to be fixtures. Today so great are the technical skills of affixing and removing objects to land or buildings that the second test is more likely than the first to be decisive. Perhaps the enduring significance of the first test is a reminder that there must be some degree of physical annexation before a chattel can be treated as part of the realty. . . .

The 7th Earl decided in the early part of the 20th century to install in the two rooms the panelling and so designed it that there were recesses for pictures. It is this feature which lends plausibility to the suggestion that the pictures, fitted into the recesses left for them, were not to be enjoyed as objects in themselves but as part of the grand architectural design of the two rooms. The Vice-Chancellor rejected this view. So do I. When the panelling was installed in the two rooms the design was either panelled walls with recesses for pictures to be enjoyed as pictures, or rooms having walls which were a composite of panelling and pictures: in other words, the pictures were to be part of a composite mural. I think the former was the truth. The panelling was Victorian, the pictures a heterogeneous collection. According to Sothebys' expert they were of different dates in the 17th and 18th centuries, of different styles, by different hands, the sort of set anyone could put together at any time — very different, I would comment, from that unity of design, the "Elizabethan Room" in the case of *Re Whaley*. There was a particular Poulett family interest in "The Return" and in the two coronation portraits, but this interest focused attention not on the design of the room but on the pictures themselves. Notwithstanding the painstaking and attractive arguments of Mr. Millett for the plaintiff, I find, applying the second test, that the pictures were not fixtures. They were put in place on the wall to be enjoyed as pictures. The panelling presented a technical problem in putting them up. The way the carpenter, or whoever it was, solved the problem is not decisive in determining their legal character. But the purpose in putting them there is.

The statue and the sundial give rise in my judgment to no difficulty. Neither was at the time of the sale physically attached to the realty. The sundial was a small object and, once the Earl had detached it (as he did many years earlier) from its pedestal, it ceased to be part of the realty. The statue was heavy. It weighed 10 cwt and stood 5 ft 7 in high on its plinth. There is an issue as to whether it was cemented into the plinth or rested on its own weight. The question is not decisive, for, even if it was attached by a cement bond, it was (as events proved) easily removable. However, upon the balance of probability, I agree with the Vice-Chancellor in thinking it was not attached. The best argument for the statue being a fixture was its careful siting in the West Lawn so as to form an integral part of the architectural design of the west elevation of the house. The design point is a good one so far as it goes: it explains the siting of the plinth, which undoubtedly was a fixture. But what was put upon the plinth was very much a matter for the taste of the occupier of the house for the time being. We know that at one time the object on the plinth had been a sundial. At the time of the sale it was this statue of a Greek athlete. The plinth's position was architecturally important: it ensured that whatever stood on it would be correctly positioned. But the object it carried could be whatever appealed to the occupier for the time being. Sundial or statue — it did not matter to the design, so long as it was in the right place — a result ensured by the plinth which was firmly fixed into the ground. Being, as I think, unattached, the statue was, *prima facie*, not a fixture, but, even if it were attached, the application of the second test would lead to the same conclusion[10].

---

[10] Cf. *Hamp v Bygrave* (1982) 266 EG 720 (stone and lead garden ornaments resting on own weight held to be fixtures because the vendors regarded them as "features of, and part and parcel of, the garden"; alternatively, if the ornaments were chattels, the vendors were estopped from denying that they formed part of the sale); [1983] LSG 1773 (H. W. Wilkinson). *Berkley v Poulett* was not cited.

B. What Fixtures may be Removed?

Even if a chattel is affixed to the land so as to become part of the land, the person who affixed it or his successors in title may have a right to remove it. At common law, a tenant for years and a tenant for life were entitled to remove trade[11], ornamental or domestic fixtures[12]. By Agricultural Holdings Act 1986, section 10, replacing earlier legislation, a tenant for years may also remove agricultural fixtures. As between devisee and personal representative, vendor and purchaser and mortgagor and mortgagee there is no right of removal, and the question of entitlement is dependent upon the question of annexation to the land[13].

---

[11] *Poole's Case* (1703) 1 Salk 368; *Climie v Wood* (1869) LR 4 Exch 328; *Penton v Robart* (1801) 2 East 88; *Wardell v Usher* (1841) 3 Scott NR 508; *Elliott v Bishop* (1854) 10 Exch 496; *Smith v City Petroleum Co Ltd* [1940] 1 All ER 260; *New Zealand Government Property Corpn v H M and S Ltd* [1982] QB 1145, [1982] 1 All ER 624. See *Mancetter Developments Ltd v Garmaston Ltd* (1986) Financial Times, 22 January.
[12] *Grymes v Boweren* (1830) 6 Bing 437; *Buckland v Butterfield* (1820) 2 Brod & Bing 54; *Beck v Rebow* (1706) 1 P Wms 94; *Leach v Thomas* (1835) 7 C & P 327; *Spyer v Phillipson* [1931] 2 Ch 183; *Colegrave v Dias Santos* (1823) 2 B & C 76, 77; *Darby v Harris* (1841) 1 QB 895; *Lyde v Russell* (1830) 1 B & Ad 394.
[13] See p. 89, ante.

2. Registered Land[1]

I. Registered Conveyancing

We have seen that the basic doctrines of land law developed at common law under a system in which title to land was proved by the production of deeds recording the history of transactions affecting the land; and that the system is steadily being overtaken by a system which is based upon the registration of title to land. In areas in which the latter system is in operation, all transfers of legal title are required to be by registration of the transferee's name in the register; and gradually title to land in the area is entered on the register. The old cumbrous method of conveyancing by title deeds is dispensed with; and a registered title is thenceforth guaranteed by the State.

C & B, pp. 99–107, 734–750; M & W, pp. 194–230; MM, pp. 111–132, 533–549. The authoritative account is Ruoff and Roper (predecessors of E. J. Pryer as Chief Land Registrar), *Law and Practice of Registered Conveyancing* (4th edn. 1979); Ruoff and West, *Concise Land Registration Practice* (3rd edn. 1982); Ruoff and West, *Land Registration Forms* (3rd edn. 1983); Encyclopaedia of Forms and Precedents (4th edn. 1970), vol. xvii, pp. 112–270 (R. B. Roper); Wolstenholme and Cherry, *Conveyancing Statutes* (13th edn. 1972), vol. 6; Barnsley, *Conveyancing Law and Practice* (2nd edn. 1982), chaps. 2, 3, 4, 12, 16; Hayton, *Registered Land* (3rd edn. 1981); Wontner's *Guide to Land Registry Practice* (15th edn. 1985). The Land Registry issues Practice Notes in conjunction with the Law Society (1982–83), and the Chief Land Registrar an Annual Report on H.M. Land Registry. The Law Commission is revising registered conveyancing. Its first report was published in 1983 (Law Com No. 125, HC 86) on Identity and Boundaries, Conversion of Title, the Treatment of Leases and the Minority Interests Index; and its second report in 1985 on Inspection of the Register (Law Com No. 148, HC 551). A third report will deal with Overriding Interests, Rectification and Indemnity and a fourth with Protection and Priority of Minor Interests. Four working papers have already been published: No. 32 (leaseholds), No. 37 (overriding interests), No. 45 (identity and boundaries: and rectification and indemnity), and No. 67 (methods of protection of interests in land, including mortgages and charges). A report on The Implications of *Williams & Glyn's Bank Ltd v Boland* (1982 Law Com No. 115) is now being reconsidered; Nineteenth Annual Report 1983–1984 (Law Com No. 140, HC 214); Law Commission Second Report on Registered Land: Inspection of the Register 1985 (Law Com No. 148, HC 551), para. 1. Eventually the Law Commission intends "to undertake a complete revision and redrafting of the Land Registration Acts 1925–1971": Twentieth Annual Report 1984–1985 (Law Com No. 155, HC 247).

A system of registration of title was introduced into England as far back as 1862, but only on an optional basis. The revised system of registration of title contained in the Land Registration Acts 1925–1971[2] and Rules of 1925[3] — which must be kept wholly distinct from systems of registration of deeds[4] and charges (such as that under the Land Charges Act 1972) — is, however, in the process of being made, area by area, compulsory over the whole of England and Wales; compulsory in the sense that dealings in land after the given date must be carried out under the new and not the old system of conveyancing. Responsibility for making an area, from a given date, one of compulsory registration in this sense, now rests with the central, and not the local authorities[5]. It is expected that this coverage will rise to some 85% of the population by 1987[6].

The 1925 registration system provides for the *registration* of legal titles to land, and the *protection* of other interests in and over land. It is important to grasp the nature of this dichotomy. Only interests capable of subsisting at law under the Law of Property Act 1925, s. 1, are *registrable*. Other interests, called "minor interests", are protected, not by registration as separate titles, but by entry on the register by means of a notice, restriction, caution or inhibition. Each legal title has a separate card in the Registry[7] and that card will contain such entries as are appropriate. In 1977 a computerised system was introduced for indexing the names of proprietors of registered land and registered charges[8], and experimental work is being carried out at the Plymouth District Registry with a view to computerisation of the register itself by the mid-1990s[9]. In addition, however, there are overriding interests that are binding on purchasers irrespective of entry on the register. Overriding interests are those which are not capable of being fitted into a system of registration. Their existence prevents the register from being the sole source of title to rights affecting land. The landowner receives from the

---

[2] LRA 1925, 1936, 1966 and Land Registration and Land Charges Act 1971, Parts I and III.

[3] For further Rules see LRR 1956, 1964, 1967, 1976 and 1978; LR (Powers of Attorney) R 1971, LR (Souvenir Land) R 1972; LR (Capital Transfer Tax) R 1975; LR (Official Searches) R 1981; LR (Matrimonial Homes) R 1983 and LR (Fee Order) 1985.

[4] The Yorkshire Deeds Registries are now closed: LPA 1969, Part II.

[5] LRA 1966, s. 1 (1). For compulsory registration areas, see Registration of Title Order 1985 (SI 1985 No. 1999), p. 96, post and for present progress, see the Annual Report for 1984–85, paras. 19–21. Voluntary registration in non-compulsory areas is possible in classes of cases specified by the Registrar, e.g. certain large building developments, or certain cases of lost or destroyed deeds; LRA 1966, s. 1 (2); [1983] Conv 169. There is compulsory registration in respect of sales or leases by local authorities to tenants exercising rights under Housing Act 1980, whether or not the dwelling-house is in an area of compulsory registration: s. 20. See also Housing Defects Act 1984, ss. 6, 50, Sch. 3, para. 2.

On 31 March 1985 there were 9,373,618 separate titles on the register, and during the year ended 31 March: 310,334 applications for first registration were completed. Annual Report 1984–85, paras. 5, 12. Of the 19.2 million dwellings in England and Wales, some 7 million have already been registered. Some 1 million registered titles exist in respect of non-residential property. The Registering files take up more than 40 miles of shelving: (1984) 128 SJ 71 (E. J. Pryer).

[6] Annual Report 1983–84, para. 27.

[7] The Headquarters is at Lincoln's Inn Fields, London. Registers of Title are kept at thirteen District Registries: LR (District Registries) Order 1984 (SI 1984 No. 1579). For a map showing their areas of responsibility, see (1985) 129 SJ 29.

[8] Annual Report for 1977–78, paras. 20–22.

[9] AJA 1982, s. 66; Annual Report for 1983–84, paras. 64–73; 1984–1985, paras. 52–68; Second Report of Conveyancing Committee: Conveyancing Simplifications 1985, paras. 4.2–4.9.

Registry a land certificate which reproduces the relevant entries on the register, but it is the register, not the land certificate, which establishes, and is, the source of title. There is no room in the registered land system for the doctrine of the bona fide purchaser of the legal estate for value without notice; but, in cases where the Act fails to provide an answer, the court, as has been seen[10], will fall back on general equitable principles.

We have already seen that the number of legal estates which can exist after 1925 is reduced to two by s. 1 of the Law of Property Act 1925. We will see in Part II that, under the 1925 legislation, equitable beneficial interests in land are not required to be disclosed in the title deeds. A purchaser knows that they exist, but does not need to know details of them, as he will "overreach" them — that is, he will buy the land free from them, and they will attach instead to the purchase money. Similarly with registered land, the purchaser will know that there are equitable interests affecting the land[11], but will not know, nor need to know, what they are. For, although equitable beneficial interests in land may be protected by entry on the register, they are "overreached" on a sale as they would be with unregistered land.

AREAS OF COMPULSORY REGISTRATION
as at 1 November 1986[12]

County (including Greater London)	Areas of compulsory registration
Avon	The whole county.
Bedfordshire	The whole county.
Berkshire	The whole county.
Buckinghamshire	The whole county.
Cambridgeshire	The districts of Cambridge, Huntingdonshire, Peterborough and South Cambridgeshire.
Cheshire	The whole county.
Cleveland	The whole county.
Clwyd	The districts of Alyn and Deeside, Delyn and Rhuddlan.
Cornwall	The districts of Caradon and Restormel.
Cumbria	The districts of Allerdale, Barrow-in-Furness and Carlisle.
Derbyshire	The districts of Amber Valley, Bolsover, Chesterfield, Derby, Erewash, North East Derbyshire and South Derbyshire.
Devon	The districts of East Devon, Exeter, Mid Devon, North Devon, Plymouth, South Hams, Teignbridge and Torbay.
Dorset	The districts of Bournemouth, Christchurch, Poole, Weymouth and Portland, and Wimborne.
Durham	The districts of Chester-le-Street, Darlington, Durham, Easington and Sedgefield.
Dyfed	The district of Llanelli.
East Sussex	The whole county.
Essex	The districts of Basildon, Braintree, Brentwood, Chelmsford, Colchester, Epping Forest, Harlow, Southend-on-Sea, Thurrock and Uttlesford.

[10] P. 25, ante; *Abigail v Lapin* [1934] AC 491 at 500–502; *Strand Securities Ltd v Caswell* [1965] Ch 958 at 991, [1965] 1 All ER 820 at 833 per RUSSELL LJ.
[11] See LRA 1925, s. 88 (1).
[12] Registration of Title Order 1985 (SI 1985 No. 1999).

County (including Greater London)	Areas of compulsory registration
Gloucestershire	The whole county.
Greater London	The whole administrative area.
Greater Manchester	The whole county.
Gwent	The whole county.
Hampshire	The districts of Basingstoke and Deane Eastleigh, Fareham, Gosport, Havant, Portsmouth, New Forest and Southampton.
Hereford and Worcester	The districts of Bromsgrove, Hereford, Redditch and Worcester.
Hertfordshire	The whole county.
Humberside	The whole county.
Isle of Wight	The whole county.
Kent	The whole county.
Lancashire	The districts of Blackburn, Blackpool, Burnley, Chorley, Fylde, Hyndburn, Pendle, Preston, Rossendale, South Ribble and West Lancashire.
Leicestershire	The whole county.
Lincolnshire	The district of Lincoln.
Merseyside	The whole county.
Mid Glamorgan	The whole county.
Norfolk	The districts of Great Yarmouth and Norwich.
Northamptonshire	The whole county.
Northumberland	The districts of Blyth Valley, Castle Morpeth and Wansbeck.
North Yorkshire	The districts of Craven, Harrogate, Selby and York.
Nottinghamshire	The whole county.
Oxfordshire	The whole county.
Shropshire	The districts of Bridgnorth and The Wrekin.
Somerset	The districts of Taunton Deane and West Somerset.
South Glamorgan	The whole county.
South Yorkshire	The whole county.
Staffordshire	The districts of Cannock Chase, Lichfield, Newcastle-under-Lyme, Stoke-on-Trent and Tamworth.
Suffolk	The districts of Ipswich and Waveney.
Surrey	The whole county.
Tyne and Wear	The whole county.
Warwickshire	The whole county.
West Glamorgan	The whole county.
West Midlands	The whole county.
West Sussex	The whole county.
West Yorkshire	The whole county.
Wiltshire	The district of Thamesdown and West Wiltshire.

LAND REGISTRATION ACT 1925

123. Effect of Act in areas where registration is compulsory. — (1) In any area in which an Order in Council declaring that registration of title to land within that area is to be compulsory on sale is for the time being in force[13], every conveyance on sale of freehold land and every grant of a term of years absolute not being less than forty years from the date of the delivery of the grant, and every assignment on sale of leasehold land held for a term of years absolute having not less than forty years to run from the date of delivery of the assignment[14], shall (save as hereinafter provided), on the expiration of two months from the date thereof or of any authorised extension of that period, become void so far as regards the grant or conveyance of the legal estate[15] in the freehold or leasehold land comprised in the conveyance, grant, or assignment, or so much of such land as is situated within the area affected, unless the grantee (that is to say, the person who is entitled to be registered as proprietor of the freehold or leasehold land) or his successor in title or assign has in the meantime applied to be registered as proprietor of such land: . . .[16].

LAND REGISTRATION RULES 1925

8. Index Map and Parcels Index. — (1) Index Maps shall be kept in the Registry which shall show the position and extent of every registered estate, provided that, where practicable, the General Map shall be used for this purpose.

LAND REGISTRATION ACT 1925

3. Interpretation. —

   (viii) "Land" includes land of any tenure (including land, subject or not to manorial incidents, enfranchised under Part V of the Law of Property Act 1922), and mines and minerals, whether or not held with the surface, buildings or parts of buildings (whether this division is horizontal, vertical or made in any other way) and other corporeal hereditaments; also a manor, an advowson, and a rent and other incorporeal hereditaments[17], and an easement, right, privilege, or benefit in, over, or derived from land[18], but not an undivided share in land; . . . .

---

[13] Compulsory registration does not apply to any area of land declared by the Registrar to be subject to a souvenir land scheme: LR & LCA 1971, s. 4; LR (Souvenir Land) Rules 1972 (SI 1972 No. 985); W & C, vol. 6, p. 130.

[14] Law Commission Report on Land Registration (Law Com No. 125 HC 86) Part IV, para. 4.30 recommends that in compulsory areas all leases granted for more than 21 years out of unregistered titles should be compulsorily registrable on grant, and existing leases with more than 21 years unexpired at the date of assignment should be compulsorily registrable on assignment.

[15] But they are valid in equity: *E. S. Schwab & Co Ltd v McCarthy* (1975) 31 P & C R 196 at 212.

[16] For the effect of failure to register, see *Mascall v Mascall* (1984) LS Gaz R 2218 (where donor had done everything to perfect gift of land in favour of donee, but transfer not yet registered, held that donor was trustee of the land for donee); (1985) 82 LSG 1629 (H. Wilkinson); Ruoff and Roper, pp. 176–179; W & C, vol. 6, pp. 104, 105.

[17] LRR 1925, r. 50. In practice, rent means rentcharge only. See C & B, pp. 613–614.

[18] P. 642, post. Legal easements may only be registered as appurtenant to the registered title of the dominant tenement: LRR 1925, r. 257.

(xi) "Legal estates" means the estates interests and charges in or over land subsisting or created at law which are by the Law of Property Act 1925, authorised to subsist or to be created at law[19]; and "Equitable interests" mean all the other interests and charges in or over land or in the proceeds of sale thereof; an equitable interest "capable of subsisting at law" means such as could validly subsist at law if clothed with the legal estate;

(xxiv) "Registered land" means land or any estate or interest in land the title to which is registered under this Act or any enactment replaced by this Act, and includes any easement[20], right, privilege, or benefit which is appurtenant or appendant thereto, and any mines and minerals within or under the same and held therewith;

2. What estates may be registered. — (1) After the commencement of this Act, estates capable of subsisting as legal estates shall be the only interests in land in respect of which a proprietor can be registered and all other interests in registered land (except overriding interests[1] and interests entered on the register at or before such commencement) shall take effect in equity as minor interests[2]. . .

69. Effect of registration on the legal estate. — (1) The proprietor of land (whether he was registered before or after the commencement of this Act) shall be deemed to have vested in him without any conveyance, where the registered land is freehold, the legal estate in fee simple in possession, and where the registered land is leasehold the legal term created by the registered lease, . . .[3]

(4) The estate for the time being vested in the proprietor shall only be capable of being disposed of or dealt with by him in manner authorised by this Act.

19. Registration of disposition of freeholds. — (1) The transfer of the registered estate in the land or part thereof shall be completed by the registrar entering on the register[4] the transferee as the proprietor of the estate transferred, but until such entry is made the transferor shall be deemed to remain proprietor of the registered estate; . . .

(3) The general words implied in conveyances under the Law of Property Act 1925[5], shall apply, so far as applicable thereto, to dispositions of a registered estate.

74. Notice of trust not to affect registered dealing. — Subject to the provisions of this Act as to settled land, neither the registrar nor any person dealing with a registered estate or charge shall be affected with notice of a trust express implied or constructive, and references to trusts shall, so far as possible, be excluded from the register.

---

[19] LPA 1925, s. 1 (1)–(4), p 6, ante.

[20] P. 642, post.

[1] P. 117, post.

[2] P. 135, post.

[3] For the "statutory magic" effected by this section, see *Argyle Building Society v Hammond* (1984) 49 P & CR 148 at 155, p. 151, post.

[4] Registration is completed as of the day on which the application is delivered to the Registrar: LRR 1925, r. 83 (2), as substituted by LRR 1978, r. 8; see letter from the Registrar, cited in (1976) 40 Conv (NS) 307; p. 115, post.

[5] LPA 1925, s. 62, p. 586, post.

101. Dispositions off register creating "minor interests". — (1) Any person, whether being the proprietor or not, having a sufficient interest or power in or over registered land, may dispose of or deal with the same, and create any interests or rights therein which are permissible in like manner and by the like modes of assurance in all respects as if the land were not registered, but subject as provided by this section.

(2) All interests and rights disposed of or created under subsection (1) of this section (whether by the proprietor or any other person) shall, subject to the provisions of this section, take effect as minor interests, and be capable of being overridden by registered dispositions for valuable consideration.

(3) Minor interests shall, subject to the express exceptions contained in this section, take effect only in equity, but may be protected by entry on the register of such notices, cautions, inhibitions and restrictions as are provided for by this Act or rules[6].

107. Power for proprietors to bind successors and to enforce contracts. — (1) Subject to any entry to the contrary on the register, the proprietor of any registered land or charge may enter into any contract in reference thereto in like manner as if the land or charge had not been registered, and, subject to any disposition for valuable consideration which may be registered or protected on the register before the contract is completed or protected on the register, the contract may be enforced as a minor interest against any succeeding proprietor in like manner and to the same extent as if the land or charge had not been registered[7].

PRECEDENT FOR TRANSFER OF FREEHOLD LAND[8]

H.M. LAND REGISTRY

Land Registration Acts 1925–1971

TRANSFER OF WHOLE

County and district: ....
   (or name of Greater London   ....
   borough where applicable)   ....
Title No.:   ....
Property: ....
Date: ....

In consideration of .... pounds (£..........) the receipt whereof is hereby acknowledged I, *AB*, of .... [*address and description*] [formerly of .... [*registered address*]] as Beneficial Owner HEREBY TRANSFER to *CD* of .... [*address and description*] the land comprised in the title above referred to

[It is hereby certified that the transaction hereby effected does not form part of a larger transaction or series of transactions in respect of which the

---

[6] P. 135, post.
[7] See (1977) 93 LQR 541 at pp. 550–552 (R. J. Smith).
[8] Reprinted from Hallett's *Conveyancing Precedents* (1965), p. 1247.

amount or value or aggregate amount or value of the consideration exceeds [£30,000]]

Signed sealed and delivered by
the said *AB*   [*Signature and seal of AB*]
in the presence of

Name ....
Address ....
....
Description ....

LAND REGISTRATION ACT 1925

63.   Issue of land and charge certificates. — (1) On the first registration of a freehold or leasehold interest in land, and on the registration of a charge, a land certificate, or charge certificate, as the case may be, shall be prepared in the prescribed form; it shall state whether the title is absolute, good leasehold, qualified or possessory, and it shall be either delivered to the proprietor or deposited in the registry as the proprietor may prefer[9].

(2) If so deposited in the registry it shall be officially endorsed from time to time, as in this Act provided, with notes of all subsequent entries in the register affecting the registered land or charge to which it relates.

64.   Certificates to be produced and noted on dealings. — (1) So long as a land certificate or charge certificate is outstanding, it shall be produced to the registrar —

(*a*) on every entry in the register of a disposition by the proprietor of the registered land or charge to which it relates; and

(*b*) on every registered transmission; and

(*c*) in every case (except as hereinafter mentioned) where under this Act or otherwise notice of any estate right or claim or a restriction is entered or placed on the register, adversely affecting the title of the proprietor of the registered land or charge, but not in the case of the lodgment of a caution or of an inhibition or of a creditors' notice, or of the entry of a notice of a lease at a rent without taking a fine, or a notice of a charge for capital transfer tax[10].

(2) A note of every such entry or transmission shall be officially entered on the certificate. . . .

---

[9] See Second Report of the Conveyancing Committee: Conveyancing Simplifications, 1985, paras. 4.60–4.61, where it is said that "it is the entry on the register which provides the essential protection, and the Certificates themselves may be regarded as rather unnecessarily glamorous receipts . . . there must be scope for reducing the size of certificates to ease storage problems."

[10] As amended by FA 1975, s. 52, Sch. 12, para. 5 (5).

SPECIMEN LAND CERTIFICATE[11]

[11] Reproduced by permission of the Chief Land Registrar.

H.M. LAND REGISTRY

SPECIMEN

Edition 1   opened 10.7.1977   **TITLE NUMBER** BLK00001   *This register consists of* 2 *pages*

A. PROPERTY REGISTER
containing the description of the registered land and the estate comprised in the Title

COUNTY	DISTRICT
BLANKSHIRE	NORTH CRUMPTON

The Freehold land shown and edged with red on the plan of the above Title filed at the Registry registered on 10 July 1977 known as 1 to 9 (odd numbers) Lincoln Way and 2 Park Road.

The land edged and numbered in green on the filed plan has been removed from this title and registered under the title number or numbers shown in green on the said plan. (15:5:1978)

NOTE:—A transfer of the land edged and numbered BLK00457 in green on the filed plan dated 6 May 1978 from Michael Moxhay (Transferor) to Percival Patman contains the following exception and reservation:—

"Except and reserving to the Transferor and the owner or owners for the time being of 7 Lincoln Way the free passage and running of water and soil therefrom through the drain at the rear of the garden under the land hereby transferred." (15:5:1978)

B. PROPRIETORSHIP REGISTER
stating nature of the Title, name, address and description of the proprietor of the land and any entries affecting the right of disposing thereof

TITLE ABSOLUTE

Entry number	Proprietor, etc
1.	MICHAEL MOXHAY of 217 Lonsdale Street, Swolford, Blankshire, Builder, registered on 10 July 1977.
2.	ERNEST ELLISTON, Solicitor, and ENIS ELLISTON, his wife, both of Tithe Barn, Lincoln Way, North Crumpton, Blankshire, registered on 18 September 1979.
3.	RESTRICTION registered on 18 September 1979:—No disposition by one proprietor of the land (being the survivor of joint proprietors and not being a trust corporation) under which capital money arises is to be registered except under an order of the Registrar or of the Court.

Any entries struck through are no longer subsisting

Demand No 8037440 11/79 W & W Ltd 131¶

SPECIMEN

TITLE NUMBER BLK00001

C. CHARGES REGISTER	
containing charges, incumbrances etc., adversely affecting the land and registered dealings therewith	

Entry number	The date at the beginning of each entry is the date on which the entry was made on this edition of the register	Remarks
1.	10 July 1977—Nos 1 Lincoln Way and 2 Park Road (numbered 1 and 2 on the filed plan) are with other land subject to a perpetual yearly rent-charge of £27.10s. 3d. created by a Conveyance dated 3 December 1884 and made between (1) Andrew Austerberry (2) Benjamin Ballard. NOTE:—The Conveyance dated 6 July 1931 referred to in entry No. 3 below contains a covenant by the Vendor to pay the said rentcharge of £27.10s. 3d. in exoneration of 1 Lincoln Way and 2 Park Road and provides that in case of her default the Purchaser shall have rights of retainer, distress and entry for perception.	Rentcharge registered under BLK00002 Abstract issued with Certificate: abstract filed.
2.	10 July 1977—Lease dated 21 November 1916 of 9 Lincoln Way (numbered 3 on the filed plan) to Frederick Formby for 99 years from 29 September 1916 at the rent of £35.	Lessee's title registered under BLK00003.
3.	10 July 1977—A Conveyance dated 6 July 1931 of the land in this title and made between (1) Dorothy Duce (Vendor) (2) Michael Moxhay (Purchaser) contains the following covenants:— "The Purchaser hereby covenants with the Vendor for the benefit of her adjoining land known as 2, 4, 6 and 8 Lincoln Way to observe the stipulations specified in the Second Schedule hereto. The Second Schedule 1. NO house is to be erected of less value than £1000 the value of a house being the amount of its first net cost in material and labour of construction only estimated at the lowest current prices. 2. The land is not to be used for the purpose of carrying on the trade or business of an innkeeper or licensed victualler nor for a beer or spirit shop or for the retail of any liquors. 3. Nothing is to be done or permitted on the land which may be a nuisance or annoyance to the adjoining houses or to the neighbourhood.	
4.	~~10 July 1977—CHARGE dated 30 June 1977 registered on 10 July 1977 to~~ secure the moneys including the further advances ~~therein mentioned.~~	
5.	~~PROPRIETOR—THE WEYFORD BUILDING SOCIETY of Society House, The Avenue, Weyford, Blankshire, WF 2AB, registered on 10 July 1977.~~	
6.	18 September 1979—NOTICE of deposit of land certificate with Eastminster Bank Limited of 989 Old Street, London EC3A 4PH, registered on 18 September 1979.	

Any entries struck through are no longer subsisting

[There is also a map]

A new design for the cover of the Land Certificate is to be introduced in 1986 to be used where the register of the title has been converted into computerised form. This process will begin at Plymouth in 1986 and certificates issued by that District Registry will be the first to be issued in the new style.

HM Land Registry

Land Certificate

This is to certify

that the land described within and shown on the official plan is registered at HM Land Registry with the title number and class of title stated in the register.

There are contained in this certificate office copies of the entries in the register and of the official plan and, where so indicated in the register, of documents filed in the Land Registry.

Under section 68 of the Land Registration Act, 1925 and rule 264 of the Land Registration Rules, 1925 this certificate shall be admissible as evidence of the matters contained herein and must be produced to the Chief Land Registrar in the circumstances set out in section 64 of the said Act.

II.   Registration of Title[12]

Registration of title is concerned basically with legal title to corporeal land. It follows that the only registrable freehold estate is the fee simple absolute in possession. An incorporeal interest at law, such as a legal easement[13], is registrable only as appurtenant to registered land. A term of years absolute can be registered, provided it is a term of more than 21 years. In this case there will be two registrations of title affecting one piece of land, that of the fee simple, and that of the term of more than 21 years[14].

The register takes the form of a card index system, based on one card for each title, but divided into three parts, the property register, the proprietorship register and the charges register.

There are four classes of title, absolute, good leasehold, possessory and qualified[15]. Provision is made for conversion from one class of title to another.

A.   What Title may be Registered

i.   FIRST REGISTRATION

(a) *Freehold*

LAND REGISTRATION ACT 1925

4.   Application for registration of freehold land. — Where the title to be registered is a title to a freehold estate in land —

  (a)   any estate owner holding an estate in fee simple (including a tenant for life, statutory owner, personal representative, or trustee for sale) whether subject or not to incumbrances; or

  (b)   any other person (not being a mortgagee where there is a subsisting right of redemption or a person who has merely contracted to buy land) who is entitled to require a legal estate in fee simple whether subject or not to incumbrances, to be vested in him;

may apply to the registrar to be registered in respect of such estate, or, in the case of a person not in a fiduciary position, to have registered in his stead any nominee, as proprietor with an absolute title or with a possessory title:

  Provided that —

  (i)   Where an absolute title is required the applicant or his nominee shall not be registered as proprietor until and unless the title is approved by the registrar;

  (ii)   Where a possessory title is required the applicant or his nominee may be registered as proprietor on giving such evidence of title and serving such notices, if any, as may for the time being be prescribed; . . .

5.   Effect of first registration with absolute title. — Where the registered land is a freehold estate, the registration of any person as first proprietor thereof with an absolute title shall vest in the person so registered

---

[12] C & B, pp. 99–104, 736–737; M & W, pp. 197–204; MM, pp. 114–120.
[13] See p. 642, post.
[14] Pp. 471–477, post.
[15] On first registration of freehold land, over 99 per cent of applications are registered with absolute title. The majority of the remainder relate to titles founded purely on adverse possession. See [1980] Conv 7–9, 96–98, 165–167.

an estate in fee simple in possession in the land, together with all rights, privileges, and appurtenances belonging or appurtenant thereto, subject to the following rights and interests, that is to say, —

(a) Subject to the incumbrances, and other entries, if any, appearing on the register[16]; and

(b) Unless the contrary is expressed on the register, subject to such overriding interests, if any, as affect the registered land; and

(c) Where the first proprietor is not entitled for his own benefit to the registered land subject, as between himself and the persons entitled to minor interests, to any minor interests of such persons of which he has notice,

but free from all other estates and interests whatsoever, including estates and interests of His Majesty[17].

6. Effect of first registration with possessory title. — Where the registered land is a freehold estate, the registration of any person as first proprietor thereof with a possessory title only shall not affect or prejudice the enforcement of any estate, right or interest adverse to or in derogation of the title of the first proprietor, and subsisting or capable of arising at the time of registration of that proprietor; but, save as aforesaid, shall have the same effect as registration of a person with an absolute title[18].

7. Qualified title. — (1) Where an absolute title is required, and on the examination of the title it appears to the registrar that the title can be established only for a limited period, or only subject to certain reservations, the registrar may, on the application of the party applying to be registered, by an entry made in the register, except from the effect of registration any estate, right, or interest —

(a) arising before a specified date; or

(b) arising under a specified instrument or otherwise particularly described in the register,

and a title registered subject to such excepted estate, right, or interest shall be called a qualified title.

(2) Where the registered land is a freehold estate, the registration of a person as first proprietor thereof with a qualified title shall have the same effect as the registration of such person with an absolute title, save that registration with a qualified title shall not affect or prejudice the enforcement of any estate, right or interest appearing by the register to be excepted.

(b) Leasehold

8. Application for registration of leasehold land. — (1) Where the title to be registered is a title to a leasehold interest in land —

(a) any estate owner (including a tenant for life, statutory owner, personal representative, or trustee for sale, but not including a mortgagee where there is a subsisting right of redemption), holding

---

[16] If an option to renew a lease is void for non-registration under LCA 1972, s. 4 (6), it cannot be revived by subsequent first registration of title under LRA 1925, s. 9, and the entry of the lease containing the option on the charges register: *Kitney v M.E.P.C. Ltd* [1977] 1 WLR 981, [1978] 1 All ER 595; (1977). 41 Conv (NS) 356; [1978] CLJ 13 (D. J. Hayton).

[17] See (1974) 38 Conv (NS) 236 (S.N.L. Palk).

[18] *Spectrum Investment Co v Holmes* [1981] 1 WLR 221, [1981] 1 All ER 6, p. 193, post.

under a lease for a term of years absolute of which more than twenty-one are unexpired, whether subject or not to incumbrances; or

(b) any other person (not being a mortgagee as aforesaid and not being a person who has merely contracted to buy the leasehold interest) who is entitled to require a legal leasehold estate held under such a lease as aforesaid (whether subject or not to incumbrances) to be vested in him,

may apply to the registrar to be registered in respect of such estate, or in the case of a person not being in a fiduciary position to have registered in his stead any nominee, as proprietor with an absolute title, with a good leasehold title or with a possessory title:

Provided that —

(i) Where an absolute title is required, the applicant or his nominee shall not be registered as proprietor until and unless the title both to the leasehold and to the freehold, and to any intermediate leasehold that may exist, is approved by the registrar;

(ii) Where a good leasehold title is required, the applicant or his nominee shall not be registered as proprietor until and unless the title to the leasehold interest is approved by the registrar;

(iii) Where a possessory title is required, the applicant or his nominee may be registered as proprietor on giving such evidence of title and serving such notices, if any, as may for the time being be prescribed;

(iv) If on an application for registration with a possessory title the registrar is satisfied as to the title to the leasehold interest, he may register it as good leasehold, whether the applicant consents to such registration or not, but in that case no higher fee shall be charged than would have been charged for registration with possessory title.

(2) Leasehold land held under a lease containing an absolute prohibition against all dealings therewith inter vivos shall not be registered in pursuance of this Act; and leasehold land held under a lease containing a restriction on any such dealings, shall not be registered under this Act unless and until provision is made in the prescribed manner for preventing any dealing therewith in contravention of the restriction by an entry on the register to that effect, or otherwise[19].

(3) Where on an application to register a mortgage term, wherein no right of redemption is subsisting, it appears that the applicant is entitled in equity to the superior term, if any, out of which it was created, the registrar shall register him as proprietor of the superior term without any entry to the effect that the legal interest in that term is outstanding, and on such registration the superior term shall vest in the proprietor and the mortgage term shall merge therein:

Provided that this subsection shall not apply where the mortgage term does not comprise the whole of the land included in the superior term, unless in that case the rent, if any, payable in respect of the superior term has been apportioned, or the rent is of no money value or no rent is reserved, and

---

[19] Law Commission Report on Land Registration Part IV Treatment of Leases (Law Com No. 125, HC 86), para. 4.30, recommends that leases should cease to be rendered non-registrable by reason of a prohibition against their assignment.

unless the covenants, if any, entered into for the benefit of the reversion have been apportioned (either expressly or by implication) as respects the land comprised in the mortgage term.

9. Effect of first registration with absolute title. — Where the registered land is a leasehold interest, the registration under this Act of any person as first proprietor thereof with an absolute title shall be deemed to vest in such person the possession of the leasehold interest described, with all implied or expressed rights, privileges, and appurtenances attached to such interest, subject to the following obligations, rights, and interests, that is to say, —

(*a*) Subject to all implied and express covenants, obligations, and liabilities incident to the registered land; and

(*b*) Subject to the incumbrances and other entries (if any) appearing on the register; and

(*c*) Unless the contrary is expressed on the register, subject to such overriding interests, if any, as affect the registered land; and

(*d*) Where such first proprietor is not entitled for his own benefit to the registered land subject as between himself and the persons entitled to minor interests, to any minor interests of such persons of which he has notice;

but free from all other estates and interests whatsoever, including estates and interests of His Majesty.

10. Effect of first registration with good leasehold title. — Where the registered land is a leasehold interest, the registration of a person as first proprietor thereof with a good leasehold title shall not affect or prejudice the enforcement of any estate, right or interest affecting or in derogation of the title of the lessor to grant the lease, but, save as aforesaid, shall have the same effect as registration with an absolute title[20].

13. Regulations as to examination of title by registrar. —

(*c*) If the registrar, upon the examination of any title, is of opinion that the title is open to objection, but is nevertheless a title the holding under which will not be disturbed, he may approve of such title, or may require the applicant to apply to the court, upon a statement signed by the registrar, for its sanction to the registration[1].

LAND REGISTRATION RULES 1925

72. Dealings by persons having right to apply for first registration.— (1) Where a person having the right to apply for registration as first proprietor desires to deal with the land in any way permitted by the Act before he is himself registered as proprietor he may do so in the manner, and subject to the conditions, which would be applicable if he was in fact the registered proprietor. In the case of a transfer, the transferee shall be deemed to be the applicant for first registration and shall be entered on the register accordingly.

---

[20] LRA 1925, ss. 11, 12 contain analogous provisions with regard to possessory and qualified title.

[1] (1976) 40 Conv (NS) 122 (C. T. Emery); *MEPC Ltd v Christian-Edwards* [1978] Ch 281, [1978] 3 All ER 795; affd. [1981] AC 205, [1979] 3 All ER 752; [1978] Conv 382 (F. R. Crane).

ii.   REGISTERED DEALINGS WITH REGISTERED LAND

LAND REGISTRATION ACT 1925

20.   Effect of registration of dispositions of freeholds[2]. — (1) In the
case of a freehold estate registered with an absolute title, a disposition of the
registered land or of a legal estate therein, including a lease thereof, for
valuable consideration shall, when registered, confer on the transferee or
grantee an estate in fee simple or the term of years absolute or other legal
estate expressed to be created in the land dealt with, together with all rights,
privileges, and appurtenances belonging or appurtenant thereto, including
(subject to any entry to the contrary in the register) the appropriate rights
and interests which would, under the Law of Property Act, 1925, have been
transferred if the land had not been registered, subject —

> (*a*) to the incumbrances and other entries, if any, appearing on the
> register and any charge for capital transfer tax subject to which the
> disposition takes effect under section 73 of this Act[3];
>
> (*b*) unless the contrary is expressed on the register, to the overriding
> interests, if any, affecting the estate transferred or created,

but free from all other estates and interests whatsoever, including estates and
interests of His Majesty, and the disposition shall operate in like manner as if
the registered transferor or grantor were (subject to any entry to the contrary
in the register) entitled to the registered land in fee simple in possession for
his own benefit.

(4) Where any such disposition is made without valuable consideration, it
shall, so far as the transferee or grantee is concerned, but subject to any
minor interests subject to which the transferor or grantor held the same, but,
save as aforesaid, shall, when registered, in all respects, and in particular as
respects any registered dealings on the part of the transferee or grantee, have
the same effect as if the disposition had been made for valuable consideration.

In *Peffer v Rigg* [1977] 1 WLR 285, [1978] 3 All ER 745[4], Peffer and Rigg
(the first defendant) purchased, in 1962, 103 Leighton Road, Kentish Town,
London, as a home for their mother-in-law. Rigg was registered as sole
proprietor, but it was agreed that Rigg should hold the house on trust for
Peffer and himself as tenants in common in equal shares. In 1967 this was
confirmed in a formal trust deed. Peffer's interest was not protected in the
register (by way of restriction, notice or caution), nor had he an overriding
interest. In 1971, as part of the financial arrangements between Mr and Mrs
Rigg on their divorce, Rigg transferred the house to Mrs Rigg (the second
defendant) for £1. Mrs Rigg, who was "perfectly well aware" of the trust in
favour of Peffer, was registered as proprietor.

---

[2] LRA 1925, s. 20 (2), (3) contains analogous provisions with regard to qualified and possessory
title. Cf. s. 23 with regard to leaseholds, p. 473, post.
[3] As amended by FA 1975, s. 52, Sch. 12, para. 5 (2); CTTA 1984, s. 276, Sch. 8, para. 1.
[4] (1977) 41 Conv (NS) 207 (F. R. Crane); 93 LQR 341 (R. J. Smith); [1977] CLJ 227 (D.
Hayton); (1977) 40 MLR 602 (S. Anderson); [1978] Conv (J. Martin). See also *Orakpo v
Manson Investments Ltd* [1977] 1 WLR 347, at 360, 370, [1977] 1 All ER 666 at 678, 687; (1978)
94 LQR 239 (D. C. Jackson).

GRAHAM J, in granting Peffer a declaration of his half-interest and an order for sale, said at 292, at 750:

"The purported transfer, however, of the whole of the beneficial interest in the property by the first defendant to the second defendant on the occasion of the divorce agreement in the light of their knowledge of the true facts as I have found them seems to me to be in a very different position. It was argued by Mr Banks, for the second defendant, that the property was transferred to her for valuable consideration as part of the divorce agreement and that, therefore, the combined effect of sections 20 and 59 of the Land Registration Act 1925 protected the second defendant against any claim or interest of the plaintiff because there is no entry on the register in his favour prior to the transfer to the second defendant. This argument would be convincing if it were not for my finding that the second defendant at the time knew perfectly well that the first defendant could not transfer to her more than a half share of the property. It is this knowledge which seems to me to cause great difficulty to her and prevents her argument succeeding for a number of different reasons put forward by Mr Poulton for the plaintiff at the second hearing. He argues first that the purported transfer from the first to the second defendant of the beneficial interest in the whole of the property, 103, Leighton Road, was expressed to be for the consideration of £1. This is nominal consideration and not valuable consideration and it follows that the second defendant is not protected by section 20 of the Land Registration Act 1925. In accordance with the provisions of section 20 (4) she can only take subject to any minor interests subject to which the first defendant held the same. He was party to the trust deed of 30 May 1968, and clearly had notice of the plaintiff's half interest in the property. The second defendant can therefore only take subject to the minor interest of the plaintiff in the property subject to which the first defendant held it.

The argument to the contrary is that the transfer was only part of the whole agreement entered into by the first and second defendants on the occasion of the divorce and it is not therefore right to limit the consideration for the transfer to the £1 expressed to be therefor. The consideration, there, was a great deal more and included all the obligations undertaken by the second defendant. Such consideration was therefore not nominal but valuable within section 20 and the second defendant received the protection of the section. I do not see why, when the parties have chosen to express a transfer as being for a nominal consideration, the court should seek to hold that the consideration was in fact otherwise than as agreed and stated. If, however, the proper view is that there was valuable consideration for the transfer, then it is argued as follows. There is a contrast between sections 20 and 59 of the Act. Section 20 (1) protects any 'transferee' for valuable consideration. By section 18 (5) 'transfer' and 'transferee' in relation to freehold land have very wide meanings but are not specifically defined in section 3. It is to be noted, however, that section 20, though it mentions valuable consideration, does not mention 'good faith' as being necessary on the part of the transferee, nor does it mention notice. It can be argued therefore that section 20 seems to be saying that a transferee whether he has good faith or not, and whether he has notice or not, takes free of all interests (other than overriding interests) provided he has given valuable consideration.

This at first sight seems a remarkable proposition and though undoubtedly the property legislation of 1925 was intended to simplify such matters of title as far as possible, I find it difficult to think that section 20 of this Act can have been intended to be as broad in scope as this. Similar doubt is expressed in *Brickdale & Stewart-Wallace's Land Registration Act 1925*, 4th edn (1939), p. 107, note (1). The provisions for rectification in section 82 as against a proprietor in possession who has been a party to a fraud, mistake or an omission in consequence of which rectification of the register is sought also seem to me to show that section 20 must be read with some limitations; see also *Ruoff & Roper, Registered Conveyancing*, 3rd edn (1972), p. 417. Section 59 (6)[5] on the other hand speaks of a 'purchaser' not being affected by matters which are not protected by a caution or other entry on the register. By definition, however (see section 3(xxi)). ' "Purchaser" means a purchaser in good faith for valuable consideration . . .' It seems clear therefore that as a matter of construction a purchaser who is not in fact one 'in good faith' *will* be concerned with matters not protected by a caution or other entry on the register, at any rate, as I hold, if he has notice thereof. If these sections 20 and 59 are read together in the context of the Act they can be reconciled by holding that if the 'transferee' spoken of in section 20 is in fact a 'purchaser' he will only be protected if he has given valuable consideration and is in good faith. He cannot in my judgment be in good faith if he has in fact notice of something which affects his title as in the present case. Of course if he and, a fortiori, if a purchaser from him has given valuable consideration and in fact has no notice he is under no obligation to go behind the register, and will in such a case be fully protected. This view of the matter seems to me to enable the two sections to be construed consistently together without producing the unreasonable result of permitting a transferee purchaser to take advantage of the Act, and divest himself of knowledge of defects in his own title, and secure to himself a flawless title which he ought not in justice to be allowed to obtain. This view of the Act produces a result which is also produced by applying the principles applicable in the case of a constructive trust which I will now consider."

His Lordship held that the second defendant was bound by a constructive trust, p. 145, post, and continued:

"On this assumption it seems to me that the ground is properly laid for granting rectification of the register under section 82. The second defendant, even though in possession, comes within the exceptions of subsection (3) and this would in my judgment be a case where rectification could properly be ordered against her. Mr Reid, for the first defendant, supported the propositions of Mr Poulton and adopted his argument. In addition he referred to *Jones v Lipman* [1962] 1 WLR 832, [1962] 1 All ER 442, which, he submitted, could only have been decided on the basis that the company in that case could not escape from, or divest itself of, its knowledge by reason of sections 20 and 59. It seems that this must be so, and Russell J mentions and rejects the argument at 837, at 445. . . .

It follows that in my judgment the second defendant holds the property in question in trust for herself and the plaintiff and that the latter is entitled to appropriate relief."

---

[5] P. 137, post.

B. Conversion to Another Title

77. Conversion of possessory into absolute or good leasehold title.—
(2) Where the registrar is satisfied as to the title he may, on a transfer for valuable consideration of land registered with a qualified, good leasehold or possessory title, enter the title of a transferee or grantee as absolute or good leasehold, as the case may require or admit, . . .

(3) The following provisions shall apply with respect to land registered with a qualified or possessory title:—

(*b*) Where the land has been registered, if freehold land, for fifteen years, or if leasehold land, for ten years, with a possessory title, the registrar shall, if satisfied that the proprietor is in possession, and after giving such notices, if any, as may be prescribed, enter the title of the proprietor of the freehold land as absolute, and the title of the proprietor of the leasehold land as good leasehold. . . .

(4) Where the land has been registered with a good leasehold title for at least ten years, the registrar may, subject to the payment of any additional insurance fee and to any advertisements or inquiries which may be prescribed, and if he is satisfied that the proprietor or successive proprietors has or have been in possession during the said period, at the request of the proprietor enter his title as absolute.

(6) Any person, other than the proprietor, who suffers loss by reason of any entry on the register made by virtue of this section shall be entitled to be indemnified under this Act as if a mistake had been made in the register.

Law Commission Report on Land Registration 1983
(Law Com No. 125 HC 86), para. 3.17.

"3.17 Our detailed recommendations are as follows:—

(1) Any inferior freehold title should be convertible to absolute title at any time if the Registrar is satisfied as to the title.

(2) Any inferior leasehold title should be convertible to absolute title at any time if the Registrar is satisfied both as to the leasehold title and as to any reversionary title; and the provisions of section 77 (4) for the conversion of good leasehold (after lapse of time) without evidence as to title should be removed.

(3) A single period of 12 years should be substituted for the periods of 15 and 10 years in section 77 (3) (*b*) after which possessory freehold and leasehold titles may be converted without documentary evidence to absolute and good leasehold titles respectively.

(4) Section 77 should be redrafted to give effect to the recommendations at (1) to (3) above and otherwise to clarify and modernise the existing provisions."

C. The Registers[6]

i.　TRIPARTITE

LAND REGISTRATION RULES 1925

2.　Parts of register and title number. — The register shall consist of three parts, called the Property Register, the Proprietorship Register, and the Charges Register. The title to each registered property shall bear a distinguishing number.

3.　Property Register. — The Property Register shall contain —
(1) The description of the land and estate comprised in the title.[7]. . .
(2) Such notes as have to be entered relating —
　(b) to exemption from any of the overriding interests mentioned in section 70 of the Act[8];
　(c) to easements[9], rights, privileges, conditions and covenants for the benefit of the land[10], and other like matters.

5.　Leasehold land, rentcharges and land subject thereto. — (1) In the case of leasehold land there shall be entered in the Property Register a reference to the registered lease, and such particulars of the lease, and of the exceptions or reservations therefrom (if any) as the applicant may desire, and the Registrar approve; and a reference to the lessor's title, if registered.
(2) In the case of rentcharges created by an instrument, that instrument shall be referred to in the Property Register.
(3) Where land is acquired in consideration of the reservation of a rentcharge and the grant of the land contains any exceptions or reservations, that grant shall be referred to in the Property Register.

6.　Proprietorship Register. — The Proprietorship Register shall state the nature of the title, and shall contain the name, address, and description of the proprietor of the land, and cautions, inhibitions, and restrictions affecting his right of disposing thereof.

7.　Charges Register. — The Charges Register shall contain —
　(a) incumbrances subsisting at the date of first registration;
　(b) subsequent charges, and other incumbrances (including notices of leases and other notices of adverse interests or claims permitted by the Act);
　(c) such notes as have to be entered relating to covenants, conditions, and other rights adversely affecting the land;
　(d) all such dealings with registered charges and incumbrances as are capable of registration.

10.[11]　List of pending applications for first registration. — Until the estate in land comprised in a pending application for first registration is shown on the Index Map, the title number and a short description of the land shall be entered in a list known as the list of pending applications for first registration.

---

[6] See Ruoff, Appx. "A" for Model Registers and Plans.
[7] See Law Commission Report on Land Registration Part I Identity and Boundaries 1983 (Law Com No. 125 HC 86); [1984] Conv 2.
[8] See pp. 118–121, post.
[9] See p. 642, post.
[10] See p. 830, post.
[11] As substituted by LRR 1978, r. 4.

ii. DELIVERY AND DATE OF APPLICATIONS

LAND REGISTRATION RULES 1925

83.[12] **Delivery of applications.** — (1) Every application shall be delivered at the proper office and, when so delivered, shall be allocated an official reference number and shall be dated as of the day on which it is deemed under rule 85 of these rules to have been delivered.

(2) The application shall be completed by registration as of the day on which and, subject to the effect of any provision of the Act or of any rules made thereunder, of the priority in which it is deemed to have been delivered.

85. Date of delivery of applications. — Every application delivered at the proper office after 11.00 hours on one day and before or at 11.00 hours on the next day shall be deemed to have been delivered at the same time, namely, immediately after 11.00 hours on the second day.

iii. PRIVACY[13]

LAND REGISTRATION ACT 1925

112. Inspection of register and other documents at land registry[14]. — (1) Subject —

(*a*) to section 112A and 112AA below[15];

(*b*) to the provisions of this Act as to furnishing information to Government departments and local authorities[16]; and

(*c*) to such exceptions as may be prescribed,

any person registered as proprietor of any land or charge, and any person authorised —

(i) by any such proprietor[15a]; or

(ii) by an order made under subsection (2) or (3) of this section; or

(iii) by general rule,

but no other person, shall have a right, on payment of a fee and in accordance with the prescribed procedure, to inspect and make copies of the

---

[12] As substituted by LRR 1978, rr. 8, 10. For priority of applications where two or more applications are deemed to have been delivered at the same time, see r. 84, as substituted by LRR 1978, r. 9.

[13] Cf. the position in unregistered land, where there is no general duty on an estate owner to produce his title deeds, but where anyone can search for possible land charges merely by paying the appropriate fee. Law Commission Second Report on Registered Land: Inspection of the Register 1985 (Law Com No. 148 HC 551) recommends that the register of title should become public. See p. 161, post.

[14] As substituted by AJA 1982, s. 67, Sch. 5 (*b*).

[15] S. 112A, as amended by Insolvency Act 1985, s. 235, Sch. 8, para. 5 (5), 5 (6), refers to inspection in connection with criminal proceedings; s. 112A, as inserted by Insolvency Act 1985, s. 215, refers to inspection in connection with involvency.

[15a] Under LRA 1925, s. 110 (1), a purchaser (other than a lessee or chargee) is entitled to the vendor's authority to inspect the register of title.

[16] LRA 1925, s. 129 (including the Commissioners of Inland Revenue); LRR 1925, rr. 287–297. The Index Maps, the General Map and the Parcels Index are open to inspection: LRR 1925, r. 12 (1), as amended by LRR 1978, r. 5. The index of proprietors' names is open to anyone who satisfies the Registrar that he "is interested generally (for instance, as trustee in bankruptcy or personal representative) in the property"; ibid., r. 9.

whole or any part of any register or document in the custody of the **registrar** relating to such land or charge.

(2) The High Court may by order authorise —

    (*a*) the inspection of a register or document in the custody of the registrar and relating to land or a charge; and

    (*b*) the making of copies of the whole or any part of any such register or document,

if —

    (i) it appears to the court that the register or any such document may contain information which is relevant to proceedings pending in the court (including proceedings for the enforcement of a judgment or order of the High Court or any other court); or

    (ii) it appears to the court, on an application made for that purpose, that such an order ought to be made for any other reason[17].

112B. Search on behalf of mortgagee for notice or caution for statutory rights of occupation. — Where registered land which consists of or includes a dwelling house is subject to a registered charge, or to a mortgage which is protected by a notice or caution in accordance with section 106 (3)[18] of this Act, the proprietor of the registered charge, or as the case may be the mortgagee, may requisition an official search of the register to ascertain whether any notice or caution affecting that land has been registered under section 2 (8) of the Matrimonial Homes Act 1983[18a], and a certificate showing the result of that search[19].

LAND REGISTRATION RULES 1925

287. Authority to inspect the register. — Subject to the provisions of sections 59, 61[20] and 112 of the Act, any entry in the register, and any document in the custody of the Registrar and referred to in the register, may be inspected by or under the authority of the proprietor of the land or of any charge or incumbrance thereon.

288. Inspection of Property Register only and of other entries after notice to proprietor. — (1) The Property Register and the filed plan of any title may be inspected by any person interested in the land or in any adjoining land or in a charge or incumbrance thereon.

(2) Other entries in the register and documents referred to therein, and the statutory declaration in support of a caution, may be inspected by any person interested, on giving three days' notice to the proprietor or on satisfying the Registrar that, by reason of the death of a sole proprietor, or for any other sufficient reason, he cannot obtain the requisite authority for or consent to such inspection, and that such inspection is reasonable and proper.

---

[17] Sub-s. (3) deals with the orders which can be made by a county court.

[18] P. 741, post.

[18a] P. 259, post.

[19] As added by Matrimonial Homes and Property Act 1981, s. 4 (4), and amended by Matrimonial Homes Act 1983, s. 12, Sch. 2.

[20] The sections entitle a judgment creditor, official receiver or trustee in bankruptcy to inspect the register.

iv. SEARCHES

LAND REGISTRATION (OFFICIAL SEARCHES) RULES 1981[1]

5. Official search by purchaser. — When a purchaser[2] has applied in accordance with these rules for an official search, any entry which is made in the register during the priority period[3] relating to that search shall be postponed to a subsequent application to register the instrument effecting the purchase and, if the purchase is dependent on a prior dealing, to a subsequent application to register the instrument effecting that dealing provided each such subsequent application:

    (i) is deemed to have been delivered at the proper office within the priority period;

    (ii) affects the same land or charge as the postponed entry; and

    (iii) is in due course completed by registration[4].

9. Official search without priority. — (1) A person (not being a purchaser requiring an official search under rule 3 of these rules) who has authority to inspect a register may apply on form 94C for an official search of that register.

(2) Form 94C shall be delivered in duplicate to the proper office and on completion of the search an official certificate of search shall be issued in form 94D or form 94E but this certificate shall not confer upon the applicant priority for the registration of any dealing.

III. Overriding Interests[5]

Interests in land which cannot be registered as separate titles fall into the category of either overriding interests or minor interests. Overriding interests are enforceable without being protected on the register, and bind a registered proprietor and his transferee even though he does not know of their existence. They thus detract from the principle that the register should be a mirror of the title. They are listed in section 70 (1) of the Land Registration Act 1925 and have been added to by later enactments[6]. They consist of third party rights which on policy grounds should bind a purchaser, but which for some reason or other do not fit into the pattern of the register. If, however, an overriding interest does appear on the register[7], then its protection under

---

[1] See (1978) 75 LS Gaz 1173–1174 (R. B. Roper). There were 3,509,531 applications for official search, office copies and other ancillary services made during 1983–1984: Annual Report for 1984–1985, para. 13.

[2] "Any person (including a lessee or chargee) who in good faith and for valuable consideration acquires or intends to acquire a legal estate in land" (r. 2). On the meaning of good faith, see *Smith v Morrison* [1974] 1 WLR 659, [1974] 1 All ER 957.

[3] Of 30 working days (r. 2).

[4] A search may be made by telephone or teleprinter (rr. 7, 8). Such a search is not an official search for the purpose of indemnity under LRA 1925, s. 83 (3), p. 150, post.

[5] C & B, pp. 104–105, 739–745; M & W, pp. 204–209; MM, pp. 121–124; Ruoff and Roper, chap. 6; W & C, vol. 6, pp. 63–67; Barnsley, pp. 44–65; Farrand (2nd edn), pp. 184–209; Hayton (3rd edn), chap. 6.

[6] LRR 1925, r. 258, p. 120, post; Tithe Act 1936, s. 13 (11), p. 119, n. 15, post; Coal Act 1938, s. 41: Coal Industry Nationalisation Act 1946, ss. 5, 8, Sch. 1.

[7] And it often does: Ruoff and Roper, pp. 112–114; (1969) 32 MLR at p. 129 (T. B. F. Ruoff). See *Re Dances Way, West Town, Hayling Island* [1962] Ch 490 at 507, [1962] 2 All ER 42 at 50, per UPJOHN LJ.

this category is superfluous; it ceases to bind as an overriding interest and its protection is then the protection of a minor interest entered on the register.

There has been criticism of the category of overriding interests[8], especially of the wide-ranging safety-net of paragraph (*g*), which accords protection to "the rights of every person in actual occupation of the land or in receipt of the rents and profits thereof, save where enquiry is made of such person and the rights are not disclosed". This paragraph protects an occupier who has failed either to register a title or to protect an interest by an entry on the register. This is diametrically opposed to the Draconian provisions of the Land Charges Act 1972 in the case of unregistered land under which a purchaser takes free of an unregistered land charge even if the person entitled thereto is in possession[9].

Section 70 (1) (*g*) is, in effect, an application of the rule in *Hunt v Luck*[10] to registered land; extended so as to include the rights of every person in receipt of the rents and profits of the land; and extended, it seems, in some of the decisions on the question of "actual occupation"[11]. On principle, this type of rule is sounder than the Land Charges Act rule. In most cases, of course, vacant possession will be given to the purchaser on completion, and the problem does not arise. Where the purchaser completes when some other person is in occupation, he will almost always, if he is careful, discover the occupation. In that situation, three solutions are possible; the purchaser takes subject to that interest; the purchaser takes free even though he has actual notice; or if he has constructive notice. The last solution would revive all the problems which registration is intended to avoid. The second solution (that of the Land Charges Act 1972) can cause great and obvious injustice. The first will nearly always produce the right result. It should not, it is submitted, be abandoned in favour of the logical symmetry of a complete system of registration.

LAND REGISTRATION ACT 1925

3. Interpretation. — (xvi) "Overriding interests" mean all the incumbrances, interests, rights, and powers not entered on the register but subject to which registered dispositions are by this Act to take effect, and in regard to land registered at the commencement of this Act include the matters which are by any enactment repealed by this Act declared not to be incumbrances; . . .

---

70. Liability of registered land to overriding interests. — (1) All registered land shall, unless under the provisions of this Act the contrary is expressed on the register, be deemed to be subject to such of the following overriding interests as may be for the time being subsisting in reference thereto, and such interests shall not be treated as incumbrances within the meaning of this Act, (that is to say):—

    (*a*) Rights of common[12], drainage rights, customary rights (until extinguished), public rights, profits à prendre, rights of sheep-walk, rights of way, watercourses, rights of water, and other easements

---

[8] Law Commission Working Paper No. 37 (1971). The Law Commission hopes to publish a report in 1986; see p. 132, post.
[9] LCA 1972, s. 4, p. 37, ante.
[10] [1901] 1 Ch 45; affd. [1902] 1 Ch 428, p. 46, ante.
[11] P. 130 et seq., post.
[12] Commons Registration Act 1965, s. 1 (1), (2), p. 58, ante.

not being equitable easements required to be protected by notice on the register[13];

(b) Liability to repair highways by reason of tenure, quit-rents, crown rents, heriots, and other rents and charges (until extinguished) having their origin in tenure;

(c) Liability to repair the chancel of any church[14];

(d) Liability in respect of embankments, and sea and river walls;

(e) . . .,[15] payments in lieu of tithe, and charges or annuities payable for the redemption of tithe rentcharges; ·

(f) Subject to the provisions of this Act, rights acquired or in course of being acquired under the Limitation Acts[16];

(g) The rights of every person in actual occupation of the land or in receipt of the rents and profits thereof[17], save where enquiry is made of such person and the rights are not disclosed[18];

---

[13] *Celsteel Ltd v Alton House Holdings Ltd* [1985] 1 WLR 204, [1985] 2 All ER 562, p. 644, post.

[14] Law Commission Report on Liability for Chancel Repairs 1985 (Law Com No. 152) recommends that liability should be abolished after 10 years; but, if not abolished promptly, it should be registered in Local Land Charges registers, and failure to register would exonerate a purchaser of the land; (1984) 100 LQR 185 (J. H. Baker). For the liability in unregistered land, see *Hauxton Parochial Church Council v Stevens* [1929] P 240; *Chivers & Sons Ltd v Air Ministry and Queen's College, Cambridge* [1955] Ch 585, [1955] 2 All ER 607.

[15] As amended by Tithe Act 1936, s. 48, Sch. IX, and Finance Act 1963, ss. 68, 73 (8) (b), Sch. 14, Pt. VI. Tithe redemption annuities were extinguished as from 2 October 1977; FA 1977 s. 56.

[16] LRA 1925, s. 75, p. 193, post; *Re Chowood's Registered Land* [1933] Ch 574 at 581; *Bridges v Mees* [1957] Ch 475, [1957] 2 All ER 577.

[17] *National Provincial Bank Ltd v Ainsworth* [1965] AC 1175, [1965] 2 All ER 472, p. 121, post (deserted wife's equity not overriding interest); *Strand Securities Ltd v Caswell* [1965] Ch 958, [1965] 1 All ER 820, p. 130, post (step-daughter's occupation on her own account of flat by gratuitous licence from step-father lessee not actual occupation); *Webb v Pollmount Ltd* [1966] Ch 584, [1966] 1 All ER 481, p. 129, post (option to purchase freehold reversion contained in lease held to be overriding interest); *London and Cheshire Insurance Co Ltd v Laplagrene Property Co Ltd* [1971] Ch 499, [1971] 1 All ER 766, p. 130, post (unpaid vendor's lien under lease-back from purchaser held to be overriding interest); *Hodgson v Marks* [1971] Ch 892, [1971] 2 All ER 684 (equitable fee simple under bare trust held to be overriding interest); *Lee-Parker v Izzet (No. 2)* [1972] 1 WLR 775, [1972] 2 All ER 800 (overriding interest conceded where purchaser-occupier expended money at request of vendor in belief induced by vendor that purchaser was beneficial owner under contract of sale, later held void for uncertainty); *Epps v Esso Petroleum Co Ltd* [1973] 1 WLR 1071, [1973] 2 All ER 465, p. 154, post (intermittent parking of car on undefined space not actual occupation); *E.S. Schwab & Co Ltd v McCarthy* (1976) 31 P & C R 196 ("receipt" means "actual receipt" of rent from a tenant); *Williams and Glyn's Bank Ltd v Boland* [1981] AC 487, [1980] 2 All ER 408, p. 121, post (wife held to be in actual occupation of matrimonial home registered in sole name of husband); *Blacklocks v JB Developments (Godalming) Ltd* [1982] Ch 183, [1981] 3 All ER 392 (right to rectify contract and conveyance for mistake [1983] Conv 169, 257 (J.T.F.) or right to rectify the register [1983] Conv 361 (D.G. Barnsley) held to be overriding interest. No reference was made to *Smith v Jones* [1954] 1 WLR 1089, [1954] 2 All ER 823, p. 47, ante; *Eden Park Estates Ltd v Longman* [1982] Conv 239 (P. H. Kenny) (payment in advance in respect of rent by tenant to original landlord held not to be overriding interest); *Kling v Keston Properties Ltd* (1983) 49 P & CR 212 (right of pre-emption held to be overriding interest; see *Pritchard v Briggs* [1980] Ch 338, [1980] 1 All ER 294, p. 86 ante); *Chhokar v Chhokar* [1984] FLR 313, p. 132, post (wife evicted by fraudulent purchaser of matrimonial home from husband held to be in actual occupation); *Celsteel Ltd v Alton House Holdings Ltd* [1985] 1 WLR 204, [1985] 2 All ER 562 (lessee exercising right of way to garage held to be in actual occupation); *City of London Building Society v Flegg* (1985) Times, 23 December, p. 128, post (equitable interests of parents as tenants in common arising from contribution to purchase price of house, registered in names of their daughter and son-in-law, held to be overriding interests; and not overreachable by mortgagees under LPA 1925, s. 2 (1) (ii), p. 205, post); *Winkworth v Edward Baron Development Co Ltd* (1985) Times, 23 December (equitable interest of wife in occupation of matrimonial home, arising from contribution to purchase price paid by husband and wife to company controlled by them both, held to be overriding interest; *Paddington Building Society v Mendelsohn* (1985) 50 P & CR 244 (only *enforceable* rights of actual occupant at date of transfer are protected under para. (g)).

See also *Bridges v Mees*, supra (overlap between para. (f) and para. (g)). For statutory exclusions from para. (g), see Matrimonial Homes Act 1983, s. 2 (8) (b) (spouse's right of occupation); Leasehold Reform Act 1967, s. 5 (5) (tenant's right to acquire freehold or apply for extended lease).

[18] On the proviso, cf. in unregistered land *Midland Bank Ltd v Farmpride Hatcheries Ltd* (1980) 260 EG 493, p. 28, ante.

(*h*) In the case of a possessory, qualified, or good leasehold title[19], all estates, rights, interests, and powers excepted from the effect of registration;

(*i*) Rights under local land charges unless and until registered or protected on the register in the prescribed manner[20];

(*j*) Rights of fishing and sporting, seignorial and manorial rights of all descriptions (until extinguished), and franchises;

(*k*) Leases for any term or interest not exceeding twenty-one years, granted[1] at a rent without taking a fine[2]; . . .

Provided that, where it is proved to the satisfaction of the registrar that any land registered or about to be registered is exempt from land tax, or tithe rentcharge or payments in lieu of tithe, or from charges or annuities payable for the redemption of tithe rentcharge, the registrar may notify the fact on the register in the prescribed manner.

(2) Where at the time of first registration any easement, right, privilege, or benefit created by an instrument and appearing on the title adversely affects the land, the registrar shall enter a note thereof on the register[3].

(3) Where the existence of any overriding interest mentioned in this section is proved to the satisfaction of the registrar or admitted, he may (subject to any prescribed exceptions) enter notice of the same or of a claim thereto on the register, but no claim to an easement, right, or privilege not created by an instrument shall be noted against the title to the servient land if the proprietor of such land (after the prescribed notice is given to him) shows sufficient cause to the contrary.

LAND REGISTRATION RULES 1925

197. Notice of freedom from or the existence of overriding interests. —
(1) Where any person desires to have an entry made in the register of the freedom from or the existence of an overriding interest mentioned in Section 70 of the Act, the application shall be made in writing and shall state the particulars of the entry required to be made[4].

(6) Any entry showing that the registered land is free from any one or more of the liabilities, rights, or interests, mentioned in Section 70 of the Act, shall be made in the Property Register.

258. Adverse easements treated as overriding interests. — Rights, privileges, and appurtenances appertaining or reputed to appertain to land or demised, occupied, or enjoyed therewith or reputed or known as part or

---

[19] LRA 1925, ss. 6, 7, 10, 11, 12, pp. 107, 109, ante.

[20] LRA, s. 49 (1) (*c*), p. 136, post; s. 59 (2), p. 137, post; p. 51, ante.

[1] This does not include an agreement for a lease: *City Permanent Building Society v Miller* [1952] Ch 840, [1952] 2 All ER 621, p. 473 post. But a person in possession under an agreement for a lease may be protected under para. (*g*). No application can be made for the entry of a notice of a lease for 21 years or less: LRA 1925, s. 48 (1). Law Commission Report on Land Registration Part IV Treatment of Leases 1983 (Law Com No. 121 HC 86) para. 4.37 recommends that the exclusion of gratuitous leases and of leases granted at a premium should be removed.

[2] Para. (*l*) specifies certain rights to mines and minerals existing before 1926.

[3] See p. 642, post.

[4] See *Re Dances Way, West Town, Hayling Island* [1962] Ch 490 at 510, [1962] 2 All ER 42 at 52, per DIPLOCK LJ; and cf. Ruoff and Roper, p. 115.

parcel of or appurtenant thereto, which adversely affect registered land, are overriding interests within section 70 of the Act, and shall not be deemed incumbrances for the purposes of the Act[5].

A. The Legal Framework of Section 70

In *National Provincial Bank Ltd v Ainsworth* [1965] AC 1175, [1965] 2 All ER 472, Lord WILBERFORCE said at 1261, at 503: "[The Land Registration] Act is a registration Act concerned (in this instance) to provide that certain rights are to be binding without registration and without the necessity for actual notice. To ascertain what 'rights' come within this provision, one must look outside the Land Registration Act and see what rights affect purchasers under the general law. To suppose that the subsection makes any right, of howsoever a personal character, which a person in occupation may have, an overriding interest by which a purchaser is bound, would involve two consequences: first that this Act is, in this respect, bringing about a substantive change in real property law by making personal rights bind purchasers; second, that there is a difference *as to the nature of the rights by which a purchaser may be bound* between registered and unregistered land; for purely personal rights including the wife's right to stay in the house (if my analysis of this is correct) cannot affect purchasers of unregistered land even with notice. One may have to accept that there is a difference between unregistered land and registered land as regards what kind of notice binds a purchaser, or what kind of inquiries a purchaser has to make. But there is no warrant in the terms of this paragraph or elsewhere in the Act for supposing that the nature of the rights which are to bind a purchaser is to be different, excluding personal rights in one case, including them in another. The whole frame of section 70, with the list that it gives of interests, or rights, which are overriding, shows that it is made against a background of interests or rights whose nature and whose transmissible character is known, or ascertainable, aliunde, i.e., under other statutes or under the common law. So, if the right of a deserted wife is a purely personal claim against her husband, not specifically related to the house in question, but merely, at its highest, to be provided with a home, there is no difficulty in seeing that this type of right cannot, any more than any purely contractual right, be an overriding interest."

WILLIAMS AND GLYN'S BANK LTD *v* BOLAND
WILLIAMS AND GLYN'S BANK LTD *v* BROWN[6]
[1981] AC 487, [1980] 2 All ER 408
(HL, Lord WILBERFORCE, Viscount DILHORNE, Lords SALMON, SCARMAN and ROSKILL)

In each of two cases the husband was registered as sole proprietor of the matrimonial home where he and his wife lived. The wife had made a substantial contribution to the purchase, which entitled her to a share in the

---

[5] *Celsteel Ltd v Alton House Holdings Ltd* [1985] 1 WLR 204, [1985] 2 All ER 562, p. 644, post.
[6] [1980] Conv 361; [1981] Conv 84 (J. Martin); (1979) 95 LQR 501; (1981) 97 LQR 12 (R. J. Smith); (1980) 130 NLJ 896 (R. L. Deech); (1980) SJ 651, 670 (P. W. Smith).

house. She had not protected her interest by entering a notice, caution or restriction on the register. The husband, without the wife's consent, charged the house to the plaintiff bank to secure his business indebtedness. The bank made no enquiry as to whether the wife had any interest in the house. It now claimed repayment of the loan and possession of the house. In both cases the wife claimed an overriding interest under Land Registration Act 1925, section 70 (1) (g).

Held. The wife had an overriding interest.

LORD WILBERFORCE. My Lords, these appeals, . . . raise for decision the same question: whether a husband or a wife, (in each actual case a wife) who has a beneficial interest in the matrimonial home, by virtue of having contributed to its purchase price, but whose spouse is the legal and registered owner, has an "overriding interest" binding on a mortgagee who claims possession of the matrimonial home under a mortgage granted by that spouse alone. Although this statement of the issue uses the words "spouse," "husband and wife," "matrimonial home," the appeals do not, in my understanding, involve any question of matrimonial law, or of the rights of married women or of women as such. Exactly the same issue could arise if the roles of husband and wife were reversed, or if the persons interested in the house were not married to each other. The solution must be derived from a consideration in the light of current social conditions of the Land Registration Act 1925 and other property statutes. . . .

The legal framework within which the appeals are to be decided can be summarised as follows:

Under the Land Registration Act 1925, legal estates in land are the only interests in respect of which a proprietor can be registered. Other interests take effect in equity as "minor interests," which are overridden by a registered transfer. But the Act recognises also an intermediate, or hybrid, class of what are called "overriding interests": though these are not registered, legal dispositions take effect subject to them. The list of overriding interests is contained in section 70 and it includes such matters as easements, liabilities having their origin in tenure, land tax and tithe rentcharge, seignorial and manorial rights, leases for terms not exceeding 21 years, and finally, the relevant paragraph being. section 70 (1) (g):

"The rights of every person in actual occupation of the land or in receipt of the rents and profits thereof, save where enquiry is made of such person and the rights are not disclosed; . . ."

The first question is whether the wife is a "person in actual occupation" and if so, whether her right as a tenant in common in equity is a right protected by this provision.

The other main element arises out of the Law of Property Act 1925. Since that Act, undivided shares in land can only take effect in equity, behind a trust for sale upon which the legal owner is to hold the land. Dispositions of the land, including mortgages, may be made under this trust and, provided that there are at least two trustees, or a trust corporation, "overreach" the trusts. This means that the "purchaser" takes free from them, whether or not he has notice of them, and that the trusts are enforceable against the proceeds of sale: see Law of Property Act 1925, section 2 (2) and (3) which lists certain exceptions.

The second question is whether the wife's equitable interest under the trust for sale, if she is in occupation of the land, is capable of being an overriding interest, or whether, as is generally the rule as regards equitable interests it can only take effect as a "minor interest." In the latter event a registered transferee, including a legal mortgagee, would take free from it.

The system of land registration, as it exists in England, which long antedates the Land Registration Act 1925, is designed to simplify and to cheapen conveyancing. It is intended to replace the often complicated and voluminous title deeds of property by a single land certificate, on the strength of which land can be dealt with. In place of the lengthy and often technical investigation of title to which a purchaser was committed, all he has to do is to consult the register; from any burden not entered on the register, with one exception, he takes free. Above all, the system is designed to free the purchaser from the hazards of notice — real or constructive — which, in the case of unregistered land, involved him in enquiries, often quite elaborate, failing which he might be bound by equities. The Law of Property Act 1925 contains provisions limiting the effect of the doctrine of notice, but it still remains a potential source of danger to purchasers. By contrast, the only provisions in the Land Registration Act 1925 with regard to notice are provisions which enable a purchaser to take the estate free from equitable interests or equities whether he has notice or not. (See, for example, section 3 (xv) s.v. "minor interests"). The only kind of notice recognised is by entry on the register.

The exception just mentioned consists of "overriding interests" listed in section 70. As to these, all registered land is stated to be deemed to be subject to such of them as may be subsisting in reference to the land, unless the contrary is expressed on the register. The land is so subject regardless of notice actual or constructive. In my opinion therefore, the law as to notice as it may affect purchasers of unregistered land, whether contained in decided cases, or in a statute (the Conveyancing Act 1882, section 3, Law of Property Act, section 199) has no application even by analogy to registered land. Whether a particular right is an overriding interest, and whether it affects a purchaser, is to be decided upon the terms of section 70, and other relevant provisions of the Land Registration Act 1925, and upon nothing else.

In relation to rights connected with occupation, it has been said that the purpose and effect of section 70 (1) (g) of the Land Registration Act 1925 was to make applicable to registered land the same rule as previously had been held to apply to unregistered land: see *per* Lord Denning MR in *National Provincial Bank Ltd v Hastings Car Mart Ltd* [1964] Ch 665 at 689, [1964] 1 All ER 688 at 697, and in this House [1965] AC 1175 at 1259, [1965] 2 All ER 472 at 501–502.

I adhere to this, but I do not accept the argument which learned counsel for the appellant sought to draw from it. His submission was that, in applying section 70 (1) (g), we should have regard to and limit the application of the paragraph in the light of the doctrine of notice. But this would run counter to the whole purpose of the Act. The purpose, in each system, is the same, namely, to safeguard the rights of persons in occupation, but the method used differs. In the case of unregistered land, the purchaser's obligation depends upon what he has notice of — notice actual or constructive. In the case of registered land, it is the fact of occupation that matters. If there is actual occupation, and the occupier has rights, the purchaser takes subject to them. If not, he does not. No further element is material.

I now deal with the first question. Were the wives here in "actual occupation"? These words are ordinary words of plain English, and should, in my opinion, be interpreted as such. Historically they appear to have emerged in the judgment of Lord Loughborough LC in *Taylor v Stibbert* (1794) 2 Ves 437 at 439–440, in a passage which repays quotation:

". . . whoever purchases an estate from the owner, knowing it to be in possession of tenants, is bound to inquire into the estates, those tenants have. It has been determined, that a purchaser being told, particular parts of the estate were in possession of a tenant, without any information as to his interest, and taking it for granted it was only from year to year, was bound by a lease, that tenant had, which was a surprise upon him. That was rightly determined; for it was sufficient to put the purchaser upon inquiry, that he was informed, the estate was not in the *actual possession* of the person, with whom he contracted; that he could not transfer the ownership and possession at the same time; that there were interests, as to the extent and terms of which it was his duty to inquire."

They were taken up in the judgment of the Privy Council in *Barnhart v Greenshields* (1853) 9 Moo PCC 18. The purpose for which they were used, in that case, was evidently to distinguish the case of a person who was in some kind of legal possession, as by receipt of the rents and profits, from that of a person actually in occupation as tenant. Given occupation, i.e., presence on the land, I do not think that the word "actual" was intended to introduce any additional qualification, certainly not to suggest that possession must be "adverse": it merely emphasises that what is required is physical presence, not some entitlement in law. So even if it were necessary to look behind these plain words into history, I would find no reason for denying them their plain meaning.

Then, were the wives in actual occupation? I ask: why not? There was physical presence, with all the rights that occupiers have, including the right to exclude all others except those having similar rights. The house was a matrimonial home, intended to be occupied, and in fact occupied by both spouses, both of whom have an interest in it: it would require some special doctrine of law to avoid the result that each is in occupation. Three arguments were used for a contrary conclusion. First, it was said that if the vendor (I use this word to include a mortgagor) is in occupation, that is enough to prevent the application of the paragraph. This seems to be a proposition of general application, not limited to the case of husbands, and no doubt, if correct, would be very convenient for purchasers and intending mortgagees. But the presence of the vendor, with occupation, does not exclude the possibility of occupation of others[7]. There are observations which suggest the contrary in the unregistered land case of *Caunce v Caunce* [1969] 1 WLR 286, [1969] 1 All ER 722, but I agree with the disapproval of these, and with the assertion of the proposition I have just stated by Russell LJ in *Hodgson v Marks* [1971] Ch 892 at 934, [1971] 2 All ER 684 at 690. Then it was suggested that the wife's occupation was nothing but the shadow of the husband's — a version I suppose of the doctrine of unity of husband and wife. This expression and the argument flowing from it was used by

---

[7] "Occupation need not be in one single person. Two persons can be in actual occupation, by themselves jointly, or each of them severally": *Williams and Glyn's Bank Ltd v Boland* [1979] Ch 312 at 331, [1979] 2 All ER 697 at 705, per Lord DENNING MR.

Templeman J in *Bird v Syme-Thomson* [1979] 1 WLR 440 at 444, [1978] 3 All ER 1027 at 1030, a decision preceding and which he followed in the present case. The argument was also inherent in the judgment in *Caunce v Caunce* which influenced the decisions of Templeman J. It somewhat faded from the arguments in the present case and appears to me to be heavily obsolete. The appellant's main and final position became in the end this: that, to come within the paragraph, the occupation in question must be apparently inconsistent with the title of the vendor. This, it was suggested, would exclude the wife of a husband-vendor because her apparent occupation would be satisfactorily accounted for by his. But, apart from the rewriting of the paragraph which this would involve, the suggestion is unacceptable. Consistency, or inconsistency, involves the absence, or presence, of an independent right to occupy, though I must observe that "inconsistency" in this context is an inappropriate word. But how can either quality be predicated of a wife, simply qua wife? A wife may, and everyone knows this, have rights of her own; particularly, many wives have a share in a matrimonial home. How can it be said that the presence of a wife in the house, as occupier, is consistent or inconsistent with the husband's rights until one knows what rights she has? And if she has rights, why, just because she is a wife (or in the converse case, just because an occupier is the husband), should these rights be denied protection under the paragraph? If one looks beyond the case of husband and wife, the difficulty of all these arguments stands out if one considers the case of a man living with a mistress, or of a man and a woman — or for that matter two persons of the same sex — living in a house in separate or partially shared rooms. Are these cases of apparently consistent occupation, so that the rights of the other person (other than the vendor) can be disregarded? The only solution which is consistent with the Act (section 70 (1) (*g*)) and with common sense is to read the paragraph for what it says. Occupation, existing as a fact, may protect rights if the person in occupation has rights. On this part of the case I have no difficulty in concluding that a spouse, living in a house, has an actual occupation capable of conferring protection, as an overriding interest, upon rights of that spouse.

This brings me to the second question, which is whether such rights as a spouse has under a trust for sale are capable of recognition as overriding interests — a question to my mind of some difficulty. The argument against this is based upon the structure of the Land Registration Act 1925 and upon specific provisions in it.

As to structure, it is said that the Act recognises three things: (*a*) legal estates, (*b*) minor interests, which take effect in equity, (*c*) overriding interests. These are mutually exclusive: an equitable interest, which is a minor interest, is incapable of being at the same time an overriding interest. The wife's interest, existing under or behind a trust for sale, is an equitable interest and nothing more. To give it the protection of an overriding interest would, moreover, contradict the principle according to which such an equitable interest can be overreached by an exercise of the trust for sale. As to the provisions of the Act, particular emphasis is placed on section 3 (xv) which, in defining "minor interests" specifically includes in the case of land held on trust for sale "all interests and powers which are under the Law of Property Act 1925 capable of being overridden by the trustees for sale" and excludes, expressly, overriding interests. Reliance is also placed on section 86, which, dealing analogously, so it is said, with settled land, prescribes that successive or other interests created by or arising under a settlement take effect as minor interests and not otherwise, and on section 101 which, it is argued, recognises the exclusive character of minor interests, which in all cases can be overridden.

My Lords, I find this argument formidable. To reach a conclusion upon it involves some further consideration of the nature of trusts for sale, in relation to undivided shares. The trusts upon which, in this case, the land is to be held are defined — as "statutory trusts" — in section 35 of the Law of Property Act 1925, i.e.:

". . . upon trust to sell the same and to stand possessed of the net proceeds of sale, after payment of costs, and of the net rents and profits until sale after payment of rates, taxes, costs of insurance, repairs, and other outgoings, upon such trusts, and subject to such powers and provisions, as may be requisite for giving effect to the rights of the persons . . . interested in the land."

In addition to this specific disposition, the general provisions as to trusts for sale in sections 23 to 31, where not inconsistent, appear to apply. The right of occupation of the land pending sale is not explicitly dealt with in these sections and the position as to it is obscure. Before the Act the position was that owners of undivided shares (which could exist at law) had concurrent rights of occupation. In *Bull v Bull* [1955] 1 QB 234, [1955] 1 All ER 253, p. 253 post it was held by the Court of Appeal, applying *Re Warren* [1932] 1 Ch 42, that the conversion of these legal estates into equitable interests by the Law of Property Act 1925 should not affect the mutual rights of the owners. Denning LJ, in a judgment which I find most illuminating, there held, at 238, at 255 in a factual situation similar to that of the instant cases, that "when there are two equitable tenants in common, then, until the place is sold, each of them is entitled concurrently with the other to the possession of the land and to the use and enjoyment of it in a proper manner." And he referred to section 14 of the Law of Property Act 1925 which provides that the Act "shall not prejudicially affect the interest of any person in possession or in actual occupation of land to which he may be entitled in right of such possession or occupation."

How then are these various rights to be fitted into the scheme of the Land Registration Act 1925? It is clear, at least, that the interests of the co-owners under the "statutory trusts" are minor interests — this fits with the definition in section 3 (xv). But I can see no reason why, if these interests, or that of any one of them, are or is protected by "actual occupation" they should remain merely as "minor interests." On the contrary, I see every reason why, in that event, they should acquire the status of overriding interests. And, moreover, I find it easy to accept that they satisfy the opening, and governing, words of section 70, namely, interests subsisting in reference to the land. As Lord Denning MR points out, to describe the interests of spouses in a house jointly bought to be lived in as a matrimonial home as merely an interest in proceeds of sale, or rents and profits until sale, is just a little unreal: see also *Elias v Mitchell* [1972] Ch 652, [1972] 2 All ER 153, p. 269, post *per* Pennycuick V-C with whose analysis I agree, and contrast, *Cedar Holdings Ltd v Green* [1981] Ch 129, [1979] 3 All ER 117 (which I consider to have been wrongly decided).

There are decisions, in relation to other equitable interests than those of tenants in common, which confirm this line of argument. In *Bridges v Mees* [1957] Ch 475, [1957] 2 All ER 577, Harman J decided that a purchaser of land under a contract for sale, who had paid the price and so was entitled to the land in equity, could acquire an overriding interest by virtue of actual occupation, and a similar position was held by the Court of Appeal to arise in relation to a resulting trust: *Hodgson v Marks* [1971] Ch 892, [1971] 2 All ER 684. These decisions (following the law as it undoubtedly existed before 1925 — see *Barnhart v Greenshields* (1853) 9 Moo PCC 18 at 32, *Daniels v Davison* (1809) 16 Ves 249, *Allen v Anthony* (1816) 1 Mer 282, 284 *per* Lord Eldon LC) provide an answer to the argument that there is a firm dividing line, or an unbridgeable gulf, between minor interests and overriding interests, and, on the contrary, confirm that the fact of occupation enables protection of the latter to extend to what without it would be the former. In my opinion, the wives' equitable interests, subsisting in reference to the land, were by the fact of occupation, made into overriding interests, and so protected by section 70 (1) (*g*). I should add that it makes no difference to this that these same interests might also have been capable of protection by the registration of a caution: see *Bridges v Mees* [1957] Ch 475 at 487, [1957] 2 All ER 577 at 582 and Land Registration Act 1925, section 59 (6).

There was finally an argument based upon section 74 of the Land Registration Act 1925. The section provides:

"Subject to the provisions of this Act as to settled land, neither the registrar nor any person dealing with a registered estate or charge shall be affected with notice of a trust express implied or constructive, and references to trusts shall, so far as possible, be excluded from the register."

The argument was that if the overriding interest sought to be protected is, under the general law, only binding on a purchaser by virtue of notice, the section has the effect of denying the protection. It is obvious — and indeed conceded — that if this is right, *Hodgson v Marks* and *Bridges v Mees* must have been wrongly decided.

I am of opinion that this section has no such effect. Its purpose is to make clear, as I have already explained, that the doctrine of notice has no application to registered conveyancing, and accordingly to establish, as an administration measure, that entries may not be made in the register which would only be appropriate if that doctrine were applicable. It cannot have the effect of cutting down the general application of section 70 (1).

I would only add, in conclusion, on the appeal as it concerns the wives a brief observation on the conveyancing consequences of dismissing the appeal. These were alarming to Templeman J, and I can agree with him to the extent that whereas the object of a land registration system is to reduce the risks to purchasers from anything not on the register, to extend (if it be an extension) the area of risk so as to include possible interests of spouses, and indeed, in theory, of other members of the family or even outside it, may add to the burdens of purchasers, and involve them in enquiries which in some cases may be troublesome.

But conceded, as it must be, that the Act, following established practice, gives protection to occupation, the extension of the risk area follows necessarily from the extension, beyond the paterfamilias, of rights of ownership, itself following from the diffusion of property and earning capacity. What is involved is a departure from an easy-going practice of dispensing with enquiries as to occupation beyond that of the vendor and accepting the risks of doing so. To substitute for this a practice of more careful enquiry as to the fact of occupation, and if necessary, as to the rights of occupiers can not, in my view of the matter, be considered as unacceptable except at the price of overlooking the widespread development of shared interests of ownership. In the light of section 70 of the Act, I cannot believe that Parliament intended this, though it may be true that in 1925 it did not foresee the full extent of this development.

In *City of London Building Society v Flegg* (1985) Times, 23 December[7a], the Court of Appeal held that the decision in *Boland* applied where there were *two* registered proprietors (a daughter and son-in-law) granting the mortgage, and that the equitable interests of the tenants in common (her parents) which arose from their contribution to the purchase price of Bleak House, Gillingham, Kent, were protected under para. (*g*) by reason of their actual occupation. Their overriding interests were not overreached under LPA 1925, s. 2 (1) (ii), p. 205, post. DILLON LJ said that "it was fundamental to every aspect of the building society's case that the occupiers' right to occupy the property as equitable tenants in common was overreached by operation of Part I of the LPA. However, LPA 1925 s. 14 provided that Part I 'shall not prejudicially affect the interest of any person in possession or in actual occupation of land to which he may be entitled in right of such possession or occupation.' Those words were apt to cover the interest of an equitable tenant in common which was reinforced by his being in possession or actual occupation of land."

B. The Rights

WEBB *v* POLLMOUNT LTD
[1966] Ch 584, [1966] 1 All ER 481 (ChD, UNGOED-THOMAS J)

The plaintiff held under a lease granted by the defendant's predecessor in title. The lease gave to the plaintiff the option to purchase the freehold but, as the register contained no mention of the option, the defendant claimed that it could not be exercised as against him. The issue was whether the option constituted an overriding interest within section 70 (1) (*g*).

Held. The option was an overriding interest[8].

UNGOED-THOMAS J. The defendant submits that overriding interests or rights in section 70 (1) (*g*) are limited to rights of a person in an estate in the land, and he makes this submission with a view to establishing that the plaintiff's overriding interest is here limited to his leasehold estate exclusive of the option to purchase. It was first sought to establish this by limiting "land" in sub-paragraph (*g*) to an estate in the land. . . .

As a matter of first impression, "land" in section 70 (1) (*g*) does not appear to me to refer to an estate in land, but to the physical land. The references which are contained in the sub-paragraph to "actual occupation" and "receipt of the rents and profits thereof" indicate this conclusion: and (*g*) is not limited to the rights of every tenant or estate owner, but extends to the rights of every person in actual occupation. "Registered land" and "land" are by definition not limited to estates in land, but include physical land. . . .

As the definition of "overriding interests" expressly excludes matters entered on the register, it indicates that matters registrable, but not registered, are not excluded. Overriding interests may include registrable matters, provided they have not been entered on the register. . . .

The opening words of section 70 (1) provide a further limit on overriding

---

[7a] (1986) 83 LSG 684 (P. H. Kenny). See also [1980] Conv 427 (A. Sydenham); [1981] Conv 219 (J. Martin); p. 50, ante; p. 254, n. 10, post.

[8] For the desirability of protecting such an option by notice, see Registered Land Practice Notes (1982–1983), pp. 37–38.

interests within the section, namely, that they be "for the time being subsisting in reference" to the registered land. The result is that, so far as material to this case, rights within section 70 (1) (*g*) must fall within such rights as (1) are "not entered on the register", (2) are "affecting the estate transferred" to the defendant, (3) "may be for the time being subsisting in reference" to the registered land. The option was not entered on the register, and there is no difficulty about the first of these limitations. So, the question in this case is whether the option to purchase contained in the lease affects the reversion transferred to the defendant and subsists in reference to the registered land. The statute itself does not answer this question: it raises it. The answer is only to be found by reference to the general law in whose context the statute was enacted.

In *National Provincial Bank Ltd v Ainsworth* [1965] AC 1175, [1965] 2 All ER 472, the House of Lords, in considering the rights of a deserted wife in respect of the matrimonial home, dealt with section 70. Russell LJ's observations in the Court of Appeal in that case were quoted with approval in the House of Lords. He said:

"It seems to me that section 70 in all its parts is dealing with rights in reference to land which have the quality of being capable of enduring through different ownerships of the land, according to normal conceptions of title to real property."

Lord Upjohn said:

". . . notice itself does not create the right. To create a right over the land of another that right must (apart from statute) create a burden on the land, i.e., an equitable estate or interest in the land."

Thus, for a right to be within section 70 (1) (*g*), it must be an "interest in the land" "capable of enduring through different ownerships of the land according to normal conceptions of title to real property."

An option to purchase is an interest in the land in respect of which it is exercisable, whether contained in a lease or not. . . .

It was suggested for the defendant that "the right of every person in actual occupation of the land" should be construed as the right by virtue of which a person is in actual occupation of the land. The short answer to this, it seems to me, is that it does not say so; and the wording is in marked contrast with the wording in section 14 of the Law of Property Act 1925, where reference is made to the interest of a person in possession or occupation of land "to which he may be entitled in right of such possession or occupation". It is neither, in my view, consistent with the wording of section 70 (1) (*g*) of the Land Registration Act 1925, nor with the authorities from which I have quoted.

Although an option to purchase does not, like an option to renew, "touch", "concern" or "affect" "the land demised and regarded as the subject-matter of the lease" (so as, e.g., to bind the reversion under the Grantees of Reversions Act 1540), what we are concerned with here is not whether it so "affects" "the land demised" and is within the relationship of landlord and tenant as considered in the judgment of the Court of Appeal in *Woodall v Clifton* [1905] 2 Ch 257, p. 354, post, but whether within section 20 (1) (*b*)[9] it is an interest "affecting the estate transferred" to the defendant. That it is capable of affecting the estate transferred to the defendant is not disputed; e.g., if the defendant had notice of it before transfer to him. So, it seems to me to fall within Russell LJ's test in *National Provincial Bank Ltd v Ainsworth* of "being capable of enduring through different owner-ships of the land according to normal conceptions of title to real

---

[9] See p. 110, ante.

property". And if it, thus, in the circumstances of this case, is a right "affecting the estate transferred", within the requirement of section 20 (1) (*b*), it seems to me that it is "for the time being subsisting in reference to" registered land within the requirement of section 70 (1). My conclusion, therefore, is that subject to deciding the question as to the effect of section 59[10], the option to purchase appears to be an overriding interest.

In *London and Cheshire Insurance Co Ltd v Laplagrene Property Co Ltd* [1971] Ch 499, [1971] 1 All ER 766[11], the unpaid vendors of registered land who remained in occupation under a leaseback by the purchasers, had an overriding interest under section 70 (1) (*g*). This entitled the vendors to enforce their lien against chargees of the purchaser, even though they had gone out of occupation subsequent to the purchase. BRIGHTMAN J said at 505 at 771: "I can see nothing in section 20[12], read with section 70, which causes a paragraph (*g*) overriding interest, subject to which a disposition was made, to be extinguished merely because the owner of the right ceases occupation after that disposition but before there has been any other material dealing with the land. The extinction of the overriding interest in such a case, for the fortuitous benefit of the proprietor of the land, seems to me both unsupported by the wording of the Act and an unreasonable result. A right exists as an overriding interest for the very good reason that the owner of the right is in occupation of the land, ought to have been asked to define his rights by the intending transferee or grantee, but is ignored and has no inquiry made of him. In such circumstances, it is reasonable to provide that the transferee or grantee takes subject to the right as an overriding interest. The transferee or grantee has no one but himself to blame for that result. If the overriding interest were extinguished when the owner of the right went out of occupation, that would be a windfall for the transferee or grantee. He would be freed from a burden for no good reason that I can discern."

C. Actual Occupation[13]

STRAND SECURITIES LTD *v* CASWELL
[1965] Ch 958, [1965] 1 All ER 820 (CA, Lord DENNING MR and HARMAN and RUSSELL LJJ)

The first defendant was the sub-lessee of a flat, the 42-year head lease of which had been registered with good leasehold title. The sub-lease of 39¼ years, less three days, was not, at the material date, entered in any way on the register. The question arose whether the first defendant had an overriding interest within section 70 (1) (*g*) which prevailed against a purchaser from the freeholders[14]. He lived in the country but used the flat as a London base. He allowed his step-daughter, the second defendant (who had been deserted by her husband) to live in the flat rent free.

---

[10] See p. 144, post.

[11] (1971) 35 Conv (NS) 188 (F. R. Crane).

[12] P. 110, ante.

[13] The relevant date for occupation is that of the registration of the title of the transferee: *Re Boyle's Claim* [1961] 1 WLR 339, [1961] 1 All ER 620; or more specifically when the application for registration is delivered at the registry: LRR 1925, s. 83 (2), as substituted by LRR 1978, r. 8, p. 115, ante. See, however, *Paddington Building Society v Mendelsohn* (1985) 50 P & CR 244 at 247, per BROWNE-WILKINSON, LJ.

[14] LRA 1925, s. 70 (1) (*k*) did not apply; the first defendant's sub-lease exceeded 21 years; the second defendant was a gratuitous licensee.

Held. The first defendant had no overriding interest.

RUSSELL LJ: It is to be remarked that if [the first defendant] . . . had moved up to London and occupied the bedroom or received from or demanded of his step-daughter . . . a penny a week for the privilege of remaining there, he would have had an unanswerable claim to his sublease being an overriding interest under section 70 (1) (*g*) as he would be in the one case a person in actual occupation and in the other in receipt of the rents and profits. Of course he did neither of these things. Their possibility, however, serves to show how rare it must be that an actual sublessee entitled to possession is not a person either in actual occupation or in receipt of the rents and profits. . . .

On the facts, was the first defendant . . . a person in actual occupation, though he was not in any ordinary sense residing there or treating it as his home, and the second defendant and her family were allowed by him to reside there? As a matter of the ordinary use of language I would not consider the first defendant to be such. For him it was argued that the phrase "in actual occupation" derives from cases in which "actual occupation" and "actual possession" are used indifferently to describe a condition of enjoyment of the land itself, and that the phrase "actual occupation" here involves that form of the legal concept of possession as distinct from the other or notional forms of that concept consisting of the receipt of money payments derived from land, or of the right to possession though the land be vacant. And it was argued that "actual possession" was avoided by the draftsman as a phrase because of the difficulty which would flow from the definition of "possession" in section 3 (xviii) of the Land Registration Act, 1925. Reference was made to a number of authorities, including cases in the fields of rating, poor law, and landlord and tenant, with a view to showing that possession, and therefore occupation, may be had through the medium of another. Suppose, it was said, that the first defendant employed a resident caretaker to look after the flat in question, would the first defendant not be a person in actual occupation? I think that is correct. Then, it was argued, that is because the caretaker would be his licensee, bound to go at his will, and that was the position of the second defendant. But I think that here is the distinction between occupation by the caretaker as a matter of duty on behalf of the first defendant and the occupation of the second defendant on her own behalf; both were licensees, but the former, by her occupation for which she was employed, was the representative of the first defendant and her occupation may therefore be regarded as his. The proposition that in each case the first defendant was in actual occupation because neither the caretaker nor the second defendant had a right to occupy independently of him seems to me too broadly stated and to ignore that distinction. I do not say that a contract of employment or agency with the person residing there is essential to actual occupation by the other person. I think that it might well be that if a house was used as a residence by a wife, separated from the tenant, her husband (whether or not in desertion), he could also be regarded as in actual occupation through her; the question whether the husband was also a person in actual occupation did not, of course, arise in *National Provincial Bank Ltd v Hastings Car Mart Ltd* [1964] Ch 665, [1964] 3 All ER 93n. But this conception, even if valid, could not extend to the relationship in the present case.

Nor, it seems to me, can the presence on the premises of some of the first defendant's furniture[15], nor the previously mentioned use by him and others of the family of the flat, nor the fact, which I am prepared to assume though

---

[15] See *Chhokar v Chhokar* [1984] FLR 313, infra, where furniture was relevant.

it was not proved, that he had a key, nor a combination of those matters, constitute actual occupation by him[16].

In *Chhokar v Chhokar* [1984] FLR 313, [1984] Fam Law 269, a husband and wife purchased the registered freehold of 5 Lady Margaret Road, Southall, as a matrimonial home in 1977. Both contributed to the purchase price and upkeep of the house which was registered in the name of the husband only. In 1978 the husband and wife went to India, where the husband deserted his wife and returned home. She followed him a few weeks later, being seven months' pregnant. In December the husband, without the knowledge of his wife, arranged to sell the house to a Mr Parmar at a price well below market value. As CUMMING-BRUCE LJ said in the Court of Appeal "there was an obvious similarity between this discussion and a discussion that might take place in similar circumstances in relation to property which was asserted to have fallen off the back of a lorry". EWBANK J said at 317:

"On 19 February 1979, the date of completion, the husband made special arrangements to have the net proceeds of sale in cash in his hands. He paid his debts and then he set off for India. That was the last the wife saw of him for some 2 years. The wife and the baby were discharged from hospital on 22 February. They went home. They found the locks had been changed and so they went to spend the night with an aunt with whom the elder child had been staying while the wife was in hospital. On the following day, 23 February, the wife went home. Mr Parmar, who had bought the house, ejected her. On 1 March 1979 Mr Parmar registered the conveyance to him at the Land Registry. The wife on that date was not in the house because he had put her out, but some of her furniture was there. I have to consider whether she was in actual occupation on the day of the registration of the conveyance. I have no difficulty in deciding that she was in actual occupation. Her interest, accordingly, in the house is an overriding interest and Mr Parmar, in my judgment, took the conveyance of the house into his name subject to her overriding interest. He accordingly has held the house since then, subject to a half share belonging to the wife."

This part of the judgment was not challenged in the Court of Appeal. For the application by the purchaser for a sale of the house under section 30 of the Law of Property Act 1925, see p. 254, post.

D. Law Reform

The Law Commission hopes to publish a report on overriding interests in 1986[17]. There have, however, been interim developments.

---

[16] The first defendant succeeded on another ground, when he had made application for first registration of his sub-lease, he was unable to produce the head-lessor's land certificate. CA held that there was no need to produce it (p. 474, post), and that the register should be rectified. This gave the sub-lease priority over the transfer of the head-lease to the purchaser, which had not been registered until after the date of the first defendant's application.

[17] Nineteenth Annual Report 1983–84 (Law Com No. 140, HC 214), para. 2.44; Twentieth Annual Report 1984–1985 (Law Com No. 155, HC 247), para. 2.36.

Law Commission Seventeenth Annual Report 1981–1982 (Law Com No. 119, HC 203), paras. 2.52–2.54.

"2.52 [The Law Commission Report on The Implications of *Williams and Glyn's Bank Ltd v Boland* 1982 (Law Com No. 115 Cmnd 8636)] points out that the law in this field is now in a most unsatisfactory state. Although the effect of the *Boland* decision is to confer some protection on co-owners in the event of an unauthorised dealing in the land, this protection is far from complete. Purchasers and mortgagees, moreover, are positively put at risk: they now need to take special precautions in every conveyancing transaction for detecting the existence of a co-ownership interest. These precautions tend to create delays and expense in conveyancing, and even the most stringent precautions may prove inadequate for their purpose. The situation is worsened by the obscurity of the law on the question of the existence, or extent, of a co-ownership interest.

2.53 The conclusions of the report are that purchasers and mortgagees need to be properly protected against the possibility of undisclosed co-ownership interests; that married co-owners need to be further protected in their enjoyment of the matrimonial home; and that there should be clear and fair rules as to co-ownership of the matrimonial home. To give effect to these conclusions, the report makes three central recommendations, the first primarily for overcoming the present conveyancing difficulties of purchasers and mortgagees, and the second and third primarily for protecting and establishing the interests of married co-owners in the matrimonial home. These recommendations are as follows:—

   (i) co-ownership interests in land should be registrable at H.M. Land Registry and should be protected against purchasers and mortgagees if, and only if, they are so registered;

  (ii) the interest of every married co-owner in the matrimonial home should carry with it a right to prevent any dealing being made without that co-owner's consent or a court order;

 (iii) as a general rule married couples should, in the absence of agreement to the contrary, have an equal ownership of the matrimonial home.

2.54 The report further proposes that these recommendations should be implemented by legislation based upon the draft Matrimonial Homes (Co-ownership) Bill annexed to our third report on family property and indicates that we intend to put in hand the drafting of a new Bill when it seems helpful to do so. The report points out that the *Boland* decision provides an added reason for the introduction of equal co-ownership of the matrimonial home."

In a debate on the Report in the House of Lords in 1982, Lord HAILSHAM OF ST. MARYLEBONE LC firmly pigeon-holed the recommendations[18]. On the registration requirements, he said (HL Deb December 15 col 662):

"While not wishing to minimise the difficulties created by the *Boland* case, or the prejudice that might result from its reversal, it must be said that it has been part of our law for over a year now, and that in fact conveyancers have come to terms with it fairly well. Contrary to their predictions, the world has

---

[18] [1983] Conv 87 46 MLR 330 (W. T. Murphy).

not come to an end as a result of the decision in *Boland* in the Court of Appeal
and the House of Lords."

Similarly Lord TEMPLEMAN[19] who said (Col 649):
"It is asking a lot of a wife to go and register what appears to be a hostile
notice in the Land Registry against her loving husband."

In 1985 the Land Registration and Law of Property Bill was introduced
into the House of Lords. The intention was that the interest of a *spouse* in the
Boland situation would continue to be overriding, but not that of any other
person e.g. a co-habitee or a parent who may have contributed to the
purchase price of the dwelling-house[20]. The Bill attracted hostile criticism
and was withdrawn — and rightly so.

QUESTION

You are advising the mortgagee bank in a *Boland* situation.

(*a*) How would you set about discovering whether there is a "person in
actual occupation"? And when would you inspect the property?
Hayton, pp. 88–91. See the criticisms of VINELOTT J in *Kling v
Keston Properties Ltd* (1983) 49 P & CR 212 at 221–222.

(*b*) You discover an actual occupant who discloses to you a beneficial
interest under a trust. The mortgagee nevertheless still wishes to
lend money to the registered proprietor. How would you seek to
neutralise the occupant's rights?

Consider in particular

(i) The appointment of an additional trustee.

Would this entitle the bank to overreach the occupant's interest? *City of
London Building Society v Flegg* (1985) Times, 23 December, p. 128, ante;
[1980] Conv 427 (A. Sydenham) [1981] Conv 219 (J. Martin).

(ii) The release of rights by the occupant.

Are there any difficulties if —

1. The occupant is a minor?

2. You do not warn the occupant to consult an independent legal
adviser? *Kings North Trust Ltd v Bell* [1986] 1 W.LR 119 expecially at
125, per DILLON LJ; [1985] LSG 1320 (P. H. Kenny); *Cornish v
Midland Bank plc* [1985] 3 All ER 513; cf. *National Westminster Bank plc
v Morgan* [1985] AC 686, [1985] 1 All ER 821. (1985) 48 MLR 579
(D. Tiplady); [1985] Conv 387 (C. J. Barton and P. M. Rank). See
also *Avon Finance Co Ltd v Bridger* [1985] 2 All ER 281.

(1983) 80 LSG 2197 (T. D. Putnam); 3139 (J. E. Adams); Law Commission Report on *The Implications of Williams & Glyn's Bank Ltd v Boland* 1982
(Law Com No. 115, Cmnd 8636), Part III, pp. 14–19.

(iii) The editorial Draft Practice Note suggested in [1980] Conv 85;
[1981] Conv 313, 317, 323.

---

[19] As TEMPLEMAN J, he had decided *Boland* at first instance in favour of this mortgagee-bank with
a view to avoiding inconvenient conveyancing consequences: (1978) 36 P & CR 448.

[20] And likewise for unregistered land, by proposing that only possession by a *spouse* would affect a
purchaser of the legal estate with notice of the beneficial interest.

IV. Minor Interests[1]

As we have seen, overriding interests do not stand in need of protection on the register, but minor interests do need entry on the register of the land affected if they are to bind purchasers for value. As in unregistered land, actual notice of the interest which should be protected, but is not so protected, is irrelevant[2]. An entry on the register may be made by way of notice, restriction, caution or inhibition[3].

A notice is entered on the charges register of the land affected, and gives protection to and information about such interests as leases, agreements for leases, restrictive covenants and estate contracts[4]. Before a notice can be entered, the land certificate must be lodged at the Registry[5], and for this the registered proprietor's co-operation is required. But production is not necessary where the land is subject to a registered charge; in this case the land certificate will already be deposited at the Registry[6]. Nor is it necessary where a lease has been granted at a rent without taking a fine[7]. If a notice has been entered, any disposition of the land affected takes effect subject to the estate or interest protected by the notice, but only if and so far as such estate or interest may be valid[8].

A restriction is an entry on the proprietorship register, which prevents dealings in registered land until certain conditions and requirements have been complied with[9]. A common example of a restriction is when it is used to ensure that a purchaser of the land complies with the rules relating to the overreaching provisions of the Settled Land Act 1925[10] and the Law of Property Act 1925[11], thereby protecting the interests of the beneficiaries. Normally only the registered proprietor may enter a restriction, but other persons may do so, if they can persuade him to produce the land certificate[12].

A caution against dealings is entered on the proprietorship register. The land certificate need not be produced[13] and therefore the co-operation of the registered proprietor is unnecessary. Its effect is merely to achieve "no dealing with the land", without notice being first served on the cautioner, so as to give him an opportunity to object[14].

An inhibition rarely occurs, except where a bankruptcy inhibition is automatically entered by the Registrar[15].

---

[1] C & B, pp. 101–102, 104–105, 745–750; M & W, pp. 209–216; MM, pp. 125–130; Ruoff and Roper, chaps. 7, 34–39. For detailed discussion of priorities of minor interests, see [1976] CLP 26 at p. 37 et seq. (D. J. Hayton); (1977) 93 LQR 541 (R. J. Smith); p. 745, post.

[2] P. 45, ante; LRA 1925, s. 59 (6); *Hodges v Jones* [1935] Ch 657 at 671, per Luxmoore J; *De Lusignan v Johnson* (1973) 117 SJ 854; see, however, *Peffer v Rigg* [1977] 1 WLR 285, [1978] 3 All ER 745, p. 110, ante.

[3] LRA 1925, s. 101 (3), p. 100, ante; (1953) 17 Conv (NS) 105 (T. B. F. Ruoff); (1958) 22 Conv (NS) 14 (F. R. Crane). For a chart showing the registration machinery which replaces that of LCA 1972, see Ruoff and Roper, pp. 702–703, pp. 140–141, post.

[4] LRA 1925, ss. 48–51, 59 (2), 59 (5), pp. 136–138, post.

[5] LRA 1925, s. 64, p. 101, ante.

[6] LRA 1925, s. 65, p. 743, post.

[7] LRA 1925, s. 64 (1) (*c*), p. 101, ante.

[8] LRA 1925, s. 52 (1), p. 137, post.

[9] LRA 1925, s. 58 (1), p. 138, post.

[10] P. 310, post.

[11] P. 240, post.

[12] LRA 1925, s. 58 (5); LRR 1925, r. 236, p. 138, post.

[13] LRA 1925, s. 64 (1) (*c*).

[14] LRA 1925, ss. 54, 56, p. 139, post.

[15] LRA 1925, s. 57, p. 138, post.

LAND REGISTRATION ACT 1925

3. Interpretation. —

(xv) "Minor interests" mean the interests not capable of being disposed of or created by registered dispositions and capable of being overridden (whether or not a purchaser has notice thereof) by the proprietors unless protected as provided by this Act, and all rights and interests which are not registered or protected on the register and are not overriding interests, and include —

(*a*) in the case of land held on trust for sale, all interests and powers which are under the Law of Property Act, 1925, capable of being overridden by the trustees for sale, whether or not such interests and powers are so protected; and

(*b*) in the case of settled land, all interests and powers which are under the Settled Land Act, 1925, and the Law of Property Act, 1925, or either of them, capable of being overridden by the tenant for life or statutory owner, whether or not such interests and powers are so protected as aforesaid.

A.   Notices

LAND REGISTRATION ACT 1925

48 (1).   Registration of notice of lease. — P. 473, post.

49.   Rules to provide for notices of other rights, interests and claims. — (1) The provisions of the last foregoing section shall be extended by the rules[16] so as to apply to the registration of notices of or of claims in respect of —

(*a*) The grant or reservation of any annuity or rentcharge in possession, either perpetual or for a term of years absolute:

(*b*) The severance of any mines or minerals from the surface, except where the mines and minerals severed are expressly included in the registration:

(*c*) Land charges[17] until the land charge is registered as a registered charge:

(*d*) The right of any person interested in the proceeds of sale of land held on trust for sale or in land subject to a settlement to require that (unless a trust corporation is acting as trustee) there shall be at least two trustees of the disposition on trust for sale or of the settlement:

(*e*) The rights of any widow in respect of dower or under the Intestates' Estates Act, 1890, and any right to free bench or other like right saved by any statute coming into force concurrently with this Act (which rights shall take effect in equity as minor interests):

(*f*) Creditors' notices and any other right, interest, or claim which it may be deemed expedient to protect by notice instead of by caution, inhibition, or restriction:

---

[16] LRR 1925, r. 190.

[17] "Land charge" means a land charge of any class described in LCA 1972, s. 2 or a local land charge: LRA 1925, s. 3 (ix), as substituted by LLCA 1975, s. 17, Sch. 1.

(g) Charging orders (within the meaning of the Charging Orders Act 1979) which in the case of unregistered land may be protected by registration under the Land Charges Act 1972 and which, notwithstanding section 59 of this Act, it may be deemed expedient to protect by notice instead of by caution[18].

(2) A notice shall not be registered in respect of any estate, right, or interest which (independently of this Act) is capable of being overridden by the proprietor under a trust for sale or the powers of the Settled Land Act, 1925, or any other statute, or of a settlement, and of being protected by a restriction in the prescribed manner:

Provided that notice of such an estate right or interest may be lodged pending the appointment of trustees of a disposition on trust for sale or a settlement, and if so lodged, shall be cancelled if and when the appointment is made and the proper restriction (if any) is entered.

50. Notices of restrictive covenants. — P. 831, post.

52. Effect of notices. — (1) A disposition by the proprietor shall take effect subject to all estates, rights, and claims which are protected by way of notice on the register at the date of the registration or entry of notice of the disposition, but only if and so far as such estates, rights, and claims may be valid[19] and are not (independently of this Act) overridden by the disposition.

(2) Where notice of a claim is entered on the register, such entry shall operate by way of notice only, and shall not operate to render the claim valid whether made adversely to or for the benefit of the registered land or charge.

59. Writs, orders, deeds of arrangement, pending actions, &c. — (1) A writ, order, deed of arrangement, pending action[20], or other interest which in the case of unregistered land may be protected by registration under the Land Charges Act, 1925, shall, where the land affected or the charge securing the debt affected is registered, be protected only by lodging a creditor's notice, a bankruptcy inhibition or a caution against dealings with the land or the charge.

(2) Registration of a land charge (other than a local land charge) shall, where the land affected is registered, be effected only by registering under this Act a notice caution or other prescribed entry: . . .

(5) The foregoing provisions of this section shall apply only to writs and orders, deeds of arrangement, pending actions and land charges which if the land were unregistered would for purposes of protection be required to be registered or re-registered after the commencement of this Act under the Land Charges Act 1925[1], and for the purposes of this section a land charge does not include a puisne mortgage[1a].

(6) Subject to the provisions of this Act relating to fraud and to the title of a trustee in bankruptcy, a purchaser acquiring title under a registered disposition, shall not be concerned with any pending action, writ, order, deed of arrangement, or other document, matter, or claim (not being an

---

[18] As added by Charging Orders Act 1979, s. 3 (3). See also s. 7 (4); pp. 271–272, post.
[19] *Cator v Newton and Bates* [1940] 1 KB 415, [1939] 4 All ER 457 (entry that freehold land is subject to positive covenant does not make covenant enforceable).
[20] *Greenhi Builders Ltd v Allen* [1979] 1 WLR 156, [1978] 3 All ER 1163.
[1] Now LCA 1972.
[1a] As amended by FA 1975, s. 59 (5), Sch. 13, Part I.

overriding interest) or a charge for capital transfer tax subject to which its disposition takes effect under section 73 of this Act[2] which is not protected by a caution or other entry on the register, whether he has or has not notice thereof, express, implied, or constructive[3].

LAND REGISTRATION RULES 1925

199.   Entry as to trivial rights not required. — The Registrar shall not be required to enter notice of any liability, right, or interest which shall appear to him to be of a trivial or obvious character, or the entry of which on the register is likely to cause confusion or inconvenience.

B.   Restrictions

LAND REGISTRATION ACT 1925

58.   Power to place restrictions on register. — (1) Where the proprietor of any registered land or charge desires to place restrictions on transferring or charging the land or on disposing of or dealing with the land or charge in any manner in which he is by this Act authorised to dispose of or deal with it, or on the deposit by way of security of any certificate, the proprietor may apply to the registrar to make an entry in the register that no transaction to which the application relates shall be effected, unless the following things, or such of them as the proprietor may determine, are done —

    (*a*)   unless notice of any application for the transaction is transmitted by post to such address as he may specify to the registrar;

    (*b*)   unless the consent of some person or persons, to be named by the proprietor, is given to the transaction;

    (*c*)   unless some such other matter or thing is done as may be required by the applicant and approved by the registrar: . . .

(2) The registrar shall thereupon, if satisfied of the right of the applicant to give the directions, enter the requisite restrictions on the register, and no transaction to which the restriction relates shall be effected except in conformity therewith; . . .

(5) Rules may be made to enable applications to be made for the entry of restrictions by persons other than the proprietor[4].

C.   Inhibitions

57.   Power for court or registrar to inhibit registered dealings. — (1) . . . The registrar . . . may . . . issue an order or make an entry inhibiting for a time, or until the occurrence of an event to be named in such order or entry, or generally until further order or entry, the registration or entry of any-dealing with any registered land or registered charge.

(2) The court or registrar may make or refuse to make any such order or entry, and annex thereto any terms or conditions the court or registrar may

---

[2] As amended by FA 1975, s. 52, Sch. 12, para. 5 (4); CTTA 1984, s. 276, Sch. 8, para. 1.
[3] See *Peffer v Rigg* [1977] 1 WLR 285 at 294, [1978] 3 All ER 745 at 752, per GRAHAM J.
[4] LRR 1925, r. 236.

think fit, and discharge such order or cancel such entry when granted, with or without costs, and generally act in the premises in such manner as the justice of the case requires.

(4) The court or the registrar may, in lieu of an inhibition, order a notice or restriction to be placed on the register.

D.   Cautions

53.   Cautions against first registration. — (1) Any person having or claiming such an interest in land not already registered as entitles him to object to any disposition thereof being made without his consent, may lodge a caution with the registrar to the effect that the cautioner is entitled to notice in the prescribed form, and to be served in the prescribed manner, of any application that may be made for the registration of an interest in the land affecting the right of the cautioner.

(3) After a caution has been lodged in respect of any estate, which has not already been registered, registration shall not be made of such estate until notice has been served on the cautioner to appear and oppose, if he thinks fit, such registration, and the prescribed time has elapsed since the date of the service of such notice, or the cautioner has entered an appearance, whichever may first happen.

54.   Cautions against dealings. — (1) Any person interested under any unregistered instrument, or interested as a judgment creditor, or otherwise howsoever, in any land or charge registered in the name of any other person, may lodge a caution with the registrar to the effect that no dealing with such land or charge on the part of the proprietor is to be registered until notice has been served upon the cautioner[5]:

Provided that a person whose estate, right, interest, or claim has been registered or protected by a notice or restriction shall not be entitled (except with the consent of the registrar) to lodge a caution in respect of such estate, right, interest, or claim, but this provision shall not operate to prevent an incumbrancer or assignee of a life interest, remainder, reversion or executory interest, from lodging a priority caution in a specially prescribed form.

55.   Effect of cautions against dealings. — (1) After any such caution against dealings has been lodged[6] in respect of any registered land or charge, the registrar shall not, without the consent of the cautioner, register any dealing or make any entry on the register for protecting the rights acquired under a deposit of a land or charge certificate or other dealing by the proprietor with such land or charge until he has served notice on the cautioner, warning him that his caution will cease to have any effect after the expiration of the prescribed number of days next following the date at which such notice is served; and after the expiration of such time as aforesaid the caution shall cease unless an order to the contrary is made by the registrar, and upon the caution so ceasing the registered land or charge may be dealt with in the same manner as if no caution had been lodged.

---

[5] *Re White Rose Cottage* [1965] Ch 940, [1965] 1 All ER 11 (equitable charge), p. 141, post; *Parkash v Irani Finance Ltd* [1970] Ch 101, [1969] 1 All ER 930 (charging order), p. 143, post; *Elias v Mitchell* [1972] Ch 652, [1972] 2 All ER 153 (equitable tenant in common under trust for sale), p. 269, post; cf. *Myton Ltd v Schwab-Morris* [1974] 1 WLR 331, [1974] 1 All ER 326.
[6] *Smith v Morrison* [1974] 1 WLR 659 at 682, [1974] 1 All ER 957 at 978.

Ruoff and Roper: *Law and Practice of Registered Conveyancing* (4th edn., 1979), pp. 702–703:

REGISTRATION MACHINERY REPLACING THAT OF THE LAND CHARGES ACT

Instrument or matter as defined in the Land Charges Act 1972	Normal method of protection against registered land	Some other possible alternative methods	Reference to the Land Registration Act 1925
Pending land action.	Caution.	Inhibition if the court so orders.	ss. 59 (1), 54, 57.
Petition in bankruptcy.	Creditor's notice entered automatically by Chief Land Registrar.	None other necessary.	ss. 59 (1), 61 (1).
Writ or order for enforcing judgment against land.	Caution.	Notice, if the land certificate can be produced.	ss. 49, 59 (1) (3), 54.
Receiving order in bankruptcy.	Bankruptcy inhibition entered automatically by Chief Land Registrar.	None other necessary.	ss. 59 (1), 61 (3).
Deed of arrangement affecting land.	Substantive registration of the trustee as proprietor pursuant to a transfer.	Caution.	ss. 59 (1), 54.
Land charge, class A (created by applicant).	Substantive registration of the charge.	Notice or caution.	ss. 26, 49 (1) (c), 59 (2), 54.
Land charge, class B (arising automatically).	Substantive registration of the charge.	Notice or caution.	ss. 26, 49 (1) (c), 59 (2), 54.
Land charge, class C (i) (puisne mortgage).	Substantive registration of the charge.	Notice or caution.	ss. 26, 49 (1) (c), 54, 59 (5), and 106.
Land charge, class C (ii) (limited owner's charge).	Caution or restriction.	Presumably a notice cannot be used as the charge can be overridden.	ss. 49 (1) (c), 49 (2), 54, 58 (1).
Land charge, class C (iii) (generally equitable charge).	Notice.	Caution or notice of [intended] deposit.	ss. 49 (1) (c), 59 (2), 54, 66 and 106 (as amended)
Land charge, class C (iv) (estate contract).	Notice; but it is usually considered that no protection is necessary if possession is taken immediately or if completion is to be soon.	Caution or restriction.	ss. 49 (1) (c), 59 (2), 54, 58 (1).
Land charge, class D (i) (Inland Revenue charge for capital transfer tax).	Notice.	None.	ss. 73, 59 (5)[7].

[7] LRA 1925, ss. 59 (5) and 73 have been amended by FA 1975, ss. 52, 59, Schs. 12 and 13; and s. 73 also by CTTA 1984, s. 276, Sch 8, para. 1. LRA 1925, s. 106 has been amended by AJA 1977, s. 26 (which substituted a new section), p. 741, post.

Instrument or matter as defined in the Land Charges Act 1972	Normal method of protection against registered land	Some other possible alternative methods	Reference to the Land Registration Act 1925
Land charge, class D (ii) (restrictive covenant).	Notice (entered automatically by Chief Land Registrar if the covenant is disclosed on first registration, and if created by a transfer of registered land, entered on registration of the transfer).	Caution.	ss. 5, 19 (2), 20 (1), 50 and 54.
Release or modification of restrictive covenant.	Notice.	None; unless the effectiveness of the release, etc., is strictly proved, when the original entry may be cancelled.	ss. 40, 50.
Land charge, class D (iii) (equitable easement).	Notice.	Caution.	ss. 49 (1) (c), 70 (1) (a), 59 (2), 54.
Land charge, class E (old annuities).	Notice, provided the annuity cannot be overridden.	Caution.	ss. 49 (1) (c), 49 (2), 59 (2), 54.
Land charge, class F (rights of occupation of matrimonial home[8]).	Applicant applies for notice. Chief Land Registrar will enter notice when the property is subject to a registered charge or, if it is not, when the land certificate is produced.	None.	ss. 49 (1) (c), 54.
Renewal of class F charge[9].	Notice or caution, according to method already in use.	None.	ss. 49 (1) (c), 54.

RE WHITE ROSE COTTAGE
[1965] Ch 940, [1965] 1 All ER 11 (CA, Lord DENNING MR, HARMAN and SALMON LJJ)

The proprietor of land registered with an absolute title executed a memorandum of deposit of the land certificate with a bank to secure advances, and undertook to execute a legal charge on request. Notice of the deposit was entered on the charges register. The bank later wished to enter on the register notice of the equitable charge created by the memorandum, but Chippendale Workshops Ltd (the contractors), who were creditors of the proprietor of the land, and had meanwhile lodged cautions, objected.

Held. The contractors were not entitled to object to the registration.

---

[8] Matrimonial Homes Act 1983, ss. 1 (1), 2 (1) (8) (9).

[9] Matrimonial Homes Act 1983, s. 5 (3); Land Registration (Matrimonial Homes) Rules 1983 (SI 1983 No. 40), r. 4.

LORD DENNING MR: Once the bank got the equitable charge, together with the land certificate, on 3 May 1962, the position about registration was as follows:

(1) The bank could not register the charge as a *substantive charge* on the property[10]. In order to make a substantive registration, so as to get special priority, one must have a *legal* charge. An equitable charge will not do: see sections 25 to 36 of the Land Registration Act, 1925. . . .

(2) The bank could apply to the registrar to register *notice* of the charge as a *land charge*, provided they produced the land certificate to him as well: see sections 48 (1)[11], 49 (1) (c)[12] and 64 (1)[13] of the Act of 1925. Where the charge is protected by a *notice* of this kind, it means that every subsequent purchaser or incumbrancer is deemed to be affected with notice of the charge: see section 52[14].

(3) The bank could lodge a *caution* with the registrar: see section 54 of the Act[15]. A caution gives the cautioner this right: he is entitled to have notice, and to be heard, before any subsequent dealing is registered. After a hearing "the registrar shall make such order in the matter as he shall think just" (see rule 220 (3)); bearing in mind that a caution gives a protection to the cautioner in that it gives notice of his interest: see section 59[16].

(4) The bank could give a *notice* that the land certificate had been *deposited* with them. It is true that they had an equitable charge by deed. But they had also the land certificate. It had been deposited with them as security. And I see no reason why they should not give notice of the deposit. Indeed rule 239 (1) is quite clear and contemplates it. Such a notice operates as a caution: see rule 239 (4).

In this case, on 7 May 1962, the bank chose course (4). They gave notice of deposit of the land certificate. I think it was open to them to do so. It operated as a caution at the land registry warning all persons who looked at the register that the land certificate had been deposited with them as security for money. I think it took effect in priority to the subsequent charges by the contractors. The contractors are not entitled to object to the registration by the bank of notice of their charge.

HARMAN LJ: It is, I think, quite right to say that the deposit of the land certificate did not create the charge: that was done by the memorandum and the correct course would have been to seek to enter notice of the memorandum under section 49 of the Act of 1925. Nevertheless the entry on the register was in my opinion a sufficient notice to all the world that the land certificate was in the hands of someone as security for money and this is enough to put the subsequent encumbrancer on enquiry which can only lead to ascertaining the true facts[17].

---

[10] For an account of the types of mortgage and charge allowed in registered and unregistered land, see pp. 740–741, 655–658 respectively, post.

[11] P. 473, post.

[12] P. 136, ante.

[13] P. 101, ante.

[14] P. 137, ante.

[15] P. 139, ante.

[16] P. 137, ante.

[17] It would seem that the deposit of the land certificate alone would have been sufficient to give notice to a subsequent purchaser: *Barclays Bank Ltd v Taylor* [1974] Ch 137, [1974] 1 All ER 752, p. 745, post.

PARKASH *v* IRANI FINANCE LTD
[1970] Ch 101, [1969] 1 All ER 930 (ChD, PLOWMAN J)

In January 1967 one Kalra, who was registered as proprietor of No. 205 Wexham Road, Slough, with an absolute title, agreed to sell it to the plaintiff, subject to contract. No formal contract was ever signed. On 2 July the plaintiff went into possession. On 7 July the defendants obtained a charging order on the property under the County Courts Act 1959, to secure a judgment debt, and on 10 July lodged a caution with the Land Registry. On 27 July the Land Registry issued to the plaintiff's solicitors an official search without mentioning the caution. On 10 August Kalra transferred the property to the plaintiff and on 14 August the transfer was lodged for registration. The defendant then received notice of this application and objected.

The Chief Land Registrar referred to the court the question whether the caution should continue to have effect or be cancelled.

Held. The defendant's caution continued to have effect.

PLOWMAN J: The plaintiff's case, in a nutshell, is this: while conceding that he could not establish any prior equity as against Irani (since he never had a specifically enforceable contract for the purchase of the property), he submits that he is entitled to pray in aid the doctrine of purchaser of a legal estate for value without notice and therefore to take free of the equitable charge created by the charging order. At first sight this submission is a little surprising, since one of the essential features of registration of title is to substitute a system of registration of rights for the doctrine of notice. In the circumstances it is necessary to examine the statutory provisions affecting the present case in order to see whether cautions are anomalous.

[His Lordship then referred to ss. 54 (1), 55, 56 (2) and 59 (1) Land Registration Act 1925 and continued:]

The effect of the registration of a caution, therefore, is that the cautioner's order (in this case a charging order) is "protected" (to quote section 59 (1))[18] by the fact that no dealing can be registered without notice to him so that he can, if he wishes, assert his right and challenge the proposed registration. Conversely, a purchaser of the property, who has a statutory right to an authority from his vendor to inspect the register (see section 110 (1) of the Land Registration Act 1925), will find that no transfer can be registered in his favour without notice to the cautioner. He will not know the precise nature of the cautioner's rights, nor will he probably inquire; his course, in the ordinary way, will be to call upon his vendor to procure either the withdrawal of the caution or the consent of the cautioner to the registration of the intended transfer. No doubt that is what would have happened here, if the plaintiff had made a personal instead of an official search. If the vendor had failed to comply, the plaintiff would presumably have declined to go on with his purchase.

There is one further provision in the Land Registration Act 1925, to which I must refer and that is section 59 (6)[19].

It is true, as was stressed in the argument before me, that what the subsection says is that a purchaser is *not* affected by notice, express, implied

---

[18] P. 137, ante.
[19] P. 137, ante.

or constructive, of matters capable of protection by a caution and not so protected and that (unlike the case of a notice of lease under section 48 (1) of the Act)[20] it does not say in terms that a purchaser *is* affected by a notice of matters capable of protection by caution, which *are* so protected, but that, in my judgment, is implicit in the scheme of the Act and in the subsection.

The effect of the statutory provisions to which I have referred is, in my judgment, this: first, that the appropriate form of protection for a charging order is a caution; secondly, that once the caution is registered, the cautioner can only lose his protection either by virtue of section 55 (1)[1] or by withdrawing his caution, or consenting to its cancellation or by order of the Chief Land Registrar or this court; and, thirdly, that therefore he does not lose it merely because a purchaser of the property does not know of its existence, even if the purchaser's ignorance is the result of a mistake of the Land Registry, short of a failure to act on an application to register the caution in the first place.

There are certain dicta in the Court of Appeal which, even if they be obiter, seem to me to support the view which I have expressed. The case in question is *Re White Rose Cottage* [1965] Ch 940, [1965] 1 All ER 11.

I, therefore, reach the conclusion that . . . Irani has not lost the protection given to it by its caution.

In *Webb v Pollmount Ltd* [1966] Ch 584, [1966] 1 All ER 481[2], UNGOED-THOMAS J said at 599, at 487: "So, I come to section 59[3]. The defendant's submission is that it provides that an option to purchase can only be protected by registration. But it will be convenient, by way of introduction to it, to refer briefly to certain provisions relating to the registration of options under the Land Charges Act 1925[4], and the Land Registration Act 1925. An option to purchase relating to unregistered land is an estate contract within section 10 (1), Class C (iv), of the Land Charges Act 1925[4], and may thus under section 10 (1) be registered as a land charge and under section 13 (2)[5] it is void against a purchaser of the land unless registered before completion of the purchase. Section 23[6] excludes (inter alia) land charges, not including local land charges, from the Act so far as they can be protected under the Land Registration Act 1925, 'by lodging or registering a creditor's notice, restriction, caution, inhibition or other notice'. All land charges can be so protected under the Land Registration Act 1925, by notice, under section 49 (1)[7] until registered as a registered charge, or by caution under section 54[8]. Therefore, the Land Charges Act 1925[9], does not apply to this option to purchase. . . .

---

[20] P. 473, post.
[1] P. 139, ante.
[2] P. 128, ante. The question was whether an option to purchase held by a tenant in actual occupation was valid as an overriding interest.
[3] P. 137, ante.
[4] Now LCA 1972, s. 2 (4).
[5] Now LCA 1972, s. 4 (6).
[6] Now LCA 1972, s. 14.
[7] P. 136, ante.
[8] P. 139, ante.
[9] Now LCA 1972.

The crucial word in section 59 (1), for the purposes of the defendant's argument, is the word 'only' which is relied on to establish that an option to purchase cannot be protected otherwise than by a caution, the creditor's notice or bankruptcy inhibition which it mentions being inapplicable.

Subsection (1) is curiously worded in view of subsection (5). . . .

. . . no explanation seems clearly convincing. But it does seem reasonably clear that if section 59 were read as an exhaustive statement of the only exclusive methods of protecting land charges, it would be inconsistent with other substantial specific sections, and I am convinced that it should not be so read. . . .

I, therefore, respectfully agree with the conclusion of Harman J in *Bridges v Mees* [1957] Ch 475 at 487, [1957] 2 All ER 577 at 582, that section 59 (1) does not establish that it is only by registration in accordance with the subsection that any of the interests, therein mentioned, even though they would otherwise be overriding interests, can be protected."[10]

QUESTION

Legal and equitable estates in land existed for centuries. Since 1925, we speak of legal estates and equitable interests. To what extent is this nomenclature meaningful in the context of:

    (*a*) Interests and charges registered under the Land Charges Act 1972;

    (*b*) Registered Land?

See Maitland, *Equity*, pp. 210–215.

V.   Registered Land and Constructive Trust

The constructive trust has been used in two cases at first instance to avoid the consequences of the failure to register a right as a minor interest under the Land Registration Act 1925.

A. Purchaser With Notice

In *Peffer v Rigg* [1977] 1 WLR 285, [1978] 3 All ER 745 p. 110, ante, a purchaser with notice of an interest under a trust for sale was held to take subject to it, applying general equitable principles. By section 20 (1) of the Land Registration Act 1925, a transferee for valuable consideration takes free from unprotected minor interests. GRAHAM J held that the requirement of good faith could be read into this provision, so that a transferee with notice of the minor interest could not rely on it; but that the same result could be achieved by the device of a constructive trust. He said at 294, at 752:

"On the evidence in this case I have found that the second defendant knew quite well that the first defendant held the property on trust for himself and the plaintiff in equal shares. The second defendant knew this was so and that the property was trust property when the transfer was made to her, and therefore she took the property on a constructive trust in accordance with

---

[10] Followed in *Kling v Keston Properties Ltd* (1983) 49 P & CR 212.

general equitable principles: see *Snell's Principles of Equity* 27th edn. (1973), pp. 98–99. This is a new trust imposed by equity and is distinct from the trust which bound the first defendant. Even if, therefore, I am wrong as to the proper construction of sections 20 and 59, when read together, and even if section 20 strikes off the shackles of the express trust which bound the first defendant, this cannot invalidate the new trust imposed on the second defendant."

In *Williams and Glyn's Bank Ltd v Boland* [1981] AC 487 at 504, [1980] 2 All ER 408 at 412, the House of Lords has confirmed that the doctrine of notice has no relevance to registered land. As Lord WILBERFORCE said: "The only kind of notice recognised is by entry on the register."[11]

B.   A Statute Cannot be Used as an Instrument of Fraud

In *Lyus v Prowsa Developments Ltd* [1982] 1 WLR 1044, [1982] 2 All ER 953, a development company was the registered proprietor of St Martin's Green Estate, Trimley, Suffolk. In 1978 it mortgaged the estate to the bank, and in 1979 contracted to build a house on Plot 29 and sell it to the plaintiffs. It then went insolvent, leaving the house unfinished. The bank, although not subject to the plaintiffs' contract, sold Plot 29 as mortgagees to Prowsa Developments Ltd (the first defendants) "subject to and with the benefit of" the plaintiffs' contract. Prowsa Developments Ltd then contracted to re-sell Plot 29 to the second defendants, subject to the plaintiffs' contract of 1978 "so far, if at all, as it may be enforceable against" Prowsa Developments Ltd. The second defendants were registered as proprietors after a transfer which did not mention the contract of 1978.

The plaintiffs claimed for a declaration that the 1978 contract was binding on Prowsa Developments Ltd and on the second defendants, and for an order for specific performance.

DILLON J held that the defendants were bound by a constructive trust on the ground that the Land Registration Act was not to be used as an instrument of fraud. Having applied *Bannister v Bannister* [1948] 2 All ER 133 and a dictum of Lord DENNING MR in *Binions v Evans* [1972] Ch 359 at 368, [1972] 2 All ER 70 at 76, p. 499, post, he said at 1054, at 962:

"This does not, however, conclude the matter since I also have to consider the effect of the provisions of the Land Registration Act 1925, Plot 29 having at all material times, as I have mentioned, been registered land. In the course of the argument, emphasis was laid on the effect of section 34 (4) (p. 743, post) of the Land Registration Act 1925, which is concerned with the effect on subsequent interests of a transfer of registered land by a mortgagee. Section 34 has, however, to be read with section 20 (p. 110, ante), which is concerned with the effect of the registration of a transfer of registered land by the registered proprietor. The protection conferred by section 34 on a transfer by a mortgagee is thus additional to the protection which is

---

[11] *Peffer v Rigg* was not cited.

conferred by section 20 on registration of a transfer by a registered proprietor.

It has been pointed out by Lord Wilberforce in *Midland Bank Trust Co Ltd v Green* [1981] AC 513 at 531, [1981] 1 All ER 153 at 159, p. 41, ante, that it is not fraud to rely on legal rights conferred by Act of Parliament. Under section 20, the effect of the registration of the transferee of a freehold title is to confer an absolute title subject to entries on the register and overriding interests, but, "free from all other estates and interests whatsoever, including estates and interests of His Majesty . . ." In *Miles v Bull (No 2)* [1969] 3 All ER 1585, Bridge J expressed the view that the words which I have quoted embraced, prima facie, not only all kinds of legal interests, but all kinds of equitable interests: see p. 1589. He therefore held, at p. 1590, as I read his judgment, that actual or constructive notice on the part of a purchaser of an unregistered interest would not have the effect of imposing a constructive trust on him. The interest in *Miles v Bull (No 2)* was the interest in the matrimonial home of a deserted wife who had failed to protect her interest by registration under the Matrimonial Homes Act 1967[12]. The contract for sale between the husband, who was the registered proprietor, and the purchaser provided that the house concerned was sold subject to such rights of occupation as might subsist in favour of the wife, with a proviso that this was not to imply that the wife had, or would after completion have any such rights as against the purchaser. Plainly, therefore, the clause was only included in the contract for the protection of the husband who was the vendor. The wife was to get no fresh rights, and it was not in *Miles v Bull (No 2)* a stipulation of the bargain between the vendor and the purchaser that the purchaser should give effect to the rights as against the vendor of the deserted wife. *Miles v Bull (No 2)* is thus distinguishable from the facts of the present case as I interpret those facts.

It seems to me that the fraud on the part of the defendants in the present case lies not just in relying on the legal rights conferred by an Act of Parliament, but in the first defendant reneging on a positive stipulation in favour of the plaintiffs in the bargain under which the first defendant acquired the land. That makes, as it seems to me, all the difference. It has long since been held, for instance, in *Rochefoucauld v Boustead* [1897] 1 Ch 196, that the provisions of the Statute of Frauds 1677 now incorporated in certain sections of the Law of Property Act 1925, cannot be used as an instrument of fraud, and that it is fraud for a person to whom land is agreed to be conveyed as trustee for another to deny the trust and relying on the terms of the statute to claim the land for himself. *Rochefoucauld v Boustead* was one of the authorities on which the judgment in *Bannister v Bannister* [1948] 2 All ER 133[13] was founded.

It seems to me that the same considerations are applicable in relation to the Land Registration Act 1925. If, for instance, the agreement of October 18, 1979, between the bank and the first defendant had expressly stated that the first defendant would hold Plot 29 upon trust to give effect for the benefit of the plaintiffs to the plaintiffs' agreement with the vendor company, it would be difficult to say that that express trust was over-reached and rendered nugatory by the Land Registration Act 1925. The Land Registra-

---

[12] Now Matrimonial Homes Act 1983, p. 257, post.
[13] See generally [1984] CLJ 306 (T. G. Youdan).

tion Act 1925 does not, therefore, affect the conclusion which I would otherwise have reached in reliance on *Bannister v Bannister* and the judgment of Lord Denning MR in *Binions v Evans* [1972] Ch 359, [1972] 2 All ER 70 had Plot 29 been unregistered land.

The plaintiffs are, therefore, entitled to succeed in this action. The appropriate relief in that event is that specific performance should be ordered as against the second defendants of the sale to the plaintiffs of Plot 29, with the completed house thereon, on the terms of the agreement of January 30, 1978, made between the plaintiffs and the vendor company.''

(1983) 46 MLR 96 (P. H. Kenny), at p. 98:

"The case is as important for what was omitted as for what was decided. Key sections of the Land Registration Act were not referred to: section 74 which states that no "person dealing with a registered estate or charge shall be affected with notice of a trust express implied or constructive" was ignored. Similarly, section 59 (1) providing that matters registerable in the case of unregistered land under the Land Charges Act 1972 are to be "protected only by lodging a creditor's notice, a bankruptcy inhibition or a caution against dealings with the land or charge" was ignored[14]. Presumably, the same sweeping principles of equity would have sidestepped these provisions.

The court here showed the usual judicial reluctance to grapple firmly with the mechanics of land registration. This arm's-length approach to the registration system led it not to give effect to the prescriptive system of registration in the Land Registration Act 1925. In the same way that the effect of non-registration of an estate contract is prescribed by section 4 of the Land Charges Act 1972 and had to be given effect to in *Midland Bank Trust Co Ltd v Green*, so the need to register an equivalent interest in registered land is prescribed by section 59 (1) of the Land Registration Act 1925 which, with section 20 and section 34 (4), should have been given effect to by the court. The legislation for both registered and unregistered land makes mandatory provision for registration and is specific on the effect of non-registration. The estate contract could, under the Land Registration Act, have been protected against the charge only by registration giving priority over the charge with the bank's consent. If there is a principle of equity which allows such transparently clear provisions to be sidestepped it should at least be described with greater precision and result from a less cavalier treatment of the relevant legislation[15].''

---

[14] *De Lusignan v Johnson* (1973) 230 EG 499 was also ignored although it could have been distinguished in the same way as *Miles v Bull (No 2)*.

[15] See Oakley, *Constructive Trusts* (1978), p. 28 "the imposition of a constructive trust on the joint and equitable grounds may well seriously undermine established principles of property law". For further criticism, see [1982] All ER Rev (P. J. Clarke); [1983] CLJ 54 (C. J. Harpum); [1983] Conv 64 (P. Jackson); (1983) 133 NLJ 798 (C. T. Emery and B. Smythe); cf. (1984) 47 MLR 476 (P. Bennett). On constructive trusts generally, see H & M, chap. 12.

VI.   Rectification of the Register and Indemnity[16]

LAND REGISTRATION ACT 1925

82.   Rectification of the register. — (1) The register may be rectified pursuant to an order of the court or by the registrar, subject to an appeal to the court, in any of the following cases, but subject to the provisions of this section:—

(*a*) Subject to any express provisions of this Act to the contrary, where a court of competent jurisdiction has decided that any person is entitled to any estate right or interest in or to any registered land or charge, and as a consequence of such decision such court is of opinion that a rectification of the register is required, and makes an order to that effect[17];

(*b*) Subject to any express provision of this Act to the contrary, where the court, on the application in the prescribed manner of any person who is aggrieved by any entry made in, or by the omission of any entry from, the register, or by any default being made, or unnecessary delay taking place, in the making of any entry in the register, makes an order for the rectification of the register[18];

(*c*) In any case and at any time with the consent of all persons interested;

(*d*) Where the court or the registrar is satisfied that any entry in the register has been obtained by fraud[19];

(*e*) Where two or more persons are, by mistake, registered as proprietors of the same registered estate or of the same charge;

(*f*) Where a mortgagee has been registered as proprietor of the land instead of as proprietor of a charge and a right of redemption is subsisting[20];

(*g*) Where a legal estate has been registered in the name of a person who if the land had not been registered would not have been the estate owner[1]; and

(*h*) In any other case where, by reason of any error or omission in the register, or by reason of any entry made under a mistake, it may be deemed just to rectify the register[2].

---

[16] C & B, pp. 104, 731–739; M & W, pp. 225–230; MM, p. 130, chap. 15; Barnsley, chap. 4; Farrand (2nd edn.), pp. 209–220; Hayton, chap. 9; Ruoff and Roper, chap. 40; (1968) 84 LQR 528 (S. M. Cretney and G. Dworkin); (1969) 32 MLR 138–141 (T. B. F. Ruoff); (1971) 35 Conv (NS) 390 (T. B. F. Ruoff and P. Meehan); Law Commission Working Paper No. 45 (1972), pp. 36–74.

[17] *Chowood Ltd v Lyall (No 2)* [1930] 2 Ch 156 (rectification ordered to give effect to overriding interest acquired by adverse possession to part of land registered in name of proprietor); *Calgary and Edmonton Land Co Ltd v Discount Bank (Overseas) Ltd* [1971] 1 WLR 81, [1971] 1 All ER 551 (caution removed). See also *Spectrum Investment Co v Holmes* [1981] 1 WLR 221, [1981] 1 All ER 6, p. 193, post.

[18] *Chowood Ltd v Lyall (No 2)*, supra at 168–169, per LAWRENCE LJ; *Calgary and Edmonton Land Co Ltd v Discount Bank (Overseas) Ltd*, supra; *Lester v Burgess* (1973) 26 P & C R 536 (caution removed).

[19] *Re Leighton's Conveyance* [1936] 1 All ER 667 (fraudulent misrepresentation and undue influence); *Argyle Building Society v Hammond* (1984) 49 P & C R 148 (forgery), p. 151, post. LRA 1925, s. 114.

[20] Cf. for unregistered land LPA 1925, ss. 85 (2), (3), 86 (2), (3), p. 655, post.

[1] *Chowood Ltd v Lyall (No 2)*, supra.

[2] *Re Dances Way, West Town, Hayling Island* [1962] Ch 490, [1962] 2 All ER 42, p. 646, post (notice of adverse easement cancelled).

(2) The register may be rectified under this section, notwithstanding that the rectification may affect any estates, rights, charges, or interests acquired or protected by registration, or by any entry on the register, or otherwise[3].

(3)[4] The register shall not be rectified, except for the purpose of giving effect to an overriding interest[5] or an order of the court so as to affect the title of the proprietor who is in possession — .

   (*a*) unless the proprietor has caused or substantially contributed to the error or omission by fraud or lack of proper care; or

   (*c*) unless for any other reason, in any particular case, it is considered that it would be unjust not to rectify the register against him[6].

83. Right to indemnity in certain cases[7].

— (1) Subject to the provisions of this Act to the contrary, any person suffering loss by reason of any rectification of the register under this Act shall be entitled to be indemnified[8].

(2) Where an error or omission has occurred in the register, but the register is not rectified, any person suffering loss by reason of such error or omission, shall, subject to the provisions of this Act, be entitled to be indemnified.

(3) Where any person suffers loss by reason of the loss or destruction of any document lodged at the registry for inspection or safe custody or by reason of an error in any official search, he shall be entitled to be indemnified under this Act.

(4) Subject as hereinafter provided, a proprietor of any registered land or charge claiming in good faith under a forged disposition shall, where the register is rectified, be deemed to have suffered loss by reason of such rectification and shall be entitled to be indemnified under this Act.

(5) No indemnity shall be payable under this Act in any of the following cases:—

   (*a*) Where the applicant or a person from whom he derives title (otherwise than under a disposition for valuable consideration which is registered or protected on the register) has caused or substantially contributed to the loss by fraud or lack of proper care[9];

---

[3] *Freer v Unwins Ltd* [1976] Ch 288, [1976] 1 All ER 634 (where it was held that the rectification of the register of title to servient land by the entry of a notice of restrictive covenants does not operate retrospectively so as to bind a person taking under a prior registered disposition for valuable consideration). See (1976) 40 Conv (NS) 304 (F. R. Crane); 126 NLJ 523 (S. M. Cretney); Ruoff & Roper, pp. 793–794.

[4] As amended by AJA 1977, s. 24, which came into force on 29 August 1977; see Law Com Working Paper No. 45 (1972), pp. 36–74.

[5] *Re Chowood's Registered Land* [1933] Ch 574, p. 159, post; *Epps v Esso Petroleum Co Ltd* [1973] 1 WLR 1071, [1973] 2 All ER 465, p. 154, post.

[6] *Epps v Esso Petroleum Co Ltd*, supra.

[7] The indemnity is payable by the Chief Land Registrar out of moneys provided by Parliament: LR & LCA 1971, s. 1. See (1971) 35 Conv (NS) 390 (T. B. F. Ruoff and P. Meehan). During 1984–1985, £107,489 was paid in respect of 233 claims; these included twenty-four claims for erroneous inclusion of land on first registration. Annual Report for 1984–1985, paras. 36–38. Viewed against a fee revenue of about £102 million for the year 1984–1985, the sums paid by way of indemnity "fade almost into insignificance".

[8] *Re Chowood's Registered Land* [1933] Ch 574.

[9] As substituted by LR & LCA 1971, s. 3 (1); (1971) 35 Conv (NS) 390.

(11) ... when a claim to indemnity arises in consequence of the registration of an estate in land with an absolute or good leasehold title, the claim shall be enforceable only if made within six years from the date of such registration, ...[10].

A. Fraud: Forgery

ARGYLE BUILDING SOCIETY *v* HAMMOND
(1984) 49 P & CR 148
(CA, LAWTON and SLADE LJJ and Sir DAVID CAIRNS)[11]

In 1964 Mr Steed (the appellant and third defendant) became the registered freehold proprietor of 2 Arlow Road, Winchmore Hill, London. In 1976 he went to the United States, leaving in the house his mother, and his sister and her husband, Mr and Mrs Hammond (the first and second defendants). He alleged that in 1979 his sister induced him to sign a power of attorney to enable his mother to sell the house on his behalf; and that a transfer of the house took place by way of a forged deed in favour of the sister and her husband who were then registered as joint proprietors. They borrowed £15,000 by way of registered legal charge from the Argyle Building Society. On default the Building Society brought an action for possession. Mr Steed was given leave to be joined as the third defendant so that he could apply to have the registered charge rectified against the Building Society. The County Court judge held that he had no jurisdiction to order rectification and granted an order for possession.

Held. The Court had power to rectify. New trial ordered.

SLADE LJ: We now turn to the substantive issues arising on this appeal. If the title to the house were not registered and the appellant's signature on the transfer of the house to Mr and Mrs Hammond was a forgery, there would in our judgment, at least prima facie, be no possible question of the ... charge of the respondent ... binding the appellant. At least prima facie, the appellant could assert that the transfer was a nullity and that nothing had occurred to divest him of the freehold title to the house, unincumbered by any charge in favour of the respondent ... (compare *Re Cooper* (1882) 20 ChD 611). However, as Mr Leckie has stressed, the fact that the title to the house in the present case is registered necessitates a somewhat different approach to the legal problems. The effect of the registration of Mr and Mrs Hammond as proprietors of the freehold interest in the house must have been to vest in them the legal fee simple, whether or not the purported signature of Mrs Mary Steed on the transfer to them was forged. This is by virtue of the "statutory magic" effected by section 69 (1) of the 1925 Act p. 99, ante, to which *Ruoff & Roper* refer (4th edn. 1979, p. 498). We have already quoted that subsection, but should mention that the word "proprietor", which appears in it, is defined by section 1 (XX) as meaning "the registered proprietor for the time being of an estate in land or a charge." The

---

[10] Then follow special provisions for the date at which the six years start in cases of minors, settlements, covenants, and mortgages.
[11] [1985] Conv 135 (A. Sydenham). On forgeries and registered land generally, see (1985) 101 LQR 79 (R. J. Smith).

relevant provisions of the 1925 Act relating to charges are to be found in sections 25 to 27 (pp. 741–742, post). . . .

It follows that once a person has been registered as the proprietor of freehold land, he has, so long as he remains so registered, the statutory power to create valid charges (through the combined effect of sections 69 (1), 25, 26 and 27), even though the purported transfer of the freehold under which he himself claims is a forged instrument. Likewise, so long as he remains so registered, he has the power to transfer the freehold title itself. The 1925 Act thus contains striking exceptions to the general principle "*Nemo dat quod non habet.*". . .

Nevertheless, it is clear that any protection enjoyed by a proprietor or mortgagee under the 1925 Act is conferred subject to the provisions for rectification of the Register contained in section 82, of which subsection (1), so far as material, reads as follows:

[His Lordship read s. 82 (1), p. 149 ante, and continued.]

We pause to make two points in relation to this subsection. First, registers of title made pursuant to the 1925 Act consist of three parts, namely the property register, the proprietorship register and the charges register. The jurisdiction to rectify under the subsection plainly extends to all or any of these parts. Secondly, on the assumed facts in the present case, the court would, in our judgment, have clear jurisdiction to rectify the proprietorship register of the house by substituting the name of the appellant for that of Mr and Mrs Hammond, since the case would fall within all or any of sub-paragraphs (*a*), (*b*), (*d*), (*g*) and (*h*) of section 82 (1). The present argument relates to the possibility or otherwise of rectification of the charges register.

Section 82 (2) of the 1925 Act provides as follows:

"The register may be rectified under this section, notwithstanding that the rectification may affect any estates, rights, charges, or interests acquired or protected by registration, or by any entry on the register, or otherwise."

This subsection, which reversed the position under section 95 of the Land Transfer Act 1875, is important in the present context. It makes it clear that the court has jurisdiction in any proper case to rectify the charges register, even though the rectification may affect a charge acquired or protected by registration. . . .

In the light of the very wide discretion given to the court by the 1925 Act, we found it at first sight surprising that the judge should have concluded that on the assumed facts and as a matter of law, there was no possibility of the appellant's obtaining rectification of the charges register against the mortgagee. . . .

In reaching this conclusion he relied heavily, not only on the statements of law in *Ruoff & Roper*, but on the decision in *Re Leighton's Conveyance* [1936] 1 All ER 667.

The facts of the latter case, as summarised in the headnote to the report, were as follows:

A daughter without her mother's knowledge arranged for the sale of certain registered land from the mother to herself. Without explaining the true nature of the document, the daughter secured the execution of the necessary transfer by her mother and her own registration as owner with an absolute title. The daughter subsequently created charges upon the property, the chargees being ignorant of the fraud upon the mother, and giving full consideration for their charges.

The mother sought both rectification of the proprietorship register with regard to the house, and rectification of the charges register, by removing the registered charges. Though a plea that the transfer was forged was not proceeded with, she asserted that the deed which purported to convey the property to her daughter was not her deed upon the basis of the doctrine known as *"non est factum"*. Though Luxmoore J had no doubt that the daughter had adopted a course of conduct which was "wholly improper" (at 671), he considered it important to determine whether or not this was in truth a case where the doctrine applied. For, as he pointed out at 672:

"If a party who executes a document can read but does not do so, it is good even if contrary to their mind. But if it is read falsely or its contents falsely declared and then signed, the deed is not his deed."

Luxmoore J however concluded that the relevant deed was the deed of the mother. As he said at 672:

"There is little doubt that she had no understanding of the nature of the documents, but I am equally satisfied that she knew she was doing *some*thing, and if she had made inquiries she would have found out that it had to do with No. 167 Camden Road. She made no such inquiries . . ."

On the basis of these facts, the conclusion which Luxmoore J reached was that the proprietorship register should be rectified by substituting the name of the mother for that of the daughter, but that there were no grounds for interfering with the charges by rectifying the charges register. . . .

The decision of Luxmoore J went to appeal on a question relating to costs: [1936] 3 All ER 1033. Lord Wright MR, referred to his decision on the rectification issue with apparent approval, but we think that for present purposes nothing turns on what was said in the Court of Appeal.

[His Lordship discussed *Re Leighton's Conveyance* and continued:]

There is no doubt whatever that in the present case, on the basis of the assumed facts, the court would have jurisdiction, in the proper exercise of its discretion, to rectify the charges register as against the chargees. The wording of section 82 (1), which issues the permissive word "may," and reported decisions to which we have been referred such as *Claridge v Tingey* [1967] 1 WLR 134 at 141, [1966] 3 All ER 935 at 941 and *Epps v Esso Petroleum Co Ltd* [1973] 1 WLR 1071, [1973] 2 All ER 465, p. 154, post, leave no doubt that the jurisdiction to rectify in a case falling within one or more of the sub-paragraphs of the subsection, is of a discretionary nature. And section 82 (2) makes it clear that the jurisdiction is exercisable against persons claiming through a registered proprietor. The decision in the *Leighton* case, in our judgment, affords little useful guidance, certainly no conclusive guidance, as to the manner in which the court's discretion would fall to be exercised in the instant case, since in at least one crucial respect it is clearly distinguishable from the present case on its facts. In a case such as the present, on its assumed facts, where the registered proprietor has been deprived of his freehold estate as a result of a forged transfer followed by a new registration of the freehold title at the Land Registry, quite different considerations may fall to be applied when the court comes to exercise its discretion. For, unlike the plaintiff in the *Leighton* case, the person seeking rectification will be able to assert that the written instrument which most directly led to such deprivation was not his own deed or instrument in any sense, but was a complete nullity. The passage already cited from the judgment of Luxmoore J in the *Leighton* case makes it clear that he regarded it as highly material that the relevant deed was the deed of the misguided plaintiff. The court, in exercising its discretion in the present case, would no doubt also bear in mind that, if the title to the house were unregistered, there would, at least prima facie, be no question of the mortgagees' being entitled to assert any equity which, on the assumed facts, would prevail over the appellant's legal title. It would also have in mind that section 83 (4) of the 1925 Act would give the mortgagees, as persons claiming in good faith under a forged disposition, an express right to an indemnity.

We draw attention to these various points, not meaning to suggest that, on the assumed facts, an application by the appellant for rectification of the charges register would be bound to succeed; the court still would have to exercise its discretion, having regard to all the relevant evidence before it.

B.   Double Conveyance. Overriding Interest

EPPS *v* ESSO PETROLEUM CO LTD
[1973] 1 WLR 1071, [1973] 2 All ER 465[12] (ChD, TEMPLEMAN J)

In 1935 Alfred Clifford owned 4 Darland Avenue, Gillingham, Kent, and, on the north side of it, the adjoining Darland Garage. In that year he leased both to Mr Jones. In 1955 his personal representatives conveyed the house to Mrs Jones in fee simple, together with an extra 11 foot strip of frontage on the north side of the wall dividing the home from the garage. The object was to provide space for a garage at the home. Mrs Jones covenanted to erect a new wall on the new boundary, but never did. In 1956 Clifford's personal representatives granted a new lease of Darland Garage to Mr Jones, and in error the plan included the 11 foot strip. In 1959 they conveyed the garage, subject to the lease, to Julian Ball, and included the strip. The Land Registration Act 1925 had become applicable, and Ball became first registered proprietor of the garage and strip, with the consequence that LRA 1925, section 5 deprived Mrs Jones of the strip and vested it in Ball, subject to any overriding interests affecting the strip. In 1964 Ball conveyed the garage and strip to the defendants who became the second registered proprietors with absolute title. In 1968 the personal representatives of Mrs Jones conveyed 4 Darland Avenue and the strip to Mr and Mrs Epps, who obtained first registration of the house without the strip.

On a summons by Mr and Mrs Epps for rectification of the register, so as to exclude the strip from the defendant's title on the register, the plaintiffs argued that Mrs Jones was in possession of the strip at the time of the conveyance to the defendant in 1964; and, therefore, Mrs Jones and her estate had an overriding interest under LRA 1925, section 70 (1) (*g*) by virtue of that possession.

Held. Rectification refused.

TEMPLEMAN J: Section 82 (1) of the Land Registration Act provides that the register may be rectified where, inter alia, as in the present case, a legal estate has been registered in the name of a person who, if the land had not been registered, would not have been the estate owner. That describes the defendants. Section 82 (3), limits the exercise of the power of rectification conferred by section 82 (1). The limitation is in these terms:

---

[12] (1973) 37 Conv (NS) 284 (F. R. Crane).

"The register shall not be rectified, except for the purpose of giving effect to an overriding interest, so as to affect the title of the proprietor who is in possession — unless . . ."
and then it specifies three conditions[13], one of which must be satisfied, if rectification is to be granted. . . .

Condition (c) provides for rectification — and I quote:

"unless for any other reason, in any particular case, it is considered that it would be unjust not to rectify the register against . . ." [the registered proprietor.]

Mr Cullen, for the plaintiffs, submitted that when Mrs Jones was deprived of her legal estate in fee simple by the mistaken registration of Mr Ball as proprietor, Mrs Jones retained or acquired, and her successors in title, down to and including the plaintiffs, acquired an equitable interest in fee simple. The registered proprietor, first Mr Ball and now the defendants, acquired the legal estate, subject to the equitable interest of Mrs Jones and her successors. Effect should be given to that equitable interest by rectification. The limitation on the exercise of the power of rectification, which is to be found in section 82 (3), does not apply where rectification is required to give effect to an overriding interest. The equitable interest of Mrs Jones and her successors in title is an overriding interest.

By section 70 (1) (g) overriding interests include the rights of every person in actual occupation of the land or in receipt of the rents and profits thereof, save where inquiry is made of such person and the rights are not disclosed. Mrs Jones and her successors in title were in actual occupation, because Mr Jones, and later the plaintiffs, parked a car on the disputed strip. Mr Ball and the defendants acquired the disputed strip subject to the overriding interests of Mrs Jones and her successors constituted by an equitable interest protected by actual occupation. The defendants never were in possession or, at any rate, ceased to be in possession when the plaintiffs erected their fence in 1968. Thus far Mr Cullen. . . .

The claim put forward by Mr Cullen on behalf of the plaintiffs to an overriding interest depends on whether Mr Jones was in actual occupation of the disputed strip when the defendants became the registered proprietor of the disputed strip in 1964. The contention put forward by Mr Cullen that the defendants were not in possession depends on whether they went into possession of the disputed strip when they became the registered proprietor and remained in possession until after the plaintiffs completed their purchase in 1968. Mr Brodie for the defendants took up a position at the opposite pole. He submitted that even if Mr Jones was in actual occupation he occupied in his capacity as tenant of Mr Ball. Alternatively, the occupation of Mr Jones could not protect any equitable interest vested in the probate judge at the date when the defendants became the registered proprietors of the disputed strip in 1964.

I reject these submissions of Mr Brodie. If Mr Jones was in actual occupation when the defendants completed their purchase of the disputed strip then his occupation in the present circumstances sufficed to assert and protect any equitable interest of Mrs Jones and her estate so as to constitute an overriding interest, and sufficed also to defeat the claim by the defendants to be in possession. . . .

---

[13] Now only two. AJA 1977, s. 24, p. 150, ante.

In my judgment, the fact that the defendants were not the original proprietors, but subsequent transferees, is only one element to be considered in the exercise of the discretion conferred by section 82 (1) and section 82 (3) (c) of the Land Registration Act 1925. In the confrontation envisaged by section 82 (1) and in particular by section 82 (1) (g), between, on the one hand, the registered proprietor, who is a victim of double conveyancing, and the first purchaser or his successors, deprived of the legal estate by registration, the court must first determine whether the registered proprietor is in possession. If the registered proprietor is not in possession then section 82 (3) does not apply, and the court will normally grant rectification: see *Chowood Ltd v Lyall (No 2)* [1930] 2 Ch 156. A fortiori if the registered proprietor is not in possession but the applicant has an overriding interest constituted by an equitable interest protected by actual occupation, the court will grant rectification: see *Bridges v Mees* [1957] Ch 475 at 486, [1957] 2 All ER 577 at 581, 582. However, the power of rectification given by section 82 (1) never ceases to be discretionary, so that where section 82 (3) does not apply there may still be circumstances which defeat the claim for rectification.

If the registered proprietor is in possession, the applicant for rectification will not normally be in actual occupation, and one of the conditions specified in section 82 (3) must be satisfied if rectification is to be granted. . . .

It follows that the crucial questions in the present case are, first, whether Mr Jones was in actual occupation of the disputed strip when the defendants completed purchase in 1964; secondly, whether the defendants were in possession at the date when the plaintiffs completed their purchase of 4 Darland Avenue in 1968; and if those questions are decided in favour of the defendants, thirdly, whether it would be unjust not to rectify against them.

In *Hodgson v Marks* [1971] Ch 892 at 931, [1971] 2 All ER 684 at 688, Russell LJ said, on actual occupation as an ingredient of an overriding interest, that he was prepared for the purpose of that case to assume, without necessarily accepting, that section 70 (1) (g) of the Land Registration Act 1925 is designed only to apply to a case in which the occupation is such in point of fact as would in the case of unregistered land affect a purchaser with constructive notice of the rights of the occupier. Then Russell LJ said, at 932, at 688:

"I do not think it desirable to attempt to lay down a code or catalogue of situations in which a person other than the vendor should be held to be in occupation of unregistered land for the purpose of constructive notice of his rights, or in actual occupation of registered land for the purposes of section 70 (1) (g). It must depend on the circumstances, and a wise purchaser or vendor will take no risks. Indeed, however wise he may be he may have no ready opportunity of finding out; but, nevertheless, the law will protect the occupier."

In my judgment Mr Jones was not in actual occupation of the disputed strip when the defendants completed their purchase of Darland Garage and was not thereafter in actual occupation.

Mr Jones gave evidence that every night he parked his car on the disputed strip, and sometimes the car was there during the day. Mr Jones's recollection, not unnaturally, was not very reliable, and I find that he sometimes parked his car on the disputed strip, but how often and when no one can now determine with any certainty. But even if Mr Jones regularly parked his car on the disputed strip I do not consider that this constituted actual occupation of the disputed strip in the circumstances of the present case. I reach this conclusion for the following reasons: first, the parking of a car on a strip 11 feet wide by 80 feet long does not actually occupy the whole, or a substantial, or any defined part of that disputed strip for the whole or any defined time. Secondly, the parking of a car on an unidentified piece of land, apparently comprised in garage premises, is not an assertion of actual occupation of anything.

In addition to these two reasons there are circumstances which show that, not only was Mr Jones not in actual occupation, but on the contrary that the defendants were.

[His Lordship reviewed the evidence and continued:]

In my judgment, therefore, section 82 (3) does apply because the Jones's and the plaintiffs had no overriding interest protected by actual occupation and because the defendants were in possession. There remains the question, under condition (c) of section 82 (3) whether it would be unjust not to rectify against the defendants.

In my judgment, justice in the present case lies wholly with the defendants and not with the plaintiffs. . . .

In my judgment, whereas the defendants bought the disputed strip, the plaintiffs bought a law suit, thanks to the default of their vendor in not taking steps to assert ownership and possession of the disputed strip, and thanks to the failure of the plaintiffs to make before completion the inquiries which they made immediately after completion.

Mr Cullen put forward one additional circumstance which he argued, with some force, tilted the balance of justice in favour of rectification. That circumstance, he submitted, was that if the register is rectified the defendants can recover compensation based on the 1973 value of the disputed strip, but if the register is not rectified the plaintiffs cannot recover compensation. This argument is founded on section 83 of the Land Registration Act 1925 which deals with compensation. Section 83 (1) provides that, subject to the provisions of the Act to the contrary, any person suffering loss by reason of any rectification of the register under the Act shall be entitled to be indemnified. That will be the position of the defendants if I rectify. Section 83 (2) provides that where an error or omission has occurred in the register but the register is not rectified, any person suffering loss by reason of such error or omission shall, subject to the provisions of the Act, be entitled to be indemnified. That is the position of the plaintiffs, if I do not rectify.

By section 83 (6) where indemnity is paid in respect of the loss of an estate or interest in or charge on land the amount so paid shall not exceed (a), where the register is not rectified the value of the estate interest or charge at the time when the error or omission which caused the loss was made. In other words, if I do not rectify then the plaintiffs' indemnity is reduced to the value of the disputed strip as at 1959 when the error was made. Subsection (6) (b), on the other hand, says that where the register is rectified the indemnity is not to exceed the value if there had been no rectification of the estate, interest or charge immediately before the time of rectification. This would apply to the defendants. So that the legislature provides 1959 values for the plaintiffs and 1973 values for the defendants. The matter does not end there, however, because by subsection (11) there is a further limitation on indemnity. Subsection (11) provides that a liability to pay indemnity under the Act shall be deemed a simple contract debt and for the purposes of the Limitation Act the cause of action shall be deemed to arise at the time when the claimant knows or, but for his own default, might have known of the existence of his claim. Whether or not that applies to the plaintiffs, it clearly does not affect the defendants; first, because they are not claimants; and, secondly, because they must have been in complete innocence of anything wrong until the plaintiffs came on the scene and raised the question of where the true boundary lay. Then there is a proviso:

"Provided that, when a claim to indemnity arises in consequence of the registration of an estate in land with an absolute or good leasehold title, the claim shall be enforceable only if made within six years from the date of such registration, except in the following cases . . ."

and then it sets out cases involving infants or settled land, which plainly do not apply. Clearly, that proviso operates to deprive the plaintiffs of compensation, because their claim to indemnity is made more than six years from the date of the 1959 registration. Mr Cullen submits that it does not apply to the defendants. First, he says that the proviso only applies to section 83 (2); and, secondly, he says that the claim to indemnity will only arise so far as the defendants are concerned in consequence of the registration which will follow upon any order for rectification.

Mr Brodie, on the other hand, submits that the proviso applies to the defendants and that if it does not, the matter is obscure, and any decision I make on it will not be binding, and the defendants should not be left in the uncertainty of knowing whether that decision is right.

I can only peer through my own spectacles and, in my judgment, the proviso does not apply to the defendants. It is intended only to apply to a claimant who has the means and opportunity of finding out and asserting his claim, and therefore there is no reason why the six-year period should not operate. In the case of the defendants, however, who are in possession and who have got the title, I do not consider that the proviso applies: they will not suffer and their claim to indemnity will not arise unless and until an order for rectification is made. Accordingly, the foundation for Mr Cullen's submission is established. This is a case, in my judgment, in which if an order for rectification is made the defendants will be entitled to indemnity on 1973 values, and if the claim for rectification is refused then they will keep the land, but the plaintiffs will not get compensation.

The question I have to determine is whether that is sufficient to upset the justice of the defendants' claim that there should not be rectification in the present instance. Is it sufficient — and this is the test — to make it unjust not to rectify the register against the defendants? Mr Cullen pointed out that as far as the defendants are concerned the disputed strip formed, he calculated, 4 per cent of the garage premises. He said it could not make a lot of difference to the defendants' garage; on the other hand, it was of importance to 4 Darland Avenue because it provided a private garage, an asset which is important in commuter territory.

In my judgment, however, this cannot be solved merely on the question of money. The defendants bought the land; they bought it to exploit for their commercial purposes; they did not buy it in order to sell a strip for a 1973 value, which in real terms will not, in my judgment, adequately indemnify them. Although the strip is at the back of the garage, in the same way as it could be used as a private garage for 4 Darland Avenue, so it could be used by the defendants for commercial purposes, and in fact they say now they intend to use it in connection with a car wash; if they are deprived of it they will be in considerable difficulty, and will not have all the facilities which a modern garage requires. I think that may be putting it a bit high, but the fact of the matter is that this strip is worth more to the defendants than the pounds, shillings and pence which they will receive by indemnity, even on a 1973 basis.

Accordingly, in my judgment, that argument is not sufficient to overturn all the other arguments in favour of the defendants, and I decline to order rectification of the register.

RE CHOWOOD'S REGISTERED LAND[14]
[1933] Ch 574 (ChD, CLAUSON J)

Lyall had, before the registration of Chowood Ltd (the purchaser of certain freeholds from Ralli) as proprietor of those freeholds with an absolute title, acquired a right under the Limitation Acts to a part thereof. The register was rectified and Chowood Ltd claimed an indemnity under section 83.

Held. Chowood Ltd was not entitled to be indemnified.

CLAUSON J: Chowood's title was all along subject to the rights which Lyall has succeeded in establishing; and the loss, if it may properly be so called, which Chowood has suffered is that they have not got, and since the Act of 1925 came into force (whatever may have been the position before) have never had title to the strip, except subject to an overriding right in Lyall. That loss was occasioned by Chowood failing to ascertain that, when they bought, Lyall was in possession, and in possession under such circumstances that Ralli could not make a title to the strip. The loss was occasioned by paying Ralli for a strip to which Ralli could not make title. The rectification of the register merely recognized the existing position, and put Chowood in no worse a position than they were in before.

In these circumstances I must hold that Chowood have suffered no loss by reason of the rectification of the register.

VII.   Powers of Registrar[15]

The Chief Land Registrar has wide administrative and judicial powers under the Act. They are contained in a number of sections scattered throughout the Act[16]. Those of a general nature are set out below.

LAND REGISTRATION ACT 1925

127. Conduct of business by registrar. — Subject to the provisions of this Act, the Chief Land Registrar shall conduct the whole business of registration under this Act, and shall frame and cause to be printed and circulated or otherwise promulgated such forms and directions as he may deem requisite or expedient for facilitating proceedings under this Act.

---

[14] Followed in *Re Boyle's Claim* [1961] 1 WLR 339, [1961] 1 All ER 620.
[15] Curtis and Ruoff, chap. 41.
[16] E.g. LRA 1925, ss. 13, 17, 82, 128.

140. Power of registrar to state case for the court[17]. —(1) Whenever, upon the examination of the title to any interest in land, the registrar entertains a doubt as to any matter of law or fact arising upon such title, he may (whether or not the matter has been referred to a conveyancing counsel in the prescribed manner), upon the application of any party interested in such land —

  (*a*) refer a case for the opinion of the High Court and the court may direct an issue to be tried before a jury for the purpose of determining any fact;

  (*b*) name the parties to such case;

  (*c*) give directions as to the manner in which proceedings in relation thereto are to be brought before the court.

(2) The opinion of any court to whom any case is referred by the registrar shall be conclusive on all the parties to the case, unless the court permits an appeal.

LAND REGISTRATION RULES 1925

298. Hearing before the Registrar. — (1) If any question, doubt, dispute, difficulty or complaint arises before the Registrar upon any application or during any investigation of title —

  (*a*) as to the registration of a title, incumbrance, or charge,

  (*b*) as to any dealing with any registered title, incumbrance, or charge, or any matter entered or noted in or omitted from the register, or

  (*c*) as to the amendment or withdrawal from the register or production to the Registrar of any certificate or other document, or

  (*d*) in any registration or other proceedings in the Registry, or

  (*e*) as to any claim for indemnity[18],

(whether such questions relate to the construction, validity, or effect of any instrument, or the persons interested, or the nature or extent of their respective interests or powers, or as to order of priority, or the mode in which any entry should be made or dealt with in the register or otherwise), the Registrar shall hear and determine the matter and, subject to appeal to the Court, make such order in the matter as he shall think just.

(2) But the Registrar may, if he thinks fit, instead of deciding the question himself, refer the matter at any stage, or any question thereon, for the decision of the Court[19].

299. Appeal to the Court. — Any person aggrieved by an order or decision of the Registrar may appeal to the Court.

322. Power to relax regulations, etc. — (1) The Registrar, if he so thinks fit, may, in any particular case, extend the time limited, or relax the regulations made by general rules, for any purpose; and may at any time adjourn any proceeding, and make any new appointment[20].

---

[17] For the registrar's power to summon witnesses and compel production of documents, see LRA 1925, s. 128.

[18] See now LR & LCA 1971, s. 2 (4).

[19] LRR 1925, r. 220 (4). See *Re White Rose Cottage* [1965] Ch 940, [1965] 1 All ER 11, p. 141, ante; *Barclays Bank Ltd v Taylor* [1974] Ch 137, [1973] 1 All ER 752; (1956) 20 Conv (NS) 194 (G. H. Curtis).

[20] *Morelle Ltd v Wakeling* [1955] 2 QB 379, [1955] 1 All ER 708; *Smith v Morrison* [1974] 1 WLR 659, [1974] 1 All ER 957.

(2) If at any time he is of opinion that the production of any further documents, or evidence, or the giving of any further notices is necessary or desirable, he may refuse to complete or proceed with a registration, or to do any act, or make any entry until such further documents, or evidence, or notices have been supplied or given.

QUESTIONS

1. Compare the position of a purchaser under the registered and the unregistered systems. Should there be any differences? If not, how should the existing differences be resolved? C & B, pp. 105–107, 744–745; M & W, pp. 196–197; (1977) 41 Conv (NS) 405 (J. G. Riddall); [1978] Conv 248 (P. R. Gelling); (1976) CLP 26 (D. J. Hayton); *Spectrum Investment Co v Holmes* [1981] 1 WLR 221, [1981] 1 All ER 6, p. 193, ante; (1985) 82 LSG 2399 (J. E. Adams); 2719 (P. H. Kenny), and subsequent correspondence: 2964 (R. T. Oerton); 3135 (J. E. Adams); 3311 (E. J. Pryer and J. T. Farrand); (1986) 83 LSG 6 (R. T. Oerton).

2. How far is a purchaser bound, and how far should he be bound, by an unregistered registrable interest of which he actually knows?

    (a) Unregistered Land. LPA 1925, s. 199; LCA 1972, s. 4; *Hollington Bros Ltd v Rhodes* [1951] 2 TLR 691, p. 45, ante; *Industrial Properties (Barton Hill Ltd) v Associated Electrical Industries Ltd* [1977] QB 580 at 608–609, [1977] 2 All ER 293 at 312–313, per ROSKILL LJ; *Midland Bank Trust Co Ltd v Green* [1981] AC 513, [1981] 1 All ER 153, p. 37, ante.

    (b) Registered Land. *Hodges v Jones* [1935] Ch 657 at 671, per LUXMOORE J; *De Lusignan v Johnson* (1973) 117 SJ 854, p. 135 ante; *Peffer v Rigg* [1977] 1 WLR 285, [1978] 3 All ER 745, pp. 110, 145, ante; *Lyus v Prowsa Developments Ltd* [1982] 1 WLR 1044, [1982] 2 All ER 953, p. 146, ante.

3. Compare the meaning in registered land of transferee (LRA 1925, s. 20 (1)) and purchaser (s. 59 (6)) with that of purchaser in unregistered land (LCA 1925, ss. 4, 17 (1)); *Peffer v Rigg*, supra; *Midland Bank Trust Co Ltd v Green*, supra.

4. In 1984 the Law Commission distributed nearly 50,000 copies of a pamphlet "Who Owns That House?" through public libraries and the branches of one of the large building societies, in which members of the public were asked whether the register should be open to public inspection. About 400 replies were received (**Law Commission Second Report on Land Registration: Inspection of the Register 1985 (Law Com No. 148 HC 551), para. 7, Annex II**).

    How would you have answered the question?

    LRA 1925, ss. 112, 112A, 112B; LRR 1925, rr. 287, 288; LR (Official Searches) Rules 1981, p. 117, ante; Law Commission Report, supra; (1984) 134 NLJ 736; [1985] Conv 73 ("A person in financial straits with several mortgages on his house would not like his local Hilda Ogden to be able to find out and spread the news").

3. Limitation of Actions[1]

I. Introduction

The Limitation Act 1980 consolidates the law of limitation of civil actions[2]. The general principle is that no action may be brought for the recovery of land after the expiration of a prescribed period from the time when the right of action first accrues. This period is now in general twelve years[3], and the Act deals specifically with the accrual of the right of action in the case of present interests, future interests, settled land and land held under trust for sale, forfeiture or breach of condition, and tenancies. For an action to accrue, and consequently for time to start running, there must be an "adverse possessor" against whom an action can be brought[4].

The policy of limitation was stated by Streatfeild J in *R B Policies at Lloyd's v Butler*[5]: "It is a policy of the Limitation Acts that those who go to sleep upon their claims should not be assisted by the courts in recovering their property, but another, and, I think, equal policy behind these Acts, is that there shall be an end of litigation . . ."[6] What is the effect of such a policy? What is the effect of the expiration of the limitation period on D (the person who has been dispossessed or has discontinued his possession) and on A (the adverse possessor)[7]?

---

[1] C & B, pp. 823–849; M & W, pp. 1030–1057; MM, pp. 520–531. See the annotation of the Limitation Act 1980 in Current Law Statutes (D. Morgan), and generally Preston and Newsom, *Limitation of Actions* (3rd edn, 1953); Franks, *Limitation of Actions* (1959). For the history of the old law: Holdsworth, vol. iv, pp. 484–486, vol. vii, p. 29, et seq.; Simpson, *Introduction to History of Land Law* (1961), pp. 141–145; Hayes, *Introduction to Conveyancing* (5th edn.), pp. 222 et seq.

[2] Previous statutes on the land law were: Limitation Act 1623; Real Property Limitation Acts 1833, 1874. Limitation Act 1939 (based upon Law Revision Committee Fifth Interim Report (Statutes of Limitation) 1936 (Cmd. 5334)); Limitation Amendment Act 1980 (based upon Law Reform Committee 21st Report (Final Report on Limitations of Actions) 1977 (Cmnd 6923) which contains a valuable discussion of all aspects of limitation).

[3] Limitation Act 1980, s. 15 (1); the general period of 20 years, fixed by the Real Property Limitation Act 1833, was reduced to 12 years by the Real Property Limitation Act 1874.

[4] Limitation Act 1980, s. 17 (6), Sch. 1, para. 8; *Leigh v Jack* (1879) 5 Ex D 264, p. 000, post; *Treloar v Nute* [1976] 1 WLR 1295, [1977] 1 All ER 230, p. 000, post.

[5] [1950] 1 KB 76 at 81, [1949] 2 All ER 226 at 229; *A'Court v Cross* (1825) 3 Bing 329 at 332, per BEST CJ "It is . . . an Act of peace. Long dormant claims have often more of cruelty than of justice in them."

[6] See [1985] Conv 272 (M. Dockray).

[7] C & B, pp. 840–844; M & W, pp. 102–109, 1050–1056; MM, pp. 133–134, 528–531; Pollock and Wright, *Possession* (1888), pp. 93–100; Preston and Newsom, pp. 77–84; Franks,

(a) On D

The effect of the Limitation Act is purely negative. Not only is D's right of action to recover the land from A extinguished, but also his title to the land[8]. D cannot revive his title by a later acknowledgment or payment made to him[9], or by a judgment obtained by default[10]. He cannot restore his position by re-entry on the land (in this case, he can only regain it by lapse of time as an adverse possessor), and if he brings an action for recovery of the land, A need not plead the Limitation Act[11].

(b) On A

Here the Act is silent. It is now clear that D's title is not transferred to A: there is no "Parliamentary Conveyance"[12]. But by a combination of the negative effect of the Act on D's title, and the positive effect of his adverse possession, A has a new estate of his own, a fee simple subject to the unextinguished rights of other persons[13]. If D is a fee simple owner, then, as Megarry and Wade say[14], "A's possession at once gives all the rights and powers of ownership[15]. A has, in fact, a legal estate, a fee simple absolute in possession. But so also has D, until such time as his title is extinguished by limitation. . . . There is thus no absurdity in speaking of two or more[16] adverse estates in the land, for their validity is relative. If D allows his title to become barred by lapse of time, A's title becomes the better, and A then becomes 'absolute owner'. But if D brings his action within the time allowed, he can successfully assert his better title based on his prior possession; as against D, A's legal estate is nothing."

If D is a lessee of L, and A has been in adverse possession for twelve years, A's possession extinguishes D's title. This has no effect on L's title, because L's right of action does not accrue until the end of the lease[17]. "A has a legal estate (probably a fee simple) subject to L's right of entry at the end of the original term[18]." But A may be evicted before then (a) by L, if he has taken a surrender of the lease from D[19], or if he has forfeited the lease[20], (b) by D, if he

---

pp. 131–133, 141–143; (1925) 41 LQR 139 (S. A. Wiren); (1940) 56 LQR 376 (A. D. Hargreaves), 479 (W. S. Holdsworth); (1962) 78 LQR 541 (H. W. R. Wade); (1964) 80 LQR 63 (B. Rudden); (1973) 32 Conv (NS) 85 (J. A. Omotola); Section VII, post.

[8] Limitation Act 1980, s. 17, p. 186, post; s. 25 (3) (advowsons).

[9] *Sanders v Sanders* (1881) 19 ChD 373, p. 185, post; *Nicholson v England* [1926] 2 KB 93.

[10] *Irish Land Commission v Ryan* [1900] 2 IR 565.

[11] *Dawkins v Lord Penrhyn* (1878) 4 App Cas 51; *Dismore v Milton* [1938] 3 All ER 762; Franks, pp. 131, 265.

[12] *Tichborne v Weir* (1892) 67 LT 735, p. 191, post.

[13] Co Litt 271a (also 2a, 297a) "For a disseisor, abator, intruder, usurper, etc., have a fee simple, but it is not a lawful fee"; *Leach v Jay* (1878) 9 ChD 44 at 45; *Rankin v M'Murtry* (1889) 24 LR Ir 290; (1962) 78 LQR at 543–5.

[14] At p. 107. The symbols have been changed.

[15] If A dies, the land passes under his will or intestacy; *Asher v Whitlock* (1865) LR 1 QB 1, p. 186, post; *Allen v Roughley* (1955) 94 CLR 98; [1956] CLJ 177 (H. W. R. Wade).

[16] In the case of successive adverse possessors, the last in possession may be evicted by an earlier adverse possessor, until that possessor's title has itself been extinguished by lapse of time.

[17] Limitation Act 1980, s. 15 (2), p. 174, post.

[18] M & W, p. 1053.

[19] *Fairweather v St. Marylebone Property Co Ltd* [1963] AC 510, [1962] 2 All ER 288; p. 187, post. For a different solution in registered land, see *Spectrum Investment Co v Holmes* [1981] 1 WLR 221, [1981] 1 All ER 6, p. 193, post.

[20] *Tickner v Buzzacott* [1965] Ch 426, [1964] 1 All ER 131 (adverse possessor not entitled to apply to court for relief against forfeiture of lease for non-payment of rent).

has taken a conveyance of the fee simple from L[1]. If, however, A acknowledges L as the freeholder, he may become a tenant for a term of years, or a yearly tenant or a tenant at will[2].

Whatever interest A gets, it is subject to the legal and equitable rights of third parties which run with the land and have not themselves been independently extinguished e.g. easements and restrictive covenants[3]. If the land is leasehold and A has extinguished the title of the lessee but not that of the lessor, he is not an assignee of the lease, and so is not bound by any covenants in the lease, unless they are enforceable as restrictive covenants. If A pays rent to the lessor and becomes a yearly tenant, he is not, by the mere payment of rent, estopped from denying that he is bound by the terms of the original lease[4].

The Limitation Act 1980, then, operates negatively; not positively as does the Prescription Act 1832. It does not create a title in A, it merely prevents D from enforcing his. The effect of this as between vendor and purchaser is that a title based on adverse possession alone for the limitation period or longer is not necessarily a good title. The claims of a reversioner or a remainderman may have yet to be extinguished[5]: the reversion may be on a 99 year lease, the remainderman's interest may not vest in possession for over 100 years[6]. But if a vendor can establish that the flaw in an otherwise good title is one that can be cured by the running of time in his favour under the Act, he can force a purchaser to take the title[7]. Proof that rival claims have been extinguished by the lapse of time may be very difficult, and in practice a purchaser often agrees to accept an imperfect title.

LIMITATION ACT 1980

15. Time limit for actions to recover land. — (6) Part I of Schedule 1[8] to this Act contains provisions for determining the date of accrual of rights of action to recover land in the cases there mentioned.

(7) Part II of that Schedule[9] contains provisions modifying the provisions of this section in their application to actions brought by, or by a person claiming through, the Crown or any spiritual or eleemosynary corporation sole.

---

[1] *Taylor v Twinberrow* [1930] 2 KB 16.
[2] For an analysis of the situation where A is a tenant for life, see M & W, p. 1051.
[3] *Re Nisbet and Potts' Contract* [1906] 1 Ch 386, p. 192, post; *Scott v Scott* (1854) 4 HL Cas 1065.
[4] *Tichborne v Weir* (1892) 67 LT 735, p. 191, post and p. 191, n. 15, post.
[5] Limitation Act 1980, s. 15 (2). Time runs against the landlord even if the lease is immediately renewed: p. 180, post.
[6] *Cadell v Palmer* (1833) 1 Cl & Fin 372: vesting postponed for over 100 years (note to *Re Villar* [1928] Ch 471 at 478).
[7] *Re Atkinson's and Horsell's Contract* [1912] 2 Ch 1; *Re Spencer and Hauser's Contract* [1928] Ch 598, distinguished in *George Wimpey & Co Ltd v Sohn* [1967] Ch 487, [1966] 1 All ER 232; Farrand, *Contract and Conveyance* (4th edn, 1983), pp. 108–109.
[8] Paras. 1–9.
[9] Paras. 10–13.

SCHEDULE I

Right of action not to accrue or continue unless there is adverse possession

8.—(1) No right of action to recover land shall be treated as accruing unless the land is in the possession of some person in whose favour the period of limitation can run (referred to below in this paragraph as "adverse possession"); and where under the preceding provisions of this Schedule any such right of action is treated as accruing on a certain date and no person is in adverse possession on that date, the right of action shall not be treated as accruing unless and until adverse possession is taken of the land.

(2) Where a right of action to recover land has accrued and after its accrual, before the right is barred, the land ceases to be in adverse possession, the right of action shall no longer be treated as having accrued and no fresh right of action shall be treated as accruing unless and until the land is again taken into adverse possession[10].

(3) For the purposes of this paragraph —

(*a*) possession of any land subject to a rentcharge by a person (other than the person entitled to the rentcharge) who does not pay the rent shall be treated as adverse possession of the rentcharge; and

(*b*) receipt of rent under a lease by a person wrongfully claiming to be entitled to the land in reversion immediately expectant on the determination of the lease[11] shall be treated as adverse possession of the land[12].

(4) For the purpose of determining whether a person occupying any land is in adverse possession of the land it shall not be assumed by implication of law that his occupation is by permission of the person entitled to the land merely by virtue of the fact that his occupation is not inconsistent with the latter's present or future enjoyment of the land.

This provision shall not be taken as prejudicing a finding to the effect that a person's occupation of any land is by implied permission of the person entitled to the land in any case where such a finding is justified on the actual facts of the case[13]. In this Act, unless the context otherwise requires "land" includes corporeal hereditaments, tithes and rentcharges and any legal or equitable estate or interest therein, including an interest in the proceeds of the sale of land held upon trust for sale, but except as provided above in this definition does not include any incorporeal hereditament.

(5) Subject to subsection (6) below, a person shall be treated as claiming through another person if he became entitled by, through, under, or by the act of that other person to the right claimed, and any person whose estate or

---

[10] Enacting the rule in *Trustees, Executors and Agency Co Ltd v Short* (1888) 13 App Cas 793.
[11] See p. 173, post.
[12] *Bligh v Martin* [1968] 1 WLR 804, [1968] 1 All ER 1157.
[13] As added by Limitation Amendment Act 1980, s. 4. This reverses the doctrine of implied or hypothetical licence suggested by Lord DENNING MR in "*Wallis's Cayton Bay Holiday Camp Ltd v Shell Mex and BP Ltd* [1975] 1 QB 94, [1974] 3 All ER 575; *Gray v Wykeham-Martin and Goode* [1977] Bar Library Transcript No 10A (CA, affirming the decision of GOULDING J, who had followed *Wallis* by implying a licence without any factual basis); *Powell v McFarlane* (1979) 38 P & CR 452 — SLADE J held he was bound by these cases if necessary to find an implied or hypothetical licence, but actually found that possession had not been taken. The contrary approach, along traditional lines, was demonstrated in *Treloar v Nute* [1976] 1 WLR 1295, [1977] 1 All ER 230." Law Reform Committee 21st Report (1977), paras. 3.47–3.52, n. 24. See (1980) 77 LSG 270 (P.A. Kay).

interest might have been barred by a person entitled to an entailed interest in possession shall be treated as claiming through the person so entitled.

(6) A person becoming entitled to any estate or interest by virtue of a special power of appointment shall not be treated as claiming through the appointor.

38. Interpretation — (1) In this Act, unless the context otherwise requires — "land" includes corporeal hereditaments, tithes and rentcharges and any legal or equitable estate or interest therein, including an interest in the proceeds of the sale of land held upon trust for sale, but except as provided above in this definition does not include any incorporeal hereditament.

II. Accrual of Right of Action[14]

A. Present Interests

LIMITATION ACT 1980

SCHEDULE I

Accrual of right of action in case of present interests in land

1.   Where the person bringing an action to recover land, or some person through whom he claims, has been in possession of the land, and has while entitled to the land been dispossessed or discontinued his possession, the right of action shall be treated as having accrued on the date of the dispossession or discontinuance.

2.   Where any person brings an action to recover any land of a deceased person (whether under a will or on intestacy) and the deceased person —
   (*a*) was on the date of his death in possession of the land or, in the case of a rentcharge created by will or taking effect upon his death, in possession of the land charged; and
   (*b*) was the last person entitled to the land to be in possession of it; the right of action shall be treated as having accrued on the date of his death.

3.   Where any person brings an action to recover land, being an estate or interest in possession assured otherwise than by will to him, or to some person through whom he claims, and —
   (*a*) the person making the assurance was on the date when the assurance took effect in possession of the land or, in the case of a rentcharge created by the assurance, in possession of the land charged; and

---

[14] C & B, pp. 826–838; M & W, pp. 1033–1045; MM, pp. 521–526. For the accrual of the cause of action (and limitation generally) in negligence cases involving latent defects, see *Pirelli General Cable Works Ltd v Oscar Faber & Partners Ltd* [1983] 2 AC 1, [1983] 1 All ER 65, which held that a cause of action for negligent construction or design of a building accrues at the date when physical damage occurs to the building, irrespective of whether or not the damage is or could reasonably be discovered at that date; *Ketteman v Hansel Properties Ltd* [1984] 1 WLR 1274, [1985] 1 All ER 352; cf. *Kamloops v Neilsen, Hughes and Hughes* [1984] 5 WWR 1, where *Pirelli* was not followed by the Supreme Court of Canada. See the subsequent report by the Law Reform Committee 24th Report on Latent Damage (1984 Cmnd 9390); (1985) 48 MLR 564 (M. A. Jones); and also Law Reform Committee 21st Report (1977 Cmnd 6923), paras. 2.1–2.38. See the Latent Damage Bill 1986 which is based on the 24th Report. See also Defective Premises Act 1972, s. 1 (5).

(*b*) no person has been in possession of the land by virtue of the assurance;

the right of action shall be treated as having accrued on the date when the assurance took effect.

LEIGH *v* JACK
(1879) 5 Ex D 264 (CA, Cockburn CJ, Bramwell and Cotton LJJ)

In 1854 J. S. Leigh conveyed to the defendant a plot of land on the South side of an intended street, on which the defendant built an iron foundry. In 1857 Leigh conveyed to the Mersey Dock Trustees the plot of land on the North side of the intended street, which in 1872 was conveyed by them to the defendant. The intended street was never dedicated to the public as a highway. From 1854 the defendant placed on it materials used at the foundry so as to close it to all except pedestrians: in 1865 he enclosed an oblong portion of it, and in 1872 fenced in the ends. In 1876 the plaintiff, who was tenant for life of all Leigh's lands, brought an action to recover the site of the intended street.

Held. The plaintiff's title was not barred by the Real Property Limitation Act 1883: there had been no dispossession or discontinuance of possession.

Bramwell LJ: The second point relates to the true construction of the Statute of Limitations, section 3[15]. Two things appear to be contemplated by that enactment, dispossession and discontinuance of possession. It is difficult to suppose a case where it can be doubtful whether there has been a discontinuance of possession as to a house; if any chair or table, or other small article of furniture be left, there is strong evidence of an intention that there shall be no discontinuance of possession; but it is possible to conceive a case of discontinuance of possession as to a piece of land where the former owner does nothing to it for the space of twenty years. In the present case, if the plaintiff and her predecessors had done nothing for twenty years to Grundy Street and Napier Place, it might have been possible to argue that there had been a discontinuance of possession. But, after all, it is a question of fact, and the smallest act would be sufficient to shew that there was no discontinuance. . . . The circumstance that J. S. Leigh within twenty years before suit repaired the fence separating Grundy Street from Regent Road is strong to shew that there was no discontinuance. I do not think that there was any dispossession of the plaintiff by the acts of the defendant; . . . in order to defeat a title by dispossessing the former owner, acts must be done which are inconsistent with his enjoyment of the soil for the purposes for which he intended to use it: that is not the case here, where the intention of the plaintiff and her predecessors in title was not either to build upon or to cultivate the land, but to devote it at some future time to public purposes. The plaintiff has not been dispossessed, nor has she discontinued possession, her title has not been taken away, and she is entitled to our judgment[16].

---

[15] Now Limitation Act 1980, s. 15 (6), Sch. 1, para. 1, p. 166, ante.
[16] *See Williams Bros Direct Supply Co Ltd v Raftery* [1958] 1 QB 159, [1957] 3 All ER 593; *Wallis's Cayton Bay Holiday Camp Ltd v Shell-Mex and BP Ltd* [1975] QB 94, [1974] 3 All ER 575.

TRELOAR *v* NUTE
[1976] 1 WLR 1295, [1977] 1 All ER 230[17]
(CA, STAMP, ORMROD LJJ and Sir John PENNYCUICK)

In 1961 the plaintiff owned a derelict plot of land at Halwin, Cornwall, comprising about one-seventh of an acre. In the same year the defendant's father bought adjacent land, believing that the derelict plot formed part of the purchase. The plot was included in the conveyance of September 1962. Between 1961 and September 1962 (when the limitation period began), the defendant's father had used the plot for grazing a couple of cows and a yearling, storing timber and stone, and filling in a gully, and his children rode motor cycles on it. In 1963 he erected a fence, and when the plaintiff removed it, re-erected it. In 1965 the defendant conveyed it to his son as a gift, and in 1974 the son started to build a bungalow on it. The plaintiff had made no use of the land since the father took possession in 1961, and there was no evidence of her having any special purpose in mind for the future use of the plot. She sought an injunction, damages for trespass and a declaration of her title. The defendant pleaded the Limitation Act.

Held (reversing the County Court judge). The plaintiff's title was barred by Limitation Act 1939, section 10 (now Limitation Act 1980, s. 15 (6), Sch. 1, para. 8 (1), p. 165, ante).

SIR JOHN PENNYCUICK: The particular acts found by the judge are we think rather on the borderline of what can properly be regarded as constituting possession, always apart from the consideration of adverse possession. Whether or not a person has taken possession of land is a question of fact depending on all the particular circumstances. The test is well put by Lord O'Hagan in *Lord Advocate v Lord Lovat* (1880) 5 App Cas 273 (a case not otherwise in point) in the following words, at 288:

"As to possession, it must be considered in every case with reference to the peculiar circumstances. The acts, implying possession in one case, may be wholly inadequate to prove it in another. The character and value of the property, the suitable and natural mode of using it, the course of conduct which the proprietor might reasonably be expected to follow with a due

---

[17] *Seddon v Smith* (1877) 36 LT 168; *Littledale v Liverpool College* [1900] 1 Ch 19; *George Wimpey & Co Ltd v Sohn* [1967] Ch 487, [1966] 1 All ER 232 (where the plaintiff had an easement over this land in question); *Bligh v Martin* [1968] 1 WLR 804, [1968] 1 All ER 1157; *Tecbild Ltd v Chamberlain* (1969) 20 P & CR 633 (playing by children and tethering of ponies held to be acts too trivial for adverse possession); *Basildon District Council v Manning* (1975) 237 EG 878 (erecting fence and dumping poultry manure held not to be adverse possession); *Red House Farms (Thorndon) Ltd v Catchpole* (1976) 244 EG 295 (shooting over marshy ground held to be adverse possession); *Treloar v Nute*, supra (grazing of two cows and a yearling, storing timber and stone and filling in a gully held to be adverse possession); *Hyde v Pearce* [1982] 1 WLR 560, [1982] 1 All ER 1029 (continued occupation by purchaser, after termination of licence to occupy pending completion, held not to be adverse possession since "he had at no time made it clear that he was no longer bound by the contract of sale") cf. *Bridges v Mees* [1957] Ch 475, [1957] 2 All ER 577 (contracting purchaser having equitable ownership held adverse possessor); [1982] Conv 383 (J.E.M.); 46 MLR 89 (M. Dockray); *Bills v Fernandez-Gonzalez* (1981) 132 NLJ 66 (compost pens, bonfires, free-ranging chickens and planting trees and shrubs, together with adjoining owner's walking along line of fence for purposes of *his* garden, held not to be adverse possession); *Williams v Usherwood* (1981) 45 P & CR 235 (enclosure of land by fence, parking of three cars in enclosed curtilage of private dwelling-house and paving of driveway with decorative crazy-paving stones held to be adverse possession); [1983] Conv 398 (M. Dockray); (1984) 134 NLJ 144 (H. Wilkinson). See also (1978) 75 LS 769 (D. Brahams).

regard to his own interests — all these things, greatly varying as they must, under various conditions, are to be taken into account in determining the sufficiency of a possession."

In the present case the disputed land is extremely small, about one-seventh of an acre and admitted of very limited agricultural use, but would be a convenient site for a small house or bungalow. The defendant's father did put it to some small agricultural use by grazing two cows and a yearling. Much more important, in our view, is the change in the surface of the land by placing soil in the gully, thereby setting in train the levelling of the land upon which a bungalow could be built. It seems to us that these acts were sufficient to support a finding of possession and indeed on the material before us we would be disposed to reach the same conclusion. The other acts relied upon are of very little weight.

We turn then to the law. We will quote from three sections of the Limitation Act 1939:

[His Lordship quoted from sections 4 (3), 5 (1) and 10 (1) (now Limitation Act 1980, ss. 15 (1), 15 (6), Sch. 1, para. 1, para. 8 (1)), and continued:]

It is not in doubt that under the Act of 1939 as under the previous law, the person claiming by possession must show either (1) discontinuance by the paper owner followed by possession or (2) dispossession (or as it is some-times called "ouster") of the paper owner. Clearly, possession concur-rent with the paper owner is insufficient. On the other hand, where the person claiming by possession establishes possession in the full sense of exclusive possession, that by itself connotes absence of possession on the part of the paper owner and I doubt if there is any real difference in the concept of taking possession and the concept of dispossession except in the special type of case where the owner, although not technically in possession, has some purpose to which he intends to put the land in the future. We will refer to this special type of case in a moment.

The law, as we understand it, always apart from that special type of case, is that if a squatter takes possession of land belonging to another and remains in possession for 12 years to the exclusion of the owner that represents adverse possession and accordingly at the end of the 12 years the owner's title is extinguished. That is the plain meaning of the statutory provisions which I have quoted and no authority to the contrary has been quoted to us. The simple question is, "Did the squatter acquire and remain in exclusive possession?"

The literal application of the statutory provisions has been adapted by this court to meet one special type of case. It sometimes happens that the owner of a piece of land retains it with a view to its utilisation for some specific purpose in the future and that meanwhile some other person has physical possession of it. When that state of affairs exists, the owner is not treated as dispossessed: see *Leigh v Jack* (1879) 5 Ex D 264, where factory materials were placed upon a strip of land intended by the owner to be dedicated as a road; in particular per Cockburn CJ at 271 and per Bramwell LJ, where the latter said, at 273:

"In order to defeat a title by dispossessing the former owner, acts must be done which are inconsistent with his enjoyment of the soil for the purposes for which he intended to use it: that is not the case here, where the intention of the plaintiff and her predecessors in title was not either to build upon or to cultivate the land, but to devote it at some future time to public purpose."

See also *Williams Bros Direct Supply Ltd v Raftery* [1958] 1 QB 159, [1957] 3 All ER 593 where a strip of land intended by the owner for development was used during and after the war for growing vegetables and keeping greyhounds.

The principle was restated and applied by the majority of the Court of Appeal in the recent case, *Wallis's Cayton Bay Holiday Camp Ltd v Shell-Mex and BP Ltd* [1975] QB 94, [1974] 3 All ER 575. In that case a strip of land was intended by the owner to be the site of a garage which would front upon a projected road, which in fact never materialised, and meanwhile was occupied successively as part of a farm and part of a holiday camp. The Court of Appeal held that the owner had not been dispossessed. Lord Denning MR stated the principle in the following terms, at 103, at 580:

"There is a fundamental error in that argument. Possession by itself is not enough to give a title. It must be *adverse* possession. The true owner must have discontinued possession or have been dispossessed and another must have taken it adversely to him. There must be something in the nature of an ouster of the true owner by the wrongful possessor. That is shown by a series of cases in this court which, on their very facts, show this proposition to be true. When the true owner of land intends to use it for a particular purpose in the future, but meanwhile has no immediate use for it, and so leaves it unoccupied, he does not lose his title to it simply because some other person enters on it and uses it for some temporary purpose, like stacking materials; or for some seasonal purpose, like growing vegetables. Not even if this temporary or seasonal purpose continues year after year for 12 years, or more: see *Leigh v Jack* (1879) 5 Ex D 264; *Williams Bros Direct Supply Ltd v Raftery* [1958] 1 QB 159, [1957] 3 All ER 593; and *Tecbild Ltd v Chamberlain* (1969) 20 P & CR 633. The reason is not because the user does not amount to actual possession. The line between acts of user and acts of possession is too fine for words."

The subsequent passage has clearly no application to the facts of the present case. Stamp LJ dissented, holding that upon the facts the case could not be brought within the principle of *Leigh v Jack*. Ormrod LJ in company with Lord Denning MR held that applying the principle of *Leigh v Jack* there was upon the facts no dispossession of the owner. He makes a rather broad statement at 114, at 589. But the theme of purpose, i.e. the purpose to which the owner intends to put the land in the future, runs throughout his judgment and we do not read him as saying that in the absence of such purpose there can be no dispossession merely by reason that the owner has no present use for the land. We have referred at length to this case because it was much relied upon by counsel for the plaintiff and although the judge does not specifically mention it we think it is clear that he had it in mind in the critical passage where he refers to the defendant's possession as not being adverse.

It is worth observing that all these cases were concerned with a narrow strip of land of such a character that the acquisition of a possessory title to it would not fall within the ordinary purview of the statute and the court was clearly anxious not to put too literal a construction upon the words of the statute. The same observation applies to *Littledale v Liverpool College* [1900] 1 Ch 19, a case distinguishable on other grounds.

A full statement of the law as it stood before *Wallis's Cayton Bay Holiday Camp Ltd v Shell-Mex and BP Ltd* will be found in *Preston and Newsom's*

Limitation of Actions 3rd edn. (1953), pp. 88 et seq., and in *Halsbury's Laws of England* 3rd edn. vol. 24 (1958), pp. 251 et seq.

We return then to the present case. The judge found, as we read his judgment, that the defendant's father took possession of the disputed land outside the limitation period but that this possession was not adverse by reason that it caused no inconvenience to the plaintiff. In our judgment the second part of this finding is contrary to the plain terms of section 10 of the Act of 1939 which in effect defines adverse possession as possession of some person in whose favour the period of limitation can run. It is not permissible to import into this definition a requirement that the owner must be inconvenienced or otherwise affected by that possession. Apart from the case relating to special purpose no authority has been cited to us which would support the requirement of inconvenience to the owner and we are not ourselves aware of any such authority. On the contrary, so far as our own experience goes, the typical instance in which a possessory title is treated as having been acquired is that in which a squatter establishes himself upon a piece of land for which the owner has no use. Indeed, if inconvenience to the owner had to be established it would be difficult indeed ever to acquire a possessory title since the owner if inconvenienced would be likely to take proceedings.

We conclude that, once it is accepted that the judge found, and could properly find, that the defendant's father took possession of the disputed land before the commencement of the limitation period, and in the absence of any evidence of special purpose on the part of the plaintiff, time began to run from such taking of possession, irrespective of whether the plaintiff suffered inconvenience from the possession, and that the defendant must be treated as having acquired a possessory title before the commencement of this action. . . .

We would allow the appeal.

In *Powell v McFarlane* (1977) 38 P & CR 452[18], the plaintiff claimed a possessory title to some three acres of land near Reigate in Surrey. The adverse possession relied on included the grazing by the plaintiff at the age of 14 of a "remarkable cow" called Kashla, otherwise known as Ted's cow, the cutting of growing hay, the repair of boundary fences to make them stock-proof, and the cutting of brambles and fifty Christmas trees. In holding that the plaintiff failed, SLADE J said at 470:

"It will be convenient to begin by restating a few basic principles relating to the concept of possession under English law:

(1) In the absence of evidence to the contrary, the owner of land with the paper title is deemed to be in possession of the land, as being the person with the prima facie right to possession. The law will thus, without reluctance, ascribe possession either to the paper owner or to persons who can establish a title as claiming through the paper owner.

(2) If the law is to attribute possession of land to a person who can establish no paper title to possession, he must be shown to have both factual possession and the requisite intention to possess (*animus possidendi*).

(3) Factual possession signifies an appropriate degree of physical control. It must be a single and conclusive possession, though there can be a single possession exercised by or on behalf of several persons jointly. Thus an owner

---

[18] (1980) 96 LQR 332 (P. Jackson); [1982] Conv 256, 345 (M. Dockray).

of land and a person intruding on that land without his consent cannot both be in possession of the land at the same time. The question what acts constitute a sufficient degree of exclusive physical control must depend on the circumstances, in particular the nature of the land and the manner in which land of that nature is commonly used or enjoyed. In the case of open land, absolute physical control is normally impracticable, if only because it is generally impossible to secure every part of a boundary so as to prevent intrusion. 'What is a sufficient degree of sole possession and user must be measured according to an objective standard, related no doubt to the nature and situation of the land involved but not subject to variation according to the resources or status of the claimants': *West Bank Estates Ltd v Arthur* [1967] AC 665 at 678, 679 per Lord Wilberforce. It is clearly settled that acts of possession done on parts of land to which a possessory title is sought may be evidence of possession of the whole. Whether or not acts of possession done on parts of an area establish title to the whole area must, however, be a matter of degree. It is impossible to generalise with any precision as to what acts will or will not suffice to evidence factual possession. On the particular facts of *Cadija Umma v S Don Manis Appu* [1939] AC 136 the taking of a hay crop was held by the Privy Council to suffice for this purpose; but this was a decision which attached special weight to the opinion of the local courts in Ceylon owing to their familiarity with the conditions of life and the habits and ideas of the people: at 141–142. Likewise, on the particular facts of the *Red House Farms* case, mere shooting over the land in question was held by the Court of Appeal to suffice; but that was a case where the court regarded the only use that anybody could be expected to make of the land as being for shooting (1976) 244 EG 295: per Cairns, Orr and Waller LJJ. Everything must depend on the particular circumstances, but broadly, I think what must be shown as constituting factual possession is that the alleged possessor has been dealing with the land in question as an occupying owner might have been expected to deal with it and that no-one else has done so.

(4) The *animus possidendi*, which is also necessary to constitute possession, was defined by Lindley MR in *Littledale v Liverpool College* [1900] 1 Ch 19 at 23 (a case involving an alleged adverse possession) as 'the intention of excluding the owner as well as other people.' This concept is to some extent an artifical one, because in the ordinary case the squatter on property such as agricultural land will realise that, at least until he acquires a statutory title by long possession and thus can invoke the processes of the law to exclude the owner with the paper title, he will not for practical purposes be in a position to exclude him. What is really meant, in my judgment, is that the *animus possidendi* involves the intention, in one's own name and on one's own behalf, to exclude the world at large, including the owner with the paper title if he be not himself the possessor, so far as is reasonably practicable and so far as the processes of the law will allow.

The question of *animus possidendi* is, in my judgment, one of crucial importance in the present case. An owner or other person with the right to possession of land will be readily assumed to have the requisite intention to possess, unless the contrary is clearly proved. This, in my judgment, is why the slightest acts done by or on behalf of an owner in possession will be found to negative discontinuance of possession. The position, however, is quite different from a case where the question is whether a trespasser has acquired possession. In such a situation the courts will, in my judgment, require clear and affirmative evidence that the trespasser, claiming that he has acquired possession, not only had the requisite intention to possess, but made such intention clear to the world. If his acts are open to more than one interpretation and he has not made it perfectly plain to the world at large by his actions or words that he has intended to exclude the owner as best he can, the courts will treat him as not having had the requisite *animus possidendi* and consequently as not having dispossessed the owner.

A number of cases illustrate the principle just stated and show how heavy an onus of proof falls on the person whose alleged possession originated in a trespass.

[His Lordship referred to *Leigh v Jack* (1879) 5 Ex D 264, p. 167, ante; *Williams Bros Direct Supply Ltd v Raftery* [1958] 1 QB 159, [1957] 3 All ER 593 and *Tecbild Ltd v Chamberlain* (1969) 20 P & CR 633, and continued:]

In my judgment it is consistent with principle as well as authority that a person who originally entered another's land as a trespasser, but later seeks to show that he has dispossessed the owner, should be required to adduce compelling evidence that he had the requisite *animus possidendi* in any case where his use of the land was equivocal, in the sense that it did not necessarily, by itself, betoken an intention on his part to claim the land as his own and exclude the true owner. The status of possession, after all, confers on the possessor valuable privileges *vis-à-vis* not only the world at large, but also the owner of the land concerned. It entitles him to maintain an action in trespass against anyone who enters the land without his consent, save only against a person having a better title to possession than himself. Furthermore it gives him one valuable element of protection even against the owner himself. Until the possession of land has actually passed to the trespasser, the owner may exercise the remedy of self-help against him. Once possession has passed to the trespasser, this remedy is not available to the owner, so that the intruder's position becomes that much more secure; if he will not then leave voluntarily, the owner will find himself obliged to bring proceedings for possession and for this purpose to prove his title.

Against this background, it is not in the least surprising that over many years in cases such as *Leigh v Jack*, the *Williams* case and *Tecbild Ltd v Chamberlain* the courts have been reluctant to infer the necessary *animus possidendi* on the part of a squatter, even where the acts relied on could have sufficed to constitute factual possession."

B. Future Interests

LIMITATION ACT 1980

SCHEDULE I

PART I

Accrual of right of action in case of future interests

4. The right of action to recover any land shall, in a case where —
    (a) the estate or interest claimed was an estate or interest in reversion or remainder or any other future estate or interest; and

(b) no person has taken possession of the land by virtue of the estate or interest claimed;

be treated as having accrued on the date on which the estate or interest fell into possession by the determination of the preceding estate or interest.

15. Actions to recover land and rent. — (2) Subject to the following provisions of this section, where —

(a) the estate or interest claimed was an estate or interest in reversion or remainder or any other future estate or interest and the right of action to recover the land accrued on the date on which the estate or interest fell into possession by the determination of the preceding estate or interest; and

(b) the person entitled to the preceding estate or interest (not being a term of years absolute) was not in possession of the land on that date;

no action shall be brought by the person entitled to the succeeding estate or interest after the expiration of twelve years from the date on which the right of action accrued to the person entitled to the preceding estate or interest or six years from the date on which the right of action accrued to the person entitled to the succeeding estate or interest, whichever period last expires.

(3) Subsection (2) above shall not apply to any estate or interest which falls into possession on the determination of an entailed interest and which might have been barred by the person entitled to the entailed interest[19].

SCHEDULE I

PART II

13. Section 15 (2) of this Act shall apply in any case where the Crown or a spiritual or eleemosynary corporation sole is entitled to the succeeding estate or interest with the substitution —

(a) for the reference to twelve years of a reference to thirty years; and

(b) for the reference to six years of a reference to twelve years.

C. Settlements and Trusts for Sale

LIMITATION ACT 1980

18. Settled land and land held on trust. — (1) Subject to section 21 (1) and (2) of this Act, the provisions of this Act shall apply to equitable interests in land, including interests in the proceeds of the sale of land held upon trust for sale, as they apply to legal estates.

Accordingly a right of action to recover the land shall, for the purposes of this Act but not otherwise, be treated as accruing to a person entitled in possession to such an equitable interest in the like manner and circumstances, and on the same date, as it would accrue if his interest were a legal estate in the land (and any relevant provision of Part I of Schedule 1 to this Act shall apply in any such case accordingly).

---

[19] See also ss. 15 (1), (3) and 38 (5); M & W, p. 1037. The combined effect of these three sections is that a "reversioner or remainderman expectant upon an entail in possession is not entitled to the alternative six-year period, if his interest could have been barred by the tenant in tail".

(2) Where the period prescribed by this Act has expired for the bringing of an action to recover land by a tenant for life or a statutory owner of settled land —

> (a) his legal estate shall not be extinguished if and so long as the right of action to recover the land of any person entitled to a beneficial interest in the land either has not accrued or has not been barred by this Act; and
>
> (b) the legal estate shall accordingly remain vested in the tenant for life or statutory owner and shall devolve in accordance with the Settled Land Act 1925;

but if and when every such right of action has been barred by this Act, his legal estate shall be extinguished.

(3) Where any land is held upon trust (including a trust for sale) and the period prescribed by this Act has expired for the bringing of an action to recover the land by the trustees, the estate of the trustees shall not be extinguished if and so long as the right of action to recover the land of any person entitled to a beneficial interest in the land or in the proceeds of sale either has not accrued or has not been barred by this Act; but if and when every such right of action has been so barred the estate of the trustees shall be extinguished.

(4) Where —

> (a) any settled land is vested in a statutory owner; or
>
> (b) any land is held upon trust (including a trust for sale);

an action to recover the land may be brought by the statutory owner or trustees on behalf of any person entitled to a beneficial interest in possession in the land or in the proceeds of sale whose right of action has not been barred by this Act, notwithstanding that the right of action of the statutory owner or trustees would apart from this provision have been barred by this Act.

SCHEDULE I

PART I

*Possession of beneficiary not adverse to others interested
in settled land or land held on trust for sale*

9.   Where any settled land or any land held on trust for sale is in the possession of a person entitled to a beneficial interest in the land or in the proceeds of sale (not being a person solely or absolutely entitled to the land or the proceeds), no right of action to recover the land shall be treated for the purposes of this Act as accruing during that possession to any person in whom the land is vested as tenant for life, statutory owner or trustee, or to any other person entitled to a beneficial interest in the land or the proceeds of sale[1].

21.   Time limit for actions in respect of trust property. —(1) No period of limitation prescribed by this Act shall apply to an action by a beneficiary under a trust, being an action —

> (a) in respect of any fraud or fraudulent breach of trust to which the trustee was a party or privy; or

---

[1] *Bridges v Mees* [1957] Ch 475, [1957] 2 All ER 577; *Re Cussons Ltd* (1904) 73 LJ Ch 296; M & W, p. 1043.

(*b*) to recover from the trustee trust property or the proceeds of trust property in the possession of the trustee, or previously received by the trustee and converted to his use.

(2) Where a trustee who is also a beneficiary under the trust receives or retains trust property or its proceeds as his share on a distribution of trust property under the trust, his liability in any action brought by virtue of sub-section (1) (*b*) above to recover that property or its proceeds after the expiration of the period of limitation prescribed by this Act for bringing an action to recover trust property shall be limited to the excess over his proper share.

This subsection only applies if the trustee acted honestly and reasonably in making the distribution.

(3) Subject to the preceding provisions of this section, an action by a beneficiary to recover trust property or in respect of any breach of trust, not being an action for which a period of limitation is prescribed by any other provision of this Act, shall not be brought after the expiration of six years from the date on which the right of action accrued.

For the purposes of this subsection, the right of action shall not be treated as having accrued to any beneficiary entitled to a future interest in the trust property until the interest fell into possession.

D.　Forfeiture

LIMITATION ACT 1980

SCHEDULE I
Part I

*Accrual of right of action in case of forfeiture or
breach of condition*

7.—(1) Subject to sub-paragraph (2) below, a right of action to recover land by virtue of a forfeiture or breach of condition shall be treated as having accrued on the date on which the forfeiture was incurred or the condition broken.

(2) If any such right has accrued to a person entitled to an estate or interest in reversion or remainder and the land was not recovered by virtue of that right, the right of action to recover the land shall not be treated as having accrued to that person until his estate or interest fell into possession, as if no such forfeiture or breach of condition had occurred.

E.　Tenancies

i.　PERIODIC TENANCIES

LIMITATION ACT 1980

15.　Time limit for actions to recover land. — (2) p. 174, ante.

SCHEDULE I
Part I

Accrual of right of action in case of future interests

4.　p. 173, ante.

5.—(1) Subject to sub-paragraph (2) below, a tenancy from year to year or other period, without a lease in writing, shall for the purposes of this Act be treated as being determined at the expiration of the first year or other period; and accordingly the right of action of the person entitled to the land subject to the tenancy shall be treated as having accrued at the date on which in accordance with this sub-paragraph the tenancy is determined[2].

(2) Where any rent has subsequently been received in respect of the tenancy, the right of action shall be treated as having accrued on the date of the last receipt of rent.

6.—(1) Where —

    (a) any person is in possession of land by virtue of a lease in writing by which a rent of not less than ten pounds a year is reserved; and

    (b) the rent is received by some person wrongfully claiming to be entitled to the land in reversion immediately expectant on the determination of the lease; and

    (c) no rent is subsequently received by the person rightfully so entitled; the right of action to recover the land of the person rightfully so entitled shall be treated as having accrued on the date when the rent was first received by the person wrongfully claiming to be so entitled and not on the date of the determination of the lease.

(2) Sub-paragraph (1) above shall not apply to any lease granted by the Crown.

In *Hayward v Chaloner* [1968] 1 QB 107, [1967] 3 All ER 122, the Saville Estate leased in 1938 to the rector of the parish of Bilsthorpe part of Redcote Farm for use as a garden on an oral tenancy at a rent of 10s. a year. The rent was paid by successive rectors until 1942, but not subsequently. In 1955 the plaintiffs purchased Redcote Farm including the part let to the rector.

In 1966 the incumbent rector, the defendant, claimed title under the Limitation Act 1939. The plaintiffs' application for possession failed before the Court of Appeal (Lord DENNING dissenting). RUSSELL LJ said at 122, at 127:

"In the present case there was a periodic tenancy, not in writing: the last payment of rent was in May, 1942, by the then rector, Mr McCormick, so that the right of action must by section 9 (2)[3] for the purposes of the Limitation Act be deemed to have then accrued, and the plaintiffs' action in 1966 to recover possession was clearly forbidden by section 4 (3)[4].

It was argued for the plaintiffs, and the argument found favour with the county court judge, that section 10 (1)[5] operated to prevent the right of action being deemed to accrue at any time because no person was in adverse possession at any time, adverse possession being the label applied by section 10 to 'the possession of some person in whose favour the period of limitation can run.' I do not think it necessary to discuss here the history of the conception of 'adverse possession' beyond a reference to Preston and Newsom's Limitation of Actions, 3rd edn. (1953), p. 86. I have no doubt that for this purpose the possession of a tenant is to be considered adverse once

---

[2] *Moses v Lovegrove* [1952] 2 QB 533, [1952] 1 All ER 1279 (rent-book is not a lease in writing: and the Rent Acts do not prevent time from running); *Jessamine Investment Co v Schwartz* [1978] QB 264, [1976] 3 All ER 521.
[3] Now Limitation Act 1980, s. 15 (6), Sch. 1, para. 5, supra.
[4] Ibid., s. 15 (1), p. 181, post.
[5] Ibid., s. 15 (6), Sch. 1, para. 8 (1), p. 165, ante.

the period covered by the last payment of rent has expired so that section 10
(1) does not bear further upon section 9 (2). Nor do I doubt the applicability
of section 9 (2) to the present case just because the freeholders were content
that the rector should not pay his rent and did not bother to ask for it for all
those years. In *Moses v Lovegrove* [1952] 2 QB 533, [1952] 1 All ER 1279, in
this court it was assumed on all hands that when section 9 apparently
operates, adverse possession starts: see especially Lord Evershed, and Romer
LJ, at 538–540, 543, at 1282–1283, 1285. The principle clearly accepted was
that once the period covered by the last payment of rent expired, the tenant
ceased to be regarded by the Limitation Acts as the tenant. This case was not
cited to the county court judge. A similar assumption was made in *Nicholson v
England* [1926] 2 KB 93 under the then existing principles which section 10
(1) was designed to embody. Textbooks to the same effect include Cheshire's
Modern Law of Real Property, 9th edn. (1962), pp. 797, 798; Megarry and
Wade's Textbook of the Law of Real Property, 3rd edn. (1966), p. 1010; and
Preston and Newsom on Limitation of Actions, 3rd edn. (1953), p. 89. I am
not aware that the contrary view has been anywhere expressed, and in my
judgment the cases relied upon by the county court judge of *Leigh v Jack*
(1879) 5 ExD 264, and *Williams Bros Direct Supply Ltd v Raftery* [1958] 1 QB
159, [1957] 3 All ER 593, have no bearing on a question arising under section
9 (2) of the Act. In my judgment, therefore, a possessory title has been
acquired to this property. . . .

The generous indulgence of the plaintiffs and their predecessors in title,
loyal churchmen all, having resulted in a free accretion at their expense to
the lands of their church, their reward may be in the next world. But in this
jurisdiction we can only qualify them for that reward by allowing the appeal
and dismissing their action.''

ii.   OCCUPATION FOR BENEFIT OF LANDLORD

SMIRK *v* LYNDALE DEVELOPMENTS LTD
[1975] Ch 317, [1975] 1 All ER 690
(ChD, PENNYCUICK V-C, and CA, CAIRNS and LAWTON LJJ and
WALTON J)

A tenant of a house, first of British Railways, and, from 1967, of the
defendants, occupied other land belonging to British Railways which
adjoined the house (the blue land) and enclosed it. The defendants in 1973
began to develop the blue land, and the plaintiff brought this action claiming
(i) that he had a good possessory title to the land, or alternatively (ii) that he
held it as an extension of the tenanted land.

Held. (i) (expressly agreeing with PENNYCUICK V-C) the plaintiff held the
land as an addition to the demised land; and (ii) (reversing PENNYCUICK
V-C) the purchase of the blue land by the defendants in 1967 did not, on the
facts, operate as a surrender and regrant of the lease.

PENNYCUICK V-C[6]: I turn now to the law applicable where a tenant takes
possession of adjoining land — a tenant, during the currency of his tenancy,
who takes possession of adjoining land belonging to his landlord. The law on
this point, if I may respectfully say so, has got into something of a tangle.

---

[6] The present extract covers the judgment of PENNYCUICK V-C on the first point.

[His Lordship referred to *Kingsmill v Millard* (1855) 11 Exch 313 and quoted from the judgments of Alderson and Parke BB and continued:]

It will be observed that in his judgment Parke B in terms states that the presumption that the tenant has inclosed for the benefit of the landlord applies, irrespective of whether the inclosed land is part of the waste or belongs to the landlord; and indeed he uses the word "encroachment" as appropriate in either case. He then goes on to state in terms, following and agreeing what Alderson B said in the course of the argument, that in order to displace the presumption there must be communication to the landlord. That decision of high authority seems to me to be in accordance with justice and common sense, and unless I were compelled to do otherwise by subsequent authority, I would certainly adopt it. I should add, as is perhaps obvious, as appears in some of the later cases, that the presumption may be rebutted by any form of express or implied agreement or, in some cases, as Parke B says, by estoppel.

The next case is *Whitmore v Humphries* (1871) LR 7 CP 1, where Willes J says, at 4–5:

"This case raises a question upon a branch of the law which involves considerations of some nicety. By the rule of law applicable to this subject the landlord is entitled at the determination of the tenancy to recover from the tenant, not only the land originally demised, but also any land which the tenant may have added to it by encroachment from the waste, such encroachment being deemed to be made by him as tenant as an addition to his holding, and consequently for the benefit of his landlord, unless it is made under circumstances which show an intention to hold it for his own benefit alone, and not as part of his holding under the landlord. This rule undoubtedly applies when the encroachment is made over land belonging to the landlord, and no inquiry appears ever to have been made in such cases, whether it was made with the consent of the landlord or not. In such cases the reasonableness of the rule is very obvious; it only gives back to the landlord that which is rightly his, and prevents the tenant, who has taken advantage of his tenancy to encroach, from keeping that which it would be a breach of the duty arising from the relation of landlord and tenant not to give up. The rule, however, goes further than this. It is not confined to cases where the encroachment is upon land to which the landlord is entitled, it applies to cases where the land encroached upon does not belong to the landlord"

and he then goes on to deal with the position where the encroachment is upon land to which the landlord is not entitled. Willes J continues, at 5:

"The rule is based upon the obligation of the tenant to protect his landlord's rights, and to deliver up the subject of his tenancy in the same condition, fair wear and tear excepted, as that in which he enjoyed it. There is often great temptation and opportunity afforded to the tenant to take in adjoining land which may or may not be his landlord's and it is considered more convenient and more in accordance with the rights of property that the tenant who has availed himself of the opportunity afforded him by his tenancy to make encroachments, should be presumed to have intended to make them for the benefit of the reversioner, except under circumstances pointing to an intention to take the land for his own benefit exclusively. The result is to avoid questions which would otherwise frequently arise as to the property in land, and to exclude persons who have come in as tenants, and who are likely to encroach, from raising such questions. The reason of the rule appears on the one hand to be entirely independent of any notion of encroachment being a wrong done, and so also on the other hand it appears to be quite independent of the question, whether the encroachment was made with the assent of the landlord."

[His Lordship said that this principle was applied also in *Tabor v Godfrey* (1895) 64 LJQB 245. But statements in other cases (*Lord Hastings v Saddler* (1898) 79 LT 355 and *J.F. Perrott & Co Ltd v Cohen* [1951] 1 KB 705, [1950] 2 All ER 939) apply the presumption only to cases where the land occupied by the tenant is waste and adjacent to the demised land.]

Having been through the authorities I propose, as I have said earlier, to adopt and apply the principle laid down in *Kingsmill v Millard* (1855) 11 Exch 313.

To return to the present case, there is nothing on the facts which could in any way rebut the presumption, which it seems to me is applicable here, namely, that the tenant, the plaintiff, was occupying the plots by way of an addition to land comprised with his tenancy, and not otherwise adversely to the landlord. I need only add on this point that if, contrary to my view, the unilateral intention of the plaintiff was relevant, the plaintiff's very candid evidence of intention would be fatal to his own case.

iii.   TIME RUNS EVEN IF THE LEASE IS IMMEDIATELY RENEWED

In *Gray v Wykeham-Martin and Goode* [1977] Bar Library Transcript No. 10A GEOFFREY LANE LJ said: "A person coming to this type of situation freshly may well wonder by what possible rule of law a life tenant[7] could be affected [where there have been continual renewals]. It would seem to the uninitiated that the land has been in the possession of tenants throughout and that even if the freeholder had wanted to remove the chicken houses or the rabbit hutches from the land and to ensure thereby that the plaintiff had no claim to the land, he could not have done so. Such it seems is not the case; because it is not disputed by the defendants that the decision of the House of Lords in *Ecclesiastical Comrs of England and Wales v Rowe* (1880) 5 App Cas 736 governs the situation and that, where a tenancy comes to an end, even if it is followed immediately by a fresh tenancy, there is a moment of time, however short, in which the freeholder notionally regains possession of the land and a moment when time can start to run against the freeholder or life tenant; . . . Consequently if during that moment of time, or one of those moments of time, the squatter is in the necessary adverse possession of the disputed land, time under the Limitation Act starts to run against the life tenant."

III.   Limitation Period[8]

LIMITATION ACT 1980

2.   Time limit for actions founded on tort. — An action founded on tort shall not be brought after the expiration of six years from the date on which the cause of action accrued.

---

[7] The landlord.
[8] C & B, pp. 825–826; M & W, pp. 1032–1033; MM, p. 521.

5. Time limit for actions founded on simple contract. — An action founded on simple contract shall not be brought after the expiration of six years from the date on which the cause of action accrued.

8. Time limit for actions on a specialty. — (1) An action upon a specialty[9] shall not be brought after the expiration of twelve years from the date on which the cause of action accrued.

(2) Subsection (1) above shall not affect any action for which a shorter period of limitation is prescribed by any other provision of this Act.

36. Equitable jurisdiction and remedies. — (1) The following time limits under this Act, that is to say —

> (*a*) the time limit under section 2 for actions founded on tort;
> (*b*) the time limit under section 5 for actions founded on simple contract; . . .
> (*d*) the time limit under section 8 for actions on a specialty; . . .

shall not apply to any claim for specific performance of a contract or for an injunction or for other equitable relief, except in so far as any such time limit may be applied by the court by analogy in like manner as the corresponding time limit under any enactment repealed by the Limitation Act 1939 was applied before 1st July 1940.

(2) Nothing in this Act shall affect any equitable jurisdiction to refuse relief on the ground of acquiescence or otherwise[10].

15. Time limit for actions to recover land. — (1) No action shall be brought by any person to recover any land after the expiration of twelve years from the date on which the right of action accrued to him or, if it first accrued to some person through whom he claims, to that person[11].

SCHEDULE I

PART II

Modifications of Section 15 where Crown or
Certain Corporations Sole are involved

10. Subject to paragraph 11 below, section 15 (1) of this Act shall apply to the bringing of an action to recover any land by the Crown or by any spiritual or eleemosynary corporation sole with the substitution for the reference to twelve years of a reference to thirty years.

11.—(1) An action to recover foreshore may be brought by the Crown at any time before the expiration of sixty years from the date mentioned in section 15 (1) of this Act. . . .

12. Notwithstanding section 15 (1) of this Act, where in the case of any action brought by a person other than the Crown or a spiritual or eleemosynary corporation sole the right of action first accrued to the Crown

---

[9] This includes a covenant under seal: *Re Compania de Electricidad de la Provincia de Buenos Aires Ltd* [1980] Ch 146, [1978] 3 All ER 668 (the obligation must be created or secured by the specialty); *Collin v Duke of Westminster* [1985] QB 581, [1985] 1 All ER 463 (tenant's claim to enfranchisement under Leasehold Reform Act 1967 held to be a claim upon a specialty).

[10] This preserves the equitable doctrine of laches; Snell, pp. 34–37.

[11] The same period applies in the case of a spiritual or eleemosynary corporation sole. On advowsons, see Limitation Act 1980, s. 25.

or any such corporation sole through whom the person in question claims, the action may be brought at any time before the expiration of —

- (a) the period during which the action could have been brought by the Crown or the corporation sole; or
- (b) twelve years from the date on which the right of action accrued to some person other than the Crown or the corporation sole;

whichever period first expires.

16. Time limit for redemption actions. — When a mortgagee of land has been in possession of any of the mortgaged land for a period of twelve years, no action to redeem the land of which the mortgagee has been so in possession shall be brought after the end of that period by the mortgagor or any person claiming through him[12].

19. Time limit for actions to recover rent. — No action shall be brought, or distress made, to recover arrears of rent, or damages in respect of arrears of rent, after the expiration of six years from the date on which the arrears became due.

20. Time limit for actions to recover money secured by a mortgage or charge or to recover proceeds of the sale of land. — (1) No action shall be brought to recover —

- (a) any principal sum of money secured by a mortgage or other charge on property (whether real or personal); or
- (b) proceeds of the sale of land;

after the expiration of twelve years from the date on which the right to receive the money accrued.

(3) The right to receive any principal sum of money secured by a mortgage or other charge and the right to foreclose on the property subject to the mortgage or charge shall not be treated as accruing so long as that property comprises any future interest or any life insurance policy which has not matured or been determined.

(4) Nothing in this section shall apply to a foreclosure action in respect of mortgaged land, but the provisions of this Act relating to actions to recover land shall apply to such an action.

(5) Subject to subsections (6) and (7) below, no action to recover arrears of interest payable in respect of any sum of money secured by a mortgage or other charge or payable in respect of proceeds of the sale of land, or to recover damages in respect of such arrears shall be brought after the expiration of six years from the date on which the interest became due.

(6) Where —

- (a) a prior mortgagee or other incumbrancer has been in possession of the property charged; and
- (b) an action is brought within one year of the discontinuance of that possession by the subsequent incumbrancer;

the subsequent incumbrancer may recover by that action all the arrears of interest which fell due during the period of possession by the prior incumbrancer or damages in respect of those arrears, notwithstanding that the period exceeded six years.

---

[12] *Young v Clarey* [1948] Ch 191, [1948] 1 All ER 197.

(7) Where —
- (*a*) the property subject to the mortgage or charge comprises any future interest or life insurance policy; and
- (*b*) it is a term of the mortgage or charge that arrears of interest shall be treated as part of the principal sum of money secured by the mortgage or charge;

interest shall not be treated as becoming due before the right to recover the principal sum of money has accrued or is treated as having accrued.

IV.   Effect of Disability[13]

LIMITATION ACT 1980

28.   Extension of limitation period in case of disability. — (1) Subject to the following provisions of this section, if on the date when any right of action accrued for which a period of limitation is prescribed by this Act, the person to whom it accrued was under a disability, the action may be brought at any time before the expiration of six years from the date when he ceased to be under a disability or died (whichever first occurred) notwithstanding that the period of limitation has expired.

(2) This section shall not affect any case where the right of action first accrued to some person (not under a disability) through whom the person under a disability claims.

(3) When a right of action which has accrued to a person under a disability accrues, on the death of that person while still under a disability, to another person under a disability, no further extension of time shall be allowed by reason of the disability of the second person.

(4) No action to recover land or money charged on land shall be brought by virtue of this section by any person after the expiration of thirty years from the date on which the right of action accrued to that person or some person through whom he claims.

38.   Interpretation. — (2) For the purposes of this Act a person shall be deemed to be under a disability while he is an infant, or of unsound mind. . . .

V.   Effect of Fraud, Concealment and Mistake[14]

LIMITATION ACT 1980

32.   Postponement of limitation period in case of fraud, concealment or mistake. — (1) Subject to subsection (3) below, where in the case of any action for which a period of limitation is prescribed by this Act, either —
- (*a*) the action is based upon the fraud of the defendant[15]; or

---

13 C & B, p. 845; M & W, pp. 1045–1046; MM, pp. 526–527.
14 C & B, pp. 845–846; M & W, pp. 1046–1048; MM, p. 527.
15 *Beaman v ARTS Ltd* [1949] 1 KB 550 at 558, [1949] 1 All ER 465 at 467, per Lord GREENE MR.

(*b*) any fact relevant to the plaintiff's right of action has been deliberately concealed from him by the defendant[16]; or

(*c*) the action is for relief from the consequences of a mistake[17];

the period of limitation shall not begin to run until the plaintiff has discovered the fraud, concealment or mistake (as the case may be) or could with reasonable diligence have discovered it[18].

References in this subsection to the defendant include references to the defendant's agent and to any person through whom the defendant claims[19] and his agent.

(2) For the purposes of subsection (1) above, deliberate commission of a breach of duty in circumstances in which it is unlikely to be discovered for some time amounts to deliberate concealment of the facts involved in that breach of duty.

(3) Nothing in this section shall enable any action —

(*a*) to recover, or recover the value of, any property; or

(*b*) to enforce any charge against, or set aside any transaction affecting, any property;

to be brought against the purchaser of the property or any person claiming through him in any case where the property has been purchased for valuable consideration by an innocent third party since the fraud or concealment or (as the case may be) the transaction in which the mistake was made took place.

(4) A purchaser is an innocent third party for the purposes of this section —

(*a*) in the case of fraud or concealment of any fact relevant to the plaintiff's right of action, if he was not a party to the fraud or (as the case may be) to the concealment of that fact and did not at the time of the purchase know or have reason to believe that the fraud or concealment had taken place; and

(*b*) in the case of mistake, if he did not at the time of the purchase know or have reason to believe that the mistake had been made.

VI.   Effect of Acknowledgement and Part Payment[20]

LIMITATION ACT 1980

29.   Fresh accrual of action on acknowledgement or part payment. — (1) Subsections (2) and (3) below apply where any right of action (including a foreclosure action) to recover land or an advowson[21]. . . has accrued.

---

[16] *Rains v Buxton* (1880) 14 Ch D 537, 49 LJ Ch 473; *Vane v Vane* (1872) 8 Ch App 383, 42 LJ Ch 299; *Clark v Woor* [1965] 1 WLR 650, [1965] 2 All ER 353; *Applegate v Moss* [1971] 1 QB 406, [1971] 1 All ER 747; *King v Victor Parsons & Co* [1973] 1 WLR 29, [1973] 1 All ER 206; *Tito v Waddell (No 2)* [1977] Ch 106 at 224–225, [1977] 3 All ER 129 at 244–245; *Lewisham London Borough v Leslie & Co Ltd* (1978) 250 EG 1289; *Bartlett v Barclays Bank Trust Co Ltd (No 1)* [1980] Ch 515 at 537, [1980] 1 All ER 139 at 154–155.

[17] See *Phillips-Higgins v Harper* [1954] 1 QB 411, [1954] 1 All ER 116, per PEARSON J.

[18] See *Peco Arts Inc v Hazlitt Gallery Ltd* [1983] 1 WLR 1315 at 1322–1323, [1983] 3 All ER 193 at 199 (drawing Études Pour le Bain Turc by Ingres) per WARNER J.

[19] *Eddis v Chichester Constable* [1969] 2 Ch 345, [1969] 2 All ER 912 (painting attributed to Caravaggio).

[20] C & B, pp. 847–848; M & W, pp. 1048–1049; MM, pp. 521–528.

[21] Limitation Act 1980, s. 25.

(2) If the person in possession of the land . . . acknowledges the title of the person to whom the right of action has accrued —

    (*a*) the right shall be treated as having accrued on and not before the date of the acknowledgement . . .

(3) In the case of a foreclosure or other action by a mortgagee, if the person in possession of the land, . . . or the person liable for the mortgage debt makes any payment in respect of the debt (whether of principal or interest) the right shall be treated as having accrued on and not before the date of the payment.

(4) Where a mortgagee is by virtue of the mortgage in possession of any mortgaged land and either —

    (*a*) receives any sum in respect of the principal or interest of the mortgage debt; or

    (*b*) acknowledges the title of the mortgagor, or his equity of redemption;

an action to redeem the land in his possession may be brought at any time before the expiration of twelve years from the date of the payment or acknowledgment.

(5) Subject to subsection (6) below, where any right of action has accrued to recover —

    (*a*) any debt or other liquidated pecuniary claim[1]; or

    (*b*) any claim to the personal estate of a deceased person or to any share or interest in any such estate;

and the person liable or accountable for the claim acknowledges the claim[2] or makes any payment in respect of it the right shall be treated as having accrued on and not before the date of the acknowledgment or payment.

(6) A payment of a part of the rent or interest due at any time shall not extend the period for claiming the remainder then due, but any payment of interest shall be treated as a payment in respect of the principal debt.

(7) Subject to subsection (6) above, a current period of limitation may be repeatedly extended under this section by further acknowledgments or payments, but a right of action, once barred by this Act, shall not be revived by any subsequent acknowledgment or payment[3].

30. Formal provisions as to acknowledgments and part payments. — (1) To be effective for the purposes of section 29 of this Act, an acknowledgment must be in writing and signed by the person making it.

(2) For the purposes of section 29, any acknowledgment or payment —

    (*a*) may be made by the agent of the person by whom it is required to be made under that section; and

    (*b*) shall be made to the person, or to an agent of the person, whose title or claim is being acknowledged or, as the case may be, in respect of whose claim the payment is being made[4].

---

[1] As, for example, rent due under a lease.

[2] *Good v Parry* [1963] 2 QB 418, [1963] 2 All ER 59; *Dungate v Dungate* [1965] 1 WLR 1477, [1965] 3 All ER 818; *Surrendra Overseas Ltd v Government of Sri Lanka* [1977] 1 WLR 565, [1977] 2 All ER 481; *Kamouh v Associated Electrical Industries International Ltd* [1980] QB 199; *Re Overmark Smith Warden Ltd* [1982] 1 WLR 1195, [1982] 3 All ER 513.

[3] *Sanders v Sanders* (1881) 19 ChD 373; *Nicholson v England* [1926] 2 KB 93.

[4] *Edginton v Clark* [1964] 1 QB 367, [1963] 3 All ER 468 (letter to owner's agent offering to purchase land held to be effective acknowledgement); *Re Compania de Electricidad de la Provincia de Buenos Aires Ltd* [1980] Ch 146, [1978] 3 All ER 668 (balance sheet effective acknowledgement if received by creditor).

31. Effect of acknowledgment or part payment on persons other than the maker or recipient. — (1) An acknowledgment of the title to any land . . . by any person in possession of it shall bind all other persons in possession during the ensuing period of limitation.

(2) A payment in respect of a mortgage debt by the mortgagor or any other person liable for the debt, or by any person in possession of the mortgaged property, shall, so far as any right of the mortgagee to foreclose or otherwise to recover the property is concerned, bind all other persons in possession of the mortgaged property during the ensuing period of limitation.

VII.   Effect of Expiration of Limitation Period[5]

LIMITATION ACT 1980

17. Extinction of title to land after expiration of time limit. — Subject to —

(*a*) section 18 of this Act[6]; and

(*b*) section 75 of the Land Registration Act 1925[7];

at the expiration of the period prescribed by this Act for any person to bring an action to recover land (including a redemption action)[8] the title of that person to the land shall be extinguished.

ASHER *v* WHITLOCK
(1865) LR 1 QB 1 (Ct Exch Ch, Cockburn CJ and Mellor and Lush JJ)

In 1842 Williamson enclosed some manorial land, which he occupied until his death in 1860. At that time (the period of limitation being 20 years) the title of the Lord of the Manor was not yet extinguished. He devised the land by will to his widow so long as she remained unmarried, with remainder to his daughter in fee simple. After his death the widow remained in possession, and in 1861 married the defendant, who came to live with the widow and daughter. The daughter died in February and the widow in May 1863. The defendant remained in possession of the property, and in 1865 the daughter's heir-at-law brought ejectment against him.

Held. The heir-in-law was entitled to recover the property.

Cockburn CJ: Assuming the defendant's possession to have been adverse, we have then to consider how far it operated to destroy the right of the devisee and her heir-at-law. . . . I take it as clearly established, that possession is good against all the world except the person who can shew a good title: and it would be mischievous to change this established doctrine. In *Doe d. Hughes v Dyeball* (1829) Mood & M 346 one year's possession by the plaintiff was held good against a person who came and turned him out; and there are other authorities to the same effect. Suppose the person who originally inclosed the land had been expelled by the defendant, or the

---

[5] See p. 162, n. 7, ante.
[6] See p. 174, ante.
[7] See p. 193, post.
[8] Limitation Act 1980, s. 16, p. 182, ante.

defendant had obtained possession without force, by simply walking in at the open door in the absence of the then possessor, and were to say to him, "You have no more title than I have, my possession is as good as yours", surely ejectment could have been maintained by the original possessor against the defendant. All the old law on the doctrine of disseisin was founded on the principle that the disseisor's title was good against all but the disseisee. It is too clear to admit of doubt, that if the devisor had been turned out of possession he could have maintained ejectment. What is the position of the devisee? There can be no doubt that a man has a right to devise that estate, which the law gives him against all the world but the true owner. Here the widow was a prior devisee, but *durante viduitate* only, and as soon as the testator died, the estate became vested in the widow; and immediately on the widow's marriage the daughter had a right to possession; the defendant however anticipates her, and with the widow takes possession. But just as he had no right to interfere with the testator, so he had no right against the daughter, and had she lived she could have brought ejectment; although she died without asserting her right, the same right belongs to her heir. Therefore I think the action can be maintained, inasmuch as the defendant had not acquired any title by length of possession. The devisor might have brought ejectment, his right of possession being passed by will to his daughter, she could have maintained ejectment, and so therefore can her heir, the female plaintiff. We know to what extent encroachments on waste lands have taken place; and if the lord has acquiesced and does not interfere, can it be at the mere will of any stranger to disturb the person in possession? I do not know what equity may say to the rights of different claimants who have come in at different times without title; but at law, I think the right of the original possessor is clear. On the simple ground that possession is good title against all but the true owner, I think the plaintiffs entitled to succeed[9]. . . .

FAIRWEATHER *v* ST MARYLEBONE PROPERTY CO LTD
[1963] AC 510, [1962] 2 All ER 288 (HL, Lords RADCLIFFE, DENNING, MORRIS OF BORTH-Y-GEST[10] and GUEST)

LORD DENNING: My Lords, at the back of a leasehold house in Hampstead there is a shed. In the year 1920 the next-door neighbour, Mr Millwood, saw it was unused and out of repair. He went in and repaired it and has treated it as his own ever since. Mr Millwood has actually sub-let it as part of his own house. Now a property company has bought the freehold of the property on which the shed stands and wants to recover possession of the shed. Can it do so? or is it barred by the Statutes of Limitation? There are three important persons to consider:

(1) The *freeholder* who, in 1893, let the premises on which the shed stands on a lease for 99 years at a ground rent with a repairing covenant and a proviso for re-entry. The 99 years will not expire till 1992.

(2) The *leaseholder* who has taken no steps for more than 12 years to recover possession of the shed which stands on part of his leasehold premises.

---

[9] *Perry v Clissold* [1907] AC 73.
[10] Lord MORRIS dissented. For criticism of the majority view, see (1962) 78 LQR 541 (H. W. R. Wade).

His right of action first accrued in 1920. So the 12 years for him to sue expired in 1932.

(3) The *squatter*, who has been in possession of the shed since 1920, by himself or his sub-tenants.

And there is one important event to consider: The *surrender* in 1959 by the *leaseholder* to the *freeholder* of the rest of the term of 99 years. Whereupon the freeholder claims that he is entitled to possession of the shed. But the *squatter* says he is entitled to stay in it until 1992.

It is quite clear from the Statutes of Limitation that in the year 1932 the "title" of the leaseholder to the land was "extinguished". What does this mean? There are four suggestions to consider.

The first suggestion is that the title of the leaseholder to the shed is extinguished completely, not only against the squatter, but also against the freeholder. So that the leasehold interest disappears altogether, and the freeholder becomes entitled to the land. I reject this suggestion completely. It would mean in this case that the freeholder would have become entitled to possession of the shed in the year 1932 and time would have begun to run against him from 1932. So that 12 years later the title of the freeholder to the shed would have been extinguished, that is, in 1944. That cannot be right, and it was not seriously suggested. In 99 cases out of 100, the freeholder has no knowledge that the squatter is on the premises at all. It would be utterly wrong if the title of the freeholder could be eroded away during the lease without his knowledge. The correct view is that the freehold is an estate in reversion within section 6 (1) of the Act of 1939[11], and time does not run against the freeholder until the determination of the lease: see *Doe d Davy v Oxenham* (1840) 7 M & W 131.

The second suggestion is that the title of the leaseholder to the shed is extinguished so far as the leaseholder is concerned — so that he is no longer entitled to the shed — but that the leasehold interest itself persists and is vested in the squatter. In other words, the squatter acquired a title which is "commensurate" with the leasehold interest which has been extinguished. This suggestion was made in 1867 in the first edition of Darby and Bosanquet's book [Statutes of Limitation] at p. 390, and it was accepted in 1889 as correct by the court in Ireland in *Rankin v M'Murtry* (1889) 24 LR Ir 290. But it has since been disapproved. If it were correct, it would mean that the squatter would be in the position of a statutory assignee of the shed, and he would by reason of privity of estate, be liable on the covenants and subject to the conditions of the lease. I reject this suggestion also: for the simple reason that the operation of the Statutes of Limitation is merely negative. It destroys the leaseholder's title to the land but does not vest it in the squatter. The squatter is not liable on the repairing covenants: see *Tichborne v Weir* (1892) 67 LT 735, p. 191, post. Nor, when the leasehold is a tenancy from year to year, does he step into the shoes of the tenant so as to be himself entitled to six months' notice to quit: see *Taylor v Twinberrow* [1930] 2 KB 16.

The third suggestion is that the *title* of the leaseholder is extinguished but that his *estate* in the land is not. This is too fine a distinction for me. And so it was for Parliament. For Parliament itself uses the two words as if they meant the same: see section 16 of the Limitation Act 1939, and section 75 of the Land Registration Act 1925.

---

[11] Now Limitation Act 1980, s. 15 (6), Sch. 1, para. 4, p. 173, ante.

The fourth suggestion is that the title of the leaseholder to the shed is extinguished as *against the squatter*, but remains good as *against the freeholder*. This seems to me the only acceptable suggestion. If it is adopted, it means that time does not run against the freeholder until the lease is determined — which is only just. It also means that until that time the freeholder has his remedy against the leaseholder on the covenants, as he should have; and can also re-enter for forfeiture, as he should be able to do: see *Humphry v Damion* (1612) 3 Cro Jac 300, and can give notice to determine on a "break" clause or notice to quit, as the case may be. Further, it means that if the leaseholder should be able to induce the squatter to leave the shed — or if the squatter quits and the leaseholder resumes possession — the leaseholder is at once in the same position as he was originally, being entitled to the benefits and subject to the burdens of the lease in regard to the shed. All this seems to me eminently reasonable but it can only be achieved if, despite the presence of the squatter, the title of the leaseholder remains good as against the freeholder.

On this footing it is quite apparent that at the date of the surrender, the leaseholder had something to surrender. He still had his title to the shed as against the freeholder and was in a position to surrender it to him. The maxim nemo dat quod non habet has no application to the case at all.

But there still remains the question: What was the effect of the surrender? There are here two alternatives open:

(1) On the one hand, it may be said that the surrender operated to *determine* the term, just as a forfeiture does. If this is correct, it would mean that the freeholder would be entitled to possession at once as soon as the leaseholder surrendered the house. He could evict the squatter by virtue of his freehold estate against which the squatter could say nothing. And time would begin to run against the freeholder as soon as the surrender took place. This view is based on *Ecclesiastical Comrs of England and Wales v Rowe* (1880) 5 App Cas 736, and section 6 (1) of the Limitation Act 1939.

(2) On the other hand, it may be said that the surrender operated as an *assignment* by the leaseholder to the freeholder of the rest of the 99 years. If this is correct, it would mean that the freeholder could not evict the squatter because the freeholder would be "claiming through" the leaseholder and would be barred for the rest of the 99 years, just as the leaseholder would be: see section 4 (3) of the Limitation Act. Time would not begin to run against the freeholder until the 99 years expired. This view is based on *Walter v Yalden* [1902] 2 KB 304.

My Lords, I have come to the clear conclusion that a surrender operates as a determination of the term. It is not an assignment of it. I am aware that no less an authority than Lindley LJ once said that "the surrender of the term only operated as an assignment of the surrenderor's interest in it": see *David v Sabin* [1893] 1 Ch 523, 533. But if that be true, it is not by any rule of the common law, only by force of statute: and then only in the case of underleases, not in the case of trespasser or squatter.

At common law, if a leaseholder made an underlease and afterwards surrendered his term to the freeholder, then the freeholder could not evict the underlessee during the term of the underlease: see *Pleasant (Lessee of Hayton) v Benson* (1811) 14 East 234. But this was not because there was any assignment from surrenderor to surrenderee. It is clear that, upon the surrender, the head term was determined altogether. It was extinguished completely, so much so that the freeholder could not sue the underlessee on the covenants or enforce the proviso for re-entry: see *Webb v Russell* (1789) 3 Term Rep 393. The underlessee could enjoy the property without payment of rent and without performance of the covenants and conditions until the end of the term of the underlease: see *Ecclesiastical Comrs for England v Treemer* [1893] 1 Ch 166. This was remedied by the statutes of 1740 and 1845, which have been re-enacted in sections 139 and 150 of the Law of Property Act 1925. Under those statutes, on a surrender of the head lease, an underlessee becomes a direct tenant of the freeholder on the terms of his underlease. So that the surrender does operate as if it were an assignment of the surrenderor's interest. But those statutes have no application to trespassers or squatters.

The question may be asked: why did the common law on a surrender protect the underlessee from eviction? The answer is to be found in Coke upon Littleton II, p. 338b, where it is said that "having regard to the parties to the surrender, the estate is absolutely drowned . . . But having regard to strangers, who were not parties or privies thereunto, lest by a voluntary surrender they may receive prejudice touching any right or interest they had before the surrender, the estate surrendered hath in consideration of law a continuance." This passage applies in favour of an underlessee so as to protect him from eviction during the term of his underlease: but it does not apply in favour of a trespasser. The reason for the difference is because the underlessee comes in under a grant from the lessee; and the lessee cannot, by a surrender, derogate from his own grant: see *Davenport's* case (1608) 8 Co Rep 144b and *Mellor v Watkins* (1874) LR 9 QB 400 at 405, by Blackburn J. But a trespasser comes in by wrong and not by grant of the lessee. If the lessee surrenders his term, the freeholder is at once entitled to evict the trespasser for the simple reason that, on the surrender, the lease is determined, and there is no bar whatever to the freeholder recovering possession: see *Ecclesiastical Comrs of England and Wales v Rowe* (1880) 5 App Cas 736. And I see no reason why the same reasoning should not apply even though, at the date of the surrender, the trespasser is a squatter who has been there more than 12 years. For, as against the freeholder, he is still a trespasser. The freeholder's right to possession does not arise until the lease is determined by the surrender. It then comes into being and time begins to run against him under section 6 (1) of the Limitation Act, 1939.

The only reason, it seems to me, which can be urged against this conclusion is that it means that a squatter's title can be destroyed by the leaseholder and freeholder putting their heads together. It is said that they can by a surrender — or by a surrender and regrant — destroy the squatter's title completely and get rid of him. So be it. There is no way of preventing it. But I would point out that, if we were to deny the two of them this right, they could achieve the same result in another way. They could easily do it by the leaseholder submitting to a forfeiture. If the leaseholder chooses not to pay the rent, the freeholder can determine the lease under the proviso for re-entry. The squatter cannot stop him. He cannot pay the rent without the authority of the leaseholder. He cannot apply for relief against forfeiture. The squatter's title can thus be defeated by a forfeiture — or by a forfeiture and regrant — just as it can by a surrender — or by a surrender and regrant. So there is nothing in the point.

My Lords, so far as these questions under the Limitation Acts are concerned, I must say that I see no difference between a surrender or merger or a forfeiture. On each of those events the lease is determined and the freeholder is entitled to evict the squatter, even though the squatter has been on the land during the lease for more than 12 years: and on the determination of the lease, time then begins to run against the freeholder. It follows that, in my opinion, *Walter v Yalden* [1902] 2 KB 304 was wrongly decided and *Taylor v Twinberrow* [1930] 2 KB 16 was rightly decided. . . . I would dismiss this appeal[12].

In *Tichborne v Weir* (1892) 67 LT 735[13] KAY LJ, said, at 737: "On the occasion of the conveyance [between Giraud and Weir] Giraud made a statement that he had no assignment of the lease, but only a title by a possession of forty years. The question is, what is the effect of that title. There is no doubt that covenants running with the land would bind anyone coming into possession of the estate which Baxter had, and if the lease is anyhow vested in the defendant, he would be bound by such covenants. Therefore the question is, whether Baxter's estate is vested in the defendant. It was argued that the effect of the statute was to transfer the term from Baxter to Giraud, and so it would be vested in the defendant. Under section 34 of 3 & 4 Will 4, c 27[14], 'the right and title' of Baxter to 'the land' (which by the interpretation clause includes chattel interest) was 'extinguished'. That is the operation of the section, and we are now asked to construe the Act of Parliament so as to make it say that Baxter's right and title was transferred to Giraud. . . . The defendant got an estate in the land which he has admitted, by paying rent, is not the fee simple, and by operation of the statute Baxter's right to claim the term was extinguished. It follows that Giraud during the rest of the term was free from liability to Baxter or anyone claiming under him, but it does not follow that he acquired Baxter's estate. There is another point as to whether the defendant is estopped from denying that he was in possession of Baxter's lease. He admits he is in possession of the land, he and Giraud have paid rent agreed on in the lease of 1802, and they have claimed possession for the rest of the term. The landlord's title to the land has been completely admitted, but there is no other evidence of the defendant's being bound by all the terms of the lease, or of his holding all Baxter's estate. There being no such admission, either express or implied, we must hold that there is no evidence of such an extensive estoppel as that which has been contended for[15]. I think that the defendant, for the reasons I have stated, is not liable on the covenants of the lease, and that this appeal should be dismissed."

---

[12] *Jessamine Investment Co v Schwartz* [1978] QB 264, [1976] 3 All ER 521 (sub-tenant, protected as statutory tenant under Rent Acts, acquired possessory title against his immediate landlord, whose title continued to exist as against the freeholder until head lease expired. Sub-tenant held still protected under Rent Acts thereafter against freeholder); (1977) 41 Conv (NS) 213 (F. R. Crane).

[13] See p. 766, post, where the facts are given.

[14] Reproduced with amendments as Limitation Act 1980, s. 17, p. 186, ante.

[15] *Tickner v Buzzacott* [1965] Ch 426, [1964] 1 All ER 131 (payment of rent due under lease not estoppel); *Ashe v Hogan* [1920] 1 IR 159; *O'Connor v Foley* [1906] 1 IR 20.

In *Re Nisbet and Potts' Contract* [1906] 1 Ch 386[16], COZENS-HARDY LJ said at 409:

"The suggestion which is at the root of the appellant's argument is this, that a squatter can wholly disregard restrictive covenants affecting a building estate. That is so startling a proposition, and so wide-reaching, that it must be wrong. The value of estates in the neighbourhood of London and all large towns, and the amenity of those estates, depend almost entirely upon the continuance of the mutual restrictive covenants affecting the user and the enjoyment of the property; and when we are told that the squatter, notwithstanding that he is a mere trespasser, is to be in a better position than that occupied by a person deriving a title strictly through the original covenantor, one feels that there must be an answer to the argument; and I think the authorities, when carefully examined, make the answer quite plain. The benefit of a restrictive covenant of this kind is a paramount right in the nature of a negative easement not in any way capable of being affected by the provisions of the Statute of Limitations on which the squatter relies. The only rights extinguished for the benefit of the squatter under section 34[17] are those of persons who might, during the statutory period, have brought, but did not in fact bring, an action to recover possession of the land. But the person entitled to the benefit of a restrictive covenant like this never had any cause of action which he could have brought, because unless and until there is a breach, or a threatened breach, of such a covenant, it is impossible for the person entitled to the benefit of it to bring any action. It appears, therefore, so far as the squatter is himself concerned, that both during the currency of the twelve years and after the expiration of the twelve years, there could be no possible answer to the claim of anyone seeking to enforce the covenant. In fact, there would, so far as he is concerned, be no difference between this covenant, which is in the nature of an equitable easement, and a legal easement strictly and properly so called. But although the squatter took the property subject to this equitable burden, it may be that the present vendor, who purchased from or through the squatter, is able to say that the burden does not affect the property in his hands. But what must he prove in order to claim this exemption? He must prove that he is a purchaser for value of the legal estate without notice. . . . Now can the present vendor allege and prove that he was a purchaser for value without notice? I think not."

VIII.   Registered Land[18]

LAND REGISTRATION ACT 1925

70.   Liability of registered land to overriding interests. — (1) (*f*) p. 117, ante[19].

---

[16] P. 766, post, where the facts are given.
[17] Reproduced with amendments as Limitation Act 1980, s. 17.
[18] C & B, pp. 848–849; M & W, pp. 222–223, 1053; MM, pp. 528–529; Ruoff and Roper, pp. 648–656.
[19] For overlap with para. (*g*), see *Bridges v Mees* [1957] Ch 475, [1957] 2 All ER 577.

75. Acquisition of title by possession. — (1) The Limitation Acts shall apply to registered land in the same manner and to the same extent as those Acts apply to land not registered, except that where, if the land were not registered, the estate of the person registered as proprietor would be extinguished, such estate shall not be extinguished but shall be deemed to be held by the proprietor for the time being in trust for the person who, by virtue of the said Acts, has acquired title against any proprietor, but without prejudice to the estates and interests of any other person interested in the land whose estate or interest is not extinguished by those Acts.

(2) Any person claiming to have acquired a title under the Limitation Acts to a registered estate in the land may apply to be registered as proprietor thereof.

(3) The registrar shall, on being satisfied as to the applicant's title, enter the applicant as proprietor either with absolute, good leasehold, qualified, or possessory title, as the case may require, but without prejudice to any estate or interest protected by any entry on the register which may not have been extinguished under the Limitation Acts, and such registration shall, subject as aforesaid, have the same effect as the registration of a first proprietor; but the proprietor or the applicant or any other person interested may apply to the court for the determination of any question arising under this section.

SPECTRUM INVESTMENT CO *v* HOLMES
[1981] 1 WLR 221, [1981] 1 All ER 6 (ChD, BROWNE-WILKINSON J)[20]

In 1902 the registered freeholder of 43 Mount Pleasant Lane, London granted a 99 year lease to K; the leasehold interest was registered. In 1939 K granted a monthly tenancy to Mrs Holmes who lived there with her daughter. In 1944 K assigned her lease to Mrs David who was registered as proprietor of it. Subsequent tenders of rent by Mrs Holmes were refused, and after her death in 1951, Miss Holmes remained in the house without paying rent. In 1968 Miss Holmes, who had acquired a possessory title against Mr David under the Limitation Act 1939, was registered as proprietor of the leasehold interest with possessory title, and Mrs David's registered title was closed.

In 1975 Mrs David "woke up" and purported to surrender her lease to the plaintiff (a company controlled by her family), who were the freeholder's successor in title. The plaintiff claimed possession of the house from Miss Holmes; and Mrs David, who was joined as plaintiff, claimed rectification of the register by the cancellation of Miss Holmes's possessory title and the restoration of her own.

Held. Both claims fail. Since Mrs David's title had been closed, she was no longer the registered proprietor of the lease and was therefore unable to surrender it. Rectification failed because the registrar had registered Miss Holmes's possessory title under the mandatory duty imposed on him by the Land Registration Act, s. 75.

BROWNE-WILKINSON J: I can now shortly state the contentions of the plaintiff. The plaintiff submits that the Land Registration Act 1925 introduces mere machinery for proving title to and transferring land and does not

---

[20] [1981] Conv 155 (R. E. Annand); (1981) 131 NLJ 718 (P. F. Smith), 774 (E. G. Nugee); [1982] Conv 201 (P. H. Kenny).

affect the substantive rights which parties enjoy under the general law. Accordingly, it is said that the rights of the plaintiff (as established by *Fairweather v St Marylebone Property Co Ltd* [1963] AC 510, [1962] 2 All ER 288, p. 187, ante) must be reflected in the provisions of the Act of 1925 and are preserved by the words in section 11 which expressly provide that registration with possessory title "shall not affect or prejudice the enforcement of any estate, right, or interest (whether in respect of the lessor's title or otherwise) adverse to or in derogation of" the proprietor with possessory title. So, it is said, having obtained a surrender of the lease from Mrs David, the plaintiff's right to possession as against the defendant is preserved.

There is in my judgment a short answer to the claim by the plaintiff. Accepting for the moment the broad proposition that the Act of 1925 was not intended to alter substantive rights, it undoubtedly was intended to alter the manner in which such rights were to be established and transferred. The surrender by Mrs David to the plaintiff is the linchpin of the plaintiff's claim. But in my judgment that surrender has not been effected by the only means authorised by the Land Registration Act 1925 for the disposal of a registered leasehold interest by act of the parties. At the date of the alleged surrender the lease was registered under title no. NGL 65073 in the name of the defendant. Mrs David was not registered as proprietor, her title no. LN 66166 having been taken off the register. By virtue of section 69 (1) the effect of the registration of the defendant as proprietor of the lease was, as against Mrs David, to vest the term or deem it to be vested in the defendant.

Section 69 (4) provides: "The estate for the time being vested in the proprietor shall only be capable of being disposed of or dealt with by him in manner authorised by this Act."

In my judgment the effect of these provisions is that, so long as the defendant is registered as proprietor of the lease, only she can dispose of it. Moreover by virtue of sections 21 and 22, even the defendant can only do so by a registered disposition. Accordingly, in my judgment there has, as yet, been no valid surrender of the lease and the plaintiff's claim fails in limine.

Mr Tager for the plaintiff sought to avoid this result by saying that a surrender was not a registrable disposition and referred me to section 46 of the Act. This argument does not meet the point that Mrs David was not registered as proprietor when she purported to surrender the lease. But even if she had been, in my judgment the surrender would have had to be effected by a registered disposition. Section 69 (4) makes it clear that even a registered proprietor only has power to deal with any estate vested in him in the manner authorised by the Act. The only powers of disposition are those conferred by section 21 of the Act which authorises the transfer of the registered estate. In my judgment the word "transfer" in this section must include surrendering the term, otherwise the Act does not authorise a surrender. Any disposition under section 21 has to be completed by registration: section 22. Section 46 on which Mr Tager relied merely directs the registrar to note on the register the determination of the lease, however that occurs, which will include determination by effluxion of time or operation of law. Section 46 does not purport to lay down the ways in which the determination can be effected by disposition of one of the parties.

Mr Tager submitted further that there ought to have been two registered titles to the lease, of which Mrs David was the proprietor of one and the defendant was the proprietor of the other. This suggestion seems to have no warrant in any provision of the Act and in my judgment runs contrary to the whole scheme of the Act, which is intended to ensure that there shall be one title for any interest in registered land and anyone dealing with that land can treat the registered proprietor of that interest as the owner of that interest.

For these reasons, in my judgment there has, as yet, been no surrender of the term by Mrs David to the plaintiff. Therefore, the plaintiff's claim fails since, so long as the term exists, it has no immediate right to possession. However, in order to determine the real issue between the parties I gave leave for Mrs David to be joined as co-plaintiff. If she is entitled to rectification of the register, she may thereafter be able to execute the necessary registered surrender and, if she can, the plaintiff's claim to possession would be unanswerable.

Mr Charles's submissions for the defendant were very far-reaching. He submitted that the whole scheme of the Land Registration Act 1925 shows that the position of the squatter on registered land is totally different from that of a squatter on unregistered land as laid down by the House of Lords in *Fairweather v St Marylebone Property Co Ltd*. He submits that section 75 (2) makes it clear that the squatter who has obtained title against the documentary lessee is entitled to apply to be registered as proprietor of the documentary lessee's registered estate in the land, i.e. as proprietor of the lease itself. Section 75 (3) then requires the registrar, if satisfied of the facts, to effect such registration. Accordingly it is said that what was done in the present case was quite correct: the defendant is rightly registered as proprietor of the lease itself. As a result, it is said, the legal term of years is vested in the defendant by a parliamentary conveyance contained in section 69 of the Act. By virtue of sections 9 and 11 of the Act the defendant as registered proprietor is deemed to have vested in her the possession of the leasehold interest, subject to the express and implied obligations in the lease and subject to any rights of the freeholder adverse to her interest. Therefore, Mr Charles submits, the scheme of the Land Registration Act 1925 is to produce exactly the result which the House of Lords held was not the result in relation to unregistered land, namely, to make the squatter the successor in title to the documentary lessee by parliamentary conveyance, the squatter taking subject to and with the benefit of the covenants in the lease.

This is a formidable and far-reaching submission. But, on the other side I was strongly pressed with authority suggesting that squatter's rights were the same over both registered and unregistered land.

[His Lordship referred to *Fairweather v St Marylebone Property Co Ltd* at 542–543, at 296, per Lord RADCLIFFE, at 548, at 299, per Lord DENNING, and to *Jessamine Investment Co v Schwartz* [1978] QB 264 at 275, [1976] 3 All ER 521 at 530, per Sir John PENNYCUICK, and continued:]

Finally, the words of section 75 (1) itself state that the Limitation Acts shall apply to registered land "in the same manner and to the same extent" as it applies to unregistered land, and then goes on to state exceptions.

On the other hand, I take into account the recent decision of the House of Lords in *Williams & Glyn's Bank Ltd v Boland* (decided since the conclusion of the argument in this case) [1981] AC 487, [1980] 2 All ER 408, p. 121, ante which shows that, if the words of the Land Registration Act 1925 are clear, they are to be given their natural meaning and not distorted so as to seek to produce uniformity in the substantive law as between registered and unregistered land. I therefore approach this question on the basis that one would expect that substantive legal rights would be the same whether the land is registered or unregistered but that clear words in the Act of 1925 must be given their natural meaning even if this leads to a divergence.

I do not find it necessary to reach any conclusion on the far-reaching propositions which Mr Charles put forward, since I think that I can decide this case on quite a narrow ground, leaving it to others to resolve the more fundamental questions. In my judgment, if Mrs David is to succeed in any claim to have the defendant deleted from the register as proprietor of the lease, she (Mrs David) must show at least that the registration of the defendant was not a mandatory requirement of the provisions of the Land Registration Act 1925. It is clear from the references in section 75 (3) that section 75 applies to a leasehold interest. Under section 75 (3) the registrar is under a mandatory duty to register the squatter on the application made by the squatter under section 75 (2) if the registrar is satisfied as to the squatter's title. For what does the squatter make application? I will read section 75 (2) again: "Any person claiming to have acquired a title under the Limitation Acts to a registered estate in the land may apply to be registered as proprietor thereof."

To my mind the words are clear and unequivocal: the squatter claims to have acquired a title to "a registered estate in the land" (i.e. the leasehold interest) and applies to be registered as a proprietor "*thereof*" (my emphasis). Therefore under section 75 (2), references to the squatter having acquired title to a registered estate must include the rights which under the Limitation Act 1939 the squatter acquires in relation to leasehold interests. Section 75 (2) then refers to the squatter applying to be registered as proprietor "thereof." This word can, in my judgment, only refer back to the registered estate in the land against which the squatter has acquired title under the Act of 1939, i.e. the leasehold interest. The clear words of the Act therefore seem to require that, once the 12 years have run, the squatter is entitled to be registered as proprietor of the lease itself, and is bound to be so registered if he applies for registration. It follows that in my judgment the defendant (as the squatter) is correctly registered as proprietor of the lease itself in accordance with the clear requirements of section 75. If that is right, Mrs David cannot be entitled to rectification of the register as against the defendant, and she can therefore never get into a position in which she is competent to surrender the lease to the plaintiff.

I am conscious that in so deciding I am reaching a conclusion which produces at least a limited divergence between squatter's rights over registered and unregistered land. Once the squatter is rightly registered as proprietor under section 75 (3) the documentary lessee and the freeholder can no longer defeat the squatter's rights by a surrender. But I am not deciding anything as to the position during the period between the date when the squatter obtains his title by adverse possession and the date on which he obtains registration of it. This is the period covered by section 75 (1) which is the subsection on which Lord Radcliffe in *Fairweather v St Marylebone Property Co Ltd* [1963] AC 510 at 542, [1962] 2 All ER 588 at 296 and Sir John Pennycuick in *Jessamine Investment Co v Schwartz* [1978] QB 264 at 275, [1976] 3 All ER 521 at 530, were commenting. It may well be, as their dicta suggest, that during the period preceding any registration of the squatter's rights, the documentary lessee (as registered proprietor of the lease) and the freeholder can deal with the legal estate without reference to a person whose rights are not recorded on the register. But once the Act provides for registration of the squatter's title, it must in my judgment follow that the squatter's rights (once registered) cannot be overriden. The difference between registered and unregistered land in this respect is an inevitable consequence of the fact that the Land Registration Act 1925 provides for registration of the squatter as proprietor and that registered proprietors have rights.

I can summarise my conclusions as follows:

(*a*) The plaintiff cannot, under section 11 of the Act, have any estate right or interest adverse to or in derogation of the title of the defendant (as registered proprietor of the lease with possessory title) unless and until the lease has come to an end.

(*b*) The lease has not come to an end by virtue of the purported surrender of May 7, 1975, since at that date the leasehold interest was registered land and the surrender was not made in accordance with the provisions of the Act.

(*c*) Mrs David is not entitled to rectification of the register reinstating her as registered proprietor of the lease, since the defendant is registered in accordance with the mandatory requirements of section 75 of the Act.

Therefore (*d*) Mrs David can never surrender the term so as to merge it in the freehold, and accordingly the plaintiff cannot become entitled to possession by reason of such a surrender.

In these circumstances it is not necessary for me to consider the argument that in exercising my discretion whether or not to rectify the register, I should not in any event order rectification against the defendant, the registered proprietor in possession, at the suit of those whose disregard of their own property interest has led to the defendant's registration.

I therefore dismiss the claim by the plaintiff.

QUESTIONS

1. What weight do you think should be given, in determining whether adverse possession has been taken, to the fact that
    (*a*) the owner did not currently need the land but had plans for future development
    (*b*) the trespasser did or did not intend to acquire the land as his own
    (*c*) the owner knew or did not know or should have known of the trespass?

2. Consider the very difficult questions which arise in determining whether the owner (plaintiff) impliedly permitted the defendant to occupy; and whether an earlier express permission is still operative. A similar question arises in connection with the acquisition of easements by prescription. *Healy v Hawkins* [1968] 1 WLR 1967, [1968] 3 All ER 836, p. 608, *post*; Limitation Act 1980, s. 15 (6), Sch. 1, para. 8 (4), p. 165, *ante*; Law Reform Committee 21st Report (1977), paras. 3.47–3.52.

Part Two. Family Interests

4. Trusts for Sale[1]

I. Successive and Concurrent Interests

A system of private ownership of property must provide for something more sophisticated than absolute ownership of the property by one person. A property owner needs to be able to do more than own it during his lifetime and pass it on to someone else on his death. He may wish to give it to his children, subject to an annuity for his widow, or to give a life interest to the widow and a remainder to the children; or to provide, on his son's marriage, a life interest for his son, and after his death for the daughter-in-law and after her death for their children. He may wish to set up a form of family dynasty, such as was popular among the aristocracy in the 17th, 18th and 19th centuries. The law should make possible the satisfaction of an owner's reasonable wishes on these lines. Limits are imposed on the extent to which property can be tied up in this way. We will see that dispositions are void unless they vest within the period of a life in being plus twenty-one years, or, if a fixed period of years is chosen, a period not exceeding eighty years.

But a system which allows successive interests in property necessarily raises a number of problems. Who is to manage the property during the period of the working out of the various interests? Above all, who is the person to take the decision to sell the property and to transfer title? And what is to happen, when the land is sold, to the interests of the beneficiaries?

The problem is simplest with a fund of money. The common law never developed a system of limited estates in personalty. But in equity a fund

---

[1] C & B, pp. 69–80, 94–96, 193–205, 165–166, 755–764; M & W, pp. 314–317, 322–324, 385–397, 403–410; MM, pp. 236–237, 241–242, 277–283, 286–292; H & M, chap. 11; Harvey, *Settlements of Land* (1973). See Bonfield, *Marriage Settlements 1601–1740* (1983); English and Saville, *Strict Settlement* (1983), which contains details of several dynastic settlements of land. The Law Commission is reviewing the whole subject of trusts of land and published a working paper in 1985 (No. 94), p. 311, post. It contains a useful outline of the problems arising from the present system of successive and concurrent interests.

could be vested in trustees, who would receive the income and pay it to the income beneficiary and hand over the capital to the person who was absolutely entitled at the conclusion of the limited interests. Similarly there was no problem in equity with investments. The trustees could buy and sell them, the purchaser taking a good title from the trustees, and the purchase money being added as capital to the trust fund. Chattels can be held in trust; but there has always been doubt as to the forms of limited ownership which could exist in personalty; and heirlooms used to be settled on trusts conforming as far as possible to the devolution of the land with which they were connected[2]. In a trust, it is important to state what powers are to be given to the trustees; powers of management and investment, and the power to sell and to give a good receipt to the purchaser free from the trusts of the settlement. Much of this is now covered by statute.

Successive interests in land of course provided a special case. The common law system of estates provided for life estates, fees tail, remainders and reversions. When uses and trusts of land developed, equity, generally speaking, followed the law, and allowed similar interests in equity behind a use or a trust. But, when the legal fee simple of land was split up between successive limited owners, there was no provision for the proper management of the land and, above all, no provision for selling. If land were limited to A for life, with remainder to B for life, with remainder to C in fee simple, who would sell the land? The same problem arose if similar limitations were created behind a trust; for, unless special powers were given to the trustees, they could not give a clear title to anyone other than a purchaser of the legal estate for value without notice, because any other purchaser would take the legal estate with notice of the trusts and would be bound by them[3]. Of course, all the legal estate owners in the case of a limitation of legal estates, or all the beneficiaries in the case of a trust, could combine to sell. That might not be difficult where there was a simple limitation, such as one to A for life with remainder to B. But it becomes highly impracticable if there is a long series of limitations, and impossible if the limitations include an entail in a minor or if they create interests which are designed to vest on the happening of some contingencies which have not yet been worked out[4].

What is needed therefore is a system which meets both these difficulties; which allows a property owner to create future successive and contingent interests in the property (always within the perpetuity rule[3]) and, at the same time, provides for proper management of the fund and the power to sell and to pass a good title to the purchaser free from the trusts affecting the property. The problem is most acute where the capital consists of one single unique piece of property, like a piece of land. How can the interests of the beneficiaries and those of a purchaser be reconciled?

The solution is found by the application of the principle of "overreaching", and this is applied in each of two forms of procedure used for the purpose, the strict settlement and the trust for sale. "Overreaching" is a principle by which, on a sale of property which is subject to successive interests, the

---

[2] *Shelley v Shelley* (1868) LR 6 Eq 540; *Re Morrison's Settlement* [1974] Ch 326, [1973] 3 All ER 1094.

[3] P. 24, ante.

[4] [1972] Duke Law Journal 517 (W. M. Fratcher); (1977) 42 Missouri LR 355 (R. H. Maudsley).

[5] Chap. 7, p. 312, post.

interests of the beneficiaries leave the property and attach to the purchase money. The interests of the beneficiaries are said to be overreached. The beneficiaries do not lose economically out of the sale. A ton of feathers weighs the same as a ton of lead. A life interest in remainder in £50,000 worth of land is worth exactly the same as the same interest in £50,000; indeed, more valuable if the money is invested more profitably; less valuable, though, if the land proved to be the better investment. The question is one of choice of investment of the family capital.

The two procedures or methods by which this result can be achieved are the strict settlement and the trust for sale. In the context of family holdings of land, the strict settlement is historically the more significant; because it was in this way that the great families held their ancestral lands. Legislation providing for the application of the overreaching principle to successive interests in land first came in 1882[6]. Now, under the Settled Land Act 1925, where there are successive interests in land, the legal estate is to be vested in the tenant for life (the income beneficiary) and he has the powers of management and of sale of the fee simple; and on such a sale the beneficial interests in the land are overreached and thus transferred from the land to the proceeds of sale.

Our emphasis will however be upon the other method, the trust for sale. Land held on trust for sale is vested in trustees upon trust to sell and to hold the income until sale and the proceeds of the sale on trust for the beneficiaries according to their interests under the terms of the limitation. Under the doctrine of conversion, by which land subject to a trust for sale is treated in equity as being personalty, the interests of the beneficiaries are already interests in personalty. Overreaching is therefore automatic, but the Law of Property Act 1925 section 2 makes express provision for it[7]. The existence of the trust for sale does not mean that the trustees must sell forthwith, for they are given by statute a discretionary power to postpone sale; and they can retain the land under this power as long as they wish. They are also given the same powers of management and sale as the tenant for life in the case of a settlement. The trust for sale is thus an alternative method of dealing with successive interests in land. It is more convenient than a strict settlement for various reasons, the most important of which are: land and personalty can be held together, and most family trusts contain each; decisions are taken by a group of persons in a fiduciary position and not by one interested beneficiary; it is equally convenient where there are concurrent as opposed to successive interests; and it proved more flexible and able to accommodate special forms of trusts developed to reduce taxation[8]. Income tax, estate duty (replaced by capital transfer tax in 1974) and capital gains tax have all played their part in developing the modern law of settlements[9].

---

[6] SLA 1882.

[7] It makes provision also for overreaching interests prior to the trust for sale where the trustees are either two or more individuals approved or appointed by the court or a trust corporation: LPA 1925, s. 2 (2), p. 206, post.

[8] C & B, pp. 199–205; M & W, pp. 410, 1059; MM, pp. 290–292; (1928) 166 LT 45; (1938) 85 LJ News 353 (J.M.L.); (1938) 54 LQR 576 (M. M. Lewis); (1944) 8 Conv (NS) 147 (H. Potter); (1957) CLP 152 (E. H. Scamell); (1961) 24 MLR 123 (G. A. Grove); (1962) CLP 104 (E. C. Ryder).

[9] See generally C & B, pp. 199–204; H & M, chap. 9; M & B, *Trusts and Trustees* (3rd edn, 1984), Part III; Thomas, *Taxation and Trusts* (1981).

Concurrent interests used to create a similar problem for a purchaser. To get a good title, he had to buy from all the co-owners. This problem is overcome in 1925 by providing that all concurrent interests, other than landholding by trustees, exist only behind a trust for sale[10]. There cannot be more than four trustees of land[11]. So, even if land is beneficially owned by 130 tenants in common, the purchaser buys from not more than four trustees for sale, who pass the title, as with successive interests, free from the beneficial interests of the co-owners. Their interests attach to the purchase money. A statutory trust for sale is imposed also in the case of intestacy[12].

All cases of successive or concurrent ownership are thus subject to either a trust for sale or a strict settlement. Conveyancers use the trust for sale almost exclusively at the present day, and, for this reason, it will be given prominence here. But many titles, especially those deriving from large family landholdings, are still dependent upon the Settled Land Act conveyancing, and each of the methods needs to be understood.

The interests of the beneficiaries under the strict settlement are by statute treated as interests in land after the sale[13]; while, under a trust for sale they are, by the operation of the doctrine of conversion, interests in personalty even before the land is sold. But the logic of the theory is not always followed with land subject to a trust for sale. This is a complex matter which will best be considered after concurrent interests and statutory trusts for sale have been examined[14].

II.   Express and Statutory Trusts for Sale[15]

Trusts for sale may be created expressly or by statute. In the former case, it is important to distinguish between a trust for sale, and a mere power of sale. The overreaching provisions apply only in the case of a trust for sale. The distinction is simple in most cases, but difficult questions can arise[16].

Statutory trusts for sale can arise in various situations. The most important are[17] —

Co-ownership: Law of Property Act 1925, sections 34–36 (p. 243, post).

Intestacy: Administration of Estates Act 1925, sections 33, 47.

LAW OF PROPERTY ACT 1925

35.   Meaning of the statutory trusts. — For the purposes of this Act land held upon the "statutory trusts" shall be held upon the trusts and subject to

---

[10] Chap. 5, p. 243, post.

[11] TA 1925, s. 34.

[12] AEA 1925, s. 33.

[13] SLA 1925, s. 75 (5).

[14] Pp. 266–273, post.

[15] C & B, pp. 198–199; M & W, pp. 389–391; MM, pp. 278–279; H & M, chap. 11.

[16] C & B, pp. 193–194; M & W, pp. 323–324, 386; MM, pp. 277–278; *Re Newbould* (1913) 110 LT 6; *Re Smith and Lonsdale's Contract* (1934) 78 SJ 173; *Re White's Settlement* [1930] 1 Ch 179; LPA 1925, s. 25 (4); SLA 1925, s. 30 (1) (i).

[17] See also LPA 1925, s. 19 (2) (infant entitled to legal estate with person of full age); s. 28 (4) (infant entitled under partition); s. 31 (right of redemption barred); s. 32 (personalty settlement).

the provisions following, namely, upon trust to sell the same and to stand possessed of the net proceeds of sale, after payment of costs, and of the net rents and profits until sale after payment of rates, taxes, costs of insurance, repairs, and other outgoings, upon such trusts, and subject to such powers and provisions, as may be requisite for giving effect to the rights of the persons (including an incumbrancer of a former undivided share or whose incumbrance is not secured by a legal mortgage) interested in the land [and the right of a person who, if the land had not been made subject to a trust for sale by virtue of this Act, would have been entitled to an entailed interest in an undivided share in the land, shall be deemed to be a right to a corresponding entailed interest in the net proceeds of sale attributable to that share[18].]

[Where —

    (*a*) an undivided share was subject to a settlement, and

    (*b*) the settlement remains subsisting in respect of other property, and

    (*c*) the trustees thereof are not the same persons as the trustees for sale,

then the statutory trusts include a trust for the trustees for sale to pay the proper proportion of the net proceeds of sale or other capital money attributable to the share to the trustees of the settlement to be held by them as capital money arising under the Settled Land Act 1925[19].]

III.   Effect of Sale. Overreaching[20]

LAW OF PROPERTY ACT 1925

2. Conveyances overreaching certain equitable interests and powers. — (1) A conveyance to a purchaser of a legal estate in land shall overreach any equitable interest or power affecting that estate, whether or not he has notice thereof, if —

    (ii) the conveyance is made by trustees for sale and the equitable interest or power is at the date of the conveyance capable of being overreached by such trustees under the provisions of subsection (2) of this section or independently of that subsection[1], and the statutory requirements respecting the payment of capital money arising under a disposition upon trust for sale are complied with;

    (iii) the conveyance is made by a mortgagee or personal representative in the exercise of his paramount powers, and the equitable interest or power is capable of being overreached by such conveyance, and any capital money arising from the transaction is paid to the mortgagee or personal representative;

    (iv) the conveyance is made under an order of the court and the equitable interest or power is bound by such order, and any capital money arising from the transaction is paid into, or in accordance with the order of, the court.

---

[18] The words in square brackets were added by LP (Entailed Interests) A 1932, s. 1.

[19] The words in square brackets were added by LP (A) A 1926, Sch.

[20] C & B, pp. 78–79, 761–764; M & W, pp. 403–410; MM, pp. 283–290.

[1] *Re Ryder and Steadman's Contract* [1927] 2 Ch 62.

(2)[2] Where the legal estate affected is subject to a trust for sale, then if at the date of a conveyance made after the commencement of this Act under the trust for sale or the powers conferred on the trustees for sale, the trustees (whether original or substituted) are either —

    (*a*) two or more individuals approved or appointed by the court or the successors in office of the individuals so approved or appointed; or

    (*b*) a trust corporation[3],

any equitable interest or power having priority to the trust for sale, shall, notwithstanding any stipulation to the contrary, be overreached by the conveyance, and shall, according to its priority, take effect as if created or arising by means of a primary trust affecting the proceeds of sale and the income of the land until sale.

(3) The following equitable interests and powers are excepted from the operation of subsection (2) of this section, namely —

    (i) Any equitable interest protected by a deposit of documents relating to the legal estate affected;

    (ii) The benefit of any covenant or agreement restrictive of the user of land;

    (iii) Any easement, liberty, or privilege over or affecting land and being merely an equitable interest (in this Act referred to as an "equitable easement");

    (iv) The benefit of any contract (in this Act referred to as an "estate contract") to convey or create a legal estate, including a contract conferring either expressly or by statutory implication a valid option to purchase, a right of pre-emption, or any other like right;

---

[2] This subsection was amended by LP (A) A 1926, Sch. The trust for sale then becomes "ad hoc" with additional overreaching powers. See SLA 1925, s. 21, p. 285, post for "ad hoc" settlements.

[3] Defined in LPA 1925, s. 205 (1) (xxviii) as follows: "Trust corporation" means the Public Trustee or a corporation either appointed by the court in any particular case to be a trustee or entitled by rules made under subsection (3) of section four of the Public Trustee Act, 1906, to act as custodian trustee.

Corporations which are entitled under the Public Trustee Rules 1912, r. 30, as substituted by the Public Trustee (Custodian Trustee) Rules 1975 (S.I. 1975 No. 1189, as amended by S.I. 1976 No. 836; S.I. 1981, No. 358; S.I. 1984, No. 109; S.I. 1985, No. 132), include "any corporation constituted under the law of the United Kingdom and empowered by its constitution to undertake trust business and having one or more places of business there", and being a registered company "having a capital (in stock or shares) for the time being issued of not less than £250,000, of which not less than £100,000, has been paid up in cash".

The definition was extended by LP (A) A 1926, s. 3 to include the "Treasury Solicitor, the Official Solicitor, and any person holding any other official position prescribed by the Lord Chancellor, and, in relation to the property of a bankrupt and property subject to a deed of arrangement, includes the trustee in bankruptcy and the trustee under the deed respectively, and, in relation to charitable, ecclesiastical and public trusts, also includes any local or public authority so prescribed, and any other corporation constituted under the laws of the United Kingdom or any part thereof which satisfies the Lord Chancellor that it undertakes the administration of any such trusts without remuneration, or that by its constitution it is required to apply the whole of its net income after payment of outgoings for charitable, ecclesiastical or public purposes, and is prohibited from distributing, directly or indirectly, any part thereof by way of profits amongst any of its members, and is authorised by him to act in relation to such trusts as a trust corporation." See also SLA 1925, s. 117 (1) (xxx); TA 1925, s. 68 (18); AEA 1925, s. 55 (1) (xxvi); Supreme Court Act 1981, s. 128.

(v) Any equitable interest protected by registration under the Land Charges Act, 1925[4], other than —
   (a) an annuity within the meaning of Part II of that Act;
   (b) a limited owner's charge or a general equitable charge within the meaning of that Act.

(4) Subject to the protection afforded by this section to the purchaser of a legal estate, nothing contained in this section shall deprive a person entitled to an equitable charge of any of his rights or remedies for enforcing the same.

(5) So far as regards the following interests, created before the commencement of this Act (which accordingly are not within the provisions of the Land Charges Act 1925[4]), namely —
   (a) the benefit of any covenant or agreement restrictive of the user of the land;
   (b) any equitable easement;
   (c) the interest under a puisne mortgage within the meaning of the Land Charges Act, 1925, unless and until acquired under a transfer made after the commencement of this Act;
   (d) the benefit of an estate contract, unless and until the same is acquired under a conveyance made after the commencement of this Act;

a purchaser of a legal estate shall only take subject thereto if he has notice thereof, and the same are not overreached under the provisions contained or in the manner referred to in this section.

IV.   Definition[5]

LAW OF PROPERTY ACT 1925

205.   General definitions. — (1)
   (xxix) "Trust for sale", in relation to land, means an immediate binding trust for sale, whether or not exercisable at the request or with the consent of any person, and with or without a power at discretion to postpone the sale; "trustees for sale" mean the persons (including a personal representative) holding land on trust for sale; and "power to postpone a sale" means power to postpone in the exercise of a discretion.

The definition of a trust for sale has created a number of problems. It is vital to distinguish a trust for sale from a settlement; for the trustees in the former and the tenant for life in the latter are the persons to make title, and to exercise the powers of management until sale. It will be seen that wherever there are successive interests in land, or where a fee simple is subject to a family rentcharge, there is a settlement unless the land is held upon trust for sale[6]. The definition of trust for sale in terms of itself is not helpful, and problems have arisen on the construction of the words "immediate" and "binding".

---

[4] Now LCA 1972. The annuity referred to in (a) is one created before 1926 and registered in the Register of Annuities which then existed: LCA 1972, Sch. 1.
[5] C & B, pp. 193–195; M & W, pp. 385–389; MM, pp. 277–278.
[6] SLA 1925, s. 1 (7), p. 276, post.

A. Immediate[7]

RE HERKLOTS' WILL TRUSTS
[1964] 1 WLR 583, [1964] 2 All ER 66 (ChD, UNGOED-THOMAS J)

By clauses 4 and 5 of her will, the testatrix left the residue of her estate on trust for sale, and by clause 7 directed the income to be paid to Miss Gordon for life with permission to "reside in my said house during her life for so long as she wishes". A codicil directed that the plaintiff could, if he wished, claim the house instead of a share of the residue given to him by the will. Miss Gordon proposed to sell the house, and the plaintiff brought this action to restrain her.

Held. Injunction granted. The house was held under a trust for sale subject to the consent of both Miss Gordon and the plaintiff.

UNGOED-THOMAS J: It is submitted on behalf of the plaintiff that with regard to the house, 8 Cannon Place, first, there was a trust for sale with a prohibition against sale in the lifetime of Miss Gordon without the plaintiff's consent and, secondly, that, even if that were not so, nonetheless the will and codicil declared a purpose, namely, that the plaintiff should on Miss Gordon's death have the house if he wished to have it, and that purpose must prevail over the trust for sale with the result that the property cannot be sold in the plaintiff's lifetime without his consent.

On the other hand, it is submitted on behalf of the defendants that, on the proper construction of this will, and having regard to the law which is applicable to it, the house is settled land and not subject to a trust for sale at all. The result of it being settled land would be that Miss Gordon, as tenant for life, could sell the property under her Settled Land Act powers, and that the proceeds of sale would constitute capital and, it is submitted for the trustees, consequently become subject to the option which the plaintiff was given by the . . . codicil of the testatrix's will in exactly the same way as if the house had not been sold. . . .

I was referred to *Re Hanson* [1928] Ch 96 which dealt with the question whether or not a provision for residence requires that the property should be treated as settled land rather than as being subject to a trust for sale. In that case the testator directed the trustees of his will to purchase a dwelling-house for his wife as a residence for herself until his son David should attain 25 "if she should so long continue the testator's widow". On David attaining 25, or on the second marriage of his widow (whichever happened first) the house was to fall into and form part of the testator's residuary estate, and it was devised to trustees upon trust for sale. There was no provision in the terms of the will for a trust for sale followed by a direction that the donee should have the power to reside in the house for a specified period. There was simply a direction that a house should be bought followed by a provision that at the end of the specified period there should be a trust for sale. That case turned largely on the application in those circumstances of section 32 of the Law of Property Act 1925, which provides by subsection (1): "Where a settlement of personal property or of land held upon trust for sale contains a power to invest money in the purchase of land, such land shall, unless the settlement otherwise provides, be held by the trustees on trust for sale." In *Re Hanson* there was a settlement of personal property; there was a power to invest

---

[7] See also *Re Hanson* [1928] Ch 96; *Bacon v Bacon* [1974] P 151, [1974] 2 All ER 327.

money in the purchase of land, namely, the house for the widow, and, therefore, it would follow that the land would, under the provisions of section 32 (1), be held by the trustees upon trust for sale "unless the settlement otherwise provides". Astbury J, in the course of his judgment, said (at p. 99): "The only question therefore is whether the will settlement 'otherwise provides'. . . . I imagine that the testator's direction to the trustees to purchase a dwelling-house for the widow's residence until David attained 25 or she remarried is inconsistent with there being an immediate trust for sale. Such a trust for sale would no doubt oust the Settled Land Act 1925. But in my view the testator has otherwise provided within section 32 of the Law of Property Act 1925. He could not have intended that a dwelling-house, expressly directed to be purchased for the widow's residence, should be liable to be sold over her head." What he was considering there was whether or not, on the construction of that will, the will otherwise provided. He held, that on the construction of that will, there was a contrary intention, in that the testator had himself provided that no trust for sale should operate before the time indicated in the will.

Here, on the other hand, the testatrix provided, by clauses 4 and 5, for there to be a trust for sale. The question here, therefore, is different, namely, whether, on the construction of this will, the testatrix takes out of the trust for sale, which she has declared, the house which was the subject of the gift in this case. Looking again at clause 7 of the will, it does not appear to me that the provision that Miss Gordon should be permitted to reside in this house so long as she wished is inconsistent with the trust for sale for which the testatrix had expressly provided. I have to construe the will and, so far as is possible, to reconcile the provisions of the will in accordance with what, so far as I can gather from the terms of the will and codicil, are the testatrix's intentions. Reading this provision for residence in clause 7 of the will, coming as it does in the clause which deals with the income of the investments of the trust, it does not appear to me that the testatrix there contemplated that the provision for residence should take this property out of the trust for sale. It is certainly reconcilable with the trust for sale because the effect would simply be that if Miss Gordon wished to reside in this house, it was not to be sold. I find nothing in the fact that her consent to the sale was required in that way inconsistent with the definition of trust for sale contained in section 205 (1) (xxix) of the Law of Property Act 1925.

[His Lordship then held that the intention of the testatrix was that the house should not be sold without the plaintiff's consent.]

B. Binding

The basic problem has been to know whether or not the word "binding" means merely that the trust is valid as a binding trust to sell, as opposed to a power of sale, or whether it has greater significance.

The difficulty usually arises where the fee simple in land, subject to family charges, is left by will to trustees on trust for sale. Is there a binding trust for sale subject to the family charges? Or is it a settlement within the Settled Land Act 1925, section 1 (1) (v)?

Re Leigh's Settled Estates [1926] Ch 852 was a case of this type. Mrs Tenison was tenant in tail of land which was subject to an equitable jointure rentcharge in favour of her mother. In 1923, Mrs Tenison disentailed and conveyed the fee simple, subject to the charge, to trustees on trust for sale. The question was whether or not, on 1 January 1926, the land was settled land or was subject to "an immediate binding trust for sale". TOMLIN J held that it was settled land because the trust for sale was not "binding" on every interest in the land. He said at 859: "The question is what is meant by 'an immediate binding trust for sale'. Of course an immediate trust for sale is an intelligible conception where immediate is used as distinct from future; a binding trust for sale in its simplest form would be something the opposite of one that was not binding, but it is difficult to suppose that this is the contrast which was intended to be indicated by the use of this phrase. There must be, it seems to me, some significance in the word 'binding' here. It is incredible that the word should have no meaning. It has presumably been inserted for some definite purpose, and it is the duty of the Court to attribute to it some intelligible meaning. The expression 'unless the land is subject to an immediate binding trust for sale' must I think mean unless the land that is the total subject matter of the settlement is subject to a trust for sale which operates in relation to the whole subject matter of the settlement and is immediately exercisable, although possibly with the limitation, that it is treated as immediately exercisable 'whether or not exercisable at the request or with the consent of any person and with or without a power at discretion to postpone the sale'. If that be the meaning of the phrase it may well be that, where the subject matter of the settlement is the whole unencumbered fee simple, there is no immediate binding trust for sale so long as there is not a trust for sale which is capable of overriding all charges having under the settlement priority to the trust for sale. In the present case there is no trust for sale capable of overriding all prior charges."[8]

In *Re Parker's Settled Estates* [1928] Ch 247[9], the question was whether land held by trustees on trust for sale, subject to prior *legal* charges to secure portions, was settled land, or land subject to an immediate binding trust for sale. ROMER J disapproved TOMLIN J's construction of the definition of "trust for sale", but held that, because there were prior legal charges, the land was settled land. He said at 257: "Now 'trust for sale' is defined as meaning, in relation to land, an immediate binding trust for sale whether or not exercisable at the request or with the consent of any person, and it was contended before me that the land is not held upon an immediate binding trust for sale within the meaning which it was said had been given to those words by Tomlin J in *Re Leigh's Settled Estates* [1926] Ch 852. In that case the learned judge came to the conclusion that where the subject-matter of a settlement is the whole unincumbered fee simple, 'the land' is not 'subject to an immediate binding trust for sale', so long as there is not a trust for sale

---

[8] The case was tried a second time after the trustees for sale had been approved by the court. The trustees for sale were thus given powers to overreach the rentcharge (LPA 1925, s. 2 as amended by LP (A) A 1926, Sch.) and TOMLIN J then held that it was a binding trust for sale: *Re Leigh's Settled Estates (No 2)* [1927] 2 Ch 13.

[9] (1928) 65 LJ News 248, 272, 293 (J.M.L.).

which is capable of overriding all charges having, under the settlement, priority to the trust for sale. At the time that this decision was given the Law of Property (Amendment) Act 1926 had not been passed, so that the learned judge was not dealing with subsection 7 of section 1 of the Settled Land Act[10]. He was merely dealing with section 20, subsection 1 (viii), of the Act. But I feel some little doubt as to whether the learned judge held that 'the land' in the case before him was not subject to any trust for sale, inasmuch as the subject-matter of the trust was merely the fee simple subject to the incumbrance, or whether he held that no land can ever be subject to a binding trust for sale, unless the trustees have power to overreach prior equitable interests. If the latter be the real reason of his decision, I find myself, with the greatest respect, unable to follow it. For it means that there cannot be, within the meaning of the Settled Land Act, any trust for sale of land that is subject to equitable interests, unless the trustees have a legal estate and are either two or more individuals approved or appointed by the court, or the successors in office of such individuals or a trust corporation. . . .

The conclusion, however, that I come to as a result of a consideration of all the Acts is that the words 'trust for sale', when used in reference to land that is subject to a prior equitable interest, are not confined to cases where that equitable interest can be overreached by the trustees. It may be said that in that case no effect is given to the word 'binding'. But the word may quite conceivably have been inserted to meet a case of a revocable trust for sale such as existed in *Re Goodall's Settlement* [1909] 1 Ch 440, and even if this be not so I should prefer to treat the word as mere surplusage, inserted ex majore cautela, rather than to give it a meaning that would exclude from being trusts for sale innumerable trusts which are indubitably trusts for sale, as that phrase has always been understood by lawyers hitherto, and which would either exclude them without any apparent reason from a very large number of the general provisions of the Acts relating to 'trusts for sale' or would necessitate the court holding that the context required some other meaning to be attributed to that expression.

There is therefore, in my opinion, a trust for sale in the present case affecting the legal estate in fee simple vested in the trustees of the 1924 deed. But is there a trust for sale that brings the present case within the exception to section 1 of the Settled Land Act introduced by the new subsection 7? In my opinion there is not. It is, I think, reasonably clear that that subsection only applies where 'the land' that would otherwise be the subject of a settlement under subsection 1 is held upon trust for sale.

[Here however, because there was an outstanding legal term of 1,000 years to secure portions] the whole legal estate which is the subject-matter of the settlement is not therefore subjected to a trust for sale, and in my opinion subsection 7 has no application to the case."

RE NORTON[11]
[1929] 1 Ch 84 (ChD, ROMER J)

On 31 December 1925, lands stood limited to Lord Norton for life and, after his death, subject to certain equitable charges, to trustees on trust for sale. A

---

[10] P. 276, post.
[11] (1929) 67 LJ News 24, 44 (J.M.L.).

vesting deed was executed in favour of Lord Norton. He died in December 1926, and probate, limited to settled land, was granted to the trustees of the compound settlement[12] as his special representatives. One question was whether the land remained settled or was held upon trust for sale.

Held. The legal estate was vested in Lord Norton as tenant for life under the Settled Land Act[13].

ROMER J: The first question that arises upon this summons is whether the compound settlement came to an end on the death of the second Lord Norton. The solution of that question depends upon the answer to be given to the further question whether, on the death of Lord Norton, the land, which previously had been the subject-matter of the settlement, was held upon trust for sale within the meaning of section 3 of the Settled Land Act 1925[14]. [His Lordship read section 3 and continued:] It is quite clear from that, that this land remains settled land after the death of the second Lord Norton, unless upon the happening of that event the land became held upon trust for sale. I had occasion recently in the case of *Re Parker's Settled Estates* [1928] Ch 247 to consider the meaning of the phrase "trust for sale" as used in subsection 7 of section 1 of the Settled Land Act, and for reasons that I then gave I came to the conclusion that land was not settled land where the whole legal estate, which would be otherwise subject to a settlement, was held upon trust for sale. But I also came to the conclusion that the land in question there was settled land, because there was outstanding in certain trustees a legal estate in a term of years for securing portions. The whole legal estate subject to the settlement was not therefore held upon trust for sale.

That being so, what I have to consider here is whether, on the death of Lord Norton, the legal estate in the whole subject-matter of the settlement, which undoubtedly had existed up to that date, was thereafter held upon trust for sale. Up to his death he had had the legal estate in fee simple, and that was the legal estate which was the subject of the settlement. On his death it vested in his personal representatives, his special representatives to whom probate had been granted, and was not vested in the trustees for sale. I must accordingly turn to section 7 of the Act which is the section that provides what is to be done with the legal estate which becomes vested in his personal representatives on the death of a tenant for life, and for the purposes of the present case I need only refer to subsection 5, which is in these terms: "If any person of full age becomes absolutely entitled to the settled land (whether beneficially, or as personal representative, or as trustee for sale, or otherwise) free from all limitations, powers, and charges taking effect under the settlement, he shall be entitled to require the trustees of the settlement, personal representatives, or other persons in whom the settled land is vested, to convey the land to him". But the trustees for sale in this case have not become absolutely entitled to the settled land free from all charges taking effect under the settlement. There are certain equitable rentcharges which take effect in priority to the trust for sale. That being so, it appears to me that not only was the whole legal estate the subject-matter of the settlement not held upon trust for sale upon the death of the second Lord Norton, but that

[12] P. 276, post.
[13] P. 286, post.
[14] See p. 309, post.

the trustees for sale as such had not, and have not now, a right to call for the legal estate. So far, I must, as it seems to me, come to the conclusion that on the death of the second Lord Norton, the land did not cease to be settled land, but continued to be settled land and is still settled land[15].

V.   Powers of Trustees for Sale[16]

A.   Postponement of Sale

LAW OF PROPERTY ACT 1925

25.   Power to postpone sale. — (1) A power to postpone sale shall, in the case of every trust for sale of land, be implied unless a contrary intention appears.

(2) Where there is a power to postpone the sale, then (subject to any express direction to the contrary in the instrument, if any, creating the trust for sale) the trustees for sale shall not be liable in any way for postponing the sale, in the exercise of their discretion, for any indefinite period; nor shall a purchaser of a legal estate be concerned in any case with any directions respecting the postponement of a sale.

(3) The foregoing provisions of this section apply whether the trust for sale is created before or after the commencement or by virtue of this Act.

(4) Where a disposition or settlement coming into operation after the commencement of this Act contains a trust either to retain or sell land the same shall be construed as a trust to sell the land with power to postpone the sale.

In *Re Rooke* [1953] Ch 716, [1953] 2 All ER 110, the testator directed his trustees to sell his farm "as soon as possible after my death", the proceeds of sale to fall into residue. In spite of the fact that the will contained an express power to retain "investments" not authorised by law, HARMAN J held that the earlier direction constituted a "contrary intention" under section 25 (1) as regards the farm[17].

In *Re Mayo* [1943] Ch 302, [1943] 2 All ER 440, an application was made by the testator's son, one of three trustees holding land on statutory trusts for sale, asking the court to exercise its discretion under the Law of Property Act 1925, section 30[18] to order a sale. The other two trustees were not willing to agree to sell.

---

[15] See also *Re Ryder and Steadman's Contract* [1927] 2 Ch 62; *Re Beaumont's Settled Estates* [1937] 2 All ER 353; *Re Sharpe's Deed of Release* [1939] Ch 51, [1938] 3 All ER 449; (1928) 65 LJ News 294; (1929) 67 LJ News 24, 44.

[16] C & B, pp. 195–198, 270–272; M & W, pp. 391–395; MM, pp. 279–281. A power to act by a majority may be given in the trust deed, but it will be strictly construed: *Re Butlin's Settlement Trusts* (1974) 118 SJ 757. See also [1976] Ch 251 at 253, 259, [1976] 2 All ER 483 at 486.

[17] Referring to *Scriven v Sandom* (1862) 2 John & H 743; *Re Doherty-Waterhouse* [1918] 2 Ch 269; *Re Smith* [1896] 1 Ch 171; *Re Ball* (1930) 74 SJ 298. See also *Re Atkins' Will Trusts* [1974] 1 WLR 761, [1974] 2 All ER 1, p. 332, post.

[18] See p. 222, post.

SIMONDS J made the order, saying: "The result of the residuary devise, having regard to the provisions of section 36 of the Settled Land Act 1925, was that the property was held on trust for sale, but, superadded to that trust, there is a statutory power of postponement. It appears to me that the judicial discretion conferred by section 30 of the Law of Property Act 1925 must be exercised in the same way as the discretion which is exercisable by the court in the case of an instrument containing an express trust for sale. The trust for sale will prevail, unless all three trustees agree in exercising the power to postpone. The principle is established by *Re Roth* (1896) 74 LT 50, and *Re Hilton* [1909] 2 Ch 548. Here there is no suggestion of mala fides on the part of the testator's son, who claims that the sale should not be postponed. If that were established, the position would be different, but in the present case I think that the son is reasonable in asking for the property to be sold. It has been urged that the same considerations should influence the court as those by which it would have been influenced before 1925 on applications under the Partition Acts. I do not think that the analogy is in any way of assistance. Here there is an express trust for sale imposed by the statute with a power to postpone the sale. I cannot exercise the discretion in any other way than I should have exercised it if there had been an express trust for sale, with a power of postponement, in the will. I must direct the trustees to concur with the testator's son in taking all necessary steps for the sale of the property."

B. Management and Sale

i. SETTLED LAND ACT POWERS GIVEN TO TRUSTEES FOR SALE

LAW OF PROPERTY ACT 1925

28. Powers of management, &c. conferred on trustees for sale. — (1) Trustees for sale shall, in relation to land . . . and to the proceeds of sale, have all the powers of a tenant for life and the trustees of a settlement under the Settled Land Act, 1925[19], including in relation to the land the powers of management conferred by that Act during a minority[20]: [and where by statute settled land is or becomes vested in the trustees of the settlement upon the statutory trusts, such trustees and their successors in office shall also have all the additional or larger powers (if any) conferred by the settlement on the tenant for life, statutory owner, or trustees of the settlement[1]], and (subject to any express trust to the contrary) all capital money arising under the said

---

[19] Pp. 289–298, et seq., post; the question arises whether the powers of the trustees for sale are indefeasible like those of a tenant for life under SLA 1925, s. 106, p. 289, post. Apart from the possibility of the powers being restricted by the imposition of a requirement of consents to a sale under LPA 1925, s. 26, p. 220, post, it would appear that they are. See *Re Davies' Will Trusts* [1932] 1 Ch 530, holding that a life interest to a nephew, "so long as he shall reside upon and assist in the management of the . . . farm", would not be forfeited by the exercise of powers inconsistent with such condition. The decision related to statutory trusts under LPA 1925, s. 35, but there appears to be no reason why the powers given to the trustees should not be irreducible powers like those of the tenant for life under a settlement; [1978] Conv 229 (P. Smith).

[20] SLA 1925, s. 26, p. 286, post; s. 102.

[1] The words in square brackets were added by LP (A) A 1926, Sch.

powers shall, unless paid or applied for any purpose authorised by the Settled Land Act, 1925[2], be applicable in the same manner as if the money represented proceeds of sale arising under the trust for sale.

All land acquired under this subsection shall be conveyed to the trustees on trust for sale.

The powers conferred by this subsection shall be exercised with such consents (if any) as would have been required on a sale under the trust for sale[3], and when exercised shall operate to overreach any equitable interests or powers which are by virtue of this Act or otherwise made to attach to the net proceeds of sale as if created by a trust affecting those proceeds[4].

(2) Subject to any direction to the contrary in the disposition on trust for sale in the settlement of the proceeds of sale, the net rents and profits of the land until sale, after keeping down costs of repairs and insurance and other outgoings shall be paid or applied, except so far as any part thereof may be liable to be set aside as capital money under the Settled Land Act, 1925, in like manner as the income of investments representing the purchase money would be payable or applicable if a sale had been made and the proceeds had been duly invested.

ii.　POWERS OF THE TENANT FOR LIFE UNDER THE SETTLED LAND ACT 1925[5]

SETTLED LAND ACT 1925

38.　Powers of sale and exchange. — A tenant for life —
- (i) May sell the settled land, or any part thereof, or any easement, right or privilege of any kind over or in relation to the land; and
- (iii) May make an exchange of the settled land, or any part thereof, or of any easement, right, or privilege of any kind, whether or not newly created, over or in relation to the settled land, or any part thereof, for other land, or for any easement, right or privilege of any kind, whether or not newly created, over or in relation to other land, including an exchange in consideration of money paid for equality of exchange[6].

41.　Power to lease for ordinary or building or mining or forestry purposes. — A tenant for life may lease the settled land, or any part thereof, or any easement, right, or privilege of any kind over or in relation to the land, for any purpose whatever, whether involving waste or not, for any term not exceeding —
- (i) In case of a building lease, nine hundred and ninety-nine years;
- (ii) In case of a mining lease, one hundred years;
- (iii) In case of a forestry lease, nine hundred and ninety-nine years;
- (iv) In case of any other lease, fifty years[7].

51.　Power to grant options. — (1) A tenant for life may at any time, either with or without consideration, grant by writing an option to purchase

---

[2] E.g., for certain improvements, p. 302, post.
[3] LPA 1925, s. 26, p. 220, post.
[4] LPA 1925, s. 2 (1) (ii), p. 205, ante.
[5] See the whole of SLA 1925, Part II.
[6] For further details concerning the powers of sale and exchange, see ss. 39, 40.
[7] For further details concerning the power of leasing, see ss. 42–48. As to whether a tenant for life has power to insert a rent renewal clause in the lease, see [1979] Conv 258 (M. Dockray).

or take a lease of the settled land, or any part thereof, or any easement, right, or privilege over or in relation to the same at a price or rent fixed at the time of the granting of the option[8].

(2) Every such option shall be made exercisable within an agreed number of years not exceeding ten.

71. Power to raise money by mortgage. — (1) Where money is required for any of the following purposes namely:—

    (i) Discharging an incumbrance on the settled land or part thereof;

    (ii) Paying for any improvement authorised by this Act or by the settlement;

    (iii) Equality of exchange;

    (vi) Redeeming a compensation rentcharge in respect of the extinguishment of manorial incidents and affecting the settled land;

    (vii) Commuting any additional rent made payable on the conversion of a perpetually renewable leasehold interest into a long term;

    (viii) Satisfying any claims for compensation on the conversion of a perpetually renewable leasehold interest into a long term by any officer, solicitor, or other agent of the lessor in respect of fees or remuneration which would have been payable by the lessee or under-lessee on any renewal;

    (ix) Payment of the costs of any transaction authorised by this section or either of the two last preceding sections;

the tenant for life may raise the money so required, on the security of the settled land, or of any part thereof, by a legal mortgage, and the money so raised shall be capital money for that purpose, and may be paid or applied accordingly.

Law Reform Committee 23rd Report (The Powers and Duties of Trustees) 1982 Cmnd. 8733, para. 9.1. VIII. 52–56.

"52.   A tenant for life of settled land should be empowered to grant a lease of that land or any part of it at a rent initially ascertained by arbitration or valuation, or any other generally recognised method of arriving at the best rent. (para. 8.4)

53.   A tenant for life should be given statutory authority to grant concurrent leases[9]. (para. 8.5)

54.   Section 41 of the Settled Land Act 1925 should be amended to give the tenant for life the power to grant ordinary leases of 99 years. (para. 8.6)

55.   Trustees of a settlement should be empowered to require a tenant for life to obtain valuations in respect of transactions under section 101 of the Settled Land Act 1925[10] so enabling them to control transactions with the settled land more effectively. (para. 8.9)

56.   Section 51 of the Settled Land Act 1925 should be amended so as to enable the tenant for life of a settlement to grant options at a price to be fixed by valuation, arbitration or any other generally recognised method. (para. 8.10)"

---

[8] *Re Morgan's Lease* [1972] Ch 1, [1971] 2 All ER 235.
[9] P. 422, post.
[10] P. 289, post.

iii.   DELEGATION

LAW OF PROPERTY ACT 1925

29.   Delegation of powers of management by trustees for sale. —
(1) The powers of and incidental to leasing, accepting surrenders of leases
and management, conferred on trustees for sale whether by this Act or
otherwise, may, until sale of the land, be revocably delegated from time to
time, by writing, signed by them, to any person of full age (not being merely
an annuitant) for the time being beneficially entitled in possession to the net
rents and profits of the land during his life or for any less period: and in
favour of a lessee such writing shall, unless the contrary appears, be sufficient
evidence that the person named therein is a person to whom the powers may
be delegated, and the production of such writing shall, unless the contrary
appears, be sufficient evidence that the delegation has not been revoked.

(2) Any power so delegated shall be exercised only in the names and on
behalf of the trustees delegating the power.

(3) The persons delegating any power under this section shall not, in
relation to the exercise or purported exercise of the power, be liable for the
acts or defaults of the person to whom the power is delegated, but that person
shall, in relation to the exercise of the power by him, be deemed to be in the
position and to have the duties and liabilities of a trustee.

(4) Where, at the commencement of this Act, an order made under section
seven of the Settled Land Act, 1884, is in force, the person on whom any
power is thereby conferred shall, while the order remains in force, exercise
such power in the names and on behalf of the trustees for sale in like manner
as if the power had been delegated to him under this section[11].

C.   General Powers for the Benefit of the Settled Land

SETTLED LAND ACT 1925

**64.   General power for the tenant for life to effect any transaction
under an order of the court.** — (1) Any transaction affecting or concerning the settled land, or any part thereof, or any other land (not being a
transaction otherwise authorised by this Act, or by the settlement) which in
the opinion of the court could be for the benefit of the settled land, or any
part thereof, or the persons interested under the settlement, may, under an
order of the court, be effected by a tenant for life, if it is one which could have
been validly effected by an absolute owner.

(2) In this section "transaction" includes any sale, . . . grant, lease . . . or
other disposition, and any purchase or other acquisition, and any covenant,
contract, or option, and any application of capital money . . ., and any
compromise or other dealing, or arrangement[12]. . .;

This section is applicable both to settlements and trusts for sale[13].

---

[11] C & B, p. 197, n. 5; M & W, pp. 322–323, 396; MM, p. 241.
[12] Sub-s. 2 has been amended by Settled Land and Trustee Acts (Court's General Powers) Act
1943, s. 2. See also s. 1.
[13] *Re Simmons' Trusts* [1956] Ch 125, [1955] 3 All ER 818.

The wide definition of "transaction" has enabled the power given by the section to be exercised in the following situations:

In *Re White-Popham Settled Estates* [1936] Ch 725, [1936] 2 All ER 1486, approval was given to a scheme for paying off debts incurred in keeping up the estate. The Court of Appeal (reversing EVE J) held that the section was wide enough to cover schemes which were for the benefit of persons interested under the settlement as well as those for the benefit of the settled land.

In *Re Scarisbrick Re-settlement Estates* [1944] Ch 229, [1944] 1 All ER 404, approval was given to a scheme to raise £10,000 out of capital to enable the tenant for life to continue to live in the mansion house.

In *Re Earl of Mount Edgcumbe* [1950] Ch 615, [1950] 2 All ER 242, approval was given to the expenditure of £10,000, being compensation for chattels and heirlooms destroyed by war, upon such furniture and chattels for a rebuilt mansion house as the trustees (other than the tenant for life) thought suitable.

In *Re Rycroft's Settlement* [1962] Ch 263, [1961] 3 All ER 581, intended leases were held to be outside the statutory powers of the tenant for life, and WILBERFORCE J said at 273, at 587: "Therefore it must either be discarded altogether or it must be brought forward by means of some individual scheme justified on its merits and sanctioned by the court, either under the general provisions of section 64 of this Act, or . . . the rather more special provisions which apply to building leases contained in section 46."

This section also enables the court to approve on behalf of those who, because minor, incompetent or unborn, cannot consent to schemes which adjust beneficial interests under a settlement[14], where the object of the adjustment is to reduce liability to taxation. Its jurisdiction is wider than that of the Trustee Act 1925, section 57[15]. However, the Variation of Trusts Act 1958, section 1 gives the court power to approve an "arrangement" varying the trusts or the powers of the trustees on behalf of persons covered by the section: this section is now most commonly used for the ordinary case of adjustment or re-distribution of capital for the purpose of reducing liability to taxation[16]. If the 1958 Act does not apply to a particular case, and if the settlement includes land, Settled Land Act 1925, section 64 may be used.

VI.　Capital Money[17]

A.　Rights and Duties of Purchasers
LAW OF PROPERTY ACT 1925

27.　Purchaser not to be concerned with the trusts of the proceeds of sale which are to be paid to two or more trustees or to a trust corporation. — (1) A purchaser of a legal estate from trustees for sale shall not be concerned with the trusts affecting the proceeds of sale of land subject

---

[14] *Re Downshire Settled Estates* [1953] Ch 218, [1953] 1 All ER 103.
[15] *Chapman v Chapman* [1954] AC 429, [1954] 1 All ER 798.
[16] H & M, chap. 21; Snell, pp. 240–244; M & B, *Trusts and Trustees* (3rd edn, 1984), chap. 19; Harris, *Variation of Trusts* (1975).
[17] C & B, pp. 189–192, 762; M & W, pp. 376, 404–405; MM, pp. 273, 286–287.

to a trust for sale (whether made to attach to such proceeds by virtue of this Act or otherwise), or affecting the rents and profits of the land until sale, whether or not those trusts are declared by the same instrument by which the trust for sale is created.

(2) Notwithstanding anything to the contrary in the instrument (if any) creating a trust for sale of land or in the settlement of the net proceeds, the proceeds of sale or other capital money shall not be paid to or applied by the direction of fewer than two persons as trustees for sale, except where the trustee is a trust corporation, but this subsection does not affect the right of a sole personal representative as such to give valid receipts for, or direct the application of, proceeds of sale or other capital money, nor, except where capital money arises on the transaction, render it necessary to have more than one trustee[18].

B. Investment

LAW OF PROPERTY ACT 1925

28. Powers of management, &c., conferred on trustees for sale. — (1), (2), pp. 214–215, ante.

The Settled Land Act 1925, section 73 gives a list of investments or other authorised applications of capital money under the Act[19]. There are 21 such headings, of which the most important are:

(i) In investment in Government securities, or in other securities in which the trustees of the settlement are by the settlement or by law authorised to invest trust money of the settlement;

(ii) In discharge, purchase, or redemption of incumbrances affecting the whole estate the subject of the settlement . . .

(iii) In payment for any improvement authorised by this Act;

(xi–xii) In purchase of land in fee simple, or of leasehold land held for sixty years or more unexpired at the time of purchase, or with or without mines and minerals; or mines and minerals separately, convenient to be held or worked with the settled land;

(xxi) In any other mode authorised by the settlement with respect to money produced by the sale of the settled land.

The Trustee Investments Act 1961 gives wider powers of investment to trustees. In short, it allows trustees to divide the fund into two parts "equal in value at the time of the division" and to invest one part in "narrower-range" investments (those falling within Parts I and II of the First Schedule, and consisting of a modernised form of the old trustee investments); and the other part in "wider-range" investments (those falling within Part III and permitting investment in ordinary shares of companies quoted on a recognised stock exchange[20], having a paid up share capital of at least one million

---

[18] Sub-s. 2 was substituted by LP (A) A 1926, s. 7 and Sch. See also TA 1925, s. 14.
[19] See also Coal Mining (Subsidence) Act 1957, s. 11 (7); Leasehold Reform Act 1967, s. 6 (5), Sch. 2, para. 9.
[20] As defined by Prevention of Frauds (Investments) Act 1958.

pounds, and which have in each of the immediately preceding five years paid a dividend). The Act should be consulted for further details[1].

In *Re Wakeman* [1945] Ch 177, [1945] 1 All ER 421, UTHWATT J held that trustees for sale who sold *all* the land which was subject to the trust for sale did not have power to apply the proceeds of sale in the purchase of land. Such a purchase would not be an authorised investment for ordinary trustees; and the trustees in *Re Wakeman*, having sold all the land, could not rely upon Law of Property Act 1925, section 28 because they were no longer "persons holding land on trust for sale", and therefore not trustees for sale[2].

In *Re Wellsted's Will Trusts* [1949] Ch 296, the Court of Appeal held that trustees for sale who do retain some land may, under section 28, apply the proceeds of sale of land, and investments traceable to such proceeds, in the purchase of land; and COHEN LJ desired "to reserve the question of what the position would be if at the time when the question of investment arose no land was held upon the trusts of the settlement"[3].

VII.   Consents to Sale[4]

LAW OF PROPERTY ACT 1925

26.   Consents to the execution of a trust for sale. — (1) If the consent of more than two persons is by the disposition made requisite to the execution of a trust for sale of land, then, in favour of a purchaser, the consent of any two of such persons to the execution of the trust or to the exercise of any statutory or other powers vested in the trustees for sale shall be deemed sufficient.

(2) Where the person whose consent to the execution of any such trust or power is expressed to be required in a disposition is not sui juris or becomes subject to disability, his consent shall not, in favour of a purchaser, be deemed to be requisite to the execution of the trust or the exercise of the power; but the trustees shall, in any such case, obtain the separate consent of the parent or testamentary or other guardian of an infant or of the receiver (if any) of a person suffering from mental disorder[5].

(3) p. 221, post.

28.   Powers of management, &c., conferred on trustees for sale. — (1) p. 214, ante.

30.   Powers of court where trustees for sale refuse to exercise powers. — p. 222, post.

---

[1] H & M, pp. 504–517; Snell, pp. 214–225; M & B, *Trusts and Trustees* (3rd edn, 1984), pp. 598–629. The Law Reform Committee 23rd Report (The Powers and Duties of Trustees) 1982 Cmnd. 8733, paras. 9.1. II 6–10 recommends that the Trustee Investments Act 1961 be replaced by an up-to-date statute.
[2] LPA 1925, s. 205 (1) (xxix) p. 207, ante.
[3] At p. 319, Lord GREENE MR analysed LPA 1925, s. 28 in detail and considered some of the difficulties to which it gives rise. See also *Re Gray* [1927] 1 Ch 242; *Re Smith* [1930] 1 Ch 88.
[4] C & B, p. 197; M & W, pp. 394–395; MM, pp. 316–317.
[5] As amended by Mental Health Act 1959, s. 149, Sch. 7, Part I.

In *Re Inns* [1947] Ch 576, [1974] 2 All ER 308 there was an application by a widow under the Inheritance (Family Provision) Act 1938, section 1 for an increased provision from her deceased husband's very substantial estate. The widow argued that it was the testator's intention that she should reside during widowhood in a luxurious mansion "Springfield" which was expensive to run and would consume more than the financial provision made for her. The house was held on trust for sale, but could only be sold with the consent both of the widow and of the Stevenage Urban District Council, to whom the house was to be offered, on the widow's remarriage or death, for use as a hospital, with £10,000 in addition for maintenance and equipment if they accepted the gift.

WYNN-PARRY J refused to hold, on the facts, that the financial provision for the widow was unreasonable, but at no stage was doubt cast upon the validity of the requirement of the consent of the widow and of the Council. WYNN-PARRY J said at 582, at 312:

"After an exhaustive consideration of all the circumstances I come to the conclusion that while, if I had been sitting in the testator's armchair, I might well have avoided tying up 'Springfield' so that only the plaintiff's consent to its sale in her lifetime would have been required, and I might well have provided a somewhat larger fund than the 85,000*l* in view of the size of the estate; yet, bearing in mind the principles upon which I am directed to proceed by the authorities which I regard as binding on me, and with which I am respectfully in agreement, I cannot bring myself to the conclusion that what has been provided is so little as to be unreasonable. From the plaintiff's point of view the provisions regarding 'Springfield' are unfortunate in that neither she nor the trustees can bring about a sale during her lifetime."

VIII.   The Beneficiaries under a Trust for Sale[6]

A.   Consultation

LAW OF PROPERTY ACT 1925

26.   Consents to the execution of a trust for sale. — (3)[7] Trustees for sale shall so far as practicable consult the persons of full age for the time being beneficially interested in possession in the rents and profits of the land until sale, and shall, so far as consistent with the general interest of the trust, give effect to the wishes of such persons, or, in the case of dispute, of the majority (according to the value of their combined interests) of such persons, but a purchaser shall not be concerned to see that the provisions of this subsection have been complied with.

In the case of a trust for sale, not being a trust for sale created by or in pursuance of the powers conferred by this or any other Act, this subsection shall not apply unless the contrary intention appears in the disposition creating the trust[8].

---

[6] C & B, pp. 197–198, 223–224; M & W, pp. 391–392, 397, 441–442; MM, pp. 282, 313–317.

[7] Substituted for the original subsection by LP (A) A 1926, Sch.; *Waller v Waller* [1967] 1 WLR 451, [1967] 1 All ER 305; *Caunce v Caunce* [1969] 1 WLR 286, [1969] 1 All ER 722.

[8] I.e. the rule relating to consultation of the beneficiaries applies to statutory trusts for sale. In an express trust for sale, the trustees are bound by the testator's wishes. If there are no special provisions, apart from the trust to sell, the trustees may, if they wish, postpone the sale: LPA 1925, s. 25. But, unless they all agree to do so, they must sell: *Re Mayo* [1943] Ch 302, p. 213, ante; see also *Bull v Bull* [1955] 1 QB 234 at 238–239, [1955] 1 All ER 253 at 256; (1973) 117 SJ 518 (A. M. Prichard).

B.   Application to Court for Exercise of Powers

LAW OF PROPERTY ACT 1925

30.[9] **Powers of court where trustees for sale refuse to exercise powers.** — (1) If the trustees for sale refuse to sell or to exercise any of the powers conferred by either of the last two sections[10], or any requisite consent cannot be obtained, any person interested[11] may apply to the court for a vesting or other order for giving effect to the proposed transaction or for an order directing the trustees for sale to give effect thereto, and the court may make such order as it thinks fit.

Cretney, *Principles of Family Law* (4th edn. 1984), pp. 670–673

The Statutory Provisions

"The statutory framework governing the exercise of the trust for sale is section 30 of the Law of Property Act 1925. This provides that if the trustees for sale refuse to sell the property, or any requisite consent cannot be obtained, any person interested may apply to the court and the court may make such order as it thinks fit. Thus, if the legal title to the property is vested in husband and wife (or in a cohabiting couple) either of them may apply to the court for an order for sale under this section. Again, if the beneficial interest of either the husband or the wife has vested in a trustee in bankruptcy[12], the trustee in bankruptcy is a person interested who may apply to the court for an order for sale. It should, however, be noted that if the legal estate is vested in only one of the partners (say the husband) on trust for himself and the wife an application under section 30 by the wife will only be appropriate if the husband *refuses* to sell; if he intends to sell (or otherwise deal with the property) against the wife's wishes she should apply to the court for an injunction to restrain him from doing so, at least until a second trustee has been appointed to protect her interests[13].

Exercise of the Court's Discretion

How then will the court exercise its discretion on such an application? Two preliminary points must be stressed. First, the court has no power on an application under section 30 to *adjust* the parties' property rights; it is only concerned to give effect to existing property rights. The court thus has a much more restricted function than it has in the exercise of its adjustive

---

[9] As renumbered by County Courts Act 1984, s. 148 (1), Sch. 2, para. 2 (2). Sub-s. (2) gives jurisdiction to the county court. See Law Commission Working Paper: Trusts of Land No. 94 (1985), paras. 10.3–10.5; p. 311, post.

[10] LPA 1925, s. 28, p. 214, ante; s. 29, p. 217, ante.

[11] *Stevens v Hutchinson* [1953] Ch 299 at 305, [1953] 1 All ER 699 at 701 per UPJOHN J ("a person interested in some proprietary right under the trust for sale"); *Re Solomon* [1967] Ch 573, [1966] 3 All ER 255.

[12] See p. 234, post.

[13] *Waller v Waller* [1967] 1 WLR 451, [1967] 1 All ER 305. It should also be noted that the court would apparently have jurisdiction to make an order for sale with vacant possession on the husband's application if the wife refused to vacate the premises. Since the wife is a co-owner, the husband is not entitled to turn her out; she would therefore be a person whose consent to the sale was requisite within the terms of s. 30: *Bull v Bull* [1955] 1 QB 234, [1955] 1 All ER 253.

jurisdiction in divorce and other matrimonial proceedings[14], even though it may be that the approach of the courts to the exercise of its discretions under section 30 has been to some extent affected by the existence of the broader adjustive jurisdiction[15], of which it will take notice. Secondly, there has now developed an important distinction between those cases in which the dispute is between the partners themselves, and those cases in which the order is sought by the trustee in bankruptcy[16]. We therefore consider, first, the principle applied by the courts in cases between the partners; we then consider the extent to which those principles are affected by the fact that the application is made by a trustee in bankruptcy.

Disputes Between the Partners

Although the basic principle of trust law is that the trustees (i.e. the spouses if they both hold the legal estate) must be unanimous if they are to exercise their discretionary power to postpone a sale, so that if either wishes to sell there should be a sale, it has now come to be accepted that the trust for sale is often simply a convenient conveyancing technique used in a variety of situations in which an actual sale was far from the original intentions of the parties. Accordingly, in exercising its discretionary powers under section 30 the court will have regard to the *underlying purpose* for which the trust was created[17]. It has traditionally been said that the question therefore becomes whether the trust itself or the circumstances in which it was made show that there was a 'secondary or collateral' object besides sale[18]; and where the property in question is a family home that fact by itself suffices to show that the purpose of the trust was the provision of a home for the parties, and not a sale. More recently, it has come to be accepted that a *primary* object of the trust is the provision of a home for the parties[19]. In such cases, so long as the purpose remains alive, the court will not order a sale. However, where the

---

[14] *Re Evers' Trust* [1980] 1 WLR 1327 at 1330, [1980] 3 All ER 399 at 401, p. 225, post, per ORMROD LJ; *Dennis v McDonald* [1981] 1 WLR 810, [1981] 2 All ER 632, per PURCHAS J (Court on application under s. 30 not required to take into account all the circumstances of the parties, as it could do on application for ancillary relief under s. 25 MCA 1973). It has, however, been suggested that applications relating to the family home should (unless the application is by a trustee in bankruptcy: *Re Holliday* [1981] Ch 405, [1980] 3 All ER 385, p. 229, post or otherwise relates to the enforcement of a debt: *First National Securities Ltd v Hegerty* [1985] QB 850, [1984] 1 All ER 139) be started in the Family Division of the High Court rather than the Chancery Division: see *Williams v Williams* [1976] Ch 278, [1977] 1 All ER 28; *Bernard v Josephs* [1982] Ch 391 at 401, [1982] 3 All ER 162 at 168, per Lord DENNING MR. The court may order the transfer of a case started in the Chancery Division to the Family Division, as was done in *Dennis v McDonald*, supra. It is possible for the Family Division to exercise jurisdiction under s. 30, LPA, by reason of a *Practice Direction (High Court: Divisions)* [1973] 1 WLR 627, [1973] 2 All ER 233; see generally *Bothe v Amos* [1976] Fam 46, [1975] 2 All ER 321).

[15] See e.g. *Williams v Williams*, supra, at 285–286, at 31, per Lord DENNING MR ("The truth is that the approach to these cases has been transformed since the legislation has given the power to the court after a divorce to order the transfer of property").

[16] See *Re Holliday*, supra; *Re Lowrie* [1981] 3 All ER 353, p. 236, post.

[17] *Re Evers' Trust*, supra at 1330, at 401, per ORMROD LJ.

[18] *Jones v Challenger* [1961] 1 QB 176, [1960] 1 All ER 785.

[19] *Williams v Williams*, supra at 285, at 31; *Dennis v McDonald*, supra at 814, at 636; cf. *Jones v Challenger*, supra at 183, at 789, per DEVLIN J ("investment . . . is the primary object of the trust").

marriage (or relationship[20]) has come to an end (for example, by divorce) then the court will, at least if there are no children, normally order a sale unless there are special circumstances[1].

What is to be the position if the relationship comes to an end, but there are still young children for whom a house has to be provided? There are, unfortunately, conflicting dicta in different decisions of the Court of Appeal[2]. On the one hand, it is said that a purpose of the trust in such a case would be to provide a home for them during their infancy, so that a sale would not generally be ordered whilst that purpose still existed[3]; in this view, the purpose of the trust is to provide a *family* home. On the other, it is urged that the children are not beneficiaries of the trust for sale, and that their interests are only to be taken into account 'so far as they affect the equities in the matter as between the two persons entitled to the beneficial interests in the property'[4]; on this view, the purpose of the trust is to provide a *matrimonial* (or cohabitational) home. It will thus be noted that there is no dispute that the interests of the children *are* to be taken into account; and it is submitted that in most cases the distinction will not lead to any difference of result[5]. Husband and wife are obliged to support their children; and it seems difficult to believe that the court would order a sale unless they were able to provide alternative accommodation for them. It is true that an unmarried man is not obliged to support his partner's children unless he has been adjudged to be their father[6]; so that it may be possible to envisage cases in which the court will hold it to be reasonable for him to insist on the sale of a house in which he has lived with his partner and her still-dependent children. It most cases, however, where a sale is sought by one of the partners[7] it is submitted that the courts would now hold that the provision of a home for the children had been a primary purpose or the

[20] *Re Evers' Trust*, supra; *Bernard v Josephs*, supra. See generally (1982) 12 Fam Law 108 (R. Schuz).

[1] See, for example, *Jones v Challenger*, supra at 183, at 789, per DEVLIN J: "with the end of the marriage, that purpose was dissolved and the primacy of the duty to sell was restored. No doubt there is still a discretion. If the husband wanted time to obtain alternative accommodation, the sale could be postponed for that purpose, but he has not asked for that. If he was prepared to buy out the applicant's interest it might be proper to allow it". Cf. the more widely expressed view of Lord DENNING MR, that sale may be postponed if "it would be unduly harsh to require the remaining party to vacate": *Bernard v Josephs*, supra at 400, at 168.

[2] See [1981] Conv 404, 407–408 (Hayes and Battersby); (1982) 98 LQR 519 (F. Webb).

[3] *Rawlings v Rawlings* [1964] P 398 at 419, [1964] 2 All ER 804 at 814, per SALMON LJ; *Burke v Burke* [1974] 1 WLR 1063, [1974] 2 All ER 944, per LAWTON LJ; *Williams v Williams*, supra at 285, at 31; *Re Evers' Trust*, supra; *Dennis v McDonald*, supra.

[4] *Burke v Burke*, supra at 1067, at 947–948, per BUCKLEY LJ; *Re Holliday*, supra at 417, 421, at 393, 395.

[5] See e.g. *Dennis v McDonald*, supra at 814, at 636; *Cousins v Dzosens* (1981) Times, 12 December, p. 233, post; and see now *Chhokar v Chhokar* [1984] FLR 313; cf. (1982) 98 LQR 519 (F. Webb). It is not satisfactory to distinguish the cases on the basis that the courts now have ample powers to safeguard the children's interests by the exercise of the adjustive proceedings, since if the couple are unmarried such adjustive power will not be available: cf. *Re Holliday*, supra at 418, 421, at 393, 395.

[6] A married man is obliged to support any "children of the family," a class which may include children of whom neither he nor his wife is the parent.

[7] A different approval may be accepted where in cases where the application is by a trustee in bankruptcy: see infra.

underlying purpose of the trust[8], and thus refuse to order a sale during their infancy[9].

It should also be mentioned that the court may in any case refuse to order a sale if it would be inequitable to do so[10]. Thus, in *Bedson v Bedson*[11] the husband was carrying on a business in the house and sale would have ruined him. Since it would have been inequitable to order a sale, the court refused to do so. The husband was ordered to pay the wife £1 a week in respect of her interest in the house[12]."

i.   GENERAL PRINCIPLES. CONFLICTING APPROACHES IN COURT OF APPEAL

RE EVERS' TRUST
[1980] 1 WLR 1327, [1980] 3 All ER 399 (CA, ORMROD, EVELEIGH and TEMPLEMAN LJJ)[12]

In 1974 M and W, who were not married to one another, began to co-habit. In 1976 they had a child, and in the same year they were joined by two of W's children from a former marriage. In 1978 M and W purchased a cottage for £13,950, of which £10,000 was obtained on mortgage, £2,400 paid by W and £1,050 plus expenses by M. The cottage was conveyed into their joint names on trust for sale as joint tenants in equity. In 1979 they separated, M leaving W and the children in the cottage.

M applied under section 30 for an order for the sale of the cottage. The trial judge held that there should be no sale until the child of M and W should attain the age of 16 or until further order. On appeal by M

Held. M's appeal dismissed on W's undertaking to discharge the liability under the mortgage, to pay the outgoings and to indemnify M so long as she occupied the cottage; with leave to either party to reapply if there was a change in circumstances.

ORMROD LJ (delivering the judgment of the court): The appeal in relation to the section 30 application raises questions of general importance, because it appears to be the first time that this court has had to consider the application of section 30 in relation to a property purchased as a home and held in joint names, by two persons who are not married to one another. This is a situation which is occurring much more frequently now than in the past, and is a social development of considerable importance with which the courts are now likely to have to deal from time to time.

The usual practice in these cases has been to order a sale and a division of the proceeds of sale, thus giving effect to the express purpose of the trust. But the trust for sale has become a very convenient and much used conveyancing technique. Combined with the statutory power in the trustees to postpone the sale, it can be used to meet a variety of situations, in some of which an actual sale is far from the intentions of the parties at the time when the trust for sale comes into existence. So, when asked to exercise its discretionary

---

[8] *Re Evers' Trust*, supra at 1332–1334, at 402–404; cf. *Re Holliday*, supra (a bankruptcy case, and, it is submitted, to be distinguished by that fact. For the view that the two cases are irreconcilable, see (1982) 98 LQR 519 (F. Webb)).

[9] In practice, the courts prefer to dismiss the application for a sale, rather than making an order postponed, e.g. until the children have ceased to be dependent. The applicant may then apply again if there is a material change of circumstances, (e.g. respondent's marriage).

[10] *Re·Buchanan-Wollaston's Conveyance* [1939] Ch 738 at 747, [1939] 2 All ER 302 at 305; *Jones v Challenger*, supra at 184, at 789.

[11] [1965] 2 QB 666, [1965] 3 All ER 307.

[12] As to the power to make such order, see p. 239, post.

[13] Leave to appeal was refused by HL Appeal Committee.

powers under section 30 to execute the trust, the court must have regard to its underlying purpose: see *Re Buchanan-Wollaston's Conveyance* [1939] Ch 217, and in this court at 738, [1939] 2 All ER 302. In that case four adjoining landowners purchased a plot of land to prevent it being built on and held it on trust for sale. They also covenanted with one another that the land would not be dealt with except with the unanimous agreement of the trustees. Subsequently one of them wished to sell, but some of the other trustees objected so the plaintiff applied to the court under section 30 for an order for sale. At first instance, Farwell J refused the order, saying, at 223:

"The question is this: will the court assist the plaintiff to do an act which would be directly contrary to his contract with the other parties, since it was plainly the intention of the parties to the contract that the land should not be sold save with the consent of them all?"

His decision was upheld in this court, but on a broader basis. Sir Wilfrid Greene MR said, at 747, at 308:

". . . it seems to me that the court of equity, when asked to enforce the trust for sale, whether one created by a settlement or a will or one created by the statute, must look into all the circumstances of the case and consider whether or not, at the particular moment and in the particular circumstances when the application is made to it, it is right and proper that such an order shall be made. In considering a question of that kind, in circumstances such as these, the court is bound to look at the contract into which the parties have entered and to ask itself the question whether or not the person applying for execution of the trust for sale is a person whose voice should be allowed to prevail."

Some 20 years later, in *Jones v Challenger* [1961] 1 QB 176, [1960] 1 All ER 785, Devlin LJ reviewed the authorities and affirmed this principle. He said, at 181, at 787:

"But this simple principle" i.e., that in a trust for sale there is a duty to sell "cannot prevail where the trust itself or the circumstances in which it was made show that there was a secondary or collateral object besides that of sale. Simonds J, in his judgment in *Re Mayo* [1943] Ch 302, [1943] 2 All ER 440, said that if there were mala fides, the position would be different. If it be not mala fides, it is at any rate wrong and inequitable for one of the parties to the trust to invoke the letter of the trust in order to defeat one of its purposes, whether that purpose be written or unwritten, and the court will not permit it."

In that case a house had been purchased by a husband and wife jointly as a home. Subsequently, the marriage broke down, the wife left and committed adultery and applied to the court for an order for sale of the property, a leasehold with only a few years to run. The husband continued to live in the house on his own; there were no children. In these circumstances the court decided that the house should be sold. Devlin LJ said, at 183, at 789:

"In the case we have to consider, the house was acquired as the matrimonial home. That was the purpose of the joint tenancy and, for so long as that purpose was still alive, I think that the right test to be applied would be that in *Re Buchanan-Wollaston's Conveyance* [1939] Ch 738, [1939] 2 All ER 302. But with the end of the marriage, that purpose was dissolved and the primacy of the duty to sell was restored."

Had there been children whose home was still in the property, the conclusion in that case might have been different. Later Devlin LJ said, at

184, at 789: "The true question is whether it is inequitable for the wife, once the matrimonial home has gone, to want to realise her investment."

In *Burke v Burke* [1974] 1 WLR 1063, [1974] 2 All ER 944, however, children were involved. On the husband's application under section 17 of the Married Women's Property Act 1882 the registrar ordered a sale, but postponed it for a year or so to give the wife, who had custody of the children, an opportunity to find an alternative home for them. This court upheld the registrar's order. The application was actually made under section 17 of the Married Women's Property Act 1882. That section is purely procedural and the principles are the same as under section 30 of the Law of Property Act 1925. In giving the leading judgment Buckley LJ took the view that the trust for sale was an immediate binding trust subject to the discretionary power in the court to postpone the execution of the trust for sale, and that the court must have regard to all the relevant circumstances of the case and to the situation of both the beneficial owners. The interests of the children in that case, he thought, were:

". . . interests which are only incidentally to be taken into consideration in that sort of way. They are proper to be taken into consideration so far as they affect the equities in the matter as between the two persons entitled to the beneficial interests in the property. But it is not, I think, right to treat this case as though the husband was obliged to make provision for his children by agreeing to retain the property unsold. To do so is, as I think, and as was urged upon us by Mr Matheson, to confuse with a problem relating to property considerations which are relevant to maintenance." (See [1974] 1 WLR 1063 at 1067, at 947.)

He expressed disagreement with an obiter dictum of Salmon LJ in the earlier case of *Rawlings v Rawlings* [1964] P 398 at 419, [1964] 2 All ER 804 at 814, where he said:

"If there were young children the position would be different. One of the purposes of the trust would no doubt have been to provide a home for them, and whilst that purpose still existed a sale would not generally be ordered."

Buckley LJ was plainly anxious to make it clear that the children themselves in such circumstances were not objects of the trust and, therefore, had no beneficial interests in the property, and so were in that sense, only "incidental" to the problem, but we do not think that Salmon LJ thought otherwise. The court in *Burke v Burke* was not referred to *Re Buchanan-Wollastan's Conveyance*, so Buckley LJ does not seem to have considered, in so many words, whether or not the primary purpose of the trust, i.e., for sale, ("the letter of the trust," in Devlin LJ's words) had been affected by the underlying purpose (quoting Devlin LJ again, "written or unwritten") of providing a home, not only for the parents, but also for the children. Salmon LJ's dictum appears, therefore, to be more in line with the judgments of this court in *Re Buchanan-Wollaston's Conveyance*, and in *Jones v Challenger*. Moreover, it is now supported by a dictum of Lord Denning MR in *Williams v Williams* [1976] Ch 278 at 285, [1977] 1 All ER 28 at 30: "The court, in executing the trust should regard the primary object as being to provide a home and not a sale."

This approach to the exercise of the discretion given by section 30 has considerable advantages in these "family" cases. It enables the court to deal with substance, that is reality, rather than form, that is, convenience of conveyancing; it brings the exercise of the discretion under this section, so far as possible, into line with exercise of the discretion given by section 24 of the Matrimonial Causes Act 1973; and it goes some way to eliminating differences between legitimate and illegitimate children in accordance with present legislative policy: see, for example Part II of the Family Law Reform Act 1969.

The relevant facts in the present case must now be examined. [His Lordship examined the facts and continued:]

The irresistible inference from these facts is that, as the judge found, they purchased this property as a family home for themselves and the three children. It is difficult to imagine that the mother, then wholly responsible for two children, and partly for the third, would have invested nearly all her capital in the purchase of this property if it was not to be available to her as a home for the children for the indefinite future. It is inconceivable that the father, when he agreed to this joint adventure, could have thought otherwise, or contemplated the possibility of an early sale without the consent of the mother. The underlying purpose of the trust was, therefore, to provide a home for all five of them for the indefinite future. Unfortunately, the relationship between the father and the mother broke down very soon, and the parties separated.

It was . . . argued that the father ought to be allowed to "take his money out" or "to realise his investment." In point of fact, his investment amounted to less than one-fifth of the purchase price of the property, and was smaller than the mother's investment. The major part of the purchase price was provided by the mortgagees, and the mother is prepared to accept full responsibility for paying the interest on the mortgage, and keeping up the capital re-payments. The father has a secure home with his mother. There is no evidence that he has any need to realise his investment. It is an excellent one, combining complete security with considerable capital appreciation in money terms. His share is now said to be worth about £5,000, i.e., it has more than doubled in value in two years. On the other hand, a sale of the property now would put the mother into a very difficult position because she cannot raise the finance to rehouse herself or meet the cost of borrowing money at present rates. So there is no justification for ordering a sale at the present time.

For these reasons the judge was right not to order an immediate sale but the form of his actual order is not satisfactory. Under section 30, the primary question is whether the court should come to the aid of the applicant at the "particular moment and in the particular circumstances when the application is made to it . . .": see *Re Buchanan-Wollaston's Conveyance* [1939] Ch 738 at 747, [1939] 2 All ER 302 at 308. In the present case, at the present moment and in the existing circumstances, it would be wrong to order a sale. But circumstances may change unpredictably. It may not be appropriate to order a sale when the child reaches 16 years — a purely arbitrary date — or it may become appropriate to do so much sooner, for example on the mother's remarriage, or on it becoming financially possible for her to buy the father out. In such circumstances it will probably be wiser simply to dismiss the application while indicating the sort of circumstances which would, prima facie, justify a further application. The ensuing uncertainty is unfortunate but, under this section, the court has no power to adjust property rights or to re-draft the terms of the trust. Ideally, the parties should now negotiate a settlement on the basis that neither of them is in a position to dictate terms. We would therefore, dismiss the father's appeal, but would vary the order to dismiss the application on the mother's undertaking to discharge the liability under the mortgage, to pay the outgoings and maintain the property, and to indemnify the father so long as she is occupying the property.

RE HOLLIDAY (A BANKRUPT)
[1981] Ch 405, [1980] 3 All ER 385 (CA, BUCKLEY and GOFF LJJ and Sir David CAIRNS)[14]

In 1962 H and W married, and in 1970 purchased 9 Woodgrange Close, Thorpe Bay, Essex as their matrimonial home for £7,850, of which £6,500 was raised on mortgage. It was conveyed on trust for sale to H and W as joint legal and beneficial owners. In 1974 W was granted a divorce, and on 3 March 1976 gave notice of her intention to apply for ancillary relief. On the same day H successfully petitioned for an immediate adjudication order in bankruptcy under section 6 of the Bankruptcy Act 1914[15] (by which the petitioner is not required to verify his statement that he is unable to pay his debts). H later filed a statement, verifying that he was unable to pay £1,260 to his former solicitors and £5,000 to his bank. In May 1976 W was given custody of the three children born in 1965, 1968 and 1973.

H's trustee in bankruptcy applied in the County Court for an order under section 30 for the sale of 9 Woodgrange Close. W cross-appealed for the annulment of the adjudication order on the ground that it was an abuse of the process of the court, being a device to prevent her from obtaining a property transfer order. The proceedings were transferred to the High Court but not consolidated with the matrimonial proceedings, on the ground that there was no jurisdiction to do so.

In 1978 FOSTER J dismissed W's application for annulment and granted the trustee in bankruptcy's application for an immediate sale.

Held. (1) bankruptcy adjudication order affirmed
(2) the proceedings within the High Court were not transferable to the Family Division, but must remain within the Chancery Division
(3) (after further evidence) order for sale varied. Sale of 9 Woodgrange Close deferred until 1985 by which time the two elder children would be over 17 years of age.

GOFF LJ: By an order dated 4 July 1977, Browne-Wilkinson J transferred the bankruptcy proceedings to the High Court, but he refused to consolidate them with the matrimonial proceedings on the ground that he had no jurisdiction to do so, and that is not challenged. Accordingly, we could not, even if asked to do so, make any order under the Matrimonial Causes Act 1973. The most we could do would be to transfer the trustee's summons

---

[14] The final judgment was delivered on the day after *Re Evers' Trust* was heard, and neither case refers to the other. (1980) 77 LSG 288 (A. J. Oakley and D. Marks); [1981] Conv 79 (A. Sydenham); (1981) 97 LQR 200 (C. Hand); (1982) 98 LQR 519 (F. Webb); [1984] Conv 103 (M. P. Thompson).
[15] Now Insolvency Act 1985, ss. 122, 123.

under section 30 of the Law of Property Act 1925 to the Family Division or adjourn it until after the hearing by that division of the wife's application.

I turn now to the second appeal. Where property is held on trust for sale and any person interested desires a sale but that is opposed, then the court has in all cases a discretion whether to order a sale or not, but the exercise of that discretion may be very much limited and controlled by the facts and circumstances of the case.

I shall first consider the position as it was before *Williams v Williams* [1976] Ch 278, [1977] 1 All ER 28, and then consider the impact of that case. Where the property in question is a matrimonial home, then the provision of a home for both parties is a secondary or collateral object of the trust for sale (see per Devlin LJ in *Jones v Challenger* [1961] 1 QB 176 at 181, [1960] 1 All ER 785 at 787) and the court will not ordinarily order a sale if the marriage be still subsisting and no question of bankruptcy has supervened.

Where, however, the marriage has come to an end by divorce or death of one of the parties or is dead in fact, though still subsisting at law, then apart from any question how far the secondary or collateral object can be said to be still subsisting if there are young or dependent children, though there remains a discretion it is one in which, as I see it, some very special circumstances need to be shown to induce the court not to order a sale: see *Jones v Challenger* and *Rawlings v Rawlings* [1964] P 398, [1964] 2 All ER 804.

[His Lordship also referred to *Burke v Burke* [1974] 1 WLR 1063 at 1067, [1974] 2 All ER 944 at 947, p. 227, ante and continued:]

So the question is whether to adopt Salmon LJ's view expressed in *Rawlings v Rawlings* at 419, at 814, that the existence of young or dependent children prolongs the secondary or collateral purpose, or Buckley LJ's view expressed in *Burke v Burke* at 1067, at 947, that the purpose is ended, but the existence of the children is a factor incidentally to be taken into account so far as they affect the equities in the matter as between the persons entitled to the beneficial interests in the property.

With all respect to both the Lords Justices concerned, I would prefer the view of Buckley LJ to that of Salmon LJ because, as Devlin LJ pointed out in *Jones v Challenger* at 184, at 789:

"The conversion of the property into a form in which both parties can enjoy their rights equally is the prime object of the trust; the preservation of the house as a home for one of them singly is not an object at all. If the true object of the trust is made paramount, as it should be, there is only one order that can be made . . . ,"

and in my view the preservation of the house as a home for the children can be no more an object than its preservation as a home for the spouse.

At this stage, however, I must turn to consider *Williams v Williams*. There, according to the headnote, *Jones v Challenger* and *Burke v Burke* were distinguished. When, however, one looks at the judgments it was said that the approach in those cases was outdated: per Lord Denning MR, at 285E–F, at 31 or "a rather narrow, old-fashioned way": per Roskill LJ, at 286F–G, at 31. This seems to me not so much to be distinguishing cases as saying that having regard to modern thinking and circumstances the court should have regard to different considerations in exercising its discretion.

Whether and how far that makes the authorities conflicting I need not pause to consider for *Jones v Challenger* and *Burke v Burke* on the one hand, and *Williams v Williams* and also *Browne (formerly Pritchard) v Pritchard* [1975] 1

WLR 1366, [1975] 3 All ER 721 on the other, are in truth in my judgment distinguishable, since at the time when the first was decided the Matrimonial Proceedings and Property Act 1970 and of course its replacement, the Matrimonial Causes Act 1973, had not been passed, and in the second no argument was based upon those statutes.

The distinction clearly appears in this passage in the judgment of Lord Denning MR in *Williams v Williams* [1976] Ch 278 at 285–286, [1977] 1 All ER 28 at 31:

"The truth is that the approach to these cases has been transformed since the Matrimonial Proceedings and Property Act 1970 and the Matrimonial Causes Act 1973 which have given the power to the court after a divorce to order the transfer of property. In exercising any discretion under section 30 of the Law of Property Act 1925, those Acts must be taken into account. The discretion should be exercised on the principles stated by this court in *Jackson v Jackson* [1971] 1 WLR 1539 at 1543, [1971] 3 All ER 774 at 778. I would add this: An application about a matrimonial home should not be restricted to section 30 of the Law of Property Act 1925. In view of the wide powers of transfer and adjustment which are available under the new matrimonial property legislation it seems to me that the applications should be made to the Family Division under the relevant provisions. If taken out in another division, they should be transferred to a judge of the Family Division. In this very case it seems to me that the right course (which the wife's advisers ought to have taken before) is that they should now, and at once, take out the appropriate application under section 24 of the Matrimonial Causes Act 1973 for any necessary orders and so on to be made with regard to the house and the property. That application should be brought on together with an application under section 30."

Where then the matrimonial jurisdiction is available I would agree that today a spouse wishing to obtain an order for sale should apply to the Family Division and if he or she applies in the Chancery Division the other spouse should apply for an order for transfer to that division and for any ancillary relief he or she may wish to seek under sections 23 and 24 of the Act of 1973. That division may then dispose of the problem by a transfer of property order, or may consider the question of sale in combination with an exercise of its powers under section 23 and section 24, and will have regard to the guidelines laid down in section 25.

I need not consider how the matter will stand if a party applies in the Chancery Division for a sale and the other does not seek ancillary relief, since here the wife has done so.

In my judgment, however, *Williams v Williams* itself is clearly distinguishable from the present and this case falls within *Jones v Challenger* because of the intervention of the trustee in bankruptcy. . . .

The Family Division has no jurisdiction to make an order against him under section 24, because he is not a party to the marriage, and its power to make an order under section 23 against the debtor is at this stage much circumscribed by the fact that he is bankrupt. . . .

It seems to me, therefore, that we ought to decide the present case overselves and not refer it back to the Family Division and that our discretion should be exercised in accordance with the law as established and as I have adumbrated it apart from *Williams v Williams* [1976] Ch 278, [1977] 1 All ER 28; so, as it seems to me, we have to decide this case according to the principle of *Jones v Challenger* [1961] 1 QB 176 at 181, [1960] 1 All ER 785 at 787, as applied by me in the bankruptcy cases *Re Solomon* [1967] Ch 573, [1966] 3 All ER 255; *Re Turner* [1974] 1 WLR 1556, [1975] 1 All ER 5 and *Re Densham* [1975] 1 WLR 1519, [1975] 3 All ER 726. I laid down the relevant principle where there is a bankruptcy in *Re Turner* at 1558C, at 7:

"In my judgment, the guiding principle in the exercise of the court's discretion is not whether the trustee or the wife is being reasonable but, in all the circumstances of the case, whose voice in equity ought to prevail . . . ,"

and I would apply that test to this case. So we have to decide having regard to all the circumstances, including the fact that there are young children and that the debtor was made bankrupt on his own petition, whose voice, that of the trustee seeking to realise the debtor's share for the benefit of his creditors or that of the wife seeking to preserve a home for herself and the children, ought in equity to prevail. In all those cases I held that the trustee must prevail as did the Divisional Court in *Re Bailey* [1977] 1 WLR 278, [1977] 2 All ER 26.

Nevertheless there is a discretion, and I would hear argument according to these principles on the question whose voice in the circumstances of this case ought to prevail, and in this connection it will be necessary to consider the schooling arrangements at present obtaining, and what could be done if the house were sold, but the evidence at present does not cover this very adequately.

While the appeal was stood over to enable further evidence to be filed, GOFF LJ died and this matter was disposed of by BUCKLEY J and Sir David CAIRNS.

SIR DAVID CAIRNS: I agree with Buckley LJ that in all the circumstances here the voice of the wife, on behalf of herself and the children, should prevail to the extent that the sale of the house should be deferred for a substantial period. I reach that view because I am satisfied that it would at present be very difficult, if not impossible, for the wife to secure another suitable home for the family in or near Thorpe Bay; because it would be upsetting for the children's education if they had to move far away from their present schools, even if it were practicable, having regard to the wife's means, to find an alternative home at some more distant place; because it is highly unlikely that postponement of the payment of the debts would cause any great hardship to any of the creditors; and because none of the creditors thought fit themselves to present a bankruptcy petition and it is quite impossible to know whether any one of them would have done so if the debtor had not himself presented such a petition.

Although there is apparently no previous reported case in which the interests of a debtor's family have been held to prevail over those of creditors in a bankruptcy, there have certainly been earlier cases in which family interests have been considered and set against those of the creditors: see *Re Turner* [1974] 1 WLR 1556, [1975] 1 All ER 5, where it was the wife's interest that was considered; and *Re Bailey* [1977] 1 WLR 278, [1977] 2 All ER 26, where it was the interests of a son of the family.

In the earlier cases the trustee has succeeded, because no sufficiently substantial case of hardship of dependants was established. That is where, in my judgment, this case differs from the earlier ones. It may well be, however, that the hardship for the wife and children would be much less, or would have disappeared altogether, in five years' time or possibly even earlier. I therefore agreed that it is appropriate that we should not at this stage defer sale for longer than five years or thereabouts, and that we should leave a loophole for earlier sale to be applied for if the circumstances change in such a way as to warrant it.

In *Cousins v Dzosens* (1981) Times, 12 December[15], Mr D and Miss C had lived together for many years and had an adult son. The quasi-matrimonial home was vested in Mr D, but Miss C was held to be entitled to a third share in equity. On the break-up of the relationship, Mr D left the home and applied for a sale under section 30. Waite QC, sitting as a deputy judge of the Chancery Division, held that the purpose of the trust was deemed to continue beyond the date of the separation of the parties until Miss C could find alternative accommodation. The Axioın Housing Association would be able to house Miss C in eight months time and sale was postponed until then. Waite QC said that: "the discretion which the court was required to exercise under section 30 was a very wide one but guidelines were provided by *Re Buchanan-Wollaston's Conveyance* [1939] Ch 738, [1939] 2 All ER 302; *Jones v Challenger* [1961] 1 QB 176, [1960] 1 All ER 785; *Re Evers' Trust* [1980] 1 WLR 1327, [1980] 3 All ER 399, p. 225, ante; and *Re Holliday* [1981] Ch 405, [1980] 3 All ER 385, p. 229, ante. At first reading those authorities gave an impression of some divergence of view. Mr Speaight contended that the court had no jurisdiction at all to postpone sale, beyond fixing a reasonable period for the plaintiff to pack up and go. Accordingly the court's first task was to decide whether the court did have a discretion in the matter.

His Lordship did not believe the authorities were really in conflict, and thought that while there were differences in language and emphasis, they were really attributable to the choice of language influenced by differing circumstances.

One court might ask itself whether the original trust purpose had wholly failed; another might inquire whose voice in equity should prevail, but in reality the questions were really one and the same. If there was still some outstanding equity to be satisfied, it had necessarily to follow that the trust purposes could not yet have been wholly exhausted, and if the entire purpose of the trust had not yet been accomplished, then there had to be scope for equity to determine whether or not a sale should proceed.

That view depended of course on the notion of a trust being treated flexibly, it being for the judge to say in his discretion in what circumstances the original purpose had been or would be extinguished. In *Hall v Hall*

---

[15] (1982) 98 LQR 519, 523 (F. Webb). See also *Chhokar v Chhokar* [1984] FLR 313 at 327, p. 132, ante (CA refused to order sale where a third party acquired the legal estate by means of a fraudulent conspiracy with the husband, and also refused to order the wife to pay a rent to him. "Is there any room for crocodile tears because his unlawful enterprise did not succeed? I can see no room for giving him anything more than the court in an unreported case gave to the money-lender who had rights over a debtor. The proceedings are recorded in a play of Shakespeare," per CUMMING-BRUCE LJ at 331.

(1981) Times, 4 April the Court of Appeal held that the judge did indeed have exactly such a discretion. The law did not entitle the defendant here to a sale order as of right. The court had to determine whether his voice or the plaintiff's should prevail in equity, or to put it another way, whether the original purpose was to be treated as including a right of the plaintiff to go on living alone in a property bought for the occupation of them both.

After consideration of the pros and cons, his Lordship concluded, on balance, that the equity of the case required the plaintiff to take advantage of Axiom's offer and allow Lawn Avenue to be sold, or expressed another way that the purposes of the particular trust had to be deemed to extend beyond the date of separation to such date as the plaintiff could move to suitable alternative accommodation and would not until then be fully discharged.''

ii. BANKRUPTCY
Cretney, *Principles of Family Law* (4th edn, 1984), pp. 673–674

Bankruptcy Cases

"Many applications under section 30 of the Law of Property Act 1925 are made by one of the parties to a relationship which has broken down; but there is a significant number of reported cases[17] in which the application is made, consequent on the bankruptcy of one partner (say the husband) by his trustee in bankruptcy. The trustee is under an obligation to realise the husband's assets (including his share of the matrimonial home) for the benefit of his creditors[18]; and the court in exercising its discretion is not concerned solely with the interests of the family. This is because it is the policy of the law that a man has an obligation to pay his debts and to pay them promptly, even if this affects his ability to maintain his wife and family[19]. Bankruptcy has its own claim to protection and it is not the case that the trustee will fail in an application to sell merely because the husband would have done so[20]. It has accordingly been held that in exercising its discretion whether or not to order a sale of the family home the guiding principle is not whether the trustee (seeking a sale for the benefit of the creditors) or the wife (seeking to preserve a home for the family) is being reasonable, but rather 'whose voice in equity ought, in all the circumstances to prevail[21]?' The court therefore has to take into account and weigh against each other the conflicting legal and moral claims of the creditors asserted through the trustee in bankruptcy on the one hand and those of the wife on the other[22]. Such a comparison is in its nature very difficult, because the position of the creditors and the wife are hard to compare; and the opinions of individual judges may reasonably differ as to the relative weight of the different considerations in a particular case[1]. The fact that there are young

---

[17] *Re Solomon* [1967] Ch 573, [1966] 3 All ER 255; *Re Turner* [1974] 1 WLR 1556, [1975] 1 All ER 5; *Re Densham* [1975] 1 WLR 1519, [1975] 3 All ER 726; *Re Bailey* [1977] 1 WLR 278, [1977] 2 All ER 26; *Re Holliday* [1981] Ch 405, [1980] 3 All ER 385, p. 229, ante; *Re Lowrie* [1981] 3 All ER 353, p. 236, post.
[18] See generally Williams and Muir Hunter, *Bankruptcy* (19th edn, 1979), pp. 265–266; [1983] Conv 219 (C. Hand).
[19] *Re Bailey*, supra at 284, at 32, per WALTON J.
[20] *Re Holliday*, supra at 419, at 394.
[21] *Re Turner*, supra at 1558, at 7, per GOFF J; approved in *Re Holliday*, supra.
[22] *Re Holliday*, supra at 421, at 395, per BUCKLEY LJ.
[1] *Re Lowrie*, supra at 359, per GOULDING J.

children is a relevant factor in deciding how to exercise the discretion[2]; but the usual result is that a sale will be ordered unless a very substantial degree of hardship to the family or other exceptional circumstances can be shown[3]. In *Re Bailey*[4], for instance, it was held that the wife's claim to stay in the matrimonial home until her son had taken his 'A' level examinations did not outweigh the claims of the husband's creditors to an immediate realisation: and in *Re Lowrie*[5] it was said that the fact that a family (including very young children) would be rendered homeless by the sale was not an exceptional circumstance, but a normal circumstance which was the 'all too obvious result' of a husband having conducted the financial affairs of the family in a way which had led to bankruptcy. It is not the case that the courts will always prefer the claim of the trustee to that of the family, but there appears to be only one reported decision[6] in which the making of an order has been postponed for any length of time, and that decision involved a wholly exceptional set of facts[7]."

INSOLVENCY ACT 1985

Chapter VI

Effect of Bankruptcy on Certain Rights, Transactions Etc.

Rights of occupation

171. Rights of occupation etc. of bankrupt's spouse. — (3) Where a person and his spouse or former spouse are trustees for sale of a dwelling house and that person is adjudged bankrupt, any application by the trustee of the bankrupt's estate for an order under section 30 of the Law of Property Act 1925 (powers of court where trustees for sale refuse to exercise powers) shall be made to the court having jurisdiction in relation to the bankruptcy.

(4) On such an application as is mentioned in subsection . . . (3) above the court shall make such order under the said . . . section 30 as it thinks just and reasonable having regard to the interests of the bankrupt's creditors, to the conduct of the spouse or former spouse so far as contributing to the bankruptcy, to the needs and financial resources of the spouse or former spouse, to the needs of any children and to all the circumstances of the case other than the needs of the bankrupt.

(5) Where such an application is made after the end of the period of one year beginning with the first vesting, under Chapter V of this Part, of the bankrupt's estate in a trustee, the court shall assume, unless the circumstances of the case are exceptional, that the interests of the bankrupt's creditors outweigh all other considerations.

---

[2] *Re Holliday*: the existence of such children does not prolong the "secondary or collateral purpose of the trust for sale".

[3] *Re Holliday*, supra; *Re Lowrie*, supra; and see also *Re Tobman (A Bankrupt)* (1982) Times, 3 March.

[4] See also *Re Turner*, supra.

[5] At 356, per WALTON J.

[6] *Re Holliday*, supra, where sale was postponed for five years, by which time the youngest child would have attained the age of 17.

[7] *Re Lowrie*, supra at 355, per WALTON J.

RE LOWRIE (A BANKRUPT)
[1981] 3 All ER 353 (Div Ct, GOULDING and WALTON JJ)[7a]

In 1974 H and W were married, and H purchased a house in Maidenhead, Berkshire, in his own name as the matrimonial home for £12,000 with a mortgage from the local authority of £11,500. There were two children born in 1977 and 1980. In 1979 H became bankrupt, and £9,600 was needed to pay his debts (other than the mortgage) and the costs of the bankruptcy. H's only asset was the matrimonial home, by then worth £30,000, less £10,000 outstanding under the mortgage.

In 1981 H's trustee in bankruptcy applied for an order for sale under section 30. The county court judge held that the wife was entitled to a half share in the house on the basis of her contributions to the household. He made an order that the house should be sold with vacant possession, but that the sale should be suspended for thirty months. On appeal by the trustee in bankruptcy.

Held. Order for an immediate sale, subject to completion not taking place before three months from the court's decision.

WALTON J: What is the position when a trustee in bankruptcy asks for an order for the sale of property which is held, as the present property is held, on trust for the bankrupt husband and the innocent wife in equal shares? I think that the deputy judge correctly appreciated the drift of what I think all the cases quite uniformly laid down to date when he said in his judgment:

"It is quite right to say that the effect of these cases is that there is a discretion to order a sale, and the fact that there is going to be a sale should be regarded as just and proper because the creditors should in fact be paid. The approach of the court as I understand it is that the trustee has certain presumptions in his favour except in exceptional circumstances. The presumption that there are debts outstanding, a sale should be ordered. A short period of suspension so that the bankrupt and his family should make their arrangements."

I would not, speaking for myself, quarrel with a word of that. But of course one must always look at the whole of the circumstances of the case, and in exceptional circumstances there is no doubt that the trustee's voice will not be allowed to prevail in equity and the sale will not be ordered. A brilliant example of just such a situation is to be found in *Re Holliday* [1981] Ch 405, [1980] 3 All ER 385, p. 229, ante, where the petition in bankruptcy had been presented by the husband himself as a tactical move, and quite clearly as a tactical move, to avoid a transfer of property order in favour of his wife, or ex-wife, at a time when no creditors whatsoever were pressing and he was in a position in the course of a year or so out of a very good income to discharge whatever debts he had. He had gone off leaving the wife in the matrimonial home, which was the subject matter of the application, with responsibility for all the children on her own. One can scarcely, I think, imagine a more exceptional set of facts, and the court gave effect to those exceptional facts.

Before one looks at the conclusion of the judge, since he had rightly in the beginning set out what the law was, I think it is desirable to step back for a moment and look at the situation which must in these cases inevitably occur, or at any rate must occur so frequently as to be almost inevitable. The first one is of course that the whole family are going to be rendered homeless.

[7a] [1982] Conv 374 (A. Sydenham); [1983] Conv 219 (C. Hand).

That is not an exceptional circumstance. It is a normal circumstance and is the result, the all too obvious result, of a husband having conducted the financial affairs of the family in a way which has led to bankruptcy. The second result almost invariably is that it is going to be incredibly hard and incredibly bad luck on the co-owner, the wife, who is in most cases a totally innocent person who has done nothing to bring about the bankruptcy. Of course, as against that, one has to realise that she has been enjoying over whatever period it may be the fruits of the debts which the bankrupt has contracted and which debts are not at the moment being paid. So that although it may be very bad luck on her, she at any rate has had some enjoyment of the fruits which led to the bankruptcy.

That being so, let us now look and see what the judge said:

"I look to see all the circumstances. I of course have very much in mind in cases of a sale the bankrupt comes along and says it is going to be a great hardship. It is not a submission which finds much favour with me as regards [the bankrupt] himself. However, when I look at all the circumstances of the persons who occupy this house my judgment is that I am justified in suspending the order for sale. The position is that the wife has worked throughout the marriage and she had to give up work to look after the children. One of the children has medical treatment and is getting better. The two children are extremely young. It is going to be a situation that [if the wife] were ordered to leave she is going to be in a position that is unenviable: she is not going to be in a good position to get alternative accommodation. She would rely on the resources of the local authority. The local authority will not be sympathetic with a husband earning an income of £9,500. The hope of obtaining accommodation on the private market would in my view be difficult given the fact that there are two young children."

Pausing there, it appears to me that nothing in that circumstance is a matter which is either unusual or of exceptional hardship. Indeed, one can very well see the case that is from time to time put up where the children are going to be interrupted at a sensitive stage in their schooling, for example taking O levels, or more particularly, because O levels or CSE are not in general all that important, when taking their A levels. There the court, I think, has always hitherto been sympathetic if it can be shown that the eviction will necessarily entail the children having to change schools. The court will always be sympathetic to the extent of allowing a year or something of that nature before the order for sale is carried out. But here we are dealing with two young children, children who are going to remain young for a long period and who will still be extremely young even after the expiration of 30 months. And it does not seem to me that so far as such children are concerned there is any grave hardship in their being evicted from a place which they barely recognise at the moment. Then it is said in addition that the bankrupt is going to be in a bad position with regard to raising a loan or mortgage because it is well known that bankrupts are not well regarded by mortgagees. Again, pausing there, that is a universal circumstance. It cannot, even if it can be classified as hardship, be regarded as exceptional hardship. Also one must take into account that the wife throughout this sad episode has shown responsibility. She is the mainstay of this family. That I think is up to a point true in that I think she is the one who is keeping the family together, and indeed the bankrupt very sensibly, and it is a thousand pities that he did not do this before, is now placing the whole of his earnings under the wife's control so that the family will not find themselves in this sort of situation again. But to suggest that she is the mainstay of this family in the sense that she brings in the greater income is palpably not true. On the latest affidavit sworn by her the bankrupt's monthly salary is £650 net and her salary is between £200 and £250 monthly net. . . .

The matter is indeed in some ways ironic. The only reason why either the bankrupt or his wife has an asset of any value is because of inflation taking place steadily since the purchase of the property in the year 1974 and continuing ever since. Apart from that the equity, the difference between the mortgage and the worth of the property, would be very little indeed. At the same time the money which the bankrupt owes to his creditors year by year is steadily diminishing in value as the worth of the property increases, and the princely rate of interest laid down under the bankruptcy legislation of 4% was a rate laid down in times when the value of money was stable, and bears no relation to what is happening today. So the situation undoubtedly is that there will be totally unlooked-for and unnecessary hardship on the creditors if they are kept out of their money for any appreciable length of time. Eighteen months has already elapsed between the date of the order for adjudication and the order of the deputy circuit judge. Of course I suppose the trustee in bankruptcy might have made an application earlier, but he did not do so, and the bankrupt and his wife have had the benefit of the property during all that time.

Looking at the other side of the coin, it seems to me that if a sale is ordered the wife will have in her hands the not inconsiderable sum of £10,000 which should go at any rate some way towards providing for a deposit on another house even if that house has to be obtained on her sole income without the income of her husband. The husband informed us that he had been told that as a bankrupt there would be precious little chance of his obtaining any mortgage. That I can undoubtedly see. But of course if, as I confidently expect, as a result of the sale of the property the whole of his debts are discharged and he obtains a discharge from his bankruptcy the matter may very well be of a totally different complexion thereafter. But be that as it may this is not a case where the family would be being thrown out in the gutter without anything. They will be thrown out as it were with a sum of £10,000 which is, as I have already said, due not to any merit of either of them but due to the passage of time and the rate of inflation that we have been enjoying. But at any rate it is sufficient to ensure that they do not get totally cast out without any resources of any description with which to rehouse themselves.

Therefore it seems to me at the end of the day that the deputy circuit judge went so plainly wrong that this court is in a position to come to a different conclusion. He went wrong because after having correctly cited the approach laid down in all the cases he then did not so frame the remainder of his judgment as to bring himself within the law so laid down, and he did not do so because he treated matters which are as it were, however regrettably, of everyday incidence and occurrence in this type of jurisdiction as if they were exceptional circumstances where none of them in fact were. Therefore for those reasons I would be in favour of allowing the appeal.

iii. ANCILLARY ORDERS

Cratney, *Principles of Family Law* (4th edn, 1984), p. 675

"If the court makes an order for sale, it may if it considers it appropriate impose terms on the parties (for example, that it be not enforced for a period of time). However, there may well be cases in which a sale will be an unsatisfactory result, particularly for the party in occupation. The question therefore arises whether, in order to achieve justice between the parties, the court could refuse to order a sale, but order the one party to grant to the party left in possession a tenancy at an occupation rent. In at least one case[8] the Court of Appeal has made an order for payment of an occupation rent; but it seems very doubtful whether there is any jurisdiction to do so under section 30. This is because, although section 30 empowers the court to 'make such order as it thinks fit' these words only envisage the making of orders ancillary to an order for sale which are necessary to implement such an order[9] (for example, orders that the one party should have the carriage of the sale). The court may, of course, indicate to the defendant that an order for sale *will* be made unless he is prepared to pay an occupation rent[10], but if the other party is not prepared to accept such an undertaking the court probably cannot compel him to do so instead of ordering the sale to which, as a matter of trust law, he is entitled[11]. This unsatisfactory result is one of the consequences of utilising the trust for sale as a conveyancing device, in circumstances to which it is not really appropriate."

IX. Termination of Trusts for Sale[12]

LAW OF PROPERTY ACT 1925

23. Duration of trusts for sale. — Where land has, either before or after the commencement of this Act, become subject to an express or implied trust for sale, such trust shall, so far as regards the safety and protection of any purchaser thereunder, be deemed to be subsisting until the land has been conveyed to or under the direction of the persons interested in the proceeds of sale.

This section applies to sales whether made before or after the commencement of this Act, but operates without prejudice to an order of any court restraining a sale.

---

[8] *Bedson v Bedson* [1965] 2 QB 666, [1965] 3 All ER 307; see particularly, per Lord DENNING MR at 682, at 314; cf. per RUSSELL LJ dissenting; cf. also *Re John's Assignment Trusts* [1970] 1 WLR 955, [1970] 2 All ER 210, where *Bedson* was distinguished on the basis that only an interim order was made in that case.

[9] *Dennis v McDonald* [1981] 1 WLR 810 at 819, [1981] 2 All ER 632 at 640, per PURCHAS J.

[10] Ibid.

[11] *Bernard v Josephs* [1982] Ch 391 at 411, [1982] 3 All ER 162 at 175, per KERR LJ; but cf. generally *Chhokar v Chhokar* [1984] FLR 313. See generally (1980) 132 NLJ 526 (R.E. Annand); (1982) 46 Conv (NS) 305 (J. Martin); Law Commission Working Paper: Trusts of Land No. 94 (1985), paras. 8.10–8.11; p. 311, post.

[12] C & B, p. 761; M & W, p. 397; MM, p. 292.

Law Reform Committee 23rd Report (The Powers and Duties of Trustees) 1982 Cmnd 8733, paras. 5.5–6.

"Termination of Trusts for Sale of Land

5.5 Our attention has been drawn to a particular problem arising out of the law relating to trusts for sale. In general, the device of declaring a trust for sale of land and settling the future proceeds of sale is nowadays used rather than a settlement of the land itself. One important advantage which exists in the case of settled land is, however, that the Settled Land Act 1925 and the Administration of Estates Act 1925 provide specific machinery for the termination of the settlement, whereas no such machinery is provided for the termination of a settlement by way of trust for sale. This means that where the trust for sale comes to an end otherwise than by sale of the land, the trusts of the proceeds have to be brought onto the title in order to show that they are at an end. This is contrary to the general policy of the 1925 legislation of keeping beneficial trusts off the title.

5.6 We suggest that legislation be introduced corresponding to section 36 (7) of the Administration of Estates Act 1925[13] to the effect that a conveyance of a legal estate by trustees for sale not expressly made subject to the trust for sale should, in favour of a purchaser, be taken as sufficient evidence that the person to whom the conveyance is made is entitled to the legal estate conveyed free and discharged from any trust for sale and upon and subject to any other trusts declared or referred to in the conveyance, but should not otherwise prejudicially affect the claim of any other person rightfully entitled to or interested in the estate conveyed, the proceeds of sale thereof or any charge thereon."

X.   Registered Land[14]

Title to land subject to a trust for sale must be registered in the name of the trustees for sale (not exceeding four in number), and the purchaser is informed of the necessity to pay capital moneys to at least two trustees for sale or to a trust corporation by entry of a restriction in Form 62[15] (as amended from the statutory form by the Chief Land Registrar[16]).

LAND REGISTRATION ACT 1925

74.   Notice of trust not to affect registered dealing. — Subject to the provisions of this Act as to settled land, neither the registrar nor any person dealing with a registered estate or charge shall be affected with notice of a trust express, implied or constructive, and references to trusts shall, so far as possible, be excluded from the register.

94.   Land held on trust for sale. — (1) Where registered land is subject to a trust for sale, express or implied, whether or not there is power to

---

[13] See also SLA 1925, s. 17 (3), p. 309, ante; Conv Precedents, pp. 6511–6513.
[14] C & B, p. 199; M & W, pp. 215, 219–220; MM, pp. 294–295; Ruoff and Roper, chap. 20.
[15] P. 241, post.
[16] Ruoff and Roper, p. 380.

postpone the sale, the land shall be registered in the names of the trustees for sale.

95. Restriction on number of trustees. — The statutory restrictions affecting the number of persons entitled to hold land on trust for sale and the number of trustees of a settlement apply to registered land[17].

49. Rules to provide for notices of other rights, interests and claims. — (2) p. 137, ante.

58. Power to place restrictions on register. — (3) In the case of joint proprietors the restriction may be to the effect that when the number of proprietors is reduced below a certain specified number no disposition shall be registered except under an order of the court, or of the registrar after inquiry into title, subject to appeal to the court, and, subject to general rules, such an entry under this subsection as may be prescribed, shall be obligatory unless it is shown to the registrar's satisfaction that the joint proprietors are entitled for their own benefit, or can give valid receipts for capital money, or that one of them is a trust corporation.

(5) Rules may be made to enable applications to be made for the entry of restrictions by persons other than the proprietor[18].

LAND REGISTRATION RULES 1925

Statutory Form 62

Entry restraining a disposition by a sole surviving proprietor

No disposition by one proprietor of the land (being the survivor of joint proprietors and not being a trust corporation) under which capital money arises is to be registered except under an order of the registrar or of the court.

QUESTIONS

1. Having read so far, would you suppose that an interest under a trust for sale:
    (i) passed under a testamentary gift of realty or of personalty? *Re Newman* [1930] 2 Ch 409, p. 246, post.
    (ii) came within LPA 1925, s. 40, requiring evidence in writing of contracts concerning an interest in land? *Cooper v Critchley* [1955] Ch 431, [1955] 1 All ER 520, p. 268, post.
    (iii) was a minor interest if the legal title is registered? *Elias v Mitchell* [1972] Ch 652, [1972] 2 All ER 153, p. 269, post.
    (iv) was an overriding interest if the legal title is registered? LRA 1925, s. 70 (1) (*g*); *Williams and Glyn's Bank Ltd v Boland* [1981] AC 487, [1980] 2 All ER 408, p. 121, ante, p. 270, post.
    (v) was binding on a purchaser of a legal estate for value if in possession, with constructive notice? LPA 1925, s. 27 (2); TA

---

[17] TA 1925, s. 34; LPA 1925, s. 27 (2), p. 219, ante; SLA 1925, ss. 18 (1), 94 (1), pp. 281, 282, post.
[18] See LRR 1925, rr. 235, 236.

1925, s. 14 (1); *Caunce v Caunce* [1969] 1 WLR 286, [1969] 1 All ER 722, p. 255, post.

2. Is it possible to reconcile the different approaches of the Court of Appeal in *Re Evers' Trust* [1980] 1 WLR 1327, [1980] 3 All ER 399, p. 225, ante, and *Re Holliday* [1981] Ch 405, [1981] 3 All ER 385, p. 229, ante. Do you think that the CA in *Re Holliday* would have decided *Re Evers' Trust* differently? *Cousins v Dzosens* (1981) Times, 12 December, p. 233, ante; (1982) 98 LQR 519 (F. Webb); *Chhokar v Chhokar* [1984] FLR 313 at 327, pp. 132, 233, n. 14, ante; *Dennis v McDonald* [1981] 1 WLR 810, [1981] 2 All ER 632.

5. Concurrent Interests After 1925[1]

I. The Scheme of the 1925 Legislation

The sections of the 1925 legislation applicable to concurrent interests are a further manifestation of the basic principles of that legislation. They attempt to· simplify conveyancing by presenting to the purchaser a single title, however numerous and complicated the beneficial interests are, and by applying the overreaching principle to beneficial interests. In short, this is achieved by providing that the only form of co-ownership that can exist *at law* is a form of un-severable joint tenancy such as trustees hold. This is held on trust for sale, and every form of *beneficial* co-ownership can only exist behind the trust for sale.

LAW OF PROPERTY ACT 1925

1. Legal estates and equitable interests. — (6) p. 7, ante.

26. Consents to the execution of a trust for sale. — (3) p. 221, ante.

34. Effect of future dispositions to tenants in common. — (1) An undivided share in land shall not be capable of being created except as provided by the Settled Land Act, 1925[2], or as hereinafter mentioned.

(2) Where, after the commencement of this Act, land is expressed to be conveyed to any persons in undivided shares and those persons are of full age, the conveyance shall (notwithstanding anything to the contrary in this Act) operate as if the land had been expressed to be conveyed to the grantees, or, if there are more than four grantees, to the four first named in the conveyance, as joint tenants upon the statutory trusts hereinafter mentioned

---

[1] C & .B, pp. 207–235; M & W, pp. 417–464; MM, pp. 299–331. For the nature and characteristics of different types of co-ownership, and for the pre-1926 law, see C & B, pp. 210–220; M & W, pp. 417–433, 449–450, 456–462; MM, pp. 299–305. The present chapter assumes an understanding of this material.

[2] SLA 1925, s. 36 (1), (2), p. 245, post.

and so as to give effect to the rights of the persons who would have been entitled to the shares had the conveyance operated to create those shares:

Provided that, where the conveyance is made by way of mortgage the land shall vest in the grantees or such four of them as aforesaid for a term of years absolute (as provided by this Act) as joint tenants subject to cesser on redemption in like manner as if the mortgage money had belonged to them on a joint account, but without prejudice to the beneficial interests in the mortgage money and interest.

(3) A devise bequest or testamentary appointment, coming into operation after the commencement of this Act, of land to two or more persons in undivided shares shall operate as a devise bequest or appointment of the land to the trustees (if any) of the will for the purposes of the Settled Land Act, 1925, or, if there are no such trustees, then to the personal representatives of the testator, and in each case (but without prejudice to the rights and powers of the personal representatives for purposes of administration) upon the statutory trusts hereinafter mentioned.

35.   Meaning of the statutory trusts. — p. 204, ante.

36.   Joint tenancies. — (1) Where a legal estate (not being settled land)[3] is beneficially limited to or held in trust for any persons as joint tenants, the same shall be held on trust for sale, in like manner as if the persons beneficially entitled were tenants in common, but not so as to sever their joint tenancy in equity.

(2) No severance of a joint tenancy of a legal estate, so as to create a tenancy in common in land, shall be permissible, whether by operation of law or otherwise, but this subsection does not affect the right of a joint tenant to release his interest to the other joint tenants, or the right to sever a joint tenancy in an equitable interest whether or not the legal estate is vested in the joint tenants:

Provided that, where a legal estate (not being settled land) is vested in joint tenants beneficially, and any tenant desires to sever the joint tenancy in equity[4], he shall give to the other joint tenants a notice in writing[5] of such desire or do such other acts or things as would, in the case of personal estate, have been effectual to sever the tenancy in equity, and thereupon under the trust for sale affecting the land the net proceeds of sale, and the net rents and profits until sale, shall be held upon the trusts which would have been requisite for giving effect to the beneficial interests if there had been an actual severance.

[Nothing in this Act affects the right of a survivor of joint tenants, who is solely and beneficially interested, to deal with his legal estate as if it were not held on trust for sale.][6]

---

[3] The definition of settled land is the same as that in SLA 1925, s. 1, p. 274, post; *Re Gaul and Houlston's Contract* [1928] Ch 689.

[4] See *Bedson v Bedson* [1965] 2 QB 666 at 678, [1965] 3 All ER 307 at 311; *Re Draper's Conveyance* [1969] 1 Ch 486, [1967] 3 All ER 853, p. 247, post; *Burgess v Rawnsley* [1975] Ch 429, [1975] 3 All ER 142, p. 250, post; *Harris v Goddard* [1983] 1 WLR 1203, [1983] 3 All ER 242, p. 250, n. 19, post.

[5] *Re 88 Berkeley Road, NW 9* [1971] Ch 648, [1971] 1 All ER 254 (notice properly served by recorded delivery, even if not received by addressee); LPA 1925, s. 196 (4); (1971) 87 LQR 155.

[6] The words in square brackets were added by LP (A) A 1926, s. 7 and Sch.

37. Rights of husband and wife. — A husband and wife shall, for all purposes of acquisition of any interest in property, under a disposition made or coming into operation after the commencement of this Act, be treated as two persons.

SETTLED LAND ACT 1925

36. Undivided shares to take effect behind a trust for sale of the land. — (1) If and when, after the commencement of this Act, settled land is held in trust for persons entitled in possession under a trust instrument[7] in undivided shares, the trustees of the settlement (if the settled land is not already vested in them) may require the estate owner in whom the settled land is vested (but in the case of a personal representative subject to his rights and powers for purposes of administration), at the cost of the trust estate, to convey the land to them, or assent to the land vesting in them as joint tenants, and in the meantime the land shall be held on the same trusts as would have been applicable thereto if it had been so conveyed to or vested in the trustees.

(2) If and when the settled land so held in trust in undivided shares is or becomes vested in the trustees of the settlement, the land shall be held by them (subject to any incumbrances affecting the settled land which are secured by a legal mortgage, but freed from any incumbrances affecting the undivided shares or not secured as aforesaid, and from any interests, powers and charges subsisting under the trust instrument which have priority to the trust for the persons entitled to the undivided shares) upon the statutory trusts.

(4) An undivided share in land shall not be capable of being created except under a trust instrument or under the Law of Property Act, 1925, and shall then only take effect behind a trust for sale.

(6) For the purposes of this section land held upon the statutory trusts shall be held upon the trusts and subject to the provisions following, namely, upon trust to sell the same, with power to postpone the sale of the whole or any part thereof, and to stand possessed of the net proceeds of sale, after payment of costs, and of the net rents and profits until sale, after payment of rates, taxes, costs of insurance, repairs, and other outgoings, upon such trusts and subject to such powers and provisions as may be requisite for giving effect to the rights of the persons interested in the settled land, [and the right of a person who, if the land had not been made subject to a trust of sale by virtue of this Act, would have been entitled to an entailed interest in an undivided share in the land, shall be deemed to be a right to a corresponding entailed interest in the net proceeds of sale attributable to that share[8]].

The scheme of the Act is to subject to a trust for sale all forms of concurrent ownership except for joint owners taking as tenants for life, in which case the land remains settled land[9]. The question arises, however, of the position of a form of concurrent ownership which does not come within

---

[7] P. 277, post.
[8] The words in square brackets were added by LP (Entailed Interests) Act 1932, s. 1 (1).
[9] SLA 1925, s. 19 (2), p. 286, post.

the terms of the Law of Property Act 1925, sections 34 and 36[10]. For example, land conveyed in undivided shares to an adult and an infant; or where a tenancy in common exists although the land is not "expressed to be conveyed in undivided shares".

In *Bull v Bull* [1955] 1 QB 234, [1955] 1 All ER 253, land was conveyed to X, the purchase money being paid partly by him and partly by his mother. The Court of Appeal (DENNING, HODSON and PARKER LJJ) treated this as a case of beneficial tenancy in common; the Settled Land Act 1925, section 36 (4) permitted tenancy in common only behind a trust for sale[11].

In *Re Buchanan-Wollaston's Conveyance* [1939] Ch 217 (FARWELL J), *affd* [1939] Ch 738, [1939] 2 All ER 302, a conveyance to purchasers as joint tenants (who provided the purchase money in unequal shares) was treated as coming within the Law of Property Act 1925, section 36 (1), although this does violence to the requirement for the application of that section that the legal estate should be "beneficially limited to . . . persons as joint tenants."

In *Re Kempthorne* [1930] 1 Ch 268[12], the testator, by a will dated 1911, left "all my freehold and copyhold property" to A, and ". . . all my personal estate and effects . . ." to B. He died in 1928, entitled to undivided shares in freehold land and freehold minerals. The Court of Appeal (Lord HANWORTH MR, LAWRENCE and RUSSELL LJJ) held that the undivided shares, being subjected to the statutory trusts by the Law of Property Act 1925, section 36 on 1 January 1926, passed as personalty to B.

A different construction might have been possible if the words of the will had shown an intention to give to A his interests in the freeholds, whatever they might be[13]; and such a construction would be easier to apply if the will were executed after 1925, or, if executed before 1926, was republished by a codicil dated after 1925[14].

II.   Severance[14a]

LAW OF PROPERTY ACT 1925

36.   Joint Tenancies. — (1), (2) p. 244, ante.

The provision in Law of Property Act 1925, section 36 (2) for the severance of equitable joint tenancies by the giving of notice to the other joint tenants was new in 1925; and is additional to other methods of severance.

---

[10] (1945) 9 Conv (NS) 37; (1963) 27 Conv (NS) 51 (B. A. Rudden).
[11] A similar situation arises where a matrimonial home, to whose purchase both spouses contribute, is conveyed to one, p. 252, post.
[12] *Re Newman* [1930] 2 Ch 409.
[13] *Re Mellish* [1929] 2 KB 82n ("All his share and interest in an estate known as the Rushall Estate"); *Re Wheeler* [1929] 2 KB 81n ("My interest in an undivided moiety of the real estate in the county of York").
[14] *Re Warren* [1932] 1 Ch 42 (codicil expressly confirming); *Re Harvey* [1947] Ch 285, [1947] 1 All ER 349 (codicil impliedly confirming).
[14a] See Law Commission Working Paper: Trusts of Land No. 94, paras. 6.11–6.14; p. 311, post.

RE DRAPER'S CONVEYANCE[15]
[1969] 1 Ch 486, [1967] 3 All ER 853 (ChD, PLOWMAN J)

A house was conveyed to a husband and wife as joint tenants. The wife obtained a divorce, and issued a summons under section 17 of the Married Women's Property Act 1882, asking for an order that the house be sold and the proceeds distributed according to the interests of the spouses. The order was made but the husband remained in occupation. The husband died and the question was whether the wife was entitled to the house absolutely by survivorship or whether she and her husband's estate were entitled in equal shares.

Held. The wife held the legal estate on trust for herself and her husband's estate in equal shares.

PLOWMAN J: It is common ground that the answer to the question asked by originating summons in this case depends upon whether a beneficial joint tenancy which subsisted between two persons who were formerly husband and wife in a certain house was severed in the lifetime of the husband. . . . Mr Cooke, on behalf of the defendants, submits that the joint tenancy was severed, and he puts the matter in two ways, either that it was severed by notice in writing, or it was severed by conduct, and in order to explain those submissions I should, I think, refer to section 36 (2) of the Law of Property Act 1925. . . .

Mr Cooke, as I say, puts it in two ways: first, he submits that the wife's conduct was such as to effect a severance of the joint tenancy, and in relation to that matter he relies on the summons of 11 February 1966, in the Probate, Divorce and Admiralty Division, coupled with the orders which were made by that court, coupled with the plaintiff's solicitor's letter of 7 June 1966. And he says, either as a result of those three matters or as a result of any of them, the joint tenancy became severed by conduct, and he referred me to the decision of Havers J in *Hawkesley v May* [1956] 1 QB 304, [1955] 3 All ER 353. The part of that case which is relevant for present purposes depends upon these facts, which I read from the headnote: "A settled fund was held by trustees upon trusts under which on attaining the age of 21 the plaintiff and his younger sister became absolutely entitled as joint tenants." The question was whether that joint tenancy had become severed, and Havers J said:

"The joint tenancy was capable of being severed by the plaintiff on attaining the age of 21. There are a number of ways by which a joint tenancy may be severed. In *Williams v Hensman* (1861) 1 John & H 546 Page Wood V-C, in the course of his judgment, said: 'A joint-tenancy may be severed in three ways: in the first place, an act of any one of the persons interested operating upon his own share may create a severance as to that share[16]. The right of each joint-tenant is a right by survivorship only in the event of no severance having taken place of the share which is claimed under the jus accrescendi. Each one is at liberty to dispose of his own interest in such manner as to sever it from the joint fund — losing, of course, at the same

---

[15] (1968) 84 LQR 462 (PVB).
[16] E.g. by sale or mortgage or settlement of the share; *First National Securities Ltd v Hegerty* [1985] QB 850, [1984] 1 All ER 139, 641 (joint tenancy held to be severed where husband purported to mortgage jointly-owned property by forging wife's signature).

time, his own right of survivorship. Secondly, a joint-tenancy may be severed by mutual agreement. And, in the third place, there may be a severance by any course of dealing sufficient to intimate that the interests of all were mutually treated as constituting a tenancy in common. When the severance depends on an inference of this kind without any express act of severance, it will not suffice to rely on an intention, with respect to the particular share, declared only behind the backs of the other persons interested'."

Havers J continued:

"The first method indicated, namely, an act of any one of the persons interested operating upon his own share, obviously includes a declaration of intention to sever by one party."

Then, after referring to *Walmsley v Foxhall* (1870) 40 LJ Ch 28 he said:

"This being the state of the authorities, I hold that on the plaintiff attaining the age of 21 he was entitled to the income of his share of the fund. As regards the severance, I hold that when the sister wrote the letter dated 18 March 1942, in which she said: 'Thank you for your letter of 17th instant with the particulars of the investments. I should like the dividends to be paid into my account at Martins Bank, 208 Kensington High Street' (which was a letter in reply to the first defendant), that was a sufficient act on her part to constitute a severance of the joint tenancy. If I am wrong about that, there clearly was a severance when her share of the trust funds were transferred to her in September 1942."

So from that case I derive this; a declaration by one of a number of joint tenants of his intention to sever operates as a severance. Mr Cooke also, as I have said, relied upon the notice in writing which under section 36 (2) of the Law of Property Act, 1925, is allowed in the case of a joint tenancy in land, although not in personalty, and he submits that the summons to which I have already referred, although not signed, amounted to a notice in writing on the part of the wife that she desired to sever the joint tenancy in equity. I say "although not signed by the wife or by anybody on her behalf" because there is no requirement in the subsection of a signature.

Dealing with the matter there, and ignoring for a moment certain matters which were submitted by Mr McCulloch, it seems to me that Mr Cooke's submissions are right whether they are based on the new provision in section 36 (2) of the Law of Property Act, 1925, or whether they are based on the old law which applied to severing a joint tenancy in the case of a personal estate. It seems to me that that summons, coupled with the affidavit in support of it, clearly evinced an intention on the part of the wife that she wished the property to be sold and the proceeds distributed, a half to her and a half to the husband. And if that is right then it seems to me that that is wholly inconsistent with the notion that a beneficial joint tenancy in that property is to continue, and therefore, apart from these objections to which I will refer in a moment, I feel little doubt that in one way or the other this joint tenancy was severed in equity before the end of February 1966, as a result of the summons which was served on the husband and as a result of what the wife stated in her affidavit in support of the summons.

But then certain matters were submitted to me by Mr McCulloch on behalf of the wife, which I think fall under two heads. In the first place I was referred to certain observations which were made by Lord Denning MR in *Bedson v Bedson* [1965] 2 QB 666, [1965] 3 All ER 307. That was a case in which a wife, in September 1964, applied to the county court under section

17 of the Married Women's Property Act 1882, for an order that the property together with the fixtures, fittings, car, stock and goodwill be sold, and the proceeds divided between herself and her husband in equal shares. And then the headnote goes on to state that no matrimonial proceedings had at any relevant date been begun.

But Lord Denning in the course of his judgment had certain things to say about the severance of the joint tenancy in the matrimonial home. He said:

"(3) So long as the house is in the possession of the husband and wife as joint tenants or one of them, there can be no severance of their equitable interests: see section 36 (1) (3)." That is a reference to the Law of Property Act 1925. "Neither of them can sell his or her equitable interest separately. If he or she could do so, it would mean that the purchaser could insist on going into possession himself — with the other spouse there — which is absurd. It would mean also that one of them could, of his own head, destroy the right of survivorship which was the essence of the joint tenancy. That cannot be correct."

If I may say so, it is not easy to understand what it is in section 36 (1) and (3) of the Law of Property Act 1925, on which Lord Denning was relying as authority for the proposition that so long as the house is in the possession of the husband and wife as joint tenants or one of them there can be no severance of their equitable interests.

Then Lord Denning MR added:

"One further point: I am of opinion that, while the husband is in possession of the house, there can be no severance of the joint tenancy. The wife cannot sell her interest separately. In case I am wrong about this, I think we should make an order restraining the wife from doing so. It would be quite intolerable that she should, for instance, be able to sell her interest to her mother and get her to turn him out. The jurisdiction in this behalf is amply covered by *Lee v Lee* [1952] 2 QB 489n, [1952] 1 All ER 1299, which has been approved by the House of Lords."

Mr McCulloch points out that in the present case the husband continued in possession until January of 1967 which was some time after the orders of the Divorce court had been made. However, Russell LJ in the same case took a different view about the severance of beneficial joint tenancies. He said:

"I am unable to accept the legal proposition of Lord Denning MR, that when husband and wife are joint tenants of the legal estate in the matrimonial home and also beneficial joint tenants in respect of it, neither can, so long as one is in possession, sell his or her beneficial interest therein or otherwise sever the beneficial joint tenancy. The proposition is, I think, without the slightest foundation in law or in equity. If anything, it appears to be an attempt to revive to some extent the long defunct tenancy by entireties which, as I have already remarked, was doomed by the Married Women's Property Act, 1882, itself. It may indeed be that either the wife's claim in this case, or the notation in the business accounts of the husband of her interest has long since operated as a severance."

If I have to choose between those two statements I respectfully express my preference for that of Russell LJ[17]. It is interesting to note that he referred to the possibility that the wife's claim in that case might have operated by itself

---

[17] See also (1966) 82 LQR 29 (R.E.M.); (1976) 40 Conv (NS) 77 (J. F. Garner).

as a severance, and, as I have already stated, I take the view that in this case the summons issued by the wife in the Divorce Division coupled with the affidavit which she swore in support of that summons did operate to sever her beneficial joint tenancy[18].

BURGESS v RAWNSLEY
[1975] Ch 429, [1975] 3 All ER 142 (CA, Lord DENNING MR,
BROWNE LJ and Sir John PENNYCUICK)[19]

Lord DENNING MR: In 1966 there was a scripture rally in Trafalgar Square. A widower, Mr Honick, went to it. He was about 63. A widow, Mrs Rawnsley, the defendant, also went. She was about 60. He went up to her and introduced himself. He was not much to look at. "He looked like a tramp," she said. "He had been picking up fag-ends." They got on well enough, however, to exchange addresses. His was 36 Queen's Road, Waltham Cross, Hertfordshire. Hers was 74 Downton Avenue, Streatham Hill, London, SW2. Next day he went to her house with a gift for her. It was a rose wrapped in a newspaper. Afterwards their friendship grew apace. She was sorry for him, she said. She smartened him up with better clothes. She had him to meals. She went to his house: he went to hers. They wrote to one another in terms of endearment. We were not shown the letters, but counsel described them as love letters.

A few months later Mr Honick had the opportunity of buying the house where he lived at 36 Queen's Road, Waltham Cross. He had been the tenant of it for some years, but his wife had died and his married daughter had left; so that he was alone there. He talked it over with Mrs Rawnsley. He told her that the owner was willing to sell the house to him for £800. Mrs Rawnsley said she would go half shares: she would have the upper flat and he the lower flat.

[In 1967 they bought the house in their joint names "as joint tenants", each providing half the purchase price. Mr Honick was minded to marry Mrs Rawnsley, but it was clear that she was not minded to marry him. In fact they did not marry and Mrs Rawnsley did not move into the house. There was evidence of an oral agreement between them in 1968 whereby she agreed to sell her share to him for £750 but that she later refused to sell. Mr Honick died and the question was whether his estate was entitled to a half share in the house. In holding that it was, because there had been a severance of the joint tenancy, Lord DENNING MR continued:]

"Was there a severance of the beneficial joint tenancy? The judge said:
'I hold that there has been a severance of the joint tenancy brought about by the conduct of the defendant in asking £750 for her share which was agreed to.'

---

[18] Cf. *Harris v Goddard* [1983] 1 WLR 1203, [1982] 3 All ER 242 (where CA held that a wife's prayer in a divorce petition for a property adjustment order to be made in respect of the former matrimonial home did not operate); [1984] Conv 148 (S. Coneys).

[19] (1975) 39 Conv (NS) 443 (F. R. Crane); [1976] CLJ 20 (D. J. Hayton); (1977) 41 Conv (NS) 243 (S. M. Bandali).

In making that statement the judge made a little slip. She did not ask £750. But it was a slip of no importance. The important finding is that there was an agreement that she would sell her share to him for £750. Almost immediately afterwards she went back upon it. Is that conduct sufficient to effect a severance?

Mr Levy submitted that it was not. He relied on the recent decision of Walton J in *Nielson-Jones v Fedden* [1975] Ch 222, [1974] 3 All ER 38, given subsequently to the judgment of the judge here. Walton J held that no conduct is sufficient to sever a joint tenancy unless it is irrevocable. Mr Levy said that in the present case the agreement was not in writing. It could not be enforced by specific performance. It was revocable and was in fact revoked by Mrs Rawnsley when she went back on it. So there was, he submitted, no severance.

Walton J founded himself on the decision of Stirling J in *Re Wilks* [1891] 3 Ch 59. He criticised *Hawkesley v May* [1956] 1 QB 304, [1955] 3 All ER 353 and *Re Draper's Conveyance* [1969] 1 Ch 486, [1967] 3 All ER 853, and said that they were clearly contrary to the existing well-established law. He went back to *Coke upon Littleton*, 189a, 299b and to *Blackstone's Commentaries*. Those old writers were dealing with legal joint tenancies. *Blackstone* said, 8th edn. (1778), vol. II, pp. 180, 185:

"The properties of a joint estate are derived from its unity, which is fourfold; the unity of interest, the unity of title, the unity of time, and the unity of possession: . . . an estate in joint tenancy may be severed and destroyed . . . by destroying any of its constituent unities."

and he gives instance of how this may be done. Now that is all very well when you are considering how a legal joint tenancy can be severed. But it is of no application today when there can be no severance of a legal joint tenancy; and you are only considering how a beneficial joint tenancy can be severed. The thing to remember today is that equity leans against joint tenants and favours tenancies in common.

Nowadays everyone starts with the judgment of Sir William Page Wood V-C in *Williams v Hensman* (1861) 1 John & H 546, 557, where he said:

"A joint tenancy may be severed in three ways: in the first place, an act of any one of the persons interested operating upon his own share may create a severance as to that share. . . . Secondly, a joint tenancy may be severed by mutual agreement. And, in the third place, there may be a severance by any course of dealing sufficient to intimate that the interests of all were mutually treated as constituting a tenancy in common. When the severance depends on an inference of this kind without any express act of severance, it will not suffice to rely on an intention, with respect to the particular share, declared only behind the backs of the other persons interested. You must find in this class of cases a course of dealing by which the shares of all the parties to the contest have been affected, as happened in the cases of *Wilson v Bell* (1843) 5 I Eq R 501 and *Jackson v Jackson* (1804) 9 Ves 591."

In that passage Page Wood V-C distinguished between severance 'by mutual agreement' and severance by a 'course of dealing.' That shows that a 'course of dealing' need not amount to an agreement, expressed or implied, for severance. It is sufficient if there is a course of dealing in which one party makes clear to the other that he desires that their shares should no longer be held jointly but be held in common. I emphasise that it must be made clear to the other party. That is implicit in the sentence in which Page Wood V-C says:

'it will not suffice to rely on an intention, with respect to the particular share, declared only behind the backs of the other persons interested.'

Similarly it is sufficient if both parties enter on a course of dealing which evinces an intention by both of them that their shares shall henceforth be held in common and not jointly. As appears from the two cases to which Page Wood V-C referred of *Wilson v Bell* (1843) 5 I Eq R 501 and *Jackson v Jackson* (1804) 9 Ves 591.

I come now to the question of notice. Suppose that one party gives a notice in writing to the other saying that he desires to sever the joint tenancy. Is that sufficient to effect a severance? I think it is.

[His Lordship read LPA 1925, section 36 (2), p. 244, ante, and continued:]

The word 'other' is most illuminating. It shows quite plainly that, in the case of personal estate one of the things which is effective in equity to sever a joint tenancy is 'a notice in writing' of a desire to sever. So also in regard to real estate.

Taking this view, I find myself in agreement with Havers J in *Hawkesley v May* [1956] 1 QB 304, 313–314, [1955] 3 All ER 353, 356, and of Plowman J in *Re Draper's Conveyance* [1969] 1 Ch 486, [1967] 3 All ER 853. I cannot agree with Walton J in *Nielson-Jones v Fedden* [1975] Ch 222 at 234–235, [1974] 3 All ER 38 at 48–49, that those cases were wrongly decided. It would be absurd that there should be a difference between real estate and personal estate in this respect. Suppose real estate is held on a joint tenancy on a trust for sale and is sold and converted into personal property. Before sale, it is severable by notice in writing. It would be ridiculous if it could not be severed afterwards in like manner. I look upon section 36 (2) as declaratory of the law as to severance by notice and not as a new provision confined to real estate. A joint tenancy in personal estate can be severed by notice just as a joint tenancy in real estate.

[His Lordship referred to *Nielson-Jones v Fedden* and *Re Wilks* [1891] 3 Ch 59, and continued:]

It remains to apply these principles to the present case. I think there was evidence that Mr Honick and Mrs Rawnsley did come to an agreement that he would buy her share for £750. That agreement was not in writing and it was not specifically enforceable. Yet it was sufficient to effect a severance. Even if there was not any firm agreement but only a course of dealing, it clearly evinced an intention by both parties that the property should henceforth be held in common and not jointly.

On these grounds I would dismiss the appeal[20].

III.   Legal Estate in One Person with Beneficial Interest in Two or More

Complicated situations arise where the legal estate in land is held by one person, but the beneficial interest is held by two or more. Such a case occurs usually, but not exclusively, in the context of the matrimonial home. A

---

[20] Cf. *Greenfield v Greenfield* (1979) 38 P & CR 570 (where the plaintiff failed to establish severance by a course of dealing); *Barton v Morris* [1985] 1 WLR 1257, [1985] 2 All ER 1032 (inclusion of property as a partnership asset in the partnership accounts for tax purposes held not severance by a course of dealing).

number of problems can arise, and it will sometimes be relevant to determine the true nature of the beneficiary's interest. Thus, a husband takes a conveyance, in his own name, of a house which is paid for partly by him and partly by his wife, or where there has been an agreement to hold to joint names[1]. Or, as in *Bull v Bull* [1955] 1 QB 234, [1955] 1 All ER 253, where a house was conveyed to the plaintiff who provided the bulk of the purchase money, but his mother, the defendant, also contributed. The plaintiff married, and he attempted to evict his mother. Or, as in *Barclay v Barclay* [1970] 2 QB 677, [1970] 2 All ER 676, where a trust for sale in a will provided for the sale of a bungalow and division of the proceeds. The sole trustee was a daughter-in-law of the testator. She wished to sell with vacant possession, but one of the beneficiaries, the testator's son, remained in possession throughout.

A. Co-ownership in Equity

In these situations, the first question is whether there is co-ownership in equity of the house. In *Bull v Bull*, there was, because the mother had provided part of the purchase money, and was entitled in equity to a share of the beneficial ownership, which related to her share of the purchase money. Similarly, in the matrimonial situation[2]. A spouse may obtain a beneficial interest by making a contribution directly or indirectly, in money or money's worth, to the purchase price, whether towards the initial deposit[3] or to the mortgage instalments; or by substantially contributing in money or money's worth to the improvement of the property[4]. If some person, other than the legal estate owner, is entitled to a beneficial proprietary interest in the house, there is co-ownership in equity.

B. Statutory Trust for Sale

The next question is whether or not such co-ownership in equity creates a statutory trust for sale. We have seen that the courts are willing to hold that it does; even though the provisions of Law of Property Act 1925, section 34 or section 36 may have to be strained in order to reach this result[5]. Beneficial joint tenancy or tenancy in common can only exist in equity; and we have seen that a tenancy in common can only take effect behind a trust for sale[6].

---

[1] *Caunce v Caunce* [1969] 1 WLR 286, [1969] 1 All ER 722; *Williams and Glyn's Bank Ltd v Boland* [1981] AC 487, [1980] 2 All ER 408.

[2] See generally Cretney, *Principles of Family Law* (4th edn, 1984), chap. 21; Miller, *Family Property and Financial Provision* (2nd edn, 1983) and, where the parties are unmarried, Parker, *Cohabitation* (1981), chaps. 8, 9; Parry, *Cohabitation* (1981), chap. 2; *Burns v Burns* [1984] Ch 317, [1984] 1 All ER 244 (where the parties had lived for 197 days as man and wife but at the end of their relationship had no rights in respect of their common home: "the unfairness of that is not a matter which the courts can control. It is a matter for Parliament", per Fox LJ at 332, at 255); Law Commission 19th Annual Report 1983–1984 (Law Com No. 140 HC 214), para. 2.35; [1984] Conv 381 (S. Coneys); *Bristol and West Building Society v Henning* [1985] 1 WLR 778, [1985] 2 All ER 606, p. 495, n. 7, post.

[3] See Cretney, pp. 644–645.

[4] Matrimonial Proceedings and Property Act 1970, s. 37.

[5] P. 245, ante.

[6] SLA 1925, s. 36 (4), p. 245, ante.

C. Right to Possession Against Trustee

Assuming that there is a trust for sale, express, as in *Barclay v Barclay* [1970] 2 QB 677, [1970] 2 All ER 676, or statutory, a further question is whether the equitable co-owners can remain in possession as against the trustee. In *Bull v Bull* [1955] 1 QB 234, [1955] 1 All ER 253, and in *Barclay v Barclay*, the sole trustee sued for possession. The action failed in the former case because Mrs Bull, it was said, had an interest in the land; but succeeded in the latter because, it was said, the brother-in-law had an interest only in the proceeds of sale[7]. Thus, a conceptual analysis can reach either result. The question is whether a beneficiary under a trust for sale is entitled to possession as against the trustee. Before 1926, this depended very much on the discretion of the trustees.

(1955) 19 Conv (NS) 146, at p. 147 (F. R. Crane)

"Before 1926 beneficiaries with equitable interests in land under trusts were not entitled to possession as of right[8] but only in the discretion of the trustees, duly controlled by the court, which was fairly ready to give possession (see *Re Earl of Stamford and Warrington* [1925] Ch 162, reviewing the earlier authorities). The same rules applied to beneficiaries under trusts for sale (*Re Bagot's Settlement* [1894] 1 Ch 177). . . .

It is therefore respectfully submitted that the law laid down in *Re Bagot* now applies to both express and statutory trusts for sale; beneficiaries are not entitled to possession as of right, though the trustee should give it in proper cases, especially where section 26 (3) of the Law of Property Act applies[9]."

D. Overreaching on Sale

Where a trustee for sale is suing a beneficiary for possession, he usually does so in order to be able to sell with vacant possession. He does not need possession in order to be able to sell. For a sale by trustees for sale over-reaches the interests of the beneficiaries, including the interest of a beneficiary in possession; even if that interest is valid against the trustee's claim for possession, it would have no effect against the purchaser. But, to effect a sale as trustees for sale, there must be at least two trustees[10]. A second trustee therefore needs to be appointed. A sale could then be made; though it would leave the purchaser with the unattractive problem of evicting the remaining beneficiary, and that would reduce the price which could be obtained.

E. Order of Court under Law of Property Act 1925, section 30

The 1925 legislation on co-ownership assumes that the beneficial co-owners (or the first four mentioned) are the trustees[11]. This assumption fails in this

---

[7] At 684, at 678, per Lord DENNING MR. See *Irani Finance Ltd v Singh* [1971] Ch 59 at 79–80, [1970] 3 All ER 199 at 203–204; (1970) 34 Conv (NS) 344 (F. R. Crane).

[8] Nor can one tenant in common claim rent from another who is in possession, unless there is an "ouster"; rent received from a stranger will be shared: *M'Mahon v Burchell* (1846) 2 Ph 127; *Jones v Jones* [1977] 1 WLR 438, [1977] 2 All ER 231; (1978) 41 MLR 208 (J. Alder); *Dennis v McDonald* [1982] Fam 63, [1982] 1 All ER 590.

[9] P. 221, ante. See also [1984] Conv 198 (R. Cocks).

[10] LPA 1925, s. 27, p. 218, ante. See, however, *City of London Building Society v Flegg* (1985) Times, 23 December, p. 128 ante, where, in the case of registered land, CA held that an overriding interest of an equitable tenant in common arising from actual occupation under LRA 1925, s. 70 (1) (*g*), was not overreached by two trustees. This decision runs counter to the whole point of the doctrine of overreaching, and may apply also in the case of unregistered land where the beneficiary is in possession.

[11] LPA 1925, s. 34 (2), p. 243, ante.

type of case because the trust for sale is imposed without, as has been seen, direct statutory language to require it. If the house had been conveyed to the Bulls or the Barclays as joint tenants, or had been expressed to be conveyed in undivided shares, then they would have been the trustees.

They would have to agree upon a sale. If they disagreed, there could be an application to the court under the Law of Property Act 1925, section 30, and on the principles which have emerged in its operation[12].

If there is one trustee for sale only and more than one beneficial owner, as where the legal title is in a husband and he and his wife are beneficial owners, a second trustee for sale should be appointed in order to effect a sale. The wife would be appropriate. But if there is disagreement, she cannot insist on being appointed. She may, however, as a "person interested", apply to the court under Law of Property Act 1925, section 30 for an order for sale.

F. Sale by Single Owner

i. UNREGISTERED LAND

A further problem arises if the sale is made by one trustee only. The overreaching provisions do not apply[13]. This was illustrated in *Caunce v Caunce* [1969] 1 WLR 286, [1969] 1 All ER 722, where a husband and wife agreed that the wife would make a capital payment towards the purchase of a house, that the husband would pay the instalments to the building society, and that the conveyance would be in their joint names. The house was, however, conveyed to the husband alone, and, without the wife's knowledge, he further charged it in favour of Lloyds Bank. On the husband's bankruptcy, one question was whether the bank took subject to, or free from, the wife's equitable interest. STAMP J held that the bank took free, as a bona fide purchaser of a legal estate for value without notice. Thus, in that situation, whether or not a purchaser is bound by the interest of the beneficial co-owner depends upon the application of the old doctrine of the bona fide purchaser without notice[14]. Presumably, if the bank had had notice, actual or constructive, of the wife's interest, the mortgage would have been subject to it; though that assumes that the wife's interest as tenant in common in equity behind a trust for sale is an interest in the land. If it were treated as an interest in the proceeds of sale only, the bank would take free of that interest, even if it had notice.

ii. REGISTERED LAND

This type of situation arises in a different form in the case of registered land. Notice there is irrelevant; or should be. The question is whether the wife has

---

[12] P. 222 et seq., ante.

[13] See *Williams and Glyn's Bank Ltd v Boland* [1979] Ch 312 at 330, [1979] 2 All ER 697 at 703–704, per Lord DENNING MR.

[14] *Caunce v Caunce* was disapproved in *Williams and Glyn's Bank Ltd v Boland* [1981] AC 487, [1980] 2 All ER 408: Lord SCARMAN at 511, at 418 "was by no means certain that *Caunce v Caunce* was rightly decided." So too RUSSELL LJ in *Hodgson v Marks* [1971] Ch 892 at 924–925, [1971] 2 All ER 684 at 690. See the instructive decision of the Eire Supreme Court in *Northern Bank Ltd v Henry* [1981] IR 1 (noted *Emmet on Title*, pp. 180–181) where a bank mortgagee from a husband was held to have constructive notice of resident wife's equitable interest: apart from a deeds registry search, it had made no enquiries or investigation of title. See also (1980) 15 Ir Jur 211 (R. A. Pearce).

an overriding interest under Land Registration Act 1925, section 70 (1) (g)[15].
Such an interest must be in the nature of a proprietary interest "subsisting in
reference to" the land, and not merely in the notional purchase money; and
the spouse claiming it must be in actual occupation. On the first point, Lord
WILBERFORCE said in *Williams and Glyn's Bank Ltd v Boland* [1981] AC 487 at
507, [1980] 2 All ER 408 at 414, p. 126, ante:

"I find it easy to accept that they satisfy the opening, and governing,
words of section 70, namely, interests subsisting in reference to the land. As
Lord Denning MR points out, to describe the interests of spouses in a house
jointly bought to be lived in as a matrimonial home as merely an interest in
proceeds of sale, or rents and profits until sale, is just a little unreal: see also
Elias v Mitchell [1972] Ch 652, [1972] 2 All ER 153, per Pennycuick V-C with
whose analysis I agree, and contrast, *Cedar Holdings Ltd v Green* [1981] Ch
129, [1979] 3 All ER 117, p. 269, n. 1, post (which I consider to have been
wrongly decided)."

In the Court of Appeal [1979] Ch 312, [1979] 2 All ER 697, ORMROD LJ
said at 336, at 709:

"In my judgment, the rights of an equitable tenant in common are not
accurately described as an interest in a sum of money, simpliciter. So long as
the land remains unsold he has the same rights against his co-tenant in
respect of the land as a legal tenant in common before the legislation of 1925
came into effect: *Bull v Bull* [1955] 1 QB 234. Such rights include the right
not to be dispossessed by his co-tenant and the right, if his share is 50 per
cent or more, to prevent the land from being sold, subject to the overriding
power of the court to order a sale, which power may not and will not be
exercised if to do so would defeat the object of the trust: see again Farwell J in
Re Buchanan-Wollaston's Conveyance [1939] Ch 217. In the instant cases the
object of the trust was to provide a joint home and the last thing the parties
contemplated was that the house would be sold and the cash divided between
them.

In converting such a relationship into a trust for sale the legislation of 1925
created, in effect, a legal fiction, at least in so far as the implied trusts are
concerned. This may have been an inescapable consequence of the method
adopted to achieve its primary objective, that is, the simplification of
conveyancing. But to press this legal fiction to its logical conclusion and
beyond the point which is necessary to achieve the primary objective is not
justifiable, particularly when it involves the sacrifice of the interests of a class
or classes of person. The consequence is that the interests of persons in the
position of the wives ought not to be dismissed as a mere interest in the
proceeds of sale except where it is essential to the working of the scheme to do
so.

It follows that in construing this, and other legislation closely connected
with it, it is permissible, and indeed necessary, to construe the relevant
phraseology so as to do the least possible violence to the rights of holders of
equitable interests in the property.

---

[15] P. 117, ante. Interests under a strict settlement can never be overriding interests: LRA 1925, s.
86 (2); (1958) 22 Conv (NS) 14, at pp. 23–24 (F. R. Crane); p. 310, post.

[His Lordship referred to *Irani Finance Ltd v Singh* [1971] Ch 59, [1970] 3 All ER 199, p. 266 post, and *Elias v Mitchell* [1972] Ch 652, [1972] 2 All ER 153, p. 269 post, and continued:]

In the present case the relevant words (combining paragraph (g) and the opening words of section 70 (1)) are 'Rights subsisting in reference to registered land.' In my judgment, these words are apt to include the interests of a co-owner or equitable tenant in common whose rights are not fully described, for reasons already stated, as an interest in the proceeds of sale."

G. Right of Occupation. Matrimonial Homes Act 1983

A wife however has a further means of protection. She may rely, not upon her ownership, but upon the statutory right of occupation given to a spouse under the Matrimonial Homes Act 1983, section 1[17]. She may protect this against purchasers by registration of a land charge. Class F in the case of unregistered land. With registered land, the right must be protected by entry of a notice[18]. In these situations, that is to say, in respect of the statutory protection given to the wife under the Matrimonial Homes Act 1983, all depends on following the correct procedure for protection. Failure to register or to protect by notice involves the loss of the right against a purchaser. But the loss of that right still leaves open any claim which the wife may have in respect of her beneficial ownership.

MATRIMONIAL HOMES ACT 1983[19]

1. Rights concerning matrimonial home where one spouse has no estate, etc. — (1) Where one spouse is entitled to occupy a dwelling house by virtue of a beneficial estate or interest or contract or by virtue of any enactment[20] giving him or her the right to remain in occupation, and the

---

[17] Consolidating Matrimonial Homes Act 1967, as amended by Matrimonial Proceedings and Property Act 1970, s. 38, Domestic Violence and Matrimonial Proceedings Act 1976, ss. 3 and 4 and Matrimonial Homes and Property Act 1981. See *Richards v Richards* [1984] AC 174 at 217–221, [1983] 2 All ER 807 at 826–829, per Lord BRANDON of OAKBROOK; Law Commission 19th Annual Report 1983–1984 (Law Com No. 140 HL 214), para. 2.35: "With regard to the courts' power to adjust the parties' respective rights of occupation, we have noted the observation of Lord SCARMAN in *Richards v Richards* at 207, at 818 that 'the sooner the range, scope and effect of these powers are rationalised into a coherent and comprehensive body of statute law, the better' ".

In 1977–78 there were 10,687 applications to register Class F land charges, and a further 6,300 or so applications in respect of registered land. Figures for subsequent years relating to registered land are not available. In 1984–1985 there were 5,873 registrations against unregistered land. Cretney, p. 259 n. 93; Annual Report of Chief Land Registrar 1984–1985, para. 47; Law Commission Report Implications of *Williams and Glyn's Bank Ltd v Boland* 1982 (Law Com No. 115, Cmnd 8636) p. 34, n. 190.

[18] It cannot be an overriding interest under LRA 1925, s. 70 (1) (g), even if the spouse is in actual occupation. The difference between a wife who has an equitable interest (protected as an overriding interest: *Williams and Glyn's Bank Ltd v Boland* [1981] AC 487, [1980] 2 All ER 408) and a wife who has only her rights of occupation under the Act is therefore considerable.

[19] Bromley, *Family Law* (6th edn, 1981), pp. 456–469; Cretney, *Principles of Family Law* (4th edn, 1984), pp. 243–262; (1968) 32 Conv (NS) 85 (F. R. Crane); *Wroth v Tyler* [1974] Ch 30, [1973] 1 All ER 897. See Law Commission Third Report on Family Property 1978 (Law Com No. 86, HC 450), pp. 241–334.

[20] E.g. Rent Act 1977; *Penn v Dunn* [1970] 2 QB 686, [1970] 2 All ER 858.

other spouse is not so entitled, then, subject to the provisions of this Act, the spouse not so entitled shall have the following rights (in this Act referred to as "rights of occupation") —

> (a) if in occupation, a right not to be evicted or excluded from the dwelling house or any part thereof by the other spouse except with the leave of the court given by an order under this section;
>
> (b) if not in occupation[1], a right with the leave of the court so given to enter into and occupy the dwelling house[2].

(2) So long as one spouse has rights of occupation, either of the spouses may apply to the court for an order —

> (a) declaring, enforcing, restricting or terminating those rights, or
>
> (b) prohibiting, suspending or restricting the exercise by either spouse of the right to occupy the dwelling house, or
>
> (c) requiring either spouse to permit the exercise by the other of that right.

(3) On an application for an order under this section, the court may make such order as it thinks just and reasonable having regard to the conduct of the spouses in relation to each other and otherwise, to their respective needs and financial resources, to the needs of any children and to all the circumstances of the case[3]. . . .

(5) Where a spouse is entitled under this section to occupy a dwelling house or any part thereof, any payment or tender made or other thing done by that spouse in or towards satisfaction of any liability of the other spouse in respect of rent, rates, mortgage payments or other outgoings affecting the dwelling house shall, whether or not it is made or done in pursuance of an order under this section, be as good as if made or done by the other spouse.

(10) This Act shall not apply to a dwelling house which has at no time been a matrimonial home of the spouses in question; and a spouse's rights of occupation shall continue only so long as the marriage subsists and the other spouse is entitled as mentioned in subsection (1) above to occupy the dwelling house, except where provision is made by section 2 of this Act for those rights to be a charge on an estate or interest in the dwelling house.

(11) It is hereby declared that a spouse who has an equitable interest in a dwelling house or in the proceeds of sale thereof, not being a spouse in whom is vested (whether solely or as a joint tenant) a legal estate in fee simple or a legal term of years absolute in the dwelling house, is to be treated for the purpose only of determining whether he or she has rights of occupation under this section as not being entitled to occupy the dwelling house by virtue of that interest.

2. Effect of rights of occupation as charge on dwelling house. — (1) Where, at any time during the subsistence of a marriage, one spouse is entitled to occupy a dwelling house by virtue of a beneficial

---

[1] *Hoggett v Hoggett* (1979) 39 P & CR 121 at 127.

[2] *Watts v Waller* [1973] QB 153, [1972] 3 All ER 257 (spouse out of occupation can register before getting leave of court to re-enter); *Barnett v Hassett* [1981] 1 WLR 1385, [1982] 1 All ER 80 (spouse having no intention to occupy not permitted to register in attempt to freeze proceeds of intended sale).

[3] These criteria apply equally to applications under the Domestic Violence and Matrimonial Proceedings Act 1976 for ouster orders: *Richards v Richards*, supra. They are also applicable under that Act where the parties are unmarried: *Lee v Lee* [1984] FLR 243.

estate or interest, then the other spouse's rights of occupation shall be a charge on that estate or interest, having the like priority as if it were an equitable interest created at whichever is the latest of the following dates, that is to say —

(*a*) the date when the spouse so entitled acquires the estate or interest,

(*b*) the date of the marriage, and

(*c*) the 1st January 1968 (which is the date of commencement of the Act of 1967).

(2) If, at any time when a spouse's rights of occupation are a charge on an interest of the other spouse under a trust, there are, apart from either of the spouses, no persons, living or unborn, who are or could become beneficiaries under the trust, then those rights shall be a charge also on the estate or interest of the trustees for the other spouse, having the like priority as if it were an equitable interest created (under powers overriding the trusts) on the date when it arises.

(3) In determining for purposes of subsection (2) above whether there are any persons who are not, but could become, beneficiaries under the trust, there shall be disregarded any potential exercise of a general power of appointment exercisable by either or both of the spouses alone (whether or not the exercise of it requires the consent of another person).

(4) Notwithstanding that a spouse's rights of occupation are a charge on an estate or interest in the dwelling house, those rights shall be brought to an end by —

(*a*) the death of the other spouse, or

(*b*) the termination (otherwise than by death) of the marriage,

unless in the event of a matrimonial dispute or estrangement the court sees fit to direct otherwise by an order made under section 1 above during the subsistence of the marriage . . .[4]

(7) Where a spouse's rights of occupation are a charge on the estate or interest of the other spouse or of trustees for the other spouse, and the other spouse —

(*a*) is adjudged bankrupt or makes a conveyance or assignment of his or her property (including that estate or interest) to trustees for the benefit of his or her creditors generally, or

(*b*) dies and his or her estate is insolvent,

then, notwithstanding that it is registered under section 2 of the Land Charges Act 1972[4] or subsection (8) below, the charge shall be void against the trustee in bankruptcy, the trustees under the conveyance or assignment or the personal representatives of the deceased spouse, as the case may be.

(8) Where the title to the legal estate by virtue of which a spouse is entitled to occupy a dwelling house (including any legal estate held by trustees for that spouse) is registered under the Land Registration Act 1925 or any enactment replaced by that Act —

(*a*) registration of a land charge affecting the dwelling house by virtue of this Act shall be effected by registering a notice under that Act[5], and

---

[4] On the rights of a bankrupt spouse, see now Insolvency Act 1985, s. 171, p. 262, post.

[5] *Miles v Bull (No. 2)* [1969] 3 All ER 1585 (where wife failed to register right of occupation purchaser with notice took free under LRA 1925, s. 20 (1), pp. 110, 145, ante). Cf. *Lyus v Prowsa Developments Ltd* [1982] 1 WLR 1044, [1982] 2 All ER 953, p. 146, ante.

(*b*) a spouse's rights of occupation shall not be an overriding interest within the meaning of that Act affecting the dwelling house notwithstanding that the spouse is in actual occupation of the dwelling house.

(9) A spouse's rights of occupation (whether or not constituting a charge) shall not entitle that spouse to lodge a caution under section 54 of the Land Registration Act 1925[6].

(10) Where —

(*a*) a spouse's rights of occupation are a charge on the estate of the other spouse or of trustees for the other spouse, and

(*b*) that estate is the subject of a mortgage within the meaning of the Law of Property Act 1925[7],

then, if, after the date of creation of the mortgage, the charge is registered under section 2 of the Land Charges Act 1972, the charge shall, for the purposes of section 94[8] of that Act of 1925 (which regulates the rights of mortgagees to make further advances ranking in priority to subsequent mortgages), be deemed to be a mortgage subsequent in date to the first-mentioned mortgage.

(11) It is hereby declared that a charge under subsection (1) or (2) above is not registrable under section 2 of the Land Charges Act 1972 or subsection (8) above unless it is a charge on a legal estate.

6. Release of rights of occupation and postponement of priority of charge.

— (1) A spouse entitled to rights of occupation may by a release in writing release those rights or release them as respects part only of the dwelling house affected by them[9].

(3) A spouse entitled by virtue of section 2 above to a charge on an estate or interest may agree in writing that any other charge on, or interest in, that estate or interest shall rank in priority to the charge to which that spouse is so entitled.

8. Dwelling house subject to mortgage.

— (1) In determining for the purposes of the foregoing provisions of this Act (including Schedule 1) whether a spouse or former spouse is entitled to occupy a dwelling house by virtue of an estate or interest, there shall be disregarded any right to possession of the dwelling house conferred on a mortgagee of the dwelling house under or by virtue of his mortgage, whether the mortgagee is in possession or not; but the other spouse shall not by virtue of the rights of occupation conferred by this Act have any larger right against the mortgagee to occupy the dwelling house than the one first mentioned has by virtue of his or her estate or interest and of any contract with the mortgagee, unless under section 2 above those rights of occupation are a charge, affecting the mortgagee, on the estate or interest mortgaged.

(2) Where a mortgagee of land which consists of or includes a dwelling house brings an action in any court for the enforcement of his security, a

---

[6] P. 139, ante. The land certificate need not be produced: LRA 1925, s. 64 (5). Until the Matrimonial Homes and Property Act 1981, registration was by a notice or a caution. Land Registration (Matrimonial Homes) Rules 1983 (SI 1983 No. 40).

[7] Pp. 655, et seq, post.

[8] P. 739, post.

[9] *Holmes v H Kennard & Son* (1984) 49 P & CR 202; [1985] Conv 293 (N.S. Price), where purchaser's solicitors were held liable in negligence for failure to obtain release of vendor's wife's right of occupation by correct conveyancing procedure.

spouse who is not a party to the action and who is enabled by section 1 (5) or
(8) above to meet the mortgagor's liabilities under the mortgage, on applying
to the court at any time before the action is finally disposed of in that court,
shall be entitled to be made a party to the action if the court —

   (*a*) does not see special reason against it, and

   (*b*) is satisfied that the applicant may be expected to make such
      payments or do such things in or towards satisfaction of the
      mortgagor's liabilities or obligations as might affect the outcome of
      the proceedings or that the expectation of it should be considered
      under section 36 of the Administration of Justice Act 1970[10].

   (3) Where a mortgagee of land which consists or substantially consists of a
dwelling house brings an action for the enforcement of his security, and at the
relevant time there is —

   (*a*) in the case of unregistered land, a land charge of Class F registered
      against the person who is the estate owner at the relevant time or
      any person who, where the estate owner is a trustee, preceded him
      as trustee during the subsistence of the mortgage, or

   (*b*) in the case of registered land, a subsisting registration of a notice
      under section 2 (8) above or a notice or caution under section 2 (7)
      of the Act of 1967,

notice of the action shall be served by the mortgagee on the person on whose
behalf the land charge is registered or the notice or caution entered, if that
person is not a party to the action[11].

   (4) For the purposes of subsection (3) above, if there has been issued a
certificate of the result of an official search made on behalf of the mortgagee
which would disclose any land charge of Class F, notice or caution within
subsection (3) (*a*) or (*b*) above, and the action is commenced within the
priority period, the relevant time is the date of that certificate; and in any
other case the relevant time is the time when the action is commenced.

   (5) In subsection (4) above, "priority period" means, for both registered
and unregistered land, the period for which, in accordance with section 11
(5) and (6) of the Land Charges Act 1972[12], a certificate on an official search
operates in favour of a purchaser.

**9. Rights concerning matrimonial home where both spouses have
estate, etc.** — (1) Where each of two spouses is entitled, by virtue of a legal
estate vested in them jointly, to occupy a dwelling house in which they have
or at any time have had a matrimonial home, either of them may apply to the
court, with respect to the exercise during the subsistence of the marriage of
the right to occupy the dwelling house, for an order prohibiting, suspending
or restricting its exercise by the other or requiring the other to permit its
exercise by the applicant.

   (2) In relation to orders under this section, section 1 (3), (4) and (9) above
shall apply as they apply in relation to orders under that section.

   (3) Where each of two spouses is entitled to occupy a dwelling house by
virtue of a contract, or by virtue of any enactment giving them the right to
remain in occupation, this section shall apply as it applies where they are
entitled by virtue of a legal estate vested in them jointly.

---

[10] P. 695, post.

[11] The mortgagee is entitled to search without authority from the registered proprietor: LRA
1925, s. 112B, p. 116, ante.

[12] P. 31, n. 8, ante.

(4) In determining for the purposes of this section whether two spouses are entitled to occupy a dwelling house, there shall be disregarded any right to possession of the dwelling house conferred on a mortgagee of the dwelling house under or by virtue of his mortgage, whether the mortgagee is in possession or not.

INSOLVENCY ACT 1985

171.   Rights of occupation etc. of bankrupt's spouse. — (2) Where a spouse's rights of occupation under the said Act of 1983 are a charge on the estate or interest of the other spouse or of trustees for the other spouse and the other spouse is adjudged bankrupt —

(*a*) the charge shall continue to subsist notwithstanding the bankruptcy and, subject to the provisions of that Act, shall bind the trustee of the bankrupt's estate and persons deriving title under that trustee; and

(*b*) any application for an order under section 1 of that Act shall be made to the court having jurisdiction in relation to the bankruptcy.

In *Wroth v Tyler* [1974] Ch 30, [1973] 1 All ER 897, MEGARRY J said at 46, at 909: "At this stage I may summarise my conclusions as to the essentials of the right given by the Act to an occupying spouse as follows. The right is in essence a personal and non-assignable statutory right not to be evicted from the matrimonial home in question during marriage or until the court otherwise orders; and this right constitutes a charge on the estate or interest of the owning spouse which requires protection against third parties by registration. For various reasons, the right may be said to be one which readily fits into no category known to conveyancers before 1967; the phrase sui generis seems apt, but of little help."

H.   Law Reform

Cheshire and Burn, *Modern Law of Real Property* (13th edn, 1982), pp. 233–234.

"The Law Commission Third Report on Family Property 1978 (Law Com No. 86, HC 450)[13] proposes automatic statutory co-ownership of the matrimonial home, whereby, subject to various exceptions, it is to be held upon trust for sale for both spouses as beneficial joint tenants[14]. Thus a wife (or husband) who, under the existing law, owns less than a half share (or has no proprietary interest at all in the home) will acquire an equitable interest equal to that of her husband.

'The present law about the ownership of the matrimonial home during marriage is not only highly technical and sometimes uncertain in application, but inappropriate in substance. The rules now applied to determine the ownership of the home are essentially the same as those which determine the ownership of a commercial investment property; they ignore the fact that the home is the residence of a family as well as being, in many cases, its major capital asset. Husband and wife each contribute to the home in their different ways — the wife's contributions are no less real because they may not be

---

[12a] Replacing Matrimonial Homes Act 1983, s. 7, which was repealed by Insolvency Act 1985, s. 235, Sch. 10, Part III.

[13] The scheme, which applies only to married couples, was previously proposed in the First Report on Family Property (1973) (Law Com No. 52, HC 274).

[14] Para. 1. See [1978] Conv 194 (H. Forrest).

financial — and the home is essential to the well-being of the family as a whole. In our view these factors make the matrimonial home a unique item of property, and one to which a unique law of co-ownership should apply[15]'.

Under the new proposals, the wife will not automatically acquire the legal estate, but may apply for it to be vested in joint names. While the legal estate remains vested in one spouse only, he or she will be unable to dispose of the property unless the other spouse consents. Subject to the registration provisions mentioned below, any disposition entered into without the spouse's consent will be of no effect.

In the case of unregistered land, the 'acquiring' spouse's equitable interest under the trust for sale is to be protected by a new Class G land charge. This will also ensure that the purchaser complies with the rule requiring payment to two trustees for sale, and with the consent requirement mentioned above. The charge fails against a purchaser of any interest unless registered by completion. If not so registered the purchaser will take free of the spouse's interest even if there is only one trustee for sale and no consent. The proposed Class G land charge is to be confined to spouses, the general law continuing to apply to other co-owners.

In the case of registered land, the equivalent protection is to be the entry of a restriction, which will not, however, require production of the land certificate[16]."

In 1979 Lord SIMON OF GLAISDALE introduced the Matrimonial Homes (Co-ownership) Bill into the House of Lords for giving effect to the Law Commission's proposals, but it was not enacted. It now appears that the scheme will not be put into effect in the foreseeable future, especially since the Family Law (Scotland) Act 1985 implements the Report of the Scottish Law Commission on Matrimonial Property 1984 (Scot Law Com No. 86, HC 467), which recommended against any scheme for automatic co-ownership of the matrimonial home. Furthermore the Law Commission Report on *The Implications of Williams and Glyn's Bank Ltd v Boland* 1982 (Law Com No. 115, Cmnd 8636) appears to have been rejected, and the controversial Land Registration and Law of Property Bill which was introduced into the House of Lords in 1985, restricting protection under Land Registration Act 1925, s. 70 (1) (*g*), p. 134, ante, to spouses only, was withdrawn.

IV. Conveyance to Joint Tenants, One of Whom Dies

From the purchaser's position, this situation is the converse of that in the previous section. If land were conveyed to A and B as joint tenants a purchaser would see that a trust for sale was created by virtue of Law of Property Act 1925, section 36. He would therefore expect to deal with two trustees and to hand the purchase money over to them[17]. Suppose A dies. The absence of two trustees was met, as has been seen[18] by the addition to section 36 of the words: "Nothing in this Act affects the right of a survivor of joint

---

[15] Para. 0.9.
[16] Where there is no such entry, the report recommends that the owner of a trust for sale (or settlement) will not have an overriding interest under LRA, s. 70 (1) (*g*) even if in occupation. This is at variance with the decision of the House of Lords in *Williams and Glyn's Bank Ltd v Boland* [1981] AC 487, [1980] 2 All ER 408.
[17] LPA 1925, s. 27, p. 218, ante.
[18] See p. 244, ante.

tenants, who is solely and beneficially interested, to deal with his legal estate as if it were not held on trust for sale." The successor, B, will only be "solely and beneficially interested" if he remains a joint tenant until A's death; and he can only satisfy the purchaser of this by establishing the negative proposition that there has been no severance of the joint tenancy in equity. This problem is dealt with, as will be seen, by the Law of Property (Joint Tenants) Act 1964.

RE COOK

[1948] Ch 212, [1948] 1 All ER 231 (ChD, HARMAN J)

Before 1926 a freehold house was conveyed to H and W as joint tenants. H died in January 1944 and W, by her will made in March 1944, left "all my personal estate" to her nephews and nieces, and died in September 1944 still possessed of the house.

The question was whether the house passed under the gift of personalty in the will.

Held. Although the freehold was subjected to a trust for sale on 1 January 1926 under the Law of Property Act 1925, section 36, it was reconverted to its natural state on the death of H and did not pass as personalty under the will of W.

HARMAN J: The question to be decided is this: Did the trust for sale imposed by section 36 come to an end on the husband's death? After that date there is no doubt that the entire interest in the property, both legal and equitable, became vested in the testatrix. It is said by Mr Danckwerts for the Custodian of Enemy Property that, according to the ordinary and well-known rule in *Re Selous* [1901] 1 Ch 921 per Farwell J, the legal estate swallows up the equitable, that there is a merger between the two, and that from January, 1944, onwards the testatrix was merely the owner of this property and no trust for sale could exist, because A cannot be trustee for A. I think Mr Alcock, who argued on behalf of the beneficiaries under the will of the testatrix, would admit that to be so if this were anything but what is known as a statutory trust, but he submits that, this trust being the creature of statute, statute must put an end to it and without any statutory ending it goes on, and he points out that under section 23 of the Law of Property Act 1925, a trust for sale may, at any rate so far as protection of a purchaser is concerned, be deemed to go on indefinitely. Even so, I think he would be in great difficulty but for the addition to section 36 of the Law of Property Act 1925 made by the Law of Property (Amendment) Act 1926 in these terms: "Nothing in this Act affects the right of a survivor of joint tenants, who is solely and beneficially interested" — that is the position of the testatrix in this case — "to deal with his legal estate as if it were not held on trust for sale".

Mr Alcock argues, and I think with force, that the inference from that is inevitable, namely, that the legal estate is held on trust for sale, although the owner of it is given leave by the Act to deal with it as if it were not. If that were the true meaning of it, he says it follows that a trust for sale still does affect the property until it is dealt with in some way inconsistent with that position. I feel the force of that, but I do not think it is enough to alter the view which I should have taken if it were not there. This sentence is an afterthought introduced into the Act ex cautela because of some danger, real or imaginary, that was thought to exist after the Act of 1925 had come into force, and in my judgment it is not enough to alter the prima facie rule that you cannot have a trust existing when nobody is interested under it except the trustee, because nobody can enforce it and there is, in fact, no trust in existence.

I get some assistance also from section 36, subsection 1 itself, because there are found the words "shall be held on trust for sale, in like manner as if the persons beneficially entitled were tenants in common". As soon as only one person is beneficially entitled there are no persons who would be tenants in common, because there is only one person interested. The phrase "persons beneficially entitled" must, as Mr Freeman submitted to me, mean what it says, namely, "persons", in the plural, and therefore the subsection does not apply as soon as there is but one person interested in the entirety of the property. Consequently, I hold that upon the death of the husband the testatrix became the absolute owner of this property and there was no trust for sale subsisting beyond that date. . . .

If I am right so far, this property was at the time of her will and at the time of her death real estate to which she was entitled in fee simple. . . . It may well be that she thought "personal estate" meant "all my worldly goods"; I do not know. In the absence of something to show that the phrase ought not to be so construed, I must suppose that she used the term "personal estate" in its ordinary meaning as a term of art. Consequently, I hold that the testatrix only succeeded in disposing of what the lawyers would call her "personal estate" and she did not dispose of this house, . . . which therefore devolves as on an intestacy.

LAW OF PROPERTY (JOINT TENANTS) ACT 1964[19]

1. Assumptions on sale of land by survivor of joint tenants. — (1) For the purposes of section 36 (2) of the Law of Property Act 1925, as amended by section 7 of and the Schedule to the Law of Property (Amendment) Act 1926, the survivor of two or more joint tenants shall in favour of a purchaser of the legal estate, be deemed to be solely and beneficially interested if he conveys as beneficial owner or the conveyance includes a statement that he is so interested.

Provided that the foregoing provisions of this subsection shall not apply if, at any time before the date of the conveyance by the survivor —

(*a*) a memorandum of severance (that is to say a note or memorandum signed by the joint tenants or one of them and recording that the joint tenancy was severed in equity on a date therein specified) had been endorsed on or annexed to the conveyance by virtue of which the legal estate was vested in the joint tenants; or

(*b*) a bankruptcy order[20] made against any of the joint tenants, or a petition for such an order, had been registered under the Land Charges Act 1925[1], being an order or petition of which the purchaser has notice, by virtue of the registration, on the date of the conveyance by the survivor.

---

[19] W & C, vol. 2, pp. 149–151; (1964) 28 Conv (NS) 329; (1966) 30 Conv (NS) 27 (P. Jackson).
[20] As amended by Insolvency Act 1985, s. 235, Sch. 8, para. 13.
[1] Now LCA 1972.

(2) The foregoing provisions of this section shall apply with the necessary modifications in relation to a conveyance by the personal representatives of the survivor of joint tenants as they apply in relation to a conveyance by such a survivor.

2.   Retrospective and transitional provisions. — Section 1 of this Act shall be deemed to have come into force on 1st January 1926, and for the purposes of that section in its application to a conveyance executed before the passing of this Act a statement signed by the vendor or by his personal representatives that he was solely and beneficially interested shall be treated as if it had been included in the conveyance.

3.   Exclusion of registered land. — This Act shall not apply to any land the title of which has been registered under the provisions of the Land Registration Acts 1925 and 1936.

V.   Nature of Interests of Beneficiaries under a Trust for Sale

As we have seen[2], the doctrine of conversion applies as soon as a trust for sale comes into operation; the interests of the beneficiaries are thus automatically interests in the proceeds of sale of land and not in the land itself. CROSS LJ said in *Irani Finance Ltd v Singh* [1971] Ch 59 at 80, [1970] 3 All ER 199 at 204: "The whole purpose of the trust for sale is to make sure, by shifting the equitable interests away from the land and into the proceeds of sale, that a purchaser of the land takes free from the equitable interests. To hold these to be equitable interests in the land itself would be to frustrate this purpose. Even to hold that they have equitable interests in the land for a limited period, namely, until the land is sold, would, we think, be inconsistent with the trust for sale being an 'immediate' trust for sale working an immediate conversion, which is what the Law of Property Act, 1925, envisages (see section 205 (1) (xxix))[3]."

But this view has given rise to difficulties and in certain situations it has been found undesirable to apply the full logic of the doctrine of conversion.

A.   General[4]

(1971) 34 MLR 441 (S. M. Cretney)

"A beneficiary under a trust for sale of land can be said to have an interest in the land itself at least in the following ways. (1) He may, with the concurrence of the other beneficiaries, compel the transfer of the land to himself[5]. (2) If the trust is imposed by law, he has a right to be consulted by the trustees as to the exercise of their powers over the land; they are obliged

---

[2] Pp. 203, 205, ante.

[3] P. 207, ante.

[4] See also [1971] CLJ 44 (M. J. Prichard); [1978] Conv 194 (H. Forrest); [1981] Conv 108 (A. E. Boyle). See generally (1984) 100 LQR 86 (S. Anderson); Law Commission Working Paper: Trusts of Land No. 94 (1985), para. 16.4; p. 311, post.

[5] *Saunders v Vautier* (1841) 4 Beav 115; cf. the trustees' power to partition land held on trust for tenants in common: LPA 1925, s. 28 (3).

to give effect to the beneficiaries' wishes[6]. (3) Even if some of the trustees wish to execute the trust (rather than use their power to postpone sale) the court may refuse to permit this (contrary to the general principle that even a minority may compel the execution of an imperative obligation[7]) if some particular purpose for which the land was acquired still subsists, or it would be inequitable to do so[8]. (4) For purposes of construction, although a devise of 'all my freehold and copyhold land' is inapt to carry an interest under a trust for sale[9] yet a gift of a 'share and interest' in land has been held to suffice[10].

It is thus chimerical to suppose that a single 'correct' answer can be given to the problem whether the beneficiary's interest is or is not an 'interest in land': in some ways it is, in others it is not. It is submitted that the right approach is therefore to ask for what purposes the land has been subjected to the trust, and what is the policy of the legislation under which the question arises.

The realistic process of considering the purpose of the settlement is well illustrated by the three cases[11] in which the Court of Appeal has held that a person jointly interested in a dwelling-house had a right to possession (or at least a right not to be ousted from possession). It is quite clear that an equitable beneficiary had no such right prior to 1926[12], when it was a matter of choice[13] whether to interpose a trust between the legal estate and the beneficiaries. It is incredible to suppose that the legislature could, in pursuance of its aim of simplifying conveyancing, have intended to deprive all existing owners of undivided shares in land of their right to possession, leaving this to the discretion of a trustee (perhaps even the Public Trustee)[14]. If the clear intention is that a dwelling-house should be occupied by the joint purchasers it is absurd to deny them, because of conveyancing

---

[6] LPA 1925, s. 26 (3), which applies only to trusts imposed by statute: LP (A) A 1926, Sch. It could be argued that this shows legislative recognition of the need to distinguish between cases where the trust for sale should be regarded as machinery, on the one hand, and those where it has been expressly chosen, when its logical consequences may be implemented.

[7] *Re Mayo* [1943] Ch 302, [1943] 2 All ER 440; cf. *Re 90 Thornhill Road, Tolworth, Surrey* [1970] Ch 261, [1969] 3 All ER 685.

[8] *Re Buchanan-Wollaston's Conveyance* [1939] Ch 738, [1939] 2 All ER 302; *Re Hyde's Conveyance* (1950) noted in 102 LJo 58; *Bedson v Bedson* [1965] 2 QB 666, [1965] 3 All ER 307; *Rawlings v Rawlings* [1964] P 398, [1964] 2 All ER 804.

[9] *Re Kempthorne* [1930] 1 Ch 268.

[10] *Re Newman* [1930] 2 Ch 409, see particularly per FARWELL J at 414; and see also *Re Warren* [1932] 1 Ch 42.

[11] *Bull v Bull* [1955] 1 QB 234, [1955] 1 All ER 253; *Cook v Cook* [1962] P 235, [1962] 2 All ER 811; *Gurasz v Gurasz* [1970] P 11, [1969] 3 All ER 822; *Bull v Bull* was a controversial decision: see (1955) 19 Conv (NS) 146 (Crane); (1970) 34 Conv (NS) 344 (Crane); (1955) 18 MLR 303 (Latham); ibid 408 (Gray); (1956) 19 MLR 312 (Forrest); [1955] CLJ 156. The view that an equitable beneficiary might be held "entitled to occupy a dwelling-house by virtue of any estate or interest . . ." (Matrimonial Homes Act 1967, s. 1) led the Law Commission, *ex abundante cautela*, to recommend an amendment of the Act; Matrimonial Proceedings and Property Act 1970, s. 38; Law Com No. 25, para. 59, and explanatory note to draft cl. 28.

[12] *Re Wythes* [1893] 2 Ch 369 at 374; *Re Newen* [1894] 2 Ch 297; *Re Bagot* [1894] 1 Ch 177; *Re Earl of Stamford and Warrington* [1925] Ch 162.

[13] There is evidence in the old cases that the intention of the settlor was of paramount importance in determining whether the beneficiary be allowed into possession or not: thus in *Tidd v Lister* (1820) 5 Madd 429 Sir J. LEACH V-C, pointed out that the nature of the property (e.g., a family residence) might indicate that the beneficiary should not be excluded.

[14] LPA 1925, Sch. 1, Part IV, paras. 1 (3), 1 (4).

machinery, any sufficient interest in the house: *Bull v Bull*[15]; if, on the other hand, there is an express trust for sale (not created on the purchase of the property), and it is clear that the intention was that the property be sold and the proceeds divided, it is equally absurd to claim that any single beneficiary is entitled to frustrate this object by retaining possession as against the trustee: *Barclay v Barclay*[16].

This is a more attractive approach than simply to ask the abstract question whether the beneficiaries have an interest in the land itself. Unfortunately it did not attract the division of the Court of Appeal which decided *Irani Finance Ltd v Singh. . .*"[17]

B.   Statutory Definitions of Land

The question whether a reference in a statute to "land" includes an interest under a trust for sale is primarily one of statutory interpretation. Sometimes a statute deals expressly with the point. Under the Limitation Act 1980, for example, land includes "an interest in the proceeds of the sale of land held upon trust for sale[18]".

Questions of interpretation have arisen in connection with the following statutes.

i.   LAW OF PROPERTY ACT 1925, SECTION 40[19]

In *Cooper v Critchley* [1955] Ch 431, [1955] 1 All ER 520[20], the question arose whether a contract by one of two tenants in common in equity to sell his interest to the other was a contract for the sale of "land or any interest in land", and, to be enforceable, needed a memorandum in writing. VAISEY J and the Court of Appeal (EVERSHED MR, JENKINS and HODSON LJJ) held that there was no contract, and then considered what the position would have been if there had been one. JENKINS LJ said at 439, at 524: "The definition of land in section 205 (1) (ix) of this Act does, in so many words, exclude an undivided share in land; but that does not, to my mind, conclude the matter. The interest here in question is not an undivided share in land: it is a right to a share of the proceeds to arise from a sale of land, and paragraph (ix) does not say that such a right is not an interest in land, while paragraph (x) classes together as 'equitable interests' interests in land or the proceeds of sale thereof. Moreover, the definitions in section 205 of the Act of 1925 are assigned subject to the qualification 'unless the context otherwise requires.' Section 40 of the Act of 1925, as is well known, replaced section 4 of the Statute of Frauds, and there is to my mind little doubt that, before the Law of Property Act, 1925, an interest in the proceeds to arise from a sale of land would, notwithstanding the equitable doctrine of conversion, have ranked as an interest in land for the purposes of section 4 of the old statute. I am reluctant to construe section 40 of the Act of 1925 as altering the law in this respect.

---

[15] See p. 267, n. 11.
[16] [1970] 2 QB 677, [1970] 2 All ER 676; (1970) 34 Conv (NS) 344.
[17] [1971] Ch 59, [1970] 3 All ER 1455, p. 266, ante.
[18] S. 38 (1). See also AEA 1925, s. 3 (1) (ii).
[19] P. 63, ante.
[20] (1955) 71 LQR 177 (R.E.M.); Farrand (4th edn, 1983), pp. 33–35; *Steadman v Steadman* [1974] QB 161, [1973] 3 All ER 977; affd [1976] AC 536, [1974] 2 All ER 977.

Accordingly, I would be disposed to hold that a share in the proceeds to arise from a sale of land is an interest in land within the meaning of section 40. But if I am wrong in my inclination to accept the proposition in these general terms, I think that in a case such as this, where the transaction to which the contract relates is a sale by one to the other of two legal joint tenants of land, each of whom is beneficially entitled to one-half of the proceeds to arise from its sale, and who, moreover, as joint lessors under a lease to which the property is subject, and by virtue of the transaction the purchaser will acquire, subject to and with the benefit of the lease, the whole estate, legal and beneficial, in the entirety of the land, the contract cannot well be regarded as anything else than a contract for the sale of an interest in land and, were it necessary for us to do so, I would so hold[1]."

ii. LAND REGISTRATION ACT 1925, SECTION 54 (1)

In *Elias v Mitchell* [1972] Ch 652, [1972] 2 All ER 153[2], PENNYCUICK V-C was asked to decide in interlocutory proceedings whether a person interested in the proceeds of sale of registered land had a minor interest which could be protected by the entry of a caution. Under a partnership deed of 1967 Elias and Mitchell were business partners of freehold property in Ealing. Mitchell was registered as sole proprietor. The deed provided that the partners would stand possessed of the property for themselves in equal shares. In August 1970, Mitchell determined the partnership, and in October executed a transfer of the property to Mohammed Yousaf Dar, who, having no notice of the partnership, paid the purchase price to Mitchell as registered proprietor. Mohammed unfortunately did not present the transfer for registration until March 1971. Meanwhile in December 1970 Elias lodged a caution in respect of the property. Mohammed thereupon sought to remove the caution on the ground that Elias had no locus standi to lodge it. PENNYCUICK V-C, in holding that Elias was a person interested in land within section 54 (1) and so was entitled to lodge a caution, said at 659, at 155:

"I will first consider this matter apart from authority. When one reads the definition of 'minor interests' in section 3 (xv)[3] it seems to me perfectly clear that although what is defined is simply 'minor interests,' that is intended as a definition of minor interests in land. The opening words 'interests not capable of being disposed of or created by registered dispositions and capable of being overridden . . . by the proprietors unless protected as provided by

---

[1] Cf. *Re Rayleigh Weir Stadium* [1954] 1 WLR 786, [1954] 2 All ER 283 (such a contract held not registrable under LCA 1925 where the definition of land expressly excludes an undivided share in land: s. 17 (1)).

In *Cedar Holdings Ltd v Green* [1981] Ch 129, [1979] 3 All ER 117, Mr and Mrs G were joint legal and beneficial owners of their matrimonial home. Mr G wished to raise money by a mortgage of the home. Mr G and a woman, who impersonated Mrs G, executed a legal charge in favour of CH Ltd. The question was whether this transaction charged Mr G's share of his beneficial interest in the home. CH Ltd argued that it did, since under LPA 1925, s. 63, "every conveyance is effectual to pass all the interest which the conveying parties respectively have in the property conveyed or expressed or intended so to be." CA rejected this argument because under the doctrine of conversion Mr H's interest was not "an interest in the property conveyed". On this point the CA decision was considered to have been wrongly decided in *Williams and Glyn's Bank Ltd v Boland* [1981] AC 487, [1980] 2 All ER 408, p. 126, ante. See *Thames Guaranty Ltd v Campbell* [1985] QB 210, [1984] 2 All ER 585.

[2] (1972) 36 Conv (NS) 206 (D. J. Hayton).

[3] P. 136, ante.

this Act . . .' relate straight back to section 2 (1): '. . . all other interests in registered land . . . shall take effect in equity as minor interests. . . .' Reading those two subsections together it seems to me clear that the entire subject matter of the definition of 'minor interests' consists of interests in land. Then one finds in section 3 (xv) (a) that interests under a trust for sale are expressly included among minor interests; and it follows that those particular interests under a trust for sale are treated, for the purpose of this Act, as being minor interests in land.

Then one comes to section 54 (1): 'Any person interested . . . howsoever, in any land . . . may lodge a caution. . . .' If it is right to say that an interest in the proceeds of sale being by definition a minor interest is, within the intendment of this Act, an interest in land, then there is no doubt that a person interested in the proceeds of sale is a person interested in land for the purpose of section 54 (1) and can accordingly lodge a caution. If there were any doubt on this point, it would, I think, be set at rest by section 102 (3) which provides that minor interests may be protected by entry on the register of cautions. So that subsection in terms provides that minor interests, which by definition include interests under a trust for sale, may be protected by entry on the register, and that means that such interests are interests in land within the scope of section 54. . . .

Apart from authority then, I conclude that the plaintiff, having an interest in the proceeds of sale under this trust for sale, is a person interested in the land within the meaning of section 54 and as such is in a position to lodge a caution. That seems to me an entirely sensible provision in accordance with the general scheme of the Act. Indeed, it would be strange if a person having an interest in the proceeds of sale of land were not in a position to obtain a protection against some threatened misapplication of the land by the registered proprietor.

I turn now to the authorities which I propose to go through fairly briefly. They deal with comparable provisions contained in other parts of the legislation of 1925.

[His Lordship referred to *Stevens v Hutchinson* [1953] Ch 299, [1953] 1 All ER 699; *Cooper v Critchley* [1955] Ch 431, [1955] 1 All ER 520, p. 268, ante; *Georgiades v Edward Wolfe & Co Ltd* [1965] Ch 487, [1964] 3 All ER 433; *Taylor v Taylor* [1968] 1 WLR 378, [1968] 1 All ER 843; *Thomas v Rose* [1968] 1 WLR 1797, [1968] 3 All ER 765; *Irani Finance Ltd v Singh* [1971] Ch 59, [1970] 3 All ER 1455, and continued:]

It seems to me that the general principle to be applied in this connection is, if I may say so, correctly set out in the obiter statement made by Jenkins LJ in *Cooper v Critchley* [1955] Ch 431 at 439, [1955] 1 All ER 520 at 524, p. 268, ante. One must look at the particular Act and see whether in the context of that particular Act an expression such as 'interest in land' is or is not apt to cover an interest in the proceeds of sale of land. I do not find anything in the other authorities which I have cited which leads me to a different conclusion from that which I have expressed on the construction of the relevant sections of the Land Registration Act viewed in the context of that Act."

iii.   LAND REGISTRATION ACT 1925, SECTION 70 (1)

In *Williams and Glyn's Bank Ltd v Boland* [1981] AC 487, [1980] 2 All ER 408, p. 121, ante, the House of Lords held that an interest under a trust for sale was an "interest subsisting in reference to" registered land for the purposes of an overriding interest under section 70 (1) (*g*). See the judgments of Lord WILBERFORCE at 507, at 415, and of ORMROD LJ in the Court of Appeal [1979] Ch 312 at 336, [1979] 2 All ER 697 at 709, p. 256, ante.

iv. ADMINISTRATION OF JUSTICE ACT 1956, SECTION 35
Section 35 (1) gave power to the High Court or County Court to make a charging order on, inter alia, "any such land or interest in land of the debtor as may be specified in the order". The question arose whether the Court's power applied in relation to an interest under a trust for sale. A distinction was drawn between the case where the charging order was made against the separate interest of one beneficiary[4], and that where the order was made against both joint tenants together[5]. Section 35 has been repealed[6], and the jurisdiction is now widened to cover both cases[7].

CHARGING ORDERS ACT 1979

1. Charging orders. — (1) Where, under a judgment or order of the High Court or a county court, a person (the "debtor") is required to pay a sum of money to another person (the "creditor") then, for the purpose of enforcing that judgment or order, the appropriate court may make an order in accordance with the provisions of this Act imposing on any such property of the debtor as may be specified in the order a charge for securing the payment of any money due or to become due under the judgment or order.

(5) In deciding whether to make a charging order the court shall consider all the circumstances of the case and, in particular, any evidence before it as to —
   (*a*) the personal circumstances of the debtor, and
   (*b*) whether any other creditor of the debtor would be likely to be unduly prejudiced by the making of the order[8].

2. Property which may be charged. — (1) Subject to subsection (3) below, a charge may be imposed by a charging order only on —
   (*a*) any interest held by the debtor beneficially —
         (i) in any asset of a kind mentioned in subsection (2) below, or
         (ii) under any trust; or

---

[4] Where there was no jurisdiction: *Irani Finance Ltd v Singh* [1971] Ch 59, [1970] 3 All ER 1455.
[5] Where there was jurisdiction: *National Westminster Bank Ltd v Allen* [1971] 2 QB 718, [1971] 3 All ER 201.
[6] Charging Orders Act 1979, s. 7 (2). The Act was based on the Law Commission Report on Charging Orders 1976 (Law Com No. 74 Cmnd 6412). See generally (1980) 124 SJ 91, 110, 136 (A. J. Shipwright); [1981] Conv 69 (A. Sydenham).
[7] *National Westminster Bank Ltd v Stockman* [1981] 1 WLR 67, [1981] 1 All ER 800.
[8] See *Roberts Petroleum Ltd v Bernard Kenny Ltd* [1983] 2 AC 192, [1983] 1 All ER 564. If a charging order is obtained, the judgment creditor may then apply to the court under LPA 1925, s. 30, p. 222, ante, for an order for sale of the property. For the reluctance of the court to anticipate this application, see *First National Securities Ltd v Hegerty* [1985] QB 850, [1984] 3 All ER 641; cf. *Harman v Glencross* [1985] Fam 49, [1984] 2 All ER 577 (competition between one co-owning spouse and judgment creditors of the other); affd (1986) 136 NLJ 69, where BALCOMBE LJ sets out guidelines for the solution of this type of problem; [1985] Conv 129 (P. F. Smith); (1985) 5 OJLS 132 (N. P. Gravells).

    (*b*) any interest held by a person as trustee of a trust ("the trust"), if the interest is in such an asset or is an interest under another trust and —

        (i) the judgment or order in respect of which a charge is to be imposed was made against that person as trustee of the trust, or

        (ii) the whole beneficial interest under the trust is held by the debtor unencumbered and for his own benefit, or

        (iii) in a case where there are two or more debtors all of whom are liable to the creditor for the same debt, they together hold the whole beneficial interest under the trust unencumbered and for their own benefit.

(2) The assets referred to in subsection (1) above are —

    (*a*) land,

    (*b*) securities of any of the following kinds —

        (i) government stock,

        (ii) stock of any body (other than a building society) incorporated within England and Wales,

        (iii) stock of any body incorporated outside England and Wales or of any state or territory outside the United Kingdom, being stock registered in a register kept at any place within England and Wales,

        (iv) units of any unit trust in respect of which a register of the unit holders is kept at any place within England and Wales, or

    (*c*) funds in court.

(3) In any case where a charge is imposed by a charging order on any interest in an asset of a kind mentioned in paragraph (*b*) or (*c*) of subsection (2) above, the court making the order may provide for the charge to extend to any interest or dividend payable in respect of the asset.

3. Provisions supplementing sections 1 and 2. — (2) The Land Charges Act 1972[9] and the Land Registration Act 1925[10] shall apply in relation to charging orders as they apply in relation to other orders or writs issued or made for the purpose of enforcing judgments[11].

QUESTIONS

1.   What effect would the abolition of the doctrine of conversion have on the nature of beneficial interests under a trust for sale? (1970) 34 Conv (NS) 50, 421 (F. R. Crane); (1955) 71 LQR 179 (R.E.M.); (1971) 34 MLR 441 (S. M. Cretney); Survey of the Land Law of Northern Ireland (1971), para. 359.

2.   Compare the protection accorded to beneficiaries under a trust for sale of unregistered and registered land; (1958) 22 Conv (NS) 14, 22–26; Wolstenholme and Cherry, vol. 6, pp. 65–66; Barnsley, *Conveyancing Law and Practice* (2nd edn. 1982), pp. 326–328, 362–363, 378–379; (1973) 117 SJ 115, 136 (G. Miller); LRA 1925, ss. 74 (p. 240, ante), 86 (2),

---

[9] P. 30, ante.
[10] P. 137, ante.
[11] See also (1976) 40 Conv NS 394 on the now repealed (FA 1985, s. 93, Sch. 25, Part I, Sch. 27, Part X) Development Land Tax Act 1976, ss. 28 (4) (*a*), 46 (4); [1984] Conv 9 (J.E.A.) on Consumer Credit Act 1974, s. 189 (1).

p. 310, n. 6, post; *Elias v Mitchell* [1972] Ch 652, [1972] 2 All ER 153, p. 269, ante; *Caunce v Caunce* [1969] 1 WLR 286, [1969] 1 All ER 722, p. 255, ante; *Williams and Glyn's Bank Ltd v Boland* [1981] AC 487, [1980] 2 All ER 408, p. 121, ante; *City of London Building Society v Flegg* (1985) Times, 23 December, p. 128, ante; C & B, pp. 234–235.

3. Consider the difficulties arising from the registrability of Class F land charges in *Wroth v Tyler* [1974] Ch 30, [1973] 1 All ER 897, p. 262, ante; and in *Watts v Waller* [1973] QB 153, [1972] 3 All ER 257. Do you think that registration is a suitable mechanism for the protection of interests of a family character? Cretney, *Principles of Family Law* (4th edn.), pp. 259–260; Megarry and Wade, *Law of Real Property* (5th edn.), pp. 443, 811, 812; [1974] 38 Conv (NS) 110; (1975) 39 Conv (NS) 78 (D. J. Hayton); [1974] CLP 76 (D. G. Barnsley); (1976) CLP 26 at pp. 31–33, 43–50 (D. J. Hayton).

6. Strict Settlements[1]

A settlement exists whenever successive interests exist in land (not being land held upon trust for sale). Successive interests are interests less than a fee simple, and cannot exist as legal estates. They are therefore equitable interests, existing behind a trust. These elementary propositions are the key to understanding the definition of a settlement for the purposes of the Settled Land Act 1925. With a single exception, it will be seen that the definition in section 1 includes an element of successive ownership. The exception is the case where land is held by a minor; the Settled Land Act machinery is then imposed in order to make possible dealings with the legal estate.

It should also be noted that by virtue of subsection 7 of section 1, settlements and trusts for sale are alternatives.

I. Definition of a Settlement under the Settled Land Act 1925[2]

SETTLED LAND ACT 1925

1. What constitutes a settlement. — (1) Any deed, will, agreement for a settlement or other agreement[3], Act of Parliament, or other instrument[4], or

---

[1] C & B, pp. 69–80, 94–96, 165–173, 755–761, 762–764; M & W, pp. 311–374, 317–322, 324–385, 398–403, 405–410; MM, pp. 234–236, 237–241, 242–277, 283–298; Harvey, *Settlements of Land* (1973); Bonfield, *Marriage Settlements 1601–1740* (1983); English and Saville, *Strict Settlement* (1983); and essays in Rubin and Sugarman, *Law, Economy and Society* (1984) at pp. 1–123 (D. Sugarman and G. R. Rubin), 124–167 (M. R. Chesterman), 168–191 (E. Spring) and 209–210 (B. English).

[2] C & B, pp. 166–169; M & W, pp. 343–350; MM, pp. 238, 257–262.

[3] *Bacon v Bacon* [1947] P 151, [1947] 2 All ER 327 (a separation agreement giving the wife the right to remain in the house for her life).

[4] *Martin v Martin* [1978] Fam 12, [1977] 3 All ER 762; [1978] Conv 229 (P. Smith); *Griffiths v Williams* (1977) 248 EG 947, p. 550, post.

any number of instruments, whether made or passed before or after, or partly before and partly after, the commencement of this Act, under or by virtue of which instrument or instruments any land, after the commencement of this Act, stands for the time being —

(i) limited in trust[4a] for any persons by way of succession; or

(ii) limited in trust for any person in possession —

    (*a*) for an entailed interest whether or not capable of being barred or defeated;

    (*b*) for an estate in fee simple or for a term of years absolute subject to an executory limitation, gift, or disposition over on failure of his issue or in any other event;

    (*c*) for a base or determinable fee or any corresponding interest in leasehold land;

    (*d*) being an infant, for an estate in fee simple or for a term of years absolute; or

(iii) limited in trust for any person for an estate in fee simple or for a term of years absolute contingently on the happening of any event; or . . .

(v) charged, whether voluntarily or in consideration of marriage or by way of family arrangement, and whether immediately or after an interval, with the payment of any rentcharge for the life of any person, or any less period[5], or of any capital, annual, or periodical sums for the portions, advancement, maintenance, or otherwise for the benefit of any persons, with or without any term of years for securing or raising the same;

creates or is for the purposes of this Act a settlement and is in this Act referred to as a settlement, or as the settlement, as the case requires:

Provided that, where land is the subject of a compound settlement, references in this Act to the settlement shall be construed as meaning such compound settlement, unless the context otherwise requires.

(2) Where an infant is beneficially entitled to land for an estate in fee simple or for a term of years absolute and by reason of an intestacy or otherwise there is no instrument under which the interest of the infant arises or is acquired, a settlement shall be deemed to have been made by the intestate, or by the person whose interest the infant has acquired.

(4) An estate or interest not disposed of by a settlement and remaining in or reverting to the settlor, or any person deriving title under him, is for the purposes of this Act an estate or interest comprised in the subject of the settlement and coming to the settlor or such person under or by virtue of the settlement.

[4a] It need not be expressly limited. The trust may arise by operation of law, as, for instance, where there is a constructive trust under which the court gives protection to a licensee for the period of his life: pp. 499–504, post: *Bannister v Bannister* [1948] 2 All ER 133, p. 499, post; *Binions v Evans* [1972] Ch 359, [1972] 2 All ER 70, p. 503, post (Lord DENNING MR dissented on this point at 366, at 74); cf. *Ivory v Palmer* [1975] ICR 340. See Harvey, pp. 54, 82 et seq.; *Emmet on Title* (18th edn.), pp. 649–650; (1977) 93 LQR 561 (J. A. Hornby). On SLA avoidance of an unintentional creation of a strict settlement in this situation, see *Griffiths v Williams* (1977) 248 EG 947, p. 550, post; [1978] Conv 250. For similar problems arising in connection with settlements on divorce, see p. 287, n. 17, post. See also Law Commission Working Paper No. 94 Trusts of Land 1985, paras. 16.16–16.18.

[5] See *Re Austen* [1929] 2 Ch 155.

(5) Where —

    (*a*) a settlement creates an entailed interest which is incapable of being barred or defeated, or a base or determinable fee, whether or not the reversion or right of reverter is in the Crown, or any corresponding interest in leasehold land; or

    (*b*) the subject of a settlement is an entailed interest, or a base or determinable fee, whether or not the reversion or right of reverter is in the Crown, or any corresponding interest in leasehold land;

the reversion or right of reverter upon the cesser of the interest so created or settled shall be deemed to be an interest comprised in the subject of the settlement, and limited by the settlement.

(6) Subsections (4) and (5) of this section bind the Crown.

(7) This section does not apply to land held upon trust for sale.[5a]

2. What is settled land. — Land which is or is deemed to be the subject of a settlement is for the purposes of this Act settled land, and is in relation to the settlement referred to in this Act as the settled land.

The Law of Property (Amendment) Act 1926, Schedule, amending Law of Property Act 1925, section 7 (1), provides that "a fee simple subject to a legal or equitable right of entry or re-entry is for the purposes of this Act a fee simple absolute[6]".

Other types of settlement also arise:

i. Compound settlements[7]: Where new trusts are declared of land which is already subject to a settlement, as, for example, where a settlement is followed by a resettlement, the land is subject to a compound settlement. Normally the same person would be tenant for life under both settlements; but, even if he was tenant for life under the resettlement only, he could act as tenant for life under the compound settlement. The Settled Land Act 1925, section 31 (1)[8] provides that the trustees of the original settlement or, if there are none[9], the trustees of the resettlement shall be trustees of the compound settlement.

ii. Referential settlements: i.e. a settlement which incorporates by reference an earlier settlement[10].

iii. Derivative settlements: i.e. a settlement which is created out of the beneficial interest of one of the beneficiaries of another settlement.

In *Re Ogle's Settled Estates* [1927] 1 Ch 229, Romer J held that where the owner of an estate subject to family charges sold plots subject to the charges, the land retained and the plots sold were subject to separate settlements. Romer J said at 232: "In some parts of the Act no doubt 'settlement' means

---

[5a] Sub-s. 7 was added by LP (A) A 1926, Sch.

[6] See p. 8, n. 4, *ante*, where this amendment is commented upon.

[7] C & B, pp. 168, 188; M & W, pp. 357–358; MM, pp. 264–266.

[8] See p. 299, *post*. The section is retrospective: *Re Symons* [1927] 1 Ch 344.

[9] This provision was added by LP (A) A 1926, Sch.

[10] SLA 1925, s. 32, also retrospective.

merely the document or documents creating the settlement: see, for example, sections 1 subsection 4, 47 and 64. But in general a settlement, for the purposes of the Act, is a state of affairs in relation to certain land, brought about, or deemed to have been brought about by one or more documents, the particular state of affairs being one or more of those specified in subsections (i) to (v) of section 1 subsection 1. A document may, therefore, create more than one settlement. If by means of one and the same document, Blackacre and Whiteacre stand limited in trust for A. and his children in strict succession, and for B. and his children in strict succession respectively, there are two settlements."

II.   Machinery. The Curtain Principle[11]

The Settled Land Act 1925 introduced the "curtain principle", shutting off the purchaser's view of matters which do not concern him, such as the beneficial interests, and providing him with all the information he needs for the purpose of being certain to obtain the legal estate.

Dealings with the legal estate and equitable interests are contained in separate documents.

SETTLED LAND ACT 1925

4. Authorised method of settling land inter vivos. — (1) Every settlement of a legal estate in land inter vivos, shall, save as in this Act otherwise provided, be effected by two deeds, namely, a vesting deed and a trust instrument and if effected in any other way shall not operate to transfer or create a legal estate.

(2) By the vesting deed the land shall be conveyed to the tenant for life or statutory owner (and if more than one as joint tenants) for the legal estate the subject of the intended settlement:

Provided that, where such legal estate is already vested in the tenant for life or statutory owner, it shall be sufficient, without any other conveyance, if the vesting deed declares that the land is vested in him for that estate.

(3) The trust instrument shall —

  (*a*) declare the trusts affecting the settled land;
  (*b*) appoint or constitute trustees of the settlement;
  (*c*) contain the power, if any, to appoint new trustees of the settlement;
  (*d*) set out, either expressly or by reference, any powers intended to be conferred by the settlement in extension of those conferred by this Act;
  (*e*) bear any ad valorem stamp duty which may be payable (whether by virtue of the vesting deed or otherwise) in respect of the settlement.

TRUST INSTRUMENT ON THE SETTLEMENT OF LAND[12]

This Trust Instrument is made [&c.] between *John H.* of [&c.] (hereinafter called the Settlor) of the first part, *Jane W.* of [&c.] of the second part, and *X*

---

[11] C & B, pp. 169–173, 755–761; M & W, pp. 327–334; MM, pp. 244–254.
[12] SLA 1925, 1st Sch Form No. 3.

of [&c.], *Y* of [&c.], and *Z* of [&c.] (hereinafter called the trustees) of the third part.

Whereas by a deed (hereinafter called the Vesting Deed) bearing even date with but executed contemporaneously with these presents, and made between the same parties and in the same order as these presents, certain hereditaments situated at . . . . in the county of . . . . were vested in the Settlor Upon the trusts declared concerning the same by a trust instrument of even date therein referred to (meaning these presents).

Now in consideration of the intended marriage between the Settlor and *Jane W.*, this Deed witnesseth as follows:—

1.   The Settlor hereby agrees that he will hold the hereditaments and property comprised in the Vesting Deed In trust for himself until the solemnisation of the said marriage and thereafter Upon the trusts following, that is to say:—

2.   Upon trust for the Settlor during his life without impeachment of waste with remainder Upon trust if *Jane W.* survives him that she shall receive out of the premises during the residue of her life a yearly jointure rentcharge of [&c.] and subject thereto Upon trust for the trustees for a term of 800 years from the date of the death of the Settlor without impeachment of waste Upon the trusts hereinafter declared concerning the same. And subject to the said term and the trusts thereof Upon trust for the first and other sons of the said intended marriage successively according to seniority in tail male with remainder [&c.] *with an ultimate remainder in trust for the Settlor in fee simple.*

[*Here add the requisite trusts of the portions term, and any other proper provisions including the appointment of the trustees to be trustees of the settlement for the purposes of the Settled Land Act, 1925, extension of Settled Land Act powers, and a power for the tenant for life for the time being of full age to appoint new trustees of the settlement.*]

In witness [&c.].

[NOTE.—The Vesting Deed and the Trust Instrument can be executed as escrows till the marriage.]

---

5.   Contents of vesting deeds. — (1) Every vesting deed for giving effect to a settlement or for conveying settled land to a tenant for life or statutory owner during the subsistence of the settlement (in this Act referred to as a "principal vesting deed") shall contain the following statements and particulars, namely:—

(*a*)   A description, either specific or general, of the settled land;

(*b*)   A statement that the settled land is vested in the person or persons to whom it is conveyed or in whom it is declared to be vested upon the trusts from time to time affecting the settled land;

(*c*)   The names of the persons who are the trustees of the settlement;

(*d*)   Any additional or larger powers conferred by the trust instrument relating to the settled land which by virtue of this Act operate and are exercisable as if conferred by this Act on a tenant for life;

(*e*)   The name of any person for the time being entitled under the trust instrument to appoint new trustees of the settlement.

(2) The statements or particulars required by this section may be incorporated by reference to an existing vesting instrument, and, where there

is a settlement subsisting at the commencement of this Act, by reference to that settlement and to any instrument whereby land has been conveyed to the uses or upon the trusts of that settlement, but not (save as last aforesaid) by reference to a trust instrument nor by reference to a disentailing deed.

(3) A principal vesting deed shall not be invalidated by reason only of any error in any of the statements or particulars by this Act required to be contained therein[13].

VESTING DEED ON THE SETTLEMENT OF LAND[14]

This Vesting Deed made [&c.] between *John H.* of [&c.] of the first part, *Jane W.* of [&c.] of the second part, and *X* of [&c.], *Y* [&c.], and *Z* of [&c.] (hereinafter called the trustees) of the third part.

Witnesseth and it is hereby declared as follows:—

1. In consideration of the intended marriage between *John H.* and *Jane W.* the said *John H.* as Settlor hereby declares that

All that (*setting out the parcels by reference to a schedule or otherwise*) are vested in *John H.* in fee simple (*or in the case of leaseholds refer to the terms*).

Upon the trusts declared concerning the same by a Trust Instrument bearing even date with but intended to be executed contemporaneously with these presents and made between the same parties and in the same order as these presents or upon such other trusts as the same ought to be held from time to time.

2. The trustees are the trustees of the settlement for the purposes of the Settled Land Act, 1925.

3. The following additional or larger powers are conferred by the said trust instrument in relation to the settled land and by virtue of the Settled Land Act, 1925, operate and are exercisable as if conferred by that Act on a tenant for life. [*Here insert the additional powers.*]

4. The power of appointing a new trustee or new trustees of the settlement is vested in the said [*John H.*] during his life.

In witness [&c.].

---

6. Procedure in the case of settlements by will. — Where a settlement is created by the will of an estate owner who dies after the commencement of this Act —

    (*a*) the will is for the purposes of this Act a trust instrument; and

    (*b*) the personal representatives of the testator shall hold the settled land on trust, if and when required so to do, to convey it to the person who, under the will, or by virtue of this Act, is the tenant for life[15] or statutory owner[16], and, if more than one, as joint tenants[17].

8. Mode and costs of conveyance, and saving of rights of personal representatives and equitable chargees. — (1) A conveyance by personal

---

[13] SLA 1925, s. 110 (2); see p. 304, post.
[14] SLA 1925, 1st Sch. Form No. 2.
[15] SLA 1925, ss. 19, 20; see pp. 286–288, post.
[16] SLA 1925, s. 20.
[17] SLA 1925, s. 19 (2).

representatives under either of the last two preceding sections[18] may be made by an assent in writing signed by them which shall operate as a conveyance[19].

9.   Procedure in the case of settlements and of instruments deemed to be trust instruments. — (1) Each of the following settlements or instruments shall for the purposes of this Act be deemed to be a trust instrument, and any reference to a trust instrument contained in this Act shall apply thereto, namely:—

    (i) An instrument executed, or, in case of a will, coming into operation, after the commencement of this Act which by virtue of this Act is deemed to be a settlement;

    (ii) A settlement which by virtue of this Act is deemed to have been made by any person after the commencement of this Act[20];

    (iii) An instrument inter vivos intended to create a settlement of a legal estate in land which is executed after the commencement of this Act, and does not comply with the requirements of this Act with respect to the method of effecting such a settlement; and

    (iv) A settlement made after the commencement of this Act (including a settlement by the will of a person who dies after such commencement) of any of the following interests —

        (*a*) an equitable interest in land which is capable, when in possession, of subsisting at law; or

        (*b*) an entailed interest; or

        (*c*) a base or determinable fee or any corresponding interest in leasehold land,

    but only if and when the interest settled takes effect free from all equitable interests and powers under every prior settlement (if any).

(2) As soon as practicable after a settlement, or an instrument which for the purposes of this Act is deemed to be a trust instrument, takes effect as such, the trustees of the settlement may, and on the request of the tenant for life or statutory owner shall, execute a principal vesting deed, containing the proper statements and particulars, declaring that the legal estate in the settled land shall vest or is vested in the person therein named, being the tenant for life or statutory owner, and including themselves if they are the statutory owners, and such deed shall, unless the legal estate is already so vested, operate to convey or vest the legal estate in the settled land to or in the person or persons aforesaid and, if more than one, as joint tenants.

(3) If there are no trustees of the settlement, then (in default of a person able and willing to appoint such trustees) an application under this Act shall be made to the court for the appointment of such trustees.

III.   Dispositions of Settled Land[1]

A.   No Vesting Instrument. Paralysis

SETTLED LAND ACT 1925

13.   Dispositions not to take effect until vesting instrument is made. — Where a tenant for life or statutory owner has become entitled to

---

[18] For s. 7, see p. 302, post.

[19] The vesting assent performs the same function as a vesting deed; but it need not be sealed: AEA 1925, s. 36.

[20] For instruments deemed to be settlements or settlements deemed to have been made after the commencement of the Act, see SLA 1925, ss. 1 (2), (3), 20 (3), 29 (1).

[1] C & B, pp. 172–173, 759–761; M & W, pp. 321–334, 341–342; MM, pp. 246–252.

have a principal vesting deed or a vesting assent executed in his favour, then until a vesting instrument is executed or made pursuant to this Act in respect of the settled land, any purported disposition thereof inter vivos by any person, other than a personal representative (not being a disposition which he has power to make in right of his equitable interests or powers under a trust instrument), shall not take effect except in favour of a purchaser of a legal estate [without notice of such tenant for life or statutory owner having become so entitled as aforesaid][2], but, save as aforesaid, shall operate only as a contract for valuable consideration to carry out the transaction after the requisite vesting instrument has been executed or made, and a purchaser of a legal estate shall not be concerned with such disposition unless the contract is registered as a land charge[3].

By virtue of Law of Property (Amendment) Act 1926, section 1, a person beneficially entitled in possession to land for an estate in fee simple or term of years absolute subject to charges[4] which would normally make the land settled land[5] may sell the land subject to such charges without complying with the Settled Land Act procedure and section 13. Alternatively he can overreach the charges by complying with the statutory procedure.

B. Subject to Vesting Instrument

SETTLED LAND ACT 1925

18. Restrictions on dispositions of settled land where trustees have not been discharged. — (1) Where land is the subject of a vesting instrument and the trustees of the settlement have not been discharged under this Act, then —

  (*a*) any disposition by the tenant for life or statutory owner of the land, other than a disposition authorised by this Act or any other statute, or made in pursuance of any additional or larger powers mentioned in the vesting instrument, shall be void, except for the purpose of conveying or creating such equitable interests as he has power, in right of his equitable interests and powers under the trust instrument, to convey or create; and

  (*b*) if any capital money is payable in respect of a transaction, a conveyance to a purchaser of the land shall only take effect under this Act if the capital money is paid to or by the direction of the trustees of the settlement or into court; and

  (*c*) notwithstanding anything to the contrary in the vesting instrument, or the trust instrument, capital money shall not, except where the trustee is a trust corporation, be paid to or by the direction of fewer persons than two as trustees of the settlement[6].

---

[2] As amended by LP (A) A 1926, Sch.
[3] See W & C, vol. 3, pp. 54–57.
[4] SLA 1925, s. 20 (1) (ix).
[5] SLA 1925, s. 1 (1) (v).
[6] See also SLA 1925, s. 94; and as to receipts, s. 95, p. 300, post. For the definition of a trust corporation, see p. 206, n. 3, ante.

(2) The restrictions imposed by this section do not affect —

    (*a*) the right of a personal representative in whom the settled land may be vested to convey or deal with the land for the purposes of administration;

    (*b*) the right of a person of full age who has become absolutely entitled (whether beneficially or as trustee for sale or personal representative or otherwise) to the settled land, free from all limitations, powers, and charges taking effect under the trust instrument, to require the land to be conveyed to him.

The question arises of the position of the purchaser if he fails to comply with these requirements in circumstances in which he did not know and could not have known that the land was subject to a settlement. Is the conveyance "void" under section 18? Or, should a purchaser be protected under section 110 (1) (p. 304, post)?

In *Weston v Henshaw* [1950] Ch 510, three generations of Westons, W 1, W 2, and W 3, were successively interested in Blackacre. In 1921 W 1 sold Blackacre to W 2, who in 1927 sold it back to W 1. By his will W 1 settled it on Mrs W 1 for life and then on W 2 for life and to a grandson (W 3) contingently on attaining the age of 25. W 1 died in 1931, and Mrs W 1 in 1940, and on her death the fee simple was vested by vesting assent in W 2.

W 2 charged Blackacre to the defendants by way of legal mortgage to secure a number of personal advances, making title on each occasion by showing the deeds up to the sale to him in 1921, and suppressing all subsequent documents. Thus, W 2 appeared to be the absolute owner of the fee simple. In reality, he was only a tenant for life. There was no way in which the defendant, by enquiries, could have found out.

W 3 brought this action, after the death of W 2, as his administrator, for a declaration that the charges were void against him.

DANCKWERTS J held that they were, because the land was settled land, and the mortgagee had not complied with the provisions of section 18. The mortgagee was by any standards a bona fide purchaser of the legal estate for value without notice; and, if the decision is correct, his position, under an Act which was intended to help him, is worse than it was before 1926.

The decision was doubted in *Re Morgan's Lease* [1972] Ch 1, [1971] 2 All ER 235[7], where UNGOED-THOMAS J said at 7, at 241: "I come now to the third issue on the first question, whether section 110 of the Settled Land Act 1925 only applies if the purchaser knows that the other party to the transaction is a tenant for life. The landlords' submission was founded on *Weston v Henshaw* [1950] Ch 510.

[His Lordship referred to *Mogridge v Clapp* [1892] 3 Ch 382, which "unfortunately was not brought to DANCKWERTS J's notice" and continued:]

Here Kay LJ, sitting in the Court of Appeal with Lindley LJ and Bowen LJ, seems to me to treat it as self-evident that a person dealing with a life

---

[7] (1971) 87 LQR 338 (D. W. Elliott); (1973) 36 MLR 25 at p. 28 (R. H. Maudsley).

tenant without knowing that he was a life tenant would be entitled to rely on section 110 of the Settled Land Act 1925; and, with the greatest respect for the decision in *Weston v Henshaw* [1950] Ch 510, that is the conclusion to which I would come independently of authority. There is, in the section, no express provision limiting its benefit to a purchaser who knows that the person with whom he is dealing is a tenant for life. On its face it reads as free of limitation and as applicable to a person without such knowledge as to a person who has it. There is a limitation, namely, that the purchaser must act in good faith; but that limitation reads as applicable to a purchaser with such knowledge as without. So, despite the insertion of the limitation of good faith on the part of the purchaser, there is no insertion of the limitation for which the landlords contend. Thus my conclusion is that section 110 applies whether or not the purchaser knows that the other party to the transaction is tenant for life."

IV. Overreaching[8]

A. Under an Ordinary Conveyance

If the correct machinery is used, a sale by a tenant for life "overreaches" the beneficial interests under the settlement and passes the title to a purchaser free from them. The beneficial interests are transferred from the land to the purchase money[9].

LAW OF PROPERTY ACT 1925

2. Conveyances overreaching certain equitable interests and powers. — (1) A conveyance to a purchaser of a legal estate in land shall overreach any equitable interest or power affecting that estate, whether or not he has notice thereof, if —

> (i) the conveyance is made under the powers conferred by the Settled Land Act, 1925[10], or any additional powers conferred by a settlement, and the equitable interest or power is capable of being overreached thereby, and the statutory requirements respecting the payment of capital money arising under the settlement are complied with[11];

SETTLED LAND ACT 1925

72. Completion of transactions by conveyance. — (1) On a sale, exchange, lease, mortgage, charge, or other disposition, the tenant for life may, as regards land sold, given in exchange, leased, mortgaged, charged, or otherwise disposed of, or intended so to be, or as regards easements or other rights or privileges sold, given in exchange, leased, mortgaged, or otherwise disposed of, or intended so to be, effect the transaction by deed to the extent of the estate or interest vested or declared to be vested in him by the last or

---

[8] C & B, pp. 79, 757–759, 762–764; M & W, pp. 136–139, 398–403, 405–409; MM, pp. 107–108, 283–286, 287–290.
[9] SLA 1925, s. 75 (5), p. 301, post.
[10] SLA 1925, s. 72.
[11] SLA 1925, s. 18 (1) (*b*), p. 281, ante.

only vesting instrument affecting the settled land or any less estate or interest, in the manner requisite for giving effect to the sale, exchange, lease, mortgage, charge, or other disposition, but so that a mortgage shall be effected by the creation of a term of years absolute in the settled land or by charge by way of legal mortgage, and not otherwise.

(2) Such a deed, to the extent and in the manner to and in which it is expressed or intended to operate and can operate under this Act, is effectual to pass the land conveyed, or the easements, rights, privileges or other interests created, discharged from all the limitations, powers, and provisions of the settlement, and from all estates, interests, and charges subsisting or to arise thereunder, but subject to and with the exception of —

    (i) all legal estates and charges by way of legal mortgage having priority to the settlement; and

    (ii) all legal estates and charges by way of legal mortgage which have been conveyed or created for securing money actually raised at the date of the deed; and

    (iii) all leases and grants at fee-farm rents or otherwise, and all grants of easements, rights of common, or other rights or privileges which —

        (*a*) were before the date of the deed granted or made for value in money or money's worth, or agreed so to be, by the tenant for life or statutory owner, or by any of his predecessors in title, or any trustees for them, under the settlement, or under any statutory power, or are at that date otherwise binding on the successors in title of the tenant for life or statutory owner; and

        (*b*) are at the date of the deed protected by registration under the Land Charges Act, 1925[12], if capable of registration thereunder.

(3) Notwithstanding registration under the Land Charges Act, 1925[12], of —

    (*a*) an annuity within the meaning of Part II of that Act;

    (*b*) a limited owner's charge or a general equitable charge within the meaning of that Act;

a disposition under this Act operates to overreach such annuity or charge which shall, according to its priority, take effect as if limited by the settlement.

(4) Where a lease is by this Act authorised to be made by writing under hand only, such writing shall have the same operation under this section as if it had been a deed.

B. Ad Hoc Settlements

SETTLED LAND ACT 1925

21. Absolute owners subject to certain interests to have the powers of tenant for life. — (1) Where a person of full age is beneficially entitled in possession to a legal estate subject to any equitable interests or powers, then, for the purpose of overreaching such interests or powers, he may, notwithstanding any stipulation to the contrary, by deed (which shall have effect as a principal vesting deed within the meaning of this Act) declare that the legal estate is vested in him on trust to give effect to all equitable interests and powers affecting the legal estate, and that deed shall be executed by two or

---

[12] Now LCA 1972.

more individuals approved or appointed by the court or a trust corporation[13], who shall be stated to be the trustees of the settlement for the purposes of this Act.

Thereupon so long as any of the equitable interests and powers are subsisting the following provisions shall have effect:—

(a) The person so entitled as aforesaid and each of his successors in title being an estate owner shall have the powers of a tenant for life and the land shall be deemed to be settled land;

(b) The instrument (if any) under which his estate arises or is acquired, and the instrument (if any) under which the equitable interests or powers are subsisting or capable of taking effect shall be deemed to be the trust instrument:

Provided that where there is no such instrument as last aforesaid then a deed (which shall take effect as a trust instrument) shall be executed contemporaneously with the vesting deed, and shall declare the trusts affecting the land;

(c) The persons stated in the principal vesting deed to be the trustees of the settlement for the purposes of this Act shall also be the trustees of the trust instrument for those purposes; and

(d) Capital money arising on any disposition of the land shall be paid to or by the direction of the trustees of the settlement or into court, and shall be applicable towards discharging or providing for payment in due order of any principal money payable in respect of such interests or charges as are overreached by such disposition, and until so applied shall be invested or applied as capital money under the trust instrument, and the income thereof shall be applied as the income of such capital money, and be liable for keeping down in due order any annual or periodical sum which may be overreached by the disposition.

(2) The following equitable interests and powers are excepted from the operation of subsection (1) of this section, namely —

(i) an equitable interest protected by a deposit of documents relating to the legal estate affected;

(ii) the benefit of a covenant or agreement restrictive of the user of land;

(iii) an easement, liberty or privilege over or affecting land and being merely an equitable interest;

(iv) the benefit of a contract to convey or create a legal estate, including a contract conferring either expressly or by statutory implication a valid option of purchase, a right of pre-emption, or any other like right;

(v) any equitable interest protected by registration under the Land Charges Act 1925[14], other than —

(a) an annuity within the meaning of Part II of that Act;

(b) a limited owner's charge or a general equitable charge within the meaning of that Act.

(3) Subject to the powers conferred by this Act on a tenant for life, nothing contained in this section shall deprive an equitable chargee of any of his rights or of his remedies for enforcing those rights.

---

[13] See p. 260, n. 3, ante.
[14] Now LCA 1972.

V. The Tenant for Life[15]

A.   Who is Tenant for Life and Who has Powers of Tenant for Life

i.   TENANT FOR LIFE AND OTHER LIMITED OWNERS

SETTLED LAND ACT 1925

19.   Who is tenant for life. — (1) The person of full age who is for the time being beneficially entitled under a settlement to possession of settled land for his life is for the purposes of this Act the tenant for life of that land and the tenant for life under that settlement.

(2) If in any case there are two or more persons of full age so entitled as joint tenants, they together constitute the tenant for life for the purposes of this Act.

(3) If in any case there are two or more persons so entitled as joint tenants and they are not all of full age, such one or more of them as is or are for the time being of full age is or (if more than one) together constitute the tenant for life for the purposes of this Act, but this subsection does not affect the beneficial interests of such of them as are not for the time being of full age.

(4) A person being tenant for life within the foregoing definitions shall be deemed to be such notwithstanding that, under the settlement or otherwise, the settled land, or his estate or interest therein, is incumbered or charged in any manner or to any extent, and notwithstanding any assignment by operation of law or otherwise of his estate or interest under the settlement, whether before or after it came into possession, other than an assurance which extinguishes that estate or interest.

20.   Other limited owners having powers of tenant for life. — (1) Each of the following persons being of full age shall, when his estate or interest is in possession, have the powers of a tenant for life under this Act, (namely):—

(i) A tenant in tail, including a tenant in tail after possibility of issue extinct, and a tenant in tail who is by Act of Parliament restrained from barring or defeating his estate tail, and although the reversion is in the Crown, but not including such a tenant in tail where the land in respect whereof he is so restrained was purchased with money provided by Parliament in consideration of public services;

(ii) A person entitled to land for an estate in fee simple or for a term of years absolute with or subject to, in any of such cases, an executory limitation, gift, or disposition over on failure of his issue or in any other event;

(iii) A person entitled to a base or determinable fee, although the reversion or right of reverter is in the Crown, or to any corresponding interest in leasehold land;

(iv) A tenant for years determinable on life, not holding merely under a lease at a rent;

(v) A tenant for the life of another, not holding merely under a lease at a rent;

(vi) A tenant for his own or any other life, or for years determinable on life, whose estate is liable to cease in any event during that life, whether by expiration of the estate, or by conditional limitation,

---

[15] C & B, pp. 173–186; M & W, pp. 350–354, 358–384; MM, pp. 239, 242–244, 262, 266–276.

or otherwise, or to be defeated by an executory limitation, gift, or disposition over, or is subject to a trust for accumulation of income for any purpose;

(vii) A tenant by the curtesy;

(viii) A person entitled to the income of land under a trust or direction for payment thereof to him during his own or any other life, whether or not subject to expenses of management or to a trust for accumulation of income for any purpose, or until sale of the land, or until forfeiture, cesser or determination by any means of his interest therein, unless the land is subject to an immediate binding trust for sale;

(ix) A person beneficially entitled to land for an estate in fee simple or for a term of years absolute subject to any estates, interests, charges, or powers of charging, subsisting or capable of being exercised under a settlement[16].

117. Definitions. — (1) . . .

(xxviii) "Tenant for life" includes a person (not being a statutory owner) who has the powers of a tenant for life under this Act, and also (where the context requires) one of two or more persons who together constitute the tenant for life, or have the powers of a tenant for life[17]; . . .

ii. STATUTORY OWNERS

SETTLED LAND ACT 1925

23. Powers of trustees, &c., when there is no tenant for life. — (1) Where under a settlement there is no tenant for life, nor, independently of this section, a person having by virtue of this Act the powers of a tenant for life then —

(a) any person of full age on whom such powers are by the settlement expressed to be conferred[18]; and

(b) in any other case the trustees of the settlement;

---

[16] Such persons may, however, convey the land subject to a prior interest as if the land had not been settled land: LP(A)A 1926, s. 1.

[17] *Re Jefferys* [1939] Ch 205, [1938] 4 All ER 120 (an annuitant is not tenant for life); *Re Carne's Settled Estates* [1899] 1 Ch 324 ("to occupy the land rent free so long as she might wish to do so," held to be a tenant for life); *Ayer v Benton* (1967) 204 EG 359; *Re Catling* [1931] 2 Ch 359 (wife as tenant at a nominal annual sum, the tenancy not to be determined so long as she made the property her principal place of residence held, not to be a tenant for life; and indeed there was no settlement); *Re Waleran Settled Estates* [1927] 1 Ch 522 (a term to a woman "for 99 years if she should so long live", held to be a tenant for life); *Re Ogle's Settled Estates* [1927] 1 Ch 229, p. 276, ante; *Re Cayley and Evans' Contract* [1930] 2 Ch 143; *Re Gallenga Will Trusts* [1938] 1 All ER 106. Questions also arise in connection with settlements on divorce: *Morss v Morss* [1972] Fam 264, [1972] 1 All ER 1121 (agreement incorporated in court order allowing a wife the use of house "rent free for her life or until . . . debarred by court from access to the children"; held a licence); *Martin v Martin* [1978] Fam 12, [1977] 3 All ER 762 (court order giving house on trust to wife for life or until remarriage or such earlier date as she should cease to live there, and thereafter on trust for the parties in equal shares. This would presumably make the wife a tenant for life; the inconveniences of such a decision are pointed out in [1978] Conv 229 (P. Smith)). See also *Allen v Allen* [1974] 1 WLR 1171, [1974] 3 All ER 385, where a similar result was achieved through the machinery of a trust for sale. A similar problem arises where the court gives protection to a licensee for the period of his life; p. 275, n. 4a, ante, p. 550, post.

[18] *Re Craven Settled Estates* [1926] Ch 985; *Re Norton* [1929] 1 Ch 84, p. 211, ante; *Re Beaumont's Settled Estates* [1937] 2 All ER 353.

shall have the powers of a tenant for life under this Act[19].

26.   Infants, how to be affected[20]. — (1) Where an infant is beneficially entitled in possession to land for an estate in fee simple or for a term of years absolute or would if of full age be a tenant for life of or have the powers of a tenant for life over settled land, then, during the minority of the infant —

   (*a*)   if the settled land is vested in a personal representative, the personal representative, until a principal vesting instrument has been executed pursuant to the provisions of this Act; and

   (*b*)   in every other case, the trustees of the settlement;

shall have, in reference to the settled land and capital money, all the powers conferred by this Act and the settlement on a tenant for life, and on the trustees of the settlement.

117.   Definitions. — (1) . . .

(xxvi)   "Statutory owner" means the trustees of the settlement or other persons who, during a minority, or at any other time when there is no tenant for life, have the powers of a tenant for life under this Act, but does not include the trustees of the settlement, where by virtue of an order of the court or otherwise the trustees have power to convey the settled land in the name of the tenant for life;

B.   Powers of the Tenant for Life

i.   TENANT FOR LIFE AND TRUSTEES FOR SALE

The tenant for life's powers are given in detail in Settled Land Act 1925, Part II. The same powers are given to trustees for sale by Law of Property Act 1925, section 28, and the most important sections are set out at pp. 215–216, ante.

ii.   NOTICE TO TRUSTEES

When a tenant for life exercises his powers of sale, exchange, leasing, mortgaging, charging or granting an option, he is usually required to give notice to the trustees[1]. In the case of the sale of a mansion house, their consent is required.

---

[19] SLA 1925, s. 104 (1) provides that the powers of a tenant for life are not capable of assignment or release. A person who becomes a "statutory owner" under s. 23 (1) may release his powers, and the trustees then become statutory owners: *Re Craven Settled Estates* [1926] Ch 985, p. 292, post.

[20] SLA 1925, ss. 1 (1) (ii) (*d*), 1 (2), 102. The Family Law Reform Act 1969, s. 1 provides that as from January 1, 1970, "a person shall attain full age on attaining the age of eighteen instead of on attaining the age of twenty-one; and a person shall attain full age on that date if he has then already attained the age of eighteen but not the age of twenty-one". On minors generally, see C & B, pp. 857–864; M & W, pp. 1015–1019, MM, pp. 182–185. A minor cannot hold a legal estate in land, although he may hold an equitable interest: LPA 1925, s. 1 (6); LRA 1925, s. 3 (iv). For the effect of a conveyance of a legal estate to a minor: LPA 1925, s. 19; SLA 1925, s. 27; LRA 1925, s. 111. See Law Commission Report on Minors' Contracts 1984 (Law Com No. 134, HC 494), paras. 5.13–5.16 on leases granted to minors. He cannot be appointed a trustee: LPA 1925, s. 20, nor an executor: Supreme Court Act 1981, s. 118; nor an administrator: *Re Manuel* (1849) 13 Jur 664. He cannot make a will: Wills Act 1837, s. 7, except as provided by Wills (Soldiers and Sailors) Act 1918. Any disposition by a minor of any interest in land is voidable at his option, on his attaining his majority, or within a reasonable time thereafter.

[1] SLA 1925, s. 101.

iii.   SPECIAL CONSENTS[2]

SETTLED LAND ACT 1925

65.   Power to dispose of mansion. — (1) The powers of disposing of settled land conferred by this Act on a tenant for life may be exercised as respects the principal mansion house, if any, on any settled land, and the pleasure grounds and park and lands, if any, usually occupied therewith:

Provided that those powers shall not be exercised without the consent of the trustees of the settlement or an order of the court —

(a) if the settlement is a settlement made or coming into operation before the commencement of this Act and the settlement does not expressly provide to the contrary; or

(b) if the settlement is a settlement made or coming into operation after the commencement of this Act and the settlement expressly provides that these powers or any of them shall not be exercised without such consent or order.

(2) Where a house is usually occupied as a farmhouse, or where the site of any house and the pleasure grounds and park and lands, if any, usually occupied therewith do not together exceed twenty-five acres in extent, the house is not to be deemed a principal mansion house within the meaning of this section, and may accordingly be disposed of in like manner as any other part of the settled land.

C.   Reductions from and Additions to the Powers of the Tenant for Life

SETTLED LAND ACT 1925

106[3].   Prohibition or limitation against exercise of powers void, and provision against forfeiture. — (1) If in a settlement, will, assurance, or other instrument executed or made before or after, or partly before and partly after, the commencement of this Act a provision is inserted —

(a) purporting or attempting, by way of direction, declaration, or otherwise, to forbid a tenant for life or statutory owner to exercise any power under this Act, or his right to require the settled land to be vested in him; or

(b) attempting, or tending, or intended, by a limitation, gift, or disposition over of settled land, or by a limitation, gift, or disposition of other real or any personal property, or by the imposition of any condition, or by forfeiture, or in any other manner whatever, to prohibit or prevent him from exercising, or to induce him to abstain from exercising, or to put him into a position inconsistent with his exercising any power under this Act, or his right to require the settled land to be vested in him;

that provision, as far as it purports, or attempts, or tends, or is intended to have, or would or might have, the operation aforesaid, shall be deemed to be void.

(2) For the purposes of this section an estate or interest limited to continue so long as a person abstains from exercising any such power or right as aforesaid shall be and take effect as an estate or interest to continue for the

---

[2] See also s. 66 (1) (cutting and sale of timber by tenant for life impeachable for waste); s. 58 (compromising claims); s. 67 (3) (order of the court needed for the sale of settled chattels); s. 64 (general power to effect any transaction under a court order: p. 218, ante).

[3] [1978] Conv 229 (P. Smith).

period for which it would continue if that person were to abstain from exercising the power or right, discharged from liability to determination or cesser by or on his exercising the same.

(3) Notwithstanding anything in a settlement, the exercise by the tenant for life or statutory owner of any power under this Act shall not occasion a forfeiture.

108.   Saving for and exercise of other powers. — (1) Nothing in this Act shall take away, abridge, or prejudicially affect any power for the time being subsisting under a settlement, or by statute or otherwise, exercisable by a tenant for life, or (save as hereinafter provided) by trustees with his consent, or on his request, or by his direction, or otherwise, and the powers given by this Act are cumulative.

(2) In case of conflict between the provisions of a settlement and the provisions of this Act, relative to any matter in respect whereof the tenant for life or statutory owner exercises or contracts or intends to exercise any power under this Act, the provisions of this Act shall prevail; and, notwithstanding anything in the settlement, any power (not being merely a power of revocation or appointment) relating to the settled land thereby conferred on the trustees of the settlement or other persons exercisable for any purpose, whether or not provided for in this Act, shall, after the commencement of this Act, be exercisable by the tenant for life or statutory owner as if it were an additional power conferred on the tenant for life within the next following section of this Act and not otherwise.

109.   Saving for additional or larger powers under settlement. — (1) Nothing in this Act precludes a settlor from conferring on the tenant for life, or (save as provided by the last preceding section) on the trustees of the settlement, any powers additional to or larger than those conferred by this Act.

(2) Any additional or larger powers so conferred shall, as far as may be, notwithstanding anything in this Act, operate and be exercisable in the like manner, and with all the like incidents, effects, and consequences, as if they were conferred by this Act, and, if relating to the settled land, as if they were conferred by this Act on a tenant for life.

In *Re Jefferys* [1939] Ch 205, [1938] 4 All ER 120, Farwell J held that a power given to an annuitant to restrain a sale by trustees of the settlement as statutory owners was not a "power exercisable by trustees with" the consent of the tenant for life[4] and was not therefore saved by section 108 (1); the annuitant's power to restrain a sale was thus in conflict with the powers given to the statutory owners by the Act[5]. The statutory power of sale thus prevailed under section 108 (2); and, even if the annuitant consented, sales by the statutory owners were sales under their statutory power, and the provisions of the Settled Land Act 1925 as to capital money must be complied with[6].

---

[4] See p. 287, n. 17, ante.
[5] See p. 289, ante.
[6] SLA 1925, s. 18 (1), p. 281, ante; s. 73, p. 219, ante; s. 75, p. 301, post; (1939) 55 **LQR** 22 (H.P.).

In *Re Ames* [1893] 2 Ch 479, personalty was bequeathed for the upkeep of settled land; the surplus income being applicable to the tenant for life, but, if the tenant for life should become disentitled to the possession or income of the settled land, the settled personalty should fall into residue.

NORTH J held the proviso void under the Settled Land Act 1882, section 51 (the predecessor of section 106) and the tenant for life continued to be entitled to the income of the personalty after the sale of the settled land.

In *Re Acklom* [1929] 1 Ch 195, the testator gave his leasehold house and its contents on trust for Mrs Hawkins for life; with a direction to the trustees that if "and when she shall not wish to reside or continue to reside there", the house should be sold, and the proceeds divided between certain charities.

The testator died in 1918 and Mrs Hawkins went into possession. In 1925, she went abroad for health reasons, and her return was delayed by a serious illness in the spring of 1926. In 1927 she sold the premises in exercise of her Settled Land Act powers and the trustees sold the contents.

In holding that she had not forfeited her interest in the property, and could receive the income from the proceeds of sale, MAUGHAM J said at 198: "There is no doubt at all that under section 106 of the Settled Land Act, 1925, which applies to the provisions of wills made before or after the Act, a provision which limits or prevents the tenant for life from exercising his power of sale is void. Accordingly it is reasonably clear to my mind in this case that if Mrs Hawkins was in a position to exercise the powers of a tenant for life on 29 June 1927, a provision whereby the proceeds of sale should under the terms of the will pass to the charities is void. If authority were needed for that it would be found in *Re Paget's Settled Estates* (1885) 30 ChD 161, *Re Trenchard* [1902] 1 Ch 378 and *Re Gibbons* [1920] 1 Ch 372. By parity of reasoning it cannot be denied that so long as Mrs Hawkins was a person having the powers of a tenant for life she was entitled to let Wiseton Court without incurring any forfeiture even if she ceased thereupon to reside or to continue to reside within the meaning of the words contained in the clause I have read. The argument for the charities does not dispute this proposition. They maintain that on the evidence and in the events which happened Mrs Hawkins must be taken to have ceased to reside or to continue to reside at a date considerably anterior to the sale, and accordingly that she had forfeited her interest in the property prior to the sale, and therefore that they are entitled to the proceeds of sale. Now the evidence as to this is unsatisfactory; ... I have no evidence that at any particular date it can be established that prior to the sale she had finally and irrevocably decided not only not to continue to reside, but not to let the house under her powers as tenant for life. The question of intention is affected by section 106; and if a tenant for life or person entitled to possession, so long as he enjoys it, is careful to exercise the powers as under the Act so that section 106 applies, the intention is wholly immaterial. I hold that Mrs Hawkins was entitled temporarily to give up possession if it was for the purpose of exercising her powers under the Settled Land Act or of procuring a tenant or effecting a sale, and that on the evidence before me Mrs Hawkins has so acted that the trustees had not the power of sale of the property. Of course it is material in that connection to bear in mind that they never purported to exercise any such power. They are to be presumed to have allowed her to sell without interference by any one. Accordingly I answer the first question by saying that she has not forfeited her interest in the proceeds of sale of the leasehold property[7]."

D. Non-Assignability
SETTLED LAND ACT 1925

104. Powers not assignable, and contract not to exercise powers void. — (1) The powers under this Act of a tenant for life are not capable of assignment or release, and do not pass to a person as being, by operation of law or otherwise, an assignee of a tenant for life, and remain exercisable by the tenant for life after and notwithstanding any assignment, by operation of law or otherwise, of his estate or interest under the settlement.

This subsection applies notwithstanding that the estate or interest of the tenant for life under the settlement was not in possession when the assignment was made or took effect by operation of law.

(2) A contract by a tenant for life not to exercise his powers under this Act or any of them shall be void.

(4) Where such an assignment for value[8] is made or comes into operation after the commencement of this Act, the consent of the assignee shall not be requisite for the exercise by the tenant for life of any of the powers conferred by this Act:

Provided that —

> (*a*) the assignee shall be entitled to the same or the like estate or interest in or charge on the land, money, or securities for the time being representing the land, money, or securities comprised in the assignment, as he had by virtue of the assignment in the last-mentioned land, money, or securities; and
>
> (*b*) if the assignment so provides, or if it takes effect by operation of the law of bankruptcy, and after notice thereof to the trustees of the settlement, no investment or application of capital money for the time being affected by the assignment shall be made without the consent of the assignee, except an investment in securities authorised by statute for the investment of trust money[9], and
>
> (*c*) notice of the intended transaction shall, unless the assignment otherwise provides, be given to the assignee, but a purchaser shall not be concerned to see or inquire whether such notice has been given.

(10) An assignment by operation of the law of bankruptcy, where the assignment comes into operation after the commencement of this Act, shall be deemed to be an assignment for value for the purposes of this section.

105. Effect of surrender of life estate to the next remainderman. — (1) Where the estate or interest of a tenant for life under the settlement has been or is absolutely assured with intent to extinguish the same, either before or after the commencement of this Act, to the person next entitled in remainder or reversion under the settlement[10], then, the statutory powers of

---

[7] See also *Re Orlebar* [1936] Ch 147; and *Re Aberconway's Settlement Trusts* [1953] Ch 647, [1953] 2 All ER 350.

[8] I.e., an assignment for value of the beneficial interest of the tenant for life (sub-s. 3).

[9] SLA 1925, ss. 73, 74; Trustee Investments Act 1961, p. 219, *ante*; LPA 1925, s. 28 (2), p. 215, *ante*.

[10] A remainderman or reversioner does not qualify if there is an intervening limitation which may take effect: *Re Maryon-Wilson's Instruments* [1971] Ch 789, [1969] 3 All ER 558.

the tenant for life under this Act shall, in reference to the property affected by the assurance, and notwithstanding the provisions of the last preceding section, cease to be exercisable by him, and the statutory powers shall thenceforth become exercisable as if he were dead, but without prejudice to any incumbrance affecting the estate or interest assured, and to the rights to which any incumbrancer would have been entitled if those powers had remained exercisable by the tenant for life. . . .

In *Re Shawdon Estates Settlement* [1930] 2 Ch 1, it was held by the Court of Appeal (Lord HANWORTH MR, LAWRENCE and ROMER LJJ, affirming EVE J) that section 105 (1) applied also to the case where the "assurance" was made by the trustee in bankruptcy of the tenant for life. The tenant for life refused to execute a vesting deed in favour of the tenant in tail in remainder, the "person next entitled", who was held to be entitled to call for a vesting order in his favour under the Settled Land Act 1925, section 12 (1) (*a*).

SETTLED LAND ACT 1925

24. As to a tenant for life who has parted with his interest. — (1) If it is shown to the satisfaction of the court that a tenant for life, who has by reason of bankruptcy, assignment, incumbrance, or otherwise ceased in the opinion of the court to have a substantial interest in his estate or interest in the settled land or any part thereof, has unreasonably refused to exercise any of the powers conferred on him by this Act, or consents to an order under this section, the court may, on the application of any person interested in the settled land or the part thereof affected, make an order authorising the trustees of the settlement, to exercise in the name and on behalf of the tenant for life, any of the powers of a tenant for life under this Act, in relation to the settled land or the part thereof affected, either generally and in such manner and for such period as the court may think fit, or in a particular instance, and the court may by the order direct that any documents of title in the possession of the tenant for life relating to the settled land be delivered to the trustees of the settlement.

(2) While any such order is in force, the tenant for life shall not, in relation to the settled land or the part thereof affected, exercise any of the powers thereby authorised to be exercised in his name and on his behalf, but no person dealing with the tenant for life shall be affected by any such order, unless the order is for the time being registered as an order affecting land[11].

(3) An order may be made under this section at any time after the estate or interest of the tenant for life under the settlement has taken effect in possession, and notwithstanding that he disposed thereof when it was an estate or interest in remainder or reversion.

RE THORNHILL'S SETTLEMENT

[1941] Ch 24, [1940] 4 All ER 83, 249 (ChD, BENNETT J, affirmed in five lines by CA Sir Wilfrid GREENE MR, CLAUSON and GODDARD LJJ).

Michael Christopher Wright McCreagh, the tenant for life, was bankrupt. He neglected the management of the property, and the mansion house and three farms were derelict.

---

[11] LCA 1972, s. 6, p. 43, ante.

The summons asked that the Public Trustee, as trustee of the settlement, should be authorised by order under the Settled Land Act 1925, section 24 (1) to exercise the tenant for life's powers of leasing and sale.

Held. The tenant for life had unreasonably refused to exercise his powers, and the order should be made.

BENNETT J: The real question which I have to determine is whether the applicant has satisfied me that the tenant for life, the bankrupt, has unreasonably refused to exercise the powers which the Settled Land Act 1925 gives to him as a tenant for life. . . .

There is evidence which satisfies me that for some years past the land comprised in the settlement has been neglected. . . .

The fact that the land has been allowed to fall into this deplorable condition is not a ground for exercising the jurisdiction which section 24 of the Settled Land Act 1925 confers on this court. I have to be satisfied by evidence that the tenant for life has unreasonably refused to exercise the powers which that Act gives him — namely, the powers of sale and the powers of leasing and other powers concerned with the disposal of the land comprised in the settlement.

There are three respects in which, in my judgment, the applicant has proved that the bankrupt has unreasonably refused to exercise his powers . . .

[His Lordship referred to occasions on which the bankrupt unreasonably refused to let farms, to sell to the War Office land which they had requisitioned, and to let some allotments. The tenant for life was acting in this way because he felt aggrieved that the settlor, his mother, had given him only a life interest under the settlement.]

On the evidence I think that it is plain that in the interests of everybody interested in the settled land an order should be made authorizing the trustees of the settlement to exercise on behalf of the tenant for life some of the tenant for life's powers. I do not propose, as at present advised and on the evidence before me, to make an order which will authorize the trustees of the settlement to exercise powers of sale over the whole of the settled land, because, as I understand it, the settled land has been in the possession of the ancestors of the present tenant for life since the days of King John. It may well be that the bankrupt might have objections founded on reason against the whole of the estate being disposed of. The order which I propose to make under the section is one which will enable the Public Trustee, as trustee of the settlement, to exercise in the name and on behalf of the tenant for life the powers of sale in relation to any of the land comprised in the settlement and requisitioned by or on behalf of the War Office, and the powers of the tenant for life to lease any part of the settled land and to exercise all powers conferred on a tenant for life by the Act ancillary to the powers of leasing. I will also make an order on the tenant for life to deliver to the trustee documents of title in his possession relating to the settled land. I will authorize the trustee to exercise the powers of the tenant for life to make a contract to sell the land requisitioned by the War Office and to sell it, and I will vest in the trustee the power to direct investment.

E. Fiduciary Nature of the Powers of the Tenant for Life

SETTLED LAND ACT 1925

107. Tenant for life trustee for all parties interested. — (1) A tenant for life or statutory owner shall, in exercising any power under this Act, have regard to the interests of all parties entitled under the settlement, and shall, in relation to the exercise thereof by him, be deemed to be in the position and to have the duties and liabilities of a trustee for those parties.

In *Wheelwright v Walker* (1883) 23 ChD 752, the defendant was tenant for life of land which was settled within the Settled Land Act 1882, and his daughter was entitled in remainder[12]. The daughter sold her interest in remainder to the plaintiff. The defendant intended to sell under his Settled Land Act powers, the result of such sale being to deprive the plaintiff of his right to occupy the land when the defendant died[13]. No Settled Land Act trustees had been appointed.

PEARSON J granted an injunction on the ground that, since no Settled Land Act trustees had been appointed, the provisions of the Act would not be complied with. On the question of the tenant for life's power to sell, he said at 758:

"So far as I can see, there is no restriction whatever in the Act on the power of a tenant for life to sell. There is nothing that I can see in the Act to enable the Court to restrain him from selling, whether he desires to sell because he is in debt, and wishes to increase his income; or whether, without being in debt, he thinks he can increase his income; or whether he desires to sell from mere unwillingness to take the trouble involved in the management of landed property; or whether he acts from worse motives, as from mere caprice or whim, or because he is desirous of doing that which he knows would be very disagreeable to those who expect to succeed him at his death. There is not, so far as I can see, any power either in the Court or in trustees to interfere with his power of sale[14]. . . . Now if *Elizabeth France*, instead of selling the property to the Plaintiff *J. W. Wheelwright*, had simply settled it, on her marriage, on herself as tenant for life, with remainder to her children, I am of opinion that this Act would have applied, and her father, as tenant for life under the will, could have exercised the power of sale as tenant for life under the Act. I think it makes no difference that *Elizabeth France* simply sold to the Plaintiff *J. W. Wheelwright* instead of settling her interest. I find nothing whatever in the Act which gives any person entitled in remainder any power of any sort or description to interfere with the right of the tenant for life to sell. So far as I can see, the object of the Act is to enable the tenant for life of real estate comprised in a settlement to take it out of the settlement, and to substitute for it, *ex mero motu*, the value of it in pounds, shillings, and pence. I come now to the next question which has been raised. It was said that the tenant for life may have a power to sell, but that there are no trustees here; that trustees are required to be in existence under the Act, and that the

---

[12] Subject to partial divestment if, as was most unlikely, her father had further children.

[13] The plaintiff's interest would be overreached on sale and transferred to the purchase money: SLA 1882, s. 22 (5); SLA 1925, s. 75 (5), p. 301, post.

[14] See also *Cardigan v Curzon-Howe* (1885) 30 ChD 531 at 540, per CHITTY J.

tenant for life cannot sell unless there be trustees under the Act, because he is required to give them notice. . . . Although I do not see exactly what power or control they have over the tenant for life in regard to selling the property, it is quite plain from the whole scope of the Act that the trustees are considered as having an important duty to perform; at all events, I think it clear that even as regards a sale they have this important duty to perform, that if a tenant for life attempted to commit what may be called a fraud, and proposed to sell the property for something infinitely below its real value, it would be the duty of the trustees to come to the Court and ask for an injunction to restrain a sale. I do not think it would be right for them to leave the remainderman to take the objection at some remote period when the evidence might be very conflicting as to the circumstances under which the sale was made, and as to the value of the property; but I think it would be the trustees' duty to bring the matter before the Court, and the Court would have power in that case of controlling the sale, and the more so because the 53rd section of the Act[15] states that 'a tenant for life shall in exercising any power under this Act . . . be deemed to be in the position and to have the duties and liabilities of a trustee for' all parties. I assent to Mr *William Pearson's* argument that a tenant for life in selling under the Act must sell as fairly as trustees must sell for the tenant for life and for those in remainder. . . . Now, there are certainly no trustees here who come within the meaning of the Act. But by the 38th section[16] power is given to 'the tenant for life', or any other person having an interest in the settled land, to come to the Court, and then the Court 'may, if it thinks fit, . . . appoint fit persons to be trustees under the settlement for the purposes of this Act'. I think, therefore, that *John Walker*, the tenant for life, has himself power to sell the fee simple and inheritance of this property if he should comply with the provisions of the Act, but I also think that he has been proceeding, up to the present moment, precipitately, because there are no trustees to whom he can give notice, and therefore I shall grant an injunction to restrain him from selling or offering for sale the property until such time as there shall have been appointed proper trustees of the will for the purposes of the Act, to whom notice can be given and until due notice shall have been given to them of the intention to sell."

In *Middlemas v Stevens* [1901] 1 Ch 574, the defendant was entitled under her deceased husband's will to the enjoyment of a house during widowhood and so long as she resided therein. Intending to marry again, she proposed to grant, under her Settled Land Act powers, a 21 year lease to her intended husband. The remainderman objected, and JOYCE J held that her proposed action was not a bona fide exercise of her powers.

JOYCE J said at 577: "I have no doubt in this case. A tenant for life in exercising any of the powers conferred by the Settled Land Acts must have regard to the interests of all parties entitled under the settlement. Here is a lady who is tenant for life during widowhood. Apart from any question as to her relationship to the gentleman who is the intended lessee, if I found a person, whose interest in the settled property would come to an end to-morrow, persisting in granting a lease which was objected to by all those

---

[15] Replaced by SLA 1925, s. 107 (1), p. 295, ante.
[16] Replaced by SLA 1925, s. 34, p. 299, post.

entitled in remainder, I should regard the case with considerable suspicion. But this case goes beyond suspicion. It is clear from the correspondence that the real object of the lady in granting the lease is that she may herself continue in occupation of the premises. That, in my opinion, is not a bona fide exercise of her powers as tenant for life. But it does not rest there, because it is admitted by the correspondence that she has no intention of granting the lease in the event of her not marrying the gentleman in question. I think the plaintiffs are entitled to an injunction restraining the defendant from granting the lease without their consent or the sanction of the Court[17]."

Subject to restrictions, the tenant for life may however deal with the settled land for his own purposes.

SETTLED LAND ACT 1925

68. Provision enabling dealings with tenant for life. — (1) In the manner mentioned and subject to the provisions contained in this section —

    (*a*) a sale, grant, lease, mortgage, charge or other disposition of settled land, or of any easement, right, or privilege over the same may be made to the tenant for life; or

    (*b*) capital money may be advanced on mortgage to him; or

    (*c*) a purchase may be made from him of land to be made subject to the limitations of the settlement; or

    (*d*) an exchange may be made with him of settled land for other land; and

    (*e*) any such disposition, advance, purchase, or exchange as aforesaid may be made to, from, or with any persons of whom the tenant for life is one.

(2) In every such case the trustees of the settlement shall, in addition to their powers as trustees, have all the powers of a tenant for life in reference to negotiating and completing the transaction, and shall have power to enforce any covenants by the tenant for life, or, where the tenant for life is himself one of the trustees, then the other or others of them shall have such power, and the said powers of a tenant for life may be exercised by the trustees of the settlement in the name and on behalf of the tenant for life[18].

(3) This section applies, notwithstanding that the tenant for life is one of the trustees of the settlement, or that an order has been made authorising the trustees to act on his behalf, or that he is [suffering from mental disorder][19], but does not apply to dealings with any body of persons which includes a trustee of the settlement, not being the tenant for life, unless the transaction is either previously or subsequently approved by the court.

---

[17] See also later proceedings in *Wheelwright v Walker* (1883) 31 WR 912, where a malicious attempt to sell at a deflated price was restrained; *Re Handman and Wilcox's Contract* [1902] 1 Ch 599 (best rent not obtained as required by SLA 1882, s. 7, now SLA 1925, s. 42); *Re Earl Somers* (1895) 11 TLR 567 (lease of public house by teetotal tenant for life containing a term that intoxicating liquors should not be sold).

[18] See *Re Pennant's Will Trusts* [1970] Ch 75, [1969] 2 All ER 862.

[19] Amended by Mental Health Act 1959, s. 149 (1) and Sch. 7, Part I.

VI.   Trustees of the Settlement[20]

SETTLED LAND ACT 1925

30. Who are trustees for purposes of Act. — (1) Subject to the provisions of this Act, the following persons are trustees of a settlement for the purposes of this Act, and are in this Act referred to as the "trustees of the settlement" or "trustees of a settlement", namely —

  (i) the persons, if any, who are for the time being under the settlement, trustees with power of sale of the settled land (subject or not to the consent of any person), or with power of consent to or approval of the exercise of such a power of sale, or if there are no such persons; then

 (ii) the persons, if any, for the time being, who are by the settlement declared to be trustees thereof for the purposes of the Settled Land Acts 1882 to 1890, or any of them, or this Act, or if there are no such persons; then

(iii) the persons, if any, who are for the time being under the settlement trustees with power of or upon trust for sale of any other land comprised in the settlement and subject to the same limitations as the land to be sold or otherwise dealt with, or with power of consent to or approval of the exercise of such a power of sale, or, if there are no such persons; then

 (iv) the persons, if any, who are for the time being under the settlement trustees with future power of sale, or under a future trust for sale of the settled land, or with power of consent to or approval of the exercise of such a future power of sale, and whether the power or trust takes effect in all events or not, or, if there are no such persons; then

  (v) the persons, if any, appointed by deed to be trustees of the settlement by all the persons who at the date of the deed were together able, by virtue of their beneficial interests or by the exercise of an equitable power, to dispose of the settled land in equity for the whole estate the subject of the settlement.

  (2) Paragraphs (i), (iii) and (iv) of the last preceding subsection take effect in like manner as if the powers therein referred to had not by this Act been made exercisable by the tenant for life or statutory owner.

  (3) Where a settlement is created by will, or a settlement has arisen by the effect of an intestacy, and apart from this subsection there would be no trustees for the purposes of this Act of such settlement, then the personal representatives of the deceased shall, until other trustees are appointed, be by virtue of this Act the trustees of the settlement, but where there is a sole personal representative, not being a trust corporation, it shall be obligatory on him to appoint an additional trustee to act with him for the purposes of this Act, and the provisions of the Trustee Act, 1925[1], relating to the appointment of new trustees and the vesting of trust property shall apply accordingly.

---

[20] C & B, pp. 186–189; M & W, pp. 354–358, 384–385, 480–485; MM, pp. 262–266, 276–277.
[1] TA 1925, ss. 36–44.

31. As to trustees of compound settlements. — (1) Persons who are for the time being trustees for the purposes of this Act of an instrument which is a settlement, or is deemed to be a subsisting settlement for the purposes of this Act, shall be the trustees for the purposes of this Act of any settlement constituted by that instrument and any instruments subsequent in date or operation.

[Where there are trustees for the purposes of this Act of the instrument under which there is a tenant for life or statutory owner but there are no trustees for those purposes of a prior instrument, being one of the instruments by which a compound settlement is constituted, those trustees shall, unless and until trustees are appointed of the prior instrument or of the compound settlement, be the trustees for the purposes of this Act of the compound settlement[2].]

34. Appointment of trustees by court. — (1) If at any time there are no trustees of a settlement, or where in any other case it is expedient, for the purposes of this Act, that new trustees of a settlement be appointed, the court may, if it thinks fit, on the application of the tenant for life, statutory owner, or of any other person having, under the settlement, an estate or interest in the settled land, in possession, remainder or otherwise, or, in the case of an infant, of his testamentary or other guardian or next friend, appoint fit persons to be trustees of the settlement.

(2) The persons so appointed, and the survivors and survivor of them, while continuing to be trustees or trustee, and, until the appointment of new trustees, the personal representatives or representative for the time being of the last surviving or continuing trustee, shall become and be the trustees or trustee of the settlement.

35. Procedure on appointment of new trustees. — (1) Whenever a new trustee for the purposes of this Act is appointed of a trust instrument or a trustee thereof for the purposes aforesaid is discharged from the trust without a new trustee being appointed, a deed shall be executed supplemental to the last or only principal vesting instrument containing a declaration that the persons therein named, being the persons who after such appointment or discharge, as the case may be, are the trustees of the trust instrument for the purposes aforesaid, are the trustees of the settlement for those purposes; and a memorandum shall be endorsed on or annexed to the last or only principal vesting instrument in accordance with the Trustee Act, 1925.

(2) Every such deed as aforesaid shall, if the trustee was appointed or discharged by the court, be executed by such person as the court may direct, and, in any other case, shall be executed by —

(i) the person, if any, named in the principal vesting instrument as the person for the time being entitled to appoint new trustees of the settlement, or if no person is so named, or the person is dead or unable or unwilling to act, the persons who if the principal vesting instrument had been the only instrument constituting the settlement would have had power to appoint new trustees thereof;

(ii) the persons named in the deed of declaration as the trustees of the settlement; and

(iii) any trustee who is discharged as aforesaid or retires.

---

[2] The words in square brackets were added by LP (A) A 1926, Sch.

(3) A statement contained in any such deed of declaration as is mentioned in this section to the effect that the person named in the principal vesting instrument as the person for the time being entitled to appoint new trustees of the settlement is unable or unwilling to act, or that a trustee has remained outside the United Kingdom for more than twelve months, or refuses or is unfit to act, or is incapable of acting, shall in favour of a purchaser of a legal estate be conclusive evidence of the matter stated.

95. Trustees' receipts. The receipt or direction in writing of or by the trustees of the settlement, or where a sole trustee is a trust corporation, of or by that trustee, or of or by the personal representatives of the last surviving or continuing trustee, for or relating to any money or securities, paid or transferred to or by the direction of the trustees, trustee, or representatives, as the case may be, effectually discharges the payer or transferor therefrom, and from being bound to see to the application or being answerable for any loss or misapplication thereof, and, in case of a mortgagee or other person advancing money, from being concerned to see that any money advanced by him is wanted for any purpose of this Act, or that no more than is wanted is raised.

Provisions relating to the protection of trustees are contained in Settled Land Act 1925, sections 96–98.

VII.   Capital Money[3]

A.   Application

SETTLED LAND ACT 1925

75. Regulations respecting investment, devolution, and income of securities, &c.[4] — (1) Capital money arising under this Act[5] shall, in order to its being invested or applied as aforesaid, be paid either to the trustees of the settlement or into court at the option of the tenant for life, and shall be invested or applied by the trustees, or under the direction of the court, as the case may be, accordingly.

(2) The investment or other application by the trustees shall be made according to the direction of the tenant for life, and in default thereof according to the discretion of the trustees, but in the last-mentioned case subject to any consent required or direction given by the settlement with respect to the investment or other application by the trustees of trust money of the settlement, and any investment shall be in the names or under the control of the trustees.

(3) The investment or other application under the direction of the court shall be made on the application of the tenant for life, or of the trustees.

(4) Any investment or other application shall not during the subsistence of the beneficial interest of the tenant for life be altered without his consent.

(5) Capital money arising under this Act while remaining uninvested or unapplied, and securities on which an investment of any such capital money

---

[3] C & B, pp. 189–192; M & W, pp. 372–376, 402–403; MM, pp. 272–273, 285–286.
[4] As to investment of capital money, see SLA 1925, ss. 73, 74 and Trustee Investments Act 1961, p. 219, ante.
[5] For the meaning of capital money, see W & C, vol. 2, pp. 156–157.

is made shall for all purposes of disposition, transmission and devolution be treated as land, and shall be held for and go to the same persons successively, in the same manner and for and on the same estates, interests, and trusts, as the land wherefrom the money arises would, if not disposed of, have been held and have gone under the settlement.

(6) The income of those securities shall be paid or applied as the income of that land, if not disposed of, would have been payable or applicable under the settlement.

(7) Those securities may be converted into money, which shall be capital money arising under this Act.

(8) All or any part of any capital money paid into court may, if the court thinks fit, be at any time paid out to the trustees of the settlement.

B. Improvements
SETTLED LAND ACT 1925

83. Description of improvements authorised by Act. — Improvements authorised by this Act are the making or execution on, or in connexion with, and for the benefit of settled land, of any of the works mentioned in the Third Schedule to this Act, or of any works for any of the purposes mentioned in that Schedule, and any operation incident to or necessary or proper in the execution of any of those works, or necessary or proper for carrying into effect any of those purposes, or for securing the full benefit of any of those works or purposes.

84. Mode of application of capital money. — (1) Capital money arising under this Act may be applied in or towards payment for any improvement authorised by this Act or by the settlement, without any scheme for the execution of the improvement being first submitted for approval to, or approved by, the trustees of the settlement or the court.

The Third Schedule is divided into three Parts:
I   Improvements, the costs of which are not liable to be replaced by instalments.
II   Improvements, the costs of which the trustees of the settlement or the court may require to be replaced by instruments.
III Improvements, the costs of which the trustees of the settlement or the court must require to be replaced by instalments[6].

C. Receipts
SETTLED LAND ACT 1925

94. Number of trustees to act. — (1) Notwithstanding anything in this Act, capital money arising under this Act shall not be paid to fewer than two persons as trustees of the settlement, unless the trustee is a trust corporation[7].

---

[6] Law Reform Committee 23rd Report (The Powers and Duties of Trustees) 1982 (Cmnd 8733), paras. 8–11, suggested that the provisions of the Third Schedule "undoubtedly require modernisation".
[7] See SLA 1925, s. 95, p. 300, ante.

D. Investment (Pp. 219–220, ante)

VIII.   Change of Ownership

SETTLED LAND ACT 1925

7. Procedure on change of ownership. — (1) If, on the death of a tenant for life or statutory owner, or of the survivor of two or more tenants for life or statutory owners, in whom the settled land was vested, the land remains settled land, his personal representatives shall hold the settled land on trust, if and when required to so do, to convey it to the person who under the trust instrument or by virtue of this Act becomes the tenant for life or statutory owner and, if more than one, as joint tenants.

(2) If a person by reason of attaining full age becomes a tenant for life for the purposes of this Act of settled land, he shall be entitled to require the trustees of the settlement, personal representatives, or other persons in whom the settled land is vested, to convey the land to him.

(3) If a person who, when of full age, will together with another person or other persons constitute the tenant for life for the purposes of this Act of settled land attains that age, he shall be entitled to require the tenant for life, trustees of the settlement, personal representatives or other persons in whom the settled land is vested to convey the land to him and the other person or persons who together with him constitute the tenant for life as joint tenants.

(4) If by reason of forfeiture, surrender, or otherwise the estate owner of any settled land ceases to have the statutory powers of a tenant for life and the land remains settled land, he shall be bound forthwith to convey the settled land to the person who under the trust instrument, or by virtue of this Act, becomes the tenant for life or statutory owner and, if more than one, as joint tenants.

(5) If any person of full age becomes absolutely entitled to the settled land (whether beneficially, or as personal representative, or as trustee for sale, or otherwise) free from all limitations, powers, and charges taking effect under the settlement, he shall be entitled to require the trustees of the settlement, personal representatives, or other persons in whom the settled land is vested, to convey the land to him, and if more persons than one being of full age become so entitled to the settled land they shall be entitled to require such persons as aforesaid to convey the land to them as joint tenants.

8. Mode and costs of conveyance, and saving of rights of personal representatives and equitable chargees. — (1) A conveyance by personal representatives under either of the last two preceding sections may be made by an assent in writing signed by them which shall operate as a conveyance.

(4) Where the land is or remains settled land a conveyance under either of the last two preceding sections[8] shall —

(a) if by deed, be a principal vesting deed; and

(b) if by an assent, be a vesting assent, which shall contain the like statements and particulars as are required by this Act in the case of a principal vesting deed.

---

[8] For s. 6, see p. 279, ante.

ADMINISTRATION OF ESTATES ACT 1925

22. Special executors as respects settled land. — (1) A testator may appoint, and in default of such express appointment shall be deemed to have appointed, as his special executors in regard to settled land, the persons, if any, who are at his death the trustees of the settlement thereof, and probate may be granted to such trustees specially limited to the settled land.

In this subsection "settled land" means land vested in the testator which was settled previously to his death and not by his will[9].

(2) A testator may appoint other persons either with or without such trustees as aforesaid or any of them to be his general executors in regard to his other property and assets.

24. Power for special personal representatives to dispose of settled land. — (1) The special personal representatives may dispose of the settled land without the concurrence of the general personal representatives, who may likewise dispose of the other property and assets of the deceased without the concurrence of the special personal representatives.

(2) In this section the expression "special personal representatives" means the representatives appointed to act for the purposes of settled land and includes any original personal representative who is to act with an additional personal representative for those purposes.

IX. Protection of Purchasers[10]

SETTLED LAND ACT 1925

110. Protection of purchasers, &c. — (1) On a sale, exchange, lease, mortgage, charge, or other disposition, a purchaser dealing in good faith with a tenant for life or statutory owner shall, as against all parties entitled under the settlement, be conclusively taken to have given the best price, consideration, or rent, as the case may require, that could reasonably be obtained by the tenant for life or statutory owner, and to have complied with all the requisitions of this Act[11].

(2) A purchaser of a legal estate in settled land shall not, except as hereby expressly provided, be bound or entitled to call for the production of the trust instrument or any information concerning that instrument or any ad valorem stamp duty thereon, and whether or not he has notice of its contents he shall, save as hereinafter provided, be bound and entitled if the last or only principal vesting instrument contains the statements and particulars required by this Act to assume that —

(a) the person in whom the land is by the said document vested or declared to be vested is the tenant for life or statutory owner and has all the powers of a tenant for life under this Act, including such additional or larger powers, if any, as are therein mentioned;

---

[9] *Re Bridgett and Hayes' Contract* [1928] Ch 163, p. 306, post. For similar result in the case of intestacy, see Supreme Court Act 1981, s. 116. See too W & C, vol. 5, pp. 36–38.

[10] C & B, pp. 757–761; M & W, pp. 335–339; MM, pp. 249–256.

[11] See *Weston v Henshaw* [1950] Ch 510, p. 282, ante; *Re Morgan's Lease* [1972] Ch 1, [1971] 2 All ER 235, p. 282, ante; see also *Gilmore v O'Conor* [1947] IR 462; *Davies v Hall* [1954] 1 WLR 855, [1954] 2 All ER 330, raising the question whether the purchaser can claim to be acting in good faith when the tenant for life's failure to observe the statutory requirements was discoverable; *Re Handman and Wilcox's Contract* [1902] 1 Ch 599 (transferee from lessee).

(*b*) the persons by the said instrument stated to be the trustees of the settlement, or their successors appearing to be duly appointed, are the properly constituted trustees of the settlement;

(*c*) the statements and particulars required by this Act and contained (expressly or by reference) in the said instrument were correct at the date thereof;

(*d*) the statements contained in any deed executed in accordance with this Act declaring who are the trustees of the settlement for the purposes of this Act are correct;

(*e*) the statements contained in any deed of discharge, executed in accordance with this Act, are correct;

Provided that, as regards the first vesting instrument executed for the purpose of giving effect to —

(*a*) a settlement subsisting at the commencement of this Act; or

(*b*) an instrument which by virtue of this Act is deemed to be a settlement[12]; or

(*c*) a settlement which by virtue of this Act is deemed to have been made by any person after the commencement of this Act; or

(*d*) an instrument inter vivos intended to create a settlement of a legal estate in land which is executed after the commencement of this Act and does not comply with the requirements of this Act with respect to the method of effecting such a settlement;

a purchaser shall be concerned to see —

(i) that the land disposed of to him is comprised in such settlement or instrument;

(ii) that the person in whom the settled land is by such vesting instrument vested, or declared to be vested, is the person in whom it ought to be vested as tenant for life or statutory owner;

(iii) that the persons thereby stated to be the trustees of the settlement are the properly constituted trustees of the settlement.

(3) A purchaser of a legal estate in settled land from a personal representative shall be entitled to act on the following assumptions:—

(i) If the capital money, if any, payable in respect of the transaction is paid to the personal representative, that such representative is acting under his statutory or other powers and requires the money for purposes of administration;

(ii) If such capital money is, by the direction of the personal representative, paid to persons who are stated to be the trustees of a settlement, that such persons are the duly constituted trustees of the settlement for the purposes of this Act, and that the personal representative is acting under his statutory powers during a minority;

(iii) In any other case, that the personal representative is acting under his statutory or other powers.

(4) Where no capital money arises under a transaction, a disposition by a tenant for life or statutory owner shall, in favour of a purchaser of a legal estate, have effect under this Act notwithstanding that at the date of the transaction there are no trustees of the settlement.

(5) If a conveyance of or an assent relating to land formerly subject to a vesting instrument does not state who are the trustees of the settlement for

---

[12] See p. 280, n. 20, ante.

the purposes of this Act, a purchaser of a legal estate shall be bound and entitled to act on the assumption that the person in whom the land was thereby vested was entitled to the land free from all limitations, powers, and charges taking effect under that settlement, absolutely and beneficially, or, if so expressed in the conveyance or assent, as personal representative, or trustee for sale or otherwise, and that every statement of fact in such conveyance or assent is correct.

The scheme of the Settled Land Act 1925 with the exceptions as shown in the proviso to section 110 (2), is based on the assumption that the purchaser of settled land is unaffected by the beneficial interests of the settlement. The scheme assumes that the appropriate machinery is correctly used; and the Act does not provide answers to the problems that will arise if mistakes are made[13]. Problems are most likely to arise in connection with a vesting instrument. Fraudulent suppression of deeds is another hazard, not however confined to settled land[14].

(1946) 62 LQR 167, at pp. 168–169 (A. H. Withers)
"Conveyancers also assume that, in connexion with settled land, abstracted documents purporting to be vesting deeds, vesting assents by personal representatives of deceased tenants for life, deeds of declaration and deeds of discharge operate according to their tenor, except (1) in the case of the first vesting instrument made to give effect to a pre-1926 settlement, and (2) where facts or events are disclosed which suggest that some mistake has been made. In practice conveyancers must make these assumptions, though . . . unless section 110 of the Settled Land Act 1925 is benevolently construed by the court, such assumptions are not justified."

RE BRIDGETT AND HAYES' CONTRACT
[1928] Ch 163 (ChD, Romer J)

At the date of her death on 17 January 1926, Mrs Thornley was tenant for life of settled land, and Jackson was sole surviving trustee of the settlement, which came to an end on Mrs Thornley's death.

Mrs Thornley appointed Bridgett as her sole executor, and he entered into an agreement to sell the land to Hayes. Hayes objected on the ground that title should have been made by Mrs Thornley's special representative under the Administration of Estates Act, 1925, section 22 (1).

Held. Bridgett was able to give a good title to the land.

Romer J: It is common ground that up to the date of her death Mrs Emily Margaret Thornley, who was the tenant for life of the property now in question, had vested in her the legal estate in the property. It is common ground that, that being so, on her death this legal estate passed to her personal representative by virtue of subsections 1 and 3 of section 1 of the Administration of Estates Act, 1925. But then it is said that by virtue of

---

[13] Similar problems have arisen in connection with AEA 1925, s. 36 (1): *Re Duce and Boots Cash Chemists (Southern) Ltd's Contract* [1937] Ch 642, [1937] 3 All ER 788; *Re Alefounder's Will Trusts* [1927] 1 Ch 360.
[14] *Pilcher v Rawlins* (1872) 7 Ch App 259, p. 26, ante; *Weston v Henshaw* [1950] Ch 510, p. 282, ante.

section 22, subsection 1, of that Act, in such a case as this the lady must be deemed to have appointed as her special executor in regard to this land the person who up to the date of her death was sole surviving trustee for the purposes of the Settled Land Act. Let me assume that that was so. On 17 January 1926, she died, and on 7 April 1926, a general grant of probate of her will was made to Thomas William Bridgett, a person whom she had thereby appointed as executor. As from that date, at any rate, wherever the legal estate in this property may have been as between the date of her death and this act of probate, the legal estate in this land vested in Thomas William Bridgett, and, while that act of probate remains unrevoked, he can in my opinion properly convey the legal estate to the purchaser. Section 204 of the Law of Property Act, 1925, subsection 1, says this: "An order of the Court under any statutory or other jurisdiction shall not, as against a purchaser, be invalidated on the ground of want of jurisdiction, or of want of any concurrence, consent, notice, or service, whether the purchaser has notice of any such want or not." Section 22, subsection 1 (if the purchaser is right as to its application at all to this case), provided that probate might have been granted to this sole surviving trustee. In point of fact the Court of Probate did not grant probate to him, but granted probate to Thomas William Bridgett. That being so, it appears to me that section 204 of the Law of Property Act applies to the case with regard to the taking of a conveyance from the legal personal representative. Further, the purchaser would be protected in the event of any subsequent revocation of that grant of probate by section 37, subsection 1, of the Administration of Estates Act, 1925. It can hardly be doubted that in this case, if the purchaser does take a conveyance from the person to whom the grant of probate was granted, he would be acting in good faith, within the meaning of section 55, subsection 1 (xviii), of the Act. . . .

The point still remains as to whether section 22, subsection 1, applies to the present case, it being conceded on both sides that on the death of this lady the settlement came to an end.

[His Lordship read section 22 (1) and continued:]

Section 22 is the first of three sections which are introduced under the general heading "Special Provisions as to Settled Land". In sections 23 and 24 it is I think reasonably clear that "settled land" means land which after the death of the testator continues to be settled land, and the words in section 22, subsection 1, " 'settled land' means land vested in the testator which was settled previously to his death and not by his will" refer in terms only to that particular subsection. I cannot help thinking that these words were merely designed for the purpose of making it clear that section 22, subsection 1, did not apply to a case where the land was settled by the will of a testator. However, I have to deal with the words as I find them, and that being so I must read the earlier part of the sub-section as follows: "A testator may appoint and in default of such express appointment shall be deemed to have appointed as his special executors in regard to land vested in the testator which was settled previously to his death the persons if any who are at his death the trustees of the settlement thereof." So far down to the words "previously to his death" the section applies to the present case, because here land was vested in the testatrix and it had been settled previously to her death. Then the sub-section says she shall be deemed to have appointed as her special executors the persons, if any, who are at her death the trustees of the settlement. Now before any one can go to the Court of Probate and get probate specially limited to the settled land granted to him, he must be in a position to say to the Court that he is to be deemed to have been appointed special executor of this land, because at the death of the testator he was trustee of the settlement thereof. But in my opinion he is not in a position to make that statement if the settlement comes to an end the moment the testator dies. It is to be observed that the sub-section does not refer to the persons who immediately before the death of the testator were the trustees of the settlement, but to the persons who at his death are the trustees of the settlement.

The words "persons who are at his death the trustees of the settlement" connote to my mind persons who are trustees notwithstanding his death, especially when it is realized that the section is dealing with the testator's will, which comes into operation only when he is dead.

For these reasons I think this sub-section does not apply in a case like the present, where, upon the death of the testatrix in question, the settlement existing up to that date comes to an end.

It has been seen that difficulties can arise where a vesting instrument is executed by those who appear to the purchaser to be the wrong persons. Similarly there may be doubt as to whether or not the land is settled land and whether, if it is settled, it has been vested in the right person as tenant for life. There seems little doubt that a purchaser who follows the correct Settled Land Act machinery is intended to be protected; but, as he is a purchaser with notice of the existence of trusts affecting the land, statutory authority is needed to protect him. And if he discovers the flaw on the title by extraneous enquiries or by chance and objects to the title, it will be odd if he is compelled to take a bad title[15].

Megarry and Wade, *Law of Real Property* (5th edn.), p. 335:

"Suppose, for example, that a testator leaves his land by his will to his widow, W, for life or until remarriage, with remainder to X in fee simple; and that the widow remarries, and then nevertheless purports (as tenant for life) to sell the land to P, P duly paying the purchase-money to the trustees. If P had been allowed to inspect the trust instrument he would have discovered that W was no longer tenant for life and consequently had no power to sell to him. But he cannot discover it from the vesting deed or assent, which is all he is allowed to see. He must assume what is untrue, that W is still tenant for life. He probably obtains the legal estate, for that was vested in W and should pass by her conveyance[16]. But it seems unlikely that P can rely upon section 110 (2), mentioned above, for on W's remarriage the settlement came to an end, and P is not 'a purchaser of a legal estate in settled land.' P is a

---

[15] See (1939) 83 SJ 45 (A. H. Withers); (1946) 10 Conv (NS) 135 (H. Potter); (1947) 11 Conv (NS) 91 (H. Potter), 159 (B. B. Benas); (1958) 22 Conv (NS) 78 (F. R. Crane).

[16] Notwithstanding s. 18 for that applies only to a conveyance by a tenant for life, and W ceased to be tenant for life when she remarried.

purchaser with constructive notice of the trust in favour of X, which W (not being tenant for life) has no power to overreach[17]. P therefore takes a bad title. This disaster would be avoided only if 'settled land' could be held to mean 'land which appears to be settled land but is not[18]'. If that were possible, P could plead purchase of a legal estate without notice that W was not still tenant for life and so empowered to sell[19]."

X.   Termination of Settlements[20]

A.   Duration

SETTLED LAND ACT 1925

3.   Duration of settlements. — Land [not held upon trust for sale][1] which has been subject to a settlement shall be deemed for the purposes of this Act to remain and be settled land, and the settlement shall be deemed to be a subsisting settlement for the purposes of this Act so long as —

(a)   any limitation, charge, or power of charging under the settlement subsists, or is capable of being exercised; or

(b)   the person who, if of full age, would be entitled as beneficial owner to have that land vested in him for a legal estate is an infant.

7.   Procedure on change of ownership. — (5), p. 303, ante.

B.   Deed of Discharge

SETTLED LAND ACT 1925

17.   Deed of discharge on termination of settlement. — (1) Where the estate owner of any settled land holds the land free from all equitable interests and powers under a trust instrument, the persons who in the last or only principal vesting instrument or the last or only endorsement on or annex thereto are declared to be the trustees of the settlement or the survivors of them shall, save as hereinafter mentioned, be bound to execute, at the cost of the trust estate, a deed declaring that they are discharged from the trust so far as regards that land: . . .

Where the land is affected by a derivative settlement or trust for sale, the deed of discharge shall contain a statement that the land is settled land by virtue of such vesting instrument as aforesaid and the trust instrument therein referred to, or is held on trust for sale by virtue of such conveyance as aforesaid, as the case may require.

(3) Where a deed or order of discharge contains no statement to the contrary, a purchaser of a legal estate in the land to which the deed or order relates shall be entitled to assume that the land has ceased to be settled land, and is not subject to any trust for sale[2].

---

[17] SLA 1925, s. 72: cf. ss. 7 (4), 19. In Wolst. & C. ii, 44 it is said that "title can be made by the *de facto* estate owner," but no such general rule is laid down in the Act. See A. H. Withers in 83 SJ 45, and (1946) 62 LQR 168, 169; (1958) 22 Conv (NS) at p. 78 (F. R. Crane).

[18] "For a somewhat similar interpretation of another section of the Act (s. 36), see p. 452": (M & W, p. 336, n. 7).

[19] For further analysis, see [1984] Conv 354 (P. A. Stone); [1985] Conv 377 (R. Warrington).

[20] C & B, pp. 756–757; M & W, pp. 339–341; MM, pp. 256–257.

[1] The words in square brackets were inserted by LP (A) A 1926, s. 7 and Sch.

[2] For the unsatisfactory position of a termination of a trust for sale of land, see p. 240, ante.

110. Protection of purchasers, &c. — (5), p. 305, ante.

QUÈSTIONS

(*a*) T died in 1916, having appointed the Public Trustee sole trustee of her will, and devising land to her husband for life, and after his death to her sister A, and on A's death to the Public Trustee on trust to sell and divide the proceeds between six nieces of her husband. Her husband died in 1929. A vesting assent duly vested the legal estate in A as tenant for life. A, after giving notice to the Public Trustee, sold the land to various purchasers at a time of rapidly rising prices and in circumstances which showed that the sales were commercially most imprudent. The nieces did not know of the sales until A's death. Advise the nieces whether they have a basis of complaint against A's estate, the Public Trustee, or the purchasers.

If the nieces had known of the intention to sell, could they have prevented the sale?

See *England v Public Trustee* (1967) 205 EG 651, where SELLERS LJ suggested that it would be desirable to provide that notice of an intended sale should be given to the beneficiaries under a settlement. See also SLA 1925, ss. 30 (3), 97, 101.

(*b*) What arguments would you put forward on behalf of the purchaser in the hypothetical case on p. 308, ante?

(*c*) Would a purchaser from personal representatives obtain a good title on facts which were identical with those of *Re Bridgett and Hayes' Contract* except for the fact that, as the purchaser later discovered, the settlement had not come to an end?

(*d*) A purported to convey land to B for life and after B's death to C in fee. Later A executed a vesting deed vesting the land in B as tenant for life under the settlement and executed also a trust instrument. B, relying on the vesting deed, sold the land to X. Is X entitled to the protection of SLA 1925, s. 110 (2)? See SLA, ss. 4, 5, 9, 18, 110 (2); (1946) 10 Conv (NS) 139–140.

XI. Registered Land[3]

Settled land is registered in the name of the estate owner. The beneficial interests under the settlement are included in the definition of minor interests (LRA 1925, section 3 (xv), p. 136, ante), but they will be overridden (i.e. overreached) on a sale by the estate owner in the same way as they would be with unregistered land. A purchaser will discover that the land is settled land by means of a restriction[4] which, in whatever form is appropriate (Statutory Forms 9, 10, 11, Land Registration Rules 1925. See Form 9, p. 311, post), is required to be entered on the register.

LAND REGISTRATION ACT 1925

74. Notice of trust not to affect registered dealing. — P. 99, ante.

---

[3] C & B, pp. 192–193; M & W, pp. 215, 219–220; MM, pp. 292–294; Ruoff and Roper, Chap. 19.

[4] P. 138, ante.

86.   Registration of settled land. — (1) Settled land shall be registered in the name of the tenant for life or statutory owner.

(2) The successive or other interests created by or arising under a settlement shall (save as regards any legal estate which cannot be overridden under the powers of the Settled Land Act, 1925[5], or any other statute) take effect as minor interests and not otherwise . . .[6]

(3) There shall also be entered on the register such restrictions[7] as may be prescribed, or may be expedient, for the protection of the rights of the persons beneficially interested in the land, and such restrictions shall (subject to the provisions of this Act relating to releases by the trustees of a settlement and to transfers by a tenant for life whose estate has ceased in his lifetime)[8] be binding on the proprietor during his life, but shall not restrain or otherwise affect a disposition by his personal representative.

(5) References in this Act to the "tenant for life" shall, where the context admits, be read as referring to the tenant for life, statutory owner, or personal representative who is entitled to be registered.

49.   Rules to provide for notices of other rights, interests and claims. — (2) A notice shall not be registered in respect of any estate, right, or interest which (independently of this Act) is capable of being overridden by the proprietor under a trust for sale[9] or the powers of the Settled Land Act, 1925[10], or any other statute, or of a settlement, and of being protected by a restriction in the prescribed manner: . . .

LAND REGISTRATION RULES 1925

104.   Duty to apply for restrictions when land is settled. — (1) On the creation of a settlement it shall be the duty of the proprietor, or (if there is no proprietor) the personal representatives of a deceased proprietor, to apply to the Registrar for the entry of such restrictions or inhibitions or notices as may be appropriate to the case.

The application shall state that they are required for the protection of the minor interests under the settlement.

Statutory Form 9

Restriction where Tenant for Life is registered as proprietor

No disposition under which capital money arises is to be registered unless the money is paid to . . . (the trustees of the settlement . . .), or into Court.

Except under an order of the Registrar, no disposition is to be registered, unless authorised by the Settled Land Act, 1925.

---

[5] SLA 1925, s. 72 (2), p. 284, ante.
[6] See (1958) 22 Conv (NS) 14 at pp. 23–24 (F. R. Crane), where it is suggested that, if no restriction is entered, a beneficiary in possession of settled land cannot claim an overriding interest under LRA 1925, s. 70 (1) (*g*).
[7] P. 138, ante.
[8] LRA 1925, s. 87 (4), (6).
[9] LPA 1925, s. 2, p. 205, ante; s. 27, p. 218, ante.
[10] SLA 1925, s. 72, p. 284, ante; s. 110, p. 304, ante.

XII. Law Reform

In 1985 the Law Commission Working Paper No. 94: Trusts of Land made the following proposals for reform:

I. A New Trust of Land. The trustees would hold the legal estate in the land with a *power* to sell and a *power* to retain. It would be used for both successive and concurrent interests. The two existing systems of strict settlement and trust for sale would be abolished, and the new trust would apply to all existing strict settlements and trusts for sale. (paras. 6.1–12.1)

II. Conversion of All Settlements into Trusts for Sale. SLA 1925 would be repealed, and all successive and concurrent interests would exist behind a trust for sale. (paras. 13.1–13.10)

III. Changing the Burden of Proof. All settlements would exist behind a trust for sale, unless expressly made under SLA 1925. (para. 14.1)

IV. A New Form of Co-ownership. It would only operate where the legal and equitable interests are identical i.e. where land is held by joint tenants on trust for themselves as joint tenants (and not as tenants in common). It would not involve a trust, and the joint owners would be treated as a single owner.

V. Miscellaneous Reforms. These include the reform and codification of the law of severance (p. 246 ante), the prevention of the inadvertent settlement under SLA 1925 which arises from a right to reside on land for life (p. 275, n. 4a, ante), and the abolition of the doctrine of conversion in relation to trusts for sale (p. 266 ante). (paras. 16.1–16.18)

The Law Commission has some preference for I (the more radical proposal) than II. The proposals are not all mutually exclusive, and the miscellaneous reforms in V, which do not alter the basic structure, could be combined with II, III and IV. Proposal I stands alone. (paras. 5.1, 17.1)

QUESTION
Which proposal do you prefer? Law Commission Working Paper No. 94 (1985); C & B, pp. 199–205; articles at p. 203, n. 8, ante.

7. Perpetuities and Accumulations[1]

I. General

The policy of the law has always been to prevent property from being tied up in perpetuity. The problem has been met in various forms. Conditions

---

[1] C & B, pp. 291–319; M & W, pp. 231–310; MM, pp. 196–233; Gray, *Rule Against Perpetuities* (4th edn. 1942); Maudsley, *Modern Law of Perpetuities* (1979); Morris and Leach, *Rule Against Perpetuities* (2nd edn., 1962 and supplement, 1964); *Theobald on Wills* (14th edn 1982), chap. 44; Holdsworth, HEL, vol. vii, pp. 81–144, 193–238; Simpson, *Introduction to the History of the Land Law*, pp. 195–224.

preventing alienation are void[2], as are non-charitable trusts of perpetual duration[3]; estates tail have been barrable since *Taltarum's Case* in 1472[4], in which a condition against barring was held void[5]; and the subsequent device of the creation of successive life estates was prevented by a rule which is one aspect of the rule against double possibilities, but which is better known under its 19th century title of the rule in *Whitby v Mitchell*[6]. The emergence of the modern rule against perpetuities was inevitable once it was established that executory limitations were valid at law, and were indestructible by a tortious feoffment by the tenant in possession[7]; the power to project estates into the future was unlimited.

The rule was therefore concerned with the extent to which estates could be made to vest in the future, and the period finally established was that of a life or lives in being plus 21 years plus a period of gestation in respect of a life in being or of a beneficiary if a posthumous child were born[8].

A. Relationship between Vesting and Living Persons

Gray's famous and authoritative statement of the Rule is: "No interest is good unless it must vest, if at all, not later than twenty-one years after some life in being at the creation of the interest". This is one author's formulation and not a statute. There are special situations, dealt with below[9], where exceptions have to be made. It does not mean, of course, that an interest will be invalid, unless it is certain to vest within the period of a life in being plus 21 years. The Rule is concerned with contingent interests, and, by definition, such an interest may never vest at all. The point is that, to comply with the Rule, the interest must be such that, if it does vest in the future, it must necessarily do so within the period. Put another way, and in a way which is sometimes thought to be easier to comprehend, an interest is void if it might by any possibility vest outside the period.

It is amazing that the Rule, so simple on its face, has caused such difficulty in its operation. What has to be appreciated is that the Rule requires the *recognition of a relationship* between the vesting and the lives of living people. The question is: is it certain that the interest must vest, if it vest at all, within 21 years of the death of some person now living? That is a simple legal formulation. The difficulty is in the recognition of the *relationship* between the vesting and the lives, that is, in being able to say for certain whether a

---

[2] Litt s. 306; Co Litt 206b, 223a; and cases quoted in C & B, pp. 349–351; M & W, pp. 72–73; MM, p. 42.
[3] *Carne v Long* (1860) 2 De GF & J 75; *Gilmour v Coats* [1949] AC 426, [1949] 1 All ER 848; *Leahy v A-G for New South Wales* [1959] AC 457, [1959] 2 All ER 300; *Macaulay v O'Donnell* [1943] Ch 435 n; M & B, *Trusts and Trustees* (3rd edn, 1984), chap. 8; H & M, chap. 14; Maudsley, pp. 166–178; Morris and Leach, pp. 307–327.
[4] (1472) YB 12 Edw 4 Ed 19.
[5] *Corbet's Case* (1600) 1 Co Rep 83b; *Mildmay's Case* (1605) 6 Co Rep 40a; *Portington's Case* (1613) 10 Co Rep 35b.
[6] (1889) 42 ChD 494; *affd.* (1890) 44 ChD 85. The rule was abolished in 1925: LPA 1925, s. 161.
[7] *Pells v Brown* (1620) Cro Jac 590; Gray, s. 159; Morris and Leach, chap. 1.
[8] *Duke of Norfolk's Case* (1681) 3 Cas in Ch 1; *Lloyd v Carew* (1697) Show Parl Cas 137, 1 Moo PCC 133n; *Stephens v Stephens* (1736) Cas temp Talb 228; *Thellusson v Woodford* (1805) 11 Ves 112; *Cadell v Palmer* (1883) 1 Cl & Fin 372; *Re Wilmer's Trusts* [1903] 2 Ch 411; *Re Stern* [1962] Ch 732, [1961] 3 All ER 1129.
[9] P. 357, post.

particular contingent interest is certain to vest within 21 years of someone's death; or, to put it the other way, whether the contingent interest might vest outside the period.

As will be seen in the discussion which follows, there is no need to attempt to define who the "lives in being" may be. Anyone will do; so long as the interest must vest, if at all, within 21 years of the dropping of that life. The life (or lives) in being is (are), therefore, that person (those persons) within 21 years of whose death (deaths) the interest must vest, if it vest at all. They are the lives who validate the gift. There are no "lives in being" in the case of void gifts. The only problems in relation to "lives in being" are those in which the settlor has himself expressly selected the persons whose lives are to be used for the purpose.

Thus a gift

   (i) to the first child of A (who is alive) to marry was void at common law, because the first child of A to marry might be a future born child, and that future born child was not certain to marry, if at all, within 21 years of the death of a person living at the date of the gift.

  (ii) to the first child of A to attain the age of 21. This is valid whether A is alive or dead. If A is alive, it is valid because A's first child must attain the age of 21 within 21 years of A's death (a period of gestation is added in the case of posthumous children). A is the "life in being". If A is dead, the first child to attain the age of 21 must be a child of A living at the date of the gift. The child is the "life in being".

 (iii) to the first great-grandchild of A to go for a walk with X. This is valid, because it must happen, if at all (and however unlikely in fact), during X's lifetime. X is the "life in being".

  (iv) to the first child of A (who is alive) to marry a person now living. This is valid, because the marriage must take place, if at all, within the lifetime of a living person (though not yet identified).

   (v) to the first grandchild of A (who is alive) to attain the age of 21. This is void, because the first grandchild of A to attain the age of 21 might be a child of a future born child of A, and may attain the age of 21 more than 21 years after the death of any person alive at the date of the gift.

  (vi) to the first grandchild of A (who is deceased) to attain the age of 21. This is valid, because any grandchild of A, whether born at the date of the gift or not, must attain the age of 21 within 21 years of the death of a child of A. A's children are the "lives in being". If a child (or all the children) of A be dead, his (their) children must be alive and they would be the "lives in being".

B.   Vesting in Interest. Vesting in Possession

The requirement of vesting is that the gift must vest in interest but not necessarily in possession. This means that the beneficiary or beneficiaries must be ascertained and that all prior conditions have been satisfied[10]. In the case of class gifts, the size and the share of each beneficiary must be known

---

[10] Maudsley, p. 10; Morris and Leach, p. 1.

before the class gift is considered to vest for the purposes of the perpetuity rule[11]; a class gift does not therefore vest for this purpose until there can be no possibility of the membership of the class increasing or decreasing. Thus, a gift "to the children of A" does not "vest", as a class gift in this context, until A dies; for A may have further children after the date of the gift. And a gift "to the children of A who survive both their parents" does not vest, as a class gift in this context, until the death of both parents; for, although there can be no more children of those parents after the death of either of them, the number of members of the class may be reduced at any time before the death of the survivor, and this possibility prevents vesting until that time.

C. Remorseless Application

The rule has been applied remorselessly[12], defeating the intention of the testator, and has invalidated many gifts because of the recognition of the most extreme and unlikely possibilities, which would allow an interest to vest outside the period. This converted the rule into an object of ridicule; and one of the worst aspects of arbitrary application is, as Professor Leach has pointed out, that the vice of a void limitation is one that could have been prevented by competent drafting. The fault is the lawyer's, but the intended beneficiary is the sufferer[13]. However, apart from these anomalous cases which have become well-known draftsman's "traps", the rule has by and large performed a useful function in holding a balance between the claims of the property owner to control the disposition of his property, and the policy in favour of free alienation[14].

D. Subject Matter

A remarkable feature of its history is that it was established in the context of the control and disposition of family land, and has survived the change from land to stocks and shares as the basic form of capitalistic wealth. In this new context, the question of the tying up of property appears in a new light; in the old context of the tying up of land, the particular piece of land was inalienable during the period of the family settlement. In a settlement of stocks and shares, no property is tied up or made inalienable; for, even if successive interests under the settlement continued in perpetuity, the stocks and shares which formed the trust would remain alienable by the trustees, and would be bought and sold as the trustees decided to vary the investments.

E. Reform

In spite of much criticism, the rule proved itself obstructive to reform, and various attempts over the years to amend it in the United States have met with difficulties, and many states abandoned the attempt and re-established

---

[11] See p. 339, post; *Pearks v Moseley* (1880) 5 App Cas 714; *Re Dawson* (1888) 39 ChD 155; *Ward v Van der Loeff* [1924] AC 653.
[12] See pp. 326, et seq., post; Maudsley, p. 36.
[13] (1952) 68 LQR 35 (W. B. Leach).
[14] Simes, *Public Policy and the Dead Hand*; (1953) 52 Mich LR 179; (1955) 103 U of Penn LR 707.

the common law rule[15]. In recent years, largely through Leach's influence, various jurisdictions in the Commonwealth and the United States have, in various ways, passed legislation reforming the Rule[16]. The methods selected are basically of three types, though some jurisdictions combine the methods —

(i) Patching Up: that is to say, to provide specific solutions to the specific situations which have caused problems in the working of the Rule. The most common situation is that in which the vesting is postponed to an age greater than 21 and the interest thereby invalidated. England dealt with this case in 1925[17].

(ii) Cy-Près: that is, to give to a court the power, on the analogy of the cy-près power in connection with charitable trusts, to alter the terms of a void gift so as to make it conform to the Rule. After all, the testator did not intend to make a void gift. Altering the terms would meet his intention. This solution was considered by the Law Reform Committee in 1956, and rejected.

(iii) Wait and See. This, on its face, is the most attractive solution. Much of the criticism directed at the common law rule related to cases where the interest was held void on the ground that it might conceivably vest outside the period, but did in fact vest next year. Thus, to return to example (i) above, assume that A is a lady of 56 and has three children, all engaged to be married. They all marry within the year. But the gift would be void at common law because of the possibility that A's present children may die, A may have another child, and the first child of A to marry may do so outside the period. The policy behind the Rule is to prevent remote vesting; not to hold void gifts which vest within the period merely because they might have vested outside. Why not, therefore, wait and see whether or not the gift vests within the period; and hold it valid if it does, but void if it does not? This is the principle recommended by the Law Reform Committee and adopted by the Perpetuities and Accumulations Act 1964; along with some "patching up" provisions also.

Canada has provided the first example of legislation to abolish, and not merely to reform, the rule against perpetuities. In 1983 Manitoba abolished the rule, and in its place widened the jurisdiction of the court to vary trusts[18].

F.   Perpetuities and Accumulations Act 1964

The Perpetuities and Accumulations Act 1964 came into force on 16 July 1964, and applies only to instruments coming into effect on or after that

---

[15] Morris and Leach, pp. 13, 33.

[16] Maudsley, Appendix D.

[17] LPA 1925, s. 163; p. 337, post.

[18] Perpetuities and Accumulations Act 1983 (SM 1982–1983, c 43); Manitoba Law Reform Commission Report on the Rules against Accumulations and Perpetuities (1982 No. 49), which was largely the work of D.W.M. Waters; see (1984) OJLS 454 (R. Deech) for a detailed review and criticism of this legislation p. 368, post; (1983) Manitoba LJ 245 (A. I. McClean) "Abolition is a great step into the unknown . . . the Manitoba Law Reform Commission and the Manitoba Legislature are not to be numbered amongst the law's timorous souls"; (1984) 62 Can Bar Rev 618 (J. M. Glenn), criticizing the legislation.

date[19]. The common law rule still applies to other limitations. Litigation on pre-1964 dispositions will become less likely as the years go by; but will remain possible for many years because questions for decision do not arise until the time for payment arrives, and this may await the termination of a life interest or the attainment of a specified age by beneficiaries.

Further, Wait and See applies, according to the terms of the Act, to void gifts; that is, to dispositions which are void under the common law rule on the ground that they might vest outside the period. To follow this method, it is necessary to apply the common law rule first, in order to discover whether the disposition is valid or void under the common law rule. Thus, there are two rules to apply; and the common law rule still survives in spite of the introduction of Wait and See.

The question is whether the retention of the common law rule was necessary or sensible; whether, in other words, there is any advantage in knowing that a disposition complies with the common law rule. It is submitted here that compliance with the common law rule is irrelevant once Wait and See is enacted; and it should be noted that all jurisdictions which have enacted Wait and See, except those which have effectively copied the English Act, have abolished the common law rule and relied solely on Wait and See. In these circumstances, the common law rule would phase peacefully out, and validity would depend on Wait and See alone.

The issue turns on the question whether or not, in a Wait and See jurisdiction, there is any advantage in knowing whether a disposition complies with the common law rule. The legislators assumed that there was. The contrary view, argued in detail elsewhere[20], can only be presented shortly here. The point is that a contingent interest which is valid under the common law rule remains contingent; the beneficiary does not take until the contingency occurs. Thus, before paying out, even with "valid" gifts, you have to wait and see whether they do in fact vest. If the gift is to the first child of A to attain the age of 21, and A has a child of 16, then, you wait and see if the child attains 21. If he does, you pay out; if he does not, the gift fails. The current value of the gift depends on the statistical likelihood of vesting. Similarly with all gifts under a Wait and See system. Treat the gift as valid until it is known that it will not vest within the period, and in the meantime wait and see whether it vests within the period. The value of the interest depends on the statistical likelihood of vesting within the period. Presumably, "valid" gifts are more likely to vest within the period than "void" gifts; but the added value which they acquire is due to their increased likelihood of vesting, and not to their happening to comply with the Rule. Compare two gifts:—

  (i) To such of the children and grandchildren of A as shall return from the Moon within 21 years of the death of X. A has 2 children and 4 grandchildren (none of them astronauts).

  (ii) To the first grandchild of A (who is alive) to attain the age of 21. A has 2 children and also 4 grandchildren, all healthy and aged 20.

---

[19] Section 15 (5). An arrangement under the Variation of Trusts Act 1958 will, with the court order approving it, constitute an "instrument" for the purposes of the subsection: *Re Holt's Settlement* [1969] 1 Ch 100, [1968] 1 All ER 470.

[20] Maudsley, chap. 4.

The first gift is valid under the common law rule, because it must vest, if at all, during X's lifetime; but it would be valueless to the children and grandchildren, because the trustees would be unlikely to make an advancement, and the grandchildren would be unable to offer it as security for a loan. The second gift is void (see above), but would have value, especially in the case of the eldest grandchild. In the era of Wait and See, compliance with the common law rule is irrelevant. Likelihood of vesting is crucial.

The common law rule is logically irrelevant, because Wait and See necessarily takes it over. The common law rule asks and answers the question: Is the limitation one which must vest, if at all, within the period? Wait and See asks whether it does in fact vest within the period. If an interest *must* vest, if at all, within the period, then it *will* vest, if at all, within the period. Wait and See takes over the common law rule. Unless, that is, you can detect situations in which the periods are different: as where a life in being might validate the gift at common law, but is not a person whom the statute allows to be used as a measuring life under Wait and See. There are, tragically, a few such situations under the English Act. That should be dealt with either by adding such lives to the statutory list of measuring lives applicable to Wait and See; or by letting the disposition stand or fall by the use of the statutory lives alone. It makes no sense to perpetuate for ever the learning of the common law rules just to deal with such situations. We should look, one way or another, to a system in which we have to deal with Wait and See alone.

G.   Impact of Taxation

However you look at it, the great days of the perpetuity rule are over. There is a further reason for simplification. It is indeed paradoxical that, after waiting so long for reform of the law of perpetuities, the Act eventually comes when wealthy families no longer attempt to provide a series of successive limited interests projecting into the future. It was noted above that the problem of perpetuity became less acute when family settlements became settlements of variable securities rather than a specific piece of land; and, in the last few decades, the severity of the rates of estate duty, coupled with the rule that duty was payable at a life tenant's death upon the full value of the capital sum, greatly decreased the attractiveness of settlements containing successive limited interests. Discretionary settlements in various forms, which had substantial fiscal attractions prior to the Finance Act 1969, involve the use of the perpetuity rule only in respect of the measurement of the duration of the discretionary trust; and the provision of an alternative period of 80 years in section 1 of the Perpetuities and Accumulations Act 1964 is most welcome in this respect as an escape from a period based upon royal lives. The capital transfer tax system, introduced in the Finance Act 1975 (and consolidated in the Capital Transfer Tax Act 1984), makes the tying-up of property in family settlements even less attractive.

H.   Common Law Rule To-day

But, for the present, it remains necessary to understand the working of the common law rule. Questions may still arise relating to dispositions taking effect before 16 July 1964, to which the Act does not apply[1]. And, as has been

---

[1] PAA 1964, s. 15 (5).

seen, the form of the Act does not follow the line of reasoning in this text. The Act was based on the contrary assumption; namely that it is still important to test every disposition by the common law rule; and to introduce Wait and See only if the disposition is void under the common law rule. An outline of the working of the common law rule is therefore included here, along with the provisions of the Act.

II. The Perpetuity Period

A. At Common Law[2]

In *Cadell v Palmer* (1833) 1 Cl & Fin 372, BAYLEY B, in tendering advice to the House of Lords, discussed a number of cases[3] and continued at 416: "We would not wish the House to suppose, that there were not expressions in other cases about the same period, from which it might clearly be collected, that minority was originally the foundation of the limit[4], and to raise some presumption that the limit of 21 years after a life in being was confined to cases in which there was such a minority; but the manner in which the rule was expressed in the instances to which I have referred, as well as in text writers, appears to us to justify the conclusion, that it was at length extended to the enlarged limit of a life or lives in being, and 21 years afterwards. It is difficult to suppose, that men of such discriminating minds, and so much in the habit of discrimination, should have laid down the rule, as they did, without expressing minority as a qualification of the limit, particularly when, in many of the instances, they had minority before their eyes, had it not been their clear understanding, that the rule of 21 years was general, without the qualification of minority.

[His Lordship then referred to *Beard v Westcott* (1813) 5 Taunt 393, in which the Court of Common Pleas upheld an executory limitation which was not to take effect until 21 years after a life in being; but Lord ELDON sent the case to the King's Bench (1822) 5 B & Ald 801 where it was held void, on the ground however that it followed a prior void limitation. He continued:]

Upon the direct authority, therefore, of the decision of the Court of Common Pleas, in *Beard v Westcott*, and the *dicta* by L. C. Justice Willes, Lord Mansfield and Lord Kenyon, and the rules laid down in Blackstone and Fearne, we consider ourselves warranted in saying that the limit is a life or lives in being, and 21 years afterwards, without reference to the infancy of any person whatever. This will certainly render the estate unalienable for 21 years after lives in being, but it will preserve in safety any limitations which may have been made upon authority of the *dicta* or text writers I have mentioned; and it will not tie up the alienation an unreasonable length of time.

---

[2] C & B, pp. 294–296; M & W, pp. 240–242; MM, pp. 196–197; Maudsley, pp. 42–45; Morris and Leach, pp. 56–70; *Duke of Norfolk's Case* (1681) 3 Cas in Ch 1; *Lloyd v Carew* (1697) Show Parl Cas 137; *Stephens v Stephens* (1736) Cas temp Talb 228; *Thellusson v Woodford* (1805) 11 Ves 112.

[3] *Lloyd v Carew*, supra; *Marks v Marks* (1719) 10 Mod Rep 419; *Taylor v Biddal* (1677) 2 Mod Rep 289; *Stephens v Stephens*, supra; *Goodtitle d Gurnall v Wood* (1740) Willes 211; *Thellusson v Woodford*, supra; *Goodman v Goodright* (1759) 2 Burr 873; *Buckworth v Thirkell* (1785) 3 Bos & P 652n; *Jee v Audley* (1787) 1 Cox Eq Cas 324; *Long v Blackall* (1797) 7 Term Rep 100; *Wilkinson v South* (1798) 7 Term Rep 555.

[4] To 21 years.

Upon the second and third questions proposed by your Lordships, whether a limitation by way of executory devise is void, as too remote, or otherwise, if it is not to take effect until after the determination of a life or lives in being, and upon the expiration of a term of 21 years afterwards, together with the number of months equal to the ordinary or longest period of gestation, but the whole of such years and months to be taken as a term in gross, and without reference to the infancy of any person whatever, born or *en ventre sa mere*, the unanimous opinion of the Judges is, that such a limitation would be void, as too remote. They consider 21 years as the limit, and the period of gestation to be allowed in those cases only in which the gestation exists."

Their Lordships affirmed the decision of the court below[5].

B.   Perpetuities and Accumulations Act 1964

PERPETUITIES AND ACCUMULATIONS ACT 1964

1.   Power to specify perpetuity period[6]. — (1) Subject to section 9 (2) of this Act and subsection (2) below, where the instrument by which any disposition is made so provides, the perpetuity period applicable to the disposition under the rule against perpetuities, instead of being of any other duration, shall be of a duration equal to such number of years not exceeding eighty as is specified in that behalf in the instrument.

(2) Subsection (1) above shall not have effect where the disposition is made in exercise of a special power of appointment, but where a period is specified under that subsection in the instrument creating such a power the period shall apply in relation to any disposition under the power as it applies in relation to the power itself.

15.   Short title, interpretation and extent. — (2) In this Act —
   "disposition" includes the conferring of a power of appointment and any other disposition of an interest in or right over property, and references to the interest disposed of shall be construed accordingly[7];
(6) This Act shall apply in relation to a disposition made otherwise than by an instrument as if the disposition had been contained in an instrument taking effect when the disposition was made.

In *Re Green's Will Trusts* [1985] 3 All ER 455, Mrs Green made a codicil to her will stating that "the period from the date of my death to the 1st day of January 2020 is hereby specified as the Perpetuity Period for the purpose of the trusts of the residue of my estate contained in my said Will". She died on 1 February 1976. In holding that this was a valid specification, Nourse J said at 460:

---

[5] *Sub nom Bengough v Edridge* (1827) 1 Sim 173. See note to Astbury J's judgment in *Re Villar* [1928] Ch 471, p. 324, n. 13, post.
[6] This section does not apply to options: s. 9 (2); C & B, pp. 319–320; M & W, p. 253; MM, p. 207; Maudsley, pp. 111–115; Morris and Leach, Supplement, pp. 2–3.
[7] *Re Thomas Meadows & Co Ltd and Subsidiary Companies (1960) Staff Pension Scheme Rules* [1971] Ch 278, [1971] 1 All ER 239 (entry of employees' names in register for pension purposes held to be a disposition).

"That was an attempt to attract the operation of s. 1 (1) of the Perpetuities and Accumulations Act 1964, . . .

Counsel submits that the attempt was unsuccessful, on the ground that what was here specified was not a number of years but a period expiring on a particular date. He did not go so far as to submit that a number of years plus a fraction of another, for example 79½, could not be a number of years for this purpose. What he said was that a period which can only be reduced to a number of years by making a calculation is not a specified number of years. For that he relied on *White v Whitcher* [1928] 1 KB 453, a once well-known authority on the meaning of 'some specified age' in what later became s. 228 of the Income Tax Act 1952. I find that authority to be of no assistance in the present case. There is plenty of other authority, including that of common sense, to the effect that 'specified' merely means 'unambiguously identified' or 'made clear'. Speaking from Mrs Green's death on 1 February 1976 and looking forward to 1 January 2020, I think that the codicil unambiguously identified, or made clear, a period of 43$\frac{11}{12}$ years as the perpetuity period for the purposes of the trusts of residue. In my judgment that was a specified number of years within s. 1 (1) of the 1964 Act."

III.   Lives in Being at Common Law[8]

A.   Validating Lives

(1955) University of Florida LR at p. 470 (B. M. Sparks)[9]

"There are possibly those who will say . . . that they can never figure out this business about lives in being. They will ask how they are to determine who are the measuring lives. The best answer to that is that you may determine the measuring lives any way you desire. Do the lives have to be named in the instrument? No. Do the lives have to be lives of persons taking an interest under the will or deed? No. Is there a limit to the number of lives? No, not so long as they are reasonably ascertainable. Instead of searching for measuring lives it will probably be more profitable to concentrate on an examination of the property interest you are creating. The proper question to ask is: Can I point to some person or persons now living and say that this interest will by the very terms of its creation be vested in an identified individual within twenty-one years after that person dies?"

American Bar Association Legislation Handbook (3rd edn, 1967), p. 4

". . . at common law, if vesting were certain to occur within 21 years after *any* life in being, it was valid. But if *no* person could be identified, within 21 years of whose death an interest was certain to vest, the interest was void."

---

[8] C & B, pp. 297–301; M & W, pp. 250–253; MM, pp. 201–203; Maudsley, pp. 88–92; Morris and Leach, pp. 60–63, 67–68.
[9] Used by permission; Copyright 1955, by the University of Florida Law Review.

RE GAITE'S WILL TRUSTS
[1949] 1 All ER 459 (ChD, ROXBURGH J)

A testatrix left gifts by will in favour of such of the grandchildren of Mrs Gaite "as shall be living at my death or born within five years therefrom who shall attain the age of 21 years or being female marry under that age in equal shares". At the date of the death, there were two children and one grandchild of Mrs Gaite alive.

Held. The gifts were valid as no grandchildren could take outside the perpetuity period unless that grandchild was born, within 5 years of the testatrix's death, of a child of Mrs Gaite born after the testatrix's death; this was legally impossible as it is not lawful to marry under the age of 16 years.

ROXBURGH J: I must assume that Mrs Hagar Gaite, who was alive at the date of the death of the testatrix, might have had a child within five years after the death of the testatrix. What is impossible is that the child of Mrs Hagar Gaite, *ex hypothesi* born after the death of the testatrix, could itself have had a child within that period of five years, and that is essential to qualify for membership of the class. I do not base my judgment on physical impossibility. I leave all questions of that sort open for consideration when they arise because the matter is, in my judgment, concluded — and counsel for the second defendant admitted it was concluded — by the Age of Marriage Act 1929, section 1 (1)[10], which provides:

"A marriage between persons either of whom is under the age of sixteen shall be void."

Ex hypothesi, the child of Mrs Hagar Gaite born after the death of the testatrix must be under the age of 16 years at the expiration of five years from the death of the testatrix, and, therefore, that child could not lawfully be married and have lawful children. In construing the rule, I must have regard to the statute law of England, and, therefore, I hold that the rule is not infringed[11].

Who were the lives in being? Who were the persons within 21 years of whose death (children of future-born children being eliminated) the interest must vest if at all?

Mrs Gaite's living children were the lives in being, though nowhere mentioned in the instrument (nor in the judgment). Further grandchildren of Mrs Gaite might attain the age of 21 more than 21 years after the death of the testatrix and Mrs Gaite; but it was certain that they would do so, if at all, within 21 years of the death of the living children of Mrs Gaite.

B. Expressly Selected Lives

The same principle applies where the settlor or testator selects the persons within 21 years of whose death the interest must vest, if at all. It will be seen

---

[10] Now Marriage Act 1949, s. 2.
[11] For criticisms of the reasoning of ROXBURGH J, see (1949) 13 Conv (NS) 289 (J. H. C. Morris); Morris and Leach, pp. 85–86; *Theobald on Wills* (14th edn. 1982), p. 587; (1952) 68 LQR 35, 46 (W. B. Leach). In respect of dispositions made on or after 1 January 1970, Family Law Reform Act 1969, s. 15, provides that, in the absence of a contrary intention, references to children and other relatives include references to illegitimate persons and persons descended through illegitimate persons.

that this was done in the following cases in this section. A gift would be void if it were made, for example, to "such of the great-grandchildren of A (who is alive) as shall attain the age of 25. The measuring lives for the purposes of this limitation shall be X, Y and Z." The vesting is not, in that situation, *related* to the lives. Where it is so related, there is the further question of the number and complexity of the lives who may be selected.

RE VILLAR

[1928] Ch 471 (Ch, ASTBURY J); affirmed [1929] 1 Ch 243
(CA, Lord HANWORTH, LAWRENCE and RUSSELL LJJ)

By a will dated 1921 and confirmed by a codicil of 1926 the testator, who died in 1926, left his property upon certain trusts and provided that interests in the capital should not vest until the termination of the period of restriction which was defined as "the period ending at the expiration of 20 years from the day of the death of the last survivor of all the lineal descendants of Her late Majesty Queen Victoria who shall be living at the time of my death".

It was established that, in view of the fact that there were about 120 known descendants of Queen Victoria, some of whom had been dispersed and might be living in obscurity, and some whose fate was unknown[12], the ascertainment of the date of the dropping of these lives would be extremely difficult and expensive. The question was whether the testator could properly select such lives in 1926.

Held. The ascertainment of the lives was not impracticable and the trust was valid.

ASTBURY J: The real question is whether the period of restriction is one that can be given effect to in the circumstances. I feel the gravest doubt as to the validity of this will, having regard to the period of restriction and the circumstances now surrounding the lineal descendants of the late Queen Victoria. This form of restriction has appeared in many books of forms for many years, and the testator in 1921 adopted this form, which having regard to the war and the events during the war and subsequent thereto, is extremely difficult to carry out . . .

The whole matter turns upon the true meaning of the law as explained in *Thellusson v Woodford*. In that case the judges were called in to advise the House of Lords, and their unanimous opinion was pronounced by Macdonald CB. It is upon the true meaning of that opinion and that of Lord Eldon LC that the question must be decided . . .

The joint effect [of the tests applied by Lord Eldon LC and Macdonald CB in *Thellusson v Woodford* (1799) 4 Ves 227; *affd.* (1805) 11 Ves 112] is that, if, in the circumstances of the particular gift and the lives selected, it is substantially impracticable to ascertain the date of the extinction of the lives described, the gift is bad; but if, although the lives are numerous and the ascertainment of the date of the survivor's death is or may be difficult and expensive, the gift will not be rendered invalid if ordinary legal testimony can be applied, and will be available to determine that date.

---

[12] For example, the Grand Duchess Anastasia.

Now in this case the testator has in 1921 used an old form or precedent, restraining the distribution of his estate to a period expiring twenty years from the death of the last survivor of all the lineal descendants of the late Queen Victoria living on 6 September 1926. That must postpone the vesting for a very long period, but having regard to the character of this class, I have come to the conclusion that I cannot say it will be impracticable, having regard to the legal testimony probably available, to ascertain the period when the capital becomes distributable twenty years after the survivor's death. The expense involved will probably be very great. The trust operates very hardly upon the testator's five children. If I could have seen my way to hold this tying up invalid I would gladly have done so, but in my opinion I am not at liberty to do so.

It must be borne in mind that there are probably many other gifts and trusts now in existence with similar limitations. Years ago this was a very common form of limitation. Its application has presented increasing difficulties as time has gone on, and now, having regard to the war, the difficulties are still more serious. But I feel myself unable to hold that the determination of the period of vesting is beyond the scope of legal testimony in the ordinary sense, and for these reasons this capital gift is good. There will be liberty to apply for an inquiry to ascertain the existing descendants, but that inquiry will be unnecessary if, as I hope, my judgment is reversed on appeal[13].

In *Re Moore* [1901] 1 Ch 936, an attempt was made to stretch the period of perpetuity to the utmost: "for the longest period allowed by law, that is to say, until the period of twenty-one years from the death of the last survivor of all persons who shall be living at my death". JOYCE J held the gift void for uncertainty[14]. The gift was for the maintenance of a tomb.

In *Re Kelly* [1932] IR 255, the question concerned the validity of a bequest to expend "£4 sterling on the support of each of my dogs per year . . . and on the death of the last of my dogs" any balance to charitable purposes. MEREDITH J held that the gift was void for remoteness, and said at 260:

"It will be more convenient to deal first with the gift of any possible surplus remaining over on the death of the last of the dogs. Here the question, so far as there can be any question, is strictly one of remoteness. If the lives of the dogs or other animals could be taken into account in reckoning the maximum period of 'lives in being and twenty-one years

---

[13] It was not. A footnote to the case at [1928] Ch 478 adds: "For a somewhat similar impracticability argument see *Cadell v Palmer* (1833) 1 Cl & F 372, 397; *Tudor's Real Property Cases* 3rd edn., pp. 424, 443. In that case the testator died in April 1818, and on 16 May 1918, his estate was finally wound up by Astbury J, in *Bengough v Edridge*, a few months after the period of 28 lives and 20 years had expired." For other cases on royal lives, see *Re Leverhulme (No. 2)* [1943] 2 All ER 274 (testator died in 1925 and life tenant in 1943. MORTON J held the gift valid, but warned testators not to use the descendants of Queen Victoria in the future); *Re Warren's Will Trusts* (1961) 105 SJ 511 (gift upheld in spite of MORTON J's warning. Testator died in 1944). Modern precedents use the descendants of King George V (or, preferably a period not exceeding 80 years; p. 320, ante).
[14] And not even valid for 21 years, e.g., *Muir v IRC* [1966] 1 WLR 1269 at 1282, [1966] 3 All ER 38 at 44.

afterwards' any contingent or executory interest might be properly limited, so as only to vest within the lives of specified carp, or tortoises, or other animals that might live for over a hundred years, and for twenty-one years afterwards, which, of course, is absurd. 'Lives' means human lives. It was suggested that the last of the dogs could in fact not outlive the testator by more than twenty-one years. I know nothing of that. The court does not enter into the question of a dog's expectation of life. In point of fact neighbour's dogs and cats are unpleasantly long-lived; but I have no knowledge of their precise expectation of life. Anyway the maximum period is exceeded by the lives of specified butterflies and twenty-one years afterwards. And even, according to my decision — and, I confess, it displays this weakness on being pressed to a logical conclusion — the expiration of the life of a single butterfly, even without the twenty-one years, would be too remote, despite all the world of poetry that may be thereby destroyed. In *Robinson v Hardcastle* (1786) 2 Bro CC at 30 Lord Thurlow defined a perpetuity in these words: 'What is a perpetuity, but the extending the estate beyond a life in being, and twenty-one years after?' Of course by a 'life' he means lives; and there can be no doubt that 'lives' means lives of human beings, not of animals or trees in California.

[His Lordship then considered the gift for the support of the dogs and said:] I adhere to the view that in the present case there is a valid severable trust for twenty-one years succeeding the death of the testator, provided any of the dogs live so long."

———————

If there are no lives in being, the period of 21 years may be allowed. In *Re Hooper* [1932] 1 Ch 38, a gift for the upkeep of certain monuments "so far as [the trustees] legally can do so . . ." was upheld by MAUGHAM J for a period (in respect of non-charitable objects) of 21 years.

———————

A child en ventre sa mère[15] may be a life in being, and a period of gestation, if it exists[16], may also be added to the perpetuity period of a life in being plus 21 years. BUCKLEY J, in *Re Wilmer's Trusts* [1903] 1 Ch 874; *affd.* [1903] 2 Ch 411, said at 886: "*Thellusson v Woodford* is to be found again reported in 11 Ves 112, and at 143 Macdonald CB says: 'The case of *Long v Blackall* (1797) 7 Term Rep 100 seems to have decided that an infant in ventre matris is a life in being. The established length of time, during which the vesting may be suspended, is during a life or lives in being, the period of gestation, and the infancy of such posthumous child'."

———————

[15] "In simple English, it is an unborn child inside the mother's womb": *Royal College of Nursing of the United Kingdom v Department of Health and Social Security* [1981] AC 800 at 802, [1981] 1 All ER 545 at 554, per Lord DENNING MR. For the effect on the rule against perpetuities of delayed posthumous births by means of sperm banks or other devices, see (1979) 53 ALJ 311 (C. Sappideen).

[16] *Cadell v Palmer* (1833) 1 Cl & Fin 372, p. 319, ante; *Re Stern* [1962] Ch 732, [1961] 3 All ER 1129 (conception equivalent to birth).

IV.   Possible Not Actual Events: The Requirement of Certainty[17]

The rule requires that the interest must be certain to vest, if it vest at all, within the period. This requirement has been applied remorselessly; and limitations have been struck down where the only chance of vesting outside the period is fantastic, and even physically impossible. A number of such limitations are now well known.

A.   The Fertile Octogenarian[18]; or the Conclusive Presumption of Fertility[19]

i.   THE COMMON LAW RULE

In *Jee v Audley* (1787) 1 Cox Eq Cas 324, the testator gave £1,000 "unto my niece Mary Hall and the issue of her body lawfully begotten, and to be begotten, and in default of such issue, I give the same £1,000 to be equally divided between the daughters then living of my kinsman John Jee and his wife Elizabeth Jee".

Mary Hall was about 40 and the Jees were 70, and had four living daughters. But, because the provision related to a general failure of issue (i.e. failure at any time in the future) it was theoretically possible that Mary Hall's issue might die at a time in the future, and because the daughters of the Jees *then* living might include a future born daughter of that old couple, the gift was held void[20].

WARD *v* VAN DER LOEFF
[1924] AC 653 (HL, Viscounts HALDANE LC and CAVE,
Lords DUNEDIN, PHILLIMORE and BLANESBURGH)

By his will the testator devised and bequeathed his residuary real and personal estate on trust for his widow for life and then for their children, and, if none (as happened), on trust for the children of his brothers and sisters.

By a codicil he declared that his widow's life interest should be terminable on her remarriage unless such remarriage should be with a natural born British subject; and that on her death the trustees should hold the residuary estate on trust for the children of his brothers and sisters who should be living at the death of his wife or born at any time afterwards before any one of them . . . attained a vested interest and who being a son attained 21 or being a daughter attained that age or married. The widow married a Dutchman.

---

[17] C & B, pp. 300–304; M & W, pp. 244–247; MM, pp. 198–199; Maudsley, pp. 35, 45–56; Morris and Leach, pp. 70–95.

[18] Prof. Barton Leach labelled these categories: (1938) 51 HLR 1329; (1952) 65 HLR 721; (1952) 68 LQR 44; *Re Dawson* (1888) 39 ChD 155, p. 340, post.

[19] On the law's different approach to this matter in a non-perpetuity context, see *Re Widdow's Trusts* (1871) LR 11 Eq 408; *Re White* [1901] 1 Ch 570; *Re Eve* [1909] 1 Ch 796; *Re Fletcher* [1949] Ch 473, [1949] 1 All ER 732; *Re Wohlgemuth* [1949] Ch 12, [1948] 2 All ER 882; *Re Herwin* [1953] Ch 701, [1953] 2 All ER 782; *Re Gilpin* [1954] Ch 1, [1953] 2 All ER 1218; *Re Westminster Bank's Declaration of Trust* [1963] 1 WLR 820, [1963] 2 All ER 400n; *Re Pettifor's Will Trusts* [1966] Ch 257, [1966] 1 All ER 913.

[20] *Re Sayer's Trusts* (1868) LR 6 Eq 319; *Re Deloitte* [1926] Ch 56.

At the date of the testator's death (without issue) his parents were both aged 66. All his brothers and sisters were over 30 years old and all had infant children, one of whom was born after the remarriage of the widow.

Held. (i) The gift in the codicil was void for perpetuity. (ii) The codicil did not revoke the gift in the will which was valid.

Viscount Haldane LC: On the construction of the will and codicil, two questions arise. The first is, whether the limitation in favour of children, contained in the concluding words of the codicil, is valid, having regard to the rule against perpetuities. The second is whether, if invalid, this new limitation and the wording of the codicil have been at all events efficacious as expressing a revocation of his bequest to children contained in the will. If the limitation to children in the codicil be invalid, and that in the will has not been revoked, then a further question arises, whether the gift in the will operated in favour of any children of the brothers and sisters who were not born until after the testator's death. Philip Ponsonby Burnyeat, who is one of the parties to these appeals, was a son of the testator's brother, Myles Fleming Burnyeat, but was not born until after the testator's death and the remarriage of his widow. It is argued against his claim that the life interest of the widow was effectively determined by the provision in the codicil and that the class of children to take was finally ascertained at that date as the time of distribution. If this be so, Philip Ponsonby Burnyeat is excluded.

P. O. Lawrence J was the judge before whom this summons came in the first instance. He decided that the gift in the codicil in favour of the children of the testator's brothers and sisters was so framed as to be void for perpetuity. He held further, that the codicil operated to revoke the residuary gift in the will only so far as the substituted provision in the codicil was valid, and that the gift in the will in favour of these children, therefore, took effect, but merely in favour of such of the children as were born before the remarriage of the testator's widow. Philip Ponsonby Burnyeat was thus excluded. A majority of the Court of Appeal, Lord Sterndale MR and Warrington LJ, agreed with him in holding that the gift in the codicil in favour of the children of brothers and sisters was void for perpetuity, but held that the codicil revoked the gift in their favour contained in the will, and that there was an intestacy as regarded the residuary estate of the testator as from the remarriage of his widow. Atkin LJ dissented, holding that the testator must be taken, as matter of construction, to have been referring in his codicil only to the brothers and sisters of the whole blood in existence when he died, just as if he had designated them individually. The provision in the codicil was therefore valid, that in the will having been revoked.

My Lords, the principle to be applied in construing instruments for the purpose of ascertaining whether the direction they contain infringes the rule against perpetuity is a well settled one. It was repeated with emphasis in this House in *Pearks v Moseley* (1880) 5 App Cas 714, where it was laid down that in construing the words the effect of the rule must in the first instance be left out of sight, and then, having in this way defined the intention expressed, the court had to test its validity by applying the rule to the meaning thus ascertained. It is only therefore if, as matter of construction, the words in the codicil, taken in the natural sense in which the testator used them, do not violate the rule that they can be regarded as giving a valid direction. Looking at the language of the testator here, I am wholly unable to read it as not postponing the ascertainment of possible members of the class beyond the period of a life in being and twenty-one years afterwards. No doubt if we were warranted in interpreting the testator as having referred only to the children of those of his brothers and sisters who were alive at his death we might read his language in a way which would satisfy the law. But for so restricting the natural meaning of his words there is no justification in the language used in the context. He speaks of his brothers and sisters generally, and there is no expression which excludes the children of other possible brothers and sisters of the whole or half blood who might in contemplation of law be born. He has nowhere indicated an intention that his words are not to be construed in this, their natural meaning. I think, therefore, that the class to be benefited was not one all the members of which were, as a necessary result of the words used, to be ascertained within the period which the law prescribes, and that the gift in the codicil in favour of children of brothers and sisters is wholly void.

The next question is whether the codicil, although inoperative to this extent, was yet operative to revoke the gift to children of brothers and sisters contained in the will. After consideration, I have come to the conclusion that it was not so operative. There is indeed a revocation expressed in the codicil, but it is confined to the power of appointment given to the wife. It does not extend to what follows. That is, in terms, an attempt at a substantive and independent gift, and, as it is wholly void, I think, differing on this point from the Court of Appeal, that the provision in the will stands undisturbed. There is nothing else in the codicil which purports to affect it. It can make no difference that the class of children is a new and different class if the constitution of the new class is wholly inoperative in law. If it fails, then unless an independent and valid intention to revoke has been independently of it expressed, no revocation can take place. There is no such independent expression of intention here.

The only other point is at what period the class of children of brothers and sisters who took under the will is to be ascertained. I think that according to a well-known rule, the period is that of distribution; in other words, taking the valid alteration in the codicil into account, the remarriage of the widow with a foreign subject. Philip Ponsonby Burnyeat is thus excluded.

The result is that the judgment of P. O. Lawrence J should be restored. As the difficulty has been entirely caused by the testator himself, I think that the costs here and below should be taxed as between solicitor and client and paid out of the residuary estate.

LORD BLANESBURGH: My Lords, I too have arrived at the same conclusions as the rest of your Lordships. I am of opinion that the ultimate gift of residue contained in this testator's codicil is void as transgressing the rule against perpetuities, and I think it is also inoperative to revoke those residuary dispositions of his will which rank subsequent to the interest thereby given to his widow.

We have in this case, my Lords, an extreme but by no means uncommon illustration of the stringency — I might even describe it as the penal character — of this rule. At no time was there here any practical possibility that a perpetuity could eventuate as a result of the complete fulfilment of the terms of the gift in question; while, by the time any contest as to the validity of the gift arose, it had become, by reason of the death of the testator's father, inconceivable that any infraction of the rule could be involved in it. If we consider matters as they stood at the testator's death, which is, of course, the really relevant date, it was necessary before anything obnoxious to the rule could take place in connection with this residuary gift, that the following remarkable conjunction of events should supervene. The testator's father and mother were then each upwards of sixty-six years of age; to them, after a family of five, no child had been born for more than thirty years. It was, nevertheless, necessary that they should have another child. Alternatively it was necessary that their marriage should be dissolved otherwise than by the death of the father, and that he should marry again, and have a child by the second marriage. That child, in turn, had to have a child born after the death of the testator's widow — one born in her lifetime would not have been excluded by the rule. And even a child so born would have brought about an infraction of the rule, only if it had also eventuated that no one of the already substantial and apparently increasing families of the testator's four living brothers and sisters had survived his widow having married or attained twenty-one.

So much, as matters stood at the testator's death, had to happen before any nephew or niece excluded by the rule could appear. By the date of the summons on which the orders under appeal were made, this new event had to take place before the rule could be infringed. The testator's mother had survived her husband; she, then a widow lady of upwards of seventy-two years of age, had to marry again and have issue.

It is, I think, only fair to the draftsman of this codicil, manifestly prepared under severe pressure of time, to give this indication of the apparent remoteness of any provision contained in it from the danger of a perpetuity. It is quite certain, I make bold to say, that no idea of such a possibility entered anybody's mind. In its application to the present case, the rule has been really a snare, useless so far as its legitimate purpose is concerned, but operative in the view of the Court of Appeal and operative also in the view of this House (but for a fortunate accident for which the rule is entitled to no credit), to produce an intestacy under which certainly one person would greatly benefit, whose interests it was the permissible and express purpose of the testator by his codicil to circumscribe and reduce.

In my own experience nearly all modern manifestations of the rule are of this character, and have this result. The rule has so schooled testators into compliance with, perhaps even into approval of, its requirements, that deliberate attempts to push their privileges beyond its strict limits are now rarely made. So far as the Courts are concerned, the existence of the rule in these days is usually made manifest only in cases where nothing of the kind having been desired or suspected, and where by nothing short of a miracle could a perpetuity at any time have supervened, even that possibility has, by the time of the contest, ceased to be existent. All the same in these cases the rule is fatal even to gifts so innocuous, and I cannot doubt that such a result is both mischievous and unfortunate, in many directions — in this notably, that it brings a sound principle into entirely gratuitous discredit. Nevertheless I most fully agree that the rule is not to be whittled away by the Courts even for such a reason as that. It is too well authenticated in all its recognized incidents to be any longer under the control of any Court. It is the Legislature alone, which, maintaining the salutary purpose of the rule in its proper application, can, if it pleases, remove from it those incidents or excrescences which, without assisting to achieve its legitimate object, have done much mischief in other directions.

In the present case, and notwithstanding the actual conditions to which I have referred, I am, like the rest of your Lordships, satisfied that on the construction of the words here used by the testator, it is impossible to say that this gift is not within the prohibition of the rule as we have inherited it. It is agreed that the only conceivable means of escape is, either by construction or otherwise, to confine the apparently general expression "my brothers and sisters" to the brothers and sisters of the testator in being at the date of his codicil. On construction it is not, I think, open to your Lordships so to limit these words. Nor is it, in my judgment, permissible, by reference to surrounding circumstances, to confine them, as Atkin LJ thought he could, to those same brothers and sisters as being the only brothers and sisters the testator knew, and as being in consequence and in the circumstances those with reference to whom alone he must be taken to have spoken[1].

The problem of the "precocious toddler", dealing with the minimum age of reproduction, is dealt with in *Re Gaite's Will Trusts* [1949] 1 All ER 459, p. 322, ante.

ii.   PERPETUITIES AND ACCUMULATIONS ACT 1964[2]

PERPETUITIES AND ACCUMULATIONS ACT 1964

2.   Presumptions and evidence as to future parenthood. — (1) Where in any proceedings there arises on the rule against perpetuities a question which turns on the ability of a person to have a child at some future time, then —

    (a) subject to paragraph (b) below, it shall be presumed that a male can have a child at the age of fourteen years or over, but not under that age, and that a female can have a child at the age of twelve years or over, but not under that age or over the age of fifty-five years; but

    (b) in the case of a living person evidence may be given to show that he or she will or will not be able to have a child at the time in question.

(2) Where any such question is decided by treating a person as unable to have a child at a particular time, and he or she does so, the High Court may make such order as it thinks fit for placing the persons interested in the property comprised in the disposition, so far as may be just, in the position they would have held if the question had not been so decided.

(3) Subject to subsection (2) above, where any such question is decided in relation to a disposition by treating a person as able or unable to have a child at a particular time, then he or she shall be so treated for the purpose of any question which may arise on the rule against perpetuities in relation to the same disposition in any subsequent proceedings.

(4) In the foregoing provisions of this section references to having a child are references to begetting or giving birth to a child, but those provisions (except subsection (1) (b)) shall apply in relation to the possibility that a person will at any time have a child by adoption[3], legitimation[4] or other

---

[1] *Cooper v Laroche* (1881) 17 ChD 368; *Re Dawson* (1888) 39 ChD 155, p. 340, post.
[2] C & B, pp. 320–321; M & W, p. 250; MM, pp. 199–200; Maudsley, pp. 116–118; (1964) 80 LQR 489–491; Morris and Leach Supp., pp. 3–4.
[3] Children Act 1975, s. 8, Sch. 1, paras. 3–5. See Adoption Act 1976, s. 39 (the Act is not yet in force).
[4] Legitimacy Act 1976, ss. 5, 11, Schs., 1, 2.

means[5] as they apply to his or her ability at that time to beget or give birth to a child.

QUESTIONS
1. As a lawyer who is trained to construe a will in accordance with the intention of the testator, how would you have construed the will in *Ward v Van der Loeff?*
    See Morris and Leach 79; Restatement of Property, vol. 4, section 377, comment (*c*); *Re Powell* [1898] 1 Ch 227; *Re Cockle's Will Trusts* [1967] Ch 690, [1967] 1 All ER 391.
2. Redraft the codicil in *Ward v Van der Loeff* so as to comply with the testator's true intention.
3. (For thought now; answer later). If the codicil was void in *Ward v Van der Loeff*, why was the will not void too?
4. What would be the decision on the facts of *Re Gaite's Will Trusts* if the testatrix had died in 1970 — i.e. after the coming into force of Family Law Reform Act 1969, section 15?

B. The Unborn Widow under the Common Law Rule

RE FROST
(1889) 43 ChD 246 (ChD, KAY J)

The testator devised a freehold estate to his spinster daughter Emma for life, and after her decease, to the use of any husband she may hereafter marry for his life and, subject to a power of appointment, to the use of such of Emma's children as should be living at the death of the survivor of Emma and such husband . . . with further gifts over. The question was whether, on the death of Emma and her husband, without issue, the subsequent limitations were valid.

Held. All the limitations subsequent to the life interests to the spouses were void.

KAY J: [Emma] might have married after the death of the testator a person who was not born in his lifetime, and it might therefore have been a limitation to *Emma Frost* for life, remainder to an unborn person for his life, with a contingent remainder over to the children of *Emma Frost* living at the death of that unborn person, or such of them as should be then dead leaving issue then living, and an alternative limitation to other persons, still to be living at the death of that unborn person, or leaving issue then living. That clearly would be a limitation which would offend against the rule of perpetuity, because it would tie up the estate, not merely during the life of *Emma Frost*, who was in existence at the death of the testator, but during the life of *Emma Frost's* husband, who might possibly not be living at the death of the testator. So that it would not merely be tied up for a life in being and twenty-one years after, but for a life in being, with remainder for a life not in being, with a contingent gift over[6].

---

[5] See, for illegitimate children, Family Law Reform Act 1969, ss. 14, 15; Law Commission Report on Family Law: Illegitimacy 1982 (Law Com No. 118, HC 98).
[6] The limitation was void also under the rule in *Whitby v Mitchell* (1890) 44 ChD 85. If Emma was married at the date of the gift, it would be a question of construction whether the gift to the husband was limited to her present husband, who would be a life in being, or would include other future husbands who might not be.

In *Re Garnham* [1916] 2 Ch 413, the limitation was to A (a bachelor) for life, then to any woman he might marry for life, and then to the children of A at 21 or on marriage, and in default of children (as happened) then to certain other persons. The gift was upheld. It differed from *Re Frost*, in that, as NEVILLE J, at 416, said: "It seems to me that upon the determination of the tenancy for life given to an existing person the class is ascertained, although the enjoyment may be postponed during a life tenancy of a person who may have been unborn at the date of the gift." In other words, in this case, the limitation vested in interest on the death of A, and not, as in *Re Frost*, on the death of the survivor. The vesting in possession would be the same in either case, but this is not relevant in the application of the perpetuity rule.

This distinction was further illustrated in *Re Garnham*. The land was to be held on trust for sale on the death of the survivor of A and such wife. NEVILLE J decided that the trust for sale was void and that the property was received by those entitled to it in its unconverted form.

The Perpetuities and Accumulations Act 1964 makes provision for dealing with the unborn widow problem in section 5[7]. The section however applies only where the gift has not been saved under the "wait and see" principle introduced in section 3. The sections will be considered in the order in which they are to be applied.

C.   Administrative Contingencies under the Common Law Rule

In *Re Wood* [1894] 2 Ch 310; *affd.* [1894] 3 Ch 381[8], the testator, a gravel contractor, directed his trustees to "carry on my said business of a gravel contractor until my gravel-pits are worked out," and then to sell them and to hold the proceeds of sale among his children "then living" and the living issue of (deceased) children who being sons attain 21, or, being daughters, attain 21 or marry.

At the date of the will it was clear that the testator knew that the gravel pits would soon be worked out and they were in fact worked out within six years. KEKEWICH J and the Court of Appeal held the gift void for perpetuity because the gravel pits might not have been worked out within the perpetuity period.

In *Re Atkins' Will Trusts* [1974] 1 WLR 761, [1974] 2 All ER 1, a testator, who died in 1957, devised his farm on trust to allow his stepson, Ernest Alexander Double, to have the full use and enjoyment thereof and on his death or his ceasing to work the farm the trustees were directed to sell it "and to divide the net proceeds of sale equally and per capita amongst such of the following as shall be living at the date of the completion of the said sale", namely, the grandchildren of a deceased brother of the testator, a niece of the

---

[7] P. 344, post; C & B, p. 329; M & W, p. 260; MM, pp. 206–207; Maudsley, pp. 146–148; (1964) 80 LQR 512–515; Morris and Leach Supp., pp. 12–13.

[8] *Thomas v Thomas* (1902) 87 LT 58. This is so, even if the gift is charitable; *Re Lord Stratheden and Campbell* [1894] 3 Ch 265 (annuity of £100 to be provided to the Central London Rangers on the appointment of the next lieutenant-colonel).

testator and the four children of another niece. After the death of the stepson on 30 March 1972, the bulk of the farm was sold on 7 September 1972. In holding that the remainder was valid, PENNYCUICK V-C said at 767, at 6:

"Having reached the conclusion which I have expressed on the first two points — namely, that the proceeds of sale of the farm became divisible amongst the beneficiaries living at the date of completion of the sale and that the duty of the bank was to sell within one year, at latest, from the death of Ernest Alexander Double — then one comes to the question: was such a disposition void on the ground of perpetuity, namely, that the interests of the beneficiaries might not vest within 21 years from the death of Ernest Alexander Double, who was a life in being at the death of the testator?

Counsel for the last two defendants stressed, as is undoubtedly true, that in applying the rule against perpetuities as it stood before the Perpetuities and Accumulations Act 1964, one must look at possible and not actual events (see, for instance, *Theobald, Wills*, 13th edn. (1971), para. 1483), and there is no doubt that the court over the years has sometimes taken into account some very remote possibilities. Counsel relied in particular on *Re Wood* [1894] 3 Ch 381, in the Court of Appeal, a decision which has come in for a good deal of textbook criticism since, but which I suppose in comparable circumstances I should be bound to follow. It seems to me, however, that there is a critical distinction to be made between the possibility of delay owing to physical causes such as were considered in *Re Wood* and the possibility of delay owing to a breach of trust on the part of the trustee concerned. In the former case one must, I suppose, take into account anything physically capable of happening. I should myself wish to reserve consideration on that matter in relation to certain highly improbable events. On the other hand, where there is a possibility that delay can arise only should there be a breach of trust, that is a possibility which it seems to me the court must clearly disregard. The court will act on the basis that equity regards that as done which ought to be done, and it will treat the trustees as having done whatever they were bound to do. It will not allow the rights of beneficiaries to be defeated because the trustees failed to carry out their fiduciary duties.

So, in the present case, the duty of the trustee was to sell this farm immediately, and that means at the latest, as I have held, within one year of the death of Ernest Alexander Double, and the court.should not and cannot properly take into account the possibility that the bank, in breach of trust, might fail to realise within the time in which it was bound to realise. The result is that one must treat the sale as something which must be completed within, at the most, 12 months from the death of Ernest Alexander Double, and accordingly the vesting of the interests of the beneficiaries would take effect within one year of the death of Ernest Alexander Double, and there can be no question of a perpetuity."

V. Wait and See

A. General

It will be observed that all of the limitations in the examples given which failed did so because they *might* have vested outside the perpetuity period; not because they did so. This was necessitated by the common law rule's requirement of certainty; an interest is valid under the common law rule only if it is possible to postulate, at the date when the gift takes effect, that *if* the gift ever vests, it *must* do so within the perpetuity period. Of course, it may never vest at all. This is the risk of all contingent interests. The common law rule is concerned with the time within which it *must* vest if it ever does.

We have seen that, by making a judicious selection of measuring lives, a competent draftsman can extend the rule to its fullest extent. It will be observed that all the illustrations so far given could have been validated if the draftsman had made use of the opportunities available to him. He could have made use of selected lives; or, he could have included a simple catch-all provision, such as "provided that no beneficiary shall be entitled to take unless his interest shall vest within 21 years of the death of . . ."[9]. Such a provision would not restrict the donor's freedom of disposition, because in nearly all the cases the interests given will in fact vest within the period. It should be appreciated that, however many lives are selected, the period is the same: a life in being plus 21 years. For, as Twisden used to say, "the candles are all lighted at once"[10].

What, then, is the sense in holding void a gift which vests within the period, merely because it might have vested outside; but did not? We saw that a gift to the first child of A to marry is void, if A is alive and has no married child; because A's first child to marry *might* do so more than 21 years after the death of any persons now living. But if the gift is made on the eve of A's eldest daughter's wedding day, and she does marry on that day, why should the gift be held void for perpetuity?

In other words, why insist on certainty of vesting, if at all, within the period? Why not wait and see whether the disposition does in fact vest within the period? The adoption of a wait and see rule was enacted by the Perpetuities and Accumulations Act 1964, section 3.

PERPETUITIES AND ACCUMULATIONS ACT 1964

3.[11]   **Uncertainty as to remoteness.** — (1) Where, apart from the provisions of this section and sections 4 and 5 of this Act, a disposition would be void on the ground that the interest disposed of might not become vested until too remote a time, the disposition shall be treated, until such time (if any) as it becomes established that the vesting must occur, if at all, after the end of the perpetuity period, as if the disposition were not subject to the rule against perpetuities; and its becoming so established shall not affect the validity of anything previously done in relation to the interest disposed of by way of advancement, application of intermediate income or otherwise.

(2) Where, apart from the said provisions, a disposition consisting of the conferring of a general power of appointment would be void on the ground that the power might not become exercisable until too remote a time, the disposition shall be treated, until such time (if any) as it becomes established

---

[9] (1961) 74 HLR 1141 (W. B. Leach and J. K. Logan).

[10] *Scatterwood v Edge* (1699) 1 Salk 229.

[11] C & B, pp. 321–325; M & W, pp. 247–250; MM, pp. 200–201; Maudsley, pp. 120–122; (1964) 80 LQR 492–495; Morris and Leach Supp., pp. 5–8. For the first judicial application, see *Re Thomas Meadows & Co Ltd and Subsidiary Companies (1960) Staff Pension Scheme Rules* [1971] Ch 278, [1971] 1 All ER 239.

that the power will not be exercisable within the perpetuity period, as if the disposition were not subject to the rule against perpetuities.

(3) Where, apart from the said provisions, a disposition consisting of the conferring of any power, option or other right would be void on the ground that the right might be exercised at too remote a time, the disposition shall be treated as regards any exercise of the right within the perpetuity period as if it were not subject to the rule against perpetuities and, subject to the said provisions, shall be treated as void for remoteness only if, and so far as, the right is not fully exercised within that period.

B. Measuring Lives[12]

The introduction of the Wait and See principle requires a total reconsideration of the question of measuring lives. The common law lives obviously will not do; because the only persons recognised as common law lives are those who have already validated the gifts. If we only used them, we "would never wait and see at all"[13]. If the statute does not make some selection, it could be argued that any living person would do[14]; but this "would send potential beneficiaries ransacking the registers of births and deaths throughout the world" in order to find a centenarian capable of validating a gift which vested after 121 years.

It is obvious that the lives to be used should be known, and known precisely. If gifts are to be held valid or void, dependent on whether or not they do in fact vest within a period of lives in being plus 21 years, the system can only operate if you know how long the period is, and you only know that, if you know whose lives are to be used. The statute enacting Wait and See must lay down who the measuring lives are. They need have no relation to common law lives; it is best to discard all thoughts based on the common law situation; and to consider what, in the new situation, is required of the measuring lives. The new situation is trying to allow a limitation to be effective if it vests within a life in being plus 21 years (or 80 years). Any life? No, because of the inconvenience of following up every life; but the policy is to include every life that is reasonably connected with the limitation and identifiable at the date of the gift. In a gift "to the grandchildren of A" (a living person) why not include a present living grandchild if such inclusion enables the limitation to be valid, or allows the testator's intention to be more accurately followed; or, indeed, the donee of a power? On the other hand, an "unborn widow" is not included even if she turns out to have been alive at the date of the gift, because of the clearly sound principle that lives in being must be ascertainable at the beginning of the period. The Act of 1964 was the first in the world to recognise the problem and to produce a workable list[15].

---

[12] Maudsley, pp. 87–109, 123–139.

[13] (1965) 81 LQR 106, 108 (D. E. Allan).

[14] (1953) 52 Mich LR 179 (L. M. Simes); (1963) 6 U of WALR 21 (L. M. Simes); 27 (D. E. Allan); (1965) 81 LQR 106 (D. E. Allan); (1970) 86 LQR 357 (R. H. Maudsley); (1981) 97 LQR 593 (R. L. Deech) which contains a useful summary and discussion of the conflicting views.

[15] And followed, with or without minor changes, in Northern Ireland, Alberta, British Columbia and New Zealand; Maudsley, Appendix D.

PERPETUITIES AND ACCUMULATIONS ACT 1964[16]

3.   Uncertainty as to remoteness. —

(4) Where this section applies to a disposition and the duration of the perpetuity period is not determined by virtue of section 1 or 9 (2) of this Act, it shall be determined as follows:—

(*a*) where any persons falling within subsection (5) below are individuals in being and ascertainable at the commencement of the perpetuity period the duration of the period shall be determined by reference to their lives and no others, but so that the lives of any description of persons falling within paragraph (*b*) or (*c*) of that subsection shall be disregarded if the number of persons of that description is such as to render it impracticable to ascertain the date of death of the survivor;

(*b*) where there are no lives under paragraph (*a*) above the period shall be twenty-one years.

(5) The said persons are as follows:—

(*a*) the person by whom the disposition was made;

(*b*) a person to whom or in whose favour the disposition was made, that is to say —

(i) in the case of a disposition to a class of persons, any member or potential member of the class;

(ii) in the case of an individual disposition to a person taking only on certain conditions being satisfied, any person as to whom some of the conditions are satisfied and the remainder may in time be satisfied;

(iii) in the case of a special power of appointment exercisable in favour of members of a class, any member or potential member of the class;

(iv) in the case of a special power of appointment exercisable in favour of one person only, that person or, where the object of the power is ascertainable only on certain conditions being satisfied, any person as to whom some of the conditions are satisfied and the remainder may in time be satisfied;

(v) in the case of any power, option or other right, the person on whom the right is conferred;

(*c*) a person having a child or grandchild within sub-paragraphs (i) to (iv) of paragraph (*b*) above, or any of whose children or grandchildren, if subsequently born, would by virtue of his or her descent, fall within those sub-paragraphs;

(*d*) any person on the failure or determination of whose prior interest the disposition is limited to take effect. —

15.   Short title, interpretation and extent. —

(3) For the purposes of this Act a person shall be treated as a member of a class if in his case all the conditions identifying a member of the class are satisfied, and shall be treated as a potential member if in his case some only

---

[16] C & B, pp. 325–328; M & W, pp. 253–258; MM, pp. 204–205; Maudsley, pp. 123–139; (1964) 80 LQR 495–508; Morris and Leach Supp., pp. 8–10.

of those conditions are satisfied but there is a possibility that the remainder will in time be satisfied.

With this compare:

(i) Victoria Perpetuities and Accumulations Act 1968, section 6 (4):
"Nothing in this section[17] makes any person a life in being for the purposes of ascertaining the perpetuity period unless the life of that person is one expressed or implied as relevant for this purpose by the terms of the disposition and would have been reckoned a life in being for such purpose if this section had not been enacted:

Provided however that in the case of a disposition to a class of persons or to one or more members of a class, any person living at the date of the disposition whose life is so expressed or implied as relevant for any member of the class may be reckoned a life in being in ascertaining the perpetuity period."

(ii) Kentucky Rev. Stats. § 381.216[18].

381.216 Wait-and-see doctrine; reformation. In determining whether an interest would violate the rule against perpetuities the period of perpetuities shall be measured by actual rather than possible events; provided, however, the period shall not be measured by any lives whose continuance does not have a causal relationship to the vesting or failure of the interest. Any interest which would violate said rule as thus modified shall be reformed, within the limits of that rule, to approximate most closely the intention of the creator of the interest.

VI.   Reduction of Age Contingencies

A.   Before 1964[19]

A common cause of violation of the rule was the postponement of vesting until an age greater than 21.

LAW OF PROPERTY ACT 1925

163.   Validation of certain gifts void for remoteness. — (1) Where in a will, settlement or other instrument the absolute vesting either of capital or income of property, or the ascertainment of a beneficiary or class of beneficiaries, is made to depend on the attainment by the beneficiary or members of the class of an age exceeding twenty-one years, and thereby the gift to that beneficiary or class or any member thereof, or any gift over, remainder, executory limitation, or trust arising on the total or partial failure of the original gift, is, or but for this section would be, rendered void for remoteness, the will, settlement, or other instrument shall take effect for the purposes of such gift over, remainder, executory limitation, or trust as if the

---

[17] Introducing a "wait and see" rule.
[18] (1960) 49 Kentucky LR 62 (J. Dukeminier); Dukeminier, *Perpetuities in Action*; Maudsley, p. 107, nn. 13, 14.
[19] C & B, pp. 301–302; M & W, pp. 266–268; MM, pp. 203–204; Morris and Leach, pp. 52–56.

absolute vesting or ascertainment aforesaid had been made to depend on the beneficiary or member of the class attaining the age of twenty-one years, and that age shall be substituted for the age stated in the will, settlement, or other instrument.

(2) This section applies to any instrument executed after the commencement of this Act and to any testamentary appointment (whether made in exercise of a general or special power), devise, or bequest contained in the will of a person dying after such commencement, whether the will is made before or after such commencement.

(3) This section applies without prejudice to any provision whereby the absolute vesting or ascertainment is also made to depend on the marriage of any person, or any other event which may occur before the age stated in the will, settlement, or other instrument is attained.

B.　Perpetuities and Accumulations Act 1964[20]

A different solution was needed after the introduction of a principle of "wait and see" into the perpetuity rule by the 1964 Act.

PERPETUITIES AND ACCUMULATIONS ACT 1964

4.　Reduction of age and exclusion of class members to avoid remoteness. — (1) Where a disposition is limited by reference to the attainment by any person or persons of a specified age exceeding twenty-one years, and it is apparent at the time the disposition is made or becomes apparent at a subsequent time —

(*a*) that the disposition would, apart from this section, be void for remoteness, but

(*b*) that it would not be so void if the specified age had been twenty-one years,

the disposition shall be treated for all purposes as if, instead of being limited by reference to the age in fact specified, it had been limited by reference to the age nearest to that age which would, if specified instead, have prevented the disposition from being so void.

(2) Where in the case of any disposition different ages exceeding twenty-one years are specified in relation to different persons —

(*a*) the reference in paragraph (*b*) of subsection (1) above to the specified age shall be construed as a reference to all the specified ages, and

(*b*) that subsection shall operate to reduce each such age so far as is necessary to save the disposition from being void for remoteness.

(6) Section 163 of the Law of Property Act 1925 (which saves a disposition from remoteness arising out of a condition requiring the attainment of an age exceeding twenty-one years) is hereby repealed.

(7)[1] For the avoidance of doubt it is hereby declared that a question arising under section 3 of this Act or subsection (1) (*a*) above of whether a

---

[20] C & B, pp. 329–330; M & W, pp. 268–270; MM, pp. 205–206; Maudsley, pp. 139–143; (1964) 80 LQR 508–510; Morris and Leach Supp., pp. 10–12.

[1] As added by Children Act 1975, s. 108, Sch. 3, para. 43; (1965) 81 LQR 346 (J. D. Davies); (1976) 120 SJ 498 (F. A. R. Bennion).

disposition would be void apart from this section is to be determined as if subsection (6) above had been a separate section of this Act.

VII.   Class Gifts[2]

A.   The Common Law Rule

Many of the gifts which have been held void, in the illustrations so far discussed, have been class gifts; and they have been held void because there was a theoretical possibility that the interest of a member of the class might vest outside the period. The fact that the interests of most (and probably all) the members of the class vested well within the period did not help the gift, nor did it help the prospects of those whose interests did in fact vest. When the rule says that "an interest . . . must vest", it refers in the case of a class gift to the vesting of the class and not to the interests of individual members[3]. It means that the composition of the class and the share of each member must be known within the period. The gift is void if, outside the period, the number of members of the class might increase and the size of each share thus be reduced; or if the number of members of the class might be reduced, and the size of each share be increased[4].

It is important to appreciate that the question of "vesting", when asked in a perpetuity context, is different from that asked in the more usual context unaffected by the perpetuity rule; when, for example, the question is whether or not one member is yet qualified to claim an admittedly valid gift, and whether it is therefore safe for an executor or trustee to pay a share to him. For example: "To the children of A at 21." When A's eldest son is 21, he will have a "vested" interest and can be paid his share. If the question were whether or not the gift had "vested" in a perpetuity context, however, the answer would have to be "no; the gift will not vest until 21 years from the death of A". For until A's death, there may be more children so as to increase the class; and, after A's death, there may be fewer, if some die under 21, and this would reduce the membership.

To return to the trustee paying out under the gift to the children of A at 21. What share can he properly pay to the eldest son? There may be more children. Either the eldest must wait until A's death, at which time the maximum number of claimants would be known; and for this purpose it does not matter that the number may be later reduced[5]; or the eldest must be allowed to claim his share now, based upon the existing number of children, and to the exclusion of later born children. The problem would be presented more dramatically if the limitation were "to all the grandchildren of X at

---

[2] C & B, pp. 304–307; M & W, pp. 260–263; MM, pp. 210–212; Maudsley, pp. 15–25, 36–39; Morris and Leach, pp. 101–133; (1938) 51 HLR 1329 (W. B. Leach).

[3] Lord SELBORNE LC in *Pearks v Moseley* (1880) 5 App Cas 714 said at 723: "A gift is said to be to a 'class' of persons, when it is to all those who shall come within a certain category or description defined by a general or collective formula, and who, if they take at all, are to take one divisible subject in proportionate shares; and the rule is, that the vice of remoteness affects the class as a whole, if it may affect an unascertained number of its members." See also Restatement of Property, chap. 22.

[4] *Jee v Audley* (1787) 1 Cox Eq Cas 324; *Leake v Robinson* (1817) 2 Mer 363; *Pearks v Moseley*, supra; *Ward v Van der Loeff* [1924] AC 653 and cases cited in this section.

[5] For the share of each would then be increased.

21." X has died, leaving a grandchild Y who is 21, and a son Z who is 10. Must Y wait until the death of all his uncles and aunts, including Z, and perhaps a further 21 years before claiming? For only then will it be known how many grandchildren of X will attain 21.

The law solves the problem by closing the class of potential takers to those possible claimants who are alive at the period of distribution — i.e. when the trustees wish to start paying out. This provides a maximum number of takers and the smallest possible share; and this is what the trustees need to know. Those who are alive at that time will be paid when they vest; future born are excluded. The rule is only a rule of construction, and gives way to an expression of contrary intention and it seems that the courts are becoming more ready to find such contrary intention[6]. It is known as the rule of convenience; it is highly convenient for the trustees and for those who are alive at the period of distribution; highly inconvenient for future born. The class-closing rules have been much criticized[7]. It is important to appreciate that they are arbitrary; and inevitable.

Finally, let it be noted that the rule against perpetuities and the class-closing rules sometimes inter-act. Sometimes, as it were by a fluke, a class artificially closed must vest, if at all, within the period, although if left to close naturally, members might join outside. Some of these cases will be examined at p. 344 et seq., post.

RE DAWSON
(1888) 39 ChD 155 (ChD, CHITTY J)

A testator, by his will, provided an annuity for the plaintiff, his daughter, and after her death the residue was to be held on trust for her children at 21, or (being daughters) at that age or marriage, and also for such child or children of any son of the plaintiff who should die under 21 as shall live to attain the age of 21, or being daughters live to attain that age or marry, such children to take their parent's share.

The plaintiff was 60 years of age on the testator's death, and her children were all over 21.

She brought this action claiming that the trusts of the will subsequent to her death were void for remoteness.

---

[6] *Re Bleckly* [1951] Ch 740, [1951] 1 All ER 1064; *Re Cockle's Will Trusts* [1967] Ch 690, [1967] 1 All ER 391; *Re Kebty-Fletcher's Will Trusts* [1969] 1 Ch 339, [1967] 3 All ER 1076; *Re Harker's Will Trusts* [1969] 1 WLR 1124, [1969] 3 All ER 1; *Re Henderson's Trusts* [1969] 1 WLR 651, [1969] 3 All ER 769; *Re Edmondson's Will Trusts* [1972] 1 WLR 183, [1972] 1 All ER 444; *Re Deeley's Settlement* [1974] Ch 454, [1973] 3 All ER 1127; (1970) 34 Conv (NS) 393 (J. G. Riddall); *Re Chapman's Settlement Trusts* [1977] 1 WLR 1163, [1978] 1 All ER 1122; [1978] Conv 73 (F. R. Crane); *Re Clifford's Settlement Trusts* [1981] Ch 63, [1980] 1 All ER 1013.
[7] For a statement of the class-closing rules, see C & B, pp. 305–306, 794–795; M & W, pp. 263–265, 532–535; MM, pp. 211–212; Maudsley, pp. 17–25; Morris and Leach, pp. 109–125; (1954) 70 LQR 61 (J. H. C. Morris); [1958] CLJ 39 (S. J. Bailey); *Theobald on Wills* (14th edn, 1982), chap. 32, and note that, where the members of a class are to take vested interests at birth and no member of the class exists at the time when the property is available for distribution, the class remains open indefinitely: *Shepherd v Ingram* (1764) Amb 448; (1954) 70 LQR 66, 67. Otherwise the first born would automatically take the whole at birth. On balance that would be less satisfactory than the inconvenience of allowing the class to remain open: *Re Bleckly*, supra.

Held. Since the plaintiff could in law give birth to further children, membership of the class would not be determined until a time beyond the period and the whole class gift was void.

CHITTY J: The question in this case is whether the trust in favour of the children and grandchildren of the testator's daughter, the Plaintiff *Mary Elizabeth Johnston,* is or is not void for remoteness.

Putting aside for a moment the question that has been argued as to the admissibility of evidence to shew that the daughter was at the time of the testator's death past child-bearing, it appears to me to be clear this trust is void. The gift is in favour of one class, but made up of two generations. The first generation is the daughter's own children. As to that no objection can be raised. The children are to take at twenty-one as to sons and as to daughters on attaining twenty-one or marriage. But the limitation in favour of the next generation, that is the daughter's grandchildren, is plainly void. The gift, to read it shortly, is for such children of any son of the daughter who should die under the age of twenty-one as shall live to attain the age of twenty-one years, or being a daughter or daughters live to attain that age or marry. Admitting the possibility of the testator's daughter having a son born after the testator's death, then I should get to a life not in being at his death; and as that child might die under twenty-one more than twenty-one years after the death of the testator that limitation to his children at twenty-one is obviously too remote[8]. . . .

Then it is argued that the Court in applying the rule against perpetuities looks at the state of things as they existed at the testator's death, and it appears that the testator's daughter at his death was sixty years and three months old, or thereabouts; and thereupon it is said that she was past child-bearing, and consequently that there could be no son of hers born after the testator's death. . . .

[His Lordship, relying especially on *Jee v Audley* (1787) 1 Cox Eq Cas 324, p. 326, *ante,* and *Re Sayer's Trusts* (1868) LR 6 Eq 319, held that evidence as to capacity for child-bearing was inadmissible, and then continued:]

Another argument was adduced with reference to what appears to be the practice of the Court of Chancery in former times and of the Chancery Division of the High Court in the present day with reference to payment out where there is a married woman whose children are to take and the lady has attained a certain age. Those are cases I think, when examined from the beginning down to the present time, in which the Court does not assume the impossibility of issue, but as a mere matter of convenience of administration regards the high degree of improbability, and it has come now to be fixed somewhere about the age of fifty-four, although the circumstances may still be inquired into[9]. But with regard to the rule against perpetuities a high degree of probability or improbability will not do. The rule with regard to perpetuities is that the limitation must be such that every member of the class, where it is a question of a class gift, must of necessity take within the time allowed.

---

[8] The question so far was the same as that decided by the House of Lords in *Pearks v Moseley* (1880) 5 App Cas 714, where however there was not the complication of the physical impossibility of the appearance of new members.

[9] See p. 326, n. 19, *ante.*

In *Re Hooper's Settlement Trusts* [1948] Ch 586, [1948] 2 All ER 261[10], the same fate befell a gift where the limitation was for the sons and daughters of the settlor . . . "provided always that if any son of the settlor shall die . . . leaving surviving him a child or children who shall attain the age of twenty-one years . . ." JENKINS J held that the fact that the grandchildren were introduced by way of proviso was not sufficient to distinguish the case from *Pearks v Moseley* (1880) 5 App Cas 714.

However, a different construction may save parts of the gift.

In *Cattlin v Brown* (1853) 11 Hare 372, WOOD V-C said at 373: "The question arises on a short devise to *Thomas Bannister Cattlin* for life, and after his decease to all and every his children or child, for their lives, in equal shares, and after the decease of any or either of them, the part or share of the child so dying unto his, her, or their children or child, and his, her or their heirs for ever . . .

The fifth and last rule to which I need to advert is this, — that where there is a gift or devise of a given sum of money or property to each member of a class, and the gift to each is wholly independent of the same or similar gift to every other member of the class, and cannot be augmented or diminished whatever be the number of the other members, then the gift may be good as to those within the limits allowed by law. This was settled in the case of *Storrs v Benbow*[11]. . . .

The testator devises the estate to *Thomas Bannister Cattlin* for life, with remainder to all his children as tenants in common for life, with remainder as to every share of every child to the children of that child in fee. Now, to follow the respective shares of the property, suppose *Thomas Bannister Cattlin* to have four sons, A. B. C. and D. and A. and B. to be living at the testator's death and the others to be born afterwards. A. and B. on the testator's death take an immediate vested interest in remainder for life, expectant on their father's death, with remainder to their respective children in fee, subject to their respective moieties being diminished on the birth of C. and D., but their exact shares are ascertained within the legal limits at the death of their father, and neither their life interests nor the remainder in fee are capable of being wholly divested in favour of any party beyond the legal limits, neither could any one intended by the testator to take an interest, but at a period beyond the legal limits, possibly take in lieu of A. or B.; their shares are not therefore within the third rule, or governed by the judgment in the case of *Lord Dungannon v Smith* (1846) 12 Cl & Fin 546 as might have been the case if the devise had been to the sons of *Thomas Bannister Cattlin* living at his decease, with remainder to their sons in fee, for then there might possibly, at the death of *Thomas Bannister Cattlin*, have been no son who was in existence at the testator's death. Neither, again, can any possible event happening after the death of *Thomas Bannister Cattlin*, augment or diminish the share of A. or B. Here then A. and B. are respectively persons in esse at the death of the testator, who are to take a share that must be ascertained in a manner incapable of augmentation or diminution at the expiration of another life in esse. What is there to prevent the limitation of that share to him for life, with

---

[10] *Re Lord's Settlement* [1947] 2 All ER 685; *Haworth v IRC* [1974] STC 378.
[11] (1853) 3 De GM & G 390; *Wilkinson v Duncan* (1861) 30 Beav 111.

remainder to his children in fee? For this share must of necessity vest, if at all, within the legal limits, and complies, therefore, with the rule. It is in reality the case of *Storrs v Benbow*, substituting a given share for a given sum of money. . . .

The limitation as to the shares of C. and D. in the case I have supposed would be clearly void, as their children might be born at a period exceeding the limits which the law allows, they themselves not being in esse at the death of the testator. . . .

The declaration will be that the estate was by the will of the testator well limited in fee to the children of those children of *Thomas Bannister Cattlin* who were living at the death of the testator."

In *Re Russell* [1895] 2 Ch 698[12], there was a gift to all the daughters of Mary Dorrell who shall attain 21 . . . provided that . . . the share of any daughter shall be held on trust for her for life and after her death on trust for her children.

Mary Dorrell's only daughter, the plaintiff, who was born in the testator's lifetime and had attained 21, claimed that the proviso was void and that she was entitled absolutely.

The Court of Appeal (Lord HALSBURY LC, LINDLEY and RIGBY LJJ) construed the proviso as being a condition of defeasance of the original gift to the daughters; and held it to apply independently to the separate share of each daughter; so that, while it would have been void in the case of a daughter born after the testator's death, it was valid in the plaintiff's case.

B. Perpetuities and Accumulations Act 1964[13]

PERPETUITIES AND ACCUMULATIONS ACT 1964

4. Reduction of age and exclusion of class members to avoid remoteness. —

(2) p. 338, ante.

(3) Where the inclusion of any persons, being potential members of a class or unborn persons who at birth would become members or potential members of the class, prevents the foregoing provisions of this section[14] from operating to save a disposition from being void for remoteness, those persons shall thenceforth be deemed for all the purposes of the disposition to be excluded from the class, and the said provisions shall thereupon have effect accordingly.

(4) Where, in the case of a disposition to which subsection (3) above does not apply, it is apparent at the time the disposition is made or becomes apparent at a subsequent time that, apart from this subsection, the inclusion of any persons, being potential members of a class or unborn persons who at birth would become members or potential members of the class, would cause the disposition to be treated as void for remoteness, those persons shall,

---

[12] *Re Morrison's Will Trusts* [1940] Ch 102, [1939] 4 All ER 332.
[13] C & B, pp. 329–331; M & W, pp. 268–270; MM, pp. 212–214; Maudsley, pp. 140–143; (1964) 80 LQR 510–512; Morris and Leach Supp., pp. 10–12.
[14] Section 4 (1), (2), p. 318, ante, relating to reduction of age contingencies.

unless their exclusion would exhaust the class, thenceforth be deemed for all the purposes of the disposition to be excluded from the class.

(5) Where this section has effect in relation to a disposition to which section 3 above applies[15], the operation of this section shall not affect the validity of anything previously done in relation to the interest disposed of by way of advancement, application of intermediate income or otherwise.

5. Condition relating to death of surviving spouse. — Where a disposition is limited by reference to the time of death of the survivor of a person in being at the commencement of the perpetuity period and any spouse of that person, and that time has not arrived at the end of the perpetuity period, the disposition shall be treated for all purposes, where to do so would save it from being void for remoteness, as if it had instead been limited by reference to the time immediately before the end of that period.

QUESTIONS
1. Do you prefer the English, or the Victorian or the Kentucky treatment of the problem of the selection of measuring lives for the purposes of the perpetuity rule in a "wait and see" context?
2. Which limitations, if any, are valid at common law, but may be void under "wait and see"? Should the statutory list be made to include everyone who would be implied as a life in being at common law? If this were done, would there be any need to apply to instruments coming into operation after 15 July 1964, any parts of the common law rule, other than those relating to the selection of "express" lives in being. See Maudsley, pp. 156–160; (1975) 60 Cornell LR 355; C & B, pp. 325–328; M & W, pp. 253–258.
3. Which measuring lives do you think should be used for Wait and See?

VIII.   Class Closing Rules[16]

It may sometimes happen that a class gift is saved at common law by the fortuitous operation of the class closing rules discussed above[17]. It cannot be emphasised too strongly that the purpose of the class closing rules is to do something quite different. But it sometimes has this effect.

PICKEN *v* MATTHEWS
(1878) 10 ChD 264 (ChD, MALINS V-C)

The testator gave real and personal property on trust for the children of his daughters Helen and Charlotte who should attain 25. At the date of the testator's death Helen had three children, one of whom had attained 25 and Charlotte had two infant children.

Held. A valid gift to such of the daughters' children living at the testator's death who should attain 25.

---

[15] P. 336, ante.
[16] See p. 340, n. 7, ante.
[17] See pp. 339–340, ante.

MALINS V-C: If the two daughters of the testator had had no children living at his death, the gift would have been void for remoteness; because it would not be certain that the property would vest within a life or lives in being and twenty-one years after. But this is a gift to living grandchildren. . . . Now, the rules . . . applicable to this case are, first, that a gift to a class not preceded by any life estate is a gift to such of the class as are living at the death of the testator. . . .

The second rule is, that where you have a gift for such of the children of *A*. as shall attain a specified age, only those who are in esse when the first of the class attains the specified age can take. All afterborn children are excluded. This also is a rule of convenience . . .

Here there is a gift to such of a class as shall attain twenty-five. The class was ascertained at the death of the testator because one of them had then attained twenty-five. The two infant children of *Charlotte* . . . who were alive at the death of the testator are entitled to take provided they attain the age of twenty-five years . . .

Here I hold that there is a valid gift because one of the children of *Helen* . . . had attained twenty-five at the death of the testator; the maximum number to take was, therefore, then ascertained, and the gift in question is not void for remoteness.

A class may be closèd by the existence of the estate of a deceased member of the class who held a vested interest before his death.

In *Re Chartres* [1927] 1 Ch 466, the testator gave two-fifths of the residue, after the expiration of 21 years, in trust for the children or remoter issue of his son Richard as Richard should by will appoint, and in default of appointment in trust for all Richard's children who being sons attain 21 or being daughters attain 21 or marry.

On 11 March 1905 the testator died, so that the 21 year period expired on 11 March 1926.

On 18 March 1916, Richard's only child, Archibald, attained 21.

On 12 March 1924, Richard released his testamentary power.

On 26 February 1925, Archibald died having bequeathed his property to Richard.

Richard was still alive and the question was whether, having released his testamentary power, he could claim the two-fifths of the estate given to his children. ASTBURY J held that the class closed at the period of distribution, which would be at the expiry of the 21 year period, or the attainment of 21 by one of Richard's children, whichever was the later. Archibald's interest had "vested"; the period of distribution was therefore the expiry of the 21 year period on 11 March 1926, and the trustees were to pay the money over to Archibald's estate, to the exclusion of possible future born children of Richard[18]. The two-fifths share thus passed under Archibald's will to Richard.

---

[18] See the criticism of the application of the class-closing rules to a case where a life interest is released: *Re Kebty-Fletcher's Will Trusts* [1969] 1 Ch 339, [1967] 3 All ER 1076; *Re Harker's Will Trusts* [1969] 1 WLR 1124, [1969] 3 All ER 1; (1970) 34 Conv (NS) 393, 398, 407 (J. G. Riddall).

The Perpetuities and Accumulations Act 1964 makes no reference to the class closing rules. They will apply in exactly the same way as they did before the Act. Where they would previously have saved a gift from invalidity, their effect now is to avoid the necessity of applying the Act.

Where a limitation is void at common law and consequently the wait and see rule applies under section 3 (1), there is new scope for the operation of the class closing rules. A class gift which comes within section 3 (1) may remain open for lives in being plus 21 years, and after that time potential members who have not yet joined the class will be excluded: section 4 (4). Many class gifts will not however wait so long; for, at the period of distribution, the class will close to include only those potential members who are in being at the time.

Thus, suppose a gift: "To such of the grandchildren of A. (a living person), as shall attain the age of 21." A. has two sons, B. and C., and a grandson X., all of whom will be measuring lives under section 3 (5). Without rules for artificial closing of the class, any grandchildren could join it who attained 21 within 21 years of the dropping of the last of those lives. However on X.'s 21st birthday, he will be able to demand payment of his share; and the class will close to include only those grandchildren who are alive at the time[19].

QUESTIONS

1. On what principle was the gift in the will in *Ward v Van der Loeff* [1924] AC 653, p. 326, ante, held valid?

2. What alteration in the facts would have enabled the gift in the codicil to be upheld on the same ground as that on which the gift in the will was upheld? (1954) 70 LQR 61, 84 (J. H. C. Morris); *Re Cockle's Will Trusts* [1967] Ch 690, [1967] 1 All ER 391; Maudsley, pp. 53–56.

3. A testator bequeathed his residuary estate upon trust to be divided equally between such of his nephews and nieces as were living at the date of his death for their lives and after the death of any such nephew or niece upon trust for the child or children of such nephews or nieces who shall attain the age of 21 years.

   One nephew, Geoffrey, having no need of the income, released to the trustees all his interest to the intent that the trustees should hold the income on the same trusts as would be applicable if he were dead. The elder of Geoffrey's two daughters attained the age of 21. Is she entitled to claim half of the fund? See *Re Kebty-Fletcher's Will Trusts* [1969] 1 Ch 339, [1967] 3 All ER 1076; *Re Harker's Will Trusts* [1969] 1 WLR 1124, [1969] 3 All ER 1.

4. What would be the solution to *Ward v Van der Loeff* if the testator had died after 1964?

---

[19] If there is no grandchild alive at the testator's death, there is some doubt whether or not the class closes when the first grandchild attains 21. The better view is that it does: *Pearse v Catton* (1839) 1 Beav 352; Morris and Leach, p. 114; (1954) 70 LQR 61, 68–69 (J. H. C. Morris); *Re Bleckly* [1951] Ch 740 at 749, [1951] 1 All ER 1064 at 1069.

IX. Powers of Appointment

A. Before 1964[20]

i. GENERAL POWERS

(a) Validity of Power

A general power is one by which the donee of the power may appoint to any person, including himself. Thus, the giving of a general power to a donee is, in a sense, equivalent to giving the property to him. Hence, a general power is valid if it must become exercisable by the donee, if at all, within the perpetuity period. It is not relevant that he may exercise it outside the period.

(b) Validity of Exercise of Power

In the case of a general power, the perpetuity period runs from the time of the exercise of the power.

ii. SPECIAL POWERS

(a) Validity of Power

A special power is one in which the class of appointees is restricted. The donor of the power is exercising an element of control over the appointment. A stricter rule applies.

In *Re De Sommery* [1912] 2 Ch 622, PARKER J said at 630: "A special power which, according to the true construction of the instrument creating it, is capable of being exercised beyond lives in being and twenty-one years afterwards is, by reason of the rule against perpetuities, absolutely void; but if it can only be exercised within the period allowed by the rule, it is a good power, even although some particular exercise of it might be void because of the rule.

If a power be given to a person alive at the date of the instrument creating it, it must, of course, if exercised at all, be executed during his life, and is therefore valid. Again, if a power can be exercised only in favour of a person living at the date of the instrument creating it, it must, if exercised at all, be exercised during the life of such person, and is therefore unobjectionable. Further, the instrument itself may expressly limit a period, not exceeding the legal limits, for the exercise of the power. Lastly, where the settlor has used language from which the Court may fairly infer that he contemplated the creation, not of a single power, but of two distinct powers, one of which only is open to objection because of the rule against perpetuities, the Court will avoid the latter only and will give effect to the power which is not open to this objection. Thus, although a power vested in the trustees for the time being of a settlement has, so far as I can discover, been uniformly looked on as a single and indivisible power, it may be otherwise if the power be limited to A. and B. or other the trustees of the settlement for the time being. In this case the Court may treat the settlor as having created one power vested in A. and B. while trustees, and a distinct power vested in their successors, in which

---

[20] C & B, pp. 307–310; M & W, pp. 279–287; MM, pp. 216–221; Maudsley, pp. 59–64; Morris and Leach, pp. 134–163.

case the power vested in A. and B. would be open to no objection on the ground of remoteness: *Attenborough v Attenborough* (1855) 1 K & J 296.

In the present case the testatrix devised all her real and residuary personal estate to two named persons, thereinafter called her 'trustees', upon trust for sale, and, after payment of her debts and funeral and testamentary expenses and a certain charitable legacy, to divide the proceeds into thirteen parts, and, as to two such parts, to hold the same, upon trust to pay the capital and income thereof, or neither, to her nephew Eugene de Sommery, or to apply the capital or income thereof for his benefit, or for the benefit of his wife or any child or children of his, as her trustees should consider advisable, and, subject thereto, to pay any capital or income which might remain in their hands under that trust to such of her nephews and nieces, and in such shares, as her trustees should think proper. In my opinion, the power or powers thus created in favour of Eugene de Sommery, his wife and children, are conferred on the trustees of the will for the time being, and not on the original trustees only (see *Re Smith* [1904] 1 Ch 139); and this being so, there is, I think, no possibility of applying the principle of *Attenborough v Attenborough*. Further, if there be one power only vested in these trustees, it is fairly obvious that it may, according to the true construction of the will, be exercised during the life of any child of Eugene de Sommery, whether alive at the testatrix's death or born afterwards, and would therefore be avoided by the rule against perpetuities. I have come to the conclusion, however, that there are in fact two powers vested in the trustees for the time being of the will — first, a power of paying either capital or income to Eugene de Sommery, which is only capable of being exercised during his life, and, secondly, a power of applying either capital or income for the benefit of Eugene de Sommery, his wife or children, which is capable of being exercised beyond the period allowed by law. I see no reason on principle which precludes me from upholding the former and rejecting the latter power."

(b) Validity of Exercise of Power

The appointment must be read back into the instrument containing the power; that is the perpetuity period must run from the date of the creation of the power.

RE BROWN AND SIBLY'S CONTRACT
(1876) 3 ChD 156 (ChD, MALINS V-C)

By a marriage settlement of 1821, land was conveyed to trustees to the use of W.M. for life and after his death as he shall appoint among his issue with a gift over in default.

W.M. appointed by will in 1867 to his son W.E.M. in fee; but in case W.E.M. should have no child who should attain 21, then in fee to W.M.B. (a grandson through a daughter, and unborn at the date of the settlement).

W.E.M. sold part of the land to Brown, who then entered into a contract with Sibly to sell part of the land to him. The question was whether W.E.M. could give a good title to the fee simple without the concurrence of W.M.B.

Held. He could; because the executory gift over to W.M.B. was void for remoteness.

MALINS V-C: The point I have to decide under this settlement is free from doubt. The law is settled, that where a person takes property by virtue of the execution of a special or limited power of appointment, he takes directly under the instrument creating the power. Consequently, when *W. Metford* made his will, it was the same as if the words he there used had formed part of the settlement, and as if the property had been conveyed by that settlement to trustees to the use of himself for life, with remainder to the use of his (unborn) son in fee, with a direction that in case his son should have no child who should attain twenty-one, then that the estate should, after the son's death, go over to the settlor's grandson in fee. That is an attempt to make the property inalienable for a period which might extend to twenty-one years after the determination of the life of a person not in being at the date of the settlement. The law does not allow a man to tie up property for longer than a life or lives in being and twenty-one years; and this is clearly an attempt to do what is contrary to the law.

I need not do more than refer to my decision in *Stuart v Cockerell* (1869) LR 7 Eq 363, afterwards affirmed on appeal (1870) 5 Ch App 713, which shews that the law is as I have stated it. My opinion, therefore, is that the appointment by the testator to his son in fee is good, and the attempt to give the estate over is void. It is precisely the same as if a man were to give property to his son for life, and after his decease to his son's children, as tenants in common in fee, with a proviso that if any of the children should die under twenty-five the property should go over. In that case the proviso carrying over the shares would be void. The gift to the son in fee is therefore good, and the executory devise over is void[1].

But the court will take into consideration certain facts existing at the date on which the appointment is made.

In *Re Paul* [1921] 2 Ch 1, a testator who died in 1895 left a share of his residuary estate to his daughter Mrs. A. for life and after her death as she should appoint by will among her children.

Mrs. A., by will, appointed the share to her son A.J.A. on attaining 25 years. She died in 1919 when A.J.A. was 18 or 19.

SARGANT J upheld the appointment and said at 5: "There is ample and quite conclusive authority in favour of the appointment being good. *Wilkinson v Duncan* (1861) 30 Beav 111 and *Von Brockdorff v Malcolm* (1885) 30 ChD 172 are direct decisions in favour . . . Having regard to the fact that the son in this case was 18 or 19 years old at the time of his mother's death, so that his interest must vest in him in six or seven years after her death, I decide that the gift to him is good, contingently, of course, on his attaining the age of 25 years. . . ."

---

[1] The same principle was applied to a statutory power of advancement (TA 1925, s. 32) in *Pilkington v IRC* [1964] AC 612 at 642, [1962] 3 All ER 622 at 632: "I think that the important point for the purpose of the rule against perpetuities is that the new settlement is only effected by the operation of a fiduciary power which itself 'belongs' to the old settlement"; *Re Hastings-Bass* [1975] Ch 25, [1974] 2 All ER 193.

In *Wilkinson v Duncan* (1861) 30 Beav 111[2], there was a bequest to such of the children of George Wilkinson as he should appoint. He appointed the fund upon trust to pay £2,000 to each of his daughters as and when they attained 24, and to divide the residue among his sons equally as and when they attained 24. George Wilkinson left ten children, two of whom were under the age of three years at his death. Sir John ROMILLY MR held that the gift to the sons was void; but the gift to the daughters was valid in respect of such of the daughters as were three years old at his death.

B.   Perpetuities and Accumulations Act 1964[3]

PERPETUITIES AND ACCUMULATIONS ACT 1964

1.   Power to specify perpetuity period. — (2) p. 320, ante.

3.   Uncertainty as to remoteness. — (2) p. 334, ante.
(3) p. 345, ante.

7.   Powers of appointment. — For the purposes of the rule against perpetuities, a power of appointment shall be treated as a special power unless —

(*a*) in the instrument creating the power it is expressed to be exercisable by one person only, and

(*b*) it could, at all times during its currency when that person is of full age and capacity, be exercised by him so as immediately to transfer to himself the whole of the interest governed by the power without the consent of any other person or compliance with any other condition, not being a formal condition relating only to the mode of exercise of the power:

Provided that for the purpose of determining whether a disposition made under a power of appointment exercisable by will only is void for remoteness, the power shall be treated as a general power where it would have fallen to be so treated if exercisable by deed[4].

15.   Short title, interpretation and extent. — (2) In this Act . . . "power of appointment" includes any discretionary power to transfer a beneficial interest in property without the furnishing of valuable consideration; . . .

(5) The foregoing sections of this Act . . . in the case of an instrument made in the exercise of a special power of appointment shall apply only where the instrument creating the power takes effect after [the commencement of the Act].

Provided that section 7 above shall apply in all cases for construing the foregoing reference to a special power of appointment.

---

[2] *Permanent Trustee Co of New South Wales Ltd v Richardson* (1948) 48 SR NSW 313.
[3] C & B, pp. 331–332; M & W, pp. 279–287; MM, pp. 216–221; Maudsley, pp. 162–166; (1964) 80 LQR 518–521; Morris and Leach Supp., pp. 7, 14–15.
[4] Thus avoiding the difficulties in cases such as *Re Churston Settled Estate* [1954] Ch 334, [1954] 1 All ER 725; *Re Earl of Coventry's Indentures* [1974] Ch 77, [1973] 3 All ER 1 (joint power and consent power held special power for purposes of the rule).

X. Administrative Powers of Trustees[5]

PERPETUITIES AND ACCUMULATIONS ACT 1964

8. Administrative powers of trustees. — (1) The rule against perpetuities shall not operate to invalidate a power conferred on trustees or other
persons to sell, lease, exchange or otherwise dispose of any property for full
consideration, or to do any other act in the administration (as opposed to the
distribution) of any property, and shall not prevent the payment to trustees
or other persons of reasonable remuneration for their services.

(2) Subsection (1) above shall apply for the purpose of enabling a power
to be exercised at any time after the commencement of this Act notwithstanding that the power is conferred by an instrument which took effect
before that commencement.

XI. Expectant and Dependent Limitations

A. Before 1964[6]

In *Re Hubbard's Will Trusts* [1963] Ch 275, [1962] 2 All ER 917, the testator
gave a share of the "sisters' fund" to each of his sisters and their issue (clause
9 (iv)) by trusts which included discretionary trusts in favour of the sisters'
grandchildren, which were void for remoteness (clause 9 (v)). The will, by
clause 9 (vi), directed that, on the failure or determination of any of the
sisters' shares, there should be an accruer to the other shares, and, subject
thereto, the property was given to charity.

The question was whether the gifts over on the failure of the discretionary
trusts were valid. BUCKLEY J held that the accruer provision, being dependent upon the same provision as that which terminated the trusts, was void.
But the gift to charity was a vested gift, not dependent, and was valid. He
said at 283, at 920: "It is said that it is settled law that any limitation
dependent or expectant on a prior limitation which is void for remoteness is
itself invalid *Re Abbott* [1893] 1 Ch 54, and *Re Canning's Will Trusts* [1936] Ch
309, but it is not very easy to discover from the authorities what is meant by
the expression 'dependent or expectant on' in this context. In *Re Thatcher's
Trusts* Sir John Romilly MR used the following language (1859) 26 Beav 365
at 370: 'On the other hand if the limitations are ulterior to or expectant upon
limitations which are too remote, they are void also, although made to a
person in existence at the date of the will.'

It is clear from the comparatively modern decision of *Re Coleman* [1936]
Ch 528, [1936] 2 All ER 225 that the mere fact that a trust is ulterior to
another which is invalid for remoteness, in the sense that the benefit under
the former trust can only fall into possession when any possible benefit under
the latter, had it been valid, would have ceased, is not sufficient to render the
ulterior trust invalid. Accordingly, I think that it is necessary to look at the
cases to see to what kind of case the rule applies. . . .

---

[5] C & B, pp. 317–318, 334; M & W, p. 281; MM, pp. 216–217; Maudsley, pp. 58–59, 183–185;
Morris and Leach, pp. 232–242.

[6] C & B, pp. 310–313; M & W, pp. 270–274; MM, pp. 207–209; Maudsley, pp. 64–67; Morris
and Leach, pp. 173–181; (1950) 10 CLJ 392 (J. H. C. Morris); (1950) 14 Conv (NS) 148 (A.
K. Kiralfy).

I think that the cases in which the problem with which I am concerned has been considered, where the trusts were such that successive interests existed or could have come into existence, can be divided into three categories.

If a testator or other settlor settles property in such a way as to create a series of successive interests, each intended to take effect upon and only upon the exhaustion or termination of all antecedent interests in the chain, and one of those interests is void for remoteness, all the ulterior interests will fail, and this will be so even in the case of such an interest as a life interest given to a living person which, if it were ever to take effect at all, would necessarily do so within the limits of perpetuity. In such a case the invalidity of one of the successive interests for perpetuity breaks the chain and all interests below the point of fracture fall away. This rule seems to be based on the intention of the settlor demonstrated by the nature of the trusts. It was explained by Stirling J in *Re Abbott* [1893] 1 Ch 54 at 57, as follows: 'The reason appears to be that the persons entitled under the subsequent limitation are not intended to take unless and until the prior limitation is exhausted; and as the prior limitation which is void for remoteness can never come into operation, much less be exhausted, it is impossible to give effect to the intentions of the settlor in favour of the beneficiaries under the subsequent limitation.'

In such a case, if an ulterior interest were accelerated to fill the void created by the failure of the preceding interest on the ground of perpetuity, the result would be that some one would be in possession whom the settlor did not mean to be in possession in the existing circumstances. Alternatively, the gap might be left void. Each alternative would be contrary to the intention of the settlor.

The leading case on this subject is *Beard v Westcott* (1822) 5 B & Ald 801, explained in *Monypenny v Dering* (1852) 2 De GM & G 145. Sir John Romilly MR in *Re Thatcher's Trusts* (1859) 26 Beav 365 treated himself as following *Beard v Westcott*, and Astbury J in *Re Hewett's Settlement* [1915] 1 Ch 810 purported to follow both *Beard v Westcott* and *Re Thatcher's Trusts*. *Re Backhouse* [1921] 2 Ch 51, was presumably decided on similar grounds; and see *Re Mortimer* [1905] 2 Ch 502 where a vested legal remainder subsequent to a remote estate tail was held to fail. So far as these authorities result in an interest which, if it ever falls into possession, must do so within the perpetuity period being rendered invalid by the remoteness of some earlier interest in the chain, they have been subjected to criticism in Gray on Perpetuities, 4th edn., pp. 276–281, paras. 252–257, which seems to me to be cogent, but there is no doubt that they are binding on me. In such cases the ulterior interest may truly be said to fail by reason of contagion with or of dependency on the remote interest if, as in *Beard v Westcott*, the ulterior interest is one which is expressed to take effect on some contingency which is not itself remote. This is, I believe, the only kind of case to be found in the books in which this rule has been applied. They are to be distinguished from the kinds of cases which I now proceed to notice.

Where the testator or settlor so frames his trusts as to create an interest which will not take effect in possession until a future date but must vest in interest within the perpetuity limit, either on a stated date or on some event which must occur within that limit, and the enjoyment of that interest in possession is not dependent on the prior exhaustion of the antecedent interests, such future interest will be unaffected by remoteness in any of the antecedent interests. Thus in *Re Coleman* [1936] Ch 528, [1936] 2 All ER 225, where a testator settled a share of his residue on discretionary trusts for his son W. during his life, and after his death on similar discretionary trust for any widow W. might leave and for all or any of the children of W. and after the death of such widow on trust for the children of W. at 21 or marriage, in equal shares, it was held that though the discretionary trust in favour of W.'s widow was void for remoteness, as W. might marry a woman who was not born at the death of the testator, the ultimate trust in favour of W.'s children being vested, and not contingent or dependent on the void trust, was valid. . . .

Another case falling within this class is *Re Allan* [1958] 1 WLR 220, [1958] 1 All ER 401, where although the interest there in question was expressed to take effect 'on the determination of the trusts hereinbefore declared,' Danckwerts J construed those words as equivalent to 'on the death of such widow'.

A third class of cases is exemplified by *Re Abbott* [1893] 1 Ch 54, and *Re Canning's Will Trusts* [1936] Ch 309. Where a testator or settlor gives property to A. either immediately or at some future date which is not too remote, but so frames his trusts that the interest of A. may be displaced by the exercise of some power or discretion, the interest of A. will be unaffected by any invalidity of that power or discretion on the ground of remoteness.

[His Lordship referred to *Re Abbott* and to *Re Canning's Will Trusts* and continued:]

I now return to considering the testator's will. As I have pointed out, the accruer provision in clause 9 (vi) must take effect, if at all, while the trusts declared by clause 9 (iv) and (v) remain in operation in respect of the appropriated share of one of the testator's sisters. That is to say, it must take effect, if at all, while a sister of the testator or a child of a sister of the testator is alive. It must and could only take effect in respect of a particular share upon there ceasing to be a sister of the testator or any child of hers entitled in respect of that share under clause 9 (iv) and, ignoring perpetuity for the present purpose, any grandchild of that sister entitled in respect of that share under clause 9 (v). In other words, it could only take effect upon the exhaustion of the objects of the preceding trusts. The accruer provision is, in my judgment, dependent on the preceding trusts and expectant on their failure, as indeed the opening words of clause 9 (vi) suggest.

The disposition of capital in the second half of clause 9 (vi)[7], however, appears to me to stand on a different footing. The earlier trusts are trusts for a limited period which must end on or before an ascertainable date, namely, the death of the last survivor of the testator's sisters and their children. This event is not dependent on the exhaustion of objects of the antecedent trusts. The fact that theoretically this date might be more than 21 years after the end of a life in being at the testator's death is, I think, irrelevant: *Re Coleman*. The gift of the capital of the sisters' fund contained at the end of clause 9 (vi) is the only disposition of the capital of this fund, it vested in interest immediately on the death of the testator, and the enjoyment by the charities of that interest in possession is merely postponed because and to the extent that the testator has for a limited time given the income elsewhere. I see no ground upon which this gift could be said itself to fail for perpetuity, nor do I

---

[7] I.e., the gift over to charity.

think that the facts of the case bring it within the principle of what I may call dependent invalidity.

The only case which may perhaps be said to be awkward to reconcile with this view is *Re Backhouse* [1921] 2 Ch 51. . . .

If *Re Backhouse* and *Re Coleman* conflict, I prefer the decision of Clauson J in *Re Coleman*. At any rate, *Re Backhouse* is clearly distinguishable on its facts from the present case, and as Eve J gave no reasons for the relevant part of his decision in that case I am not embarrassed by it[8]."

B. Perpetuities and Accumulations Act 1964

PERPETUITIES AND ACCUMULATIONS ACT 1964[9]

6. Saving and acceleration of expectant interests. — A disposition shall not be treated as void for remoteness by reason only that the interest disposed of is ulterior to and dependent upon an interest under a disposition which is so void, and the vesting of an interest shall not be prevented from being accelerated on the failure of a prior interest by reason only that the failure arises because of remoteness.

XII. Contracts and Options

A. Before 1964[10]

In *Woodall v Clifton* [1905] 2 Ch 257, the question was whether the rule applied to a covenant in a 99 year lease to purchase the fee simple, in such a way as to prevent the assignee of the lease from being able to enforce the covenant against an assignee of the freehold.

WARRINGTON J held that it did. In the Court of Appeal the result was affirmed on the ground that the covenant did not run with the reversion under 32 Hen 8, c 34[11]; the perpetuity question was not referred to in the judgments on appeal.

LONDON AND SOUTH WESTERN RAILWAY CO *v* GOMM
(1882) 20 ChD 562 (CA, JESSEL MR, Sir James HANNEN, LINDLEY LJ)

In 1865 the London and South Western Railway Co conveyed to Powell for £100 the fee simple of certain land which was no longer required for the purposes of the railway. Powell covenanted with the company that he, his heirs and assigns would at any time thereafter whenever the land might be

---

[8] On the question whether "failure" of the trusts includes failure because of the application of the perpetuity rule, see *Re Robinson's Will Trusts* [1963] 1 WLR 628, [1963] 1 All ER 777 (held to include); *Re Buckton's Settlement Trusts* [1964] Ch 497, [1964] 2 All ER 487 (held not to include); (1964) 80 LQR 323 (R. E. Megarry).

[9] C & B, pp. 333–334; M & W, pp. 273–274; MM, p. 209; Maudsley, p. 185; (1964) 80 LQR 517–518. Morris and Leach Supp., pp. 13–14.

[10] C & B, pp. 314–315; M & W, pp. 287–292; MM, pp. 221–222; Maudsley, pp. 72–75; Morris and Leach, pp. 219–228; (1954) 18 Conv (NS) 576 (J. H. C. Morris and W. B. Leach).

[11] See p. 461, post.

required for the railway and upon receiving £100, reconvey the land to the company. In 1879 Gomm purchased the land from Powell's heir with notice of the covenant, and in 1880 the company brought an action for specific performance of the covenant.

Held (inter alia). The covenant was void, as it created an interest in land and might be exercised outside the perpetuity period.

JESSEL MR: If then the rule as to remoteness applies to a covenant of this nature, this covenant clearly is bad as extending beyond the period allowed by the rule. Whether the rule applies or not depends upon this as it appears to me, does or does not the covenant give an interest in the land? If it is a bare or mere personal contract it is of course not obnoxious to the rule, but in that case it is impossible to see how the present Appellant can be bound. He did not enter into the contract, but is only a purchaser from *Powell* who did. If it is a mere personal contract it cannot be enforced against the assignee. Therefore the company must admit that it somehow binds the land. But if it binds the land it creates an equitable interest in the land. The right to call for a conveyance of the land is an equitable interest or equitable estate. In the ordinary case of a contract for purchase there is no doubt about this, and an option for repurchase is not different in its nature[12]. A person exercising the option has to do two things, he has to give notice of his intention to purchase, and to pay the purchase-money; but as far as the man who is liable to convey is concerned, his estate or interest is taken away from him without his consent, and the right to take it away being vested in another, the covenant giving the option must give that other an interest in the land.

It appears to me therefore that this covenant plainly gives the company an interest in the land, and as regards remoteness there is no distinction that I know of (unless the case falls within one of the recognised exceptions, such as charities) between one kind of equitable interest and another kind of equitable interest. In all cases they must take effect as against the owners of the land within a prescribed period.

Specific performance was held to be obtainable between the original contracting parties: *Hutton v Watling*[13] [1948] Ch 26, [1947] 2 All ER 641; affirmed on other grounds [1948] Ch 398, [1948] 1 All ER 803; and even if the defendant is no longer in possession of the land, damages for breach of contract could be obtained: *Worthing Corpn v Heather* [1906] 2 Ch 532[14].

B. Perpetuities and Accumulations Act 1964[15]

PERPETUITIES AND ACCUMULATIONS ACT 1964

9. Options relating to land. — (1) The rule against perpetuities shall not apply to a disposition consisting of the conferring of an option to acquire for

---

[12] *Mountford v Scott* [1975] Ch 258, [1974] 1 All ER 248; *affd.* [1975] 1 All ER 198 (option to purchase); *George Wimpey & Co Ltd v IRC* [1974] 1 WLR 975, [1974] 2 All ER 602; cf. *Murray v Two Strokes Ltd* [1973] 1 WLR 823, [1973] 3 All ER 357 (right of pre-emption); *Pritchard v Briggs* [1980] Ch 338, [1980] 1 All ER 294; Barnsley, *Land Options* (1978), chap. 7; p. 86, ante.

[13] (1948) 12 Conv (NS) 258 (E. O. Walford).

[14] See also *South Eastern Rly Co v Associated Portland Cement Manufacturers (1900) Ltd* [1910] 1 Ch 12; *Dunn v Blackdown Properties Ltd* [1961] Ch 433, [1961] 2 All ER 62.

[15] C & B, pp. 324–325, 333–334; M & W, pp. 290–292; MM, p. 222; Maudsley, pp. 186–189; (1964) 80 LQR 522–525; Morris and Leach Supp., pp. 16–17.

valuable consideration an interest reversionary (whether directly or indirectly) on the term of a lease if —

> (*a*) the option is exercisable only by the lessee or his successors in title, and
>
> (*b*) it ceases to be exercisable at or before the expiration of one year following the determination of the lease.

This subsection shall apply in relation to an agreement for a lease as it applies in relation to a lease, and "lessee" shall be construed accordingly.

(2) In the case of a disposition consisting of the conferring of an option to acquire for valuable consideration any interest in land, the perpetuity period under the rule against perpetuities shall be twenty-one years, and section 1 of this Act shall not apply:

Provided that this subsection shall not apply to a right of pre-emption conferred on a public or local authority in respect of land used or to be used for religious purposes where the right becomes exercisable only if the land ceases to be used for such purposes.

10. Avoidance of contractual and other rights in cases of remoteness. — Where a disposition inter vivos would fall to be treated as void for remoteness if the rights and duties thereunder were capable of transmission to persons other than the original parties and had been so transmitted, it shall be treated as void as between the person by whom it was made and the person to whom or in whose favour it was made or any successor of his, and no remedy shall lie in contract or otherwise for giving effect to it or making restitution for its lack of effect.

XIII.   Possibilities of Reverter and Conditions Subsequent[16]

A.   Before 1964[17]

LAW OF PROPERTY ACT 1925

4. Creation and disposition of equitable interests. — (3) All rights of entry affecting a legal estate which are exercisable on condition broken or for any other reason may after the commencement of this Act, be made exercisable by any person and the persons deriving title under him, but, in regard to an estate in fee simple (not being a rentcharge held for a legal estate) only within the period authorised by the rule relating to perpetuities[18].

The rule was usually held not to apply to a possibility of reverter[19]. An executory gift over, outside the period, will of course be void; the interest reverts to the grantor who can dispose of it by a grant *inter vivos* or by his will

---

[16] For the distinction between a determinable and a conditional fee, see C & B, pp. 341–344; M & W, pp. 67–75; MM, pp. 39–43; see also p. 23, ante.

[17] C & B, pp. 317, 342, 347; M & W, pp. 275–279; MM, pp. 214–216; Maudsley, pp. 69–71; Morris and Leach, pp. 209–219.

[18] *Re Trustees of Hollis' Hospital and Hague's Contract* [1899] 2 Ch 540; *Re Da Costa* [1912] 1 Ch 337; *Re Bowen* [1893] 2 Ch 491; *Re Peel's Release* [1921] 2 Ch 218.

[19] *Re Randell* (1888) 38 ChD 213; *Re Blunt's Trusts* [1904] 2 Ch 767; *Re Chardon* [1928] Ch 464; *Re Wightwick's Will Trusts* [1950] Ch 260, [1950] 1 All ER 689; *Re Chambers' Will Trusts* [1950] Ch 267; *Re Cooper's Conveyance Trusts* [1956] 1 WLR 1096, [1956] 3 All ER 28.

Brown v Independent Baptist Church of Woburn[20]. The view was strongly held before 1964 that the rule ought to be applied to possibilities of reverter; and in *Hopper v Liverpool Corpn* (1944) 88 SJ 213, the Vice-Chancellor of the Lancaster County Palatine Court held that it did.

B. Perpetuities and Accumulations Act 1964[1]

PERPETUITIES AND ACCUMULATIONS ACT 1964

12. Possibilities of reverter, conditions subsequent, exceptions and reservations. — (1) In the case of —

> (a) a possibility of reverter on the determination of a determinable fee simple, or
>
> (b) a possibility of a resulting trust on the determination of any other determinable interest in property,

the rule against perpetuities shall apply in relation to the provision causing the interest to be determinable as it would apply if that provision were expressed in the form of a condition subsequent giving rise, on breach thereof, to a right of re-entry or an equivalent right in the case of property other than land, and where the provision falls to be treated as void for remoteness the determinable interest shall become an absolute interest.

(2) Where a disposition is subject to any such provision, or to any such condition subsequent, or to any exception or reservation, the disposition shall be treated for the purposes of this Act as including a separate disposition of any rights arising by virtue of the provision, condition subsequent, exception and reservation.

XIV. Exceptions to the Rule[2]

Morris and Leach, *The Rule Against Perpetuities* (2nd edn.), pp. 242–243

"It may be useful to enumerate here some of the more important exceptions to the Rule. Most of these have already been considered[3].

> (1) Gifts over from one charity to another[86].
>
> (2) Limitations which must vest at or before the termination of an entailed interest[87].
>
> (3) Contracts, unless they create contingent interests in land or other property[88].
>
> (4) Covenants for renewal in leases[89].
>
> (5) Mortgages[90].
>
> (6) Certain easements[91].

---

[20] 325 Mass 645, 91 NE (2d) 922 (1950); (1952) 65 HLR 721, 741 (W. B. Leach) (a residuary gift held in Massachusetts to include such an interest).

[1] C & B, pp. 342–343, 347–348; M & W, pp. 277–279; MM, p. 216; Maudsley, pp. 190–191; (1964) 80 LQR 525–527; Morris and Leach Supp., p. 18.

[2] C & B, pp. 314–319, 334; M & W, pp. 292–295; MM, pp. 222–224.

[3] The footnotes refer to pages in Morris and Leach.

[86] Ante, pp. 189–194.

[87] Ante, pp. 195–196.

[88] Ante, pp. 219, 227, 228.

[89] Ante, p. 223.

[90] Ante, p. 227.

[91] Ante, pp. 229–230.

(7) Certain rights of entry for non-payment of rentcharges[92].

(8) Trusts for the payment of debts[93].

(9) Accumulations for reducing the National Debt[94].

(10) Trusts of 'registered funds' the main purpose of which is to provide superannuation allowances or widows' pensions or children's allowances for employees or the assurance of capital sums on the death of employees[95]."

XV.   Accumulations[4]

A.   Introduction

The rule against accumulations was introduced by the Accumulations Act 1800, as a result of *Thellusson v Woodford* (1799) 4 Ves 227; affirmed (1805) 11 Ves 112; see p. 359, post, and these statutory provisions were re-enacted and amended by sections 164–166 Law of Property Act 1925. The general effect is to limit those accumulations, to which the Act applies[5], to any one of four periods: first, the life of the grantor or settlor; second, twenty-one years from the death of the grantor, settlor or testator, and third and fourth, two alternative periods of certain specified minorities. The main differences between the third and fourth periods[6] are that the third is limited to persons alive at the death of the testator or settlor, while the fourth period includes accumulations (a) during the minorities of persons born after the death of the grantor, settlor or testator, provided that accumulation is not directed to begin until such person is born and (b) during successive minorities; but it is confined to the minorities of those who would, if of full age, have been entitled to the income which is being accumulated[7].

Two further periods of accumulation were added by the Perpetuities and Accumulations Act 1964, section 13 (1)[8] for the benefit of a living settlor, namely twenty-one years from the date of the disposition, and the minority or respective minorities of any person or persons in being at that date. This provision offered considerable advantages to a settlor who wished to establish an inter vivos discretionary trust for his family. Previously the only periods applicable to inter vivos trusts were accumulations during minorities

---

[92] LPA 1925, ss. 121 (6), 162; ante, p. 218.

[93] Ante, pp. 240–241.

[94] Superannuation and Other Trust Funds (Validation) Act 1927, s. 9 (now replaced by Social Security Act 1973; Maudsley, p. 191).

[95] Social Security Act 1973, s. 69. Similar legislation is in force in many other parts of the British Commonwealth.

[4] C & B, pp. 334–339; M & W, pp. 300–310; MM, pp. 226–233; Gray, ss. 671–679. 1; Appendix B, ss. 686–714: Maudsley, chap. 7; Morris and Leach, pp. 266–306; Simes, *Public Policy and the Dead Hand*, chap. 4; *Theobald on Wills* (14th edn, 1982), pp. 615–621; (1953) 17 Conv (NS) 199 (G. B. Graham); [1958] CLJ 39 (S. J. Bailey); Law Reform Committee Fourth Report 1958 (Cmnd. 18), Section C.

[5] For exceptions, see LPA 1925, s. 164 (2), p. 364, post.

[6] *Re Cattell* [1914] 1 Ch 177, p. 362, post. For the relationship between LPA 1925, s. 165, as interpreted in *Re Maber* [1928] Ch 88 and the fourth period under s. 164, see Morris and Leach, pp. 276–278.

[7] *Re Cattell* [1914] 1 Ch 177 at 189, p. 362, post.

[8] Following the recommendation of the Law Reform Committee Fourth Report, paras. 56, 57; (1964) 80 LQR 529–530; Morris and Leach Supp., 19.

(third and fourth periods); or during the life of the settlor (first period) which attracted estate duty on the settlor's death[9]. Under the new tax system, capital transfer tax is payable when a capital distribution is made from a trust. In the case of discretionary trusts, there is deemed to be a distribution of the whole of the capital of the trust on each tenth anniversary of the transfer of the property to the trust; but tax is chargeable at only 30% of the rate which would be chargeable upon actual distribution[10].

The effect of a direction which breaks the rule against accumulations depends on whether it also breaks the rule against perpetuities. If it breaks both rules, then the direction is totally void i.e. there is no accumulation at all. If, however, it satisfies the rule against perpetuities but only breaks the rule against accumulations, then it is good pro tanto and only void as to the excess beyond the appropriate statutory period. There is, then, a gap from the end of the statutory period until the end of the period chosen during which the income is in effect undisposed of; during this gap the income so released either reverts to the settlor or his representatives or falls into residue or goes to the next of kin. There is no acceleration of the interests of those entitled after the accumulation is over[11].

B. Before 1964

THELLUSSON *v* WOODFORD[12]
(1805) 11 Ves 112 (HL, Lord ELDON LC)

Peter Thellusson, who died in 1797, devised real estates of the annual value of about £1,000, and other estates, directed to be purchased with the residue of the personal estate, amounting to above £600,000 to trustees upon trust to accumulate the rents and profits at compound interest during the lives of his sons, grandsons and great-grandsons living at his death or born in due time[13] afterwards, and on the death of the survivor to divide the said estates into three lots, each of which was to be strictly settled on the eldest male lineal descendant then living of each of his three sons. He directed that the trustees should stand seised, upon the failure of male lineal descendants, upon trust to sell and pay the produce to His Majesty, his heirs, and successors, to the use of the Sinking Fund: and that all the persons becoming entitled should use the surname of Thellusson only. At the time of the testator's death, there were alive his widow, three sons and four grandsons: two more grandsons, who were en ventre at the time of his death, were born later.

Held (affirming the decision of Lord LOUGHBOROUGH (1799) 4 Ves 227). The limitations and the direction to accumulate were valid, being confined to lives in being.

Counsel for the appellants: "Mr. *Thellusson's* will is morally vicious; as it was a contrivance of a parent to exclude every one of his issue from the enjoyment even of the produce of his property during almost a century; and it

---

[9] FA 1894, s. 2 (1) (*b*); FA 1969, s. 36 (The "substituted section 2 (1) (*b*) (iv).").
[10] CTTA 1984, ss. 64, 66. See also s. 71, excluding accumulation and maintenance trusts from this provision.
[11] *Green v Gascoyne* (1864) 4 De GJ & Sm 565, p. 366, post.
[12] For a general history of the Thellusson family litigation, see (1970) 21 NILQ 131 (G. W. Keeton).
[13] I.e., the period of gestation.

is politically injurious; as during the whole of that period it makes an immense property unproductive both to individuals and the community at large; and by the time, when the accumulation shall end, it will have created a fund, the revenue of which will be greater than the civil list; and will therefore give its possessor the means of disturbing the whole economy of the country. The probable amount of the accumulated fund, in the events, which have happened, is stated in the Appellant's bill, and admitted in the answer, to be 19,000,000*l*; and in case any of the persons, answering the description of heir male, when the period of suspense ends, should be a minor, and his minority should continue 10 years, it would increase the amount of that third to the sum of 10,802,373*l*; so that, if the whole property should centre in one person, and that person should have a minority of 10 years, after the end of the period of suspense (a circumstance by no means improbable, particularly as Mr. *George Woodford Thellusson* has been long married and has no son), the whole accumulated fund will amount to 32,407,120*l*[14]."

LORD ELDON LC: Another question arises out of this will; which is a pure question of equity: Whether a testator can direct the rents and profits to be accumulated for that period, during which he may direct, that the title shall not vest, and the property shall remain unalienable; and, that he can do so, is most clear law. A familiar case may be put. If this testator had given the residue of his personal estate to such person as should be the eldest male descendant of *Peter Isaac Thellusson* at the death of the survivor of all the lives, mentioned in this will, without more, that simple bequest would in effect have directed accumulation, until it should be seen, what individual would answer the description of that male descendant; and the effect of the ordinary rule of law, as applied in equity, would have supplied everything, that is contained in this will, as to accumulation; for the first question would be, Is the executory devise of the personal estate to the future individual, so described, good? If it is, wherever a residue of personal estate is given, the interest goes with the bulk; and there is no more objection to giving that person, that, which is only forming another capital, than to giving the capital itself. But the constant course of a Court of Equity is to accumulate interest from time to time without a direction, and to hand over the accumulation to that person, who is to take the capital. Take another instance of accumulation: Suppose, the nine persons, named in this will, had been lunatics: without any direction there would have been an accumulation of the interest and profits of all these estates. In truth there is no objection to accumulation upon the policy of the law, applying to perpetuities: for the rents and profits are not to be locked up, and made no use of, for the individuals, or the public. The effect is only to invest them from time to time in land: so that the fund is, not only in a constant course of accumulation, but also in a constant course of circulation. To that application what possible objection can there be in law? . . . Therefore, as to giving the property at the expiration of nine lives and the accumulation, I never could doubt upon these points.

---

[14] "On the death of the last surviving grandson in 1856, the estate was divided (not without more litigation) between the two male representatives of the two of Peter Thellusson's sons who had left issue. But owing to mismanagement and costs of litigation, the estate realised a comparatively small amount": Holdsworth, vii, p. 230; (1970) 21 NILQ at pp. 169–174.

LAW OF PROPERTY ACT 1925

164. General restrictions on accumulation of income. — (1) No person[15] may by any instrument or otherwise settle or dispose of any property in such manner that the income thereof shall, save as hereinafter mentioned, be wholly or partially accumulated for any longer period than one of the following, namely:—

(a) the life of the grantor or settlor; or

(b) a term of twenty-one years from the death of the grantor, settlor or testator; or

(c) the duration of the minority[16] or respective minorities of any person or persons living or en ventre sa mere at the death of the grantor, settlor or testator; or

(d) the duration of the minority[16] or respective minorities only of any person or persons who under the limitations of the instrument directing the accumulations would, for the time being, if of full age, be entitled to the income directed to be accumulated[17].

In every case where any accumulation is directed[18] otherwise than as aforesaid, the direction shall (save as hereinafter mentioned) be void; and the income of the property directed to be accumulated shall, so long as the same is directed to be accumulated contrary to this section, go to and be received by the person or persons who would have been entitled thereto if such accumulation had not been directed.

(3) The restrictions imposed by this section apply to instruments made on or after the twenty-eighth day of July, eighteen hundred, but in the case of wills only where the testator was living and of testamentary capacity after the end of one year from that date.

165. Qualification of restrictions on accumulation. — Where accumulations of surplus income are made during a minority under any statutory power or under the general law, the period for which such accumulations are made is not (whether the trust was created or the accumulations were made before or after the commencement of this Act) to be taken into account in determining the periods for which accumulations are permitted to be made by the last preceding section, and accordingly an express trust for accumulation for any other permitted period shall not be deemed to have been invalidated or become invalid, by reason of accumulations also having been made as aforesaid during such minority[19].

166. Restriction on accumulation for the purchase of land. — (1) No person may settle or dispose of any property in such manner that the income thereof shall be wholly or partially accumulated for the purchase

---

[15] A corporate settlor is not a "person" within the section: *Re Dodwell & Co Ltd's Trust Deed* [1979] Ch 301, [1978] 3 All ER 738.

[16] In the case of dispositions taking effect after 1969, minority ends at the age of 18; Family Law Reform Act 1969, s. 1. There are transitional provisions so that the change from 21 to 18 shall not invalidate any direction for accumulation in a settlement or other disposition made by a deed, will or other instrument, which was made before 1970: ss. 1, 4, Sch. 3, para. 7.

[17] See *Re Cattell* [1914] 1 Ch 177, p. 362, post.

[18] This includes a power to accumulate: PAA 1964, s. 13 (2), p. 364, post; affirming *Re Robb* [1953] Ch 459, [1953] 1 All ER 920. The same point was so decided in Scotland under Trusts (Scotland) Act 1961, s. 5 (2); *Baird v Lord Advocate* [1979] AC 666, [1979] 2 All ER 28.

[19] See n. 16, supra.

of land only, for any longer period than the duration of the minority or respective minorities of any person or persons who, under the limitations of the instrument directing the accumulation, would for the time being, if of full age, be entitled to the income so directed to be accumulated.

(2) This section does not, nor do the enactments which it replaces, apply to accumulations to be held as capital money for the purposes of the Settled Land Act, 1925, or the enactments replaced by that Act, whether or not the accumulations are primarily liable to be laid out in the purchase of land.

(3) This section applies to settlements and dispositions made after the twenty-seventh day of June eighteen hundred and ninety-two.

In *Re Cattell* [1914] 1 Ch 177, the question was whether an accumulation was limited to the minority of persons born in the lifetime of the testator. The Court of Appeal (LORD PARKER OF WADDINGTON, LORD SUMNER and WARRINGTON J) held that the fourth period extended to the minorities of persons born after the testator's death and to successive minorities. Lord PARKER OF WADDINGTON said at 186: "In construing the Thellusson Act, it must be remembered that it is not an enabling but a disabling Act. Prior to the passing of the Act a testator had the right to direct an accumulation for any period he chose, provided he did not exceed the time which was allowed by the perpetuity rule — that is to say, lives in being, and twenty-one years afterwards. The Act was passed in order to disable testators from taking full advantage of the liberty which they had hitherto enjoyed in that respect. The terms of the Act are 'That no person or persons shall after the passing of this Act, by any deed or deeds, surrender or surrenders, will, codicil or otherwise howsoever, settle or dispose of any real or personal property so and in such manner that the rents, issues, profits or produce thereof shall be wholly or partially accumulated for any longer term than' — then there are four alternative periods given, and it has been held, and I think rightly held, that of those four periods one only can be selected by the testator. The difficulty arises in this case in regard to the fourth period. The first contemplates the case of a man who settles property otherwise than by will, in which case he may direct that the rents and profits be accumulated during his life. The settlor cannot direct an accumulation during his life and some further period. The second period contemplates an accumulation which is to commence from the death of the settlor, and includes the case of a settlor by will. No such accumulation is to go on for more than twenty-one years. Then the third alternative is a period — almost the same period of twenty-one years from the death of the settlor — during the minority or respective minorities of any person or persons 'who shall be living or en ventre sa mère' at the time of the death of the settlor. That of course must be limited to twenty-one years, and some further period representing gestation in the case of a child yet unborn. Then there is the fourth alternative, which gives rise to the difficulty in the present case . . . [His Lordship read the fourth period[20] and continued:] It is to be observed that this last alternative clause closely follows and seems to be contrasted with the alternative with regard to the minority or respective minorities of any person or persons who should be living or en ventre sa mère at the time of the death of the settlor. One would not therefore

---

[20] Which is in substance the same as LPA 1925, s. 164 (1) (*d*), p. 361, ante.

expect it to be limited (as contended by the appellant) to children living or en ventre sa mère at the settlor's death. Indeed if so limited it would in effect add nothing to the preceding alternative. The reason urged in support of the appellant's contention rests mainly on certain decisions which it is said we ought to follow and to which I will now refer.

[His Lordship referred to *Haley v Bannister* (1819) 4 Madd 275, *Ellis v Maxwell* (1841) 3 Beav 587 and *Bryan v Collins* (1852) 16 Beav 14 and continued:] In my opinion the fourth alternative period covers not only children who are born or en ventre sa mère at the death of the settlor, but children who are subsequently born, and I think the fact that the fourth alternative comes immediately after, and in contrast with, the third alternative, which refers only to born children, and children en ventre sa mère, at the time of the death of the settlor, points strongly to this conclusion. . . .

It is said — and I think said with some truth — that in this case if we adopt the construction which allows a child who is not born at the death of the settlor to be one of the children during whose minority or respective minorities the accumulations are directed to be made, then we allow successive accumulations to be made of what practically, if not theoretically, is the same fund, which accumulations taken together may last for a considerable time. I think that may be true, but at the same time it is worth bearing in mind that though these periods may when added together amount to a considerable time, yet the periods in question are not really within the vice against which the Act is directed . . . and there being nothing in the express words of the Act to prevent us giving effect to the old powers which were possessed by testators before the Act, there is no reason to construe the fourth alternative in any other way than I have suggested. It is well known that settlements are and have been drawn up on this footing. A testator may often direct a settlement of property upon A. for life, and after his death upon his children on attaining twenty-one, and if he goes on to provide that during the minority or respective minorities of his children the income of the property shall be accumulated, it is only a clause in common form. I have never known any doubt to be thrown on the validity of such a clause, but if the appellant's contention prevailed its validity would be open to question. It seems to me, therefore, that Neville J was right in his decision, and that this appeal ought to be dismissed."

See also Trustee Act 1925, section 31, which gives power to trustees to apply income for the maintenance of beneficiaries, vested or contingent, during their minority, and requires the unapplied part of the income to be accumulated[1].

C. Perpetuities and Accumulations Act 1964[2]

PERPETUITIES AND ACCUMULATIONS ACT 1964

13. Amendment of s. 164 of Law of Property Act 1925. — (1) The periods for which accumulations of income under a settlement or other

---

[1] H & M, pp. 553–559; Snell, pp. 301–302; M & B, *Trusts and Trustees* (3rd edn, 1984), pp. 676–686.

[2] C & B, p. 336; M & W, pp. 301–302; MM, pp. 227–229; Maudsley, pp. 204–211; (1964) 80 LQR 529–530; Morris and Leach Supp., p. 19.

disposition are permitted by section 164 of the Law of Property Act 1925 shall include —

    (*a*) a term of twenty-one years from the date of the making of the disposition, and

    (*b*) the duration of the minority or respective minorities[3] of any person or persons in being at that date.

(2) It is hereby declared that the restrictions imposed by the said section 164 apply in relation to a power to accumulate income whether or not there is a duty to exercise that power, and that they apply whether or not the power to accumulate extends to income produced by the investment of income previously accumulated.

14. Right to stop accumulations. — Section 2 above shall apply to any question as to the right of beneficiaries to put an end to accumulations of income under any disposition as it applies to questions arising on the rule against perpetuities[4].

————————

Compare, with these provisions:

VICTORIA PERPETUITIES AND ACCUMULATIONS ACT 1968

19. Accumulation of income.—

(1) Where property is settled or disposed of in such manner that the income thereof may be or is directed to be accumulated wholly or in part the power or direction to accumulate that income shall be valid if the disposition of the accumulated income is or may be valid but not otherwise.

D. Exemptions from Restrictions on Accumulation

i. BY STATUTE

LAW OF PROPERTY ACT 1925

164. General restrictions on accumulation of income.—

(2) This section does not extend to any provision —

    (i) for payment of the debts of any grantor, settlor, testator or other person;

    (ii) for raising portions for —

        (*a*) any child, children or remoter issue of any grantor, settlor or testator; or

        (*b*) any child, children or remoter issue of a person taking any interest under any settlement or other disposition directing the accumulations or to whom any interest is thereby limited;

—————————————————————————

[3] See p. 361, n. 16, ante.
[4] Beneficiaries of full age holding an absolute beneficial interest in a trust fund may terminate the accumulation and the trust and require the trustees to pay the capital of the fund to them: *Saunders v Vautier* (1841) Cr & Ph 240. *Re Deloitte* [1926] Ch 56 had held that evidence of infertility was inadmissible to help beneficiaries to terminate a trust under this' rule.

(iii) respecting the accumulation of the produce of timber or wood; and accordingly such provisions may be made as if no statutory restrictions on accumulation of income had been imposed.

ii.   OTHER EXEMPTIONS

Maudsley, *Modern Law of Perpetuities*, pp. 210–211

"COMMERCIAL ARRANGEMENTS; CONTRACTS OF INSURANCE; UNIT TRUSTS

Various commerical arrangements have been held to be outside the Act, even though they involve in some sense an accumulation. Thus, in the leading case of *Bassil v Lister*[5] a testator directed his trustees to pay the premiums on a policy of insurance on his son's life out of the income of the residuary estate. Turner V-C held that this was not an accumulation of the type to which the Thellusson Act was directed; and that it was valid for the son's life, and not merely for a period of 21 years. In *Re AEG Unit Trust (Managers) Ltd's Deed*[6], the question concerned a provision in a trust deed to the effect that surplus income in any accounting period, over and above that available for distribution to unit holders, should be added to capital and should thereupon cease to be available for distribution. Again, this, in a sense, involved an accumulation of such income. Wynn-Parry J held that the Law of Property Act 1925, section 164, did not apply. An investor, purchasing units in a unit trust, did not 'settle or dispose' of property, nor was such a transaction within the scope of the section. Nor could the section be applicable where the unit holders were able at any time to amend or terminate the trust[7]. Nor does the section apply where a corporation is the settlor[8].

MAINTENANCE OF PROPERTY[9]

A provision for the application of income for the upkeep of property is also outside the scope of the Act. This is not really an exception; for it covers only the maintenance of the value of depreciating property, whether by way of provision for repairs[10], or by way of provision for the replacement of leaseholds as they expire[11]. It does not include a fund for the accumulation of income for the improvement of land, or by the construction of buildings on it[12]. Where the exception applies, the provision must of course comply with the perpetuity period[13]."

---

[5] (1851) 9 Hare 177; similarly with a partnership agreement: (1851) 9 Hare at 184; *Re AEG Unit Trust (Managers) Ltd's Deed* [1957] Ch 415 at 421, [1957] 2 All ER 506 at 508.
[6] Supra.
[7] At 421, at 508; *Wharton v Masterman* [1895] AC 186.
[8] *Re Dodwell & Co Ltd's Trust Deed* [1979] Ch 301, [1978] 3 All ER 738.
[9] See generally M & W, pp. 309–310; Morris and Leach, p. 280.
[10] *Vine v Raleigh* [1891] 2 Ch 13; *Re Mason* [1891] 3 Ch 467.
[11] *Re Gardiner* [1901] 1 Ch 697; *Re Hurlbatt* [1910] 2 Ch 553.
[12] *Vine v Raleigh* [1891] 2 Ch 13 at 26; *Re Gardiner* [1901] 1 Ch 697 at 700.
[13] *Curtis v Lukin* (1842) 5 Beav 147.

E. Excessive Accumulations

GREEN *v* GASCOYNE
(1864) 4 De GJ & Sm 565 (Lord WESTBURY LC)

LORD WESTBURY LC: The case is that of a testator directing an accumulation during the lives of his wife and sister and the life of the survivor of them of the rents and profits of certain freehold estates.

The first question is, what is the operation of the statute upon that trust for accumulation? The second, what will be its effect upon the construction and interpretation of the will?

The first effect of the statute I apprehend to be that the trust for accumulation is reduced to a term of twenty-one years, and that I must take the trust as if it had been expressed "for a period of twenty-one years, provided my wife and my sister *Sarah* or the survivor of them shall so long live". Secondly, I take it that the words of the statute which direct that the rents released by its effect from the operation of the trust for accumulation shall "go to and be received by such person or persons as would have been entitled thereto if such accumulation had not been directed", must be construed to mean "if such excessive accumulation had not been directed". The meaning of the words therefore is brought to be the same as it would have been had the accumulations been directed for twenty-one years only.

I am not at liberty to apply or use the statute so as in any manner to accelerate the enjoyment of any gift or disposition contained in the will, nor can I use the statute for the purpose of giving to any term or description contained in the will a meaning which it would not have had had the trust for accumulation been good instead of bad. Although the trust for accumulation is cut down and reduced to a limited period, the whole of the rest of the will remains in point of disposition, in point of the meaning, effect and true interpretation of its language, precisely as if there had been no such operation performed by the statute. . . .

The result is that there is a hiatus between the period when the accumulation ceases by law and the period when the accumulation is directed to cease by the will; there is nothing in the will to catch the rents which arise during that hiatus; and those rents accordingly belong to the heir at law.

Sometimes the problem is to know which of the permitted periods should be applied.

In *Re Ransome* [1957] Ch 348, [1957] 1 All ER 690, there was a testamentary direction in a will coming into operation in 1935 that "the income . . . shall be accumulated until the youngest child of my [living grandson R] shall attain the age of 21 years." R had by his first marriage a son D, who attained 21 in 1951. By R's second marriage in 1953, there were no children at the date of the proceedings. UPJOHN J held that the gift did not vest absolutely in D on his attaining 21. This meant that the direction to accumulate was excessive, and one question was the proper period of accumulation.

UPJOHN J said at 361, at 696: "The next question is as to the impact of the rule against accumulations on the direction to accumulate until the youngest child attains 21. Plainly, that direction infringes the rule and it is necessary to determine for what period the term is valid. The test is stated to be that you have first to determine which of the four periods set out in section 164 the testatrix has seemingly selected, determining that question according to the language employed and the facts of the case; see *Re Watt's Will Trusts* [1936] 2 All ER at 1562. That seems to me an artificial and difficult test. The trouble in this case and in most cases dealing with the rule against accumulations is that the testatrix has given directions clearly not having the rule in mind at all. The competing periods in this case are section 164 (1) (*b*), a term of 21 years from the death of the testatrix, which brings the period of valid accumulation to an end on 6 July 1956, on the one hand, and, on the other, sub-paragraph (*c*) of the section, the duration of the minority or respective minorities of anyone living at the death of the testatrix. If that period is selected, it is submitted that it came to an end when the eldest child, David, attained 21 on 24 June 1951.

Neither sub-paragraph fits in, in the least degree, with the directions of the testatrix. However, in directing accumulations until Robert's youngest child should attain 21, the testatrix can hardly have contemplated that the period of accumulations would in fact come to an end by the attainment by Robert's eldest child of the age of 21 years, and I propose to hold that sub-paragraph (*b*) is the relevant paragraph; the difference is not of great importance."

QUESTIONS

1. What periods would you expect to be applied in the following testamentary dispositions:

   (*a*) ". . . during the minority of the children of Gerald.": *Re Watt's Will Trusts* [1936] 2 All ER 1555.

   (*b*) ". . . so much of the dividends as shall accrue due to Elizabeth Mary Griffiths (a beneficiary) during the life of John Griffiths, her husband, . . . shall be accumulated.": *Griffiths v Vere* (1803) 9 Ves 127.

   (*c*) "to be accumulated . . . until the decease of the last survivor of the said several annuitants, or during such portion of such surviving annuitant's life as the rules of law will permit . . .": *Talbot v Jevers* (1875) LR 20 Eq 255.

   (*d*) Upon trust "to invest the same in the Funds, so as the same might accumulate, by way of Compound Interest until (the testator's) Great Nephew, Philip Crawley, [aged 3] shall attain 25.": *Longdon v Simson* (1806) 12 Ves 295; *Crawley v Crawley* (1835) 7 Sim 427.

   (*e*) "To my wife during widowhood, but if she should marry again, then from and after such marriage, I direct that all bequests in her favour shall cease, and that in lieu thereof the trustees shall pay to my wife an annuity of £500 and shall accumulate the surplus income during the remainder of the life of my wife": *Weatherall v Thornburgh* (1878) 8 ChD 261.

   (*f*) ". . . as and when each of them the said Ann Webb and William Adams shall respectively die, the annuity and annuities so given by me to or for her or him respectively as aforesaid, shall be laid out from time to time, until the death of the last survivor of them the said two last-named annuitants, as an addition to the said capital of the said rest, residue, and remainder of my said stock of three per cent consolidated Bank annuities . . . shall be and shall be taken as an increase and accumulation to the said capital stock, until the death of the last survivor of them, the said two last-mentioned annuitants.": *Webb v Webb* (1840) 2 Beav 493.

(g) And a gift inter vivos:

". . . to receive and accumulate the dividends . . . during the joint lives of James Campbell and Jane, his wife, and, after the death of James Campbell, if his wife should survive him . . . for her life, and, after her decease, whether the same should happen in the lifetime or after the decease of her husband, to stand possessed of the capital and accumulations in trust for their daughter, Charlotte Campbell . . .": *Re Lady Rosslyn's Trust* (1848) 16 Sim 391.

(h) By a settlement dated 6 December 1951 "to accumulate the income during the life of the settlor or until the beneficiary [born 1950] attains the age of 22.": *Re Erskine's Settlement Trusts* [1971] 1 WLR 162, [1971] 1 All ER 572. Would the answer be different if all the facts had taken place after 1964?

2. Do you think that restrictive rules, such as those currently applicable, are required? The present trend in countries abroad is to return to the common law rule: or even to abolish the rule altogether: PAA 1983 of Manitoba (SM 1982–83, c. 43); p. 316, ante, p. 368, post. Maudsley p. 202, Appendix D.

3. Does Wait and See apply to the question of the validity, under the Perpetuity rule, of a provision for the accumulation of income? Can you see any reason why, if Wait and See is introduced in respect of disposition generally, it should not also apply to accumulations? C & B, p. 337, n. 18; M & W, pp. 304–305; Maudsley; pp. 206–208. See Victoria Perpetuities and Accumulations Act 1968, s. 19 (1), p. 364, ante; and others included in Maudsley, Appendix D.

XVI. Abolition or Retention and Reform of the Two Rules

(1984) 4 OJLS 454 (R. Deech) at pp. 454, 458–463:

"The Perpetuities and Accumulations Act 1983 of Manitoba (SM 1982–83, c. 43) has abolished the rule against perpetuities, the rule in *Whitby v Mitchell* and the Thellusson Act as they applied in that province (sections 2, 3) and it has transformed successive legal interests into equitable interests, belatedly following section 1 of the Law of Property Act 1925. Coming into force on the same day, 1 October 1983, was an Act to Amend the Trustee Act 1983 (SM 1982–83, c. 38), which abolishes the rule in *Saunders v Vautier* (1841) 4 Beav 115, and subjects any proposal to vary a trust to the approval of the court. . . .

Is there still a case for retention and reform of the rule rather than abolition? The case for reform, but never for abolition, has been exhaustively argued by writers and law reform reports. The 1956 Law Reform Committee Report simply stated that it was 'beyond argument' that there should be a time limit on the vesting of future interests (para. 4); the case for abolition was not argued by Morris and Leach, *The Rule Against Perpetuities* (2nd edn.), both of whom had assisted in the preparation of the Fourth Report. . . . Maudsley (*The Modern Law of Perpetuities* 221) considered abolition briefly but was daunted by the risk of dynastic trusts created by testators unafraid of tax liability. This risk was considered remote by the Manitobans: whatever social conditions might prevail in England to make this a genuine problem, they were absent in Canada, and even if a few offenders emerged after abolition of the rule, they could not be numerous enough to outweigh the disadvantages of its complications and unforeseeable effect. The harm, if any, in long delayed vesting would be to the taxpayer himself, and not widespread. In Manitoba the days are long gone when an owner wished to keep a fortune in his family over as many generations as possible. In a country of immigration, of nuclear families and of marriage breakdowns calling for property reallocation, it was estimated that there was no significant risk of any ill effect if the rule were to be abolished and, moreover, with retroactive effect. Legislation would deal with specific problems when and if they arose and the balancing of the interests of the living and the dead would henceforth be achieved more satisfactorily by the power of the courts to consent to variation and revocation of trust.

Among the weightiest arguments in favour of abolition were the internal inconsistencies of wait and see itself. To repair is to assert that the rule is the right response to a genuine problem; yet the need to remove well known traps and to provide a safety net, as in the English statute, is an indictment of the rule. Wait and see creates uncertainty for lawyer and client; it also tends to prolong the actual period allowed for vesting and may well validate all gifts. If wait and see is so praiseworthy in its removal of restraint and in achieving closer fulfilment of the testator's wishes, then abolition must be even more acceptable. As Mechem said, if there is a widespread desire to liberalize the rule and a feeling of triumph when a limitation escapes its clutches, then abandonment must be the welcome culmination of the trend. If the law permits, at least to a limited extent, that a testator may make bequests that appear unreasonable to his family then, the rule having been abolished, it can be no worse to allow present disinheritance in favour of beneficiaries living a century hence.

The arguments for keeping the rule, reformed or otherwise, are undeniably less forceful. Partly it is fear; the attitude of Simes: 'I do not think there is any way in which the property institutions of a civilised country can be completely wiped out and a new set of institutions established at one stroke of the legislative pen' (103 *U Pa L Rev* 707, 732), to which the 1925 Acts must stand as a refutation. More specifically, Gray in *The Rule Against Perpetuities* (4th edn., s. 871): 'It is a dangerous thing to make such a radical change in a part of the law which is concatenated with almost mathematical precision.' American jurisdictions that had substantially amended the rule admittedly had to revert to the original, but these experiments were confined to length of perpetuity period, not the concept itself. There is also disquiet about the legislative or other response to new problems emerging if the rule is abolished, whether it be retrospective legislation or the courts' reformulation of a rule against perpetuities, thus starting the historical cycle afresh. The most solid reason for keeping the rule is its alleged power of restraint. The dissenting view in the *Report* was that the rule regulated remoteness of vesting in a fair and intelligible form, and any occasional inappropriate result could be avoided by amending legislation. The frustration of the intentions of settlors is no good argument for abolition for the rule exists precisely in order to thwart certain intentions. After all, many wills are defeated because the testator failed to comply with essential formalities, such as the signature of acceptable witnesses, yet there is no demand for wholesale relaxation of the law of wills because it embodies sound policy. It is unlikely that evidence of success would be found because the rule would, if properly applied, prevent the emergence of perpetuities problems and, so far as can be estimated, it has performed its role successfully for three centuries.

Manitoba's abolition of the rule is linked to a widened jurisdiction to vary trusts, which is to take its place and fulfil such balancing effect as the rule might be claimed to have had. If the arguments for abolition cannot be resisted, then the crucial test for the new law is whether variation of trusts can do all that is expected of it. The *Report* assumed that a combination of the rule in *Saunders v Vautier* and the Variation of Trusts Act 1958 already ensured that trusts could only remain in effect in England with the consent of the beneficiaries and the court's consent on behalf of the incapacitated[14]: the parallel legislation in Manitoba was section 61 of the Trustee Act (CCSM, T160), derived from the Sixth Report of the English Law Reform Committee, (Cmnd 310 (1957), *Court's Power to Sanction Variation of Trusts*). The Manitoba *Report* recommended amendment of section 61 to define the 'benefit' that the court must find in the proposed arrangement on behalf of the beneficiary and to make it clear that the court must also consider the intentions of the settlor or testator in creating the trust and the circumstances that prevail at the time of application under section 61.

What would motivate courts to give or to withhold approval of variation remains to be seen. There could be problems in this. The existing English law, although of a different scope, works in tandem with perpetuities: once gone, would considerations such as postponed vesting or length of trust and restrictions on spending affect Manitoban or English courts? The nature of the term 'benefit' is chameleon-like — if perpetuities cease to be an issue, it is hard to predict whether the court would regard it as of benefit to future possible beneficiaries to end a trust now and divide the capital amongst those presently alive, the difficulty being that one cannot assume that future 'beneficiaries' do *not* have a right to enjoy capital once the rule against perpetuities has been abolished. There would arise the question of compensation of remote future beneficiaries. The issue is overshadowed by clouds of possibly unborn entitled persons, and their entitlement would complicate valuation of future shares of capital. Since the settlor's intentions are relevant under the new Manitoba law, his possible desire to establish a dynastic trust will be influential and perhaps weigh so heavily that there will appear no way to terminate it. The moral and social issues involved in trusts (Harris, *Variation of Trusts* 47; *Re Remnant's Settlement Trusts* [1970] Ch 560, [1970] 2 All ER 554) will lose what certainty they have if the perpetuity period is removed as a guideline.

The tax assumptions also bear questioning. The accepted wisdom is that tax laws serve to curb a man's otherwise greedily dynastic instincts and that tax avoidance dominates *inter vivos* trust establishment. It must nevertheless be conceded that settlements will continue to be deployed when the settlor's prime purpose is not so much tax avoidance but rather control over his capital and beneficiaries. So far at least it is evident that existing tax laws have not prevented large fortunes from descending through the generations,

---

[14] See generally H & M, chap. 21; M & B, *Trusts and Trustees* (3rd edn, 1984), chap. 19, p. 364, n. 4, ante.

although it is still too early to judge the effect of capital transfer tax. There is, moreover, no foundation for the assumption that tax laws do, and always will, bite on long delayed future interests so as to act as an alternative to or a reinforcement of the perpetuities rule.

Capital transfer tax and capital gains tax[15] may be payable on the making of a 'settlement' (as defined for tax purposes) and generally the legislation treats in turn each holder of an interest in possession as if he were beneficial owner of the fund in which his interest subsists. In the case of a fixed trust there is a charge to CTT on the full value of the settled property whenever the beneficial enjoyment changes hands. In the case of a discretionary trust there is a periodic charge every ten years and when the property ceases to be held on trust. Looking at the tax implications, it is as if all present and future interests were arrayed on a conveyor belt which bore them up to the hand of the taxman at regular intervals. Viewed in this way it can make little difference taxwise whether there is a long chain of future interests moving to the point of taxation or a short one, for the tax law will bite on them rhythmically until they come to an end. The abolition of the rule against perpetuities might even have tax advantages as there would be no need to resettle, which usually has adverse tax consequences. On the other hand, no doubt something like the ten-year periodic charge would remain and if variation under the Variation of Trusts Act were deemed to create a new trust, the usual charges to CGT and CTT would arise, and this might serve as a disincentive to variation: *Re Holt's Settlements* [1969] 1 Ch 100, [1968] 1 All ER 470. Little difference would be made to planning whether remote interests were permitted or not, for it is the mode of settlement and changes in tax legislation that are important and would remain so. Flexibility would probably be increased and the abolition of the rule might even clear the way to a simpler and more consistent method of taxation on trusts. The conclusion must be that tax avoidance might not constitute a curb in substitution of the rule against perpetuities, if such a control is deemed necessary.

Tax efficiency is at the moment regarded as an important reason for variation, even if the House of Lords is less generous than hitherto in approving tax avoidance schemes: *WT Ramsay Ltd v IRC* [1982] AC 300, [1981] 1 All ER 865; *IRC v Burmah Oil Co Ltd* (1981) 54 TC 200; *Furniss v Dawson* [1984] AC 474, [1984] 1 All ER 530. The combination of tax legislation and the abolition of the rule against perpetuities could lead to the establishment of lengthy trusts with resort to the court every generation for variation to suit the demands of the moment. The uncertainties of this process might produce a result even less acceptable than the rule against perpetuities, whose common law rigidities, once mastered, had much to commend them from the point of view of certainty. The unanswerable question is whether the courts would assume that delayed vesting was a good or bad thing in deciding variation questions without the rule, which has provided a framework for trusts questions in the past. The American verdict on such a scheme is adverse; (Sparks, 45 *Va L Rev* 493, considering the parallel *Claflin* doctrine, 20 NE 454 (1889)); but only practice can tell. It could be that a few early cases concerning variation of long-running trusts established by wealthy Manitobans will set the pattern for future attitudes. If

---

[15] See generally H & M, chap 9; M & B, *Trusts and Trustees* (3rd edn. 1984), Part III.

abolition of the rule against perpetuities were to be considered in this country then, likewise, the Variation of Trusts Act would have to be altered in scope.

Accumulations law has also been reformed in Manitoba and in the rest of Canada. The arguments against lengthy accumulations were treated by Manitoba in the same way as those relating to perpetuities with the result that restrictive legislation is to be dispensed with and tax laws relied on to deter over-ambitious plans. Accumulation was regarded as a sensible plan in certain cases and the old Thellusson Act applying in Manitoba unsatisfactorily frustrating. Elsewhere in Canada there has been a reversion to the common law rule that accumulation is acceptable as long as the accumulated fund vests within the perpetuity period, following the suggestions of Simes (Alberta: Perpetuities Act, RSA 1980, cP-4, section 240; British Columbia: Perpetuity Act 1975, c. 53, section 24 (1); see also W. Australia: Law Reform (Property, Perpetuities and Succession) Act 1962, section 17) but in Ontario six accumulation periods have been provided (Accumulations Act, RSO 1980, c. 5) in emulation of English law. In Manitoba the Accumulations Act has simply been repealed and not replaced (section 2).''

Part Three. Commercial Interests

8. Terms of Years[1]

---

[1] C & B, pp. 35–37, chap. 17; M & W, pp. 40–44, 628–760; MM, pp. 17–19, 332–370, 378–388; Aldridge, *Leasehold Law* (1980); Foa, *Law of Landlord and Tenant* (8th edn, 1957); Hill and Redman, *Law of Landlord and Tenant* (17th edn, 1982); Woodfall, *Landlord and Tenant* (28th edn, 1978); Evans, *Law of Landlord and Tenant* (2nd edn, 1985); Partington, *Landlord and Tenant* (2nd edn, 1980); Yates and Hawkins, *Landlord and Tenant Law* (1980).

The Law Commission has published three reports on the general law of landlord and tenant (a) The Obligations of Landlords and Tenants 1975 (Law Com No. 67, HC 377); (b) Covenants Restricting Dispositions, Alterations and Change of User 1985 (Law Com No. 141, HC 278); (1985) 135 NLJ 991, 1015 (P. F. Smith); (c) Forfeiture of Tenancies (1985) (Law Com No. 142, HC 279). Further reports are planned on the rule which makes the original parties to a lease responsible for the performance of their covenants even after they have parted with all interest in the property, and on the remedy of Distress for Rent, on which the Payne Committee reported in 1969 (Cmnd 3909); Nineteenth Annual Report 1983–1984 (Law Com No. 140, HC 214), para. 2.49–52. See also (1980) 96 LQR 515 at p. 529 (Sir Michael Kerr).

I.　General Background

Other than the estate in fee simple absolute in possession, the only *legal* estate which can subsist after 1925 is the term of years absolute[2]. These two legal estates are different in nature, in that the former is a freehold, the latter a leasehold estate; the former, in other words, is held, theoretically, of a feudal superior by freehold tenure, the latter is held of the freeholder by leasehold tenure. The two estates can therefore exist contemporaneously in one piece of land[3], the fee simple being held by the freeholder (commonly called owner), the leasehold estate by the leaseholder (commonly called the tenant).

It was essential for the feudal system of landholding that one person or a group of feoffees to uses should be responsible for each piece of land; as freeholders they were protected, in the days before the action of trespass, by the Real Actions, the Writs of Right, Writs of Entry and the Possessory Assizes, all of which were available to, and only to, persons seised[4]. The leaseholder's position was not important to the feudal system, and he never received the protection of the Real Actions; his interest never became "Real" property, and is, to the present day, personalty; he was never seised; he was originally left to his action on the covenant against his landlord, the freeholder, if he were evicted[5].

Better remedies became available to the leaseholder as soon as remedies dependent on *possession*, as opposed to *seisin*, were developed in the King's Court. Trespass was such an action, and a leaseholder, being *possessed* of the land, could bring the writ of trespass, without being *seised*[6]. By the thirteenth century[7], the action of trespass *quare clausum fregit* was available to persons in possession of land and lay for damages against anyone who was guilty of unlawful physical interference with land. This was an improvement, but the leaseholder needed something more than damages; he needed an action by which he could recover his lease. This came with Ejectment at the end of the fifteenth century[8]. From that time a leaseholder has had a "real" remedy; but leasehold property was already established as "personalty" and it was too late then for it to become "realty" for the purposes of the general law.

The tables were now turned on the freeholder. He had a "real" remedy, but it was cumbrous and old-fashioned. The leaseholder now had a modern action for specific recovery, the action of Ejectment. Freeholders began to use this action by alleging a fictitious lease. This practice began in the sixteenth century, and continued until the abolition of the old Real Actions in the first half of the nineteenth century. Ejectment now lies in respect of any wrongful deprivation of possession of land[9].

This chapter deals with some of the principles of the law relating to leases. Superimposed upon the general law is a large body of statutory material

---

[2] LPA 1925, s. 1 (1), p. 378, post.

[3] LPA 1925, s. 1 (5).

[4] Maitland, *Forms of Action at Common Law*, pp. 20 et seq; Simpson, *Introduction to the History of the Land Law*, pp. 24–43; M & W, pp. 1155–1156.

[5] Pollock and Maitland, *History of English Law* (2nd edn. reissued 1968), vol. ii, pp. 106–117; Plucknett, *Concise History of the Common Law* (5th edn. 1956), pp. 570–574; Jouon des Longrais, *La Conception Anglaise de la Saisine*, pp. 141–148; Simpson, pp. 68–73.

[6] In the ordinary case of land being owned by A, the freeholder, and leased to B, the leaseholder, A is seised and B possessed of the land.

[7] Maitland, *Forms of Action*, p. 48; C & B, pp. 27–30; M & W, pp. 1155–1156.

[8] *Trespass de ejectione firmae*, Pollock and Maitland, p. 109: Simpson, pp. 135–136.

[9] Maitland, *Forms of Action*, pp. 57–60; C & B, p. 86; M & W, pp. 1158–1160: Simpson, pp. 136–141. On the modern law, see Prichard, *Squatting* (1981).

dealing with specialised topics. The general policy of these statutes is to limit the rent which a landlord can obtain, and restrict his right to recover possession of the premises at the end of the lease. The Leasehold Reform Act 1967 goes further, and grants to certain long leaseholders of residential premises at low rents the right to acquire their freehold or an extended lease[10]. These statutes and books dealing with them must be consulted before a working knowledge of the law of leaseholds can be obtained; but lack of space forbids their treatment here[11].

Central Statistical Office Social Trends 16 (1986 edn.), p. 133

"The trend towards more owner-occupation continues. Factors in this trend in recent years have been sales of local authority housing and more building in the private sector than by local authorities and new towns. Other

---

[10] See p. 757, post.

[11] C & B, pp. 449–483; M & W, pp. 1085–1143; MM, pp. 566–594; Aldridge, *Leasehold Law* (1980) paras. 1.004–1.109, 3.031–3.043, 4.055–4.089, 5.001–5.096, 6.095–6.135, 7.065–7.089.

The main statutes are:

(a) The Agricultural Holdings Act 1986 consolidating previous legislation with amendments. See Law Commission Report on Agricultural Holdings Bill 1985 (Law Com No. 153, Cmnd. 9665) on security of tenure for agricultural workers housed by their employees, and their successors, see Rent (Agricultural) Act 1976, Rent (Agriculture) Amendment Act 1977. Muir Watt, *Agricultural Holdings* (12th edn. 1967); Scammell and Densham's *Law of Agricultural Holdings* (6th edn. 1978); Woodfall, chap. 21; Hill and Redman, Part VI.

(b) Business Tenancies. Landlord and Tenant Act 1954, Part II; LPA 1969, Part I. Woodfall, chap. 22; Hill and Redman, Part II; Aldridge, *Letting Business Premises* (5th edn. 1985); Williams, *Handbook of Business Tenancies* (1985).

The Department of the Environment is carrying out a review of the Act.

(c) Private Residential Lettings. Rent Act 1977; Housing Act 1980; Rent (Amendment) Act 1985. Aldridge, *Housing Act 1980*, Part II; Megarry, *Rent Acts* (10th edn, 1967); Woodfall, chap. 23; Hill and Redman, Part III; Farrand and Arden, *Rent Acts and Regulations Amended and Annotated* (2nd edn. 1981); Pettit, *Private Sector Tenancies* (1981); Report of the Committee on the Rent Acts (Francis Report) 1971 (Cmnd. 4609).

In 1977 the Department of the Environment initiated a review of the Rent Acts; in 1985 the Nugee Committee of Inquiry on the Management of Privately Owned Blocks of Flats issued its report, recommending measures designed "to redress the balance for tenants who find that their landlord or managing agent is persistently unresponsive or unhelpful."; [1986] Conv 12 (A. J. Hawkins). In 1985 the Secretary of State for the Environment announced that the Government hoped to introduce legislation to encourage the supply of more houses for renting in the private sector, but probably not during the lifetime of the present Parliament: HC Deb. 1985, col. 890, June 12.

(d) Public Sector Housing. Housing Act 1985, Parts IV and V; Hill and Redman, Part IV; Woodfall, paras. 3.0314–3.0320; Aldridge, *Housing Act 1980*, Part II.

(e) Long Tenancies. Landlord and Tenant Act 1954, Part I; Leasehold Reform Act 1967, Part I; Leasehold Reform Act 1979. Barnes. *Leasehold Reform Act 1967*; Hague, *Leasehold Enfranchisement* (1967); Megarry, *Rent Acts*, pp. 130–132, 235–243; Woodfall, chap. 24; Hill and Redman, Part V.

See *James v United Kingdom* (1986) Application No. 8793/79, Times, 22 February, where the European Court of Human Rights held that the Leasehold Reform Act 1967 was not in breach of the European Convention on Human Rights. The trustees of the Grosvenor Estate in Mayfair had been compelled under the Act to sell 80 houses to long-lease tenants at a loss of £2,529,903.

(f) Mobile Homes. Caravan Sites and Control of Development Act 1960; Caravan Sites Act 1968; Mobile Homes Act 1983. Gordon, *Mobile Homes and Caravans* (1985).

significant features of the housing scene were an exceptionally high number of grants in 1983 and 1984 for renovation and improvement of property, and growing numbers of recipients homeless households accepted by local authorities.

The housing stock in the United Kingdom totalled more than 22 million dwellings in 1984, more than one and a half times the figure of a little over 14 million in 1951. More people owned their own homes; the number öf owner-occupied dwellings more than trebled, from just over 4 million in 1951 to 13½ million in 1984. The expansion of the owner-occupied sector, from 29 to 61 per cent of the housing stock, more than accounted for the overall increase in stock. The number of dwellings in the rented sector declined by 14 per cent over the period, the net result of the dramatic fall in private rented sector dwellings from 7½ million to 2½ million (11 per cent of the stock in 1984) and substantial growth of 3½ million in local authority and new town dwellings. The number of homes rented from local authorities and new towns rose from 2½ million dwellings in 1951 to almost 7 million in 1979, but then fell to just over 6 million in 1984 (28 per cent of total stock). Of the estimated 2½ million private rented sector dwellings in England and Wales in 1984, ½ million were Housing Association tenancies and slightly fewer were job or business-related tenancies. A majority of the remainder were 'regulated tenancies' (for which a 'fair' rent can be registered, as it can for Housing Association tenants). At the end of 1984 an estimated 470 thousand regulations were in force for regulated tenancies, of which almost 95 per cent were unfurnished lettings; there were a further 400 thousand Housing Association regulations[12]."

II.   General Characteristics

A.   A Lease may be a Legal Estate
LAW OF PROPERTY ACT 1925

1.   Legal estates and equitable interests. — (1) The only estates in land which are capable of subsisting or of being conveyed or created at law are —
>   (a) An estate in fee simple absolute in possession[13];
>   (b) A term of years absolute.

205.   General definitions. — (1) ... (xxvii) "Term of years absolute" means a term of years (taking effect either in possession or in reversion whether or not at a rent) with or without impeachment for waste[14], subject or not to another legal estate, and either certain or liable to determination by notice, re-entry[15], operation of law, or by a provision for cesser on redemption[16], or in any other event (other than the dropping of a life, or the determination of a determinable life interest); but does not include any term of years determinable with life or lives or with the cesser of a determinable life interest[17], nor, if created after the commencement of this Act, a term of

---

[12] See also House of Commons First Report from the Environment Committee 1981–1982: The Private Rented Housing Sector 1982 (HC 40); Duke of Edinburgh, *Inquiry into British Housing*, especially chap. 5.
[13] See p. 6, ante.
[14] See p. 18, ante.
[15] See p. 428, post.
[16] See pp. 655–656, post.
[17] LPA 1925, s. 149 (6), p. 383, post.

years which is not expressed to take effect in possession within twenty-one years after the creation thereof where required by this Act to take effect within that period[18]; and in this definition the expression "term of years" includes a term for less than a year[19], or for a year or years and a fraction of a year or from year to year.

B. "Time Certain"[1]

A lease must commence at[2], and exist for, a "time certain", or at or for a time which can be rendered certain. It may also be for a single discontinuous term[3].

LACE *v* CHANTLER
[1944] KB 368 (CA, Lord GREENE MR, MACKINNON and LUXMOORE LJJ)

In a sublease of furnished premises for 16s. 5d. a week, the rent-book stated certain conditions, one of which was that the premises were taken "furnished for duration", meaning the duration of the war. A notice to quit was served and was valid to determine a weekly tenancy, but not to determine a lease for the duration of the war. The question was whether such a lease could be, and had been, created.

Held. It was not possible to create a lease for the duration of the war.

LORD GREENE MR: Normally there could be no question that this was an ordinary weekly tenancy, duly determinable by a week's notice, but the parties in the rent-book agreed to a term which appears there expressed by the words "furnished for duration", which must mean the duration of the war. The question immediately arises whether a tenancy for the duration of the war creates a good leasehold interest. In my opinion, it does not. A term created by a leasehold tenancy agreement must be expressed either with certainty and specifically or by reference to something which can, at the time when the lease takes effect, be looked to as a certain ascertainment of what the term is meant to be. In the present case, when this tenancy agreement took effect, the term was completely uncertain. It was impossible to say how long the tenancy would last. Mr Sturge in his argument has maintained that such a lease would be valid, and that, even if the term is uncertain at its beginning when the lease takes effect, the fact that at some future time it will be rendered certain is sufficient to make it a good lease. In my opinion, that argument is not to be sustained.

---

[18] LPA 1925, s. 149 (3), p. 381, post.

[19] See *Re Land and Premises at Liss, Hants* [1971] Ch 986 at 991, [1971] 3 All ER 380 at 382 per GOULDING J; *Trustees of Henry Smith's Charity Trustees v Willson* [1983] QB 316 at 326–328, [1983] 1 All ER 73 at 81–82, per SLADE J.

[1] C & B, pp. 362–365, 368–370; M & W, pp. 645–648, 657–660; MM, pp. 335, 340–341, 345–346.

[2] *Harvey v Pratt* [1965] 1 WLR 1025, [1965] 2 All ER 786 (a contract for a lease failed to specify the date of its commencement); *James v Lock* (1977) 246 EG 395; cf. *Secretary of State for Social Services v Beavington* (1981) 262 EG 551.

[3] *Smallwood v Sheppards* [1895] 2 QB 627 (a single letting for three successive bank holidays); *Cottage Holiday Associates Ltd v Customs and Excise Comrs* [1983] QB 735 (lease of holiday cottage on time sharing basis of one week a year for 80 years held to be lease for a discontinuous term of 80 weeks); [1983] All ER Rev. 229 (P. J. Clarke).

I do not propose to go into the authorities on the matter, but in Foa's Landlord and Tenant (6th edn.), p. 115, the law is stated in this way, and, in my view, correctly: "The habendum in a lease must point out the period during which the enjoyment of the premises is to be had; so that the duration, as well as the commencement of the term, must be stated. The certainty of a lease as to its continuance must be ascertainable either by the express limitation of the parties at the time the lease is made, or by reference to some collateral act which may, with equal certainty, measure the continuance of it, otherwise it is void. If the term be fixed by reference to some collateral matter, such matter must either be itself certain (e.g., a demise to hold for 'as many years as A. has in the manor of B.') or capable before the lease takes effect of being rendered so (e.g., for 'as many years as C. shall name')." The important words to observe in that last phrase are the words "before the lease takes effect". Then it goes on: "Consequently, a lease to endure for 'as many years as A. shall live', or 'as the coverture between B. and C. shall continue', would not be good as a lease for years, although the same results may be achieved in another way by making the demise for a fixed number (ninety-nine for instance) of years determinable upon A.'s death, or the dissolution of the coverture between B. and C." In the present case, in my opinion, this agreement cannot take effect as a good tenancy for the duration of the war. . . .[4]

In *Re Midland Rly Co's Agreement*[5] [1971] Ch 725, [1971] 1 All ER 1007, the Midland Railway Company in 1920 granted a half-yearly tenancy at £1 a year of 100 square yards of land in Luton, Bedfordshire. Clause 2 provided that the lease could be determined by either party on giving to the other three months' written notice. A proviso to clause 2 stated that "this agreement shall not be so terminated by the company until they shall require the said premises for the purposes of their undertaking". In 1969 the British Railways Board, the successors to the landlords, gave notice to the tenant to terminate the tenancy under Landlord and Tenant Act 1954, section 25. They did not require the premises for the purpose of their undertaking, but claimed that clause 2 was void, on the ground of uncertainty of duration and repugnancy. The Court of Appeal held that the clause was valid, and the notice of termination void.

RUSSELL LJ said at 732, at 1009:

"Now it appears to us that [*Lace v Chantler*] is confined to a case in which that which was purported to be done was simply to create a leasehold interest for a single and uncertain period. The applicability of this matter of certainty to a periodic tenancy was not under consideration. If *Lace v Chantler* had been a case in which there was simply a periodic tenancy with a proviso that the landlord would not give notice during the continuance of the war, this court might not have concluded that such an agreement, which would of course have left the tenant free to determine on notice at any time, was inoperative to create a leasehold. There is nothing in the reasoning of the judgments to lead to the necessary conclusion that such must have been so.

---

[4] Leases and agreements for a lease for the duration of the Second World War were converted by Validation of War-time Leases Act 1944, s. 1 into leases, or agreements for a lease, for ten years, subject (usually) to determination by one month's notice given after the end of the war.
[5] [1971] CLJ 198 (D. Macintyre).

If you have an ordinary case of a periodic tenancy (for example, a yearly tenancy), it is plain that in one sense at least it is uncertain at the outset what will be the maximum duration of the term created, which term grows year by year as a single term springing from the original grant. It cannot be predicated that in no circumstances will it exceed, for example, 50 years; there is no previously ascertained maximum duration for the term; its duration will depend upon the time that will elapse before either party gives notice of determination. The simple statement of the law that the maximum duration of a term must be certainly known in advance of its taking effect cannot therefore have direct reference to periodic tenancies."

i. INTERESSE TERMINI

LAW OF PROPERTY ACT 1925

149. Abolition of interesse termini, and as to reversionary leases and leases for lives. — (1) The doctrine of interesse termini is hereby abolished.

(2) As from the commencement of this Act all terms of years absolute shall, whether the interest is created before or after such commencement, be capable of taking effect at law or in equity, according to the estate interest or powers of the grantor, from the date fixed for commencement of the term, without actual entry.

ii. REVERSIONARY LEASES[6]

LAW OF PROPERTY ACT 1925

149. Abolition of interesse termini, and as to reversionary leases and leases for lives. — (3) A term, at a rent or granted in consideration of a fine[7], limited after the commencement of this Act to take effect more than twenty-one years from the date of the instrument purporting to create it, shall be void, and any contract made after such commencement to create such a term shall likewise be void; but this subsection does not apply to any term taking effect in equity under a settlement, or created out of an equitable interest under a settlement, or under an equitable power for mortgage, indemnity or other like purposes.

RE STRAND AND SAVOY PROPERTIES LTD[8]
[1960] Ch 582, [1960] 2 All ER 327 (ChD, BUCKLEY J)

A 35 year lease contained a provision that the lessors would "at the written request of the lessee made 12 months before the expiration of the term hereby created" grant a further term of 35 years at the same rent.

The tenants took out a summons to determine whether the Law of Property Act 1925, section 149 (3) invalidated their option to renew the lease on the ground that it was a contract to take effect more than 21 years from the date of the lease granting the option.

---

[6] I.e., a lease which is to take effect at a future time. This must not be confused with a lease of the reversion (or a concurrent lease); p. 422, post.

[7] P. 79, n. 17, ante.

[8] (1960) 76 LQR 352 (R. E. M.).

ʰ   *Held*. The option for renewal was valid.

BUCKLEY J: Sir Milner Holland, who appears for the tenants, . . . says that
subsection (3) makes it impossible for any man to create a reversionary term
— that is to say, a term to take effect more than 21 years from the date of the
instrument creating the term — and that it also invalidates any contract by
which a man undertakes to create a reversionary term, that is to say, a term
which will not commence until 21 years after the date of the instrument
creating such a term. He says that the subsection does not invalidate a
contract to create a lease, at however remote a date in the future, which,
when it is granted, will create a term which will take effect within 21 years of
the date of that lease. . . .

Mr Albery, on the other hand, points out that the contention advanced by
Sir Milner really gives no operative effect to that part of subsection (3) which
deals with contracts at all, because if a lease granting a term to commence at
a date later than 21 years from the date of the lease is void, a contract to
grant such a lease must also necessarily be void without any express
provision to that effect in the statute. . . .

On [its true] terms the subsection is confined, so far as contracts are
concerned, to contracts to create terms which, when created, will only take
effect more than 21 years from the dates of the instruments creating them;
that is to say, it invalidates contracts for the granting of leases which will,
when granted, be reversionary leases, the postponement of the commencement of the term being for more than 21 years from the date of the lease.

WEG MOTORS LTD *v* HALES

[1962] Ch 49, [1961] 3 All ER 181 (CA, Lord EVERSHED MR, HARMAN
and DONOVAN LJJ)

In July 1938 the plaintiffs were granted a lease of premises for a term of 21
years from December 1938, with an option of "taking a further lease" of the
premises for a period of 21 years from the date of the exercise of the option;
and the option was expressed to be exercisable at any time before 25
December 1959. The defendants claimed that the option agreement was void
under section 149 (3).

Held. The option agreement was valid.

LORD EVERSHED MR: The question is, in our judgment, an extremely short
one — namely, does the option agreement of July, 1938, fall within the scope
of the language in subsection (3) of section 149 of the Act of 1925 as being a
contract "to create such a term" as therein mentioned? The view of the
learned author of the note to the section in volume 1 of Wolstenholme and
Cherry's *Conveyancing Statutes*, 12th edn. (1932), p. 497, appears clearly to
have been that a contract to create a term of years, which might begin to take
effect more than 21 years from the date of the contract, fell within the vice of
the subsection. It was this view that Buckley J rejected in the case already
cited[9]; and he did so upon the basis that the phrase "such a term" could in its
context refer, and refer only, to a term commencing more than 21 years from
the instrument purporting to create the term, that is to say, the lease
executed in pursuance of the contract and not the contract itself. We must

---

[9] *Re Strand and Savoy Properties Ltd* [1960] Ch 582, [1960] 2 All ER 327, p. 381, ante.

not be taken to be expressing any doubt of the correctness of Buckley J's decision. But in the present case we are concerned not with a contract, that is a binding agreement, to grant and take a lease but with an option which might never be exercised and cannot, until exercised, be in any event said, in our judgment, to create a term of years at all. It follows, therefore, in our view, that the option agreement with which we are concerned cannot be said to be such a contract as is comprehended in section 149 (3) of the Act of 1925. The challenge to the plaintiffs based upon that section must, therefore, fail.

iii.   LEASES FOR LIVES

LAW OF PROPERTY ACT 1925

149.   Abolition of interesse termini, and as to reversionary leases and leases for lives. — (6) Any lease or underlease, at a rent, or in consideration of a fine[10], for life or lives or for any term of years determinable with life or lives, or on the marriage of the lessee, or any contract therefor, made before or after the commencement of this Act, or created by virtue of Part V of the Law of Property Act, 1922, shall take effect as a lease, underlease or contract therefor, for a term of ninety years determinable after the death or marriage (as the case may be) of the original lessee, or of the survivor of the original lessees, by at least one month's notice in writing given to determine the same on one of the quarter days applicable to the tenancy, either by the lessor or the persons deriving title under him, to the person entitled to the leasehold interest, or if no such person is in existence by affixing the same to the premises, or by the lessee or other persons in whom the leasehold interest is vested to the lessor or the persons deriving title under him:
Provided that —

> (a)   this subsection shall not apply to any term taking effect in equity under a settlement or created out of an equitable interest under a settlement for mortgage, indemnity, or other like purposes; . . .

> (d)   if there are no quarter days specially applicable to the tenancy, notice may be given to determine the tenancy on one of the usual quarter days[10a].

iv.   PERPETUALLY RENEWABLE LEASES

Perpetually renewable leases are converted into terms of 2,000 years; those existing on 1 January 1926 date from the commencement of the existing tenancy, and those created after 1925 from the date fixed for the commencement of the tenancy. Perpetually renewable subleases are converted into terms of 2,000 years less one day[11].

In *Caerphilly Concrete Products Ltd v Owen* [1972] 1 WLR 372, [1972] 1 All ER 248[12], a grant in 1963 of a five year term of 4,800 square feet in an industrial area of Caerphilly at £10 a year contained a provision that "the

---

[10] Thus excluding beneficial life tenancies under a settlement. These are equitable interests and subject to SLA 1925, p. 274, ante; *Binions v Evans* [1972] Ch 359 at 366, [1972] 2 All ER 70 at 74, p. 499, post; *Ivory v Palmer* [1975] ICR 340.

[10a] Lady Day (March 25), Midsummer Day (June 24), Michaelmas Day (September 29) or Christmas Day (December 25).

[11] LPA 1922, s. 145 and Sch. 15.

[12] (1972) 88 LQR 173.

landlord will on the written request of the tenant . . . grant to him a lease of the said demised land for the further term of five years from the expiration of the said term hereby granted at the same rent and containing the like covenants and provisos as are herein contained (including an option to renew such lease for the further term of five years at the expiration thereof)". The Court of Appeal (RUSSELL, SACHS and STAMP LJJ) held that the grant took effect as a lease for 2,000 years.

RUSSELL LJ said at 374, at 251: "The approach to the question whether a lease is perpetually renewable is not in doubt. The language used must plainly lead to that result: though the fact that an argument is capable of being sustained at some length against that result does not of course suffice. As a matter of history, when a covenant by a lessor conferred a right to renewal of the lease, the new grant to contain the same or the like covenants and provisos as were contained in the lease, the courts refused to give literal effect to that language, which if taken literally would mean that the second lease would contain the same covenant (or option) to renew, totidem verbis, and so on perpetually. The reference to the same covenants was construed as not including the option covenant itself. This limited the tenant's right to one renewal. In order therefore to make it plain that the covenants to be contained in the second lease (to be granted under the exercise of the option to renew) were to include also the covenant to renew, draftsmen were accustomed to insert phrases such as (including this covenant,) so as to achieve a perpetually renewable lease. As I have indicated, if they did not do this, the second lease would not contain any option clause.

The operation of the words of inclusion was not limited to requiring the second lease to contain a covenant to renew once more only, which would have been the outcome if the words of inclusion had been omitted in the second lease. This was because the words of inclusion could not properly be construed as requiring the second lease to contain the same covenants other than the covenant to renew but additionally to include an option to renew once more only — a total of three terms. The words of inclusion defined or explained what was meant by 'the same covenants,' that is to say, as including the covenant to renew. Consequently in the second lease, in order to comply with the words of definition or explanation, the covenants referred to therein to be contained in the second lease must contain the same wording including the inclusion.

In the present case the brackets make it abundantly plain that the parties are explaining that 'containing the like covenants and provisos' is a phrase intended to embrace an option. That is to say that the covenants and provisos contained in the first lease, which the first lease requires the second lease to contain, are not to be construed as a reference to those covenants and provisos other than an option to renew, but as a reference to all those covenants including an option to renew. If the words . . . are repeated in the second lease without the words in parenthesis the second lease will not be carrying out the requirement of the first lease: it will not be granting an option for a further lease containing 'the like covenants' as defined."

SACHS LJ said at 375, at 252: "I, too, have underlined the words in brackets. It is trite to say that when construing a document such as a lease it is the prime purpose of the courts to seek to adopt a meaning that conforms to the intentions of the parties. Not even the most impeccable conveyancing logic, however neatly expressed, can convince me that in the instant case it was the mutual intention of the parties that the lease should be perpetually renewable. So far as the landlord is concerned it seems to me highly unlikely that he really intended that this particular lease could or should be 'for ever'. My doubts on that question of intention extend also to the tenant — for I would acquit him of any intent to lay a trap through the operation of the words enclosed in the brackets, which we know to have been added to the draft at the very last moment by his solicitors. It is difficult indeed, at any rate so far as I am concerned, to think that two business men would be talking in terms of five years if both — or indeed either — of them truly meant that a lease should be granted which went on ad infinitum.

Were I in a position to give effect to the views just expressed that would result in the landlord succeeding in this appeal: but it is necessary to consider whether the authorities which were so fully and so helpfully cited to us permit such a result. An examination of the relevant decisions discloses an area of law in which the courts have manoeuvred themselves into an unhappy position . . . [They] appear to have bound themselves to hold that the use of a certain set of words (to which I will refer as 'the formula') causes the lease to be perpetually renewable, even when no layman — at least if he has some elementary knowledge of business — would dream of granting such a lease and, if aware of the technical meaning of the particular phraseology would almost certainly be aghast at its devastating effect and refuse to sign. One reason for the courts so binding themselves is said to be that the formula is one the effect of which is well known to trained conveyancers, and that this is advantageous, however much of a trap it may constitute for others.

As already mentioned, the prime purpose of the courts when construing a lease is to interpret it according to the true intentions of the parties. Already 20 years ago judicial unease at having to determine those intentions in cases of the instant type by a blinkered approach is reflected in the judgments in *Parkus v Greenwood*, both at first instance [1950] Ch 33, [1949] 2 All ER 743 and on appeal [1950] Ch 644, [1950] 1 All ER 436.

[His Lordship referred to *Green v Palmer* [1944] Ch 328, [1944] 1 All ER 670 and continued:]

The judicial unease of 1950 is, so far as I am concerned, by now increased by two factors. First, more and more leases over the two succeeding decades have tended to come from pens not fully trained in the art of conveyancing. Secondly, over the same period the value of the pound sterling has been decreasing rapidly, thus making it even more unlikely that a man of business in the course of a normal transaction would knowingly part 'for ever' with his rights over land in return for a static rent. Moreover, when residential property is concerned a landlord could indeed now find himself in the position of having to relinquish a freehold when the document which he signed appeared on the face of it to be a lease for relatively short periods of years.

In those circumstances I, too, have great sympathy with the line of approach adopted by Uthwatt J in *Green v Palmer* and Harman J in *Parkus v Greenwood*. I could wish that the courts had followed the apparent preference of Lord FitzGerald in *Swinburne v Milburn* (1884) 9 App Cas 844 at 855 for confining interpretations of perpetual renewability to leases where words such as 'for ever' or 'from time to time for ever hereafter' or some equivalent were used in the relevant document. This approach would have avoided that sort of path by which good logic can on occasion make bad law, and would have been in accord with the aphorism that at times 'logic is only the art of going wrong with confidence'.

Having, however, examined the authorities, I feel bound in this court to say that the matter is concluded by them in that the words in brackets, as inserted at the last moment, have in law the same effect as those considered in *Parkus v Greenwood*."

In *Marjorie Burnett Ltd v Barclay* (1980) 258 EG 642[13], there was a grant in 1971 of a seven year lease of a shop with residential accommodation above in Boscombe at a yearly rent of £650. Clause 6 contained a covenant to renew. The plaintiff sought a declaration that this was not perpetually renewable. In holding that it was not, NOURSE J said:

"[Clause 6] reads as follows:

'If the tenant shall be desirous of taking a new lease of the demised premises after the expiration of the term hereby granted . . .'

There are then provisions which are in a not very elegant form, but the effect of them is clear enough. It is that the tenant can give the landlord notice of the desire to take a new lease. Then clause 6 goes on as follows:

'Then the landlord will at or before the expiration of the term hereby granted, if there shall then be no subsisting breach of any of the tenant's obligations under this present lease' — and now I come to some important words — 'grant to the tenant a new lease of the premises hereby demised for a further term of seven years, to commence from and after the expiration of the term hereby granted at a rent to be agreed between the parties.'

There are then provisions for the rent to be fixed in default of agreement. Then come the final words of the clause, which are also important. They read as follows:

'And such lease shall also contain a like covenant for renewal for a further term of seven years on the expiration of the term thereby granted. . . .'

[His Lordship referred to *Parkus v Greenwood* [1950] Ch 33, [1949] 2 All ER 743 and, *Caerphilly Concrete Products Ltd v Owen* [1972] 1 WLR 372, [1972] 1 All ER 248 and continued:]

In construing clause 6 of the lease in the present case I must therefore approach the matter in this way. I must bear in mind that the leaning of the courts has been against perpetual renewals. I have to find expressly in the lease a covenant or obligation for perpetual renewal. And I have to look ahead to see what the second lease will contain when the requirements of the covenant for renewal in the first have been duly observed.

I now return to clause 6 of the lease. What the landlord has to do, if the tenant gives it notice of his desire to take a new lease, is to grant to the tenant a new lease of the demised premises for a further term of seven years at a rent to be agreed, and if not agreed to be fixed in the manner specified. Then it is provided that such lease shall also contain a like covenant for renewal for a further term of seven years on the expiration of the term thereby granted.

Mr Henty really puts his case on this primary question in two ways. First, he takes the simple course of asking me to see what provisions the second lease would contain if it were to be granted pursuant to clause 6. He says that

---

[13] (1981) 131 NLJ 683 (H. W. Wilkinson).

it would inevitably be at a different rent from the £650 reserved by the first lease. Then he says that the second lease would contain a like covenant for renewal for a further term of seven years as that contained in clause 6 of the first lease. But that covenant ends with the part of clause 6 which deals with the provisions for fixing the rent in default of agreement. It does not seem to me that the second lease could possibly contain the words 'and such lease shall also contain a like covenant for renewal for a further term of seven years on the expiration of the term thereby granted,' because those words are not part of the covenant for renewal and to include them would be to go further than clause 6 requires. And so I agree with Mr Henty that the second lease would be at a new rent and that it would contain the whole of clause 6, except for the last three lines or so which I have just quoted. On that footing it is clear that there is no express covenant or obligation for perpetual renewal. Indeed the contrary is the case. There is an express provision in the lease to the effect that it can be renewed twice only.

That would in itself be enough to dispose of the primary question in these proceedings. But Mr Henty goes on to take a second point, which appears to me to be one of equal force, and that is this. He says that even supposing his first argument were wrong I must bear in mind that what will happen if this is a perpetually renewable lease is that it will be converted by the 1922 Act into a lease for a term of 2,000 years. He says, and I can see no answer to this, that the notion of a 2,000-year term is completely inimical to a lease which contains provisions for rent review every seven years. And so again he says that as a matter of construction clause 6 could not possibly have the effect for which the defendant has contended. I agree with that contention also."

C. Certainty of Rent

The rent must be certain. That does not mean that it must be certain at the date of the lease. Rent is sufficiently certain if it can be calculated with certainty at the time when payment comes to be made[14]. This problem has recently been considered in connexion with options to renew a lease and rent revision at the time of renewal[15].

---

[14] *Greater London Council v Connolly* [1970] 2 QB 100, [1970] 1 All ER 870 ("rent liable to be increased or decreased on notice being given" held to be valid); *C. H. Bailey Ltd v Memorial Enterprises Ltd* [1974] 1 WLR 728, [1974] 1 All ER 1003 (increased rent ascertained retrospectively); *Bradshaw v Pawley* [1980] 1 WLR 10, [1979] 3 All ER 273 (rent payable from a date prior to execution of lease).

[15] See *United Scientific Holdings Ltd v Burnley Borough Council* [1978] AC 904, [1977] 2 All ER 62, where HL held that there was a presumption that time was not of the essence in construing clauses which specify time limits for the operation of the rent review procedure. See generally C & B, pp. 394–397; Aldridge, *Leasehold Law*, paras. 4.038–48; Bernstein and Reynolds, *Handbook of Rent Review* (1981); Clarke and Adams, *Rent Reviews and Variable Rents* (2nd edn. 1984); Emmet, pp. 834–847; Barnsley, *Land Options* (1978), chap. 10; Rent Review Journal (which began in 1981). For precedents, see (1964) 28 Conv (NS) 663, (1965) 29 Conv (NS) 722; Conv. Precedents vol. 1, 2108–9. And for revised model forms by the Joint Working Party of the Law Society and the Royal Institution of Chartered Surveyors (2nd edn. 1986), see Conv Precedents 5.61–5.61B.

i.   OPTION TO RENEW LEASE

BROWN v GOULD[16]
[1972] Ch 53, [1971] 2 All ER 1505 (ChD, MEGARRY J)

In 1949 Margaret Gould leased part of Albion Granaries, 250 High Road, Loughton, Essex to Frank Brown[17] for 21 years from 29 September 1949, at a rent of £500 a year. Clause 3 (*c*) of the lease granted to the tenant an option to renew the tenancy for a further term of 21 years at a rent "to be fixed having regard to the market value of the premises at the time of exercising the option taking into account to the advantage of the tenant any increased value of such premises attributable to structural improvements made by the tenant during the currency of this present lease". Frank Brown spent nearly £30,000 rebuilding the premises, and in 1969 served notice in accordance with the terms of the lease purporting to exercise the option. The trustees of Margaret Gould, in whom the reversion had vested on her death, contended that the option was void for uncertainty.

Held. The option was valid.

MEGARRY J: The landlords . . . contend that the option for renewal contained in the lease is void for uncertainty. That is the sole question that I have to determine. Stated briefly, the proper approach, I think, is that the court is reluctant to hold void for uncertainty any provision that was intended to have legal effect. In this case it is very properly accepted that the option was intended to have business efficacy.

In an unreported case, *Re Lloyd's Trust Instruments* (1970) 24th June, to which I referred counsel, I endeavoured to state the basic principles applicable in cases of uncertainty. What I said there was:

"I think the starting point on any question of uncertainty must be that of the court's reluctance to hold an instrument void for uncertainty. Lord Hardwicke LC once said 'A court never construes a devise void, unless it is so absolutely dark, that they cannot find out the testator's meaning': *Minshull v Minshull* (1737) 1 Atk 411 at 412. Lord Brougham said: 'The difficulty must be so great that it amounts to an impossibility, the doubt so grave that there is not even an inclination of the scales one way': *Doe d Winter v Perratt* (1843) 9 Cl & F 606 at 689. In a well-known statement, Sir George Jessel MR said that the court would not hold a will void for uncertainty 'unless it is utterly impossible to put a meaning upon it. The duty of the court is to put a fair meaning on the terms used, and not, as was said in one case, to repose on the easy pillow of saying that the whole is void for uncertainty': *Re Roberts* (1881) 19 ChD 520 at 529. That this is not a doctrine confined to wills but is one which applies to other instruments, such as planning permissions, is shown by cases such as *Fawcett Properties Ltd v Buckingham County Council* [1961] AC 636, [1960] 3 All ER 503, where, by a majority, the delphic language of a condition in a planning permission escaped from being held void for uncertainty largely because of its resemblance to a section to be found in a modern Act of Parliament. The second question is that of the types of uncertainty. The basic type (and on one view the only true type) is uncertainty of concept, as contrasted with mere difficulty of application: see,

---

[16] (1972) 36 Conv (NS) 317 (P. Robertshaw).
[17] "He had the good fortune to live at Arabin House, High Beech, Essex", at 55, at 1506. See Megarry, *Arabinesque-at-law* (1969), p. xi.

for example, *Re Gape* [1952] Ch 418, affirmed at 743, where the question was one of a condition subsequent, in which special considerations apply. In *Fawcett's* case [1961] AC 636 at 670, [1960] 3 All ER 503 at 513, Lord Keith of Avonholm said: 'The point is one of uncertainty of concept. If it is impossible, on construction of the condition, to reach a conclusion as to what was in the draftsman's mind, the condition is meaningless and must be read as pro non scripto.' Putting it another way, the question is one of linguistic or semantic uncertainty, and not of difficulty of ascertainment: see *Re Baden's Deed Trusts* [1971] AC 424 at 457, [1970] 2 All ER 228 at 427, per Lord Wilberforce. If there is a trust for 'my old friends,' all concerned are faced with uncertainty as to the concept or idea enshrined in these words. It may not be difficult to resolve that 'old' means not 'aged' but 'of long standing'; but then there is the question how long is 'long'. Friendship, too, is a concept with almost infinite shades of meaning. Where the concept is uncertain, the gift is void. Where the concept is certain, then mere difficulty in tracing and discovering those who are entitled normally does not invalidate the gift."

To the authorities mentioned in that passage must now be added *Greater London Council v Connolly* [1970] 2 QB 100, [1970] 1 All ER 870, a landlord and tenant case concerning a condition on the rent card of a council tenant. This condition provided that the rent and other sums shown on the rent card "are liable to be increased or decreased on notice being given"; and the Court of Appeal unanimously held that the condition was not void for uncertainty. Lord Denning MR said, at 108, at 874: "The courts are always loath to hold a condition bad for uncertainty. They will give it a reasonable interpretation whenever possible. It is possible here." . . . No doubt there may be cases in which the draftsman's ineptitude will succeed in defeating the court's efforts to find a meaning for the provision in question; but only if the court is driven to it will it be held that a provision is void for uncertainty.

With that in mind, I approach the attack made on the present clause. Mr Scamell [counsel for the defendants] concentrated on three phrases in the clause, the words "a rent to be fixed", the words "having regard to" the market value of the premises at the time of exercising the option, and the words "taking into account" to the advantage of the tenant any increased value of the premises attributable to his structural improvements. In addition, he pointed to the absence of any machinery for working out this formula, by contrast with the other provisions in the lease that I have mentioned. Taken together, he said, these considerations showed that the clause provided neither a clear basis for determining the rent nor any means of quantifying that basis, and accordingly the option was void for uncertainty.

At least three types of option may be distinguished. First, the option may be for renewal simply "at a rent to be agreed". In that case, no formula for quantifying the rent is laid down, and prima facie the option will, as in *King's Motors (Oxford) Ltd v Lax* [1970] 1 WLR 426, [1969] 3 All ER 665, be void as being a mere contract to make a contract, or, perhaps more properly, as being an agreement to make a contract, or a contract dependent upon the making of an agreement[18]. In *Smith v Morgan* [1971] 1 WLR 803, [1971] 2

---

[18] See also *Courtney and Fairbairn Ltd v Tolaini Bros (Hotels) Ltd* [1975] 1 WLR 297, [1975] 1 All ER 716 (agreement "to negotiate fair and reasonable contract sums" held to be void for uncertainty); *Bushwall Properties Ltd v Vortex Properties Ltd* [1976] 1 WLR 591, [1976] 2 All ER 283 (contract for sale of 51½ acres of land for £50,000 payable in three unequal instalments held unenforceable because of provision that on each payment "a proportionate part of the land shall be released").

All ER 1500, my brother Brightman held that a right of pre-emption in a conveyance "at a figure to be agreed upon" was not void for uncertainty, but imposed upon the person granting it an obligation to offer the land to the grantee at the price at which she was willing to sell it. On this, I would make two comments. First, it illustrates the attitude of the court in striving to avoid holding a provision void for uncertainty. Second, it illustrates one of the differences between an option and a right of pre-emption. Under an option, only one step is normally needed to constitute a contract, namely, the exercise of the option. Under a right of pre-emption, two steps will usually be necessary, the making of the offer in accordance with the right of pre-emption, and the acceptance of that offer. The failure to provide either a price or a formula for ascertaining the price is accordingly far more serious in the case of an option than under a pre-emption: he who exercises such an option may well be virtually signing a blank cheque, whereas he who is entitled to a right of pre-emption can at least refrain from accepting the grantor's offer if the price be too high[18a].

The second type of option is one that is expressed to be exercisable at a price to be determined according to some stated formula, without any effective machinery being in terms provided for the working out of that formula. That is the present case. Thirdly, the option may be one which provides both a formula and the machinery, as, for example, arbitration. In this last case, it may be that the machinery can do something to cure defects in the formula: I do not have to decide that. What is before me is a formula that is assailed for its uncertainty, and the absence of any specified machinery that can do anything to cure that uncertainty. I shall consider the question of machinery first.

[His Lordship rejected the landlords' argument that there was no adequate machinery for determining the rent, and continued:]

I readily accept that the words of clause 3 (*c*) might have been more precise. But that is not the point: the point is whether it is void for uncertainty. If one approaches the formula stated in the clause with reasonable goodwill, as I think I am entitled and, indeed, required to do, does it appear to embody such uncertainty of concept as to make it void? Without saying that there is no room for argument on the details, I would answer No to that question, or, indeed, to any other reasonable way of formulating the question that I can conceive. The question is not, I think, whether the clause is proof against wilful misinterpretation, but whether someone genuinely seeking to discover its meaning is able to do so. To that question I would answer Yes.

SUDBROOK TRADING ESTATE LTD *v* EGGLETON
[1983] 1 AC 444, [1982] 3 All ER 1[19] (HL, Lords DIPLOCK, FRASER OF TULLYBELTON, RUSSELL OF KILLOWEN, SCARMAN and BRIDGE OF HARROW)

In a series of leases of industrial properties in Gloucester, the lessees were granted an option "to purchase the reversion in fee simple in the premises hereby demised . . . at such price not being less than £12,000 as may be

---

[18a] See pp. 86–88, ante.
[19] [1983] Conv 76 (K. Hodkinson); (1982) 98 LQR 539 (J. Murdoch).

agreed upon by two valuers one to be nominated by the lessor and the other by the lessee and in default of such agreement by an umpire appointed by the valuers." The lessees purported to exercise the option, but the lessors refused to appoint a valuer, claiming that machinery for the ascertainment of the option price was defectively uncertain. The lessees sought specific performance of the options.

Held. (Lord RUSSELL OF KILLOWEN dissenting). Specific performance granted.

LORD FRASER OF TULLYBELTON: I recognise the logic of the reasoning which has led to the courts' refusing to substitute their own machinery for the machinery which has been agreed upon by the parties. But the result to which it leads is so remote from that which parties normally intend and expect, and is so inconvenient in practice, that there must in my opinion be some defect in the reasoning. I think the defect lies in construing the provisions for the mode of ascertaining the value as an essential part of the agreement. That may have been perfectly true early in the 19th century, when the valuer's profession and the rules of valuation were less well established than they are now. But at the present day these provisions are only subsidiary to the main purpose of the agreement which is for sale and purchase of the property at a fair or reasonable value. In the ordinary case parties do not make any substantial distinction between an agreement to sell at a fair value, without specifying the mode of ascertaining the value, and an agreement to sell at a value to be ascertained by valuers appointed in the way provided in these leases. The true distinction is between those cases where the mode of ascertaining the price is an essential term of the contract, and those cases where the mode of ascertainment, though indicated in the contract, is subsidiary and non-essential: see *Fry on Specific Performance*, 6th edn. (1921), pp. 167, 169, paragraphs 360, 364. The present case falls, in my opinion, into the latter category. Accordingly when the option was exercised there was constituted a complete contract for sale, and the clause should be construed as meaning that the price was to be a fair price. On the other hand where an agreement is made to sell at a price to be fixed by a valuer who is named, or who, by reason of holding some office such as auditor of a company whose shares are to be valued, will have special knowledge relevant to the question of value, the prescribed mode may well be regarded as essential. Where, as here, the machinery consists of valuers and an umpire, none of whom is named or identified, it is in my opinion unrealistic to regard it as an essential term. If it breaks down there is no reason why the court should not substitute other machinery to carry out the main purpose of ascertaining the price in order that the agreement may be carried out.

In the present case the machinery provided for in the clause has broken down because the respondents have declined to appoint their valuer. In that sense the breakdown has been caused by their fault, in failing to implement an implied obligation to co-operate in making the machinery work. The case might be distinguishable in that respect from cases where the breakdown has occurred for some cause outside the control of either party, such as the death of an umpire, or his failure to complete the valuation by a stipulated date. But I do not rely on any such distinction. I prefer to rest my decision on the general principle that, where the machinery is not essential, if it breaks down for any reason the court will substitute its own machinery.

The appropriate means for the court to enforce the present agreements is in my opinion by ordering an inquiry into the fair value of the reversions. That was the method used in *Talbot v Talbot* [1968] Ch 1, [1967] 2 All ER 920 [option to purchase "at a reasonable valuation" held valid by CA]. The alternative of ordering the respondents to appoint a valuer would not be suitable because in the event of the order not being obeyed, the only sanction would be imprisonment for contempt of court which would clearly be inappropriate.

For these reasons the decisions in *Agar v Macklew* (1825) 2 Sim & St 418 and *Vickers v Vickers* (1867) LR 4 Eq 529 should in my opinion be overruled. I agree with the order proposed by my noble and learned friend, Lord Diplock, allowing this appeal.

LORD RUSSELL OF KILLOWEN (dissenting): I felt considerable sympathy for counsel for the respondents when he was told that he had all the law on his side, but was (in effect) facing the prophets. (This is a paraphrase of my own remark in argument, when he was told that he had all equity behind him and I intervened to suggest that he had less in front of him.)

In the result I would dismiss this appeal. I can only exclaim with Macduff — "What! All my pretty chickens and their dam, at one fell swoop?" (Macbeth, Act IV, Sc. 3)[20].

ii.   RENT REVIEW

In *Beer v Bowden* [1981] 1 WLR 522n, [1981] 1 All ER 1070, a lease was granted in 1956 for 14 years. The rent was £1,250 for the first five years and was to be reviewed every five years thereafter, being "such rent as shall thereupon be agreed between the landlord and the tenant". The lease contained no machinery for fixing the rent in default of agreement. On failure to agree at the end of the first five years, the question arose as to what rent was payable. The Court of Appeal held that the rent should be a fair rent.

GOFF LJ said at 525, at 1074: "*King's Motors (Oxford) Ltd v Lax* [1970] 1 WLR 426, [1969] 3 All ER 665 . . ., in my judgment, is wholly distinguishable and does not really assist at all. That was a case of an option to renew, and the exercise of the option could operate, if at all, only to create a contract. Valid contract it could not be, because an essential term — namely, the rent — was neither agreed nor ascertainable. That, in my judgment, poses an entirely different problem from that which arises where one starts with the premise that there is a subsisting lease which creates an estate in the land and with the premise that the court must imply some term, because it is conceded that rent is payable."

---

[20] Followed in *Re Malpass* [1985] Ch 42, [1984] 2 All ER 313 (testamentary option to purchase farm "at the agricultural value thereof determined for agricultural purposes . . . as agreed with the District Valuer"; the valuer declined to act). See also *Trustees of National Deposit Friendly Society v Beatties of London Ltd* (1985) 275 EG 54, where GOULDING J held valid an option agreement for a new lease in favour of tenants who had carried on a business of selling model railways for 75 years "the rent payable . . . to be the greater of £33,000 per annum exclusive or such rent as may be agreed as from the architects certificate of completion". In rejecting claims that it was void for uncertainty in regard to the date of the commencement of the term, the amount of rent and the covenants and conditions, he said at 56: "There has been such performance on the tenant's side as to justify the court in a much more liberal approach to the validity of the document than in the case of a purely executory option where nothing but perhaps a nominal consideration has been given on either side."

BUCKLEY LJ said at 528, at 1076: "It appears to me that the introduction by implication of a single word in the clause in the lease relating to the rent to be payable solves the problem of this case; that is, the insertion of the word 'fair' between the words 'such' and 'rent.' If some such implication is not made, it seems to me that this would be a completely inoperative rent review provision, because it is not to be expected that the tenant would agree to an increase in the rent if the rent to be agreed was absolutely at large. Clearly the parties contemplated that at the end of five years some adjustment might be necessary to make the position with regard to the rent a fair one, and the rent review provision with which we are concerned was inserted in the lease to enable such an adjustment to be made. The suggestion that upon the true construction of the clause it provides that the rent shall continue to be at the rate of £1,250 a year unless the parties otherwise agree would, in my opinion, render the provision entirely inoperative, because, as I say, one could not expect the tenant voluntarily to agree to pay a higher rent."

In *Thomas Bates & Son Ltd v Wyndham's (Lingerie) Ltd* [1981] 1 WLR 505, [1981] 1 All ER 1077, a seven year lease was granted in 1970 with an option for a further lease "of the demised premises . . . at a rent to be agreed between the lessor and the lessees but in default of such agreement at a rent to be fixed by a single arbitrator appointed by the President for the time being of the Royal Institution of Chartered Surveyors." In 1963 the option was exercised and a further lease was granted with an option in terms identical to the original lease. In 1970, when the lessees exercised the option, the lessor sought to introduce a review clause. A new lease was executed for 14 years with a review at the fifth and tenth years. By a mistake, the lease contained no provision for arbitration in default of agreement on the rent review, and merely provided that the rent during the second five years and the final four years should be "such rents as shall have been agreed between the Lessor and the Lessees." The lessees, though aware of the omission, did not bring it to the lessor's notice.

In proceedings for rectification, the Court of Appeal held:
  (i) the rent review clause should be rectified by inserting a reference to arbitration;
  (ii) the arbitrator should assess not the market rent but the rent which it would have been reasonable for the parties themselves to have agreed under the lease.

BUCKLEY LJ said at 519, at 1088: "In my judgment, in default of agreement between the parties, the arbitrator would have to assess what rent it would have been reasonable for these landlords and these tenants to have agreed under this lease having regard to all the circumstances relevant to any negotiations between them of a new rent from the review date.

If I were wrong on a point of rectification, then, on construction and by a process of implication, the rent to be ascertained in default of agreement must, I think, be a fair rent as between the landlords and the tenants. It would be most unjust that the landlords should receive no rent because of failure of the parties to agree. The landlords have granted a 14-year term and the court must endeavour to fill any gap in the terms of the lease by means of a fair and reasonable implication as to what the parties must have intended their bargain to be. See in this connection the decision of this court in *F & G Sykes (Wessex) Ltd v Fine Fare Ltd* [1967] 1 Lloyd's Rep 53, which was a case very different on its facts from the present, but in which the court explained the function of any court of construction where parties have embarked upon any commercial relationship but under terms that are not altogether adequate to cover the eventualities. The court would ascertain by inquiry what rent the landlords and the tenants, as willing negotiators anxious to reach agreement, would arrive at for each of the two rent review periods. In short, the standard would be the same, as I see it, as would have to be adopted by an arbitrator under the clause if it is rectified in the way in which I consider that it should be rectified[1]."

D.   Lease and Licence[2]

i.   THE DISTINCTION

In the 19th century the critical issue was whether the party in question had exclusive possession of the land[3]; if a person were in exclusive possession (other than a freeholder or copyholder) he was a tenant, if not he was a licensee[4]. During the last thirty years the emphasis shifted from the simple test of exclusive possession to that of the intention of the parties to be inferred from all the circumstances. Contrary to views expressed in many of the older cases, exclusive possession did not necessarily mean that the person in enjoyment must be a tenant and not a licensee. As SACHS LJ said in *Barnes v Barratt* [1970] 2 QB 657 at 669, [1970] 2 All ER 483 at 487: "In this case, as always, it is necessary to give weight to the fact that exclusive possession has been given to the occupiers . . . That, however, is a factor which is no longer conclusive and, indeed, appears nowadays to have diminishing weight . . . The law has adapted itself so as to deal with the complexities of the Rent Acts

---

[1] *Lear v Blizzard* [1983] 3 All ER 662 where there was an option to renew a lease for a further term of 21 years "at a rent to be agreed between the parties or in default of agreement at a rent to be determined by a single arbitrator." TUDOR EVANS J held that the rent to be determined by the arbitrator was to be a fair rent for the particular tenant and the particular landlord, account being taken of all considerations which would affect the mind of either party to negotiations between them. Cf. *Ponsford v HMS Aerosols Ltd* [1979] AC 63, [1978] 2 All ER 837, where HL, by a majority of 3 to 2, applied an objective test; "a reasonable rent for the demised premises" was construed as that which was reasonable for the premises and not what would be reasonable for the tenant to pay. See [1983] All ER Rev 239 (P. H. Pettit).

[2] C & B, pp. 365–368, 470; M & W, pp. 632–635; MM, pp. 334–335; Megarry, *Rent Acts* (10th edn.), pp. 53–64; Dawson and Pearce, *Licences Relating to the Occupation or Use of Land* (1979), pp. 3–13; Pettit, *Private Sector Tenancies* (1981), pp. 12–16 Lewison, *Lease or Licence* (1985).

[3] The giving of a right of exclusive possession should be distinguished from the giving of an exclusive or sole right to use the premises for a particular purpose which has never been held to create a tenancy: *Hill v Tupper* (1863) 2 H & C 121, p. 564, post; *Wilson v Tavener* [1901] 1 Ch 578; *Clore v Theatrical Properties Ltd and Westby & Co Ltd* [1936] 3 All ER 483.

[4] In *Lynes v Snaith* [1899] 1 QB 486, LAWRENCE J said: "As to the first question, I think it is clear [the defendant] was a tenant at will and not a licensee; for the admissions state that she was in exclusive possession, a fact which is wholly inconsistent with her having been a mere licensee" ; *Allan v Liverpool Overseers* (1874) LR 9 QB 180, p. 400, post; *Glenwood Lumber Co Ltd v Phillips* [1904] AC 405, p. 399, post. Cf. *Taylor v Caldwell* (1863) 3 B & S 826, p. 400, post.

without causing patently unintended injustice to landlords, whilst guarding against improper avoidance by the latter of the provisions of those Acts[6]".

The high water-mark of this approach was seen in the line of Court of Appeal decisions which began with *Somma v Hazelhurst* [1978] 1 WLR 1014, [1978] 2 All ER 1011, in which agreements were drafted as licences and exclusive possession was denied to the occupier by the device of reserving to the licensor the right to enter upon the premises himself or to introduce other licensees. The general principle was stated by CUMMING-BRUCE LJ at 1024, at 1020: "We can see no reason why an ordinary landlord should not be able to grant a licence to occupy an ordinary house. If that is what both he and the licensee intend and if they can frame any written agreement in such a way as to demonstrate that it is not really an agreement for a lease masquerading as a licence, we can see no reason in law or justice why they should be prevented from achieving that object." The House of Lords Appellate Committee refused leave to appeal from the decision in *Somma v Hazelhurst*[7], and subsequent decisions in the Court of Appeal continued to re-state the principle, even when the agreement was held to be a sham[8].

In *Street v Mountford* [1985] AC 809, [1985] 2 All ER 289, infra, the House of Lords (in the first case to be heard there on the distinction) decisively rejected this approach. In this case there was a licence agreement, under which the occupant was given exclusive possession but had signed a statement at the end of the agreement that she accepted that it "does not and is not intended to give me a tenancy protected under the Rent Acts". As SLADE LJ said in the Court of Appeal (1984) 271 EG 1261 at 1262: "It was a plain expression of the intentions of both parties that what she was being given was a licence rather than a tenancy. There is no plea by her of misrepresentation, undue influence or *non est factum* and no claim for rectification." The House of Lords reversed the Court of Appeal and held that the agreement was a tenancy.

The effect of this decision is that "where the only circumstances are that residential accommodation is offered and accepted with exclusive possession for a term at a rent, the result is a tenancy . . . The courts will, save in exceptional circumstances, only be concerned to inquire whether as a result of an agreement relating to residential accommodation the occupier is a lodger or a tenant": at 827, at 300[9]. Lord TEMPLEMAN (who delivered the only speech) identified as exceptional cases those where:

---

[6] The distinction is also relevant in the application of the Landlord and Tenant Act 1954 (business tenancies); the duty of care owed to an occupier in respect of his chattels by a licensor but not by a landlord: *Appah v Parncliffe Investments Ltd* [1964] 1 WLR 1064, [1964] 1 All ER 838; and the warranty of suitability of premises for their intended purpose implied into a licence: *Wettern Electric Ltd v Welsh Development Agency* [1983] QB 796, [1983] 2 All ER 629; (1983) 80 LSG 2195 (H. W. Wilkinson); there is no such warranty in respect of a lease, apart from express guarantee by the landlord. A difference was removed by *National Carriers Ltd v Panalpina Ltd* [1981] AC 675, [1981] 1 All ER 161, where HL held that the doctrine of frustration is applicable to a lease; for licences, see *Krell v Henry* [1903] 2 KB 740; C & B, p. 445.

[7] [1978] 2 All ER 1011 at 1025 (Lords WILBERFORCE, SALMON and FRASER OF TULLYBELTON).

[8] Followed in *Aldrington Garages Ltd v Fielder* (1978) 247 EG 557; *Sturolson & Co v Weniz* (1984) 272 EG 326. Cf. *O'Malley v Seymour* (1978) 250 EG 1083; *Walsh v Griffiths-Jones* [1978] 2 All ER 1002, where the agreements were held to be sham. For a detailed review, see (1980) 130 NLJ 939, 959 (A. Waite).

[9] "He will be a lodger if the landlord provides attendance or services which require the landlord or his servants to have unrestricted access to the premises". *Royal Philanthropic Society v County* (1985) 276 EG 1068 at 1071, per Fox LJ.

(*a*) the occupancy is within one of a number of special categories i.e. "under a contract for the sale of land[10], or pursuant to a contract of employment or referable to the holding of an office[11]": at 827, at 300.

(*b*) the circumstances show that there is no intention to create legal relationships as, for example, "where there has been something in the circumstances such as a family arrangement, an act of friendship or such like, to negative any intention to create a tenancy[12]". It would appear that the test of intention is relevant in deciding whether there is an intention to create a legal relationship, but irrelevant in deciding which legal relationship is created.

Further, the House of Lords disapproved obiter of "the sham device and artificial transaction" in *Somma v Hazelhurst*[13]. No reference was made to cases involving businessmen and business premises, where the occupant has exclusive possession, but the parties expressly state that the agreement is a licence and not a tenancy within the Landlord and Tenant Act 1954. The decisions which hold that such agreements are licences are presumably no longer good law[14].

The crux of the matter is that an owner of residential property is reluctant to grant a lease to a tenant who will be protected under the Rent Act 1977 with the consequence of rent control and of security of tenure after the contractual term is ended. A status of irremovability is particularly unattractive to an owner. In 1977 the Department of the Environment initiated a review of the Rent Acts, and in 1985 the Nugee Committee of Inquiry on the Management of Privately Owned Blocks of Flats issued its

---

[10] See *Bretherton v Paton* (1986) Times, 14 March, where CA interpreted this exception narrowly, in holding that a *potential* purchaser of a dwelling house who had entered into exclusive possession for a term at a rent under an arrangement for its sale was held to be a tenant. See also *Emmet on Title* (18th edn. 1983), pp. 219–221; *Errington v Errington and Woods* [1952] 1 KB 290, [1952] 1 All ER 149, p. 402, post.

[11] *Mayhew v Suttle* (1854) 4 E & B 347; *Smith v Seghill Overseers* (1875) LR 10 QB 422, p. 401, post. Distinguish a service occupant who is a licensee from a service tenant who is not. The latter is a person to whom a dwelling-house is let in consequence of his employment, but who is not required to live there for the better performance of his duties: *Torbett v Faulkner* [1952] 2 TLR 659. See *Royal Philanthropic Society v County* (1985) 276 EG 1068; Rent Act 1977, Sch. 15, Case 8.

[12] *Facchini v Bryson* [1952] 1 TLR 1386 at 1389–1390, per DENNING LJ, cited *Street v Mountford* at 821, at 296, p. 403, post. See *Booker v Palmer* [1942] 2 All ER 674, p. 402, post; *Marcroft Wagons Ltd v Smith* [1951] 2 KB 496, [1951] 2 All ER 271; p. 402, post; *Heslop v Burns* [1974] 1 WLR 1241, [1974] 3 All ER 406, p. 406, post. See also *Abbeyfield (Harpenden) Society v Woods* [1968] 1 WLR 374, [1968] 1 All ER 352n, p. 405, post; *Barnes v Barratt* [1970] 2 QB 657, [1970] 2 All ER 483 (house-sharing arrangement without rent or fixed term held to be licence).

[13] At 825, at 299. Cf. the recent similar approach in the House of Lords to tax avoidance schemes which involve "a pre-ordained series of transaction (whether or not they include the achievement of a legitimate commercial end) into which there are inserted steps which have no commercial purpose apart from the avoidance of a liability to tax which in the absence of those particular steps would have been payable": *IRC v Burmah Oil Co Ltd* [1982] STC 30 at 32, per Lord DIPLOCK. See also *WT Ramsay Ltd v IRC* [1982] AC 300, [1981] 1 All ER 865; *Furniss v Dawson* [1984] AC 474, [1984] 1 All ER 530. These cases made very severe inroads on the ambit within which the earlier doctrine of *IRC v Duke of Westminster* [1936] AC 1 at 19 had been applied. See M & B, *Trusts and Trustees* (3rd edn, 1984), pp. 469–472.

[14] *Euston Centre Properties Ltd v H & J Wilson Ltd* (1982) 262 EG 1079; *Matchams Park (Holdings) Ltd v Dommett* (1984) 272 EG 549 (stock-car racing stadium; the occupant was "obviously an experienced businessman and throughout had the benefit of solicitors' advice" per SLADE LJ).

Report. In 1985 also the Secretary of State for the Environment announced that the Government hoped to introduce legislation to encourage the supply of more homes for renting in the private sector, but probably not during the lifetime of the present Parliament[15]. The Housing Act of 1980 introduced the protected shorthold tenancy as a method of letting residential premises without security of tenure after the end of the contractual term[16]. What is needed, however, is a major review of the Rent Act 1977, and *Street v Mountford* may well provide the necessary impetus[17].

STREET *v* MOUNTFORD[18]
[1985] AC 809, [1985] 2 All ER 289 (HL, Lords SCARMAN, KEITH OF KINKEL, BRIDGE OF HARWICH, BRIGHTMAN and TEMPLEMAN)

LORD TEMPLEMAN: My Lords, by an agreement dated 7 March 1983, the respondent Mr Street granted the appellant Mrs Mountford the right to occupy the furnished rooms numbers 5 and 6 at 5, St. Clements Gardens, Boscombe, from 7 March 1983 for £37 per week, subject to termination by 14 days' written notice and subject to the conditions set forth in the agreement. The question raised by this appeal is whether the agreement created a tenancy or a licence.

A tenancy is a term of years absolute. This expression, by section 205 (1) (xxvii) of the Law of Property Act 1925, reproducing the common law, includes a term from week to week in possession at a rent and liable to determination by notice or re-entry. Originally a term of years was not an estate in land, the lessee having merely a personal action against his lessor. But a legal estate in leaseholds was created by the Statute of Gloucester 1278 and the Act of 1529 21 Hen VIII, c 15. Now by section 1 of the Law of Property Act 1925 a term of years absolute is an estate in land capable of subsisting as a legal estate. In the present case if the agreement dated 7 March 1983 created a tenancy, Mrs Mountford having entered into possession and made weekly payments acquired a legal estate in land. If the agreement is a tenancy, the occupation of Mrs Mountford is protected by the Rent Acts.

A licence in connection with land while entitling the licensee to use the land for the purposes authorised by the licence does not create an estate in the land. If the agreement dated 7 March 1983 created a licence for Mrs Mountford to occupy the premises, she did not acquire any estate in the land. If the agreement is a licence then Mrs Mountford's right of occupation is not protected by the Rent Acts. Hence the practical importance of distinguishing between a tenancy and a licence.

---

[15] HC Deb 1985 col. 890, June 12. On the political considerations, see (1985) 273 EG 369 (B. J. Pearce).

[16] Pp. 409–412, post.

[17] See also *Eastleigh Borough Council v Walsh* [1985] 1 WLR 525, [1985] 2 All ER 112, where HL, reversing CA, held that a person let into occupation of a council house under Housing (Homeless Persons) Act 1977 pending inquiries as to whether he had a priority need was a licensee and not a tenant.

[18] [1985] Conv 328 (R. Street); [1985] CLJ 351 (S. Tromans); 48 MLR 712 (S. Anderson); Lewison, *Lease or Licence* (1985); (1986) 130 SJ 3, 27 (P. M. Rank); [1986] Conv 39 (D. N. Clarke).

In the course of argument, nearly every clause of the agreement dated 7 March 1983 was relied upon by the appellant as indicating a lease and by the respondent as indicating a licence. The agreement, in full, was in these terms:

"I Mrs Wendy Mountford agree to take from the owner Roger Street the single furnished room number 5 and 6 at 5 St. Clements Gardens, Boscombe, Bournemouth, commencing 7 March 1983 at a licence fee of £37 per week.

"I understand that the right to occupy the above room is conditional on the strict observance of the following rules:

"1.   No paraffin stoves, or other than the supplied form of heating, is allowed in the room.

"2.   No one but the above-named person may occupy or sleep in the room without prior permission, and this personal licence is not assignable.

"3.   The owner (or his agent) has the right at all times to enter the room to inspect its condition, read and collect money from meters, carry out maintenance works, install or replace furniture or for any other reasonable purpose.

"4.   All rooms must be kept in a clean and tidy condition.

"5.   All damage and breakages must be paid for or replaced at once. An initial deposit equivalent to 2 weeks' licence fee will be refunded on termination of the licence subject to deduction for all damage or other breakages or arrears of licence fee, or retention towards the cost of any necessary possession proceedings.

"6.   No nuisance or annoyance to be caused to the other occupiers. In particular, all music played after midnight to be kept low so as not to disturb occupiers of other rooms.

"7.   No children or pets allowed under any circumstances whatsoever.

"8.   Prompt payment of the licence fee must be made every Monday in advance without fail.

"9.   If the licence fee or any part of it shall be seven days in arrear or if the occupier shall be in breach of any of the other terms of this agreement or if (except by arrangement) the room is left vacant or unoccupied, the owner may re-enter the room and this licence shall then immediately be terminated (without prejudice to all other rights and remedies of the owner).

"10.   This licence may be terminated by 14 days' written notice given to the occupier at any time by the owner or his agent, or by the same notice by the occupier to the owner or his agent.

"Occupier's signature

"Owner/agent's signature

"Date 7 March 1983

"I understand and accept that a licence in the above form does not and is not intended to give me a tenancy protected under the Rent Acts.

"Occupier's signature."

On 12 August 1983 on Mrs Mountford's application a fair rent was registered. Mr Steet then made application under section 51 (*a*) of the County Courts Act for a declaration that Mrs Mountford's occupancy was a licence and not a tenancy. The recorder in the county court held that Mrs Mountford was a tenant entitled to the protection of the Rent Acts and made a declaration accordingly. The Court of Appeal held that Mrs Mountford was a licensee not entitled to the protection of the Rent Acts. Mrs Mountford appeals.

On behalf of Mrs Mountford her counsel, Mr Hicks QC seeks to reaffirm and re-establish the traditional view that an occupier of land for a term at a rent is a tenant providing the occupier is granted exclusive possession. It is conceded on behalf of Mr Street that the agreement dated 7 March 1983 granted exclusive possession to Mrs Mountford. The traditional view that the grant of exclusive possession for a term at a rent creates a tenancy is consistent with the elevation of a tenancy into an estate in land. The tenant possessing exclusive possession is able to exercise the rights of an owner of land, which is in the real sense his land albeit temporarily and subject to certain restrictions. A tenant armed with exclusive possession can keep out strangers and keep out the landlord unless the landlord is exercising limited rights reserved to him by the tenancy agreement to enter and view and repair. A licensee lacking exclusive possession can in no sense call the land his own and cannot be said to own any estate in the land. The licence does not create an estate in the land to which it relates but only makes an act lawful which would otherwise be unlawful.

On behalf of Mr Street his counsel, Mr Goodhart QC, relies on recent authorities which, he submits, demonstrate that an occupier granted exclusive possession for a term at a rent may nevertheless be a licensee if, in the words of Slade LJ in the present case (1984) 271 EG 1261 at 1264: "there is manifested the clear intention of both parties that the rights granted are to be merely those of a personal right of occupation and not those of a tenant."

In the present case, it is submitted, the provisions of the agreement dated 7 March 1983 and in particular clauses 2, 4, 7 and 9 and the express declaration at the foot of the agreement manifest the clear intention of both parties that the rights granted are to be those of a personal nature and not those of a tenant.

My Lords, there is no doubt that the traditional distinction between a tenancy and a licence of land lay in the grant of land for a term at a rent with exclusive possession. In some cases it was not clear at first sight whether exclusive possession was in fact granted. For example, an owner of land could grant a licence to cut and remove standing timber. Alternatively the owner could grant a tenancy of the land with the right to cut and remove standing timber during the term of the tenancy. The grant of rights relating to standing timber therefore required careful consideration in order to decide whether the grant conferred exclusive possession of the land for a term at a rent and was therefore a tenancy or whether it merely conferred a bare licence to remove the timber.

In *Glenwood Lumber Co Ltd v Phillips* [1904] AC 405, the Crown in exercise of statutory powers "licensed" the respondents to hold an area of land for the purpose of cutting and removing timber for the term of 21 years at an annual rent. Delivering the advice of the Judicial Committee of the Privy Council, Lord Davey said, at 408–409:

"The appellants contended that this instrument conferred only a licence to cut timber and carry it away, and did not give the respondent any right of occupation or interest in the land itself. Having regard to the provisions of the Act under the powers of which it was executed and to the language of the document itself, their Lordships cannot adopt this view of the construction or effect of it. In the so-called licence itself it is called indifferently a licence and a demise, but in the Act it is spoken of as a lease, and the holder of it is described as the lessee. It is not, however, a question of words but of substance. If the effect of the instrument is to give the holder an exclusive right of occupation of the land, though subject to certain reservations or to a restriction of the purposes for which it may be used, it is in law a demise of the land itself. By [the Act] it is enacted that the lease shall vest in the lessee the right to take and keep exclusive possession of the lands described therein subject to the conditions in the Act provided or referred to, and the lessee is empowered (amongst other things) to bring any actions or suits against any party unlawfully in possession of any land so leased, and to prosecute all trespassers thereon. The operative part and habendum in the licence is framed in apt language to carry out the intention so expressed in the Act. And their Lordships have no doubt that the effect of the so-called licence was to confer a title to the land itself on the respondent.''

This was a case in which the court after careful consideration of the purposes of the grant, the terms of the grant and the surrounding circumstances, came to the conclusion that the grant conferred exclusive possession and was therefore a tenancy.

A contrary conclusion was reached in *Taylor v Caldwell* (1863) 3 B & S 826 in which the defendant agreed to let the plaintiff have the use of the Surrey Gardens and Music Hall on four specified days giving a series of four concerts and day and night fetes at the gardens and hall on those days, and the plaintiff agreed to take the gardens and the hall and to pay £100 for each day. Blackburn J said, at 832:

"The parties inaccurately call this a 'letting,' and the money to be paid a 'rent,' but the whole agreement is such as to show that the defendants were to retain the possession of the hall and gardens so that there was to be no demise of them, and that the contract was merely to give the plaintiffs the use of them on those days.''

That was a case where the court after considering the purpose of the grant, the terms of the grant and the surrounding circumstances came to the conclusion that the grantee was not entitled to exclusive possession but only to use the land for limited purposes and was therefore a licensee.

In the case of residential accommodation there is no difficulty in deciding whether the grant confers exclusive possession. An occupier of residential accommodation at a rent for a term is either a lodger or a tenant. The occupier is a lodger if the landlord provides attendance or services which require the landlord or his servants to exercise unrestricted access to and use of the premises. A lodger is entitled to live in the premises but cannot call the place his own. In *Allan v Liverpool Overseers* (1874) LR 9 QB 180 at 191–192 Blackburn J said:

"A lodger in a house, although he has the exclusive use of rooms in the house, in the sense that nobody else is to be there, and though his goods are stowed there, yet he is not in exclusive occupation in that sense, because the landlord is there for the purpose of being able, as landlords commonly do in the case of lodgings, to have his own servants to look after the house and the furniture, and has retained to himself the occupation, though he has agreed to give the exclusive enjoyment of the occupation to the lodger.''

If on the other hand residential accommodation is granted for a term at a rent with exclusive possession, the landlord providing neither attendance nor services, the grant is a tenancy; any express reservation to the landlord of limited rights to enter and view the state of the premises and to repair and maintain the premises only serves to emphasise the fact that the grantee is entitled to exclusive possession and is a tenant. In the present case it is conceded that Mrs Mountford is entitled to exclusive possession and is not a lodger. Mr Street provided neither attendance nor services and only reserved the limited rights of inspection and maintenance and the like set forth in clause 3 of the agreement. On the traditional view of the matter, Mrs Mountford not being a lodger must be a tenant.

There can be no tenancy unless the occupier enjoys exclusive possession; but an occupier who enjoys exclusive possession is not necessarily a tenant. He may be owner in fee simple, a trespasser, a mortgagee in possession, an object of charity or a service occupier. To constitute a tenancy the occupier must be granted exclusive possession for a fixed or periodic term certain in consideration of a premium or periodical payments. The grant may be express, or may be inferred where the owner accepts weekly or other periodical payments from the occupier.

Occupation by service occupier may be eliminated. A service occupier is a servant who occupies his master's premises in order to perform his duties as a servant. In those circumstances the possession and occupation of the servant is treated as the possession and occupation of the master and the relationship of landlord and tenant is not created; see *Mayhew v Suttle* (1854) 4 E & B 347. The test is whether the servant requires the premises he occupies in order the better to perform his duties as a servant:

"Where the occupation is necessary for the performance of services, and the occupier is required to reside in the house in order to perform those services, the occupation being strictly ancillary to the performance of the duties which the occupier has to perform, the occupation is that of a servant"; per Mellor J in *Smith v Seghill Overseers* (1875) LR 10 QB 422 at 428.

The cases on which Mr Goodhart relies begin with *Booker v Palmer* [1942] 2 All ER 674. The owner of a cottage agreed to allow a friend to install an evacuee in the cottage rent free for the duration of the war. The Court of Appeal held that there was no intention on the part of the owner to enter into legal relationships with the evacuee. Lord Greene MR said at 677:

"To suggest there is an intention there to create a relationship of landlord and tenant appears to me to be quite impossible. There is one golden rule which is of very general application, namely, that the law does not impute intention to enter into legal relationships where the circumstances and the conduct of the parties negative any intention of the kind. It seems to me that this is a clear example of the application of that rule."

The observations of Lord Greene MR were not directed to the distinction between a contractual tenancy and a contractual licence. The conduct of the parties (not their professed intentions) indicated that they did not intend to contract at all.

In the present case, the agreement dated 7 March 1983 professed an intention by both parties to create a licence and their belief that they had in fact created a licence. It was submitted on behalf of Mr Street that the court cannot in these circumstances decide that the agreement created a tenancy without interfering with the freedom of contract enjoyed by both parties. My Lords, Mr Street enjoyed freedom to offer Mrs Mountford the right to occupy the rooms comprised in the agreement on such lawful terms as Mr Street pleased. Mrs Mountford enjoyed freedom to negotiate with Mr Street to obtain different terms. Both parties enjoyed freedom to contract or not to contract and both parties exercised that freedom by contracting on the terms set forth in the written agreement and on no other terms. But the consequences in law of the agreement, once concluded, can only be determined by consideration of the effect of the agreement. If the agreement satisfied all the requirements of a tenancy, then the agreement produced a tenancy and the parties cannot alter the effect of the agreement by insisting that they only created a licence. The manufacture of a five-pronged implement for manual digging results in a fork even if the manufacturer, unfamiliar with the English language, insists that he intended to make and has made a spade.

It was also submitted that in deciding whether the agreement created a tenancy or a licence, the court should ignore the Rent Acts. If Mr Street has succeeded, where owners have failed these past 70 years, in driving a coach and horses through the Rent Acts, he must be left to enjoy the benefit of his ingenuity unless and until Parliament intervenes. I accept that the Rent Acts are irrelevant to the problem of determining the legal effect of the rights granted by the agreement. Like the professed intention of the parties, the Rent Acts cannot alter the effect of the agreement.

In *Marcroft Wagons Ltd v Smith* [1951] 2 KB 496, [1951] 2 All ER 271 the daughter of a deceased tenant who lived with her mother claimed to be a statutory tenant by succession and the landlords asserted that the daughter had no rights under the Rent Acts and was a trespasser. The landlords expressly refused to accept the daughter's claims but accepted rent from her while they were considering the position. If the landlords had decided not to apply to the court for possession but to accept the daughter as a tenant, the moneys paid by the daughter would have been treated as rent. If the landlords decided, as they did decide, to apply for possession and to prove, as they did prove, that the daughter was not a statutory tenant, the moneys paid by the daughter were treated as mesne profits. The Court of Appeal held with some hesitation that the landlords never accepted the daughter as tenant and never intended to contract with her although the landlords delayed for some six months before applying to the court for possession. Roxburgh J said, at 507, at 277:

"Generally speaking, when a person, having a sufficient estate in land, lets another into exclusive possession, a tenancy results, and there is no question of a licence. But the inference of a tenancy is not necessarily to be drawn where a person succeeds on a death to occupation of rent-controlled premises and a landlord accepts some rent while he or the occupant, or both of them, is or are considering his or their position. If this is all that happened in this case, then no tenancy would result."

In that case, as in *Booker v Palmer* the court deduced from the conduct of the parties that they did not intend to contract at all.

Errington v Errington and Woods [1952] 1 KB 290, [1952] 1 All ER 149 concerned a contract by a father to allow his son to buy the father's house on payment of the instalments of the father's building society loan. Denning LJ referred, at 297, at 154, to the judgment of Lord Greene MR in *Booker v Palmer* [1942] 2 All ER 674 at 677 where, however, the circumstances and the conduct of the parties negatived any intention to enter into legal relationships. Denning LJ continued, at 297–298, at 154–155:

"We have had many instances lately of occupiers in exclusive possession who have been held to be not tenants, but only licensees. When a requisitioning authority allowed people into possession at a weekly rent: . . . when a landlord told a tenant on his retirement that he could live in a cottage rent free for the rest of his days: . . . when a landlord, on the death of the widow of a statutory tenant, allowed her daughter to remain in possession, paying rent for six months: *Marcroft Wagons Ltd v Smith* [1951] 2 KB 496; when the owner of a shop allowed the manager to live in a flat above the shop, but did not require him to do so, and the value of the flat was taken into account at £1 a week in fixing his wages: . . . in each of those cases the occupier was held to be a licensee and not a tenant. . . . The result of all these cases is that, although a person who is let into exclusive possession is prima facie to be considered a tenant, nevertheless he will not be held to be so if the circumstances negative any intention to create a tenancy. Words alone may not suffice. Parties cannot turn a tenancy into a licence merely by calling it one. But if the circumstances and the conduct of the parties show that all that was intended was that the occupier should be granted a personal privilege, with no interest in the land, he will be held to be a licensee only."

In *Errington v Errington and Woods* and in the cases cited by Denning LJ at 297, at 154 there were exceptional circumstances which negatived the prima facie intention to create a tenancy, notwithstanding that the occupier enjoyed exclusive occupation. The intention to create a tenancy was negatived if the parties did not intend to enter into legal relationships at all, or where the relationship between the parties was that of vendor and purchaser, master and service occupier, or where the owner, a requisitioning authority had no power to grant a tenancy. These exceptional circumstances are not to be found in the present case where there has been the lawful, independent and voluntary grant of exclusive possession for a term at a rent.

If the observations of Denning LJ are applied to the facts of the present case it may fairly be said that the circumstances negative any intention to create a mere licence. Words alone do not suffice. Parties cannot turn a tenancy into a licence merely by calling it one. The circumstances and the conduct of the parties show that what was intended was that the occupier should be granted exclusive possession at a rent for a term with a corresponding interest in the land which created a tenancy.

In *Cobb v Lane* [1952] 1 TLR 1037, [1952] 1 All ER 1199, an owner allowed her brother to occupy a house rent free. The county court judge, who was upheld by the Court of Appeal, held that there was no intention to create any legal relationship and that a tenancy at will was not to be implied. This is another example of conduct which negatives any intention of entering into a contract, and does not assist in distinguishing a contractual tenancy from a contractual licence.

In *Facchini v Bryson* [1952] 1 TLR 1386, an employer and his assistant entered into an agreement which, inter alia, allowed the assistant to occupy a house for a weekly payment on terms which conferred exclusive possession. The assistant did not occupy the house for the better performance of his duty and was not therefore a service occupier. The agreement stipulated that "nothing in this agreement shall be construed to create a tenancy between the employer and the assistant." Somervell LJ said, at 1389:

"If, looking at the operative clauses in the agreement, one comes to the conclusion that the rights of the occupier, to use a neutral word, are those of a lessee, the parties cannot turn it into a licence by saying at the end 'this is deemed to be a licence;' nor can they, if the operative paragraphs show that it is merely a licence, say that it should be deemed to be a lease."

Denning LJ referred to several cases including *Errington v Errington and Woods* and *Cobb v Lane* and said, at 1389–1390:

"In all the cases where an occupier has been held to be a licensee there has been something in the circumstances, such as a family arrangement, an act of friendship or generosity, or such like, to negative any intention to create a tenancy. . . . In the present case, however, there are no special circumstances. It is a simple case where the employer let a man into occupation of a house in consequence of his employment at a weekly sum payable by him. The occupation has all the features of a service tenancy, and the parties cannot by the mere words'of their contract turn it into something else. Their relationship is determined by the law and not by the label which they choose to put on it: . . ."

The decision, which was thereafter binding on the Court of Appeal and on all lower courts, referred to the special circumstances which are capable of negativing an intention to create a tenancy and reaffirmed the principle that the professed intentions of the parties are irrelevant. The decision also indicated that in a simple case a grant of exclusive possession of residential accommodation for a weekly sum creates a tenancy.

In *Murray Bull & Co Ltd v Murray* [1953] 1 QB 211, [1952] 2 All ER 1079 a contractual tenant held over, paying rent quarterly. McNair J found at 217, at 1082:

"both parties intended that the relationship should be that of licensee and no more . . . The primary consideration on both sides was that the defendant, as occupant of the flat, should not be a controlled tenant."

In my opinion this case was wrongly decided. McNair J citing the observations of Denning LJ in *Errington v Errington and Woods* [1952] 1 KB 290 at 297, [1952] 1 All ER 149 at 154–155 and *Marcroft Wagons Ltd v Smith* [1951] 2 KB 496, [1951] 2 All ER 271 failed to distinguish between first, conduct which negatives an intention to create legal relationships, secondly, special circumstances which prevent exclusive occupation from creating a tenancy and thirdly, the professed intention of the parties. In *Murray Bull & Co Ltd v Murray* the conduct of the parties showed an intention to contract and there were no relevant special circumstances. The tenant holding over continued by agreement to enjoy exclusive possession and to pay a rent for a term certain. In those circumstances he continued to be a tenant notwithstanding the professed intention of the parties to create a licence and their desire to avoid a controlled tenancy.

In *Addiscombe Garden Estates Ltd v Crabbe* [1958] 1 QB 513, [1957] 3 All ER 563, the Court of Appeal considered an agreement relating to a tennis club carried on in the grounds of a hotel. The agreement was:

"described by the parties as a licence . . . the draftsman has studiously and successfully avoided the use either of the word 'landlord' or the word 'tenant' throughout the document" per Jenkins LJ at 522, at 567.

On analysis of the whole of the agreement the Court of Appeal came to the conclusion that the agreement conferred exclusive possession and thus created a tenancy. Jenkins LJ said, at 522, at 565:

"The whole of the document must be looked at; and if, after it has been examined, the right conclusion appears to be that, whatever label may have been attached to it, it in fact conferred and imposed on the grantee in substance the rights and obligations of a tenant, and on the grantor in substance the rights and obligations of a landlord, then it must be given the appropriate effect, that is to say, it must be treated as a tenancy agreement as distinct from a mere licence."

In the agreement in the *Addiscombe* case it was by no means clear until the whole of the document had been narrowly examined that exclusive possession was granted by the agreement. In the present case it is clear that exclusive possession was granted and so much is conceded. In these circumstances it is unnecessary to analyse minutely the detailed rights and obligations contained in the agreement.

In the *Addiscombe* case Jenkins LJ referred, at 528, at 571, to the observations of Denning LJ in *Errington and Errington and Woods* to the effect that "The test of exclusive possession is by no means decisive." Jenkins LJ continued:

"I think that wide statement must be treated as qualified by his observations in *Facchini v Bryson* [1952] 1 TLR 1386 at 1389; and it seems to me that, save in exceptional cases of the kind mentioned by Denning LJ in that case, the law remains that the fact of exclusive possession, if not decisive against the view that there is a mere licence, as distinct from a tenancy, is at all events a consideration of the first importance."

Exclusive possession is of first importance in considering whether an occupier is a tenant; exclusive possession is not decisive because an occupier who enjoys exclusive possession is not necessarily a tenant. The occupier may be a lodger or service occupier or fall within the other exceptional categories mentioned by Denning LJ in *Errington v Errington and Woods*.

In *Isaac v Hotel de Paris Ltd* [1960] 1 WLR 239, [1960] 1 All ER 348 an employee who managed a night bar in a hotel for his employer company which held a lease of the hotel negotiated "subject to contract" to complete the purchase of shares in the company and to be allowed to run the nightclub for his own benefit if he paid the head rent payable by the company for the hotel. In the expectation that the negotiations "subject to contract" would ripen into a binding agreement, the employee was allowed to run the nightclub and he paid the company's rent. When negotiations broke down the employee claimed unsuccessfully to be a tenant of the hotel company. The circumstances in which the employee was allowed to occupy the premises showed that the hotel company never intended to accept him as a tenant and that he was fully aware of that fact. This was a case, consistent with the authorities cited by Lord Denning in giving the advice of the Judicial Committee of the Privy Council, in which the parties did not intend to enter into contractual relationships unless and until the negotiations "subject to contract" were replaced by a binding contract.

In *Abbeyfield (Harpenden) Society Ltd v Woods* [1968] 1 WLR 374, [1968] 1 All ER 352 n the occupier of a room in an old peoples' home was held to be a licensee and not a tenant. Lord Denning MR said, at 376, at 353:

"The modern cases show that a man may be a licensee even though he has exclusive possession, even though the word 'rent' is used, and even though the word 'tenancy' is used. The court must look at the agreement as a whole and see whether a tenancy really was intended. In this case there is, besides the one room, the provision of services, meals, a resident housekeeper, and such like. The whole arrangement was so personal in nature that the proper inference is that he was a licensee."

As I understand the decision in the *Abbeyfield* case the court came to the conclusion that the occupier was a lodger and was therefore a licensee not a tenant.

In *Shell-Mex and BP Ltd v Manchester Garages Ltd* [1971] 1 WLR 612, [1971] 1 All ER 841 the Court of Appeal after carefully examining an agreement whereby the defendant was allowed to use a petrol company's filling station for the purposes of selling petrol, came to the conclusion that the agreement did not grant exclusive possession to the defendant who was therefore a licensee. At 615, at 843 Lord Denning MR in considering whether the transaction was a licence or a tenancy said:

"Broadly speaking, we have to see whether it is a personal privilege given to a person (in which case it is a licence), or whether it grants an interest in land (in which case it is a tenancy). At one time it used to be thought that exclusive possession was a decisive factor. But that is not so. It depends on broader considerations altogether. Primarily on whether it is personal in its nature or not: see *Errington v Errington and Woods*."

In my opinion the agreement was only "personal in its nature" and created "a personal privilege" if the agreement did not confer the right to exclusive possession of the filling station. No other test for distinguishing between a contractual tenancy and a contractual licence appears to be understandable or workable.

Heslop v Burns [1974] 1 WLR 1241, [1974] 3 All ER 406 was another case in which the owner of a cottage allowed a family to live in the cottage rent free and it was held that no tenancy at will had been created on the ground that the parties did not intend any legal relationship. Scarman LJ cited with approval, at 1252, at 415, the statement by Denning LJ in *Facchini v Bryson* [1952] 1 TLR 1386, at 1389:

"In all the cases where an occupier has been held to be a licensee there has been something in the circumstances, such as a family arrangement, an act of friendship or generosity, or such like, to negative any intention to create a tenancy."

In *Marchant v Charters* [1977] 1 WLR 1181, [1977] 3 All ER 918, a bedsitting room was occupied on terms that the landlord cleaned the rooms daily and provided clean linen each week. It was held by the Court of Appeal that the occupier was a licensee and not a tenant. The decision in the case is sustainable on the grounds that the occupier was a lodger and did not enjoy exclusive possession. But Lord Denning MR said, at 1185, at 922:

"What is the test to see whether the occupier of one room in a house is a tenant or a licensee? It does not depend on whether he or she has exclusive possession or not. It does not depend on whether the room is furnished or not. It does not depend on whether the occupation is permanent or temporary. It does not depend on the label which the parties put upon it. All these are factors which may influence the decision but none of them is conclusive. All the circumstances have to be worked out. Eventually the answer depends on the nature and quality of the occupancy. Was it intended that the occupier should have a stake in the room or did he have only permission for himself personally to occupy the room, whether under a contract or not? In which case he is a licensee."

But in my opinion in order to ascertain the nature and quality of the occupancy and to see whether the occupier has or has not a stake in the room or only permission for himself personally to occupy, the court must decide whether upon its true construction the agreement confers on the occupier exclusive possession. If exclusive possession at a rent for a term does not constitute a tenancy then the distinction between a contractual tenancy and a contractual licence of land becomes wholly unidentifiable.

In *Somma v Hazlehurst* [1978] 1 WLR 1014, [1978] 2 All ER 1011, a young unmarried couple H. and S. occupied a double bedsitting room for which they paid a weekly rent. The landlord did not provide services or attendance and the couple were not lodgers but tenants enjoying exclusive possession. But the Court of Appeal did not ask themselves whether H. and S. were lodgers or tenants and did not draw the correct conclusion from the fact that H. and S. enjoyed exclusive possession. The Court of Appeal were diverted from the correct inquiries by the fact that the landlord obliged H. and S. to enter into separate agreements and reserved power to determine each agreement separately. The landlord also insisted that the room should not in form be let to either H. or S. or to both H. and S. but that each should sign an agreement to share the room in common with such other persons as the landlord might from time to time nominate. The sham nature of this obligation would have been only slightly more obvious if H. and S. had been married or if the room had been furnished with a double bed instead of two single beds. If the landlord had served notice on H. to leave and had required S. to share the room with a strange man, the notice would only have been a disguised notice to quit on both H. and S. The room was let and taken as residential accommodation with exclusive possession in order that H. and S. might live together in undisturbed quasi-connubial bliss making weekly payments. The agreements signed by H. and S. constituted the grant to H. and S. jointly of exclusive possession at a rent for a term for the purposes for which the room was taken and the agreement therefore created a tenancy. Although the Rent Acts must not be allowed to alter or influence the construction of an agreement, the court should, in my opinion, be astute to detect and frustrate sham devices and artificial transactions whose only object is to disguise the grant of a tenancy and to evade the Rent Acts. I would disapprove of the decision in this case that H. and S. were only licensees and for the same reason would disapprove of the decision in *Aldrington Garages Ltd v Fielder* (1978) 37 P & CR 461 and *Sturolson & Co v Weniz* (1984) 272 EG 326.

In the present case the Court of Appeal, 271 EG 1261 held that the agreement dated 7 March 1983 only created a licence. Slade LJ at 1262 accepted that the agreement and in particular clause 3 of the agreement "shows that the right to occupy the premises conferred on the defendant was intended as an exclusive right of occupation, in that it was thought necessary to give a special and express power to the plaintiff to enter. . . ." Before your Lordships it was conceded that the agreement conferred the right of exclusive possession on Mrs Mountford. Even without clause 3 the result would have been the same. By the 'agreement Mrs Mountford was granted the right to occupy residential accommodation. The landlord did not provide any services or attendance. It was plain that Mrs Mountford was not a lodger. Slade LJ proceeded to analyse all the provisions of the agreement, not for the purpose of deciding whether his finding of exclusive possession was correct, but for the purpose of assigning some of the provisions of the agreement to the category of terms which he thought are usually to be found in a tenancy agreement and of assigning other provisions to the category of terms which he though are usually to be found in a licence. Slade LJ may or may not have been right that in a letting of a furnished room it was "most unusual to find a

provision in a tenancy agreement obliging the tenant to keep his rooms in a
'tidy condition' ": at 1262. If Slade LJ was right about this and other
provisions there is still no logical method of evaluating the results of his
survey. Slade LJ reached the conclusion that "the agreement bears all the
hallmarks of a licence, rather than a tenancy, save for the one important
feature of exclusive occupation": at 1262. But in addition to the hallmark of
exclusive occupation of residential accommodation there were the hallmarks
of weekly payments for a periodical term. Unless these three hallmarks are
decisive, it really becomes impossible to distinguish a contractual tenancy
from a contractual licence save by reference to the professed intention of the
parties or by the judge awarding marks for drafting. Slade LJ was finally
impressed by the statement at the foot of the agreement by Mrs Mountford
"I understand and accept that a licence in the above form does not and is not
intended to give me a tenancy protected under the Rent Acts." Slade LJ said,
at 1262:

"it seems to me that if the defendant is to displace the express statement of
intention embodied in the declaration, she must show that the declaration
was either a deliberate sham or at least an inaccurate statement of what was
the true substance of the real transaction agreed between the parties; . . ."

My Lords, the only intention which is relevant is the intention demonstrated by the agreement to grant exclusive possession for a term at a rent.
Sometimes it may be difficult to discover whether, on the true construction of
an agreement, exclusive possession is conferred[19]. Sometimes it may appear
from the surrounding circumstances that there was no intention to create
legal relationships. Sometimes it may appear from the surrounding circumstances that the right to exclusive possession is referable to a legal relationship
other than a tenancy. Legal relationships to which the grant of exclusive
possession might be referable and which would or might negative the grant of
an estate or interest in the land include occupancy under a contract for the
sale of the land, occupancy pursuant to a contract of employment or
occupancy referable to the holding of an office. But where as in the present
case the only circumstances are that residential accommodation is offered
and accepted with exclusive possession for a term at a rent, the result is a
tenancy.

The position was well summarised by Windeyer J sitting in the High
Court of Australia in *Radaich v Smith* (1959) 101 CLR 209 at 222, where he
said:

"What then is the fundamental right which a tenant has that distinguishes
his position from that of a licensee? It is an interest in land as distinct from a
personal permission to enter the land and use it for some stipulated purpose
or purposes. And how is it to be ascertained whether such an interest in land
has been given? By seeing whether the grantee was given a legal right of
exclusive possession of the land for a term or from year to year or for a life or
lives. If he was, he is a tenant. And he cannot be other than a tenant, because
a legal right of exclusive possession is a tenancy and the creation of such a
right is a demise. To say that a man who has, by agreement with a landlord,
a right of exclusive possession of land for a term is not a tenant is simply to

---

[19] See *Appah v Parncliffe Investments Ltd* [1964] 1 WLR 1064, [1964] 1 All ER 838; *University of
Reading v Johnson-Houghton* (1985) 276 EG 1353; *Wigan Borough Council v Green & Son (Wigan) Ltd*
[1985] 2 EGLR 242; p. 409, n. 21.

contradict the first proposition by the second. A right of exclusive possession is secured by the right of a lessee to maintain ejectment and, after his entry, trespass. A reservation to the landlord, either by contract or statute, of a limited right of entry, as for example to view or repair, is, of course, not inconsistent with the grant of exclusive possession. Subject to such reservations, a tenant for a term or from year to year or for a life or lives can exclude his landlord as well as strangers from the demised premises. All this is long established law: see *Cole on Ejectment* (1857) pp. 72, 73, 287, 458.''

My Lords, I gratefully adopt the logic and the language of Windeyer J. Henceforth the courts which deal with these problems will, save in exceptional circumstances, only be concerned to inquire whether as a result of an agreement relating to residential accommodation the occupier is a lodger or a tenant. In the present case I am satisfied that Mrs Mountford is a tenant, that the appeal should be allowed, that the order of the Court of Appeal should be set aside and that the respondent should be ordered to pay the costs of the appellant here and below[20].

In *Bracey v Read* [1963] Ch 88, [1962] 3 All ER 472[21], the plaintiff, in 1957, agreed to lease to the defendant land at Lambourn in Berkshire, on which to train and exercise racehorses. The lease was to be for a term of three years, after which it was to continue on a yearly tenancy. The plaintiff gave notice ending the right on 31 December 1961. The notice was adequate if the agreement of 1957 created a licence, but inadequate under the Landlord and Tenant Act 1954, Part II, if a lease[1].

Cross J, holding that the agreement of 1957 created a lease, referred to ''the question whether the defendant is entitled to protection under legislation which applies to tenancies, but does not apply to licences'', and said [1962] 3 All ER at 475: ''In the case of a business transaction like this I think that the question whether a man ought to be considered as a licensee or a tenant depends principally, if not entirely, on whether he has exclusive possession of the property in question. Under arrangements which are not of an ordinary business character, one very often has a man in exclusive possession of the property in question, who is yet not a tenant but only a licensee; but no case was cited to me, and I do not know of any case, where a man who is in exclusive possession under an ordinary business agreement has been held not to be a tenant but only a licensee. . . . I think, on the whole, that the proper conclusion from the facts is that the defendant was in possession of the gallops as tenant.''

---

[20] "The original rent of £37 per week was a compromise between Mr Street's suggestion for £39 and Mrs Mountford's suggestion for £35. The rent officer then fixed a 'fair' rent of £14. Costs as claimed (but not yet taxed) at the county court, Court of Appeal and House of Lords amount to some £40,000. Meanwhile, Mrs Mountford has vacated in return for a cash sum of £1,800. This can, in effect, be deducted from the £2,410 rent she paid whilst occupying the flat for 2½ years." (1985) 129 SJ 852 in a letter from G. Cutting, Chairman, Small Landlords Association.

[21] *University of Reading v Johnson-Houghton* (1985) 276 EG 1353 (grant of right to "gallops for racehorses at Blewbury in Berkshire held to be a lease" on the balance of probabilities . . . despite its title ('licence') and much of its language), per Leonard J at 1356; *Wigan Borough Council v Green & Son (Wigan) Ltd* [1985] 2 EGLR 242 ("permission to use exclusively" stalls in covered market for "a very substantial butcher's shop" held to be tenancy).

[1] A lease of an incorporeal hereditament is not within Part II; *Land Reclamation Co Ltd v Basildon District Council* [1979] 1 WLR 106 at 111, [1978] 2 All ER 1162 at 1166.

ii.   PROTECTED SHORTHOLD TENANCY

In order to encourage short-term leases of residential accommodation, the Housing Act 1980 created the protected shorthold tenancy. This is a regulated tenancy granted for a term certain of not less than one but not more than five years. It is subject to the ordinary machinery for determining maximum rent under the Rent Act 1977[2], but its advantage is that upon the termination of the tenancy the landlord (provided that he has given the appropriate notice) will be entitled to a mandatory order for possession.

HOUSING ACT 1980

51. Preliminary. — Sections 53 to 55 below modify the operation of the 1977 Act in relation to protected shorthold tenancies as defined in section 52 below.

52. Protected shorthold tenancies. — (1) A protected shorthold tenancy is a protected tenancy granted after the commencement of this section which is granted for a term certain of not less than one year nor more than five years and satisfies the following conditions, that is to say, —

(a) it cannot be brought to an end by the landlord before the expiry of the term, except in pursuance of a provision for re-entry or forfeiture for non-payment of rent or breach of any other obligation of the tenancy; and

(b) before the grant the landlord has given the tenant a valid notice stating that the tenancy is to be a protected shorthold tenancy; and

(c) either a rent for the dwelling-house is registered at the time the tenancy is granted or —

(i) a certificate of fair rent has, before the grant, been issued under section 69 of the 1977 Act in respect of the dwelling-house and the rent payable under the tenancy, for any period before a rent is registered for the dwelling-house, does not exceed the rent specified in the certificate; and

(ii) an application for the registration of a rent for the dwelling-house is made not later than 28 days after the beginning of the term and is not withdrawn.

(2) A tenancy of a dwelling-house is not a protected shorthold tenancy if it is granted to a person who, immediately before it was granted, was a protected or statutory tenant of that dwelling-house.

(3) A notice is not valid for the purposes of subsection (1) (b) above unless it complies with the requirements of regulations made by the Secretary of State.

(4) The Secretary of State may by order direct that subsection (1) above shall have effect, either generally or in relation to any registration area specified in the order, as if paragraph (c) were omitted.

(5) If a protected tenancy is granted after the commencement of this section —

(a) for such a term certain as is mentioned in subsection (1) above, to be followed, at the option of the tenant, by a further term; or

---

[2] See C & B, pp. 454–455. This requirement was removed for tenancies outside Greater London as from December 1981 by the Protected Shorthold Tenancies (Rent Registration) Order 1981 (SI No. 1578). See also Protected Shorthold Tenancies (Notice to Tenant) Regulations 1981 (SI No. 1579); [1982] Conv 29 (P. F. Smith); 126 SJ 3, 24, 41 (G. N. Prentice); (1982) 132 NLJ 55 (V. Fisher).

(*b*) for such a term certain and thereafter from year to year or some other period;

and satisfies the conditions stated in that subsection, the tenancy is a protected shorthold tenancy until the end of the term certain.

53. Right of tenant to terminate protected shorthold tenancy. — (1) A protected shorthold tenancy may be brought to an end (by virtue of this section and notwithstanding anything in the terms of the tenancy) before the expiry of the term certain by notice in writing of the appropriate length given by the tenant to the landlord; and the appropriate length of the notice is —

(*a*) one month if the term certain is two years or less; and

(*b*) three months if it is more than two years.

(2) Any agreement relating to a protected shorthold tenancy (whether or not contained in the instrument creating the tenancy) shall be void in so far as it purports to impose any penalty or disability on the tenant in the event of his giving a notice under this section.

54. Subletting or assignment. — (1) Where the whole or part of a dwelling-house let under a protected shorthold tenancy has been sublet at any time during the continuous period specified in subsection (3) below, and, during that period, the landlord becomes entitled, as against the tenant, to possession of the dwelling-house, he shall also be entitled to possession against the sub-tenant and section 137 of the 1977 Act shall not apply.

(2) A protected shorthold tenancy of a dwelling-house and any protected tenancy of the same dwelling-house granted during the continuous period specified in subsection (3) below shall not be capable of being assigned, except in pursuance of an order under section 24 of the Matrimonial Causes Act 1973.

(3) The continuous period mentioned in subsections (1) and (2) above is the period beginning with the grant of the protected shorthold tenancy and continuing until either —

(*a*) no person is in possession of the dwelling-house as a protected or statutory tenant; or

(*b*) a protected tenancy of the dwelling-house is granted to a person who is not, immediately before the grant, in possession of the dwelling-house as a protected or statutory tenant.

55. Orders for possession. — (1) The following Case shall be added to the Cases in Part II of Schedule 15 to the 1977 Act (mandatory orders for possession):

"Case 19

Where the dwelling-house was let under a protected shorthold tenancy (or is treated under section 55 of the Housing Act 1980 as having been so let) and —

(*a*) there either has been no grant of a further tenancy of the dwelling-house since the end of the protected shorthold tenancy or, if there was such a grant, it was to a person who immediately before the grant was in possession of the dwelling-house as a protected or statutory tenant; and

(*b*) the proceedings for possession were commenced after appropriate notice by the landlord to the tenant and not later than 3 months after the expiry of the notice.

A notice is appropriate for this Case if —

(i) it is in writing and states that proceedings for possession under this Case may be brought after its expiry; and

(ii) it expires not earlier than 3 months after it is served nor, if, when it is served, the tenancy is a periodic tenancy, before that periodic tenancy could be brought to an end by a notice to quit served by the landlord on the same day;

(iii) it is served —

(a) in the period of 3 months immediately preceding the date on which the protected shorthold tenancy comes to an end; or

(b) if that date has passed, in the period of 3 months immediately preceding any anniversary of that date; and

(iv) in a case where a previous notice has been served by the landlord on the tenant in respect of the dwelling-house, and that notice was an appropriate notice, it is served not earlier than 3 months after the expiry of the previous notice."

(2) If, in proceedings for possession under Case 19 set out above, the court is of opinion that, notwithstanding that the condition of paragraph (b) or (c) of section 52 (1) above is not satisfied, it is just and equitable to make an order for possession, it may treat the tenancy under which the dwelling-house was let as a protected shorthold tenancy.

QUESTIONS

1. Is there any good reason why freedom of contract should not prevail in:
   (a) a *Street v Mountford* situation;
   (b) a *Somma v Hazelhurst* situation? Is the unlikely but possible intrusion into quasi-connubial bliss (*Street v Mountford* [1985] AC 809 at 825, [1985] 2 All ER 289 at 299) a sufficient reason for preventing the parties from being held to a genuine bargain?

2. In the light of *Street v Mountford*, what advice would you now give to an owner of private residential accommodation who wants to let it but to avoid the security of tenure and rent control given to a tenant under the Rent Act 1977?

   Consider the following possibilities:
   (a) Draft the agreement as a licence. How do you avoid granting exclusive possession to the occupant?
   (b) Grant a protected shorthold tenancy under the Housing Act 1980, ss. 51–55, p. 409, ante.
   (c) Grant a tenancy under which the exceptions to the Rent Act apply: Rent Act 1977, ss. 4–16A. In particular:
      (i) Houses let by an exempted body: s. 8; Housing Act 1980, Sch. 3, para. 11.
      (ii) Lettings by resident landlords: s. 12. Such a tenancy is a restricted contract and subject to a different system of control under which there is far less security of tenure: s. 19.
      (iii) Lettings with board or attendance: s. 7.
      (iv) Holiday lettings: s. 9; [1984] Conv 286 (T. J. Lyons).
   (d) Abandon the idea of letting in any form, and sell to a purchaser who will probably be buying on mortgage as an owner-occupier, and thereby remove a unit from the pool of private rented accommodation. See C & B, pp. 450–465, and other references at p. 377, n. 11, ante.

III.   Creation[3]

A.   Statutory Requirements

LAW OF PROPERTY ACT 1925

54.   Creation of interest in land by parol. — (1) p. 77, ante.
(2) p. 79, ante.

52.   Conveyances to be by deed. — (1) p. 76, ante.
(2) (d) p. 77, ante[4].

Special provisions relate to the creation and disposition of leaseholds in registered land and these are set out below[5].

B.   Tenancies at Common Law

i.   TENANCIES AT WILL AND AT SUFFERANCE
Entry into possession as a tenant, or holding over with the landlord's consent after the expiration of the tenancy, creates a tenancy at will[6].

A tenant who holds over without the landlord's consent becomes a tenant at sufferance. There is a presumption that such tenancies expand to become weekly, monthly or yearly tenancies where rent is paid and accepted, the length of the tenancy being related to the period in respect of which the rent is paid[7].

In *Wheeler v Mercer* [1957] AC 416, [1956] 3 All ER 631 Viscount SIMONDS said at 426, at 634: "It may, I think, be truly said that, since a tenant at will is regarded at law as being in possession by his own will and at the will, express or implied, of his landlord, he is a tenant by their mutual agreement. . . . He is distinguished from a tenant at sufferance in that such a tenant is said to be in possession without either the agreement or disagreement of the landlord. . . . A tenancy at will . . . has been properly described as a personal relation between the landlord and his tenant: it is determined by the death of either of them or by any one of a variety of acts, even by an involuntary alienation, which would not affect the subsistence of any other tenancy[8]."

In *Heslop v Burns* [1974] 1 WLR 1241, [1974] 3 All ER 406, SCARMAN LJ said at 1253, at 416:

---

[3] C & B, pp. 370–387; M & W, pp. 636–665; MM, pp. 344–348.
[4] This includes a lease for a period exceeding three years even though it may be determinable within the period: *Kushner v Law Society* [1952] 1 KB 264, [1952] 1 All ER 404.
[5] See pp. 107–109, ante, pp. 471–477, post.
[6] It is occasionally created by express agreement; *Morgan v William Harrison Ltd* [1907] 2 Ch 137; *Manfield & Sons Ltd v Botchin* [1970] 2 QB 612, [1970] 3 All ER 143; *Hagee (London) Ltd v A B Erikson and Larson* [1976] QB 209, [1975] 3 All ER 234 (a tenancy at will avoids the provisions of L & T A 1954 Part II).
[7] *Clayton v Blakey* (1798) 8 Term Rep 3; *Dougal v McCarthy* [1893] 1 QB 736; *Marcroft Wagons Ltd v Smith* [1951] 2 KB 496, [1951] 2 All ER 271; *Longrigg, Burrough and Trounson v Smith* (1979) 251 EG 847.
[8] C & B, pp. 380–382; M & W, pp. 654–655; MM, pp. 343–344.

"It may be that the tenancy at will can now serve only one legal purpose, and that is to protect the interests of an occupier during a period of transition. If one looks to the classic cases in which tenancies at will continue to be inferred, namely, the case of someone who goes into possession prior to a contract of purchase, or of someone who, with the consent of the landlord, holds over after the expiry of his lease, one sees that in each there is a transitional period during which negotiations are being conducted touching the estate or interest in the land that has to be protected, and the tenancy at will is an apt legal mechanism to protect the occupier during such a period of transition: he is there and can keep out trespassers: he is there with the consent of the landlord and can keep out the landlord as long as that consent is maintained."

ii. YEARLY BASIS

ADLER v BLACKMAN
[1952] 2 All ER 41 (QBD, ORMEROD J)[9]

Blackman had held shop premises under a weekly tenancy until December 1947, from which date the tenancy was changed to a yearly tenancy on the following terms: "To hold for the term of one year . . . at the exclusive weekly rent of £3 payable weekly . . .". After the expiration of the year, Blackman held over and Adler served on him a notice to quit, which was valid if he held a weekly, void if he held a yearly, tenancy. The notice to quit was first accepted by Blackman, whose first reaction was to claim compensation or a new lease under the Landlord and Tenant Act 1927. He subsequently claimed that the notice was invalid.

Held. Notice valid, as Blackman was a weekly tenant.

ORMEROD J: The questions to be decided are: Was the tenant holding these premises as a tenant from year to year, in which case, of course, this notice was invalid, or was he holding them on a weekly tenancy, in which case admittedly the notice is good? Secondly, even if the notice was invalid, as the tenant elected to treat it as valid by taking proceedings under the Landlord and Tenant Act, 1927, can he now say that the notice was invalid and that he is entitled to remain in possession of the premises? So far as the first point is concerned, it is clearly established that, if a tenant holds over with the consent of the landlord at the expiration of a period reserved by a lease or tenancy agreement, an implied tenancy is set up, and the presumption is that that tenancy is a yearly tenancy on the terms of the instrument creating the original tenancy so far as they are consistent with a yearly tenancy, but that presumption may be rebutted by various circumstances including, of course, the terms of the agreement itself. I am asked by the landlord to say that the fact that the original tenancy was admittedly a weekly tenancy is a circumstance which should be taken into account in rebutting this presumption. The agreement for a tenancy for twelve months, in which the rent was expressed to be payable by the week and was calculated by the week and not by the year, says the landlord, is also a very strong circumstance to take into account. Further, he says that the conduct of the parties after the expiration

---

[9] Affirmed by CA (SOMERVELL, JENKINS and HODSON LJJ) [1953] 1 QB 146, [1952] 2 All ER 945, where the decision of MACNAGHTEN J in *Covered Markets Ltd v Green* [1947] 2 All ER 140 was overruled.

of the period of tenancy, and, particularly, when the notice to quit was served by the landlord on the tenant, establishes beyond doubt the inference that the tenancy was not a tenancy from year to year. . . .

In *Covered Markets Ltd v Green* [1947] 2 All ER 140 a tenant held over at the expiration of a tenancy for seven years at a rent of £3, payable weekly. Macnaghten J decided that the presumption was that the tenancy was a yearly one, and he saw no reason to rebut that presumption. He distinguished that case from Maugham J's decision on the ground that the premises were a fishmonger's shop, whereas the premises in the *Ladies' Hosiery* case [1930] 1 Ch 304 were merely a piece of ground. I find it difficult to appreciate the distinction, but Macnaghten J very clearly held that the proper inference from the circumstances was that there was a yearly tenancy on the termination of the seven years.

I have to consider whether in the present case there is a yearly tenancy or whether the circumstances are such that the presumption of a yearly tenancy has been rebutted and the tenant holds the premises on a weekly tenancy only. I have come to the conclusion that I ought to hold that the presumption has been rebutted and that the tenancy is a weekly one. I am not influenced by the situation before the agreement for a yearly tenancy was entered into. I do not think I ought to regard that as relevant to the consideration of the circumstances because it may well be that the parties decided that they would have the tenancy on an entirely new basis. There is no evidence about that one way or the other. The terms of the tenancy under the agreement were very different from the terms of the tenancy before it, including the rent, the terms relating to repairs, and so on, but I do take into consideration strongly the fact that the rent was expressed to be the rent of £3 per week and was never calculated by reference to a yearly sum. It was always paid weekly, and, after the term of the agreement had expired, it continued to be paid weekly right up to the time when the notice to quit was given. . . . The notice to quit was served on the basis that the tenancy was a weekly one, and was accepted without question by the tenant. Clearly the tenant's view was that he was holding on a weekly tenancy and not on a yearly tenancy, and I see no reason why that should not be taken into account in deciding whether the presumption of a yearly tenancy has been rebutted. Even if that were not the case, however, I think that, where as here, the original tenancy is not for a period of years, but is for only one year, and where the rent payable is expressed as a weekly sum and not by reference to a yearly rent, the presumption is rebutted that there is a yearly tenancy and the tenant must be taken to be holding over on the basis of a weekly tenancy on the terms of the agreement so far as they are consistent therewith. It follows that the notice was valid and the landlord is entitled to succeed in this action.

[ORMEROD J found it unnecessary to decide the second question. If it had been necessary to decide it, he would have held that the tenant, by claiming a new lease under the Landlord and Tenant Act 1927, had elected to accept the notice and could not now say that it was invalid.]

iii.   THE TERMS OF A YEARLY TENANCY

Where a tenant obtains a yearly (or other periodic) tenancy by entry followed by payment of rent in pursuance of an agreement to grant a lease or of a purported grant which is void for lack of a seal, the terms of the tenancy include such of those of the void grant as are consistent with a tenancy for the period in question[10].

iv.   CERTAINTY OF TIME. REPUGNANCY

CENTAPLOY LTD v MATLODGE LTD
[1974] Ch 1, [1973] 2 All ER 720 (ChD, WHITFORD J)

In 1968 the defendant landlords' predecessors in title agreed to let to the plaintiffs a lock-up garage and workshop premises in Ashburn Mews, London on the written terms: "Ground floor garage. Received from Centaploy Ltd the sum of £12 being one week's rent on 25 Ashburn Mews, S.W.7, the tenancy to continue thus on the same terms until determined by the lessee."

In 1971 the defendants purported to determine the tenancy by giving the plaintiffs a week's notice to quit. The question was whether, in view of the terms of the agreement, they were entitled to do so.

Held. The agreement was void for repugnancy, and the notice to quit was valid.

WHITFORD J: The Court of Appeal has held in *Re Midland Railway Co's Agreement* [1971] Ch 725, [1971] 1 All ER 1007[11], that the simple statement of the law that if a term is to be validly created the maximum duration of that term must be ascertained before the term takes effect, cannot have direct application to periodic tenancies. It is, apparently, enough if you know when it could be brought to an end even if you do not know exactly when it will be brought to an end.

The law is evolutionary. In the evolution of life it is common enough to find that forms which were at one time successful have died out completely or changed radically. The defendants accept that a fetter can be placed on the right to determine a periodic tenancy for a certain period. They also accept, in this court, though they expressly reserve the point for a higher court, that, on the authority of *Re Midland Railway Co's Agreement*, it must be accepted here such a fetter can be placed upon the right to determine for an uncertain period. The defendants base themselves further on a decision given by the Court of King's Bench in *Doe d Warner v Browne* (1807) 8 East 165, where it was decided that it was repugnant to the nature of a tenancy from year to year that the right to determine should rest solely with the tenant, a decision approved by the Court of Appeal in *Cheshire Lines Committee v Lewis & Co* (1880) 50 LJQB 121.

Uncertainty and repugnancy were the defendants' main ground of attack assuming agreements in other respects unimpeachable. The submission of the plaintiffs on repugnancy was basically that this must be considered to be a ghost of the past and I was urged to pass on unafraid. In fact both the plaintiffs and the defendants relied upon the judgment of the Court of Appeal in *Re Midland Railway Co's Agreement* . . .

In the present case the position on uncertainty is somewhat different. Here we have a period growing week by week and there is never going to be any

---

[10] *Doe d Rigg v Bell* (1793) 5 Term Rep 471; *Doe d Thomson v Amey* (1840) 12 Ad & El 476; C & B, p. 385; M & W, pp. 639, 649–650; MM, pp. 336, 341–342.

[11] P. 360, ante.

possibility of knowing, on the landlord's side, its maximum length, for there is never going to be a right in the landlords to determine.

In *Re Midland Railway Co's Agreement*, counsel for the defendants submitted that a periodic tenancy is only an exception to the uncertainty rule, because if both sides are going to be able to determine there is no relevant uncertainty: see [1971] Ch 725 at 730, [1971] 1 All ER 1007 at 1008. In the present case a stronger case can be made out on the defendants' side than was made out in *Re Midland Railway Co's Agreement*. It can be urged that as the landlord cannot ever be certain when the agreement is going to be brought to an end there must be a relevant uncertainty. As I understand the judgment in the Court of Appeal, what has been held in relation to the issue of uncertainty is that it is better to enforce a clearly expressed bargain than to attempt to introduce yet further refinements into a field where the lines have perhaps already been rather over-finely drawn. On this basis I have reached the conclusion, having regard to what was said in the Court of Appeal in *Re Midland Railway Co's Agreement*, that I must reject the defendants' argument on the basis of uncertainty which, but for *Re Midland Railway Co's Agreement*, I would have been prepared to accept. . . .

In *Re Midland Railway Co's Agreement* the point which I have to consider — the ghost of the past — was expressly left unlaid. Here we have a case where the tenant is saying that on the bargain struck the landlord cannot ever determine the tenancy.

Now counsel for the plaintiffs was able to say, and to say quite rightly, that great inroads have been made on the application of this idea of repugnancy since 1807, as the passage I have just read shows, and there is no need for me to go into the cases between *Doe d Warner v Browne* and *Re Midland Railway Co's Agreement*, for it is now plain that a fetter for a period, even a period of uncertain duration, cannot necessarily be considered as repugnant to the grant of a periodic tenancy. It nevertheless appears to me that it must be basic to a tenancy that at some stage the person granting the tenancy shall have the right to determine and a tenancy in which the landlord is never going to have the right to determine at all is, as I see it, a complete contradiction in terms. Unless, therefore, some greater estate than a weekly tenancy was created by the agreements, the determination provisions must, in my view, be regarded as repugnant and on this aspect the defendants are entitled to succeed.

V.   TENANCY BY ESTOPPEL[12]

In *Webb v Austin* (1844) 7 Man & G 701, TINDAL CJ said at 724: "The doctrine on this subject, as it has been generally understood by the profession, may be collected from Mr *Preston's Treatise on Abstracts*, vol. ii, p. 210, and the authorities there cited. That general understanding appears to be, that 'An indenture of lease, or a fine *sur concessit*, for years, will be an estoppel only during the term. It first operates by way of estoppel, and finally, when the grantor obtains an ownership, it attaches on the seisin and

[12] Spencer Bower and Turner, *The Law Relating to Estoppel by Representation* (3rd edn, 1977), pp. 191–211; C & B, pp. 385–387; M & W, pp. 660–663; MM, pp. 346–348; (1964) 80 LQR 370 (A. M. Prichard); *Industrial Properties (Barton Hill) Ltd v Associated Electrical Industries Ltd* [1977] QB 580, [1977] 2 All ER 293, p. 82, ante, p. 418, post; (1977) 40 MLR 718 (P. Jackson); [1978] Conv 137 (J. Martin).

creates an interest, or produces the relation of landlord and tenant; and there is a term *commencing* by estoppel, but *for all purposes* it becomes an estate or interest. It binds the estate of the lessor, &c., and therefore continues in force against the lessor, his heirs, &c. It also binds the assigns of the lessor and of the lessee'."

(a) Determination of the Tenant's Estate

INDUSTRIAL PROPERTIES (BARTON HILL) LTD *v* ASSOCIATED ELECTRICAL INDUSTRIES LTD
[1977] QB 580, [1977] 2 All ER 293 (CA, LORD DENNING MR, ROSKILL and LAWTON LJJ)[13]

LORD DENNING MR: In the course of the discussion we were referred to many authorities, old and new. I have considered them all[14] — and others, too — but the result can be stated thus: If a landlord lets a tenant into possession under a lease, then, so long as the tenant remains in possession *undisturbed by any adverse claim* — then the tenant cannot dispute the landlord's title. Suppose the tenant (not having been disturbed) goes out of possession and the landlord sues the tenant on the covenant for rent or for breach of covenant to repair or to yield up in repair. The tenant cannot say to the landlord: "You are not the true owner of the property." Likewise, if the landlord, on the tenant's holding over, sues him for possession or for use and occupation or mesne profits, the tenant cannot defend himself by saying: "The property does not belong to you, but to another."

But if the tenant is disturbed *by being evicted by title paramount or the equivalent* of it, then he can dispute the landlord's title. Suppose the tenant is actually turned out by the third person — or if the tenant, without going out, acknowledges the title of the third person by attorning to him — or the tenant contests the landlord's claim on an indemnity from the third person — or there is anything else done which is equivalent to an eviction by title paramount — then the tenant is no longer estopped from denying the landlord's title: see *Wilson v Anderton* (1830) 1 B & Ad 450 at 457, per Littledale J. The tenant, being thus disturbed in his possession, can say to the landlord: "You were not truly the owner at the time when you demanded and received the rent from me. I am liable to pay mesne profits to this other man. So you must repay me the rent which I overpaid you. Nor am I liable to you on the covenants during the time you were not the owner." See *Newsome v Graham* (1829) 10 B & C 234, *Mountnoy v Collier* (1853) 1 E & B 630 and *Watson v Lane* (1856) 11 Exch 769. The tenant can also claim damages for the eviction if there is, as here, an express covenant for quiet enjoyment covering interruption by title paramount.

Short of eviction by title paramount, or its equivalent, however, the tenant is estopped from denying the title of the landlord. It is no good his saying: "The property does not belong to you but to a third person" unless that third person actually comes forward and successfully makes an adverse claim —by

---

[13] The facts are stated at p. 82, ante. (1977) 40 MLR 718 (P. Jackson); [1978] Conv 137 (J. Martin).
[14] His Lordship approved *Cuthbertson v Irving* (1859) 4 H & N 742; affd (1860) 6 H & N 135, and overruled *Harrison v Wells* [1967] 1 QB 263, [1966] 3 All ER 524, on the ground that it was decided per incuriam.

process in the courts or by the tenant's attornment; or acknowledgment of it as by the tenant defending on an indemnity. If the third person, for some reason or other, makes no adverse claim or is debarred from making it, the tenant remains estopped from denying the landlord's title. This is manifestly correct: for, without an adverse claim, it would mean that the tenant would be enabled to keep the property without paying any rent to anybody or performing any covenants. That cannot be right. That was the reasoning adopted by the Court of Queen's Bench in *Biddle v Bond* (1865) 6 B & S 225, a case of a bailor and bailee, but the court treated it as the same as landlord *v* tenant. . . .

In the present case the tenants, A.E.I., are not subject to any adverse claim whatever. The lessor to A.E.I. was the plaintiff company which was the equitable owner. The legal owners were the Parker trustees. They were also the directors and shareholders of the plaintiff company. They acquiesced in the lease being made by the plaintiff company to A.E.I. They could not by any possibility make any adverse claim against A.E.I. on their own account. Not only that. They have actually come in as plaintiffs in these proceedings jointly with the plaintiff company — so as to make sure that the benefit of these proceedings goes to the plaintiff company only.

Seeing that A.E.I. are absolved from any adverse claim by the legal owners, it is a very proper case for the doctrine of tenancy by estoppel. A.E.I. have had the full benefit of the lease for the stipulated term of years. They should perform the covenants — or pay damages in lieu — to the only persons entitled to sue them, namely, the plaintiff company. Even though A.E.I. have gone out of possession, they cannot avoid their responsibilities by reliance on a technical rule of law — which on investigation is found to be groundless.

(*b*) *Determination of the Landlord's Estate*

NATIONAL WESTMINSTER BANK LTD *v* HART
[1983] QB 773, [1983] 2 All ER 177 (CA, WALLER LJ and
SIR DAVID CAIRNS)[15]

42 Haggard Road, Twickenham, was let under a 99 year lease expiring in 1967. In 1921 Cowles acquired the residue of the lease, and in 1947 sub-let the house to Hart. The sub-lease expired in 1965. Thereafter Hart continued to pay rent to Cowles until 1978, when, on the death of Cowles, he claimed that Cowles's title had expired in 1967. He refused to pay rent to Cowles's executor, the plaintiff bank, until it proved title. In the county court the plaintiff recovered arrears of rent on the ground that Hart was estopped from denying its title, since there was no third party claim to a better title.

Held (reversing the county court judge). Hart was not estopped from denying the bank's title.

WALLER LJ: The defendants submit that they became tenants of this house before 1965, at which time they became tenants of the Cowles, and that the Cowles made no communication to them in 1967 when the headlease expired. The defendants cannot be estopped by the fact that they paid rent from March 1967 until August 1978, because they did not know the facts, and the Cowles did not tell them. They submit that neither the Cowles nor

---

[15] [1984] Conv 64 (J. W. Price).

their personal representatives have title to 42, Haggard Road. They rely on *Fenner v Duplock* (1824) 2 Bing 10 and *Serjeant v Nash, Field & Co* [1903] 2 KB 304, and submit that the judge was in error in his conclusions.

The bank submit that the defendants are not entitled to succeed because they are unable to prove an adverse claim by a third party. They rely on *Carlton v Bowcock* (1884) 51 LT 659 and *Hindle v Hick Bros Manufacturing Co Ltd* [1947] 2 All ER 825.

The judge, being of opinion that the reasoning in *Carlton's* case and *Hindle's* case was inconsistent with *Fenner's* case and *Serjeant's* case, preferred *Carlton* and *Hindle*, and since there was no adverse claim by a third party on the facts of this case, gave judgment for the bank. . . .

Can the reasoning of these two lines of cases be reconciled? The bank submit that they are not inconsistent because in *Fenner v Duplock*, and in *Serjeant v Nash, Field & Co* although in neither case did the judges mention it, there was in each case a third party claimant. There was in each case a possible third party claimant, but in my judgment the existence of such a person was not regarded by the judge as important. In *Fenner's* case, Best CJ, having said that a tenant may show that his title has expired, said, at 11, that the rule was founded on good sense, "because if it were otherwise, the tenant might be called on to pay his rent twice over." And in *Serjeant v Nash, Field & Co* the observations of each member of the court were quite specific, and I cannot believe that the necessity would have gone unmentioned by each member of the court if it was regarded as a requirement.

Mr Parker, on behalf of the defendants, submits that the decisions are quite consistent because when considering estoppel there is a great difference between the case of the landlord's title determining without informing a tenant so that the tenant in ignorance continues to pay rent, and the case of the landlord assigning his interest and the tenant, aware that there has been an assignment, paying rent to the assignee. In the latter case he is on notice that there has been a change of landlord and it is for him to decide whether to pay his rent to the assignee or not. If he does, he cannot be heard to complain about the assignee's title unless there is somebody else claiming title. It is clear from the care with which Cave J set out the receipts in his judgment that he regarded them as important because they gave notice of the change. In the former case of the landlord's title determining, the tenant does not know because nothing has happened to give him notice of the change. There can be no estoppel unless the tenant knows the facts or he has had notice which should have warned him.

As Mr Parker pointed out, there is a logical difference between the assignee and the landlord whose title has determined. When the tenant has freely entered into a tenancy agreement with the landlord and has as a consequence entered into possession, so long as he is in possession he is estopped from denying his landlord's title. However, the tenant whose landlord has assigned the tenancy and he, with notice, has accepted the assignee, cannot challenge the assignee's title unless there is a third party claiming to be the landlord.

Finally, in the case of the landlord whose title has determined and who has not informed the tenant:

"It is clear law that though a tenant cannot deny the title of his landlord to deal with the premises, he may prove that the title has determined." (See per Sir Richard Henn Collins MR in *Serjeant's* case [1903] 2 KB 304 at 312.)

In the present case in my opinion if the Cowles had told the defendants in 1967 that title had determined, the tenants would have been under no obligation to pay rent to them. The Cowles not having disclosed the fact that their title had determined, the defendants cannot now be estopped from relying on the determination. I have come to the conclusion that the defendants are not liable to pay rent to the bank, and I would allow this appeal.

Sir David Cairns: I would add that it seems to me that the bank in this case might have contended that they and their predecessors had been in possession of the rents and profits for more than 12 years, paying no rent and in no way recognising the rights of whoever may have been the freeholder, and that in that way they might have acquired a possessory title. But no such case was open to them on the pleadings, nor discussed in the court below.

(c) Feeding the Estoppel

CHURCH OF ENGLAND BUILDING SOCIETY v PISKOR
[1954] Ch 553, [1954] 2 All ER 85 (CA, Evershed MR, Birkett and Romer LJJ)

In September 1946, the defendants contracted to purchase leasehold premises at No. 32, Harold Road, Croydon, and were allowed to go into possession before completion. Early in November they purported to grant a weekly tenancy of part of No. 32 to a Captain Hamilton. On 25 November the purchase was completed by an assignment of the lease to the defendants. On the same day they executed a legal charge in favour of the plaintiffs, which stated that No. 32 "is now vested in the mortgagors free from incumbrances for the unexpired residue of the term", and also that the mortgagor's power of leasing under Law of Property Act 1925, section 99 (1) was excluded. Captain Hamilton then sub-let to Miss Hunnex, who was protected by the Rent Acts. The plaintiffs (the mortgagees) claimed possession on the ground that they had a legal title paramount to her tenancy.

Held (affirming Vaisey J). The plaintiffs were not entitled to possession.

Romer LJ: I agree. The theory that a purchase, which is completed by payment of money which has been provided in part by a third party, and a mortgage by the purchaser of the property sold to secure the repayment of that money to the lender, constitutes only one transaction, if the instruments are executed at more or less the same time, is a conception which has a prima facie appeal, but it does not, on analysis, in my opinion, truly reflect the legal effect of what takes place. The mortgage of the purchased property cannot have any operation in law (whatever rights it may give rise to in equity or by estoppel) unless and until the purchaser is in a position to vest a legal term in the property, as security, in the mortgagee, and he is not and cannot be in a position to do this until he himself has acquired from the vendor the legal estate out of which the mortgage term is capable of being created. From this it follows that the execution and delivery of the conveyance (if the property is freehold) or of the assignment (in the case of a leasehold) by the vendor to the purchaser must of necessity constitute an essential preliminary to the vesting in the mortgagee of a subsidiary interest in the property. Mr Lightman pressed upon us the necessity of looking at the substance rather than the form of the transaction which took place in the present case and referred us to such cases as *Meux v Smith* (1843) 11 Sim 410 in support of that proposition. I am very willing to do so, but the substance of the transaction was that the purchasers were to purchase property with money lent in part by the building society and give the society a mortgage on the property for the loan. All this has in fact been done and the society has got its security but, look at it how one will, the fact remains that the purchasers could not have given the society the legal charge which the society required unless, at the time when the charge was executed, the purchasers were the owners of the legal interest in the property charged. That this was recognised by the society itself is sufficiently shown by the fact that there appears in the schedule to the charge the statement that the premises were then (that is to say, at the moment of the delivery of the charge) vested in the mortgagors — a circumstance of evidence upon which Danckwerts J relied in *Woolwich Equitable Building Society v Marshall* [1952] Ch 1, [1951] 2 All ER 769. I agree with Danckwerts J that the plaintiffs, having inserted that statement in the charge, cannot very well complain if the statement is regarded as true. Even without this element, however, I should still regard the legal interest in the purchased premises as having become vested in the purchasers prior to the execution of the charge for, as I say, unless this sequence of interests is observed, the charge would have been wholly ineffective in law to achieve its immediate purpose. I agree with Mr Alcock's submission that a composite transaction cannot be regarded as being one transaction, unless it is not only one but one and indivisible; and that two transactions, each possessing a legal individuality of its own, do not coalesce into one merely because they are dependent on each other.

The whole object of the plaintiffs in trying to displace the view which is both logical and in conformity with conveyancing practice, namely, that the completion of the purchase preceded by however short a time the execution and delivery of the mortgage, is to defeat the claim of the sitting tenants. But for the Rent Restriction Acts the point would have had no importance and would, I suppose, never have been taken at all, for the society could have determined the tenancies by the service of notices to quit; and I find myself unable to treat as one what were, in law, two palpably distinct transactions merely for the purpose of enabling the society to evict persons, who were already in occupation, but whose existence or rights the society had never troubled to inquire about at all. . . .

For the above reasons, and those given by the Master of the Rolls, I agree that the appeal should be dismissed[16].

vi.　CONCURRENT LEASES[17]

LAW OF PROPERTY ACT 1925

149. Abolition of interesse termini, and as to reversionary leases and leases for lives. —

(2) See p. 381, ante.

(5) Nothing in this Act affects the rule of law that a legal term, whether or not being a mortgage term, may be created to take effect in reversion expectant on a longer term, which rule is hereby confirmed.

---

[16] See *Security Trust Co v Royal Bank of Canada* [1976] AC 503, [1976] 1 All ER 381.
[17] M & W, pp. 664–665.

When a landlord grants a lease, and then later grants another lease of the same land (for more or less than the period of the first lease), there are concurrent leases, and he is said to have granted a lease of the reversion[18]. This creates the relationship of landlord and tenant between the first and second lessees; the second lessee does not need to go into possession[19], but, by virtue of his legal estate, he can as reversioner claim rent, distrain, and enforce covenants. This is so, even if the second lease is for a term shorter than the first one[20]. If his lease continues after the end of the first lease, he is entitled to possession when the first lease terminates.

In *Re Moore and Hulm's Contract* [1912] 2 Ch 105, leaseholds were mortgaged by sub-demise for the residue of the original term less one day. Afterwards by another mortgage they were sub-demised to a second mortgagee (Worrell) for the same period, subject to the first mortgate. The second mortgage was paid off during the continuance of the first mortgage and the deed effecting the second mortgage was handed back to the mortgagor. A purchaser of the freeholds from the mortgagor declined to complete without a formal surrender being obtained of the term created by the second mortgage. JOYCE J held that a surrender was necessary and said at 109: "[Counsel for the vendor] says, first, that there was no necessity or reason for Worrell, the second mortgagee, to surrender the term granted to him by the second mortgage because no legal term or interest passed to him. Bearing in mind, however, the cases cited to me by [counsel for the purchaser], I think that a legal estate or interest did pass to the second mortgagee. I think that Worrell acquired a legal reversion upon the term created by the first mortgage. I think that he got a legal term under his mortgage. If the money secured by the earlier mortgage had been paid to the first mortgagee on the date fixed for payment I think that the second mortgagee would have had a right to the actual possession of the leasehold premises[1], and if the lease granted by the first mortgage had been terminated in any manner during the continuance of the second mortgage, the second mortgagee would have been entitled to possession for the rest of the term created by his mortgage. Therefore I think that the argument for the vendor on the first point fails. . . .

There must be a declaration that the vendor is bound to obtain a surrender of the term created by the second mortgage."

C. Lease to Self

LAW OF PROPERTY ACT 1925

72. Conveyances by a person to himself, &c. —
(3) See p. 77, ante.
(4) See p. 77, ante.

---

[18] Distinguish a reversionary lease, p. 381, ante.
[19] LPA 1925, s. 149 (2), p. 381, ante.
[20] *Neale v Mackenzie* (1836) 1 M & W 747; *Re Moore and Hulm's Contract* [1912] 2 Ch 105.
[1] For a mortgagee's right to possession, see p. 689, post.

RYE *v* RYE[2]
[1962] AC 496, [1962] 1 All ER 146 (HL, Viscount SIMONDS,
Lords MACDERMOTT, REID, RADCLIFFE and DENNING)

In 1942 Arthur Rye, the appellant, and his brother Frank, who were in
partnership as solicitors, became owners of freehold premises in London as
tenants in common in equal shares. They decided to transfer the practice
there and orally agreed that the firm should be granted a yearly tenancy of
the premises at a rent of £500 a year to be paid out of the partnership assets.
In 1948 Frank died, and the freehold was vested in Arthur and the two
trustees of Frank's will, one of whom was Frank's son, Ralph, the respondent. In 1950 Arthur took Ralph into a partnership, which was dissolved in
1957. Ralph refused to leave the premises, where he continued to occupy a
room. Arthur claimed possession of the room, on the ground that the firm
was the tenant under the oral yearly tenancy of 1942, and that he was the
surviving partner.

Held (affirming CA). No tenancy was created in 1942, and, therefore, the
claim for possession failed.

VISCOUNT SIMONDS: The first [question] is whether it is competent for two
persons orally to grant to themselves an annual tenancy of premises of which
they are the owners. . . .

It is common ground, my Lords, that before the Law of Property Act 1925
came into force it could not [be granted]. But the appellant claims that the
law has been altered by the combined effect of sections 72 and 205 of that
Act. In the courts below the meaning and effect of section 205 (1) (ii)[3] has
been the main topic of discussion, and it appears to have been readily
assumed that, if "conveyance" includes the oral grant (or agreement to make
a grant) of an annual tenancy, then either subsection (3) or subsection (4) of
section 72 validates the transaction. I do not differ from those of your
Lordships who think that section 205 (1) (ii) has not this effect, nor do I
think that any assistance is given by section 52 or section 54. But I would
briefly examine the position if the contrary view prevails and an oral grant of
a tenancy is a "conveyance" within the meaning of the Act and "convey" has
a corresponding meaning.

I turn, then, to section 72 . . . Let me take subsection (4) first. In this
subsection I do not find it provided that two persons may convey property to
themselves or three persons to themselves. On the contrary, I read the
subsection literally as meaning that where property is vested in two persons
they may convey it to one of themselves and where it is vested in three
persons they may convey it to one or two of themselves. I see no reason for
giving a more extended meaning to this subsection, and I would point out
that, if it did have the meaning claimed for it, it would add nothing to
subsection (3) except to provide a plain inconsistency in respect of the date of
commencement. I come back to subsection (3). I accept that in this
subsection the singular "person" must include the plural so that two persons
may now convey land to, or vest land in, themselves. What, then, is the scope
of this subsection? It is said on behalf of the appellant that it enables A., the
owner of property, to grant a lease of it to himself and similarly enables A.

---

[2] (1962) 78 LQR 175 (P. V. B.); 177 (R. E. M.).
[3] See p. 9, ante.

and B., the joint owners of property, to grant a lease of it to themselves. It was not, I think, suggested that A. and B. could do what A. could not do. The question, then, can conveniently be examined by asking whether the subsection enables A. to grant a lease to himself of land of which he is the owner, or, in other words, to carve out of his larger estate a lesser estate which creates (I know not how to put it otherwise) the relationship of landlord and tenant between himself and himself. I find this a strange conception. In *Grey v Ellison* (1856) 1 Giff 438, 444, Stuart V-C describes as fanciful and a whimsical transaction the proposal that a man should grant a lease to himself. He had, no doubt, in mind that a lease is in one aspect contractual. Of things necessary to a lease, says Sheppard's Touchstone of Assurances (see 7th edn., vol. II, p. 268), one is that: "There must be an acceptance, [actual or presumed], of the thing demised." Yet it is meaningless to say that a man accepts from himself something which is already his own. I recognise that a lease not only has a contractual basis between lessor and lessee, but operates also to vest an estate in the lessee. But what sort of estate is in these circumstances vested in the lessee? I will assume that it will not at once merge in the higher estate from which it springs, though I see no reason why it should not. Yet it must be an estate hitherto unknown to the law. Even a bare demise implies certain covenants at law: but to such an estate as this no covenants can be effectively attached. Nor can the common law remedy of distress operate to enable the lessor to distrain on his own goods. Again, at law in the absence of some special provision the lessee is entitled to exclusive possession of the demised premises. What meaning is to be attributed to this where the lessee is also the lessor? My Lords, my mind recoils against an interpretation of the Act which leads to so fanciful and whimsical a result, and it appears to me to be quite unnecessary.

If, then, it is asked what meaning can be given to the subsection, I think that the answer is that it is intended partly to supersede the old conveyancing device of a conveyance to uses or of a grant and regrant and partly to provide an essential step in the new machinery set up by the series of Acts passed in 1925. To the latter the word "vest" itself supplies a clue. It appears to refer to the statutory provisions for vesting the legal estate in a tenant for life or statutory owner, which are to be found, for example, in Schedule II, paragraph 1, to the Settled Land Act 1925.

Thirty-five years have now passed since the Law of Property Act came into operation. I have not found in any of the textbooks that I have been able to consult dealing with real property or the relation of landlord and tenant any suggestion that section 72 of the Act has given birth to such a monstrous child . . . I am not prepared in this case to give it currency, and for this reason I would dismiss this appeal.

D.   The Position in Equity

Where there is an enforceable agreement to grant a lease, of which equity is prepared, in the circumstances, to grant specific performance, equity (following the maxim that equity looks on that as done which ought to be done) will treat the intended tenant as having already, in equity, a lease. This is so where there is:

> (i) an agreement evidenced in writing as required by the Law of Property Act 1925, section 40, p. 63, ante; or

(ii) a "void" lease, i.e. a lease in writing for more than three years which is void at law owing to the lack of a seal, but is construed in equity as an agreement for a lease[4], or

(iii) an agreement proved by oral evidence and supported by acts of part performance[5].

E.   The Doctrine of *Walsh v Lonsdale*[6]

This doctrine is one aspect of the general doctrine of estate contracts which is discussed in detail above[7]. A question which is commonly discussed is the extent to which an agreement for a lease is as good as a lease.

F.   The Differences between a Lease and an Agreement for a Lease[8]

i.   THE BONA FIDE PURCHASER

An agreement for a lease is an equitable interest, and, as such, liable to destruction by a bona fide purchaser of a legal estate for value without notice[9]. The doctrine of the bona fide purchaser is modified, in the case of unregistered land, by the introduction of a system of registration of land charges by the Land Charges Acts 1925[10]; and has no part to play in the context of registered land[11].

ii.   LAW OF PROPERTY ACT 1925, SECTION 62

An agreement for a lease is not a "conveyance" within the meaning of the Law of Property Act 1925, section 62[12].

BORMAN *v* GRIFFITH
[1930] 1 Ch 493 (ChD, Maugham J)

In 1923 James agreed to grant a lease to Borman of a house which was situated in a large park containing a mansion. The house was approached only by the drive leading to the mansion and not by a public road. The agreement contained no express grant of a right of way over the drive. In 1926 James leased the mansion to Griffith for 14 years.

Subsequent to the agreement of 1923, James constructed an unmetalled road to the rear of Borman's house. The road was not adequate for heavy traffic, and was unsuitable for Borman's trade as a poultry dealer, and Borman continued to use the drive. In 1928 Griffith obstructed Borman's use of the drive, and Borman sued to establish his right of way.

---

[4] *Parker v Taswell* (1858) 2 De G & J 559; *Bond v Rosling* (1861) 1 B & S 371; *Tidey v Mollett* (1864) 16 CBNS 298.

[5] See p. 68, ante.

[6] (1882) 21 ChD 9, p. 81, ante.

[7] See p. 80 et seq., ante.

[8] C & B, pp. 375–380; M & W, pp. 640–644; MM, pp. 336–339.

[9] *Pilcher v Rawlins* (1872) 7 Ch App 259, p. 26, ante; Maitland, p. 158; p. 85, ante.

[10] P. 30, ante.

[11] P. 26, ante.

[12] "Conveyance" is defined in LPA 1925, s. 205 (1) (ii), p. 9, ante. For s. 62, see pp. 586–597, post.

Held. (i) Section 62 of the Law of Property Act 1925 did not apply to an agreement for a lease, and the plaintiff could not claim an easement on that ground.

(ii) The plaintiff was entitled to claim the right of way under the rule in *Wheeldon v Burrows* (1879) 12 ChD 31, p. 582, post.

MAUGHAM J: . . . The date of the contract is a date before the coming into force of the Law of Property Act 1925, and is a date at which the Conveyancing Act, 1881, was still in force. The plaintiff relies on section 62, subsections 1 and 2 of the Law of Property Act, 1925, under which certain general words are deemed to be included in a conveyance, and, in particular, the words "ways . . . reputed to appertain to the land, houses, etc." and "reputed or known as part or parcel of or appurtenant to, the land, houses, etc.": and he asserts that the way along the drive in the front of his house, and the branch drive leading directly to the back of his house, were ways enjoyed with the premises demised by the contract; and he points out that under subsection 6, the section applies to conveyances executed after 31 December 1881, and that "conveyance" is defined in section 205, subsection 1 (ii), to include "a lease . . . and every other assurance of property or of an interest therein by any instrument, except a will". . . .

On the whole, I think that it is not a "conveyance", because it is not an "assurance of property or of an interest therein". It is true that, under the decision in *Walsh v Lonsdale* (1882) 21 ChD 9 at 14, p. 81, ante it has been held that, where there is an agreement for a lease under which possession has been given, the tenant holds, for many purposes, as if a lease had actually been granted. [His Lordship then quoted from the judgment of Jessel MR and continued:] That is the well known judgment of Sir George Jessel MR, with which Cotton and Lindley LJJ agreed. But no court has yet declared that an agreement for a lease for a term of more than three years is an "assurance". It has to be borne in mind that a lease for any term of more than three years must be by deed, and it is well known that, under section 3 of the Real Property Act, 1845, ". . . a lease, required by law to be in writing, of any tenements or hereditaments . . . shall . . . be void at law unless made by deed." (See now section 52 of the Law of Property Act, 1925, and the repeal section.)

In my opinion, a contract for a lease exceeding a term of three years does not come within the meaning of the phrase "assurance of property or of an interest therein" as that phrase is used in section 205, subsection 1 (ii), of the Law of Property Act, 1925: and accordingly I am unable to construe the agreement of 10 October 1923, as if the general words of section 62 of that Act were included in it . . .

In my view, the principles laid down in such cases as *Wheeldon v Burrows* (1879) 12 ChD 31; *Brown v Alabaster* (1887) 37 ChD 490; and *Nicholls v Nicholls* (1899) 81 LT 811 are applicable. Without going through all those cases in detail, I may state the principle as follows — namely, that where, as in the present case, two properties belonging to a single owner and about to be granted are separated by a common road, or where a plainly visible road exists over the one for the apparent use of the other, and that road is necessary for the reasonable enjoyment of the property, a right to use the road will pass with the quasi-dominant tenement, unless by the terms of the contract that right is excluded: and in my opinion, if the present position were that the plaintiff was claiming against the lessor specific performance of the agreement of 10 October 1923, he would be entitled to be given a right of way for all reasonable purposes along the drive, including the part that passes the farm on the way to the orchard.

iii.   AVAILABILITY OF SPECIFIC PERFORMANCE[13]

The doctrine of *Walsh v Lonsdale* is dependent upon the availability of specific performance, which is discretionary.

iv.   THE EFFECT OF AN ASSIGNMENT.

See p. 428, post[14].

IV.   Remedies of the Landlord

It is not possible, in the available space, to deal with all the landlord's remedies. This section will be confined to a consideration of some of the restrictions upon the landlord's right to recover possession of the demised premises.

A.   Statutory Restrictions on Recovery of Possession[15]

When a lease comes to an end, whether by the expiry of the term or by notice to quit, the landlord's common law right to recover possession is subject to certain statutory restrictions.

(a) The landlord may be liable criminally, under Criminal Law Act 1977, section 6[16], and under Protection from Eviction Act 1977, section 1[17], for unlawful eviction and harassment.

(b) The tenant may be protected under the Rent (Agriculture) Act 1976 or Agricultural Holdings Act 1986, the Landlord and Tenant Act 1954, the Leasehold Reform Act 1967, the Rent Act 1977 and the Housing Act 1980.

(c) Or, more generally, under the following provisions:

---

[13] *Coatsworth v Johnson* (1886) 55 LJQB 220, p. 84, ante; *Foster v Reeves* [1892] 2 QB 255; *Cornish v Brook Green Laundry Ltd* [1959] 1 QB 394, [1959] 1 All ER 373; (1959) 75 LQR 168 (R. E. M.); *Kingswood Estate Co Ltd v Anderson* [1963] 2 QB 169, [1962] 3 All ER 593; (1963) 79 LQR 19 (R. E. M.); *Rushton v Smith* [1976] QB 480, [1975] 2 All ER 905; *Industrial Properties (Barton Hill) Ltd v Associated Electrical Industries Ltd* [1977] QB 580, [1977] 2 All ER 293, p. 82, ante; *Warmington v Miller* [1973] QB 877 at 887, [1973] 2 All ER 372 at 377; *Bell Street Investments v Wood* (1970) 216 EG 585; *Henry Smith's Charity Trustees v Hemmings* (1982) 265 EG 383.

[14] A further difference was removed by *National Carriers Ltd v Panalpina (Northern) Ltd* [1981] AC 675, [1981] 1 All ER 161, where HL held that the doctrine of frustration is applicable to a lease; for an agreement for a lease, see *Rom Securities Ltd v Rogers (Holdings) Ltd* (1967) 205 EG 427.

[15] C & B, pp. 443, 449–450, 460–461; M & W, pp. 672, 701, 1141–1142; MM, pp. 592–593; Report of the Committee on the Rent Acts (1971) (Cmnd 4609), pp. 105–106.

[16] The Forcible Entry Acts 1381–1623 were abolished by s. 13. See Law Com. Report, Conspiracy and Criminal Law Reform, Part II (Law Com. No. 76, 1976).

[17] *R v Phekoo* [1981] 1 WLR 1117, [1981] 3 All ER 84; *R v Yuthiwattana* (1984) 80 Cr App Rep 55. The section does not give rise to a civil cause of action for damages in addition to the causes of action which the tenant would ordinarily have for the torts or breaches of contract constituted by the acts of harassment: *McCall v Abelesz* [1976] QB 585, [1976] 1 All ER 727; *Drane v Evangelou* [1978] 1 WLR 455, [1978] 2 All ER 437 (exemplary damages for landlord's "monstrous behaviour"); *Guppys (Bridport) Ltd v Brookling* (1983) 269 EG 846, 942.

PROTECTION FROM EVICTION ACT 1977[18]

2. Restriction on re-entry without due process of law. — Where any premises are let as a dwelling on a lease which is subject to a right of re-entry or forfeiture it shall not be lawful to enforce that right otherwise than by proceedings in the court while any person is lawfully residing in the premises or part of them.

3. Prohibition of eviction without due process of law. — (1) Where any premises have been let as a dwelling under a tenancy which is not a statutorily protected tenancy and —

    (*a*) the tenancy (in this section referred to as the former tenancy) has come to an end, but

    (*b*) the occupier continues to reside in the premises or part of them,

it shall not be lawful for the owner to enforce against the occupier, otherwise than by proceedings in the court, his right to recover possession of the premises[19].

(2) In this section "the occupier", in relation to any premises, means any person lawfully residing in the premises or part of them at the termination of the former tenancy.

(2A)[20] Subsections (1) and (2) above apply in relation to any restricted contract (within the meaning of the Rent Act 1977) which —

    (*a*) creates a licence; and

    (*b*) is entered into after the commencement of section 69 of the Housing Act 1980;

as they apply in relation to a restricted contract which creates a tenancy.

(3) This section shall, with the necessary modifications, apply where the owner's right to recover possession arises on the death of the tenant under a statutory tenancy within the meaning of the Rent Act 1977 or the Rent (Agriculture) Act 1976[1].

5. Validity of notices to quit. — (1) No notice by a landlord or a tenant to quit any premises let (whether before or after the commencement of this Act) as a dwelling shall be valid unless —

    (*a*) it is in writing and contains such information as may be prescribed, and

    (*b*) it is given not less than 4 weeks before the date on which it is to take effect[2].

(2) In this section "prescribed" means prescribed by regulations made by the Secretary of State by statutory instrument, and a statutory instrument containing any such regulations shall be subject to annulment in pursuance of a resolution of either House of Parliament[3].

(3) Regulations under this section may make different provision in relation to different descriptions of lettings and different circumstances.

---

[18] Farrand, *Protection from Eviction Act 1977* (1978).

[19] *Warder v Cooper* [1970] Ch 495, [1970] 1 All ER 1112.

[20] Added by Housing Act 1980, s. 69 (1).

[1] S. 4 contains special provisions for agricultural employees.

[2] This section does not apply to a licence; a tenancy at will: *Crane v Morris* [1965] 1 WLR 1104, [1965] 3 All ER 77; a tenancy arising under an attornment clause in a mortgage: *Alliance Building Society v Pinwill* [1958] Ch 788, [1958] 2 All ER 408; *Peckham Mutual Building Society v Registe* (1980) 42 P & CR 186.

[3] See Notice to Quit (Prescribed Information) Regulations 1980 (S.I. 1980 No. 1624).

8. Interpretation. — (1) In this Act "statutorily protected tenancy" means —

    (*a*) a protected tenancy within the meaning of the Rent Act 1977 or a tenancy to which Part I of the Landlord and Tenant Act 1954 applies;

    (*b*) a protected occupancy or statutory tenancy as defined in the Rent (Agriculture) Act 1976;

    (*c*) a tenancy to which Part II of the Landlord and Tenant Act 1954 applies;

    (*d*) a tenancy of an agricultural holding within the meaning of the Agricultural Holdings Act 1986[3a].

(2) For the purposes of Part I of this Act a person who, under the terms of his employment, had exclusive possession of any premises other than as a tenant shall be deemed to have been a tenant and the expressions "let" and "tenancy" shall be construed accordingly.

(3) In Part I of this Act "the owner", in relation to any premises, means the person who, as against the occupier, is entitled to possession thereof.

9. The court for purposes of Part I. — (3) Nothing in this Act shall affect the jurisdiction of the High Court in proceedings to enforce a lessor's right of re-entry or forfeiture[4] or to enforce a mortgagee's right of possession in a case where the former tenancy was not binding on the mortgagee[5].

B.   Forfeiture and Relief against Forfeiture[6]

A lease usually includes a forfeiture clause which provides for the landlord's right to forfeit the remainder of the lease if there is a breach by the tenant of any covenants in the lease[7].

Unlimited application of such a clause could inflict hardship on the tenant out of all proportion to the damage suffered by the landlord. For example, a tenant, who is in arrears with his rent, may subsequently pay everything that is due with interest; a breach of a covenant to insure may cause no loss to the landlord, but it used to be treated as sufficient to produce forfeiture under a forfeiture clause.

It has long been settled that equity will relieve a tenant against forfeiture in respect of non-payment of rent, but as a general rule not in other cases. The position is now regulated by statute.

i.   NON-PAYMENT OF RENT

COMMON LAW PROCEDURE ACT 1852

210. Proceedings in ejectment by landlord for non-payment of rent. — In all cases between landlord and tenant, as often as it shall happen that one half year's rent shall be in arrear, and the landlord or lessor, to

---

[3a] As amended by the Agricultural Holdings Act 1986, Sch. 14, para. 61.

[4] *Borżak v Ahmed* [1965] 2 QB 320, [1965] 1 All ER 808.

[5] See p. 687, post.

[6] C & B, pp. 416–429; M & W, pp. 670–683; MM, pp. 349–356.

[7] See *Richard Clarke & Co Ltd v Widnall* [1976] 1 WLR 845, [1976] 3 All ER 301, where a clause in a lease under which the landlord was entitled to serve a notice to terminate for breach of covenant was construed as a forfeiture clause. Cf. *Clays Lane Housing Co-operative Ltd v Patrick* (1984) 49 P & CR 72 (for a clause to be a forfeiture clause it must bring the lease to an end earlier than the actual termination date).

whom the same is due, hath right by law to re-enter for the non-payment thereof, such landlord or lessor shall and may without any formal demand or re-entry, serve a writ in ejectment for the recovery of the demised premises, which service shall stand in the place and stead of a demand and re-entry[8]; and in case of judgment against the defendant for non-appearance, if it shall be made appear to the court where the said action is depending, by affidavit, or be proved upon the trial in case the defendant appears, that half a year's rent was due before the said writ was served, and that no sufficient distress was to be found on the demised premises, countervailing the arrears then due, and that the lessor had power to re-enter, then and in every such case the lessor shall recover judgment and execution, in the same manner as if the rent in arrear had been legally demanded, and a re-entry made; and in case the lessee or his assignee, or other person claiming or deriving under the said lease, shall permit and suffer judgment to be had and recovered on such trial in ejectment, and execution to be executed thereon, without paying the rent and arrears, together with full costs, and without proceeding for relief in equity within six months after such execution executed, then and in such case the said lessee, his assignee, and all other persons claiming and deriving under the said lease, shall be barred and foreclosed from all relief or remedy in law or equity, other than by bringing error for reversal of such judgment, in case the same shall be erroneous, and the said landlord or lessor shall from thenceforth hold the said demised premises discharged from such lease . . .

211. Lessee proceeding in equity not to have injunction or relief without payment of rent and costs. — In case the said lessee, his assignee, or other person claiming any right, title, or interest, in law or equity, of, in, or to the said lease, shall, within the time aforesaid, proceed for relief in any court of equity, such person shall not have or continue any injunction against the proceedings at law on such ejectment, unless he does or shall, within forty days next after a full and perfect answer shall be made by the claimant in such ejectment, bring into court, and lodge with the proper officer such sum and sums of money as the lessor or landlord shall in his answer swear to be due and in arrear over and above all just allowances, and also the costs taxed in the said suit, there to remain till the hearing of the cause, or to be paid out to the lessor or landlord on good security, subject to the decree of the court; and in case such proceedings for relief in equity shall be taken within the time aforesaid, and after execution is executed, the lessor or landlord shall be accountable only for so much and no more as he shall really and bona fide, without fraud, deceit, or wilful neglect, make of the demised premises from the time of his entering into the actual possession thereof; and if what shall be so made by the lessor or landlord happen to be less than the rent reserved on the said lease, then the said lessee or his assignee, before he shall be restored

---

[8] See *Canas Property Co Ltd v KL Television Services Ltd* [1970] 2 QB 433, [1970] 2 All ER 795; *Richards v De Freitas* (1975) 29 P & CR 1. The forfeiture does not become final until the landlord has obtained unconditional judgment for possession. Until then the covenants in the lease remain potentially good in favour of the tenant: *Driscoll v Church Comrs for England* [1957] 1 QB 330, [1956] 3 All ER 802; *Peninsular Maritime Ltd v Padseal Ltd* (1981) 259 EG 860 (landlord's covenant to repair lift held enforceable by tenant while seeking relief against forfeiture). See also *Meadows v Clerical Medical and General Life Assurance Society* [1981] Ch 70, [1980] 1 All ER 454; *Associated Deliveries Ltd v Harrison* (1984) 50 P & CR 91; [1985] Conv 285 (J. E. Martin).

to his possession, shall pay such lessor or landlord what the money so by him made fell short of the reserved rent for the time such lessor or landlord held the said lands[9].

212.   Tenant paying all rent, with costs, proceedings to cease. — If the tenant or his assignee do or shall, at any time before the trial in such ejectment, pay or tender to the lessor or landlord, his executors or administrators, or his or their attorney in that cause, or pay into the court where the same cause is depending, all the rent and arrears[10], together with the costs, then and in such case all further proceedings on the said ejectment shall cease and be discontinued; and if such lessee, his executors, administrators, or assigns, shall, upon such proceedings as aforesaid, be relieved in equity, he and they shall have, hold, and enjoy the demised lands, according to the lease thereof made, without any new lease.

LAW OF PROPERTY ACT 1925

146.   Restrictions on and relief against forfeiture of leases and underleases. — (4) p. 436, post.

SUPREME COURT ACT 1981

38.   Relief against forfeiture for non-payment of rent. — (1) In any action in the High Court for the forfeiture of a lease for non-payment of rent, the court shall have power to grant relief against forfeiture in a summary manner, and may do so subject to the same terms and conditions as to the payment of rent, costs or otherwise as could have been imposed by it in such an action immediately before the commencement of this Act.

(2) Where the lessee or a person deriving title under him is granted relief under this section, he shall hold the demised premises in accordance with the terms of the lease without the necessity for a new lease.

In *Belgravia Insurance Co Ltd v Meah* [1964] 1 QB 436, [1963] 3 All ER 828, Lord DENNING MR reviewed the law relating to the right to relief for non-payment of rent and said at 443, at 831:

"The first thing to notice is that the ground of forfeiture was *for non-payment of rent*. Relief from such a forfeiture is treated differently from relief for other breaches, such as disrepair and so forth. In case of non-payment of rent, relief is still based fundamentally on the jurisdiction of Courts of Equity to grant relief, subject to the limitations imposed by sections 210 and 212 of the Common Law Procedure Act 1852. In case of other breaches, relief is based on section 146 of the Law of Property Act 1925.

In the case of a *lessee* himself seeking relief from forfeiture for non-payment of rent, the relevant principles have been stated recently by this court in *Gill v Lewis* [1956] 2 QB 1, [1956] 1 All ER 844. But here we are concerned with the position of an *under-lessee* to whom somewhat different considerations

---

[9] The granting of relief is discretionary: *Stanhope v Haworth* (1886) 3 TLR 34.
[10] *Standard Pattern Co Ltd v Ivey* [1962] Ch 432, [1962] 1 All ER 452 (limiting the tenant's right to cases where at least half a year's rent is in arrear); (1962) 78 LQR 168 (R. E. Megarry).

apply. I say an *under-lessee* because, although the applicant is a *mortgagee* holding a charge by way of legal mortgage, he is to be treated as if he held a mortgage by sub-demise (see section 87 of the Law of Property Act, 1925, and *Grand Junction Co Ltd v Bates* [1954] 2 QB 160, [1954] 2 All ER 385, p. 657, post), that is, as if he was an under-lessee.

When an under-lessee or a mortgagee by sub-demise (as all mortgagees are now) claims relief from *forfeiture for non-payment of rent*, he can *either* claim under the equitable jurisdiction (which is preserved by section 46 of the Judicature Act of 1925)[11] *or* under section 146 (4) of the Law of Property Act, 1925. The applicant claimed under both. It was suggested before us that there was some difference between the principles applicable. I do not think there is. I will deal with them separately.

First, the application under section 46 of the Judicature Act of 1925.

The jurisdiction to give relief under section 46 of the Judicature Act of 1925 is founded on the jurisdiction of the old Court of Chancery. The Court of Chancery from its earliest days held that, wherever the court could fully compensate the party entitled for breach of a condition, i.e., wherever it could ensure that the party would get all that was due to him, it would grant relief against a forfeiture. It was so held in 1682 by Lord Nottingham LC in *Popham v Bampfeild* (1682) 1 Vern 79, 83, and in 1707 by Lord Cowper LC in *Grimston v Lord Bruce* (1707) 1 Salk 156. In accordance with this principle it granted relief not only to lessees, but also to under-lessees and to mortgagees by assignment or by sub-demise, provided always that all the covenants were performed. A good instance was in 1689 when the then Lord Salisbury granted a lease at a certain rent and the lessee covenanted to repair. The lessee granted a hundred under-leases to a hundred sub-tenants. The lessee did not pay the rent nor perform the covenant to repair. So Lord Salisbury re-entered. Six out of the one hundred sub-tenants applied for relief, joining the lessee and Lord Salisbury as parties. The court granted relief on the terms that the six sub-tenants *paid the whole rent in arrear and repaired the premises:* see *Webber v Smith* (1689) 2 Vern 103[12]. It would seem that the principle of that case was applied to mortgagees, whether by assignment or by sub-demise. For it was expressly recognised by the legislature in the Landlord and Tenant Act 1730 . . . In 1852 the statute was re-enacted in virtually the same terms in section 210 of the Common Law Procedure Act, 1852. In 1860, by section 1 of the Common Law Procedure Act, 1860, the courts of common law were given the same powers as the Court of Chancery. And in 1895, when the common law courts came to apply these powers, they applied them in precisely the same way as the Courts of Chancery had done. In *Newbolt v Bingham* (1895) 72 LT 852 the lessee was in arrear with his rent and had let the premises fall into disrepair. The landlord forfeited the lease for non-payment of rent. A mortgagee by sub-demise applied for relief and he was granted it *on condition that he paid all rent in arrear and did all the repairs and paid all the costs.* . . .

The principle was thus clearly established that, in case of forfeiture for non-payment of rent, a Court of Chancery would, in the ordinary way, grant

---

[11] Now Supreme Court Act 1981, s. 38.
[12] Compare *Chatham Empire Theatre (1955) Ltd v Ultrans Ltd* [1961] 1 WLR 817, [1961] 2 All ER 381, where SALMON J, without referring to *Webber v Smith*, granted relief on payment of a proportionate share by the applicant sub-lessees.

relief to an under-lessee or a mortgagee by sub-demise, if he paid all the rent in arrear and performed all the covenants and paid all the costs. The court, however, as a rule only granted relief if the original lessee was made a party (see *Hare v Elms* [1893] 1 QB 604) though this rule could be relaxed for good cause: see *Humphreys v Morten* [1905] 1 Ch 739.

Secondly, the application under section 146 (4) of the Law of Property Act, 1925.

During the nineteenth century it was held (following Lord Eldon LC's views in *Hill v Barclay* (1810) 16 Ves 402, 405, p. 453, post) that the Court of Chancery had no jurisdiction to grant a lessee relief from forfeiture for any breaches except non-payment of rent. This was remedied in 1881 by section 14 of the Conveyancing Act, 1881 (which did not apply to non-payment of rent). But that section did not apply to under-lessees. So Parliament enacted section 4 of the Conveyancing Act, 1892, so as to include them. But this section was held to apply, not only to other breaches, but also to non-payment of rent: see *Gray v Bonsall* [1904] 1 KB 601. In 1925 the whole law, as so evolved, was consolidated in section 146 of the Law of Property Act, 1925. Section 146 (4) enabled the court to grant relief to an under-lessee, not only in case of other breaches but also non-payment of rent, on such conditions 'as the court in the circumstances of each case may think fit'. It seems to me that, in exercising this discretion, the court will, in the ordinary way, grant relief to an under-lessee on the terms of paying the rent in arrear, performing the covenants, and paying all the costs: see *Gray v Bonsall* at 608, per Romer LJ. In short, on the same terms as the old Court of Chancery would have done. The only difference is that it is not necessary to make the lessee a party.

Thirdly, power to refuse relief.

In any case, whether under the old Chancery jurisdiction or under section 146 (4) of the Law of Property Act, 1925, it is clear that the court may always refuse relief, if the conduct of the applicant is such as to make it inequitable that relief should be given to him: see *Bowser v Colby* (1841) 1 Hare 109, 134 per Wigram V-C, and *Gill v Lewis* [1956] 2 QB 1 at 17, [1956] 1 All ER 844 at 854, per Hodson LJ[13]."

ii.   BREACH OF COVENANTS OTHER THAN NON-PAYMENT OF RENT

(a) *Law of Property Act 1925, section 146*

Before a landlord can enforce a right of forfeiture for breach of covenant other than one for the payment of rent, he must serve a notice on the tenant under section 146 (1) of the Law of Property Act 1925. Whether a breach is capable of remedy under para. (*b*) has given rise to difficulty. If the covenant is positive, e.g. to repair, the breach is clearly capable of remedy[14]. In the case

---

[13] See *Howard v Fanshawe* [1895] 2 Ch 581. *Lovelock v Margo* [1963] 2 QB 786, [1963] 2 All ER 13, holding that, under the ancient jurisdiction of the Court of Chancery, the court has power, independent of statute, to grant relief from forfeiture where there has been a peaceable entry; *Thatcher v CH Pearce & Sons (Contractors) Ltd* [1968] 1 WLR 748 (tenant granted relief, in spite of bringing action six months and four days after landlord regained possession).

For the similar jurisdiction of the county court to grant relief, see County Courts Act 1984, s. 138 as amended by AJA 1985, s. 55, reversing the effect of *Di Palma v Victoria Square Property Co Ltd* [1985] 3 WLR 207, [1985] 2 All ER 676.

[14] *Expert Clothing Service and Sales Ltd v Hillgate House Ltd* [1985] 3 WLR 359, [1985] 2 All ER 998, p. 443, post.

of a negative covenant, the Court of Appeal held in *Scala House and District Property Co Ltd v Forbes* [1974] QB 575, [1973] 3 All ER 308, p. 439, post, that the breach of a covenant not to assign, underlet or part with possession was incapable of remedy. "It is a complete breach once for all[15]." The Court also considered that the breach of a user covenant, e.g. not to use the premises for illegal or immoral purposes, where the user has ceased before the service of a section 146 notice, is also incapable of remedy. Hitherto the test applicable to such breaches had been whether or not the stigma attaching to the premises could be removed by mere cesser of the immoral or illegal user[16]. It might be preferable to revert to the "attractive and easy[17]" ratio of MACKINNON J in *Rugby School (Governors) v Tannahill*[18] and to hold that all negative covenants are incapable of remedy, and that recovery of possession by the landlord depends solely on whether the tenant can persuade the court to grant relief from forfeiture under section 146 (2).

The effect of the grant of relief to a tenant by the court is to reinstate the old lease, which is deemed to have been continuously in force. The court may impose conditions on granting relief. Where a lease is forfeited, any under-leases created out of it automatically come to an end. But an under-lessee or mortgagee has the same right of applying to the court for relief against forfeiture of the head lease as the tenant has under the head lease. In this case, however, the effect of granting relief to an under-lessee is to grant and vest a new term in him; the lease forfeited by the landlord is not revived and continued[19].

LAW OF PROPERTY ACT 1925

146. Restrictions on and relief against forfeiture of leases and under-leases. — (1) A right of re-entry or forfeiture under any proviso or stipulation in a lease for a breach of any covenant or condition in the lease shall not be enforceable, by action or otherwise, unless and until the lessor serves on the lessee[20] a notice —

---

[15] At 588, at 315, per RUSSELL LJ, p. 442, post.

[16] *Rugby School (Governors) v Tannahill* [1935] 1 KB 87, p. 438, post; *Egerton v Esplanade Hotels, London Ltd* [1947] 2 All ER 88; *Hoffmann v Fineberg* [1949] Ch 245, [1948] 1 All ER 592, p. 441, post; *Borthwick-Norton v Romney Warwick Estates Ltd* [1950] 1 All ER 798; *Glass v Kencakes Ltd* [1966] 1 QB 611, [1964] 3 All ER 807, p. 441, post; *Dunraven Securities Ltd v Holloway* (1982) 264 EG 709 (keeping in tenant's Soho sex shop obscene articles for publication for gain contrary to Obscene Publications Act 1959); (1983) 133 NLJ 485 (H. W. Wilkinson); *British Petroleum Pension Trust Ltd v Behrendt* (1985) 276 EG 199, p. 438, n. 12, post.

[17] *Hoffmann v Fineberg* [1949] Ch 245 at 254, [1948] 1 All ER 592 at 596, per HARMAN J.

[18] [1934] 1 KB 695 at 700–701.

[19] The new term cannot be any longer than the one forfeited, and the words "any longer term . . . sub-lease" in PA 1925 s. 146 (4) refer to the position immediately before forfeiture: *Cadogan v Dimovic* [1984] 1 WLR 609, [1984] 2 All ER 168 (sub-lease terminated by forfeiture of head lease, which was a business tenancy subject to extension under L & T Act 1954 (see C & B, pp. 476–479); sub-lessee granted a new term of appropriate duration but within the limits of the extension imposed by the 1954 Act); *Official Custodian for Charities v Mackey* [1985] Ch 168, [1984] 3 All ER 689 (rent for under-leases payable to lessor during period between forfeiture of the old lease and the creation of the new one); [1985] Conv 50 (J. Martin).

[20] Where a lessee assigns his lease in breach of covenant, the assignment is effective, and the notice must be served on the assignee and not on the original lessee: *Old Grovebury Manor Farm Ltd v W Seymour Plant Sales and Hire Ltd (No 2)* [1979] 1 WLR 1397, [1979] 3 All ER 504; *Governors of the Peabody Donation Fund v Higgins* [1983] 1 WLR 1091, [1983] 3 All ER 122.

(a) specifying the particular breach complained of; and

(b) if the breach is capable of remedy, requiring the lessee to remedy the breach; and

(c) in any case, requiring the lessee to make compensation in money for the breach[1];

and the lessee fails, within a reasonable time thereafter, to remedy the breach, if it is capable of remedy, and to make reasonable compensation in money, to the satisfaction of the lessor, for the breach.

(2) Where a lessor is proceeding[2], by action[3] or otherwise[4], to enforce such a right of re-entry or forfeiture, the lessee[5] may, in the lessor's action, if any, or in any action brought by himself, apply to the court for relief; and the court may grant or refuse relief, as the court, having regard to the proceedings and conduct of the parties under the foregoing provisions of this section, and to all the other circumstances, thinks fit; and in case of relief may grant it on such terms, if any, as to costs, expenses, damages, compensation, penalty, or otherwise, including the granting of an injunction to restrain any like breach in the future, as the court, in the circumstances of each case, thinks fit[6].

(4) Where a lessor is proceeding by action or otherwise to enforce a right of re-entry or forfeiture under any covenant, proviso, or stipulation in a lease, or for non-payment of rent, the court may, on application by any person claiming as under-lessee[7] any estate or interest in the property comprised in the lease or any part thereof, either in the lessor's action (if any) or in any action brought by such person for that purpose, make an order vesting, for the whole term of the lease or any less term, the property comprised in the lease or any part thereof in any person entitled as under-lessee to any estate or interest in such property upon such conditions as to execution of any deed or other document, payment of rent, costs, expenses, damages, compensation, giving security, or otherwise, as the court in the circumstances of each case may think fit, but in no case shall any such under-lessee be entitled to

---

[1] This does not make it necessary for the lessor to claim compensation if he does not want it: *Lock v Pearce* [1893] 2 Ch 271; *Rugby School (Governors) v Tannahill*, supra.

[2] The right to relief, unlike that in respect of breach of a covenant to pay rent, terminates upon re-entry by the lessor: *Rogers v Rice* [1892] 2 Ch 170. The lessor may not, of course, re-enter without serving the notice required by sub-s. (1).

[3] Such an action is a pending land action under LCA 1972, s. 17 (1) and is registrable under s. 5; and, in the case of registered land, is required to be protected by a caution under LRA 1925, s. 59 (1), (5). *Selim Ltd v Bickenhall Engineering Ltd* [1981] 1 WLR 1318, [1981] 3 All ER 210.

[4] I.e., by the service of a notice under s. 146: *Pakwood Transport Ltd v 15 Beauchamp Place Ltd* (1978) 36 P & CR 112.

[5] Where there are joint lessees, relief cannot be granted on the application of only one of them: *TM Fairclough & Sons Ltd v Berliner* [1931] 1 Ch 60.

[6] In some circumstances the court may be able to grant relief as to part of the demised premises by restricting the order for possession to a part only: *GMS Syndicate Ltd v Gary Elliott Ltd* [1982] Ch 1, [1981] 1 All ER 619. NOURSE J said at 12, at 626: "I emphasise that I do not intend to go beyond the circumstances of the present case, where the two parts of the demised property are physically separated one from the other and are capable of being distinctly enjoyed, and where the breaches complained of were committed on one part of the property and on that part alone."

[7] See *Grand Junction Co Ltd v Bates* [1954] 2 QB 160, [1954] 2 All ER 385, p. 657, post, where it was held that a mortgagee by way of legal charge can claim as under-lessee. So can an equitable chargee: *Re Good's Lease* [1954] 1 WLR 309, [1954] 1 All ER 275.

require a lease to be granted to him for any longer term than he had under his original sub-lease[8].

(5) For the purposes of this section —

(a) "Lease" includes an original or derivative under-lease; also an agreement for a lease where the lessee has become entitled to have his lease granted; also a grant at a fee farm rent, or securing a rent by condition;

(b) "Lessee" includes an original or derivative under-lessee, and the persons deriving title under a lessee; also a grantee under any such grant as aforesaid and the persons deriving title under him;

(c) "Lessor" includes an original or derivative under-lessor, and the persons deriving title under a lessor; also a person making such grant as aforesaid and the persons deriving title under him;

(d) "Under-lease" includes an agreement for an under-lease where the under-lessee has become entitled to have his under-lease granted;

(e) "Under-lessee" includes any person deriving title under an under-lessee.

(8) This section does not extend —

(i) To a covenant or condition against assigning, underletting, parting with the possession, or disposing of the land leased where the breach occurred before the commencement of this Act; or

(ii) In the case of a mining lease, to a covenant or condition for allowing the lessor to have access to or inspect books, accounts, records, weighing machines or other things, or to enter or inspect the mine or the workings thereof.

(9) This section does not apply to a condition for forfeiture on the bankruptcy of the lessee[9] or on taking in execution of the lessee's interest if contained in a lease of —

(a) Agricultural or pastoral land;

(b) Mines or minerals;

(c) A house used or intended to be used as a public-house or beershop;

(d) A house let as a dwelling-house, with the use of any furniture, books, works of art, or other chattels not being in the nature of fixtures;

(e) Any property with respect to which the personal qualifications of the tenant are of importance for the preservation of the value or character of the property[10], or on the ground of neighbourhood to the lessor, or to any person holding under him.

(10) Where a condition of forfeiture on the bankruptcy of the lessee or on taking in execution of the lessee's interest is contained in any lease, other

---

[8] For the inherent jurisdiction of the court to grant relief outside sub-s. (4) where the lessor has re-entered for breach of covenant to pay a sum of money other than payment of rent and is therefore no longer "proceeding by action or otherwise", see *Abbey National Building Society v Maybeech Ltd* [1985] Ch 190, [1984] 3 All ER 262. Cf. *Smith v Metropolitan City Properties Ltd* (1985) 277 EG 753, where WALTON J held that the inherent jurisdiction has been replaced by s. 146 (2) (otherwise "it would make complete nonsense of subsection (2)"); *Official Custodian for Charities v Parway Estates Developments Ltd* [1985] Ch 151, [1984] 3 All ER 679, where CA held that it had no inherent jurisdiction where the lessee was outside the time limits for relief under sub-s. 10, infra; [1984] All ER Rev 195 (P. H. Pettit). But the mortgagee can apply outside the time limits under sub-s. (4); *Official Custodian for Charities v Mackey (No 2)* [1985] 2 All ER 1016, 274 EG 398.

[9] But it does apply on the bankruptcy of a lessee's surety: *Halliard Property Co Ltd v Jack Segal Ltd* [1978] 1 WLR 377, [1978] 1 All ER 1219.

[10] *Earl of Bathurst v Fine* [1974] 1 WLR 905, [1974] 2 All ER 1160; (1974) 90 LQR 441.

than a lease of any of the classes mentioned in the last subsection, then —

    (*a*) if the lessee's interest is sold within one year from the bankruptcy or taking in execution, this section applies to the forfeiture condition aforesaid;

    (*b*) if the lessee's interest is not sold before the expiration of that year, this section only applies to the forfeiture condition aforesaid during the first year from the date of the bankruptcy or taking in execution[11].

(11) This section does not, save as otherwise mentioned, affect the law relating to re-entry or forfeiture or relief in case of non-payment of rent.

(12) This section has effect notwithstanding any stipulation to the contrary.

LAW OF PROPERTY (AMENDMENT) ACT 1929

1. Relief of under-lessees against breach of covenant. — Nothing in subsection (8), subsection (9) or subsection (10) of section one hundred and forty-six of the Law of Property Act, 1925 . . . shall affect the provisions of subsection (4) of the said section.

1. BREACH OF NEGATIVE COVENANT

RUGBY SCHOOL (GOVERNORS) *v* TANNAHILL

[1935] 1 KB 87 (CA, GREER, MAUGHAM and ROCHE LJJ)[12]

The Governors of Rugby School let premises in London to tenants who assigned them with their consent to the defendant, a woman who was convicted of using the premises for the purpose of habitual prostitution. The lease contained a covenant that the premises should not be used for illegal or immoral purposes, and contained a proviso for re-entry for breach of covenant. The Governors served a notice under Law of Property Act 1925, s. 146, requiring the defendant to surrender possession. The defence was that the notice to quit was bad in that it did not require the defendant to remedy the breach under s. 146 (1) (*b*), nor to make compensation in money under s. 146 (1) (*c*).

Held. (i) The breach was not capable of remedy and omission to require it to be remedied did not invalidate the notice;

(ii) As the landlords did not require compensation, omission to demand it did not invalidate the notice.

GREER LJ: The first point is, whether this particular breach is capable of remedy. In my judgment MacKinnon J was right in coming to the conclusion that it was not. I think perhaps he went further than was really necessary for the decision of this case in holding that a breach of any negative covenant — the doing of that which is forbidden — can never be capable of remedy[13]. It is unnecessary to decide the point on this appeal; but in some

---

[11] See *Official Custodian for Charities v Parway Estates Developments Ltd* [1985] Ch 151, [1984] 3 All ER 679, p. 437, n. 8, ante.

[12] *British Petroleum Pension Fund Trust Ltd v Behrendt* (1985) 276 EG 199, where PURCHAS LJ said at 204: "I have found nothing in the recent authorities which enables me to accede to Mr Brook's submissions that the concept that breaches of the negative covenant in 'stigma' cases are irremediable has in any way been relaxed."

[13] [1934] 1 KB 695 at 701: "A promise to do a thing, if broken, can be remedied by the thing being done. But breach of a promise not to do a thing cannot in any sense be remedied; that which was done cannot be undone. There cannot truly be a remedy; there can only be abstention, perhaps accompanied with apology."

cases where the immediate ceasing of that which is complained of, together with an undertaking against any further breach, it might be said that the breach was capable of remedy. This particular breach, however — conducting the premises, or permitting them to be conducted, as a house of ill-fame — is one which in my judgment was not remedied by merely stopping this user. I cannot conceive how a breach of this kind can be remedied. The result of committing the breach would be known all over the neighbourhood and seriously affect the value of the premises. Even a money payment together with the cessation of the improper use of the house could not be a remedy. Taking the view as I do that this breach was incapable of remedy, it was unnecessary to require in the notice that the defendant should remedy the breach.

The further question is whether the absence of any statement in the notice requiring compensation in money in respect of the breach is fatal to the validity of the notice. As to that, the decision of the Court of Appeal in *Lock v Pearce* [1893] 2 Ch 271 binds us to hold that the plaintiffs were under no obligation to require compensation in money. I can well understand that a body like the plaintiffs would be averse to touch money coming from a tenant in such circumstances. In any event, whatever might have been our view in the absence of authority, it is plain from the judgments in *Lock v Pearce* that the point is not open in this court. Lindley LJ there used these words at 279: "Then, as regards the notices required by s. 14, sub-s. 1 [of the Conveyancing Act 1881], the statute requires notice to be given specifying the breach complained of, as the first thing, and, if the breach is capable of remedy, requiring the lessee to remedy it, and 'in any case requiring the lessee to make compensation in money for the breach.' Supposing the lessor does not want compensation, is the notice to be held bad because he does not ask for it? There is no sense in that. The meaning is to be found by looking a little further on. The sub-section begins by saying that the right of re-entry or forfeiture shall not be enforceable unless proper notice is given and the lessee fails within a reasonable time afterwards to remedy the breach and to make reasonable compensation in money to the satisfaction of the lessor. The sense of that is that the lessor must tell the lessee what he wants done. The lessee is entitled to know what his landlord complains of, and, if his landlord is entitled to compensation, whether he wants compensation." The Lord Justice there concluded his judgment in a paragraph of two sentences which are specially applicable to the present case; he said: "On these grounds I am of opinion that this appeal fails. Upon the merits as well as upon the technicalities, all the points are against the appellants." In the later case of *Civil Service Co-operative Society Ltd v McGrigor's Trustee* [1923] 2 Ch 347, Russell J followed *Lock v Pearce* as applicable to a case where the breach was incapable of remedy. The appeal must be dismissed.

SCALA HOUSE AND DISTRICT PROPERTY CO LTD *v* FORBES[14]
[1974] QB 575, [1973] 3 All ER 308 (CA, RUSSELL and JAMES LJJ and PLOWMAN J)

By a lease dated 8 February 1968, the lessees covenanted not to assign underlet or part with the possession of a shop in Dean Street, London, without the permission of the landlords. The lease contained a proviso for

---

[14] (1973) 89 LQR 460 (P.V.B.); (1973) 57 Conv (NS) 445 (D. Macintyre).

re-entry on breach of covenant. In March the lease was assigned to the first defendant with the landlords' consent. He used the premises as a restaurant, and then in November entered into an agreement with Pierto and Elisa Delpoio, the second and third defendants, to manage the restaurant for him. This agreement, which was intended to be a management agreement, in fact created a sub-lease in breach of the covenant. The plaintiff, who had acquired the reversion of the lease, served on the defendants a notice under Law of Property Act 1925, section 146 (1), requiring them to remedy the breach, and 14 days later then issued a writ for possession. NIELD J held that the breach was capable of remedy, and since 14 days was insufficient time for the defendants to remedy the breach, dismissed the action. On appeal by the plaintiff.

Held. (i) The breach was not capable of remedy, and therefore 14 days was a sufficient time.

(ii) Relief from forfeiture was granted to the first defendant.

RUSSELL LJ: It is a remarkable fact that this case raises questions under section 146 of the Law of Property Act 1925, which, except in a case at first instance reported only in the Estates Gazette Digest[15], have never been considered for decision. . . .

So the first question is whether a breach of covenant such as is involved in the present case is capable of remedy. If it is capable of remedy, and is remedied in reasonable time, the lessor is unable to prove that a condition precedent to his ability to seek to forfeit by action or otherwise has been fulfilled. Here at once is a problem. An unlawful subletting is a breach once and for all. The subterm has been created.

I turn to the authorities. In *Jackson v Simons* [1923] 1 Ch 373 there was a breach of a covenant against sharing the premises let: such a breach was not excluded from section 14 of the Act of 1881: no notice at all was served before the writ for possession issued and this was fatal to the action. The sharing apparently ended shortly after the writ: but there was no discussion whether a subsequent notice based on a "past" breach, followed by a writ, would have resulted in either forfeiture or relief. *Rugby School (Governors) v Tannahill* [1935] 1 KB 87 was a case of user by the lessee for immoral purposes contrary to covenant in the lease sought to be forfeited. Apparently before the section 146 notice the prostitutes had left and the premises had ceased to be used for immoral purposes. The notice did not call upon the lessee to remedy the breach. At first instance the judge decided in favour of the lessor on the short ground that breach of a negative covenant could never be remedied. This court did not call upon counsel for the lessor, who thus had no opportunity to support the judge's short ground: this court expressed the view that breach of negative covenants might be capable of remedy, but not this one, on the ground that the stigma attaching to the premises would not be removed by mere cesser of the immoral user. I observe that it does not appear to have been considered whether the breach in that case was incapable of remedy on another ground, viz.: that the wrongful user had ceased before the section 146 notice. It might perhaps be argued that reliance

---

[15] *Capital and Counties Property Co Ltd v Mills* [1966] EGD 96.

by this court on the "stigma" point suggests that it was considered that a wrongful user in breach wholly in the past, without continuing adverse effect, would not entitle the lessor to seek to forfeit at all. But the question does not seem to have been canvassed.

[His Lordship referred to *Borthwick-Norton v Romney Warwick Estates Ltd* [1950] 1 All ER 798, and continued:]

In *Hoffmann v Fineberg* [1949] Ch 245, [1948] 1 All ER 592 (Harman J), the lessee, in breach of user covenants, allowed the premises to be used for illegal gambling, for which there were convictions. The section 146 notice did not call for the breach to be remedied. It is not clear whether the illegal user continued at the date of the notice. Again the decision was based on the "stigma" aspect as making the breach incapable of remedy within a reasonable time. Harman J said, at 257 at 597: ". . . on the facts of this case this is a breach where mere cesser is no remedy." The judgment referred to another immoral user case of *Egerton v Esplanade Hotels London Ltd* [1947] 2 All ER 88 (Morris J), in which the notice did not call for the breach to be remedied: it was decided on the stigma point, on the facts of that case, that the breach was not capable of remedy within a reasonable time. Morris J said, at 91: "Merely desisting from the wrongful user or not continuing to commit further breaches is not, . . . on the facts of this case, a way of remedying the breach." Neither case was considered on the possible shorter ground that a user covenant breach when the user had ceased before the section 146 notice was incapable of remedy for that very reason.

Glass v Kencakes Ltd [1966] 1 QB 611, [1964] 3 All ER 807, a decision of Paull J, was of this nature. The lease forbade the use of the upper part of the premises otherwise than for residential purposes. The lessee sublet that part to D, who caused and permitted their use for the business of prostitution unknown to the lessee. The sublease contained a similar covenant. The section 146 notice was simply based upon the fact of business use. It asserted that the breach was incapable of remedy. The judge held that the breach of the sublease by D was incapable of remedy by him: apparently he considered that the person who caused or permitted such a use could not, by the cesser of such use, remedy the breach, because the stigma on the premises could not be blotted out within a reasonable time so long as the man responsible remained subtenant. He therefore could not remedy his breach. Paull J pointed out that in the *Rugby School* case [1934] 1 KB 695, in *Egerton v Esplanade Hotels London Ltd* [1947] 2 All ER 88 (both cases of immoral user) and in *Hoffmann v Fineberg* [1949] Ch 245, [1948] 1 All ER 592 (the illegal gambling case) it was in each case the tenant under the lease sought to be forfeited who was directly responsible for the breach: and that in the *Borthwick-Norton* case [1950] 1 All ER 798 the lessee had in breach suffered and permitted the immoral user by a subtenant. Paull J decided, however, that where the breach alleged was merely of a user by a subtenant for which the lessee whose lease was sought to be forfeited could not be said to have permitted or suffered or to be in any way responsible for, the breach was not incapable of remedy by that lessee, the remedy required being not only the cesser of the user in breach but also the ending of the subterm with all expedition by forfeiture. Paull J was much impressed by the argument that where there was a lease for a large block of flats, one of which, without any fault of the lessee, was used for a short time in breach of the user covenant in the lease by a subtenant, he should not be put in the situation that he was not capable of remedying the breach and must therefore be put to the expense of seeking relief from forfeiture. He held in that case that the notice was bad since it asserted that the breach was not capable of remedy[16].

Two points are to be noticed in that case. First: Paull J did not address his mind, particularly in the case of the large block of flats mentioned, to the possible situation of the lessee if the subletting in question, and therefore the unlawful user, had come to an end before discovery by the head lessor, when no remedial step would have been available to the lessee, and whether in such case the lessee could only have sought relief. Second: the decision in terms says nothing of a case (other than "stigma" cases) where the lessee is directly responsible for the breach by a business user contrary to covenant. . . .

In summary upon the cases we have therefore a number of cases of user of premises in breach of covenant in which the decision that the breach is not capable of remedy has gone upon the "stigma" point, without considering whether a short answer might be — if the user had ceased before the section 146 notice — that it was ex hypothesi incapable of remedy, leaving the lessee only with the ability to seek relief from forfeiture and the writ unchallengeable as such. If a user in breach has ceased before the section 146 notice (quite apart from the stigma cases) then either it is incapable of remedy and after notice there is nothing in the way of a writ: or the cesser of use has somehow deprived the lessor of his ability to seek to forfeit though he has done nothing to waive the breach, a situation in law which I find extremely difficult to spell out of section 146. But whatever may be the position in user breach cases, which are of a continuing nature, there is no authority, other than that of *Capital and Counties Property Co Ltd v Mills* [1966] EGD 96 to suggest that the creation of a subterm in breach of covenant is capable of remedy. I would make two particular comments on that decision, as reported. First: I find it difficult to see how a breach is said to be capable of remedy because the lessor can waive the breach, which would be involved in the suggestion that he could post hoc consent to the subletting. Second: I do not see how a breach by unlawful subletting can be said to be remedied by the lessee when he does nothing except wait for the subterm to come to an end by effluxion of time.

After this review of the cases I come to the conclusion that breach by an unlawful subletting is not capable of remedy at all. In my judgment the introduction of such breaches into the relevant section for the first time by section 146 of the Act of 1925 operates only to confer a statutory ability to relieve the lessee from forfeiture on that ground. The subterm has been effectively created subject only to risks of forfeiture: it is a complete breach once for all: it is not in any sense a continuing breach. If the law were otherwise a lessee, when a subtenancy is current at the time of the section 146 notice, would have a chance of remedying the situation without having to apply for relief. But if the unlawful subletting had determined before the notice, the lessee could only seek relief from forfeiture. The only escape from that wholly unsatisfactory difference would be to hold that in the second

---

[16] Cf. *British Petroleum Pension Trust Ltd v Behrendt* (1985) 276 EG 199, where "the tenant either knew of or deliberately shut his eyes to the use of the premises for prostitution" by his licensee.

example by some analogy the lessor was disabled from issuing a writ for possession. But I can find nothing in the section to justify that limitation on the common law right of re-entry, bearing especially in mind that a lessor might discover a whole series of past expired unlawful sublettings which might well justify a refusal to grant relief in forfeiture proceedings.

I stress again that where there has been an unlawful subletting which has determined (and which has not been waived) there has been a breach which at common law entitles the lessor to re-enter: nothing can be done to remedy that breach: the expiry of the subterm has not annulled or remedied the breach: in such case the lessor plainly need not, in his section 146 notice, call upon the lessee to remedy the breach which is not capable of remedy, and is free to issue his writ for possession, the possibility of relief remaining. Can it possibly be that, while that is the situation in such case, it is otherwise if the lessee has failed to get rid of the subterm until after a notice served? Is the lessee then in a stronger position and the lessor in a weaker position? In my judgment not so. These problems and questions arise only if such a breach is capable of remedy, which in my judgment it is not[17]. I consider that *Capital and Counties Property Co Ltd v Mills* [1966] EGD 96, if correctly reported, was wrongly decided. I should add that I find some support for my opinion in the comments of Fraser J in *Abrahams v Mac Fisheries Ltd* [1925] 2 KB 18, 35, who expressed the view that the exceptions in section 14 (6) of the Act of 1881 (as to, inter alia, subletting) were made to cover cases where the breach cannot be remedied specifically.

In those circumstances in judging whether the 14 days that here elapsed between the section 146 notice and the writ, the time which it might reasonably take the lessee to come to terms with the subtenants, the second and third defendants, so as to end the subterm, which in fact was done in June 1972, is irrelevant. In those circumstances it is in my view plain that the writ was not prematurely issued, even assuming, as with all familial piety I must having regard to *Civil Service Co-operative Society Ltd v McGrigor's Trustee* [1923] 2 Ch 347, citing *Horsey Estate Ltd v Steiger* [1899] 2 QB 79, that reasonable time in the case of an irremediable breach is related to something other than making compensation in money, notwithstanding the language of the section.

2.   BREACH OF POSITIVE COVENANT

EXPERT CLOTHING SERVICE AND SALES LTD *v* HILLGATE HOUSE LTD
[1985] 3 WLR 359, [1985] 2 All ER 998 (CA, O'CONNOR and SLADE LJJ and BRISTOW J)

In 1972 the plaintiff landlords granted a 25 year lease of Hillgate House, London W 8 to the defendants, who covenanted to reconstruct the premises into a gymnasium and health club and to make them ready for occupation by

---

[17] See the general criticism of this reasoning in *Expert Clothing Service and Sales Ltd v Hillgate House Ltd* [1985] 3 WLR 359 at 380, [1985] 2 All ER 998 at p. 1015, per O'CONNOR LJ: "It seems to me that it cannot be right to describe a breach which has been remedied as a breach which *is* incapable of remedy, and thereafter to say that it was incapable of remedy before it was remedied. To my mind a breach which has been remedied has been demonstrated to have been a breach which was ab initio capable of remedy."

or before 28 September 1982. The defendants failed to carry out the work. The plaintiffs served a s. 146 notice, alleging the breach of covenant and stating that the breach was incapable of remedy. They then brought proceedings claiming possession of the premises.

Held (reversing Judge Paul Baker QC). Claim for possession refused. The breach was capable of remedy, and, therefore the notice was invalid[19].

SLADE LJ: In a case where the breach is "capable of remedy" within the meaning of the section, the principal object of the notice procedure provided for by section 146 (1), as I read it, is to afford the lessee two opportunities before the lessor actually proceeds to enforce his right of re-entry, namely (1) the opportunity to remedy the breach within a reasonable time after service of the notice, and (2) the opportunity to apply to the court for relief from forfeiture. In a case where the breach is not "capable of remedy," there is clearly no point in affording the first of these two opportunities; the object of the notice procedure is thus simply to give the lessee the opportunity to apply for relief.

Unfortunately the authorities give only limited guidance as to what breaches are capable of remedy within the meaning of the section. As Harman J pointed out in *Hoffman v Fineberg* [1949] Ch 245 at 253:

"In one sense, no breach can ever be remedied, because there must always, ex concessis, be a time in which there has not been compliance with the covenant, but the section clearly involves the view that some breaches are remediable, and therefore it cannot mean that."

[His Lordship referred to MACKINNON J in *Rugby School (Governors) v Tannahill* [1934] 1 KB 695 at 701, p. 438, n. 13, ante, and to GREER LJ in [1935] 1 KB 87 at 90–91, p. 438, ante, and MAUGHAM LJ at 93, and continued:]

In supporting the judge's conclusion that the breach relating to reconstruction of the premises was irremediable, Mr Collins, on behalf of the plaintiffs, has submitted to us three principal arguments. First, he pointed out that (as is common ground) the first defendant's failure to build by 28 September 1982 was a "once and for all" breach of the relevant covenant, and not a continuing breach: see, for example, *Stephens v Junior Army and Navy Stores Ltd* [1914] 2 Ch 516 at 523, per Lord Cozens-Hardy MR. He submitted that the breach of a covenant such as this, which can only be broken once, is ex hypothesi in no case capable of remedy.

Some superficial support for this conclusion is perhaps to be found in the judgments in *Scala House and District Property Co Ltd v Forbes* [1974] QB 575, [1973] 3 All ER 308, p. 439, ante, in which the Court of Appeal held that the breach of a covenant not to assign, underlet or part with possession was not a breach capable of remedy within the meaning of section 146 (1). . . .

[His Lordship referred to RUSSELL LJ at 588, at 315, p. 442, ante, and continued:]

It might well be regarded as anomalous if the once and for all breach of a negative covenant not to sublet were to be regarded as "capable of remedy" within section 146, provided that the unlawful subtenancy was still current at the date of the section 146 notice, but (as Russell LJ considered) were not to be regarded as "capable of remedy" if the unlawful subtenancy had been

---

[19] The court further held that the plaintiffs had not waived their right to forfeit the lease.

determined at that date. Russell LJ and James LJ who agreed with his reasoning (see particularly at p. 591c–d), were clearly much influenced by this anomaly in reaching the conclusion that the breach of a covenant against underletting is never capable of remedy.

However, in the *Scala House* case this court was addressing its mind solely to the once and for all breach of a negative covenant. No corresponding anomaly arises if the once and for all breach of a positive covenant is treated as capable of remedy. While the *Scala House* decision is, of course, authority binding on this court for the proposition that the breach of a negative covenant not to assign, underlet or part with possession is never "capable of remedy," it is not, in my judgment, authority for the proposition that the once and for all breach of a positive covenant is never capable of remedy.

Mr Neuberger, on behalf of the defendants, did not feel able to go so far as to support the view of MacKinnon J that the breach of a positive covenant is *always* capable of remedy. He accepted, for example, that the breach of a covenant to insure might be incapable of remedy at a time when the premises had already been burnt down. Another example might be the breach of a positive covenant which in the event would be only capable of being fully performed, if at all, after the expiration of the relevant term.

Nevertheless, I would, for my part, accept Mr Neuberger's submission that the breach of a positive covenant (whether it be a continuing breach or a once and for all breach) will ordinarily be capable of remedy. As Bristow J pointed out in the course of argument, the concept of capability of remedy for the purpose of section 146 must surely be directed to the question whether the harm that has been done to the landlord by the relevant breach is for practicable purposes capable of being retrieved. In the ordinary case, the breach of a promise to do something by a certain time can for practical purposes be remedied by the thing being done, even out of time. For these reasons I reject the plaintiffs' argument that the breach of the covenant to reconstruct by 28 September 1982 was not capable of remedy *merely* because it was not a continuing breach. . . .

[His Lordship rejected the second main argument that the breach of covenant was incapable of remedy because of the operation of a rent review clause and continued:]

I therefore turn to the third, and far the most important point, relied on by Mr Collins in support of the decision of the court below. His submissions in this context were to the following effect. The judgment of Maugham LJ in the *Rugby School* case [1935] 1 KB 87 at 93 and other judicial dicta indicate that if a breach is to be "capable of remedy" at all within the meaning of section 146, it must be capable of remedy *within a "reasonable time."* As was observed by Lord Herschell LC in *Hick v Raymond and Reid* [1893] AC 22 at 29: "there is of course no such thing as a reasonable time in the abstract. It must always depend upon circumstances." In the present case, it was submitted, what was a reasonable time was a question of fact. In deciding that the breach of the covenant to reconstruct was not capable of remedy within a reasonable time, the judge expressed himself as "having regard to the facts as I have found them.". . . .

In my opinion, in considering whether or not remedy within a reasonable time is possible, a crucial distinction (which I infer from the judgment did not feature prominently in argument before the judge) falls to be drawn between breaches of negative user covenants, such as those under consideration in the *Rugby School* and the *Esplanade Hotels* [1947] 2 All ER 88 cases, and breaches of positive covenants. In the two last-mentioned cases, where the relevant breaches consisted of allowing premises to be used as a brothel, even full compliance with the covenant within a reasonable time and for a reasonable time would not have remedied the breach. As Maugham LJ pointed out in the *Rugby School* case, at 94:

"merely ceasing for a reasonable time, perhaps a few weeks or a month, to use the premises for an immoral purpose would be no remedy for the breach of covenant which had been committed over a long period."

On the facts of cases such as those, mere cesser by the tenant of the offending use within a reasonable period and for a reasonable period of time could not have remedied the breaches because it could not have removed the stigma which they had caused to attach to the premises. The harm had been irretrievably done. In such cases, as Harman J pointed out in *Hoffmann v Fineberg* [1949] Ch 245 at 257, [1948] 1 All ER 592 at 597, mere cesser will not enable the tenant to "make his record clean, as he could by complying, though out of time, with a failure to lay on the prescribed number of coats of paint."

In contrast with breaches of negative user covenants, the breach of a positive covenant to do something (such as to decorate or build) can ordinarily, for practical purposes, be remedied by the thing being actually done if a reasonable time for its performance (running from the service of the section 146 notice) is duly allowed by the landlord following such service and the tenant duly does it within such time.

In the present case there is no question of the breach of the covenant to reconstruct having given rise to any "stigma" against the lessors or the premises. Significantly, the lease in 1982 still had 20 years to run. Mr Collins has, I think, been able to suggest no convincing reasons why the plaintiffs would still have suffered irremediable damage if (i) the section 146 notice had required the lessee to remedy the breach and (ii) the lessors had then allowed a reasonable time to elapse sufficient to enable the lessee to comply with the relevant covenant, and (iii) the lessee had complied with the covenant in such reasonable time and had paid any appropriate monetary compensation. Though he has submitted that a requirement directed to the defendants to remedy the breach would have been purposeless, on the grounds that they had neither the financial means nor the will to do the necessary work, these are matters which, in my opinion, a landlord is not entitled to prejudge in drafting his notice. An important purpose of the section 146 procedure is to give even tenants who have hitherto lacked the will or the means to comply with their obligations one last chance to summon up that will or find the necessary means before the landlord re-enters. In considering what "reasonable time" to allow the defendants, the plaintiffs, in serving their section 146 notice, would, in my opinion, have been entitled to take into account the fact that the defendants already had enjoyed 15 months in which to fulfil their contractual obligations to reconstruct and to subject the defendants to a correspondingly tight timetable running from the date of service of the notice, though, at the same time, always bearing in mind that the contractual obligation to reconstruct did not even arise until 29 June 1981, and that as at 8 October 1982 the defendants had been in actual breach of it for only some 10 days. However, I think they were not entitled to say, in effect: "We are not going to allow you any time at all to remedy the breach, because you have had so long to do the work already."

In my judgment, on the remediability issue, the ultimate question for the court was this: if the section 146 notice had required the lessee to remedy the breach and the lessors had then allowed a reasonable time to elapse to enable the lessee fully to comply with the relevant covenant, would such compliance, coupled with the payment of any appropriate monetary compensation, have effectively remedied the harm which the lessors had suffered or were likely to suffer from the breach? If, but only if, the answer to this question was "No," would the failure of the section 146 notice to require remedy of the breach have been justifiable. In *Rugby School (Governors) v Tannahill* [1935] 1 KB 87; *Egerton v Esplanade Hotels, London Ltd* [1947] 2 All ER 88 and *Hoffman v Fineberg* [1949] Ch 245, [1948] 1 All ER 592 the answer to this question plainly would have been "No." In the present case, however, for the reasons already stated, I think the answer to it must have been "Yes."

My conclusion, therefore, is that the breach of the covenant to reconstruct . . . was "capable of remedy." In reaching this conclusion, I find it reassuring that no reported case has been brought to our attention in which the breach of a positive covenant has been held incapable of remedy, though I do not suggest that cases of this nature, albeit perhaps rarely, could not arise.

In *Plymouth Corporation v Harvey* [1971] 1 WLR 549, [1971] 1 All ER 623, the tenant executed an undated deed of surrender in escrow. When he was in breach, the landlord dated the deed and demanded possession. The deed was held void as being a device to circumvent section 146. The statutory notices were required. "A forfeiture in the guise of a surrender . . . remains a forfeiture for the purposes of section 146," said PLOWMAN J.

(b) Covenants to Repair

LANDLORD AND TENANT ACT 1927

18. Provisions as to covenants to repair. — (2) A right of re-entry or forfeiture for a breach of any such covenant or agreement as aforesaid shall not be enforceable, by action or otherwise, unless the lessor proves that the fact that such a notice as is required by section one hundred and forty-six of the Law of Property Act, 1925, had been served on the lessee was known either —

    (*a*) to the lessee; or
    (*b*) to an under-lessee holding under an under-lease which reserved a nominal reversion only to the lessee; or
    (*c*) to the person who last paid the rent due under the lease either on his own behalf or as agent for the lessee or under-lessee;

and that a time reasonably sufficient to enable the repairs to be executed had elapsed since the time when the fact of the service of the notice came to the knowledge of any such person.

Where a notice has been sent by registered post[20] addressed to a person at his last known place of abode in the United Kingdom, then, for the purposes of this subsection, that person shall be deemed, unless the contrary is proved, to have had knowledge of the fact that the notice had been served as from the

---

[20] The recorded delivery service may be used as an alternative to registered post; Recorded Delivery Service Act 1962, s. 1 (1).

time at which the letter would have been delivered in the ordinary course of post.

This subsection shall be construed as one with section one hundred and forty-six of the Law of Property Act, 1925.

Where the landlord sues for damages or to enforce a forfeiture in respect of a covenant to keep or put the premises in repair, he is subject to a further statutory restriction under the Leasehold Property (Repairs) Act 1938[1].

LEASEHOLD PROPERTY (REPAIRS) ACT 1938

1[2].   Restriction on enforcement of repairing covenants in long leases of small houses. — (1) Where a lessor serves on a lessee under subsection (1) of section one hundred and forty-six of the Law of Property Act, 1925, a notice that relates to a breach of a covenant or agreement to keep or put in repair[3] during the currency of the lease all or any of the property comprised in the lease, and at the date of the service of the notice three years or more of the term of the lease remain unexpired, the lessee may within twenty-eight days from that date serve on the lessor a counter-notice to the effect that he claims the benefit of this Act.

(2) A right to damages[1] for a breach of such a covenant as aforesaid shall not be enforceable by action commenced at any time at which three years or more of the term of the lease remain unexpired unless the lessor has served on the lessee not less than one month before the commencement of the action such a notice as is specified in subsection (1) of section one hundred and forty-six of the Law of Property Act, 1925[3], and where a notice is served under this subsection, the lessee may, within twenty-eight days from the date of the service thereof, serve on the lessor a counter-notice to the effect that he claims the benefit of this Act.

(3) Where a counter-notice is served by a lessee under this section, then, notwithstanding anything in any enactment or rule of law, no proceedings, by action or otherwise, shall be taken by the lessor for the enforcement of any right of re-entry or forfeiture under any proviso or stipulation in the lease for breach of the covenant or agreement in question, or for damages for breach thereof, otherwise than with the leave of the court.

(4) A notice served under subsection (1) of section one hundred and forty-six of the Law of Property Act, 1925, in the circumstances specified in

---

[1] For the special provisions relating to internal decorative repair, see LPA 1925, s. 147.

[2] As amended by Landlord and Tenant Act 1954, s. 5 (2), (5).

[3] *Starrokate Ltd v Burry* (1982) 265 EG 871 ("an obligation to cleanse is not an obligation to repair").

[4] A landlord's action to recover a sum expended on carrying out repairs for which the tenant was liable was held to be for debt and not for damages: *Hamilton v Martell Securities Ltd* [1984] Ch 266, [1984] 1 All ER 665; *Colchester Estates (Cardiff) v Carlton Industries plc*, [1984] 3 WLR 693 [1984] 2 All ER 601; *Swallow Securities Ltd v Brand* (1981) 45 P & CR 328 was not followed; (1984) 134 NLJ 791 (H. W. Wilkinson).

[5] A notice cannot be served after the breach has been remedied, even if it is remedied by the landlord, since the s. 146 notice cannot then require the tenant to remedy the breach: *SEDAC Investments Ltd v Tanner* [1982] 1 WLR 1342, [1982] 3 All ER 646 ("a conclusion reached" by Michael Wheeler QC "with surprise and regret"): In *Hamilton v Martell Securities Ltd*, VINELOTT J was "not persuaded that the decision was wrong." [1983] Conv 72 (P. F. Smith).

subsection (1) of this section, and a notice served under subsection (2) of this section shall not be valid unless it contains a statement, in characters not less conspicuous than those used in any other part of the notice[6], to the effect that the lessee is entitled under this Act to serve on the lessor a counter-notice claiming the benefit of this Act, and a statement in the like characters specifying the time within which, and the manner in which, under this Act a counter-notice may be served and specifying the name and address for service of the lessor[7].

(5) Leave for the purposes of this section shall not be given unless the lessor proves[8] —

   (*a*) that the immediate remedying of the breach in question is requisite for preventing substantial diminution in the value of his reversion, or that the value thereof has been substantially diminished by the breach;

   (*b*) that the immediate remedying of the breach is required for giving effect in relation to the premises to the purposes of any enactment, or of any byelaw or other provision having effect under an enactment, or for giving effect to any order of a court or requirement of any authority under any enactment or any such byelaw, or other provision as aforesaid;

   (*c*) in a case in which the lessee is not in occupation of the whole of the premises as respects which the covenant or agreement is proposed to be enforced, that the immediate remedying of the breach is required in the interests of the occupier of those premises or of part thereof;

   (*d*) that the breach can be immediately remedied at an expense that is relatively small in comparison with the much greater expense that would probably be occasioned by postponement of the necessary work; or

   (*e*) special circumstances which in the opinion of the court, render it just and equitable that leave should be given.

(6) The court may, in granting or in refusing leave for the purposes of this section, impose such terms and conditions on the lessor or on the lessee as it may think fit.

iii.   WAIVER

(*a*) *The Doctrine*

In *Matthews v Smallwood* [1910] 1 Ch 777, PARKER J said at 786: "I think that the law on the subject of waiver is reasonably clear. The right to re-enter is a legal right which, apart from release or abandonment or waiver, will exist and can be exercised, at any time within the period fixed by the Statutes of Limitation; and if a defendant in an action of ejectment based upon that right of re-entry alleges a release or abandonment or waiver, logically speaking the onus ought to lie on him to shew the release or the abandonment or the

---

[6] To be read as "equally readable": *Middlegate Properties Ltd v Messimeris* [1973] 1 WLR 168, [1973] 1 All ER 645.

[7] *Middlegate Properties Ltd v Messimeris*, supra; *BL Holdings Ltd v Marcolt Investments Ltd* (1978) 249 EG 849.

[8] The landlord has only to show a prima facie or arguable case: *Sidnell v Wilson* [1966] 2 QB 67, [1966] 1 All ER 681; *Land Securities plc v Metropolitan Police District Receiver* [1983] 1 WLR 439, [1983] 2 All ER 254 (Scotland Yard).

waiver. Waiver of a right of re-entry can only occur where the lessor, with knowledge of the facts upon which his right to re-enter arises, does some unequivocal act recognizing the continued existence of the lease. It is not enough that he should do the act which recognizes, or appears to recognize, the continued existence of the lease, unless, at the time when the act is done, he has knowledge of the facts under which, or from which, his right of entry arose. Therefore we get the principle that, though an act of waiver operates with regard to all known breaches, it does not operate with regard to breaches which were unknown to the lessor at the time when the act took place. It is also, I think, reasonably clear upon the cases that whether the act, coupled with the knowledge, constitutes a waiver is a question which the law decides, and therefore it is not open to a lessor who has knowledge of the breach to say 'I will treat the tenancy as existing, and I will receive the rent, or I will take advantage of my power as landlord to distrain; but I tell you that all I shall do will be without prejudice to my right to re-enter, which I intend to reserve'. That is a position which he is not entitled to take up. If, knowing of the breach, he does distrain, or does receive the rent, then by law he waives the breach, and nothing which he can say by way of protest against the law will avail him anything. Logically, therefore, a person who relies upon waiver ought to shew, first, an act unequivocally recognizing the subsistence of the lease, and, secondly, knowledge of the circumstances from which the right of re-entry arises at the time when the act is performed[9]."

LAW OF PROPERTY ACT 1925

148.   Waiver of a covenant in a lease. — (1) Where any actual waiver by a lessor or the persons deriving title under him of the benefit of any covenant or condition in any lease is proved to have taken place in any particular instance, such waiver shall not be deemed to extend to any instance, or to any breach of covenant or condition save that to which such waiver specially relates, nor operate as a general waiver of the benefit of any such covenant or condition.

(2) This section applies unless a contrary intention appears and extends to waivers effected after the twenty-third day of July, eighteen hundred and sixty.

---

[9] *Goodright d Charter v Cordwent* (1795) 6 Term Rep 219; *Dendy v Nicholl* (1858) 4 CBNS 376; *Ward v Day* (1864) 5 B & S 359; *Grimwood v Moss* (1872) LR 7 CP 360; *Segal Securities Ltd v Thoseby* [1963] 1 QB 887, [1963] 1 All ER 500 (demand for rent made without prejudice held to be waiver); cf. *Expert Clothing Service and Sales Ltd v Hillgate House Ltd* [1985] 3 WLR 359, [1985] 2 All ER 998, p. 443, ante (proferring of negotiating document held not to be waiver where no acceptance of rent or demand for rent involved); *Church Commissioners for England v Nodjoumi* (1985) 135 NLJ 1185 (service of s. 146 notice held not to be waiver of right to forfeit lease on grounds other than those set out in notice); *Central Estates (Belgravia) Ltd v Woolgar (No 2)* [1972] 1 WLR 1048, [1972] 3 All ER 610 (clerk of landlord's agents accepted rent by mistake); *David Blackstone Ltd v Burnetts (West End) Ltd* [1973] 1 WLR 1487, [1973] 3 All ER 782, p. 451, post (demand for future rent); *Welch v Birrane* (1975) 29 P & CR 102; (1976) 40 Conv (NS) 327; (1977) 41 Conv (NS) 220 (E. L. G. Tyler); *Metropolitan Properties Co Ltd v Cordery* (1979) 39 P & CR 10 (landlords' acceptance of rent for flat with knowledge, through their porters, of facts which pointed to breach of covenant held to be waiver). Cf. *Trustees of Henry Smith's Charity v Willson* [1983] QB 316, [1983] 1 All ER 73 (uncommunicated rent demand); *Official Custodian for Charities v Parway Estates Developments Ltd* [1985] Ch 151, [1984] 3 All ER 679, CA (publication in London Gazette of compulsory liquidation held not to be imputed knowledge so as to constitute waiver).

In *David Blackstone Ltd v Burnetts (West End) Ltd* [1973] 1 WLR 1487, [1973] 3 All ER 782, SWANWICK J, in holding that there had been waiver by a landlord who was demanding future rent, said at 1498, at 792:

"My view, both on principle and on such persuasive authority as has been cited to me, is that an unambiguous demand for future rent in advance such as was made here does in law amount to an election and does constitute a waiver if, at the time when it is made, the landlord has sufficient knowledge of the facts to put him to his election. To my perhaps simple mind there is a fundamental inconsistency between contending that a lease has been determined and demanding rent on the basis of its future continuance.

This leads me to the second main issue in this case: what knowledge must the landlord or his agent be proved to have had in order that a demand for rent should amount to a waiver; what is the point in time at which such knowledge is to be assessed; and, therefore, are the second plaintiffs proved to have had the necessary knowledge at the relevant time so as to make their demand a waiver?

I will deal first with the appropriate point in time. . . .

I consider that . . . for there to be a valid election to waive a breach, the landlord or his agent must have sufficient knowledge of the breach before despatching the document making the election, but that such election does not become effective until it is communicated to the tenant. . . .

This leaves the final branch of the final question. At the relevant time, did the second plaintiffs possess sufficient knowledge of the breach to render the demand a waiver in law? . . .

In my judgment, again without the guidance of any direct authority, the knowledge required to put a landlord to his election is knowledge of the basic facts which in law constitute a breach of covenant entitling him to forfeit the lease. Once he or his agent knows those facts an appropriate act by himself or any agent will in law effect a waiver or a forfeiture. His knowledge or ignorance of the law is, in my judgment, irrelevant. If it were not so, a vast gap would be opened in the administration of the law of landlord and tenant and a facile escape route for landlords would be provided. Indeed, if this were the position unscrupulous landlords could hardly have failed in the past to take advantage of it long before now."

(b) Waiver of Continuing Breach

In *City and Westminster Properties (1934) Ltd v Mudd* [1959] Ch 129, [1958] 2 All ER 733[10] a lease contained a covenant by the tenant "to use the demised premises as showrooms, workrooms and offices only". The tenant admitted that he was sleeping there. In an action for forfeiture for breach of covenant, the tenant alleged, inter alia, a release or waiver by the landlord by reason of his knowledge of the breach prior to and during the currency of the lease. In refusing the claim of waiver, HARMAN J said at 143, at 741:

"The next issue is that of waiver. Now residence, contrary to the covenants of the lease, is a continuing breach and therefore prima facie it is only waived by the acceptance of rent down to the date of that acceptance and there is a new breach immediately thereafter which is not waived. My attention was called to a number of cases which show that acts of waiver may be so continuous that the court is driven to the conclusion that there has been a

---

[10] *Cooper v Henderson* (1982) 263 EG 592.

new agreement for letting or a licence or a release of the covenant. The cases cited on this subject show acquiescence continuing for a very long period of years. For instance, in *Gibson v Doeg* (1857) 2 H & N 615 the period was 20 years, in *Gibbon v Payne* (1905) 22 TLR 54 it was 40 years, and in *Hepworth v Pickles* [1900] 1 Ch 108, 24 years. In the more recent case of *Lloyds Bank Ltd v Jones* [1955] 2 QB 298, [1955] 2 All ER 409, Singleton LJ points out that no particular period such as 20 years is required. . . .

Again, in *Wolfe v Hogan* [1949] 2 KB 194, [1949] 1 All ER 570 I find this in the headnote: 'The mere acceptance of rent by the landlord from the tenant, after he had knowledge of the change of user by the tenant, though it continues for some time, does not, by itself, constitute such acceptance by the landlord of the changed position as to show that the house has been let as a separate dwelling'; and Denning LJ, after dealing with the facts, says this at 205, at 575: 'A house or a part of a house originally let for business purposes does not become let for dwelling purposes unless it can be inferred from the acceptance of rent that the landlord has affirmatively consented to the change of user. Let me illustrate that from the common law doctrine as to waiver of forfeiture. A breach of covenant not to use premises in a particular way is a continuing breach. Any acceptance of rent by the landlord, after knowledge, only waives the breaches up to the time of the acceptance of rent. It does not waive the continuance of the breach thereafter and, notwithstanding his previous acceptance of rent, the landlord can still proceed for forfeiture on that account. Indeed, in the case of a continuing breach, the acceptance of rent, after knowledge, is only a bar to a claim for forfeiture if it goes on for so long, or is accepted in such circumstances, that it can be inferred that the landlord has not merely waived the breach but has affirmatively consented to the tenant continuing to use the premises as he has done. I cannot think that anything proved here amounts to a release by the landlord of his rights. He knew, indeed, that the tenant was using the property to sleep in, but I do not think he knew more than that. At that he was willing to wink, but I am unable to find a release of the covenant or an agreement for a new letting. In my judgment, therefore, the plea of waiver fails.'

iv. RELIEF AGAINST FORFEITURE

In *Shiloh Spinners Ltd v Harding* [1973] AC 691, [1973] 1 All ER 90[11], Lord WILBERFORCE said at 722, at 100: "There cannot be any doubt that from the earliest times courts of equity have asserted the right to relieve against the forfeiture of property. The jurisdiction has not been confined to any particular type of case. The commonest instances concerned mortgages, giving rise to the equity of redemption, and leases, which commonly contained re-entry clauses; but other instances are found in relation to copyholds, or where the forfeiture was in the nature of a penalty. Although the principle is well established, there has undoubtedly been some fluctuation of authority as to the self-limitation to be imposed or accepted on this

---

[11] P. 34, ante. See also *Scala House and District Property Co Ltd v Forbes* [1974] QB 575 at 584, [1973] 3 All ER 308, p. 439, ante. For a case where CA was prepared to grant relief in wholly exceptional circumstances in favour of a tenant who was in breach of a covenant against immoral user, see *Central Estates (Belgravia) Ltd v Woolgar (No 2)* [1972] 1 WLR 1048, [1972] 3 All ER 610; cf. *British Petroleum Pension Trust Ltd v Behrendt* (1985) 276 EG 199.

power. There has not been much difficulty as regards two heads of jurisdiction. First, where it is possible to state that the object of the transaction and of the insertion of the right to forfeit is essentially to secure the payment of money, equity has been willing to relieve on terms that the payment is made with interest, if appropriate, and also costs (*Peachy v Duke of Somerset* (1721) 1 Stra 447 and cases there cited). Yet even this head of relief has not been uncontested: Lord Eldon LC in his well-known judgment in *Hill v Barclay* (1811) 18 Ves 56 expressed his suspicion of it as a valid principle, pointing out, in an argument which surely has much force, that there may be cases where to oblige acceptance of a stipulated sum of money even with interest, at a date when receipt had lost its usefulness, might represent an unjust variation of what had been contracted for: see also *Reynolds v Pitt* (1812) 19 Ves 140. Secondly there were the heads of fraud, accident, mistake or surprise, always a ground for equity's intervention, the inclusion of which entailed the exclusion of mere inadvertence and a fortiori of wilful defaults.

Outside of these there remained a debatable area in which were included obligations in leases such as to repair and analogous obligations concerning the condition of property, and covenants to insure or not to assign. As to covenants to repair and cases of waste, cases can be quoted before the 19th century in which relief was granted: see *Webber v Smith* (1689) 2 Vern 103 and *Nash v Earl of Derby* (1705) 2 Vern 537. There were hostile pronouncements. In *Wadman v Calcraft* (1804) 10 Ves Jun 67 both Sir William Grant MR and Lord Eldon LC are found stating it to be clear that relief cannot be given against the breach of other covenants — i.e. than covenants to pay rent.

It was soon after that the critical divide or supposed divide occurred, between the liberal view of Lord Erskine LC in *Sanders v Pope* (1806) 12 Ves Jun 282 and the strict view of Lord Eldon LC in *Hill v Barclay*. The latter case came to be followed as the true canon; the former was poorly regarded in Lincoln's Inn, but it is important to observe where the difference lay. This was not, as I understand it, in any disagreement as to the field in which relief might be granted, for both cases seem to have accepted that, in principle, relief from forfeiture might be granted when the covenant was to lay out a sum of money on property: but rather on whether equity would relieve against a wilful breach. The breach in *Sanders v Pope* was of this kind but Lord Erskine LC said at 293: 'If the covenant is broken with the consciousness, that it is broken, that is, if it is wilful, not by surprise, accident, or ignorance, still if it is a case, where full compensation can be made, these authorities say, not that it is imperative upon the court to give the relief, but that there is a discretion.' To this Lord Eldon LC answers, 18 Ves Jun 56, 63: '. . . with regard to other cases,' (sc. waste or omitting repairs) 'the doctrine I have repeatedly stated is all wrong, if it is to be taken, that relief is to be given in case of a wilful breach of covenant.' The emphasis here, and the root of disagreement, clearly relates to wilful breaches, and on this it is still Lord Eldon LC's view which holds the field.

The suggestion that relief could not be granted against forfeiture for breach of other covenants was not one that followed from either case: relief was so granted in *Bargent v Thomson* (1864) 4 Giff 473. Equally in *Barrow v Isaacs & Son* [1891] 1 QB 417, a case of a covenant against underletting without consent, a high water mark of the strict doctrine, the emphasis is not so much on the nature of the breach which may or may not be relieved against, but on the argument that it is enough to show that compensation can be given: '. . . it was soon recognised that there would be great difficulty in estimating the proper amount of compensation; and, since the decision of Lord Eldon LC in *Hill v Barclay* it has always been held that equity would not relieve, merely on the ground that it could give compensation, upon breach of any covenant in a lease except the covenant for payment of rent' (per Kay LJ at 425).

We are not bound by these decisions, certainly not by every shade of opinion they may reflect, but I am entirely willing to follow them in their main lines.

As regards the present appeal it is possible to disengage the following considerations. In the first place there should be put on one side cases where the court has been asked to relieve against conditions contained in wills or gifts inter vivos. These raise considerations of a different kind from those relevant to contractual stipulations. Secondly, no decision in the present case involves the establishment or recognition directly or by implication of any general power — that is to say, apart from the special heads of fraud, accident, mistake or surprise — in courts exercising equitable jurisdiction to relieve against men's bargains. Lord Eldon LC's firm denial of any such power in *Hill v Barclay* does not call for any revision or review in this case. Equally there is no need to qualify Kay LJ's proposition in *Barrow v Isaacs & Son* (cited above). I would fully endorse this: it remains true today that equity expects men to carry out their bargains and will not let them buy their way out by unconvenanted payment. But it is consistent with these principles that we should reaffirm the right of courts of equity in appropriate and limited cases to relieve against forfeiture for breach of covenant or condition where the primary object of the bargain is to secure a stated result which can effectively be attained when the matter comes before the court, and where the forfeiture provision is added by way of security for the production of that result[12]. The word 'appropriate' involves consideration of the conduct of the applicant for relief, in particular whether his default was wilful, of the gravity of the breaches, and of the disparity between the value of the property of which forfeiture is claimed as compared with the damage caused by the breach.

Both as a matter of history and by the nature of things, different considerations apply to different covenants. As regards covenants to pay rent, in spite of Lord Eldon LC's reservations, the matter has, subject to qualifications which need not be discussed, been taken over by statute, first by 4 Geo 2 c 28 then by later Acts leading up to the Law of Property Act 1925. The same is true of covenants to insure and other covenants in leases. I shall consider shortly the implications of the legislation as regards other covenants than those expressly mentioned. As regards covenants to repair and analogous covenants concerning the condition of property, other than

---

[12] The effect of the decisions of the House of Lords in *Scandinavian Trading Tanker Co AB v Flota Petrola Ecuatoriana* [1983] 2 AC 694, [1983] 2 All ER 763, and *Sport International Bussum BV v Inter-Footwear Ltd* [1984] 1 WLR 776, [1984] 1 All ER 376, is to confine the court's jurisdiction to grant relief against forfeiture to contracts concerning the transfer of proprietary or possessory rights; it will not be granted where the right is merely a contractual licence. See also *BICC plc v Burndy Corpn* [1985] Ch 232, [1985] 1 All ER 417, where DILLON LJ considered that, in the absence of "clear authority", relief in the form of an extension of time to pay was available in respect of an interest in personal property. See [1984] CLJ 134; [1985] CLJ 204 (C. J. Harpum); (1984) 100 LQR 427 (A. G. Long).

those now dealt with by Act of Parliament, it is not necessary to overrule *Hill v Barclay* any more than it was necessary for Lord Eldon LC to do more than to distinguish *Sanders v Pope*. Lord Eldon LC's decision was in fact based partly upon the circumstance that he was concerned with a wilful default and partly upon the impossibility of speculating whether the later doing of the repairs would compensate the landlord: such considerations remain relevant. Where it is necessary, and, in my opinion, right, to move away from some 19th century authorities, is to reject as a reason against granting relief, the impossibility for the courts to supervise the doing of work. The fact is a reality, no doubt, and explains why specific performance cannot be granted of agreements to this effect but in the present context it can now be seen (as it was seen by Lord Erksine LC in *Sanders v Pope*) to be an irrelevance: for what the court has to do is to satisfy itself, ex post facto, that the convenanted work has been done, and it has ample machinery, through certificates, or by enquiry, to do precisely this. This removes much of the support from one of the more formidable authorities, viz.: the majority judgment in *Bracebridge v Buckley* (1816) 2 Price 200.

There remain two other arguments which cannot be passed over. First it is said that the strict view (that there should be no relief except under the two classical headings) has been endorsed in this House in *Hughes v Metropolitan Rly Co* (1877) 2 App Cas 439. There is no substance in this. The basis of decision in this House was that the landlord's notice was suspended in operation by acquiescence, so that there was no effective breach. The opinion invoked is that of Lord Cairns LC, in which there appears this portion of a sentence, at 448: 'it could not be argued, that there was any right of a court of equity, . . . to give relief in cases of this kind, by way of mercy, or by way merely of saving property from forfeiture, . . .' words which have only to be re-read to show that they are no sort of denial of the jurisdiction now invoked.

Secondly, a point of more difficulty arises from the intervention of Parliament in providing specific machinery for the granting of relief against forfeiture of leases: see Law of Property (Amendment) Act 1859 (22 & 23 Vict c 35), Common Law Procedure Act 1852, Law of Property Act 1925, Leasehold Property (Repairs) Act 1938 and other statutes. This, it is said, negatives an intention that any corresponding jurisdiction should exist outside the case of leases. I do not accept this argument. In my opinion where the courts have established a general principle of law or equity, and the legislature steps in with particular legislation in a particular area, it must, unless showing a contrary intention, be taken to have left cases outside that area where they were under the influence of the general law. To suppose otherwise involves the conclusion that an existing jurisdiction has been cut down by implication, by an enactment moreover which is positive in character (for it amplifies the jurisdiction in cases of leases) rather than negative. That legislation did not have this effect was the view of Kay LJ in *Barrow v Isaacs & Son* [1891] 1 QB 417, 430, when he held that covenants against assigning — excluded from the Conveyancing Act 1881 — were left to be dealt with according to the ordinary law[13]. The Occupiers' Liability Act

---

[13] See *Official Custodian for Charities v Parway Estates Developments Ltd* [1985] Ch 151, [1984] 3 All ER 679, p. 437, n. 8, ante, where DILLON LJ cited that passage in refusing to hold that the court had an inherent jurisdiction to grant relief where LPA 1925, s. 146 (10) had not been complied with; *Smith v Metropolitan City Properties Ltd* (1985) 277 EG 753, p. 437, n. 8, ante.

1957 gave rise to a similar problem since it legislated as to one part of a larger total field; I may perhaps refer to what I said in *Herrington v British Railways Board* [1972] AC 877, [1972] 1 All ER 749.

The present case, in my opinion, falls within the class of case in which it would be possible for a court of equity to intervene. When the appellants assigned a portion of their leased property, retaining the rest, which adjoined and was supported by the portion assigned, they had an essential interest in securing adequate protection for their buildings, in having the entire site fenced, in preventing unauthorised access through the assigned property. The covenants were drafted accordingly. The power of re-entry was inserted by way of reinforcement of the contractual obligation which it must have been perceived might cease to be enforceable as such. Failures to observe the covenants having occurred, it would be right to consider whether the assignor should be allowed to exercise his legal rights if the essentials of the bargain could be secured and if it was fair and just to prevent him from doing so. It would be necessary, as stated above, to consider the conduct of the assignee, the nature and gravity of the breach, and its relation to the value of the property which might be forfeited. Established and, in my opinion, sound principle requires that wilful breaches should not, or at least should only in exceptional cases, be relieved against, if only for the reason that the assignor should not be compelled to remain in a relation of neighbourhood with a person in deliberate breach of his obligations.

In this light should relief have been granted? The respondent's difficulty is that the Vice-Chancellor, who heard the witnesses and went into all the facts, clearly took the view that the case was not one for relief. I should be reluctant, in any event, except on clear conviction to substitute a different view of my own. But I have examined in detail the evidence given, the correspondence over a period of four years, the photographs and plans of the site. All this material establishes a case of clear and wilful breaches of more than one covenant which, if individually not serious, were certainly substantial: a case of continuous disregard by the respondent of the appellants' rights over a period of time, coupled with a total lack of evidence as to the respondent's ability speedily and adequately to make good the consequences of his default, and finally a failure to show any such disproportion between the expenditure required and the value of the interest involved as to amount to a case of hardship. In my opinion the case is not, on established principles, one for relief.

For all these reasons I would allow the appeal."

V.   LAW REFORM

The Law Commission Report on Forfeiture of Tenancies 1985 (Law Com No. 142, HC 279) recommends radical changes in the law of forfeiture. "It is complex and confused; its many features fit together awkwardly; and it contains a number of uncertainties, anomalies and injustices." (para. 3.2) The Report identifies two major defects.

Firstly, the doctrine of re-entry under which a landlord forfeits a tenancy by re-entry upon the property let, and the tenancy terminates on the date on which re-entry takes place. As a result, the obligations which the tenancy imposes upon the tenant terminate also at that time. So, although the tenant may remain in posession for several months afterwards, he is not obliged to pay rent[14] or to perform any of his other covenants, unless he is granted relief, in which case the tenancy is taken never to have ended at all, and his liability revives retrospectively. (paras. 3.3–3.10)

Secondly, in relation to relief against forfeiture, there are two almost entirely separate regimes, one for cases involving non-payment of rent and the other for all other cases. There are also uncertainties, including the fact that the courts' ancient equitable jurisdiction to grant relief exists, though to an extent not altogether certain, side by side with their statutory powers). (paras. 3.11–3.13, 3.16)

The Report recommends that the present law of forfeiture, both statutory and non-statutory, be swept away, and with it, the doctrine of re-entry. They are to be replaced by a scheme under which there is to be no distinction between termination for non-payment of rent and termination for other reasons, and under which the tenancy is to continue in force until the date on which the court orders that it should terminate. "The landlord's right to terminate is merged with the tenant's right to resist termination so as to produce one single rule that the court has a primary discretion as to whether the tenancy should terminate or not." The court is to have power to make a *termination order* which can be applied for only on the occasion of a *termination order event* i.e. (*a*) Breach of covenant by the tenant, or (*b*) Disguised breach of covenant, that is, broadly, a breach by the tenant of an obligation imposed on him otherwise than by covenant, or (*c*) Insolvency of the tenant. The order may be either *absolute* (to terminate the tenancy unconditionally on a date specified) or *remedial* (to terminate the tenancy on a date specified unless the tenant takes remedial action by that time). In both cases the court may grant or refuse to grant the order according to a discretion exercisable within guidelines. (paras. 3.25–3.71)

Finally a tenant is given a new right to terminate a tenancy in cases of fault on the part of the landlord. The right is analogous to the landlord's right to terminate, and the tenant exercising this right is given a right to claim damages from the landlord for the loss of his tenancy. (paras. 3.72–3.93)

The new scheme applies to existing tenancies as well as to those created in the future. (para. 3.29)

V.   The Title to the Freehold[15]

LAW OF PROPERTY ACT 1925

44.   Statutory commencements of title. — (2) Under a contract to grant or assign a term of years, whether derived or to be derived out of freehold or leasehold land, the intended lessee or assign shall not be entitled to call for the title to the freehold.

(3) Under a contract to sell and assign a term of years derived out of a leasehold interest in land, the intended assign shall not have the right to call for the title to the leasehold reversion.

---

[14] The court may order the tenant to make interim payments to the landlord on account of mesne profits.

[15] C & B, pp. 705–706; M & W, pp. 723–727; MM pp. 101–102.

(4) On a contract to grant a lease for a term of years to be derived out of a leasehold interest, with a leasehold reversion, the intended lessee shall not have the right to call for the title to that reversion.

(5) Where by reason of any of the three last preceding subsections, an intending lessee or assign is not entitled to call for the title to the freehold or to a leasehold reversion, as the case may be, he shall not, where the contract is made after the commencement of this Act, be deemed to be affected with notice of any matter or thing of which, if he had contracted that such title should be furnished, he might have had notice.

SHEARS *v* WELLS
[1936] 1 All ER 832 (ChD, Luxmoore J)

The first defendant was the owner, and the second defendant, Cooper, the tenant of premises under a tenancy commencing in 1929[16]. The plaintiff brought this action for an injunction to restrain the breach of a restrictive covenant contained in the conveyance to the first defendant. The second defendant pleaded that he had no notice of the restrictive covenant. On the question of his liability.

Held. By virtue of the Law of Property Act 1925, section 44 (5), the second defendant was only bound by matters of which the plaintiff could prove he had notice at the commencement of his tenancy.

Luxmoore J: I think that Cooper is not liable under the covenant at all. He took the tenancy of the garage in 1929 after the passing of the Law of Property Act 1925. Section 44 enacts as follows:—

[His Lordship read section 44 (2), (4), (5):] It follows that the onus of proving that the defendant Cooper had notice when he took the tenancy is on the plaintiff. There is no evidence here that he had notice and the onus is not discharged. The defendant Cooper is therefore not subject to the covenants in the deed.

This case illustrates the reversal of the rule in *Patman v Harland* (1881) 17 ChD 353, where Sir George Jessel MR held that a tenant had constructive notice of a restrictive covenant affecting the freehold, which covenant was disclosed in the deeds. The tenant was not protected even if the lessor told her that there was no such covenant, nor by the Vendor and Purchaser Act 1874, section 2 which provides "subject to any stipulation to the contrary" that "under a contract to grant or assign a term of years, whether derived or to be derived out of a freehold or leasehold estate, the intended lessee or assign shall not be entitled to call for the title to the freehold."

Shears v Wells does not, however, solve all the problems. The person entitled to the benefit of the covenant needs to ensure that the lessee has notice of the covenant. Presumably he could do this by registration and rely on the provisions of the Law of Property Act 1925, section 198 (1) that registration is deemed to constitute "actual notice . . . to all persons . . . connected with the land affected[17]." The result is not satisfactory; for the

---

[16] In the statement of facts this date is given as 1931 but this is at variance with the date given in the judgment which is used here.

[17] In *White v Bijou Mansions* [1937] Ch 610 at 619, [1937] 3 All ER 269 at 273, Simonds J suggested "that s. 198 . . . appears, notwithstanding the unqualified language of s. 44, sub-s. 5, to affect a lessee with notice of all those charges which are registered under the Land Charges Act 1925". For registered land, see p. 831, n. 1, post.

procedure for registration under the Land Charges Act 1925 provides for registration under personal names and not under the land concerned. Unless therefore the incumbrance is registered against the present lessor, the tenant (a fortiori, a sub-tenant), not seeing the earlier deeds, will not know under whose name to search. And neither pre-1926 covenants nor covenants originally entered into between landlord and tenant are registrable[18].

VI.   The Effect of Assignment on Covenants[19]

A.   Covenants which "Touch and Concern" the Land

The only covenants which can be enforced by or against assignees of the leasehold estate or the reversion, are those which touch and concern the land[20]; or (which means the same thing) have "reference to the subject-matter of the lease[1]." In Lord Ellenborough's words, the test is satisfied if the covenant "affected the nature, quality or value of the thing demised, independently of collateral circumstances; or if it affected the mode of enjoying it[2]." The simplest test is that put forward by Cheshire[3], that is to consider whether the covenant affects "the landlord *qua* landlord or the tenant *qua* tenant". No single definition seems adequate to explain all the cases. Textbooks commonly list examples of covenants falling on either side of the line, and it is not proposed to enter into details here[1].

B.   Covenants Running with the Leasehold Estate

The common law rule was that covenants which touched and concerned the land were enforceable by and against the assignee of the tenant. There was however an exception to the effect that a covenant relating to something not in esse at the date of the covenant only ran with the leasehold estate if assigns were expressly mentioned; this exception was abolished in 1925[5].

SPENCER'S CASE
(1583) 5 Co Rep 16a (KB)

Spencer and his wife leased land to S for 21 years. S covenanted for him, his executors and administrators that he, his executors, administrators, or assigns would build a brick wall thereon. He assigned his lease to J, who

---

[18] (1940) 56 LQR 361 (D. W. Logan); [1956] CLJ 230–234 (H. W. R. Wade).
[19] C & B, pp. 429–440; M & W, pp. 643–644, 665–668, 742–760; MM, pp. 348, 378–388.
[20] *Spencer's Case* (1583) 5 Co Rep 16a; *Smith's Leading Cases* (13th edn. 1929), vol. 1, p. 51.
[1] LPA 1925, ss. 141, 142; *Davis v Town Properties Investment Corpn Ltd* [1903] 1 Ch 797.
[2] *Congleton Corpn v Pattison* (1808) 10 East 130 at 135.
[3] C & B, p. 431, and approved in *Breams Property Investment Co Ltd v Stroulger* [1948] 2 KB 1 at 7, [1948] 1 All ER 758 at 759. For a detailed discussion, see *Pinemain Ltd v Welbeck International Ltd* (1984) 272 EG 1166, where E. G. Nugee QC held that a covenant by a surety in a lease did not touch and concern the land, and therefore the benefit did not pass under LPA 1925, s. 62, p. 586, post; decisions of the High Court of Australia in *Consolidated Trust Ltd v Naylor* (1936) 55 CLR 423 and of Supreme Court of New South Wales in *Sacher Investments Pty Ltd v Forma Stereo Consultants Pty Ltd* [1976] 1 NSWLR 5 followed; [1985] Conv 246 (J.E.A.).
[4] Aldridge, paras. 1.010–1.012; Woodfall, paras. 1.1130–1131; C & B, pp. 431–433; M & W, pp. 743–746; MM, p. 379.
[5] LPA 1925, s. 79, p. 461, post.

assigned it to the defendant Clark. The question is as to the liability of Clark on the covenant to build.

Held. Since the covenant was in respect of something to be done on the land demised, and was not made expressly on behalf of the assigns the defendant was not liable.

The report records that after many arguments at the Bar, the case was excellently argued and debated by the Justices at the Bench. Three of the resolutions were:

"1. When the covenant extends to a thing *in esse*, parcel of the demise, the thing to be done by force of the covenant is *quodammodo* annexed and appurtenant to the thing demised, and shall go with the land, and shall bind the assignee although he be not bound by express words: but when the covenant extends to a thing which is not in being at the time of the demise made, it cannot be appurtenant or annexed to the thing which hath no being: as if the lessee covenants to repair the houses demised to him during the term, that is parcel of the contract, and extends to the support of the thing demised, and therefore is *quodammodo* annexed appurtenant to houses, and shall bind the assignee although he be not bound expressly by the covenant: but in the case at bar, the covenant concerns a thing which was not *in esse* at the time of the demise made, but to be newly built after, and therefore shall bind the covenantor, his executors, or administrators, and not the assignee, for the law will not annex the covenant to a thing which hath no being.

2. It was resolved that in this case, if the lessee had covenanted for him and his assigns, that they would make a new wall upon some part of the thing demised, that for as much as it is to be done upon the land demised, that it should bind the assignee; for although the covenant doth extend to a thing to be newly made, yet it is to be made upon the thing demised, and the assignee is to take the benefit of it, and therefore shall bind the assignee by express words. So on the other side, if a warranty be made to one, his heirs and assigns, by express words, the assignee shall take benefit of it, and shall have a *Warrantia chartae*. . . . But although the covenant be for him and his assigns, yet if the thing to be done be merely collateral to the land, and doth not touch or concern the thing demised in any sort, there the assignee shall not be charged. As if the lessee covenants for him and his assigns to build a house upon the land of the lessor which is no parcel of the demise, or to pay any collateral sum to the lessor, or to a stranger, it shall not bind the assignee, because it is merely collateral, and in no manner touches or concerns the thing that was demised, or that is assigned over; and therefore in such case the assignee of the thing demised cannot be charged with it, no more than any other stranger.

4. It was resolved, that if a man makes a feoffment by this word *dedi*, which implies a warranty, the assignee of the feoffee shall not vouch; but if a man makes a lease for years by this word *concessi* or *demisi*, which implies a covenant, if the assignee of the lessee be evicted, he shall have a writ of covenant; for the lessee and his assignee hath the yearly profits of the land which shall grow by his labour and industry for an annual rent, and therefore it is reasonable when he hath applied his labour, and employed his cost upon the land, and be evicted (whereby he loses all), that he shall take such benefit of the demise and grant, as the first lessee might, and the lessor hath no other prejudice than what his special contract with the first lessee hath bound him to."

LAW OF PROPERTY ACT 1925[6]

78. Benefit of covenants relating to land. — (1) A covenant relating to any land of the covenantee shall be deemed to be made with the covenantee and his successors in title and the persons deriving title under him or them, and shall have effect as if such successors and other persons were expressed.

For the purposes of this subsection in connexion with covenants restrictive of the user of land "successors in title" shall be deemed to include the owners and occupiers for the time being of the land of the covenantee intended to be benefited.

(2) This section applies to covenants made after the commencement of this Act, but the repeal of section fifty-eight of the Conveyancing Act, 1881, does not affect the operation of covenants to which that section applied.

79. Burden of covenants relating to land. — (1) A covenant relating to any land of a covenantor or capable of being bound by him, shall, unless a contrary intention is expressed, be deemed to be made by the covenantor on behalf of himself his successors in title and the persons deriving title under him or them, and, subject as aforesaid, shall have effect as if such successors and other persons were expressed.

This subsection extends to a covenant to do some act relating to the land, notwithstanding that the subject-matter may not be in existence when the covenant is made.

(2) For the purposes of this section in connexion with covenants restrictive of the user of land "successors in title" shall be deemed to include the owners and occupiers for the time being of such land.

(3) This section applies only to covenants made after the commencement of this Act.

C. Covenants Running with the Reversion

At common law the benefit and burden of covenants other than "usual" or "implied" covenants did not run with the landlord's reversion. Statutory provision was made in 32 Hen 8 c 34 and in the Conveyancing Act 1881. These provisions were superseded by the Law of Property Act 1925.

LAW OF PROPERTY ACT 1925

141. Rent and benefit of lessee's covenants to run with the reversion. — (1) Rent reserved by a lease, and the benefit of every covenant or provision therein contained, having reference to the subject-matter thereof, and on the lessee's part to be observed or performed, and every condition of re-entry and other condition therein contained, shall be annexed and incident to and shall go with the reversionary estate in the land, or in any part thereof, immediately expectant on the term granted by the lease, notwithstanding severance of that reversionary estate[7], and without prejudice to any liability affecting a covenantor or his estate.

---

[6] See also pp. 767–768, 768–772, 777–785, 787–788, post.

[7] When the reversion is severed i.e. different parts come into different ownerships, the benefit of any covenant, condition or right of entry is apportioned and annexed to the severed parts: LPA 1925, s. 140. The severance must be genuine: *Persey v Bazley* (1983) 267 EG 519 (landlord conveyed part of reversion to bare trustees for himself); [1985] Conv 292 (J. Martin). The tenancy itself remains a single tenancy: *Jelley v Buckman* [1974] QB 488, [1973] 3 All ER 853; *Nevill Long & Co (Boards) Ltd v Firmenich & Co* (1983) 268 EG 572.

(2) Any such rent, covenant or provision shall be capable of being recovered, received, enforced, and taken advantage of, by the person from time to time entitled, subject to the term, to the income of the whole or any part, as the case may require, of the land leased.

(3) Where that person becomes entitled by conveyance or otherwise, such rent, covenant or provision may be recovered, received, enforced or taken advantage of by him notwithstanding that he becomes so entitled after the condition of re-entry or forfeiture has become enforceable, but this subsection does not render enforceable any condition of re-entry or other condition waived or released before such person becomes entitled as aforesaid.

(4) This section applies to leases made before or after the commencement of this Act, but does not affect the operation of —
    (*a*) any severance of the reversionary estate; or
    (*b*) any acquisition by conveyance or otherwise of the right to receive or enforce any rent covenant or provision;
effected before the commencement of this Act.

142. Obligation of lessor's covenants to run with reversion.— (1) The obligation under a condition or of a covenant entered into by a lessor with reference to the subject-matter of the lease shall, if and as far as the lessor has power to bind the reversionary estate immediately expectant on the term granted by the lease, be annexed and incident to and shall go with that reversionary estate, or the several parts thereof, notwithstanding severance of that reversionary estate, and may be taken advantage of and enforced by the person in whom the term is from time to time vested by conveyance, devolution in law, or otherwise; and, if and as far as the lessor has power to bind the person from time to time entitled to that reversionary estate, the obligation aforesaid may be taken advantage of and enforced against any person so entitled.

(2) This section applies to leases made before or after the commencement of this Act, whether the severance of the reversionary estate was effected before or after such commencement:

Provided that, where the lease was made before the first day of January eighteen hundred and eighty-two, nothing in this section shall affect the operation of any severance of the reversionary estate effected before such commencement.

This section takes effect without prejudice to any liability affecting a covenantor or his estate.

RE KING[8]
[1963] Ch 459, [1963] 1 All ER 781 (CA, Lord DENNING MR, UPJOHN and DIPLOCK LJJ)

In 1895 Edward Graves-Tagg granted a lease of land and a factory in Bethnal Green to Mrs Elven, who covenanted for herself, her executors, administrators and assigns (*a*) to keep the premises in repair, (*b*) to insure the premises and keep them insured against loss or damage by fire and (*c*) to lay out all moneys received under any such policy in rebuilding or repairing

---

[8] (1966) 30 Conv (NS) 429 (D. Macintyre). On the construction of a covenant to insure, see *Farimani v Gates* (1984) 271 EG 887; *Beacon Carpets Ltd v Kirby* [1985] QB 755, [1984] 2 All ER 726.

the premises destroyed or damaged by fire and, if necessary, to reinstate the premises. In 1907 the lease was assigned to King. In 1944 the factory was severely damaged by fire, but could not be repaired or rebuilt owing to wartime restrictions. The insurance moneys were duly paid. In 1946 Edward Graves-Tagg assigned his reversion to Edward Ernest Graves-Tagg ("Tagg") and in 1949 King died. The factory had never been repaired or rebuilt. In 1960 Tagg assigned his reversion to the London County Council as a result of a compulsory purchase order. In 1961, during negotiations between the London County Council and King's executors for the transfer of the lease to the London County Council, King's executors issued a summons to determine, inter alia, whether Tagg could still sue them for the breach of the covenant to repair and to reinstate, which had occurred before the assignment of 1960. If he could, then King's executors argued that an indemnity by the London County Council should be included in the transfer of the lease.

Held. King's executors were not liable to Tagg.

UPJOHN LJ: The first question may be briefly stated in this way: Can a landlord, who has assigned his reversion to a lease, after the date of such assignment, sue the lessee in respect of breaches of covenant which occurred before the assignment? . . .

This case is concerned with express covenants in a lease, and in such case it cannot possibly be doubted that section 141 of the Law of Property Act 1925 governs the situation. [His Lordship read sections (1) and (2) and continued:]

I turn, then, to a consideration of the meaning of section 141 and construe the language used in its ordinary and natural meaning, which seems to me quite plain and clear. To illustrate this, consider the case of a lease containing a covenant to build a house according to certain detailed specifications before a certain day. Let me suppose that after that certain day the then lessor assigns the benefit of the reversion to an assignee, and at the time of the assignment the lessee has failed to perform the covenant to build. Who can sue the lessee for breach of covenant? It seems to me clear that the assignee alone can sue. Upon the assignment the benefit of every covenant on the lessee's part to be observed and performed is annexed and incident to and goes with the reversionary estate. The benefit of that covenant to build, therefore, passed; as it had been broken, the right to sue also passed as part of the benefit of the covenant and, incidentally, also the right to re-enter, if that has not been waived. I protest against the argument that because a right to sue is itself a chose in action it, therefore, has become severed from, and independent of, the parent covenant; on the contrary it remains part of it. The right to sue on breach is merely one of the bundle of rights that are contained in the concept "benefit of every covenant". . . . To return to my example. Suppose the right to sue for breach of that covenant did not pass, and that right remained in the assignor, then the assignee would take the lease without the benefit of that covenant and he could never enforce it. So he has not got the benefit of every covenant contained in the lease and the words of the section are not satisfied. That cannot be right. . . .

Then suppose the lease contains a covenant to keep in repair which is broken at the date of the assignment, and that at all material times the premises were out of repair; that is, a continuing breach. It is an a fortiori case to the example I have just dealt with. Indeed, with all respect to the argument to the contrary, you cannot give any sensible meaning to the words of the section unless the entire benefit of a repairing covenant has passed, leaving the assignor without remedy against the lessee. Look at the absurd results if that were not so. The assignor of the reversion remains at liberty to sue the lessee for breaches down to the moment of the assignment. After assignment he sues and obtains judgment for certain damages. But then the premises are still out of repair and the breach continues. The assignee claims to re-enter or to sue because the premises are out of repair. What is the situation of the lessee? Either he has to pay damages twice or pay damages to the assignor and then reinstate the premises because otherwise the assignee will re-enter. This is impossible. Alternatively, the assignee's right to re-enter or to sue in respect of post-assignment breaches is in some way adversely affected by reason of the fact that the assignor has recovered a judgment for damages for pre-assignment breaches; therefore, the benefit of the covenant to keep in repair did not pass wholly to him even in respect of post-assignment breaches. That directly contradicts the words of the section. . . .

In my judgment Tagg's claims fail and I would allow this part of the appeal.

In *London and County (A and D) Ltd v Wilfred Sportsman Ltd* [1971] Ch 764, [1970] 2 All ER 600 the Court of Appeal held that section 141 should be similarly interpreted in the case of a covenant to pay rent. Russell LJ said at 784, at 606: "The language of section 141 (substantially re-enacting the earlier legislation from 1881 onwards) is such as, in my judgment, to indicate plainly that an assignee of the reversion may sue and re-enter for rent in arrear at the date of the assignment when the right of re-entry has arisen before the assignment[9]. The decision in *Rickett v Green* [1910] 1 KB 253, p. 469, post was, therefore, correct."

D. Privity of Estate

i. ASSIGNEES AND SUB-TENANTS

Subject to the situation discussed in ii below, liability under, and the right to sue upon, covenants running with the land or the reversion exists only between persons between whom there is privity of estate. The original contracting parties are liable to each other contractually and remain so liable[10]: assignees are liable and able to sue only if, and so long as, they hold

---

[9] *Arlesford Trading Co Ltd v Servansingh* [1971] 1 WLR 1080, [1971] 3 All ER 113 (assignee of reversion recovered rent against lessee who had assigned his lease before the reversion was assigned).

[10] On the continuing liability of an original lessee to the lessor for rent which falls due after assignment of the lease, see *Warnford Investments Ltd v Duckworth* [1979] Ch 127, [1978] 2 All ER 517. The lessee remains liable to the lessor, even though there has been a post-assignment agreement between lessor and assignee for increased rent under a rent review clause in the lease: *Centrovincial Estates plc v Bulk Storage Ltd* (1983) 268 EG 59; *Selous Street Properties Ltd v Oronel Fabrics Ltd* (1984) 270 EG 643; and even though the lessor has released a guarantor of the assignee: *Allied London Investments Ltd v Hambro Life Assurance Ltd* (1983) 269 EG 41. For the liability of a lessee to the lessor for breach by assignee of covenants to repair and to deliver up possession at end of lease, see *Thames Manufacturing Co Ltd v Perrotts (Nichol & Peyton) Ltd* (1984) 271 EG 284. See generally (1984) 81 LSG 2214 (K. Reynolds and S. Fogel); [1984] Conv 443 (P. McLaughlin).

the estate with which the covenant runs; and such persons must be assignees and not sub-lessees[11] or squatters[12].

In *South of England Dairies v Baker* [1906] 2 Ch 631, the freeholder of certain property demised it for 21 years and covenanted to pay all rates and taxes (except one third of the water rate). In the following year, the lessee sub-demised the premises to the plaintiff (a company formed by the lessee) for the remainder of his term less three days. Seven years later the freeholder sold the fee simple subject to the lease to the defendant, who in the following year accepted the surrender of the lease from the original lessee. The plaintiff, the sub-tenant, was compelled by the Local Authority to pay the rates, and sought to recover damages from the defendant under the landlord's covenant to pay all rates and taxes. JOYCE J held that the defendant was not liable since the plaintiff was not an assignee of the original lessee and was unable therefore to enforce the covenant originally given to the lessee.

In *Milmo v Carreras* [1946] KB 306, [1946] 1 All ER 288, the plaintiff was tenant of a flat under a 7 year lease, expiring on 28 November 1944. In October 1943, he agreed to sublet the flat to the defendant for one year from 1 November 1943, "and thereafter quarterly until such time as" one of the parties should give three months' notice to terminate. The plaintiff gave such notice on returning from active service in 1945.

The Court of Appeal (Lord GREENE MR, MORTON and BUCKNILL LJJ) held that the notice was bad because the plaintiff retained no reversion. Lord GREENE MR said at 310, at 290:

"For the purposes of this case, I think it is sufficient to say that, in accordance with a very ancient and established rule, where a lessee, by a document in the form of a sub-lease, divests himself of everything that he has got (which he must necessarily do if he is transferring to his so-called sub-lessee an estate as great as, or purporting to be greater than, his own) he from that moment is a stranger to the land, in the sense that the relationship of landlord and tenant, in respect of tenure, cannot any longer exist between him and the so-called sub-lessee. That relationship must depend on privity of estate. I myself find it impossible to conceive of a relationship of landlord and tenant which has not got that essential element of tenure in it, and that implies that the tenant holds of his landlord, and he can only do that if the landlord has a reversion. You cannot have a purely contractual tenure. Tenure exists by reason of privity of estate. That seems to me to be the effect of all the decisions, and that position is recognised by all the decisions."

ii. AGREEMENTS FOR LEASES

The question of the enforcement of covenants after assignment raises different issues where there has been no grant of a lease, but merely an agreement for a lease[13]. First, it used to be said that covenants could run with land at common law only if created under seal[14], but this rule has since been

---

[11] *South of England Dairies Ltd v Baker* [1906] 2 Ch 631.
[12] *Tichborne v Weir* (1892) 67 LT 735, p. 766, post.
[13] See pp. 80, 425, ante.
[14] *Manchester Brewery Co v Coombs* [1901] 2 Ch 608, p. 467, post.

changed[15]. Secondly, there is no privity of estate between persons who have entered into a contract for a lease or between their assigns[16]; nor between the lessor and one who has contracted to take an assignment from a lessee[17].

Since the benefit of a covenant can be assigned at law, there is no difficulty in holding that the benefit of a covenant runs with the freehold reversion[18]; and it appears that the benefit will run also by virtue of Law of Property Act 1925, section 141[19], and, if this is so, the burden will run also with the reversion under section 142. It is usually held that the benefit but not the burden of covenants will run on the assignment of an agreement for a lease[20]; an assignee may be liable under an implied agreement if he enters into possession and pays rent[1]; or on grounds of estoppel[2]. His freedom from liability under the covenant may cause great hardship to the lessor, and the question is whether this is a necessary limitation.

The rule seems to have developed from the independence of law and equity before the Judicature Act. There could be no liability at law after the assignment because there was no privity of estate; in equity, the question was whether or not specific performance of the agreement would be given, and the question of monetary liability under the covenants pending the grant of specific performance did not arise. There appears to be no reason why, since the Judicature Act, the doctrine of *Walsh v Lonsdale* should not be applied and the monetary liability of the defendant determined *as if* the decree of specific performance had been granted. The dicta in *Boyer v Warbey* [1953] 1 QB 234, [1952] 2 All ER 976, p. 470, post indicate that "nowadays" the rules relating to the running of covenants should be the same, whether the lease which has been assigned is legal or equitable. Further, as has been seen, the Court of Appeal in *Industrial Properties (Barton Hill) Ltd v Associated Electrical Industries Ltd* [1977] QB 580, [1977] 2 All ER 293, p. 82, ante held, as an alternative ground for supporting the judgment, that the doctrine of *Walsh v Lonsdale* applied where an equitable owner had purported to grant a lease; the effect was to treat the equitable lease as a legal lease, and thus enable the owner to sue for damages for breach of covenant in the lease.

The older cases are to the contrary. The only case in which the issue appears to have arisen since the Judicature Act is *Purchase v Lichfield Brewery* [1915] 1 KB 184, which was, however, one of assignment by way of mortgage. It is submitted that the trend of the modern cases should be supported, and that the court should hold that the liability, both of the assignee of an equitable lease and that of the equitable assignee of a legal lease, is the same as it would be if specific performance had been granted[3].

---

[15] LPA 1925, s. 154; *Boyer v Warbey* [1953] 1 QB 234, [1952] 2 All ER 976, p. 470, post.
[16] *Purchase v Lichfield Brewery Co* [1915] 1 KB 184, p. 469, post.
[17] *Cox v Bishop* (1857) 8 De GM & G 815; *Friary, Holroyd, and Healey's Breweries Ltd v Singleton* [1899] 1 Ch 86.
[18] *Manchester Brewery Co v Coombs*, supra.
[19] *Rickett v Green* [1910] 1 KB 253; *Rye v Purcell* [1926] 1 KB 446; *London and County (A and D) Ltd v Wilfred Sportsman Ltd* [1971] Ch 764, [1970] 2 All ER 600.
[20] *Marquis of Camden v Batterbury* (1860) 7 CBNS 864; *Purchase v Lichfield Brewery Co*, supra.
[1] *Buckworth v Simpson* (1835) 1 Cr M & R 834; *Cornish v Stubbs* (1870) LR 5 CP 334 at 338–339.
[2] *Ashe v Hogan* [1920] 1 IR 159; *Rodenhurst Estates Ltd v WH Barnes Ltd* [1936] 2 All ER 3.
[3] [1978] CLJ 98 (R. J. Smith).

(a) Benefit

MANCHESTER BREWERY CO *v* COOMBS
[1901] 2 Ch 608 (ChD, FARWELL J)

By an agreement under seal dated 10 December 1892 between the defendant and Broadbents Ltd, who were brewers, the defendant, who alone executed the deed, undertook to take a yearly tenancy of a hotel, and covenanted with "Broadbents Ltd and their successors in business" to buy all his liquor from them. The covenant did not mention "assigns".

In June 1899, Broadbents sold their business to the plaintiffs, who gave notice of the purchase to the defendant. The defendant continued to take his supplies from the plaintiffs until December, when he ceased to buy from them. They brought this action for an injunction to restrain a breach of the covenant contained in the deed of 1892.

Held. The plaintiffs were entitled to the benefit of the covenant.

FARWELL J (after holding that the covenant was not, on its construction, a mere personal covenant confined to beer brewed at the original brewery which no longer operated): The last point taken by Mr Younger rests on the fact that the agreement of 10 December 1892 was not executed by the landlords. Having regard to the construction that I have put on the covenant, it could not be contended that it is not of such a nature as to run with the land. But it is said that, in order to arrive at the conclusion that it does run with the land, the Court must first find that an estate has been duly created at law in the land with which the covenant can run, or, in other words, that there must be privity of estate between lessor and lessee, and that such estate can only be created by deed duly executed by the lessor, and that this is borne out by 32 Hen 8, c 34, which applies only to leases by deed. This is undoubtedly sound — e.g., it has been held that a lease by mortgagor and mortgagee, in which the covenants to repair were with the mortgagor and his assigns, did not enable an assign of the mortgagee to maintain an action on the covenant: [His Lordship referred to *Webb v Russell* (1789) 3 Term Rep 393 per Lord Kenyon at 402, and to *Standen v Chrismas* (1847) 10 QB 135, and continued:] . . . But it by no means follows that the plaintiffs would have failed in every form of action, even before the Judicature Acts; still less that they must fail now. Before the Judicature Acts the plaintiffs might have succeeded if they had sued on the new contract implied from the conduct of the tenant and the assignee of the landlord, instead of suing on the original contract between the tenant and the landlord.

[His Lordship then found that the defendant agreed that the plaintiffs should occupy the position of landlords to him in the same way as Broadbents Ltd had done, and conunued:]

There is, moreover, another point which is fatal to the defendant. The defendant holds under an agreement for a lease from Broadbents Limited, under which he has been in possession and paid rent for several years. The whole contract has been performed up to the present time, except that the legal estate has not been actually demised. The defendant would have no defence to an action for specific performance, the sole object of which would be to compel him to accept the legal estate. If Broadbents Limited had not parted with the legal estate, I see no reason why they should not now execute the deed in order to complete the transaction. The present plaintiffs are the assigns of the benefit of the agreement both by implication from the conveyance of the land subject to the lease, and by the express words of clause 26 of the agreement of 29 March 1899. The plaintiffs could, therefore, obtain specific performance in this court of the contract so far as it is incomplete . . . Holding, therefore, as I do, that the plaintiffs could obtain specific performance against the defendant, I find it laid down by the Court of Appeal that since the Judicature Acts there are not in such a case as this two estates as there were formerly, one at common law by reason of the payment of the rent, and another in equity under the agreement, but the tenant holds under the same terms, and has the same rights and liabilities as if a lease had been granted: *Walsh v Lonsdale* (1882) 21 ChD 9, approved by Cotton LJ in *Lowther v Heaver* (1889) 41 ChD 248 at 264, and explained by Lord Esher in *Swain v Ayres* (1888) 21 QBD 289 at 292 and *Foster v Reeves* [1892] 2 QB 255. Although it has been suggested that the decision in *Walsh v Lonsdale* takes away all differences between the legal and equitable estate, it, of course, does nothing of the sort, and the limits of its applicability are really somewhat narrow. It applies only to cases where there is a contract to transfer a legal title, and an act has to be justified or an action maintained by force of the legal title to which such contract relates. It involves two questions: (1) Is there a contract of which specific performance can be obtained? (2) If Yes, will the title acquired by such specific performance justify at law the act complained of, or support at law the action in question? It is to be treated as though before the Judicature Acts there had been, first, a suit in equity for specific performance, and then an action at law between the same parties; and the doctrine is applicable only in those cases where specific performance can be obtained between the same parties in the same court, and at the same time as the subsequent legal question falls to be determined. Thus, in *Walsh v Lonsdale*, the landlord under an agreement for a lease for a term of seven years distrained. Distress is a legal remedy and depends on the existence at law of the relation of landlord and tenant; but the agreement between the same parties, if specifically enforced, created that relation. It was clear that such an agreement would be enforced in the same court and between the same parties: the act of distress was therefore held to be lawful. So in the present case I have already stated that specific performance can be granted between the parties to this action. I must treat it therefore as granted, and I then find that the result justifies this action. It is not necessary to call in aid this doctrine in matters that are purely equitable; its existence is due entirely to the divergence of legal and equitable rights between the same parties, nor does it affect the rights of third parties. Thus, a contract by a landowner to sell the fee simple of land in possession to A. would not enable A. to maintain an action of ejectment or trespass against a third person, because such actions are purely legal actions requiring the legal estate and possession respectively to support them, and the contract relied on is not made with the defendant. . . .

I hold, therefore, on this point, that the plaintiffs, being clearly entitled in this court against the defendant to specific performance of the agreement under which the defendant has been for years and still is in possession of the land, can sue him on the covenants in the same manner as they could have done if Broadbents had actually executed the original agreement. . . .

The result is that I grant the injunction as asked, and order the defendant to pay the costs of the action.

In *Rickett v Green* [1910] 1 KB 253, one of the questions was whether or not the plaintiff, as assignee of the freehold, was entitled to demand rent from the defendant who held the premises under an agreement for a lease. DARLING and PHILLIMORE JJ held that he was entitled to sue by virtue of the Conveyancing Act 1881, section 10 (now Law of Property Act 1925, section 141). DARLING J said at 259: "the question occurred to [the county court judge] whether this tenancy agreement was a 'lease' within the meaning of section 10 of the Act of 1881, inasmuch as the agreement was dated 19 December 1907, and the three years were to run from 25 December 1907, so that the lease was one exceeding three years from the making thereof and, not being under seal, was void at law under section 3 of the Real Property Act 1845. Though at law it may be void as a lease, still in equity it is looked upon as a lease, and in my judgment it must be treated, as between the parties, as if it were a lease under seal. A Court of Equity would look upon the matter as if a lease under seal had been granted. Upon the case to which we have been referred the county court judge came to a right conclusion upon this point, and the agreement must be treated as a 'lease' for the purposes of section 10 of the Act of 1881, and for other purposes also."

(b) Burden

In *Cox v Bishop* (1857) 8 De G M & G 815, the freeholder brought an action for rent due and for breaches of covenant in a lease. The lessees had contracted to assign the lease to persons who assigned to the defendants. KNIGHT BRUCE and TURNER LJJ held that the defendants were not liable on the covenants, TURNER LJ, saying at 823: "If, on the other hand, these Defendants are not at law liable to the Plaintiffs, what are the grounds alleged by this bill upon which they are in equity to be made liable? Simply that they have contracted to purchase interests in the lease and have been in possession. The contracts to purchase, however, are not contracts with the Plaintiffs, and there is nothing in the bill to shew that the Plaintiffs are in any manner entitled to the benefit of those contracts, and if the Defendants are liable by virtue of their possession, the liability, as I apprehend, is to be enforced at law and not in equity. Courts of equity do not, as I think, in ordinary cases, decree the payment of rent or the performance of covenants upon a mere agreement for a lease. In such cases the Court does not treat the relation of landlord and tenant as completed by the agreement, and decree the rent to be paid and the covenants to be performed accordingly, but it decrees the execution of the lease, and leaves the parties to their remedies at law consequent upon the relation created by the execution of it. To take, however, a case more near to the present, suppose, in the case of an agreement for a lease, the intended lessee has assigned the benefit of the contract, can this Court, at the instance of the intended lessor, enforce the payment of the rent or the performance of the covenants by the assignee of the contract. I take it most clearly not; for there is no privity of contract between the lessor and the assignee; but if this cannot be done where there is a mere contract for a lease, upon what principle it is to be done where there is an actual lease and the lessee has agreed to assign."

PURCHASE *v* LICHFIELD BREWERY CO
[1915] 1 KB 184 (KBD, HORRIDGE and LUSH JJ)

The plaintiff, in writing but not under seal, purported to grant to Lunnis a 15-year lease of a house, the agreement containing a proviso that Lunnis would not assign the term without the plaintiff's consent, such consent not to be unreasonably refused.

On the following day Lunnis assigned by way of mortgage his interest to the defendant, who never went into possession. The rent being unpaid, the plaintiff claimed from the defendant (mortgagee) the rent due under the agreement.

Held. In the absence of privity of contract or estate the defendant was not liable.

LUSH J (agreeing with HORRIDGE J): I am of the same opinion. The only point which the county court judge decided was that the present case was governed by *Williams v Bosanquet* (1819) 1 Brod & Bing 238. In my view that case does not apply. The lease in question there was under seal. It was assigned by deed to mortgagees. That was a valid assignment. The only question was whether the mortgagees, not having taken possession, were bound by the covenants in the lease. It was held that they were bound. In this case there was no lease under seal. No term was created as between lessor and lessee. Therefore the question decided in *Williams v Bosanquet* does not arise in this case. Consequently the judgment of the county court judge cannot stand on the grounds on which he has based it.

Then can the judgment be supported on other grounds? I do not think it is necessary to say how the case might have stood if the defendants had ever taken possession. They are liable, if at all, on the principle of *Walsh v Lonsdale* (1882) 21 ChD 9. In that case the tenant was in possession under the agreement. In the present case the defendants never did take possession. The agreement contained a provision against assigning. The defendants were only mortgagees. It does not follow from *Walsh v Lonsdale* that a court of equity would decree specific performance against mere mortgagees who only took an assignment by way of security. In my opinion it would leave the parties to their position at law. Accordingly the matter stands thus: A tenant under an agreement, whose only title to call himself a lessee depends on his right to specific performance of the agreement, assigns his right to assignees. The assignees never had a term vested in them because no term was ever created; therefore there was never privity of estate. They never went into possession or were recognised by the landlord; therefore there was never privity of contract. It is impossible that specific performance of a contract can be decreed against a person with whom there is neither privity of contract nor privity of estate. Therefore these assignees are not liable to perform the terms of the agreement and this appeal must be allowed.

In *Boyer v Warbey* [1953] 1 QB 234, [1952] 2 All ER 976 (CA, EVERSHED MR, DENNING and ROMER LJJ), one question was whether a covenant by a tenant in a written lease of a flat within the Rent Restriction Acts to pay £40 towards the cost of redecoration "immediately after the expiration or determination of the tenancy" was binding on an assignee of the tenant.

The lease was for 3 years; within nine days of the expiration of the term, the lessee assigned the lease to the defendant who, on the expiry of the nine days, became a statutory tenant, subject to all the terms of the original tenancy "so far as the same are consistent with the provisions of this Act⁴."

---

⁴ Increase of Rent and Mortgage Interest (Restrictions) Act 1920, s. 15 (1); now Rent Act 1977, s. 3 (1).

It was held, inter alia, that the covenant to pay the £40 became a term of the statutory tenancy.

DENNING LJ said at 245: "Seeing that the agreement touched and concerned the thing demised, it ran with the land so as to bind the assignee, the tenant, as soon as he entered into possession. I know that before the Judicature Act 1873, it was said that the doctrine of covenants running with the land only applied to covenants under seal and not to agreements under hand. See *Elliot v Johnson* (1868) LR 2 QB 120. But since the fusion of law and equity, the position is different. The distinction between agreements under hand and covenants under seal has been largely obliterated. There is no valid reason nowadays why the doctrine of covenants running with the land — or with the reversion — should not apply equally to agreements under hand as to covenants under seal; and I think we should so hold, not only in the case of agreements for more than three years which need the intervention of equity to perfect them, but also in the case of agreements for three years or less which do not."

QUESTION

A. agreed to grant a lease for 99 years to B. of valuable land at a rent of £25,000 a year. B. assigned his interest to C., and disappeared. C. has not yet taken possession. Is he liable for the rent? See C & B, p. 378; M & W, pp. 643–644, 746–747; MM, pp. 338, 381; *Purchase v Lichfield Brewery Co* [1915] 1 KB 184; (1978) 37 CLJ 90 (R. J. Smith).

VII.   Registered Land[5]

We have already seen that a term of years absolute can be registered as a separate title, provided that it is a term of more than 21 years[6]. In addition, a notice of the lease itself must be entered on the register of the lessor's title[7]. Where the lease is registered as a separate title, the notice is entered automatically by the Registrar at the time of registration[8]. But where a lease is incapable of registration, because it is a lease of 21 years or less, a distinction is drawn between leases granted at a rent without taking a fine, and other leases, such as are granted with a premium (or fine). With the latter, the lessee must apply for the entry of a notice on the register[9]. The former are overriding interests under section 70 (1) (*k*) of the Land Registration Act 1925[10], and no other protection is necessary. "To prevent the register from being cluttered by notices of leases which are overriding interests the Chief Land Registrar can refuse to enter such notices[11]. In practice it is very rarely that application is made to register notice of leases

---

[5] C & B, pp. 101, 483–486; M & W, pp. 199–203, 206; MM, pp. 339–340; Barnsley, *Conveyancing Law and Practice* (2nd edn, 1982), pp. 456–464; Ruoff and Roper, chap. 23; Law Commission Report on Land Registration Part IV: Treatment of Leases 1983 (Law Com No. 125, HC 86).

[6] P. 107, ante.

[7] LRA 1925, s. 19 (2), p. 472, post; s. 22 (2).

[8] LRR 1925, r. 46.

[9] LRA 1925, s. 48, p. 473, post.

[10] P. 120, ante.

[11] LRA 1925, ss. 19 (2) (*a*), 22 (2) (*a*); LRR 1925, r. 199; cf. LRA 1925, s. 70 (3), p. 120, ante.

that are overriding interests[12]." Where the lease has not been noted on the register, a lessee who is in actual occupation will also be protected by virtue of an overriding interest under section 70 (1) (*g*) of the Land Registration Act 1925[13].

LAND REGISTRATION. ACT 1925

3. Interpretation. — (x) "Lease" includes an under-lease and any tenancy or agreement for a lease, under-lease or tenancy[14].

8. Application for registration of leasehold land. — p. 107, ante.

9. Effect of first registration with absolute title. — p. 109, ante.

10. Effect of first registration with good leasehold title. — p. 109, ante.

123. Effect of Act in areas where registration is compulsory. — (1) p. 98, ante.

19. Registration of disposition of freeholds[15]. — (2) All interests transferred or created by dispositions by the proprietor, other than a transfer of the registered estate in the land, or part thereof, shall, subject to the provisions relating to mortgages, be completed by registration in the same manner and with the same effect as provided by this Act with respect to transfers of registered estates and notice thereof shall also be noted on the register:

Provided that nothing in this subsection —

    (*a*) shall authorise the registration of a lease granted for a term not exceeding twenty-one years, or require the entry of a notice of such a lease if it is granted at a rent without taking a fine[16]; or

    (*b*) shall authorise the registration of a mortgage term where there is a subsisting right of redemption; . . .

Every such disposition shall, when registered, take effect as a registered disposition, and a lease made by the registered proprietor under the last foregoing section which is not required to be registered or noted on the register shall nevertheless take effect as if it were a registered disposition immediately on being granted.

    (*c*) shall render necessary the registration of any easement, right, or privilege except as appurtenant to registered land, or the entry of notice thereof except as against the registered title of the servient land.

22. Registration of dispositions of leaseholds. — (1) A transfer of the registered estate in the land or part thereof shall be completed by the registrar entering on the register the transferee as proprietor of the estate transferred, but until such entry is made the transferor shall be deemed to remain the proprietor of the registered estate; and where part only of the land is transferred, notice thereof shall also be noted on the register.

---

[12] Ruoff and Roper, p. 452.

[13] P. 119, ante.

[14] Accordingly, notice of a sub-lease is properly entered on the intermediate lessor's title: *Strand Securities Ltd v Caswell* [1965] Ch 958, [1965] 1 All ER 820, p. 474, post. The subsection is misleading, however, in including an agreement for a lease: *City Permanent Building Society v Miller* [1952] Ch 840, [1952] 2 All ER 621, p. 120, n. 1, ante, p. 473, post; [1981] Conv 396.

[15] For almost identical provisions relating to dispositions by registered proprietors of leaseholds, see LRA 1925, s. 22 (2).

[16] This is protected as an overriding interest under LRA 1925, s. 70 (1) (*k*), p. 120, ante.

(3) The general words implied in conveyances under the Law of Property Act, 1925[17], shall apply, so far as applicable thereto, to transfers of a registered leasehold estate.

23. Effect of registration of dispositions of leaseholds[18]. — (1) In the case of a leasehold estate registered with an absolute title, a disposition (including a subdemise thereof) for valuable consideration shall, when registered, be deemed to vest in the transferee or underlessee the estate transferred or created to the extent of the registered estate, or for the term created by the subdemise, as the case may require, with all implied or expressed rights, privileges, and appurtenances attached to the estate transferred or created, including (subject to any entry to the contrary on the register) the appropriate rights and interests which would under the Law of Property Act, 1925, have been transferred if the land had not been registered, but subject as follows:—

(*a*) To all implied and express covenants, obligations, and liabilities incident to the estate transferred or created; and

(*b*) To the incumbrances and other entries (if any) appearing on the register and any charge for capital transfer tax subject to which the disposition takes effect under section 73 of this Act[19];

(*c*) Unless the contrary is expressed on the register, to the overriding interests, if any, affecting the estate transferred or created,

but free from all other estates and interests whatsoever, including estates and interests of His Majesty; and the transfer or subdemise shall operate in like manner as if the registered transferor or sublessor were (subject to any entry to the contrary on the register) absolutely entitled to the registered lease for his own benefit.

(5) Where any such disposition is made without valuable consideration it shall, so far as the transferee or underlessee is concerned, be subject to any minor interests subject to which the transferor or sublessor held the same; but, save as aforesaid, shall, when registered, in all respects, and in particular as respects any registered dealings on the part of the transferee or underlessee, have the same effect as if the disposition had been made for valuable consideration.

48. Registration of notice of lease. — (1) Any lessee or other person entitled to or interested in a lease of registered land, where the term granted is not an overriding interest[20], may apply to the registrar to register notice of such lease in the prescribed manner, and when so registered, every proprietor and the persons deriving title under him shall be deemed to be affected with notice of such lease, as being an incumbrance on the registered land in respect of which the notice is entered. . . .

70. Liability of registered land to overriding interests. — (1) (*k*) p. 120, ante.

In *City Permanent Building Society v Miller* [1952] Ch 840, [1952] 2 All ER 621, the Court of Appeal held that an agreement for a lease was not within LRA 1925, s. 70 (1) (*k*). JENKINS LJ said at 852, at 628:

----

[17] LPA 1925, s. 62, p. 586, post.
[18] Sub-ss. (2), (3) and (4) contain analogous provisions with regard to good leasehold, qualified, and possessory titles. Cf. s. 20 with regard to freeholds, p. 110, ante.
[19] As amended by FA 1975, s. 52, Sch. 12, para. 5 (3).
[20] I.e. under LRA, s. 70 (1) (*k*), p. 120, ante.

"Mr Marsh relied on the definition of 'lease' contained in section 3 (x) of the Land Registration Act, 1925, which is in these terms: 'Lease' includes an underlease and any tenancy 'or agreement for a lease, underlease or tenancy.' He argued that the word 'leases' in section 70 (1) (*k*) of the same Act must accordingly be construed as including agreements for leases; but, as my Lord has pointed out, the definitions in section 3 are prefaced by the familiar form of words. 'In this Act, unless the context otherwise requires, the following expressions have the meanings hereby assigned to them respectively, that is to say.' In my view, the context afforded in section 70 (1) (*k*) does 'otherwise require.' It refers to 'leases for any term or interest not exceeding 21 years, granted at a rent without taking a fine.' In my judgment, the use there of the word granted clearly imports the actual creation of a term of years, whether it is done by deed or by an agreement under hand only, in that class of case in which a legal term can be created by a document not under seal, or indeed by parol in any case in which an actual tenancy taking effect at law may be created without writing. But in my judgment the word 'granted' necessarily imports the actual creation of a term, and that excludes, by force of the context, the case of a mere agreement for a lease, having no more than a contractual effect. To include such a case, in my judgment, section 70 (1) (*k*) should have read 'granted or agreed to be granted.' "

STRAND SECURITIES LTD *v* CASWELL[1]
[1965] Ch 958, [1965] 1 All ER 820 (CA, Lord DENNING MR, HARMAN and RUSSELL LJJ)

LORD DENNING MR: The case raises the question: What is the proper course for the Land Registrar to take when he is asked to register a leasehold interest (for more than 21 years) which has never been registered before? The present case concerns a sublease derived out of a superior lease, but the question is the same in the case of a lease derived out of the freehold. Sections 4, 19 and 20 of the Land Registration Act 1925 (which relate to freeholds) are in all material respects the same as sections 8, 22 and 23 (which relate to leaseholds). It is, however, much more simple to state the position when a freeholder grants a lease: and I will, therefore, take that case. These are the steps which, in my opinion, should be taken on first registration of a lease:

(1) The lessee must apply to be registered as the first proprietor of his leasehold interest. His application must be accompanied by his own lease, but it need not be accompanied by the freeholder's land certificate. We are told that the registrar insists that the lessee shall produce the freeholder's land certificate showing the freeholder's title to his freehold. If it is not produced, the registrar treats the application by the lessee as insufficient and incomplete. In my opinion that practice is wrong. In the absence of express agreement, a lessee has no right to call for his lessor's title. Likewise he has no right to call for his lessor's land certificate. The registrar should not insist on the lessee producing a document to which he has no right. The application is complete without it. . . .

The judge was much influenced by the practice of the Land Registry. He thought he ought to give weight to it, just as to the practice of conveyancers. I

---

[1] P. 130, ante; (1965) 62 LSG 507 (T. B. F. Ruoff).

do not agree with this. We cannot allow the registrar by his practice to make bad law and it is bad law to insist on the lessee producing his landlord's land certificate — to which he has no right[2].

(2) As soon as the application to register the leasehold interest is received, the registrar must enter it in the list of pending applications, which is open to the public, see rules 10 and 12 of the Land Registration Rules 1925[3]. Thereafter anyone who makes a search of the freeholder's register is told that there is a pending application affecting it and the nature of the application, namely, to register a lease. . . .

(3) It is desirable, however, that before the lease is registered, some enquiry should be made of the freeholder, so as to see that the lease is genuine. If it is genuine, it is desirable that an entry should be made in the freeholder's register. Else a purchaser might buy the freehold without knowledge of the lease. The Act and rules make provision for this. As soon as the registrar receives the application from the lessee to register the lease, he must give notice to the freeholder. This appears from rule 46 where "is registered" clearly means "is being registered". The freeholder has seven days in which to object. In the ordinary way he will not object because it will be he who has granted the lease. In that case, there being no objection, the registrar should proceed to enter the lease as a first registration. He should give it a new title number, and enter the lessee as the proprietor of this new leasehold interest. But he should also, at the same time, enter a notice in the charges section of the freeholder's register (see rule 7 (b)) to the effect that the lease has been granted out of the freehold. The lease then is an incumbrance on the freehold and the freeholder, and all persons deriving title under him, are affected by notice of it, see rule 46 (2) and section 48.

(4) The important thing to notice is that, when the registration is eventually effected of the lease, it takes effect as of the date on which the application was delivered at the Land Registry, see rule 83, and the note on the freeholder's register also takes effect as a notice effected on that day. The reason is because section 19 (2) for freeholds (the corresponding section for leaseholds is section 22 (2)) treats the registration and the noting as contemporaneous and rule 46 (2) equates the noting under that rule with a notice under section 48 which takes effect as of the date of application, see rule 83[4].

(5) Thus far we have got the note about the lease on the freeholder's register which is kept in the Land Registry. But it is desirable that this note about the lease should also be entered on the freeholder's land certificate. The freeholder holds this himself and the registrar has no right to call for this. Section 64 (1) (c) makes it clear that it need not be produced. There is no reason, however, why the registrar should not ask the freeholder to produce it voluntarily and, if it is forthcoming as it usually will be, he can enter the notice on it. If it is not forthcoming, all that the registrar can do is to wait until the freeholder's land certificate comes into the Land Registry on some other matter and then enter the notice on it.

---

[2] Annual Report of Chief Registrar for 1980–1981, para. 15; [1981] Conv 395.
[3] See LRR 1925, rr. 7A (entry in the day list) and 10 (list of pending applications for first registration), p. 115, ante. R. 7A was added, and r. 10 substituted, by LRR 1978.
[4] See r. 83, as substituted by LRR 1978, r. 8.

(6) Here I will go back a little to paragraph 3 above. If the freeholder within the seven days, objects to the lease being entered on the freeholder's register, then the registrar should hear and determine the objection, subject to an appeal to the court, see rule 298. If the objection is disallowed, the registration and noting will proceed and will take effect as of the date of application. If the objection is upheld, then the lease should not be registered and no note be made on the freeholder's register.

(7) It is obvious that some time may elapse between the date of the application to register the lease and the eventual registration and the noting on the freeholder's register. Suppose in the interval the freeholder agrees to transfer his freehold or to grant a lease to someone else. The transferee or lessee, before completing, will of course search at the registry. Upon this search, he will be told of any pending application which affects the land. In particular he will be told that there is an application to register a lease as a first registration and he will know that, if this application is granted, it will date back to the date of the original application. So it will take priority over the transfer or lease which is then in contemplation. So it does appear that under the steps I have stated there is good protection against fraud.

Registered Land Practice Notes (1982–1983), pp. 18–21

"Protection of lessee where lease not an overriding interest — registration of leases and assignments of leases

(a) *Where the freehold or superior leasehold is registered (whether in the compulsory areas or not)*

Subject to paragraphs (d) and (e) below, a grant of a term of more than twenty-one years by the registered proprietor must be completed by registration if the grantee is to obtain a legal estate (sections 20 and 23). It is emphasised that this refers to substantive registration of the lessee's term under section 19 (2) or 22 (2).

Notice of the grant must be entered against the freehold or superior leasehold title (section 48) and it is desirable that the land certificate of the title of the freeholder or superior leaseholder should be produced. The land certificate must be produced if the lessor takes a premium (section 64 (1) (c)).

(b) *Where the freehold or superior leasehold is not registered (compulsory areas only)*
Subject to paragraphs (d) and (e) below:
    (i) a grant of a term of forty years or more or an assignment on sale of leasehold land where the lease has not less than forty years to run at the date of the delivery of the assignment *must* be completed by registration within two months from the date of the grant or the assignment (section 123).
    (ii) a grant of a term of more than twenty-one years but less than forty years and of which more than twenty-one years are unexpired, or an assignment of a term having less than forty years but more than twenty-one years unexpired, *may* be registered.

(c) *Position where lessee fails to register*
    (i) In the case of a lease falling within paragraph (a) above, the lessee will not obtain the legal estate. However, he may nevertheless have an overriding interest under section 70 (1) (g) whilst in actual occupation of the land or in receipt of the rents and profits thereof

but, if these circumstances change, the overriding interest may well cease (see *Strand Securities Ltd v Caswell* [1965] Ch 958, [1965] 1 All ER 820).

(ii) In the case of leases falling within paragraph (*b*) (i) above, the lessee or assignee will, on the expiry of the two months' period prescribed by section 123 (1), lose the legal estate. Thus, if a head lessee fails to register in any case where registration is compulsory, he cannot confer a legal estate on a sub-lessee (*British Maritime Trust v Upsons Ltd* [1931] WN 7).

(*d*) *The following interests are incapable of registration:*

    (i) A lease with only twenty-one years (or less) to run at the time of application (section 8 (1) (*a*)).

    (ii) A lease originally granted for twenty-one years (or less) (section 19 (2), proviso (*a*)).

    (iii) A mortgage term where there is a subsisting right of redemption (section 8 (1) and section 19 (2), proviso (*b*)).

    (iv) A lease containing an absolute prohibition against alienation *inter vivos* (section 8 (2)).

    (v) an agreement for a lease (section 8 (1) (*b*)).

The interests referred to in items (i), (iv) and (v) should be protected on the register by notice, but such protection is neither authorised nor required in the case of the lease mentioned in (ii), if it was granted at a rent without taking a fine (section 19 (2), proviso (*a*), section 48 (1) and section 70 (1) (*k*)).

(*e*) *Registration out of time: Registrar's discretion*

    (i) If a lessee has failed to register in accordance with paragraph (*a*) above, the Chief Land Registrar would normally consider favourably an application to register that lease even though more than twenty-one years of the term do not remain.

    (ii) If a lessee or assignee has failed to register within the two months' period in accordance with paragraph (*b*) (i) above, application may be made to the Chief Land Registrar to make an order pursuant to the proviso to section 123 (1) for an extension of that period. Any such application, which states briefly the reasons why the matter has been overlooked, will be viewed sympathetically."

9. Licences[1]

I. Introduction[2]

In its simplest form, a licence is a permission to enter upon land. It makes lawful what would otherwise be a trespass[3]; and, in the absence of special circumstances, is revocable at the will of the licensor. It is not a proprietary interest, and is not the subject matter of a grant.

But there are many ways in which a licence has progressed from this simplistic form. Since the Judicature Act 1873, equitable remedies became available to protect a licensee in suitable cases. The years since World War II have seen a rapid development of their use, and this development is not fully worked out. The earlier cases focussed on the question whether the licensee was to be protected against the licensor, by an injunction restraining the licensor from revoking the licence. Protection of the licensee against the licensor inevitably gave rise to the next question; whether the licensee was also to be protected against third parties, who would usually be the successors in title of the licensor. Protection against third parties further gave rise to the question whether such a licence had acquired proprietary characteristics. It may be that a licence which protects the licensee against third parties should be regarded as "proprietary" in nature, or it may be that an interest should only be regarded as proprietary[4] if it is capable of being

---

[1] C & B, pp. 553–570; M & W, pp. 798–808; MM, pp. 370–376; H & M, chap. 27; Dawson and Pearce, *Licences Relating to the Occupation or Use of Land* (1979).

[2] (1954) 70 LQR 326 (Lord EVERSHED).

[3] VAUGHAN CJ in *Thomas v Sorrell* (1673) Vaughan 330 at 351.

[4] *National Provincial Bank Ltd v Ainsworth* [1965] AC 1175 at 1247–1248, [1965] 2 All ER 472 at 494–495.

assigned, bought and sold, and of passing through the estate of a deceased person. There have not yet been cases in which a protected licensee has purported to "sell" his licence. But there are cases in which licensees have been held to be entitled to an order transferring to them an easement, or a life interest, or a fee simple in the land[5]; or have been held, even in the absence of such order, to be entitled to compensation, in their capacity as licensees, under statutory provisions authorising the payment of compensation to persons having interests in the land[6]. The question of the proper nature of a licence in modern law will not be answered in this book; but it is one which should be borne in mind in reading the cases.

The facts of the cases will show in what a wide variety of circumstances questions of protection of licensees can arise. And it will not be a matter of surprise to recognise that a large percentage of current cases are dealing with arrangements for the occupation of family homes, using "family" in a sense wide enough to include mistresses. This question is related to that discussed in the context of Trusts for Sale[7]. Where a proprietary interest is found by the application of trust doctrines (usually resulting or constructive trust) in the party who is not the legal owner, a beneficial co-ownership is created; and various questions then arise as to the determination of the rights of the parties, as by sale of the premises, or by their retention as a home for (usually) the woman and children. Where a non-owner has no such proprietary interest, protection may be given, by restraining the legal owner from evicting the licensee.

The litigation on the protection of licensees has generally concerned licences of four main types: contractual licences; licences by estoppel; licences arising under a constructive trust; and, for the short period of their recognition, the deserted wife's licence[8]. Each of these will be looked at in turn; but it will be useful, first of all, to lay down some of the basic propositions of the common law. The modern development has been by way of the application of equitable principles and remedies to that situation.

II.   The Common Law Rules[9]

A.   A Bare and Gratuitous Licence is Revocable at the Will of the Licensor

The licensee here avoids being a trespasser only because of the licensor's permission to enter. Such is the position of a guest at dinner, or of a picnic party in a friend's garden. The licensor is free to withdraw his permission, as is a bailor in the case of gratuitous bailment. The licensee then becomes a

---

[5] P. 545, post.
[6] P. 533, post.
[7] P. 252, ante.
[8] Dawson and Pearce use nine categories of licences: Bare Licences; Contractual Licences; Licences by Estoppel; Licences arising under the doctrine of benefit and burden; Licences arising under the doctrine against derogation from grant; Licences and s. 62 LPA 1925; Licences arising by operation of law; Licences coupled with an interest; Licences as interests under a constructive trust.
[9] C & B, pp. 554–555; M & W, pp. 798–804; MM, pp. 370–371; **Dawson and Pearce**, pp. 22–24, 68–73.

trespasser, but is first allowed a reasonable time in which to collect his goods, if any, and to leave the land[10].

B.   Entry upon a Licence does not make it Irrevocable

There is also a doctrine[11] of long standing, little relied on, to the effect that, if a licence has been acted upon, it is not revocable. Such an argument would prove too much, for it disregards the many cases in which licensees are permitted to be evicted after entry[12], and also disregards the reasoning in other cases in which the licensee has been protected on other grounds. *Tayler v Waters* (1816) 7 Taunt 374, one of the leading cases in support of this theory, was disapproved in *Wood v Leadbitter* and described as being "to the last degree unsatisfactory" (1845) 13 M & W 838 at 852, p. 481, post. If the principle of *Tayler v Waters* had developed, it "would go close to reversing the general rule of the revocability of licences"[13]. The cases have been explained as illustrations of the principle of estoppel, discussed below[14]. But there is no indication that the judges in the cases so thought, and no express reference to that principle. A related but distinct concept appears in modern law in the rule formulated by Lord EVERSHED in *Armstrong v Sheppard and Short Ltd* [1959] 2 QB 384 at 399, [1959] 2 All ER 651 at 658: "If A gives authority to B for the doing of an act on A's land, and the act is done and completed, then, whatever be the strict description of the authority . . . it is, generally speaking at any rate, too late for A . . . to complain of it.[15]"

C.   A Licence is not the Subject Matter of a Grant

This and the following proposition are closely related, and are both based upon the elementary rule that a grant of property is not revocable. A conveyance transfers to the grantee the subject matter of the grant, and it is beyond the grantor's power to recall.

But, of course, to be effective, the conveyance must have concerned something which the law recognises as being the subject matter of a grant and capable of being conveyed. A licensee, as stated above, is merely "not a trespasser". A licence is not a piece of property. But a licence may be coupled with a grant of an interest in property, real or personal, and, as shown in D below, p. 483, post, it will then be irrevocable.

---

[10] *Minister of Health v Bellotti* [1944] KB 298, [1944] 1 All ER 238; *Canadian Pacific Rly Co v R* [1931] AC 414; *Australian Blue Metal Ltd v Hughes* [1963] AC 74, [1962] 3 All ER 335.

[11] *Webb v Paternoster* (1619) Palm 71; *Wood v Lake* (1751) Say 3; *Winter v Brockwell* (1807) 8 East 308; *Tayler v Waters* (1816) 7 Taunt 374; *Wallis v Harrison* (1838) 4 M & W 538 at 544; *Feltham v Cartwright* (1839) 5 Bing NC 569; *Wood v Manley* (1839) 11 Ad & El 34 where, however, the licence was coupled with an interest, for the licensee was the owner of the hay; *Bendall v McWhirter* [1952] 2 QB 466 at 479, [1952] 1 All ER 1307 at 1312, per DENNING LJ; *Armstrong v Sheppard and Short Ltd* [1959] 2 QB 384, [1959] 2 All ER 651; *Hounslow London Borough Council v Twickenham Garden Developments Ltd* [1971] Ch 233 at 255, [1970] 3 All ER 326 at 344; (1965) 29 Conv (NS) 19 (M. C. Cullity).

[12] E.g. *Winter Garden Theatre (London) Ltd v Millennium Productions Ltd* [1948] AC 173, [1947] 2 All ER 331, p. 486, post.

[13] (1965) 29 Conv (NS) 19 at p. 31.

[14] P. 510, post. See Dawson and Pearce, p. 31.

[15] See *Hounslow London Borough Council v Twickenham Garden Developments Ltd* [1971] Ch 233 at 255, [1970] 3 All ER 326 at 344.

In *Wood v Leadbitter* (1845) 13 M & W 838, the plaintiff bought a ticket entitling him to enter the grandstand at Doncaster racecourse. On account of alleged malpractices on a previous occasion, he was ordered by the defendant, who was the servant of Lord Eglintoun, the steward of the course, to leave the racecourse. On his refusal, he was physically removed, no more force being used than was reasonably necessary. His action for assault and false imprisonment failed. He was a licensee only; and not a grantee of an interest in land. ALDERSON B, delivering the judgment of the Court of Exchequer, said at 845: "It may further be observed, that a license under seal (provided it be a mere license) is as revocable as a license by parol; and, on the other hand, a license by parol, coupled with a grant, is as irrevocable as a license by deed, provided only that the grant is of a nature capable of being made by parol. But where there is a license by parol, coupled with a parol grant, or pretended grant, of something which is incapable of being granted otherwise than by deed, there the licence is a mere licence; it is not an incident to a *valid* grant, and it is therefore revocable."

This may be logical; but hardly satisfactory. Where a licensee has paid to enter premises for a period of time, and he observes the terms and conditions of the licence, is it right that the licensor should be allowed to break the contract and turn the licensee into a trespasser?

In *Hurst v Picture Theatres Ltd* [1915] 1 KB 1, the plaintiff bought a ticket for 6d. to watch a cinema show at a theatre of the defendants. During the performance, the plaintiff was requested to leave on the ground, as the defendants incorrectly believed, that he had not paid for his ticket. He refused, and was ejected forcibly, but without the use of unnecessary violence. His action for assault and false imprisonment succeeded by a majority of 2 to 1. The majority (BUCKLEY and KENNEDY LJJ) found that he had an interest in the land. Since the Judicature Act, an interest in land could be granted without a deed. A contract for valuable consideration of which equity would decree specific performance would suffice.

The fallacy of this reasoning was shown by PHILLIMORE LJ, dissenting. The doctrine of *Walsh v Lonsdale* (1882) 21 Ch D 9, p. 80, ante, he said, is that a man "has the estate which equity thinks he ought to have. That has no bearing on the question if there is no estate, and no interest in land given by the document relied on".

In short, contractual licences are not grants. They are contracts, and should be treated as such.

In *Cowell v Rosehill Racecourse Co Ltd* (1937) 56 CLR 605, LATHAM CJ said at 616:

"The doctrine of *Wood v Leadbitter* is clear and coherent. If a man creates a proprietary right in another and gives him a licence to go upon certain land in order that he may use or enjoy that right, the grantor cannot divest the grantee of his proprietary right and revest it in the grantor, or simply determine it, by breaking the agreement under which the licence was given. The grantee owns the property to which the licence is incident, and this ownership, with its incidental licence, is unaffected by what purports to be a revocation of the licence. The revocation of the licence is ineffectual. Easements and *profits à prendre* supply examples of interests to which licences to enter and remain upon land may be incidental.

The majority judgment in *Hurst's* case modified, if it did not reject, the law of *Wood v Leadbitter* by holding that a 'right to see' a spectacle was an interest which could be granted so that a licence to go into a theatre or a racecourse to see a play or to witness races was, when given for value, irrevocable because it was a licence coupled with an interest. Further, the majority judgment held that, in so far as *Wood v Leadbitter* rested upon the rule that no incorporeal hereditament affecting land can be created or transferred otherwise than by deed, the Judicature Act had radically changed the position. The court was now bound to give effect to equitable doctrines and would therefore ignore the absence of a seal and would (as in *Frogley v Earl of Lovelace* (1859) John 333) grant an injunction to protect the right granted.

The first ground of the decision, in my opinion, ignores the distinction between a proprietary right and a contractual right. In *Wood v Leadbitter* there was obviously a contractual 'interest.' The plaintiff had bought and paid for a contractual right to go upon land for the purpose of witnessing a spectacle. But this fact, which was treated as irrelevant in *Wood v Leadbitter*, is made the foundation of the first ground of the judgment in *Hurst's Case*. In that case *Buckley* LJ at 5–9 interpreted 'interest' in a sense quite different from that in which the word was used in *Wood v Leadbitter*. The learned judge said that there was a grant of a right to come to see a spectacle. The licence is described as 'only something granted to him for the purpose of enabling him to have that which had been granted to him, namely, the right to see.' The 'right to see' is treated as the 'interest' which has been 'granted.'

It is clear that the learned judge used the word 'grant' in a sense very different from that in which it was used in *Wood v Leadbitter*. It was there used in relation to interests in land which were, if they existed at all, clearly proprietary interests. The right to see a spectacle cannot, in the ordinary sense of legal language, be regarded as a proprietary interest. Fifty thousand people who pay to see a football match do not obtain fifty thousand interests in the football ground.

The second ground of the decision in *Hurst's* case is based upon the opinion that the plaintiff in *Wood v Leadbitter* failed because he did not have a grant under seal of the right which he claimed. It is true that the absence of a seal was a complete reply, in an action at law, to the contention of the plaintiff that he had an interest in the land upon which a race meeting was being held. But in fact the presence of a seal would not have assisted the plaintiff to establish the impossible proposition that he had an easement in gross. It is true that, as the majority judgments in *Hurst's* case state, a grant of an interest in land need not, in order to be effective in a court of equity, be made by deed, and that, since the Judicature Act, this rule is enforced in all divisions of the High Court in England: *Walsh v Lonsdale* (1882) 21 Ch D 9, p. 81, ante. But this proposition does not justify the assertion that interests in land can, since the Judicature Act, be created by simple contract even though, before that Act, they were of such a character that they could not be created by deed as interests in land. *Buckley* LJ applies to the facts of *Hurst's* case the statement of *Parker* J in *James Jones & Sons Ltd v Earl of Tankerville* [1909] 2 Ch 440 at 443 that an injunction restraining the revocation of a licence 'merely prevents' the defendant 'from breaking his contract, and protects a right in equity which but for the absence of a seal would be a right at law, and since the *Judicature Act* it may well be doubted whether the absence of a seal in such a case can be relied on in any court.' This statement was made with respect to a proprietary right (a *profit à prendre*) and it is a begging of the question to apply it to a case in which the matter in dispute is whether the alleged interest is such that it can be an interest in land, whether created by deed or not. *Frogley v Earl of Lovelace*, which is relied upon in *Hurst's* case, was a case of an agreement for a *profit à prendre*, an incorporeal hereditament. Thus the second ground for the majority judgments in *Hurst's* case cannot, in my opinion, be supported. I regard the dissenting judgment of *Phillimore* LJ as a convincing statement of the true position both at law and in equity."

D.   A Licence Coupled with a Grant (or an Interest) is Irrevocable

It is an anciently established rule that a licence coupled with a proprietary interest (in land or in a chattel) is irrevocable[16]. The interest must, of course, have been correctly granted[17]. In the grant of incorporeal hereditaments in realty at common law, a seal was needed; but, since the Judicature Act, an agreement for valuable consideration suffices[18]. It is, indeed, somewhat artificial to speak of a licence coupled with an interest in realty; for if the interest is properly granted and is one which involves entry upon another's land, the grantee enters by force of the grant and does not need to rely on a licence.

In the case of licences coupled with a chattel interest, that interest must again be properly granted, usually by gift or sale. Thus, where the occupier gives or sells a stack of coal on the land to a purchaser, the donee or purchaser is entitled to enter the land to take away the coal, and the donor or seller cannot deny him the right[19]. And a contract to cut and carry away timber on the Earl of Tankerville's Estate[20] created a chattel interest in the cut timber and a realty interest in the growing trees.

III.   Licences for Consideration: Contractual Licences[1]

A.   Damages for Breach of Contract

It has been seen that much confusion has been caused by the inability of the common law to give protection to a contractual licensee unless he has a proprietary interest in the land or chattels upon it. This position, based upon

---

[16] *Webb v Paternoster* (1619) Palm 71; *Wood v Manley* (1839) 11 Ad & El 34; *James Jones & Sons Ltd v Earl of Tankerville* [1909] 2 Ch 440.

[17] On the question whether certain interests need to be regarded as realty or personalty for the purpose of a grant or of compliance with LPA 1925, s. 40, see M & W, pp. 573–575; MM, p. 137; see also p. 63, ante.

[18] *Walsh v Lonsdale* (1882) 21 ChD 9, p. 81, ante.

[19] *Wood v Manley* (1839) 11 Ad & El 34.

[20] *James Jones & Sons Ltd v Earl of Tankerville* [1909] 2 Ch 440.

[1] C & B, pp. 555–559; M & W, pp. 800–804; MM, pp. 371–374; Dawson and Pearce, pp. 24–38, 73–97, 133–144, 153–161, 167. See MEGARRY J's summary in *Hounslow London Borough Council v Twickenham Garden Developments Ltd* [1971] Ch 233 at 254, [1970] 3 All ER 326 at 343; *Chandler v Kerley* [1978] 1 WLR 693, [1978] 2 All ER 942.

Wood v Leadbitter, meant that the licensor could, without giving any reason, turn out at will any watchers of a cinema show, horse race or football match[2]. The only difference between a contractual and a gratuitious licence was that, in the former, the licensor must pay damages. These were commonly assumed to be the price which the licensee had paid to enter. But there seems to be no reason why the damages should not reflect the loss of the licensee's expectation under the contract[3].

B.   Restitution

An alternative basis for compensation is the licensor's obligation to restore to the licensee the unjust benefit which he has received as a result of his wrongful termination of the contract.

In *Tanner v Tanner* [1975] 1 WLR 1346, [1975] 3 All ER 776[4], the plaintiff and defendant had baby daughters. They were not married. The plaintiff purchased a house for the defendant, and she accordingly left her rent-controlled flat. The time came when the plaintiff, having changed his affections, decided to turn out the defendant and the children. She stayed, claiming that she should be allowed to remain in the house with the children until they had finished school. In the county court, an order for possession was made, and the defendant was rehoused by the local authority.

The Court of Appeal held that she was a licensee entitled to protection. She should have been entitled to stay in the house with the children until they left school, if the house continued to be needed for that purpose. But, as they had left, damages were awarded, compensating her for her loss. Lord DENNING MR said at 1350, at 780: "It seems to me that enables an inference to be drawn, namely that in all the circumstances it is to be implied that she had a licence — a contractual licence — to have accommodation in the house for herself and the children so long as they were of school age and the accommodation was reasonably required for her and the children. There was, it is true, no express contract to that effect, but the circumstances are such that the court should imply a contract by the plaintiff — or, if need be impose the equivalent of a contract by him — whereby they were entitled to have the use of the house as their home until the girls had finished school. . . . . .

If therefore the defendant had sought an injunction restraining the plaintiff from determining the licence, it should have been granted. The order for possession ought not to have been made."

[But the order for possession had been made and the defendant had moved out. His Lordship continued at 1351, at 780:] "What is to be done? The judge ordered possession in six weeks. Thereupon the local housing authority (as they usually do when an order for possession is made) provided accommodation for the defendant and the children. She moved out in pursuance of the order and does not ask to be put back now. Seeing that the order ought not to have been made and we reverse it, what is to be done? It seems to me that this court has ample power, when it reverses an order of the court below,

---

[2] Per PHILLIMORE LJ in *Hurst v Picture Theatres Ltd* [1915] 1 KB 1, p. 481, ante; *Cowell v Rosehill Racecourse Co Ltd* (1937) 56 CLR 605 p. 481, ante.
[3] *Kerrison v Smith* [1897] 2 QB 445.
[4] (1976) 92 LQR 168 (J.L. Barton).

to do what is just and equitable to restore the position as fairly as it can in the circumstances. The plaintiff has obtained an unjust benefit and should make restitution. In the circumstances the court can and should assess compensation to be payable by him. . . . . It seems to me a reasonable sum for loss of this licence (which the defendant ought not to have lost) would be £2,000[5]."

C. Injunction To Restrain Breach of Contract

The more realistic question, however, is whether a licensee may obtain a remedy to prevent the revocation of the licence; as the defendant in *Tanner v Tanner* would have done if she had not previously been rehoused. The plain fact is that the common law had no appropriate remedy; and this may explain the development of the tenuous and unsatisfactory common law doctrine that a licence, once entered upon, was irrevocable[6].

After the Judicature Act, equitable remedies became available. We saw that, in *Hurst's Case*[7], the Court of Appeal found that the licensee should be protected; but only by reasoning the weakness of which is shown in the dissenting judgment of PHILLIMORE LJ. The availability of equitable rights and remedies is vital in this situation. The normal way of protecting a contractual licensee against wrongful revocation is by issuing an injunction to restrain the breach by the licensor. And, as we shall see, the Court of Appeal has recently held that a contractual licence may also be enforceable by a decree of specific performance[8].

The crucial question in considering the revocability of contractual licences is whether the licence is revocable according to the proper construction of the contract[9]. Express provision will often be made. In its absence, the right to revoke will depend upon the intention of the parties as gathered from all the surrounding circumstances. There is no presumption one way or the other[10]; but it will presumably be more difficult to establish the non-revocability of a licence unlimited in time than it would be in the case of a licence for a specific period. The court may find that the licensor has a right to revoke upon giving reasonable notice, and will determine what that period is. If the licensor has no right to revoke, the question is whether the case is one in which it is appropriate to protect the licensee by an injunction restraining the licensor from breaking the contract, or whether the licensee should be left to his remedy in damages.

A licensee who is himself in breach of the terms of the contractual licence will not be protected[11]; nor presumably if the effect of the injunction would be

---

[5] No contract was implied in similar circumstances in *Horrocks v Forray* [1976] 1 WLR 230, [1976] 1 All ER 737 (described in (1976) 40 Conv (NS) 362 (M. Richards) as "*Tanner v Tanner* in a middle class setting").

[6] P. 480, ante.

[7] [1915] 1 KB 1, p. 481, ante. The plaintiff received £150 as damages for assault and false imprisonment.

[8] *Verrall v Great Yarmouth Borough Council* [1981] QB 202, [1980] 1 All ER 839, p. 493, post.

[9] *Winter Garden Theatre (London) Ltd v Millennium Productions Ltd* [1948] AC 173, [1947] 2 All ER 331.

[10] Ibid at 203, at 344, per Lord MACDERMOTT. Lord PORTER said at 195, at 339, that a licence was prima facie revocable. See also *Re Spenborough UDC's Agreement* [1968] Ch 139, [1967] 1 All ER 959; *Beverley Corpn v Richard Hodgson & Sons Ltd* (1972) 225 EG 799.

[11] *Thompson v Park* [1944] KB 408, [1944] 2 All ER 477, where the defendant had "been guilty at least of riot, affray, wilful damage, forcible entry, and, perhaps, conspiracy", per GODDARD LJ at 409. The defendant was a preparatory school master who had moved, with his pupils, to the plaintiff's school when the defendant's premises were unavailable because of the war.

to compel people to live together in intolerable circumstances[12]. And it has been held that a licensee, whose occupation of premises was dependent upon his employment, was not protected where he was dismissed in breach of contract[13].

In *Winter Garden Theatre (London) Ltd v Millennium Productions Ltd* [1948] AC 173, [1947] 2 All ER 331, the appellants granted to the respondents a licence to use and present plays in the Winter Garden Theatre in Drury Lane for a period of six months, from 6 July 1942, with an option to renew for a further six months at an increased payment. The licence provided that on the expiration of these periods the respondents should have the option to continue the licence for an unstated period, terminable by them at a month's notice. No provision was made for termination by the appellants. The options were duly exercised. The appellants retained possession of the bars and cloakrooms. After three years the appellants wished to terminate the licence, and on 11 September 1945 served a notice requiring the respondents to vacate the theatre on 13 October 1945. The respondents refused to leave and brought an action for a declaration that the licence was not revocable; or, alternatively, if it was, that a reasonable period after the service of the notice had not expired.

The House of Lords held that, on the proper construction of the contract, the licence was terminable on giving reasonable notice, and that the notice given was reasonable. The question of wrongful revocation did not arise. But, on that subject, Lord UTHWATT said at 202, at 343:

"My view as to the construction of the agreement renders it unnecessary to consider whether *Hurst v Picture Theatres Ltd* [1915] 1 KB 1, p. 481, ante was rightly decided, or to express any concluded opinion on the question of the remedies now open in every court to a bare licensee who claims that the licensor has in breach of his bargain affected to revoke it. I merely confess my present inability to see any answer to the propositions of law stated by the Master of the Rolls in his judgment in the case under appeal[14]. The settled practice of the courts of equity is to do what they can by an injunction to preserve the sanctity of a bargain. To my mind, as at present advised, a licensee who has refused to accept the wrongful repudiation of the bargain which is involved in an unauthorised revocation of the licence is as much entitled to the protection of an injunction as a licensee who has not received any notice of revocation; and, if the remedy of injunction is properly available in the latter case against unauthorised interference by the licensor, it is also available in the former case. In a court of equity, wrongful acts are no passport to favour."

The Court of Appeal in this case had been faced with the question of the proper solution to the problem of the protection of a contractual licensee under a contract which was construed as irrevocable; it had taken a different

---

[12] Ibid, per GODDARD LJ at 409, at 478–479.
[13] *Ivory v Palmer* [1975] ICR 340. For a consideration of the question of the circumstances in which misbehaviour by a licensee by estoppel will allow his licence to be terminated, see *Williams v Staite* [1979] Ch 291, [1978] 2 All ER 928; *Brynowen Estates Ltd v Bourne* (1981) 131 NLJ 1212; *Willis & Son v Willis* (1985) 277 EG 1133; p. 559, post.
[14] Infra.

view from the House of Lords of the construction of the contract. The statement of the law by Lord GREENE MR, referred to by Lord Uthwatt is as follows [1946] 1 All ER 678 at 684:

"The next question which I must mention is this. The respondents[15] have purported to determine the licence. If I have correctly construed the contract their doing so was a breach of contract. It may well be that, in the old days, that would only have given rise to a right to sue for damages. The licence would have stood revoked, but after the expiration of what was the appropriate period of grace the licensees would have been trespassers and could have been expelled, and their right would have been to sue for damages for breach of contract, as was said in *Kerrison v Smith* [1897] 2 QB 445. But the matter requires to be considered further, because the power of equity to grant an injunction to restrain a breach of contract is, of course, a power exercisable in any court. The general rule is that, before equity will grant such an injunction, there must be, on the construction of the contract, a negative clause express or implied. In the present case it seems to me that the grant of an option which, if I am right, is an irrevocable option, must imply a negative undertaking by the licensor not to revoke it. That being so, in my opinion, such a contract could be enforced in equity by an injunction. Then the question would arise, at what time can equity interfere? If the licensor were threatening to revoke, equity, I apprehend, would grant an injunction to restrain him from carrying out that threat. But supposing he has in fact purported to revoke, is equity then to say: 'We are now powerless. We cannot stop you from doing anything to carry into effect your wrongful revocation?' I apprehend not. I apprehend equity would say: 'You have revoked and the licensee had no opportunity of stopping you doing so by an injunction; but what the court of equity can do is to prevent you from carrying that revocation into effect and restrain you from doing anything under it.' In the present case, nothing has been done. The appellants are still there. I can see no reason at all why, on general principles, equity should not interfere to restrain the licensors from acting upon the purported revocation, that revocation being, as I consider, a breach of contract.

Looking at it in that rather simple way, one is not concerned with the difficulties which are suggested to arise from the decision of this court in *Hurst v Picture Theatres Ltd* [1915] 1 KB 1, p. 481, ante. Counsel for the respondents agreed that in this court he could not ask us to take a different view to the view there taken. It is a decision which has not satisfied everybody, but, quite apart from that decision, the simple propositions which I have just enunciated, which I cannot help thinking are right, would appear to me to get round any difficulties which might be felt as to the reasoning in *Hurst v Picture Theatres Ltd*. We are not concerned here with a licence coupled with a grant. Nothing of that kind is suggested. It is not suggested that that type of licence is in question here. It is a pure licence and nothing else, and the breach of the licence contract by the licensor could be restrained by a court of equity, and a court of equity would interfere to prevent the licensor taking steps pursuant to this wrongful revocation. That seems to me to put the matter right so far as this case is concerned[16]."

---

[15] I.e., *Winter Garden Theatre (London) Ltd* who became the appellants in the House of Lords.
[16] See also *Hounslow London Borough Council v Twickenham Garden Developments Ltd* [1971] Ch 233 at 254, [1970] 3 All ER 326 at 343, where MEGARRY J summarises the law relating to contractual licenses; (1971) 87 LQR 309; *Mayfield Holdings Ltd v Moana Reef Ltd* [1973] 1 NZLR 309.

CHANDLER *v* KERLEY
[1978] 1 WLR 693, [1978] 2 All ER 942 (CA, Lord SCARMAN, MEGAW and ROSKILL LJJ)[17]

LORD SCARMAN: This appeal is concerned with the right to occupy a dwelling-house, 300 Salisbury Road, Testwood, Totton, in Hampshire. The plaintiff owns it: the defendant, with her two children, occupies it. She will not leave, because she says the plaintiff has agreed that she may stay there as long as she pleases. The plaintiff went to the Southampton County Court with a claim for possession, alleging that the defendant was a trespasser, her licence having been terminated. The defendant not only resisted the claim, but also counterclaimed for a declaration that she is a tenant for life, alternatively that "she is the beneficiary under a trust. . . upon terms that she is entitled to remain therein with her children for as long as she wishes." In this court the defendant was allowed, the plaintiff not opposing, to amend her counterclaim by adding in the further alternative that she is a licensee for life, or for so long as her children remain in her custody and the younger is of school age and so long as she does not remarry, or for a period terminable only by reasonable notice.

On 26 May 1977, Judge McCreery dismissed the plaintiff's claim and gave judgment for the defendant on the counterclaim, declaring that the defendant is a beneficiary under a trust upon terms that she is entitled to occupy the house for her life or for so long as she pleases. The plaintiff now appeals.

The facts are unusual. The plaintiff, Mr Chandler, acquired the house from the defendant, Mrs Kerley, and her husband in the following circumstances. In 1972 Mr and Mrs Kerley jointly bought the house for £11,000, intending it to be their family home. The purchase was partly financed by a building society mortgage for £5,800. Mr Kerley paid the mortgage instalments. They have two children, both of whom are now living with their mother. In 1974 the marriage broke down. In May of that year Mr Kerley left home, not to return. However, he continued to pay the building society instalments. The defendant and the children continued to live in the house.

At about the time Mr Kerley left home, the defendant met the plaintiff. They became friends: sexual intercourse followed, and the defendant became the plaintiff's mistress. This relationship continued until January 1976, when it ended.

Early in 1975 Mr Kerley stopped paying the building society: he said he could not afford it. He and his wife put the house on the market for £14,950, but failed to find a buyer — even when in the autumn they reduced the asking price to £14,300. Meanwhile the building society was threatening to foreclose. The defendant naturally told the plaintiff of her anxieties. He wanted to help, and said he could afford £10,000, but no more. Finally it was agreed that the Kerleys should sell the house to the plaintiff for that figure, and the house was sold to him in December 1975. The net proceeds of sale, after they had paid off the debt to the building society, were divided —£1,000 to the defendant and £1,800 to Mr Kerley. The defendant accepted less than

---

[17] *Roach v Johannes* [1976] CLY 1549 (licence of "paying guest" terminable on giving reasonable notice, which in the circumstances was not less than 21 days); *Piquet v Tyler* [1978] CLY 119 (irrevocable licence for life of defendants, who had, by arrangement with plaintiff, surrendered protected tenancy to look after plaintiff's aged mother).

her half-share because she understood that the plaintiff was going to let her live in the house.

The arrangement between the plaintiff and the defendant which made all this possible was, according to the judge's findings, the following. The plaintiff agreed to buy the house for £10,000 (a figure substantially less than the asking price) upon the understanding that the defendant would continue to live in it indefinitely till he moved in. For at this time, 1975, they contemplated living together in the house as man and wife once they were free to do so, that is to say, after a divorce between Mr and Mrs Kerley. The defendant, very sensibly, did ask the plaintiff what would happen if they parted: he replied that he could not put her out.

Within six weeks of the purchase of the house, the plaintiff had brought their relationship to an end. It was not suggested, however, that he did so in order to get the defendant out of the house. Nevertheless he did purport in 1976 to serve a notice terminating her licence. It was given by solicitors' letter dated April 29 requiring the lady to quit on May 28.

The judge found that the plaintiff had granted the defendant an express licence and that the notice was not effectual to terminate it. There is now no challenge to these findings. The defendant is, therefore, a licensee whose right to occupy has not yet been terminated. In so far, therefore, as the appeal is against the dismissal of the plaintiff's claim for possession, it must fail. The true dispute, however, between the parties arises on the counter-claim. There are two substantial issues: (1) the terms of the licence; and (2) whether the defendant has an equitable interest arising under a constructive trust; and, if so, what is the extent of the interest.

The judge's findings as to the terms of the licence are obscure. He rejected the submission made on behalf of the defendant that she had an implied licence to remain in the house all her life: yet he also held (and I quote from the notes of judgment) "that there was an express agreement between the two and, as a result, there was a constructive trust with Mr Chandler as trustee and Mrs Kerley being the beneficiary." It is possible, though certainly not clear to me, that the judge is here finding an express agreement that she may remain for life: for he certainly granted her a declaration that she had an equity to that effect. But, whatever the finding as to the terms of the agreement, the reasoning of the judge in this passage is, in my judgment, unsound. If the defendant can establish a licence for life, there is neither room nor need for an equitable interest. Since the fusion of law and equity, such a legal right can be protected by injunction: see *Hurst v Picture Theatres Ltd* [1915] 1 KB 1, p. 481, ante, *Winter Garden Theatre (London) Ltd v Millennium Productions Ltd* [1948] AC 173, [1947] 2 All ER 331, p. 486, ante and *Foster v Robinson* [1951] 1 KB 149, [1950] 2 All ER 342, per Lord Evershed MR, at 156, at 346. If she cannot establish such a licence (express or implied), she cannot establish an equity: for no question of estoppel arises in this case. It is simply a case of what the parties envisaged by their arrangement: see *Dodsworth v Dodsworth* (1973) 228 EG 1115, p. 548, post, where the Court of Appeal considered it not right to confer upon the defendants a greater interest than was envisaged by the parties. In the present case the parties certainly intended that the arrangement between them should have legal consequences. If, therefore, they agreed upon a right of occupation for life, there is a binding contract to that effect: if they did not so agree, there is nothing to give rise to an equity to that effect.

In a case such as the present, the role of equity is supportive and supplementary. Where the parties have contracted for a licence, equity will today provide an equitable remedy to protect the legal right, for example by injunction, which may be by interlocutory order, if the court considers it just and convenient: see section 45, Supreme Court of Judicature (Consolidation) Act 1925[18]. If, however, the legal relationship between the parties is such that the true arrangement envisaged by the parties will be frustrated if the parties are left to their rights and duties at law, an equity will arise which the courts can satisfy by appropriate equitable relief. An old illustration of equity at work in this way was given by Parker J in *Jones v Earl of Tankerville* [1909] 2 Ch 440 at 443 (quoted in *Hurst's* case [1915] 1 KB 1 at 9). Likewise in another old case, *Frogley v Earl of Lovelace* (1859) John 333, Page Wood V-C granted an injunction to restrain the defendant from interfering with the plaintiff shooting over his land "until the defendant shall have executed a proper legal grant of the right claimed by the plaintiff."

The judge in the present case believed he was constrained by the decision in *Bannister v Bannister* [1948] 2 All ER 133, p. 503, post to declare the existence of a right of occupation for life, even though he had rejected an implied contractual right to that effect. But, when analysed, *Bannister v Bannister* is no more than an illustration of the supportive and supplementary role of equity. It was a case in which the plaintiff gave an oral undertaking that the defendant would be allowed to live in the cottage rent-free for as long as she desired. The defendant could not show a legal right: but she did establish the existence of an understanding or arrangement with the plaintiff which, though giving rise to no legal right, brought into existence an equity which the court thought it just to satisfy by declaring the defendant had an equitable life interest in the cottage with the plaintiff as her trustee. The court treated this life interest as the equivalent to a tenancy for life under the Settled Land Act 1925.

Errington v Errington and Woods [1952] 1 KB 290, [1952] 1 All ER 149, p. 496, post is a decision which follows the same pattern. The arrangement in that case was oral. The father bought a house, put his son and daughter-in-law into occupation and promised them that if they paid the instalments on the mortgage the house would be theirs when the last instalment was paid. The Court of Appeal held that the arrangement conferred upon the daughter-in-law (father having died, son having left his wife and she continuing to pay the instalments) a contractual right of occupation which carried with it an equity which on payment of the last instalment would give her a good equitable title to the house. The case may be said to be a classic illustration of equity supplementing a contractual right so as to give effect to the intention of the parties to the arrangement. *Binions v Evans* [1972] Ch 359, [1972] 2 All ER 70, p. 499, post, is to the same effect.

The defendant in this appeal, however, relied strongly on *Bannister v Bannister* to support a submission that she has a tenancy for life. Like Megaw LJ in *Binions v Evans* at 370, at 78, I find great difficulty in understanding how the court in *Bannister's* case came to conclude that there was in that case a tenancy for life under the Act. It was, however, a matter which depended upon the particular facts of the case.

---

[18] Now Supreme Court Act 1981, s. 37.

As Russell LJ commented in *Dodsworth v Dodsworth* (1973) 228 EG 1115, there is a risk that such an inference may fall foul of the Settled Land Act 1925, which confers a power of sale and of leasing upon the tenant — powers which cannot, for instance, have been in the minds of the parties in the present case. The present is *not*, in my judgment, a case of life tenancy: and in this respect *Bannister v Bannister* is a decision to be treated as turning on the particular facts of that case.

The most recent case to which we were referred is the decision of the Court of Appeal in *Tanner v Tanner* [1975] 1 WLR 1346, [1975] 3 All ER 776, p. 484, ante. It is close on its facts to the present case, in that the defendant was found to have no proprietary interest in the house but did have a contractual right to live in it until her two children, of whom the plaintiff was the father, were no longer of school age. The defendant had been the mistress of the plaintiff, who had bought the house (when she had been a tenant protected by the Rent Act) to provide accommodation for her and their two children. The court held it to be a case of contractual licence, Lord Denning MR saying at 1350, at 780:

"It was a contractual licence of the kind which is specifically enforceable on her behalf: and which he can be restrained from breaking: and he could not sell the house over her head so as to get her out in that way."

It is yet another case of a contractual licence supported by equity so far, and only so far, as is necessary to give effect to the expectations of the parties when making their arrangement.

Accordingly, the task in this case is to determine what were the terms of the arrangement, express and implied, between the parties. I agree with the judge that it is not possible to imply a licence to the defendant to occupy the house for her life. The plaintiff had invested £10,000 in the house and, in the absence of express stipulation, cannot be supposed in the circumstances to have frozen his capital for as long as the defendant pleased or for the duration of her life. On the other hand, the plaintiff was well aware that the defendant wanted the house as a home for her children as well as for herself. It would be wrong, however, to infer, in the absence of an express promise, that the plaintiff was assuming the burden of housing another man's wife and children indefinitely, and long after his relationship with them had ended. The balance of these factors leads me to the conclusion that the defendant's contractual licence was terminable upon reasonable notice, and that the notice must be such as to give the defendant ample opportunity to re-house herself and her children without disruption. In my judgment 12 calendar months' notice is reasonable in the circumstances.

For these reasons I do not think this is a case in which it is necessary to invoke the support of any equitable doctrine. The defendant is entitled to 12 months' notice. It follows that the appeal against the dismissal of the claim to possession fails in my judgment, the licence not yet having been determined. The order upon the counterclaim should, in my judgment, be varied so as to substitute for the declaration granted by the judge a declaration that the defendant's licence is terminable upon reasonable notice and that reasonable notice is one of 12 calendar months from its service.

In *Hardwick v Johnson* [1978] 1 WLR 683, [1978] 2 All ER 935, a mother purchased a house for occupation by her son and daughter-in-law as their home. Rent of £7 per week was payable, but it ceased to be paid after a month or two, and the mother did not demand it. Within a year the marriage was collapsing, and the son was about to leave his wife. The mother sued for possession and arrears of rent. The daughter-in-law gave birth to a child, and claimed to be entitled to remain in possession on paying £7 a week. The Court of Appeal held that the licence was irrevocable. The daughter-in-law was not in breach in respect of the arrears because the mother had indicated no desire to claim the rent. ROSKILL LJ said at 690, at 940:

"When one looks at the correspondence before action brought and indeed at the pleadings, one sees an ever increasing number of legal arguments being founded upon a perfectly simple family arrangement; but in my judgment this case can be decided upon one very short ground. It is plain, as the deputy judge said, that there was here never any tenancy. It is equally plain, in my judgment, that there was here a licence; and for my part, with respect to Lord Denning MR, I prefer to call it a contractual licence rather than an equitable licence.

The only question we have to decide is what was the nature of that contractual licence. Was it a licence to both the son and his future wife as joint licensees or was it a licence to the son alone? Nobody contemplated the possibility that this marriage would break down as soon as it did. Nobody contemplated that the son would within a couple of years or so go off and have an affair with another woman, abandoning his wife with the child of the marriage who remained in the house. What the parties would have agreed upon if they had thought of that possibility in March 1973 no one can tell; but the court, as Lord Denning MR has said and as has been said many times before (and Lord Diplock also said it in *Pettitt v Pettitt* [1970] AC 777 at 821–823, [1969] 2 All ER 385 at 413–414), has in those circumstances to impute to the parties a common intention to make some arrangement in the events which have occurred, albeit unexpectedly. I cannot, for my part, think that anybody would impute to these parties an intention that if the marriage broke down as soon as it did and the husband went off with another woman the wife would be liable to be ejected from the home together with the child of the marriage. It seems to me that the arrangement was perfectly straight-forward: it was a joint contractual licence to the husband and wife to live there. It was not conditional upon the marriage succeeding. It was not conditional upon a number of other possibilities.

I am disinclined to express any opinion on what if any events that licence is now determinable. Suffice it to say that in my judgment it is not determinable in the event which has occurred, namely, that the husband has left the wife — no divorce proceedings are pending, as Lord Denning MR has said — since that licence was not given only to the husband. It seems to me that no event has yet taken place which justifies the bringing to an end of this contractual licence; and therefore, for that reason, I think the deputy circuit judge reached the right conclusion in a careful and closely reasoned judgment."

Lord DENNING said that the licence was a personal equitable licence. BROWNE LJ delivered a judgment agreeing with ROSKILL LJ.

D. Specific Performance

VERRALL v GREAT YARMOUTH BOROUGH COUNCIL
[1981] QB 202, [1980] 1 All ER 839 (CA, Lord DENNING MR, ROSKILL and CUMMING-BRUCE LJJ)

The Conservative council of Great Yarmouth agreed in April 1979 to a two-day hiring of the Wellington Pier Pavilion by the National Front for its annual conference in October. In May 1979 the council, following a change in its political control to Labour, purported to repudiate the contract. An action was brought on behalf of the National Front for specific performance.

Held. Specific performance granted.

LORD DENNING MR: Since the *Winter Garden* case, it is clear that once a man has entered under his contract of licence, he cannot be turned out. An injunction can be obtained against the licensor to prevent his being turned out. On principle it is the same if it happens before he enters. If he has a contractual right to enter, and the licensor refuses to let him come in, then he can come to the court and in a proper case get an order for specific performance to allow him to come in. An illustration was taken in the course of the argument. Supposing one of the great political parties — say, the Conservative Party — had booked its hall at Brighton for its conference in September of this year: it had made all its arrangements accordingly: it had all its delegates coming: it had booked its hotels, and so on. Would it be open to the local council to repudiate that agreement, and say that the Conservative Party could not go there? Would the only remedy be damages? Clearly not. The court would order the council in such a case to perform its contract. It would be the same in the case of the Labour Party, or whoever it may be. When arrangements are made for a licence of this kind of such importance and magnitude affecting many people, the licensors cannot be allowed to repudiate it and simply pay damages. It must be open to the court to grant specific performance in such cases. . . . The newly constituted council is bound by what the old constituted council did. The newly constituted council must honour the contract. I see no sufficient reason for not holding the council to their contract. In the interests of our fundamental freedoms — freedom of speech, freedom of assembly, and the importance of holding people to their contracts — we ought to grant specific performance in this case, as the judge did.

E. Enforcement of Contractual Licences Against Third Parties[19]

The next question is whether a contractual licence, which is irrevocable by the licensor, is binding on a third party. On the one hand, it is well settled that, subject to exceptions, contractual rights are binding on, and enforceable by, the parties to the contract only[20]. On the other hand, the protection given to the licensee may be of little use if a transfer of the land to a third party leaves that third party free to claim possession, and leaves the licensee to his remedy in damages against the original licensor. Further, a licensee's

---

[19] Dawson and Pearce, pp. 153–161.

[20] *Tweddle v Atkinson* (1861) 1 B & S 393; *Dunlop Pneumatic Tyre Co Ltd v Selfridge & Co Ltd* [1915] AC 847; *Beswick v Beswick* [1968] AC 58, [1967] 2 All ER 1197; Cheshire and Fifoot, *Law of Contract* (10th edn, 1981), chap. 14; Treitel, *Law of Contract* (6th edn, 1983), pp. 473–477.

right to protection by injunction against the licensor gives him some sort of equity, and it is arguable that such an equity should give him protection against all but bona fide purchasers for value without notice.

Whether or not contractual licences should be held to be binding on third parties is ultimately a policy question. So it has been in other areas of the law. Contractual restrictions on the use of chattels have been held not to be binding on third parties even though they have express notice of the restriction[1]. The great case of *Tulk v Moxhay*[2] decided that a convenant restricting the user of land was binding on successors in title of the covenantor taking with notice. It was soon found that so wide a doctrine would create burdens on land for which there was no justification, and the basis of the doctrine was later changed so as to limit the running of the burden to cases in which the continuation of the covenant was necessary to protect land capable of benefiting; more like a negative equitable easement[3]. The point is that the whole question whether an equity enforceable against one contracting party is enforceable against third parties is determined, not by a rule of thumb, but by an examination of the policy questions applicable to the particular situation.

On this basis, it would seem clear that contractual licences should not, in the ordinary case, be binding on third parties. Otherwise, thousands of minor personal arrangements, like hotel bookings, contracts for lodgings, car parking contracts, and a host of other minor non-proprietary arrangements would in effect come on to the title; with no effective way of determining the question whether or not the third party had notice. After all, the contractual licensee has his remedy in damages.

Authority is to the same effect[4]. In spite of the privity of contract rule, however, a contractual licensee may be able to enforce a right against a third party, if the facts give rise to some other legal relationship outside the sphere of contract, i.e. under the doctrine of proprietary estoppel or of the constructive trust. In both these spheres, which require different criteria of proof and give rise to different remedies, the licensee acquires an equitable interest, either as an estoppel licensee or as a beneficiary under a trust, which is enforceable against a third party with notice. *Errington v Errington and Woods* [1952] 1 KB 290, [1952] 1 All ER 149, p. 496, post is generally accepted as being a case of a contractual licence. But there is clearly an estoppel situation also, and it will be discussed under that heading. In *Binions v Evans* [1972] Ch 359, [1972] 2 All ER 70, p. 499, post, the conveyance was made expressly subject to the contractual right of the licensee; and this was held to create a constructive trust. In *DHN Food Distributors Ltd v Tower Hamlets London Borough Council* [1976] 1 WLR 852, [1976] 3 All ER 462[5], an irrevocable

---

[1] *De Mattos v Gibson* (1859) 4 De G & J 276; *Lord Strathcona SS Co Ltd v Dominion Coal Co Ltd* [1926] AC 108; *Port Line Ltd v Ben Line Steamers Ltd* [1958] 2 QB 146, [1958] 1 All ER 787. See, however, *Swiss Bank Corpn v Lloyds Bank Ltd* [1979] Ch 548 at 569–575, [1979] 2 All ER 853 at 869–874; revsd. on different grounds [1982] AC 584, [1981] 2 All ER 449; (1982) 98 LQR 279 (S. Gardner).

[2] (1848) 2 Ph 774, p. 761, post.

[3] P. 765, post.

[4] *Clore v Theatrical Properties Ltd and Westby & Co Ltd* [1936] 3 All ER 483; *King v David Allen & Sons, Billposting Ltd* [1916] 2 AC 54, infra. See also *Midland Bank Ltd v Farm Pride Hatcheries Ltd* (1980) 260 EG 493, p. 28, ante, where the issue of the binding effect of a contractual licence on a third party was not raised.

[5] (1977) 93 LQR 170 (D. Sugarman and F. Webb); (1977) 41 Conv (NS) 73.

contractual licence was said, as one of three rationes in the case, to give rise to a constructive trust, and to "give to D.H.N. a sufficient interest in the land to qualify them for compensation for disturbance" upon compulsory purchase by the local authority. And in *Re Sharpe* [1980] 1 WLR 219, [1980] 1 All ER 198, p. 506, post, an irrevocable licence to occupy a house until a loan was repaid, "whether it be called a contractual licence or an equitable licence or an interest under a constructive trust", was held to be binding on the trustee in bankruptcy of the licensor[6].

It will be obvious that this possibility of the multiple characterisation of the right gives to the court the powers which it needs to reach a just solution[7].

i. THIRD PARTIES TAKING WITH NOTICE

KING *v* DAVID ALLEN AND SONS, BILLPOSTING LTD
[1916] 2 AC 54 (HL, Lord BUCKMASTER LC, Earl LOREBURN and Lord ATKINSON)

By an agreement of 1 July 1913, the appellant gave the respondents an exclusive permission to affix advertisements for a stated period to the walls of a cinema which was to be built.

In September 1913 the appellant executed a lease of the property to the cinema company, but the lease, disregarding arrangements previously made, contained no reference to the agreement of 1 July. The company refused to allow the advertisement to be posted and the respondents brought an action against the appellant King, for breach of the agreement of 1 July.

Held. The appellant (the licensor) was liable in damages.

EARL LOREBURN: My Lords, I agree in the opinion expressed by the Lord Chancellor, and with him I greatly regret the position in which Mr King has been placed, which seems to me to be hard upon him. He has behaved perfectly honestly in the whole business, and one cannot help regretting the expense to which he has been put.

I have very little to add to what has been said, but I look at the case in this way. The plaintiffs say that Mr King promised them for four years the use of a certain wall for advertising purposes by the agreement of 1 July 1913, and they say that after that Mr King demised that land, and that Mr King's lessees refused to make good the promise in regard to advertisement. Well, if the agreement of 1 July, which purports to be on the face of it a licence, was equivalent to creating an incorporeal hereditament or a sufficient interest in land, Mr King did not break his contract in making the lease, and would not be responsible for any trespasses that were committed by his licensees. But we must look at the document itself, and it seems to me that it does not create any interest in land at all; it merely amounts to a promise on the part of Mr King that he would allow the other party to the contract to use the wall for

---

[6] On the relationship between contractual and estoppel licences, see the controversy between [1981] Conv 212, [1983] Conv 285 (A. Briggs) and [1983] Conv 50, 471 (M. P. Thompson).

[7] An interest under a constructive trust or under an estoppel licence may either not arise, or, if it does arise, it may be subject to that of a purchaser from the constructive trustee/licensor, if such was the express or presumed common intention of trustee/licensor and beneficiary/licensee: *Bristol and West Building Society v Henning* [1985] 1 WLR 778, [1985] 2 All ER 606; [1985] Conv 361 (P. Todd). See also *Paddington Building Society v Mendelsohn* (1985) 50 P & CR 244; [1985] CLJ 354 (M. Welstead).

advertising purposes, and there was an implied undertaking that he would not disable himself from carrying out his contract. Now Mr King has altered his legal position in respect of his control of this land. Those to whom he granted the lease have disregarded his wishes and refused to allow his bargain to be carried out, and they have been practically enabled to do so by reason of the demise that he executed. In these circumstances it seems to me that there has been a breach in law of the contract of 1 July, and Mr King has disabled himself from giving effect to it as intended by parting with his right to present possession. That is enough to establish a case for damages against Mr King. There may be a remedy over against the lessees. I say nothing of that, because they are not here, and I do not wish either to encourage or to discourage any further proceedings; but this I think is clear: that the existence of such a remedy, if remedy there be, does not release Mr King from his liability to answer for breaking the contract which he made.

In *Clore v Theatrical Properties Ltd and Westby & Co Ltd* [1936] 3 All ER 483, an indenture provided that "the lessor doth hereby demise and grant unto the lessee the free and exclusive use of all the refreshment rooms . . . of the theatre . . . for the purpose only of the supply to and the accommodation of the visitors to the theatre and for no other purpose whatsoever". The definition clause stated that the terms "lessor" and "lessee" should include their executors, administrators and assigns. Both parties assigned and the assignees of the lessor sought to prevent the assignees of the lessee from exercising any of the rights conferred upon the lessee by the indenture. The action was brought by the plaintiff (Clore) for a declaration that the defendants could not exercise rights given to the licensees by the indenture.

The Court of Appeal (Lord WRIGHT MR, ROMER and GREENE LJJ) held that the indenture was not a lease, but a licence, and that it could only be enforced between the parties to it. They upheld CLAUSON J in making the declaration.

Lord WRIGHT MR said at 485: "I think that this court is bound by the decisions in previous cases[8] to hold that this document does not convey any interest in land but is merely a personal contract embodying a licence. On that ground the learned judge decided this matter and I agree with him and in particular with his final conclusion in that the rights mentioned in the document are purely contractual. It follows from this that there is no circumstance which enables the present appellants to assert any rights against the present respondent because there is no contractual nexus between them".

ii. PROPRIETARY ESTOPPEL; CONSTRUCTIVE TRUST

ERRINGTON *v* ERRINGTON AND WOODS
[1952] 1 KB 290, [1952] 1 All ER 149 (CA, SOMERVELL, DENNING and HODSON LJJ)

In 1936 a father bought a house through a building society, paying a lump sum of £250 and leaving the balance of £500 on mortgage. He told his

---

[8] *Edwardes v Barrington* (1901) 85 LT 650, HL, affirming *sub nom Daly v Edwardes* (1900) 83 LT 548; *Frank Warr & Co Ltd v LCC* [1904] 1 KB 713.

daughter-in-law shortly after her marriage to his son, that the property would be theirs when they had paid the last instalment on the mortgage, gave the daughter-in-law the building society's book, and allowed them to go into occupation. The father, however, took the conveyance in his own name and paid the rates. The young couple paid the instalments as they became due, but the payments were not all completed when the father died in 1945 leaving all his property, including the house in question, to his widow. The son then left his wife and went to live with his mother; his mother now claimed possession of the house from her daughter-in-law, who had remained in the house with her sister, the second defendant, and continued to pay the instalments.

Held. The daughter-in-law was a licensee who was entitled to protection against the plaintiff.

DENNING LJ: It is to be noted that the couple never bound themselves to pay the instalments to the building society; and I see no reason why any such obligation should be implied. It is clear law that the court is not to imply a term unless it is necessary; and I do not see that it is necessary here. Ample content is given to the whole arrangement by holding that the father promised that the house should belong to the couple as soon as they paid off the mortgage. The parties did not discuss what was to happen if the couple failed to pay the instalments to the building society, but I should have thought it clear that, if they did fail to pay the instalments, the father would not be bound to transfer the house to them. The father's promise was a unilateral contract — a promise of the house in return for their act of paying the instalments. It could not be revoked by him once the couple entered on performance of the act, but it would cease to bind him if they left it incomplete and unperformed, which they have not done. If that was the position during the father's lifetime, so it must be after his death. If the daughter-in-law continues to pay all the building society instalments, the couple will be entitled to have the property transferred to them as soon as the mortgage is paid off; but if she does not do so, then the building society will claim the instalments from the father's estate and the estate will have to pay them. I cannot think that in those circumstances the estate would be bound to transfer the house to them, any more than the father himself would have been.

What is the result in law of those facts? The relationship of the parties is open to three possible legal constructions: (i) That the couple were tenants at will paying no rent. That is what the judge thought they were. He said that, in this case, just as in *Lynes v Snaith* [1899] 1 QB 486, the defendant "was in exclusive possession and was therefore not a mere licensee but in the position of a tenant at will". But in my opinion it is of the essence of a tenancy at will that it should be determinable by either party on demand, and it is quite clear that the relationship of these parties was not so determinable. The father could not eject the couple as long as they paid the instalments regularly to the building society. It was therefore not a tenancy at will. . . . (ii) That the couple were tenants at a rent of 15s. 0d. a week, that rent being for convenience paid direct to the building society instead of to the father, and the tenancy being either a weekly tenancy or a tenancy for the duration of the mortgage repayments. But I do not think that the 15s. 0d. can possibly be regarded as rent, for the simple reason that the couple were not bound to pay it. If they did not pay it, the father could not sue for it or distrain for it.

He could only refuse to transfer the house to them. If the 15s. 0d. was not rent, then it affords no ground for inferring a tenancy. (iii) That the couple were licensees, having a permissive occupation short of a tenancy, but with a contractual right, or at any rate, an equitable right to remain so long as they paid the instalments, which would grow into a good equitable title to the house itself as soon as the mortgage was paid. This is, I think, the right view of the relationship of the parties. I will explain how I arrive at it.

The classic definition of a licence was propounded by Vaughan CJ in the seventeenth century in *Thomas v Sorrell* (1673) Vaugh 330 at 351: "A dispensation or licence properly passeth no interest nor alters or transfers property in any thing, but only makes an action lawful, which without it had been unlawful." The difference between a tenancy and a licence is, therefore, that, in a tenancy, an interest passes in the land, whereas, in a licence, it does not. . . .

The result of all these cases is that, although a person who is let into exclusive possession is prima facie to be considered to be a tenant, nevertheless he will not be held to be so if the circumstances negative any intention to create a tenancy. Words alone may not suffice. Parties cannot turn a tenancy into a licence merely by calling it one. But if the circumstances and the conduct of the parties show that all that was intended was that the occupier should be granted a personal privilege, with no interest in the land, he will be held to be a licensee only. In view of these recent cases I doubt whether *Lynes v Snaith* [1899] 1 QB 486, and the case of the gamekeeper referred to therein (unreported case; Kennedy J), would be decided the same way today.

Applying the foregoing principles to the present case, it seems to me that, although the couple had exclusive possession of the house, there was clearly no relationship of landlord and tenant. They were not tenants at will but licensees. They had a mere personal privilege to remain there, with no right to assign or sub-let. They were, however, not bare licensees. They were licensees with a contractual right to remain[9]. As such they have no right at law to remain, but only in equity, and equitable rights now prevail. I confess, however, that it has taken the courts some time to reach this position. At common law a licence was always revocable at will, notwithstanding a contract to the contrary: *Wood v Leadbitter* (1845) 13 M & W 838, p. 481, ante. The remedy for a breach of the contract was only in damages. That was the view generally held until a few years ago: see, for instance, what was said in *Booker v Palmer* [1942] 2 All ER 674, 677, and *Thompson v Park* [1944] KB 408, 410, [1944] 2 All ER 477, 479. The rule has, however, been altered owing to the interposition of equity.

Law and equity have been fused for nearly 80 years, and since 1948 it has been clear that, as a result of the fusion, a licensor will not be permitted to eject a licensee in breach of a contract to allow him to remain: see *London Millennium Productions Ltd v Winter Garden Theatre* per Lord Greene [1946] 1 All ER 678 at 680, p. 487, ante, and in the House of Lords per Lord Simon [1948] AC 173 at 191, [1947] 2 All ER 342 at 336; nor in breach of a promise on which the licensee has acted, even though he gave no value for it: see *Foster v Robinson* [1951] 1 KB 149 at 156, [1950] 2 All ER 342 at 346, where Sir

---

[9] See *Street v Mountford* [1985] AC 809 at 820, [1985] 2 All ER 289 at 295, p. 403, ante, where Lord TEMPLEMAN cites this analysis.

Raymond Evershed MR said that as a result of the oral arrangement to let the man stay, he was entitled as licensee to occupy the premises without any payment of rent for the rest of his days. This infusion of equity means that contractual licences now have a force and validity of their own and cannot be revoked in breach of the contract. Neither the licensor nor anyone who claims through him can disregard the contract except a purchaser for value without notice. . . .

In the present case it is clear that the father expressly promised the couple that the property should belong to them as soon as the mortgage was paid, and impliedly promised that so long as they paid the instalments to the building society they should be allowed to remain in possession. They were not purchasers because they never bound themselves to pay the instalments, but nevertheless they were in a position analogous to purchasers. They have acted on the promise, and neither the father nor his widow, his successor in title, can eject them in disregard of it. The result is that in my opinion the appeal should be dismissed and no order for possession should be made.

BINIONS *v* EVANS[10]
[1972] Ch 359, [1972] 2 All ER 70 (CA, Lord DENNING MR, MEGAW and STEPHENSON LJJ)

The trustees of the Tredegar Estate in Monmouthshire and South Wales entered into an agreement with Mrs Evans, the 79 year old widow of an employee of the Estate. The trustees agreed to permit her to reside in and occupy a cottage on the estate for the remainder of her life as tenant at will rent free. She agreed to keep it in a proper manner and "personally occupy and live in it as a private residence only and not assign, sub-let or part with the possession" of it. Two years later the trustees sold the cottage to the plaintiffs expressly subject to Mrs Evans's tenancy agreement, a copy of which was handed to the purchasers. Six months later the plaintiffs gave Mrs Evans notice to quit as a mere tenant at will and claimed possession of the cottage.

Held. Order for possession refused. Per MEGAW and STEPHENSON LJJ: Mrs Evans was tenant for life under the Settled Land Act 1925[11].

LORD DENNING MR (having held that Mrs Evans was not a tenant at will, nor a lessee nor a tenant for life under the Settled Land Act):

An equitable interest
Seeing that the defendant has no legal estate or interest in the land, the question is what right has she? At any rate, she has a contractual right to reside in the house for the remainder of her life or as long as she pleases to stay. I know that in the agreement it is described as a tenancy: but that does not matter. The question is: What is it in reality? To my mind it is a licence, and no tenancy. It is a privilege which is personal to her. On all the modern cases, which are legion, it ranks as a contractual licence, and not a tenancy:

---

[10] (1972) 88 LQR 336 (P.V.B.); (1972) 36 Conv (NS) 266 (J. Martin); 277 (D.J. Hayton); [1973] CLJ 123 (R.J. Smith); (1973) 117 SJ 23 (B.W. Harvey); (1977) 93 LQR 561 (J.A. Hornby).
[11] See pp. 550–555, post.

see *Shell-Mex and BP Ltd v Manchester Garages Ltd* [1971] 1 WLR 612, [1971] 1 All ER 841.

What is the status of such a licence as this? There are a number of cases in the books in which a similar right has been given. They show that a right to occupy for life, arising by contract, gives to the occupier an equitable interest in the land: just as it does when it arises under a settlement: see *Re Carne's Settled Estates* [1899] 1 Ch 324 and *Re Boyer's Settled Estates* [1916] 2 Ch 404. The courts of equity will not allow the landlord to turn the occupier out in breach of the contract: see *Foster v Robinson* [1951] 1 KB 149 at 156, [1950] 2 All ER 342 at 346; nor will they allow a purchaser to turn her out if he bought with knowledge of her right — *Errington v Errington and Woods* [1952] 1 KB 290, 299, [1952] 1 All ER 149, p. 496, ante.

It is instructive to go back to the cases before the Supreme Court Judicature Act 1873. They show that, if a landlord, by a memorandum in writing, let a house to someone, let us say to a widow, at a rent, for her life or as long as she pleased to stay, the courts of equity would not allow the landlord to turn her out in breach of his contract. If the landlord were to go to the courts of law and obtain an order in ejectment against her, as in *Doe d Warner v Browne* (1807) 8 East 165, the courts of equity would grant an injunction to restrain the landlord from enforcing his rights at law, as in *Browne v Warner* (1808) 14 Ves 409. The courts of equity would give the agreement a construction, which Lord Eldon LC called an "equitable construction," and construe it as if it were an agreement to execute a deed granting her a lease of the house for her life — *Browne v Warner* (1807) 14 Ves 156 at 158. They would order the landlord specifically to perform the contract, so construed, by executing such a deed. This court did so in *Zimbler v Abraham* [1903] 1 KB 577. This means that she had an equitable interest in the land. So much so that if a purchaser wished to buy her interest from her, he had to pay her its full value as such. Malins V-C so held in *Re King's Leasehold Estate* (1873) LR 16 Eq 521 at 527, where he described it as an "equitable interest." It follows that, if the owner sold his reversion to another, who took with notice of the widow's interest, his successor could not turn her out any more than he could. She would have, I should have thought, at least as strong a case as the occupier in *Webb v Paternoster* (1619) Poph 151, which received the blessing of Lord Upjohn in *National Provincial Bank Ltd v Hastings Car Mart Ltd* [1965] AC 1175 at 1239, [1965] 2 All ER 472 at 489.

Suppose, however, that the defendant did not have an equitable interest at the outset, nevertheless it is quite plain that she obtained one afterwards when the Tredegar Estate sold the cottage. They stipulated with the plaintiffs that they were to take the house "subject to" the defendant's rights under the agreement. They supplied the plaintiffs with a copy of the contract: and the plaintiffs paid less because of her right to stay there. In these circumstances, this court will impose on the plaintiffs a constructive trust for her benefit: for the simple reason that it would be utterly inequitable for the plaintiffs to turn the defendant out contrary to the stipulation subject to which they took the premises. That seems to me clear from the important decision of *Bannister v Bannister* [1948] 2 All ER 133, p. 503, post, which was applied by the judge, and which I gladly follow.

The imposing of a constructive trust is entirely in accord with the precepts of equity. As Cardozo J once put it: "A constructive trust is the formula through which the conscience of equity finds expression," see *Beatty v*

Guggenheim Exploration Co 225 NY 380, 386 (1919): or, as Lord Diplock put it quite recently in *Gissing v Gissing* [1971] AC 886 at 905, [1970] 2 All ER 780 at 790, a constructive trust is created "whenever the trustee has so conducted himself that it would be inequitable to allow him to deny to the cestui que trust a beneficial interest in the land acquired".

I know that there are some who have doubted whether a contractual licensee has any protection against a purchaser, even one who takes with full notice. We were referred in this connection to Professor Wade's article Licences and Third Parties in (1952) 68 LQR 337, and to the judgment of Goff J in *Re Solomon* [1967] Ch 573, [1966] 3 All ER 255. None of these doubts can prevail, however, when the situation gives rise to a constructive trust. Whenever the owner sells the land to a purchaser, and at the same time stipulates that he shall take it "subject to" a contractual licence, I think it plain that a court of equity will impose on the purchaser a constructive trust in favour of the beneficiary. It is true that the stipulation (that the purchaser shall take it subject to the rights of the licensee) is a stipulation for the benefit of one who is not a party to the contract of sale; but, as Lord Upjohn said in *Beswick v Beswick* [1968] AC 58 at 98, [1967] 2 All ER 1197 at 1219, that is just the very case in which equity will "come to the aid of the common law." It does so by imposing a constructive trust on the purchaser. It would be utterly inequitable that the purchaser should be able to turn out the beneficiary. It is to be noticed that in the two cases which are said to give rise to difficulty *King v David Allen & Sons, Billposting Ltd* [1916] 2 AC 54, p. 495, ante and *Clore v Theatrical Properties Ltd and Westby & Co Ltd* [1936] 3 All ER 483, p. 496, ante there was no trace of a stipulation, express or implied, that the purchaser should take the property subject to the right of the contractual licensee. In the first case, if Mr King had protected himself by stipulating that the company should take the lease "subject to the rights of David Allen," I cannot think that he would have been held liable to damages. In the second case the documents were exceedingly complicated, but if Mr Clore had acquired the theatre "subject to the rights of the licensees," I cannot suppose that this court would have allowed him to disregard those rights.

In many of these cases the purchaser takes *expressly* "subject to" the rights of the licensee. Obviously the purchaser then holds the land on an imputed trust for the licensee. But, even if he does not take expressly "subject to" the rights of the licensee, he may do so *impliedly*. At any rate when the licensee is in actual occupation of the land, so that the purchaser must know he is there, and of the rights which he has: see *Hodgson v Marks* [1971] Ch 892, [1971] 2 All ER 684. Whenever the purchaser takes the land impliedly subject to the rights of the contractual licensee, a court of equity will impose a constructive trust for the beneficiary. So I still adhere to the proposition I stated in *Errington v Errington and Woods* [1952] 1 KB 290 at 299, [1952] 1 All ER 149 at 155, and elaborated in *National Provincial Bank Ltd v Hastings Car Mart Ltd* [1964] Ch 665 at 686–689, [1964] 1 All ER 688 at 695–697, namely, that, when the licensee is in actual occupation, neither the licensor nor anyone who claims through him can disregard the contract except a purchaser for value without notice.

Conclusion
In my opinion the defendant, by virtue of the agreement, had an equitable interest in the cottage which the court would protect by granting an

injunction against the landlords restraining them from turning her out. When the landlords sold the cottage to a purchaser "subject to" her rights under the agreement, the purchaser took the cottage on a constructive trust to permit the defendant to reside there during her life, or as long as she might desire. The courts will not allow the purchaser to go back on that trust. I entirely agree with the judgment of Judge Bulger. I would dismiss this appeal.

STEPHENSON LJ: Apart from authority, I would not have thought that such an interest could be understood to amount to a tenancy for life within the meaning of the Settled Land Act 1925, and I would have thought that the other terms of her tenancy (as I think it ought properly to be called) are inconsistent with a power to ask for the legal estate to be settled on her or to sell the cottage. But *Bannister v Bannister* [1948] 2 All ER 133, p. 503, post, is a clear decision of this court that such words as have been used in this agreement (excepting, I must concede, the words "as tenant at will of them") create a life interest determinable (apart from the special considerations introduced by the Settled Land Act 1925) on the beneficiary ceasing to occupy the premises and the landlords hold the cottage on trust to permit her to occupy it "during her life or as long as she lives," as Judge Bulger held, and subject thereto in trust for them.

I therefore find it unnecessary to consider or decide the vexed questions (1) whether this agreement is or creates an irrevocable contractual licence to occupy, and (2) whether such a licence has been elevated to a status equivalent to an estate or interest in land by decisions of this court such as *Errington v Errington and Woods* [1952] 1 KB 290, [1952] 1 All ER 149 or *Foster v Robinson* [1951] 1 KB 149, [1950] 2 All ER 342 or still awaits legislation before it can so achieve transmissibility to subsequent purchasers with notice: see the rival views set out by Goff J in *Re Solomon* [1967] Ch 573 at 582–586, [1966] 3 All ER 255 at 259–262[12].

QUESTION

Have contractual licences become interests in land? (1953) 16 MLR 1 (G. C. Cheshire); (1952) 16 Conv (NS) 323 (F. R. Crane); (1953) 17 Conv (NS) 440 (L. A. Sheridan); (1984) 100 LQR 376 (S. Moriarty); Dawson and Pearce, chap. 11.

IV.   Constructive Trusts[13]

Before dealing with the major topic of Licences by Estoppel, it will be useful to refer to the doctrine, which has already been met in *Binions v Evans* [1972] Ch 359, [1972] 2 All ER 70, p. 499, ante and *DHN Food Distributors Ltd v Tower Hamlets London Borough Council* [1976] 1 WLR 852, [1976] 3 All ER 462, p. 494, ante (both of which cases could be included in this section), and

---

[12] MEGAW LJ also suggested at 371, at 78 that the plaintiffs would be guilty of the tort of interference with existing contractual rights if they were to evict the defendant; (1977) 41 Conv (NS) 318 (R.J. Smith).

[13] C & B, pp. 560–561. On constructive trusts generally, see H & M, chap. 14; Snell, pp. 192–196; Underhill, pp. 293–346; M & B, *Trusts and Trustees* (3rd edn, 1984), chap. 7; Oakley, *Constructive Trusts* 1978).

which will appear again in many of the estoppel cases: that of the constructive trust in favour of the licensee. Equity finds a constructive trust, in various circumstances, on the principle of unjust enrichment. In the present context, the finding of a constructive trust in favour of the licensee creates an equitable interest in his favour. This solution has sometimes been too readily applied; without appreciating the conveyancing problems which follow; as has been explained. This development stems back to *Bannister v Bannister* [1948] 2 All ER 133, where the facts provided a compelling situation for the protection of an old lady who had no proprietary interest in the premises. This was before the doctrine of promissory estoppel in *Central London Property Trust Ltd v High Trees House Ltd* [1947] KB 130, [1956] 1 All ER 256n had been widely recognised, and before licensees were protected on the ground of estoppel. The advantage of an estoppel theory is that, as will be seen, the court has available to it a much wider choice of remedy. *Bannister v Bannister* would probably be so treated at the present day[14].

BANNISTER *v* BANNISTER
[1948] 2 All ER 133 (CA, Scott and Asquith LJJ and Jenkins J)

The defendant was the owner of two cottages, Nos. 30 and 31. In 1943, she sold them to the plaintiff, her brother-in-law, for £250 (£150 below the market price) under an oral arrangement by which the brother-in-law would "let you stay [in No. 30] as long as you like, rent free". No mention of this arrangement was made in the conveyance. The defendant lived in the cottage until 1945 when she gave up possession of all except one downstairs room. In 1947, the plaintiff claimed possession of that, on the ground that she was a tenant at will only.

Held. The defendant was entitled to a life interest determinable upon her ceasing to reside in the cottage under a constructive trust created by the oral agreement.

Scott LJ: It is, we think, clearly a mistake to suppose that the equitable principle on which a constructive trust is raised against a person who insists on the absolute character of a conveyance to himself for the purpose of defeating a beneficial interest, which, according to the true bargain, was to belong to another, is confined to cases in which the conveyance itself was fraudulently obtained. The fraud which brings the principle into play arises as soon as the absolute character of the conveyance is set up for the purpose of defeating the beneficial interest, and that is the fraud to cover which the Statute of Frauds or the corresponding provisions of the Law of Property Act, 1925, cannot be called in aid in cases in which no written evidence of the real bargain is available. Nor is it, in our opinion, necessary that the bargain on which the absolute conveyance is made should include any express stipulation that the grantee is in so many words to hold as trustee. It is enough that the bargain should have included a stipulation under which some sufficiently

---

[14] (1977) 93 LQR 561 (J.A. Hornby); [1980] Conv 250; *Binions v Evans* [1972] Ch 359, [1972] 2 All ER 70, p. 499, ante; *DHN Food Distributors Ltd v Tower Hamlets London Borough Council* [1976] 1 WLR 852, [1976] 3 All ER 462, p. 494, ante; *Re Sharpe* [1980] 1 WLR 219, [1980] 1 All ER 198, p. 506, post.

defined beneficial interest in the property was to be taken by another. The above propositions are, we think, clearly borne out by the cases to which we were referred of *Booth v Turle* (1873) LR 16 Eq 182, *Chattock v Muller* (1878) 8 ChD 177, *Re Duke of Marlborough* [1894] 2 Ch 133, and *Rochefoucauld v Boustead* [1897] 1 Ch 196.

We see no distinction in principle between a case in which property is conveyed to a purchaser on terms that the entire beneficial interest in some part of it is to be retained by the vendor (as in *Booth v Turle*) and a case, like the present, in which property is conveyed to a purchaser on terms that a limited beneficial interest in some part of it is to be retained by the vendor. We are, accordingly, of opinion that the third ground of objection to the learned county court judge's conclusion also fails. His finding that there was no fraud in the case cannot be taken as meaning that it was not fraudulent in the plaintiff to insist on the absolute character of the conveyance for the purpose of defeating the beneficial interest which he had agreed the defendant should retain. The conclusion that the plaintiff was fraudulent, in this sense, necessarily follows from the facts found, and, as indicated above, the fact that he may have been innocent of any fraudulent intent in taking the conveyance in absolute form is for this purpose immaterial. . . . The plaintiff holds No. 30 in trust during the life of the defendant to permit the defendant to occupy the same for so long as she may desire to do so, and subject thereto in trust for the plaintiff. A trust in this form has the effect of making the beneficiary a tenant for life within the meaning of the Settled Land Act, 1925.

In *Hussey v Palmer* [1972] 1 WLR 1286, [1972] 3 All ER 744[15], Mrs Hussey, an elderly widow, was invited to live with her daughter and son-in-law. To accommodate her, an additional bedroom was built on to the house, and Mrs Hussey paid £607, the cost of the construction.

Differences arose, and Mrs Hussey left. She claimed recovery of the money. Lord DENNING MR, in upholding the claim, said at 1289, at 747: "If there was no loan, was there a resulting trust? and, if so, what were the terms of the trust?

Although the plaintiff alleged that there was a resulting trust, I should have thought that the trust in this case, if there was one, was more in the nature of a constructive trust: but this is more a matter of words than anything else. The two run together. By whatever name it is described, it is a trust imposed by law whenever justice and good conscience require it. It is a liberal process, founded upon large principles of equity, to be applied in cases where the legal owner cannot conscientiously keep the property for himself alone, but ought to allow another to have the property or the benefit of it or a share in it. The trust may arise at the outset when the property is acquired, or later on, as the circumstances may require. It is an equitable remedy by which the court can enable an aggrieved party to obtain restitution. It is comparable to the legal remedy of money had and received which, as Lord Mansfield said, is 'very beneficial and therefore, much encouraged' [*Moses v MacFerlan* (1760) 2 Burr 1005 at 1012]. Thus we have repeatedly held that, when one person contributes towards the purchase price of a·house, the owner holds it on a constructive trust for him, proportionate to his

---

[15] (1973) 89 LQR 2.

contribution, even though there is no agreement between them, and no declaration of trust to be found, and no evidence of any intention to create a trust. Instances are numerous where a wife has contributed money to the initial purchase of a house or property; or later on the payment of mortgage instalments; or has helped in a business: see *Falconer v Falconer* [1970] 1 WLR 1333, [1970] 3 All ER 449; *Heseltine v Heseltine* [1971] 1 WLR 342, [1971] 1 All ER 952 and *Re Cummins* [1972] Ch 62, [1971] 3 All ER 782. Similarly, when a mistress has contributed money, or money's worth, to the building of a house: *Cooke v Head* [1972] 1 WLR 518, [1972] 2 All ER 38. Very recently we held that a purchaser, who bought a cottage subject to the rights of an occupier, held it on trust for her benefit: *Binions v Evans* [1972] Ch 359, [1972] 2 All ER 70, p. 499, ante. In all those cases it would have been quite inequitable for the legal owner to take the property for himself and exclude the other from it. So the law imputed or imposed a trust for his or her benefit.

The present case is well within the principles of those cases. Just as a person, who pays part of the purchase price, acquires an equitable interest in the house, so also he does when he pays for an extension to be added to it. Mr Owen has done a lot of research and has found a case in 1858 to that very effect. It is *Unity Joint Stock Mutual Banking Association v King* (1858) 25 Beav 72. A father had land on which he built a granary. His two sons built two other granaries on it at a cost of £1,200. Sir John Romilly MR held that the two sons had a lien or charge on the property as against the father, and any person claiming through him. The father had never promised to pay the sons £1,200. He was not indebted to them in that sum. He had never engaged or promised to make over the land to them or to give them a charge on it. Yet they had a lien or charge on the land. That case was approved by the Privy Council in *Chalmers v Pardoe* [1963] 1 WLR 677 at 681–682, [1963] 3 All ER 552 at 555, where it was said to be based on the 'general equitable principle that . . . it would be against conscience' for the owner to take the land without repaying the sums expended on the buildings. To this I would add *Inwards v Baker* [1965] 2 QB 29, [1965] 1 All ER 446, p. 528, post, when a son built a bungalow on his father's land in the expectation that he would be allowed to stay there as his home, though there was no promise to that effect. After the father's death, his trustees sought to turn the son out. It was held that he had an equitable interest which was good against the trustees. In those cases it was emphasised that the court must look at the circumstances of each case to decide in what way the equity can be satisfied. In some by an equitable lien. In others by a constructive trust. But in either case it is because justice and good conscience so require.

In the present case Mrs Hussey paid £607 to a builder for the erection of this extension. It may well be, as the defendant says, that there was no contract to repay it at all. It was not a loan to the son-in-law. She could not sue him for repayment. He could not have turned her out. If she had stayed there until she died, the extension would undoubtedly have belonged beneficially to the son-in-law. If, during her lifetime, he had sold the house, together with the extension, she would be entitled to be repaid the £607 out of the proceeds. He admits this himself. But he has not sold the house. She has left, and the son-in-law has the extension for his own benefit and could sell the whole if he so desired. It seems to me to be entirely against conscience that he should retain the whole house and not allow Mrs Hussey any interest in it, or any charge upon it. The court should, and will, impose or impute a trust by which Mr Palmer is to hold the property on terms under which, in the circumstances that have happened, she has an interest in the property proportionate to the £607 which she put into it. She is quite content if he repays her the £607. If he does not repay the £607, she can apply for an order for sale, so that the sum can be paid to her. But the simplest way for him would be to raise the £607 on mortgage and pay it to her. But, on the legal point raised, I have no doubt there was a resulting trust, or, more accurately, a constructive trust, for her, and I would so declare. I would allow the appeal, accordingly."

In *Re Sharpe* [1980] 1 WLR 219, [1980] 1 All ER 198[16], an aunt lent £12,000 to her nephew to enable him to purchase a property in Hampstead for £17,000. She also spent over £2,000 on its decorations and fittings, and paid off some of the nephew's debts in order to stave off his bankruptcy. The understanding was that the aunt should live there and be looked after by the nephew and his wife. The aunt moved in, the nephew finally went bankrupt, and his trustee in bankruptcy made a contract to sell the property with vacant possession for £17,000. In holding that the circumstances gave rise to a constructive trust in the aunt's favour, which conferred on her an interest binding on the trustee in bankruptcy, BROWNE-WILKINSON J said at 223, at 201:

"I turn then to the alternative claim that Mrs Johnson is entitled to something less than an aliquot share of the equity in the premises, namely, the right to stay on the premises until the money she provided indirectly to acquire them has been repaid. This right is based upon the line of recent Court of Appeal decisions which has spelt out irrevocable licences from informal family arrangements, and in some cases characterised such licences as conferring some equity or equitable interest under a constructive trust. I do not think that the principles lying behind these decisions have yet been fully explored and on occasion it seems that such rights are found to exist simply on the ground that to hold otherwise would be a hardship to the plaintiff. It appears that the principle is one akin to or an extension of a proprietary estoppel stemming from Lord Kingsdown's well-known statement of the law in *Ramsden v Dyson* (1866) LR 1 HL 129 at 170, p. 512, post. In a strict case of proprietary estoppel the plaintiff has expended his own money on the defendant's property in an expectation encouraged by or known to the defendant that the plaintiff either owns the property or is to have some interest conferred on him. Recent authorities have extended this doctrine and, in my judgment, it is now established that, if the parties have proceeded on a common assumption that the plaintiff is to enjoy a right to reside in a particular property and in reliance on that assumption the plaintiff has expended money or otherwise acted to his detriment, the defendant will not be allowed to go back on that common assumption and the court will imply an irrevocable licence or trust which will give effect to that common assumption. Thus in *Errington v Errington and Woods* [1952] 1 KB 290, [1952] 1 All ER 149, p. 496, ante, Denning LJ held that the son,

---

[16] [1980] Conv 207 (J. Martin), suggesting estoppel licence as a preferable basis for the decision; (1980) 96 LQR 336 (G. Woodman).

who had paid the instalments under the mortgage in the expectation that the property would eventually become his, had an equitable right to stay in occupation until the mortgage was paid off. In *Tanner v Tanner* [1975] 1 WLR 1346, [1975] 3 All ER 776, p. 484, ante, the plaintiff was held entitled to a licence to occupy a house bought in contemplation of it being a home for herself and her children, there being no express contract to that effect. In *Hardwick v Johnson* [1978] 1 WLR 683, [1978] 2 All ER 935, p. 491, ante, where the plaintiff's house had been occupied by the plaintiff's son and his first wife under an informal family arrangement, the Court of Appeal imputed an intention to grant an irrevocable licence to the wife on payment by her of a weekly sum.

Applying those principles to the present case, I have little doubt that as between the debtor on the one hand and Mrs Johnson on the other, the circumstances in which she provided the money by way of loan in order to enable the premises to be bought do give rise to some right in Mrs Johnson. It is clear that she only loaned the money as part of a wider scheme, an essential feature of which was that she was to make her home in the property to be acquired with the money loaned. Say that immediately after the property had been bought the debtor had tried to evict Mrs Johnson without repaying the loan; can it be supposed that the court would have made an order for possession against her? In my judgment, whether it be called a contractual licence or an equitable licence or an interest under a constructive trust, Mrs Johnson would be entitled as against the debtor to stay in the house. *Dodsworth v Dodsworth* (1973) 228 EG 1115, p. 548, post shows that there are great practical difficulties in finding that she is entitled to a full life interest: but there is no reason why one should not imply an intention that she should have the right to live there until her loan is repaid, which was the result reached in *Dodsworth v Dodsworth*.

Unfortunately, this case does not arise for decision simply between Mrs Johnson on the one hand and the debtor on the other. She has to show some right good against the trustee in bankruptcy and the purchaser from the trustee in bankruptcy. Due to an unfortunate procedural position, the purchaser is not a party to this application and nothing I can say can, or is intended to, bind him. As an antidote to the over-indulgence of sympathy which everyone must feel for Mrs Johnson, I put on record that the purchaser's plight is little better. He apparently had no reason to suspect that there was any flaw in the trustee's right to sell with vacant possession. As a result of the trustee's inability to complete the sale he cannot open the business he intended and he and his wife and two children are being forced to live in a small motorised caravan parked in various places on or near Hampstead Heath.

Is then Mrs Johnson's right against the debtor binding on the trustee in bankruptcy? This is an important and difficult point and, were it not for the urgency of the matter and the late stage of the term, I would like to have given it longer consideration. In general the trustee in bankruptcy steps into the shoes of the debtor and takes the debtor's property subject to all rights and equities affecting it: see *Halsbury's Laws of England*, 4th edn, vol. 3 (1973), para. 594. However, the trustee in bankruptcy is free to break any merely contractual obligation of the debtor, leaving the other party to his remedy in damages, which damages will only give rise to a right to prove in the bankruptcy.

Are rights of the kind spelt out in the cases I have referred to merely contractual licences or do they fetter the property and create some right over it? On the authorities as they stand, I think I am bound to hold that the rights under such an irrevocable licence bind the property itself in the hands of the trustee in bankruptcy. Lord Denning MR has, on a number of occasions, said that these licences arise under a constructive trust and are binding on the third party's acquiring with notice. These statements are for the most part obiter dictá with which other members of the court have not associated themselves, preferring to rest their decision on there being a contractual licence. But in *Binions v Evans* [1972] Ch 359, [1972] 2 All ER 70, p. 499, ante, a third party taking with notice of, and expressly subject to, such a licence was held bound by it. In that case the liability could not have depended merely on contract. Closer to the present case is a decision which was not referred to in argument and therefore any comments on it must be treated with some reserve. In *DHN Food Distributors Ltd v Tower Hamlets London Borough Council* [1976] 1 WLR 852, [1976] 3 All ER 462, p. 494, ante, certain premises were legally owned by one company (Bronze) but occupied by an associated company (DHN) under an informal arrangement between them. The premises were compulsorily acquired and the question was whether any compensation for disturbance was payable, it being said that Bronze had not been disturbed. The Court of Appeal held that DHN had an irrevocable licence to remain in the premises indefinitely and this gave DHN a compensatable interest in the land. Lord Denning MR said, at 859, at 466–467:

'It was equivalent to a contract between the two companies whereby Bronze granted an irrevocable licence to DHN to carry on their business on the premises. In this situation Mr Dobry cited to us *Binions v Evans*, to which I would add *Bannister v Bannister* [1948] 2 All ER 133 and *Siew Soon Wah v Yong Tong Hong* [1973] AC 836, p. 503, ante. Those cases show that a contractual licence (under which a person has the right to occupy premises indefinitely) gives rise to a constructive trust, under which the legal owner is not allowed to turn out the licensee. So, here. This irrevocable licence gave to DHN a sufficient interest in the land to qualify them for compensation for disturbance.'

Goff LJ also made this a ground of his decision: see pp. 860 to 861, pp. 467–468.

It seems to me that this is a decision that such contractual or equitable licence does confer some interest in the property under a constructive trust. Accordingly, in my judgment, it follows that the trustee in bankruptcy takes the property subject to Mrs Johnson's right to live there until she is repaid the moneys she provided to acquire it.

Mr Moss, for the trustee in bankruptcy, argued that this was the wrong approach. He said that the species of constructive trust which Lord Denning MR was considering in the cases was different from the traditional constructive trust known to equity lawyers. It is not, Mr Moss says, a substantive right but an equitable remedy: see per Lord Denning MR in *Hussey v Palmer* [1972] 1 WLR 1286 at 1290, [1972] 3 All ER 744 at 747, p. 504, ante and in *Binions v Evans* [1972] Ch 359 at 368, [1972] 2 All ER 70 at 76. Then, says Mr Moss, the time to decide whether to grant such a remedy is when the matter comes before the court in the light of the then known circumstances. In the present case those circumstances are that the debtor is a bankrupt and

Mrs Johnson has failed to put forward her claim until after the trustee has contracted to sell the property to an innocent third party, notwithstanding two inquiries as to whether she had a claim. Accordingly, he says, it would not be equitable to grant her an interest under a constructive trust at this time.

I cannot accept that argument in that form. Even if it be right to say that the courts can impose a constructive trust as a remedy in certain cases — which to my mind is a novel concept in English law — in order to provide a remedy the court must first find a right which has been infringed. So far as land is concerned an oral agreement to create any interest in it must be evidenced in writing: see section 40 of the Law of Property Act 1925. Therefore if these irrevocable licences create an interest in land, the rights cannot rest simply on an oral contract. The introduction of an interest under a constructive trust is an essential ingredient if the plaintiff has any right at all[17]. Therefore in cases such as this, it cannot be that the interest in property arises for the first time when the court declares it to exist. The right must have arisen at the time of the transaction in order for the plaintiff to have any right the breach of which can be remedied. Again, I think the *DHN Food Distributors Ltd* case shows that the equity predates any order of the court. The right to compensation in that case depended on substantive rights at the date of compulsory acquisition, not on what remedy the court subsequently chose to grant in the subsequent litigation.

Accordingly, if I am right in holding that as between the debtor and Mrs Johnson she had an irrevocable licence to remain in the property, authority compels me to hold that that gave her an interest in the property before the bankruptcy and the trustee takes the property subject to that interest. In my judgment the mere intervention of the bankruptcy by itself cannot alter Mrs Johnson's property interest. If she is to be deprived of her interest as against the trustee in bankruptcy, it must be because of some conduct of hers which precludes her from enforcing her rights, that is to say, the ordinary principles of acquiescence and laches which apply to all beneficiaries seeking to enforce their rights apply to this case.

I am in no way criticising the trustee in bankruptcy's conduct; he tried to find out if she made any claim relating to the £12,000 before he contracted to sell the property. But I do not think that on ordinary equitable principles Mrs Johnson should be prevented from asserting her rights even at this late stage. She is very old and in bad health. No one had ever advised her that she might have rights to live in the property. As soon as she appreciated that she was to be evicted she at once took legal advice and asserted her claim. This, in my judgment, is far removed from conduct which precludes enforcement by a beneficiary of his rights due to his acquiescence, the first requirement of acquiescence being that the beneficiary knows his or her rights and does not assert them.

Accordingly, I hold that Mrs Johnson is entitled as against the trustee in bankruptcy to remain in the property until she is repaid the sums she advanced. I reach this conclusion with some hesitation since I find the present state of the law very confused and difficult to fit in with established

---

[17] See Sir Christopher SLADE's Child & Co Oxford Lecture 1984 on *The Informal Creation of Interests in Land* at p. 12. As M & W say at p. 508 n. 73, "many decisions on contractual licences turn a blind eye to this problem".

equitable principles. I express the hope that in the near future the whole question can receive full consideration in the Court of Appeal, so that, in order to do justice to the many thousands of people who never come into court at all but who wish to know with certainty what their proprietary rights are, the extent to which these irrevocable licences bind third parties may be defined with certainty. Doing justice to the litigant who actually appears in the court by the invention of new principles of law ought not to involve injustice to the other persons who are not litigants before the court but whose rights are fundamentally affected by the new principles.

Finally, I must reiterate that I am in no way deciding what are the rights of the purchaser from the trustee as against Mrs Johnson. It may be that as a purchaser without express notice in an action for specific performance of the contract his rights will prevail over Mrs Johnson's. As to that, I have heard no argument and express no view. I do, however, express my sympathy for him in the predicament in which he finds himself.

I therefore dismiss the trustee's application for possession against Mrs Johnson."

V.   Licences by Estoppel[18]

The doctrine of estoppel, which is of general application at law and in equity, has played a significant part in the modern development of the law of licences. The basic principle of the doctrine is that a person who makes, by words or conduct, a representation to another, intending that other to act on it, and the other does so to his detriment[19], will not be allowed subsequently to take a position inconsistently with the representation. At common law, the representation had to be one of existing fact[20]. The estoppel acted as a rule of evidence. The representor could not subsequently allege, in dealings with the representee, that the facts were different from those represented. The estoppel did not however give rise to any independent cause of action.

The doctrine widened in equity so as to cover a representation, not only of fact, but of intention, or a promise. This is promissory estoppel; which became well known through *Central London Property Trust Ltd v High Trees House Ltd* [1947] KB 130, [1946] 1 All ER 256, and was firmly established in later years. Promissory estoppel also gives negative protection only, and is not a cause of action[1].

The past few years have seen a remarkable growth, in the context of licences, of a different, but related doctrine: called proprietary estoppel. The doctrine deals with the equities arising out of a situation in which one party (O) knowingly encourages another (A) to act, or acquiesces in his acting to his detriment and in infringement of O's rights, so that it would be unconscionable for O to insist on his strict legal rights. O will be unable to

---

[18] C & B, pp. 561–569; M & W, pp. 804–808; MM, pp. 74–77, 374–375; Spencer Bower and Turner, *Estoppel by Representation* (3rd edn, 1977) passim, and especially chap. 12; Dawson and Pearce, pp. 29–36, 97–99, 144–145, 161–163; Snell, chap. 5; [1981] Conv 347 (P.N. Todd); [1981] Conv 118 at pp. 125–132 (A.R. Everton); (1984) 100 LQR 376 (S. Moriarty); Sir Christopher SLADE, *The Informal Creation of Interests in Land* (1984) Child & Co Oxford Lecture; Finn, Essays in Equity (1985), pp. 59–94.

[19] As by expenditure of money, or giving up present accommodation.

[20] *Jorden v Money* (1854) 5 HL Cas 185.

[1] *Combe v Combe* [1951] 2 KB 215, [1951] 1 All ER 767.

complain later of the infringement; and may indeed be required to make good A's expectations in respect of the rights exercised. Thus, unlike other estoppels, this doctrine may create a claim, and an entitlement to property rights in or over land[2]. Authoritative statements laying down the requirements for the operation of the doctrine appear below.

These estoppel doctrines have been applied to many cases involving licences. The licence may be gratuitous or contractual. The categories of licences may therefore overlap[3]. If the licence is contractual, the licensee may be protected under the doctrines relating to contractual licences, discussed above; and it may be unnecessary to invoke the doctrine of estoppel[4]. Where, however, the licensee is seeking protection against a third party, a licence by estoppel is more effective. It will be seen that the courts appear to have these factors in mind in categorising licences.

Decisions to protect licensees of all kinds raise a number of difficulties. Some of these have been seen in the context of contractual licences. With licences by estoppel, the courts recognise their power and duty in these cases as being to "look at the circumstances in each case to decide in what way the equity can be satisfied"[5]. The court may decide to protect the licensee by means of an injunction restraining the licensor from interfering; and in cases of estoppel by representation, this may be the only choice[6]. Such a solution produces conveyancing difficulties; for it leaves the licensee in possession with no title. His equity is good, not only against the licensor, but also against third parties other than a bona fide purchaser for value without notice[7]. In such a situation, it seems that, in the case of unregistered land, the licence not being registrable, we are thrown back on the hazards of notice[8]. With registered land, a licensee in occupation will presumably have an overriding interest, and may be able to acquire protection by entering a caution or a notice[9].

The negative protection under the classical estoppel principle has advantages in situations where the time is not yet ripe for a final settlement; as where a licensee is protected in occupation which may only be temporary and something less than a permanent solution is required; as where a son builds a bungalow on his father's land in the expectation of being allowed to stay there for the rest of his life[10]; or parents give up a home and move in to

---

[2] *Western Fish Products Ltd v Penwith District Council* [1981] 2 All ER 204, p. 514, post.
[3] In *Hardwick v Johnson* [1978] 1 WLR 683, [1978] 2 All ER 935, p. 491, ante, the Court of Appeal divided 2–1 on the question of the type of licence. But that made no difference to the result. See also *Re Sharpe* [1980] 1 WLR 219, [1980] 1 All ER 198, p. 506, ante.
[4] *Tanner v Tanner* [1975] 1 WLR 1346, [1975] 3 All ER 776, p. 484, ante.
[5] *Plimmer v Wellington Corpn* (1884) 9 App Cas 699 at 714; *Chalmers v Pardoe* [1963] 1 WLR 677 at 682, [1963] 3 All ER 552 at 555; *Inwards v Baker* [1965] 2 QB 29 at 37, [1965] 1 All ER 446 at 449; *ER Ives Investment Ltd v High* [1967] 2 QB 379 at 395, [1967] 1 All ER 504 at 507, p. 542, post; *Crabb v Arun District Council* [1976] Ch 179 at 188, [1975] 3 All ER 865 at 871, p. 536, post.
[6] Unless a constructive trust is found: *Bannister v Bannister* [1948] 2 All ER 133, p. 503, ante; *Hussey v Palmer* [1972] 1 WLR 286, [1972] 3 All ER 744, p. 504, ante; *Re Sharpe* [1980] 1 WLR 219, [1983] 1 All ER 198, p. 506, ante.
[7] *Hopgood v Brown* [1955] 1 WLR 213, [1955] 1 All ER 550, p. 530, post.
[8] Which may not be a serious problem if the licensee is in occupation; but could be if the licensee's rights were only exercisable periodically: (1956) 20 Conv (NS) 281 (R.H. Maudsley); Dawson and Pearce, p. 162.
[9] C & B, pp. 569–570; Dawson and Pearce, pp. 194–200.
[10] *Inwards v Baker* [1965] 2 QB 29, [1965] 1 All ER 446, p. 528, post.

look after an aged grandparent[11]; or a mistress requires a home until the children are of school age[12]; or a garage is built which overlaps a neighbour's boundary[13]; or a housekeeper remains in a house looking after a family in the expectaton of being allowed to stay there rent free for the rest of her life[14].

In several of the recent cases, the court, applying the doctrine of proprietary estoppel, has found it best to declare that some interest is to be vested in the licensee. If the proper documentation follows, the conveyancing difficulties are avoided: but until that time, they exist as before; perhaps more acutely; for it is one thing for a purchaser to buy land which is subject to a licensee's temporary rights of protection; and another to find that he has taken title from a non-owner, or has bought settled land from someone other than the tenant for life. Some of these difficulties were not foreseen in the earlier cases; but the courts, as will be seen from the cases, are now aware of the problems, especially that of the application of the Settled Land Act 1925[15] and attempt to avoid them[16].

The court exercises wide discretionary powers in seeking the just solution. Negative protection may be hazardous and inadequate. A positive solution, ordering a transfer of the land to the licensee, may do injustice to the legal owner; as where a prior owner promised a gift, failed to make it, and a conveyance is ordered, without payment, by the successor owner[17]. The court has power to order a transfer, subject to payment by the licensee of the value of the site; or to order compensation to the licensee for his expenditure; and it may in some circumstances be best to give to the licensee the choice. This situation indeed "displays equity at its most flexible[18]". The court has to bear in mind the equities between the parties involved in all the circumstances; and also the effect of its order upon the conveyancing system. The extent to which these principles have been observed should be considered in the cases which follow.

In *Ramsden v Dyson* (1866) LR 1 HL 129, Lord KINGSDOWN in a dissenting speech, where however the difference of opinion was on the application of the principle to the facts, and not on the statement of the principle, said at 170:

"If a man, under a verbal agreement with a landlord for a certain interest in land, or, what amounts to the same thing, under an expectation, created or encouraged by the landlord, that he shall have a certain interest, takes possession of such land, with the consent of the landlord, and upon the faith of such promise or expectation, with the knowledge of the landlord, and without objection by him, lays out money upon the land, a Court of equity will compel the landlord to give effect to such promise or expectation."

---

[11] *Piquet v Tyler* [1978] CLY 119; *Dodsworth v Dodsworth* (1973) 228 EG 1115, p. 548, post; *Williams v Staite* [1979] Ch 291, [1978] 2 All ER 928; *Griffiths v Williams* (1978) 248 EG 947, p. 550, post.
[12] *Tanner v Tanner* [1975] 1 WLR 1346, [1975] 3 All ER 776, p. 484, ante a contractual licence also; damages were awarded because the licensee had already been rehoused.
[13] *Hopgood v Brown*, supra.
[14] *Greasley v Cooke* [1980] 1 WLR 1306, [1980] 3 All ER 710, p. 524, post.
[15] See (1977) 93 LQR 561 (J.A. Hornby); [1978] Conv 250; p. 275, n. 4a, ante.
[16] *Griffiths v Williams* (1977) 248 EG 947, p. 550, post.
[17] *Dillwyn v Llewelyn* (1862) 4 De GF & J 517; *Pascoe v Turner* [1979] 1 WLR 431, [1979] 2 All ER 945, p. 545, post.
[18] Snell, p. 562.

In *Willmott v Barber* (1880) 15 Ch D 96 at 105, p. 517, post, FRY J specified the detailed requirements in what have come to be called "the five probanda", and nearly a century later SCARMAN LJ was listing them in *Crabb v Arun District Council* [1976] Ch 179 at 194–195, [1975] 3 All ER 865 at 876–877, p. 538, post. FRY J said:

"A man is not to be deprived of his legal rights unless he has acted in such a way as would make it fraudulent for him to set up those rights. What, then, are the elements or requisites necessary to constitute fraud of that description? In the first place the plaintiff must have made a mistake as to his legal rights. Secondly, the plaintiff must have expended some money or must have done some act (not necessarily upon the defendant's land) on the faith of his mistaken belief. Thirdly, the defendant, the possessor of the legal right, must know of the existence of his own right which is inconsistent with the right claimed by the plaintiff. If he does not know of it he is in the same position as the plaintiff, and the doctrine of acquiescence is founded upon conduct with a knowledge of your legal rights. Fourthly, the defendant, the possessor of the legal right, must know of the plaintiff's mistaken belief of his rights. If he does not, there is nothing which calls upon him to assert his own rights. Lastly, the defendant, the possessor of the legal right, must have encouraged the plaintiff in his expenditure of money or in the other acts which he has done, either directly or by abstaining from asserting his legal right. Where all these elements exist, there is fraud of such a nature as will entitle the court to restrain the possessor of the legal right from exercising it, but, in my judgment, nothing short of this will do."

In recent years, however, the principle in *Ramsden v Dyson* has been expressed in much broader terms. In *Taylors Fashions Ltd v Liverpool Victoria Trustees Co Ltd* (1979) [1982] QB 133n, [1981] 1 All ER 897, OLIVER J said at 151, at 915:

"The more recent cases indicate, in my judgment, that the application of the *Ramsden v Dyson* principle — whether you call it proprietary estoppel, estoppel by acquiescence or estoppel by encouragement is really immaterial —. requires a very much broader approach which is directed rather at ascertaining whether, in particular individual circumstances, it would be unconscionable for a party to be permitted to deny that which, knowingly, or unknowingly, he has allowed or encouraged another to assume to his detriment than to inquiring whether the circumstances can be fitted within the confines of some preconceived formula serving as a universal yardstick for every form of unconscionable behaviour[19]."

The effect of this approach is that the court now regards the five probanda no longer as rigid criteria to be satisfied, but as being "guidelines, which will probably prove to be the necessary and essential guidelines, to assist the court to decide the question whether it is unconscionable for the plaintiffs to

---

[19] Approved by OLIVER LJ in *Habib Bank Ltd v Habib Bank AG Zurich* [1981] 1 WLR 1265 at 1285, [1981] 2 All ER 650 at 666; (1981) 97 LQR 513. See also SCARMAN LJ in *Crabb v Arun District Council* [1976] Ch 179 at 194, [1975] 3 All ER 865 at 876, p. 536, post; MEGARRY V-C in *Appleby v Cowley* (1982) Times, 14 April, p. 555, post; ROBERT GOFF LJ in *Amalgamated Investment and Property Co Ltd v Texas Commerce International Bank Ltd* [1982] QB 84 at 103, [1981] 1 All ER 923 at 935; affd [1982] QB 84, [1981] 3 All ER 577; (1982) 79 LSG 662 (P. Matthews); *Esso Petroleum Co Ltd v Anthony Gibbs Financial Services Ltd* (1981) 262 EG 661; *Pacol Ltd v Trade Lines Ltd and R/I Sif IV* [1982] 1 Lloyd's Rep 456.

assert their legal rights by taking advantage of the defendant[20]". OLIVER J had suggested at 146, at 911, that the five probanda might be necessary where the defendant has done no positive act, and merely "stands by without protest".

On the other hand an important limitation was placed on the principle in 1978 by the Court of Appeal in *Western Fish Products v Penwith District Council* [1981] 2 All ER 204[1], where MEGAW LJ said at 218:

"We know of no case, and none has been cited to us, in which the principle set out in *Ramsden v Dyson* and *Crabb v Arun District Council* has been applied otherwise than to rights and interests created in and over land. It may extend to other forms of property[2]: see Lord Denning MR in *Moorgate Mercantile Co Ltd v Twitchings* [1976] QB 225 at 242, [1975] 3 All ER 314 at 323. In our judgment there is no good reason for extending the principle further."

A.   Establishment of the Equity

i   GENERAL PRINCIPLES

TAYLORS FASHIONS LTD v LIVERPOOL VICTORIA TRUSTEES CO LTD

OLD & CAMPBELL LTD v LIVERPOOL VICTORIA FRIENDLY SOCIETY
[1982] QB 133n, [1981] 1 All ER 897 (ChD, Oliver J)

The first plaintiffs (Taylors) sought to exercise an option to renew a lease, granted in 1948, of commercial premises at No 22 Westover Road, Bournemouth. The option had not been registered as a Class C (iv) Land Charge under the Land Charges Act 1925, and, following *Beesly v Hallwood Estates Ltd* [1960] 1 WLR 549, [1960] 2 All ER 314, p. 32, n. 20, ante, was void as against the defendants. The question was whether the defendants were estopped from asserting their strict legal rights against Taylors, who had spent some £12,000 on improving the premises, including the installation of a •lift, in the expectation that the option would be enforceable. The defendants acquiesced in the works carried out by Taylors, and at the time did not suspect that they might have any reason for challenging the validity of the option. The fourth of FRY J's five probanda (see p. 513, ante) was therefore not fulfilled.

The second plaintiffs (Olds) had been granted a lease in 1949 of No 21 (adjacent to Taylors' premises), and a further lease in 1963 of No 20. The 1949 lease contained a clause permitting the defendants to determine that lease, if Taylors did not exercise their option in regard to No 22. The 1963 lease contained in Clause 4 an option enabling Olds to renew, if Taylors in fact exercised their option.

Held. Taylors were not entitled to obtain a renewal of their lease, but the defendants were estopped from denying that Olds were entitled to exercise their option.

---

[20] *Swallow Securities Ltd v Isenberg* (1985) 274 EG 1028 at 1030, per CUMMING-BRUCE LJ (no evidence to induce in the defendant an expectation that she had legal rights more extensive than was in fact the case).

[1] It was held not to apply where an owner spent money on his own land in the expectation encouraged by a local authority that he would acquire a planning permission.

[2] *Re Foster* [1938] 3 All ER 610 (life insurance policy).

OLIVER J: The points which arise for decision, therefore, are these. (1) Is Taylors' option, as the defendants claim and as the plaintiffs contest, void against the defendants for want of registration? (2) If it is, are the defendants estopped as against Taylors from relying upon this ground of invalidity having regard to the expenditure by Taylors made with the defendants' concurrence in 1959 and 1960? (3) If the option is indeed unenforceable against the defendants, has it nevertheless been "exercised" for the purposes of the break and renewal clauses in the lease to Olds? (4) If it has not, are the defendants estopped as against Olds from relying upon the invalidity of an option which their own grants assert to be subsisting?

[His Lordship considered the first point, concluded that he must follow the decision of BUCKLEY J in *Beesly v Hallwood Estates Ltd* [1960] 1 WLR 549, [1960] 1 All ER 314, and continued:]

I approach the case, therefore, on the footing that, whatever the parties may have thought, the option was in fact void as against the defendants (although of course still contractually binding as between the original parties) from the moment when they completed their purchase. This brings me to the second and fourth questions which I have postulated above. As regards the general principles applicable I can treat the two questions together, although there are certain circumstances peculiar to Olds and some additional arguments of law in their case to which I shall have to refer later on. The starting point of both Mr Scott's and Mr Essayan's arguments on estoppel is the same and was expressed by Mr Essayan in the following proposition: if A under an expectation created or encouraged by B that A shall have a certain interest in land, thereafter, on the faith of such expectation and with the knowledge of B and without objection by him, acts to his detriment in connection with such land, a Court of Equity will compel B to give effect to such expectation. This is a formulation which Mr Millett accepts but subject to one important qualification, namely that at the time when he created and encouraged the expectation and (I think that he would also say) at the time when he permitted the detriment to be incurred (if those two points of time are different) B not only knows of A's expectation but must be aware of his true rights and that he was under no existing obligation to grant the interest.

This is the principal point upon which the parties divide. Mr Scott and Mr Essayan contend that what the court has to look at in relation to the party alleged to be estopped is only his conduct and its result, and not — or, at any rate, not necessarily — his state of mind. It then has to ask whether what that party is now seeking to do is unconscionable. Mr Millett contends that it is an essential feature of this particular equitable doctrine that the party alleged to be estopped must, before the assertion of his strict rights can be considered unconscionable, be aware both of what his strict rights were and of the fact that the other party is acting in the belief that they will not be enforced against him.

The point is a critical one in the instant case and it is one upon which the authorities appear at first sight to be divided. The starting point is *Ramsden v Dyson* (1866) LR 1 HL 129 where a tenant under a tenancy at will had built upon the land in the belief that he would be entitled to demand a long lease. The majority in the House of Lords held that he would not, but Lord Kingsdown dissented on the facts. There was no — or certainly no overt — disagreement between their Lordships as to the applicable principle, but it was stated differently by Lord Cranworth LC and Lord Kingsdown and the real question is how far Lord Cranworth was purporting to make an exhaustive exposition of principle and how far what he stated as the appropriate conditions for its application are to be treated, as it were, as being subsumed sub silentio in the speech of Lord Kingsdown. Lord Cranworth expressed it thus, at 140–141:

"If a stranger begins to build on my land supposing it to be his own, and I, perceiving his mistake, abstain from setting him right, and leave him to persevere in his error, a court of equity will not allow me afterwards to assert my title to the land on which he had expended money on the supposition that the land was his own. It considers that, when I saw the mistake into which he had fallen, it was my duty to be active and to state my adverse title; and that it would be dishonest in me to remain wilfully passive on such an occasion, in order afterwards to profit by the mistake which I might have prevented. But it will be observed that to raise such an equity two things are required, first, that the person expending the money supposes himself to be building on his own land; and, secondly, that the real owner at the time of the expenditure knows that the land belongs to him and not to the person expending the money in the belief that he is the owner. For if a stranger builds on my land knowing it to be mine, there is no principle of equity which would prevent my claiming the land with the benefit of all the expenditure made on it. There would be nothing in my conduct, active or passive, making it inequitable in me to assert my legal rights."

So here, clearly stated, is the criterion upon which Mr Millett relies. Lord Kingsdown stated the matter differently and rather more broadly although in the narrower context of landlord and tenant. He says, at 170:

"The rule of law applicable to the case appears to me to be this: If a man, under a verbal agreement with a landlord for a certain interest in land, or, what amounts to the same thing, under an expectation, created or encouraged by the landlord, that he shall have a certain interest, takes possession of such land, with the consent of the landlord, and upon the faith of such promise or expectation, with the knowledge of the landlord, and without objection by him, lays out money upon the land, a court of equity will compel the landlord to give effect to such promise or expectation. This was the principle of the decision in *Gregory v Mighell* (1811) 18 Ves 328, and as I conceive, is open to no doubt."

So here, there is no specific requirement, at any rate in terms, that the landlord should know or intend that the expectation which he has created or encouraged is one to which he is under no obligation to give effect.

Mr Millett does not — nor could he in the light of the authorities — dispute the principle. What he contends is that even if (which he contests) this is a case where the defendants could be said to have encouraged the plaintiffs' expectations — and that it is not necessarily the same as having encouraged or acquiesced in the expenditure — the principle has no application to a case where, at the time when the expectation was encouraged, both parties were acting under a mistake of law as to their rights.

There is, he submits, a clear distinction between cases of proprietary estoppel or estoppel by acquiescence on the one hand and promissory estoppel or estoppel by representation (whether express or by conduct) on the other. In the latter case, the court looks at the knowledge of the party who has acted and the effect upon him of his having acted. The state of mind of the promissor or representor (except to the extent of knowing, either actually or inferentially, that his promise or representation is likely to be acted upon) is largely irrelevant. In the former case, however, it is essential, Mr Millett submits, to show that the party alleged to have encouraged or acquiesced in the other party's belief himself knew the true position, for if he did not there can be nothing unconscionable in his subsequently seeking to rely upon it. Mr Millett concedes that there may be cases which straddle this convenient dichotomy — cases which can be put either as cases of encouragement or proprietary estoppel on Lord Kingsdown's principle or as estoppel by representation, express or implied. But, he submits, the party alleging the estoppel must, whichever way he elects to put his case or even if he runs them as alternatives, demonstrate the presence of all the essential ingredients of whatever type of estoppel he relies on. He cannot manufacture a third and new hybrid type of estoppel by an eclectic application of some of the ingredients of each. So, if he wishes to put his case as one of estoppel by representation, he must, for instance, show an unequivocal representation of existing fact. Equally, if he wants to rely upon the circumstances of the case as raising a proprietary estoppel arising from acquiescence in his having acted upon an erroneous supposition of his legal rights, then he must accept the burden of showing that the error was known to the other party.

So far as proprietary estoppel or estoppel by acquiescence is concerned, he supports his submission by reference to the frequently cited judgment of Fry J in *Willmott v Barber* (1880) 15 ChD 96 which contains what are described as the five "probanda". The actual case was one where what was alleged was a waiver by acquiescence. A lease contained a covenant against assigning, subletting or parting with possession without the lessor's consent and the lessee had let a sublessee into possession of part of the land under an agreement with him which entitled him to occupy that part for the whole term and conferred an option to purchase the remaining land for the balance of the term outstanding when the option was exercised. The sublessee built on the land and the head landlord was aware that he was in possession and was expending money. It was, however, proved that he did not then know that his consent was required to a sub-letting or assignment. The question arose between the sublessee and the head landlord when the sublessee tried to exercise his option over the remaining land and found himself met with the response that the head landlord refused consent to the assignment. The case was, on Fry J's finding of fact, one simply of acquiescence by standing by and what was being argued was that the landlord was estopped by his knowledge of the plaintiff's expenditure on the part of the land of which the plaintiff *was* in possession from withholding his consent to an assignment of that part of which he was not. It having been found as a fact that the landlord did not, at the time of the plaintiff's expenditure, know about the covenant against assignment and that there was nothing in what had passed between them to suggest either that the landlord was aware that the plaintiff was labouring under the belief that no consent was necessary or to encourage that belief, Fry J dismissed the plaintiff's claim. It has to be borne in mind, however, in reading the judgment, that this was a pure acquiescence case where what was relied on was a waiver of the landlord's rights by standing by without protest. It was a case of mere silence where what had to be established by the plaintiff was some duty in the landlord to speak. The passage from the judgment in *Willmott v Barber* most frequently cited is where Fry J says, at 105–106:

[His Lordship cited the passage set out at p. 513, ante, and continued:]

Mr Millett's submission is that when one applies these five probanda to the facts of the instant case it will readily be seen that they are not all complied with. In particular, Mr Millett submits, the fourth probandum involves two essential elements, viz., (i) knowledge by the possessor of the legal right of the other party's belief; and (ii) knowledge that that belief is mistaken. In the instant case the defendants were not aware of their inconsistent right to treat the option as void and equally they could not, thus, have been aware that the plaintiffs' belief in the validity of the option was a mistaken belief. The alternative approach via estoppel by representation is not, he submits, open to the plaintiffs in this case because so far as Taylors were concerned the defendants made no representation to them at all and so far as Olds were concerned the representation of the continuing validity of the option, if there was one at all, was a representation of law.

Now, convenient and attractive as I find Mr Millett's submissions as a matter of argument, I am not at all sure that so orderly and tidy a theory is really deducible from the authorities — certainly from the more recent authorities, which seem to me to support a much wider equitable jurisdiction to interfere in cases where the assertion of strict legal rights is found by the court to be unconscionable. It may well be (although I think that this must now be considered open to doubt) that the strict *Willmott v Barber* probanda are applicable as necessary requirements in those cases where all that has happened is that the party alleged to be estopped has stood by without protest while his rights have been infringed. It is suggested in *Spencer Bower and Turner, Estoppel by Representation*, 3rd edn. (1977), para. 290 that acquiescence, in its strict sense, is merely an instance of estoppel by representation and this derives some support from the judgment of the Court of Appeal in *De Bussche v Alt* (1878) 8 ChD 286 at 314. If that is a correct analysis then, in a case of mere passivity, it is readily intelligible that there must be shown a duty to speak, protest or interfere which cannot normally arise in the absence of knowledge or at least a suspicion of the true position. Thus for a landowner to stand by while a neighbour lays drains in land which the landowner does not believe that he owns (*Armstrong v Sheppard & Short Ltd* [1959] 2 QB 384, [1959] 2 All ER 651) or for a remainderman not to protest at a lease by a tenant for life which he believes he has no right to challenge (*Svenson v Payne* (1945) 71 CLR 531) does not create an estoppel. Again, where what is relied on is a waiver by acquiescence, as in *Willmott v Barber* itself, the five probanda are no doubt appropriate. There is, however, no doubt that there are judicial pronouncements of high authority which appear to support as essential the application of all the five probanda over the broader field covering all cases generally classified as estoppel by "encouragement" or "acquiescence": see, for instance, the speech of Lord Diplock in *Kammins Ballrooms Co Ltd v Zenith Investments (Torquay) Ltd* [1971] AC 850 at 884, [1970] 2 All ER 871 at 875.

Mr Scott submits, however, that it is historically wrong to treat these probanda as holy writ and to restrict equitable interference only to those cases which can be confined within the strait-jacket of some fixed rule governing the circumstances in which, and in which alone, the court will find that a party is behaving unconscionably. Whilst accepting that the five probanda may form an appropriate test in cases of silent acquiescence, he submits that the authorities do not support the absolute necessity for compliance with all five probanda, and, in particular, the requirement of knowledge on the part of the party estopped that the other party's belief is a mistaken belief, in cases where the conduct relied on has gone beyond mere silence and amounts to active encouragement. In Lord Kingsdown's example in *Ramsden v Dyson*, for instance, there is no room for the literal application of the probanda, for the circumstances there postulated do not presuppose a "mistake" on anybody's part, but merely the fostering of an expectation in the minds of *both* parties at the time but from which, once it has been acted upon, it would be unconscionable to permit the landlord to depart. As Scarman LJ pointed out in *Crabb v Arun District Council* [1976] Ch 179, [1975] 3 All ER 865, the "fraud" in these cases is not to be found in the transaction itself but in the subsequent attempt to go back upon the basic assumptions which underlay it.

[His Lordship considered *Stiles v Cowper* (1748) 3 Atk 692; *Jackson v Cator* (1800) 5 Ves 688; *Gregory v Mighell* (1811) 18 Ves 328; *Plimmer v Wellington Corpn* (1884) 9 App Cas 699, p. 533, post; *Sarat Chunder Dey v Gopal Chunder Laha* (1892) 19 LR Ind App 203; *Craine v Colonial Mutual Fire Insurance Co Ltd* (1920) 28 CLR 305; *Re Eaves* [1940] Ch 109, [1939] 4 All ER 260; *Hopgood v Brown* [1955] 1 WLR 213, [1955] 1 All ER 550; *Electrolux Ltd v Electrix Ltd* (1953) 71 RPC 23, and continued:]

Furthermore the more recent cases indicate, in my judgment, that the application of the *Ramsden v Dyson* principle — whether you call it proprietary estoppel, estoppel by acquiescence or estoppel by encouragement is really immaterial — requires a very much broader approach which is directed rather at ascertaining whether, in particular individual circumstances, it would be unconscionable for a party to be permitted to deny that which, knowingly, or unknowingly, he has allowed or encouraged another to assume to his detriment than to inquiring whether the circumstances can be fitted within the confines of some preconceived formula serving as a universal yardstick for every form of unconscionable behaviour.

So regarded, knowledge of the true position by the party alleged to be estopped, becomes merely one of the relevant factors — it may even be a determining factor in certain cases — in the overall inquiry. This approach, so it seems to me, appears very clearly from the authorities to which I am about to refer. In *Inwards v Baker* [1965] 2 QB 29, [1965] 1 All ER 446, p. 528, post, there was no mistaken belief on either side. Each knew the state of the title, but the defendant had been led to expect that he would get an interest in the land on which he had built and, indeed, the overwhelming probability is that that was indeed the father's intention at the time. But it was not mere promissory estoppel, which could merely be used as a defence, for, as Lord Denning MR said, at 37, at 449, "it is for the court to say in what way the equity can be satisfied." The principle was expressed very broadly both by Lord Denning MR and by Danckwerts LJ. Lord Denning said at 37, at 449:

"But it seems to me, from *Plimmer's* case, 9 App Cas 699, 713–714 in particular, that the equity arising from the expenditure on land need not fail 'merely on the ground that the interest to be secured has not been expressly indicated . . . the court must look at the circumstances in each case to decide in what way the equity can be satisfied.'"

And a little further down he said:

"All that is necessary is that the licensee should, at the request or with the encouragement of the landlord, have spent the money in the expectation of being allowed to stay there. If so, the court will not allow that expectation to be defeated where it would be inequitable so to do."

And Danckwerts LJ said, at 38, at 449:

"It seems to me that this is one of the cases of an equity created by estoppel, or equitable estoppel, as it is sometimes called, by which the person who has made the expenditure is induced by the expectation of obtaining protection, and equity protects him so that an injustice may not be perpetrated."

An even more striking example is *ER Ives Investment Ltd v High* [1967] 2 QB 379, [1967] 1 All ER 504, p. 542, post. Here again, there does not appear to have been any question of the persons who had acquiesced in the defendant's expenditure having known that his belief that he had an enforceable right of way was mistaken. Indeed, at the stage when the expenditure took place, both sides seem to have shared the belief that the agreement between them created effective rights. Nevertheless the successor in title to the acquiescing party was held to be estopped. Lord Denning MR said, at 394–395:

"The right arises out of the expense incurred by Mr High in building his garage, as it is now, with access only over the yard: and the Wrights standing by and acquiescing in it, knowing that he believed he had a right of way over the yard. By so doing the Wrights created in Mr High's mind a reasonable expectation that his access over the yard would not be disturbed. That gives rise to an 'equity arising out of acquiescence.' It is available not only against the Wrights but also their successors in title. The court will not allow that expectation to be defeated when it would be inequitable so to do. It is for the court in each case to decide in what way the equity can be satisfied . . ."

It should be mentioned that the Wrights themselves clearly also believed that Mr High had a right of way, because when they came to sell, they sold expressly subject to it. So, once again, there is an example of the doctrine of estoppel by acquiescence being applied without regard to the question of whether the acquiescing party knew that the belief of the other party in his supposed rights was erroneous.

Mr Scott and Mr Essayan have also drawn my attention to the Privy Council decision in *Bank Negara Indonesia v Hoalim* (1973) 2 MLJ 3 where again, it seems that the misconception of the legal position which gave rise to the assurance creating the estoppel seems to have been shared by both parties. This is, however, rather a case of promissory estoppel than of the application of the *Ramsden v Dyson* principle. More nearly in point is *Crabb v Arun District Council* [1976] Ch 179, [1975] 3 All ER 865, p. 536, post, where the plaintiff had altered his legal position in the expectation, encouraged by the defendants, that he would have a certain access to a road. Now there was no mistake here. Each party knew that the road was vested in the defendants and each knew that no formal grant had been made. Indeed I cannot see why in considering whether the defendants were behaving unconscionably, it should have made the slightest difference to the result if, at the time when the plaintiff was encouraged to open his access to the road, the defendants had thought that they were bound to grant it. The fact was that he had been encouraged to alter his position irrevocably to his detriment on the faith of a belief, which was known to and encouraged by the defendants, that he was going to be given a particular right of access — a belief which, for all that appears, the defendants probably shared at that time.

The particularly interesting features of the case in the context of the present dispute are, first, the virtual equation of promissory estoppel and proprietary estoppel or estoppel by acquiescence as mere facets of the same principle and secondly the very broad approach of both Lord Denning MR and Scarman LJ, both of whom emphasised the flexibility of the equitable doctrine. It is, however, worth noting that Scarman LJ adopted and applied the five probanda in *Willmott v Barber*, which he described as "a valuable guide." He considered that those probanda were satisfied and it is particularly relevant here to note again the fourth one — namely that the defendant, the possessor of the legal right, must know of the plaintiff's mistaken belief. If Scarman LJ had interpreted this as meaning — as Mr Millett submits that it does mean — that the defendant must know not only of the plaintiff's belief but also that it was mistaken, then he could not, I think, have come to the conclusion that this probandum was satisfied, for it seems clear from Lord Denning's recital of the facts that, up to the critical moment when the plaintiff acted, *both* parties thought that there *was* a firm assurance of access. The defendants had, indeed, even erected a gate at their own expense to give effect to it. What gave rise to the necessity for the court to intervene was the defendants' attempt to go back on this subsequently when they fell out with the plaintiff. I infer therefore that Scarman LJ must have construed this probandum in the sense which Mr Scott and Mr Essayan urge upon me, namely that the defendant must know merely of the plaintiff's belief which, in the event, turns out to be mistaken.

Finally, there ought to be mentioned the most recent reference to the five probanda which is to be found in *Shaw v Applegate* [1977] 1 WLR 970, [1978] 1 All ER 123. That was a case where the plea of estoppel by acquiescence failed on appeal, but it is significant that two members of the court expressed serious doubt whether it was necessary in every case of acquiescence to satisfy the five probanda. Buckley LJ said at 977–978, at 130:

"As I understand that passage" and there he is referring to the passage from the judgment of Fry J in *Willmott v Barber* to which I have already referred, "what the judge is there saying is that where a man has got a legal right — as the plaintiffs have in the present case, being legal assignees of the benefit of the covenant binding the defendant — acquiescence on their part will not deprive them of that legal right unless it is of such a nature and in such circumstances that it would really be dishonest or unconscionable of the plaintiffs to set up that right after what has occurred. Whether in order to reach that stage of affairs it is really necessary to comply strictly with all five tests there set out by Fry J may, I think, still be open to doubt, although no doubt if all those five tests were satisfied there would be shown to be a state of affairs in which it would be dishonest or unconscionable for the owner of the right to insist upon it. In *Electrolux Ltd v Electrix Ltd* (1953) 71 RPC 23 Sir Raymond Evershed MR said, at 33: 'I confess that I have found some difficulty — or should find some difficulty if it were necessary to make up my mind and express a view whether all five requisites which Fry J stated in *Willmott v Barber* must be present in every case in which it is said that the plaintiff will be deprived of his right to succeed in an action on the ground of acquiescence. All cases (and this is a trite but useful observation to repeat) must be read in the light of the facts of the particular case.' So I do not, as at present advised, think it is clear that it is essential to find all the five tests set out by Fry J literally applicable and satisfied in any particular case. The real test, I think, must be whether upon the facts of the particular case the situation has become such that it would be dishonest or unconscionable for the plaintiff, or the person having the right sought to be enforced, to continue to seek to enforce it."

And Goff LJ referred again to the judgment in *Willmott v Barber* and said, at 980, at 132:

"But for my part, I share the doubt entertained by Sir Raymond Evershed MR in the *Electrolux* case, whether it is necessary in all cases to establish the five tests which are laid down by Fry J, and I agree that the test is whether, in the circumstances, it has become unconscionable for the plaintiff to rely upon his legal right."

So here, once again, is the Court of Appeal asserting the broad test of whether in the circumstances the conduct complained of is unconscionable without the necessity of forcing those incumbrances[2a] into a Procrustean bed constructed from some unalterable criteria.

The matter was expressed by Lord Denning MR in *Moorgate Mercantile Co Ltd v Twitchings* [1976] QB 225 at 241 [1975] 3 All ER 314 at 323 as follows:

"Estoppel is not a rule of evidence. It is not a cause of action. It is a principle of justice and of equity. It comes to this: when a man, by his words or conduct, has led another to believe in a particular state of affairs, he will not be allowed to go back on it when it would be unjust or inequitable for him to do so. Dixon J put it in these words: 'The principle upon which estoppel in pais is founded is that the law should not permit an unjust departure by a party from an assumption of fact which he has caused another party to adopt or accept for the purpose of their legal relations.' Sir Owen said so in 1937 in *Grundt v Great Boulder Proprietary Gold Mines Ltd* (1937) 59 CLR 641 at 674. In 1947 after the *High Trees* case (*Central London Property Trust Ltd v High Trees House Ltd* [1947] KB 130, [1956] 1 All ER 256 n), I had some correspondence with Sir Owen about it: and I think I may say that he would not limit the principle to an assumption of fact, but would extend it, as I would, to include an assumption of fact or law, present or future. At any rate, it applies to an assumption of ownership or absence of ownership. This gives rise to what may be called proprietary estoppel. There are many cases where the true owner of goods or of land had led another to believe that he is not the owner, or, at any rate, is not claiming an interest therein, or that there is no objection to what the other is doing. In such cases it has been held repeatedly that the owner is not to be allowed to go back on what he has led the other to believe. So much so that his own title to the property, be it land or goods, has been held to be limited or extinguished, and new rights and interests have been created therein. And this operates by reason of his conduct — what he has led the other to believe — even though he never intended it."

The inquiry which I have to make therefore, as it seems to me, is simply whether, in all the circumstances of this case, it was unconscionable for the defendants to seek to take advantage of the mistake which, at the material time, everybody shared, and, in approaching that, I must consider the cases of the two plaintiffs separately because it may be that quite different considerations apply to each.

So far as Taylors are concerned there seem to me to be two difficulties in counsel's way. In the first place, whilst it is, no doubt, true that at the time

---

[2a] Presumably circumstances in intended.

when the work of putting in the lift was commenced with the defendants' knowledge and co-operation — co-operation, at least, to the extent of entering into discussions with regard to the siting of the lift — all parties shared the common belief that there was a valid and enforceable option, it is difficult to see how that belief had been in any way created or encouraged by the defendants. . . . So far as acquiescence pure and simple is concerned the defendants could not lawfully object to the work and could be under no duty to Taylors to communicate that which they did not know themselves, namely that the non-registration of the option rendered it unenforceable. So far as encouragement is concerned, it is not in my judgment possible fairly to say that the mere presence of the defendants' representative at a site meeting "encouraged" Taylors in their belief that the option was valid. No doubt it did nothing to discourage such a belief, but their representative would, I venture to think, have been present even if Taylors had already made up their minds that the option was not going to be exercised. . . .

The second difficulty in Mr Scott's way seems to me to be this. The work which was carried out was work which was referable to the unexpired term which Taylors then held and was no doubt undertaken with a view to making the premises more attractive and convenient for customers of the business which, after all, was going to be carried on for another 18 years before any question of exercising the option even arose. By that time, the initial expense would long since have been written off by normal depreciation. Taylors believed that the option was a valid option — that is to say that they had, potentially, a longer term than they had in fact. But what is there to indicate that the work was undertaken "on the faith of" that belief rather than merely "in" that belief?

[His Lordship referred to Lord Eldon LC in *Dann v Spurrier* (1802) 7 Ves 231 at 235–236; and Lord Hardwicke LC in *A-G v Baliol College, Oxford* (1744) 9 Mod Rep 407 at 411, and continued:]

It is conceivable that Taylors might not have done the work, although I find it difficult to believe that they would have contemplated operating a ladies' store on three floors in a fashionable Bournemouth shopping centre for 18 years without the convenience of a lift. It is conceivable that, if they had known the true position, they might have sought to re-negotiate a fresh option with the defendants rather than rely upon their rights under the Landlord and Tenant Act 1954. But what Mr Taylor was unable to say was that they would not have done the work if they had not thought that option was available, much less that the defendants were or must have been aware that they would not have done it.

Whilst, therefore, it may not seem very admirable for the defendants to avail themselves of a technicality which runs counter to the common assumption entertained by all the parties to the transaction, that is what the law permits them to dò; and I cannot find, in the cicumstances of this case, and even given the flexibility of the equitable principles, that Taylors have discharged the burden of showing that it is dishonest or unconscionable for them to do so. I must, therefore, dismiss Taylors' claim for specific performance of the option, although I do so with some regret.

Turning now to the case of Olds, the position appears to me to be very different. . . .

Mr Essayan puts his case . . . upon the *Ramsden v Dyson* principle. Here Olds were encouraged by the defendants to alter their legal position irrevocably upon the faith of the belief or expectation, of which the defendants knew and which they themselves fostered by the terms of the lease, that they would be getting a term which was to be cut down only upon a particular supposition, namely that Taylors would be either unwilling or would disentitle themselves from exercising their option.

But it is, I think, unnecessary for Mr Essayan to rely solely upon the transaction in 1949. The 1963 transaction presents an even clearer picture, because Olds were encouraged by the defendants to expend a very large sum on the premises and to take a lease of the adjoining premises, upon the faith of the expectation, encouraged by the defendants that they would be entitled to renew in a particular event which, whether it was probable or not, Olds were at least invited to believe was possible. That they acted upon that supposition cannot I think be doubted. One has only to refer to Mr Old's statement in the correspondence leading up to the lease that "this is no 14-year project." Nor, equally, can it be doubted that the defendants were aware of, and indeed, shared that supposition. Again, I do not think that it really matters whether the case is put as one of estoppel by acquiescence or of estoppel by representation. Clause 4 of the 1963 lease, in its entirety, is without sense except on the footing that the reference to the tenants of the neighbouring premises known as no. 22 Westover Road exercising "their option to have granted to them by the landlords," i.e., by the defendants, "a further term" is construed as a reference to an option between those tenants and the defendants subsisting and still capable of being exercised at the date of the lease. On any other footing the clause never could have any sphere of operation at all. . . .

It would, in my judgment, be most inequitable that the defendants, having put forward Taylors' option as a valid option in two documents, under each of which they are the grantors, and having encouraged Olds to incur expenditure and to alter their position irrevocably by taking additional premises on the faith of that supposition, should now be permitted to resile and to assert, as they do, that they are and were all along entitled to frustrate the expectation which they themselves created and that the right which they themselves stated to exist did not, at any material time, have any existence in fact. . . .

In the result, therefore, the claim of Taylors for specific performance must be dismissed and there will be in favour of Olds a declaration as regards the non-operation of the break clause in the 1949 lease and a decree of specific performance of the renewal option in the 1963 lease.

ii.   BURDEN OF PROOF

In *Greasley v Cooke* [1980] 1 WLR 1306, [1980] 3 All ER 710[3], Doris Cooke aged 16 went as a maid servant in 1938 to help in the house of a widower Arthur Greasley and was paid 10 shillings a week. From 1946 she co-habited with one of his sons until the son died in 1975. She was paid wages until Arthur's death in 1948, and thereafter continued, without wages, to live in the house and to look after it and the family, including a mentally ill

---

[3] [1981] Conv 154 (R.E. Annand); 44 MLR 461 (G. Woodman); 125 NLJ 539 (M.P. Thompson). Detriment was required by CA in *Christian v Christian* (1981) 131 NLJ 43. See also *Watkins v Emslie* (1981) 261 EG 1192; *Dann v Spurrier* (1802) 7 Ves 231 at 235–236, per Lord ELDON LC, cited in *Taylors Fashions Ltd v Liverpool Victoria Trustees Co Ltd* [1982] QB 133 at 156, [1981] 1 All ER 897 at 919; *Watts v Story* [1983] CA Transcript 319, p. 526, post.

daughter. After Arthur's death, members of the family led Doris to believe that she could regard the property as her home for the rest of her life and accordingly did not ask for any payment.

The Court of Appeal held that Doris was entitled to occupy the house rent-free so long as she wished to stay there. Lord DENNING MR said at 1311, at 713:

"The first point is on the burden of proof. Mr Weeks referred us to many cases, such as *Reynell v Sprye* (1852) 1 De GM & G 660 at 708; *Smith v Chadwick* (1882) 20 ChD 27 at 44 and *Brikom Investments Ltd v Carr* [1979] QB 467 at 482–483, [1978] 2 All ER 753 at 759, where I said that when a person makes a representation intending that another should act on it:

'It is no answer for the maker to say: "You would have gone on with the transaction anyway." That must be mere speculation. No one can be sure what he would, or would not, have done in a hypothetical state of affairs which never took place. . . . Once it is shown that a representation was calculated to influence the judgment of a reasonable man, the presumption is that he was so influenced[4].'

So here. These statements to Miss Cooke were calculated to influence her — so as to put her mind at rest — so that she should not worry about being turned out. No one can say what she would have done if Kenneth and Hedley had not made those statements. It is quite possible that she would have said to herself: 'I am not married to Kenneth. I am on my own. What will happen to me if anything happens to him? I had better look out for another job now: rather than stay here where I have no security'.

So, instead of looking for another job, she stayed on in the house looking after Kenneth and Clarice. There is a presumption that she did so, relying on the assurances given to her by Kenneth and Hedley. The burden is not on her, but on them, to prove that she did not rely on their assurances. They did not prove it, nor did their representatives. So she is presumed to have relied on them. So on the burden of proof it seems to me that the judge was in error.

The second point is about the need for some expenditure of money — some detriment — before a person can acquire any interest in a house or any right to stay in it as long as he wishes. It so happens that in many of these cases of proprietary estoppel there has been expenditure of money. But that is not a necessary element. I see that in *Snell's Principles of Equity*, 27th ed. (1973), p. 565, it is said: 'A must have incurred expenditure or otherwise have prejudiced himself.' But I do not think that that is necessary. It is sufficient if the party, to whom the assurance is given, acts on the faith of it — in such circumstances that it would be unjust and inequitable for the party making the assurance to go back on it: see *Moorgate Mercantile Co Ltd v Twitchings* [1976] QB 225, [1975] 3 All ER 314 and *Crabb v Arun District Council* [1976] Ch 179 at 188, [1976] 3 All ER 865 at 871. Applying those principles here it can be seen that the assurances given by Kenneth and Hedley to Doris Cooke — leading her to believe that she would be allowed to stay in the house as long as she wished — raised an equity in her favour. There was no need for her to prove that she acted on the faith of those assurances. It is to be presumed that she did so. There is no need for her to prove that she acted to her detriment or to her prejudice. Suffice it that she stayed on the house — looking after Kenneth and Clarice — when otherwise she might have left and

---

[4] Similarly for the requirement of reliance where there is a material representation to another to induce him to enter into a contract: *Redgrave v Hurd* (1881) 20 Ch D 1 at 21, per JESSEL MR.

got a job elsewhere. The equity having thus been raised in her favour, it is for the courts of equity to decide in what way that equity should be satisfied. In this case it should be by allowing her to stay on in the house as long as she wishes."

DUNN LJ said at 1313, at 715:

"There is no doubt that for proprietary estoppel to arise the person claiming must have incurred expenditure or otherwise have prejudiced himself or acted to his detriment. The only question before us is as to the burden of proof of the detriment. The judge thought that the onus lay on the claimant to prove it. I agree that in that he fell into error for the reasons given by Lord Denning MR, and I also would allow this appeal."

In *Watts v Story* [1983] CA Transcript 319, the Court of Appeal (DUNN and SLADE LJJ) held that an action for possession succeeded against a grandson aged 30 who had not shown "that when the benefits derived by him from his rent free occupation of Apple House, Woodborough, Nottingham (owned by his grandmother whose mind was 'as sharp as a razor') are set against any detriments suffered by him as a result of making the move from his Rent Act protected flat in Leeds, he has on balance suffered any detriment in financial or material terms."

DUNN LJ said:

"There was some discussion at the Bar as to what Lord Denning MR meant in the passage which I have cited from *Greasley v Cooke* [1980] 1 WLR 1306, [1980] 3 All ER 710. In that case there was no doubt on the evidence that Miss Cooke had been given assurances by the Greasley family that she could regard the property as her home for the rest of her life. Equally, there was no doubt on the facts that she had suffered a detriment, because she had devoted her life to looking after the Greasley family without payment instead of getting a paid job. The only question in the case was whether that admitted detriment was caused by the assurances, or whether she would have continued to look after the family anyway because she was fond of Kenneth Greasley. The judge held that the onus was on her to prove that the detriment was caused by the assurances and that she had failed to discharge the burden of proof. That is clear from, in particular, the judgment of Waller LJ at 1312, at 714. It is in that context that the words of Lord Denning cited by the judge in this case should be read. . . .

Lord Denning was not saying that there was no need for detriment in order to establish proprietary estoppel. On the facts of the case detriment spoke for itself, and was admitted. All that Lord Denning was saying was that, the assurances having been established, there was no need for Doris Cooke to prove that the obvious detriment had resulted from them.

The law is well stated in Snell's Principles of Equity (28th Edition) at page 561 in the following passage: 'Once it is shown that O gave assurances or other encouragement to A, and A suffers detriment, it will readily be inferred that the detriment was suffered as a result of the encouragement; the burden of proof is on O to show that A's conduct was not induced by the assurances.'

Nor, if that passage from Lord Denning's judgment is read as a whole, was he stating any new proposition of law. As the judge said, it matters not whether one talks in terms of detriment or whether one talks in terms of it being unjust or inequitable for the party giving the assurance to go back on it. It is difficult to envisage circumstances in which it would be inequitable for the party giving an assurance alleged to give rise to a proprietary estoppel, i.e., an estoppel concerned with the positive acquisition of rights and interests in the land of another, unless the person to whom the assurance was given had suffered some prejudice or detriment."

B.   Satisfaction of the Equity

Snell's Principles of Equity (28th edn, 1982), pp. 562–563

"If the equity is established, effect is given to it in whatever is the most appropriate way[5]. Often it suffices merely to dismiss an action brought by O to enforce his legal rights. Thus a claim for possession may be dismissed[6] or a claim to enforce a mortgage may be restrained[7]. Similarly, where O and A are trustees for sale, O's application to have the trust executed may be refused[8]. In such cases the equity is given effect as a defence like any other estoppel. Often, however, more positive action is required[9].

(1) INJUNCTIONS.   O may be restrained by injunction from interfering with possession of land[10], or from exercising a right to cut down trees and so destroy the beauty of improvements made by A in which he acquiesced[11], or from obstructing ancient lights altered by A with O's acquiescence[12]. Further, the injunction may be granted subject to an undertaking by A, e.g. to exercise compulsory powers of acquisition[13].

(2) CHARGE FOR EXPENDITURE.   A may be given an equitable lien on the property for his expenditure[14], or for the value of his improvements[15]; and in such a case he will be treated as a mortgagee in possession[16]. Alternatively, an order for possession against A may be made conditionally upon O repaying the cost of improvements effected by A[17]. Or it may appear that A has already had 'sufficient satisfaction' for his expenditure, and so is entitled to no relief[18].

(3) CONFERMENT OF TITLE.   In many cases justice cannot be done by the mere use of the doctrine by way of defence, or by the recoupment of

---

[5] See *Lord Cawdor v Lewis* (1835) 1 Y & C Ex 427 at 433; *Plimmer v Wellington Corpn* (1884) 9 App Cas 699 at 713, 714.

[6] *Forbes v Ralli* (1925) LR 52 Ind App 178; *Inwards v Baker* [1965] 2 QB 29, [1965] 1 All ER 446, p. 528, post; *Williams v Staite* [1979] Ch 291, [1978] 2 All ER 928; and see *Powell v Thomas* (1848) 6 Hare 300 (injunction restraining action for ejectment).

[7] *Steed v Whitaker* (1740) Barn Ch 220.

[8] *Jones (AE) v Jones (FW)* [1977] 1 WLR 438, [1977] 2 All ER 231, p. 532, post.

[9] *Quaere* why in *Cullen v Cullen* [1962] IR 268 the equity was held to give no more than a defence.

[10] *Duke of Devonshire v Eglin* (1851) 14 Beav 530 (obstruction of water course).

[11] *Jackson v Cator* (1800) 5 Ves 688.

[12] *Cotching v Bassett* (1862) 32 Beav 101.

[13] *Somersetshire Coal Canal Co v Harcourt* (1858) 2 De G & J 596.

[14] *Unity Joint Stock Mutual Banking Association v King* (1858) 25 Beav 72 (land); *Re Foster* [1938] 3 All ER 610 (life insurance policy): and see *Veitch v Caldicott* (1945) 173 LT 30; *Taylor v Taylor* [1956] NZLR 99; *Neesom v Clarkson* (1845) 4 Hare 97 (form of account); *Hussey v Palmer* [1972] 1 WLR 1286, [1972] 3 All ER 744, p. 504, ante (trust interest proportionate to expenditure); *sed quaere:* see (1973) 89 LQR 2.

[15] *Raffaele v Raffaele* [1962] WAR 29, discussed by D.E. Allan (1963) 79 LQR 238.

[16] *Neesom v Clarkson* (1845) 4 Hare 97.

[17] *Dodsworth v Dodsworth* (1973) 228 EG 1115, p. 548, post.

[18] *A-G v Baliol College, Oxford* (1744) 9 Mod Rep 407 at 412, per Lord HARDWICKE LC (expenditure by lessee).

expenditure, even where this is small[19], but A must be granted some right. Thus if O has made an imperfect gift of the land to A, as by merely signing an informal memorandum[20] or uttering words of abandonment[1], the court will compel O to perfect the gift by conveying the land to A[2]. In such cases the court may act by analogy with the specific performance of contracts: A's expenditure with O's knowledge plays the part both of valuable consideration and of part performance[3]. If the circumstances do not suggest a gift, O may be compelled to convey the land on being paid its unimproved value[4], or to hold the land on trust for sale, and to hold the proceeds after discharge of the respective expenditure of A and O to divide the residue between them[5]. Or the circumstances may indicate that A is to have a lease[6], a perpetual easement[7], a perpetual licence[8] or a licence as long as he desires to use the premises as his home[9] or a licence to remain until a loan is repaid[10], and a lessor may be compelled to grant a licence to assign[11]. Interests created by the doctrine are not registrable as land charges[12]."

i.   NEGATIVE PROTECTION[13]

INWARDS *v* BAKER[14]
[1965] 2 QB 29, [1965] 1 All ER 446 (CA, Lord DENNING MR, DANCKWERTS and SALMON LJJ)

In 1931, the younger Mr Baker wished to build a bungalow for himself on land which he hoped to purchase, but the project was beyond his means. His father said "Why not put the bungalow on my land and make the bungalow

---

[19] See *Pascoe v Turner* [1979] 1 WLR 431 at 438, [1979] 2 All ER 945 at 951, p. 545, post.
[20] *Dillwyn v Llewelyn* (1862) 4 De GF & J 517.
[1] *Thomas v Thomas* [1956] NZLR 785 (husband and wife).
[2] *Pascoe v Turner*, supra.
[3] See *Dillwyn v Llewelyn*, supra, at 521, 522; and see Lord RUSSELL OF KILLOWEN's restrictive interpretation of *Ramsden v Dyson*, (1866) LR 1 HL 129, in *Ariff v Rai Jadunath Majumdar Bahadur* (1931) LR 58 Ind App 91 at 102, 103.
[4] *Duke of Beaufort v Patrick* (1853) 17 Beav 60.
[5] *Holiday Inns Inc v Broadhead* (1974) 232 EG 951 (proposed joint venture to build and operate hotel on O's land).
[6] *Stiles v Cowper* (1748) 3 Atk 692; *Siew Soon Wah v Yong Tong Hong* [1973] AC 836; *Griffiths v Williams* (1977) 248 EG 947, p. 550, post, and see *Gregory v Mighell* (1811) 18 Ves 328; *Ramsden v Dyson*, supra; *Taylors Fashions Ltd v Liverpool Victoria Trustees Co Ltd* [1982] QB 133n, [1981] 1 All ER 897, p. 514, ante.
[7] *Ward v Kirkland* [1967] Ch 194, [1966] 1 All ER 609; *ER Ives Investment Ltd v High* [1967] 2 QB 379, [1967] 1 All ER 504, p. 542, post; *Crabb v Arun District Council* [1976] Ch 179, [1975] 3 All ER 865, p. 536, post (where payment was considered but not imposed in the circumstances).
[8] *Plimmer v Wellington Corpn* (1884) 9 App Cas 699.
[9] *Inwards v Baker* [1965] 2 QB 29, [1965] 1 All ER 446, p. 528, post (son builds a bungalow on father's land).
[10] *Re Sharpe* [1980] 1 WLR 219, [1980] 1 All ER 198, p. 506, ante.
[11] *Willmott v Barber* (1880) 15 Ch D 96 (where the claim failed).
[12] *ER Ives Investment Ltd v High*, supra; and see J.F. Garner (1967) 31 Conv (NS) 332.
[13] (1976) 40 Conv (NS) 416 (A.M. Everton). See also *Jones v Jones* [1977] 1 WLR 438, [1977] 2 All ER 231, p. 532, post. It is not clear whether the case fits best into this category or the later one.
[14] (1965) 81 LQR 183 (R.H. Maudsley); *Ward v Kirkland* [1967] Ch 194 at 235–243, [1966] 1 All ER 609 at 621–627; *ER Ives Investment Ltd v High* [1967] 2 QB 379, [1967] 1 All ER 504; *Siew Soon Wah v Yong Tong Hong* [1973] AC 836.

a little bigger?'' The son did so, building the bungalow largely through his own labour and expense. He lived there continuously until his father's death in 1951, and also from his father's death until the proceedings began.

The land was left elsewhere in a will dated 1922, and in 1963 the trustees for sale of the land brought proceedings for possession.

Held. The son could not be disturbed.

LORD DENNING MR: The trustees say that at the most Jack Baker had a licence to be in the bungalow but that it had been revoked and he had no right to stay. The judge has held in their favour. He was referred to *Errington v Errington and Woods* [1952] 1 KB 290, [1952] 1 All ER 149, p. 496, ante but the judge held that that decision only protected a contractual licensee. He thought that, in order to be protected, the licensee must have a contract or promise by which he is entitled to be there. The judge said: "I can find no promise made by the father to the son that he should remain in the property at all — no contractual arrangement between them. True the father said that the son could live in the property, expressly or impliedly, but there is no evidence that this was arrived at as the result of a contract or promise — merely an arrangement made casually because of the relationship which existed and knowledge that the son wished to erect a bungalow for residence.'' Thereupon, the judge, with much reluctance, thought the case was not within *Errington's* case, and said the son must go.

The son appeals to this court. We have had the advantage of cases which were not cited to the county court judge, — cases in the last century, notably *Dillwyn v Llewelyn* (1862) 4 De GF & J 517, p. 547, post, and *Plimmer v Wellington Corpn* (1884) 9 App Cas 699, p. 533, post. This latter was a decision of the Privy Council which expressly affirmed and approved the statement of the law made by Lord Kingsdown in *Ramsden v Dyson* (1866) LR 1 HL 129, 170, p. 512, ante. It is quite plain from those authorities that if the owner of land requests another, or indeed allows another, to expend money on the land under an expectation created or encouraged by the landlord that he will be able to remain there, that raises an equity in the licensee such as to entitle him to stay. He has a licence coupled with an equity. Mr Goodhart urged before us that the licensee could not stay indefinitely. The principle only applied, he said, when there was an expectation of some precise legal term. But it seems to me, from *Plimmer's* case in particular, that the equity arising from the expenditure on land need not fail "merely on the ground that the interest to be secured has not been expressly indicated . . . the court must look at the circumstances in each case to decide in what way the equity can be satisfied."

So in this case, even though there is no binding contract to grant any particular interest to the licensee, nevertheless the court can look at the circumstances and see whether there is an equity arising out of the expenditure of money. All that is necessary is that the licensee should, at the request or with the encouragement of the landlord, have spent the money in the expectation of being allowed to stay there. If so, the court will not allow that expectation to be defeated where it would be inequitable so to do. In this case it is quite plain that the father allowed an expectation to be created in the son's mind that this bungalow was to be his home. It was to be his home for his life or, at all events, his home as long as he wished it to remain his home. It seems to me, in the light of that equity, that the father could not in 1932 have turned to his son and said: "You are to go. It is my land and my house." Nor could he at any time thereafter so long as the son wanted it as his home.

Mr Goodhart put the case of a purchaser. He suggested that the father could sell the land to a purchaser who could get the son out. But I think that any purchaser who took with notice would clearly be bound by the equity. So here, too, the present plaintiffs, the successors in title of the father, are clearly themselves bound by this equity. It is an equity well recognised in law. It arises from the expenditure of money by a person in actual occupation of land when he is led to believe that, as the result of that expenditure, he will be allowed to remain there. It is for the court to say in what way the equity can be satisfied. I am quite clear in this case it can be satisfied by holding that the defendant can remain there as long as he desires to as his home.

I would allow the appeal accordingly and enter judgment for the defendant.

DANCKWERTS LJ: I agree and I will add only a few words. It seems to me the claim of the defendant in respect of this property is amply covered by *Errington v Errington and Woods, Dillwyn v Llewelyn,* and *Plimmer v Wellington Corpn.* Further, it seems to me to be supported by the observations of Lord Kingsdown in *Ramsden v Dyson.* It is true that in that case Lord Kingsdown reached a result on the facts of the case which differed from that reached by the other members of the House of Lords, but Lord Kingsdown's observations which are relevant in the present case have received support since that case was decided; and, in particular, I would like to refer to the observations in the judgment of the Privy Council in *Plimmer v Wellington Corpn.* It is said there (1884) 9 App Cas 699 at 713: "Their Lordships consider that this case falls within the principle stated by Lord Kingsdown as to expectations created or encouraged by the landlord, with the addition that in this case the landlord did more than encourage the expenditure, for he took the initiative in requesting it."

There are similar circumstances in the present case. The defendant was induced to give up his project of building a bungalow on land belonging to somebody else other than his father, in which case he would have become the owner or tenant of the land in question and thus have his own home. His father induced him to build on his, the father's, land and expenditure was made by the defendant for the purpose of the erection of the bungalow.

In my view the case comes plainly within the proposition stated in the cases. It is not necessary, I think, to imply a promise. It seems to me that this is one of the cases of an equity created by estoppel, or equitable estoppel, as it is sometimes called, by which the person who has made the expenditure is induced by the expectation of obtaining protection, and equity protects him so that an injustice may not be perpetrated.

I am clearly of opinion that the appeal should be allowed and judgment should be entered for the defendant.

In *Hopgood v Brown*[15] [1955] 1 WLR 213, [1955] 1 All ER 550, adjoining plots of land (here called plots A and B) were conveyed to a purchaser in 1932 by separate conveyances. The common boundary was not precisely

[15] *Penfold and Penfold v Cooke* (1978) NLJ 736, not following *Hopgood v Brown* because there was no sufficient reason, on the facts, to raise the equity.

indicated, reference being made in each conveyance to a plan "for the purpose of facilitating identification only". Both plots were later sold, B to the defendant, and A, to the North of it, to a company of which the defendant was a director. The defendant engaged the company to build a bungalow and a garage on his plot, which, in accordance with plans agreed with the company, encroached on plot A beyond the line which would form the boundary between these plots if the boundary between them were a line drawn parallel to their other lateral boundaries. When the garage had been built, it gave the appearance of forming the boundary, but, if the boundary were such a parallel line, it covered also a wedge shaped area belonging to plot A. Plot A was sold to one Lester in April 1952 and by him to the plaintiff, in November 1952, and these conveyances described the plot in the same terms as the conveyance of 1932 had done. The plaintiff began to build a bungalow on plot A, and, after the building had reached an advanced stage, he discovered that it was not possible for a car to pass between his bungalow and the southern boundary of his plot because of the encroachment made by the defendant's garage.

The plaintiff sought to eject the defendant from the encroachment, and to require him to remove the garage, and damages.

The Court of Appeal (Lord EVERSHED MR, JENKINS and MORRIS LJJ) held that the defendant was entitled to remain. Lord EVERSHED MR said at 224, at 559:

"In my judgment, there was, beyond a peradventure, a representation by the company to the defendant which has all the qualities which Mr Spencer Bower[16] enumerated, and which had, therefore, all its consequences. In effect, and by way of paraphrase only, the defendant was saying to his northern neighbour, the company: 'Our boundary shown on the small plan has never been marked out on the land. I want to build a bungalow and garage. I have made plans, and I believe that the boundary goes as it is shown on my plans. I want to build accordingly. It may be that I shall take a little bit of your land or that you will take a little bit of mine, or both, but do you assent to the boundary being so assumed and fixed?' and the company said: 'Yes. What is more, we will assist you to carry out your purpose and build for you at your cost your house and garage' . . . . Is it really suggested (for this must, I think, follow from an argument to the contrary) that the company, having assented to what had been proposed, having participated in what followed, and having taken the sum of £2,200 from the defendant for building the garage and his house in the places which he had identified, could tell the defendant next day that they had now measured the plot more accurately, and that he must take down that part of the garage which encroached upon the company's land, and which they had just built at his entire expense? It seems to me that such a suggestion would, indeed, shock common sense and be contrary to the realities of the case.

If that is right, the only other question is whether the disability on the company's part from averring the boundary to be in any place other than that where they, with the defendant, had put it, is equally binding on the plaintiff. In my judgment, that can also be answered in favour of the defendant; and I accept the passage which Mr Holdsworth [counsel for the

---

[16] Spencer Bower, *The Law Relating to Estoppel by Representation* (1923), pp. 9–10; (3rd edn, 1977), pp. 4–6.

defendant] read from the judgment of Mansfield CJ in *Taylor v Needham* (1810) 2 Taunt 278. That was a case of estoppel between lessor and lessee, but the principle is the same. Mansfield CJ said at 282: 'Then the question comes, whether the assignee of the lease may be allowed to controvert the title of the lessor, when the lessee, under whom he derives, could not controvert the title of the lessor; so that the assignee should have a better right than he from whom he derives it. Exclusive of all the dicta, it would be a very odd thing in the law of any country, if A could take, by any form of conveyance, a greater or better right than he had who conveys it to him; it would be contrary to all principle. But it does not rest merely on the general principle; for if you look into all the books upon estoppel, you find it laid down that parties and privies are estopped, and he who takes an estate under a deed, is privy in estate, and therefore never can be in a better situation than he from whom he takes it.' My conclusion, therefore, is that Mr Lester has failed to satisfy me that there are any good grounds for differing from the judge's decision.''

Jones (AE) v Jones (FW) [1977] 1 WLR 438, [1977] 2 All ER 231[17] is difficult to classify. The Court of Appeal avoided a decision on the question whether the defendant should be given a life interest. He already owned $\frac{1}{4}$ share as tenant in common. In that case, Mr Jones encouraged his son Frederick to move from Kingston-upon-Thames to Blundeston in Suffolk in order to have the family closer. He purchased a house there for £4,000. Frederick gave up his job at Kingston, moved to the house at Blundeston, and paid £1,000 to his father. He paid the rates, but no rent.

The father's will, made before these circumstances took place, left his residuary estate to his second wife, Alice, stepmother to Frederick. She unsuccessfully attempted to evict Frederick, and that litigation established that Frederick owned a 25% interest in the house by reason of the money paid, and that Alice owned 75%. Alice now sued for rent, to be calculated on the basis of 75% of the market rental. This claim failed, on the ground that one tenant in common is not entitled to claim rent from another. The Court of Appeal held that Frederick was entitled, as against his co-tenant in common, to remain in possession of the house rent free for the rest of his life. Lord DENNING MR said at 442, at 235:

"Second, the order for sale. Here comes into play the doctrine of proprietary estoppel. It has been considered by this court in *Inwards v Baker* [1965] 2 QB 29, [1965] 1 All ER 446, p. 528, ante and *Crabb v Arun District Council* [1976] Ch 179, [1975] 3 All ER 865, p. 536, post. It is quite plain that the principles of those cases apply here.

Old Mr Jones' conduct was such as to lead his son Frederick reasonably to believe that he could stay there and regard Philmona as his home for the rest of his life. On the basis of that reasonable expectation, the son gave up his work at Kingston-upon-Thames and moved to Blundeston. He paid the £1,000 too in the same expectation. He did work on the house as well. It was all because he had been led to believe that his father would never turn him out of the house: it would be his family's home for the rest of his life. He and the rest of the family thought that the father would alter his will or make over

---

[17] (1977) 41 Conv (NS) 279 (F.R. Crane); (1978) 41 MLR 208 (J. Alder).

the house to the son. The father did not do it, but nevertheless he led the son to believe that he could stay there for the rest of his life. On those two cases it is clear that old Mr Jones would be estopped from turning the son out. After his death the plaintiff is equally estopped from turning the defendant out.

Similarly, the plaintiff is not entitled to an order for the property to be sold. Nor for any payment to be made by Frederick to her pending sale. Even though there is an implied trust for sale, nevertheless, the courts will not allow it to be used so as to defeat the purposes contemplated by the parties. That appears from *Bedson v Bedson* [1965] 2 QB 666, [1965] 3 All ER 307: see what I said at 679, at 312, and per Russell LJ at 697 and 698, at 324. No order for the sale of this property should be made because that would defeat the very purpose of the acquisition, namely that the son Frederick would be able to be there for his life and remain in it as his home.

The two doctrines go hand in hand to show that no order should be made so as to disturb the son in his possession of the house: nor should he be made to pay anything for staying there.

The ultimate result of the case is that the son has a proprietary interest of a one-quarter share in the house. He is able to stay there for life by virtue of his interest in it, and the plaintiff is estopped from turning him out. Nor can it be sold without his consent. The appeal should be allowed and an order made accordingly."

ROSKILL LJ said at 443, at 237:

"I would mention one other thing. It was suggested by Mr Sunnucks that if we took the view which we do we ought to order a life interest to be created in favour of the defendant. In my judgment, at this stage it would be wrong so to do. This does not seem to have been the subject of argument below, and it seems to me that the defendant's real case was that he should not pay the rent, and not to seek the creation of a life interest."

ii. ACQUISITION OF PROPRIETARY INTERESTS

(a) *Acquisition of Interest for Purposes of Statute*

PLIMMER *v* WELLINGTON CORPORATION[18]
(1884) 9 App Cas 699 (PC, Lord WATSON, Sir Barnes PEACOCK, Sir Robert P COLLIER, Sir Richard COUCH and Sir Arthur HOBHOUSE)

Plimmer moored an old hulk on the foreshore of Wellington Bay and used it as a wharf and store by permission of the Crown. An earthquake raised the level of the land and necessitated the building of a jetty, which Plimmer built. Between 1856 and 1861, at the instance of the Provincial Government, Plimmer extended the jetty. Subsequently the Government took possession of the jetty under statutory powers, and Plimmer and another claimed compensation under the Public Works Loans Act 1882 under which any person who "had any estate or interest in, to or out of the lands . . . vested in the Corporation . . . shall be entitled to . . . compensation".

---

[18] Cf. *DHN Food Distributors Ltd v Tower Hamlets London Borough Council* [1976] 1 WLR 852, [1976] 3 All ER 462, p. 494, ante (a case of a contractual licence). See also *Pennine Raceway Ltd v Kirklees Metropolitan Council* [1983] QB 382, [1982] 3 All ER 628, where a licensee of land was held entitled to compensation under TCPA 1971, s. 164 as a person "interested in the land" on withdrawal of planning permission; [1982] All ER Rev 173 (P.J. Clarke).

Held. The equitable right so acquired is an "estate or interest in, to or out of land" within the meaning of the Act of 1882.

SIR ARTHUR HOBHOUSE: The law relating to cases of this kind may be taken as stated by Lord Kingsdown in the case of *Ramsden v Dyson* (1866) LR 1 HL 129. The passage is at 170: "If a man, under a verbal agreement with a landlord for a certain interest in land, or, what amounts to the same thing, under an expectation created or encouraged by the landlord that he shall have a certain interest, takes possession of such land with the consent of the landlord, and upon the faith of such promise or expectation, with the knowledge of the landlord and without objection by him, lays out money upon land, a Court of Equity will compel the landlord to give effect to such promise or expectation. This was the principle of the decision in *Gregory v Mighell* (1811) 18 Ves 328, and, as I conceive, is open to no doubt. If at the hearing of the cause there appears to be such uncertainty as to the particular terms of the contract as might prevent a Court of Equity from giving relief if the contract had been in writing but there had been no expenditure, a Court of Equity will nevertheless, in the case which is above stated, interfere in order to prevent fraud, though there has been a difference of opinion amongst great judges as to the nature of the relief to be granted. Lord Thurlow seems to have thought that the Court would ascertain the terms by reference to the Master, and if they could not be ascertained would itself fix reasonable terms. Lord Alvanley and Lord Redesdale, and perhaps Lord Eldon, thought this was going too far; but I do not understand any doubt to have been entertained by any of them that, either in the form of a specific interest in the land, or in the shape of compensation for the expenditure, a Court of Equity would give relief, and protect in the meantime the possession of the tenant. If, on the other hand, a tenant being in possession of land, and knowing the nature and extent of his interest, lays out money upon it in the hope or expectation of an extended term or an allowance for expenditure, then, if such hope or expectation has not been created or encouraged by the landlord, the tenant has no claim which any Court of Law or Equity can enforce. This was the principle of the decision in *Pilling v Armitage* (1805) 12 Ves 78, and, like the decision in *Gregory v Mighell*, seems founded on plain rules of reason and justice. . . ."

In the present case, the equity is not claimed because the landowner has stood by in silence while his tenant has spent money on his land. This is a case in which the landowner has, for his own purposes, requested the tenant to make the improvements. The Government were engaged in the important work of introducing immigrants into the colony. For some reason, not now apparent, they were not prepared to make landing-places of their own, and in fact they did not do so until the year 1863. So they applied to John Plimmer to make his landing-place more commodious by a substantial extension of his jetty and the erection of a warehouse for baggage. Is it to be said that, when he had incurred the expense of doing the work asked for, the Government could turn round and revoke his licence at their will? Could they in July, 1856, have deprived him summarily of the use of the jetty? It would be in a high degree unjust that they should do so, and that the parties should have intended such a result is, in the absence of evidence, incredible. . . .

Their Lordships will not be the first to hold, and no authority has been cited to them to shew that after such a landowner has requested such a tenant to incur expense on his land for his benefit, he can without more and at his own will take away the property so improved. Their Lordships consider that this case falls within the principle stated by Lord Kingsdown as to expectations created or encouraged by the landlord, with the addition that in this case the landlord did more than encourage the expenditure, for he took the initiative in requesting it. . . .

The question still remains as to the extent of interest which Plimmer acquired by his expenditure in 1856. Referring again to the passage quoted from Lord Kingsdown's judgment, there is good authority for saying what appears to their Lordships to be quite sound in principle, that the equity arising from expenditure on land need not fail merely on the ground that the interest to be secured has not been expressly indicated.

In such a case as *Ramsden v Dyson*, the evidence (according to Lord Kingsdown's view) shewed that the tenant expected a particular kind of lease, which Vice-Chancellor Stuart decreed to him, though it does not appear what form of relief Lord Kingsdown himself would have given. In such a case as the *Duke of Beaufort v Patrick* (1853) 17 Beav 60, nothing but perpetual retention of the land would satisfy the equity raised in favour of those who spent their money on it, and it was secured to them at a valuation. In such a case as *Dillwyn v Llewelyn* (1862) 4 De G F & J 517, nothing but a grant of the fee simple would satisfy the equity which the Lord Chancellor held to have been raised by the son's expenditure on his father's land. In such a case as that of the *Unity Joint-Stock Mutual Banking Association v King* (1858) 25 Beav 72, the Master of the Rolls, holding that the father did not intend to part with his land to his sons who built upon it, considered that their equity would be satisfied by recouping their expenditure to them. In fact, the Court must look at the circumstances in each case to decide in what way the equity can be satisfied.

In this case their Lordships feel no great difficulty. In their view, the licence given by the Government to John Plimmer, which was indefinite in point of duration but was revocable at will, became irrevocable by the transactions of 1856, because those transactions were sufficient to create in his mind a reasonable expectation that his occupation would not be disturbed; and because they and the subsquent dealings of the parties cannot be reasonably explained on any other supposition. Nothing was done to limit the use of the jetty in point of duration. The consequence is that Plimmer acquired an indefinite, that is practically a perpetual, right to the jetty for the purposes of the orginal licence, and if the ground was afterwards wanted for public purposes, it could only be taken from him by the legislature.

An analogy to this process may be found in such cases as *Winter v Brockwell* (1807) 8 East 308 and *Liggins v Inge* (1831) 7 Bing 682. These cases shew that where a landowner permits his neighbour to execute works on his (the neighbour's land), and the licence is executed, it cannot be revoked at will by the licensor. If indefinite in duration, it becomes perpetual. Their Lordships think that the same consequence must follow where the licence is to execute works on the land of the licensor, and owing to some supervening equity the licence has become irrevocable.

There are perhaps purposes for which such a licence would not be held to be an interest in land. But their Lordships are construing a statute which takes away private property for compensation, and in such statutes the expression "estate or interest in, to or out of land" should receive a wide meaning. Indeed the statute itself directs that, in ascertaining the title of anybody to compensation, the Court shall not be bound to regard strict legal rights only, but shall do what is reasonable and just. Their Lordships have no difficulty in deciding that the equitable right acquired by John Plimmer is an interest in land carrying compensation under the Acts of 1880 and 1882[19].

(b) Acquisition of Incorporeal Interest

1.   AS BETWEEN THE PARTIES

CRABB *v* ARUN DISTRICT COUNCIL
[1976] Ch 179, [1975] 3 All ER 865[20] (CA, Lord DENNING MR, LAWTON AND SCARMAN LJJ)

The plaintiff owned two acres of land. The outlet to the road was through a point of access (point A) to a lane owned by the defendants, and by a right of way over that lane in a northerly direction to the road.

He decided to divide his land into two parts, and to sell them separately. This would require another point of access to the South, together with an additional right of way over the lane, to serve the Southern part. This was negotiated with the defendants at a meeting in July 1967, at which there was an oral agreement in principle that the plaintiff should have another access at point B; but no formal agreement was signed. The defendants, in accordance with the terms of the informal agreement, fenced the boundary between their land and the plaintiff's, leaving gaps at A and B, and erected gates at these points, the gateposts being set in concrete.

The plaintiff sold the Northern part, together with the right of way and access from point A. Differences arose between the plaintiff and defendants. The defendants uprooted the gatepost at point B, continued the fence to cover the gateway, and left the Southern part of the plaintiff's land landlocked. They offered access at point B and right of way for £3,000. The action was for a declaration and injunction, claiming that the defendants were estopped by their conduct from denying the plaintiff a right of access at point B and a right of way.

Held. Rights of access and way awarded to the plaintiff without payment[1].

SCARMAN LJ: I agree that the appeal should be allowed. The plaintiff and the defendants are adjoining landowners. The plaintiff asserts that he has a right of way over the defendants' land giving access from his land to the public highway. Without this access his land is in fact landlocked, but, for reasons which clearly appear from the narration of the facts already given by my Lords, the plaintiff cannot claim a right of way by necessity. The plaintiff has no grant. He has the benefit of no enforceable contract. He has no prescriptive right. His case has to be that the defendants are estopped by their conduct from denying him a right of access over their land to the public highway. If the plaintiff has any right, it is an equity arising out of the

---

[19] Cf. *Canadian Pacific Rly Co v R* [1931] AC 414 at 428–429; *Lee-Parker v Izzet (No 2)* [1972] 1 WLR 775 at 780–781, [1972] 2 All ER 800 at 804–805.

[20] (1976) 40 Conv (NS) 156 (F.R. Crane); (1976) 92 LQR 174 (P.S. Atiyah); 342 (P.J. Millett).

[1] See *Crabb v Arun District Council (No 2)* (1976) 121 SJ 86 where C was refused an enquiry as to damages. See also *Salvation Army Trustee Co Ltd v West Yorkshire Metropolitan County Council* (1980) 41 P & CR 179 (where proprietary estoppel was extended to the *disposal* of an interest in land where the disposal was closely linked by an arrangement that also involved the acquisition of an interest in land).

conduct and relationship of the parties. In such a case I think it is now well settled law that the court, having analysed and assessed the conduct and relationship of the parties, has to answer three questions. First, is there an equity established? Secondly, what is the extent of the equity, if one is established? And, thirdly, what is the relief appropriate to satisfy the equity? See *Duke of Beaufort v Patrick* (1853) 17 Beav 60; *Plimmer v Wellington Corpn* (1884) 9 App Cas 699, p. 533, ante and *Inwards v Baker* [1965] 2 QB 29, [1965] 1 All ER 446, p. 528, ante, a decision of this court, and particularly the observations of Lord Denning MR at 37, at 448–449. Such therefore I believe to be the nature of the inquiry that the courts have to conduct in a case of this sort. In pursuit of that inquiry I do not find helpful the distinction between promissory and proprietary estoppel. This distinction may indeed be valuable to those who have to teach or expound the law; but I do not think that, in solving the particular problem raised by a particular case, putting the law into categories is of the slightest assistance.

Nor do I think it necessary in a case such as this to inquire minutely into the law of agency. These defendants could, of course, only act through agents; but, as I have already made clear, from the very nature of the case, there would be no question of grant, no question of legally enforceable contract. We are in the realm of equity; and within that realm we find that equity, to its eternal credit, has developed an immensely flexible, yet perfectly clear, doctrine: see *ER Ives Investment Ltd v High* [1967] 2 QB 379, [1967] 1 All ER 504, p. 542, post, per Danckwerts LJ at 399, at 510–511. The approach of equity, when there is a question of agency in a field such as this, must I think be a very simple one. It will merely be that, within reasonable limits, those to whom a defendant entrusts the conduct of negotiations must be treated as having the authority, which, within the course of the negotiations, they purport to exercise. I put it in that way in the light of the comments of Lord Denning MR in *Moorgate Mercantile Co Ltd v Twitchings* [1976] QB 225 at 243, [1975] 3 All ER 314 at 324, comments which were themselves made upon a judgment to the same effect in *Attorney-General to the Prince of Wales v Collom* [1916] 2 KB 193 at 203. I would add only one reservation to this broad proposition. The defendant, if he thinks that an agent has exceeded his instructions, can always so inform the plaintiff before the plaintiff acts to his detriment in reliance upon what the agent has said or done. If a defendant has done so, the plaintiff cannot then establish the equity: for the defendant will have intervened to prevent him acting to his detriment. Nothing of that sort happened in this case. After the meeting in July 1967, to which both my Lords have referred, the plaintiff was left to form his own conclusions as to the intentions of the defendants.

I come now to consider the first of the three questions which I think in a case such as this the court have to consider. What is needed to establish an equity? In the course of an interesting addition to his submissions this morning, Mr Lightman cited *Ramsden v Dyson* (1886) LR 1 HL 129, 142, to support his proposition that in order to establish an equity by estoppel there must be a belief by the plaintiff in the existence of a right created or encouraged by the words or actions of the defendant. With respect, I do not think that that is today a correct statement of the law. I think the law has developed so that today it is to be considered as correctly stated by Lord Kingsdown in his dissenting speech in *Ramsden v Dyson*. Like Lord Denning MR, I think that the point of dissent in *Ramsden v Dyson* was not on the law but on the facts. Lord Kingsdown's speech, in so far as it dealt with propositions of law, has been often considered, and recently followed by this court in *Inwards v Baker*. So what is the effect of looking to Lord Kingsdown's speech for a statement of the law? Lord Kingsdown said, LR 1 HL 129, 170:

"The rule of law applicable to the case appears to me to be this: If a man, under a verbal agreement with a landlord for a certain interest in land, or, what amounts to the same thing, *under an expectation, created or encouraged by the landlord,"* — my italics — "that he shall have a certain interest, takes possession of such land, with the consent of the landlord, and upon the faith of such promise or expectation, with the knowledge of the landlord, and without objection by him, lays out money upon the land, a court of equity will compel the landlord to give effect to such promise or expectation."

That statement of the law is put into the language of landlord and tenant because it was a landlord and tenant situation with which Lord Kingsdown was concerned; but it has been accepted as of general application. While *Ramsden v Dyson* may properly be considered as the modern starting-point of the law of equitable estoppel, it was analysed and spelt out in a judgment of Fry J in 1880 in *Willmott v Barber* (1880) 15 ChD 96, a decision to which Pennycuick V-C referred in his judgment. I agree with Pennycuick V-C in thinking that the passage from Fry J's judgment, from p. 105, is a valuable guide as to the matters of fact which have to be established in order that a plaintiff may establish this particular equity. Moreover, Mr Lightman for the defendants sought to make a submission in reliance upon the judgment. Fry J said, at 105–106:

"It has been said that the acquiescence which will deprive a man of his legal rights must amount to fraud, and in my view that is an abbreviated statement of a very true proposition. A man is not to be deprived of his legal rights unless he has acted in such a way as would make it fraudulent for him to set up those rights. What, then, are the elements or requisites necessary to constitute fraud of that description? In the first place the plaintiff must have made a mistake as to his legal rights[2]. Secondly, the plaintiff must have expended some money or must have done some act (not necessarily upon the defendant's land) on the faith of his mistaken belief. Thirdly, the defendant, the possessor of the legal right, must know of the existence of his own right which is inconsistent with the right claimed by the plaintiff. If he does not know of it he is in the same position as the plaintiff, and the doctrine of acquiescence is founded upon conduct with a knowledge of your legal right. Fourthly, the defendant, the possessor of the legal rights, must know of the plaintiff's mistaken belief of his rights[3]. If he does not, there is nothing which calls upon him to assert his own rights. Lastly," — if I may digress, this is the important element as far as this appeal is concerned — "the defendant, the possessor of the legal right, must have encouraged the plaintiff in his expenditure of money or in the other acts which he has done, either directly or by abstaining from asserting his legal right."

Mr Lightman, in the course of an interesting and vigorous submission, drew the attention of the court to the necessity of finding something akin to

---

[2] In *E & L Berg Homes Ltd v Grey* (1979) 253 EG 473, the plaintiff failed because he was unable to satisfy this requirement. See also *Gloucestershire County Council v Farrow* [1983] 2 All ER 1031.
[3] Though this was said not to be essential in *Taylor Fashions Ltd v Liverpool Victoria Friendly Society* [1982] QB 133n at 147–148; [1981] 1 All ER 897 at 911–912, p. 514, ante.

fraud before the equity sought by the plaintiff could be established. "Fraud" was a word often in the mouths of those robust judges who adorned the bench in the 19th century. It is less often in the mouths of the more wary judicial spirits today who sit upon the bench. But it is clear that whether one uses the word "fraud" or not, the plaintiff has to establish as a fact that the defendant, by setting up his right, is taking advantage of him in a way which is unconscionable, inequitable or unjust. It is to be observed from the passage that I have quoted from the judgment of Fry J that the fraud or injustice alleged does not take place during the course of negotiation, but only when the defendant decides to refuse to allow the plaintiff to set up his claim against the defendants' undoubted right. The fraud, if it be such, arises after the event, when the defendant seeks by relying on his right to defeat the expectation which he by his conduct encouraged the plaintiff to have. There need not be anything fraudulent or unjust in the conduct of the actual negotiations — the conduct of the transaction by the defendants.

The court therefore cannot find an equity established unless it is prepared to go as far as to say that it would be unconscionable and unjust to allow the defendants to set up their undoubted rights against the claim being made by the plaintiff. In order to reach a conclusion upon that matter the court does have to consider the history of the negotiations under the five headings to which Fry J referred. I need not at this stage weary anyone with an elaborate statement of the facts. I have no doubt upon the facts of this case that the first four elements referred to by Fry J exist. The question before the judge and now in this court is whether the fifth element is present: have the defendants, as possessor of the legal right, encouraged the plaintiff in the expenditure of money or in the other acts which he has done, either directly or by abstaining from asserting their legal rights? The first matter to be considered is the meeting on site of 26 July 1967. Pennycuick V-C made a finding of fact about the meeting; and for myself I am not prepared to dissent from his finding. But the substance of the finding of fact has to be regarded; not its phrasing. One must not be misled by words or phrases into mis-construing the nature of the finding. Pennycuick V-C found there was no definite assurance given by the defendants' representative to the plaintiff and his architect.

[His Lordship summarised the evidence and continued:]

That was a finding that there was acceptance in principle that there should be access and a right of way over the defendants' land at point B; and I am content to go no further and to base my judgment on what I believe to be that finding of Pennycuick V-C. Clearly the plaintiff and Mr Alford came away from that meeting in the confident expectation that a right would in due course be accorded to the plaintiff. Mr Alford did foresee "further processes." Of course, there would be further processes. The nature of the legal right to be granted had to be determined. It might be given by way of licence. It might be granted by way of easement. Conditions might be imposed. Payment of a sum of money might be required. But those two men, the plaintiff and his architect, came away from the meeting in the confident expectation that such a right would be granted upon reasonable conditions. What happened? By August — a month or less, after the meeting — posts for a fence were already on the ground, though not erected. There was already an indication, at about that time, I think — if not then, certainly soon after — of the presence of a gap at point B, that being the point of access agreed in principle. During the later months of 1967 nothing relevant transpired in the conduct of the negotiations between the plaintiff and the defendants. I accept Mr Lightman's submission that relationship as well as conduct is relevant: but during this period their relationship did not develop at all. They remained adjoining landowners, one of whom had agreed in principle at a meeting upon the site that there should be a right of way from point B over his land to the public road. Yet, things were happening. In the later months of 1967 the defendants, who were the local authority, were busy developing on neighbouring land, which the plaintiff's predecessor in title had sold them, a council housing estate. Lorries were being used for carting building materials, removing debris and so forth; and these lorries were in fact going upon the land of the plaintiff. Unfortunately materials on the land, the property of the plaintiff, were being pilfered. And so there came a meeting in January 1968, the point of which was to draw the attention of the defendants' officers to the situation which was developing. By the time the meeting took place the fence, which the defendants were obliged under the conveyance of their estate to erect between their land and the plaintiff's land, was substantially in position with gaps at point A, the access to the northern land, and at point B, the access in dispute. Nobody on behalf of the defendants gave the slightest indication to the plaintiff and his representatives at that meeting that there was going to be any difficulty or was likely to be any difficulty about access at point B. The confident expectation with which the plaintiff and Mr Alford left the meeting in July remained remarkably undisturbed by the meeting of January 1968. Indeed it was reinforced because there on the ground, plain for all to see, was a fence with gaps which accorded exactly with the agreement in principle reached in the previous July. Ten days later the defendants ordered gates, and by March the gates were installed. I ask myself: as at March 1968 had these defendants encouraged the plaintiff to think that he had or was going to be given a right? To use the language of Fry J, had they done it directly or had they done it by abstaining from asserting a legal right? Their encouragement of the belief in the mind of the plaintiff and Mr Alford was both direct and indirect. It was direct because of what they had done on the ground. It was indirect because ever since the July meeting they had abstained from giving the plaintiff or his architect any indication that they were standing on their rights, or had it in mind to go back, as, of course, they were entitled at that stage to go back, upon the agreement in principle reached at that meeting. And so matters proceeded until September 1968. By now, be it observed, over a year had passed since that first meeting when there was agreement in principle. Nothing had been done to disabuse the minds of the plaintiff and Mr Alford of the expectation reasonably induced by what the defendants' engineer then said: and there had been the direct encouragement of the gates. In September 1968, without telling the defendants or giving them any notice, so far as I am aware, the plaintiff entered into a contract to sell the northern piece of land without reservation over that land of any right of way. This was the act which was detrimental to the interests of the plaintiff. He did it in the belief that he had or could enforce a right of way and access at point B in the southern land.

One of the points taken by Mr Lightman is that the defendants had no notice of the sale, and therefore no opportunity to correct what on his case was a false belief in the mind of the plaintiff. Mr Millett in the course of his submissions conceded that he had not found in the books any case in which the sort of estoppel which we are here considering had arisen when the fact known to the defendants was an intention and not the realisation of that intention. That is, of course, what differentiates this case from one such as *E R Ives Investment Ltd v High* [1967] 2 QB 379, [1967] 1 All ER 504, p. 542, post. There the party who was found to be estopped did have notice of what the other party was doing at the time he was doing it. Therefore I think Mr Lightman rightly invites us to face this question: Does the fact that the defendants had no notice of the sale of the northern land before it was completed destroy the equity? Mr Lightman will concede, as I understand this part of his argument, no more than this: that the plaintiff might have been able to establish an equity if he had referred to the defendants before binding himself to the purchaser of the northern land: for that would have given the defendants an opportunity of disabusing the mind of the plaintiff before he acted to his detriment. The point is worthy of careful consideration. I reject it because, in my judgment, in this sort of proceedings, the court must be careful to avoid generalisation. I can conceive of cases in which it would be absolutely appropriate for a defendant to say: "But you should not have acted to your detriment until you had had a word with me and I could have put you right." But there are cases in which it is far too late for a defendant to get himself out of his pickle by putting upon the plaintiff that sort of duty; and this, in my judgment, is one of those cases. If immediately following the July meeting the clerk to the defendant authority had written saying: "I have had a report of the meeting with the assistant engineer and I must inform you that whether or not there is to be an easement or a licence is a matter which can only be decided by the council," the plaintiff would not now establish his equity: in selling the northern land without reservation of a right of way, he would have acted at his own risk. But one has to look at the whole conduct of the parties and the developing relationship between them. By September 1968, 13½ months after the initial meeting, the plaintiff must really and reasonably have been attaching importance to the abstention of the defendants from declaring to him in correspondence, or by telephone to his agent, their true position, namely, that there would be no acceptance in principle of a right until the matter had been considered by the authority itself. By that time there had been, as well, the laying out of the fence and the installing of the gates. It is for those reasons — the passage of time, the abstention and the gates — that I think the defendants cannot rely upon the fact that the plaintiff acted, without referring to the defendants, on his intention — an intention of which they had had notice ever since their agent was informed of it at the meeting in July 1967. I think therefore an equity is established.

I turn now to the other two questions — the extent of the equity and the relief needed to satisfy it. There being no grant, no enforceable contract, no licence, I would analyse the minimum equity to do justice to the plaintiff as a right either to an easement or to a licence upon terms to be agreed. I do not think it is necessary to go further than that. Of course, going that far would support the equitable remedy of injunction which is sought in this action. If there is no agreement as to terms, if agreement fails to be obtained, the court can, in my judgment, and must, determine in these proceedings upon what terms the plaintiff should be put to enable him to have the benefit of the equitable right which he is held to have. It is interesting that there has been some doubt amongst distinguished lawyers in the past as to whether the court can so proceed. Lord Kingsdown refers in fact to those doubts in a passage, which I need not quote, in *Ramsden v Dyson* (1866) LR 1 HL 129 at 171. Lord Thurlow clearly thought that the court did have this power. Other lawyers of that time did not. But there can be no doubt that since *Ramsden v Dyson* the courts have acted upon the basis that they have to determine not only the extent of the equity, but also the conditions necessary to satisfy it, and they have done so in a great number and variety of cases. I need refer only to the interesting collection of cases enumerated in *Snell's Principles of Equity,* 27th edn. (1973), at pp. 567–568, para. 2 (*b*)[4].

In the present case the court does have to consider what is necessary now in order to satisfy the plaintiff's equity. Had matters taken a different turn, I would without hesitation have said that the plaintiff should be put upon terms to be agreed if possible with the defendants, and, if not agreed, settled by the court. But, as already mentioned by Lord Denning MR and Lawton LJ, there has been a history of delay, and indeed high-handedness, which it is impossible to disregard. In January 1969 the defendants, for reasons which no doubt they thought good at the time, without consulting the plaintiff, locked up his land. They removed not only the padlocks which he had put on the gates at point B, but the gates themselves. In their place they put a fence — rendering access impossible save by breaking down the fence. I am not disposed to consider whether or not the defendants are to be blamed in moral terms for what they did. I just do not know. But the effect of their action has been to sterilise the plaintiff's land; and for the reasons which I have endeavoured to give, such action was an infringement of an equitable right possessed by the plaintiff. It has involved him in loss, which has not been measured; but, since it amounted to sterilisation of an industrial estate for a very considerable period of time, it must surpass any sort of sum of money which the plaintiff ought reasonably, before it was done, to have paid the defendants in order to obtain an enforceable legal right. I think therefore that nothing should now be paid by the plaintiff and that he should receive at the hands of the court the belated protection of the equity that he has established. Reasonable terms, other than money payment, should be agreed: or, if not agreed, determined by the court.

For those reasons I also would allow the appeal.

2.   AS AGAINST A PURCHASER. THE PROBLEM OF NOTICE

E R IVES INVESTMENT LTD *v* HIGH[5]
[1967] 2 QB 379, [1967] 1 All ER 504 (CA, LORD DENNING MR, DANCKWERTS and WINN LJJ)

In 1949, the defendant, High, began to build a house on a plot of land. Soon after, Westgate, his neighbour, started to erect a block of flats in such a way that their foundations encroached by about one foot upon the defendant's land. The defendant and Westgate agreed that the foundations could remain, and that the defendant should have a right of way for his car across Westgate's yard. The agreement for the right of way was never registered.

---

[4] See now 28th edn. (1982), pp. 562–563, p. 527, ante.
[5] *Montague v Long* (1972) 24 P & CR 240.

Westgate sold the block to Flt.-Lt. and Mrs Wright who knew of the agreement, and also knew that in 1959 the defendant erected a garage so sited that it could only be approached across the yard. In 1960, the defendant contributed to the surfacing of the yard.

In 1962 the Wrights sold the flats to the plaintiffs, expressly subject to the right of way. The plaintiffs sued the defendant for trespass to the yard, claiming that the defendant had no legal right of way, and that if he was entitled to an equitable easement, it was void against them because it was not registered.

Held. The defendant was entitled to use the way across the yard.

LORD DENNING MR: One thing is quite clear. Apart from this point about the Land Charges Act 1925, Mr High would have in equity a good right of way across the yard. This right arises in two ways:

1. *Mutual benefit and burden.* The right arises out of the agreement of 2 November 1949, and the subsequent action taken on it: on the principle that "he who takes the benefit must accept the burden." When adjoining owners of land make an agreement to secure continuing rights and benefits for each of them in or over the land of the other, neither of them can take the benefit of the agreement and throw over the burden of it. This applies not only to the original parties, but also to their successors. The successor who takes the continuing benefit must take it subject to the continuing burden. This principle has been applied to neighbours who send their water into a common drainage system: see *Hopgood v Brown* [1955] 1 WLR 213, [1955] 1 All ER 550, p. 530, ante, and to purchasers of houses on a building estate who had the benefit of using the roads and were subject to the burden of contributing to the upkeep: see *Halsall v Brizell* [1957] Ch 169, [1957] 1 All ER 371, p. 757, post. The principle clearly applies in the present case. The owners of the block of flats have the benefit of having their foundations in Mr High's land. So long as they take that benefit, they must shoulder the burden. They must observe the condition on which the benefit was granted, namely, they must allow Mr High and his successors to have access over their yard: cf. *May v Belleville* [1905] 2 Ch 605. Conversely, so long as Mr High takes the benefit of the access, he must permit the block of flats to keep their foundations in his land.

2. *Equity arising out of acquiescence.* The right arises out of the expense incurred by Mr High in building his garage, as it is now, with access only over the yard: and the Wrights standing by and acquiescing in it, knowing that he believed he had a right of way over the yard. By so doing the Wrights created in Mr High's mind reasonable expectation that his access over the yard would not be disturbed. That gives rise to an "equity arising out of acquiescence." It is available not only against the Wrights but also their successors in title. The court will not allow that expectation to be defeated when it would be inequitable so to do. It is for the court in each case to decide in what way the equity can be satisfied: see *Inwards v Baker* [1965] 2 QB 29, [1965] 1 All ER 446, p. 524, ante; *Ward v Kirkland* [1967] Ch 194, [1966] 1 All ER 609 and the cases cited therein. In this case it could only be satisfied by allowing Mr High and his successors to have access over the yard so long as the block of flats has its foundations in his land.

The next question is this: was that right a land charge such as to need registration under the Land Charges Act 1925? For if it was a land charge, it was never registered and would be void as against any purchaser: see section

13 of the Act[6]. It would, therefore, be void against the plaintiffs, even though they took with the most express knowledge and notice of the right.

It was suggested that the agreement of 2 November 1949, was "an estate contract" within Class C (iv). I do not think so. There was no contract by Mr Westgate to convey a legal estate of any kind.

It was next suggested that the right was an "equitable easement" within Class D (iii). This class is defined as "any easement right or privilege over or affecting land created or arising after the commencement of this Act, and being merely an equitable interest." Those words are almost identical with section 2 (3) (iii) of the Law of Property Act 1925, and should be given the same meaning. They must be read in conjunction with sections 1 (2) (*a*), 1 (3) and 4 (1) of the Law of Property Act 1925. It then appears that an "equitable easement" is a proprietary interest in land such as would before 1926 have been recognised as capable of being conveyed or created *at law*, but which since 1926 only takes effect as an equitable interest. An instance of such a proprietary interest is a profit à prendre for life. It does not include a right to possession by a requisitioning authority: see *Lewisham Borough Council v Maloney* [1948] 1 KB 50, [1947] 2 All ER 36. Nor does it include a right, liberty or privilege arising in equity by reason of "mutual benefit and burden," or arising out of "acquiescence," or by reason of a contractual licence: because none of those before 1926 were proprietary interests such as were capable of being conveyed or created *at law*. They only subsisted *in equity*. They do not need to be registered as land charges, so as to bind successors, but take effect in equity without registration: see an article by Mr C. V. Davidge on "Equitable Easements" in (1937) 53 Law Quarterly Review, p. 259 and by Professor H. W. R. Wade in [1956] Cambridge Law Journal, pp. 225–226[7].

The right of Mr High to cross this yard was not a right such as could ever have been created or conveyed at law. It subsisted only in equity. It therefore still subsists in equity without being registered. Any other view would enable the owners of the flats to perpetrate the grossest injustice. They could block up Mr High's access to the garage, whilst keeping their foundations in his land. That cannot be right.

I am confirmed in this construction of the statute when I remember that there are many houses adjoining one another which have drainage systems in common, with mutual benefits and burdens. The statute cannot have required all these to be registered as land charges.

I know that this greatly restricts the scope of Class D (iii) but this is not disturbing[8]. A special committee has already suggested that Class D (iii) should be abolished altogether: see the report of the Committee on Land Charges ((1956) Command Paper 9825, para. 16)[9].

---

[6] Now LCA 1972, s. 2 (6).

[7] P. 32, ante; p. 577, post.

[8] See *Shiloh Spinners Ltd v Harding* [1973] AC 691 at 719–721, [1973] 1 All ER 90 at 98–99, p. 34, ante.

[9] P. 577, n. 5, post.

(c) Acquisition of Fee Simple Estate

PASCOE *v* TURNER[10]
[1979] 1 WLR 431, [1979] 2 All ER 945 (CA, ORR, LAWTON and
CUMMING-BRUCE LJJ)

The plaintiff and defendant lived together in the plaintiff's home. Later, the
plaintiff purchased another house and they moved in. He told the defendant
that the house was hers, and everything in it. In reliance on this gratuitous
promise, she expended, to the plaintiff's knowledge, her own money on
repairs, improvements and redecoration; and also on furniture.

Later, when the relationship ended, the plaintiff gave to the defendant two
month's notice to determine the licence.

Held. The defendant occupied the house as a licensee. There was a gift of
the contents, but no valid gift or declaration of trust of the house. But an
estoppel operated in her favour, and this could most properly be satisfied by
a conveyance of the house to the defendant.

CUMMING-BRUCE LJ:

The issues

The appeal raises three issues about the house: (*a*) Did the defendant prove
the trust found by the judge? (*b*) Did she prove such facts as prevented the
plaintiff by estoppel from asserting his legal title? (*c*) If the answer to that
question is yes, what is the equitable relief to which she is entitled? In respect
of the contents of the house, did the defendant prove that they were given to
her by the plaintiff's voluntary gift? . . . .

The judge found that the plaintiff had made a gift to her of the contents of
the house. I have no doubt that he was right about that. She was already in
possession of them as a bailee when he declared the gift. Counsel for the
plaintiff submitted that there was no gift because it was uncertain what he
was giving her. He pointed to a safe and to the defendant's evidence that she
had sent round an orange bedroom suite to the plaintiff so that he should
have a bed to sleep on. The answer is that he gave her everything in the
house, but later, recognising his need, she gave back some bits and pieces to
him. So much for the contents.

Her rights in the realty are not quite so simply disposed of because of
section 53 and section 54 of the Law of Property Act 1925. There was nothing
in writing. The judge considered the plaintiff's declarations, and decided
that they were not enough to found an express trust. We agree. But he went
on to hold that the beneficial interest in the house had passed under a
constructive trust inferred from words and conduct of the parties. He relied
on the passage in *Snell's Principles of Equity*, 27th edn. (1973), p. 185, in which
the editors suggest a possible definition of a constructive trust. But there are
difficulties in the way. The long and short of events in 1973 is that the
plaintiff made an imperfect gift of the house. There is nothing in the facts
from which an inference of a constructive trust can be drawn. If it had not
been for section 53 of the Law of Property Act 1925 the gift of the house
would have been a perfect gift, just as the gift of the contents was a perfect

---

[10] [1979] Conv 379 (F.R. Crane); (1979) 42 MLR 574 (B. Sufrin). Cf. *Dillwyn v Llewelyn* (1862) 4
De GF & J 517.

gift. In the event it remained an imperfect gift and, as Turner LJ said in *Milroy v Lord* (1862) 4 De G F & J 264 at 274: "there is no equity in this court to perfect an imperfect gift." So matters stood in 1973, and if the facts had stopped there the defendant would have remained a licensee at will of the plaintiff.

But the facts did not stop there. On the judge's findings the defendant, having been told that the house was hers, set about improving it within and without. Outside she did not do much: a little work on the roof and an improvement which covered the way from the outside toilet to the rest of the house, putting in a new door there, and Snowcem to protect the toilet. Inside she did a good deal more. She installed gas in the kitchen with a cooker, improved the plumbing in the kitchen and put in a new sink. She got new gas fires, putting a gas fire in the lounge. She redecorated four rooms. The fitted carpets she put in the bedrooms, the stair carpeting, and the curtains and the furniture that she bought are not part of the realty, and it is not clear how much she spent on those items. But they are part of the whole circumstances. There she was, on her own after he left her in 1973. She had £1,000 left of her capital, and a pension of some kind. Having as she thought been given the house, she set about it as described. On the repairs and improvement to the realty and its fixtures she spent about £230. She had £300 of her capital left by the date of the trial, but she did not establish in evidence how much had been expended on refurbishing the house with carpets, curtains and furniture. We would describe the work done in and about the house as substantial in the sense that that adjective is used in the context of estoppel. All the while the plaintiff not only stood by and watched but encouraged and advised, without a word to suggest that she was putting her money and her personal labour into his house. What is the effect in equity?

The cases relied upon by the plaintiff are relevant for the purpose of showing that the judge fell into error in deciding that on the facts a constructive trust could be inferred. They are the cases which deal with the intention of the parties when a house is acquired. But of those cases only *Inwards v Baker* [1965] 2 QB 29, [1965] 1 All ER 446, p. 528, ante is in point here. For this is a case of estoppel arising from the encouragement and acquiescence of the plaintiff between 1973 and 1976 when, in reliance upon his declaration that he was giving and, later, that he had given the house to her, she spent a substantial part of her small capital upon repairs and improvements to the house. The relevant principle is expounded in *Snell's Principles of Equity*, 27th edn., p. 565 in the passage under the heading "Proprietary Estoppel," and is elaborated in *Spencer Bower and Turner, Estoppel by Representation*, 3rd edn. (1977), chapter 12 entitled "Encouragement and Acquiescence."

The cases in point illustrating that principle in relation to real property are *Dillwyn v Llewelyn* (1862) 4 De G F & J 517; *Ramsden v Dyson* (1866) LR 1 HL 129 and *Plimmer v Wellington Corpn* (1884) 9 App Cas 699. One distinction between this class of case and the doctrine which has come to be known as "promissory estoppel" is that where estoppel by encouragement or acquiescence is found on the facts, those facts give rise to a cause of action. They may be relied upon as a sword, not merely as a shield. In *Ramsden v Dyson* the plaintiff failed on the facts, and the dissent of Lord Kingsdown was upon the inferences to be drawn from the facts. On the principle, however, the House was agreed, and it is stated by Lord Cranworth LC and by Lord

Wensleydale as well as by Lord Kingsdown. Likewise in *Plimmer's* case the plaintiff was granted a declaration that he had a perpetual right of occupation.

The final question that arises is: to what relief is the defendant entitled upon her counterclaim? In *Dillwyn v Llewelyn* there was an imperfect gift of land by a father who encouraged his son to build a house on it for £14,000. Lord Westbury LC said, at 521:

"About the rules of the court there can be no controversy. A voluntary agreement will not be completed or assisted by a court of equity, in cases of mere gift. If anything be wanting to complete the title of the donee, a court of equity will not assist him in obtaining it; for a mere donee can have no right to claim more than he has received. But the subsequent acts of the donor may give the donee that right or ground of claim which he did not acquire from the original gift. Thus, if A gives a house to B, but makes no formal conveyance, and the house is afterwards, on the marriage of B, included, with the knowledge of A, in the marriage settlement of B, A would be bound to complete the title of the parties claiming under that settlement. So if A puts B in possession of a piece of land, and tells him, 'I give it to you that you may build a house on it,' and B on the strength of that promise, with the knowledge of A, expends a large sum of money in building a house accordingly, I cannot doubt that the donee acquires a right from the subsequent transaction to call on the donor to perform that contract and complete the imperfect donation which was made."

In *Plimmer's* case the Privy Council pose the question, how should the equity be satisfied? (See pp. 713, 714). And the Board declare that on the facts a licence revocable at will became irrevocable as a consequence of the subsequent transactions. So in *Thomas v Thomas* [1956] NZLR 785 the Supreme Court of New Zealand ordered the defendant to execute a proper transfer of the property.

In *Crabb v Arun District Council* [1976] Ch 179, [1975] 3 All ER 865, p. 536, ante this court had to consider the principles upon which the court should give effect to the equity: see Lord Denning MR at 189, at 872. Lawton and Scarman LJJ agreed with the remedy proposed by Lord Denning MR. On the facts of that case Scarman LJ expressed himself thus at 198–199, at 880:

[His Lordship quoted the paragraph set out on p. 541, ante, beginning "I turn now to . . ." and continued:]

So the principle to be applied is that the court should consider all the circumstances, and the counterclaimant having at law no perfected gift or licence other than a licence revocable at will, the court must decide what is the minimum equity to do justice to her having regard to the way in which she changed her position for the worse by reason of the acquiescence and encouragement of the legal owner. The defendant submits that the only appropriate way in which the equity can here be satisfied is by perfecting the imperfect gift as was done in *Dillwyn v Llewelyn*.

Counsel for the plaintiff on instructions has throughout submitted that the plaintiff is entitled to possession. The only concession that he made was that the period of notice given in the letter of 9 April 1976 was too short. He made no submission upon the way the equity, if there was an equity, should be satisfied save to submit that the court should not in any view grant a remedy more beneficial to the defendant than a licence to occupy the house for her lifetime.

We are satisfied that the problem of remedy on the facts resolves itself into a choice between two alternatives: should the equity be satisfied by a licence to the defendant to occupy the house for her lifetime, or should there be a transfer to her of the fee simple?

The main consideration pointing to a licence for her lifetime is that she did not by her case at the hearing seek to establish that she had spent more money or done more work on the house than she would have done had she believed that she had only a licence to live there for her lifetime. But the court must be cautious about drawing any inference from what she did not give in evidence as the hypothesis put is one that manifestly never occurred to her. Then it may reasonably be held that her expenditure and effort can hardly be regarded as comparable to the change of position of those who have constructed buildings on land over which they had no legal rights.

This court appreciates that the moneys laid out by the defendant were much less than in some of the cases in the books. But the court has to look at all the circumstances. When the plaintiff left her she was, we were told, a widow in her middle fifties. During the period that she lived with the plaintiff her capital was reduced from £4,500 to £1,000. Save for her invalidity pension that was all that she had in the world. In reliance upon the plaintiff's declaration of gift, encouragement and acquiescence she arranged her affairs on the basis that the house and contents belonged to her. So relying, she devoted a quarter of her remaining capital and her personal effort upon the house and its fixtures. In addition she bought carpets, curtains and furniture for it, with the result that by the date of the trial she had only £300 left. Compared to her, on the evidence the plaintiff is a rich man. He might not regard an expenditure of a few hundred pounds as a very grave loss. But the court has to regard her change of position over the years 1973 to 1976.

We take the view that the equity cannot here be satisfied without granting a remedy which assures to the defendant security of tenure, quiet enjoyment, and freedom of action in respect of repairs and improvements without interference from the plaintiff. The history of the conduct of the plaintiff since 9 April 1976 in relation to these proceedings leads to an irresistible inference that he is determined to pursue his purpose of evicting her from the house by any legal means at his disposal with a ruthless disregard of the obligations binding upon conscience. The court must grant a remedy effective to protect her against the future manifestations of his ruthlessness. It was conceded that if she is granted a licence, such a licence cannot be registered as a land charge, so that she may find herself ousted by a purchaser for value without notice. If she has in the future to do further and more expensive repairs she may only be able to finance them by a loan, but as a licensee she cannot charge the house. The plaintiff as legal owner may well find excuses for entry in order to do what he may plausibly represent as necessary works and so contrive to derogate from her enjoyment of the licence in ways that make it difficult or impossible for the court to give her effective protection.

Weighing such considerations this court concludes that the equity to which the facts in this case give rise can only be satisfied by compelling the plaintiff to give effect to his promise and her expectations. He has so acted that he must now perfect the gift.

(d) Solution Adjusted to all the Circumstances

In *Dodsworth v Dodsworth* (1973) 228 EG 1115, giving the judgment of the court, RUSSELL LJ said: "In this case the plaintiff, aged over 70, owned in 1967 a bungalow near Boston, Lincolnshire, and lived there alone. Her younger brother and his wife — the two defendants — returned to England from Australia and were looking for a house to acquire as their home. The plaintiff persuaded them to join her in her bungalow. The judge held on the evidence that the defendants spent a sum of over £700 on improvements to the plaintiff's bungalow in the expectation, encouraged and induced by the plaintiff, that the defendants and the survivor of them would be able to remain in the bungalow as their home — sharing of course with the plaintiff while she lived — for as long as they wished to do so, in circumstances that raised an equity in favour of the defendants on the footing of principles exemplified in a passage from Lord Kingsdown's speech in *Ramsden v Dyson* (1866) LR 1 HL 129, and in other cases since then. The judge, however, held on the evidence that the parties did not intend to create a legal relationship. Not many months after the defendants moved into the bungalow, the plaintiff repented of her invitation for reasons, or alleged reasons, which need not be rehearsed. She started proceedings for possession: the defendants counterclaimed to assert an equity. The plaintiff did not appear at the hearing, and her claim for possession was non-suited. The question on the counterclaim was whether the proper way in which the equity should be satisfied would be to make some order which would assure the defendants in their occupation of the bungalow as their home for as long as they wished, or on the other hand to declare in effect that possession could only be obtained against them by the plaintiff if they were repaid their outlay on improvements to the bungalow.

The judge decided upon the latter as the appropriate course. His main ground was this. The plaintiff was anxious to sell the bungalow and buy a smaller and less expensive one for herself. She could not do this, having no other capital asset, if the defendants were entitled to stay rent free. She would therefore have to continue sharing her home for the rest of her life with the defendants, with whom she was, or thought she was, at loggerheads. Against this the defendants would, on leaving, recover and have available towards another home the expenditure which they laid out in the expectation, albeit encouraged by the plaintiff, of ability to stay there as their home. We think that the judge in balancing these considerations was entitled, and right, to come to that decision. We do not accept that the judge was wrong on the ground submitted to us that where the extent of the expectations was defined, though without intention to create a legal relationship, between the parties, compensation for outlay could not be an appropriate satisfaction of the equity. On the appeal, the plaintiff having died intestate after notice of appeal, leave was given to the respondents, who are her administrators under a grant of letters of administration, to be joined as parties to the appeal. They do not contend that there was not an equity. They support the view, in the changed circumstances, of the judge that it was proper to satisfy the defendants' equity by protecting their occupation unless and until their expenditure was reimbursed.

Now it is clear that the ground upon which the judge mainly decided upon the appropriate remedy has, by the plaintiff's death, disappeared. But what is the situation now? Apart from the equity, the situation is this. The estate vested in the legal personal representatives consists only of the bungalow. This is subject to a standing mortgage of some £200 to £300. Its value free of any occupation rights in the defendants might be £5,000. Under the

Administration of Estates Act 1925 the administrators hold the bungalow on trust for sale and to pay out of the proceeds of sale debts, duties, if any, and administration expenses (which must include their costs of this appeal), and then to divide among ten stirpes of beneficiaries, the first defendant in fact being one stirps. The immediate problem seems to be this. If immediate and direct effect is given to the expectations of the defendants, to take effect in priority to the respondents' entitlement and statutory duties, we cannot see but that it will lead, by virtue of the provisions of the Settled Land Act, to a greater and more extensive interest than was ever contemplated by the plaintiff and the defendants. The defendants would necessarily become joint tenants for life. As such they could sell the property, or quit and let it. In the one case, they would be entitled to the income of the invested proceeds of sale for life and the life of the survivor: in the other, they would be entitled to the net rents. None of these possibilities could conceivably have been embodied in the expectations giving rise to the equity in question, and we do not think that it can be right to satisfy such an equity by conferring upon the defendants a greater interest in the property than was envisaged by the parties. This, we should say,, is a point which appears to have been overlooked in *Inwards v Baker* [1965] 2 QB 29, [1965] 1 All ER 446, p. 528, ante.

Is it possible in the present case to give effect to the expectation without falling foul of the impact of the Settled Land Act? . . ." Yes it was. "In short therefore we do not see how we can sensibly, and without awarding to the defendants a greater interest in law than was within the induced expectation, satisfy this equity save by securing their occupation until this expenditure has been reimbursed, which was the effect of the judge's order or declaration."

GRIFFITHS *v* WILLIAMS
(1977) 248 EG 947 (CA, Megaw, Orr and Goff LJJ)

No. 1 Gordon Villa, in Hereford, was owned by Mrs Cole, who was the mother of Mrs Williams, who was the mother of Mrs Griffiths. Mrs Williams was a school teacher, who had lived most of her life at the house.

Mrs Cole had always indicated her intention of leaving Mrs Williams a life interest in the house, and made a will to that effect in 1971. But in 1974, she changed her will, and left the house absolutely to Mrs Griffiths.

Mrs Williams looked after Mrs Cole in her latter years, and expended her money on repairs and improvements to the house. She did so primarily for the care of her mother, but also in the belief that she would be entitled to live in the house for the rest of her life.

Held. Mrs Williams was protected under the doctrine of estoppel. The award of a life interest was not appropriate, because that might create a settlement under the Settled Land Act 1925. Mrs Williams should receive (with all the parties' agreement) a lease determinable upon death, with no power to assign, and at a nominal rent which did not exceed two thirds of the rateable value.

Goff LJ: [The] equity is said to arise because the grandmother had repeatedly assured Mrs Williams that she would be allowed to live in the house for the whole of her life, and because, on the faith of those assurances, Mrs Williams had expended money upon the property which otherwise she would not have done. It emerged at the trial that she had spent in all, out of her own moneys, a sum of £2,000. Part of that was spent upon improvements to the property which consisted of putting in a bathroom and an indoors toilet, rewiring for electricity, concreting the yard, and repairs to one of the walls; but part of it had been spent in paying outgoings. In so far as the expenditure was of the latter character, I doubt whether it would raise an equity in Mrs Williams' favour, because it could be regarded simply as current payment for the benefits which she was enjoying by being allowed to live in the house. But in so far as money was spent upon permanent improvements such as I have mentioned, it would be capable of creating what is known as a promissory estoppel[11]. It seems that a grant in aid towards the improvements was obtained from the local authority; but, even so, as I read the evidence Mrs Williams did incur expenditure out of her own money on improvements. But the evidence does not show how the £2,000 should be broken down between expenditure of that character and expenditure on current repairs.

In these circumstances, in my judgment, we have to determine three questions, which were propounded by Scarman LJ in his judgment in the case of *Crabb v Arun District Council* [1976] Ch 179, [1975] 3 All ER 865, p. 536, ante the relevant passage being at 193, at 875. I will read them from another case where they were cited, namely, *Jones v Jones* [1977] 1 WLR 438, [1977] 2 All ER 231, p. 532, ante, because there Roskill LJ answered those questions — of course, on the facts of the case before him, but the answers I think throw light on the nature of the questions and what the approach to answering them should be. I cite from the judgment of Roskill LJ at 443, at 236, where his Lordship said:

"As for the rest, Lord Denning MR has referred to the decision of this court, consisting of himself and Lawton and Scarman LJJ, in *Crabb v Arun District Council*. I would refer to the three questions, posed by Scarman LJ at the beginning of his judgment, which the court has to ask in relation to the now well-settled law of estoppel, at 193, at 875. 'First, is there an equity established?' The answer here is unquestionably Yes. 'Secondly, what is the extent of the equity, if one is established?' — and the answer, shortly, is that the equity is of a possessory nature entitling the defendant to remain in this house —"

and then (though not relevant for present purposes)

"but it would not, in my judgment, extend to the defendant's wife. 'And, thirdly, what is the relief appropriate to satisfy the equity?'"

Then he went on to answer that question, saying:

"All the members of the court in *Crabb v Arun District Council* thought that in some circumstances a court might impose the making of payment of some form or another as a condition of giving effect to the equity, but in the present case it seems to me that it would be wrong to impose as a condition of protecting the equity that the defendant should pay rent to the plaintiff for the following reasons. . . ."

which he then set out.

That indicates to my mind that the third question is one upon which the court has to exercise a discretion. If it finds that there is an equity, then it must determine the nature of it, and then, guided by that nature and

---

[11] Presumably proprietary estoppel is intended.

exercising discretion in all the circumstances, it has to determine what is the fair order to make between the parties for the protection of the claimant.

So I direct my mind to the first question: Was there here an equity? Mr McCarthy says that there was not, because the defendant failed to prove, and the learned judge did not find, that the grandmother at the time the improvements were effected knew that Mrs Williams was making a mistake as to her position. He relied on the passage in *Snell's Equity*, 27th edn. at p. 566, where it is said:

"Knowledge of the mistake makes it dishonest for him to remain wilfully passive in order afterwards to profit by the mistake he might have prevented. The knowledge must accordingly be proved by 'strong and cogent evidence.' "

He also points to the learned judge's judgment, where he said:

"It was clear that Mrs Williams — and I think this would apply to most sensitive people in her position — was reluctant to admit, even to herself, that in spending her own money on housekeeping and house improvement, she was thinking predominantly of her own inheritance rather than the care and comfort of her mother. What she did say, however, was that had it occurred to her that her enjoyment and benefit of these improvements, or rather of the house as improved (a house that she had always regarded as her home) would be limited to her mother's life span, she would have had to think whether she was not obliged to look more closely to her own future. . . . It was equally clear, however, that none of this occurred to her at the time, or perhaps even not until it was put to her in this court."

In so far as it is necessary to prove that Mrs Williams made a mistake, I think the mistake is to be found in her belief that she would be allowed to live in the house for the whole of her life. But I do not myself think that it really depends upon mistake. The equity is based upon the fact that where one has made a representation on the faith of which another party has expended his money, then the man who made the representation will not, to the prejudice of the other, be allowed to go back on it and assert his strict legal rights if to do so would be unconscionable. I cite this passage from the judgment of Lord Denning MR in *Inwards v Baker* [1965] 2 QB 29 at 37, [1965] 1 All ER 446 at 448:

[His Lordship quoted the paragraph set out on p. 529, ante, beginning "So in this case . . .", and continued:].

The facts in that case were different, but the principle appears to me to apply precisely to the facts of the present case. Mrs Williams' evidence, which the learned judge preferred to that of Mrs Griffiths, was as follows: "Whenever the question arose in any discussion Mrs Williams had always been assured that the house was her home for life. That was always what was said and she never expected more than a life interest." That does not read as if it was the lady giving evidence, but the notes of the evidence appear throughout in that form, and this was obviously a record which the learned judge was making of the evidence which had been given before him. Then Mr Hedley Williams, whose evidence the learned judge also accepted, said — or the effect of his evidence is recorded — as follows: "He had always understood that the house was his mother's for life, and this had been said to, or in front of, him over many years by both his grandmother and his mother"; and, again, "As to the improvements etc there was no objection by the grandmother and he had never heard any mention (prior to his grandmother's death) of his mother leaving, or being asked to leave." So when the learned judge speaks of what Mrs Williams would have thought had it occurred to her, it is clear that it would have occurred to her but for the fact that Mrs Cole, the testatrix, was throughout repeatedly assuring Mrs Williams that she could live in the house for the rest of her life. It seems to me, on this evidence, clear that Mrs Williams expended her money on the faith of those repeated assurances, and it is, I think, an irresistible inference that Mrs Cole knew that Mrs Williams was relying on the assurances which she herself was repeatedly making to her daughter. In my judgment, therefore, there is no doubt at all in this case but that an equity is made out.

I therefore pass to the second question, and that is: What is the equity? That must be an equity to have made good, so far as may fairly be done between the parties, the representation that Mrs Williams should be entitled to live in the house rent-free for the rest of her life.

So I come to the third question, which is really the one which gives rise to such difficulties as there are in this case. In *Dodsworth v Dodsworth* (1973) 228 EG 115, p. 548, ante this court unanimously decided that if an equity of this nature were implemented by giving the claimant the right to occupy the house (as it was in that case) for his life, the result would be to create a tenancy for life within the meaning of the Settled Land Act, and so the party setting up the equity would get more than it was ever represented that he should have, because he would get all the statutory powers of a tenant for life under the Act: he could sell the property and take the income of the proceeds for his life, or he could grant a long lease. In that case the court does not seem to have considered what may in such cases be a difficult problem, namely, what is the "settlement?" I think there are many authorities which establish that a right to occupy property for one's life is the equivalent of a tenancy for life under the Act. But the Act defines "settlement" in section 1 in these terms:

"Any deed, will, agreement for a settlement or other agreement, Act of Parliament, or other instrument, or any number of instruments, whether made or passed before or after, or partly before and partly after, the commencement of this Act, under or by virtue of which instrument or instruments any land, after the commencement of this Act, stands for the time being. . . ."

and then follow the various limitations which make it settled land.

Where the interest arises under a contract or other agreement, of course, there is no difficulty, because that falls fairly and squarely within the words of subsection (1) of section 1. But where what is set up is an equity arising from acting upon a representation, it is not obvious how that can be brought within the terms of section 1 (1). There are two other cases in which this type of problem was considered by this court, namely, *Binions v Evans* [1972] Ch 359, [1972] 2 All ER 70, p. 499, ante and *Bannister v Bannister* [1948] 2 All ER 133, p. 503, ante. In *Binions v Evans* the Master of the Rolls thought that such an equity would not in any event create a settlement; but, with all respect, I think his reasoning leads to difficulties, because at 367, at 75 he reached the conclusion that it created an equitable interest, and once that is established then the ground on which he said (at 366, at 74) there was no settlement appears to me to be undermined. The other two Lord Justices who heard that case, Megaw LJ and Stephenson LJ, felt that they were bound by the earlier decision in *Bannister v Bannister* to hold that there was a settlement; but they did not direct themselves to any question under section 1; nor, I think, need they have done so, because in *Binions v Evans* and the earlier case of *Bannister v Bannister* there was actually an agreement. So that the difficulty which in my view arises, on the case of *Dodsworth v Dodsworth* and upon the present case, of seeing whether there can be a settlement when you have an interest which appears to give you a tenancy for life but there does not obviously appear to be anything which is a "settlement" within the Act, did not arise in those two earlier cases. If it were necessary, we would have to decide what is, I think, a serious problem — whether *Dodsworth v Dodsworth* is binding upon us or whether it was decided strictly *per incuriam* because the learned Lord Justices who heard it did not advert to section 1 of the Settled Land Act, and, if it be not binding upon us, whether in truth it be right, and if so, what is the answer to the conundrum posed by subsection (1) of section 1. It may be that in such a case there is a settlement, and it is the order of the court declaring the equity, which is an "instrument" and, therefore, the "settlement" within the meaning of that subsection.

Happily, by the good sense of the parties in accepting a solution of the problem which I propounded for their consideration, it is unnecessary for this court to resolve those problems. In *Dodsworth v Dodsworth*, having decided that a right of occupation for the whole life of the claimant would be a wrong way of giving effect to the equity because it would create a settlement under the Settled Land Act and give the claimant too much, the court then adopted an alternative suggestion of compensation by recouping the claimant his expenditure (I think with interest) and giving him possession until payment. They recognised that that really went too far the other way; and certainly it would not be appropriate in this case — if for no other reason, because of the difficulty of quantification. But it seems to me that *Dodsworth v Dodsworth* proceeded upon the basis which I have spelt out of *Crabb's* case — that the third problem is one of discretion: the court ought to see, having regard to all the circumstances, what is the best and fairest way to secure protection for the person who has been misled by the representations made to him and subsequently repudiated.

In the present case, it seemed to me, and I suggested to the parties, that the fairest way of dealing with the matter would be to direct the plaintiffs to grant Mrs Williams a long lease, determinable upon her death, at a nominal rent, since that would give her the right of occupation for her whole life and could not in any event give her the statutory powers under the Settled Land Act. The nominal rent would be an obligation not contemplated when the representations were made to her, but perfect equity is seldom possible.

There appeared to be only two objections to this course. One was that she might assign the lease; but that can be dealt with by including in the lease an absolute covenant not to assign, and by her giving an undertaking to this court, which I understand she is prepared to do, not to assign. The other difficulty was that, if she were to marry again, her husband might be able to claim a protected tenancy under the Rent Acts. I know that to Mrs Williams that appears a flight of fantasy; but we have to take precautions to see that what we propose is something which will not go wrong in an event which is not impossible and could happen. Counsel have made inquiries and they assure us that the husband would not be entitled to protection under the Rent Acts if the rent did not exceed two-thirds of the rateable value at the relevant date; and they have ascertained that that rateable value is £46 per annum. Therefore, if we direct the lease to be at a rent of £30 per annum we will have served the two ends of keeping it below two-thirds of the rateable value and making it nominal; and that is what I would propose. I took the precaution of making it clear to counsel, and they have made it clear to the parties, that, while we might order that as a term after deciding whether or not a life interest would be a "settlement" within the meaning of the Act, if we were to decide that it was not a settlement within the Act Mrs Williams would be entitled to claim a full life interest without reservation of any rent, and therefore we could only adopt this course of a long lease at this stage if the parties consented to it, otherwise we must first determine the problem which I have mentioned and then consider what it would be right to order in the light of that determination. Counsel, having withdrawn and consulted with their clients and taken instructions, say that they are content that we should adopt the solution proposed by me.

I would therefore allow the appeal, discharge the order of the learned deputy circuit judge, and direct the plaintiffs to grant to Mrs Williams the lease which I have indicated.

In *Appleby v Cowley* (1982) Times, 14 April[12], a claim was based on proprietary estoppel, that the plaintiffs were entitled to occupy a building in Nottingham indefinitely and use it as barristers' chambers subject to indemnifying Mr Cowley the defendant for the costs of providing it. In holding that it failed, MEGARRY V-C said:

"That leaves the fourth head of expenditure, the repairs and renovations to the roof and exterior walls in 1973 at a cost of some £7,700. . . . As the law has developed, it may be that in cases in which a claim based on proprietary estoppel is made, the real question comes down simply to whether or not the assertion of strict legal rights would be unconscionable, without any detailed conditions or criteria being specified: see *Taylor Fashions Ltd v Liverpool Victoria Trustees Co Ltd* [1982] QB 133n at 151–154, [1981] 1 All ER 897 at 915–918, and *Amalgamated Investment and Property Co Ltd v Texas Commerce International Bank Ltd* [1982] QB 84 at 103–104, [1981] 1 All ER 923 at 935–936. In the present case, would it be unconscionable for the company to take the benefit of these remedial works to its building?

I think that there are circumstances in which the answer would be Yes. If soon after the works had been done the company had evicted all the members of chambers, or had required them to make payments equal to the full rental value of the chambers, then the company might well be said to be reaping the fruits of the expenditure unfairly. However, that is not what has happened. When the work was being done the rental value of the premises for which some £1,500 a year had been paid for some 10 years was about £4,300; and as events have turned out, Mr Cowley is making no claim for use and occupation at a rate greater than £1,500 a year until 30th November 1976 onwards. In those circumstances I think Mr Cowley may echo the phrase of

---

[12] The extract is taken from the Bar Library Transcript. A claim based on fiduciary or confidential relationship was also rejected. One reason was "the nature of the alleged beneficiaries. I do not think that practising barristers are in consimili casu with children, wards, patients, clients and the like. As a class they are not immature, weak, credulous creatures, easily persuaded and ready to yield their powers of decision to others."

Lord Hardwicke L C in *A-G v Baliol College, Oxford* (1744) 9 Mod Rep 407 at 412, when directing an inquiry in chambers, and say that the plaintiffs have had 'sufficient satisfaction' for their expenditure. Certainly I do not think that Mr Cowley is acting unconscionably. It may be a nice academic point whether the result is that no case of proprietary estoppel has been established, or whether it is that such a case has been established but no remedy should be granted. I shall not debate that. All I need do is to say that the claim on proprietary estoppel fails. Certainly I can see nothing which comes within measurable distance of establishing any sort of a case that because of the expenditure the plaintiffs are beneficially entitled to the building, subject to indemnifying Mr Cowley."

In *Savva v Costa and Harymode Investments Ltd* [1980] CA Transcript 723 (BUCKLEY, SHAW and OLIVER LJJ), the plaintiff, a Cypriot seamstress, and the defendant had lived together from 1967 to 1968. Thereafter the defendant assumed responsibility for the maintenance and education of their two children who lived with the plaintiff. In early 1977 the defendant suggested to the plaintiff that she should move with the children and live in a house which he owned. The plaintiff's expenditure on work carried out to the house was substantial; the defendant was aware that the work was going on, although he claimed that he had protested that some of it was extravagant and unnecessary.

In May 1977, the defendant indicated his intention to transfer the house to trustees for the two children, on terms that the plantiff would be permitted to reside there with them. The plaintiff claimed a beneficial half share in the property, or, alternatively, a lien on the property for the amount which she had expended.

In rejecting both claims, OLIVER LJ said:

"Mr Goodenday has drawn our attention to a line of authorities, starting with the well-known dictum of Lord Kingsdown in *Ramsden v Dyson* and applied in *Plimmer v Wellington Corpn* (1884) 9 App Cas 699, p. 512, ante; *Inwards v Baker* [1965] 2 QB 29, [1965] 1 All ER 446, p. 528, ante; *Ward v Kirkland* [1967] Ch 194, [1966] 1 All ER 609 and other cases. These relate to what is known as a proprietary estoppel. The effect can be summarised by saying that where A under an expectation created or encouraged by B that A shall have a certain interest in land, expends money on B's land on the faith of such expectation and to the knowledge of B, a court of equity will not allow B to take the benefit of such expenditure without giving effect to the expectation so created or encouraged. The expenditure in such circumstances gives rise to an equity to which the court will give effect in such way as may be appropriate in the circumstances of the individual case. It may be by injunction, it may be by declaring a trust of the beneficial interest or it may be by a declaration of lien for monies expended. This line of cases Mr Goodenday has conveniently referred to as "the representation cases"; but he accepts that, in the light of the learned deputy judge's findings of fact in the instant case, he cannot bring himself directly within them. What he submits is that the representation cases do not exhaust the category of cases in which equities of this type can arise. There are, he suggests, two other categories of case, under either of which he is entitled to succeed in the claim which he makes for a beneficial interest in the property.

The first category of case represents, as he submits, an extension of the *Ramsden v Dyson* principle to a situation in which there is no representation or expectation, but merely an expenditure of money with the consent of the landowner. If I have his submission aright, Mr Goodenday expresses the principle thus: Where a person expends money on the land of another with the knowledge and consent of that other but without any sort of representation, this gives rise to an equity in the person making the expenditure to have either an interest in the land commensurate with his expenditure or at least a lien for the amount expended.

In support of this Mr Goodenday relies upon two authorities.

[His Lordship referred to *Unity Joint Stock Mutual Banking Association v King* (1858) 25 Beav 72, p. 505, ante, and *Hussey v Palmer* [1972] 1 WLR 1286, [1972] 3 All ER 744, p. 504, ante, and continued:]

Now these cases do not, in my judgment at any rate, support any such broad principle as that for which Mr Goodenday contends. Mr Reid submits, and for my part I accept the submission, that on analysis they are not extensions of the *Ramsden v Dyson* principle, but merely examples of its application, and they do not support the broad proposition relied upon by Mr Goodenday that mere expenditure with the consent of the landowner is sufficient to raise an equity without any representation or expectation created by the landowner. The *Unity Joint Stock Banking* case was so treated in *Chalmers v Pardoe* [1963] 1 WLR 677, [1963] 3 All ER 552, itself a representation case, and it is clear that in *Hussey v Palmer*, the common expectation was that the plaintiff would continue to live in the house, an expectation which was not realised in the event, but on the strength of which the expenditure was made.

In my judgment these cases cannot be prayed in aid to demonstrate that the mere expenditure by A on improvements to B's land with B's knowledge without more, gives rise to some equity in the payer. . . . .

In the instant case, on the facts as found by the learned deputy judge, there was no agreement and there was no request on the part of the defendant. The plaintiff was aware that the house belonged to the defendant and if she believed that she was to get any interest in it, there is nothing to indicate that the defendant knew that that was her belief. The most that can be inferred in these circumstances is that she expended monies in improvements in the expectation that, as in fact was and is the case, she would be permitted to live there with the children.

[His Lordship rejected a claim based on "a resulting trust which arises by the establishment by evidence of conduct of a common intention on the acquisition of the property, that the beneficial interest shall be shared in some way": *Gissing v Gissing* [1971] AC 886, [1970] 2 All ER 780, and continued:]

I should perhaps add this. As the learned deputy judge pointed out, his decision in no way determined the question of the plaintiff's right to continue in occupation of the property. That was not in issue before him and it is not in issue before this court. It may very well be that, although Mr Goodenday has felt unable to rely upon the principle of *Ramsden v Dyson* to establish the equitable interest claimed by the plaintiff in this action, the plaintiff would be entitled, if her enjoyment of the property is terminated in the future, to invoke that principle in support of a claim to an irrevocable licence — an equity to which, if it is established, the court might then give effect by a declaration of lien as suggested in *Hussey v Palmer*, if the circumstances and the duration or terms of the licence were thought to render that course appropriate. That is something about which I think it safer and wiser to express no view. It was not argued below and, understandably, there are no findings by the learned deputy judge as to the terms or duration of any such licence — matters which it would be essential, as I see it, to determine before the court could give any relief. The plaintiff's occupation has not in fact been disturbed and Mr Reid, on instructions, disclaims any present intention on his client's part to disturb it. I agree with the learned deputy judge, therefore, that it would be premature for the court to intervene now, and indeed it does not, as I think, have before it the material to enable it to do so. I mention the matter only to make clear that the present appeal, which I would dismiss, is in no way determinative of such rights of occupation as the plaintiff may have, or be entitled to, or of the course which the court might think it appropriate to take if such occupation were to be disturbed in the future."

SHAW LJ said: "I only append a footnote. The questions raised and to be decided on this appeal are of course confined to the issues with which the learned deputy judge had to deal, and to his findings of fact in regard to them. It may be that there remain outside the context of the present proceedings, prospective potential rights which will accrue to Miss Savva in certain eventualities; the existence and nature of those rights may have to be determined in the future; they are not within the ambit of this appeal.

I would therefore echo Lord Justice Oliver's indication as to what the position in law might be if Miss Savva were at any time to be denied the advantage of residing in No 6 Windermere Road, having regard to the considerable expenditure by her on the improvement of the property. . . .

If at some time it should be sought to turn Miss Savva out, there would arise a serious question as to the protection of an interest in the property on her behalf commensurate with the money she has spent on improving its condition so as to provide a proper degree of amenity for the accommodation of the children, who are intended to be the ultimate proprietors of the property[13]."

QUESTIONS
1. How would you reformulate the principle of *Ramsden v Dyson?* Consider, in particular, whether
    (a) there is any difference between estoppel by acquiescence or silence, estoppel by encouragement and promissory estoppel
    (b) the principle should be confined to land or other property
    (c) proof of detriment is necessary.
2. Is the requirement of unconscionability referable to the establishment of the equity, or to its satisfaction, or to both?
3. Do the courts apply the same criteria when considering whether an equity is established in the case of
    (a) a claim by a licensee to a proprietary interest; and
    (b) a defence by a licensee to an action for possession by the licensor? *Pascoe v Turner* [1979] 1 WLR 431, [1979] 2 All ER 945, p. 545, ante; *Savva v Costa and Harymode Investments Ltd* [1980] CA Transcript 723, p. 556, ante; *Bristol and West Building Society v Henning* [1985] 1 WLR 778, [1985] 2 All ER 606, p. 495, n. 7, ante.

---

[13] See also *Bristol and West Building Society v Henning* [1985] 1 WLR 778, [1985] 2 All ER 606, p. 495, n. 7, ante.

4. Is a licence by estoppel an interest in land? Can it be sold? Does it pass with the land? Is it assignable? *Hamilton v Geraghty* (1901) 1 SR NSW Eq 81; *Lands Comr v Hussein* [1968] EA 585; (1969) ASCL 354 (E. H. Burn); C & B p. 566.

5. Consider the solutions reached in the various cases in this Section V, and compare them with those reached in sections III and IV.

6. To what extent is a licensee's right to protection affected by his conduct (*a*) before and (*b*) after his licence is established? Why are contractual licences and licences by estoppel treated differently? *Thompson v Park* [1944] KB 408; *Williams v Staite* [1979] Ch 291, [1978] 2 All ER 928; *Brynowen Estates Ltd v Bourne* (1981) 131 NLJ 1213; *Willis & Son v Willis* (1985) 277 EG 1133; Dawson and Pearce, pp. 223–224.

7. How would you solve (*a*) *Inwards v Baker* [1965] 2 QB 29, [1965] 1 All ER 446, p. 528, ante and (*b*) *E R Ives Investment Ltd v High* [1967] 2 QB 379, [1967] 1 All ER 504, p. 542, ante, if the title of the land of the licensor were registered under the Land Registration Act 1925? C & B, pp. 569–570.

8. Do you think that Parliament should intervene to give protection to a licensee for life? See the statutory protection given in Ireland: Republic of Ireland Registration of Title Act 1964, s. 81; Northern Ireland Land Registration Act 1970, s. 47; (1970) 21 NILQ 389 (B. W. Harvey); Wylie, *Irish Land Law* (1975) paras. 20.15–20.19.

9. An aged relative asks his adult child to move into his house and look after him for the rest of his days. In return the relative makes an oral promise to leave the house by will to the child or to the child and his or her spouse. The child moves in, but the aged relative fails to leave the house by will. Consider the possible legal analyses and solutions, and in particular:
   - (*a*) in contract, under the doctrine of part performance, p. 68, ante;
   - (*b*) in property, as a licence;
   - (*c*) in trust, as an express or constructive trust (or a resulting trust if the child makes any financial contribution);
   - (*d*) in succession, under the Inheritance (Provision for Family and Dependants) Act 1975;
   - (*e*) in restitution; *Deglman v Guaranty Trust Co of Canada and Constantinean* [1954] 3 DLR 785; Goff & Jones, *The Law of Restitution* (2nd edn, 1978), p. 321.

See generally [1982] CLJ 290 (S. J. Burridge); MM, pp. 375–376.

VI. Deserted Wives. A Historical Note

Brief mention should be made here of a body of doctrine which grew up in the nineteen-fifties, with the object of protecting a deserted wife in the occupation of the family home. If a husband owns the matrimonial home and deserts his wife, does the wife become a trespasser, liable to eviction by the husband; or by a third party, if the husband has transferred the title? In a number of cases, the deserted wife was protected on the theory that she was a licensee under a licence which was irrevocable by the husband, or by a transferee other than a bona fide purchaser of a legal estate for value without notice[14]. There is no need now to enter into the complexities and controversies which this situation created; for the House of Lords held in *National Provincial Bank Ltd v Ainsworth* [1965] AC 1175, [1965] 2 All ER 472 that she had no interest capable of enforcement against a third party; and the short but active career of "the deserted wife's equity" came to an end. "The deserted wife therefore", said Lord Wilberforce, "cannot resist a claim from a 'purchaser' from her husband whether the 'purchase' takes place after or before the desertion. As regards transactions subsequent to the desertion this disability is somewhat mitigated by three factors. First, if it appears that the husband is threatening to dispose of the house in such a manner as to defeat her rights, she may be able to obtain an injunction to restrain him from doing so (*Lee v Lee* [1952] 2 QB 489n, [1952] 1 All ER 1299). An injunction is, of course, a discretionary remedy and it does not follow that the wife will be granted it in every case, but in suitable circumstances she has this protection. Secondly, the courts have ample powers to detect, and to refuse to give effect to, sham or fraudulent transactions — such as that which was attempted in *Ferris v Weaven* [1952] 2 All ER 233.

A deserted wife (spouse) has, in recent years, earned protection under different theories. She is not merely a licensee of her husband in the family home. Her contributions to the establishment of the home have been more and more readily treated as an entitlement to a share in the ownership of the family home. Regardless of any property ownership, however, she has a right of occupation, and may protect this against third parties by registration, as has been seen, under the Matrimonial Homes Act 1983[15]. Further, her shared ownership, together with her occupation of the home, along with her husband, has been held to be sufficient to entitle her to an overriding interest[16]. It remains to be seen whether occupation based upon a licence by estoppel would be similarly treated. And, where the wife has protection, the mistress does not follow far behind.

---

[14] *Bendall v McWhirter* [1952] 2 QB 466, [1952] 1 All ER 1307; *Ferris v Weaven* [1952] 2 All ER 233; *Street v Denham* [1954] 1 WLR 624, [1954] 1 All ER 532; *Lee v Lee* [1952] 2 QB 489n, [1952] 1 All ER 1299; *Jess B Woodcock & Sons Ltd v Hobbs* [1955] 1 WLR 152, [1955] 1 All ER 445; *Westminster Bank Ltd v Lee* [1956] Ch 7, [1955] 2 All ER 883; *Miles v Bull* [1969] 1 QB 258, [1968] 3 All ER 632.

[15] P. 257, ante. The right of occupation was created in Matrimonial Homes Act 1967.

[16] *Williams and Glyn's Bank Ltd v Boland* [1981] AC 487, [1980] 2 All ER 408, p. 121, ante.

10. Easements and Profits A Prendre[1]

I. General

Easements and profits à prendre are interests entitling their owners to exercise certain rights over the land of another. They may be legal[2] or equitable. They are distinguishable in that a profit entitles its owner to take away something capable of ownership from the servient land, while an easement does not; and also in that a profit may exist "in gross", while an easement must always be appurtenant to land. Little will be said of profits, owing to lack of available space; or, indeed, of commons[3].

II. Nature of Easements[4]

A. General Characteristics

The detailed characteristics of an easement are discussed in the text-books and need not be repeated here. In short, an easement is a right, appurtenant

---

[1] C & B, pp. 487–551; M & W, pp. 834–912; MM, pp. 395–438; *Gale on Easements* (14th edn, 1972); Jackson, *Law of Easements and Profits* (1978); (1964) 28 Conv (NS) 450 (M.A. Peel).
[2] LPA 1925, ss. 1 (2), 187.
[3] For registration of commons under Commons Registration Act 1965, see p. 58, ante.
[4] C & B, pp. 489–499; M & W, pp. 834–855; MM, pp. 395–408; Gale, pp. 3–60; Jackson, pp. 1–27, 39–49.

to one piece of land[5] and exercisable over another piece of land, and capable of forming the subject matter of a grant. Indeed, all easements, other than those created by statute, are either granted expressly or impliedly, or are presumed to have been granted. An easement must be distinguished from a licence in that it is a proprietary interest and must be appurtenant to land; from a lease in that it does not give the owner of the easement any possessory rights over the land of another; from local customary rights in that there cannot be a grant without a capable grantee; and from natural rights in that these need no grant; from the covenant in that it must be a right capable of being granted. Thus rights which are properly licences, leases, customary rights, natural rights or covenants may look very much like easements, but they may be very different. If X, the owner of Whiteacre, tells Y, the owner of Blackacre, that Y's son may enter Whiteacre to collect a lost ball, that is clearly a licence; but if X were to permit the owner of Blackacre to enter Whiteacre at any time for pleasure and recreation, it might create an easement[6]. Again, a letting of a garage on a weekly tenancy is clearly in no sense an easement; but a right to park vehicles on a neighbour's ground without interfering with his user of the land looks more like an easement[7], and the right to fix a signboard on a neighbour's house can be an easement[8]. Again, local inhabitants of a particular area may have the right to pass across another's land on the way to church[9], or to dry their nets on someone's land[10]; but these rights rely on custom and not on grant and cannot be easements. Again, every landowner has the right of support from his neighbour to his land in its natural state[11]. A right of support to buildings on land is, however, a right which must be claimed as the result of a grant[12]. A covenant not to use land as a fish shop is clearly no easement; but an arrangement permitting the owner of neighbouring land to walk across it in perpetuity to the road is capable of being an easement. In connection with this comparison between easements and covenants, the anomalous position of the easement of light may be noted[13]. For this easement is more like a negative right; the grantor does not grant the light; he is rather under an obligation not to obstruct it. One can only suppose that in the times of narrow streets, poor lighting and small windows, some way of protecting the access of light to houses in towns was necessary. Until 1848[14], there was no way of providing that a negative covenant between freeholders should run with the land, and the only way in which a landowner could be protected was by regarding him as the owner of an easement. It seems, however, more natural to look upon that situation as one of covenant — one in which the neighbour is under an obligation not to

---

[5] See (1980) 96 LQR 557 (M.F. Sturley) for criticism of the rule that an easement cannot exist in gross. See also (1982) 98 LQR 279 at p. 305 (S. Gardner).

[6] *Horton v Tidd* (1965) 196 EG 697; *Re Ellenborough Park* [1965] Ch 131, [1955] 3 All ER 667, p. 566, post; *Miller v Jackson* [1977] QB 966, [1977] 3 All ER 338; *Newman v Jones* (22 March, 1982 unreported), p. 573, post; cf. (1977) 93 LQR 481.

[7] *Copeland v Greenhalf* [1952] Ch 488, [1952] 1 All ER 809, p. 570, post.

[8] *Re Webb's Lease* [1951] Ch 808, [1951] 2 All ER 131, p. 600, post.

[9] *Brocklebank v Thompson* [1903] 2 Ch 344.

[10] *Mercer v Denne* [1905] 2 Ch 538; *Alfred F Beckett Ltd v Lyons* [1967] Ch 449, [1967] 1 All ER 833.

[11] *Hunt v Peake* (1860) John 705; *Backhouse v Bonomi* (1851) 9 HL Cas 503.

[12] *Dalton v Angus* (1881) 6 App Cas 740; *Ray v Fairway Motors (Barnstaple) Ltd* (1969) 20 P & CR 261.

[13] See p. 634, post.

[14] *Tulk v Moxhay* (1848) 2 Ph 774, p. 761, post.

build, rather than one in which he has granted the landowner a right "not to have his light obstructed". Nevertheless it is so treated historically. A similar situation arises in the case of an easement of support[15]. A further anomaly exists in the case of an easement to repair a fence. The general principle is that the servient owner is under no obligation to expend money on the maintenance of any property over which an easement is exercised[16]. The dominant owner may enter to effect the necessary repair[16a]. Thus the easement of fencing is unusual in that the servient owner is under a duty to take positive steps to maintain the fence, including the expenditure of money[17]. There may also be cases where the parties have expressly or impliedly agreed that the servient owner shall bear the burden; as where a local authority, which owned a high-rise block of flats, let them to tenants. Easements of access over the common parts of the building retained by the local authority were implied in favour of the tenants (the dominant owners). And the authority was held liable, on an implied term of the contract, to maintain those parts[18].

While the essential characteristics of an easement are reasonably clear, and no right which fails to comply with them can exist as an easement, it is not possible to say that the law will recognise as an easement every right that does comply. An easement can be described rather than defined, and lists of those judicially recognised are collected in the books[19]. New ones may arise: "The category of servitudes and easements must alter and expand with the changes that take place in the circumstances of mankind[20]." Whether or not a new right, complying with the accepted requirements of an easement, will be judicially recognised or not is very difficult to forecast[1]. Inevitably the cases in this section are a random selection.

---

[15] *Dalton v Angus* (1881) 6 App Cas 740.

[16] See *Holden v White* [1982] QB 679, [1982] 2 All ER 328 (servient owner owed no duty of care at common law to milkman injured by disintegrating manhole cover on private footpath giving access to terraced house, nor under Occupiers Liability Act 1957. See now Occupiers' Liability Act 1984, in effect reversing the decision).

[16a] There is no *general* right. The Law Commission Report on Rights of Access to Neighbouring Land 1985 (Law Com No. 151, Cmnd 9692) recommends that any person needing access to neighbouring land for carrying out necessary preservation work to his own land should have a right to apply to the county court for an order giving him the necessary right of access.

[17] *Lawrence v Jenkins* (1873) LR 8 QB 274 (a 'spurious easement'); *Jones v Price* [1965] 2 QB 618, [1965] 2 All ER 625; *Crow v Wood* [1971] 1 QB 77, [1970] 3 All ER 425, p. 576, post; other rights cannot be easements if they involve expenditure by the servient owner: *Regis Property Co Ltd v Redman* [1956] 2 QB 612, [1956] 2 All ER 335 (covenant to supply hot water held not to be an easement so as to pass under LPA 1925, s. 62 being a personal contract to perform services); *Rance v Elvin* (1983) 49 P & CR 65 (right to metered water supply paid for by servient owner held not to be an easement, even though dominant owner agreed to reimburse water charges); (1985) 50 P & CR 9 (CA held that the right was to the uninterrupted passage of water, and not to its supply; it was therefore an easement, and the servient owner was liable in quasi-contract to reimburse). See [1985] CLJ 458 (A.J. Waite).

[18] *Liverpool City Council v Irwin* [1977] AC 239, [1976] 2 All ER 39; cf. *Duke of Westminster v Guild* [1985] QB 688, [1984] 3 All ER 144 (tenant qua dominant owner of right of drainage held to be liable for repairs). See also *Stokes v Mixconcrete (Holdings) Ltd* (1979) 38 P & CR 488.

[19] C & B, pp. 495–498; M & W, pp. 838–842, 908–909; MM, pp. 398–400, 434–435; Gale, pp. 35–37.

[20] *Dyce v Lady James Hay* (1852) 1 Macq 305 at 312–313, per Lord St. Leonards.

[1] *A-G of Southern Nigeria v John Holt & Co (Liverpool) Ltd* [1915] AC 599; *Miller v Emcer Products Ltd* [1956] Ch 304, [1956] 1 All ER 237; (1956) 72 LQR 172 (R. E. M.); *Phipps v Pears* [1965] 1 QB 76, [1964] 2 All ER 35; (1964) 80 LQR 318 (R. E. M.), p. 574, post; *Dowty Boulton Paul Ltd v Wolverhampton Corpn (No 2)* [1976] Ch 13, [1973] 2 All ER 491.

i.   CAPABILITY OF EXISTENCE AS EASEMENT

HILL *v* TUPPER
(1863) 2 H & C 121 (Exch, POLLOCK CB, MARTIN and BRAMWELL BB)

The Company of Proprietors of the Basingstoke Canal Navigation leased premises on the bank of the canal to the plaintiff, a boat proprietor. The lease to the plaintiff purported to give to him, inter alia, "the sole and exclusive right or liberty to put or use boats on the said canal, and let the same for hire for the purpose of pleasure only". It was alleged that the defendant, the landlord of an inn adjoining the canal, had interfered with the plaintiff's right by putting boats on the canal. The judge refused an application to nonsuit the plaintiff. A rule *nisi* was obtained to enter a nonsuit.

Held. Rule made absolute. The plaintiff was a licensee only and was not entitled to an easement.

POLLOCK CB: We are all of opinion that the rule must be absolute to enter the verdict for the defendant on the second plea. After the very full argument which has taken place, I do not think it necessary to assign any other reason for our decision, than that the case of *Ackroyd v Smith* (1850) 10 CB 164 expressly decided that it is not competent to create rights unconnected with the use and enjoyment of land, and annex them to it so as to constitute a property in the grantee. This grant merely operates as a licence or covenant on the part of the grantors, and is binding on them as between themselves and the grantee, but gives him no right of action in his own name for any infringement of the supposed exclusive right. It is argued that, as the owner of an estate may grant a right to cut turves, or to fish or hunt, there is no reason why he may not grant such a right as that now claimed by the plaintiff. The answer is, that the law will not allow it. So the law will not permit the owner of an estate to grant it alternately to his heirs male and heirs female. A new species of incorporeal hereditament cannot be created at the will and pleasure of the owner of property; but he must be content to accept the estate and the right to dispose of it subject to the law as settled by decisions or controlled by Act of Parliament. A grantor may bind himself by covenant to allow any right he pleases over this property, but he cannot annex to it a new incident, so as to enable the grantee to sue in his own name for an infringement of such a limited right as that now claimed.

BRYANT *v* LEFEVER
(1879) 4 CPD 172 (CA, BRAMWELL, BRETT and COTTON LJJ)

The plaintiff and defendants were occupiers of adjoining houses which were of approximately equal height. The houses had remained in the same condition for much more than twenty years before 1876 when the defendants re-built their house in such a way that a new wall structure, adjoining the plaintiff's chimneys, made it possible for the defendants to stack timber on their roof. This structure caused the plaintiff's chimneys to smoke. The plaintiff brought this action, claiming that he had a right to the free access of air to his chimneys and for nuisance.

Held. The action failed. The right claimed was not capable of existing as an easement.

COTTON LJ: This is an appeal of the defendants from a judgment of Lord Coleridge in favour of the plaintiff in respect of the interruption of air to the plaintiff's chimney caused by the defendants.

The jury have found, first, that there had been for more than twenty years free access of air to the chimneys of the plaintiff's house; secondly, that the defendants interfered with it; thirdly, that the erection of the defendants' wall sensibly and materially interfered with the comfort of human existence in the plaintiff's premises; fourthly, that the plaintiff sustained damage 40*l* by the building of the defendants' wall.

The first question is, whether the plaintiff has, either as a natural right of property or as an easement, a right as against the defendants to have the access of air to his chimney without any interruption by the defendants. In my opinion he has no such right.

In my opinion it would be a contradiction in terms to say that a man has a natural right against his neighbour in respect of a house which is an artificial addition to, and not a user of, the land. That the owner of a house has, as against his neighbour, no natural rights in respect of his house, is shewn by the cases as to subjacent and lateral support. These shew that while every owner of property has, independently of user, a natural right to support for his land, if he adds buildings to his land and thereby requires an increased support, he, in the absence of express grant, can only acquire a right to such support by user, that is, by way of easement. The right (if any) of the plaintiff to the uninterrupted flow of air to his chimney must therefore be by way of easement. Cases to prevent, or to claim damages for, intereference with ancient lights, are frequently spoken of as cases of light and air, and the right relied on as a right to the access of light and air. But this is inaccurate. The cases, as a rule, relate solely to the interference with the access of light, and in no case has any injunction been granted to restrain interference with the access of air. It is unnecessary to say whether, if the uninterrupted flow of air through a definite aperture or channel over a neighbour's property has been enjoyed as of right for a sufficient period, a right by way of easement could be acquired. No such point is made in this case, and I am of opinion that a right by way of easement to the access of air over the general unlimited surface of a neighbour cannot be acquired by mere enjoyment. For this *Webb v Bird* (1862) 13 CBNS 84 is an authority, and as the last decision in that case was in the Exchequer Chamber, it would be sufficient to rely upon the authority of that case. But I think it better to say that I entirely agree with that decision and with the reasons given in this case by Bramwell LJ. In my opinion, therefore, the plaintiff has no right in respect of the flow of air to or from his chimney.

[His Lordship held that no action lay in nuisance because the defendants had not sent impure air on to the plaintiff's land: they had merely blocked the escape of the plaintiff's own impure air[2].]

In *Cable v Bryant* [1908] 1 Ch 259, it was held that an easement could exist which entitled the dominant owner to the access of air through a defined aperture (a ventilator), although there was no defined channel across the servient tenement through which the air flowed[3].

---

[2] See also *Harris v De Pinna* (1886) 33 ChD 238. The right may arise under the doctrine of non-derogation from grant: *Aldin v Latimer, Clark, Muirhead & Co* [1894] 2 Ch 437.

[3] *Wong v Beaumont Property Trust Ltd* [1965] 1 QB 173, [1964] 2 All ER 119, p. 584, post.

RE ELLENBOROUGH PARK
[1956] Ch 131, [1955] 3 All ER 667 (ChD, DANCKWERTS J and CA,
EVERSHED MR, BIRKETT and ROMER LJJ)

In 1855 the White Cross Estate, which included Ellenborough Park, was
being developed for building purposes. Purchasers of the several plots
surrounding the Park were given in their conveyances certain rights of user
over the Park; and for the purposes of the present action it was agreed to take
as typical of all these conveyances, one dated 1864 conveying a plot to John
Porter. The material part of this conveyance was as follows: "Together
with . . . and also full enjoyment at all times hereafter in common with the
other persons to whom such easements may be granted of the pleasure
ground set out and made in front of the said plot of land . . . in the centre of
the square called Ellenborough Park . . . but subject to the payment of a fair
and just proportion of the costs charges and expenses of keeping in good
order and condition the said pleasure ground." John Porter covenanted to
pay a fair proportion of the expenses of the upkeep of the Park, and the
vendors covenanted to keep the Park as an ornamental pleasure ground. The
Park became vested in the plaintiffs on statutory trusts for sale.

During the Second World War, the Park was requisitioned, and subsequently the War Office paid sums of money in respect of compensation
rental and on account of dilapidations. Various questions arose, concerning
the rights of the original purchasers and their successors in title to use the
Park, and concerning the allocation of compensation money from the War
Office. The question was whether the surrounding owners had lost a legal
right, for which they would be entitled to be compensated.

Held (affirming DANCKWERTS J). The right of enjoyment was an easement
appurtenant to the plots bought by the original purchasers, and the plaintiffs
were therefore entitled to compensation.

EVERSHED MR: The substantial question in the case, which we have
briefly indicated, is one of considerable interest and importance. It is clear
from our brief recital of the facts that, if the house owners are now entitled to
an enforceable right in respect of the use and enjoyment of Ellenborough
Park, that right must have the character and quality of an easement as
understood by, and known to, our law. It has, therefore, been necessary for
us to consider carefully the qualities and characteristics of easements, and,
for such purpose, to look back into the history of that category of incorporeal
rights in the development of English real property law. It may be fairly
assumed that, in the case of *Duncan v Louch* (1845) 6 QB 904, the Court of
Queen's Bench in the year 1845, and particularly Lord Denman CJ, who
delivered the first judgment in the court, was of opinion that such a right as
the respondent claims was capable of fulfilling the qualifying conditions of an
easement. And Buckley J, in the case in 1904 of *Keith v Twentieth Century Club
Ltd* (1904) 73 LJ Ch 545, answered certain questions which Byrne J had
ordered to be set down to be argued before the court, themselves depending
upon the assumption that such a right could exist in law. On the other hand,
Farwell J, a judge peculiarly experienced and learned in real property law,
on two occasions, namely, in 1903 in the case of *International Tea Stores Co v
Hobbs* [1903] 2 Ch 165 at 172, and in 1905 in *A-G v Antrobus* [1905] 2 Ch 188
at 198, used language appearing to treat as axiomatic the proposition, that a
right, which should properly be described as a jus spatiandi, was a right
excluded by English law, as by Roman law, from the company of servitudes.

The four cases which we have mentioned must be considered hereafter at greater length. But it can be said at once that, with the possible exception of the first, none of them constitutes or involves a direct decision upon the question now before us: and although the existence of gardens surrounded by houses, the owners or occupiers of which enjoy in practice the amenities of the gardens, is a well-known feature of town development throughout the country, no other case appears to have come before the courts in which the validity of the rights in fact enjoyed in the gardens has ever been tested. . . .[4]

For the purposes of the argument before us, Mr Cross and Mr Goff [counsel for each side] were content to adopt, as correct, the four characteristics formulated in Dr Cheshire's *Modern Real Property* 7th edn, pp. 456[5] et seq. They are (1) there must be a dominant and a servient tenement: (2) an easement must "accommodate" the dominant tenement: (3) dominant and servient owners must be different persons[6], and (4) a right over land cannot amount to an easement, unless it is capable of forming the subject-matter of a grant. . . .

We pass, accordingly, to a consideration of the first of Dr. Cheshire's conditions — that of the accommodation of the alleged dominant tenements by the rights as we have interpreted them. For it was one of the main submissions by Mr Cross on behalf of the appellant that the right of full enjoyment of the park, granted to the purchaser by the conveyance of 23 December 1864, was insufficiently connected with the enjoyment of the property conveyed, in that it did not subserve some use which was to be made of that property; and that such a right accordingly could not exist in law as an easement. In this part of his argument Mr Cross was invoking a principle which is, in our judgment, of unchallengeable authority, expounded, in somewhat varying language, in many judicial utterances, of which the judgments in *Ackroyd v Smith* (1850) 10 CB 164 are, perhaps, most commonly cited. We think it unnecessary to review the authorities in which the principle has been applied; for the effect of the decisions is stated with accuracy in Dr. Cheshire's *Modern Real Property* 7th edn, p. 457. After pointing out that "one of the fundamental principles concerning easements is that they must be not only appurtenant to a dominant tenement, but also connected with the normal enjoyment of the dominant tenement" and referring to certain citations in support of that proposition the author proceeded: "We may expand the statement of the principle thus: a right enjoyed by one over the land of another does not possess the status of an easement unless it accommodates and serves the dominant tenement, and is reasonably necessary for the better enjoyment of that tenement, for if it has no necessary connexion therewith, although it confers an advantage upon the owner and renders his ownership of the land more valuable, it is not an easement at all, but a mere contractual right personal to and only enforceable between the two contracting parties."

[His Lordship rejected the argument, based on an observation of WILLES J in *Bailey v Stephens* (1862) 12 CB NS 91 to the effect that a right could only

---

[4] Lord EVERSHED referred to Holdsworth, *Historical Introduction to Land Law* (1927), p. 265.

[5] 13th edn., pp. 490 et seq.

[6] This is not strictly true. A tenant may grant an easement, for a period not exceeding that of his lease, in favour of another tenant of the same landlord; and an easement of light may be so acquired by prescription: *Morgan v Fear* [1907] AC 425, p. 638, post; (1949) 13 Conv (NS) 104 (A.K.R. Kiralfy); (1958) 74 LQR 82 (V.T.H. Delany); M & W, p. 837.

exist as an easement if it could benefit only the claimant to the easement and no other person, and continued:] Can it be said, then, of the right of full enjoyment of the park in question, which was granted by the conveyance of 23 December 1864, and which, for reasons already given, was, in our view, intended to be annexed to the property conveyed to Mr Porter, that it accommodated and served that property? It is clear that the right did, in some degree, enhance the value of the property, and this consideration cannot be dismissed as wholly irrelevant. It is, of course, a point to be noted; but we agree with Mr Cross's submission that it is in no way decisive of the problem; it is not sufficient to show that the right increased the value of the property conveyed, unless it is also shown that it was connected with the normal enjoyment of that property. It appears to us that the question whether or not this connexion exists is primarily one of fact, and depends largely on the nature of the alleged dominant tenement and the nature of the right granted. As to the former, it was in the contemplation of the parties to the conveyance of 1864 that the property conveyed should be used for residential and not commercial purposes. . . . As to the nature of the right granted, the conveyance of 1864 shows that the park was to be kept and maintained as a pleasure ground or ornamental garden. . . .

On these facts Mr Cross submitted that the requisite connexion between the right to use the park and the normal enjoyment of the houses which were built around it or near it had not been established. He likened the position to a right granted to the purchaser of a house to use the Zoological Gardens free of charge or to attend Lord's Cricket Ground without payment. Such a right would undoubtedly, he said, increase the value of the property conveyed but could not run with it at law as an easement, because there was no sufficient nexus between the enjoyment of the right and the use of the house. It is probably true, we think, that in neither of Mr Cross's illustrations would the supposed right constitute an easement, for it would be wholly extraneous to, and independent of, the use of a house as a house, namely, as a place in which the householder and his family live and make their home; and it is for this reason that the analogy which Mr Cross sought to establish between his illustrations and the present case cannot, in our opinion, be supported. A much closer analogy, as it seems to us, is the case of a man selling the freehold of part of his house and granting to the purchaser, his heirs and assigns, the right, appurtenant to such part, to use the garden in common with the vendor and his assigns. In such a case, the test of connexion, or accommodation, would be amply satisfied; for just as the use of a garden undoubtedly enhances, and is connected with, the normal enjoyment of the house to which it belongs, so also would the right granted, in the case supposed, be closely connected with the use and enjoyment of the part of the premises sold. Such, we think, is in substance the position in the present case. The park became a communal garden for the benefit and enjoyment of those whose houses adjoined it or were in its close proximity. Its flower beds, lawns and walks were calculated to afford all the amenities which it is the purpose of the garden of a house to provide; and, apart from the fact that these amenities extended to a number of householders, instead of being confined to one (which on this aspect of the case is immaterial), we can see no difference in principle between Ellenborough Park and a garden in the ordinary signification of that word. It is the collective garden of the neighbouring houses, to whose use it was dedicated by the owners of the estate and as such amply satisfied, in our judgment, the requirement of connexion with the dominant tenements to which it is appurtenant. The result is not affected by the circumstance that the right to the park is in this case enjoyed by some few houses which are not immediately fronting on the park. The test for present purposes, no doubt, is that the park should constitute in a real and intelligible sense the garden (albeit the communal garden) of the houses to which its enjoyment is annexed. But we think that the test is satisfied as regards these few neighbouring, though not adjacent, houses. We think that the extension of the right of enjoyment to these few houses does not negative the presence of the necessary "nexus" between the subject-matter enjoyed and the premises to which the enjoyment is expressed to belong. . . .[7]

For the reasons which we have stated, we are unable to accept the contention that the right to the full enjoyment of Ellenborough Park fails in limine to qualify as a legal easement for want of the necessary connexion between its enjoyment and the use of the properties comprised in the conveyance of 1864, and in other relevant conveyances.

We turn next to Dr Cheshire's fourth condition for an easement — that the right must be capable of forming the subject-matter of a grant. As we have earlier stated, satisfaction of the condition in the present case depends on a consideration of the questions whether the right conferred is too wide and vague, whether it is inconsistent with the proprietorship or possession of the alleged servient owners, and whether it is a mere right of recreation without utility or benefit.

To the first of these questions the interpretation which we have given to the typical deed provides, in our judgment, the answer; for we have construed the right conferred as being both well defined and commonly understood. In these essential respects the right may be said to be distinct from the indefinite and unregulated privilege which, we think, would ordinarily be understood by the Latin term "jus spatiandi", a privilege of wandering at will over all and every part of another's field or park, and which, though easily intelligible as the subject-matter of a personal licence, is something substantially different from the subject-matter of the grant in question, namely, the provision for a limited number of houses in a uniform crescent of one single large but private garden.

Our interpretation of the deed also provides, we think, the answer to the second question; for the right conferred no more amounts to a joint occupation of the park with its owners, no more excludes the proprietorship or possession of the latter, than a right of way granted through a passage, or than the use by the public of the gardens of Lincoln's Inn Fields (to take one of our former examples) amount to joint occupation of that garden with the London County Council, or involve an inconsistency with the possession or proprietorship of the council as lessees.

[His Lordship referred to *Copeland v Greenhalf* [1952] Ch 488, [1952] 1 All ER 809, p. 570, post, discussed the nature of the right claimed in the present case and continued:]

The right to full enjoyment of Ellenborough Park, which was granted by the 1864 and other relevant conveyances, was, in substance, no more than a

---

[7] *Todrick v Western National Omnibus Co Ltd* [1934] Ch 561; *Birmingham, Dudley and District Banking Co v Ross* (1888) 38 ChD 295 at 314; *Pugh v Savage* [1970] 2 QB 373, [1970] 2 All ER 353 (intervening land between dominant and servient tenements).

right to use the park as a garden in the way in which gardens are commonly used. In a sense, no doubt, such a right includes something of a jus spatiandi, inasmuch as it involves the principle of wandering at will round each part of the garden, except of course, such parts as comprise flower beds, or are laid out for some other purpose, which renders walking impossible or unsuitable. We doubt, nevertheless, whether the right to use and enjoy a garden in this manner can with accuracy be said to constitute a mere jus spatiandi. Wandering at large is of the essence of such a right and constitutes the main purpose for which it exists. A private garden, on the other hand, is an attribute of the ordinary enjoyment of the residence to which it is attached, and the right of wandering in it is but one method of enjoying it. On the assumption, however, that the right now in question does constitute a jus spatiandi, or that it is analogous thereto, it becomes necessary to consider whether the right, which is in question in these proceedings, is, for that reason, incapable of ranking in law as an easement.

[His Lordship referred to dicta of Farwell J in *International Tea Stores Co v Hobbs* [1903] 2 Ch 165 at 171, and in *A-G v Antrobus* [1905] 2 Ch 188 at 198, 199, 205, which spoke of a jus spatiandi as being a right "not known to our law". These statements were obiter and "cannot be regarded as authoritative". His Lordship continued:]

Duncan v Louch (1845) 6 QB 904, on the other hand, decided more than 100 years ago but not, as we have observed, quoted to Farwell J in either of the two cases which we have cited, is authoritative in favour of the recognition by our law as an easement of a right closely comparable to that now in question which, if it involves in some sense a jus spatiandi, is nevertheless properly annexed and appurtenant to a defined hereditament. . . .

We agree with Danckwerts J in regarding *Duncan v Louch* as being a direct authority in the defendant's favour. It has never, so far as we are aware, been since questioned, and we think it should, in the present case, be followed.

For the reasons which we have stated, Danckwerts J came, in our judgment, to a right conclusion in this case and, accordingly, the appeal must be dismissed.

ii. EXCLUSIVE OR JOINT USER

COPELAND *v* GREENHALF[8]
[1952] Ch 488, [1952] 1 All ER 809 (ChD, UPJOHN J)

The plaintiff was the owner of an orchard and an adjoining house. Access to the orchard from the road was provided by a strip of land of varying width about 150 ft. long.

The defendant was a wheelwright whose premises were across the road from the plaintiff's land. The defendant proved that for 50 years he and his father before him had to the plaintiff's knowledge used one side of the plaintiff's strip of land to store and repair vehicles in connection with his business as wheelwright; leaving always room for the plaintiff to have access to the orchard. He claimed a prescriptive right to do so. The plaintiff brought this action to restrain him.

---

[8] Gale, pp. 30–34.

Held. Such a right was not an easement, and the claim amounted to one for beneficial user of the land.

UPJOHN J: Mr Horne [for the plaintiff] . . . says that there are two reasons why this cannot be a valid easement. First, he says that it is uncertain. He says that the court is not in a position to control the exercise of this easement. He relied on *Hill v Tupper* (1863) 2 H & C 121, p. 564, ante, and he referred to the well-known passage in the judgment of Pollock CB, which says: "A new series of incorporeal hereditament cannot be created at the will and pleasure of the owner of property; but he must be content to accept the estate and the right to dispose of it subject to the law as settled by decisions or controlled by Act of Parliament. A grantor may bind himself by covenant to allow any right he pleases over his property, but he cannot annex to it a new incident, so as to enable the grantee to sue in his own name for an infringement of such a limited right as that now claimed."

He pressed me, of course, very strongly with the well-known case of *Dyce v Lady James Hay* (1852) 1 Macq 305, in the House of Lords, in which the sidenote reads as follows: "There can be no prescriptive right in the nature of a servitude or easement so large as to preclude the ordinary uses of property by the owner of the lands affected. *Semble*, that where a claim in the nature of a servitude or easement is incapable of judicial control and restriction it cannot be sustained by prescription. It does not follow that rights sustainable by grant are necessarily sustainable by prescription. The law of Scotland agrees with the law of England in holding that the right to village greens and playgrounds stands upon a principle of original dedication to the use of the public. Where new inventions come into use they may have the benefit of servitudes and easements, the law accommodating its practical operation to the varying circumstances of mankind." . . .

He contended that there is nothing novel in the business of a wheelwright, but that it is an entirely novel suggestion that a wheelwright or anyone else carrying on trade can have such a right as this. He pointed out the great width of the right claimed: vehicles can be left there for an indefinite time, for years, if necessary; they can be left in a vague and undefined part of the strip, leaving an ill-defined gangway, as it has been called, for the owner of the strip to use in getting to his land. He further pointed out that the defendant is really doing much more than an ordinary wheelwright's business; that he is doing repairs to every form of modern type of vehicle, such as motor lorries, and that that also makes the claim really too uncertain to be enforceable.

Mr Horne's second point is this, that an easement must be for the benefit of the land, and not for a business carried on in connexion with the land. . . .

I think that . . . the matter is concluded for me by the decision of Fry J in *Moody v Steggles* (1879) 12 ChD 261 in which he said: "The next point taken on behalf of the defendants is this: It is said that the easement in question relates, not to the tenement, but to the business of the occupant of the tenement, and that therefore I cannot tie the easement to the house. It appears to me that that argument is of too refined a nature to prevail, and for this reason, that the house can only be used by an occupant, and that the occupant only uses the house for the business which he pursues, and therefore in some manner (direct or indirect) an easement is more or less connected with the mode in which the occupant of the house uses it." Then he proceeds to illustrate that by reference to certain cases. I also have in mind that the Judicial Committee in the *Nigerian* case [1915] AC 599 felt no difficulty in principle in holding that there might be an easement in connexion with a right to deposit trade goods.

So far, therefore, as that point is concerned, I decide that it does not avail the plaintiff; but I must return to the point of uncertainty.

I think that the right claimed goes wholly outside any normal idea of an easement, that is, the right of the owner or the occupier of a dominant tenement over a servient tenement. This claim (to which no closely related authority has been referred to me) really amounts to a claim to a joint user of the land by the defendant. Practically, the defendant is claiming the whole beneficial user of the strip of land on the south-east side of the track there; he can leave as many or as few lorries there as he likes for as long as he likes; he may enter on it by himself, his servants and agents to do repair work thereon. In my judgment, that is not a claim which can be established as an easement. It is virtually a claim to possession of the servient tenement, if necessary to the exclusion of the owner; or, at any rate, to a joint user, and no authority has been cited to me which could justify the conclusion that a right of this wide and undefined nature can be the proper subject-matter of an easement. It seems to me that to succeed, this claim must amount to a successful claim of possession by reason of long adverse possession[9]. I say nothing, of course, as to the creation of such rights by deeds or by covenant; I am dealing solely with the question of a right arising by prescription.

In *Grigsby v Melville* [1972] 1 WLR 1355, [1973] 1 All ER 385[10], the plaintiff and the defendants were neighbours. The defendants claimed the right to store articles in a cellar beneath the plaintiff's drawing room floor. BRIGHTMAN J, in rejecting the claim to an easement of storage, said, at 1363, at 391: "There are, I think, two issues here: first, whether an easement of unlimited storage within a confined or defined space is capable of existing as a matter of law. Secondly, if so, whether such an easement was reserved in the present case.

[His Lordship referred to *Copeland v Greenhalf* [1952] Ch 488, [1952] 1 All ER 809 and continued:]

Mr Ainger countered by observing that *Copeland v Greenhalf* was inconsistent with *Wright v Macadam* [1949] 2 KB 744, [1949] 2 All ER 565, p. 587, post, an earlier decision of the Court of Appeal in which it was held that the right of a tenant to store domestic coal in a shed on the landlord's land could exist as an easement for the benefit of the demised premises. I am not convinced that there is any real inconsistency between the two cases. The point of the decision in *Copeland v Greenhalf* was that the right asserted amounted in effect to a claim to the whole beneficial user of the servient tenement and for that reason could not exist as a mere easement. The precise facts in *Wright v Macadam* in this respect are not wholly clear from the report and it is a little difficult to know whether the tenant had exclusive use of the coal shed or of any defined portion of it. To some extent a problem of this sort may be one of degree.

---

[9] (1968) 32 Conv (NS) 270 (M. J. Goodman).
[10] Affirmed [1974] 1 WLR 81, [1973] 3 All ER 455, when CA held that there was no evidence to support the claim to an easement, and declined to "embark upon an analysis of the cases"; (1973) 37 Conv (NS) 60 (D.J. Hayton).

In the case before me, it is, I think, clear that the defendant's claim to an easement would give, to all practical intents and purposes, an exclusive right of user over the whole of the confined space representing the servient tenement. I think I would be at liberty, if necessary, to follow *Copeland v Greenhalf*. I doubt, however, whether I need express any concluded view on this aspect of the case."

[His Lordship then held that an easement was not reserved in the present case].

In *Newman v Jones* (22 March, 1982 unreported); noted M & W, p. 840, n. 34, MEGARRY V-C, in holding that a right to park cars on the forecourt of a block of flats passed as an easement under LPA 1925, s. 62 (2), said: "In view of *Wright v Macadam* [1949] 2 KB 744, [1949] 2 All ER 565 (which was not cited in *Copeland v Greenhalf* [1952] Ch 488, [1952] 1 All ER 809) I feel no hesitation in holding that a right for a landowner to park a car anywhere in a defined area nearby is capable of existing as an easement."

(1973) 37 Conv (NS) 62 (D. J. Hayton)
"On this footing it would appear, for example, that a right to park a car in a particular defined space amounts to a claim to whole beneficial user of the servient space and so cannot rank as an easement, whilst a right to park a car anywhere in a large area does not amount to a claim to whole beneficial user of any servient area and so can rank as an easement. Lawyers advising companies allocating car spaces in basements of flats for flat owners should thus use leases or licences or merely grant a general easement of parking in the basement but ensure that a practical *modus vivendi* is arrived at between the car-owning flat-occupiers. However, the law would adapt itself much better to 'the conditions of modern society and trade', to use Lord Shaw's words in the *Holt* case [1915] AC 599 at 617, if it were to treat as valid easements of parking or of storage in particular defined places, as held by Judge Block in the case of parking in *Sweet and Maxwell Ltd v Michael-Michaels Advertising Ltd* [1965] CLY 2192[11]."

In *Miller v Emcer Products Ltd* [1956] Ch 304, [1956] 1 All ER 237[12], premises were demised to a tenant together with the right to use two lavatories on upper floors which were occupied by a third party. One question, inter alia, which arose was whether or not such a right could exist as an easement. As to this ROMER LJ, in a judgment with which Lord EVERSHED MR and BIRKETT LJ concurred, said at 316, at 240: "In my judgment the right had all the requisite characteristics of an easement. There is no doubt as to what were intended to be the dominant and servient tenements respectively, and the right was appurtenant to the former and calculated to enhance its beneficial use and enjoyment. It is true that during the times when the dominant owner exercised the right, the owner of the servient tenement would be excluded, but this in greater or less degree is a

---

[11] See also (1976) 40 Conv (NS) 317.
[12] (1956) 72 LQR 172 (R. E. M.).

common feature of many easements (for example, rights of way) and does not amount to such an ouster of the servient owner's rights as was held by Upjohn J to be incompatible with a legal easement in *Copeland v Greenhalf* [1952] Ch 488, [1952] 1 All ER 809, p. 570, ante[13]. No case precisely in point on this issue was brought to our attention, but the right to use a lavatory is not dissimilar, I think, to the right to use a neighbour's kitchen for washing, the validity of which as an easement was assumed without question in *Heywood v Mallalieu* (1883) 25 ChD 357. No objection can fairly be made based upon uncertainty, and it follows, in my judgment, that the right may properly be regarded as an easement which the lessors were professing to grant for a term of years; and such an easement would rank as an interest in or over land capable of being created at law by virtue of section 1 (2) of the Law of Property Act 1925."

iii. NEGATIVITY

In *Phipps v Pears* [1965] 1 QB 76, [1964] 2 All ER 35[14], the question was whether a right to make use of a neighbour's house as protection from the weather could exist as an easement.

Two houses, Nos. 14 and 16 Market St., Warwick, were owned by a single owner. No. 16 was rebuilt, "with its flank wall flat up against the old wall of No. 14," the two walls not being bonded together. No. 16 was sold and then No. 14. No. 14 was demolished, and the flank wall of No. 16 was exposed to the weather, and damage resulted.

The owner of No. 16 argued that a right to protection passed to him on the purchase of No. 16 by virtue of Law of Property Act 1925, section 62, p. 586, post.

On the question whether such a right could exist as an easement, Lord DENNING MR said at 82, at 37: "There are two kinds of easements known to the law: positive easements, such as a right of way, which give the owner of land *a right himself to do something* on or to his neighbour's land: and negative easements, such as a right of light, which gives him *a right to stop his neighbour doing something* on his (the neighbour's) own land. The right of support does not fall neatly into either category. It seems in some way to partake of the nature of a positive easement rather than a negative easement. The one building, by its weight, exerts a thrust, not only downwards, but also sideways on to the adjoining building or the adjoining land, and is thus doing something to the neighbour's land, exerting a thrust on it, see *Dalton v Angus* (1881) 6 App Cas 740, 793, per Lord Selborne LC. But a right to protection from the weather (if it exists) is entirely negative. It is a right to stop your neighbour pulling down his own house. Seeing that it is a negative easement, it must be looked at with caution. Because the law has been very chary of creating any new negative easements.

[His Lordship referred to the fact that the law recognised no easement to a view: *Bland v Moseley* (1587) cited in 9 Co Rep at 58a; nor to the passage of air through an undefined channel to the sails of a windmill[15] and continued:]

---

[13] In *Ward v Kirkland* [1967] Ch 194 at 222, [1966] 1 All ER 609 at 615, a right to enter and maintain a wall was held to be an easement and not to amount to "the possession or joint possession of part of the servient property".

[14] Criticised (1964) 80 LQR 318 (R. E. M.); 27 MLR 614; (1965) 28 MLR 264 (H.W. Wilkinson); supported in (1964) 27 MLR 768 (J.F. Garner).

[15] *Webb v Bird* (1861) 10 CB NS 268.

The reason underlying these instances is that if such an easement were to be permitted, it would unduly restrict your neighbour in his enjoyment of his own land. It would hamper legitimate development, see *Dalton v Angus* per Lord Blackburn (1881) 6 App Cas at 824. Likewise here, if we were to stop a man pulling down his house, we would put a brake on desirable improvement. Every man is entitled to pull down his house if he likes. If it exposes your house to the weather, that is your misfortune. It is no wrong on his part. Likewise every man is entitled to cut down his trees if he likes, even if it leaves you without shelter from the wind or shade from the sun, see the decision of the Master of the Rolls in Ireland in *Cochrane v Verner* (1895) 29 ILT 571. There is no such easement known to the law as an easement to be protected from the weather. The only way for an owner to protect himself is by getting a covenant from his neighbour that he will not pull down his house or cut down his trees. Such a covenant would be binding on him in contract: and it would be enforceable on any successor who took with notice of it. But it would not be binding on one who took without notice[16]."

(1964) 80 LQR 321 (R. E. Megarry)

"Finally, there seems to be at least one field in which the decision [*Phipps v Pears*] may cause difficulty, namely, that of freehold flats and maisonettes. If A sells the upper part of his house to B, the conveyance may well provide for the grant of easements of support by A to B, and for the reservation of easements of shelter and protection by A against B: see, e.g. George, *The Sale of Flats* (2nd edn, 1959), pp. 27, 128. *Phipps v Pears* now seems to mean that the reservation by A creates no easement, and that B's successors in title will not be bound by it. Yet it would be most unsatisfactory to be compelled to hold that although A's successors in title may not remove the support from B's flat, B's successors in title may freely remove any or all of their flat and leave A's flat at the mercy of the elements. Even though a right 'to protection from the weather', *totidem verbis*, may well be too indefinite to be an easement, it is still questionable why such a right, if sufficiently and clearly defined in its ambit by the instrument granting it, should be refused recognition as an easement, and left to more complex and less potent means of enforcement such as covenants of indemnity and the doctrine of *Halsall v Brizell* [1957] Ch 169, [1957] 1 All ER 371. In recent years many new rights have been accepted as easements, not least the right to use a lavatory: see *Miller v Emcer Products Ltd* [1956] Ch 304, [1956] 1 All ER 237, p. 573, ante. Is the law of

---

[16] Followed in *Merchant v Capital and Counties Property Co Ltd* (1982) 263 EG 661; (1983) 267 EG 483 (award by CA under London Building Acts (Amendment) Act 1939). Under Public Health Act 1961, s. 29 (5), a local authority may serve a notice on anyone demolishing a building, requiring him to weatherproof any surfaces of adjacent buildings exposed by the demolition.

In *Sedgwick Forbes Bland Payne Group Ltd v Regional Properties Ltd* (1978) 257 EG 64 at 70, it was suggested that a right to protection against the weather by a roof might be an easement, thereby limiting *Phipps v Pears* to an easement of protection against the weather in the vertical plane. For liability for weather proofing of party walls where there is a right of support, see *Bradburn v Lindsay* [1983] 2 All ER 408 (servient owner held liable in negligence for infestation of dominant tenement by dry rot, and in nuisance for loss of support to, and consequent exposure of, the side of the dominant tenement to rot and decay); [1984] Conv 54 (P. Jackson). See also *Brace v South East Regional Housing Association Ltd* (1984) 270 EG 1286; *Tollemache & Cobbold Breweries Ltd v Reynolds* (1983) 268 EG 52; (1984) 269 EG 200 (C.M. Brand and D.W. Williams).

easements not ample enough to match bodily relief with protection from the elements[17]?''

iv.   EXPENDITURE BY SERVIENT OWNER

In *Crow v Wood* [1971] 1 QB 77, [1970] 3 All ER 425[18], the parties farmed land adjoining a large sheep moor in the North Riding of Yorkshire. Each had the right to allow his sheep to stray on the moor. The defendant's sheep trespassed on the plaintiff's land by passing through the plaintiff's fence, which had not been repaired since 1966. There was no arrangement between the parties as to fencing, but the defendant claimed that he was entitled to an easement requiring the plaintiff to maintain the fence. Such an easement, if it existed, passed to the defendant under Law of Property Act 1925, section 62. LORD DENNING said at 84, at 428: "The question is, therefore, whether a right to have a fence or wall kept in repair is a right which is capable of being granted by law. I think it is because it is in the nature of an easement. It is not an easement strictly so called because it involves the servient owner in the expenditure of money. It was described by Gale [*Easements*, 11th edn. (1932), p. 432] as a 'spurious kind of easement'. But it has been treated in practice by the courts as being an easement. Professor Glanville Williams on *Liability for Animals* (1939), says, at p. 209: 'If we put aside these questions of theory and turn to the practice of the courts, there seems to be little doubt that fencing is an easement.' In *Jones v Price* [1965] 2 QB 618 at 633, [1965] 2 All ER 625 at 630, Willmer LJ said: 'It is clear that a right to require the owner of adjoining land to keep the boundary fence in repair is a right which the law will recognise as a quasi-easement.' Diplock LJ, at 639, at 634, points out that it is a right of such a nature that it can be acquired by prescription which imports that it lies in grant, for prescription rests on a presumed grant.

It seems to me that it is now sufficiently established — or at any rate, if not established hitherto, we should now declare — that a right to have your neighbour keep up the fences is a right in the nature of an easement which is capable of being granted by law so as to run with the land and to be binding on successors. It is a right which lies in grant and is of such a nature that it can pass under section 62 of the Law of Property Act 1925[19]."

QUESTION

Having read the cases on the nature of easements, can you set out any guide-lines to help a court decide whether or not a right which complies with the accepted requirements of an easement is to be recognised judicially? C & B, pp. 496–498; *Dowty Boulton Paul Ltd v Wolverhampton Corpn (No 2)* [1976] Ch 13 at 23, [1973] 2 All ER 491 at 495, per RUSSELL LJ: "A tendency in the past to freeze the categories of easements has been overtaken by the defrosting operation in *Re Ellenborough Park* [1956] Ch 131, [1955] 3 All ER 667".

---

[17] Many of the difficulties can be overcome by suitably drawn covenants. See p. 756, post.
[18] *Liverpool City Council v Irwin* [1977] AC 239, [1976] 2 All ER 39, p. 563, ante.
[19] An easement of fencing may also be acquired (i) as an easement by prescription: *Lawrence v Jenkins* (1873) LR 8 QB 274; *Jones v Price* [1965] 2 QB 618, [1965] 2 All ER 625 (ii) by custom: *Egerton v Harding* [1975] QB 62, [1974] 3 All ER 689.

B. Legal and Equitable Easements

LAW OF PROPERTY ACT 1925

1. Legal estates and equitable interests.

(2) (*a*), p. 6, ante.

(3), p. 7, ante.

2. Conveyances overreaching certain equitable interests and powers.

(3) (iii), p. 206, ante.

4. Creation and disposition of equitable interests.

(1), p. 12, ante.

LAND CHARGES ACT 1972

2. Register of land charges.

(4) Class C (iv), p. 32, ante.

(5) Class D (iii), p. 32, ante.

An easement is a legal interest if it (*a*) complies with section 1 (2) (*a*), Law of Property Act 1925 and is held for "an interest equivalent to an estate in fee simple absolute in possession or a term of years absolute" and (*b*) is created either by statute, deed or prescription.

An easement which fails to satisfy either (*a*) or (*b*) is not a legal, but an equitable, interest, e.g., if it is for the life of the grantee or created by an equitable owner (in which case it is registrable, if created after 1925, as a Land Charge Class D (iii)), or if it is granted informally or is the subject of a contract to grant (when it is registrable as an estate contract Class C (iv))[20].

In spite of some earlier views to the contrary[1], it is now settled that the definition of an equitable easement (which is defined in section 2 (3) (iii) of the Law of Property Act 1925 as "any easement, liberty[2], or privilege over or affecting land and being merely an equitable interest") is to be construed narrowly. This excludes such informal equitable rights as an equitable right of re-entry[3], or any rights arising in equity by reason of an estoppel licence or the doctrine of mutual benefit and burden[4]. These rights are therefore not registrable as land charges, and their enforcement against third parties depends solely on the doctrine of notice[5].

---

[20] *McManus v Cooke* (1887) 35 ChD 681 (easement), p. 83, ante; *Mason v Clarke* [1955] AC 778, [1955] 1 All ER 914 (profit à prendre), p. 83, ante; *Lowe v JW Ashmore Ltd* [1971] Ch 545 at 557–558, [1971] 1 All ER 1057 at 1068–1069 (profit à prendre).

[1] (1935) 15 Bell Yard 18 (G. Cross); see also (1948) 12 Conv (NS) 202 (J. F. Garner).

[2] The definition in LCA 1972, s. 2 (5) substitutes the word "right" for "liberty".

[3] *Shiloh Spinners Ltd v Harding* [1973] AC 691, [1973] 1 All ER 90, p. 34, ante.

[4] *ER Ives Investment Ltd v High* [1967] 2 QB 379, [1967] 1 All ER 504, p. 542, ante; followed in *Poster v Slough Estates Ltd* [1969] 1 Ch 495, [1968] 3 All ER 257 (right of entry to remove fixtures at end of lease); (1937) 53 LQR 259 (C. V. Davidge); (1969) 33 Conv (NS) 135 (P. Jackson). See also *Lewisham Borough Council v Maloney* [1948] 1 KB 50, [1947] 2 All ER 36 (requisitioning authority's right to possession).

[5] P. 24, ante. Report of the Committee on Land Charges 1956 (Cmnd 9825), para. 16 suggested that Class D (iii) might be abolished. Law Commission Report on Land Charges affecting Unregistered Land 1969 (Law Com No. 18, HC 125), para. 65, recommended its retention. Registrations in that class were then running at an annual rate of 2,500–3,500; there were 1,849 registrations during the year ended 31 March 1985; p. 33, ante.

III.   Acquisition[6]

Easements, like any other incorporeal hereditaments, lie in grant at common law. They could not, like corporeal hereditaments, pass by "livery of seisin", and, as an easement is real property, a deed of grant was required. Situations could arise, however, in which it was felt that the landowner should have an easement, but he could show no express grant. The common law, true to the basic rule that easements lie in grant, developed rules whereby the grant could be *implied* in a deed conveying land but making no mention of the easement, or could be *presumed* where there was no deed at all; this latter case deals with what is more commonly called prescription. As has been seen, an easement may be granted in equity. There are statutory provisions relating to various aspects of acquisition by grant[7]. And, on occasion, statutes have been passed specifically creating easements between adjoining owners; the common example of this type of statute is an Inclosure Act which distributed among individual owners land which had been subject to rights of common and created certain easements among these owners.

A.   Acquisition by Express Grant or Reservation[8]

i.   AT LAW

Coke (Co Litt 9a): "And here is implyed a division of fee, or inheritance, *viz*, into corporeall, . . . and incorporeall (which lie in grant, and cannot passe by livery, but by deede, as advowsons, commons &c., and of some is called haereditas incorporata, and, by the delivery of the deede, the freehold, and inheritance of such inheritance, as doth lie in grant, doth passe) comprehended in this word grant. And the deed of incorporeate inheritances doth equall the livery of corporeate."

LAW OF PROPERTY ACT 1925

52.   Conveyances to be by deed. — (1) p. 76, ante.

65.   Reservation of legal estates. — (1) A reservation of a legal estate shall operate at law without any execution of the conveyance by the grantee of the legal estate out of which the reservation is made, or any regrant by him, so as to create the legal estate reserved, and so as to vest the same in possession in the person (whether being the grantor or not) for whose benefit the reservation is made.

(2) A conveyance of a legal estate expressed to be made subject to another legal estate not in existence immediately before the date of the conveyance, shall operate as a reservation, unless a contrary intention appears[9].

(3) This section applies only to reservations made after the commencement of this Act.

---

[6] C & B, pp. 500–525; M & W, pp. 855–892; MM, pp. 408–427; Gale, pp. 75–192; Jackson, pp. 71–138, 189–194.

[7] LPA 1925, s. 62, p. 586, post.

[8] C & B, pp. 501–506; M & W, pp. 856–861; MM, pp. 408–410; Gale, pp. 76–82; Jackson, pp. 108–109.

[9] *Wiles v Banks* (1983) 50 P & CR 80.

In *St Edmundsbury and Ipswich Diocesan Board of Finance v Clark (No 2)* [1975] 1 WLR 468, [1975] 1 All ER 772, the question arose whether on the reservation of an easement by a vendor the terms of the reservation were, in case of doubt, to be construed against the vendor or against the purchaser. The Court of Appeal laid down that it should be construed against the purchaser, as on a re-grant. Sir John PENNYCUICK said at 477, at 780:

"Second, is the maxim 'omnia praesumuntur contra proferentem' applicable against the vendor or against the purchaser where there is a conveyance subject to the reservation of a new right of way? In view of the full discussion of this question by Megarry J, and of the fact that we do not agree with his conclusion, we think it right to deal fairly fully with it. But it is necessary to make clear that this presumption can only come into play if the court finds itself unable on the material before it to reach a sure conclusion on the construction of a reservation. The presumption is not itself a factor to be taken into account in reaching the conclusion. In the present case we have indeed reached a sure conclusion, and on this footing the presumption never comes into play, so that the view which we are about to express upon it is not necessary to the decision of the present case.

The point turns upon the true construction of section 65 (1) of the Law of Property Act 1925. [His Lordship read the section (p. 578, ante) and continued:] Formerly the law was that on a conveyance with words merely reserving an easement, the easement was held to be created, provided that the purchaser executed the conveyance, without the necessity for words of regrant. The law treated the language of the reservation as having the same effect as would the language of regrant though there was not in terms a regrant, and in those circumstances regarded the purchaser as the proferens for present purposes. This was a relaxation of the strict requirements for the creation of an easement. (An easement could be created without execution by the purchaser of a conveyance by reference to the Statute of Uses, once section 62 of the Conveyancing Act 1881 removed the technical objection that that statute could not operate to create an easement. This method disappeared with the repeal of the Statute of Uses in the 1925 property legislation).

Section 65 must be read in the light, therefore, of two aspects of the preceding law. First: that previously the law was sufficiently relaxed from its prima facie stringency to permit the language of mere reservation to have the effect of a regrant though it was not in truth a regrant by its language. Second: that for this purpose the purchaser must execute the conveyance if an easement was to be created; that is to say, although a regrant in terms was not required. Against that background, are the words in section 65 'without . . . any regrant by' the purchaser to be regarded as altering the law so that the purchaser is no longer to be regarded as the relevant proferens? Or are they to be regarded as merely maintaining for the avoidance of doubt the situation that had been already reached by the development of the law, viz. that mere words of reservation could be regarded as having the same effect as would the language of regrant though without there being in terms any purported regrant by the purchaser? We would, apart from authority, construe the words in the latter sense, so that the only relevant change in the law is the absence of the requirement that the purchaser should execute the conveyance. We read the section as if it were in effect saying that whereas an easement could be created by mere words of reservation without any words of regrant by the purchaser, provided that the purchaser executes the conveyance, hereafter the easement can be created by mere words of reservation without any words of regrant by the purchaser even if he does not execute the conveyance: it is not to be said that in the latter event the previous relaxation of the strict law has disappeared, so that the language of the conveyance must be more than the mere language of reservation. It will be observed that that view keeps in line, on the relevant point, a post-1925 conveyance executed by the purchaser, which is apparently not touched by section 65, and one which is executed by him.

The above is our view apart from authority. What then of authority? We start with the fact that Sir Benjamin Cherry, architect of the 1925 property legislation, made no reference to this suggested change of principle in the law in the first edition of *Wolstenholme and Cherry's Conveyancing Statutes* after the 1925 property legislation. Further, in more than one case since 1925, judges of high authority took it for granted that the old principle still prevails: see *Bulstrode v Lambert* [1953] 1 WLR 1064, [1953] 2 All ER 728 per Upjohn J at 1068, at 731; *Mason v Clarke* [1954] 1 QB 460, [1954] 1 All ER 189, in the Court of Appeal, per Denning LJ at 467, at 192 and in the House of Lords per Lord Simonds [1955] AC 778 at 786, [1955] 1 All ER 914 at 915. In these cases the contrary was not argued and the judicial statements are not of binding authority. But in *Johnstone v Holdway* [1963] 1 QB 601, [1963] 1 All ER 432 in the Court of Appeal, Upjohn LJ, giving the judgment of the court, not only in terms re-stated the old principle but made it part of the ratio decidendi of his judgment.

He said, at 612, at 436:

'that the exception and reservation of the mines and minerals was to the vendor, that is the legal owner, but the exception and reservation of the right of way was to the company, the equitable owner. If the reservation of a right of way operated strictly as a reservation, then, as the company only had an equitable title, it would seem that only an equitable easement could have been reserved. But it is clear that an exception and reservation of a right of way in fact operates by way of regrant by the purchaser to his vendor and the question, therefore, is whether as a matter of construction the purchaser granted to the company a legal easement or an equitable easement.'

The opposing view was expressed by Megarry J in *Cordell v Second Clanfield Properties Ltd* [1969] 2 Ch 9, [1968] 3 All ER 746 (upon motion and without being referred to *Johnstone v Holdway*) and in the present case (after a full review of the authorities, including *Johnstone v Holdway*). He distinguishes *Johnstone v Holdway* as a decision based on mistake and states his own conclusion in the following words [1973] 1 WLR 1572 at 1591, [1973] 3 All ER 902 at 921:

'The fair and natural meaning of section 65 (1) seems to me to be that if a vendor reserves an easement, the reservation is to be effective at law without any actual or notional regrant by the purchaser, and so without the consequences that flow from any regrant. At common law, the rule that a reservation of an easement was to be construed against the purchaser depended solely upon the notional regrant. Apart from that, the words of reservation, being the words of the vendor, would be construed against the vendor in accordance with the general principle stated in *Norton on Deeds*, 2nd edn (1928), just as an exception or a reservation of a rent would; it was the fiction of a regrant which made reservations of easements stand out of line with exceptions and reservations in the strict sense. With the statutory abolition of the fictitious regrant, reservations of easements fall into line with the broad and sensible approach that it is for him who wishes to retain something for himself to see that there is an adequate statement of what it is that he seeks to retain; and if after considering all the circumstances of the case there remains any real doubt as to the ambit of the right reserved, then that doubt should be resolved against the vendor. Accordingly, in this case I hold that the words "subject also to a right of way over the land coloured red on the said plan to and from St. Botolphs Church" in the 1945 conveyance should, if their meaning is not otherwise resolved, be construed against the church authorities and so in favour of Mr Clark.'

We see much force in this reasoning. But we find it impossible to accept Megarry J's analysis of the decision in *Johnstone v Holdway*. We are not prepared to infer from the report that experienced and responsible counsel misrepresented the terms of section 65 to the court and that the judge based his decision on the terms of the section as so misrepresented. It follows that the decision in *Johnstone v Holdway* is binding upon this court and that we ought to follow it."

ii. IN EQUITY

An agreement for valuable consideration to grant an easement or a profit à prendre is a contract which equity will specifically enforce and is registrable as an estate contract. Equity looks on that as done which ought to be done and such an agreement operates as a grant in equity of an easement. Further, equity construes an informal (unsealed) grant as a contract to grant an easement. Such a contract, being an agreement for a disposition of an interest in land, is required to be evidenced in writing; but the doctrine of part performance applies, and, as in the case of an agreement for a lease, equity will construe a purported oral or written grant as an agreement to grant an easement.

McManus v Cooke (1887) 35 ChD 681, p. 83, ante[10].

B. Acquisition by Implied Grant or Reservation[11]

When the owner of land grants part of it, or certain interests in part of it, to another person, there will be implied, in appropriate circumstances, (i) certain rights in favour of the grantee exercisable over the land retained (implied grant), and (ii) certain rights in favour of the grantor over the land granted (implied reservation). These rights are rights in the nature of easements, but which could not be easements before the grant because all the land was under single ownership. These two cases — implied grant and implied reservation — are treated differently and must be dealt with separately.

---

[10] See also *May v Belleville* [1905] 2 Ch 605; *Mason v Clarke* [1955] AC 778, [1955] 1 All ER 914 (profit à prendre), p. 83, ante.
[11] C & B, pp. 506–511; M & W, pp. 861–869; MM, pp. 410–415; Gale, pp. 82–132; Jackson, pp. 70–109; Farrand (2nd edn), pp. 377–392.

i.   EASEMENTS IMPLIED IN FAVOUR OF THE GRANTEE

(a) The Common Law Rule

Consistently with the principle that a grantor must not derogate from his grant[12], the law readily implies easements in favour of the grantee. The rule has been laid down in an obiter dictum in *Wheeldon v Burrows*, which has subsequently been accepted universally as a correct statement of the law, to the effect that in a grant of land there may be implied in favour of the grantee those rights in the nature of easements which (1) are "continuous and apparent" or "in other words all those easements which are necessary to the reasonable enjoyment of the property granted" and (2) have been and are, at the time of the grant, used by the grantor for the benefit of the part granted. Easements of necessity without which the property could not be enjoyed at all and easements which were clearly within the common intention of the parties[13] will also be implied in favour of the grantee; and sometimes in favour of the grantor also.

The doctrine of *Wheeldon v Burrows* has been shorn of much of its importance by section 62 of the Law of Property Act 1925. But it still remains available wherever, for one reason or another, a claimant cannot rely on section 62[14]. It always operates subject to the terms of the contract or conveyance[15], and to the circumstances existing at the date of the grant.

WHEELDON *v* BURROWS

(1879) 12 ChD 31 (CA, THESIGER, JAMES and BAGGALLAY LJJ)

Of land owned in 1875 by one Tetley, part was sold in January 1876 to the plaintiff's husband, William Wheeldon. Another part was sold in February 1876 to the defendant; on this part there was a shed containing, and lighted by, three windows which overlooked the plaintiff's land. In 1878 the plaintiff, then the widow and devisee of William Wheeldon, erected hoardings near the edge of her land facing the defendant's shed for the purpose of ascertaining her right to exclude the light from the shed. The defendant, claiming an easement of light, knocked down the hoardings, and this action was brought for trespass.

Held. The defendant had no right to knock down the hoardings because no right to the access of light to the windows of the shed had been reserved by Tetley on the sale of the land to the plaintiff's husband.

---

[12] (1964) 80 LQR 244 (D. W. Elliott); Gale pp. 88–92; *Ward v Kirkland* [1967] Ch 194 at 226–227, [1966] 1 All ER 609 at 617; *Sovmots Investments Ltd v Secretary of State for the Environment* [1979] AC 144 at 165, [1977] 2 All ER 385 at 391, per Lord WILBERFORCE, p. 595, post.

[13] *Pwllbach Colliery Co Ltd v Woodman* [1915] AC 634; *Keewatin Water Power Co Ltd v Lake of the Woods Milling Co Ltd* [1930] AC 640; *Wong v Beaumont Property Trust Ltd* [1965] 1 QB 173, [1964] 2 All ER 119, p. 584, post; *Nickerson v Barraclough* [1981] Ch 426, [1981] 2 All ER 369, p. 598, n. 7, post.

[14] See p. 586, post.

[15] This may be expressed by a condition of sale; see *National Conditions of Sale* (20th edn, 1981) Condition 20; Law Society's *General Conditions of Sale* (1984 Revision), Condition 5 (3) (*b*); Wilkinson, *Standard Conditions of Sale of Land* (3rd edn), pp. 26–30; Hallett's *Conveyancing Precedents*, pp. 210, para. (4), 213, para. (3); *Squarey v Harris-Smith* (1981) 42 P & CR 118 (where a standard condition that the purchaser should not acquire any rights which would restrict the free use of the vendor's other land for building was held to negative the operation of s. 62); cf. *Lyme Valley Squash Club Ltd v Newcastle under Lyme Borough Council* [1985] 2 All ER 405, in which *Squarey v Harris-Smith* was not cited, and the opposite conclusion was reached; [1985] Conv 243.

THESIGER LJ: We have had a considerable number of cases cited to us, and out of them I think that two propositions may be stated as what I may call the general rules governing cases of this kind. The first of these rules is, that on the grant by the owner of a tenement of part of that tenement as it is then used and enjoyed, there will pass to the grantee all those continuous[16] and apparent easements (by which, of course, I mean *quasi* easements), or, in other words, all those easements which are necessary to the reasonable enjoyment of the property granted, and which have been and are at the time of the grant used by the owners of the entirety for the benefit of the part granted. The second proposition is that, if the grantor intends to reserve any right over the tenement granted, it is his duty to reserve it expressly in the grant. Those are the general rules governing cases of this kind, but the second of those rules is subject to certain exceptions. One of those exceptions is the well-known exception which attaches to cases of what are called ways of necessity; and I do not dispute for a moment that there may be, and probably are, certain other exceptions, to which I shall refer before I close my observations upon this case.

Both of the general rules which I have mentioned are founded upon a maxim which is as well established by authority as it is consonant to reason and common sense, viz., that a grantor shall not derogate from his grant. It has been argued before us that there is no distinction between what has been called an implied grant and what is attempted to be established under the name of an implied reservation; and that such a distinction between the implied grant and the implied reservation is a mere modern invention and one which runs contrary, not only to the general practice upon which land has been bought and sold for a considerable time, but also to authorities which are said to be clear and distinct upon the matter. So far, however, from that distinction being one which was laid down for the first time by and which is to be attributed to Lord *Westbury* in *Suffield v Brown* (1864) 4 De GJ & Sm 185, it appears to me that it has existed almost as far back as we can trace the law upon the subject; and I think it right, as the case is one of considerable importance, not merely as regards the parties, but as regards vendors and purchasers of land generally, that I should go with some little particularity into what I may term the leading cases upon the subject.

. . . These cases in no way support the proposition for which the appellant in this case contends; but, on the contrary, support the propositions that in the case of a grant you may imply a grant of such continuous and apparent easements or such easements as are necessary to the reasonable enjoyment of the property conveyed, and have in fact been enjoyed during the unity of ownership, but that, with the exception which I have referred to of easements of necessity, you cannot imply a similar reservation in favour of the grantor of land[17].

---

[16] C & B, pp. 509–510; M & W, p. 863; MM, pp. 411–412; Gale, pp. 92–99; Jackson, pp. 77–79; Farrand (2nd edn), pp. 383–384; *Polden v Bastard* (1865) LR 1 QB 156; *Hansford v Jago* [1921] 1 Ch 322; cf. MAUGHAM J in *Borman v Griffith* [1930] 1 Ch 493, p. 426, ante; *Ward v Kirkland* [1967] Ch 194 at 224–225, [1966] 1 All ER 609 at 615, per UNGOED-THOMAS J, citing with approval Cheshire, *Modern Law of Real Property* (9th edn), p. 468.

[17] *Aldridge v Wright* [1929] 2 KB 117; *Suffield v Brown* (1864) 4 De GJ & Sm 185; *Borman v Griffith* [1930] 1 Ch 493, p. 388, ante.

In *Ward v Kirkland* [1967] Ch 194, [1966] 1 All ER 609, UNGOED-THOMAS J referred to the discrepancy in the first and last paragraphs of THESIGER LJ's judgment[18]. Of the first paragraph he said at 224, at 615: "There, it might appear that the words 'in other words' in that passage would indicate that the requirement, 'which are necessary to the reasonable enjoyment of the property granted', and the earlier words, 'continuous and apparent easements', refer to the same easements."

Of the last paragraph he said: "Reading that passage on its own, on first impression, it would appear that the 'easements which are necessary to the reasonable enjoyment of the property conveyed' might be a separate class from 'continuous and apparent easements.' . . . It has been suggested that perhaps the 'easements necessary to the reasonable enjoyment of the property conveyed' might refer to negative easements. . . . I understand that there is no case in which positive easements which are not 'continuous and apparent' have been held to come within the doctrine of *Wheeldon v Burrows*[19]."

WONG v BEAUMONT PROPERTY TRUST LTD
[1965] 1 QB 173, [1964] 2 All ER 119 (CA, Lord DENNING MR, PEARSON and SALMON LJJ)

In 1957, three cellars in Exeter were let to one Blackaby who covenanted to use the premises as a popular restaurant and to control all smells and odours according to health regulations and so as not to become a nuisance. To comply with these undertakings, it was necessary to construct a ventilation duct fixed to the outside wall of the landlords' premises. This was not realised by the parties at the time, and no duct was built.

In 1961 the plaintiff bought the remainder of the lease and developed the premises into a highly successful Chinese restaurant. The smells and odours caused the Midland Bank, who occupied the floor above, to complain and the public health inspector required the duct to be built. The defendants, assignees in 1962 of the original landlords, refused to allow the work to be done, and the plaintiff asked for a declaration of entitlement and damages.

Held (affirming Judge Pratt). Declaration that the plaintiff was entitled to an easement as an easement of necessity.

LORD DENNING MR: The question is: Has the plaintiff a right to put up this duct without the landlords' consent? If he is to have any right at all, it must be by way of easement and not merely by way of implied contract. He is not the original lessee, nor are the defendants the original lessors. Each is a successor in title. As between them, a right of this kind, if it exists at all, must be by way of an easement. In particular, an easement of necessity. The law on the matter was stated by Lord Parker of Waddington in *Pwllbach Colliery Co Ltd v Woodman* [1915] AC 634, where he said at 646, omitting immaterial words, "The law will readily imply the grant or reservation of such easements as may be necessary to give effect to the common intention of the parties to a grant of real property, with reference to the manner or purposes in and for which the land granted . . . is to be used. But it is essential for this purpose that the parties should intend that the subject of the grant . . .

---

[18] See also *Squarey v Harris-Smith* (1981) 42 P & CR 118 at 124, per OLIVER LJ.
[19] (1967) 83 LQR 240 (A. W. B. Simpson).

should be used in some definite and particular manner. It is not enough that the subject of the grant . . . should be intended to be used in a manner which may or may not involve this definite and particular use." That is the principle which underlies all easements of necessity. If you go back to Rolle's Abridgment you will find it stated in this way: "If I have a field inclosed by my own land on all sides, and I alien this close to another, he shall have a way to this close over my land, as incident to the grant; for otherwise he cannot have any benefit by the grant."

I would apply those principles here. Here was the grant of a lease to the lessee for the very purpose of carrying on a restaurant business. It was to be a popular restaurant, and it was to be developed and extended. There was a covenant not to cause any nuisance; and to control and eliminate all smells; and to comply with the Food Hygiene Regulations. That was "a definite and particular manner" in which the business had to be conducted. It could not be carried on in that manner at all unless a ventilation system was installed by a duct of this kind. In these circumstances it seems to me that, if the business is to be carried on at all — if, in the words of Rolle's Abridgment, the lessee is to "have any benefit by the grant" at all — he must of necessity be able to put a ventilation duct up the wall. It may be that in Blackaby's time it would not have needed such a large duct as is now needed in the plaintiff's time. But nevertheless a duct of some kind would have had to be put up the wall. The plaintiff may need a bigger one. But that does not matter. A man who has a right to an easement can use it in any proper way, so long as he does not substantially increase the burden on the servient tenement. In this case a bigger duct will not substantially increase the burden.

There is one point in which this case goes further than the earlier cases which have been cited. It is this. It was not realised by the parties, at the time of the lease, that this duct would be necessary. But it was in fact necessary from the very beginning. That seems to me sufficient to bring the principle into play. In order to use this place as a restaurant, there must be implied an easement, by the necessity of the case, to carry a duct up this wall. The county court judge so held. He granted a declaration. I agree with him.

In *Barry v Hasseldine* [1952] Ch 835, [1952] 2 All ER 317, DANCKWERTS J said at 839, at 319: "In my opinion, however, if the grantee has no access to the property which is sold and conveyed to him except over the grantor's land or over the land of some person or persons whom he cannot compel to give him any legal right of way, common sense demands that a way of necessity should be implied, so as to confer on the grantee a right of way, for the purposes for which the land is conveyed, over the land of the grantor; and it is no answer to say that a permissive method of approach was in fact enjoyed, at the time of the grant, over the land of some person other than the grantor because that permissive method of approach may be determined on the following day, thereby leaving the grantee with no lawful method of approaching the land which he has purchased."

QUESTION
Is there a difference between an easement of necessity, and an easement which is "necessary to give effect to the common intention of the parties?"

If there is a difference, is it relevant in either case that the parties did not realise that the necessity existed?

(1964) 80 LQR 322–323 (R. E. Megarry) and pp. 597–602, *post*; *Horn v Hiscock* (1972) 223 EG 1437 at 1441; *Nickerson v Barraclough* [1980] Ch 325 at 332, [1979] 3 All ER 312 at 320–321.

(b) Law of Property Act 1925, section 62

The Law of Property Act 1925, section 62 (replacing the Conveyancing Act 1881, section 6), has taken over much of the area formerly governed by the rule in *Wheeldon v Burrows*, p. 582, ante. Its application is wider, in that the right need not be "continuous and apparent"[20] nor "necessary for the reasonable enjoyment of the property granted"[1]; it also applies to profits à prendre[2]. On the other hand, it does not apply where the dominant owner obtains his interest without a conveyance under seal (as by will or under contract)[3], or where there was previously no diversity of occupation of the two tenements[4].

LAW OF PROPERTY ACT 1925

62.   General words implied in conveyances[5] — (1) A conveyance of land shall be deemed to include and shall by virtue of this Act operate to convey, with the land, all buildings, erections, fixtures, commons, hedges, ditches, fences, ways, waters, watercourses, liberties, privileges, easements, rights, and advantages whatsoever, appertaining or reputed to appertain to the land, or any part thereof, or, at the time of conveyance[6], demised, occupied, or enjoyed with[7] or reputed or known as part or parcel of or appurtenant to the land or any part thereof.

(2) A conveyance of land, having houses or other buildings thereon, shall be deemed to include and shall by virtue of this Act operate to convey, with the land, houses, or other buildings, all outhouses, erections, fixtures, cellars, areas, courts, courtyards, cisterns, sewers, gutters, drains, ways, passages, lights, watercourses, liberties, privileges, easements, rights, and advantages whatsoever, appertaining or reputed to appertain to the land, houses, or other buildings conveyed, or any of them, or any part thereof, or, at the time

---

[20] *Ward v Kirkland* [1967] Ch 194, [1966] 1 All ER 609 (right to enter farmyard to maintain a wall held to be not continuous and apparent, but to be an easement created under s. 62). The right must be exercised at the date of the conveyance: *Penn v Wilkins* (1974) 236 EG 203 (passage of sewage, which ceased many years before conveyance, not covered by s. 62).

[1] *Goldberg v Edwards* [1950] Ch 247, p. 590, post.

[2] *Polden v Bastard* (1865) LR 1 QB 156; *White v Williams* [1922] 1 KB 727; *White v Taylor (No 2)* [1969] 1 Ch 160, [1968] 1 All ER 1015; *Anderson v Bostock* [1976] Ch 312, [1976] 1 All ER 560; *Re Yateley Common, Hampshire* [1977] 1 WLR 840 at 850, [1977] 1 All ER 505 at 514; *Re Broxhead Common, Whitehill, Hampshire* (1977) 33 P & CR 451.

[3] *Borman v Griffith* [1930] 1 Ch 493, p. 426, ante; *Schwann v Cotton* [1916] 2 Ch 459; *Horn v Hiscock* (1972) 223 EG 1437.

[4] *Long v Gowlett* [1923] 2 Ch 177, p. 593, post; *Ward v Kirkland* [1967] Ch 194, [1966] 1 All ER 609; *Sovmots Investments Ltd v Secretary of State for the Environment* [1979] AC 144, [1977] 2 All ER 385, p. 595, post.

[5] (1966) 30 Conv (NS) 340 (P. Jackson); Jackson, pp. 92–108.

[6] This section is not concerned with future rights: *Nickerson v Barraclough* [1981] Ch 426, [1981] 2 All ER 369.

[7] This is not synonymous with user: *Re Yateley Common, Hampshire*, supra.

of conveyance, demised, occupied, or enjoyed with, or reputed or known as part or parcel of or appurtenant to, the land, houses, or other buildings conveyed, or any of them, or any part thereof.

(4) This section applies only if and as far as a contrary intention is not expressed in the conveyance, and has effect subject to the terms of the conveyance and to the provisions therein contained[8].

(6) This section applies to conveyances made after the thirty-first day of December, eighteen hundred and eighty-one.

WRIGHT *v* MACADAM[9]
[1949] 2 KB 744, [1949] 2 All ER 565 (CA, TUCKER, JENKINS and SINGLETON LJJ)

In 1940, the defendant let a top floor flat at 13 Mount Ararat Road, Richmond, to Mrs Wright for one week. After the expiration of that time Mrs Wright continued in occupation by virtue of the Rent Acts.

In 1941, the defendant gave Mrs Wright permission to use a shed in the garden for the storage of coal, and this permission was exercised.

In 1943, the defendant granted a new tenancy of the premises with an additional room to Mrs Wright and her daughter by an unsealed document which made no reference to the use of the shed. The Wrights enjoyed the use of the shed until 1947 when the defendant suggested that 1s. 6d. a week should be paid for its use. They refused, and were denied the use of the shed. This action was brought for an injunction to restrain interference with their use of it and for £10 in damages.

Held. The right to use the coal-shed passed to the Wrights as an easement under section 62 of the Law of Property Act 1925 on the grant of the tenancy in 1943.

JENKINS LJ: The plaintiffs claimed an injunction to restrain the defendant from trespassing or otherwise interfering with their lawful use of the coal shed, a declaration that their tenancy of the flat included the right to use the coal shed, and damages limited to 10*l*. I may mention that, as matters stand at present, the last of those claims appears to be the only relevant one, inasmuch as we were informed in the course of the hearing that the defendant has in fact pulled down the coal shed. The question, therefore, is simply this: whether the plaintiffs, as tenants of the top floor flat at 13, Mount Ararat Road, were entitled to the use of the coal shed in question. It is argued for the plaintiffs that they were so entitled, by virtue of section 62 of the Law of Property Act, 1925, which is the section replacing the old section 6 of the Conveyancing Act 1881, and providing by statute the general words which it was formerly customary to insert in full in the parcels of conveyances and other dispositions of land. The plaintiffs claim that this section covers the case. The defendant, on the other hand, claims that, although the coal shed was admittedly used, it was used under no sufficiently definite arrangement; that it was used purely as a matter of personal licence and precariously; and that the arrangement under which it was used could not be said to confer a

---

[8] There are restrictions upon the exclusion of the section in a conveyance of a freehold to a tenant enfranchised under the Leasehold Reform Act 1967, s. 10 (1).
[9] (1950) 66 LQR 302 (R. E. M.). Followed in *Graham v Philcox* [1984] QB 747, [1984] 2 All ER 643, p. 632, post.

right in any way appurtenant to the flat, but was an arrangement of a kind to which section 62 of the Act had no application.

[His Lordship came to the conclusion that the tenancy agreement, being sufficient by virtue of the Law of Property Act 1925, sections 52, 54, to pass a legal estate, was a "conveyance" within the meaning given to that term in section 205 (1) (ii). There was therefore a "conveyance of land" within the meaning of section 62 (1). He continued:]

The question in the present case, therefore, is whether the right to use the coal shed was at the date of the letting of 28 August 1943 a liberty, privilege, easement, right or advantage appertaining or reputed to appertain, to the land, or any part thereof, or, at the time of the conveyance, demised, occupied or enjoyed with the land — that is the flat — or any part thereof. It is enough for the plaintiffs' purposes if they can bring the right claimed within the widest part of the subsection — that is to say, if they can show that the right was at the time of the material letting demised, occupied or enjoyed with the flat or any part thereof.

The predecessor of section 62 of the Act of 1925, in the shape of section 6 of the Act of 1881 has been the subject of a good deal of judicial discussion, and I think the effect of the cases can be thus summarised. First, the section is not confined to rights which, as a matter of law, were so annexed or appurtenant to the property conveyed at the time of the conveyance as to make them actual legally enforceable rights. Thus, on the severance of a piece of land in common ownership, the quasi easements de facto enjoyed in respect of it by one part of the land over another will pass although, of course, as a matter of law, no man can have a right appendant or appurtenant to one part of his property exerciseable by him over the other part of his property[10]. Secondly, the right, in order to pass, need not be one to which the owner or occupier for the time being of the land has had what may be described as a permanent title. A right enjoyed merely by permission is enough. The leading authority for that proposition is the case of *International Tea Stores Co v Hobbs* [1903] 2 Ch 165[11]. That was a decision of Sir George Farwell as a judge of first instance. It was a case in which the defendant, who owned two houses, let one of them for business purposes and there had been a practice of giving permission to the successive managers of the property let to pass and re-pass with their servants and so forth across a yard which was part of the property and remained in the defendant's occupation. The part of the property which had been let was later sold to the tenants, nothing being said in the conveyance about the right of way. The purchasers claimed to exercise the right of way by virtue of section 6 of the Act of 1881. That claim was disputed, and the point was taken that it could not be a right which would pass under the implied general words inasmuch as it was only precariously enjoyed. The learned judge held that the fact that the way was permissive only was irrelevant for this purpose, and that by virtue of section 6 of the Act of 1881 the grant included a corresponding right of way in fee simple. Dealing with the question of licence or permission, the learned judge said this: "Unless I am prepared to say that in no case can a tenant obtain under the Conveyancing Act 1881 a right of way unless he has enjoyed it as of right, I

---

[10] Compare *Long v Gowlett* [1923] 2 Ch 177, p. 593, post.
[11] See the remarks of CROSS J in *Green v Ashco Horticulturist Ltd* [1966] 1 WLR 889 at 896–897, [1966] 2 All ER 232 at 238; *Ward v Kirkland* [1967] Ch 194, [1966] 1 All ER 609.

must hold in this case that the fact of licence makes no difference. In all these cases the right of way must be either licensed or unlicensed. If it is unlicensed it would be at least as cogent an argument to say, 'True you went there, but it was precarious, because I could have sent a man to stop you or stopped you myself any day.' If it is by licence, it is precarious, of course, in the sense that the licence, being ex hypothesi revocable, might be revoked at any time; but if there be degrees of precariousness, the latter is less precarious than the former. But, in my opinion, precariousness has nothing to do with this sort of case, where a privilege which is by its nature known to the law — namely, a right of way — has been in fact enjoyed. Lord Coleridge's argument was founded upon a misconception of a judgment of mine in *Burrows v Lang* [1901] 2 Ch 502, where I was using the argument of precariousness to show that the right which was desired to be enjoyed there was one which was unknown to the law — namely, to take water if and whenever the defendant chose to put water into a particular pond; such a right does not exist at law; but a right of way is well known to the law."

[His Lordship referred also to *Lewis v Meredith* [1913] 1 Ch 571 and *White v Williams* [1922] 1 KB 727 and continued:] There is, therefore, ample authority for the proposition that a right in fact enjoyed with property will pass on a conveyance of the property by virtue of the grant to be read into it under section 62, even although down to the date of the conveyance the right was exercised by permission only, and therefore was in that sense precarious.

The next proposition deducible from the cases is the one laid down in *Burrows v Lang*, which has been referred to in some of the passages I have already read. It is that the right in question must be a right known to the law. . . . For the purposes of section 62, it is only necessary that the right should be one capable of being granted at law, or, in other words, a right known to the law. If it is a right of that description it matters not, as the *International Tea Stores* case [1903] 2 Ch 165 shows, that it has been in fact enjoyed by permission only. The reason for that is clear, for, on the assumption that the right is included or imported into the parcels of the conveyance by virtue of section 62, the grant under the conveyance supplies what one may call the defect in title, and substitutes a new title based on the grant.

[His Lordship also referred to *Birmingham, Dudley and District Banking Co v Ross* (1888) 38 ChD 295 and continued:] I think those are all the cases to which I can usefully refer, and applying the principles deducible from them to the present case one finds, I think, this. First of all, on the evidence the coal shed was used by Mrs Wright by the permission of Mr Macadam, but *International Tea Stores Co v Hobbs* shows that that does not prevent section 62 from applying, because permissive as the right may have been it was in fact enjoyed.

Next, the right was, as I understand it, a right to use the coal shed in question for the purpose of storing such coal as might be required for the domestic purposes of the flat. In my judgment that is a right or easement which the law will clearly recognise[12], and it is a right or easement of a kind which could readily be included in a lease or conveyance by the insertion of appropriate words in the parcels. This, therefore, is not a case in which a title

---

[12] On easements of storage, cf. *Copeland v Greenhalf* [1952] Ch 488, [1952] 1 All ER 809, p. 570, ante; *Grigsby v Melville* [1972] 1 WLR 1355, [1973] 1 All ER 385, p. 572, ante.

to a right unknown to the law is claimed by virtue of section 62. Nor is it a case in which it can be said to have been in the contemplation of the parties that the enjoyment of the right should be purely temporary. No limit was set as to the time during which the coal shed could continue to be used. Mr Macadam simply gave his permission; that permission was acted on; and the use of the coal shed in fact went on down to 28 August 1943, and thereafter down to 1947. Therefore, applying to the facts of the present case the principles which seem to be deducible from the authorities, the conclusion to which I have come is that the right to use the coal shed was at the date of the letting of 28 August 1943 a right enjoyed with the top floor flat within the meaning of section 62 of the Law of Property Act 1925, with the result that (as no contrary intention was expressed in the document) the right in question must be regarded as having passed by virtue of that letting, just as it would have passed if it had been mentioned in express terms in cl. 1, which sets out the subject-matter of the lease. . . .

For these reasons I would allow the appeal and direct that, inasmuch as the coal shed is now no longer in existence, judgment should be entered for the plaintiffs for the sum of damages claimed.

GOLDBERG v EDWARDS
[1950] Ch 247 (CA, EVERSHED MR, COHEN and ASQUITH LJJ)

The first defendant was the owner of a house at Salford and of an annexe consisting of two storeys at the rear. The annexe could be reached by an uncovered passage to the East of the house, and this approach had always been used by the tenants previous to the plaintiffs. During the course of the negotiations with the plaintiffs, Isadore Goldberg and Barnett Sewelson, for the letting of the annexe, the first defendant agreed to give a personal privilege to the plaintiffs to use another approach to the annexe which led through the front door of the house, and to use the letter box in that door.

On 13 January 1947, an oral agreement for a lease of the annexe to the plaintiffs was reached, and they went into possession on 18 January 1947. On 10 July 1947, the first defendant, pursuant to this agreement, demised the annexe to the plaintiffs "with the appurtenances" for two years from 18 January 1947 with an option to renew for a further two. From the time of taking possession the plaintiffs took privileges beyond those given to them, but the first defendant was held by the Vice-Chancellor of the County Palatine Court of Lancaster to have consented to such acts for the period of time during which she should be in possession of the house.

In January 1949, the first defendant agreed to let the house to the second defendant who went into possession and obstructed the plaintiffs in the enjoyment of these privileges. The action was to restrain interference with the use of the passage through the front door to the annexe by the plaintiffs, their servants and agents.

Held (reversing in part the Vice-Chancellor of the County Palatine). The plaintiffs were entitled to the right of way because it was a right appertaining to their premises on 10 July 1947, the date of the lease; but not to the other privileges.

EVERSHED MR: The substance of the judge's finding is clearly this: he found that there was a sharp and substantial distinction between the privilege to the two plaintiffs themselves to go to and from the annexe through the front door, on the one hand, and all the other privileges on the other. [His Lordship quoted from the judge's judgment and continued:] The passage just read seems to me consistent only with the view that in the Vice-Chancellor's opinion the privilege given to the plaintiff tenants was intended to be one which otherwise was capable of annexation to the demised property and therefore capable of being caught by section 62 of the Law of Property Act 1925.

The claim of the plaintiffs . . . has been based on two grounds: first, implied grant, apart altogether from section 62 of the Law of Property Act 1925, and secondly section 62. In my judgment, the first ground cannot be sustained.

[His Lordship explained that the use of the front door and passage was not "necessary for the reasonable or convenient enjoyment" of the annexe, and a grant could not therefore be implied, and continued:] I therefore reject the argument based on implied grant, and turn to section 62.

The various rights here claimed are these: first, a right for the plaintiffs personally to pass through the front door and along the passage of the house. . . . Secondly, a right to maintain a signboard and an electric bell; thirdly, as a necessary corollary to that, a right for the plaintiffs' customers to use the front door and passage; and, fourthly, a right to use it for the passage of goods. . . . It is plain, in my view, that these rights, other than the plaintiffs' personal right of passage, were not within the language of section 62 so as to be covered by the demise to them.

That leaves only the personal right. . . . Having regard to his judgment, I think that I am bound to regard the view of the judge as having been that, in contra-distinction to the other rights, it was intended to be something which the plaintiffs should enjoy qua lessees during the term of the demise, though it should not be enjoyed by their servants, workmen or any other persons with their authority. Therefore, I think, to quote Jenkins LJ, in the recent case of *Wright v Macadam* [1949] 2 KB 744 at 752, [1949] 2 All ER 565 at 572, p. 587, ante: "It is a right or easement of a kind which could be readily included in a lease or conveyance by the insertion of appropriate words in the parcels." What those would be I will state later, because, in the view which I take, it is necessary to see that the injunction or declaration to which the plaintiffs may be entitled is properly formulated.

Wright v Macadam was decided after the Vice-Chancellor gave judgment in this case. . . . The present privilege is in some ways indeed not dissimilar to that which in *Wright v Macadam* was held to be covered by section 62, namely, a privilege for the tenant to use a shed for storing her coal. I therefore think that, if the right which I have defined was one which was being enjoyed at the time of the conveyance, it is covered by section 62.

That therefore leaves the final point: what is the "time of conveyance" within the meaning of section 62, subsections 1 and 2? The arrangement about this use of the passage appears to have been made at various dates, the last of which was 13 January 1947. The plaintiffs went into occupation of the annexe on 18 January 1947. The fitting of the bell and signboard took place after that. Several months passed (why, I know not, and it is quite immaterial) before the lease was executed on 10 July 1947, though the term was expressed to run from 18 January. It is plain that before 10 July there was no written instrument whatever. Possession may no doubt have been attributable to an oral agreement of which, having regard to the position, specific performance might have been granted; but I fail to find any instrument in writing within the meaning of section 62 before the lease of 10 July. It seems to me, therefore, that the phrase "at the time of conveyance" must mean in this case 10 July. I am unable to accept the view that one should construe that as meaning at the time when the term granted by the lease is stated to have begun. On 10 July 1947, under the privilege granted, this right of ingress and egress was being enjoyed in fact. As I have held, though it is limited to the lessees themselves and does not extend to other persons, it would be capable of formulation and incorporation as a term of the lease, and it is, in my judgment, covered by section 62. To that extent, therefore, but to that limited extent only, the plaintiffs are entitled to succeed.

In *Phipps v Pears* [1965] 1 QB 76, [1964] 2 All ER 35, p. 574, ante, Lord DENNING MR, after holding that a right to protection from the weather could not exist as an easement, added at 84, at 38: "There is a further point. It was said that when the owner . . . conveyed No. 16 to Helena Field, the plaintiff's predecessor, there was implied in the conveyance all the general words of section 62 of the Law of Property Act 1925. The conveyance included all 'easements, rights and advantages whatsoever appertaining or reputed to appertain to the land'. On the conveyance of No. 16, Market Street, to the plaintiff's predecessor, there passed to him all these 'advantages' appertaining to No. 16. One of these advantages, it was said, was the benefit of having the old No. 14 there as a protection from the weather. I do not think this argument avails the plaintiff for the simple reason that, in order for section 62 to apply, the right or advantage must be one which is known to the law, in this sense, that it is capable of being granted at law so as to be binding on all successors in title, even those who take without notice, see *Wright v Macadam* [1949] 2 KB 744, [1949] 2 All ER 565, p. 587, ante. A fine view, or an expanse open to the winds, may be an 'advantage' to a house but it would not pass under section 62. Whereas a right to use a coal shed or to go along a passage would pass under section 62. The reason being that these last are rights known to the law, whereas the others are not. A right to protection from the weather is not a right known to the law. It does not therefore pass under section 62."

Section 62 only applies, unlike the rule in *Wheeldon v Burrows*, if there has been a "diversity of occupation" before the sale or lease; that is to say that the section does not apply where a person who has been both owner and occupier of adjoining premises sells or leases one of them.

A number of problems would arise if the exercise of general rights of ownership by the common owner and occupier over the part to be sold were treated as "rights and advantages" so as to give the purchaser an easement in respect of such of them as were capable of existing as easements.

In *Long v Gowlett* [1923] 2 Ch 177[13], Mrs Nichols, the owner of land adjoining the River Granta at Linton, Cambridgeshire, sold the land in two lots by contemporaneous sales to two purchasers; Lot 1 to Gowlett and Lot 2 to Long's predecessor in title. The common owner had been accustomed to go from Lot 1, on which Hadstock Mill stood, to Lot 2 higher up the river, to repair the river bank and cut weeds therefrom, so as to ensure a free flow of water downstream to the Mill. Gowlett, the owner of Lot 1, claimed that an easement to enter Lot 2 to repair and cut had been created in his favour by the conveyance of 1909 under section 6 Conveyancing Act 1881 (now section 62 Law of Property Act 1925). Long sought an injunction and damages for trespass. In rejecting Gowlett's claim, SARGANT J said at 199:

"And on these facts it is contended for the defendant that this constituted a 'privilege easement right or advantage' over or in relation to Lot 2, which at the time of the conveyance was occupied or enjoyed with Lot 1; and accordingly, that this advantage passed to the defendant by virtue of the express words of the sub-section as included in the conveyance by virtue of the statute. The argument is not based in any way on the existence of any continuous and apparent easement existing over Lot 2 in favour of Lot 1; indeed, any such claim would be incompatible with the evidence, which clearly established that there was no defined way at all along the south bank. The claim is founded upon there having been a statutory introduction into the conveyance to the defendant of words equivalent to or identical with those either expressly contained or statutorily introduced in the corresponding conveyances in such cases as *James v Plant* (1836) 4 Ad & El 749; *Watts v Kelson* (1871) 6 Ch App 166; *Bayley v Great Western Rly Co* (1884) 26 ChD 434; and *White v Williams* [1922] 1 KB 727.

It is, therefore, necessary for the purpose of dealing with the matter on this footing to consider whether, during the common ownership and occupation of Lot 1 and Lot 2 by Mr Nichols and his widow, and therefore at the date of the conveyance, there was a 'privilege, easement, right or advantage' of the kind now claimed, which can properly be said to have been 'demised, occupied or enjoyed' with Lot 1 over Lot 2. It is very difficult to see how this can have been the case. No doubt the common owner and occupier did in fact repair the bank of Lot 2, and cut the weeds there; and no doubt also this repair and cutting would enure not solely for the benefit of Lot 2 (which comprised, amongst other things, a lawn tennis court), so as to prevent its being flooded, but also and very likely to a greater extent for the benefit of Lot 1. But there is nothing to indicate that the acts done on Lot 2 were done otherwise than in the course of the ownership and occupation of Lot 2, or that they were by way of using a 'privilege, easement or advantage' over Lot 2 in connection with Lot 1. The common owner and occupier of Whiteacre and Blackacre may in fact use Blackacre as an alternative and more convenient method of communication between Whiteacre and a neighbouring village. But it has never been held, and would I think be contrary to principle to hold, that (in default of there being a made road over Blackacre forming a continuous and apparent means of communication) a sale and conveyance of Whiteacre alone would carry a right to pass over Blackacre in the same way in which the common owner had been accustomed to pass. As

---

[13] See also *Ward v Kirkland* [1967] Ch 194 at 227–231, [1966] 1 All ER 609 at 618–620, p. 586, n. 20, ante.

it seems to me, in order that there may be a 'privilege, easement or advantage' enjoyed with Whiteacre over Blackacre so as to pass under the statute, there must be something done on Blackacre not due to or comprehended within the general rights of an occupying owner of Blackacre, but of such a nature that it is attributable to a privilege, easement, right or advantage, however precarious, which arises out of the ownership or occupation of Whiteacre, altogether apart from the ownership or occupation of Blackacre. And it is difficult to see how, when there is a common ownership of both Whiteacre and Blackacre, there can be any such relationship between the two closes as (apart from the case of continuous and apparent easements or that of a way of necessity) would be necessary to create a 'privilege, easement, right or advantage' within the words of section 6, subsection 2, of the statute. For this purpose it would seem that there must be some diversity of ownership or occupation of the two closes sufficient to refer the act or acts relied on not to mere occupying ownership, but to some advantage or privilege (however far short of a legal right) attaching to the owner or occupier of Whiteacre as such and de facto exercised over Blackacre. Let me illustrate my meaning from the latest case on the subject — namely, *White v Williams* [1922] 1 KB 727. . . .

Mr Greene for the defendant was challenged to produce from the very many cases in which, on a conveyance of Whiteacre, an easement over Blackacre has been held to pass under the statutory words or their equivalent, a single case in which both the closes in question had been in common ownership and occupation, or in which there had not been an actual enjoyment over Blackacre on the part of an owner or occupier of Whiteacre who was not the owner and occupier of Blackacre. And neither from among the cases cited to me, nor from any other case in the books, was he able (with one solitary exception) to produce such a case as required. The exception, however, is one of high authority — namely, that of *Broomfield v Williams* [1897] 1 Ch 602 — and it is necessary to examine it with some attention.

In that case the common owner of a house and of adjoining land over which light had in fact been received through the windows of the house, sold and conveyed the house by a conveyance after the date of the Conveyancing Act 1881, but retained the adjoining land. It was held by the Court of Appeal that, although the retained land was marked on the plan on the conveyance as 'building land', the vendor was not at liberty subsequently to build on the retained land so as to interfere substantially with the access of light to the windows of the house. A. L. Smith LJ, it is true, based his judgment solely on the principle that the grantor was not entitled to derogate from his grant; and this was quite sufficient to support the actual decision. But the other two members of the Court relied mainly, if not exclusively, on the express words of section 6, subsection 2, of the Act; and the decision is, therefore, undoubtedly binding on me with regard to the access of light, and also with regard to any other 'privilege, easement, right or advantage' that is on the same footing as 'light.'

But such an easement or advantage as is now claimed is, in my judgment, very different from light, or a right to light. The access of light to a window over adjoining land is a physical fact plainly visible to any one buying a house. It is extremely similar to a continuous and apparent easement. It is mentioned in the subsection in the midst of a number of physical features ending with the word 'watercourses'; and the special position of light to an existing window as compared with other easements is fully recognised in the Prescription Act, which makes the acquisition of an easement of light depend on the enjoyment of the light simpliciter, and not, as in the case of other easements, on enjoyment as of right. The fact, therefore, that the inclusion of light in the subject matter of conveyance in section 6, subsection 2, has been held to entitle the grantee to the light coming to an existing window, does not necessarily involve the further inclusion of imperceptible rights or advantages, corresponding with intermittent practice or user as between two tenements of the common owner and occupier of both. Such an intermittent and non-apparent user or practice stands, in my judgment, on a completely different footing from the visible access of light to an existing window.

The importance of such a distinction is specially obvious in a case like the present, where there is a contemporaneous sale by a common owner to two separate purchasers of adjoining lots completely divided by a physical boundary. If the contention of the defendant is correct, it would be necessary in any such case for the purchaser to inquire how the common owner and occupier had been accustomed to make use of each close in connection with the other. Would the plaintiff, for instance, in this case be entitled, as against the defendant, to an alternative way over Lot 1 to reach Lot 2, because while both lots were in common ownership and occupation, it was the practice of Mr and Mrs Nichols by way of Lot 1 to repair the south bank of Lot 2? Any number of similar puzzles would arise, if the law were as the defendant would have it. The fact that the common owner and occupier sells two adjoining closes separately is, in my mind, a negation of the intention to preserve access between them: compare such a case as *Midland Rly Co v Gribble* [1895] 2 Ch 827.

The only two exceptions to this rule appear to be those of ways of necessity and of continuous and apparent easements. Had the general words of section 6, subsection 2, any such effect as is suggested by the defendant — and it must be remembered that these words were not new, but represented conveyancing practice for many years previously — it is difficult, if not impossible, to understand how there have not been numerous cases in which, on a severance of two closes, a subsisting practice by the common owner and occupier of both has not been given effect to by way of legal easement as a result of general words of this kind."

In *Sovmots Investments Ltd v Secretary of State for the Environment* [1979] AC 144, [1977] 2 All ER 385[14], the House of Lords considered both the rule in *Wheeldon v Burrows* and section 62. The London Borough of Camden made a compulsory purchase order to acquire 36 residential maisonettes in Centre Point. The question was whether certain rights over and in respect of other parts of Centre Point, without which the maisonettes could not be used as housing accommodation, passed on the conveyance; and whether, if they did not pass, the Borough had power to make a compulsory purchase order to acquire the maisonettes which, without the additional rights, could not be used for housing purposes. In quashing the order, Lord WILBERFORCE said at 168, at 391[15]:

---

[14] (1977) 41 Conv (NS) 415; [1979] Conv 113 (C. Harpum); [1978] Conv 449 (P. Smith); 127 NLJ 695 (H. W. Wilkinson); Jackson, pp. 100–103.
[15] See also at 175–176 at 397–398, per Lord EDMUND-DAVIES.

"The main argument before the inspector and in the courts below was that in this case and under the compulsory purchase order as made no specific power to require the creation of ancillary rights was necessary because these would pass to the acquiring authority under either, or both, of the first rule in *Wheeldon v Burrows* (1879) 12 ChD 31 ("the rule") or of section 62 of the Law of Property Act 1925. Under the rule (I apologise for the reminder but the expression of the rule is important)

'on the grant by the owner of a tenement of part of that tenement *as it is then used and enjoyed*, there will pass to the grantee all those continuous and apparent easements (by which, of course, I mean quasi-easements), or, in other words, all those easements which are necessary to the reasonable enjoyment of the property granted, and *which have been and are at the time of the grant used* by the owners of the entirety for the benefit of the part granted' (see per Thesiger LJ at 49, my emphasis).

Under section 62 a conveyance of land operates to convey with the land all ways, watercourses, liberties, privileges, easements, rights and advantages whatsoever, appertaining or reputed to appertain to the land, or any part thereof, or, at the time of conveyance, demised, occupied or enjoyed with, or reputed or known as part or parcel of or appurtenant to the land or any part thereof.

My Lords, there are very comprehensive expressions here, but it does not take much analysis to see that they have no relevance to the situation under consideration.

The rule is a rule of intention, based on the proposition that a man may not derogate from his grant. He cannot grant or agree to grant land and at the same time deny to his grantee what is at the time of the grant obviously necessary for its reasonable enjoyment. To apply this to a case where a public authority is taking from an owner his land without his will is to stand the rule on its head: it means substituting for the intention of a reasonable voluntary grantor the unilateral, opposed, intention of the acquirer.

Moreover, and this point is relevant to a later argument, the words I have underlined[16] show that for the rule to apply there must be actual, and apparent, use and enjoyment at the time of the grant. But no such use or enjoyment had, at Centre Point, taken place at all.

Equally, section 62 does not fit this case. The reason is that when land is under one ownership one cannot speak in any intelligible sense of rights, or privileges, or easements being exercised over one part for the benefit of another. Whatever the owner does, he does as owner and until a separation occurs, of ownership or at least of occupation, the condition for the existence of rights, etc., does not exist: see *Bolton v Bolton* (1879) 11 ChD 968, 970 per Fry J and *Long v Gowlett* [1923] 2 Ch 177, 189, 198, in my opinion a correct decision.

A separation of ownership, in a case like the present, will arise on conveyance of one of the parts (e.g. the maisonettes), but this separation cannot be projected back to the stage of the compulsory purchase order so as, by anticipation to bring into existence rights not existing in fact."

---

[16] As printed in italics.

[1978] Conv 449, at pp. 454–455 (P. Smith)

"In fact there is a considerable body of authority against [*Long v Gowlett*], both academic and precedent based, none of which was seriously considered by the House of Lords. There is no need to consider it in any detail as most readers will be aware of it[17]. The first limitation namely that section 62 has no ambit where there is no diversity of occupation, does not stand up to precedent for a start. In *Broomfield v Williams*[18] the Court of Appeal made no such limitation as suggested by Sargant J in *Long v Gowlett* and Lord Wilberforce and Lord Edmund-Davies in the *Sovmots* case. With respect to Lord Edmund-Davies and to Mr Harpum[19], merely to state easements of light are different from other easements does not explain why section 62, apparently very widely drawn, applies to those easements and not to others when there is no diversity of occupation. There is absolutely nothing in the section to justify such a limitation. Furthermore the objection that the rights etc. do not exist at the relevant time, ignores the substantial body of case law where section 62 has turned a precarious right into a full legal easement[20]. . . .

The real problem now is what is left after *Sovmots*? It appears that one of the major opponents of the limitations imposed by the case is prepared to concede it now[1], but is such resignation necessary? Only two of the five law lords considered the point, no argument was addressed to them on the point and no cases cited."

QUESTIONS
Is there good reason in principle or authority for requiring a diversity of occupation for the operation of section 62? What bearing does the *Sovmots* case have on the matter? And is there justification for applying a different rule to easements of light?

Jackson, pp. 92 et seq; [1978] Conv 449 (P. Smith); M & W, p. 865 n. 97; *Broomfield v Williams* [1897] 1 Ch 602.

Is there good reason for differentiating in this respect between the operation of the rule in *Wheeldon v Burrows* and the Law of Property Act 1925, section 62? See JENKINS LJ in *Wright v Macadam* [1949] 2 KB 744, [1949] 2 All ER 565, p. 587, ante; C & B, pp. 505–506; M & W, p. 867; MM, p. 412; Gale, pp. 125–126; Jackson, pp. 100–103.

ii. EASEMENTS IMPLIED IN FAVOUR OF THE GRANTOR
Generally, any rights which a grantor wishes to enjoy as easements in favour of the land he retains, and exercisable over the land sold, must be expressly reserved[2] or regranted. Otherwise he may not derogate from his grant[3]. In

---

[17] For starters Jackson (1966) 30 Conv (NS) 342–348 and thence Jackson, *The Law of Easements and Profits*, pp. 97–103; Megarry and Wade, *The Law of Real Property* (4th edn.), pp. 836, note 47 and 837–838; Farrand, *Contract and Conveyance* (2nd edn.), pp. 384–386; *Emmet*, p. 515; Barnsley, *Conveyancing Law and Practice*, pp. 484–485 (perhaps?); and *Gale on Easements* (14th edn.), pp. 125–126. The last book is particularly significant as the Thirteenth Edition of that book supported *Long v Gowlett* but was changed after Professor Jackson's article supra.

[18] [1897] 1 Ch 602.

[19] (1977) 41 Conv (NS) 415.

[20] See e.g. *Wright v Macadam* [1949] 2 KB 744, [1949] 2 All ER 565; *Goldberg v Edwards* [1950] Ch 247 and *International Tea Stores v Hobbs* [1903] 2 Ch 165. None of these cases featured in the *Sovmots* case.

[1] See Jackson, p. 100.

[2] LPA 1925, s. 65, p. 578, ante.

[3] (1964) 80 LQR 244 (D. W. Elliott).

exceptional cases, however, easements will be implied in his favour. These are easements of necessity[4], and may be (*a*) "an easement without which the property retained cannot be used at all, and not one merely necessary to the reasonable enjoyment of that property[5], and (*b*) an easement which is required to carry out the common intention of the parties[6]. These are usually easements of support, and such easements can only be claimed when the intention is clear[7]. In each case the right which the grantor can claim is the minimum necessary to comply with the rule under which it is claimed.

CORPORATION OF LONDON *v* RIGGS
(1880) 13 ChD 798 (ChD, JESSEL MR)

In 1887, Heathcote, the owner of land in Essex, conveyed part of this land to London Corporation who declared that they would hold the land conveyed as an open space for ever. This land completely encircled a close of about two acres called Barn Hoppet which was owned also by Heathcote, and had been used up to that time for agricultural purposes only. No easements in favour of Barn Hoppet were reserved in the conveyance of the other land to London Corporation. In 1879 Riggs entered into possession of Barn Hoppet as tenant, and he made preparations for the erection of a house and of other buildings for the sale of refreshments to the public. The plaintiffs claimed a declaration that Riggs' right of way of necessity was limited to purposes sufficient to the use of Barn Hoppet for agricultural purposes only; and an injunction and damages. The action was tried on demurrer.

Held. The defendant's right of way was limited to the purposes for which it was used in 1877.

JESSEL MR: I am afraid that, whatever I may call my decision, it will, in effect, be making law, which I never have any desire to do; but I cannot find that the point is covered by any decided case, or even appears to have been discussed in any decided case. The only satisfaction I have in deciding the point is this, that it will in all probability be carried to a higher court, and it will be for that court to make the law, or, as we say, declare the law, and not for me.

The real question I have to decide is this — whether, on a grant of land wholly surrounding a close, the implied grant, or re-grant, of a right of way by the grantee to the grantor to enable him to get to the reserved, or excepted, or inclosed close, is a grant of a general right of way for all purposes, or only a grant of a right of way for the purpose of the enjoyment of the reserved or excepted close in its then state.

---

[4] See *Nickerson v Barraclough* [1980] Ch 325 at 332, [1979] 3 All ER 312 at 320–321.
[5] *Union Lighterage Co v London Graving Dock Co* [1902] 2 Ch 557 at 573; *Pinnington v Galland* (1853) 9 Exch 1; *Deacon v South Eastern Rly Co* (1889) 61 LT 377; *Midland Rly Co v Miles* (1886) 33 ChD 632.
[6] *Richards v Rose* (1853) 9 Exch 218; *Shubrook v Tufnell* (1882) 46 LT 886; *Re Webb's Lease* [1951] Ch 808, [1951] 2 All ER 131, p. 600, post.
[7] See *Nickerson v Barraclough* [1981] Ch 426, [1981] 2 All ER 369 (where CA, reversing MEGARRY V-C, held that "the doctrine of way of necessity is not founded upon public policy at all but upon an implication from the circumstances" (per BRIGHTMAN LJ at 440, at 379); and so if the grant implied by way of construction was negated by an express contrary provision in the conveyance, no grant could be implied by the court under a rule of public policy, for example, against land being rendered unusable by being landlocked); [1981] Conv 442 (L. Crabb).

There is, as I have said, no distinct authority on the question. It seems to me to have been laid down in very early times — and I have looked into a great number of cases, and among others several blackletter cases — that the right to a way of necessity is an exception to the ordinary rule that a man shall not derogate from his own grant, and that the man who grants the surrounding land is in very much the same position as regards the right of way to the reserved close as if he had granted the close, retaining the surrounding land. In both cases there is what is called a way of necessity; and the way of necessity, according to the old rules of pleading, must have been pleaded as a grant, or, where the close is reserved, as it is here, as a re-grant. . . .

Well, now, if we try the case on principle — treating this right of way as an exception to the rule — ought it to be treated as a larger exception than the necessity of the case warrants? That of course brings us back to the question, What does the necessity of the case require? The object of implying the re-grant, as stated by the older Judges, was that if you did not give the owner of the reserved close some right of way or other, he could neither use nor occupy the reserved close, nor derive any benefit from it. But what is the extent of the benefit he is to have? Is he entitled to say, I have reserved to myself more than that which enables me to enjoy it as it is at the time of the grant? And if that is the true rule, that he is not to have more than necessity requires, as distinguished from what convenience may require, it appears to me that the right of way must be limited to that which is necessary at the time of the grant; that is, he is supposed to take a re-grant to himself of such a right of way as will enable him to enjoy the reserved thing as it is.

That appears to me to be the meaning of a right of way of necessity. If you imply more, you reserve to him not only that which enables him to enjoy the thing he has reserved as it is, but that which enables him to enjoy it in the same way and to the same exent as if he reserved a general right of way for all purposes: that is — as in the case I have before me — a man who reserves two acres of arable land in the middle of a large piece of land is to be entitled to cover the reserved land with houses, and call on his grantee to allow him to make a wide metalled road up to it. I do not think that is a fair meaning of a way of necessity: I think it must be limited by the necessity at the time of the grant; and that the man who does not take the pains to secure an actual grant of a right of way for all purposes is not entitled to be put in a better position than to be able to enjoy that which he had at the time the grant was made. I am not aware of any other principle on which this case can be decided.

I may be met by the objection that a way of necessity must mean something more than what I have stated, because, where the grant is of the inclosed piece, the grantee is entitled to use the land for all purposes, and should therefore be entitled to a right of way commensurate with his right of enjoyment. But there again the grantee has not taken from the grantor any express grant of a right of way: and all he can be entitled to ask is a right to enable him to enjoy the property granted to him as it was granted to him. It does not appear to me that the grant of the property gives any greater right. But even if it did, the principle applicable to the grantee is not quite the same as the principle applicable to the grantor: and it might be that the grantee obtains a larger way of necessity — though I do not think he does — than the grantor does under the implied re-grant.

I am afraid that I am laying down the law for the first time — that I am for the first time declaring the law; but it is a matter of necessity from which I cannot escape.

The demurrer must, therefore, be overruled, with costs.

RE WEBB'S LEASE
[1951] Ch 808, [1951] 2 All ER 131 (CA, EVERSHED MR, JENKINS and MORRIS LJJ)

The defendant (the landlord) was head lessee of a three storey building. He occupied the ground floor for his own business as a butcher, and leased the upper two storeys to the plaintiff (the tenant). The first letting was in 1939 for three years; the tenant remained in occupation until 1949 when he was granted a 21 year lease. Throughout all this time one side of the building contained an advertisement for the defendant's business, and another side (the west wall) one for Bryant and May's matches, both of which covered all or part of the external walls of the upper two storeys. None of the leases made any reservation of the right of the landlord to use the outer walls of the demised premises for this purpose. In 1950, the tenants began to make enquiries concerning the landlord's right so to use the walls and finally issued this summons to determine the question.

Held (reversing DANCKWERTS J). Without express reservation, the landlord had no right to claim the easement in question.

JENKINS LJ: The matter therefore stands thus: The landlord did not include in the provisions of the lease as executed any reservation of advertising rights over any part of the outer walls; but, at the date of the lease, the advertisements now in dispute were in their present positions on the walls and plainly to be seen. Moreover, they had existed in their present positions continuously since before the commencement of the tenant's original tenancy in 1939; and the tenant never objected to their presence at any time during his original tenancy, or at the time of the granting of the lease of 11 August 1949, or thereafter until January 1950. There is no evidence that either party ever even mentioned the subject of the advertisements to the other during the whole of this period of more than ten years.

This being in substance the whole of the available facts, the question is whether on those bare facts without more, the court can and ought as a matter of law to imply in favour of the landlord a reservation during the term of twenty-one years granted by the lease of 11 August 1949, of advertising rights over the outer walls demised, at all events to the extent required to enable him to maintain the existing advertisements and to retain for his own benefit any periodical payments receivable from the Borough Billposting Company in respect of the site of the "Brymay" poster.

As to the law applicable to the case, it is not disputed that as a general rule a grantor, whether by way of conveyance or lease, of part of a hereditament in his ownership, cannot claim any easement over the part granted for the benefit of the part retained, unless it is expressly reserved out of the grant. See (for instance) *Suffield v Brown* (1864) 4 De GJ & Sm 185; *Crossley & Sons Ltd v Lightowler* (1867) 2 Ch App 478; *Wheeldon v Burrows* (1879) 12 ChD 31, p. 582, ante.

There are, however, certain exceptions to the general rule. Two well-established exceptions relate to easements of necessity and mutual easements such as rights of support between adjacent buildings. But it is recognised in the authorities that these two specific exceptions do not exhaust the list, which is indeed incapable of exhaustive statement, as the circumstances of any particular case may be such as to raise a necessary inference that the common intention of the parties must have been to reserve some easement to the grantor, or such as to preclude the grantee from denying the right consistently with good faith, and there appears to be no doubt that where circumstances such as these are clearly established the court will imply the appropriate reservation.

[His Lordship quoted from the judgment of THESIGER LJ, in *Wheeldon v Burrows*, at p. 582, ante, referred to *Russell v Watts* (1885) 10 App Cas 590; *Aldridge v Wright* [1929] 2 KB 117; *Liddiard v Waldron* [1934] 1 KB 435, and continued:] The most comprehensive statement of the area of potential exceptions is probably that contained in the speech of Lord Parker in *Pwllbach Colliery Co Ltd v Woodman* [1915] AC 634, where his Lordship, after referring to the exception with respect to easements of necessity, said this: "The second class of cases in which easements may impliedly be created depends not upon the terms of the grant itself, but upon the circumstances under which the grant was made. The law will readily imply the grant or reservation of such easements as may be necessary to give effect to the common intention of the parties to a grant of real property, with reference to the manner or purposes in and for which the land granted or some land retained by the grantor is to be used. See *Jones v Pritchard* [1908] 1 Ch 630, and *Lyttelton Times Co Ltd v Warners Ltd* [1907] AC 476. But it is essential for this purpose that the parties should intend that the subject of the grant or the land retained by the grantor should be used in some definite and particular manner. It is not enough that the subject of the grant or the land retained should be intended to be used in a manner which may or may not involve this definite and particular use.". . .

The question is whether the circumstances of the case as proved in evidence are such as to raise a necessary inference that the common intention of the parties was to reserve to the landlord during the twenty-one years' term some, and if so what, rights in regard to the display of advertisements over the outer walls of the demised premises, or such as to preclude the tenant from denying the implied reservation to the landlord of some such rights consistently with good faith.

That question must be approached with the following principles in mind: (i) If the landlord intended to reserve any such rights over the demised premises it was his duty to reserve them expressly in the lease of 11 August 1949: *Wheeldon v Burrows* (1879) 12 ChD 31; (ii) The landlord having failed in this duty, the onus was upon him to establish the facts to prove, and prove clearly, that his case was an exception to the rule: *Aldridge v Wright* [1929] 2 KB 117; (iii) The mere fact that the tenant knew at the date of the lease of 11 August 1949 that the landlord was using the outer walls of the demised premises for the display of the advertisements in question did not suffice to absolve the landlord from his duty of expressly reserving any rights in respect of them he intended to claim, or to take the case out of the general rule: see *Suffield v Brown* (1864) 4 De GJ & Sm 185; *Crossley & Sons Ltd v Lightowler* (1867) 2 Ch App 478.

Applying these principles to the present case, I ask myself whether the landlord has on the meagre facts proved discharged the onus which lies upon him of proving it an exception to the general rule. He can, so far as I can see, derive no assistance from the passage quoted above from Lord Parker's speech in the *Pwllbach Colliery Case* [1915] AC 634. It might, I suppose, be said to have been in the contemplation of the parties that the landlord would continue to use the ground floor of the premises for the purposes of his business as a butcher and provision merchant, but it cannot in my view be contended that the maintenance during the term of the lease of his advertisement over the door was a necessary incident of the user so contemplated. This applies a fortiori to the "Brymay" advertisement, the display of which on the outer wall of the demised premises by the Borough Billposting Company as licensees of the landlord was so far as I can see not related in any way to the use or occupation of the ground floor for the existing or any other purpose. The transaction with the Borough Billposting Company was simply a hiring out for reward of part of an outer wall of the demised premises for use as an advertising or billposting site or station.

The mere fact that the tenant knew of the presence of the advertisements at the date when the lease of 11 August 1949 was granted being, as stated above, beside the point, nothing is left beyond the bare circumstance that the advertisements were not only present at the date of the grant but had been continuously present without objection by the tenant since the commencement of his original tenancy in 1939. Does this circumstance suffice to raise a necessary inference of an intention common to both parties at the date of the lease that the landlord should have reserved to him the right to maintain these advertisements throughout the twenty-one years' term thereby granted? I cannot see that it does. The most that can be said is that the facts are consistent with such a common intention. But that will not do. The landlord must surely show at least that the facts are not reasonably consistent with any other explanation. Here he manifestly fails. . . .

In short, I can hold nothing more established by the facts proved than permissive user of the outer walls by the landlord for the display of the advertisements during the original tenancy and thereafter from the granting of the lease until the tenant's objection in January 1950; with nothing approaching grounds for inferring, as a matter of necessary inference, an intention common to both parties that such permissive user should be converted by the lease into a reservation to the landlord of equivalent rights throughout the twenty-one years' term thereby granted.

C. Acquisition by Presumed Grant, or Prescription[8]

i. PRESCRIPTION AT COMMON LAW: TIME IMMEMORIAL

In *Bryant v Foot* (1867) LR 2 QB 161[9], the question was whether the rector of Horton, Buckinghamshire, could establish a claim based on long user, to a fee of 13s. for marriages performed in the parish church. User was proved since 1808, but there was no evidence prior to that time.

---

[8] C & B, pp. 512–525; M & W, pp. 869–892; MM, pp. 415–427; Gale, pp. 133–192; Jackson, pp. 110–138; (1975) 38 MLR 641 (S. Anderson).

[9] *Duke of Norfolk v Arbuthnot* (1880) 5 CPD 390 (no prescription in respect of church built about 1380).

Cockburn CJ, Mellor and Lush JJ (Blackburn J dissenting) held that the size of the fee made it impossible to believe that it existed in the time of Richard I. The presumption of immemorial legal existence which arose from user within living memory was rebutted. In discussing the methods of proof of immemorial user, Cockburn CJ said at 179: "The law of England ever has been and still is, in respect of prescriptive rights, in a most unsatisfactory state. The common law admitted of no prescription in the matter of real estate, or of any franchise which was matter of record, as not lying in grant. In respect of things incorporeal, lying in grant, it admitted of a species of prescription, not upon the ground that possession or enjoyment for a given period gave an indefeasible right, but on the assumption, when possession or enjoyment had been carried back as far as living memory would go, that a grant had once existed which had since been lost.

Practically speaking, by means of this presumption prescriptive rights were established in respect of matters which lay in grant. Protection, in respect of real estates, after continued and peaceable enjoyment, was effected, not by the law being that after possession for a given number of years the right of property should be absolutely acquired, but by the indirect contrivance of debarring the adverse claimant from the benefit of the procedure by which alone his right could be established. And here again our ancestors, instead of fixing a given number of years as the period within which legal proceedings to recover real property must be resorted to, had recourse to the singular expedient of making the period of limitation run from particular events or dates. From the time of Henry I to that of Henry III, on a writ of right, the time within which a descent must be shewn was the time of King Henry I (Co Litt 114b). In the 20th year of Henry III, by the Statute of Merton (c. 8) the date was altered to the time of Henry II. Writs of mort d'ancestor were limited to the time of the last return of King John into England; writs of novel disseisin to the time of the king's first crossing the sea into Gascony. In the previous reign, according to Glanville (Lib 13, c. 33), the disseisin must have been since the last voyage of King Henry II into Normandy. So that the time necessary to bar a claim varied materially at different epochs. Thus matters remained till the 3 Edw I (Stat West 1 c. 39), when, as all lawyers are aware, the time within which a writ of right might be brought was limited to cases in which the seisin of the ancestor was since the time of King Richard I, which was construed to mean the beginning of that king's reign (2 Inst 238), a period of not less than eighty-six years. The legislature having thus adopted the reign of Richard I as the date from which the limitation in a real action was to run, the courts of law adopted it as the period to which, in all matters of prescription or custom, legal memory, which till then had been confined to the time to which living memory could go back, should thenceforth be required to extend. Thus the law remained for two centuries and a half, by which time the limitation imposed in respect of actions to recover real property having long become inoperative to bar claims which had their origin posterior to the time of Richard I, and having therefore ceased practically to afford any protection against antiquated claims, the legislature, in 32nd of Henry VIII (c. 2), again interfered, and on this occasion, instead of dating the period of limitation from some particular event or date, took the wiser course of prescribing a fixed number of years as the limit within which a suit should be entertained. The legislature having thus altered the period within which rights to real estate could be asserted by parties out of possession, the courts on this occasion omitted to follow the analogy of the recent statute as fixing the date from which legal memory was to commence, as they had done on the passing of the statute of the 3 Edw I, and adhered in all that related to prescription or custom to the previously established standard. It was of course impossible that as time went on the adoption of a fixed epoch, as the time from which legal memory was to run, should not be attended by grievous inconvenience and hardship. Possession, however long, enjoyment, however uninterrupted, afforded no protection against stale and obsolete claims, or the assertion of long abandoned rights. And as parliament failed to intervene to amend the law, the judges set their ingenuity to work, by fictions and presumptions, to atone for the supineness of the legislature, and to amend, so far as in them lay, the law, which I cannot but think they were bound to administer as they found it. They first laid down the somewhat startling rule that from the usage of a lifetime the presumption arose that a similar usage had existed from a remote antiquity. Next, as it could not but happen that, in the case of many private rights, especially in that of easements, which had a more recent origin, such a presumption was impossible, judicial astuteness to support possession and enjoyment, which the law ought to have invested with the character of rights, had recourse to the questionable theory of lost grants. Juries were first told that from user, during living memory, or even during twenty years, they might presume a lost grant or deed; next they were recommended to make such presumption; and lastly, as the final consummation of judicial legislation, it was held that a jury should be told, not only that they might, but also that they were bound to presume the existence of such a lost grant, although neither judge nor jury, nor any one else, had the shadow of a belief that any such instrument had ever really existed. In this manner the courts have endeavoured to supply the deficiency of the law in the matter of rights acquired by possession and enjoyment. When the doctrine of presumptions had proceeded far towards its development, the legislature at length interfered, and in respect of real property and of certain specified easements, fixed certain periods of possession or enjoyment as establishing presumptive rights. But with regard to all prescriptions or customs not provided for by statutory enactment the law remains as before.''

In advising the House of Lords in *Dalton v Angus* (1881) 6 App Cas 740 at 773–4, where a claim to an easement of support for a building based upon 27 years user was upheld, FRY J, in a famous passage, based the doctrine of prescription upon acquiescence.

"But leaving such technical questions aside, I prefer to observe that, in my opinion, the whole law of prescription and the whole law which governs the presumption or inference of a grant or covenant rest upon acquiescence. The Courts and the Judges have had recourse to various expedients for quieting the possession of persons in the exercise of rights which have not been resisted by the persons against whom they are exercised, but in all cases it appears to me that acquiescence and nothing else is the principle upon which these expedients rest. It becomes then of the highest importance to consider of what ingredients acquiescence consists. In many cases, as, for instance, in the case of that acquiescence which creates a right of way, it will be found to involve, 1st, the doing of some act by one man upon the land of another;

2ndly, the absence of right to do that act in the person doing it; 3rdly, the knowledge of the person affected by it that the act is done; 4thly, the power of the person affected by the act to prevent such act either by act on his part or by action in the Courts; and lastly, the abstinence by him from any such interference for such a length of time as renders it reasonable for the Courts to say that he shall not afterwards interfere to stop the act being done. In some other cases, as, for example, in the case of lights, some of these ingredients are wanting; but I cannot imagine any case of acquiescence in which there is not shewn to be in the servient owner: 1, a knowledge of the acts done; 2, a power in him to stop the acts or to sue in respect of them; and 3, an abstinence on his part from the exercise of such power. That such is the nature of acquiescence and that such is the ground upon which presumptions or inferences of grant or covenant may be made appears to me to be plain both from reason, from maxim, and from the cases.

As regards the reason of the case, it is plain good sense to hold that a man who can stop an asserted right, or a continued user, and does not do so for a long time, may be told that he has lost his right by his delay and his negligence, and every presumption should therefore be made to quiet a possession thus acquired and enjoyed by the tacit consent of the sufferer. But there is no sense in binding a man by an enjoyment he cannot prevent, or quieting a possession which he could never disturb."

ii. USER AS OF RIGHT[10]

In *Diment v NH Foot Ltd* [1974] 1 WLR 1427, [1974] 2 All ER 785, the plaintiff and defendant owned adjacent farms at Buckland Newton, in Dorset, known as Sanctions Farm and Bookham Farm respectively. On an outlying part, a gateway gave access from a "panhandle", or narrow tongue of land, on Bookham Farm through Field 415 on Sanctions Farm to the highway. From 1936 onwards Foot (the predecessor in title of the defendant) used this way across Mrs Diment's land six to ten times a year. From 1936 to 1967 Mrs Diment was absent from the farm, but visited it occasionally. During that time she let it on four separate agricultural tenancies, and employed a firm of chartered surveyors to act as her agent. She first heard of Foot's user on her final return in 1967, and in 1970 sought an injunction to restrain Foot's entry on her land. PENNYCUICK V-C held that Foot had not acquired an easement by prescription and said at 1433, at 791:

"Coming to the facts of the present case, I have already held that the plaintiff had never heard that the defendant company or its predecessors had been using no. 415 for access to their own land, until Mr Billen told her something in 1967. I have already made clear that I accept that evidence, so that she did not have actual knowledge at any time before 1967. Were the circumstances such that if she had followed up any clues she would have ascertained that the relevant act was being done? I have reached the clear conclusion that the plaintiff did not possess any such means of knowledge.

Mr Bradburn contended that she must be treated as having such means of knowledge by reason of the existence of the gateway at point B, considered in connection with the lie of the land which made the extreme north-west tip of

---

[10] M & W, p. 870, n. 53; "*Solomon v Mystery of Vintners* (1859) 4 H & N 585 at 602 (common law prescription); *Sturges v Bridgman* (1879) 11 ChD 852 at 863 (lost modern grant); *Tickle v Brown* (1836) 4 Ad & El 369 at 382 (prescription under the Prescription Act 1832; and see ss. 1, 2)."

the panhandle virtually inaccessible to vehicles except through that gate. I am not at all certain that the plaintiff, doing all the acts which a diligent landowner could have done, would have even seen gate B when she made her inspections of Sanctions Farm during this period from 1936 to 1967. During this period the plaintiff came down to Buckland Newton perhaps once a year to look over Sanctions Farm. No. 415 was an outlying part of a large farm and there is no reason I can see why one should infer that the plaintiff, looking over the farm as a whole, should have walked up along the boundary to this outlying field. Even if she had done so, I am not persuaded that the mere site of a gate at point B leading to the panhandle would have put her on any further inquiry as to why that gate was there. There can be all sorts of reasons why a gate stands between two pieces of land which are not at present in common ownership and I should not have thought that the mere sight of the gate would have put her on inquiry as to whether the gate was in current use by the owner/occupier for the time being of Bookham Farm for the purposes of access over no. 415. I conclude that it is not possible to impute to the plaintiff personally any means of knowledge.

Mr Bradburn put his contention of knowledge in one rather different way. I mention now the case to which I alluded earlier, namely, *Pugh v Savage* [1970] 2 QB 373, [1970] 2 All ER 353 in which Cross LJ said at 384, at 359: 'When long user — here user for 36 years — of a way has been shown, I think that the law should support it if it can, and that we ought to presume, in the absence of any evidence to the contrary, that the owners of 457 in the period 1932/1940 knew of the user and that Ralphs knew of it.' There Cross LJ — and both Harman and Salmon LJJ agreed — was stating that there is a presumption that the owner concerned knows of the relevant user of a way but, as he himself said, it is obvious that that presumption can be rebutted by evidence that the owner did not have such knowledge. The effect of that statement is to throw the burden of proof upon the owner concerned, that is to say instead of the other party having to establish affirmatively that he did have knowledge, he must establish that he did not have knowledge. That is I think an enlargement of the principle stated in the earlier case[11].

The plaintiff, herself, did not have such knowledge and so, as far as she is concerned, she has in the present case rebutted the presumption. But during these years the plaintiff employed a firm of chartered surveyors known as Henry Duke & Son of Dorchester to act for her in connection with Sanctions Farm including the making of agreements with the successive tenants in occupation of no. 415. Mr Bradburn contended that any knowledge or imputed knowledge on the part of the plaintiff's agent must be treated for this purpose as her own knowledge as principal and that the presumption of knowledge applies as regards Messrs Henry Duke & Son, and could only be rebutted by showing that Henry Duke & Son did not in fact have knowledge of the user of the way, or means of such knowledge. I do not think the presumption can legitimately be carried so far where a landowner employs an agent in connection with the property. There cannot, I think, be a presumption, merely by reason of that relation and without reference to the particular circumstances, that the agent has knowledge or means of knowledge of any particular act upon the land. That would be carrying this presumption altogether beyond anything that was said in *Pugh v Savage* and

---

[11] *Dalton v Angus* (1881) 6 App Cas 740.

would, I venture to think, lead to some very odd consequences. It seems to me that where one is concerned with an agent, the role of establishing knowledge or means of knowledge must rest on the other party concerned, who might discharge that burden by direct evidence or by inference — the inference depending upon all the particular circumstances. There was no evidence here as to the precise activities carried on by Henry Duke & Son apart from the fact that they were responsible for making the tenancies and dealing with matters of rents and so forth. There is no evidence as to what members of that firm or their representative did physically upon Sanctions Farm or no. 415 by way of inspection and I see no ground upon which I would be entitled to hold that Henry Duke & Son had knowledge or means of knowledge of the user of this way by Mr Foot or the defendant company.

That is sufficient to decide this case because the defendant company has failed to establish that the plaintiff either had knowledge of the use of this way or the means of such knowledge and that is the third of Fry J's requirements."

Davies v Du Paver [1953] 1 QB 184, [1952] 2 All ER 991, p. 615, post.

GARDNER *v* HODGSON'S KINGSTON BREWERY CO LTD
[1903] AC 229 (HL, Lords HALSBURY, ASHBOURNE, MACNAGHTEN, DAVEY, ROBERTSON and LINDLEY)

For some 70 or 80 years, the owners of the plaintiff's house had been accustomed to use a way from their stable across the yard of the defendant's inn to reach a road. The user was open and uninterrupted, but, for a long period, and certainly since 1855, an annual payment of 15*s*. had been made.

The plaintiff claimed a declaration that she was entitled to a right of way.

Held. No claim could be made under the Prescription Act or under the doctrine of lost modern grant because the user, being by permission, was not "as of right".

LORD LINDLEY: The plaintiff's statement of claim is so drawn as to entitle her to succeed if she can bring herself within the Prescription Act, or failing that, if the facts warrant the presumption of a lost grant. Cozens-Hardy J considered that she was entitled to succeed under the Prescription Act; but that if not, a lost grant in her favour ought to be presumed. It is necessary to consider both of these methods of establishing her right; for the Prescription Act has not taken away any of the modes of claiming easements which existed before that Act was passed: see *Aynsley v Glover* (1875) 10 Ch App 283.

I will take the Prescription Act first. Section 2 is the important section, and the last part of it is relied upon by the plaintiff. To bring herself within this enactment she must prove that she and her predecessors in title have enjoyed the way in question "claiming right thereto" without interruption for forty years. The difficulty is raised by the words "claiming right thereto", and by the payment of the 15*s*. a year. I understand the words "claiming right thereto" and the equivalent words "as of right", which occur in section 5, to have the same meaning as the older expression nec vi, nec clam, nec precario. A temporary permission, although often renewed, would prevent an enjoyment from being "as of right"; but a permanent, irrevocable permission attributable to a lost grant would not have the same effect. The common law doctrine is that all prescription presupposes a grant. But if the grant is proved and its terms are known, prescription has no place.

A title by prescription can be established by long peaceable open enjoyment only; but in order that it may be so established the enjoyment must be inconsistent with any other reasonable inference than that it has been as of right in the sense above explained. This, I think, is the proper inference to be drawn from the authorities discussed in the court below. If the enjoyment is equally consistent with two reasonable inferences, enjoyment as of right is not established; and this, I think, is the real truth in the present case.

The enjoyment is equally open to explanation in one of two ways, namely, by a lost grant of a right of way in consideration of a rent-charge on the plaintiff's land of 15s. a year, or by a succession of yearly licences not, perhaps, expressed every year, but implied and assumed and paid for[12].

In *Healey v Hawkins* [1968] 1 WLR 1967, [1968] 3 All ER 836, the question arose of the effect of initial oral permission on user for the 20 year period under the Prescription Act 1832. GOFF J held that the user which was permissive in origin did not so continue and thus prevent the defendant from acquiring an easement of way. He said at 1973, at 841:

"In principle it seems to me that once permission has been given, the user must remain permissive and not be capable of ripening into a right save where the permission is oral and the user has continued for 40 or 60 years, unless and until, having been given for a limited period only, it expires or, being general, it is revoked, or there is a change in circumstances from which revocation may fairly be implied. Moreover, *Gaved v Martyn* (1865) 19 CBNS 732 appears to me to be a decision expressly in point and in accordance with the conclusion in Megarry and Wade (p. 850, para. 4 (iii)). In that case, oral permission had been given to use an artificial watercourse, and a successor who did not claim under the original licensee and who had no actual knowledge of permission having been given continued to exercise the privilege, but in circumstances which ought to, or might, have put him on inquiry, and the court held that there was evidence and, as Byles J at 747 thought, abundant evidence, on which the jury could find, as it had done, that the user even by the new occupier remained permissive.

Of course, when the user has continued for 40 or 60 years a prior parol consent affords no answer, because it is excluded by the express terms of section 2 of the Prescription Act, but, even so, permission given during the period will defeat the claimant because it negatives user as of right. That is, in my judgment, the explanation of the distinction drawn by the House of Lords in *Gardner v Hodgson's Kingston Brewery* [1903] AC 229, between antecedent and current parol consents."

---

[12] *Monmouth Canal Co v Harford* (1834) 1 Cr M & R 614.

iii.   USER IN FEE SIMPLE[13]

In *Kilgour v Gaddes* [1904] 1 KB 457, a dispute arose between two neighbouring tenants of Sir James Graham in connection with the use of a pump which was situated on the land occupied by the plaintiff. The defendant and his predecessors in title had used the pump for forty years before the action was brought.

The Court of Appeal held that there was no prescriptive right to use the pump, COLLINS MR saying at 460: "The question in this case is whether, as between two persons who are termors of different tenements, a right of way to a pump has been acquired by prescription for the owner of one of the tenements over the other tenement under section 2 of the Prescription Act 1832. I say a right for the owner, for it appears to me clear that under the section the right cannot be acquired merely by a tenant as against a tenant, but must be acquired by the owner of the fee in one of the tenements as against the owner of the fee in the other. Here the respective tenants of the so-called dominant and servient tenements hold under the same landlord; and, if the proposition be correct that a prescriptive right of way under section 2 of the Act must be acquired by the owner of the fee in one of the tenements as against the owner of the fee in the other, then in this case the defendant's contention would involve the result that the tenant of one of the tenements has acquired for his landlord a right of way over the landlord's own land; which is impossible and inconsistent with the essential notion of a right by prescription, namely, that the right is acquired by the owner of land over land belonging to another owner. I limit what I am saying to such an easement as a right of way, because questions with regard to the easement of light stand on a different footing, and depend on the provisions of section 3 of the Act[14]. . . . 'If I am asked how it is consistent with the Prescription Act, I answer that such user and enjoyment is not as of right within the meaning of the 2nd section. It is a user by a termor, who, if he acquire the right, must acquire it as incident to the land of which he is termor, and thus for the benefit of his reversioner. Such user cannot be as of right, unless a reversioner can in law by user acquire a right against himself[15].' That reasoning appears to me conclusive of the present case. There was a long discussion in the course of the argument as to the possibility of a termor under one landlord acquiring for his landlord an easement by user over land in the occupation of a termor under another landlord, and as to whether an easement in such a case could be acquired, unless and until the user had continued for the period of three years after the determination of the term in the servient tenement without interference by the reversioner[16]. That no doubt raises an interesting question, which appears to have been decided in Ireland in the case of *Beggan v M'Donald* (1877) 2 LR Ir 560, contrary to the view expressed in this country in *Bright v Walker* (1834) 1 Cr M & R 211 and also in *Wheaton v Maple & Co* [1893] 3 Ch 48, in neither of which cases, however, was it necessary actually

---

[13] M & W, p. 872, n. 72; "*Bright v Walker* (1834) 1 Cr M & R 211 at 221 (prescription at common law); *Wheaton v Maple & Co* [1893] 3 Ch 48 at 63 (lost modern grant); *Kilgour v Gaddes* [1904] 1 KB 457 at 460 (Prescription Act 1832)." *Pugh v Savage* [1970] 2 QB 373, [1970] 2 All ER 353; *Davis v Whitby* [1973] 1 WLR 629, [1973] 3 All ER 403.

[14] P. 634, post.

[15] Quoting PALLES CB, in *Timmons v Hewitt* (1888) 22 LR Ir 627.

[16] Prescription Act 1832, s. 8, p. 614, post.

to decide the point. That question, however, is not the question raised in the present case. . . .

In the case of *Wheaton v Maple & Co* the view which I am expressing was very clearly stated by Lindley LJ in his judgment. He dealt first with the question of the possibility of acquiring an easement as against a tenant of land by a presumption of a lost grant as follows: 'I am not aware of any authority for presuming, as a matter of law, a lost grant by a lessee for years in the case of ordinary easements, or a lost covenant by such a person not to interrupt in the case of light, and I am certainly not prepared to introduce another fiction to support a claim to a novel prescriptive right. The whole theory of prescription at common law is against presuming any grant or covenant not to interrupt, by or with any one except an owner in fee. A right claimed by prescription must be claimed as appendant or appurtenant to land, and not as annexed to it for a term of years. Although, therefore, a grant by a lessee of the Crown, commensurate with his lease, might be inferred as a fact, if there was evidence to justify the inference, there is no legal presumption, as distinguished from an inference in fact, in favour of such a grant. This view of the common law is in entire accordance with *Bright v Walker* where this doctrine of presumption is carefully examined.' He was there dealing with the question of an implied grant."

———

Claims to easements (other than easements of light, p. 634, post) under prescription at common law (*Bright v Walker* (1834) 1 Cr M & R at 221; or under the doctrine of implied grant must be based upon user against a fee simple owner. In *Wheaton v Maple & Co* [1893] 3 Ch 48, the easement claimed was an easement of light, but the Crown was the freeholder of the servient tenement; Prescription Act 1832, section 3 (right to light) does not, as do sections 1 and 2, bind the Crown, and the plaintiff was thrown back on reliance on section 2 or upon the doctrine of lost modern grant.

Similarly, prescription (apart from easements of light) can operate only in favour of a fee simple estate, but the fee simple owner may take advantage of user enjoyed by a lessee or other limited owner in making a claim to an easement.

The rule is clear; but there appears to be no logical reason why the doctrine of the lost modern grant should not apply to cases of prescription by or against a lessee or other limited owner. The doctrine could apply so as to presume a grant to a lessee of the dominant tenement of an easement for the period of his tenancy; or to a grant either by the lessee of the servient tenement of an easement for years or by the fee simple owner of an easement in fee[17].

———

[17] (1958) 74 LQR 82 (V. T. H. Delany).

iv. THE DOCTRINE OF LOST MODERN GRANT[18]

HULBERT *v* DALE
[1909] 2 Ch 570 (ChD, JOYCE J; CA, COZENS-HARDY MR, FLETCHER
MOULTON and FARWELL LJJ)

By an Inclosure Award of 1804, a "private carriage road of the width of
thirty feet" over Crown Farm (now owned by the plaintiff) was allotted to
the predecessor in title of the defendant's lessor, owner of Fishmore Farm.
The road was never made, and trees grew and buildings were built on the
intended site. However the defendant and his predecessor in title or
occupation had, since 1804, uninterruptedly used a private road running
across the plaintiff's farm, parallel to the site of the awarded road and some
100 yards from it.

There had been unity of possession of the two farms from 1889 to 1905,
while they were in the occupation of the same tenant.

The plaintiff brought this action for an injunction to restrain the defendant
from using the road.

Held (affirming JOYCE J). A lost grant of a right of way should be
presumed.

JOYCE J: There was a considerable conflict of evidence in the case, but,
upon the whole, the result to my mind is that I come to the conclusion, and
find as a fact, that for a period as far back as living memory extends the
owners and occupiers for the time being of Fishmore Farm have openly and
without interruption had an unquestioned user until quite recently, when the
dispute arose, of the now disputed road, and I should have held such user to
have been as of right (or by persons claiming a right thereto) but for the
circumstance that during the period between the years 1889 and 1905 there
was unity of possession (not of ownership) of the two farms, Fishmore and
Crown Farms, both being in the occupation of the same tenant or tenants.

This being so, the defendant could not make good any claim to a right of
way along the disputed road by prescription under the 2nd section of the
Prescription Act. Nor could he, I think, have succeeded upon a claim by
prescription at common law, because I consider it to be tolerably plain, for
various reasons, that the existence of the right of way claimed, if it does exist,
originated and commenced at a date long subsequent to the reign of King
Richard I — in fact very little more than one hundred years ago. The
defendant, therefore, has to base his claim upon the existence of a grant not
produced, and he contends that it is a case for presuming a grant, now lost, of
the right to use the disputed road.

I must say that it seems to me that if ever there was a case in which some
such presumption ought to be made, this is the case. For I am tolerably
certain that the owners and occupiers of Fishmore Farm have had the use of
the disputed road without interruption and with the full knowledge of the
occupiers, and presumably of the owners, of Crown Farm, who have
acquiesced in such use possibly because of the existence of the right of the

---

[18] Holdsworth, vol. vii, pp. 347–349; *Healey v Hawkins* [1968] 1 WLR 1967, [1968] 3 All ER 836
(grant of right of way presumed); *Oakley v Boston* [1976] QB 270, [1975] 3 All ER 405
(incumbent of glebe land is capable grantor with consent of Ecclesiastical Commissioners);
Ward (Helston) Ltd v Kerrier District Council (1981) 42 P & CR 412 (grant of right of way
presumed).

awarded way, which right, if enforced, would have been much more disadvantageous to Crown Farm than the user of the disputed road by the owners and occupiers of Fishmore Farm.

In *Tehidy Minerals Ltd v Norman* [1971] 2 QB 528, [1971] 2 All ER 475, the defendants proved that they were accustomed to graze Tawna Down, Cardinham, Cornwall, from 19 January 1920 to 6 October 1941, a period of 21 years, eight and a half months. In holding that they had acquired a profit à prendre under the doctrine of lost modern grant, BUCKLEY LJ, in delivering the judgment of the Court of Appeal (SALMON, SACHS and BUCKLEY LJJ) said at 547, at 486: "The question is whether on the facts of this case enjoyment of this grazing for a period of upwards of 20 years preceding 6 October 1941 permits or requires us to presume that such enjoyment was had by virtue of grants made after 19 January 1920, but before 6 October 1921 (being 20 years before 6 October 1941), and subsequently lost, and whether we ought to act on such a presumption[19]. [His Lordship then analysed the judgments in *Angus v Dalton* (1877) 3 QBD 85, (1878) 4 QBD 162, (1881) 6 App Cas 740 "which in the course of its history enjoyed the attention of no less than 18 judges and members of the House of Lords, perhaps embodying a greater variety of judicial opinion than any other leading case", and continued:] In our judgment *Angus v Dalton* decides that, where there has been upwards of 20 years' uninterrupted enjoyment of an easement, such enjoyment having the necessary qualities to fulfil the requirements of prescription, then unless, for some reason such as incapacity on the part of the person or persons who might at some time before the commencement of the 20-year period have made a grant, the existence of such a grant is impossible, the law will adopt a legal fiction that such a grant was made, in spite of any direct evidence that no such grant was in fact made.

If this legal fiction is not to be displaced by direct evidence that no grant was made, it would be strange if it could be displaced by circumstantial evidence leading to the same conclusion, and in our judgment it must follow that circumstantial evidence tending to negative the existence of a grant (other than evidence establishing impossibility) should not be permitted to displace the fiction. Precisely the same reasoning must, we think, apply to a presumed lost grant of a profit à prendre as to an easement.

In the present case, if we are to presume lost grants, we must do so in respect of each of the four farms, Higher and Lower Hill, Cabilla and Pinsla Park. Each of the presumed grants must be supposed to have been made between 20 January 1920 and 5 October 1921, and to have been since lost in circumstances of which no one now has any recollection. This combination of circumstances seems to us to be exceedingly improbable, and we feel sympathy for the view expressed by Farwell J in *A-G v Simpson* [1901] 2 Ch 671 at 698: 'It cannot be the duty of a judge to presume a grant of the non-existence of which he is convinced, nor can he be constrained to hold that such a grant is reasonably possible within the meaning of the authorities.' In

---

[19] CA rejected an argument that, as the Prescription Act 1832 lays down longer periods for prescription in respect of profits than in respect of easements, so by analogy a longer period of enjoyment should be required in the case of a profit than in the case of an easement to support the prescription.

view, however, of the decision in *Angus v Dalton* we consider that it is not open to us in the present case to follow this line."

V. THE PRESCRIPTION ACT 1832[20]

PRESCRIPTION ACT 1832

Whereas the expression "time immemorial, or time whereof the memory of man runneth not to the contrary," is now by the Law of England in many cases considered to include and denote the whole period of time from the Reign of King Richard the First, whereby the title to matters that have been long enjoyed is sometimes defeated by shewing the commencement of such enjoyment, which is in many cases productive of inconvenience and injustice;

[1.] Claims to right of common[1] and other profits à prendre, not to be defeated after thirty years enjoyment by shewing the commencement; after sixty years enjoyment the right to be absolute, unless had by consent or agreement.— No claim which may be lawfully made at the common law, by custom, prescription, or grant, to any right of common or other profit or benefit to be taken and enjoyed from or upon any land of our sovereign lord the King, or any land being parcel of the duchy of Lancaster or of the duchy of Cornwall, or of any ecclesiastical or lay person, or body corporate, except such matters and things as are herein specially provided for, and except tithes, rent, and services, shall, where such right, profit, or benefit shall have been actually taken and enjoyed by any person claiming right thereto without interruption for the full period of thirty years, be defeated or destroyed by showing only that such right, profit, or benefit was first taken or enjoyed at any time prior to such period of thirty years, but nevertheless such claim may be defeated in any other way by which the same is now liable to be defeated; and when such right, profit, or benefit shall have been so taken and enjoyed as aforesaid for the full period of sixty years, the right thereto shall be deemed absolute and indefeasible, unless it shall appear that the same was taken and enjoyed by some consent or agreement expressly made or given for that purpose by deed or writing.

2. In claims of right of way or other easement the periods to be twenty years and forty years.—. . . No claim which may be lawfully made at the common law, by custom, prescription, or grant, to any way or other easement, or to any watercourse, or the use of any water, to be enjoyed or derived upon, over, or from any land or water of our said lord the King, or being parcel of the duchy of Lancaster or of the duchy of Cornwall, or being the property of any ecclesiastical or lay person, or body corporate, when such way or other matter as herein last before mentioned shall have been actually enjoyed by any person claiming right thereto without interruption for the full period of twenty years, shall be defeated or destroyed by showing only that such way or other matter was first enjoyed at any time prior to such period of twenty years, but nevertheless such claim may be defeated in any other way by which the same is now liable to be defeated; and where such way or other matter as herein last before mentioned shall have been so enjoyed as

---

[20] For the history of prescription, see Hóldsworth, vol. vii, pp. 343 et seq; Simpson, *Introduction to the History of Land Law*, pp. 248–251.

[1] P. 58, ante.

aforesaid for the full period of forty years, the right thereto shall be deemed absolute and indefeasible, unless it shall appear that the same was enjoyed by some consent or agreement expressly given or made for that purpose by deed or writing.

4². Before mentioned periods to be deemed those next before suits.— Each of the respective periods of years herein-before mentioned shall be deemed and taken to be the period next before some suit or action wherein the claim or matter to which such period may relate shall have been or shall be brought into question; and no act or other matter shall be deemed to be an interruption, within the meaning of this statute, unless the same shall have been or shall be submitted to or acquiesced in for one year after the party interrupted shall have had or shall have notice thereof, and of the person making or authorizing the same to be made.

7³. Proviso for infants, &c.— Provided also, that the time during which any person otherwise capable of resisting any claim to any of the matters before mentioned shall have been or shall be an infant, idiot, non compos mentis, feme covert, or tenant for life, or during which any action or suit shall have been pending, and which shall have been diligently prosecuted, until abated by the death of any party or parties thereto, shall be excluded in the computation of the periods hereinbefore mentioned, except only in cases where the right or claim is hereby declared to be absolute and indefeasible.

8³. What time to be excluded in computing the term of forty years appointed by this Act.— Provided always, that when any land or water upon, over, or from which any such way or other convenient[4] watercourse or use of water shall have been or shall be enjoyed or derived hath been or shall be held under or by virtue of any term of life, or any term of years[5] exceeding three years from the granting thereof, the time of the enjoyment of any such way or other matter as herein last before mentioned, during the continuance of such term, shall be excluded in the computation of the said period of forty years, in case the claim shall within three years next after the end or sooner determination of such term be resisted by any person entitled to any reversion expectant on the determination thereof.

Lord MACNAGHTEN in *Gardner v Hodgson's Kingston Brewery Co Ltd* [1903] AC 229, p. 607, ante, said at 236: "I rather doubt whether the scope and effect of the Prescription Act have been always rightly apprehended. The Act was passed, as its preamble declares, for the purpose of getting rid of the inconvenience and injustice arising from the meaning which the law of England attached to the expressions 'time immemorial' and 'time whereof the memory of man runneth not to the contrary'. The law as it stood put an intolerable strain on the consciences of judges and jurymen. The Act was an

---

[2] Prescriptive claims to rights of common are not to be defeated by reason of interruptions due to requisition of the common land by a Government Department, or to inability to exercise a right to graze animals for reasons of animal health: Commons Registration Act 1965, s. 16. See Rights of Light Act 1959, s. 3 (6), p. 640, post.

[3] See n. 2, supra.

[4] Probably a misprint for "easement": *Wright v Williams* (1836) Tyr & Gr 375 at 390; *Laird v Briggs* (1881) 19 ChD 22 at 33.

[5] *Palk v Shinner* (1852) 18 QB 568.

Act 'for shortening the time of prescription in certain cases'. And really it did nothing more. A person who claims a right of way and invokes the protection of the Act must claim 'as of right'. But when the way in question has been used without interruption, as defined in the Act, for forty years 'as of right' — whether the claimant is really entitled of right or not — the claim cannot be defeated except by shewing that the right claimed was enjoyed 'by some consent or agreement expressly given or made for that purpose by deed or writing'. No parol consent will do. I fail to understand how that provision helps the appellant. The respondents do not set up a parol consent given before the period of forty years. They rely on the acknowledgment and recognition of their dominion over the property — their right to grant or withhold the grant of the way in question — involved in and evidenced by the annual payment accompanying the use of the way, and they point out that no other reasonable explanation of that payment is forthcoming."

(a) Interruption
In *Davies v Du Paver* [1953] 1 QB 184, [1952] 2 All ER 991, a dispute arose over the question whether the plaintiff had acquired a right (profit) by prescription based upon 60 years' user to pasture sheep upon the defendant's land. Two main questions arose:

i.   The defendant in August 1950 completed a fence which excluded the sheep in spite of the plaintiff's vigorous protests. No further action was taken until the writ was issued in September 1951, and the defendant argued that the user was interrupted for more than a year.

ii.   During the first 55 of the 60 years during which user was proved, the defendant's land (servient tenement) had been in the possession of lessees.

The Court of Appeal (BIRKETT and MORRIS LJJ, SINGLETON LJ, dissenting) held that:

i.   there was no interruption within the Act, but ii. the plaintiff failed to show that the defendant had the knowledge or means of knowledge of the user and the power to object to it.

On the first point, MORRIS LJ said at 206, at 1000: "The first point raised by the defendant is that there was a fatal interruption of the enjoyment by the plaintiff of his alleged right of pasturage. In the notice of appeal this contention is formulated on the basis that there was no evidence that Mr Davies 'had asserted his alleged rights or protested at the interruption of his alleged rights of pasturage' between 1 August 1950 and 28 September 1951, and 'that accordingly the judge was wrong in law in holding that the plaintiff Davies did not acquiesce in, or submit to, any interruption which had continued for more than one year'. This language raises the question as to the meaning of an 'assertion of rights or of a protest'. But the real question is not whether there was an assertion of rights or a protest during some period, but whether there was in this case a submission or an acquiescence. It is provided by the Prescription Act 1832, that no act or other matter is deemed to be an interruption within the meaning of the Act unless submitted to, or acquiesced in, for one year after the party interrupted has notice of the interruption and of the person making it or authorising it to be made.

There is no doubt that there was an actual interruption for more than a year before 27 September 1951. The question is whether there was acquiescence in such interruption or submission to it lasting for one year. This is, in my judgment, a question of fact. If a case were being tried with a jury it would be a question for the jury to determine: see *Bennison v Cartwright* (1864) 5 B & S 1. . . .

The fence was completed on 9 August. Could it be said that the plaintiff had submitted to, or acquiesced in, the existence of the fence by that date? Having regard to the events that had happened, and to the correspondence, I would have thought, had it been for me to decide this question of fact, that the answer would be in the negative. The parties were breathing fury on each side of a newly erected fence. Could it be said that the challenging protests of the plaintiff must, as the August days passed, be deemed to have signified nothing, and that his former claims and assertions should be regarded as supplanted by submission and acquiescence? As time went by, it might well be that silence and inaction could be interpreted as submission or acquiescence. But the date when submission or acquiescence begins must be determined as a question of fact, having regard to all the circumstances. Had there been a beginning by 1 January 1951, or by 1 December 1950, or by 1 November 1950? These are all questions of fact. Unless it is held that there was submission or acquiescence by 27 September 1950, there would not be a period of one year. The judge referred to *Glover v Coleman* (1874) LR 10 CP 108, and stated: 'On the evidence I hold that neither of the plaintiffs submitted to or acquiesced in the interruption.' This was a finding of fact which the judge was, in my view, entitled to make, and accordingly I consider that the first submission fails.''

On the second point, the court appears to have treated the question of the knowledge or means of knowledge of the user as being a matter related to user as of right. BIRKETT LJ said at 206, at 1000: ''I see no evidence on which the judge could find that the common knowledge extended to the servient owner, or any evidence that the servient owner had the means of knowledge. It is on this ground that I would allow the appeal, for the claim 'as of right' cannot in these circumstances be established.''

The user, as the judge found, was common knowledge; the defendant was unaware because he was the lessor, not in possession. The question should then be, it is submitted, not whether the user was as of right, but whether it was in fee simple. The answer to that question would be that, in the case of 40 years' user for easements under the Prescription Act (60 years for profits), the fact that the servient tenement was in the occupation of a tenant for years was immaterial — unless the period of user under the tenancy was excluded under the special defence provided by section 8[6].

(*b*) *User as of Right is Necessary for Prescription under either Period.*

Gardner v Hodgson's Kingston Brewery Co Ltd [1903] AC 229, p. 607, ante.

Healey v Hawkins [1968] 1 WLR 1967, [1968] 3 All ER 836, p. 608, ante.

---

[6] *Wright v Williams* (1836) 1 M & W 77 (not cited); (1956) 72 LQR 32 (R.E.M.). Compare *Kilgour v Gaddes* (p. 609, ante) where both tenements were owned by the same landlord.

Diment v N. H. Foot Ltd [1974] 1 WLR 1427, [1974] 2 All ER 785, p. 605, ante.

In *Union Lighterage Co v London Graving Dock Co* [1902] 2 Ch 557, one question was whether the defendants could prescribe for an easement in respect of underwater support of a wharf, none of the metal supports except two nuts showing above the surface. The Court of Appeal (ROMER and STIRLING LJJ, VAUGHAN WILLIAMS LJ dissenting) held that there could be no prescription as the user was secret. ROMER LJ said at 570: "Now, on principle, it appears to me that a prescriptive right to an easement over a man's land should only be acquired when the enjoyment has been open — that is to say, of such a character that an ordinary owner of the land, diligent in the protection of his interests, would have, or must be taken to have, a reasonable opportunity of becoming aware of that enjoyment. And I think on the balance of authority that the principle has been recognised as the law, and ought to be followed by us."

(c) Next before Action Brought

HYMAN *v* VAN DEN BERGH
[1908] 1 Ch 167 (CA, COZENS-HARDY MR, FLETCHER MOULTON and FARWELL LJJ)

In 1877, one Cox, a former tenant of the plaintiff, built a cowshed with eight windows overlooking land subsequently purchased by the defendant. In 1896 and 1898, the defendant obstructed the windows by boards but these were quickly removed by the plaintiff. On 18 January 1899, Cox wrote a letter agreeing to pay 1*s.* per annum for the use of the light. In 1906, Cox left, and a dispute arose between the parties as to the right to the light.

Held. The plaintiff was not entitled to an easement although 22 years' uninterrupted user had been enjoyed before the permission was given.

COZENS-HARDY MR: It is often asserted that an absolute right is obtained to access of light by reason merely of twenty years' undisturbed enjoyment, but I think this statement is too wide. Lord Macnaghten in *Colls v Home and Colonial Stores* [1904] AC 179 at 189, after referring to certain "expressions not perhaps sufficiently guarded" which are to be found in the judgment in the House of Lords in *Tapling v Jones* (1865) 11 HL Cas 290, said: "In that case Lord Westbury, Lord Cranworth, and Lord Chelmsford all assumed that a period of twenty years' enjoyment of the access and use of light to a building creates an absolute and indefeasible right immediately on the expiration of the period of twenty years. No doubt section 3 says so in terms, but section 4 must be read in connection with section 3; and if the two sections are read together it will be seen that the period is not a period in gross, but a period next before some suit or action wherein the claim or matter to which such period may relate shall have been or shall be brought into question. Unless and until the claim or matter is thus brought into question, no absolute or indefeasible right can arise under the Act. There is what has been described as an inchoate right. The owner of the dominant tenement after twenty years' uninterrupted enjoyment is in a position to avail himself of the Act if his claim is brought into question. But in the meantime, however long the enjoyment may have been, his right is just the same, as the origin of his right is just the same, as if the Act had never been passed. No title is as yet acquired under the Act. This point seems to have been much discussed shortly after the Act was passed. It was finally settled in a series of cases at common law, beginning, I think, with *Wright v Williams* (1836) 1 M & W 77, and including *Richards v Fry* (1837) 7 Ad & El 698 and *Cooper v Hubbuck* (1862) 12 CB NS 456." If this is to be regarded as a decision upon sections 3 and 4, it is of course binding upon us. If, however, it is to be regarded only as a dictum of Lord Macnaghten, I desire respectfully to say that I agree with it, and I accept it as an accurate statement of the law.

It only remains to apply the law to the facts of the present case. No action was brought by the plaintiff or any other person until the present action was commenced on 11 July 1906. The only material period to be considered is the period of twenty years prior to that date. No evidence as to what was the condition of the windows prior to that date can be regarded. Now during that period there was undoubtedly the actual enjoyment of light through the windows in question, but at the end of 1898 the windows were for a short time obstructed by the defendant. The then tenant in occupation having a doubt whether a right to light could be established, and being desirous of avoiding litigation, signed and addressed to the defendant the letter of 18 January 1899; thereupon the boards were removed, and the lights were thenceforth actually enjoyed. Under these circumstances I think it is clear that the light was enjoyed by "consent or agreement" expressly made or given for that purpose by writing. It is true that it was made or given, not to or with the freeholder, but to or with the tenant in occupation. The tenant in occupation was the proper person to make such agreement or to obtain such consent as the section requires. In my view it is a fallacy to say that the freeholder had an absolute right which his lessee ought not to be permitted to defeat. In truth he had only an inchoate right which never became an absolute and indefeasible right. The judgment of Parker J so carefully deals with the law applicable to the case under the Prescription Act that I do not think I should be justified in saying anything more. In my opinion this appeal must be dismissed with costs.

Hulbert v Dale [1909] 2 Ch 570, p. 611, ante.

In *Reilly v Orange* [1955] 2 QB 112, [1955] 2 All ER 369, neighbouring owners in 1934 came to an agreement whereby the defendant could use a way over the plaintiff's land until the defendant should construct a way of his own; this he did in 1953. In December 1953 the plaintiff purported to terminate the defendant's right to use the way, and began proceedings for this purpose; the defendant counterclaimed for a declaration that, by reason of his user for over 19 years, he was entitled to an easement.

The Court of Appeal (SINGLETON, JENKINS and MORRIS LJJ) affirmed the county court judge in finding for the plaintiff, JENKINS LJ saying at 116, at 371: "Mr Blease, for the defendant, very properly admits that for the purpose of this appeal he must accept the deputy judge's finding as to the nature and terms of the agreement, but he says that notwithstanding this he is entitled to succeed. He says that on two grounds: (1) that he has had 20 years' uninterrupted enjoyment of the right claimed, as required by the Prescription Act 1832; (2) that although the right he claims had its origin in the agreement of 1934, and although that agreement, as found by the deputy judge, would only give him a right to use the drive for domestic purposes, and only until such time as he made a drive of his own, that permission did not prevent the 20 years' user on which he relies from establishing his right under the Prescription Act 1832. The second of those points can only arise if Mr Blease is entitled to succeed on the first. . . .

Mr Blease's argument on this part of the case is of this nature: he says that what must be shown is 20 years' uninterrupted user, and that, according to section 4, no act or matter counts as an interruption unless the same shall have been or shall be submitted to or acquiesced in for one year. It follows, says Mr Blease, that inasmuch as in this case over 19 years' user down to the commencement of the action is proved, the defendant's right is made good inasmuch as there could be no interruption acquiesced in for one year between the date of the commencement of the action and the completion of the full period of 20 years.

In support of that proposition he referred us to the well-known case of *Flight v Thomas* (1841) 8 Cl & Fin 231. In that case: 'A. had the free access of light and air through a window of his house for nineteen years and 330 days, and B. then raised a wall which obstructed the light, and the obstruction was submitted to only for 35 days, when A. brought an action to remove it.' It was held: 'that the right of action was complete; that the twenty years' enjoyment was to be reckoned from the commencement of the enjoyment to the time of bringing the action; and that an interruption of the enjoyment, in whatever period of the twenty years it may happen, cannot be deemed an interruption within the meaning of the Act, unless it is acquiesced in for a whole year.'

Mr Blease seeks to apply that to the present case in this way: he says that the commencement of the action constituted an interruption, and that, inasmuch as the action was not commenced until after the alleged easement had been enjoyed for more than 19 years, the interruption so constituted could not last for the required period of one year, so that his title was complete at the time of action brought. In my view that argument cannot prevail. What the Prescription Act requires, as appears from the combined effect of section 2 and section 4, is the full period of 20 years, being 'the period next before some suit or action wherein the claim or matter to which such period may relate shall have been or shall be brought into question'. The commencement of the suit or action in my view is clearly not an interruption within the meaning of section 4, but is the event marking the date down to which the requisite period of user must be shown. What must be shown is a full 20 years reckoned down to the date of action brought. That must be an uninterrupted period, but in considering whether it is an uninterrupted period or not, interruptions not acquiesced in for at least a year are not to be counted as interruptions."

In *Davis v Whitby* [1974] Ch 186, [1974] 1 All ER 806 (CA, LORD DENNING MR, STAMP and ORR LJJ), STAMP LJ said at 192, at 810: "As the point is a somewhat novel one, I will express my views in my own words. The basis of prescription, as Lord Denning MR has pointed out, is that if long enjoyment of a right is shown, the court will strive to uphold the right by presuming that it had a lawful origin. Here, the owner of no. 51 (which, for the purpose of convenience, I will call 'the dominant tenement') has for upwards of 30 years enjoyed access from the rear of his house over no. 49 (which I will call 'the servient tenement'). During the first 15 years it was enjoyed over one path, and during the second period of over 15 years it was enjoyed partly over that path and partly over a substituted path. Viewed as the exercise of a right to pass and re-pass over the servient tenement, it has been enjoyed for upwards of 30 years, which is more than a sufficiently long period for it to be presumed that the right had a lawful origin. Viewed as a right so to pass and re-pass over a specified path, it has not. The question, as I see it, is which is the right way of looking at it. What happened was that in 1950 the new track or path over the back garden of the servient owner's house was established; but, using it, the dominant owner still used, as he had formerly done, the path at the side of the servient owner's house. Was the dominant owner then using the new way as of right and as of the same right as formerly? I think he was. In substance, what was enjoyed as well before as after 1950 was access by the dominant owner to the back of his little house from the road in front of the terrace along the side of the servient owner's premises and across his back garden.

On the facts of this case, the use of the substituted route is, in my judgment, to be considered as substantially an exercise of the right claimed and enjoyed for the whole period of 30 years. It is not as though the servient owner had said: 'I will stop up the way you have been using over these last 15 years, but you may have a new defined way over a wholly different part of my land', a situation about which I will say nothing.

I had at one time thought that the point taken that the agreement of 1950 by the servient owner amounted to a consent by him which interrupted the enjoyment as of right and so made the user 'precario' was a good point. But I accept Mr Gidley Scott's submission that what was agreed in 1950 did not involve a simple consent to the user given by the owner of the dominant tenement, but is more consistent (as I think Burgess V-C thought) with the existence of a claim of right by the dominant owner settled by the servient owner affording a route less disadvantageous to him than a path crossing the middle of his garden; and I do not think that it was a case of consent, but rather of compromise.

I would, for these reasons, dismiss the appeal."

IV.   Content of Easements[7]

After establishing that an easement has been created, questions can still arise as to its content and extent. Such questions often relate to changes in the neighbourhood and, in connection with rights of way, to changes in methods of transportation. The principles applicable vary with the mode of creation of the easement.

---

[7] C & B, pp. 525–527. As to easements of light, see p. 634, post. As to rights of way see M & W, pp. 900–903; MM, pp. 430–432; Gale, pp. 261–286; Jackson, pp. 139–155.

A. Easements Created by Express Grant

The extent of an easement is dependent upon the proper construction of the deed of grant. This is dependent upon the circumstances surrounding its execution, and they may be sufficient to restrict an apparently unlimited grant.

WILLES J, in *Williams v James* (1867) LR 2 CP 577, said at 581: "The distinction between a grant and prescription is obvious. In the case of proving a right by prescription the user of the right is the only evidence. In the case of a grant the language of the instrument can be referred to, and it is of course for the court to construe that language; and in the absence of any clear indication of the intention of the parties, the maxim that a grant must be construed most strongly against the grantor must be applied."

In *White v Grand Hotel Eastbourne Ltd* [1913] 1 Ch 113[8], an unrestricted right of way to a public road granted to the owner of a private house was held not to be limited to the circumstances existing at the time of the grant. When the private house became the Grand Hotel, Eastbourne, the owners of the hotel were entitled to a right of way for the general purposes of the hotel.

In *Kain v Norfolk* [1949] Ch 163, [1949] 1 All ER 176, the rector of Bradwell had conveyed to a purchaser in 1919 land adjoining the rectory, together with a grant of the "right at all times hereafter with or without horses carts and agricultural machines and implements to go pass and repass" over a strip of land within the rectory grounds.

A sand and gravel pit was later opened, and substantial traffic of lorries carrying sand developed. The question was whether such user was within the terms of the grant of the easement; JENKINS J, relying on *White v Grand Hotel Eastbourne Ltd*, held that it was.

In *Bulstrode v Lambert* [1953] 1 WLR 1064, [1953] 2 All ER 728[9], a reservation in the conveyance by the plaintiff's predecessor in title to the defendant's predecessor in title in 1944 had been made of a right of way as follows — "reserving unto the vendor his tenants and workmen and others authorised by him the right to pass and repass with or without vehicles over and along the land coloured brown on the ... plan for the purpose of obtaining access to the building at the rear of the said premises and known as the auction mart."

At the date of the conveyance the route to the auction mart (coloured brown) was obstructed and could not be used by large vans. The obstructions were removed, and, on occasions when a better route was too crowded, the plaintiff made use of the route with furniture vans and pantechnicons for

---

[8] *United Land Co v Great Eastern Rly Co* (1875) 10 Ch App 586.
[9] *McIlraith v Grady* [1968] 1 QB 468, [1967] 3 All ER 625 (a right "to pass and repass through over and along" included a right for vehicles to stop for a reasonable time to load and unload).

bringing goods to the mart. The defendant objected on the ground that the parked pantechnicons interfered with his business as a café and car hire proprietor, but UPJOHN J held that the plaintiff could use the way with pantechnicons which could park as long as was necessary for loading and unloading, this being an incident of a right of way.

KEEFE v AMOR

[1965] 1 QB 334, [1964] 2 All ER 517 (CA, SELLERS, RUSSELL and DAVIES LJJ)

The plaintiff was the owner of one (No. 1) of two semi-detached houses whose only outlet to the road was a strip of land to the rear. This land and the other house (No. 2) were owned by the defendant.

The plaintiff's parents had bought No. 1 in 1930 from the previous owner of both houses and the conveyance contained an express grant of a right of way in the following terms: "Together also with a right of way over the land shown and coloured brown on the plan hereto annexed the purchasers paying a fair proportion in common with the adjoining owners of the cost of keeping the said way in good repair and condition subject to the liability of contributing (in common with the adjoining owners) to the upkeep and repair of the wall on the west side of the said right of way shown and marked with a T on the plan drawn hereon."

At the date of the transfer there was at the frontage to the highway a continuous wall, except for a gap four feet six inches wide between two brick pillars. Inside, a gravelled strip eight feet wide led to a doorway three feet wide to the plaintiff's property and to a gap some seven feet wide leading to the remainder of the defendant's property. In 1962 the defendant widened the entrance from the highway to about seven feet six inches wide by rehanging the original gate and hanging another, three feet wide, alongside, which she kept locked, claiming the right so to do. The plaintiff sought a declaration that she was entitled to a right of way for all purposes, including vehicular traffic, over the whole of the strip of land coloured brown and an injunction to restrain the defendant from interfering with her reasonable enjoyment of this right.

The defendant contended that, in accordance with the circumstances existing at the time of the grant, the right of way was a footway only, or, at most, for such use as the four feet six inch gap permitted.

Held. On the proper construction of the grant, the right of way included user by vehicular traffic.

RUSSELL LJ: What were the circumstances and the condition of the property at the time of the grant? The inward end of the "brown strip" abutted on the boundary wall of the plaintiff's property, No. 1 — presumably a wall belonging to No. 1 — in which was a doorway about three feet wide. Down one side of the "brown strip" was the wall referred to in the transfer. Down the other side was a hedge, which, at the inward end, left a gap of some seven feet or so, which afforded access between the "brown strip" and No. 2. At the highway frontage of the "brown strip" was a wall between the ends of the hedge and the other wall, continuous except for the gap of about four feet six inches between two 14-inch-square brick pillars suitable for a gateway; and from this gateway to the inward end of the "brown strip" was a gravelled strip appreciably wider than the gateway, with some kind of edging of tiles, and on each side beyond that edging were garden beds and bushes, though apparently not much kept up. In appearance it looked like a footpath rather than a roadway. During the tenancy of the plaintiff's parents (which had lasted since 1903), there did not appear to have been any vehicular use of the "brown strip" by them.

Bearing all those matters in mind, do they lead to the conclusion that the grant was of a footway only, or alternatively, if the grant was of a vehicular way, then that it was one limited as to the dimensions of the vehicle in the manner I have indicated? For myself, I think not. It is argued that that view, which I have just expressed, means that the plaintiff's parents could, had they been so minded, immediately after the transfer have insisted on the four feet six inch wide gap being widened, by pulling down a post and a part of the wall, if the vendor refused to do so, so as to enable a motor car, if they so wished, to come right up to their property, to enter and leave, and it is said that this surely would not have been a situation intended by the parties at the time of the grant. But there are several aspects of the transfer which I think lead to the conclusion that the greater right was intended.

First and foremost, the right of way was expressed to be over the strip whose whole 20-feet width was coloured brown. It would have been perfectly simple to define it more narrowly if that had been intended, or, of course, to define it as a footway, or as a right of way to and from the then existing gateway. Moreover, the fact that the whole 20-feet width was regarded as available if necessary for the exercise of the right is stressed by the reference to the wall marked with a "T" as being "on the west side of the said right of way", showing that the whole of the 20-feet strip was being referred to as the right of way. Why (I ask myself) should the whole width be regarded as being available, if necessary, for the use as a right of way, if all that was intended was the restricted right suggested by the defendant?

I further observe that there was no obligation imposed to contribute to the upkeep of the frontage wall and, further, that an express grant of the footway alone would have been quite superfluous in the circumstances. I refer, of course, to the history of previous user; and, whether one speaks of it as a way of necessity or whether one speaks of it, as I think more correctly, as a grant which would have been implied having regard to the pre-existing user, in either event an express grant in 1930 was technically a superfluity.

Finally I would add that an obligation to pay a fair proportion of the cost of keeping the way in good repair and condition is at least unusual if all that was envisaged was the impact of human feet.

The county court judge decided against the defendant because he felt himself bound so to do by the decision of Upjohn J in *Bulstrode v Lambert* [1953] 1 WLR 1064, [1953] 2 All ER 728, p. 621, ante. In that case there was at the time of the grant a gateway and an overhead bar which would have limited the size of vehicles having access to the auction room premises and prevented the entry of furniture vans or pantechnicons. Nevertheless, in the judge's view that did not restrict the scope of the grant. I do not myself think that that case is conclusive of the present case, because the terms of the grant in that case were very particular, though I think that it is of use in approaching the alternative contention (which, if I may say so, was certainly not Mr Poole's favourite of the two contentions), namely, the small-vehicle right.

Perhaps it would be desirable to stress what I have said by quoting from the judgment in that case where the judge says: "I am unable to accept that submission. Here is a perfectly plain, unambiguous reservation for 'the vendor, his tenants and workmen' — I think that is important — 'to pass and repass with or without vehicles' — there is no limitation whatever upon the vehicles — 'over and along the land coloured brown' on the plan. Pausing there, in my judgment the true effect of those words, that there is a right of way over and along the land coloured brown, cannot be affected by the circumstance that at the date of the grant there was this gate and bar across. The words of the grant are plain and unambiguous, and in my judgment the plaintiff plainly has a right over the whole of the yard coloured brown, and not merely a right to enter through the gates some six feet in width. Not only that: he has a right to enter it with vehicles. That must mean vehicles of any size appropriate to go down the yard, and as the yard is at no stage, until the garage is reached, less than eleven feet wide, there seems to be no reason why a pantechnicon should not use that yard."

The part that I have quoted there shows that there were particular considerations in the language of the grant in the *Bulstrode* case which are absent from the present case; and for my part I would not have thought that the judge was necessarily bound, simply as a result of that decision, to conclude that in the present case there was more than a footpath. However, as I say, I differ in the end from the conclusion at which, but for the *Bulstrode* decision, the judge would have arrived. . . .

I would remark that it is sometimes thought that the grant of a right of way in respect of every part of a defined area involves the proposition that the grantee can object to anything on any part of the area which would obstruct passage over that part. This is a wrong understanding of the law. Assuming a right of way of a particular quality over an area of land, it will extend to every part of that area, as a matter, at least, of theory. But a right of way is not a right absolutely to restrict user of the area by the owner thereof. The grantee of the right could only object to such activities of the owner of the land, including retention of obstruction, as substantially interfered with the use of the land in such exercise of the defined right as for the time being is reasonably required[10]. (I am, of course, talking now about private rights of way.)

This proposition is exemplified by the decision of this court in *Dyer v Mousley*[11], where the dominant owner asserted the right to clear and level the whole of the strip dedicated to the right of way, at a time when there was no need to do so for the current requirements of the dominant tenant.

For those reasons, in my judgment, this appeal fails.

In *Jelbert v Davis* [1968] 1 WLR 589, [1968] 1 All ER 1182, the plaintiff, in a conveyance of agricultural land to him in 1961, was granted "a right of way at all times and for all purposes over the driveway retained by the vendor leading to the main road in common with all other persons having the like right". In 1966 he obtained planning permission to use part of the land as a tourist and caravan site for up to 200 caravans or tents. The defendants, two neighbouring landowners, objected to the proposed use of the driveway for

---

[10] See *Celsteel Ltd v Alton House Holdings Ltd* [1985] 1 WLR 204, [1985] 2 All ER 562, p. 644, post (interference with driving in forwards and reversing out of a garage held to be substantial).
[11] (1962) unreported Transcript No. 315.

caravan traffic and put up notices warning off caravans and campers. The plaintiff sued for nuisance and slander of title, and the defendants counter-claimed for an injunction to restrain the plaintiff from using the driveway for access to the caravan site. The Court of Appeal held that the plaintiff was entitled to use the driveway for caravans, but not so as to cause substantial interference with its use by the defendants: the user by 200 caravans was excessive. DANCKWERTS LJ said at 597, at 1186: "On the authorities, it is plain that the easement so granted is in such wide terms that the use by the plaintiff of it for caravans is permissible; but it is an easement which on its terms is a right which is to be used 'in common with all other persons having the like right'. That includes the defendants. A use of the right of way which is so excessive that it renders the rights of such other persons practically impossible, therefore, is not justified. The difficulty is to fix the limit in respect of such use. The test must be whether the interference is so substantial as to interfere with the rights of other persons in an unreasonable manner. It cannot be right that the others should be swamped by the traffic created by the plaintiff so as to amount to a legal nuisance. It is impossible to quantify this in figures, particularly as the problem relates to the future. These people are neighbours and share the right of way and there must be give and take and accommodation. Time will show what is practicable, and in the interests of both parties a practical solution must be found or a deadlock will result."

In *St. Edmundsbury and Ipswich Diocesan Board of Finance v Clark (No 2)* [1975] 1 WLR 468, [1975] 1 All ER 772, land, including the former rectory of St. Botolph's Church, Iken, in Suffolk, was sold and conveyed in 1945 by the church authorities to the defendant. It then wholly surrounded the church and churchyard. Access from the village to the church porch was by Church Lane (a narrow public highway) which then became a path 100 yards long leading to the church porch. The first third of the path ("the disputed strip") crossed the rectory grounds, and the remainder ("the church path") was within the churchyard and church property. The first 7 yards of the disputed strip could be used by vehicles for access from the lane to a driveway leading to the rectory. The remainder ("the chestnut path") was not wider than 4 feet 6 inches and was a derelict gravel and sandy path covered with leaves. At the end of the chestnut path on the defendant's land was a gate between two gateposts, standing no more than 4 feet apart. There was no evidence that the path was used by vehicles before 1946.

On 31 December 1945 the land was conveyed to the defendant "subject to a right of way over the land coloured red on the said plan to and from St. Botolph's Church". The question was whether the right of way reserved by the church authorities was a right exercisable on foot only, or with vehicles also.

The Court of Appeal, construing the language of the conveyance in the light of all the surrounding circumstances, decided that it was a right of footway only. In explaining the correct approach in these matters, Sir John PENNYCUICK said at 476, at 779: "What is the proper approach upon the construction of a conveyance containing the reservation of a right of way? We feel no doubt that the proper approach is that upon which the court construes all documents; that is to say, one must construe the document according to the natural meaning of the words contained in the document as a whole, read in the light of surrounding circumstances."

A similar approach is adopted in the identification of the dominant tenement. In *Johnstone v Holdway* [1963] 1 QB 601, [1963] 1 All ER 432, George Horace Johnstone agreed in 1936 to sell land to the Trewithin Estates Company, but no conveyance was executed. In 1948 Trewithin Estates Company sold part of the land to Henry Bosustow, whereupon Johnstone as trustee and the company as beneficial owner conveyed it to Bosustow. The conveyance excepted and reserved to the company and its successors in title "a right of way at all times and for all purposes (including quarrying)" over the land conveyed from a point on its north-western boundary to a point on its south-eastern boundary. The conveyance failed to specify any dominant tenement for the right of way, but it was meant to be the quarry, retained as part of their land by the company. The plaintiffs, as successors in title of the company, claimed a right of way against the successors in title of Bosustow.

In holding that the plaintiffs were entitled to a legal easement, UPJOHN LJ said at 609, at 434: "Mr Seward, for the defendant . . . submits that it is essential to the valid creation of every easement that the dominant tenement must be defined in the deed itself and that no extrinsic evidence is admissible to define it. . . . But the question we have to determine is whether that is essential to the validity of the easement or whether it is permissible to identify the dominant tenement by inferences from facts and circumstances which must have been known to the parties at the time of the conveyance. . . .

In our judgment, it is a question of the construction of the deed creating a right of way as to what is the dominant tenement for the benefit of which the right of way is granted and to which the right of way is appurtenant. In construing the deed the court is entitled to have evidence of all material facts at the time of the execution of the deed, so as to place the court in the situation of the parties. . . . It seems to us perfectly plain that in this case the dominant tenement was the land and quarry[12]."

B. Easements Created by Implied Grant

As explained above the rules for the creation of easements by implied grant vary with the question whether or not the easement is claimed by the grantor or grantee.

Easements implied in favour of the grantor are limited to cases of necessity or to cases where the intention of the parties is clear[13]. Easements of necessity are strictly limited to the circumstances of the necessity.

---

[12] See p. 580, ante. (1963) 79 LQR 182 (R.E.M.); *The Shannon Ltd v Venner Ltd* [1965] Ch 682, [1965] 1 All ER 590; *Bracewell v Appleby* [1975] Ch 408, [1975] 1 All ER 993 (right to pass over close A to reach close B held to be not usable as access to close C lying beyond close B), following *Harris v Flower* (1904) 74 LJ Ch 127; (1975) 39 Conv (NS) 277 (F. R. Crane). Cf. the judgment of UPJOHN J in *Newton Abbot Co-operative Society Ltd v Williamson and Treadgold Ltd* [1952] Ch 286, [1952] 1 All ER 279, p. 790, post.

[13] *Corporation of London v Riggs* (1880) 13 ChD 798, p. 598, ante; *Nickerson v Barraclough* [1981] Ch 426, [1981] 2 All ER 369; *Re Webb's Lease* [1951] Ch 808, [1951] 2 All ER 131, p. 600, ante.

In the case of easements implied in favour of the grantee — where they are "continuous and apparent", "necessary for the reasonable enjoyment of the property granted", or where the common intention of the parties was clear — there seems to be little authority on the question of the extent of the easement. If tested at the time of the conveyance, no difficulty arises, for the same rules as govern implication will govern extent. But difficulties may arise if the matter is tested at a time when circumstances have changed. If, for example, a narrow track is sufficient to establish that a right of way is "continuous and apparent" in a conveyance of 1880, will this cover travellers on foot, horseback, by car or by lorry? The cases on easements by express grant would suggest that the extent of the easement will develop as circumstances change and that limitations will only be imposed where such a restriction is clearly justified[14].

C. Easements Acquired by Prescription

Easements acquired by prescription are dependent upon user and their content is limited by the user proved. Small adjustments are allowed. Whether a variation is a new form of user or an extended example of that proved may be a difficult question.

BRITISH RAILWAYS BOARD *v* GLASS
[1965] Ch 538, [1964] 3 All ER 418 (CA, Lord Denning MR, Harman and Davies LJJ)

In 1847 the Wilts, Somerset and Weymouth Railway, predecessors in title to the plaintiffs, constructed a railway line near a farm owned by X, the defendant's predecessor in title, and through a field also owned by him but occupied by a tenant Y. They purchased part of this field, and the conveyance contained the following proviso (inter alia): "Save and except that the . . . company and their successors shall and will at all times hereafter allow unto . . . my heirs and assigns at all times . . . a right of crossing the . . . railway to the extent of twelve feet in width on the level thereof with all manner of cattle to and from one part of the land . . . to the other part . . . severed by the . . . railway." To provide for this right of way, the company constructed a level crossing. For many years prior to 1942 one of the fields near the crossing, formerly owned by X and occupied by Z (called the "blue land") was used for campers and caravanners and in 1942 there were six caravans established on the site. Since then the numbers had grown, and the traffic of vehicles and people over the crossing substantially increased. The plaintiffs brought this action to limit the user of the crossing.

It was conceded that (i) the right of way was not limited to linking the separated parts of the field previously occupied by Y, but linked the farm occupied by Z (which included the "blue land") with the severed part of that field and with a highway beyond, and (iii) the way was not limited to foot passengers or cattle, but extended to vehicles.

---

[14] See, however, *Milner's Safe Co Ltd v Great Northern and City Rly Co* [1907] 1 Ch 208.

Two main questions arose:
  (i) Whether the grant of the right of way covered the traffic of the caravanners;
 (ii) Whether, if not covered by the grant, there was a prescriptive right for all the caravanners, the defendant admitting a prescriptive right since 1942 for 6 caravanners.

Held (affirming Ungoed-Thomas J; Lord Denning MR dissenting).
  (i) The right of way was general and not limited to agricultural purposes in the contemplation of the parties to the conveyance;
 (ii) A prescriptive right had been acquired for the use of the crossing by the caravanners, the increase in number of caravanners since 1942 not being an excessive user.

The construction of the express grant of the right of way was influenced by the fact that the conveyance of 1847 was stated to be in compensation for, inter alia, the right to have certain "accommodation works" carried out by the railway company in pursuance of their duties under the Railways Clauses Consolidation Act 1845, section 68. It was argued that the right of way should not be more extensive than the company's duty in respect of the "accommodation works", for it was an exception to them, and should therefore be limited to agricultural or domestic purposes and those in the contemplation of the parties in 1847. The Court of Appeal (Lord Denning MR dissenting), as stated above, rejected this argument[15]. The present extracts from the judgments are limited to the issue of prescription.

Lord Denning MR (dissenting): *The Prescriptive Right.* The defendant says that alternatively he obtained a right by prescription. The judge found that for 20 years before the action, from 1942 to 1962, there had been six caravans on the site permanently, but that there had been 10 or 11 there at times from 1942 to 1945 and thereafter, and increased to 28 or 29 immediately before the issue of the writ. It is clear that by prescription there is a right of way for six caravans. But is there a right for 28 or 29 caravans?

It is quite clear that, when you acquire a right of way by prescription, you are not entitled to change the character of your land so as substantially to increase or alter the burden upon the servient tenement. If you have a right of way for your pasture land, you cannot turn it into a manufactory and claim a right of way for the purposes of the factory. If you have a right of way by prescription for one house, you cannot build two more houses on the land and claim a right of way for the purposes of those houses also. I think this rule is not confined to the character of the property. It extends also to the intensity of the user. If you use your land for years as a caravan site for six caravans and thereby gain a prescriptive right over a level crossing, you are not thereby entitled to put 30 caravans on the site and claim a right for those 30. As Baggallay JA said in *Wimbledon and Putney Commons Conservators v Dixon* (1875) 1 ChD 362 at 374, "You must neither increase the burden on the servient tenement nor substantially change the nature of the user." This seems to me good sense. It would be very wrong that, because the plaintiffs have been so tolerant as to allow the occupants of six caravans to use the crossing, in consequence they are thereby to be saddled with the use of 30

---

[15] For a similar construction of s. 68, see *TRH Sampson Associates Ltd v British Railways Board* [1983] 1 WLR 170, [1983] 1 All ER 257 (owner of dominant tenement held entitled to alter user of bridge provided no increased burden on servient tenement).

caravans. Trains would be obstructed and delayed. Dangers would abound. After all, prescription is a presumed grant. No such grant for 30 caravans could ever be presumed from user for six.

On this part of the case, counsel for the defendant made a technical point. He said that the defendant had a prescriptive right to a "caravan site" and so phrased it in his defence: and that in the reply the plaintiffs had admitted that the field had been used "as a caravan site" since 1938. He says that, by this admission, the plaintiffs are debarred from saying that the defendant had a prescriptive right only for six caravans, and that the defendant has a right for as many caravans as the site will hold. I regard this as special pleading of the worst description. The facts and issues before the court are plain enough: and no one has been in the least misled by this verbal nicety. I would decide this case on the facts found, and I hold that the defendant had no prescriptive right to use the crossing for more than six caravans.

We were told that the local authority have taken steps to deal with this caravan site. They have exercised their statutory powers to see that it is gradually removed. All the caravans should be gone by 1966. That is satisfactory, in a way. But I do not see why the local authority should be forced to do this: or to pay compensation to the defendant. I think the plaintiffs are entitled to come to the court and ask for protection on their own account. I think they are entitled to restrain the defendant from putting this greatly increased burden on the crossing.

I would allow the appeal and grant a declaration and injunction as asked in the notice of appeal.

HARMAN LJ: It appeared from the evidence that before the last war there were three caravans and a tent dwelling permanently situated upon the "blue land", and that this number increased after the war began, when the Admiralty moved some of its departments to Bath, to six permanent caravans and five more that came and went, and there was a further increase in the spring of 1942 after the first bombs fell on Bath, and that after the war there were further increases from time to time until shortly before the writ was issued the number of caravans had increased to 29 and it was of this burden that the plaintiffs not unnaturally complained. All the caravanners and those who visited them, and their suppliers, had no access to the blue land save over the level crossing.

This part of the case has become largely academic because the local planning authority has, by exercise of its statutory powers, ordered the gradual clearance of the site from caravans. At the date of the hearing in the court below the number had been reduced to 16 and will be reduced to none by the end of the year 1966 or thereabouts. Nevertheless the judge considered the state of things when the writ was issued, and rightly so, and he came to the conclusion that the plaintiffs could not complain of the state of things as it then existed. He reached this conclusion upon the admissions appearing upon the face of the pleadings. The plaintiffs admitted that the "blue land" was used "as a caravan site", that is to say, the whole of the "blue land" and not merely such portions of it as had in fact been the standings of caravans. I understand that in fact there were no such permanent standings, but that caravans coming and going occupied any part of the field they chose. The prescriptive claim was not made in the right of individual caravans, which would have been a claim by individual caravanners, but by the defendant as the owner of the whole of the "blue land" and on the footing that it constituted "the caravan site". It may be regrettable that this part of the case should turn on a point of pleading, as this to some extent was, but I do not think the judge could have come to his conclusion upon any other footing. The fact is that this expression "caravan site" has only recently come into prominence, and it was not perhaps fully appreciated until the recent decision of this court in *Biss v Smallburgh RDC* [1965] Ch 335, [1964] 2 All ER 543, that it ought not to be used in a loose way. In that case a large area, which varied at various stages of the action from 70-odd acres to three or four, was claimed as being a "caravan site", but the court came to the conclusion that there was no caravan site at all within the meaning of that phrase in the Caravan Sites and Control of Development Act 1960, that the mere casual placing of caravans here and there on a large area did not constitute that area a "caravan site". So here, if the plaintiffs had not admitted that the "blue land" constituted a "caravan site", the defendant might have been in great difficulty in defining the area of the site. He was relieved of that difficulty by the pleadings and his case was that, admitting the whole "blue land" to be "a caravan site", the mere increase from, say, 10 to 29 caravans did not constitute such an increase in the burden of the prescriptive right as was a legitimate subject of complaint by the plaintiffs. The leading case on this subject is *Williams v James* (1867) LR 2 CP 577. The headnote reads: "The defendant being entitled by immemorial user to a right of way over the plaintiff's land from field N, used the way for the purpose of carting from field N some hay stacked there, which had been grown partly there and partly on land adjoining. The jury found in effect that the defendant in so doing had used the way bona fide, and for the ordinary and reasonable use of field N as a field: *Held*, that the mere fact that some of the hay had not been grown on field N did not make the carrying of it over the plaintiff's land an excess in the user of the right of way." Bovill CJ says this at 580: "In all cases of this kind which depend upon user the right acquired must be measured by the extent of the enjoyment which is proved. When a right of way to a piece of land is proved, then that is, unless something appears to the contrary, a right of way for all purposes according to the ordinary and reasonable use to which that land might be applied at the time of the supposed grant. Such a right cannot be increased so as to affect the servient tenement by imposing upon it any additional burthen. It is also clear, according to the authorities, that where a person has a right of way over one piece of land to another piece of land, he can only use such right in order to reach the latter place. He cannot use it for the purpose of going elsewhere." Willes J says this at 582: "I agree with the argument of Mr Jelf that in cases like this, where a way has to be proved by user, you cannot extend the purposes for which the way may be used, or for which it might be reasonably inferred that parties would have intended it to be used. The land in this case was a field in the country, and apparently only used for rustic purposes. To be a legitimate user of the right of way, it must be used for the enjoyment of the nine acre field, and not colourably for other closes. I quite agree also with the argument that the right of way can only be used for the field in its ordinary use as a field. The right could not be used for a manufactory built upon the field. The use must be the reasonable use for the purposes of the land in the condition in which it was while the user took place."

Applying that to the present case, you must do what the judge did, namely, base your conclusion on a consideration of what must have been the supposed contents of the lost grant on which the prescription rests. If this be supposed to be a grant of the right to use the "blue land" as "a caravan site", then it is clear that a mere increase in the numbers of the caravans using the site is not an excessive user of the right. A right to use a way for this purpose or that has never been to my knowledge limited to a right to use the way so many times a day or for such and such a number of vehicles so long as the dominant tenement does not change its identity. If there be a radical change in the character of the dominant tenement, then the prescriptive right will not extend to it in that condition. The obvious example is a change of a small dwelling-house to a large hotel, but there has been no change of that character according to the facts found in this case. The caravan site never became a highly organised town of caravans with fixed standings and roads and all the paraphernalia attendant on such a place and in my opinion the judge was right in holding that there had been no such increase in the burden of the easement as to justify the plaintiffs in seeking as they did by injunction to restrict the user to three caravans or six or to prevent its use as what in the statement of claim is called "a caravan camp or site".

I, accordingly, hold that the judge was right in both branches of the case and that the appeal should be dismissed.

DAVIES LJ: If any prescriptive right has been acquired, it has been acquired not by any one or more caravans but by the "blue land" as dominant tenement. And it is not easy to contemplate an express grant of a right of way in respect of a specified or limited number of caravans. The "blue land" is still being used as a caravan site. Its use as such has been intensified. But there has been no alteration in the nature of its use . . . So here, once it is admitted, as it has been admitted, that the "blue land" as "a caravan site" acquired by prescription a right of way, it does not seem to me that the plaintiffs can prevent a mere increase in the number of caravans upon the site and the consequent increase in the use of the right of way. An increase in the number of caravans on the site is quite a different thing from the erection of a number of new houses, though no doubt from the point of view of the servient tenement the effect is somewhat similar.

(1965) 81 LQR, at p. 18 (R. E. Megarry).

"Two cases that were not cited provide a little assistance on the point. First, in *Lock v Abercester Ltd* [1939] Ch 861, [1939] 3 All ER 562, the dominant owners had to rely on user for the prescriptive period mainly for horse-drawn vehicles delivering goods to the dominant tenement, a house previously used as a rectory. Within the last few years these owners had begun to keep cows, pigs and chickens on the land held with the house, and motor-vehicles brought the food stuffs for these animals as well as other goods. Despite this additional burden on the way, Bennett J held that the way established by prescription was wide enough to cover this user. The main point of the case was, of course, the question whether user by horse-drawn vehicles authorised enjoyment by horseless vehicles; but the element of the recent increase in agricultural user was mentioned in the judgment.

Secondly, there is *Cowling v Higginson* (1838) 4 M & W 245. This raised the question of the validity of a claim to a right of way for all purposes where the user proved was for a variety of purposes though not for every conceivable purpose. If the right were to be measured by the *de facto* user, then such a claim would fail; for the right would be 'confined to the identical carriages that have previously been used upon the road, and would not warrant even the slightest alteration in the carriage or the loading, or the purpose for which it was used': *Cowling v Higginson* (1838) 4 M & W at 254, per Parke B. On this footing, there might be 'a right to carry corn and manure, though not coals' (at 253). And so it was laid down that 'If a way has been used for several purposes, there may be a ground for inferring that there is a right of way for all purposes' (at 256, per Lord Abinger CB). As Parke B said during the argument, if the dominant owners 'shew that they have used [the way] time out of mind, for all the purposes that they wanted, it would seem to me to give them a general right' (at 252). If user for a limited number of purposes can be generalised into a right to use for all purposes, it would be remarkable if on a claim to use the way for one purpose only there were to be imposed a strict quantitative restriction to the amount of use for that purpose during the prescriptive period. In the end, the point seems to come down to the difference between quantity and quality. It may well be that a change in quantity may be so vast as to amount to a change in quality; but short of such extremities, the distinction seems valid."

In *Graham v Philcox* [1984] QB 747, [1984] 2 All ER 643[16], M, who owned a large house and garden and a coach house at the rear in High Rocks Lane, Tunbridge Wells, let the first floor flat of the coach house in 1960 to B for five years together with a right of way for all purposes over the entrance drive to the house and thence along the side of the garden as far as the coach house. In 1963 B assigned his lease to D who later became a statutory tenant under the Rent Act. In 1975 M's executors conveyed the freehold of the entire coach house to W, subject to D's tenancy of the first floor flat. Nothing was said in the conveyance about the means of access.

In June 1977 M's executors conveyed to the defendants, Mr and Mrs Philcox, the freehold of that part of the retained land over which the right of way had been granted in the lease of 1960. Finally in November 1970, W's interest in the coach house was conveyed to the plaintiffs, Mr and Mrs Graham, subject to D's tenancy. D later surrendered his tenancy to the plaintiffs who then occupied the whole coach house as their residence. The defendants refused to allow the plaintiffs to continue to use the right of way.

The Court of Appeal, following *Wright v Macadam* [1949] 2 KB 744, [1949] 2 All ER 565, p. 587, ante, held that, when the coach house was conveyed in 1925, the right of way had passed under LPA 1925, s. 62 (2) to the plaintiffs' predecessor in title. PURCHAS LJ said at 760; at 652:

"It was certainly an easement, right or advantage '*reputed to appertain to the first floor flat*' and was enjoyed with that part *of the* 'land, houses or other buildings conveyed.' I can find nothing in the wording of section 62 (2) of the Act to indicate that the 'land conveyed' cannot include land subject to a lease or an adverse right of occupation by a tenant protected by statute. The easement, right or advantage is enjoyed with and appertains to the land, not to the statutory right of occupation."

---

[16] [1985] Conv 60 (P. Todd); [1985] CLJ 15 (S. Tromans).

The Court of Appeal further held that the alteration of the dominant tenement by the enlargement of the first floor flat of the coach house into one dwelling did not affect the existence of the right of way. MAY LJ said at 156, at 648:

"Mr Godfrey's principal submission was that as the dominant tenement for the benefit of which the way is now claimed, namely the coach house, is not the same as and is indeed greater than the dominant tenement for the benefit of which the way was originally granted, namely only the upper flat in the coach house, therefore the plaintiffs cannot use that way now when the coach house is now one dwelling and the original two flats which it comprised have been combined into one . . . Mr Godfrey submitted further that if one substantially alters a dominant tenement, an easement theretofore enjoyed with it can no longer be used, because by the alterations one has increased the burden of the use on the servient tenement. The easement is consequently lost, or at least suspended temporarily: thus in the present case the plaintiffs must accept that they cannot enforce their use of the disputed right of way for so long as the coach house remains one dwelling . . .

In none of the judgments in any of the cases to which Mr Godfrey referred us is there suggestion that a mere alteration of a dominant tenement to which a right of way may be appurtenant is sufficient to extinguish it, or indeed to affect the entitlement to its use unless as the result of that alteration the extent of the user is thereby increased.

In my opinion, therefore, the mere alteration of the coach house into one dwelling cannot have had any effect upon the existence of the right of way. It should be borne in mind that there was no evidence whatever before the judge that the actual or anticipated user by the plaintiffs of the way was in any way excessive, either in quantity or quality.

Further, I do not think that on this issue any real distinction can be drawn between the instant case on the one hand and *Wright v Macadam* [1949] 2 KB 744, [1949] 2 All ER 565 on the other. In the latter case also the right for which the plaintiffs contended had, at the date of the conveyance relied on for the purposes of section 62 (2), been enjoyed by the occupier of only part of the whole premises in respect of which the continued enjoyment of the right was claimed in the action."

In *Woodhouse & Co Ltd v Kirkland (Derby) Ltd* [1970] 1 WLR 1185, [1970] 2 All ER 587, PLOWMAN J held that a considerable increase in the number of customers using a right of way was "a mere increase in user and not a user of a different kind or for a different purpose"[17].

In *Giles v County Building Contractors (Hertford) Ltd* (1971) 22 P & CR 978, BRIGHTMAN J referred to HARMAN LJ in *British Railways Board v Glass* [1965] Ch 538 at 562, [1964] 3 All ER 418 at 428, p. 631, ante and said at 987: "The important expressions, to my mind, are 'change of identity' and 'radical change in character'. In my view, the use of the convent site for the erection

---

[17] See also *Cargill v Gotts* [1981] 1 WLR 441, [1981] 1 All ER 682 (drawing of water from neighbour's millpond for agricultural purposes held to be mere increase in user, but not exercisable without licence under Water Resources Act 1963, s. 24 (1)). Cf. *Ward (Helston) Ltd v Kerrier District Council* (1981) 42 P & CR 412 (right of way for use in connection with slaughter house not extended to cartage of materials for house building).

of seven modern dwelling units in place of the two existing houses, cannot properly be described as 'changing the identity' or 'radically changing the character' of the convent site. I think it is evolution rather than mutation."

QUESTION

A landlord granted to his tenant a right of way "at all times and for all purposes" over a roadway leading to the tenant's factory. The landlord then started to build over the roadway and planned to construct a long bridge or tunnel through which the tenant could have access to the factory. Although this would not affect the roadway itself, the freedom of manoeuvre, during loading and unloading from the tenant's vehicles, would be restricted, both vertically and laterally. Is the tenant entitled to an injunction to restrain the landlord from building in such a way as to restrict his freedom to load and unload as he had been accustomed to do? See *VT Engineering Ltd v Richard Barland & Co Ltd* (1968) 19 P & CR 890; *Hayns v Secretary of State for the Environment* (1977) 36 P & CR 317.

V.　Easement of Light[18]

PRESCRIPTION ACT 1832

3.　Claim to the use of light enjoyed for 20 years. — When the access and use of light to and for any dwelling house, workshop, or other building[19] shall have been actually enjoyed therewith for the full period of twenty years without interruption, the right thereto shall be deemed absolute and indefeasible, any local usage or custom to the contrary notwithstanding, unless it shall appear that the same was enjoyed by some consent or agreement expressly made or given for that purpose by deed or writing.

COLLS *v* HOME AND COLONIAL STORES LTD
[1904] AC 179 (HL, Earl of HALSBURY LC, Lords MACNAGHTEN, DAVEY, ROBERTSON and LINDLEY)

The Home and Colonial Stores were the lessees of a building in Shoreditch where they carried on their business. They brought an action for an injunction against Colls to restrain him from building on the opposite side of the road. JOYCE J found as a fact that, even after the erection of the building, the Home and Colonial Stores premises would be "well and sufficiently lighted for all ordinary purposes of occupancy as a place of business". JOYCE J refused an injunction and was reversed by the Court of Appeal.

Held (reversing the Court of Appeal). Injunction refused.

LORD LINDLEY: The language of section 3 of the Prescription Act shews that in order to acquire a right to a light there must be — (1) Access and use of light, not access alone. Access here is understood to refer to free passage of light over the servient tenement (see per Fry LJ, in *Scott v Pape* (1886) 31 ChD at 575, and per Kay J, in *Cooper v Straker* (1888) 40 ChD 21). (2) Such access

---

[18] C & B, pp. 523–525; M & W, pp. 889–892, 903–906; MM, pp. 425–427, 432–434; Gale, pp. 147–152, 238–255; Jackson, pp. 133–137, 156–166.
[19] *Allen v Greenwood* [1980] Ch 119, [1979] 1 All ER 819, p. 637, post (greenhouse).

and use must be to and for some dwelling-house, workshop, or other building (as to which see *Harris v De Pinna* (1886) 33 ChD 238). (3) Such access and use must be actually enjoyed therewith. (4) Such enjoyment must be without interruption for twenty years. (5) If all these are proved, the right to the access and use of light so enjoyed becomes absolute and indefeasible, unless it can be explained by some deed or writing.

Pausing here for a moment, it will be observed that the statute does not in terms confer a right to light, but rather assumes its acquisition by use and enjoyment, and declares it to be "absolute and indefeasible".

Again, your Lordships will observe that nothing is said about enjoyment as of right; and notwithstanding section 5 of the Act, which refers to enjoyment as of right, it was early decided that as regards light claimed under section 3 enjoyment as of right need not be alleged or proved, and that the right, whatever it may be, is acquired by twenty years' use and enjoyment without interruption and without written consent: see *Truscott v Merchant Taylors' Co* (1856) 11 Exch 855 and *Frewen v Phillips* (1861) 11 CBNS 449; *Simper v Foley* (1862) 2 John & H 555 and *Harbidge v Warwick* (1849) 3 Exch 557. This was not so under the old law.

As regards use and enjoyment, there are some instructive decisions on unfinished and uninhabited houses, and on windows kept closed by shutters. These decisions shew that a right to light may be acquired in respect of a house which has stood for twenty years without being occupied or even finished so as to be fit for occupation; and that the fact that shutters have been closed for some months at a time does not prevent the acquisition of a right to light through the windows: see *Courtauld v Legh* (1869) LR 4 Exch 126; *Cooper v Straker* (1888) 40 ChD 21; *Collis v Laughter* [1894] 3 Ch 659; *Smith v Baxter* [1900] 2 Ch 138.

These decisions did not, however, turn upon or settle with any precision the amount of light to which a right is acquired by twenty years' user. Nor is the statute clear upon this point. . . .

The doctrine laid down in *Back v Stacey* (1826) 2 C & P 465, as I understand it, is the same as that laid down, although in somewhat different language, by the Court of Appeal in *Kelk v Pearson* (1871) 6 Ch App 809 and *City of London Brewery Co v Tennant* (1873) 9 Ch App 212, and must, I think, be taken as finally established and as good sound law, which your Lordships should adopt, notwithstanding the observations in the Irish case of *Mackey v Scottish Widows' Fund Assurance Society* (1877) IR 11 Eq 541. That doctrine, as stated in *City of London Brewery Co v Tennant*, is that generally speaking an owner of ancient lights is entitled to sufficient light according to the ordinary notions of mankind for the comfortable use and enjoyment of his house as a dwelling-house, if it is a dwelling-house, or for the beneficial use and occupation of the house if it is a warehouse, a shop, or other place of business (1873) 9 Ch App at 217. The expressions "the ordinary notions of mankind", "comfortable use and enjoyment", and "beneficial use and occupation" introduce elements of uncertainty; but similar uncertainty has always existed and exists still in all cases of nuisance, and in this country an obstruction of light has commonly been regarded as a nuisance, although the right to light has been regarded as a peculiar kind of easement. . . .

The expression "right to light" is sanctioned by the Prescription Act, and is convenient; but its use is apt to lead to error and to forgetfulness of the burden thrown on the servient tenement. This burden, however, ought never to be lost sight of in considering the extent of the right claimed in respect of the dominant tenement.

But the adoption of the more flexible standard of comfort and convenience has introduced difficulties of a serious nature, especially when dealing with places of business, and it is not surprising that different views on this subject should have been taken, and that the decisions upon it should be inconsistent with each other. . . .

There is no rule of law that if a person has 45 degrees of unobstructed light through a particular window left to him he cannot maintain an action for a nuisance caused by diminishing the light which formerly came through that window: *Theed v Debenham* (1876) 2 ChD 165[20]. But experience shews that it is, generally speaking, a fair working rule to consider that no substantial injury is done to him where an angle of 45 degrees is left to him, especially if there is good light from other directions as well. The late Lord Justice Cotton pointed this out in *Ecclesiastical Commissioners for England v Kino* (1880) 14 ChD 213 at 228; see also *Parker v First Avenue Hotel Co* (1883) 24 ChD 282.

As regards light from other quarters, such light cannot be disregarded; for, as pointed out by James V-C, in the *Dyers' Co v King* (1870) LR 9 Eq 438, the light from other quarters, and the light the obstruction of which is complained of, may be so much in excess of what is protected by law as to render the interference complained of non-actionable. I apprehend, however, that light to which a right has not been acquired by grant or prescription, and of which the plaintiff may be deprived at any time, ought not to be taken into account. (See the case just cited.)

The purpose for which a person may desire to use a particular room or building in future does not either enlarge or diminish the easement which he has acquired. If he chooses in future to use a well-lighted room or building for a lumber-room for which little light is required, he does not lose his right to use the same room or building for some other purpose for which more light is required. *Aynsley v Glover* (1875) 10 Ch App 283 is in accordance with this view. But if a room or building has been so built as to be badly lighted, the owner or occupier cannot by enlarging the windows or altering the purpose for which he uses it increase the burden on the servient tenement. *Martin v Goble* (1808) 1 Camp 320, where a malthouse was turned into a workhouse, may, I think, be upheld on this principle; and the observations of Wood V-C on *Martin v Goble* in *Dent v Auction Mart Co* (1866) LR 2 Eq 238 support this view. . . .

Joyce J was asked for an injunction and he refused it, and, in my opinion, quite rightly. He came to the conclusion that although there would be a sensible diminution of light and some inconvenience to the plaintiffs, yet they had not established by twenty years' user a right to all the light which they had had, and that the obstruction complained of would not amount to an actionable nuisance, and so infringe the plaintiffs' right. The Court of Appeal, taking a different view of the amount of light to which the plaintiffs were entitled, reversed this decision, and ordered a partial demolition of the buildings erected by the defendants. For the reasons already given, I have come to the conclusion that this was wrong[1].

---

[20] Nor is there a rule of law that if half a room at table height is receiving one or more lumens the room as a whole is adequately lit: *Ough v King* [1967] 1 WLR 1547, [1967] 3 All ER 859.
[1] See *Pugh v Howells* (1984) 48 P & CR 298, where a mandatory injunction was granted.

In *Allen v Greenwood* [1980] Ch 119, [1979] 1 All ER 819[2], the plaintiffs were the owners of 13 Woodtop Avenue, Rochdale, in which there was a greenhouse. After the greenhouse had been in use as an ordinary domestic greenhouse for more than 20 years, the defendants erected a fence on their adjoining property. This left sufficient light in the greenhouse for working in it, but insufficient for growing plants ("tomatoes, geraniums, stocks, antirrhinums, marigolds, zinnias, violets, pansies, the red ones that are rather tender"). The plaintiffs brought an action for injunctions to restrain the defendants from causing a nuisance by diminution of the access of the light to the greenhouse.

In granting the injunctions, the Court of Appeal (BUCKLEY, ORR and GOFF LJJ) held that the light required for the normal use of a greenhouse is ordinary, and also that a right to a specially high degree of light may be acquired by prescription. The Court rejected "an overriding argument" that "in any event one can only prescribe a right to light, whether ordinary or special in degree, for purposes of illumination, not a right to the direct rays of the sun, or to heat, or to other beneficial properties from the sun's rays". GOFF LJ said at 132, at 826:

"In my judgment, therefore, the crux of this case at the end of the day is the overriding argument, which I must now consider.

The defendants argue on this as follows. (1) In *Colls' Case* [1904] AC 179 the House of Lords was seeking to limit, or restrict, the extent of the right to light, so as to prevent undue restrictions on the development or improvement of surrounding land or buildings, and the court should be very chary of any extension of the right. (2) Although the standards prescribed by the speeches in *Colls'* case are expressed in terms susceptible of a wider interpretation, in their context they must be taken as referring to illumination only. (3) In all cases, at least since *Colls*, the right to light has been tested or measured in terms of illumination only. They refer, for example, to Mr Waldram's calculations and the theory of the 'grumble point:' see *Charles Semon & Co Ltd v Bradford Corpn* [1922] 2 Ch 737, 746–747, and to *Hortons' Estate Ltd v James Beattie Ltd* [1927] 1 Ch 75, where the question was whether the extent of the right to light should vary according to locality, and Russell J said, at 78: 'The human eye requires as much light for comfortable reading and sewing in Darlington Street, Wolverhampton, as in Mayfair.' Mr Maddocks on the defendants' behalf, in his supporting argument, referred also to *Warren v Brown* [1900] 2 QB 722, 725, where the test was stated to be 'all ordinary purposes of inhabitancy or business,' and to the test applied by the Court of Appeal in *Ough v King* [1967] 1 WLR 1547, [1967] 3 All ER 859, ordinary notions of contemporary mankind. These, however, I think, are at best neutral and possibly tell the other way, since a greenhouse is perfectly normal and ordinary in private gardens. . . . (6) In reality or in substance the injury here is not deprivation of light, but of heat or other energising properties of the sun and it is the plant life and not the human beings who are deprived.

I do not think this last point is in any case wholly accurate, as plants need light as well as heat, but it seems to me, with all respect to Blackett-Ord V-C and to counsel, to lead to an absurd conclusion. It cannot, I think, be right to say that there is no nuisance because one can see to go in and out of a

---

[2] [1979] Conv 298 (F. R. Crane); [1984] Conv 408 (A. H. Hudson); Conv Prec 19–32.

greenhouse and to pot plants which will not flourish, and to pick fruit which cannot properly be developed and ripened, still less because one can see to read a book.

The plaintiffs answer all this simply by submitting that they are entitled, by virtue of their prescriptive right to light, to all the benefits of the light, including the rays of the sun. Warmth, they say, is an inseparable product of daylight, and they stress the absurd conclusion which I have already mentioned, to which the contrary argument inevitably leads. This reply commends itself to me, and I adopt it.

So the overriding argument, in my judgment, does not prevail, and for the reasons I have already given the plaintiffs are right, both on their primary and their alternative case, and I would allow this appeal.

I desire, however, to add one important safeguarding proviso to this judgment. On other facts, particularly where one has solar heating (although that may not arise for some years) it may be possible and right to separate the heat, or some other property of the sun, from its light, and in such a case a different result might be reached. I leave that entirely open for decision when it arises. My judgment in this case is based upon the fact that this was a perfectly ordinary greenhouse, being used in a perfectly normal and ordinary manner, which user has, by the defendants' acts, been rendered substantially less beneficial than it was throughout the period of upwards of 20 years before action brought, and if necessary upon the fact that all this was known to the defendants and their predecessors for the whole of the relevant time."

In *Morgan v Fear* [1907] AC 425, it was held that a tenant could, by 20 years' enjoyment of access to light from neighbouring land in the occupation of another tenant of the same landlord, prescribe for an easement of light under section 3. The House of Lords relied upon established authority. Lord Loreburn LC said at 428:

"The question . . . is whether a right can be acquired by a termor over land held by another termor under the same reversion, by virtue of section 3 of the Prescription Act. This has been decided in the affirmative as long ago as 1861, in *Frewen v Phillips* (1861) 11 CB NS 449, and the same view was expressly indicated in *Mitchell v Cantrill* (1887) 37 ChD 56. I think it is accurate to say that that rule of law has been acted upon for forty-six years. I cannot advise your Lordships to disturb so well settled a rule."

Prescription is in favour of the fee simple owner, and even in the case of an easement of light, there cannot be prescription in favour of a leaseholder[3].

QUESTION

Why can prescription not operate in favour of a leasehold estate? Compare:

Morgan v Fear [1907] AC 425;

Kilgour v Gaddes [1904] 1 KB 457, p. 609, ante;

Wheaton v Maple & Co [1893] 3 Ch 48, p. 610, ante.

---

[3] *Wheaton v Maple & Co* [1893] 3 Ch 48.

RIGHTS OF LIGHT ACT 1959[4]

2. Registration of notice in lieu of obstruction of access of light. —
(1) For the purpose of preventing the access and use of light from being taken to be enjoyed without interruption, any person who is an owner of land (in this and the next following section referred to as "the servient land") over which light passes to a dwelling-house, workshop or other building (in this and the next following section referred to as "the dominant building") may apply to the local authority in whose area the dominant building is situated for the registration of a notice under this section[5].

3. Effect of registered notice and proceedings relating thereto. —
(1) Where, in pursuance of an application made in accordance with the last preceding section, a notice is registered thereunder, then, for the purpose of determining whether any person is entitled (by virtue of the Prescription Act, 1832, or otherwise) to a right to the access of light to the dominant building across the servient land, the access of light to that building across that land shall be treated as obstructed to the same extent, and with the like consequences, as if an opaque structure, of the dimensions specified in the application, —

    (*a*) had, on the date of registration of the notice, been erected in the position on the servient land specified in the application, and had been so erected by the person who made the application, and

    (*b*) had remained in that position during the period for which the notice has effect and had been removed at the end of that period.

(2) For the purposes of this section a notice registered under the last preceding section shall be taken to have effect until either —

    (*a*) the registration is cancelled, or

    (*b*) the period of one year beginning with the date of registration of the notice expires, or

    (*c*) [the expiry of the period specified under a special procedure where the case is one of exceptional urgency,]

and shall cease to have effect on the occurrence of any one of those events.

(3) Subject to the following provisions of this section, any person who, if such a structure as is mentioned in subsection (1) of this section had been erected as therein mentioned, would have had a right of action in any court in respect of that structure, on the grounds that he was entitled to a right to the access of light to the dominant building across the servient land, and that the said right was infringed by that structure, shall have the like right of action in that court in respect of the registration of a notice under the last preceding section:

Provided that an action shall not be begun by virtue of this subsection after the notice in question has ceased to have effect.

(4) Where, at any time during the period for which a notice registered under the last preceding section has effect, the circumstances are such that, if

---

[4] This section is based on recommendations in the Report of the Committee on Rights of Light (1958 Cmnd 473); [1959] CLJ 182 (H. W. R. Wade). See *Hawker v Tomalin* (1969) 20 P & CR 550 at 551, per HARMAN LJ.

[5] Lands Tribunal Rules 1975 (S.I. 1975 No. 299) Part VI; Local Land Charges Rules 1977 (S.I. 1977 No. 985), r. 10. The application must be accompanied by a certificate from the Lands Tribunal. 938 definitive and 211 temporary certificates were issued between 1959 and 1980; see (1978) 122 SJ 515, 534; (1981) 259 EG 123 (W. A. Greene).

the access of light to the dominant building had been enjoyed continuously from a date one year earlier than the date on which the enjoyment thereof in fact began, a person would have had a right of action in any court by virtue of the last preceding subsection in respect of the registration of the notice, that person shall have the like right of action in that court by virtue of this subsection in respect of the registration of the notice.

(6) For the purposes of section four of the Prescription Act, 1832 (under which a period of enjoyment of any of the rights to which that Act applies is not to be treated as interrupted except by a matter submitted to or acquiesced in for one year after notice thereof) —

> (*a*) as from the date of registration of a notice under the last preceding section, all persons interested in the dominant building or any part thereof shall be deemed to have notice of the registration thereof and of the person on whose application it was registered;
>
> (*b*) until such time as an action is brought by virtue of subsection (3) or subsection (4) of this section in respect of the registration of a notice under the last preceding section, all persons interested in the dominant building or any part thereof shall be deemed to acquiesce in the obstruction which, in accordance with subsection (1) of this section, is to be treated as resulting from the registration of the notice;
>
> (*c*) as from the date on which such an action is brought, no person shall be treated as submitting to or acquiescing in that obstruction:

Provided that if, in any such action, the court decides against the claim of the plaintiff, the court may direct that the preceding provisions of this subsection shall apply in relation to the notice as if that action had not been brought.

VI.   Extinguishment[6]

Easements and profits may be extinguished by statute (e.g. under an Inclosure Act or the Town and Country Planning Act 1971[7], or as a result of failure to register under the Commons Registration Act 1965[8]), by release, express or implied, and by unity of both ownership and possession.

A.   Implied Release

In *Tehidy Minerals Ltd v Norman* [1971] 2 QB 528, [1971] 2 All ER 475, BUCKLEY LJ said at 553, at 492: "Abandonment of an easement or of a profit à prendre can only, we think, be treated as having taken place where the person entitled to it has demonstrated a fixed intention never at any time thereafter to assert the right himself or to attempt to transmit it to anyone else."

---

[6] C & B, pp. 527–530, 539–542; M & W, pp. 894–900; MM, pp. 428–430; Gale, pp. 309–347; Jackson, pp. 195–200.
[7] Ss. 118, 127. See also Housing Act 1985, s. 295 (1)–(3); New Towns Act 1981, s. 19; Local Government, Planning and Land Act 1980, s. 144, Sch. 6.
[8] S. 1 (2), p. 58, ante.

MOORE *v* RAWSON[9]
(1824) 3 B & C 332 (Ct of KB, ABBOTT CJ, BAYLEY, HOLROYD and LITTLEDALE JJ)

The plaintiff's predecessor in title enjoyed easements of light and air in respect of certain windows in a wall of his house. He pulled down this wall and built another wall without any windows. Fourteen years later the defendant erected a building opposite to the plaintiff's blank wall. After another three years the plaintiff opened a window in the blank wall in the place of one of the old windows, and then brought an action for obstruction.

Held. The plaintiff failed, because he had abandoned his rights.

HOLROYD J: I am of the same opinion. It appears that the former owner of the plaintiff's premises at one time was entitled to the house with the windows, so that the light coming to those windows over the adjoining land could not be obstructed by the owner of that land. I think, however, that the right acquired by the enjoyment of the light, continued no longer than the existence of the thing itself in respect of which the party had the right of enjoyment; I mean the house with the windows; when the house and the windows were destroyed by his own act, the right which he had in respect of them was also extinguished. If, indeed, at the time when he pulled the house down, he had intimated his intention of rebuilding it, the right would not then have been destroyed with the house. If he had done some act to shew that he intended to build another in its place, then the new house, when built, would in effect have been a continuation of the old house, and the rights attached to the old house would have continued. If a man has a right of common attached to his mill, or right of turbary attached to his house, if he pulls down the mill or the house, the right of common or of turbary will prima facie cease. If he shew an intention to build another mill or another house, his right continues. But if he pulls down the house or the mill without shewing any intention to make a similar use of the land, and after a long period of time has elapsed, builds a house or mill corresponding to that which he pulls down, that is not the renovation of the old house or mill, but the creation of a new thing, and the rights which he had in respect of the old house or mill, do not in my opinion attach to the new one. In this case, I think, the building of a blank wall is a stronger circumstance to shew that he had no intention to continue the enjoyment of his light than if he had merely pulled down the house. In that case he might have intended to substitute something in its place. Here, he does in fact substitute quite a different thing, a wall without windows. There is not only nothing to shew that he meant to renovate the house so as to make it a continuance of the old house, but he actually builds a new house different from the old one, thereby shewing that he did not mean to renovate the old house. It seems to me, therefore, that the right is not renewed as it would have been, if, when he pulled down the old house, he had shewn an intention to rebuild it within a reasonable time, although he did not do so eo instanti.

---

[9] *Crossley & Sons Ltd v Lightowler* (1867) 2 Ch App 478; *Cook v Bath Corporation* (1868) LR 6 Eq 177; *Ecclesiastical Commissioners for England v Kino* (1880) 14 ChD 213; *Swan v Sinclair* [1924] 1 Ch 254; affd [1925] AC 227; *Re Yateley Common, Hampshire* [1977] 1 WLR 840, [1977] 1 All ER 505.

B. Unity of Ownership and Possession

Unity of both ownership and possession may cause extinguishment[10]. "An unity of possession merely suspends; there must be an unity of ownership to destroy a prescriptive right"[11]. Similarly unity of ownership without unity of possession does not suffice; the easement continues until there is also unity of possession[12]. If an easement is extinguished, it may nevertheless be re-created under the doctrine of *Wheeldon v Burrows*[13] if the land is later severed into its original parts.

In *Richardson v Graham* [1908] 1 KB 39, BUCKLEY LJ said at 44[14]: "On 29 March 1906, the plaintiffs were entitled to a leasehold interest for a term of years in the dominant tenement. The reversion in the dominant tenement was in one Eadie. The dominant tenement enjoyed over the servient tenement which was vested in the defendant a prescriptive right to ancient light acquired by user for more than twenty years. On 29 March 1906, Eadie conveyed to the defendant the reversion in the dominant tenement. It is said that the effect of that conveyance was to destroy the easement of ancient light; that is to say, that by acts done by the plaintiffs' lessor and by the owner of the servient tenement the rights enjoyed by the plaintiffs were destroyed.

In my opinion that is not the law. . . . So that it is perfectly plain on the authorities that if in this case the two tenements had belonged throughout, not to different owners, but to one owner, but the circumstances were such that a lessee of the dominant tenement had acquired a prescriptive right against the servient tenement, the right would have been good as against all the world. It is said, however, that this case is different because there was not a common owner of the dominant and servient tenement during the whole period, but common ownership of the two tenements arose after the right to light had been acquired. This seems to me an extravagant proposition."

VII.   Registered Land[15]

Legal easements are among the list of overriding interests but they may nevertheless appear in the property register of the dominant land. A note should also appear on the register of the servient land.

Equitable easements, however, are not overriding interests under the ill-drafted section 70 (1) (a) of the Land Registration Act 1925[16], but may

------

[10] *Buckby v Coles* (1814) 5 Taunt 311 (easement); *Tyrringham's Case* (1584) 4 Co Rep 36b at 38a (profit à prendre).
[11] *Canham v Fisk* (1831) 2 Cr & J 126, per BAYLEY B.
[12] *Richardson v Graham* [1908] 1 KB 39.
[13] But not under LPA 1925, s. 62, since there would be no diversity of occupation; p. 582, ante.
[14] This was a case on the easement of light, but, in principle, the rule should apply generally. Cf. *Buckby v Coles*, supra, at 315, 316; M & W, p. 899, n. 36.
[15] C & B, pp. 547–550; M & W, pp. 205, 223; MM, pp. 437–438; Registered Land Practice Notes (1982–1983) pp. 29–31.
[16] But equitable profits à prendre are. See Law Commission Working Paper: Land Registration 1971 (No. 37), para. 48; Ruoff and Roper, p. 97; W & C, vi, p. 64; Barnsley, *Conveyancing Law and Practice* (2nd edn, 1982), pp. 46–47; Farrand (2nd edn.), pp. 188–190; Hayton, *Registered Land* (3rd edn.), pp. 83–84; Jackson, pp. 44–45.

become so by virtue of rule 258 of the Land Registration Rules 1925, in spite of the conflict between the rule and the section[17].

LAND REGISTRATION RULES 1925

257. Positive registration. — The benefit of an easement, right, or privilege shall not be entered on the register except as appurtenant to a registered estate, and then only if capable of subsisting as a legal estate.

252. Application for entry of appurtenant right on register. — (1) Where the proprietor wishes (whether on first registration or at any other time) to have a specific entry on the register of any appurtenant right, capable of subsisting as a legal estate, to which he may be entitled, he may apply to the Registrar in writing, signed by himself or his solicitor, for such an entry to be made.

254. Entry of appurtenant right and its effect. — (1) If the Registrar is satisfied that the right is capable of subsisting as a legal estate and appurtenant to the land, he may enter it as part of the description of the land in the Property Register, and the effect of such entry shall be to confer an absolute, good leasehold, qualified or possessory title to the right, according to the nature of the title to the land.

(2) If the Registrar is not satisfied that the right is appurtenant, he shall enter it with such qualification as he may deem advisable, or he may merely enter notice of the fact that the proprietor claims it.

251. Registration vests appurtenances. — The registration of a person as proprietor of land shall vest in him, together with the land, all rights, privileges, and appurtenances appertaining or reputed to appertain to the land or any part thereof, or, at the time of registration, demised, occupied, or enjoyed therewith, or reputed or known as part or parcel of, or appurtenant to the land or any part thereof, including the appropriate rights and interests which, had there been a conveyance of the land or manor, would under section 62 of the Law of Property Act, 1925, have passed therewith.

LAND REGISTRATION ACT 1925

70. Liability of registered land to overriding interests. — 1 (*a*), p. 119, ante.

(2) Where at the time of first registration any easement, right, privilege, or benefit created by an instrument and appearing on the title adversely affects the land, the registrar shall enter a note thereof on the register.

LAND REGISTRATION RULES 1925

41. Adverse easements. — (1) Notice of an easement, right, or privilege created by an instrument and operating at law which appears to the Registrar to affect adversely the land shall, if the Registrar thinks fit, be entered in the register.

---

[17] *Celsteel Ltd v Alton House Holdings Ltd* [1985] 1 WLR 204, [1985] 2 All ER 562, p. 644, post; M & W, p. 205, n. 3.

258.   Adverse easements treated as overriding interests. — p. 120, ante.

LAND REGISTRATION ACT 1925

72.   Appurtenances. — If before the registration of any freehold or leasehold interest in land with an absolute or good leasehold title any easement, right, or privilege has been acquired for the benefit thereof, then, on such registration, the easement, right, or privilege shall, subject to any entry to the contrary on the register, become appurtenant to the registered land in like manner as if it had been granted to the proprietor who is registered as aforesaid.

LAND REGISTRATION RULES 1925

250.   Acquisition of adverse easements by prescription. — (1) ... easements, rights and privileges adversely affecting registered land may be acquired in equity by prescription in the same manner and to the same extent as if the land were not registered.

(2) If any easement, right, or privilege so acquired is of such estate and nature as is capable of taking effect at law it shall take effect at law also, and in that case —

> (*a*) if it is an overriding interest, notice of it may be entered on the register if the Registrar thinks fit under subsection (3) of section 70 of the Act[18].

In *Celsteel Ltd v Alton House Holdings Ltd* [1985] 1 WLR 204, [1985] 2 All ER 562[18a], Alton House Holdings Ltd (the first defendant) was the registered freeholder of Cavendish House, a large block of flats just North of Lord's cricket ground. The third plaintiff was the tenant of a flat and garage under a contract for a lease for 120 years from the predecessor in title of Alton House Holdings Ltd. The contract gave the third plaintiff rights of way from the garage (No. 52) to the street. The lease was never granted, nor was the right of way protected by any entry against the registered title of the freeholder. In 1982 Alton House Holdings Ltd granted to Mobil Oil Co Ltd (the second defendant) a lease of the ground floor of Cavendish House, including a part of the driveway over which the right of way had been given.

One question was whether the third plaintiff had an overriding interest in respect of his equitable easement of way. In holding that he had, Scott J said at 219, at 574:

"It is plain, also, that the third plaintiff, although in actual occupation of garage 52, was not in actual occupation of any part of the rear driveway. He cannot therefore protect his easement over the rear driveway under paragraph (*g*) of section 70 (1) and the only paragraph of section 70 (1) under which, arguably, he might protect that easement as an overriding interest is paragraph (*a*).

---

[18] P. 120, ante.
[18a] [1986] Conv 31 (M. P. Thompson).

Paragraph (*a*) of section 70 (1) protects as overriding interests the following rights:

[His Lordship read para. (*a*) and continued:]

The rights over the rear driveway which the third plaintiff acquired by virtue of the facts pleaded in the paragraphs of the statement of claim which I have mentioned were certainly rights of way. If they were legal rights of way then the second defendants are bound by them. If they were only equitable rights of way then I must decide whether or not they are excepted from paragraph (*a*) by the phrase 'not being equitable easements required to be protected by notice on the register.'

The third plaintiff's entitlement to the easements comprised in the intended lease of garage 52 for the intended 120 year term is an *equitable* entitlement. It could only become a *legal* entitlement by the grant to him of the lease contracted to be granted and the registration of that lease at Her Majesty's Land Registry. But the meaning and scope of the provision 'equitable easements required to be protected by notice on the register' is somewhat obscure. In *E R Ives Investment Ltd v High* [1967] 2 QB 379, [1967] 1 All ER 504 it was held by the Court of Appeal that easements acquired in equity by proprietary estoppel were not equitable easements for the purposes of section 10 (1) Class D (iii) of the Land Charges Act 1925. Lord Denning MR expressed the view that 'equitable easements' referred simply to that limited class of rights which before the 1925 property legislation were capable of being conveyed or created at law but thereafter were capable of existing only in equity: see at 395, at 508. In *Poster v Slough Estates Ltd* [1969] 1 Ch 495, [1968] 3 All ER 257, Cross J declined, at 506–507, at 262, to disagree with Lord Denning MR's view of the meaning of the expression and held that a right to re-enter premises after termination of a lease and to remove fixtures therefrom was not an 'equitable easement' for the purposes of the Land Charges Act 1925. These authorities might be thought to suggest by analogy that equitable easements in section 70 (1) (*a*) should be given a similarly limited meaning. I am, however, reluctant to do that because in general the clear intention of the Land Registration Act 1925 is that equitable interests should be protected either by entry on the register or as overriding interests and, if equitable easements in general are not within the exception in paragraph (*a*), it would follow that they would rank as overriding interests and be binding upon registered proprietors of servient land even though such proprietors did not have and could not by any reasonable means have obtained any knowledge of them. That result could not possibly be supported. In my view, therefore, the dicta in the two cases are not applicable to the construction of 'equitable easements' in paragraph (*a*) of section 70 (1).

Mr Purle submitted that the exception expressed in section 70 (1) (*a*) applied only to those equitable easements in respect of which a positive requirement that they be protected by notice on the register could be found in the Act. He submitted further that the Act contained no such requirement and that accordingly the expression covered nothing. It seems, however, from paragraph (*c*) of the proviso to section 19 (2) of the Act[18b] that the draftsman assumed that easements would require to be protected either by

---

[18b] P. 472, ante.

registration as appurtenant to registered land or by entry of notice against the registered title of the servient land. I do not, therefore, feel able to accept these submissions.

In my opinion, the words 'required to be protected' in paragraph (a) should be read in the sense 'need to be protected'. The exception in the paragraph was, in my view, intended to cover all equitable easements other than such as by reason of some other statutory provision or applicable principle of law, could obtain protection otherwise than by notice on the register. The most obvious example would be equitable easements which qualified for protection under paragraph (g) as part of the rights of a person in actual occupation. In my view I must examine the easement claimed by the third plaintiff and consider whether there is any statutory provision or principle of law which entitles it to protection otherwise than by entry of notice on the register.

The matter stands in my opinion thus. At the time when Mobil acquired its registered leasehold title the third plaintiff's right to an easement of way for the benefit of garage 52 over a part of the property enjoyed under that leasehold title was an equitable and not a legal right. It was, in ordinary conveyancing language, an equitable easement. It was not protected by any entry on the register. On the other hand, it was at the relevant time openly exercised and enjoyed by the third plaintiff as appurtenant to garage 52. Section 144 of the Land Registration Act 1925 contains power for rules to be made for a number of specified purposes. The Land Registration Rules 1925 were accordingly made and rule 258 provides:

[His Lordship read r. 258, p. 120, ante, and continued:]

The third plaintiff's equitable right of way over the rear driveway was, in my view, at the time when Mobil acquired its registered leasehold title, a right enjoyed with land for the purposes of this rule. It was plainly a right which adversely affected registered land including the part of the rear driveway comprised in Mobil's lease. Rule 258 categorises such a right as an overriding interest. Section 144 (2) of the Act provides that 'Any rules made in pursuance of this section shall be of the same force as if enacted in this Act.' Accordingly, in my judgment, the third plaintiff's right ranks as an overriding interest, does not need to be protected by entry of notice on the register and is binding on Mobil.

Mr Davidson submitted that there was no power under section 144 (1) for rules to add to the overriding interests specified in the various paragraphs of section 70 (1). He submitted that rule 258 was ultra vires and of no effect. I do not agree. Sub-paragraph (xxxi) of section 144 (1) enables rules to be made,

'for regulating any matter to be prescribed or in respect of which rules are to or may be made under this Act and any other matter or thing, whether similar or not to those above mentioned, in respect of which it may be expedient to make rules for the purpose of carrying this Act into execution.'

This is a power in very wide terms. In my view, it is in terms wide enough to justify rule 258 and I see no reason why it should be given a limited effect.

Accordingly, for these reasons, the third plaintiff's equitable right of way over the rear driveway enjoyed with garage 52 was and is, in my judgment, binding on Mobil."

In *Re Dances Way, West Town, Hayling Island* [1962] Ch 490, [1962] 2 All ER 42, DIPLOCK LJ said at 508, at 51: "Section 70 (2) . . . is a mandatory requirement and is not in my view qualified by rule 41 which deals with easements, rights or privileges created by an instrument, without being restricted to those which appear on the title. These shall, but only if the registrar thinks fit, be entered in the register. It seems to me that the *discretionary* power to enter easements created by an instrument is limited to those which do not appear on the title; where they do appear on the title, it is a mandatory duty under section 70 (2) to enter them. That means that the registrar, when the documents of title are submitted to him, must determine whether an instrument included among them and so appearing on the title does create an easement adversely affecting the land. That is a question of construction, and the material before him at the time that he makes the first entry will include only the documents of title and will not include evidence of surrounding circumstances which it is permissible to take into consideration in determining the question of construction. If the registrar, because of the absence of such evidence or for any other reason, misconstrues the document and so enters a note of an easement which was not created by an instrument and appearing on the title, it seems to me that there is then an error or a mistake in an entry, and section 82 (1) (*h*)[19] applies to that situation and entitles the registrar to rectify the error."

VIII.   Law Reform Committee Report on Acquisition of Easements and Profits by Prescription (1966 Cmnd 3100)[20]

There has been judicial criticism of the law relating to the acquisition of easements and profits by prescription. In *Tehidy Minerals Ltd v Norman* [1971] 2 QB 528, [1971] 2 All ER 475, BUCKLEY LJ said at 543, at 484: "The co-existence of three separate methods of prescribing is, in our view, anomalous and undesirable, for it results in much unnecessary complication and confusion. We hope that it may be possible for the Legislature to effect a long-overdue simplication in this branch of the law."

In 1966, the Law Reform Committee recommended the abolition of the prescriptive acquisition of easements (para. 32) and of profits à prendre (para. 98); in the former case by a majority of 8–6; in the latter unanimously[1].

The Committee, however, considered the ways in which prescriptive acquisition — if it should be retained for easements — should operate, and was unanimous on the new system which should be adopted.

---

[19] P. 149, ante.

[20] (1967) 30 MLR 189 (H. W. Wilkinson). The Law Commission intends to publish a series of reports on the subject of appurtenant rights. Its first report on The Law of Positive and Restrictive Covenants was published in 1984 (Law Com No. 127, HC 201), p. 834, post.

[1] In 1971 a Working Paper (No. 36) suggested that "easements and covenants should be assimilated along lines hitherto regarded as appropriate to easements" (para. 9); and, in relation to prescription, "as at present advised we are inclined to agree in principle with the majority, but only on the basis that some alternative to prescription can be found. In the meantime it will be assumed that prescription will continue" (para. 99). It should be reformed along the lines recommended by the Law Reform Committee. (Proposition 10.).

The main recommendations, in brief outline, are:

(1) All existing methods of acquisition of easements and profits by prescription should be abolished. This recommendation includes the abolition of prescription at common law and under the doctrine of a lost modern grant, and the repeal of the Prescription Act 1832 (paras. 40, 98, 99 (1)–(3)).

(2) Under the new system (for easements only) (para. 99 (6)):

    (*a*) The prescriptive period should be a period in gross of 12 years (i.e., it need not be "next before action brought") (paras. 41–43: Prescription Act 1832, section 4; *Hyman v Van den Bergh* [1908] 1 Ch 167, p. 167, ante).

    (*b*) There should be no "disabilities" (para. 44; Prescription Act 1832, sections 7, 8; p. 614, ante).

    (*c*) An easement should be capable of being acquired against the owner of a limited interest in the servient land so as to subsist as long as that servient owner's interest subsists (paras. 47–49; pp. 610, 638, ante). Prescription by the owner of a limited interest in the dominant land should continue, as at present, in favour of the freeholder (para. 50). A tenant should be able to prescribe against his landlord and vice-versa (para. 51).

(*d*) Enjoyment:

        (i) by force should not count in favour of the dominant owner (para. 57);

        (ii) must have been actually known to the servient owner or ought reasonably to have been known to him (para. 58);

        (iii) must be of such a kind and frequency as would only be justified by the existence of an easement (para. 59);

        (iv) by consent or agreement should not count. If so enjoyed for one year or more, the consent, like an interruption, would prevent earlier enjoyment being added to later enjoyment for the purpose of making up the required total of 12 years. A consent which is indefinite in duration should operate for one year (paras. 61–63).

    (*e*) Notional interruption, on the lines of the Rights of Light Act 1959 (p. 639, ante), should be extended to easements generally: this should be by registration after notice given. Interruption, notional or actual, should endure for 12 months in order to be effective (as at present: Prescription Act 1832, section 4) (para. 75).

    (*f*) An easement, acquired by prescription, should be lost by 12 years' continuous non-user (para. 81).

(3) The Committee is unanimous about provisions to facilitate, subject to compensation where appropriate, the acquisition of easements of support for buildings by land or for buildings by buildings (paras. 89–95, 99 (8)–(11)).

(4) Shelter should be treated in the same way as support (paras. 96, 99 (12): *Phipps v Pears* [1965] 1 QB 76, [1964] 2 All ER 35, p. 574, ante).

(5) The Lands Tribunal should be empowered to discharge easements or substitute more convenient ones, subject to payment of compensation where appropriate (paras. 97, 99 (13)).

QUESTIONS

1. Consider the arguments for and against the abolition of the acquisition of easements and profits à prendre by prescription. How is the matter affected by the extension of the practice of Registration of Title to land? See the Report, paras. 30–38.

2. "We do not consider that it is necessary or appropriate for the same legal rules to apply to the acquisition of easements by prolonged enjoyment as apply to the acquisition of title to land by adverse possession". (Para. 36.)

    "In spite of the differences between adverse possession and prescription, the same fundamental considerations apply to them." (Para. 38 (*d*).)

    Law Reform Committee 14th Report (Acquisition of Easements and Profits by Prescription) 1966 (Cmnd 3100).

With which of these two views do you agree?

3. How would the facts of *Copeland v Greenhalf* [1952] Ch 488, [1952] 1 All ER 809, p. 570, ante, have to be altered so as to establish a claim:
    (*a*) to an easement over the plaintiff's land;
    (*b*) to the plaintiff's land by adverse possession?
    (1968) 32 Conv (NS) 270 (M. J. Goodman).

11. Mortgages[1]

I. Introduction

The mortgage transaction has, throughout its history, been a collection of contradictions. Maitland described it as "one long suppressio veri and suggestio falsi"[2]. Before 1926, the usual form of mortgage of a fee simple was by conveyance of that fee simple subject to an undertaking by the mortgagee

---

[1] C & B, pp. 615–691; M & W, pp. 913–1014; MM, pp. 461–519. See generally Coote, *Law of Mortgages* (9th edn.); Fairest, *Mortgages* (2nd edn. 1980); Fisher and Lightwood, *Law of Mortgage* (9th edn. 1977); *Snell's Principles of Equity* (28th edn.), Part IV; Waldock, *Law of Mortgage* (2nd edn. 1950); (1978) 94 LQR 571 (P. Jackson). The Law Commission is beginning a review of the whole law of mortgages, with a view to producing a working paper in 1986. Twentieth Annual Report 1984–85, para. 2.34 (Law Com No. 155, HC 247).

[2] Maitland, p. 182; Simpson, *Introduction to the History of Land Law* (1961), pp. 132–134, 225–229.

to reconvey on payment, at a stated time in the future, of all moneys due; mortgages of leaseholds were by assignment or by sub-demise. Since 1925, mortgages of freeholds may only be by way of demise and mortgages of leaseholds by sub-demise; or, in either case by charge by deed expressed to be by way of legal mortgage in accordance with section 87 (1) of the Law of Property Act 1925. Statutory provision for the creation of charges by way of legal mortgage has at last made it possible for a mortgage transaction to appear to be what it really is — the charging of property as security for the repayment of a loan. The historical practice of conveying an estate in land to the mortgagee has hidden the true nature of the transaction, and has made it necessary for Courts of Chancery to make great exertions to prevent the mortgagee from using the property as something more than a security for the debt.

The legal mortgage before 1926 and the mortgage by demise or sub-demise were, and still are, drafted so as to appear to give the mortgagee something more than a security; they provide for reconveyance, or for cesser of the demise respectively, on repayment of all sums due at a time in the future. This is usually six months ahead, although in most cases there is no intention on the part of either party that the payment shall be made by that date. The mortgagor's legal right is then lost and the only protection that he receives is from equity; he is given an equitable right to redeem, and this right has been held by a series of cases to be absolute and inviolable[3].

In accordance with the proviso for redemption given by the mortgagee, the mortgagor has a legal, or contractual, right to redeem and to obtain a reconveyance of the property; and by virtue of his right to obtain specific performance of the mortgagee's covenant to reconvey, equity considered him to be the owner of the land subject to the mortgage. Equity's insistence upon the inviolability of the mortgagor's right to redeem, even after his contractual right had ended, led to the creation of an equitable right to redeem; and equity's willingness to enforce this right at any time on payment of all sums due meant that he continued to be the owner in equity subject to the mortgage. The equitable interest which he owns is called the Equity of Redemption; and just as, centuries earlier, equitable estates in land became proprietary by the protection given by equity to the cestui que use against everyone except the bona fide purchaser of the legal estate for value without notice[4], so also the equity of redemption was regarded as a proprietary interest which could be bought, sold, mortgaged, and, if it were personalty, pass to the Crown as bona vacantia[5].

Since the interest which the mortgagor retained after parting with the legal fee simple in a mortgage by conveyance before 1926 was merely equitable, all subsequent mortgages were of necessity equitable. In a mortgage by demise after 1925, the mortgagor retains an equitable interest in the term granted, the interest being the equity of redemption of the term; but he also retains the legal fee simple from which he can create subsequent legal mortgages taking effect subject to the prior mortgage and created either by legal charge or by demise for a period, usually a day longer than the first legal mortgage. The change introduced in 1925 is one of form rather than substance. For, "the

---

[3] See pp. 658, et seq.
[4] See p. 24, ante.
[5] *Re Sir Thomas Spencer Wells* [1933] Ch 29, p. 659, post.

equity of redemption has in no way lost its importance. A fee simple giving the right to possession of land only when a lease for three thousand years has expired is of little value compared with the right to insist that the fee simple shall forthwith be freed from the term of three thousand years on payment of the money due[6]."

Courts of Equity have looked upon a mortgage transaction as one in which the terms were likely to be dictated by the mortgagee. In early days the mortgagor was at a disadvantage in that he was in need of money and must take it on the mortgagee's terms; it was a lender's market. And, while the law followed the maxim "caveat emptor" in the affairs of merchants and trade, equity not surprisingly took a different view in the case of mortgages. The fact that mortgagors were, in the early days, often members of great families and mortgagees were professional money lenders no doubt contributed to some extent to the development. A consideration of the changed position of borrowers and lenders in the capitalist society of the present day will suggest that the old cases should be accepted with some reserve. The cases on this subject show a continual struggle between the principle of binding precedent and the requirements of a changing society; they can only be understood with this in mind. Those which were decided about the turn of the present century do not create the principle they apply. That litigation was a challenge to the validity of the principle laid down in earlier centuries, but generally it succeeded only in re-affirming the old principles; it was not until 1914[7] that substantial progress was made.

The problem at the present day is the extent to which these old rules still hold good. A modern mortgage of land is usually a transaction between an individual house-buyer and a building society, or forms part of a development project embarked upon by property financiers. The small man is protected from unfair pressure by the high standards set by building societies[8] and also by statutory safeguards, and the financiers must look after themselves.

The mortgage industry is big business. According to the Report of the Chief Registrar of Friendly Societies the total assets of the 190 Building Societies in 1984 were £102,689 million, the number of borrowers was 6,314,000 and of shareholders 39,380,000. In 1984 itself the societies made 1,658,000 advances, totalling £23,771 million[9]. An increase in the number of borrowers by a fifth since 1979 reflected mostly the increase in the stock of owner-occupied dwellings[9a]. In addition to Building Societies, there are three other substantial institutional lenders of money; Banks, Insurance Companies, and Local Authorities. The great expansion of bank loans on mortgage came in 1981 and 1982 when they took 36 per cent of the market; in 1983 this dropped to 24.5 per cent, but seems likely to be maintained on that level[10].

---

[6] M & W, p. 920.

[7] *Kreglinger v New Patagonia Meat and Cold Storage Co Ltd* [1914] AC 25, p. 673, post.

[8] P. 653, post.

[9] Report 1983–1984, Tables 2.1–3. See also the Green Paper "Building Societies: A New Framework", Appendix I, pp. 31–36 (1984) Cmnd 9316, containing a comparative summary of statistics. The paper initiated a discussion on proposals for the expansion of the commercial activities of building societies. [1985] Conv 1–7. See also *Central Statistical Office Social Trends 16* (1986 edn.), p. 145. The Government statement on the Paper in HL Deb 7 November 1985, col. 3 was followed by the Building Societies Bill 1985; (1985) 129 SJ 874.

[9a] P. 377, ante.

[10] Green Paper, supra, Table 7; (1984) 134 NLJ 413 (M. Boleat).

Furthermore a second mortgage market grew up, with householders taking advantage of the increased value of houses to borrow further from "banks, finance houses and even moneylenders"[11]. The Consumer Credit Act 1974[12] gives important protection to this type of borrower.

The rate of interest charged by Building Societies (and other lenders) is related to interest rates applicable to the market generally. The London clearing banks' base lending rate, currently $11\frac{1}{2}\%$, moves according to periodical political decisions by the Government; the present high rates place a heavy burden on borrowers.

When a borrower falls into arrears with his payments, a building society does all it can to avoid repossession[13], but if it has to take action to enforce the security, difficult social questions arise. The mortgagor has given as security, not an investment, but his home. And a mortgagor who has defaulted with one building society will have difficulty in borrowing money from another[14].

Most of the litigation is in respect of applications for possession[15]. The mortgagee is, in law, entitled to possession "before the ink is dry on the mortgage"[16]. A building society will not go into possession without a court order; but it will go into possession before sale in order to be able to give vacant possession to a purchaser. Applications for possession are thus usually a preliminary to sale by the mortgagee. It is in this context that questions arise at the present day concerning the mortgagor's need for protection, and mortgagors of dwelling houses now have statutory protection.

Cheshire and Burn: *Modern Law of Real Property* (13th edn, 1982) pp. 688–689.

"BUILDING SOCIETY MORTGAGES"[17]

Building societies are a special kind of mortgagee and have for many years been the main source of finance for the purchase of houses in owner-occupation. They are societies formed for raising, by the subscription of the

---

[11] Report of the Chief Registrar of Friendly Societies for the year 1972–73, para. 18.

[12] See p. 682, post.

[13] "Although very few people with building society loans get into serious difficulties with repayments, there was more than a fourfold increase in repossessions by building societies from $2\frac{1}{2}$ thousand in 1979 to 11 thousand in 1984; during the 1970s the number of repossessions varied between 1 thousand and $4\frac{1}{2}$ thousand": *Central Statistical Office Social Trends 16* (1986 edn.), p. 145.

[14] Lord DIPLOCK in *Pettitt v Pettitt* [1970] AC 777 at 824, [1969] 2 All ER 385 at 414 referred to "a real-property-mortgaged-to-a-building-society-owning democracy". In 1982, 58.9% of houses were owner-occupied, and 44.9% of these were subject to a building society mortgage. Appendix I, p. 36.

[15] See p. 689, post.

[16] Per HARMAN J, in *Four-Maids Ltd v Dudley Marshall (Properties) Ltd* [1957] Ch 317 at 320, [1957] 2 All ER 35 at 36.

[17] See Wurtzburg and Mills, *Building Society Law* (14th edn, 1976); Waldock, chap. 4; Fisher and Lightwood, pp. 193–197; Part II of the Annual Reports of the Chief Registrar of Friendly Societies; (1974) 118 SJ 744, 768, 785, 803, 841; (1975) 125 NLJ 1149; (1980) 124 SJ 405 (W. A. Greene); Committee to Review Functioning of Financial Institutions Report (The Wilson Committee) 1980 (Cmnd 9125), chaps. 8, 24, Appendix III.

members, a fund for making advances to members out of the funds of the society upon security by way of mortgage of land[18]. The principal Act regulating such societies is the Building Societies Act 1962; it contains detailed provisions relating to their management and gives responsibility for their prudential supervision to the Chief Registrar of Friendly Societies[19]. The general method of operation is to borrow money from the general public at interest and then to lend that money at interest by making advances to house purchasers on the security of their houses. The mortgage is usually one of two types; either an instalment or repayment mortgage, that is to say, it is paid off by monthly payments at a rate which covers payment of interest and repayment of capital, so that the capital is paid off over an agreed period of time, for example, thirty years; or an endowment mortgage, that is to say, the money is borrowed from the society and at the same time an endowment assurance policy is taken out; only interest payments are made to the society during the life of the mortgage, the outstanding debt being repaid when the policy matures. A building society has power to make advances on terms that the real value of the loan will be repaid to it by adjustments which take account of inflation[20].

The general law of mortgage applies to these transactions. The main difference between a building society mortgage and any other is that the mortgagor is a member of a society, and, accordingly, the rules of the society will be incorporated in the mortgage. The rules usually require the mortgagor to obey the rules of the society and reserve the right to increase the rate of interest after giving notice to the mortgagor. Another important difference is that there are statutory limits on the lending powers of a building society. It may not advance money by way of second mortgage, unless the prior mortgage is in favour of the society[1]. And the right of a society to lend members more than £60,000 is restricted[2].

Finally, . . . a building society, when selling as a mortgagee, must take reasonable care to ensure that the price is the best price which can reasonably be obtained[3]."

---

[18] Building Societies Act 1962, s. 1 (1). The primary object is to assist the members in obtaining a small freehold or leasehold property. See preamble to Building Societies Act 1836.

[19] For the discretion of the Chief Registrar of Friendly Societies to prevent a building society accepting money from the public under Building Societies Act 1962, s. 48 (2) and to revoke its designation as a trustee investment under House Purchase and Housing Act 1959, s. 1 (1), see *R v Chief Registrar of Friendly Societies* [1984] QB 227, [1984] 2 All ER 27.

[20] *Nationwide Building Society v Registry of Friendly Societies* [1983] 1 WLR 1226, [1983] 3 All ER 296; (1984) 134 NLJ 437 (H. Cohen), 513. For index-linking of mortgages generally, see *Multiservice Bookbinding Ltd v Marden* [1979] Ch 84, [1978] 2 All ER 489, p. 678, post.

[1] Building Societies Act 1962, s. 32. See *Nash v Halifax Building Society* [1979] Ch 584, [1979] 2 All ER 19.

[2] Ibid., ss. 21, 22; Building Societies (Special Advances) Order 1982 (S.I. 1982 No. 1056); (1985) 48 MLR 389 (M. J. Russell).

[3] Ibid., s. 36, p. 708, post.

II. Methods of Creation

A. Legal Mortgages and Legal Charges[4]

LAW OF PROPERTY ACT 1925

85. Mode of mortgaging freeholds. — (1) A mortgage of an estate in fee simple shall only be capable of being effected at law either by a demise for a term of years absolute, subject to a provision for cesser on redemption, or by a charge by deed expressed to be by way of legal mortgage:

Provided that a first mortgagee shall have the same right to the possession of documents as if his security included the fee simple.

(2) Any purported conveyance of an estate in fee simple by way of mortgage made after the commencement of this Act shall (to the extent of the estate of the mortgagor) operate as a demise of the land to the mortgagee for a term of years absolute, without impeachment for waste, but subject to cesser on redemption, in manner following, namely:—

> (a) A first or only mortgagee shall take a term of three thousand years from the date of the mortgage;
>
> (b) A second or subsequent mortgagee shall take a term (commencing from the date of the mortgage) one day longer than the term vested in the first or other mortgagee whose security ranks immediately before that of such second or subsequent mortgagee; . . .

86. Mode of mortgaging leaseholds. — (1) A mortgage of a term of years absolute shall only be capable of being effected at law either by a subdemise for a term of years absolute, less by one day at least than the term vested in the mortgagor, and subject to a provision for cesser on redemption, or by a charge by deed expressed to be by way of legal mortgage; and where a licence to subdemise by way of mortgage is required, such licence shall not be unreasonably refused:[5]

Provided that a first mortgagee shall have the same right to the possession of documents as if his security had been effected by assignment.

(2) Any purported assignment of a term of years absolute by way of mortgage made after the commencement of this Act shall (to the extent of the estate of the mortgagor) operate as a subdemise of the leasehold land to the mortgagee for a term of years absolute, but subject to cesser on redemption, in manner following, namely:—

> (a) The term to be taken by a first or only mortgagee shall be ten days less than the term expressed to be assigned;

---

[4] C & B, pp. 621–627; M & W, pp. 915–926, 929–931; MM, pp. 463–468; Waldock, pp. 19–43; Fisher and Lightwood, pp. 21–44. For a mortgagor's action in negligence against (a) his solicitor where he enters into a mortgage as a result of the solicitor's failure to give proper advice, see *Forster v Outred & Co* [1982] 1 WLR 86, [1982] 2 All ER 753; and (b) the mortgagee's surveyor on whose negligent report he relied, see *Yianni v Edwin Evans & Sons* [1982] QB 438, [1981] 3 All ER 592; [1981] Conv 435 (H. M. Brazier and G. Pople); *Stevenson v Nationwide Building Society* (1984) 272 EG 663. On the measure of damages against a negligent surveyor, see *Perry v Sidney Phillips & Son* [1982] 1 WLR 1297, [1982] 3 All ER 705; [1984] Conv 60 (K. Hodkinson); (1983) 99 LQR 10 (J. Murdoch); *London and South of England Building Society v Stone* [1983] 1 WLR 1242, [1983] 3 All ER 105.

[5] A charge probably dispenses with the need for a licence: *Gentle v Faulkner* [1900] 2 QB 267; *Matthews v Smallwood* [1910] 1 Ch 777; *Grand Junction Co Ltd v Bates* [1954] 2 QB 160, [1954] 2 All ER 385, p. 604, post; M & W, p. 925, n. 89.

(*b*) The term to be taken by a second or subsequent mortgagee shall be one day longer than the term vested in the first or other mortgagee whose security ranks immediately before that of the second or subsequent mortgagee, if the length of the last mentioned term permits, and in any case for a term less by one day at least than the term expressed to be assigned; . . .

87. Charges by way of legal mortgage. — (1) Where a legal mortgage of land is created by a charge by deed expressed[6] to be by way of legal mortgage, the mortgagee shall have the same protection, powers and remedies (including the right to take proceedings to obtain possession from the occupiers and the persons in receipt of rents and profits, or any of them) as if —

(*a*) where the mortgage is a mortgage of an estate in fee simple, a mortgage term of three thousand years without impeachment of waste had been thereby created in favour of the mortgagee; and

(*b*) where the mortgage is a mortgage of a term of years absolute, a sub-term less by one day than the term vested in the mortgagor had been thereby created in favour of the mortgagee.

FIFTH SCHEDULE

Forms of Instruments

Section 206   Form No. 1

CHARGE BY WAY OF LEGAL MORTGAGE

This Legal Charge is made [&c.] between *A.* of [&c.] of the one part and *B.* of [&c.] of the other part.

[*Recite the title of A. to the freeholds or leaseholds in the Schedule and agreement for the loan by B.*]

Now in consideration of the sum of .... pounds now paid by *B.* to *A.* (the receipt &c.) this Deed witnesseth as follows:—

1. *A.* hereby covenants with *B.* to pay [*Add the requisite covenant to pay principal and interest*].

2. *A.* as Beneficial Owner hereby charges by way of legal mortgage All and Singular the property mentioned in the Schedule hereto with the payment to *B.* of the principal money, interest, and other money hereby covenanted to be paid by *A.*

3. [*Add covenant to insure buildings and any other provisions desired.*]

In witness [&c.] [*Add Schedule*].

Note. — *B.* will be in the same position as if a mortgage had been effected by a demise of freeholds or a subdemise of leaseholds.

---

[6] Such a statement is not required in the case of registered land: *Cityland and Property (Holdings) Ltd v Dabrah* [1968] Ch 166, [1967] 2 All ER 639.

In *Regent Oil Co Ltd v J. A. Gregory (Hatch End) Ltd* [1966] Ch 402, [1965] 3 All ER 673, the Court of Appeal held that an attornment clause in a charge by way of legal mortgage enabled covenants in the charge to be enforced against successors in title of the mortgagor. HARMAN LJ said at 431, at 678:

"In my opinion, the new charge by way of legal mortgage created by section 87 was intended to be a substitute in all respects for a mortgage by demise, and anything which would be good in the one is good in the other. It would indeed be a trap if the rights of the mortgagee depended on whether his charge were created in one way or the other. Support for this view is to be found in *Grand Junction Co Ltd v Bates* [1954] 2 QB 160, [1954] 2 All ER 385; I read from the judgment of Upjohn J at 168, at 388: 'My approach to the problem is this: A charge by way of legal mortgage, as I have already said, was introduced as a conveyancing device by the Law of Property Act 1925, with a view to simplifying conveyancing, and it would be a pity to introduce subtle differences between one way of creating a charge and another way of creating a charge unless the words of the Act so required. It may be that there is the difference with regard to obtaining consent of the landlord to the charge, though that depends on the construction of the lease; but in any event that is no reason for making another difference between the two forms of creating a security, unless the Act so requires.' It was there held that the chargee by way of legal mortgage had a right to claim relief against forfeiture just as if he had been a mortgagee by sub-demise."

In *Weg Motors Ltd v Hales* [1962] Ch 49, [1961] 3 All ER 181, DONOVAN LJ said at 77, at 192:

"The section does not create even a notional term of years in the mortgagee but simply defines what protection, powers and remedies the mortgagee is to have[7]."

B. Equitable Mortgages and Equitable Charges[8]

i. MORTGAGE OF AN EQUITABLE INTEREST

This is created by assigning the equitable interest to the mortgagee with a proviso for reassignment on redemption. The assignment, if not made by will, must satisfy the requirements of section 53 (1) (c) of the Law of Property Act 1925[9].

---

[7] See also *Grand Junction Co Ltd v Bates* [1954] 2 QB 160 at 168, [1954] 2 All ER 385 at 388, where it was said that a tenant who charges his lease is probably not in breach of a covenant against sub-letting without the landlord's consent. Nor does a chargee have a term so as to effect a transfer to him under LPA 1925, s. 115: *Cumberland Court (Brighton) Ltd v Taylor* [1964] Ch 29, [1963] 2 All ER 536; nor is it necessary to serve upon a chargee a notice under LPA 1925, s. 146, p. 434, ante; nor under Leasehold Property (Repairs) Act 1938, p. 448, ante; *Church Commissioners for England v Ve-Ri-Best Manufacturing Ltd* [1957] 1 QB 238, [1956] 3 All ER 777; *Ushers Brewery v PS King & Co (Finance) Ltd* (1969) 212 EG 787; *Thompson v Salah* [1972] 1 All ER 530; *Edwards v Marshall-Lee* (1975) 235 EG 901; W & C, vol i., 177–178.

[8] C & B, pp. 627–629; M & W, pp. 926–929; MM, pp. 468–470; Waldock, pp. 43–59, 136–139; Fisher and Lightwood, pp. 44–51.

[9] See p. 79, ante.

ii.   AGREEMENT TO CREATE A LEGAL MORTGAGE

In accordance with the principle that Equity looks on that as done which ought to be done, an agreement to create a legal mortgage (or an imperfect legal mortgage) is treated as an actual mortgage[10], if it satisfies section 40 of the Law of Property Act 1925[11] or is supported by a sufficient act of part performance.

iii.   DEPOSIT OF TITLE DEEDS

Since *Russel v Russel*[12] in 1783 a deposit of title deeds, with the intention that the depositee shall hold them as a security, creates an equitable mortgage of the land. This is because such a deposit is construed as a contract to create a mortgage. No formalities are necessary, but it is usual for a memorandum of the agreement to accompany the deposit, and, if it is desired to enable the mortgagee to pass a legal estate on sale, the mortgagor will execute a deed and insert in it a power of attorney or a declaration of trust, or both[13].

iv.   EQUITABLE CHARGE

This arises where property is charged in equity with the payment of a debt or some other obligation. In *Matthews v Goodday* (1861) 31 LJ Ch 282, KINDERSLEY V-C said at 282:

"Suppose a man signed a written contract, by which he simply agreed that he thereby charged his real estate with 500*l* to A, what would be the effect of it? It would be no agreement to give a legal mortgage, but a security by which he equitably charged his land with the payment of a sum of money[14]."

III.   The Equity of Redemption[15]

A.   The Equity of Redemption as a Proprietary Interest

In *Casborne v Scarfe* (1738) 1 Atk 603, Lord HARDWICKE LC said at 605:

"An equity of redemption has always been considered as an estate in the land, for it may be devised, granted, or entailed with remainders, and such

---

[10] See p. 84, ante.

[11] See p. 63, ante.

[12] (1783) 1 Bro CC 269; *Dixon v Muckleston* (1872) 8 Ch App 155; *Re Wallis and Simmonds (Builders) Ltd* [1974] 1 WLR 391, [1974] 1 All ER 561; *Thames Guaranty Ltd v Campbell* [1985] QB 210, [1984] 2 All ER 585 (deposit of title deeds (land certificate) p. 740, post) to secure a debt by one joint tenant without consent of the other joint tenant not effective to create equitable charge of the jointly owned land; but it may create a charge of the equitable interest of the depositor, if the deposit amounts to an act of severance, p. 246, ante); *First National Securities Ltd v Hegerty* [1985] QB 850, [1984] 3 All ER 641, p. 247, n. 16, ante.

[13] See p. 715, post. The right to create this kind of equitable mortgage is saved by LPA 1925, s. 13. The mortgagee can retain the deeds until he is paid, but has no separate legal lien: *Re Molton Finance Ltd* [1968] Ch 325, [1967] 3 All ER 843; see also *Capital Finance Co Ltd v Stokes* [1969] 1 Ch 261 at 278; [1968] 3 All ER 625 at 629.

[14] *Swiss Bank Corpn v Lloyds Bank Ltd* [1982] AC 584 at 594–595, [1980] 2 All ER 419 at 425, per BUCKLEY LJ; *Thames Guaranty Ltd v Campbell*, supra; *First National Securities Ltd v Hegerty*, supra. Under Charging Orders Act 1979, s. 3 (4), p. 271, post, a charge imposed by a charging order has the same effect as "an equitable change created by the debtor by writing under his hand"; *Ladup Ltd v Williams & Glyn's Bank plc* [1985] 1 WLR 851, [1985] 2 All ER 577.

[15] C & B, pp. 618–619, 630–642; M & W, pp. 918–919, 920, 964–977; MM, pp. 463, 493–500; Waldock, pp. 170–223; Fisher and Lightwood, chap. 28.

cannot be considered as a mere right only, but such an estate whereof there may be a seisin; the person therefore entitled to the equity of redemption is considered as the owner of the land. . . . The interest of the land must be somewhere, and cannot be in abeyance, but it is not in the mortgagee, and therefore must remain in the mortgagor."

In *Re Sir Swimburne-Hanham v Howard Wells* [1933] Ch 29, the question was whether the Crown could claim, as bona vacantia, the equity of redemption of property owned by a company on its dissolution and not disposed of in its winding up. The property was leasehold land, and at the time of the dissolution, the rents received from it were insufficient to cover the interest on the mortgage money. The liquidator concluded that the equity of redemption was of no value. After a considerable time, the rents increased and were greater than the interest due on the mortgage to which the plaintiffs, as mortgagees, were entitled. All arrears of interest were paid off; the equity of redemption thus became of value. It was claimed by the plaintiffs on the ground that they were the legal owners of the term of years and that, the mortgagor having ceased to exist, no-one was entitled to redeem. The Court of Appeal (Lord HANWORTH MR, LAWRENCE and ROMER LJJ) held (reversing FARWELL J) that the equity of redemption was a proprietary interest which had never passed to the mortgagees. The Crown was therefore entitled to claim the equity of redemption as bona vacantia.

B. The Protection of the Mortgagor

Equity insists that unfair advantage shall not be taken of the mortgagor[16]. It will be seen that mortgagors have been subjected to schemes which attempt to take away the right to redeem by providing that the mortgagee may purchase the mortgaged property, or that the mortgagor shall not be permitted to redeem it for a certain period of time, or that, even after redemption, certain advantages shall still be enjoyed by the mortgagee. The rules which equity has laid down have been developed during the centuries, and have been summarised in the words: "Once a mortgage, always a mortgage[17]".

i. ONCE A MORTGAGE ALWAYS A MORTGAGE
Where a transaction is, on its proper construction, a mortgage, any provisions inserted for the advantage of the mortgagee which are inconsistent with the nature of a mortgage are void.

---

[16] For a mortgage which was set aside on the ground of undue influence by the bank mortgagee, see *Lloyds Bank Ltd v Bundy* [1975] QB 326, [1974] 3 All ER 757; cf. *National Westminster Bank plc v Morgan* [1985] AC 686, [1985] 1 All ER 821, p. 134, ante; *Woodstead Finance Ltd v Petrou* [1986] NLJ Rep 188, p. 684, post.

[17] *Seton v Slade* (1802) 7 Ves 265, 273, per Lord ELDON LC.

SAMUEL *v* JARRAH TIMBER AND WOOD PAVING
CORPORATION LTD[18]
[1904] AC 323 (HL, Earl of HALSBURY LC, Lords MACNAGHTEN
and LINDLEY)

First mortgage debenture stock of £30,000 was mortgaged to Samuel to
secure an advance of £5,000 at 6%. The principal was to become payable
with interest at thirty days' notice on either side; and the mortgagee, Samuel,
was given "the option to purchase the whole or any part of such stock at 40%
at any time within twelve months". Within that period Samuel claimed to
exercise this option in respect of the whole stock. The Company claimed to
redeem and to have a declaration that the option was illegal and void.

Held. The option was void, and the Company was entitled to redeem.

EARL OF HALSBURY LC: My Lords, I regret that the state of the authorities
leaves me no alternative other than to affirm the judgment of Kekewich J and
the Court of Appeal. A perfectly fair bargain made between two parties to it,
each of whom was quite sensible of what they were doing, is not to be
performed because at the same time a mortgage arrangement was made
between them. If a day had intervened between the two parts of the
arrangement, the part of the bargain which the appellant claims to be
performed would have been perfectly good and capable of being enforced;
but a line of authorities going back for more than a century has decided that
such an arrangement as that which was here arrived at is contrary to a
principle of equity, the sense or reason of which I am not able to appreciate,
and very reluctantly I am compelled to acquiesce in the judgments appealed
from.

LORD MACNAGHTEN: In *Vernon v Bethell* (1762) 2 Eden 110, 113, however,
Northington LC (then Lord Henley) laid down the law broadly in the
following terms: "This Court, as a Court of conscience, is very jealous of
persons taking securities for a loan and converting such securities into
purchases. And therefore I take it to be an established rule that a mortgagee
can never provide at the time of making the loan for any event or condition
on which the equity of redemption shall be discharged and the conveyance
absolute. And there is great reason and justice in this rule, for necessitous
men are not, truly speaking, free men, but to answer a present exigency will
submit to any terms that the crafty may impose upon them."

This doctrine, described by Lord Henley as an established rule nearly 150
years ago, has never, so far as I can discover, been departed from since or
questioned in any reported case. It is, I believe, universally accepted by
text-writers of authority. Speaking for myself, I should not be sorry if your
Lordships could see your way to modify it so as to prevent its being used as a
means of evading a fair bargain come to between persons dealing at arms'
length and negotiating on equal terms. The directors of a trading company in
search of financial assistance are certainly in a very different position from
that of an impecunious landowner in the toils of a crafty money-lender. At
the same time I quite feel the difficulty of interfering with any rule that has

---

[18] Followed in *Lewis v Frank Love Ltd* [1961] 1 WLR 261, [1961] 1 All ER 446; (1961) 77 LQR 163
(P. V. Baker). See also *Salt v Marquess of Northampton* [1892] AC 1, discussed by Lord DAVEY in
Noakes & Co Ltd v Rice [1902] AC 24, p. 670, post.

prevailed so long, and I am not prepared to differ from the conclusion at which the Court of Appeal has arrived.

In *Reeve v Lisle* [1902] AC 461 property was mortgaged to secure a loan of money. At a later date it was agreed between the parties to the mortgage that, if within five years the mortgagees should elect to enter into partnership with the mortgagors, they should be entitled to do so on the terms, inter alia, that the mortgagors should be relieved of the liability to repay the loan and that a ship (which was part of the security) should be transferred free from the mortgage for the purposes of the partnership. The House of Lords (Earl of HALSBURY LC, and Lords MACNAGHTEN, BRAMPTON and LINDLEY) construed these two transactions as being separate and independent, and held that the agreement was binding on the mortgagor[19].

ii. CONTRACTUAL POSTPONEMENT OF THE RIGHT TO REDEEM

This section deals with cases in which the mortgagor covenants to postpone redemption for a substantial length of time. The situations cover a wide range between two extremes. On the one hand are cases in which the mortgagee, solely for his own benefit, insists on the postponement of redemption for so long a time that the security is virtually irredeemable. On the other hand are cases in which a fair business transaction includes, at the request of the mortgagor, a term postponing redemption for a certain period of time, and the mortgagor, finding that interest rates have gone down, makes use of these rules to escape from his bargain.

It used to be said that a postponement was valid if it were for a reasonable time. It is clear, however, since the *Knightsbridge* case[20], that this is not the proper test, whether "reasonableness" is judged in terms of mere length of time or in terms of all the circumstances of the case. Sir Wilfrid GREENE MR, laid down the test in that case as follows:[1] "Equity is concerned to see two things — one that the essential requirements of a mortgage transaction are observed, and the other that oppressive and unconscionable terms are not enforced." With the second requirement no-one could quarrel; it is possible, however, that the first one may some day be held to be too wide. In that case, the mortgagor covenanted not to redeem a mortgage of freehold land for 40 years, and the covenant was held valid. There was no suggestion of hardship or oppression. An interesting situation would have arisen if the property mortgaged had been a forty-one year lease[2]; assuming again that there was no hardship or oppression, the conflict between *Fairclough v Swan Brewery Co Ltd* [1912] AC 565, p. 664, post and *Santley v Wilde* [1899] 2 Ch 474 would then have to be resolved, and there is much to be said for the view that a business transaction of that nature ought to be upheld.

---

[19] See *Alec Lobb (Garages) Ltd v Total Oil Great Britain Ltd* [1983] 1 WLR 87, [1983] 1 All ER 944 (sale and 51 year leaseback of part of property entered into between mortgagor and mortgagee after date of mortgage held valid under mortgage rules, but reversed in CA [1985] 1 WLR 173, [1985] 1 All ER 303 as being void for restraint of trade).

[20] *Knightsbridge Estates Trust Ltd v Byrne* [1939] Ch 441, [1938] 4 All ER 618; *affd.* [1940] AC 613, [1940] 2 All ER 401, p. 664, post.

[1] [1939] Ch at 457, [1938] 4 All ER 618 at 626.

[2] See the question on p. 668, post.

Cases falling within the present section should be distinguished from those dealt with in the next. The next section deals with cases where an advantage still remains to the mortgagee after redemption. Failure to appreciate this distinction has caused most of the misunderstanding of *Santley v Wilde*. The criticism which that case received in the House of Lords[3], and particularly from Lord DAVEY, was directed against it on the assumption that it concerned a collateral advantage existing after redemption. It is clear, however, from the judgment of the case itself, that Lord LINDLEY treated it as a case of contractual postponement.

SANTLEY *v* WILDE
[1899] 2 Ch 474 (CA, LINDLEY MR, Sir F. H. JEUNE AND ROMER LJ, reversing BYRNE J [1899] 1 Ch 747)

The plaintiff, as sub-lessee of a theatre, had the option to take over the head lease on payment of £2,000. She arranged to borrow this money from the defendant Wilde, and mortgaged to him her sub-lease as security. The mortgage provided that the mortgagor should repay the capital by instalments under an arrangement which was not challenged, and that she should "during the residue of the term . . . notwithstanding that all principal moneys and interest may have been paid . . . pay . . . a sum equal to one-third part of the clear net profit rent or rents to be derived" from the lease. The proviso for cesser provided that the mortgage should determine on payment of the principal sum and interest, "and all other the moneys hereinbefore covenanted . . . to be paid . . ." etc. After certain payments had fallen into arrear, the plaintiff, on payment of all arrears, and on tender of the outstanding principal, interest and costs, claimed a declaration that she was entitled to redeem on payment of principal, interest and costs and that so far as the mortgage deed provided for payment of a share of the rents and profits or precluded her from redeeming on payment of principal and interest, it was invalid.

Held. The plaintiff could not redeem except by observing all the covenants for which her property was given as security, including the covenant to pay the profits.

LINDLEY MR: The question raised on this appeal is extremely important: I do not profess to be able to decide it on any principle which will be in harmony with all the cases; but it appears to me that the true principle running through them is not very difficult to discover, and I think that it can be applied so as to do justice in this case and in all other cases on the subject that may arise. The principle is this: a mortgage is a conveyance of land or an assignment of chattels as a security for the payment of a debt or the discharge of some other obligation for which it is given. This is the idea of a mortgage: and the security is redeemable on the payment or discharge of such debt or obligation, any provision to the contrary notwithstanding. That, in my opinion, is the law. Any provision inserted to prevent redemption on payment or performance of the debt or obligation for which the security was given is what is meant by a clog or fetter on the equity of redemption and is therefore void. . . . A clog or fetter is something which is inconsistent with the

---

[3] Especially in *Noakes & Co Ltd v Rice* [1902] AC 24 at 33, p. 670, post.

idea of security: a clog or fetter is in the nature of a repugnant condition. If I convey land in fee subject to a condition forbidding alienation, that is a repugnant condition. If I give a mortgage on a condition that I shall not redeem, that is a repugnant condition. The Courts of Equity have fought for years to maintain the doctrine that a security is redeemable. But when and under what circumstances? On the performance of the obligation for which it was given. If the obligation is the payment of a debt, the security is redeemable on the payment of that debt. That, in my opinion, is the true principle applicable to the cases, and that is what is meant when it is said there must not be any clog or fetter on the equity of redemption. If so, this mortgage has no clog or fetter at all. Of course, the debt or obligation may be impeachable for fraud, oppression, or over-reaching: there the obligation is tainted to that extent and is invalid. But, putting such cases out of the question, when you get a security for a debt or obligation, that security can be redeemed the moment the debt or obligation is paid or performed, but on no other terms.

Now, let us see what the contract here is. It is not suggested that there has been fraud or undue influence or over-reaching or hard bargaining. Here is a lady who has a lease, of which there are ten years to run, subject to a rent and covenants. She wants to carry on a theatre, and she wants to borrow a sum of 2,000*l.* for the purpose. What is the security she offers? The security of the lease is probably absolutely insufficient. A security of that sort, unless it is kept up for the ten years, is very shaky. The lender took that view. He says, "I will lend you the money, and you may have five years in which to pay it; and you shall pay me a sum equal to one-third part of the net profit rents to be derived from any underleases". What is the lender's position? It is obvious that his security depends not only on the solvency of the lady, but also on the success of the theatre. This is the kind of security proposed, and the lender says he will lend upon that. Accordingly the 2,000*l.* is lent, and the mortgagor by her security covenants to repay the money by instalments; the deed then further goes on as follows: [His Lordship read the second testatum and covenant by the mortgagor for payment to the mortgagee of one-third of the net profit rents to be derived from any underleases or undertenancies, and also the provision for redemption: and continued:]

That means that this lease is granted or assigned by the mortgagor to the mortgagee as security not only for the payment of the 2,000*l.* and interest, but also for the payment of the one-third of the net profit rents to the end of the term. If I am right in the principle which I have laid down, that does not clog the right of redemption upon the performance of the obligation for which the security was given. That is the nature of the transaction, and the good sense of it.

But it is said that is not good law. Those, however, who say so lose sight of the true principle underlying the expression that there must be no clog or fetter on the equity of redemption. The plaintiff says, "I will pay off the balance of the 2,000*l.* and interest, and you will give me back the lease, and this is the end of my obligation". But the mortgagee says, "No; that is not the bargain: you cannot redeem on those terms. On the contrary, you may pay me the 2,000*l.* and interest, but if you do, you must also pay the one-third profit rents". On principle that is right: it follows from what I have said. That is the bargain, and there has been no oppression, and there is no reasonable legal ground for relieving this lady.

FAIRCLOUGH *v* SWAN BREWERY CO LTD
[1912] AC 565 (PC, Lords MACNAGHTEN, ATKINSON, SHAW OF
DUNFERMLINE, and MERSEY]

The appellant was lessee for $17\frac{1}{2}$ years of a hotel owned by the
respondent brewery. He executed a mortgage of his lease for £500
which contained a clause precluding him from redeeming the mortgage
during the remainder of his term less six weeks, and from purchasing beer
from any person other than the respondent brewery during the continuance
of the mortgage. On the appellant's offering to redeem and claiming to be
free to purchase beer elsewhere, the respondent brewery brought this action
in the Supreme Court of Western Australia for damages for breach of
covenant and an injunction to restrain further breaches. The appellant
argued that the covenant was void on the ground, inter alia, that it was a clog
on his equity of redemption, and claimed that he was entitled to redeem.

Held. The covenant was void and the appellant was entitled to redeem.

LORD MACNAGHTEN: The arguments of counsel ranged over a very wide
field[4]. But the real point is a narrow one. It depends upon a doctrine of
equity, which is not open to question.

"There is", as Kindersley V-C said in *Gossip v Wright* (1863) 32 LJ Ch 648
at 653, "no doubt that the broad rule is this: that the Court will not allow the
right of redemption in any way to be hampered or crippled in that which the
parties intended to be a security either by any contemporaneous instrument
with the deed in question, or by anything which this Court would regard as a
simultaneous arrangement or part of the same transaction." The rule in
comparatively recent times was unsettled by certain decisions in the Court of
Chancery in England which seem to have misled the learned judges in the
Full Court. But it is now firmly established by the House of Lords that the
old rule still prevails and that equity will not permit any device or
contrivance being part of the mortgage transaction or contemporaneous with
it to prevent or impede redemption. The learned counsel on behalf of the
respondents admitted, as he was bound to admit, that a mortgage cannot be
made irredeemable. That is plainly forbidden. Is there any difference
between forbidding redemption and permitting it, if the permission be a mere
pretence? Here the provision for redemption is nugatory. . . . For all practical
purposes this mortgage is irredeemable. It was obviously meant to be
irredeemable. It was made irredeemable in and by the mortgage itself.

KNIGHTSBRIDGE ESTATES TRUST LTD *v* BYRNE
[1939] Ch 441, [1938] 4 All ER 618 (CA, Sir Wilfrid GREENE MR,
SCOTT and FARWELL LJJ)

The plaintiff company was the owner of certain freehold property in London
which had been mortgaged at $6\frac{1}{2}$%. Wishing to pay off their mortgage, they
asked the defendants for a loan of £310,000 at $5\frac{1}{4}$% repayable over forty
years. The defendants agreed to make this loan, repayment to be made by
half-yearly instalments over forty years. The deed so provided, and in it the
defendant mortgagees undertook, if the instalments were promptly paid, not
to require repayment in any other way.

---

[4] Restraint of trade was also pleaded, at p. 566.

The plaintiffs claimed, less than six years later, that they were entitled to redeem on payment of all principal, interest and costs, on the ground that, in so far as the term prevented them from redeeming on making such payments, it was illegal and void as a clog on their right to redeem and that it rendered the mortgage irredeemable for an undue length of time.

Held (reversing Luxmoore J [1938] Ch 741, [1938] 2 All ER 444). The plaintiffs were bound by the agreement and could only redeem in accordance with its terms.

Sir Wilfrid Greene MR: We will deal first with the arguments originally presented on behalf of the respondents. The first argument was that the postponement of the contractual right to redeem for forty years was void in itself, in other words, that the making of such an agreement between mortgagor and mortgagee was prohibited by a rule of equity. It was not contended that a provision in a mortgage deed making the mortgage irredeemable for a period of years is necessarily void. The argument was that such a period must be a "reasonable" one, and it was said that the period in the present case was an unreasonable one by reason merely of its length. This argument was not the one accepted by the learned judge.

Now an argument such as this requires the closest scrutiny, for, if it is correct, it means that an agreement made between two competent parties, acting under expert advice and presumably knowing their own business best, is one which the law forbids them to make upon the ground that it is not "reasonable". If we were satisfied that the rule of equity was what it is said to be, we should be bound to give effect to it. But in the absence of compelling authority we are not prepared to say that such an agreement cannot lawfully be made. A decision to that effect would, in our view, involve an unjustified interference with the freedom of business men to enter into agreements best suited to their interests and would impose upon them a test of "reasonableness" laid down by the Courts without reference to the business realities of the case.

It is important to remember what those realities were. The respondents are a private company and do not enjoy the facilities for raising money by a public issue possessed by public companies. They were the owners of a large and valuable block of property, and so far as we know they had no other assets. The property was subject to a mortgage at a high rate of interest and this mortgage was liable to be called in at any time. In these circumstances the respondents were, when the negotiations began, desirous of obtaining for themselves two advantages: (1) a reduction in the rate of interest, (2) the right to repay the mortgage moneys by instalments spread over a long period of years. The desirability of obtaining these terms from a business point of view is manifest, and it is not to be assumed that these respondents were actuated by anything but pure considerations of business in seeking to obtain them. The sum involved was a very large one, and the length of the period over which the instalments were spread is to be considered with reference to this fact. In the circumstances it was the most natural thing in the world that the respondents should address themselves to a body desirous of obtaining a long term investment for its money. The resulting agreement was a commercial agreement between two important corporations experienced in such matters, and has none of the features of an oppressive bargain where the borrower is at the mercy of an unscrupulous lender. In transactions of this kind it is notorious that there is competition among the large insurance companies and other bodies having large funds to invest, and we are not prepared to view the agreement made as anything but a proper business transaction.

But it is said not only that the period of postponement must be a reasonable one, but that in judging the "reasonableness" of the period the considerations which we have mentioned cannot be regarded; that the Court is bound to judge "reasonableness" by a consideration of the terms of the mortgage deed itself and without regard to extraneous matters. In the absence of clear authority we emphatically decline to consider a question of "reasonableness" from a standpoint so unreal. To hold that the law is to tell business men what is reasonable in such circumstances and to refuse to take into account the business considerations involved, would bring the law into disrepute. Fortunately we do not find ourselves forced to come to any such conclusion. . . .

Assuming therefore, without in any way deciding, that the period during which the contractual right of redemption is postponed must be a "reasonable" one (a question which we will now proceed to examine), we are of the opinion that the respondents have failed to establish (and the burden is on them) that there is anything unreasonable in the mere extension of the period for forty years in the circumstances of the present case.

But in our opinion the proposition that a postponement of the contractual right of redemption is only permissible for a "reasonable" time is not well-founded. Such a postponement is not properly described as a clog on the equity of redemption, since it is concerned with the contractual right to redeem. It is indisputable that any provision which hampers redemption after the contractual date for redemption has passed will not be permitted. Further, it is undoubtedly true to say that a right of redemption is a necessary element in a mortgage transaction, and consequently that, where the contractual right of redemption is illusory, equity will grant relief by allowing redemption. This was the point in the case of *Fairclough v Swan Brewery Co Ltd* [1912] AC 565. . . .

Moreover, equity may give relief against contractual terms in a mortgage transaction if they are oppressive or unconscionable, and in deciding whether or not a particular transaction falls within this category the length of time for which the contractual right to redeem is postponed may well be an important consideration. In the present case no question of this kind was or could have been raised.

But equity does not reform mortgage transactions because they are unreasonable. It is concerned to see two things — one that the essential requirements of a mortgage transaction are observed, and the other that oppressive or unconscionable terms are not enforced. Subject to this, it does not, in our opinion, interfere. The question therefore arises whether, in a case where the right of redemption is real and not illusory and there is nothing oppressive or unconscionable in the transaction, there is something in a postponement of the contractual right to redeem, such as we have in the present case, that is inconsistent with the essential requirements of a mortgage transaction? Apart from authority the answer to this question would, in our opinion, be clearly in the negative. Any other answer would place an unfortunate restriction on the liberty of contract of competent parties who are at arm's length — in the present case it would have operated to prevent the respondents obtaining financial terms which for obvious reasons they themselves considered to be most desirable. It would, moreover, lead to highly inequitable results. The remedy sought by the respondents and the only remedy which is said to be open to them is the establishment of a right to redeem at any time on the ground that the postponement of the contractual right to redeem is void. They do not and could not suggest that the contract as a contract is affected, and the result would accordingly be that whereas the respondents would have had from the first the right to redeem at any time, the appellants would have had no right to require payment otherwise than by the specified instalments. Such an outcome to a bargain entered into by business people negotiating at arm's length would indeed be unfortunate, and we should require clear authority before coming to such a conclusion.

We will now turn to the relevant authorities cited in argument by counsel for the parties. The first in order of date is *Talbot v Braddill* (1683) 1 Vern 183. [His Lordship referred also to *Cowdry v Day* (1859) 1 Giff 316; *Teevan v Smith* (1882) 20 ChD 724; *Biggs v Hoddinott* [1898] 2 Ch 307 at 311, p. 669, post; *Bradley v Carritt* [1903] AC 253, p. 672, post; *Williams v Morgan* [1906] 1 Ch 804; *Morgan v Jeffreys* [1910] 1 Ch 620; and *Davis v Symons* [1934] Ch 442, and continued:]

The second ground upon which the respondents endeavoured to support the judgment of the Court below was that the postponement of the contractual right to redeem for a period of forty years offended the rule against perpetuities and was therefore invalid. The learned judge decided against the respondents on this question and in our judgment rightly.

———————

This decision was affirmed on appeal to the House of Lords [1940] AC 613, [1940] 2 All ER 401, on the ground that the mortgage was a debenture within the meaning of the Companies Act 1929, section 380[5] and, as such and by virtue of section 74 of that Act, not invalid by reason of postponement of the date for redemption. No views were expressed in the House of Lords on the reasoning of the Court of Appeal.

———————

In *Kreglinger v New Patagonia Meat and Cold Storage Co Ltd* [1914] AC 25, Lord PARKER said at 53:

"My Lords, I desire, in connection with what I have just said, to add a few words on the maxims in which attempts have been made to sum up the equitable principles applicable to mortgage transactions. I refer to the maxims, 'Once a mortgage, always a mortgage', or, 'A mortgage cannot be made irredeemable'. Such maxims, however convenient, afford little assistance where the Court has to deal with a new or doubtful case. They obviously beg the question, always of great importance, whether the particular transaction which the Court has to consider is, in fact, a mortgage or not, and if they be acted on without a careful consideration of the equitable considerations on which they are based, can only, like Bacon's idols of the market place, lead to misconception and error.

We will suppose that money is advanced to a company repayable at the expiration of fifteen years, not an unusual period, and that the company by

---

[5] Now Companies Act 1985, s. 193.

way of security subdemises (as is often the case) to trustees for the lenders a number of leaseholds, some of which are held for terms less than fifteen years. It would, in my opinion, be a serious error to argue that this was an attempt to make an irredeemable mortgage. There would be the same error in objecting on the like ground to a mortgage of leaseholds to secure an annuity for a period exceeding the term of the lease. If the mortgage is irredeemable at all, this arises from the nature of the property mortgaged, and not from any penal or repugnant stipulation on the part of the mortgagee, and the maxim properly understood is in no way infringed."

QUESTION

X owned a 99-year lease in Blackacre. He wished to raise £100,000 in order to develop the land. His calculations showed that once the buildings were erected — estimated at 5 years — the income from the land would allow him to pay interest on the loan at 8% and repay £1,000 of the capital each year. As the capital outstanding and thus the interest payable each year was reduced, a sum, increasing annually, would be available for himself. His expectation was that interest rates would rise.

With this plan in mind, he suggested to Y that he borrow £100,000 at 8%, the capital repayable at the rate of £1,000 per annum starting five years hence, and £2,000 per annum in the last six years of the lease. Y agreed, saying that the repayment of capital was longer delayed than he wished, but that he was happy to help X.

Interest rates then declined to 6½%. X claimed to be entitled to pay off the capital forthwith, on the ground that the terms of the mortgage made it irredeemable and therefore void.

Will he succeed? What assistance could Y obtain from (a) *Knightsbridge Estates Trust Ltd v Byrne*; from (b) *Santley v Wilde?*

iii.   COLLATERAL ADVANTAGES EXISTING AFTER REDEMPTION

The cases in this section show how modifications have been made in recent times to the strict rule that an advantage or benefit collateral to the mortgage and in favour of the mortgagee is void in so far as it is to continue after redemption. A covenant is collateral where an obligation is placed on the mortgagor which is independent of that for the performance of which the land is charged. *Biggs v Hoddinott* [1898] 2 Ch 307 held that such a collateral advantage was valid if it was to exist only until redemption; but covenants drafted so as to exist beyond redemption were struck down in *Noakes & Co Ltd v Rice* [1902] AC 24 and *Bradley v Carritt* [1903] AC 253, even though in the latter case the covenant was not of such a type that it could in any circumstances "run with" the property mortgaged. Inevitably the situation arose in which the strict application of this rule was not consistent with contemporary business requirements; and the speeches of Lords HALDANE and PARKER in *Kreglinger v New Patagonia Meat and Cold Storage Co Ltd*[6] [1914] AC 25 show that the law has managed to conform both to the requirements of the day and to the precedents and rules of earlier times.

---

[6] Followed in *Cityland and Property (Holdings) Ltd v Dabrah* [1968] Ch 166, [1967] 2 All ER 639, p. 678, post.

The most common method of reconciling the *Kreglinger* case with *Noakes &
Co Ltd v Rice* and *Bradley v Carritt*, is to construe the covenant to sell the skins
in the *Kreglinger* case as being a "contract, contained in the same document
as constituted the security, but in substance independent of it"'. Once it is so
construed it must stand or fall on its own merits. It is difficult to see why a
commercial contract, which is in itself valid, should become void because it is
recorded in the same document as a mortgage. Where it can be construed as
separate from the mortgage, the position is as if it were entered into on
Monday and the mortgage on Tuesday[8]; the two are separate and incapable
of affecting each other. It has already been seen that a covenant to do
something other than repay principal, interest and costs may be part of the
obligation for the performance of which the mortgage is given to secure; and
a covenant of this type is not a 'collateral advantage' and cannot be affected
by these rules[9]. Whether or not a contract is (i) part of the mortgage security,
as in *Santley v Wilde*, (ii) entirely independent of the mortgage transaction, as
in the *Kreglinger* case, or (iii) part of the mortgage transaction without being
part of the security, as in *Noakes & Co Ltd v Rice* and *Bradley v Carritt*, is a
question of construction in each particular case. If the contract is of types (i)
or (ii), it is not affected by the rules relating to collateral advantages. If it is of
type (iii), which is in its nature between types (i) and (ii), then it is subjected
to the authority of the cases declaring collateral advantages to be void. The
selection of the correct category for any particular contract is a question for
the court in each particular case, but the way is at least open now to the
courts to permit the enforcement of bona fide business deals by construing
them as falling outside the authority of *Noakes & Co Ltd v Rice* and *Bradley v
Carritt*.

BIGGS *v* HODDINOTT
[1898] 2 Ch 307 (CA, LINDLEY MR, CHITTY and COLLINS LJJ)

On 18 March 1896, the defendant Hoddinott, the owner of a public house,
mortgaged it to Biggs, a brewer. The deed contained an undertaking by
Hoddinott that during the continuance of the mortgage he would deal with
only the plaintiff in his purchase of certain liquor; an undertaking by the
plaintiff that during the continuance of the mortgage he would supply such
liquor at the scheduled prices; and a provision that redemption should not
take place, nor should the money be called in, for five years. About two years
later, the defendant ceased to purchase liquor from the plaintiff who brought
this action for an injunction, and the defendant claimed to be entitled to
redeem the mortgage. ROMER J granted an injunction and refused to allow
the defendant to redeem. On appeal on the question of the issue of the
injunction.

Held. The covenant tying the public house during the continuance of the
mortgage was valid.

---

[7] Per Lord HALDANE at 41; *Re Petrol Filling Station, Vauxhall Bridge Road, London* (1969) 20
P & CR 1, p. 681, post.
[8] See Lord HALSBURY in *Samuel v Jarrah Timber and Wood Paving Corpn Ltd* [1904] AC 323, p. 660,
ante.
[9] Because it does not continue after redemption: *Santley v Wilde* [1899] 2 Ch 474, p. 662, ante.

LINDLEY MR: We have listened to a very ingenious and learned argument with the view of inducing us under pressure to lay down a proposition of law which would be very unfortunate for business men. The proposition contended for comes to this — that while two people are engaged in a mortgage transaction they cannot enter into any other transaction with each other which can possibly benefit the mortgagee, and that any such transaction must be before or after the mortgage and be independent of it, so that it cannot be said that the mortgagee got any additional benefit from the mortgage transaction. Mr Farwell did not attempt to uphold this on any rational principle, but relied on authority. Of course, we must follow settled authorities whether we like them or not; but do they support this proposition? *Jennings v Ward* (1705) 2 Vern 520 was the first case relied upon. That was a redemption suit, and the stipulation which was in question seriously interfered with the redemption of the mortgaged property, and the Master of the Rolls (Sir J. Trevor) decreed redemption without regard to that stipulation. He is reported to have said: "A man shall not have interest for his money, and a collateral advantage besides for the loan of it, or clog the redemption with any by-agreement." That has been understood as meaning exactly what was said, without regard to the circumstances of the case, and has found its way into the text-books as establishing that a mortgagee cannot have principal, interests, and costs, and also some collateral advantage. But that supposed rule has been departed from again and again. Take the case of West India mortgages: it has been repeatedly decided that the mortgagee, if not in possession, may stipulate that he shall be appointed consignee. The proposition stated in *Jennings v Ward* is too wide. If properly guarded it is good law and good sense. A mortgage is regarded as a security for money, and the mortgagor can always redeem on payment of principal, interest, and costs; and no bargain preventing such redemption is valid, nor will unconscionable bargains be enforced. There is no case where collateral advantages have been disallowed which does not come under one of these two heads. To say that to require such a covenant as that now in question is unconscionable is asking us to lay down a proposition which would shock any business man, and we are not driven to it by authority. . . .

The appeal will be dismissed.

NOAKES & CO LTD *v* RICE
[1902] AC 24 (HL, Earl of HALSBURY LC, Lords MACNAGHTEN, SHAND, DAVEY, BRAMPTON, ROBERTSON and LINDLEY)

Rice, the plaintiff, purchased, in 1897, the lease of a public house; the lease was to expire in 1923. Before this purchase, Noakes and Co, brewers, were mortgagees of the house and advanced money to Rice to enable him to purchase the leasehold premises which were mortgaged to them as security for the loan. Both this and the prior mortgage included a covenant, "so as to charge the premises into whose-soever possession the same may come . . . and to the further intent that the obligation of this covenant may run with the land" that the mortgagor would not, during the continuance of the lease, "whether any principal moneys or interest shall or shall not be owing" under the mortgage, use any liquor that had not been purchased from Noakes and Co. Provision was made for payment of liquidated damages in case of breach.

Rice now wished to pay off the loan and claimed to redeem the property free from the covenant tying the house.

Held. On payment of all that was due, the plaintiff could recover the property free from the tie.

LORD DAVEY: My Lords, there are three doctrines of the Courts of Equity in this country which have been referred to in the course of the argument in this case. The first doctrine to which I refer is expressed in the maxim, "Once a mortgage always a mortgage". The second is that the mortgagee shall not reserve to himself any collateral advantage outside the mortgage contract; and the third is that a provision or stipulation which will have the effect of clogging or fettering the equity of redemption is void.

My Lords, the first maxim presents no difficulty: it is only another way of saying that a mortgage cannot be made irredeemable, and that a provision to that effect is void. In the case of *Salt v Marquess of Northampton* [1892] AC 1 the question was whether a certain life policy, the premiums on which were charged against the mortgagor, was comprised in the mortgage security. That question having been decided in the affirmative, it was declared to be redeemable, notwithstanding an express provision to the contrary contained in the deed.

My Lords, the second doctrine to which I refer, namely that the mortgagee shall not reserve to himself any collateral advantage outside the mortgage contract, was established long ago when the usury laws were in force. The Court of Equity went beyond the usury laws, and set its face against every transaction which tended to usury. It therefore declared void every stipulation by a mortgagee for a collateral advantage which made his total remuneration for the loan indirectly exceed the legal interest. I think it will be found that every case under this head of equity was decided either on this ground, or on the ground that the bargain was oppressive and unconscionable. The abolition of the usury laws has made an alteration in the view the Court should take on this subject, and I agree that a collateral advantage may now be stipulated for by a mortgagee, provided that no unfair advantage be taken by the mortgagee which would render it void or voidable, according to the general principles of equity, and provided that it does not offend against the third doctrine. On these grounds I think the case of *Biggs v Hoddinott* [1898] 2 Ch 307 in the Court of Appeal was rightly decided.

The third doctrine to which I have referred is really a corollary from the first, and it might be expressed in this form: Once a mortgage always a mortgage and nothing but a mortgage. The meaning of that is that the mortgagee shall not make any stipulation which will prevent a mortgagor, who has paid principal, interest, and costs, from getting back his mortgaged property in the condition in which he parted with it. I do not dissent from the opinion expressed by my noble and learned friend opposite (Lord Lindley), when Master of the Rolls, in the case of *Santley v Wilde* [1899] 2 Ch 474. He says: "A clog or fetter is something which is inconsistent with the idea of security; a clog or fetter is in the nature of a repugnant condition." But I ask, "security" for what? I think it must be security for the principal, interest, and costs, and, I will add, for any advantages in the nature of increased interest or remuneration for the loan which the mortgagee has validly stipulated for during the continuance of the mortgage. There are two elements in the conception of a mortgage: first, security for the money advanced; and, secondly, remuneration for the use of the money. When the mortgage is paid off the security is at an end, and, as the mortgagee is no longer kept out of his money, the remuneration to him for the use of his money is also at an end. I confess I should have decided the case of *Santley v Wilde* differently from the way in which it was dealt with in the Court of Appeal. After the payment of principal and interest, and everything which had become payable up to the date of redemption, the property in that case remained charged with the payment to the mortgagee of one-third share of the profits, and the stipulation to that effect should, I think, have been held to be a clog or fetter on the right to redeem. The principle is this — that a mortgage must not be converted into something else; and when once you come to the conclusion that a stipulation for the benefit of the mortgagee is part of the mortgage transaction, it is but part of his security, and necessarily comes to an end on the payment off of the loan. In my opinion, every yearly or other recurring payment stipulated for by the mortgagee should be held to be in the nature of interest, and no more payable after the principal is paid off than interest would be. I apprehend a man could not stipulate for the continuance of payment of interest after the principal is paid, and I do not think he can stipulate for any other recurring payment such as a share of profits. Any stipulation to that effect, would, in my opinion be void as a clog or fetter on the equity of redemption.

LORD LINDLEY: The conclusion thus arrived at is not inconsistent with *Santley v Wilde* on which the appellants so strongly rely. Some of your Lordships think that case went too far. I do not think so myself; but I will not trouble your Lordships with its details, which were complicated. The principle on which the Court of Appeal decided the case was, I still think, sound. Whether it was properly applied in that case is now of no importance. I believe the true principle applicable to these cases to be that expounded by the Court of Appeal in *Biggs v Hoddinott* and *Santley v Wilde*. That principle is perfectly consistent with a real pledge and with the maxim "Once a mortgage always a mortgage"; but it will not render valid the covenant which your Lordships have to consider in the present case.

In *Bradley v Carritt* [1903] AC 253, one Bradley, who was the owner of a controlling number of shares in the Sephinjuri Bheel Tea Company, mortgaged them to Carritt, a tea broker, who wished to become the sole broker for the sale of the company's teas. By a written agreement, Bradley undertook, in clause 4, to use his "best endeavours to secure that [Carritt, the plaintiff] shall always hereafter have the sale of all the company's teas as broker; and, in the event of any of the company's teas being sold otherwise than through" Carritt, to pay to him the commission which he would have earned if they had been sold through him. After the mortgage was paid off, the shares were again mortgaged to a different mortgagee, who took advantage of his voting-power to oust the plaintiff from his position as broker of the company. Carritt sued to recover, as damages for breach of contract, the amount of the commission.

By a bare majority, Lords MACNAGHTEN, DAVEY and ROBERTSON, with Lords SHAND and LINDLEY dissenting, the House of Lords reversed BIGHAM J and the Court of Appeal and held that the covenant was void as a clog on the equity of redemption, and that no action therefore lay.

The covenant was one that on its terms continued after redemption. The main question was whether or not it was a clog on the equity of redemption. It differed in this respect from the covenant in *Noakes v Rice* [1902] AC 24, for the covenant in that case was one that directly affected the property mortgaged; the mortgagor, having mortgaged a free house, would on redemption have received back a tied house. In this case, however, the covenant did not run with the tea shares; as Lord LINDLEY said at 276: "Clause 4 in no way fetters the right to redeem, nor obstructs the mortgagor in the practical exercise of that right, or of the use or enjoyment of his shares when he gets them back. He can then do what he likes with them, free from all control by the mortgagee." Lord DAVEY said at 268: ". . . Can it be said that the mortgagee does not retain a hold upon the shares which form the mortgaged property, or that the mortgagor has full redemption of it, when the latter is not free to exercise an important right in such manner as he may think most conducive to his own interests? . . . Again, the appellant could not part with or otherwise deal with his shares without losing the influence in the company's counsels which might enable him to secure the performance of the first part of the agreement, or running a serious risk of liability under the second part."

The speeches show again the different views of Lords LINDLEY and DAVEY upon the principles involved in the question of collateral advantages in particular and of the protection of the mortgagor in general.

KREGLINGER *v* NEW PATAGONIA MEAT AND COLD STORAGE CO LTD
[1914] AC 25 (HL, Viscount HALDANE LC, EARL of HALSBURY, Lords ATKINSON, MERSEY and PARKER OF WADDINGTON)

The appellants, a firm of woolbrokers agreed to lend £10,000 to the respondents, a firm of meat packers. Provided all interest was paid punctually and all the terms of the agreement observed, the appellants agreed not to call in the principal for five years, but the respondents were at liberty to pay off the loan whenever they wished. The loan was secured by a floating charge on the respondents' undertaking. Clause 8 of the agreement provided in sub-clause (A) that the respondents would not, for a period of five years, "sell any sheepskins to any person . . . other than the lenders so long as the lenders are willing to purchase the same at a price equal to the best price . . . offered . . . by any . . . other person . . .". Sub-clause (C) provided that the respondent company "will pay to the lenders a commission of 1% upon the sale price of all sheepskins sold by the company" to anyone other than the lenders.

After a few months over two years the respondents paid off the loan in accordance with the terms of the agreement, and disputed the right of the appellants to exercise their option to purchase the sheepskins. The appellants brought an action for an injunction to restrain the sale of sheepskins to other persons.

Held (reversing SWINFEN EADY J and the Court of Appeal (COZENS-HARDY MR, BUCKLEY and KENNEDY LJJ) (1913) 29 TLR 393; 464). Appellants entitled to an injunction.

VISCOUNT HALDANE LC: My Lords, the respondents have now, as they were entitled to do under the agreement, paid off the loan. They claim that such payment has put an end to the option of the appellants to buy the respondents' sheepskins. Under the terms of the agreement this option, as I have already stated, will, if it is valid, continue operative until 24 August 1915. What the respondents say is that the stipulation is one that restricts their freedom in conducting the undertaking or business which is the subject of the floating charge; that it was consequently of the nature of a clog on their right to redeem and invalid; and that, whether it clogged the right to redeem or was in the nature of a collateral advantage, it was not intended and could not be made to endure after redemption. The appellants, on the other hand, say that the stipulation in question was one of a kind usual in business, and that it was in the nature not of a clog but of a collateral bargain outside the actual loan, which they only agreed to make in order to obtain the option itself. They further say that even if the option could be regarded as within the doctrine of equity which forbids the clogging of the right to redeem, that doctrine does not in a case such as this extend to a floating charge. . . .

My Lords, before I refer to the decisions of this House which the Courts below have considered to cover the case, I will state what I conceive to be the broad principles which must govern it.

The reason for which a Court of Equity will set aside the legal title of a mortgagee and compel him to reconvey the land on being paid principal, interest, and costs is a very old one. . . .

The principle was . . . in the early days limited in its application to the accomplishment of the end which was held to justify interference of equity with freedom of contract. It did not go further. As established it was expressed in three ways. The most general of these was that if the transaction was once found to be a mortgage, it must be treated as always remaining a mortgage and nothing but a mortgage. That the substance of the transaction must be looked to in applying this doctrine and that it did not apply to cases which were only apparently or technically within it but were in reality something more than cases of mortgage, *Howard v Harris* (1683) 1 Vern 190 and other authorities shew. It was only a different application of the paramount doctrine to lay it down in the form of a second rule that a mortgagee should not stipulate for a collateral advantage which would make his remuneration for the loan exceed a proper rate of interest. The Legislature during a long period placed restrictions on the rate of interest which could legally be exacted. But equity went beyond the limits of the statutes which limited the interest, and was ready to interfere with any usurious stipulation in a mortgage. In so doing it was influenced by the public policy of the time. That policy has now changed, and the Acts which limited the rate of interest have been repealed. The result is that a collateral advantage may now be stipulated for by the mortgagee provided that he has not acted unfairly or oppressively, and provided that the bargain does not conflict with the third form of the principle. This is that a mortgage . . . cannot be made irredeemable, and that any stipulation which restricts or clogs the equity of redemption is void. It is obvious that the reason for the doctrine in this form is the same as that which gave rise to the other forms. It is simply an assertion in a different way of the principle that once a mortgage always a mortgage and nothing else.

My Lords, the rules I have stated have now been applied by Courts of Equity for nearly three centuries, and the books are full of illustrations of their application. But what I have pointed out shews that it is inconsistent with the objects for which they were established that these rules should crystallize into technical language so rigid that the letter can defeat the underlying spirit and purpose. Their application must correspond with the practical necessities of the time. The rule as to collateral advantages, for example, has been much modified by the repeal of the usury laws and by the recognition of modern varieties of commercial bargaining. . . .

[His Lordship referred to *Biggs v Hoddinott* [1898] 2 Ch 307 and to the dictum of TREVOR MR in *Jennings v Ward* (1705) 2 Vern 520 and continued:]

Unless such a bargain is unconscionable it is now good. But none the less the other and wider principle remains unshaken, that it is the essence of a mortgage that in the eye of a Court of Equity it should be a mere security for money, and that no bargain can be validly made which will prevent the mortgagor from redeeming on payment of what is due including principal, interest, and costs. He may stipulate that he will not pay off his debt, and so redeem the mortgage, for a fixed period. But whenever a right to redeem arises out of the doctrine of equity, he is precluded from fettering it. This principle has become an integral part of our system of jurisprudence and must be faithfully adhered to.

My Lords, the question in the present case is whether the right to redeem has been interfered with. And this must, for the reasons to which I have adverted in considering the history of the doctrine of equity, depend on the answer to a question which is primarily one of fact. What was the true character of the transaction? Did the appellants make a bargain such that the right to redeem was cut down, or did they simply stipulate for a collateral undertaking, outside and clear of the mortgage, which would give them an exclusive option of purchase of the sheepskins of the respondents? The question is in my opinion not whether the two contracts were made at the same moment and evidenced by the same instrument, but whether they were in substance a single and undivided contract or two distinct contracts. Putting aside for the moment considerations turning on the character of the floating charge, such an option no doubt affects the freedom of the respondents in carrying on their business even after the mortgage has been paid off. But so might other arrangements which would be plainly collateral, an agreement, for example, to take permanently into the firm a new partner as a condition of obtaining fresh capital in the form of a loan. The question is one not of form but of substance, and it can be answered in each case by looking at all the circumstances, and not by mere reliance on some abstract principle, or upon the dicta which have fallen obiter from judges in other and different cases. . . .

My Lords, if in the case before the House your Lordships arrive at the conclusion that the agreement for an option to purchase the respondents' sheepskins was not in substance a fetter on the exercise of their right to redeem, but was in the nature of a collateral bargain the entering into which was a preliminary and separable condition of the loan, the decided cases cease to present any great difficulty. In questions of this kind the binding force of previous decisions, unless the facts are indistinguishable, depends on whether they establish a principle. To follow previous authorities, so far as they lay down principles, is essential if the law is to be preserved from becoming unsettled and vague. In this respect the previous decisions of a Court of co-ordinate jurisdiction are more binding in a system of jurisprudence such as ours than in systems where the paramount authority is that of a code. But when a previous case has not laid down any new principle but has merely decided that a particular set of facts illustrates an existing rule, there are few more fertile sources of fallacy than to search in it for what is simply resemblance in circumstances, and to erect a previous decision into a governing precedent merely on this account. To look for anything except the principle established or recognized by previous decisions is really to weaken and not to strengthen the importance of precedent. . . .

It is not, in my opinion, conclusive in favour of the appellants that the security assumed the form of a floating charge. A floating charge is not the less a pledge because of its floating character, and a contract which fetters the right to redeem on which equity insists as regards all contracts of loan and security ought on principle to be set aside as readily in the case of a floating security as in any other case. But it is material that such a floating charge, in the absence of bargain to the contrary effect, permits the assets to be dealt with freely by the mortgagor until the charge becomes enforceable[10]. . . . No doubt it is the fact that on redemption the respondents will not get back their business as free from obligation as it was before the date of the security. But that may well be because outside the security and consistently with its terms there was a contemporaneous but collateral contract, contained in the same document as constituted the security, but in substance independent of it. If it was the intention of the parties, as I think it was, to enter into this contract as a condition of the respondents getting their advance, I know no reason either in morals or in equity which ought to prevent this intention from being left to have its effect. What was to be capable of redemption was an undertaking which was deliberately left to be freely changed in its details by ordinary business transactions with which the mortgage was not to interfere. Had the charge not been a floating one, it might have been more difficult to give effect to this intention.

[His Lordship referred to *Noakes & Co Ltd v Rice* [1902] AC 24, p. 670, ante, where "this difficulty is illustrated" and to *Bradley v Carritt* [1903] AC 253, p. 672, ante, and continued:]

[The decision in *Bradley v Carritt*] certainly cannot, in my opinion, be taken as authoritatively laying down that the mere circumstance that after redemption the property redeemed may not, as the result of some bargain made at the time of the mortgage, be in the same condition as it was before that time, is conclusive against the validity of that bargain. To render it invalid the bargain must, when its substance is examined, turn out to have formed part of the terms of the mortgage and to have really cut down a true right of redemption. I think that the tendency of recent decisions has been to lay undue stress on the letter of the principle which limits the jurisdiction of equity in setting aside contracts. The origin and reason of the principle ought, as I have already said, to be kept steadily in view in applying it to fresh cases. There appears to me to have grown up a tendency to look to the letter rather than to the spirit of the doctrine. The true view is, I think, that judges ought in this kind of jurisdiction to proceed cautiously, and to bear in mind the real reasons which have led Courts of Equity to insist on the free right to redeem and the limits within which the purpose of the rule ought to confine its scope. I cannot but think that the validity of the bargain in such cases as *Bradley v Carritt* and *Santley v Wilde* [1899] 2 Ch 474, p. 662, ante,

---

[10] See (1976) 40 Conv (NS) 397 (J. H. Farrar).

might have been made free from serious question if the parties had chosen to seek what would have been substantially the same result in a different form. . . .

LORD PARKER OF WADDINGTON: My Lords, the defendants in this case are appealing to the equitable jurisdiction of the Court for relief from a contract which they admit to be fair and reasonable and of which they have already enjoyed the full advantage. Their title to relief is based on some equity which they say is inherent in all transactions in the nature of a mortgage. They can state no intelligible principle underlying this alleged equity, but contend that your Lordships are bound by authority. That the Court should be asked in the exercise of its equitable jurisdiction to assist in so inequitable a proceeding as the repudiation of a fair and reasonable bargain is somewhat startling, and makes it necessary to examine the point of view from which Courts of Equity have always regarded mortgage transactions. . . .

My Lords, after the most careful consideration of the authorities I think it is open to this House to hold, and I invite your Lordships to hold, that there is now no rule in equity which precludes a mortgagee, whether the mortgage be made upon the occasion of a loan or otherwise, from stipulating for any collateral advantage, provided such collateral advantage is not either (1) unfair and unconscionable, or (2) in the nature of a penalty clogging the equity of redemption, or (3) inconsistent with or repugnant to the contractual and equitable right to redeem.

In the present case it is clear from the evidence, if not from the agreement of 24 August 1910 itself, that the nature of the transaction was as follows: The defendant company wanted to borrow 10,000*l*, and the plaintiffs desired to obtain an option of purchase over any sheepskins the defendants might have for sale during a period of five years. The plaintiffs agreed to lend the money in consideration of obtaining this option, and the defendant company agreed to give the option in consideration of obtaining the loan. The loan was to carry interest at 6 per cent per annum, and was not to be called in by the plaintiffs for a specified period. The defendant company, however, might pay it off at any time. It was to be secured by a floating charge over the defendant company's undertaking. The option was to continue for five years, whether the loan was paid off or otherwise, and if the plaintiffs did not exercise their option as to any of the defendant company's skins, a commission on the sale of such skins was in certain events payable to the plaintiffs.

I doubt whether, even before the repeal of the usury laws, this perfectly fair and businesslike transaction would have been considered a mortgage within any equitable rule or maxim relating to mortgages. The only possible way of deciding whether a transaction is a mortgage within any such rule or maxim is by reference to the intention of the parties. It never was intended by the parties that if the defendant company exercised their right to pay off the loan they should get rid of the option. The option was not in the nature of a penalty, nor was it nor could it ever become inconsistent with or repugnant to any other part of the real bargain within any such rule or maxim. The same is true of the commission payable on the sale of skins as to which the option was not exercised. Under these circumstances it seems to me that the bargain must stand and that the plaintiffs are entitled to the relief they claim[11].

---

[11] (1944) 60 LQR 191 (G. L. Williams).

In *Multiservice Bookbinding Ltd v Marden* [1979] Ch 84, [1978] 2 All ER 489[12], the plaintiffs in September 1966 charged their business premises to the defendant as security for a loan of £36,000, in order to purchase new premises in North London. The defendant was only willing to lend the money if he could be safeguarded against a decline in the purchasing power of sterling. The terms of the mortgage, which was created with solicitors' advice, were that (i) interest be payable at 2 per cent above bank rate on the full capital sum for the duration of the mortgage (ii) arrears of interest be capitalised after 21 days (thus providing for interest on interest) (iii) the loan be neither called in nor redeemed for 10 years, and (iv) the value of the capital and interest be index-linked to the Swiss franc ("the Swiss franc uplift" clause 6).

In September 1966 the Swiss franc was just over 12 to the pound but in October 1976, when a redemption statement was prepared, it had fallen to just over 4. The total capital repayment was £87,588, as against £36,000 lent, and the total interest due was £45,380 (£31,051 basic plus £14,329 uplift). The average rate of interest over the ten years would have been 16.01 per cent. On the other hand, the book value of the mortgaged property had more than doubled, and the plaintiff company's "growth had been considerable".

The plaintiffs took out a summons to determine how far the terms of the mortgage were enforceable. BROWNE-WILKINSON J held that all terms were valid. Having decided that an index-linked money obligation is not contrary to public policy, he continued at 109, at 501:

"I have dealt with these authorities [*Kreglinger v New Patagonia Meat and Cold Storage Co Ltd* [1914] AC 25, p. 673, ante; *Knightsbridge Estates Trust Ltd v Byrne* [1939] Ch 441, [1938] 4 All ER 618, p. 664, ante; *Biggs v Hoddinott* [1898] 2 Ch 307, p. 669, ante; *Davis v Symons* [1934] Ch 442] at some length because the sheet anchor of Mr Nugee's argument, that mere unreasonableness is sufficient to invalidate a stipulation, is the use of the word 'unreasonable' by Goff J in *Cityland and Property (Holdings) Ltd v Dabrah* [1968] Ch 166, [1967] 2 All ER 639. In that case the plaintiff company was the freehold owner of a house of which the defendant had been the tenant for 11 years. His lease expired and the plaintiff company sold the freehold to him for £3,500, of which the defendant paid £600 in cash and the balance of £2,900 was left by the plaintiff company on mortgage. The mortgage was in unusual terms in that it contained simply a covenant to pay, by instalments, the sum of £4,553, that is to say, a premium of 57 per cent over the sum advanced. No explanation was given as to what this premium represented. The defendant defaulted in paying his instalments after only one year, and the plaintiff was seeking to enforce his security for the full sum of £4,553 less payments actually made. Not surprisingly Goff J refused to permit this on the grounds that the excess over £2,900 was an unlawful premium. Bearing in mind the relative strength of lender and borrower, the size of the premium and the lack of any explanation or justification for it, the premium in that case was unconscionable and oppressive. . . .

I therefore approach the second point on the basis that, in order to be freed from the necessity to comply with all the terms of the mortgage, the plaintiffs must show that the bargain, or some of its terms, was unfair and unconscionable: it is not enough to show that, in the eyes of the court, it was

---

[12] [1978] Conv 346 (H. W. Wilkinson); 432 (D. W. Williams); and for an economist's view (1981) 131 NLJ 4 (R. A. Bowles). The Consumer Credit Act 1974, p. 682, post, was not applicable because the mortgagor was a body corporate.

unreasonable. In my judgment a bargain cannot be unfair and unconscionable unless one of the parties to it has imposed the objectionable terms in a morally reprehensible manner, that is to say, in a way which affects his conscience.

The classic example of an unconscionable bargain is where advantage has been taken of a young, inexperienced or ignorant person to introduce a term which no sensible well-advised person or party would have accepted. But I do not think the categories of unconscionable bargains are limited: the court can and should intervene where a bargain has been procured by unfair means.

Mr Nugee submitted that a borrower was, in the normal case, in an unequal bargaining position vis-à-vis the lender and that the care taken by the courts of equity to protect borrowers — to which Lord Parker referred in the passage I have quoted[12a] — was reflected in a general rule that, except in the case of two large equally powerful institutions, any unreasonable term would be 'unconscionable' within Lord Parker's test. I cannot accept this. In my judgment there is no such special rule applicable to contracts of loan which requires one to treat a bargain as having been unfairly made even where it is demonstrated that no unfair advantage has been taken of the borrower. No decision illustrating Mr Nugee's principle was cited. However, if, as in the *Cityland* case, there is an unusual or unreasonable stipulation the reason for which is not explained, it may well be that in the absence of any explanation, the court will assume that unfair advantage has been taken of the borrower. In considering all the facts, it will often be the case that the borrower's need for the money was far more pressing than the lender's need to lend: if this proves to be the case, then circumstances exist in which an unfair advantage could have been taken. It does not necessarily follow that what could have been done has been done: whether or not an unfair advantage has in fact been taken depends on the facts of each case.

Applying those principles to this case, first I do not think it is right to treat the 'Swiss franc uplift' element in the capital-repayments as being in any sense a premium or collateral advantage. In my judgment a lender of money is entitled to insure that he is repaid the real value of his loan and if he introduces a term which so provides, he is not stipulating for anything beyond the repayment of principal. I do not think equity would have struck down clause 6 as a collateral advantage even before the repeal of the usury laws. . . .

Secondly, considering the mortgage bargain as a whole, in my judgment there was no great inequality of bargaining power as between the plaintiffs and the defendant. The plaintiff company was a small but prosperous company in need of cash to enable it to expand: if it did not like the terms offered it could have refused them without being made insolvent or, as in the *Cityland* case, losing its home. The defendant had £40,000 to lend, but only, as he explained to the plaintiffs, if its real value was preserved. The defendant is not a professional moneylender and there is no evidence of any sharp practice of any kind by him. The borrowers were represented by independent solicitors of repute. Therefore the background does not give rise to any presupposition that the defendant took an unfair advantage of the plaintiffs.

Mr Nugee's main case is based on the terms of the mortgage itself. He points to the facts that (1) the defendant's principal and interest is fully

---

[12a] *Kreglinger v New Patagonia Meat and Cold Storage Co Ltd* [1914] AC 25 at 49–50, 54–56.

inflation proofed (2) that interest is payable at two per cent above minimum lending rate and (3) that interest is payable on the whole £36,000 throughout the term of the loan. He says that although any one of these provisions by itself might not be objectionable, when all these are joined in one mortgage they are together 'unfair and unconscionable.' He adds further subsidiary points, amongst them that it is impossible to know the sum required for redemption when notice to redeem has to be given; that interest is payable in advance; that no days of grace were allowed for paying the instalments of capital and any expenses incurred by the lender are charged on the property and therefore under clause 6 subject to the Swiss franc uplift even though incurred long after 1966. He also contends that if there were capitalised arrears of interest, the Swiss franc uplift would be applied twice: once when the arrears are capitalised and again when the capitalised sum is paid: in my opinion this is not the true construction of the mortgage.

However, Mr Nugee's other points amount to a formidable list and if it were relevant I would be of the view that the terms were unreasonable judged by the standards which the court would adopt if it had to settle the terms of a mortgage. In particular I consider that it was unreasonable both for the debt to be inflation proofed by reference to the Swiss franc and at the same time to provide for a rate of interest two per cent above bank rate — a rate which reflects at least in part the unstable state of the pound sterling. On top of this interest on the whole sum advanced was to be paid throughout the term. The defendant made a hard bargain. But the test is not reasonableness. The parties made a bargain which the plaintiffs, who are businessmen, went into with their eyes open, with the benefit of independent advice, without any compelling necessity to accept a loan on these terms and without any sharp practice by the defendant. I cannot see that there was anything unfair or oppressive or morally reprehensible in such a bargain entered into in such circumstances. The need for the defendant to invest his money in a way which preserved its real purchasing power provides an adequate explanation of all the terms of the mortgage[13]."

The problem has also arisen in connection with the distribution of petroleum products through tied garages. In general terms, the garage proprietor undertakes to deal only in the products of a particular oil company. The oil company undertakes to supply the products and to allow a special rebate. Sometimes the oil company advances money to the garage proprietor, and in such a case the mortgage of the garage will include an undertaking to observe the terms of the agreement during the continuance of the mortgage.

A garage proprietor who wishes to pay off the mortgage before the due date and to be free of its provisions may attack its validity on two grounds. First, on the ground of the doctrine, previously discussed, which protects a mortgagor against oppression. Secondly, on the ground that the agreement is void as being in restraint of trade. This second ground is a matter for the law of contract and its details must be sought elsewhere[14]. We should, however,

---

[13] A building society has power to make an index-linked mortgage: *Nationwide Building Society v Registry of Friendly Societies* [1983] 1 WLR 1226, [1983] 3 All ER 296.

[14] Cheshire and Fifoot, *Law of Contract* (10th edn, 1981), pp. 351–360; Treitel, *Law of Contract* (6th edn, 1983), pp. 341–361; (1969) 85 LQR 229 (J. D. Heydon); Heydon, *Restraint of Trade Doctrine* (1971), chaps. 3, 9.

note here an argument that the doctrine of restraint of trade has no application to mortgages; that the mortgagor, being especially protected by equity, has equity's protection but no other. As would be expected, this argument has not been accepted[15].

Thus a mortgage is open to attack on both grounds. The two grounds must be kept distinct, for different evidence is relevant to each, and different rules are applicable; and, following the doctrine of the *Kreglinger* case, the court may consider whether an operation is properly construed as a single transaction or as two separate transactions; one being a mortgage which is governed by the doctrine here discussed, and the other being a commercial agreement which is dealt with under the doctrine of restraint of trade.

RE PETROL FILLING STATION, VAUXHALL BRIDGE ROAD, LONDON
(1968) 20 P & CR 1 (ChD, UNGOED-THOMAS J)

The plaintiffs were owners of a petrol filling station, and entered into a twenty year contract on 9 April 1956 with the defendants, whereby the plaintiffs agreed to sell only the defendants' products, and were entitled to a rebate on the price in addition to the usual commission.

On 1 November 1956 the plaintiffs mortgaged their garage to the defendants in consideration of a loan which was required for the modernisation of the premises. The mortgage deed:
(1) provided for the repayment of the loan over nineteen years;
(2) gave the defendants (the mortgagees) a right of pre-emption over the premises during the continuance of the mortgage;
(3) provided that the term of the contract of 9 April 1956 tying the petrol station should remain in force during the continuance of the mortgage.

The question was whether the plaintiffs were entitled to redeem, and to be free of the restrictions contained in the contract and the mortgage.

Held. The plaintiffs were bound by the terms of the mortgage.

UNGOED-THOMAS J: It is common ground that the ties in the November agreement are, in accordance with its express provisions, limited to the continuance of the security and that, therefore, on redemption they cease to operate and no question of clog can arise with regard to them. It is also common ground that the ties contained in the sales agreement are capable of constituting a clog on an equity of redemption if they are (and I purposely use vague words) sufficiently connected with it. Therefore, the only question for my decision becomes whether the ties imposed by the sales agreement of April are sufficiently connected with the equity of redemption of the legal charge of November as to constitute a clog upon it. . . .

If, in accordance with my view, the plaintiffs executed the sales agreement without there being any contract with regard to the loan, then it seems to me to follow that the sales agreement and the legal charge were what they appear on their face to be, namely, two separate contracts. Such a conclusion would be in line with the reliance, based on *De Beer's Consolidated Mines Ltd v British South Africa Co* [1912] AC 52, on the British South Africa Company's

---

[15] *Esso Petroleum Co Ltd v Harper's Garage (Stourport) Ltd* [1968] AC 269, [1967] 1 All ER 699, per Lord WILBERFORCE at 342, at 735; *Alec Lobb (Garages) Ltd v Total Oil Great Britain Ltd* [1985] 1 WLR 173, [1985] 1 All ER 303, p. 661, n. 19, ante; [1985] Conv 141 (P. Todd).

obligation to grant the licence being absolute and immediate and their granting of the mortgage being optional. This distinction in that case was relied on as itself establishing that there were two contracts, one with regard to the licence and one with regard to the mortgage, and not one contract comprehending them both.

Secondly, even if there were, contrary to my view, a binding contract with regard to the loan and with regard to the sales agreement before or at the time of the sales agreement, the question would still remain whether they constituted one or two contracts. Having regard to authorities and the evidence, which I have already considered, including the commercial nature of the ties in the sales agreement, it seems to me that at its highest the defendants' agreement to lend "in return for the plaintiffs' agreeing to enter into a petrol sales agreement" as stated by Mr Pugh, was, in the words of Lord Haldane in the *Kreglinger* case [1914] AC 25 "in consideration of being given" a petrol sales agreement, which was "a collateral bargain the entering into which was a preliminary and separable condition of the loan".

Thirdly, even if there were one contract, as the plaintiffs contend, I, for my part, if I were driven to it, would conclude that that contract comprehending the sales agreement and the agreement to lend on the legal charge was not in its "real nature and substance", as a whole, a mortgage transaction, nor, to use Lord Haldane's words, "a mere mortgage", and so falls outside the doctrine of once a mortgage always a mortgage, of which the clog on the equity of redemption is an emanation. I again quote Lord Haldane, where he said, at 37:

"That the substance of the transaction must be looked to in applying this doctrine and that it did not apply to cases which were only apparently or technically within it but were in reality something more than cases of mortgage."

If there were the one contract, as the plaintiffs say, then it was "something more than" a mortgage — it was a commercial transaction, of which the mortgage formed part, leaving at any rate the sales agreement part of the transaction with the sales agreement ties outside the ambit of the other part of the transaction, namely, the mortgage, altogether. As I have indicated, the effect on the ties specified in the document of legal charge if those ties were expressed to endure beyond redemption, does not arise.

My conclusion, therefore, is that the defendants succeed on the issue before me.

iv. EXTORTIONATE CREDIT AGREEMENTS
Cheshire and Burn: *Modern Law of Real Property* (13th edn, 1982), pp. 689–691.

"CONSUMER CREDIT AGREEMENTS

The Consumer Credit Act 1974[16] establishes a comprehensive code which regulates the supply of credit not exceeding £15,000[17] to an individual[18]. It includes provisions on advertising and canvassing; the licensing of credit and

---

[16] See Guest and Lloyd, *Encyclopedia of Consumer Credit Law* (1975); Goode, *Consumer Credit Act* (1979); *Consumer Credit Legislation* (1981); Fisher and Lightwood, chap. 9; (1975) 34 CLJ 79 (R. M. Goode); (1975) 39 Conv (NS) 94 (J. E. Adams).

[17] Consumer Credit (Increase of Monetary Limits) Order 1983 (S.I. 1983 No. 1878), increasing the amount from £5,000.

[18] This includes sole traders and partnerships: s. 189 (1).

hire businesses; all aspects of the agreement; and judicial control over its enforcement.

To come within the Act, a mortgage must constitute a regulated consumer agreement, that is to say, a personal credit agreement by which a creditor provides a debtor with credit not exceeding £15,000[19]. There are, however, exempt agreements[20], of which the most important are loans made by a building society or local authority for house purchase. Banks are not exempt.

Owing to the financial limit of £15,000, only second mortgages are likely to come within the definition of a regulated consumer agreement. As the Crowther Report, on which the Act is based, said:[1]

'Much of the money borrowed on second mortgage is spent on improvements of various kinds to houses that are used as security. But there is no necessary tie, in most cases, between the loan and the purpose for which it is used — indeed, many of the advertisements emphasise the borrower's freedom to spend it on anything he chooses. Undoubtedly, there are people who have been led by this sort of advertising to endanger the security of their homes for the sake of some unnecessary extravagance.'

We can only notice in very general terms the main areas where the law of mortgage is affected.

(a) Creation

If the formalities prescribed by the Act are not complied with[2], section 65 provides that an agreement which is "improperly-executed" can be enforced against the debtor on an order of the court only[3].

(b) Rights of mortgagor

The most far-reaching provision for the protection of the mortgagor is the power given to the court to 're-open' a credit agreement if the credit bargain is extortionate[4]. This power extends to all credit bargains, whether regulated, exempt or above the £15,000 limit, other than those in which the debtor is a body corporate. A credit bargain is extortionate if the payments to be made under it are 'grossly exorbitant' or if it 'otherwise grossly contravenes ordinary principles of fair dealing.' The court is required to take into account.

(i) interest rates prevailing when the bargain was made

(ii) factors in relation to the debtor, such as his age, experience, business capacity and state of health, and the degree to which he was under financial pressure when he made the bargain

(iii) the creditor's relationship to the debtor and the degree of risk accepted by him, having regard to the value of the security provided, and

---

[19] S. 8.

[20] S. 16; Consumer Credit (Exempt Agreements) (No. 2) Order 1985 (S.I. 1985 No. 757), as amended by S.I. 1985 No. 1736 and No. 1918.

[1] (1971) Cmnd 4596, para. 2.4.52.

[2] Part V of the Act. See also s. 105.

[3] The County Court has exclusive jurisdiction: s. 141 (1). See also s. 127.

[4] Ss. 137–40. These sections "apply to agreements and transactions whenever made": s. 192 (1), Sch. 3, para. 42; it is for the creditor to prove that a bargain is not extortionate: s. 171 (7); *Coldunell Ltd v Gallon* [1986] 1 All ER 429 (where the creditor so proved). Cf. *Cityland and Property (Holdings) Ltd v Dabrah* [1968] Ch 166, [1967] 2 All ER 639, p. 678, ante. The County Court has jurisdiction where the credit does not exceed £5,000: s. 139 (5); County Courts (Jurisdiction) Order 1981 (S.I. No. 1123).

(iv) any other relevant considerations.

The court has wide discretion 'to do justice between the parties.'

All these matters were considered in *A. Ketley Ltd v Scott*[5], where the court refused an application to re-open a credit agreement involving a loan of £24,500, secured by a legal charge on a flat, at 12 per cent for three months; this was equal to a rate of interest of 48 per cent per annum. The mortgagor had been advised by his own solicitor, and 'judging by his earnings and business experience knew exactly what he was doing.'

Under section 94, the debtor under a regulated agreement has the right, on giving notice to the creditor, to redeem prematurely at any time. Any provision in the agreement which limits his rights in this respect is void[6]. It would seem that if a provision to postpone the contractual right to redeem were included in a regulated agreement it would be void[7].

(c) Rights of the mortgagee

Consonant with the object of the Act, these are curtailed. A security cannot be enforced by reason of any breach of a regulated agreement by the debtor, until the creditor has served a notice under section 87. This is similar to, but not identical with, the notice required by section 146 of the Law of Property Act 1925 in the case of the forfeiture of a lease[8]. Further, a land mortgage securing a regulated agreement is enforceable by an order of the court only[9]. This is a most important provision, since a mortgagee cannot exercise his rights of taking possession and of sale without such an order. If, however, he sells without an order, it would seem that he can pass a good title to the purchaser[10].

Finally, under section 113, a creditor shall not derive from the enforcement of the security any greater benefit than he would obtain from enforcement of a regulated agreement, if the security were not provided. This would seem to deny the mortgagee the full benefit of foreclosure[11]."

CONSUMER CREDIT ACT 1974

137. Extortionate credit bargains. — (1) If the court finds a credit bargain extortionate it may reopen the credit agreement so as to do justice between the parties.

(2) In this section and sections 138 to 140 —

    (a) "credit agreement" means any agreement between an individual (the "debtor") and any other person (the "creditor") by which the creditor provides the debtor with credit of any amount, and

---

[5] [1981] ICR 241; 130 NLJ 749; (1979) 8 Anglo-Am 240 (H. W. Wilkinson). See also *Castle Phillips v Khan* [1980] CCLR 1; *First National Securities v Bertrand* [1980] CCLR 5, discussed in (1982) 132 NLJ 1041 (R. G. Lawson); *Wills v Wood* (1984) Times 24 March, where Lord DENNING MR said: "The word is 'extortionate', not 'unwise'. The jurisdiction seems to me to contemplate at least a substantial imbalance in bargaining power of which one party has taken advantage."; *Woodstead Finance Ltd v Petrou* [1986] NLJ Rep 188 (interest of 42.5 per cent per annum for short term loan of £25,000 for six months held to be the normal rate, and therefore not extortionate).

[6] S. 173 (1).

[7] *Knightsbridge Estates Ltd v Byrne* [1939] Ch 441, [1938] 4 All ER 618, p. 664, ante.

[8] P. 434, ante.

[9] S. 126. For orders which the court can make, see Part IX of the Act.

[10] S. 177 (2).

[11] P. 717, post; (1975) 39 Conv (NS) 94 at p. 108.

(*b*) "credit bargain" —

    (i) where no transaction other than the credit agreement is to be taken into account in computing the total charge for credit, means the credit agreement, or

    (ii) where one or more other transactions are to be so taken into account, means the credit agreement and those other transactions, taken together.

138. When bargains are extortionate. — (1) A credit bargain is extortionate if it —

    (*a*) requires the debtor or a relative of his to make payments (whether unconditionally, or on certain contingencies) which are grossly exorbitant, or

    (*b*) otherwise grossly contravenes ordinary principles of fair dealing.

(2) In determining whether a credit bargain is extortionate, regard shall be had to such evidence as is adduced concerning —

    (*a*) interest rates prevailing at the time it was made,

    (*b*) the factors mentioned in subsections (3) to (5), and

    (*c*) any other relevant considerations.

(3) Factors applicable under subsection (2) in relation to the debtor include —

    (*a*) his age, experience, business capacity and state of health; and

    (*b*) the degree to which, at the time of making the credit bargain, he was under financial pressure, and the nature of that pressure.

(4) Factors applicable under subsection (2) in relation to the creditor include —

    (*a*) the degree of risk accepted by him, having regard to the value of any security provided;

    (*b*) his relationship to the debtor; and

    (*c*) whether or not a colourable cash price was quoted for any goods or services included in the credit bargain.

IV. Statutory Provisions Affecting the Rights of the Mortgagor[12]

LAW OF PROPERTY ACT 1925

91. Sale of mortgaged property in action for redemption or foreclosure. — (1) Any person entitled to redeem mortgaged property may have a judgment or order for sale instead of for redemption in an action brought by him either for redemption alone, or for sale alone, or for sale or redemption in the alternative[13].

(2) In any action, whether for foreclosure, or for redemption, or for sale, or for the raising and payment in any manner of mortgage money, the court, on the request of the mortgagee, or of any person interested either in the mortgage money or in the right of redemption, and, notwithstanding that —

    (*a*) any other person dissents; or

    (*b*) the mortgagee or any person so interested does not appear in the action;

---

[12] C & B, pp. 639–642; M & W, pp. 971–979; MM, pp. 497–500.

[13] He is apparently entitled to such an order as of right: *Clarke v Pannell* (1884) 29 SJ 147.

and without allowing any time for redemption or for payment of any mortgage money, may direct a sale of the mortgaged property, on such terms as it thinks fit, including the deposit in court of a reasonable sum fixed by the court to meet the expenses of sale and to secure performance of the terms[14].

95.   Obligation to transfer instead of reconveying, and as to right to take possession. — (1) Where a mortgagor is entitled to redeem, then subject to compliance with the terms on compliance with which he would be entitled to require a reconveyance or surrender, he shall be entitled to require the mortgagee, instead of re-conveying or surrendering, to assign the mortgage debt and convey the mortgaged property to any third person, as the mortgagor directs; and the mortgagee shall be bound to assign and convey accordingly.

(2) The rights conferred by this section belong to and are capable of being enforced by each incumbrancer, or by the mortgagor, notwithstanding any intermediate incumbrance; but a requisition of an incumbrancer prevails over a requisition of the mortgagor, and, as between incumbrancers, a requisition of a prior incumbrancer prevails over a requisition of a subsequent incumbrancer.

(3) The foregoing provisions of this section do not apply in the case of a mortgagee being or having been in possession.

(4) Nothing in this Act affects prejudicially the right of a mortgagee of land whether or not his charge is secured by a legal term of years absolute to take possession of the land, but the taking of possession by the mortgagee does not convert any legal estate of the mortgagor into an equitable interest.

(5) This section applies to mortgages made either before or after the commencement of this Act, and takes effect notwithstanding any stipulation to the contrary.

96.   Regulations respecting inspection, production and delivery of documents, and priorities.— (1) A mortgagor, as long as his right to redeem subsists, shall be entitled from time to time, at reasonable times, on his request, and at his own cost, and on payment of the mortgagee's costs and expenses in this behalf, to inspect and make copies or abstracts of or extracts from the documents of title relating to the mortgaged property in the custody or power of the mortgagee.

This subsection applies to mortgages made after the thirty-first day of December, eighteen hundred and eighty-one, and takes effect notwithstanding any stipulation to the contrary.

98.   Actions for possession by mortgagors. — (1) A mortgagor for the time being entitled to the possession or receipt of the rents and profits of any land, as to which the mortgagee has not given notice of his intention to take possession or to enter into the receipt of the rents and profits thereof, may sue for such possession, or for the recovery of such rents or profits, or to prevent or recover damages in respect of any trespass or other wrong relative thereto, in his own name only, unless the cause of action arises upon a lease or other contract made by him jointly with any other person.

(2) This section does not prejudice the power of a mortgagor independently of this section to take proceedings in his own name only, either in right of any legal estate vested in him or otherwise.

---

[14] *Twentieth Century Banking Corpn Ltd v Wilkinson* [1977] Ch 99, [1976] 3 All ER 361.

(3) This section applies whether the mortgage was made before or after the commencement of this Act.

V.   Rights Common to Mortgagor and Mortgagee[15]

LAW OF PROPERTY ACT 1925

91.   Sale of mortgaged property in action for redemption or fore-closure. — p. 685, ante.

99.   Leasing powers of mortgagor and mortgagee in possession. — (1) A mortgagor of land while in possession shall, as against every incumbrancer, have power to make from time to time any such lease of the mortgaged land, or any part thereof, as is by this section authorised.

(2) A mortgagee of land while in possession shall, as against all prior incumbrancers, if any, and as against the mortgagor, have power to make from time to time any such lease as aforesaid.

(3) The leases which this section authorises are —
   (i) agricultural or occupation leases for any term not exceeding twenty-one years, or, in the case of a mortgage made after the commencement of this Act, fifty years; and
   (ii) building leases for any term not exceeding ninety-nine years, or, in the case of a mortgage made after the commencement of this Act, nine hundred and ninety-nine years[16].

(5) Every lease shall be made to take effect in possession not later than twelve months after its date.

(6) Every such lease shall reserve the best rent that can reasonably be obtained, regard being had to the circumstances of the case, but without any fine being taken.

(7) Every such lease shall contain a covenant by the lessee for payment of the rent, and a condition of re-entry on the rent not being paid within a time therein specified not exceeding thirty days.

(8) A counterpart of every such lease shall be executed by the lessee and delivered to the lessor, of which execution and delivery the execution of the lease by the lessor shall, in favour of the lessee and all persons deriving title under him, be sufficient evidence.

(11) In case of a lease by the mortgagor, he shall, within one month after making the lease, deliver to the mortgagee, or, where there are more than one, to the mortgagee first in priority, a counterpart of the lease duly executed by the lessee, but the lessee shall not be concerned to see that this provision is complied with.

(13) This section applies only if and as far as a contrary intention is not expressed by the mortgagor and mortgagee in the mortgage deed, or otherwise in writing, and has effect subject to the terms of the mortgage deed or of any such writing and to the provisions therein contained.

---

[15] C & B, pp. 642–644; M & W, pp. 960–964; MM, pp. 490–493.
[16] For further details, see sub-ss. 9, 10.

(14) The mortgagor and mortgagee may, by agreement in writing, whether or not contained in the mortgage deed, reserve to or confer on the mortgagor or the mortgagee, or both, any further or other powers of leasing or having reference to leasing; and any further or other powers so reserved or conferred shall be exercisable, as far as may be, as if they were conferred by this Act, and with all the like incidents, effects, and consequences: . . .

100. Powers of mortgagor and mortgagee in possession to accept surrenders of leases. — (1) For the purpose only of enabling a lease authorised under the last preceding section, or under any agreement made pursuant to that section, or by the mortgage deed (in this section referred to as an authorised lease) to be granted, a mortgagor of land while in possession shall, as against every incumbrancer, have, by virtue of this Act, power to accept from time to time a surrender of any lease of the mortgaged land or any part thereof comprised in the lease, with or without an exception of or in respect of all or any of the mines and minerals therein, and, on a surrender of the lease so far as it comprises part only of the land or mines and minerals leased, the rent may be apportioned.

(2) For the same purpose, a mortgagee of land while in possession shall, as against all prior or other incumbrancers, if any, and as against the mortgagor, have, by virtue of this Act, power to accept from time to time any such surrender as aforesaid.

(5) No surrender shall, by virtue of this section, be rendered valid unless:—

(*a*) An authorised lease is granted of the whole of the land or mines and minerals comprised in the surrender to take effect in possession immediately or within one month after the date of the surrender; and

(*b*) The term certain or other interest granted by the new lease is not less in duration than the unexpired term or interest which would have been subsisting under the original lease if that lease had not been surrendered; and

(*c*) Where the whole of the land mines and minerals originally leased has been surrendered, the rent reserved by the new lease is not less than the rent which would have been payable under the original lease if it had not been surrendered; or where part only of the land or mines and minerals has been surrendered, the aggregate rents respectively remaining payable or reserved under the original lease and new lease are not less than the rent which would have been payable under the original lease if no partial surrender had been accepted.

(7) This section applies only if and as far as a contrary intention is not expressed by the mortgagor and mortgagee in the mortgage deed, or otherwise in writing, and shall have effect subject to the terms of the mortgage deed or of any such writing and to the provisions therein contained.

VI. Rights and Remedies of the Mortgagee[17]

A. Possession of the Mortgaged Premises[18]

i. RIGHT TO ENTER

LAW OF PROPERTY ACT 1925

95. Obligation to transfer instead of reconveying, and as to right to take possession.

(4), p. 686, ante.

FOUR-MAIDS LTD *v* DUDLEY MARSHALL (PROPERTIES) LTD
[1957] Ch 317, [1957] 2 All ER 35 (ChD, HARMAN J)[19]

The legal charge provided that, if the interest payments were made punctually, the principal would not be called in for some 2 years 10 months. Six months after the loan was made interest was late and the lender called in the principal. Arrears of interest were then paid, but the lender claimed the whole sum due and took out an originating summons asking for possession.

Held. The mortgagee was entitled to possession.

HARMAN J: This is an originating summons for possession. . . . This subject is one which is constantly being agitated in this court. I have had my attention called to some observations I made on it recently in *Hughes v Waite* [1957] 1 WLR 713, [1957] 1 All ER 603, and even more recently in *Alliance Perpetual Building Society v Belrum Investments Ltd* [1957] 1 WLR 720, [1957] 1 All ER 635, which came before me on an application to commit the editor of the "Daily Mail" for comments on a mortgagee's action for possession of a sort exactly similar to the present. The comments and, indeed, the arguments of counsel for the newspaper showed an entire misapprehension of what an originating summons for possession is about. They all assumed that it involved some kind of default on the part of the mortgagor, but I said there, and I repeat now, that the right of the mortgagee to possession in the absence of some contract has nothing to do with default on the part of the mortgagor. The mortgagee may go into possession before the ink is dry on the mortgage unless there is something in the contract, express or by implication[20], whereby he has contracted himself out of that right. He has the right because

---

[17] C & B, pp. 645–662; M & W, pp. 931–960; MM, pp. 472–490; Waldock, pp. 224–295; Fisher and Lightwood, chap. 18. The mortgagee's remedies are cumulative: *Rudge v Richens* (1873) LR 8 CP 358 (mortgagee, after exercising power of sale, may sue for balance on personal covenant); *Gordon Grant & Co Ltd v FL Boos* [1926] AC 781 (purchase of land (by leave) at auction and re-sale at a large profit still leaves personal action for balance not found at the auction sale); *Refuge Assurance Co Ltd v Pearlberg* [1938] Ch 687, [1938] 3 All ER 231 (a mortgagee in possession is not prevented from appointing a receiver). Foreclosure however puts an end to other remedies.

A mortgagee may also have an action against a valuer for a negligent valuation which causes him loss: *Corisand Investments Ltd v Druce & Co* (1978) 248 EG 315, 407. For a similar action against a surveyor, see *London and South of England Building Society v Stone* (1981) 261 EG 463; *Anglia Hastings and Thanet Building Society v House & Son* (1981) 260 EG 1128.

[18] C & B, pp. 646–649; M & W, pp. 942–947; MM, pp. 478–483; Fisher and Lightwood, chap. 19; [1979] Conv (NS) 266 (R. J. Smith); [1983] Conv 293 (A. Clarke); Report of the Committee on the Enforcement of Judgment Debts 1969 (Cmnd. 3909), paras. 1363–1427. As to the rights of an equitable mortgagee to possession, see M & W, pp. 950–952; (1955) 71 LQR 204 (H. W. R. Wade).

[19] (1957) 73 LQR 300 (R. E. M.); *Birmingham Citizens' Permanent Building Society v Caunt* [1962] Ch 883, [1962] 1 All ER 163; *Alnwick RDC v Taylor* [1966] Ch 355, [1966] 1 All ER 899.

[20] See *Esso Petroleum Co Ltd v Alstonbridge Properties Ltd* [1975] 1 WLR 1474, [1975] 3 All ER 358; *Western Bank Ltd v Schindler* [1977] Ch 1, [1976] 2 All ER 393, p. 696, post.

he has a legal term of years in the property or its statutory equivalent. If there is an attornment clause, he must give notice. If there is a provision that, so long as certain payments are made, he will not go into possession, then he has contracted himself out of his rights. Apart from that, possession is a matter of course.

[An application for possession] has become a very fashionable form of relief because, owing to the conditions now prevailing, if it is desired to realise a security by sale, vacant possession is almost essential. Where, therefore, the mortgagor is in occupation, a summons for possession is taken out, and no other relief is sought, and where the mortgagee is in a position to exercise his power of sale, that is all the help he requires from the court. . . .

The mortgagor said here that his default was of a very small order. So it was. If this were a case where there was discretion in the matter, I should feel that it was a hard case. But the mortgagor has entered into a contract with the mortgagee, and the mortgagee asks for his rights under the contract, and this court, in my judgment, has no power to refuse him those rights.

ii.   LIABILITY OF MORTGAGEE IN POSSESSION

WHITE *v* CITY OF LONDON BREWERY CO
(1889) 42 ChD 237 (CA, Lord ESHER MR, COTTON and FRY LJJ)

In 1868, the plaintiff, a publican, mortgaged his public house to the defendants in return for a loan. In 1869, when the plaintiff's financial affairs were in a serious condition, the defendants exercised their right to take possession, and leased the premises to a tenant who covenanted to purchase his ale, beer and porter from the defendants.

In 1879, the defendants sold the property, took what they claimed was due to them under the mortgage debt and paid the surplus to second mortgagees. The plaintiff, acting in the interests of the second mortgagees, brought this action for an account of what was due to the defendants. One question which arose was whether the defendants were chargeable, not merely with the rent which they received from their tenants, but with the rent which they would have obtained if the premises had been let free from the covenant to purchase ale, etc., from the defendants.

Held. The defendants were chargeable with the rent which they would have obtained if the tenant had not been so restricted.

COTTON LJ: There is then another point to be considered. A mortgagee in possession must account for the rents, which, but for his wilful default, he would have received. The plaintiff says that if he fails as to the brewers' profits yet he ought to have a larger sum in respect of the rents which the mortgagees would, but for their wilful default, have received. . . . The learned Judge has allowed an addition of £20 a year from 19 August 1874, down to the date of the sale, in addition to the rent obtained by the mortgagees. [His Lordship considered the evidence relating to the rent for which the public house could have been let, and continued:] The evidence on that question is of a somewhat doubtful character, but I think the plaintiff has not established that more should be given him than what the learned Judge has allowed, *viz.* £20 a year, which comes altogether, as the Master of the Rolls has said, to £100[1].

---

[1] See also *Hughes v Williams* (1806) 12 Ves 493; *Nelson v Booth* (1858) 3 De G & J 119; *Wrigley v Gill* [1905] 1 Ch 241; (1979) 129 NLJ 334 (H. E. Markson); [1982] Conv 345 at pp. 346–348 (J. E. Stannard).

It is possible also to take possession for the purpose of receiving the income of the property. It is more usual, however, to appoint a receiver[2] if the object is to make up income in arrear, for a mortgagee in possession is made to account not only for what he received, but also for what he could, by prudent management, have received.

iii. RELIEF OF MORTGAGOR

(a) At Common Law

In *Mobil Oil Co Ltd v Rawlinson* (1981) 43 P & CR 221, Rawlinson was the owner of the equity of redemption in respect of Heathfield Garage, North Petherton in Somerset. The mortgage on the petrol station secured a loan from, and also all sums due to, the defendants under a supply agreement. When Rawlinson fell into arrears, the plaintiffs sought possession of the filling station. Rawlinson sought to counterclaim and set off against the arrears sums alleged to be due to him from the defendants under the supply agreement. The Master made an order for possession, subject to a proviso that it was not to be enforced, if Rawlinson paid £8,000 into court within 14 days. In holding that the proviso should be deleted, NOURSE J said at 224:

"Before 1936 a mortgagee who was only asking for possession had to commence his proceedings in the Queen's Bench Division. That was because possession alone could not be sought by summons in the Chancery Division. But in 1936, R.S.C., Ord. 55, r. 5A was amended so as to make that possible. The Chancery judges of the time issued a practice direction which said, amongst other things, that when possession was sought and the defendant was in arrear with any instalments due under the mortgage or charge and the master was of the opinion that the defendant ought to be given an opportunity to pay off the arears, the master might adjourn the summons on such terms as he thought fit. The direction caused confusion. It led to a general view among the Chancery masters, no doubt assisted by the benevolent attitude which the legislature had by then assumed towards tenants faced with eviction by their landlords, that they had a discretion to adjourn a legal mortgagee's application for possession, at any rate in instalment cases, against the wishes of the mortgagee in order to enable the mortgagor to catch up on instalment arrears; and, inferentially, a right, if he did so, to continue to deny the mortgagee possession notwithstanding that on the default the whole of the mortgage money had become and thereafter remained repayable. By the end of the 1950s it had become necessary for the Chancery judges of a later generation to re-assert the legal mortgagee's right to possession. In the van of that movement was Harman J, although even he subscribed to the view that the practice direction had qualified the right in the case of an instalment mortgage: see *Four-Maids Ltd v Dudley Marshall (Properties) Ltd* [1957] Ch 317 at 321, [1957] 2 All ER 35 at 36, p. 689, ante.

In 1961 the whole question was fully argued and considered in *Birmingham Citizens Permanent Building Society v Caunt* [1962] Ch 883, [1962] 1 All ER 163, and it is on Russell J's judgment in that case that the foregoing summary of the earlier history is based. I well remember that decision and the general view of the profession that it had settled once and for all the limited extent of the court's power to adjourn a legal mortgagee's application for possession.

---

[2] See p. 716, post.

The rule in regard to instalment mortgages, and a fortiori in regard to ordinary mortgages, was stated by Russell J at the end of his judgment, in the following terms at 912, at 182:

'Accordingly, in my judgment, where (as here) the legal mortgagee under an instalment mortgage under which by reason of default the whole money has become payable, is entitled to possession, the court has no jurisdiction to decline the order or to adjourn the hearing whether on terms of keeping up payments or paying arrears, if the mortgagee cannot be persuaded to agree to this course. To this the *sole exception* is that the application may be adjourned for a short time to afford to the mortgagor a chance of paying off the mortgagee in full or otherwise satisfying him; but this should not be done if there is no reasonable prospect of this occurring. When I say the sole exception, I do not, of course, intend to exclude adjournments which in the ordinary course of procedure may be desirable in circumstances such as temporary inability of a party to attend, and so forth.'

The reason for the exception is that the court has never allowed a mortgagee to enforce his rights under the mortgage in the face of a concrete offer by the mortgagor to redeem.

Since then the court has twice been given additional powers of adjournment in cases where the mortgaged property consists of or includes a dwellinghouse: see section 36 of the Administration of Justice Act 1970 and section 8 of the Administration of Justice Act 1973. But the general rule continues to apply to other types of property, for example commercial premises of the kind with which the present case is concerned. . . .

I am prepared to assume in the defendant's favour that the amount of his cross-claims exceeds the amount of the mortgage debt. I say at once that I regard that as an assumption of extremely doubtful validity — on the Master's estimate there is a shortfall of about £8,000 — but I will make it nonetheless. However, I find it impossible to make any distinction between this case and *Samuel Keller (Holdings) Ltd v Martins Bank Ltd* [1971] 1 WLR 43 at 47–48, [1970] 3 All ER 950 at 953. Megarry J's statement of the principle which was expressly approved by the Court of Appeal, is in entirely general terms. The principle is that a mortgagor cannot unilaterally appropriate the amount of a cross-claim, even if it is both liquidated and admitted, and *a fortiori* if it is unliquidated or not admitted, in discharge of the mortgage debt. On that footing the origin and nature of the cross-claim and its relationship to the mortgage debt are wholly irrelevant.

In the circumstances this case must be approached on the footing that when the matter came before the master there were substantial arrears outstanding. Consistently with the general rule established in *Birmingham Citizens Permanent Building Society v Caunt* he ought then to have made an unconditional order for possession, unless of course he was satisfied that there was a reasonable prospect of the defendant's paying the arrears in full, not into court but to the plaintiffs, or otherwise satisfying the plaintiffs, in which case he should have adjourned the application for a short time.

I do not intend to suggest that there may not be other circumstances in which the court will refuse a mortgagee possession on terms that the mortgagor pays the full amount of the mortgage debt into court. A number of other possibilities are mentioned in the passage in Fisher and Lightwood's *Law of Mortgage*, (9th edn. 1977) p. 325 which I have already read. Without attempting to decide any point which does not arise for decision in the present case, I will only say that it seems to me that that course could only be adopted in a case where there was a substantial question as to the existence or enforceability of the right to possession, for example where it was claimed that the mortgage was void for illegality or that the mortgagee was in some way estopped from asserting his right. It appears probable that *Lidco Investments Ltd v Hale* (1971) 219 EG 715 is a case which falls within the former category."

(b) In Equity

QUENNELL *v* MALTBY
[1979] 1 WLR 318, [1979] 1 All ER 568
(CA, Lord DENNING MR, BRIDGE and TEMPLEMAN LJJ)[3]

Quennell, who owned a large house in Lewes, Sussex, worth more than £30,000, mortgaged it to Barclays Bank Ltd to secure a loan of £2,500. The mortgage deed prohibited the creation of a tenancy without the bank's consent. In breach of that covenant Quennell let the house to the defendants who became statutory tenants protected by the Rent Act 1977. This tenancy was binding on Quennell but not on the bank.

Quennell, who wanted to sell the house with vacant possession, asked the bank to bring an action for possession against the defendants. On the bank's refusal, Quennell's wife then paid off the mortgage debt, took a transfer of the mortgage from the bank and claimed possession against the defendants as mortgagee.

Held (reversing the County Court judge). The wife was not entitled to an order for possession.

LORD DENNING MR: [The decision of the judge], if right, opens the way to widespread evasion of the Rent Acts. If the owner of a house wishes to obtain vacant possession, all he has to do is charge it to the bank for a small sum. Then grant a new tenancy without telling the bank. Then get his wife to pay off the bank and take a transfer. Then get the wife to sue for possession.

That indeed was what happened here. In October 1977, when Mr Quennell went to the bank, he told them about the tenancies. They said that they did not intend to take proceedings. So he got Mrs Quennell to do it. In evidence, she said:

"I paid £2,500. This was for my husband. I took the charge to make the debt to his bank less onerous. I was aware he wanted to obtain possession of the house to sell it. I merely paid off the charge. These proceedings have been brought to get possession to sell."

So the objective is plain. It was not to enforce the security or to obtain repayment or anything of that kind. It was in order to get possession of the house and to overcome the protection of the Rent Acts.

Is that permissible? It seems to me that this is one of those cases where equity steps in to mitigate the rigour of the law. Long years ago it did the same when it invented the equity of redemption. As is said in *Snell's Principles of Equity*, 27th edn. (1973), p. 376:

"The courts of equity left the legal effect of the transaction unaltered but declared it to be unreasonable and against conscience that the mortgagee should retain as owner for his own benefit what was intended as a mere security."

---

[3] (1979) 129 NLJ 624 (H. W. Wilkinson); 38 CLJ 257 (R. A. Pearce).

So here in modern times equity can step in so as to prevent a mortgagee, or a transferee from him, from getting possession of a house contrary to the justice of the case. A mortgagee will be restrained from getting possession except when it is sought bona fide and reasonably for the purpose of enforcing the security and then only subject to such conditions as the court thinks fit to impose. When the bank itself or a building society lends the money, then it may well be right to allow the mortgagee to obtain possession when the borrower is in default. But so long as the interest is paid and there is nothing outstanding, equity has ample power to restrain any unjust use of the right to possession.

It is plain that in this transaction Mr and Mrs Quennell had an ulterior motive. It was not done to enforce the security or due payment of the principal or interest. It was done for the purpose of getting possession of the house in order to resell it at a profit. It was done so as to avoid the protection which the Rent Acts afford to tenants in their occupation. If Mr Quennell himself had sought to evict the tenants, he would not be allowed to do so. He could not say the tenancies were void. He would be estopped from saying so. They certainly would be protected against him. Are they protected against his wife now that she is the transferee of the charge? In my opinion they are protected. For this simple reason, she is not seeking possession for the purpose of enforcing the loan or the interest or anything of that kind. She is doing it simply for an ulterior purpose of getting possession of the house, contrary to the intention of Parliament as expressed in the Rent Acts.

On that simple ground it seems to me that this action fails and it should be dismissed. The legal right to possession is not to be enforced when it is sought for an ulterior motive. I would on this account allow the appeal and dismiss the action for possession.

BRIDGE LJ: I entirely agree. The situation arising in this case is one, it seems to me, in which the court is not only entitled but bound to look behind the formal legal relationship between the parties to see what is the true substance of the matter. Once one does that, on the facts of this case it is as plain as a pikestaff that the purpose of the bringing of these proceedings via Mrs Quennell is not for her own benefit to protect or enforce the security which she holds as the transferee of the legal charge but for the benefit of her husband as mortgagor to enable him to sell the property with the benefit of vacant possession. In substance she is suing as his agent. That being so, it seems to me inevitably to follow that she can be in no better position in these proceedings than her husband would be if they had been brought in his name. If they had been brought in his name, it is clear that the defendants would have had an unanswerable defence under the Rent Acts.

I agree that the appeal should be allowed[4].

(c) By Statute

Since 1970 there has been a statutory exception to the Draconian rule in *Four-Maids Ltd v Dudley Marshall Properties Ltd* [1957] Ch 317, [1957] 2 All ER 35, p. 689, ante in favour of the mortgagor. These additional powers can be exercised by the court whether or not the mortgagor is in default[5] and whether the loan is by way of an instalment or endowment mortgage[6].

---

[4] TEMPLEMAN LJ delivered a judgment concurring with BRIDGE LJ.
[5] *Western Bank Ltd v Schindler* [1977] Ch 1, [1976] 2 All ER 393, p. 696, post.
[6] *Governor and Company of the Bank of Scotland v Grimes* [1985] 3 WLR 294, [1985] 2 All ER 254, p. 702, post.

ADMINISTRATION OF JUSTICE ACT 1970

36. Additional powers of court in action by mortgagee for possession of dwelling-house.

— (1) Where the mortgagee under a mortgage of land which consists of or includes a dwelling-house[7] brings an action in which he claims possession of the mortgaged property, not being an action for foreclosure in which a claim for possession of the mortgaged property is also made, the court[8] may exercise any of the powers conferred on it by subsection (2) below if it appears to the court that in the event of its exercising the power the mortgagor is likely to be able within a reasonable period to pay[9] any sums due under the mortgage or to remedy a default consisting of a breach of any other obligation arising under or by virtue of the mortgage.

(2) The court —

    (*a*) may adjourn the proceedings, or

    (*b*) on giving judgment, or making an order, for delivery of possession of the mortgaged property, or at any time before the execution of such judgment or order, may —

        (i) stay or suspend execution of the judgment or order, or

        (ii) postpone the date for delivery of possession,

for such period or periods as the court thinks reasonable.

(3) Any such adjournment, stay, suspension or postponement as is referred to in subsection (2) above may be made subject to such conditions with regard to payment by the mortgagor of any sum secured by the mortgage or the remedying of any default as the court thinks fit.

(4) The court may from time to time vary or revoke any condition imposed by virtue of this section.

38A[10]. This part of this Act shall not apply to a mortgage securing an agreement which is a regulated agreement within the meaning of the Consumer Credit Act 1974[11].

ADMINISTRATION OF JUSTICE ACT 1973

8. Extension of powers of court in action by mortgagee of dwelling-house.

— (1) Where by a mortgage of land which consists of or includes a dwelling-house, or by any agreement between the mortgagee under such a mortgage and the mortgagor, the mortgagor is entitled or is to be permitted to pay the principal sum secured by instalments or otherwise to defer

---

[7] The fact that part is used as a shop or office or for business, trade or professional purposes does not prevent a house from being a dwelling-house: s. 39 (2).

[8] If the land is outside Greater London or the county palatine of Lancaster, and, if a County Court has jurisdiction, the action must be brought in the County Court: ss. 37–38; *Lord Marples of Wallasey v Holmes* (1975) 31 P & CR 94; *Frost Ltd v Green* [1978] 1 WLR 949, [1978] 2 All ER 206.

[9] *Royal Trust Co of Canada v Markham* [1975] 1 WLR 1416, [1975] 3 All ER 433 (an order for suspension must be for a fixed "period"; and the mortgagor must provide evidence that he is "likely to be able to pay"); *Universal Showcards and Display Manufacturing Ltd v Brunt* (1984) Times, 26 March (jurisdiction of county court is not lost where a second mortgagee "claims possession" as well as payment under s. 38 (1), when the mortgaged property has already been granted to a first mortgagee).

[10] Added by Consumer Credit Act 1974, s. 192, Sch. 4, para. 30; p. 684, ante.

[11] Where one spouse has defaulted on the mortgage of a dwelling-house, and the mortgagee brings an action for possession, the other spouse may be entitled to be made a party to the action: Matrimonial Homes Act 1983, s. 8, p. 260, ante; LRA 1925, s. 112 B.

payment of it in whole or in part, but provision is also made for earlier payment in the event of any default by the mortgagor or of a demand by the mortgagee or otherwise, then for purposes of section 36 of the Administration of Justice Act 1970 (under which a court has power to delay giving a mortgagee possession of the mortgaged property so as to allow the mortgagor a reasonable time to pay any sums due under the mortgage) a court may treat as due under the mortgage on account of the principal sum secured and of interest on it only such amounts as the mortgagor would have expected to be required to pay if there had been no such provision for earlier payment[12].

(2) A court shall not exercise by virtue of subsection (1) above the powers conferred by section 36 of the Administration of Justice Act 1970 unless it appears to the court not only that the mortgagor is likely to be able within a reasonable period to pay any amounts regarded (in accordance with subsection (1) above) as due on account of the principal sum secured, together with the interest on those amounts, but also that he is likely to be able by the end of that period to pay any further amounts that he would have expected to be required to pay by then on account of that sum and of interest on it if there had been no such provision as is referred to in subsection (1) above for earlier payment.

(3) Where subsection (1) above would apply to an action in which a mortgagee only claimed possession of the mortgaged property, and the mortgagee brings an action for foreclosure (with or without also claiming possession of the property), then section 36 of the Administration of Justice Act 1970 together with subsections (1) and (2) above shall apply as they would apply if it were an action in which the mortgagee only claimed possession of the mortgaged property, except that —

(a) section 36 (2) (b) shall apply only in relation to any claim for possession. . . .

WESTERN BANK LTD *v* SCHINDLER
[1977] Ch 1, [1976] 2 All ER 393 (CA, BUCKLEY, SCARMAN and GOFF LJJ)[13]

In 1973 the defendant mortgaged a dwelling-house to the plaintiffs to secure a loan of £32,000, and at the same time by a separate transaction took out an endowment policy in their favour as collateral security. The preliminary loan agreement provided for the payment of interest monthly in advance, and periodical payment of the premiums on the policy; also for repayment of the principal sum in 10 years time. The mortgage deed however failed to provide for monthly payments of interest, and provided instead that the principal and accrued interest be paid at the end of the 10 year period.

The defendant paid three monthly instalments of mortgage interest and three premiums under the policy, and then made no further payments. The

---

[12] Reversing the effect of *Halifax Building Society v Clark* [1973] 2 WLR 1, [1973] 2 All ER 33; but the grant of the statutory concession was unnecessary: *First Middlesbrough Trading and Mortgage Co Ltd v Cunningham* (1974) 28 P & CR 69; (1973) 37 Conv (NS) 213; (1974) 38 Conv (NS) 309. See *Centrax Trustees Ltd v Ross* [1979] 2 All ER 952; [1979] Conv 371 (F. R. Crane); *Habib Bank Ltd v Tailor* [1982] 1 WLR 1218, [1982] 3 All ER 561, p. 700, post; *Governor and Company of the Bank of Scotland v Grimes* [1985] 3 WLR 294, [1985] 2 All ER 254, p. 702, post.
[13] (1977) 40 MLR 356 (C. Harpum).

policy lapsed, and the mortgagees sought possession of the dwelling-house. The mortgagor was not in breach of any term of the mortgage. GOULDING J, in the exercise of his discretion under Administration of Justice Act 1970, section 36 (1), made an order for possession to take effect one month after the order.

Held. '(1) No term could be implied in the mortgage deed to exclude the mortgagees' common law right to possession.

(2) (GOFF LJ dubitante) section 36 (1) applied, even though the mortgagor was not in default.

SCARMAN LJ: I agree. This is an appeal by the mortgagor of a dwelling house against an order for possession within 28 days made by Goulding J in an action brought by the mortgagees. Owing to the strange but absolutely clear terms of the legal charge, the mortgagees were driven to base their claim for possession on the common law right which they enjoy by virtue of his legal estate: for they could allege no default, no arrears. Mr Lightman, for the mortgagor, has put forward the case that, in the absence of a default by the mortgagor upon an obligation under the charge, or of arrears owed by him, the mortgagees have no right to possession; alternatively, that, if they have, the court has a discretion to postpone an order under section 36 of the Administration of Justice Act 1970, and should have exercised its discretion in favour of the mortgagor.

Mr Lightman's argument for the mortgagor — presented, if I may respectfully say so, forcefully and cogently — falls into two parts. First, he submits that there should be implied into the terms of the legal charge a further term excluding the mortgagor's right to possession in the absence of arrears or default by the mortgagor. It is, he contends, a mortgage under which the mortgagee has expressly agreed to wait 10 years for repayment of his capital and for payment of interest (which, though it accrues from year to year, is not payable under this instrument until the date of repayment of capital): it is, therefore — he argues — consistent with the tenor of the parties' agreement to imply a term excluding the mortgagees' right to possession at least until that date, unless, of course, the mortgagor has defaulted upon any of his obligations. And there has been no such default. The second part of his argument raises an important question. He submits that, upon its true construction, section 36 (1) of the Administration of Justice Act 1970 (which applies only to mortgages of dwelling houses) excludes the common law right of the mortgagee to possession irrespective of default or arrears — a right which, in the absence of an agreement excluding it, a mortgagee enjoys by virtue of his estate: see *Fisher and Lightwood's Law of Mortgage*, 8th edn. (1969), p. 269.

If this construction of the subsection be not possible, he submits in the alternative that the subsection confers power upon the court by adjournment, or otherwise as specified in subsection (2), to delay the making or enforcement of an order for possession not only in cases of default or arrears, where the subsection expressly applies, but also in the case, not expressly mentioned in the subsection, where a mortgagee is relying on his common law right alone.

Mr Lightman argues that, unless one or other of these constructions is placed upon the subsection, the section fails to provide the mortgagor of a dwelling house with the protection against eviction which Parliament plainly intended him to have.

I now deal with the argument based on contract. I do not think it possible to imply into this legal charge a term excluding the mortgagee's common law right to possession. . . .

I now turn to the argument based on statute. One may suppose that the section was passed to protect the mortgagors of dwelling houses from the full rigour of the decision in *Four-Maids Ltd v Dudley Marshall (Properties) Ltd* [1957] Ch 317, [1957] 2 All ER 35, p. 689, ante and *Birmingham Citizens Permanent Building Society v Caunt* [1962] Ch 883, [1962] 1 All ER 163. If the section neither abrogates the common law right nor subjects it to the power of delay admittedly conferred upon the court in cases of default or arrears, the section fails in its purpose. The critical subsections are (1) and (2) [His Lordship read section 36 (1), (2) and continued:] Upon a first reading of these two subsections, I confess I thought it obvious that the powers conferred upon the court are exercisable only if it appears to the court that the mortgagor will be able within a reasonable time to pay off the arrears or remedy his default. In other words, there must be a default or arrears before the court can intervene. I thought so not only because of the wording of subsection (1) but because the powers of adjournment, suspension and postponement conferred by subsection (2) appear to be appropriate only to cases where there are arrears to be met or a default to be remedied. Subsection (2) does not, in terms, confer a power to adjourn generally or sine die, which is the sort of power needed to give effective protection against the unreasonable exercise of a mortgagee's common law right of possession, independent, as it is, of default or arrears. Mr Lightman has, however, convinced me that it would be making a nonsense of the law so to read the two subsections. It would mean that a mortgagee could be prevented from taking possession when there was a default or arrears, but could not be so prevented if there were neither default nor arrears. Parliament cannot have intended so foolish a result.

Three courses are open to the court. The first is to treat the section as having a "casus omissus," which only Parliament can fill. The second, and that for which Mr Lightman principally contends (since it would give him victory outright), is to treat the section as excluding the common law right to possession from mortgages of dwelling houses. The third is to treat the section as giving the court a discretion to delay making an order in all cases where, upon whatever ground, a mortgagee is seeking possession of a mortgaged dwelling house.

Judicial leglislation is not an option open to an English judge. Our courts are not required, as are, for instance, the Swiss courts (see the Swiss Civil Code, articles 1 and 2), to declare and insert into legislation rules which the judge would have put there, had he been the legislator. But our courts do have the duty of giving effect to the intention of Parliament, if it be possible, even though the process requires a strained construction of the language used or the insertion of some words in order to do so: see *Luke v IRC* [1963] AC 557, [1963] 1 All ER 655, per Lord Reid at 577, at 664. The line between judicial legislation, which our law does not permit, and judicial interpretation in a way best designed to give effect to the intention of Parliament is not an easy one to draw. Suffice it to say that before our courts can imply words into a statute the statutory intention must be plain and the insertion not too big, or too much at variance with the language in fact used by the legislature. The courts will strain against having to take the first of the three courses

I mentioned; that is to say, leaving unfilled the "casus omissus." In the case of this section, is there an acceptable reading which would enable us to give effect to Parliament's intention within the principle which I think governs the problem?

It would be going too far, in my judgment, to adopt the second course. It would, indeed, be judicial legislation to read a section conferring discretionary powers upon the court as abrogating a common law right. I am not prepared to go that far in an attempt to make sense. If one had to go that far, then it would be for the legislature, not the courts, to take the step.

If the second course is not open, can we adopt the third course? Though it is straining the language, I find no great difficulty in construing subsection (1) so that it confers a power of delay upon the court in whatever circumstances the mortgagee of a dwelling house is seeking to obtain possession. It entails reading the conditional clause in the subsection as applicable only where there are arrears or default, and not as cutting down the width of the power conferred. The greater difficulty, I think, is in the wording of subsection (2) which requires that the limit of a reasonable period be set upon the delaying power of the court: see for illustration, *Royal Trust Co of Canada v Markham* [1975] 1 WLR 1416, [1975] 3 All ER 433. It is appropriate to set such a limit when the problem is whether the mortgagor can find the necessary money or remedy the default. Nevertheless, though it is difficult, it is not impossible to envisage circumstances in which it would be appropriate to impose a time limit upon a mortgagee seeking possession by virtue only of his common law right. The danger to the security, which would be the reason for the mortgagee's application, might appear less imminent to the court than to the mortgagee; or the mortgagor might make proposals which the court would think ought to be given a chance. In either case it could be appropriate to adjourn proceedings for a period in order to see whether the mortgagee's fears were justified. For myself, I doubt whether the subsection empowers the court to adjourn a mortgagee's proceedings sine die or generally. But, upon the assumption that it does not, there is still sense, for the reasons given, in applying subsection (2) to cases where the mortgagee relies only on his estate and alleges no arrears or default.

Accordingly, I think that, within the general principle, it is open to the court to take the third course: and, in my opinion, the wording of the two subsections is not so difficult as to make it impossible to give effect to what was plainly the intention of Parliament, namely, to give the courts power, in their discretion, to protect the mortgagor of a dwelling house for a reasonable period against eviction by his mortgagee. I would therefore hold that the section applies as well where the mortgagee asserts his common law right as where he relies on arrears or default. Upon whatever ground the mortgagee of a dwelling house seeks possession, the court has, in my judgment, the discretion conferred by the section.

It follows, therefore, that the judge had the discretion which he believed he had. In ordering immediate or almost immediate possession, he cannot be shown to have exercised his discretion wrongly. I am not impressed with Mr Lightman's ingenious argument that the risk to the security arises not from anything that has happened to the security but from the mortgagee's own acceptance of a date of repayment 10 years ahead.

For these reasons, I would dismiss the appeal.

HABIB BANK LTD *v* TAILOR
[1982] 1 WLR 1218, [1982] 3 All ER 561 (CA, CUMMING-BRUCE, DUNN and OLIVER LJJ)[14]

Tailor mortgaged his dwelling-house, 142 Walton Avenue, Harlow, to Habib Bank Ltd to secure an overdraft of up to £6,000. He covenanted to pay, on demand in writing, all moneys which might become owing to the bank. When Tailor exceeded the overdraft limit, the bank made a written demand for the whole sum owing for principal, interest and bank charges, and later began proceedings for possession. The sum owing was £7,212, and there was no likelihood of Tailor being able to repay the whole sum within a reasonable period.

The question was whether Administration of Justice Act 1973, s. 8 applied, so as to bring into operation Administration of Justice Act 1970, s. 36.

Held (reversing the County Court judge). The Acts did not apply.

OLIVER LJ: The reasoning by which the judge arrived at his conclusion that the section applied was that he was referred to a decision of Goulding J in *Centrax Trustees Ltd v Ross* [1979] 2 All ER 952. It was a case in which there was a mortgage with a fixed date for repayment six months ahead of the date of the mortgage, the classic case in effect of the old type of fixed mortgage where the legal date for redemption is fixed at six months after the date of the execution of the mortgage, but there was a clear intention from other provisions in the mortgage, notably the provision for the payment of interest (which was clearly envisaged as extending beyond the period of six months limited for the repayment of the principal) which indicated that the common intention of the parties was that the mortgage would be allowed to stay out indefinitely and that the mortgagor would be entitled to defer payment of the principal sum beyond the date fixed so long as he paid interest on that principal sum. . . .

[His Lordship quoted from the judgment of GOULDING J at 955 and continued:]

He goes on to hold that the section applied in that case.

That of course was a very different case from the instant case. It was a case where there was a fixed date for repayment of the principal sum and it was a case where it was quite clearly intended that the actual payment of the principal sum should be deferred beyond that fixed date. And it was a case also where, if default was made in payment of interest, the mortgage contained a provision for calling in the whole sum.

Mr Wilmers, who appears for the bank in this case, has forcibly submitted that the reasoning of that case cannot apply here. In my judgment he is right in making that submission. I say nothing about the correctness of the decision in the *Centrax Trustees* case on the construction of the section. It is indeed difficult, I think, to escape from the conclusion that the section did apply to that case, even though I, for myself, rather question whether it was intended by the legislature to do so. But the instant case is really quite a different case. As Mr Wilmers pointed out, and indeed as was pointed out by Goulding J in the *Centrax Trustees* case, there are two necessary conditions for the application of the section: first, either the mortgage itself or some

---

[14] [1983] Conv 80 (P. H. Kenny); [1982] All ER Rev 177 (P. J. Clarke); [1984] Conv 91 (S. Tromans).

agreement made under it must have the effect that — I will quote only the relevant words — "the mortgagor . . . is to be permitted . . . otherwise to defer payment of" the principal sum "in whole or in part"; secondly, provision must be made in the mortgage or agreement "for earlier payment in the event of any default by the mortgagor or of a demand by the mortgagee or otherwise." Mr Wilmers's first submission is that there is no permission to defer payment. As he points out, this is a simple case of a bank mortgage to secure an overdraft. It is quite clear on the authorities that in these circumstances the money is not capable of being sued for by the bank until demand has been made. Indeed, the mortgage itself so provides, because it is to secure the moneys covenanted to be paid and the moneys are covenanted to be paid on demand having been made in writing. This nowhere more clearly appears than from *Lloyds Bank Ltd v Margolis* [1954] 1 WLR 644, [1954] 1 All ER 734. I think it is only necessary to read briefly from the judgment of Upjohn J at 649, at 738. . . .

When one looks at the charge in the instant case, one asks immediately: "Where is the agreement to be found that the mortgagor is to be permitted otherwise to defer payment of the principal?" because, by definition, the principal does not become due, and cannot be sued for by the bank, until a written demand has been made. Deferment, I think, involves the deferment of payment after it has become due, and quite clearly in this case there appears to me to be no provision, either in the agreement between the parties or in the mortgage itself, by which, on any realistic construction, it can be said that payment by the customer was to be "deferred," or that the customer was permitted to "defer" payment. Mr Cutting has in fact submitted that every case where the principal money does not become payable immediately the mortgage is executed is a case where the mortgagor is entitled to defer payment. That is a submission which I find is impossible to accept.

It seems to me that the defendant's case on the application of section 8 fails at that point, but it also fails, I think, on the other condition, too, because, as Mr Wilmers pointed out, the section requires that provision must be made for earlier payment, and one has to ask oneself: "Earlier than what?" In the instant case the payment was not due until the demand was made, and there is no provision for any payment earlier than that. It is the demand itself which makes the payment due.

For both those reasons, it seems to me that this is clearly a case where section 8 cannot apply to this mortgage, and that really concludes the case. I think it unnecessary to elaborate the matter further. If there had been some reasonable prospect of the defendant repaying the whole of the principal sum, then no doubt it would have been appropriate for the judge to have remitted the matter back to the registrar for a determination of whether he should exercise his power under section 36 (2) of the Act of 1970 to adjourn the proceedings or to postpone the date for the delivery of possession, but that, as Mr Cutting accepts, does not arise. Section 8 does not apply. There is then no further room for the operation of the discretion under section 36, and accordingly in my judgment the decision of the judge must be reversed and the decision of the deputy registrar restored. I would therefore allow the appeal.

In *Governor and Company of the Bank of Scotland v Grimes* [1985] 3 WLR 294, [1985] 2 All ER 254, the defendants borrowed from the plaintiffs £15,015 in order to purchase 26 Guppy Street, Swindon. The loan was secured by an endowment mortgage which provided for repayment of the principal sum at the end of 25 years, with interest payable by monthly instalments, and for the principal sum and accrued interest to be payable immediately in the case of default.

The defendants defaulted on the payments of interest, and the endowment policy lapsed. On the bank's summons for the payment of interest due and an order for possession, the County Court judge held that there was no deferred repayment of capital within section 8 of the Administration of Justice Act 1973, and that he could not exercise his discretion to postpone possession under section 36 of the 1970 Act.

In allowing the appeal, Sir John ARNOLD P said at 298, at 257:

"In certain circumstances the provisions of section 36 are amended and controlled by section 8 of the Administration of Justice Act 1973, and the principal issue in this case is whether that amendment and control extends to the present case.

[His Lordship read s. 8 and continued:]

What that effects in substance is an omission of the obligation for expedited payment which is to be found in the default clause for the purpose of the application of section 36 as a matter of the discretion of the court.

We have considered, and have been assisted by counsel, in the task of giving some meaning to the words 'or is to be permitted' following the word 'entitled' in that subsection, but we have been wholly unable to come to any conclusion as to any possible meaning of that phrase. It must have been included for some purpose, but what that purpose is, for my part at least, I find myself wholly unable to determine. If it is something which is short of a contractual obligation or a contractual right which is there intended to be referred to, the words 'is to be' are peculiarly unsuitable. If it is something distinct from being entitled, then what it is, is wholly obscure. But I do not think much turns on that in the present case; it is the presence of so impenetrable a phrase which makes one think that one has to be very careful in construing this section to feel onself free to give effect to the general tenor of the language in a purposive way so as to make it fit in with the general intention which is evidently exhibited and the context of section 36 in the Administration of Justice Act 1970 in which it has to be read rather than to be bound by a literal meaning of the language used which would not have the purposive effect which seems to be desired. There is no doubt whatever that section 36 of the Act of 1970 applies to such a case as this. It is not made any the less to apply because this is a case in which there is a fixed period for payment of the mortgage principal as a whole rather than an instalment arrangement. One might expect that in a suitable case in which that was the situation, for the purpose of effecting the mitigation which was evidently intended by section 8 of the Administration of Justice Act 1973, the two situations would be equated.

The construction which appealed to the judge was that a deferred payment was a payment which the payer was required to make under one provision of the bargain, but which he was entitled to have deferred under another provision of the bargain, so that, unless there was to be found an obligation to make the payment in question at some time earlier than the date of postponement of that obligation to be found in the relevant other provisions, section 8 of the Administration of Justice 1973 could not be made to apply. . . .

Habib Bank Ltd v Tailor [1982] 1 WLR 1218, [1982] 3 All ER 561, p. 700, ante was a case in which what was before the court was a charge to secure an ordinary banking overdraft so that the subject matter of the debt was one which was due immediately upon the making of an unconditional demand. That is a rather different case, at least socially, in regard to the purpose of this legislation, from the present case where what is primarily in question is a mortgage of a fixed sum for a fixed term. I do not find anything in *Habib Bank Ltd v Tailor* which prevents this court giving to the conception of 'deferred payment' a definition which includes any case in which there is a stated period before the end of which payment does not require to be made which extends into a defined future, and it seems to me that that condition is satisfied by the language of the agreement which, in its extended interpretation, which is not in dispute, is imported by the language 'period of loan 25 years.' It seems to be, therefore, that it can without doing violence to the language of the section and by way of giving effect and purpose to this section, be construed in that way so that there is, thus looked at, a provision here for deferred payment to be found in the agreement. There is no question but that there is also a provision for earlier payment in the event of any default, because that is to be found in clause 4 of the agreement. It seems to me, therefore, that this is a case in which section 8 of the Administration of Justice Act 1973 applies to modify and control the language of section 36 of the Administration of Justice Act 1970 and for that reason I would allow the appeal."

GRIFFITHS LJ said at 301: "It seems to me that it would be highly improbable that Parliament would intend such relief to apply only to instalment mortgages taken out with a building society and not to apply to the alternative and increasingly popular form of finance by loan from a bank, backed by an endowment policy. I am satisfied, for the reasons given by Sir John Arnold P that the wording 'or otherwise to defer payment of it in whole or in part' are deliberately inserted to cover this second type of mortgage transaction where there is no obligation to repay the capital until the end of the term of the loan."

QUESTIONS
1. How would you have decided:
    (*a*) *Western Bank Ltd v Schindler* [1977] Ch 1, [1976] 2 All ER 393, p. 696, ante.
    (*b*) *Quennell v Maltby* [1979] 1 WLR 318, [1979] 1 All ER 568, p. 693, ante.
2. If Mrs Quennell had succeeded, would the tenants have been entitled to protection under AJA 1970, s. 36? (1979) 129 NLJ 457 (A. Waite).

B. Powers to Grant and Accept Surrenders of Leases
LAW OF PROPERTY ACT 1925

99. Leasing powers of mortgagor and mortgagee in possession. — p. 687, ante.

100. Powers of mortgagor and mortgagee in possession to accept surrenders of leases. — p. 688, ante.

C. Sale, Insurance, Appointment of Receiver, Cutting and Selling of Timber[15]

LAW OF PROPERTY ACT 1925

101. Powers incident to estate or interest of mortgagee. — (1) A mortgagee, where the mortgage is made by deed, shall, by virtue of this Act, have the following powers, to the like extent as if they had been in terms conferred by the mortgage deed, but not further (namely):—

(i) A power, when the mortgage money has become due[16], to sell, or to concur with any other person in selling, the mortgaged property, or any part thereof, either subject to prior charges or not[17], and either together or in lots, by public auction or by private contract, subject to such conditions respecting title, or evidence of title, or other matter, as the mortgagee thinks fit, with power to vary any contract for sale, and to buy in at an auction, or to rescind any contract for sale, and to re-sell, without being answerable for any loss occasioned thereby; and

(ii) A power, at any time after the date of the mortgage deed, to insure[18] and keep insured against loss or damage by fire any building, or any effects or property of an insurable nature, whether affixed to the freehold or not, being or forming part of the property which or an estate or interest wherein is mortgaged, and the premiums paid for any such insurance shall be a charge on the mortgaged property or estate or interest, in addition to the mortgage money, and with the same priority, and with interest at the same rate, as the mortgage money; and

(iii) A power, when the mortgage money has become due, to appoint a receiver of the income of the mortgaged property, or any part thereof; or, if the mortgaged property consists of an interest in income, or of a rentcharge or an annual or other periodical sum, a receiver of that property or any part thereof; and

(iv) A power, while the mortgagee is in possession, to cut and sell timber and other trees ripe for cutting, and not planted or left standing for shelter or ornament, or to contract for any such cutting and sale, to be completed within any time not exceeding twelve months from the making of the contract.

(3) The provisions of this Act relating to the foregoing powers, comprised either in this section, or in any other section regulating the exercise of those powers, may be varied or extended by the mortgage deed, and, as so varied and extended, shall, as far as may be, operate in the like manner and with all

---

[15] The first mortgagee is entitled also to the custody of the title deeds: LPA 1925, ss. 85 (1), 86 (1), p. 655, ante; on redemption by the mortgagor, the mortgagee must deliver the deeds to him, unless he has notice of a later mortgage, when he must deliver them to the mortgagee next in order of priority of whom he has notice. In this context, registration is not notice: LPA 1925, s. 96 (2) as amended by LP (A) A 1926, Sch.

[16] I.e., as soon as the contractual date for redemption has passed. If the mortgage money is payable by instalments the power of sale arises as soon as any instalment is in arrear: *Payne v Cardiff RDC* [1932] 1 KB 241; cf. *Twentieth Century Banking Corpn Ltd v Wilkinson* [1977] Ch 99, [1976] 3 All ER 361 (where interest was in arrear but capital not yet due: held no power of sale). See also AJA 1973, s. 8, p. 695, ante.

[17] See *Kaolim Private Ltd v United Overseas Land Ltd* [1983] 1 WLR 472 at 476, per Lord Brightman.

[18] For amount and application of insurance money, see LPA 1925, s. 108.

the like incidents, effects, and consequences, as if such variations or extensions were contained in this Act.

(4) This section applies only if and as far as a contrary intention is not expressed in the mortgage deed, and has effect subject to the terms of the mortgage deed and to the provisions therein contained.

i. SALE[19]

(a) *Legal Mortgagees*

LAW OF PROPERTY ACT 1925

101. Powers incident to estate or interest of mortgagee.
(i) p. 703, ante.

103. Regulation of exercise of power of sale. — A mortgagee shall not exercise the power of sale conferred by this Act unless and until —
(i) Notice requiring payment of the mortgage money has been served on the mortgagor or one of two or more mortgagors, and default has been made in payment of the mortgage money, or of part thereof, for three months after such service; or
(ii) Some interest under the mortgage is in arrear and unpaid for two months after becoming due; or
(iii) There has been a breach of some provision contained in the mortgage deed or in this Act, or in an enactment replaced by this Act, and on the part of the mortgagor, or of some person concurring in making the mortgage, to be observed or performed, other than and besides a covenant for payment of the mortgage money or interest thereon.

104. Conveyance on sale. — (1) A mortgagee exercising the power of sale conferred by this Act shall have power, by deed, to convey the property sold, for such estate and interest therein as he is by this Act authorised to sell or convey or may be the subject of the mortgage, freed from all estates, interests, and rights to which the mortgage has priority, but subject to all estates, interests, and rights which have priority to the mortgage[20].

(2) Where a conveyance is made in exercise of the power of sale conferred by this Act, or any enactment replaced by this Act, the title of the purchaser shall not be impeachable on the ground —
(a) that no case had arisen to authorise the sale; or
(b) that due notice was not given; or
(c) where the mortgage is made after the commencement of this Act, that leave of the court, when so required, was not obtained[1]; or
(d) whether the mortgage was made before or after such commencement, that the power was otherwise improperly or irregularly exercised;

and a purchaser is not, either before or on conveyance, concerned to see or inquire whether a case has arisen to authorise the sale, or due notice has been

---

[19] C & B, pp. 649–653; M & W, pp. 936–942; MM, pp. 475–478; Fisher and Lightwood, chap. 20; (1976) 73 LSG 92, 654; (1977) 74 LSG 493 (H. E. Markson).

[20] Compare LPA 1925, s. 2 (1) (iii), p. 205, ante.

[1] See LPA 1925, s. 110, as amended by Insolvency Act 1985, s. 222, Sch 10, Part III (mortgagor a bankrupt and mortgage executed after 1925); (1944) 5 Conv YB, pp. 70–71.

given, or the power is otherwise properly and regularly exercised[2]; but any person damnified by an unauthorised, or improper, or irregular exercise of the power shall have his remedy in damages against the person exercising the power.

(3) A conveyance on sale by a mortgagee, made after the commencement of this Act, shall be deemed to have been made in exercise of the power of sale conferred by this Act unless a contrary intention appears.

105.   Application of proceeds of sale. — The money which is received by the mortgagee, arising from the sale, after discharge of prior incumbrances to which the sale is not made subject, if any, or after payment into court under this Act of a sum to meet any prior incumbrance, shall be held by him in trust to be applied by him, first, in payment of all costs, charges, and expenses properly incurred by him as incident to the sale or any attempted sale, or otherwise; and secondly, in discharge of the mortgage money, interest, and costs, and other money, if any, due under the mortgage; and the residue of the money so received shall be paid to the person entitled to the mortgaged property[3], or authorised to give receipts for the proceeds of the sale thereof.

106.   Provisions as to exercise of power of sale. — (1) The power of sale conferred by this Act may be exercised by any person for the time being entitled to receive and give a discharge for the mortgage money.

(2) The power of sale conferred by this Act does not affect the right of foreclosure.

88.   Realisation of freehold mortgages. — (1) Where an estate in fee simple has been mortgaged by the creation of a term of years absolute limited thereout or by a charge by way of legal mortgage and the mortgagee sells under his statutory or express power of sale —

 (a) the conveyance by him shall operate to vest in the purchaser the fee simple in the land conveyed subject to any legal mortgage having priority to the mortgage in right of which the sale is made and to any money thereby secured, and thereupon;

 (b) the mortgage term or the charge by way of legal mortgage and any subsequent mortgage term or charges shall merge or be extinguished as respects the land conveyed;

and such conveyance may, as respects the fee simple, be made in the name of the estate owner in whom it is vested.

89.   Realisation of leasehold mortgages. — (1) Where a term of years absolute has been mortgaged by the creation of another term of years

---

[2] See *Bailey v Bannes* [1894] 1 Ch 25 at 30, CA, per STIRLING J. If, however, he "becomes aware ... of any facts showing that the power of sale is not exercisable, or that there is some impropriety in the sale, then, in my judgment, he gets no good title on taking the conveyance"; *Lord Waring v London and Manchester Assurance Co Ltd* [1935] Ch 310 at 318, per CROSSMAN J. *Jenkins v Jones* (1860) 2 Giff 99; *Selwyn v Garfit* (1888) 38 Ch D 273; *Price Bros (Somerford) Ltd v J Kelly Homes (Stroke-on-Trent) Ltd* [1975] 1 WLR 1512, [1975] 3 All ER 369; *Northern Developments (Holdings) Ltd v UDT Securities Ltd* [1976] 1 WLR 1230, [1977] 1 All ER 747; and generally Emmet, pp. 777–778.

[3] M & W point out (p. 941, n. 36) that these words literally refer to the purchaser; "but plainly the phrase must be read as 'to the person who *immediately before the sale* was entitled to the mortgaged property' " and this of course includes other mortgagees. But if the rights of the mortgagor and other encumbrancers have become extinguished by lapse of time (Limitation Act 1980, s. 16, p. 182, ante) the mortgagee may keep all the purchase money himself: *Young v Clarey* [1948] Ch 191, [1948] 1 All ER 197.

absolute limited thereout or by a charge by way of legal mortgage and the mortgagee sells under his statutory or express power of sale, —

(a) the conveyance by him shall operate to convey to the purchaser not only the mortgage term, if any, but also (unless expressly excepted with the leave of the court)[4] the leasehold reversion affected by the mortgage, subject to any legal mortgage having priority to the mortgage in right of which the sale is made and to any money thereby secured, and thereupon;

(b) the mortgage term, or the charge by way of legal mortgage and any subsequent mortgage term or charge, shall merge in such leasehold reversion or be extinguished unless excepted as aforesaid;

and such conveyance may, as respects the leasehold reversion, be made in the name of the estate owner in whom it is vested.

Where a licence to assign is required on a sale by a mortgagee, such licence shall not be unreasonably refused.

2. Conveyances overreaching certain equitable interests and powers.

(1) (iii) p. 205, ante.

---

1. *Effect of Mortgagee's Contract to Sell*

In *Lord Waring v London and Manchester Assurance Co Ltd* [1935] Ch 310, the mortgagee had contracted to sell the property for £186,000. The mortgagor, who was negotiating elsewhere for a loan (on a mortgage of the property) of £200,000, sought an injunction to stop the sale.

CROSSMAN J refused, and said at 317: "After a contract has been entered into, however, it is, in my judgment, perfectly clear (subject to what has been said to me to-day) that the mortgagee (in the present case, the company) can be restrained from completing only on the ground that he has not acted in good faith and that the sale is therefore liable to be set aside. Counsel for the plaintiff, who has argued the case most excellently, submitted that, notwithstanding that the company exercised its power of sale by entering into the contract, the plaintiff's equity of redemption has not been extinguished, as there has been no completion by conveyance, and that, pending completion, the plaintiff is still entitled to redeem, that is, to have the property reconveyed to him on payment of principal, interest, and costs. Counsel is relying, to some extent, on the provisions of the Law of Property Act 1925, which creates a statutory power of sale. In my judgment, section 101 of that Act, which gives to a mortgagee power to sell the mortgaged property, is perfectly clear, and means that the mortgagee has power to sell out and out, by private contract or by auction, and subsequently to complete by conveyance; and the power to sell is, I think, a power by selling to bind the mortgagor. If that were not so, the extraordinary result would follow that every purchaser from a mortgagee would, in effect, be getting a conditional contract liable at any time to be set aside by the mortgagor's coming in and paying the principal, interest and costs. Such a result would make it impossible for a mortgagee, in the ordinary course of events, to sell unless he was in a position to promise that completion should take place immediately or on the day after the contract, and there would have to be a rush for completion in order to defeat a possible claim by the mortgagor[5]."

---

[4] This may be done to prevent the purchaser becoming liable upon the covenants in the lease.

[5] Followed in *Property and Bloodstock Ltd v Emerton* [1968] Ch 94, [1967] 3 All ER 321. For the effect of a contract of sale by the mortgagor upon the mortgagee's powers, see *Duke v Robson* [1973] 1 WLR 267, [1973] 1 All ER 481, p. 714, post.

2.   *Duty of Mortgagee to Obtain the True Market Value*

CUCKMERE BRICK CO LTD *v* MUTUAL FINANCE LTD
[1971] Ch 949, [1971] 2 All ER 633 (CA, SALMON, CROSS
and CAIRNS LJJ)

The plaintiffs owned some 2.6 acres of land on the outskirts of Maidstone,
which they mortgaged to the defendants in 1961–62 for £50,000 and other
money. The defendants put it up for sale by public auction with planning
permission for 33 houses, but without advertising the fact that there also
existed planning permission for 100 flats; and they refused to postpone the
sale when that was pointed out to them. However, they undertook to instruct
the auctioneers to mention at the sale the existence of the permission for flats.
The land was sold in June 1967 for £44,000, but was estimated by PLOWMAN
J to be worth £65,000. The plaintiffs brought an action for negligence.

Held. The mortgagees owed a duty to take reasonable care to obtain a
proper price (per SALMON LJ, the true market value); that (CROSS LJ
dissenting) there had been a breach of that duty; and that (SALMON LJ
dissenting) there should be an enquiry as to the damages sustained by the
mortgagors.

SALMON LJ: It is well settled that a mortgagee is not a trustee of the power
of sale for the mortgagor[6]. Once the power has accrued, the mortgagee is
entitled to exercise it for his own purposes whenever he chooses to do so. It
matters not that the moment may be unpropitious and that by waiting a
higher price could be obtained. He has the right to realise his security by
turning it into money when he likes. Nor, in my view, is there anything to
prevent a mortgagee from accepting the best bid he can get at an auction,
even though the auction is badly attended and the bidding exceptionally low.
Providing none of those adverse factors is due to any fault of the mortgagee,
he can do as he likes. If the mortgagee's interests, as he sees them, conflict
with those of the mortgagor, the mortgagee can give preference to his own
interests, which of course he could not do were he a trustee of the power of
sale for the mortgagor. . . .

It is impossible to pretend that the state of the authorities on this branch of
the law is entirely satisfactory. There are some dicta which suggest that
unless a mortgagee acts in bad faith he is safe. His only obligation to the
mortgagor is not to cheat him. There are other dicta which suggest that in
addition to the duty of acting in good faith, the mortgagee is under a duty to
take reasonable care to obtain whatever is the true market value of the
mortgaged property at the moment he chooses to sell it: compare, for
example, *Kennedy v de Trafford* [1896] 1 Ch 762, [1897] AC 180 with *Tomlin v
Luce* (1889) 43 ChD 191, 194.

The proposition that the mortgagee owes both duties, in my judgment,
represents the true view of the law. Approaching the matter first of all on
principle, it is to be observed that if the sale yields a surplus over the amount
owed under the mortgage, the mortgagee holds this surplus in trust for the
mortgagor. If the sale shows a deficiency, the mortgagor has to make it good
out of his own pocket. The mortgagor is vitally affected by the result of the

---

[6] But he is a trustee of the proceeds of sale: LPA 1925, s. 105, p. 706, ante. See *Garland v Ralph
Pay & Ransom* (1984) 271 EG 106, 197 (selling agent acting for mortgagee held to owe duty of
care to mortgagor when giving advice on marketing and value to mortgagee).

sale but its preparation and conduct is left entirely in the hands of the mortgagee. The proximity between them could scarcely be closer. Surely they are "neighbours". Given that the power of sale is for the benefit of the mortgagee and that he is entitled to choose the moment to sell which suits him, it would be strange indeed if he were under no legal obligation to take reasonable care to obtain what I call the true market value at the date of the sale. Some of the textbooks refer to the "proper price", others to the "best price". Vaisey J in *Reliance Permanent Building Society v Hardwood-Stamper* [1944] Ch 362 at 364, 365, [1944] 2 All ER 75 at 76, 77, seems to have attached great importance to the difference between these two descriptions of "price". My difficulty is that I cannot see any real difference between them. "Proper price" is perhaps a little nebulous, and "the best price" may suggest an exceptionally high price. That is why I prefer to call it "the true market value". . . .

I accordingly conclude, both on principle and authority, that a mortgagee in exercising his power of sale does owe a duty to take reasonable precautions to obtain the true market value of the mortgaged property at the date on which he decides to sell it. No doubt in deciding whether he has fallen short of that duty the facts must be looked at broadly, and he will be adjudged to be in default unless he is plainly on the wrong side of the line[7].

STANDARD CHARTERED BANK LTD *v* WALKER
[1982] 1 WLR 1410, [1982] 3 All ER 938
(CA, Lord DENNING MR, WATKINS and Fox LJJ)[8]

Mr and Mrs Walker were the two directors of John Walker (Developments) Ltd which dealt in large metal presses and moulding machines at Tetbury in Gloucestershire. In 1977 the company borrowed money from the plaintiff bank; the loan was secured by a debenture which gave the bank a floating charge over all the assets of the company and expressly provided that any receiver appointed by the bank was to be deemed to be the agent of the company, which was to be solely responsible for his acts or defaults. In 1978 Mr and Mrs Walker personally guaranteed the loan up to £75,000. In 1981 the amount outstanding was £88, 432, and the plaintiff appointed a receiver who said that he had been instructed to "be out of here as quickly as possible", and that he intended to sell the company's machines by auction as quickly as possible. The auctioneers estimate of the sale price was £90,000. The sale was held in February 1981.

---

[7] M & B, *Trusts and Trustees* (3rd edn, 1984), pp. 240–241; *Palmer v Barclays Bank Ltd* (1972) 23 P & CR 30; *Johnson v Ribbins* (1975) 235 EG 757; *Waltham Forest London Borough v Webb* (1974) 232 EG 461; *Bank of Cyprus (London) Ltd v Gill* (1979) 2 Lloyd's Rep 508; affd. [1980] 2 Lloyd's Rep 51; (1981) 125 NLJ 249 (H. E. Markson); *Norwich General Trust v Grierson* [1984] CLY 2306 (mortgagee held liable for diminution of purchase price due to his negligence in allowing premises to deteriorate between date of taking possession and date of sale); *Garland v Ralph Pay & Ransom* (1984) 271 EG 106, 197 (action by mortgagor against mortgagee's valuer for negligent marketing technique and valuation).

A building society must take reasonable care to ensure that the price is the best price which can be reasonably obtained: Building Societies Act 1962, s. 36.

[8] (1982) 132 NLJ 884 (H. W. Wilkinson); [1982] All ER Rev 39 (D. D. Prentice); *American Express International Banking Corpn v Hurley* [1985] 3 All ER 564.

"It was a disaster. Only about 70 persons attended — nearly all from places round about. Only one buyer from overseas — although the market for these machines was world-wide. It was a bitterly cold day. They had a few heating stoves, but these made such a noise that the auctioneer could not make himself heard. So they were turned off: and many prospective buyers left."

The sale only realised £41,864, which covered the expenses, but left nothing for the preferential creditors and nothing for the bank.

In April 1981 the bank issued a writ against the defendants claiming £75,000 under their guarantee and obtained judgment under an Order 14 summons. On appeal for leave to defend, the defendants alleged that the receiver owed them a duty to exercise reasonable care in conducting the sale, and that the bank, by instructing the receiver to sell as quickly as possible, was liable for having interfered in the conduct of the sale.

Held. Leave to defend granted.

LORD DENNING MR: When a bank lends money to a private company, it usually insists on the overdraft being guaranteed by the directors personally. Especially when a husband and wife are the directors and shareholders of the company. Then, when the company crash and are unable to meet their liabilities, the bank puts in a receiver. He realises the assets of the company. But not enough to pay off the overdraft. The bank then comes down on the directors on the guarantee. Have they any defence? The directors here say that the assets were sold at a gross undervalue. How far does that give them any defence?. . . .

We have had much discussion on the law. So far as mortgages are concerned the law is set out in *Cuckmere Brick Co Ltd v Mutual Finance Ltd* [1971] Ch 949, [1971] 2 All ER 633, p. 708, ante. If a mortgagee enters into possession and realises a mortgaged property, it is his duty to use reasonable care to obtain the best possible price which the circumstances of the case permit. He owes this duty not only to himself, to clear off as much of the debt as he can, but also to the mortgagor so as to reduce the balance owing as much as possible, and also to the guarantor so that he is made liable for as little as possible on the guarantee. This duty is only a particular application of the general duty of care to your neighbour which was stated by Lord Atkin in *Donoghue v Stevenson* [1932] AC 562 and applied in many cases since: see *Dorset Yacht Co Ltd v Home Office* [1970] AC 1004, [1970] 2 All ER 294 and *Anns v Merton London Borough Council* [1978] AC 728, [1977] 2 All ER 492. The mortgagor and the guarantor are clearly in very close "proximity" to those who conduct the sale. The duty of care is owing to them — if not to the general body of creditors of the mortgagor. There are several dicta to the effect that the mortgagee can choose his own time for the sale, but I do not think this means that he can sell at the worst possible time. It is at least arguable that, in choosing the time, he must exercise a reasonable degree of care[9].

So far as the receiver is concerned, the law is well stated by Rigby LJ in *Gaskell v Gosling* [1896] 1 QB 669, a dissenting judgment which was approved by the House of Lords [1978] AC 575. The receiver is the agent of the company, not of the debenture holder, the bank. He owes a duty to use

---

[9] See however, Fox LJ at 1418, at 945: "It is not disputed that a mortgagee can choose his own time for sale."

reasonable care to obtain the best possible price which the circumstances of the case permit. He owes this duty not only to the company, of which he is the agent, to clear off as much of its indebtedness to the bank as possible, but he also owes a duty to the guarantor, because the guarantor is liable only to the same extent as the company. The more the overdraft is reduced, the better for the guarantor. It may be that the receiver can choose the time of sale within a considerable margin, but he should, I think, exercise a reasonable degree of care about it. The debenture holder, the bank, is not responsible for what the receiver does except in so far as it gives him directions or interferes with his conduct of the realisation. If it does so, then it too is under a duty to use reasonable care towards the company and the guarantor.

If it should appear that the mortgagee or the receiver have not used reasonable care to realise the assets to the best advantage, then the mortgagor, the company, and the guarantor are entitled in equity to an allowance. They should be given credit for the amount which the sale should have realised if reasonable care had been used. Their indebtedness is to be reduced accordingly.

The only doubt on those propositions is cast by two cases at first instance. The first is *Barclays Bank Ltd v Thienel* (1978) 122 SJ 472.

[His Lordship reviewed the case and continued:]

The second case is *Latchford v Beirne* [1981] 3 All ER 705. That was a case of a receiver. A debenture holder had put in a receiver. The receiver sold the property. Again the guarantor sought to say that there had been want of reasonable care in the disposal of the assets. Milmo J went so far as to say that there was no duty of care towards the guarantor. He said that there was no duty of care towards the creditor. He treated the guarantor as though he was simply a creditor. I cannot agree with that either. Clearly the guarantor's liability is dependent upon the company's. He is in a very special position. The amount of his liability depends entirely on the amount that the stock realises when sold with proper care. To my mind he is well within the test of "proximity." The receiver owes a duty not only to the company, but also to the guarantor, to exercise reasonable care in the disposal of the assets. I say nothing about creditors. We are not concerned with them today.

Neither counsel before us sought to support the decisions in those two cases. . . .

Putting those two cases on one side, it seems to me that on the facts of this case there are these triable issues. There is a triable issue as to whether or not the bank did interfere with the sale in such a way as to take away some of the receiver's discretion, not only by directing him to sell as quickly as possible, but also in regard to publicity and so forth. On reading the affidavit of Mr Walker it seems to me that, until there has been discovery, there is an arguable case for saying that the bank did interfere not only in the timing of the sale, but also in other respects. So the matter should be investigated to determine the liability of the bank. I will not go into whether or not the receiver would be liable for any negligence of the auctioneer; but there is certainly a triable issue as to whether or not the sale was conducted with the proper degree of care which is owed to all those interested in the proceeds of it. It is clear that it was a disastrous sale which realised far less than any of the experts had anticipated. There is a triable issue as to whether that was due to any fault in the arrangements for the sale.

Those are triable issues of fact which ought to go for trial. There should be unconditional leave to defend[10].

3.   *Sale by Mortgagee to Himself*

It has long been the rule that in exercising the power of sale a "mortgagee cannot sell to himself, either alone or with others, nor to a trustee for himself, nor to anyone employed by him to conduct the sale. A sale by a person to himself is no sale at all[11]." But there is no hard and fast rule that a mortgagee may not sell to a company in which he is interested[12].

TSE KWONG LAM *v* WONG CHIT SEN

[1983] 1 WLR 1349, [1983] 3 All ER 54
(PC, Lords FRASER of TULLYBELTON, BRANDON of OAKBROOK, BRIGHTMAN and TEMPLEMAN and Sir John MEGAW)[13].

In 1963 the appellant mortgagor constructed a large building, containing shops, offices and flats at Kowloon in Hong Kong. He financed it by a loan from the respondent to whom he mortgaged the building.

In 1966 the appellant fell into arrears and the outstanding mortgage debt was $ HK 1.4 m. The respondent arranged for the building to be sold at public auction on 24 June. A few days before the auction, the respondent and his wife, as directors of a company, of which they and their children were the sole shareholders, held a directors' meeting at which they resolved that the wife should bid for the property on behalf of the company up to a price of $ HK 1.2 m. At the auction, which was attended by some 30–40 people, the respondent informed the auctioneer that $ HK 1.2 m. was the reserve price; and at that price the wife, who was the sole bidder, purchased the property for the company.

In an action by the respondent in 1966, the appellant counter-claimed that the sale should be set aside on the ground that it had been improper and at an undervalue. This counter-claim was not pursued to judgment until 1979.

Held.

(1) The respondent had failed to show that he had taken reasonable steps to obtain the best price reasonably obtainable.

(2) By reason of his inexcusable delay, the appellant was not entitled to have the sale set aside but only to damages.

LORD TEMPLEMAN: In the view of this Board on authority and on principle there is no hard and fast rule that a mortgagee may not sell to a company in which he is interested. The mortgagee and the company seeking to uphold the transaction must show that the sale was in good faith and that the mortgagee took reasonable precautions to obtain the best price reasonably obtainable at the time. The mortgagee is not however bound to postpone the sale in the hope of obtaining a better price or to adopt a piecemeal method

---

[10] Followed in *American Express Banking Corpn v Hurley* [1985] 3 All ER 564.
[11] *Farrar v Farrars Ltd* (1888) 40 ChD 395 at 409, per LINDLEY LJ; *Martinson v Clowes* (1882) 21 ChD 857 (purchase by secretary of building society mortgage); *Williams v Wellingborough Borough Council* [1975] 1 WLR 1327, [1975] 3 All ER 462 ("a see-through dress of a sale", at 1329, at 463, per RUSSELL LJ: the decision itself was reversed by Housing Act 1980, s. 112 for the benefit of existing local authority mortgagees).
[12] *Tse Kwong Lam v Wong Chit Sen* [1983] 1 WLR 1349, [1983] 3 All ER 54, infra.
[13] [1984] Conv 143 (P. Jackson); [1983] All ER Rev 57 (D. D. Prentice).

of sale which could only be carried out over a substantial period or at some risk of loss. This view of the matter is consistent with the decision of the House of Lords in *York Buildings Co v Mackenzie* (1795) 3 Pat 378.

In the present case in which the mortgagee held a large beneficial interest in the shares of the purchasing company, was a director of the company, and was entirely responsible for financing the company, the other shareholders being his wife and children, the sale must be closely examined and a heavy onus lies on the mortgagee to show that in all respects he acted fairly to the borrower and used his best endeavours to obtain the best price reasonably obtainable for the mortgaged property.

[His Lordship referred to *Hodson v Deans* [1903] 2 Ch 647; *Kennedy v De Trafford* [1897] AC 180; *McHugh v Union Bank of Canada* [1913] AC 299; and *Cuckmere Brick Co Ltd v Mutual Finance Ltd* [1971] Ch 949, [1971] 2 All ER 633, p. 708, ante, and continued:]

In the result their Lordships consider that in the present case the company was not debarred from purchasing the mortgaged property but, in view of the close relationship between the company and the mortgagee and in view in particular of the conflict of duty and interest to which the mortgagee was subject, the sale to the company for $1.2 m. can only be supported if the mortgagee proves that he took reasonable precautions to obtain the best price reasonably obtainable at the time of sale.

On behalf of the mortgagee it was submitted that all reasonable steps were taken when the mortgagee, with adequate advertisement, sold the property at a properly conducted auction to the highest bidder. The submission assumes that such an auction must produce the best price reasonably obtainable or, as Salmon LJ expressed the test, the true market value. But the price obtained at any particular auction may be less than the price obtainable by private treaty and may depend on the steps taken to encourage bidders to attend. An auction which only produces one bid is not necessarily an indication that the true market value has been achieved. . . .

The mortgagee could have consulted estate agents about the method of sale and about the method of securing the best price. At the very least he could have consulted an estate agent about the level of the reserve price. The auctioneer was not informed of the reserve price until immediately before the auction and in evidence he very properly declined to comment on the reserve because he had not valued the property. This confirms the impression that the auctioneers were not instructed to do more than put the property under the hammer, a procedure which may be appropriate to the sale of second-hand furniture but is not necessarily conducive to the attainment of the best price for freehold or leasehold property. It was not of course in the interests of the company that enthusiasm for the sale should be stimulated or that the reserve should be settled by anyone other than the mortgagee. The reserve of $1.2 m. was fixed by the mortgagee and was the price at which he advised and intended that the company should purchase. The mortgagee was a property investor and speculator. The company was his family company and he held shares in and financed the company. The mortgagee would not have advised the company to bid $1.2 m. for the property unless he thought that was an advantageous price for the company to pay. . . .

At the trial and on this appeal the mortgagee adopted the attitude that a mortgagee exercising his power of sale is entitled to secure the mortgaged property for a company in which he is interested at a price advised by the mortgagee provided that the property is properly advertised and sold by auction. A decision to this effect would expose borrowers to greater perils than those to which they are now subject as a result of decisions which enable a mortgagee to choose the date of the exercise of his power. A mortgagee who wishes to secure the mortgaged property for a company in which he is interested ought to show that he protected the interests of the borrower by taking expert advice as to the method of sale, as to the steps which ought reasonably to be taken to make the sale a success and as to the amount of the reserve. There was no difficulty in obtaining such advice orally and in writing and no good reason why a mortgagee, concerned to act fairly towards his borrower, should fail or neglect to obtain or act upon such advice in all respects as if the mortgagee were desirous of realising the best price reasonably obtainable at the date of the sale for property belonging to the mortgagee himself.

Where a mortgagee fails to satisfy the court that he took all reasonable steps to obtain the best price reasonably obtainable and that his company bought at the best price, the court will, as a general rule, set aside the sale and restore to the borrower the equity of redemption of which he has been unjustly deprived. But the borrower will be left to his remedy in damages against the mortgagee for the failure of the mortgagee to secure the best price if it will be inequitable as between the borrower and the purchaser for the sale to be set aside. In the present case. . . the mortgagee and the company submit that the delay on the part of the borrower in pursuing his counter-claim has rendered it unjust for the building to be restored to the borrower. . . .

The borrower has been guilty of inexcusable delay in prosecuting his counterclaim.

[His Lordship reviewed the evidence, and continued:]

The borrower by his delay achieved a favourable position; if the property decreased in value he could either abandon his action or seek damages in setting aside the sale. If the property increased in value he could persist with his claim to set aside the sale. In the circumstances the Board consider that the borrower is not[13a] entitled to the alternative remedy of damages. That was the view taken by the trial judge.

The measure of damages must be the difference between the best price reasonably obtainable on June 24, 1966, and the price of $1.2 m. paid by the company.

QUESTIONS
1. What restrictions, if any, should be placed on the time at which the mortgagee exercises his power of sale?
2. Do you think that the duty of care which the mortgagee owes to the mortgagor and his guarantor should be extended to the creditors of the mortgagor?
3. A mortgagor defaults and then contracts to sell the mortgaged property to X. The contract is registered as an estate contract under the Land Charges Act 1972, section 2 (4), Class C (iv). The mortgagee, under the statutory power of sale, contracts to sell the property to Y. Can X succeed in a claim for specific performance against the mortgagor and for an injunction against the mortgagee? *Duke v Robson* [1973] 1 WLR 267, [1973] 1 All ER 481; (1973) 37 Conv (NS) 210 (F.R. Crane).

[13a] The word "not" is correctly omitted in [1983] 3 All ER 54 at 64.

(b) Equitable Mortgagees

LAW OF PROPERTY ACT 1925

90. Realisation of equitable charges by the court. — (1) Where an order for sale is made by the court in reference to an equitable mortgage on land (not secured by a legal term of years absolute or by a charge by way of legal mortgage) the court may, in favour of a purchaser, make a vesting order conveying the land or may appoint a person to convey the land or create and vest in the mortgagee a legal term of years absolute to enable him to carry out the sale, as the case may require, in like manner as if the mortgage had been created by deed by way of legal mortgage pursuant to this Act, but without prejudice to any incumbrance having priority to the equitable mortgage unless the incumbrancer consents to the sale.

(2) This section applies to equitable mortgages made or arising before or after the commencement of this Act, but not to a mortgage which has been over-reached under the powers conferred by this Act or otherwise.

In the case of an equitable mortgage by deposit of title deeds, the mortgagee has no power of sale[14]. If he wishes to sell, he must apply to the court under Law of Property Act 1925, section 91 (2), p. 685, ante. The mortgagee's statutory power of sale becomes available if the mortgage is made by deed, and equitable mortgages are commonly accompanied by a memorandum under seal. Such a power, however, covers only "the mortgaged property"[15] — that is the equitable interest. In order to give the mortgagee power to sell the legal estate, the deed often includes a power of attorney[16], or a declaration of trust, or both.

In *Re White Rose Cottage* [1965] Ch 940, [1965] 1 All ER 11, one question was whether a sale by the mortgagor (the Kamerun company) and the bank (an equitable mortgagee) gave a title free from or subject to an equitable charge in favour of a later equitable chargee. The Court of Appeal construed the sale as one by the mortgagor with the concurrence of the mortgagee, and the title which passed was therefore that held by the mortgagor and the purchaser took subject to the later charge.

A different construction had been placed upon the sale by WILBERFORCE J at first instance [1964] Ch 483, [1964] 1 All ER 169; he treated it as being a sale by an equitable mortgagee.

The mortgagor had executed a memorandum under seal "in the usual form for effecting a charge to secure [an] advance. It was stated that the documents of title had been deposited as security for the money due. The liability under the charge was not to exceed £50,000. The Kamerun company gave an undertaking to execute a legal charge or mortgage on request and agreed to hold the property as trustee for executing such a charge, the bank having power to appoint a new trustee in the place of the . . . company at any time. An irrevocable power of attorney was given to the bank so that the

---

[14] C & B, pp. 660–662; M & W, pp. 950–953; MM, pp. 484–485.
[15] LPA 1925, s. 101 (1) (i).
[16] Powers of Attorney Act 1971, ss. 4 (1), 5 (3).

bank, in the name and on behalf of the . . . company, could vest the legal estate in the property in any purchaser or other person in exercise of the statutory powers conferred on mortgagees free and discharged from all rights of redemption".

Both judgments of the Court of Appeal (Lord DENNING MR and HARMAN LJ, with SALMON LJ agreeing with both) expressed the view that, if they had construed the sale, as WILBERFORCE J did, as being a sale by an equitable mortgagee under a power of sale, the legal estate would have passed; and by virtue of Law of Property Act 1925, section 104 (1), would have passed to the purchaser free from the subsequent charge.

HARMAN LJ said at 955, at 18: "In other words, I think that an equitable mortgagee under a deed in the terms of the memorandum . . . can by virtue of the power of attorney contained in it convey to a purchaser the legal estate in the mortgaged property without first going through the form of calling for the execution by the mortgagor of a legal mortgage."

Lord DENNING MR said at 951, at 15: "Wilberforce J has held that that conveyance was an exercise by the bank of their statutory power of sale as mortgagees; and that selling as mortgagees they were entitled to sell the property freed from all charges subsequent to their own. If this be the correct construction of the conveyance, I would agree with him. [His Lordship referred to Law of Property Act 1925, section 104 (1) and continued:] The subject of the mortgage here was the property itself, both the legal and equitable estate in it: and I see no reason why an equitable mortgagee, exercising his power of sale, should not be able to convey the legal estate[17]."

ii.   APPOINTMENT OF RECEIVER[18]

LAW OF PROPERTY ACT 1925

101.   Powers incident to estate or interest of mortgagee. — (1) (iii). P. 704, ante.

109.   Appointment, powers, remuneration and duties of receiver.— (1) A mortgagee entitled to appoint a receiver under the power in that behalf conferred by this Act shall not appoint a receiver until he has become entitled to exercise the power of sale conferred by this Act, but may then, by writing under his hand, appoint such person as he thinks fit to be receiver.

(2) A receiver appointed under the powers conferred by this Act, or any enactment replaced by this Act, shall be deemed to be the agent of the mortgagor; and the mortgagor shall be solely responsible for the receiver's acts or defaults unless the mortgage deed otherwise provides[19].

(4) A person paying money to the receiver shall not be concerned to inquire whether any case has happened to authorise the receiver to act.

(8) Subject to the provisions of this Act as to the application of insurance money[20], the receiver shall apply all money received by him as follows, namely:

---

[17] See W & C, vol. i., 212, where this view is doubted.
[18] C & B, pp. 648–649; M & W, pp. 947–949; MM, pp. 483–484; Fisher and Lightwood, chap. 18.
[19] See *Chatsworth Properties Ltd v Effiom* [1971] 1 WLR 144, [1971] 1 All ER 604; *Standard Chartered Bank Ltd v Walker* [1982] 1 WLR 1410, [1982] 3 All ER 938, p. 709, ante.
[20] LPA 1925, s. 108.

(i) In discharge of all rents, taxes, rates, and outgoings whatever affecting the mortgaged property; and

(ii) In keeping down all annual sums or other payments, and the interest on all principal sums, having priority to the mortgage in right whereof he is receiver; and

(iii) In payment of his commission, and of the premiums on fire, life or other insurances, if any, properly payable under the mortgage deed or under this Act, and the cost of executing necessary or proper repairs directed in writing by the mortgagee; and

(iv) In payment of the interest accruing due in respect of any principal money due under the mortgage; and

(v) In or towards discharge of the principal money if so directed in writing by the mortgagee;

and shall pay the residue, if any, of the money received by him to the person who, but for the possession of the receiver, would have been entitled to receive the income of which he is appointed receiver, or who is otherwise entitled to the mortgaged property.

D. Foreclosure[1]

LAW OF PROPERTY ACT 1925

88. Realisation of freehold mortgages. — (2) Where any such mortgagee obtains an order for foreclosure absolute, the order shall operate to vest the fee simple in him (subject to any legal mortgage having priority to the mortgage in right of which the foreclosure is obtained and to any money thereby secured), and thereupon the mortgage term, if any, shall thereby be merged in the fee simple, and any subsequent mortgage term or charge by way of legal mortgage bound by the order shall thereupon be extinguished.

89. Realisation of leasehold mortgages. — (2) Where any such mortgagee obtains an order for foreclosure absolute, the order shall, unless it otherwise provides, operate (without giving rise to a forfeiture for want of a licence to assign) to vest the leasehold reversion affected by the mortgage and any subsequent mortgage term in him, subject to any legal mortgage having priority to the mortgage in right of which the foreclosure is obtained and to any money thereby secured, and thereupon the mortgage term and any subsequent mortgage term or charge by way of legal mortgage bound by the order shall, subject to any express provision to the contrary contained in the order, merge in such leasehold reversion or be extinguished.

The mortgagee or any person interested may ask the court to order a sale instead of foreclosure; Law of Property Act 1925, section 91 (2), p. 685, ante[2].

---

[1] C & B, pp. 653–655; M & W, pp. 933–936; MM, pp. 473–475; Fisher and Lightwood, chaps. 21, 22; (1978) LS Gaz 447; (1979) 129 NLJ 33 (H. E. Markson), 225 (C. M. Pepper); (1981) 260 EG 899 (D. Brahams).

[2] For the inter-relationship between the two remedies, see *Twentieth Century Banking Corpn Ltd v Wilkinson* [1977] Ch 99, [1976] 3 All ER 361.

In *Campbell v Holyland* (1877) 7 ChD 166, Blakely mortgaged a reversionary interest in a trust fund to Campbell and died insolvent. A foreclosure decree was made in 1876 ordering payment of the money by 4 January 1877. Blakely's administrator, Holyland, transferred the equity of redemption to X and Y who negotiated for the purchase of the interest of the mortgagee, Campbell; and failed to pay on 4 January 1877 because they thought, incorrectly, that they had purchased the interest. They discovered subsequently that Campbell had sold his interest on 3 January, to Ford, who was aware of the negotiations to sell to X and Y. The foreclosure decree was made absolute.

In March 1877, X and Y's executors moved to reopen the foreclosure decree, and JESSEL MR allowed them to do so. He said at 171:

"I have no doubt that I ought to make the order asked for.

The question in dispute is really whether a mortgagor can be allowed to redeem after an order of foreclosure absolute, and I think, on looking at the authorities, that no Chancellor or Vice-Chancellor has ever laid down that any special circumstances are essential to enable a mortgagor to redeem in such a case.

Now what is the principle? The principle in a Court of Equity has always been that, though a mortgage is in form an absolute conveyance when the condition is broken, in equity it is always security; and it must be remembered that the doctrine arose at the time when mortgages were made in the form of conditional conveyance, the condition being that if the money was not paid at the day, the estate should become the estate of the mortgagee; that was the contract between the parties; yet Courts of Equity interfered with actual contract to this extent, by saying there was a paramount intention that the estate should be security, and that the mortgage money should be debt; and they gave relief in the shape of redemption on that principle. Of course that would lead, and did lead, to this inconvenience, that even when the mortgagor was not willing to redeem, the mortgagee could not sell or deal with the estate as his own, and to remedy that inconvenience the practice of bringing a foreclosure suit was adopted, by which a mortgagee was entitled to call on the mortgagor to redeem within a certain time, under penalty of losing the right of redemption. In that foreclosure suit the Court made various orders — interim orders fixing a time for payment of the money — and at last there came the final order which was called foreclosure absolute, that is, in form, that the mortgagor should not be allowed to redeem at all; but it was form only, just as the original deed was form only; for the Courts of Equity soon decided that, notwithstanding the form of that order, they would after that order allow the mortgagor to redeem. That is, although the order of foreclosure absolute appeared to be a final order of the Court, it was not so, but the mortgagee still remained liable to be treated as mortgagee and the mortgagor still retained a claim to be treated as mortgagor, subject to the discretion of the Court. Therefore everybody who took an order for foreclosure absolute knew that there was still a discretion in the Court to allow the mortgagor to redeem.

Under what circumstances that discretion should be exercised is quite another matter. The mortgagee had a right to deal with an estate acquired under foreclosure absolute the day after he acquired it; but he knew perfectly well that there might be circumstances to entitle the mortgagor to redeem, and everybody buying the estate from a mortgagee who merely acquired a title under such an order was considered to have the same knowledge, namely, that the estate might be taken away from him by the exercise, not of a capricious discretion, but of a judicial discretion by the Court of Equity which had made the order.

That being so, on what terms is that judicial discretion to be exercised? It has been said by the highest authority that it is impossible to say a priori what are the terms. They must depend upon the circumstances of each case. . . . In the first place the mortgagor must come, as it is said, promptly; that is, within a reasonable time. He is not to let the mortgagee deal with the estate as his own — if it is a landed estate, the mortgagee being in possession of it and using it — and then without any special reason come and say, 'Now I will redeem'. He cannot do that; he must come within a reasonable time. What is a reasonable time? You must have regard to the nature of the property. As has been stated in more than one of the cases, where the estate is an estate in land in possession — where the mortgagee takes it in possession and deals with it and alters the property, and so on — the mortgagor must come more quickly than where it is an estate in reversion, as to which the mortgagee can do nothing except sell it. So that you must have regard to the nature of the estate in ascertaining what is to be considered reasonable time.

Then, again, was the mortgagee[3] entitled to redeem, but by some accident unable to redeem? Did he expect to get the money from a quarter from which he might reasonably hope to obtain it, and was he disappointed at the last moment? Was it a very large sum, and did he require a considerable time to raise it elsewhere? All those things must be considered in determining what is a reasonable time.

Then an element for consideration has always been the nature of the property as regards value[4]. For instance, if an estate were worth £50,000, and had been foreclosed for a mortgage debt of £5,000, the man who came to redeem that estate would have a longer time than where the estate was worth £5,100, and he was foreclosed for £5,000. But not only is there money value, but there may be other considerations. It may be an old family estate or a chattel, or picture, which possesses a special value for the mortgagor, but which possesses not the same value for other people; or it may be, as has happened in this instance, that the property, though a reversionary interest in the funds, is of special value to both the litigants: it may possess not merely a positive money value, but a peculiar value having regard to the nature of the title and other incidents, so that you cannot set an actual money value upon it. In fact, that is the real history of this contest, for the property does not appear to be of much more money value — though it is of some more — than the original amount of the mortgage. All this must be taken into consideration.

Then it is said you must not interfere against purchasers. As I have already explained, there are purchasers and purchasers. If the purchaser buys a freehold estate in possession after the lapse of a considerable time from the order of foreclosure absolute, with no notice of any extraneous circumstances which would induce the Court to interfere, I for one should

---

[3] Presumably "mortgagor" was intended here.

[4] *Lancashire and Yorkshire Reversionary Interest Co v Crowe* (1970) 114 SJ 435 (foreclosure decree made absolute in respect of mortgage of reversionary interest; and re-opened after the interest fell into possession on life tenant's death. The sum due was £3,000, and the fund £6,100).

decline to interfere with such a title as that; but if the purchaser bought the estate within twenty-four hours after the foreclosure absolute, and with notice of the fact that it was of much greater value than the amount of the mortgage debt, is it to be supposed that a Court of Equity would listen to the contention of such a purchaser that he ought not to be interfered with? He must be taken to know the general law that an order for foreclosure may be opened under proper circumstances and under a proper exercise of discretion by the Court; and if the mortgagor in that case came the week after, is it to be supposed a Court of Equity would so stultify itself as to say that a title so acquired would stand in the way? I am of opinion it would not.

Now I come to the circumstances of this case, and I must say they are very strong in favour of opening the foreclosure. . . .

The present purchaser, Mr Ford, being very desirous to acquire the property for a collateral object[5] — I am not saying a wrong object, but a collateral object — had, before the time for foreclosure absolute had arrived, entered into a contract with the mortgagee to buy it. He was not a purchaser coming in even the day after foreclosure, but a purchaser coming in before foreclosure, and at that time of course he knew the property was redeemable. He bought a property certainly redeemable, for the day for redemption had not even arrived. That is the kind of purchase I am dealing with. He was aware on the day of redemption that it was not from unwillingness to redeem that the mortgagor failed to pay the money, but because the mortgagor was under the belief that he had acquired a right to take the property on paying less than the mortgage money, by reason of a contract of purchase with the mortgagee. . . .

I am of opinion, however, that such a sale as this ought to have no weight whatever, and that under the circumstances the mortgagor is entitled to open the foreclosure on the usual terms, that is, on payment of principal, interest, and costs."

In *Kinnaird v Trollope* (1888) 39 Ch D 636, STIRLING J said at 642: "Where a mortgagee has obtained a decree for foreclosure absolute he may still sue the mortgagor on the covenant for payment of the mortgage debt provided he retains the mortgaged property in his possession, but (as is laid down by Lord *Langdale* in *Lockhart v Hardy* (1846) 9 Beav 349 at 355) by so suing he gives the mortgagor a new right of redemption, notwithstanding the foreclosure, and the mortgagor may file a bill to redeem. If, however, the mortgagee has sold the mortgaged property, a Court of Equity will interfere to restrain an action on the covenant[6]."

E. Consolidation[7]

If the same mortgagor has mortgaged more than one property to the same mortgagee, and if one of the properties so mortgaged is worth less than the

---

[5] To obtain the property for Blakely's widow.

[6] Followed in *Lloyds and Scottish Trust Ltd v Britten* (1982) 44 P & CR 249 (guarantor of mortgagor likewise held not suable).

[7] C & B, pp. 656–660; M & W, pp. 955–960; MM, pp. 487–490; Waldock, pp. 284–295; Fisher and Lightwood, chap. 27. As to whether the right amounts to a general equitable charge within LCA 1972, s. 2 (4), Class C (iii), see (1948) 92 SJ 736; W & C, vol. 1, 189.

debt for the repayment of which it has been charged as security, it is in the mortgagor's interest to redeem the other properties but not that one. The mortgagor is, however, asking a favour of equity in being allowed to redeem any property after the contractual date for redemption has passed, and, in accordance with the maxim: "He who comes to Equity must do Equity", the mortgagor may be prevented from redeeming one mortgage without redeeming others. In other words, the mortgagee has a right in certain circumstances to consolidate the various mortgages against the mortgagor.

LAW OF PROPERTY ACT 1925

93. Restriction on consolidation of mortgages. — (1) A mortgagor seeking to redeem any one mortgage is entitled to do so without paying any money due under any separate mortgage made by him, or by any person through whom he claims, solely on property other than that comprised in the mortgage which he seeks to redeem.

This subsection applies only if and as far as a contrary intention is not expressed in the mortgage deeds or one of them.

(2) This section does not apply where all the mortgages were made before the first day of January, eighteen hundred and eighty-two.

(3) Save as aforesaid, nothing in this Act, in reference to mortgages, affects any right of consolidation or renders inoperative a stipulation in relation to any mortgage made before or after the commencement of this Act reserving a right to consolidate.

PLEDGE *v* WHITE
[1896] AC 187 (HL, LORDS HALSBURY LC, WATSON and DAVEY)

There were mortgages on seven different properties; the properties will be referred to as Nos. 1–7. They were mortgaged by James Banks to various mortgagees between 1863 and 1866.

In 1866 James Banks the mortgagor made a second mortgage of Nos. 4–7 to Brockman: and in 1868 a third mortgage of these properties and a second mortgage of Nos. 1–3 to Brockman and Harrison. In 1885, Brockman and Harrison assigned their equities of redemption in all 7 properties to Pledge, the appellant.

Between 1871 and 1890, Brockman became the transferee of all the first mortgages except that on No. 3[8]. He died in 1877, and in 1890 his executors, the respondents, took an assignment of the first mortgage on No. 3.

In 1890 the appellants claimed to redeem No. 2 alone. The respondents refused to allow him to do so without redeeming the other six.

Held. The mortgagee was entitled to consolidate.

LORD HALSBURY LC: My Lords, I have had an opportunity of considering the judgment prepared by my noble and learned friend (Lord Davey) and I am not prepared to dissent from it. I use that form of expression because I confess I lament the conclusion to which it has been found necessary to come,

---

[8] The facts as given by Lord DAVEY do not explain how Brockman obtained the mortgages on Nos. 6 and 7.

although I believe the strict principle upon which it rests is founded in our law at present, and in dealing with a technical system it is better to adhere to a principle when once established, than to create greater confusion by dissenting from it. I think the principle laid down in *Vint v Padget* (1858) 2 De G & J 611 has been so firmly established now by authority in our technical system, that I feel more mischief would be done by dissenting from it, than by acquiescing in it. . . :

LORD DAVEY: The question for your Lordships' decision is whether the respondents have the right of consolidation which they claim, notwithstanding that the mortgages which it is sought to consolidate were not united in title with the mortgage sought to be redeemed until after the assignment of the equity of redemption to the present appellant's predecessors in title. . . .

The equitable rule as to the consolidation of mortgages is not one of those doctrines of the Court of Chancery which has met with general approbation — at any rate as regards its later development. Originally it may have been a right of a mortgagee holding two separate mortgages on estates of the same mortgagor which have become absolute estates at law against the mortgagor and debtor personally to refuse to be redeemed as regards one estate without having his other debt also paid. But it has long been settled that the right of consolidation may be exercised by the transferee of the mortgages as well as by the original mortgagee, and may be exercised in respect of equitable mortgages as well as by a mortgagee holding the legal estate absolute at law; and on the other hand, that it may be asserted against the assignee of an equity of redemption from the mortgagor as well as against the mortgagor himself. . . .

The case of *Vint v Padget* came before Stuart V-C in the first instance, whose judgment may be referred to as shewing how entirely that experienced judge considered the point to be settled. "In accepting", he says, "by way of security the equity of redemption of two separate estates, Mr Lee deliberately incurred the risk of their uniting in one hand, and when that union has taken place there is only one single debt, and in order to redeem he must pay off both mortgages, each of which affects the entirety of both estates".

[His Lordship referred to: *Bovey v Skipwich* (1671) 1 Cas in Ch 201; *Titley v Davies* (1743) 2 Y & C Ch Cas 399; *Selby v Pomfret* (1861) 3 De G F & J 595; *Beevor v Luck* (1867) LR 4 Eq 537; *White v Hillacre* (1839) 3 Y & C Ex 597; *Harter v Colman* (1882) 19 ChD 630; *Jennings v Jordan* (1881) 6 App Cas 698, and continued:]

It appears to me, my Lords, that an assignee of two or more equities of redemption from one mortgagor stands in a widely different position from the assignee of one equity only. He knows, or has the opportunity of knowing, what are the mortgages subject to which he has purchased the property, and he knows that they may become united by transfer in one hand. If the doctrine of consolidation be once admitted it appears to me not unreasonable to hold that a person in such a position occupies the place of the mortgagor or assignor to him towards the holders of the mortgages, subject to which he has purchased, although it may be unreasonable to hold that he can be affected by the transfer to such holders of mortgages to other persons by the same mortgagor on property which he has not purchased, and with the equity of redemption of which he has no concern. He does not investigate the title to such other property and cannot know in the latter case to what mortgages the property is subject. If your Lordships affirm the decree now under appeal, the doctrine of consolidation will be confined within at least intelligible limits. It will be applicable where at the date when redemption is sought all the mortgages are united in one hand and redeemable by the same person, or where after that state of things has once existed the equities of redemption have become separated[9]. If the purchaser of two or more equities of redemption desires to prevent consolidation, he has it in his power to redeem any one mortgage before consolidation takes place; but if for his own convenience he delays doing so, he runs the same risk as his assignor ran of the mortgages becoming united by transfer in one hand.

I am of opinion that the application of the doctrine of consolidation to a case like the present has been too long considered part of the equitable jurisprudence of this country to be altered at the present time, and it is not so unreasonable as to demand a reversal of it by this House.

I move, therefore, that this appeal be dismissed with costs.

In *Cummins v Fletcher* (1880) 14 Ch D 699, the trustees of a building society, who were mortgagees of two properties, refused to allow a bank, the second mortgagee of one of the properties, to redeem it, without also redeeming the other. All payments due under the first mortgage were up to date, but those on the second were in arrears.

The Court of Appeal (JAMES, COTTON and THESIGER LJJ, reversing HALL V-C) refused to allow the building society to consolidate, on the ground that consolidation arose only where the mortgagor was in default and was asking a favour of the Court of Equity. JAMES LJ said at 708: "The whole doctrine of consolidation, whatever may have been the particular circumstances under which it has been applied to different cases, arises from the power of the Court of Equity to put its own price upon its own interference as a matter of equitable consideration in favour of any suitor."

A further reason, mentioned by the court, was that the mortgagors were not the same in the two mortgages. In the first mortgage, the mortgagor was Vaugham and in the second Vaugham and Neesham, partners. This point was not necessary for the decision.

In *Hughes v Britannia Permanent Building Society* [1906] 2 Ch 607, A in 1894 mortgaged Blackacre to the defendants, the mortgage providing that A should not be entitled to redeem without paying all the moneys due by A to the defendants under any other mortgage.

A then mortgaged Whiteacre to the defendants, and gave a second mortgage to the plaintiffs, the defendants having notice of this mortgage; A subsequently mortgaged two separate properties to the defendants.

The plaintiffs claimed to redeem Whiteacre, and the question was whether the defendants could consolidate against the plaintiffs all their mortgages or only those made before the second mortgage of Whiteacre to the plaintiffs.

KEKEWICH J held that the defendants could consolidate against the plaintiffs the mortgages on Blackacre and Whiteacre, but not those on the other properties. The mortgagor, by his express contract, would have been

---

[9] It will not apply where the equities of redemption separated before the mortgages united in one hand: *Harter v Colman* (1882) 19 ChD 630.

compelled to submit to consolidation of all the properties; and the plaintiffs would have been in the same position if the defendants, at the time of the later mortgages, had not had notice of the second mortgage on Whiteacre to the plaintiffs[10].

VII.   Discharge of Mortgages[11]

LAW OF PROPERTY ACT 1925

115.   Reconveyances of mortgages by endorsed receipts. — (1) A receipt endorsed on, written at the foot of, or annexed to, a mortgage for all money thereby secured, which states the name of the person who pays the money and is executed by the chargee by way of legal mortgage or the person in whom the mortgaged property is vested and who is legally entitled to give a receipt for the mortgage money shall operate, without any reconveyance, surrender, or release —

(*a*) Where a mortgage takes effect by demise or subdemise, as a surrender of the term, so as to determine the term or merge the same in the reversion immediately expectant thereon;

(*b*) Where the mortgage does not take effect by demise or subdemise, as a reconveyance thereof to the extent of the interest which is the subject matter of the mortgage, to the person who immediately before the execution of the receipt was entitled to the equity of redemption;

and in either case, as a discharge of the mortgaged property from all principal money and interest secured by, and from all claims under the mortgage, but without prejudice to any term or other interest which is paramount to the estate or interest of the mortgagee or other person in whom the mortgaged property was vested[12].

(2) Provided that, where by the receipt the money appears to have been paid by a person who is not entitled to the immediate equity of redemption, the receipt shall operate as if the benefit of the mortgage had by deed been transferred to him; unless —

(*a*) it is otherwise expressly provided; or

(*b*) the mortgage is paid off out of capital money, or other money in the hands of a personal representative or trustee properly applicable for the discharge of the mortgage, and it is not expressly provided that the receipt is to operate as a transfer.

(3) Nothing in this section confers on a mortgagor a right to keep alive a mortgage paid off by him, so as to affect prejudicially any subsequent incumbrancer; and where there is no right to keep the mortgage alive, the receipt does not operate as a transfer[13].

---

[10] See also *Andrews v City Permanent Benefit Building Society* (1881) 44 LT 641.

[11] C & B, pp. 640–641; M & W, pp. 984–986; MM, pp. 503–504.

[12] A building society may use either a reconveyance or a special statutory receipt: Building Societies Act 1962, s. 37, Sch. 6. See Wurtzburg & Mills, *Building Society Law* (14th edn, 1976), pp. 217–221.

[13] *Otter v Lord Vaux* (1856) 6 De GM & G 638; *Parkash v Irani Finance Ltd* [1970] Ch 101, [1969] 1 All ER 930.

(4) This section does not affect the right of any person to require a reassignment, surrender, release, or transfer to be executed in lieu of a receipt.

(8) This section applies to the discharge of a charge by way of legal mortgage, and to the discharge of a mortgage, whether made by way of statutory mortgage or not, executed before or after the commencement of this Act, but only as respects discharges effected after such commencement.

(10) This section does not apply to the discharge of a charge or incumbr-ance registered under the Land Registration Act 1925[14].

116. Cesser of mortgage terms. — Without prejudice to the right of a tenant for life or other person having only a limited interest in the equity of redemption to require a mortgage to be kept alive by transfer or otherwise, a mortgage term shall, when the money secured by the mortgage has been discharged, become a satisfied term and shall cease[15].

VIII. Priority of Mortgages[16]

Very substantial alterations were made by the legislation of 1925 to the rules concerning the priority of mortgages. The rules which were in force before 1926 are still of importance as there are still circumstances in which they may apply. The two systems will be considered separately.

A. Before 1926

i. MORTGAGES OF INTERESTS IN LAND

The basic rule was that priority depended on the time of creation, *"Qui prior est tempore, potior est jure."* This rule could, however, be made inapplicable by the other principle that "Where the equities are equal, the law prevails". Where, for example, a legal mortgagee has no notice, actual or constructive, of a prior equitable mortgage, the equities are equal and the legal mortgagee will take priority. However, wrongful conduct (fraud, misrepresentation or gross negligence) may deprive the earlier mortgagee, even the holder of the legal estate, of his normal priority.

These rules give rise to certain difficulties; inevitably, as they are conflicting. To decide which rule to apply is to determine the priority of the mortgages. And there is little guidance in the cases on the question of the tests to be applied in deciding whether the "equities are equal" or in defining how serious must be the conduct of the mortgagee before he will be postponed. A number of questions are not made clear.

First: it is not clear to what extent different rules for the displacement of the natural order of priority apply to the case of a prior equitable followed by a later legal mortgage from those applicable to a prior legal followed by a later equitable mortgage. Certainly the issues are different. The problem in

---

[14] Which can only be effected by a discharge entered on the register: LRA 1925, s. 35; LRR 1925, rr. 151, 267.

[15] *Edwards v Marshall-Lee* (1975) 235 EG 901 (vacating receipt on a legal charge not complying with s. 115 held a valid discharge); (1976) 40 Conv (NS) 102.

[16] C & B, pp. 662–685; M & W, pp. 986–1012; MM, pp. 504–519; Waldock, pp. 381–435; Fisher and Lightwood, chap. 24; (1949) 7 CLJ 243 (R. E. Megarry).

the one case is to determine when the first rule is to be displaced by the second; in the other case both rules may be upset and the legal mortgagee who is first in time may be postponed[17].

In the latter type of case, the reason for the postponement of the legal mortgagee is usually fraud or estoppel; but gross negligence by the legal mortgagee in respect of the title deeds is usually said to be sufficient[18]. The addition of adjectives to negligence always causes difficulty, and there is no precise test to show what is signified by the adjective "gross".

Secondly: the requirement of negligence in the case of a later legal following a prior equitable mortgage is not clear. The position is sometimes said to be that the later legal mortgagee will take priority over a prior equitable unless he was grossly negligent. Sometimes it is said that he will do so if he enquires for the deeds (deposited with the equitable mortgagee) and receives a reasonable excuse for non-production[19]. The obvious way to treat the question, one would have thought, would be to apply the ordinary rule relating to the bona fide purchaser for value and to postpone the later legal mortgagee unless he can pass that test[20]. But he has been more greatly favoured.

(a) *The Superiority of the Legal Estate*[1]

HEWITT *v* LOOSEMORE
(1851) 9 Hare 449 (Turner V-C)

Robert Loosemore, the mortgagor, was a solicitor; in 1834, he deposited his lease with the plaintiff as an equitable mortgage to secure the repayment of a sum of money. In 1838, he assigned the lease by way of legal mortgage to the defendant John Loosemore, who was a farmer, unacquainted with legal forms; John asked Robert whether the lease ought not to be delivered to him, and Robert said that it should, but that, as he was rather busy then, he would give it to John when he next came to market. The plaintiff brought this bill praying, inter alia, for a declaration that he was entitled to priority over the defendant.

Held. The defendant as legal mortgagee was entitled to priority.

Turner V-C: [The question in this case is] whether an equitable mortgagee by deposit of title deeds is entitled to priority over a subsequent legal mortgagee of the property comprised in the deeds, who has not made all the inquiries after the deeds which could or might have been made. . . .

The law, . . . as I collect it from the authorities, stands thus:— That a legal mortgagee is not to be postponed to a prior equitable one upon the ground of his not having got in the title-deeds, unless there be fraud or gross and wilful negligence on his part. That the court will not impute fraud, or gross or wilful negligence to the mortgagee if he has bona fide inquired for the deeds, and a reasonable excuse has been given for the non-delivery of them; but that the court will impute fraud, or gross and wilful negligence to the mortgagee if he

---

[17] *Perry Herrick v Attwood* (1857) 2 De G & J 21, p. 729, post.

[18] *Colyer v Finch* (1856) 5 HL Cas 905; *Perry Herrick v Attwood*, supra; *Clarke v Palmer* (1882) 21 Ch D 124; *Walker v Linom* [1907] 2 Ch 104, p. 731, post.

[19] *Hewitt v Loosemore* (1851) 9 Hare 449; *Agra Bank Ltd v Barry* (1874) LR 7 HL 135; *Oliver v Hinton* [1899] 2 Ch 264, p. 727, post.

[20] See p. 24, ante; *Pilcher v Rawlins* (1872) 7 Ch App 259.

[1] *Barnett v Weston* (1806) 12 Ves 130; *Agra Bank Ltd v Barry*, supra; *Hewitt v Loosemore*, supra; *Walker v Linom*, supra; *Hudston v Viney* [1921] 1 Ch 98.

omits all inquiry as to the deeds. And I think there is much principle both in the rule and the distinctions upon it.

When this court is called upon to postpone a legal mortgagee its powers are invoked to take away a legal right; and I see no ground which can justify it in doing so except fraud, or gross and wilful negligence, which, in the eyes of this court, amounts to fraud, and I think that in transactions of sale and mortgage of estates, if there be no inquiry as to the title-deeds, which constitute the sole evidence of the title to such property, the court is justified in assuming that the purchaser or mortgagee has abstained from making the inquiry, from a suspicion that his title would be affected if it was made, and is therefore bound to impute to him the knowledge which the inquiry, if made, would have imparted. But I think that where bona fide inquiry is made, and a reasonable excuse given, there is no ground for imputing the suspicion, or the notice which is consequent upon it.

Applying these principles to the present case, I am of opinion that the plaintiff has failed in making out a sufficient case for postponing the defendant, and that the only decree which I can make is the usual decree for redemption; but the plaintiff must pay the costs up to and including the decree.

OLIVER *v* HINTON
[1899] 2 Ch 264 (ChD, Romer J, and CA, Lindley MR, Sir F. H. Jeune and Rigby LJ)

The plaintiff, Mrs Oliver, brought this action for a declaration that she was entitled to certain premises as equitable mortgagee as against the defendant Mrs Hinton, who had purchased them. The circumstances were that in 1888, Hill, a solicitor, had deposited the deeds of the premises with the plaintiff under an equitable mortgage. In 1890, Hill conveyed the property to the defendant, who was represented by an agent who was not a solicitor. This agent asked Hill to see the deeds, but Hill replied that they could not be seen as they related also to other property.

Held. The plaintiff was entitled to priority over the defendant, the purchaser of the legal estate.

Lindley MR: In my opinion this case does not present any serious difficulty when once the facts are understood. The defendant has been cheated by Hill, but she has not been in any way cheated by the plaintiff. In 1888, Hill gave the plaintiff a mortgage of the three houses in question and two others. It was not a legal mortgage, but an equitable mortgage by deposit of title-deeds, accompanied by a memorandum of deposit, by which Hill agreed to execute a legal mortgage when requested by the plaintiff to do so. The plaintiff had a good equitable mortgage, and she cannot be charged with any neglect or breach of duty in not obtaining a legal mortgage. She ran, however, the risk of losing her priority in case the legal estate should be conveyed to a subsequent purchaser for value without notice of her charge. Who is it that now claims to override her charge? The only person who can do so, if he has acquired his title subsequently to hers, is a bona fide purchaser for value without notice of her charge. But this does not include a purchaser for value who is so grossly negligent as to take none of the ordinary precautions which ought to be taken in such a matter — who, in fact, takes no precautions whatever. He may be a bona *fide* purchaser for value without notice of a prior charge, but he is not entitled to the protection of the Court. I do not base my judgment upon constructive notice of the plaintiff's charge, nor do I mean to suggest that there was any fraud or complicity in fraud on the part of either the defendant or her agent, Price. Price gave his evidence with perfect candour. The defendant left the arrangement of the purchase entirely to him. He inquired about the title-deeds, and was told by Hill that they were in his possession, but that they would not be delivered up to the purchaser because they related also to other property. No abstract of title was asked for or delivered, and no further inquiry was made. Price in his evidence admitted that he made a mistake in not asking to see the deeds, but said that he relied upon Hill. Can a person whose agent acted in this way be regarded as a bona fide purchaser for value without notice who is entitled to the protection of the legal estate? To allow a purchaser who acts with such gross carelessness to deprive a prior innocent mortgagee of her priority would be the greatest injustice. . . .

In [*Hunt v Elmes* (1860) 2 De GF & J 578] and also in *Hewitt v Loosemore* (1857) 9 Hare 449, p. 726, ante, it was said that to deprive a man of the protection of the legal estate he must have been guilty of either fraud or gross and wilful negligence. To deprive a purchaser for value without notice of a prior incumbrance of the protection of the legal estate it is not, in my opinion, essential that he should have been guilty of fraud; it is sufficient that he has been guilty of such gross negligence as would render it unjust to deprive the prior incumbrancer of his priority.

The appeal must be dismissed.

(b) The Effect of Fraud, Misrepresentation, Gross Negligence

1. FRAUD[2]

NORTHERN COUNTIES OF ENGLAND FIRE INSURANCE CO v WHIPP

(1884) 26 ChD 482 (CA, COTTON, BOWEN and FRY LJJ)

On two occasions in 1878, Crabtree, the manager of the plaintiff company, executed legal mortgages of freehold properties to the company and delivered to the company the title deeds which were locked in the safe. Crabtree was entrusted by the company with one of the two sets of keys to the safe, and, later in 1878, extracted the deeds, and, suppressing the mortgages, deposited them with the defendant, Mrs Whipp, as security for a loan.

In an action by the company for foreclosure, Mrs Whipp claimed that her security should take priority over that of the company.

Held (reversing the Vice-Chancellor of the Court of the County Palatine of Lancaster). The mortgage to the company took priority.

FRY LJ: The question which has thus to be investigated is — What conduct in relation to the title deeds on the part of a mortgagee who has the legal estate, is sufficient to postpone such mortgage in favour of a subsequent equitable mortgagee who has obtained the title deeds without knowledge of the legal mortgage? The question is not what circumstances may as between two equities give priority to the one over the other, but what circumstances justify the Court in depriving a legal mortgagee of the benefit of the legal

---

[2] *Thatched House Case* (1716) 1 Eq Cas Abr 321.

estate. It has been contended on the part of the Plaintiffs that nothing short of fraud will justify the Court in postponing the legal estate. It has been contended by the Defendant that gross negligence is enough. . . .

The authorities which we have reviewed appear to us to justify the following conclusions:—

(1) That the Court will postpone the prior legal estate to a subsequent equitable estate: (*a*), where the owner of the legal estate has assisted in or connived at the fraud which has led to the creation of a subsequent equitable estate, without notice of the prior legal estate; of which assistance or connivance, the omission to use ordinary care in inquiry after or keeping title deeds may be, and in some cases has been, held to be sufficient evidence, where such conduct cannot otherwise be explained; (*b*), where the owner of the legal estate has constituted the mortgagor his agent with authority to raise money, and the estate thus created has by the fraud or misconduct of the agent been represented as being the first estate.

But (2) that the Court will not postpone the prior legal estate to the subsequent equitable estate on the ground of any mere carelessness or want of prudence on the part of the legal owner.

Now to apply the conclusions thus arrived at to the facts of the present case. That there was great carelessness in the manner in which the Plaintiff company through its directors dealt with their securities seems to us to admit of no doubt. But is that carelessness evidence of any fraud? We think that it is not. Of what fraud is it evidence? The Plaintiffs never combined with *Crabtree* to induce the Defendant to lend her money. They never knew that she was lending it, and stood by. They can have had no motive to desire that their deeds should be abstracted and their own title clouded. Their carelessness may be called gross, but in our judgment it was carelessness likely to injure and not to benefit the Plaintiff company, and accordingly has no tendency to convict them of fraud.

The rule, referred to in this case, which lays down that an earlier legal mortgagee may be postponed on the ground of fraud is undoubted. The rule however that an earlier legal mortgagee will never be postponed on the grounds of negligence (not amounting to fraud) is questioned by many writers and is inconsistent with some cases (p. 731, post). Much reconciliation can be effected by limiting the decision in *Whipp's* case to a situation where the negligence was in failure to *retain* the deeds. It is difficult however to justify in principle a distinction between a failure to obtain and a failure to retain the deeds.

2. MISREPRESENTATION[3]

PERRY HERRICK *v* ATTWOOD
(1857) 2 De G & J 21 (Lord CRANWORTH LC)

In 1848 John Attwood was substantially indebted to the trustees of a family marriage settlement, and also to three of his sisters, the defendants. While he

---

[3] *Briggs v Jones* (1870) LR 10 Eq 92; *Dixon v Muckleston* (1872) 8 Ch App 155 at 160; *Brocklesby v Temperance Permanent Building Society* [1895] AC 173; *Rimmer v Webster* [1902] 2 Ch 163; *Abigail v Lapin* [1934] AC 491.

was being pressed for payment by the trustees, he executed a legal mortgage for the amount due to his sisters. The deeds, other than the mortgage, were, however, retained by the sisters' solicitor in order to enable John Attwood to execute a mortgage to secure his debts to the trustees. In April 1848, Attwood deposited the deeds with the solicitors for the trustees. Later, by employing those same solicitors, Attwood made several legal mortgages of the same property to various persons including the plaintiffs; the plaintiffs were also transferees of some of those mortgages.

The plaintiffs filed a bill to establish their mortgages as having priority over the mortgage to the Misses Attwood.

Held (affirming Sir John ROMILLY MR). The plaintiffs were entitled to priority.

LORD CRANWORTH LC: This case has occupied a long time in argument, and has given rise to the agitation of questions of great importance. It has been discussed how far a mortgagee, taking a mortgage without taking the title deeds, does or does not postpone himself to persons who take a subsequent conveyance for value without notice of the mortgage, and obtain possession of the title deeds, and the cases on that subject have been referred to, the last being *Colyer v Finch* (1856) 5 HL Cas 905, in the House of Lords.

I should think it very inexpedient now to treat it as a question open to discussion whether the law has or has not been correctly laid down on this subject, for I consider it to have been established beyond doubt that the law is, that the person having the legal estate without the title deeds is not to be postponed to a subsequent incumbrancer having the title deeds, unless he has been guilty of something which the law calls fraud or gross negligence. I agree that this rule may very often lead to great hardships on persons who have taken conveyances relying on the possession of the title deeds as evidence of unincumbered ownership in the conveying party. Such, however, is the law, and I must act upon it until it is otherwise settled. Still, if the present case had involved that principle, I should have taken time to consider my judgment, for it is difficult in each particular case to say what amounts to negligence, and still more is it difficult to say what constitutes negligence with the epithet of gross connected with it.

In my opinion no such question arises in the present case. I do not think there was here any fraud or any negligence, for I do not believe that any of the parties to the transaction of *January* 1848 intended that the mortgage then taken should interfere with any subsequent dealings for value which *Attwood* might have with his estate. If the parties did so intend, the transaction was a gross fraud on the part of *Attwood* and his solicitor, and of the ladies also, if they understood it.

The case is that: Mr *Attwood* was a single man advanced in life, and living with two of his sisters, who were not young. He managed all their affairs. He was indebted to each of his three sisters, the two who lived with him and another who was married, in the sum of 10,000*l* each. At the end of 1847 and the beginning of 1848 he was pressed by creditors who were insisting on payment of large sums of money, amounting altogether to above 15,000*l*. He proposed to give them a mortgage, they refused it, and insisted on having payment of the money. That took place in the early part of *January* 1848. I do not go into the details of the evidence, but there were angry discussions going on and actions brought; and pending these proceedings, after issue of the writs and the delivery of pleas in the actions, Mr *Attwood* executed the deed in question, for giving a security to his three sisters for the 30,000*l* that he owed to them, but intentionally did not give them the title deeds. . . . What does that prove the purport of the transaction to have been? That this security was given either with the intention (to put the worse construction on the conduct of the parties) that the ladies should have a pocket security of which they could avail themselves afterwards, when those who were to claim under subsequent conveyances by Mr *Attwood* should assert their rights, or (to adopt a more favourable, and I hope and believe the true construction) that the deed was never intended to be set up against any subsequent dealing with the property by Mr *Attwood* by way of mortgage, the title deeds being returned to him to be dealt with as he thought fit. I think it is clear. . . . that at this time it was contemplated by all parties that Mr *Attwood* should raise money to pay off the creditors by whom he was then being sued. Taking that to be the intention, I agree with the view of the Master of the Rolls, in every part of whose judgment in this cause I entirely concur, that if a person taking a legal mortgage chooses to leave the deeds with the mortgagor, not through negligence or through fraud, but with the intention of enabling him to raise a sum of 15,000*l*, which is to take precedence of the legal mortgage, the mortgagee cannot, as against subsequent mortgagees, complain if, instead of 15,000*l* the mortgagor raises 50,000*l*, because he has himself put it into his power to raise any sum of money he pleases. That is the true nature of this transaction. It is not a case in which there was any negligence. It is not a case, as I am willing to believe, in which there was any fraud, but it is a case in which the mortgagees did deliberately and intentionally leave the deeds in the hands of the mortgagor, in order that he might raise money. To hold that a person who advances money on an estate, the title deeds of which are under such circumstances left in the hands of the mortgagor, is not to have preference, would be to shut our eyes to the plainest equity.

In *Clarke v Palmer* (1882) 21 ChD 124, the first mortgagee X failed to obtain possession of the deeds. Part of the property was then mortgaged to Y who believed that he was the first mortgagee, and the whole of the property to Z, who knew of Y, but not of X. HALL V-C held that both Y and Z took priority over X; X's negligence had brought the principle of *Perry Herrick v Attwood* into play.

3. GROSS NEGLIGENCE

WALKER *v* LINOM
[1907] 2 Ch 104 (ChD, PARKER J)

In 1896 Walker conveyed land to trustees to be held on the trusts of his marriage settlement. The title deeds, with the exception of the conveyance to Walker, were handed over to the trustees, who were solicitors and who negligently failed to discover the omission.

Walker subsequently mortgaged the land to X, who sold it to Y. On the question (inter alia) of the competing claims of the trustees and the purchaser.

Held. The trustees by their negligence were postponed to the equitable interest of the purchaser.

PARKER J reviewed in detail the judgment of FRY LJ in *Northern Counties of England Fire Insurance Co v Whipp* (1884) 26 ChD 482, and continued:

The conclusion he ultimately arrives at is that in order to postpone a prior legal to a subsequent equitable estate there must be fraud as apart from negligence, and this conclusion is stated in language wide enough to cover cases of postponement based upon the conduct of the holder of the legal estate in not getting possession of the title deeds as well as cases of postponement based upon the conduct of such holder in dealing with the title deeds after he has got them. It would seem at first sight that the Lord Justice uses the word "fraud" throughout this judgment as connoting a dishonest intent, notwithstanding that in the case of fraud to be gathered from conduct in relation to not getting in the title deeds he refers to such cases as *Le Neve v Le Neve* (1747) Amb 436 and *Ratcliffe v Barnard* (1871) 6 Ch App 652.

Now, as I have already said, I cannot under the circumstances of this case find that anyone concerned in the 1896 settlement, with the exception of George Church Walker, acted otherwise than honestly, and, if I treat Fry LJ's judgment as meaning that in no case can a prior legal estate be postponed to a subsequent equitable estate without the existence of fraud in its ordinary common law sense as necessarily connoting a dishonest intention, I must hold that the trustees are not postponed. There are, however, subsequent cases which suggest that at any rate in cases of postponement, based on no inquiry having been made for the deeds, fraud is not necessary. It is, for example, clear from the case of *Oliver v Hinton* [1899] 2 Ch 264, p. 727, ante that a purchaser obtaining the legal estate, but making no inquiry for the deeds, or making inquiry and failing to take reasonable means to verify the truth of the excuse made for not producing them or handing them over, is, although perfectly honest, guilty of such negligence as to make it inequitable for him to rely on his legal estate so as to deprive a prior incumbrancer of his priority. In this case Lindley MR disapproves of the passage in the judgment of James LJ, in *Ratcliffe v Barnard*, quoted by Fry LJ in *Northern Counties of England Fire Insurance Co v Whipp*, and distinctly says that to deprive a purchaser for value without notice of a prior equitable incumbrance of the benefit of the legal estate it is not essential that he should have been guilty of fraud. And Sir F. H. Jeune, referring also to the judgment of James LJ in *Ratcliffe v Barnard*, comes to the conclusion that the word "fraud", as there used, did not mean such conduct as would justify a jury or judge in finding that there had been actual fraud, but such conduct as would justify the Court of Chancery in concluding that there had been fraud in some artificial sense. Similarly in *Berwick & Co v Price* [1905] 1 Ch 632 at 640, Joyce J says: "The omission by a purchaser to investigate the title or to require delivery or production of the title-deeds is not to my mind either fraudulent or culpable, nor does it, since the judgment of Lindley MR in *Oliver v Hinton*, seem necessary to characterize it by any such epithet; but the consequence of such omission or wilful ignorance is that it is held to be unjust to prefer the purchaser to the previous mortgagee who has the deeds although such mortgage be equitable and the purchaser have the legal estate."

In both the cases last referred to the question was between a prior equitable and a subsequent legal estate, and I think the later case was actually decided on constructive or imputed notice. But the Master of the Rolls expressly refused to decide *Oliver v Hinton* on any such ground. The question, however, arises whether the principle laid down in *Oliver v Hinton* is equally applicable between the holder of the legal estate who has omitted to make inquiry for the title deeds and a subsequent equitable estate the creation of which has been rendered possible by such omission. In my opinion any conduct on the part of the holder of the legal estate in relation to the deeds which would make it inequitable for him to rely on his legal estate against a prior equitable estate of which he had no notice ought also to be sufficient to postpone him to a subsequent equitable estate the creation of which has only been rendered possible by the possession of deeds which but for such conduct would have passed into the possession of the owner of the legal estate. This must, I think, have been the opinion of Fry LJ in *Northern Counties of England Fire Insurance Co v Whipp* (1884) 26 Ch D 482; for he explains both *Worthington v Morgan* (1849) 16 Sim 547 and *Clarke v Palmer* (1882) 21 Ch D 124, as based upon the same sort of fraud. I do not think, therefore, that there is anything in the authorities to preclude me from holding, and I accordingly hold, that the trustees, although they have the legal estate, are postponed to the defendant.

In *Grierson v National Provincial Bank* [1913] 2 Ch 18, George Franklin, a leaseholder, deposited his lease with Grant and Maddison's Bank as security for a loan. Later, he granted a legal mortgage to Grierson which was expressly stated to be subject to the prior equitable mortgage.

Franklin then redeemed the equitable mortgage, recovered the lease, and deposited it with the defendant Bank as security for a further loan. The defendant Bank knew nothing of the legal mortgage.

JOYCE J held that Grierson, the legal mortgagee, retained his priority.

ii. MORTGAGES OF EQUITABLE INTERESTS IN PURE PERSONALTY

The priority of mortgages and assignments of interests in pure personalty (including interests under a trust for sale)[4] depended before 1926 upon the order in which notice was received by the legal owner of the personalty (i.e. usually, by the trustees); however, a mortgagee who had actual or constructive notice of a prior mortgage when he lent his money could not gain priority by giving his notice first. The rule in *Dearle v Hall* was made applicable in 1925 to mortgages of all equitable interests, in land as well as pure personalty.

DEARLE *v* HALL[5]
(1823) 3 Russ 1 (Sir Thomas PLUMER MR), affirmed
(1827) 3 Russ 48 (Lord LYNDHURST LC)

Zachariah Brown was entitled under his father's will to a life interest in a fund which produced £93 per annum. In 1808, he sold to William Dearle an annuity of £37 to be paid out of this life interest, and charged upon it. In 1809, he assigned in a similar manner an annuity of £27 to Sherring. In 1812, he sold his life interest in the whole £93 to Hall. Hall's solicitors made all

---

[4] *Lee v Howlett* (1856) 2 K & J 531.
[5] For comment on the rule (mostly adverse), see *Ward v Duncombe* [1893] AC 369; *Lyle v Rosher* [1959] 1 WLR 8, [1958] 3 All ER 597.

proper enquiries about Brown's title, and obtained no information concerning the prior assignments. Hall gave notice to the executors of the assignment to him. Later the executors of Brown's father's will learned of the assignments and refused to pay interest until the claimants' rights should be ascertained.

Held. The assignment to Hall took priority.

SIR THOMAS PLUMER MR: It is observable, in the first place, that the right which *Zachariah Brown* had under the will of his father was simply a right to a chose in action. The legal interest in the residue was vested in the executrix and executors. . . . Wherever it is intended to complete the transfer of a chose in action, there is a mode of dealing with it which a court of equity considers tantamount to possession, namely, notice given to the legal depository of the fund. Where a contract, respecting property in the hands of other persons, who have a legal right to the possession, is made behind the back of those in whom the legal interest is thus vested, it is necessary, if the security is intended to attach on the thing itself, to lay hold of that thing in the manner in which its nature permits it to be laid hold of — that is, by giving notice of the contract to those in whom the legal interest is. By such notice, the legal holders are converted into trustees for the new purchaser, and are charged with responsibility towards him; and the *cestui que trust* is deprived of the power of carrying the same security repeatedly into the market, and of inducing third persons to advance money upon it, under the erroneous belief that it continues to belong to him absolutely, free from incumbrance, and that the trustees are still trustees for him, and for no one else. That precaution is always taken by diligent purchasers and incumbrancers: if it is not taken, there is neglect; and it is fit that it should be understood that the solicitor, who conducts the business for the party advancing the money, is responsible for that neglect. The consequence of such neglect is, that the trustee of the fund remains ignorant of any alteration having taken place in the equitable rights affecting it: he considers himself to be a trustee for the same individual as before, and no other person is known to him as his *cestui que trust*. The original *cestui que trust*, though he has in fact parted with his interest, appears to the world to be the complete equitable owner, and remains in the order, management and disposition of the property as absolutely as ever; so that he has it in his power to obtain, by means of it, a false and delusive credit. He may come into the market to dispose of that which he has previously sold; and how can those, who may chance to deal with him, protect themselves from his fraud? Whatever diligence may be used by a *puisne* incumbrancer or purchaser — whatever inquiries he may make in order to investigate the title, and to ascertain the exact state of the original right of the vendor, and his continuing right, — the trustees, who are the persons to whom application for information would naturally be made, will truly and unhesitatingly represent to all who put questions to them that the fund remains the sole absolute property of the proposed vendor. These inconveniences and mischiefs are the natural consequences of omitting to give notice to trustees; and they must be considered as foreseen by those who, in transactions of that kind, omit to give notice; for they are the consequences which in the experience of mankind usually follow such omissions. To give notice is a matter of no difficulty: and whenever persons, treating for a chose in action, do not give notice to the trustee or executor, who is the legal holder of the fund, they do not perfect their title; they do not do all that is necessary in order to make the thing belong to them in preference to all other persons; and they become responsible, in some respects, for the easily foreseen consequences of their negligence. . . .

The ground of this claim is priority of time. They rely upon the known maxim, borrowed from the civil law, which in many cases regulates equities — *"qui prior est in tempore, potior est in jure"*. If, by the first contract, all the thing is given, there remains nothing to be the subject of the second contract, and priority must decide. But it cannot be contended that priority in time must decide, where the legal estate is outstanding. For the maxim, as an equitable rule, admits of exception and gives way, when the question does not lie between bare and equal equities. If there appears to be, in respect of any circumstances independent of priority of time, a better title in the *puisne* purchaser to call for the legal estate, than in the purchaser who precedes him in date, the case ceases to be a balance of equal equities, and the preference, which priority of date might otherwise have given, is done away with and counteracted. The question here is, — not which assignment is first in date, — but whether there is not, on the part of *Hall*, a better title to call for the legal estate than *Dearle* or *Sherring* can set up? Or rather, the question is, Shall these Plaintiffs now have equitable relief to the injury of *Hall*?

What title have they shown to call on a court of justice to interpose on their behalf, in order to obviate the consequence of their own misconduct? All that has happened is owing to their negligence (a negligence not accounted for) in forbearing to do what they ought to have done, what would have been attended with no difficulty, and what would have effectually prevented all the mischief which has followed. Is the Plaintiff to be heard in a court of equity, who asks its interposition in his behoof, to indemnify him against the effects of his own negligence at the expense of another who had used all due diligence, and who, if he is to suffer loss, will suffer it by reason of the negligence of the very person who prays relief against him? The question here is not, as in *Evans v Bicknell* (1801) 6 Ves 174, whether a court of equity is to deprive the Plaintiffs of any right — whether it is to take from them, for instance, a legal estate, or to impose any charge upon them. It is simply, whether they are entitled to relief against their own negligence. They did not perfect their securities; a third party has innocently advanced his money, and has perfected his security as far as the nature of the subject permitted him: is this Court to interfere to postpone him to them?

They say, that they were not bound to give notice to the trustees; for that notice does not form part of the necessary conveyance of an equitable interest. I admit, that, if you mean to rely on contract with the individual, you do not need to give notice; from the moment of the contract, he, with whom you are dealing, is personally bound. But if you mean to go further, and to make your right attach upon the thing which is the subject of the contract, it is necessary to give notice; and, unless notice is given, you do not do that which is essential in all cases of transfer of personal property. The law of *England* has always been, that personal property passes by delivery of possession; and it is possession which determines the apparent ownership. If, therefore, an individual, who in the way of purchase or mortgage contracts with another for the transfer of his interest, does not divest the vendor or mortgagor of possession, but permits him to remain the ostensible owner as before, he must take the consequences which may ensue from such a mode of dealing. That doctrine was explained in *Ryall v Rowles* (1749) 1 Ves Sen 348 before Lord *Hardwicke* and three of the Judges. If you, having the right of possession, do not exercise that right, but leave another in actual possession, you enable that person to gain a false and delusive credit, and put it in his power to obtain money from innocent parties on the hypothesis of his being the owner of that which in fact belongs to you. The principle has been long recognised, even in courts of law. In *Twyne's* case (1602) 3 Co Rep 80b, one of the badges of fraud was, that the possession had remained in the vendor. Possession must follow right; and if you, who have the right, do not take possession, you do not follow up the title, and are responsible for the consequences.

In *Re Wyatt* [1892] 1 Ch 188, the question arose whether notice to one of several trustees was a valid notice or not. The Court of Appeal established the rule that notice to one of several trustees was valid against incumbrancers who advanced money during the period of office of such trustee. This was held in spite of the argument of E. S. Ford, counsel for such an incumbrancer: "Now take this case: A first mortgage is made, of which notice is given to A but not to B. Then a second mortgage is made, of which notice is given to both. A then dies, and a third mortgage is made, of which notice is given to B. The respondents say, that 1 has priority over 2. But unquestionably 2 is prior to 3, for in each case complete notice was given, and priority of dates must settle the matter. Now, according to *Re Hall* (1880) 7 LR Ir 180, 3 has priority over 1. If, therefore, the respondents are right, we get this circle: 1 prior to 2, 2 prior to 3, 3 prior to 1, which is a *reductio ad absurdum*; and this absurdity appears still more clearly where 1 is an absolute assignment, 2 is a mortgage, and 3 is an absolute assignment. If an assignee gives notice to all, he makes all his trustees. If he gives notice to one only, he makes only that one his trustee, and on his death the assignee has no longer a trustee and loses his priority."

As to this, LINDLEY LJ, delivering the judgment of the Court (drawn up by FRY LJ), said: "The solution of the difficulty is probably to be found in the view that the third incumbrancer is subrogated to the rights of the first to the extent of his charge, and to that extent, and that extent only, can take in priority of the second incumbrancer, by which the latter sustains no injury, but that as to any excess of the amount claimed by the third incumbrancer, he comes in after the second, so that the fund would be distributed as follows. First, to the third incumbrancer to the extent of the claim of the first. Secondly, to the second incumbrancer. Thirdly, to the third incumbrancer to the extent to which he might remain unpaid after the money he had received whilst standing in the shoes of the first incumbrancer: see *Benham v Keane* (1861) 3 De GF & J 318 where a similar problem was similarly solved."

Re Wyatt was affirmed by the House of Lords *sub nom Ward v Duncombe* [1893] AC 369 but there was no discussion of the solution of counsel's hypothetical case.

B.   After 1925

i.   MORTGAGES OF LEGAL ESTATES

The system of priority of mortgages which is in operation at the present day is the creation of the legislation of 1925. The paucity of litigation on the subject suggests that the system has, on the whole, worked reasonably well; though it may be due more to the considerable rise in land prices than to the merits of the system. It is however open to certain theoretical objections which are fully explained elsewhere. No more will be attempted here than to give the statutory enactments on which the system is based.

LAW OF PROPERTY ACT 1925

13. Effect of possession of documents. — This Act shall not prejudicially affect the right or interest of any person arising out of or consequent on the possession by him of any documents relating to a legal estate in land, nor affect any question arising out of or consequent upon any omission to obtain or any other absence of possession by any person of any documents relating to a legal estate in land.

97. Priorities as between puisne mortgages. — Every mortgage affecting a legal estate in land made after the commencement of this Act, whether legal or equitable (not being a mortgage protected by the deposit of documents relating to the legal estate affected) shall rank according to its date of registration as a land charge pursuant to the Land Charges Act, 1925.

This section does not apply to mortgages or charges to which the Land Charges Act 1972 does not apply by virtue of section 14 (3) of that Act (which excludes certain land charges created by instruments necessitating registration under the Land Registration Act 1925), or to mortgages or charges of registered land[6]. . . .

199. Restrictions on constructive notice.
(1) (i) p. 45, ante.

LAND CHARGES ACT 1972

2. The register of land charges.
(4) Class C, p. 31, ante[7].

4. Effect of land charges and protection of purchasers.
(5) p. 37, ante.

17. Interpretation.
(1) p. 37, ante.

ii. MORTGAGES BY COMPANIES

LAND CHARGES ACT 1972

3. Registration of land charges. — (7) and (8), p. 56, ante.

COMPANIES ACT 1985

396. Charges which have to be registered. — p. 57, ante.

---

[6] As amended by LCA 1972, s. 18 (1), Sch. 3, para. 1.
[7] As to whether a protected equitable mortgage is registrable as an estate contract (Class C (iv)), see C & B, pp. 674–675; M & W, p. 998; Waldock, pp. 425–428; (1962) 26 Conv (NS) 446–449 (R. G. Rowley).

iii.   MORTGAGES OF EQUITABLE INTERESTS

LAW OF PROPERTY ACT 1925

137. Dealings with life interests, reversions and other equitable interests. — (1) The law applicable to dealings with equitable things in action which regulates the priority of competing interests therein, shall, as respects dealings with equitable interests in land, capital money, and securities representing capital money effected after the commencement of this Act, apply to and regulate the priority of competing interests therein.

This subsection applies whether or not the money or securities are in court.

(2) (i) In the case of a dealing with an equitable interest in settled land, capital money or securities representing capital money, the persons to be served with notice of the dealing shall be the trustees of the settlement; and where the equitable interest is created by a derivative or subsidiary settlement, the persons to be served with notice shall be the trustees of that settlement.

(ii) In the case of a dealing with an equitable interest in the proceeds of sale of land or in the rents and profits until sale the persons to be served with notice shall, as heretofore, be the trustees for sale.

(iii) In any other case the person to be served with notice of a dealing with an equitable interest in land shall be the estate owner of the land affected.

The persons on whom notice is served pursuant to this subsection shall be affected thereby in the same manner as if they had been trustees of personal property out of which the equitable interest was created or arose.

This subsection does not apply where the money or securities are in court.

(3) A notice, otherwise than in writing, given to, or received by, a trustee after the commencement of this Act as respects any dealing with an equitable interest in real or personal property, shall not affect the priority of competing claims of purchasers in that equitable interest.

(4) Where, as respects any dealing with an equitable interest in real or personal property —

(*a*) the trustees are not persons to whom a valid notice of the dealing can be given; or

(*b*) there are no trustees to whom a notice can be given; or

(*c*) for any other reason a valid notice cannot be served, or cannot be served without unreasonable cost or delay;

a purchaser may at his own cost require that —

(i) a memorandum of the dealing be endorsed, written on or permanently annexed to the instrument creating the trust;

(ii) the instrument be produced to him by the person having the possession or custody thereof to prove that a sufficient memorandum has been placed thereon or annexed thereto.

Such memorandum shall, as respects priorities, operate in like manner as if notice in writing of the dealing had been given to trustees duly qualified to receive the notice at the time when the memorandum is placed on or annexed to the instrument creating the trust.

(5) Where the property affected is settled land, the memorandum shall be placed on or annexed to the trust instrument and not the vesting instrument.

Where the property affected is land held on trust for sale, the memorandum shall be placed on or annexed to the instrument whereby the equitable interest is created.

(6) Where the trust is created by statute or by operation of law, or in any other case where there is no instrument whereby the trusts are declared, the instrument under which the equitable interest is acquired or which is evidence of the devolution thereof shall, for the purposes of this section, be deemed the instrument creating the trust.

In particular, where the trust arises by reason of an intestacy, the letters of administration or probate in force when the dealing was effected shall be deemed such instrument.

(7) Nothing in this section affects any priority acquired before the commencement of this Act.

(8) Where a notice in writing of a dealing with an equitable interest in real or personal property has been served on a trustee under this section, the trustees from time to time of the property affected shall be entitled to the custody of the notice, and the notice shall be delivered to them by any person who for the time being may have the custody thereof; and subject to the payment of costs, any person interested in the equitable interest may require production of the notice.

(9) The liability of the estate owner of the legal estate affected to produce documents and furnish information to persons entitled to equitable interests therein shall correspond to the liability of a trustee for sale to produce documents and furnish information to persons entitled to equitable interests in the proceeds of sale of the land[8].

C. Tacking after 1925[9]

LAW OF PROPERTY ACT 1925

94. Tacking and further advances. — (1) After the commencement of this Act, a prior mortgagee shall have a right to make further advances to rank in priority to subsequent mortgages (whether legal or equitable) —

    (a) if an arrangement has been made to that effect with the subsequent mortgagees; or

    (b) if he had no notice of such subsequent mortgages at the time when the further advance was made by him; or

    (c) whether or not he had such notice as aforesaid, where the mortgage imposes an obligation on him to make such further advances.

This subsection applies whether or not the prior mortgage was made expressly for securing further advances.

(2) In relation to the making of further advances after the commencement of this Act a mortgagee shall not be deemed to have notice of a mortgage merely by reason that it was registered as a land charge . . . if it was not so registered at the [time when the original mortgage was created][10] or when the

---

[8] This undermines *Low v Bouverie* [1891] 3 Ch 82. For the power to nominate a trust corporation to receive notices, see LPA 1925, s. 138; Law Reform Committee 23rd Report (The Powers and Duties of Trustees) 1982 (Cmnd 8733), paras. 2.17–2.24.

[9] C & B, pp. 668–669, 680–682; M & W, pp. 1005–1012; MM, pp. 513–515. The doctrine is of reduced importance after 1925. In relation to registered land, see LRA 1925, s. 30; LP (A) A 1926, s. 5, which adds sub-s. (3).

[10] The words in square brackets were substituted by LP (A) A 1926, s. 7 and Sch.

last search (if any) by or on behalf of the mortgagee was made, whichever last happened.

This subsection only applies where the prior mortgage was made expressly for securing a current account or other further advances[11].

(3) Save in regard to the making of further advances as aforesaid, the right to tack is hereby abolished:

Provided that nothing in this Act shall affect any priority acquired before the commencement of this Act by tacking, or in respect of further advances made without notice of a subsequent incumbrance or by arrangement with the subsequent incumbrancer.

(4) This section applies to mortgages of land made before or after the commencement of this Act, but not to charges registered under the Land Registration Act 1925, or any enactment replaced by that Act.

QUESTIONS
1.   Is it possible to postulate a principle governing the system of priority of mortgages after 1925?
2.   To what extent do the pre–1926 rules of priorities of mortgages still apply? In particular:
  (i)   On what basis is priority calculated in the case of two mortgagees both claiming to be protected by deposit, and each having some of the deeds?
  (ii) Is any significance now attached, in the issue of priority (whether in (i) above or otherwise) to the question whether a mortgage is legal or equitable?
  (iii) Is a first mortgagee, legal or equitable, whose mortgage is protected by deposit of the title deeds and is unregistered, liable to be defeated by a later mortgagee who is given a "reasonable" excuse for non-production of the title deeds?
3.   Is it possible to find a satisfactory solution of the problem of the three mortgagees, each of whom has priority over the others? *Re Wyatt* [1892] 1 Ch 188, p. 736 ante; (1968) 32 Conv (NS) 325 (W. A. Lee); (1961) 71 Yale LJ 53 (G. Gilmore).

IX.   Registered Land[12]

Mortgages of land may be effected in various ways:

i.   Registered Charge. This is a legal mortgage which is effected by registration in the Charges Register of the lender as the proprietor of the charge. The land certificate is deposited at the registry, and a charge certificate is issued to the mortgagee.

ii.   Mortgage of a Legal Estate by a method appropriate to unregistered land. This takes effect only in equity and needs to be protected as a

---

[11] (1958) 22 Conv (NS) 44 (R. G. Rowley).
[12] C & B, pp. 685–688; M & W, pp. 220–222; MM, pp. 470–472, 515–517; Ruoff and Roper, chaps. 25, 26; Fisher and Lightwood, chap. 3.

minor interest. Such a mortgage can be converted into a registered charge by registration.

iii.   Mortgage by Deposit of the Land Certificate. This operates as an equitable mortgage; the mortgagee can be protected by a notice on the register which will operate as an ordinary caution.

iv.   Mortgage of an Equitable Interest. As with unregistered land, such mortgages are treated quite differently from mortgages of a legal estate. Mortgages of certain equitable interests may be entered upon a supplemental register of dealings in equitable interests. This is the Index of Minor Interests[13], and is completely separate from the Land Register. It is the registered land counterpart of the rule in *Dearle v Hall*, p. 733, ante. The Law Commission has recommended that the Index should be abolished, and that the priorities regulated by it should be governed by the rule in *Dearle v Hall*[14].

v.   Equitable Charges which are, in unregistered land, capable of registration under the Land Charges Act 1972. These are minor interests, and may be protected as such[15].

LAND REGISTRATION ACT 1925

106[16].   Creation and protection of mortgages of registered land. — (1) The proprietor of any registered land may, subject to any entry to the contrary on the register, mortgage, by deed or otherwise, the land or any part of it in any manner which would have been permissible if the land had not been registered and, subject to this section, with the like effect.

(2) Unless and until the mortgage becomes a registered charge, —

(a) it shall take effect only in equity, and

(b) it shall be capable of being overridden as a minor interest unless it is protected as provided by subsection (3) below.

(3) A mortgage which is not a registered charge may be protected on the register by —

(a) a notice under section 49 of this Act,

(b) any such other notice as may be prescribed, or

(c) a caution under section 54 of this Act.

(4) A mortgage which is not a registered charge shall devolve and may be transferred, discharged, surrendered or otherwise dealt with by the same instruments and in the same manner as if the land had not been registered.

25.   Proprietor's power to create charges. — (1) The proprietor of any registered land may by deed —

(a) charge the registered land with the payment at an appointed time of any principal sum of money either with or without interest; . . .

(2) A charge may be in any form provided that —

(a) the registered land comprised in the charge is described by reference to the register or in any other manner sufficient to enable the

---

[13] LRA 1925, s. 102 (2), p. 743, post.

[14] Land Registration 1983 (Law Com No. 125, HC 86) Part V.

[15] LRA 1925, s. 59, p. 137, ante.

[16] As substituted by AJA 1977, s. 26 (1). Under s. 26 (2), the Registrar may convert into a registered charge any mortgage protected by a mortgage caution entered before 29 August 1977; LRR 1977 (S.I. 1977, No. 2089).

registrar to identify the same without reference to any other document.

PRECEDENT: REGISTERED CHARGE[17]

H.M. LAND REGISTRY

Land Registration Acts 1925–1971

County and district: . . . .
(or name of Greater London borough where applicable)

Title No[s].:   . . . .

Property: . . . .

Date: . . . .

In consideration of . . . . . pounds (£. . . . .) the receipt whereof is hereby acknowledged I, *AB* of . . . . [*address and description*] (hereinafter called "the Borrower" which expression shall where the context admits include all persons deriving title under the Borrower) as Beneficial Owner hereby charge by way of legal mortgage[18] the land comprised in the title[s] above referred to with the payment to *CD* of . . [*address and description*] (hereinafter called "the Mortgagee" which expression shall where the context admits include all persons deriving title under the Mortgagee) on the . . . . . day of . . . . of the principal sum of £. . . . . with interest thereupon from the date hereof at . . . . . per cent per annum payable half yearly on the . . . . . day of . . . . and the . . . . . day of . . . . in every year.
And it is hereby declared that:

[1.   *Reduction of interest on punctual payment:*]

2.   The Borrower HEREBY COVENANTS with the Mortgagee that at all times during the continuance of this security [*continue with Borrower's covenants*] . . .

[3.   *Warranty as to occupation:*] . . .

[To be executed by both AB and CD and attested]

LAND REGISTRATION ACT 1925

26.   Registration of charges. — (1) The charge shall be completed by the registrar entering on the register the person in whose favour the charge is made as the proprietor of such charge, and the particulars of the charge.

27.   Terms of years implied in or granted by charges. — (1) A registered charge shall, unless made or taking effect by demise or subdemise, and subject to any provision to the contrary contained in the charge, take effect as a charge by way of legal mortgage.

(2) Subject to the provisions of the Law of Property Act, 1925, a registered charge may contain in the case of freehold land, an express demise, and in

---

[17] The precedent is taken from Hallett, *Conveyancing Precedents*, p. 1207. See also LRR 1925, r. 139 and Sch.

[18] Omit "by way of legal mortgage" if desired.

the case of leasehold land an express subdemise of the land to the creditor for a term of years absolute, subject to a proviso for cesser on redemption.

(3) Any such demise or subdemise or charge by way of legal mortgage shall take effect from the date of the delivery of the deed containing the same, but subject to the estate or interest of any person (other than the proprietor of the land) whose estate or interest (whenever created) is registered or noted on the register before the date of registration of the charge.

29. Priorities of registered charges. — Subject to any entry to the contrary on the register, registered charges on the same land shall as between themselves rank according to the order in which they are entered on the register, and not according to the order in which they are created.

102. Priorities as between minor interests. — (2) Priorities as regards dealings effected after the commencement of this Act between assignees and incumbrancers of life interests, remainders, reversions and executory interests shall be regulated by the order of the priority cautions or inhibitions lodged (in a specially prescribed form)[19] against the proprietor of the registered estate affected, but, save as aforesaid, priorities as between persons interested in minor interests shall not be affected by the lodgment of cautions or inhibitions[20].

34. Powers of proprietor of charge. — (1) Subject to any entry on the register to the contrary, the proprietor of a charge shall have and may exercise all the powers conferred by law on the owner of a legal mortgage.

(4) A sale by the court or under the power of sale shall operate and be completed by registration in the same manner, as nearly as may be (but subject to any alterations on the register affecting the priority of the charge), as a transfer for valuable consideration by the proprietor of the land at the time of the registration of the charge would have operated or been completed, and, as respects the land transferred, the charge and all incumbrances and entries inferior thereto shall be cancelled.

65. Deposit at registry of certificate of mortgaged land. — Where a charge or mortgage (otherwise than by deposit) is registered, or is protected by a caution in a specially prescribed form, the land certificate shall be deposited at the registry until the charge or mortgage is cancelled.

LAND REGISTRATION RULES 1925

160. Registration of proprietor of incumbrances prior to first registration of land. — (1) Where it appears that any person is entitled to an incumbrance created prior to the first registration of land, the Registrar shall, on the application or with the consent of the person so entitled and on due proof of his title and after notice to the proprietor of the land, register such person as the proprietor of such incumbrance.

(2) Where there are two or more such incumbrances, their relative priorities shall not be affected by the registration of some or one of them only, or by the order in which such of them as are registered are entered in the register.

---

[19] In the Minor Interests Index.
[20] LRR 1925, rr. 11, 229, 290 (2).

LAND REGISTRATION ACT 1925

66. Creation of liens by deposit of certificates[1]. — The proprietor of any registered land or charge may, subject to the overriding interests, if any, to any entry to the contrary on the register, and to any estates, interests, charges, or rights registered or protected on the register at the date of the deposit, create a lien on the registered land or charge by deposit of the land certificate or charge certificate; and such lien shall, subject as aforesaid, be equivalent to a lien created in the case of unregistered land by the deposit of documents of title or of the mortgage deed by an owner entitled for his own benefit to the registered estate, or a mortgagee beneficially entitled to the mortgage, as the case may be.

LAND REGISTRATION RULES 1925

239. Notice of deposit of certificate. — (1) Any person with whom a land certificate or charge certificate is deposited as security for money may, by registered letter or otherwise, in writing give notice to the Registrar of such deposit, and of his name and address.

(3) On receipt of such notice the Registrar shall enter notice of the deposit in the Charges Register, and shall give a written acknowledgment of its receipt.

(4) Such notice shall operate as a caution under section 54 of the Act.

262. Form of charge certificate. — (1) A charge certificate shall certify the registration of the charge and shall' contain —

(*a*) an office copy of the charge,

(*b*) a description (if no description is contained in the charge) of the land affected,

(*c*) the name and address of the proprietor of the charge,

(*d*) a list of the prior incumbrances (if any) appearing on the register.

(2) There shall also be added such further particulars, if any, as the Registrar shall think fit, and the Land Registry seal shall be affixed to it.

(3) Notes of subsequent dealings affecting the charge shall from time to time be entered on the certificate, or a new certificate shall be issued in place thereof, as may be more convenient.

In *Grace Rymer Investments Ltd v Waite* [1958] Ch 831, [1958] 2 All ER 777, tenants under a lease for less than 21 years were in possession of the property at the date on which the lessor executed a legal charge in favour of a mortgagee. The charge was registered a few days later; an argument was addressed to the court as to the date from which the charge took effect.

Lord EVERSHED MR said at 849, at 783: "Apart from section 27 (3), it would appear therefore to be tolerably clear that the title of the purchaser or of the mortgagee, as the case may be, in the case of registered land is not perfected until registration, and that, when registration takes effect[2], it is

---

[1] See *Re White Rose Cottage* [1965] Ch 940, [1965] 1 All ER 11, p. 715, ante; (1966) 19 CLP 26 (E. C. Ryder); *Barclays Bank Ltd v Taylor* [1974] Ch 137, [1973] 1 All ER 752; (1973) 89 LQR 70 (P.V.B.); (1974) 124 NLJ 634 (S. Robinson); *Thames Guaranty Ltd v Campbell* [1985] QB 210, [1984] 2 All ER 585, p. 658, n. 12, ante.

[2] See LRR 1925, rr. 83–85, p. 115, ante.

subject to overriding interests which are anticipated by section 20[3], but more precisely defined by section 70. . . .[4]

The argument, as I follow it, appears to be: (1) that the time from which the mortgage shall take full effect must be treated as being the moment of the execution of the legal charge, which would put the legal estate in the chargee from that date: and (2) that the legal estate overrides all interests save those of persons whose estates or interests are registered or noted on the register. It seems to me that that cannot be right. If so, it would be inconsistent, so far as I can see, with the purpose and intention of the earlier sections to which I have already alluded, and which provide that until registration (in the case of a sale) the vendor remains the proprietor of the legal estate. I am unable to accept it that if the registered proprietor is to be treated as remaining the proprietor of the legal estate, a legal estate at the same time can also be created in favour of somebody else not on the register at all and not deriving title from someone on the register, although the earlier sections 19[5], 20[6] and 26[7] indicate that a charge is only completed by entry on the register. . . .

It would seem to me that it would be contrary to the whole tenor of the Act and indeed to general principle if, by reason of the reference in section 27[8] to estates or interests which are registered or noted on the register, you could produce the result that the plaintiffs could defeat the interests of a tenant of which they had notice when he took possession. According to general principles (and indeed it has not been contested) the plaintiffs had or must be treated as having had notice of the occupation of Mrs Hitchen and her companions since there they were in occupation for all to see."

(1977) 93 LQR 541 at pp. 542–543, 558–560 (R. J. Smith)

"[*In Barclays Bank Ltd v Taylor* [1974] Ch 137, [1973] 1 All ER 752] the owner of land mortgaged it by deed; the mortgage was protected by a notice of deposit of the land certificate. At first instance[9], Goulding J held that a notice of deposit was not appropriate to protect the mortgage[10] which consequently was treated as unprotected. Subsequently, the mortgagor contracted to sell the land and this estate contract was protected by caution. When the mortgagee later sought to register its charge, the cautioner objected. Thus the question arose as to whether the protected estate contract had priority over the earlier, but unprotected, equitable mortgage. Goulding J held in favour of the estate contract. On appeal, Russell LJ, delivering the judgment of the court, asked[11] the not unreasonable question: 'what provision is there in the Act which reverses the ordinary rule that as between equities — for the [cautioners] have only an interest in equity under their

---

[3] P. 110, ante.
[4] P. 118, ante.
[5] P. 99, ante.
[6] P. 110, ante.
[7] P. 742, ante.
[8] P. 742, ante.
[9] [1973] Ch 63, [1972] 2 All ER 752.
[10] Relying on LRA, s. 106 (2), by which a caution in a specially prescribed form was the only appropriate method of protection, short of registration of the charge under s. 26. This provision has now been repealed by AJA 1977, s. 26.
[11] At 146, at 757.

contract of purchase — priority is governed by the time sequence?' It does not appear that the question, quite apart from an answer to it, had been raised before Goulding J. In the Court of Appeal, counsel for the cautioners was unable to offer any convincing answer and thus the appeal was allowed, giving priority to the mortgage.

It may be noted that the *ratio decidendi* supports two allied propositions. First, an unprotected minor interest does not automatically lose priority to a subsequent minor interest and, second, that an interest protected by caution does not have any automatic priority over earlier unprotected minor interests. . . .

There are, perhaps, two principal impressions one obtains from this examination of priority issues. The first is how confused and uncertain the law is and how difficult it is to abstract either general principles or comprehensible detailed provisions from the legislation. This is a serious charge to be made against legislation designed to simplify the law. The major problem is that the land registration system is designed for those with registered interests; for such persons it works well. However, the impact of its provisions on the holders of other interests has never been properly sorted out — unlike the unregistered system, one does not have familiar principles to illuminate one's way forward. Instead, there is a fog of obscure and conflicting detail. The second conclusion is more palatable; it is that many of the conclusions eventually reached make good sense and are quite workable.

Nevertheless, the uncertainty in the area borders upon the intolerable[12] and is clearly a suitable subject for reform. Particular points requiring attention are: the impact of protection by notice, the effect of section 107 and the special provisions relating to section 48 leases, restrictive covenants and liens by deposit of certificate (especially the priority accorded to the last two interests on creation).

The most important point of principle is whether a general priority rule based upon the order of protection on the register ought to be introduced. Where the second interest holder has searched the register, protected his interest and either paid over money to the proprietor or otherwise acted to his detriment, it seems a mockery of the system to subject him to an earlier unprotected minor interest[13]. Yet at present he could only succeed if, as urged above, he was protected by notice or could rely on the *Abigail v Lapin*[14] line of

---

[12] This is not, however, reflected in any mass of case law. On the contrary, the lack of reported cases makes one rely on pure statutory interpretation and analysis to a disconcerting extent. Perhaps the factual situations under discussion are relatively rare. More likely, the difficulties have not yet been fully appreciated. Certainly, the approach of the Court of Appeal in *Barclays Bank Ltd v Taylor* [1974] Ch 137, [1973] 1 All ER 752 was radically different from that of GOULDING J at first instance [1973] Ch 63, [1972] 2 All ER 752 and that case involved the relatively simple problem of the effect of a caution.

[13] Cf. Robinson (1974) 124 NLJ 634, 635, who says of minor interests: "Until protected they are not and cannot be proprietary interests if the concept of a conclusive register is the plinth of the English system of title to land by registration."

[14] [1934] AC 491 (Privy Council, on appeal from the High Court of Australia). The case develops, in the registration context, the rule that as between two equitable interests the first in time only has priority if the equities are equal. The suggestion is that, if the first interest is not protected on the register, then the equities are not equal and so the second in time has priority. *Quaere* the need for detrimental reliance. In English law, the second interest, being registrable, could have had priority anyway if the register had been searched and the interest registered. The scope of *Abigail v Lapin* may well be limited by *J and H Just (Holdings) Pty Ltd v Bank of New South Wales* (1971) 45 ALJR 625.

authority. It has already been argued that the latter possibility would lead to unfortunate uncertainty. It is submitted that there is a need for a statutory priority in favour of the second interest holder, for only legislation can provide the degree of precision required.

One obvious question is whether all minor interests should be affected by failure to protect them[15]. It is urged that it would be unfortunate to discriminate so that interests not commonly protected would not be so affected. The idea of a minor interest which one does not need to protect is odd and contrary to the ethos of the land registration system[16]. Nor is it right to accord priority only to those interests where money is usually handed over to the proprietor. There will always be cases where other interest holders have parted with money and so are equally deserving. It would be justifiable to limit the priority to cases where the second interest holder has in fact paid over money or acted to his detriment, but it is submitted that to accord priority to all protected minor interests (subject to the holder not being a volunteer) would be simpler and preferable. This, then, is the reform urged: the priority of minor interests should be determined by the order of protection on the register."

QUESTION

What principles do you think are applicable to determine the priority of mortgages —
- (*a*) pre-1926
- (*b*) post 1925 in unregistered land and
- (*c*) post 1925 in registered land?

---

[15] Cf. the Law Commission's Working Paper No. 67; Hayton, *Registered Land* (2nd edn), pp. 147–157; (1976) 29 CLP 26.

[16] Cf. supra, p. 555. This is not an argument that where there is actual occupation then there should be no protection as an overriding interest under LRA, s. 70 (1) (*g*), for then there is a quite separate basis for binding the second interest holder.

Part Four. Control of Land

12.   Covenants Between Freeholders[1]

I.   Introduction

In considering to what extent covenants between freeholders may be
enforced between persons who were not original parties to the covenant, two
main distinctions must be made. First, different rules apply to the "running"
of the benefit and the "running" of the burden. And, secondly, in connection
both with the burden and the benefit, the rules of common law are different
from those of equity. This is most marked in connection with the running of
the burden, where the decision in equity of *Tulk v Moxhay* in 1848[2] provided
the basis of the modern doctrine. The common law rules for the running of
the benefit are still applicable, but they have been further developed in
equity[3]. The burden and the benefit will be considered separately.

The common law rules for the running of the benefit are ancient. As with
every case of a covenant running at common law, the covenant ran with the
estate of the covenantee and not with the land[4], and it was necessary for the

---

[1] C & B, pp. 571–602; M & W, pp. 739–741, 798; MM, pp. 439–459; Preston and Newsom,
Restrictive Covenants Affecting Freehold Land (7th edn. 1982); Elphinstone, *Covenants Affecting Land*
(1946); Farrand (2nd edn. 1973), pp. 404–429; Maitland, pp. 162–178. For a historical
account, see Simpson, *Introduction to the History of Land Law* (1961), pp. 109–111, 131–132,
238–243.
[2] (1848) 2 Ph 774, p. 761, post.
[3] See p. 772, post.
[4] For covenants in leases, see p. 459, ante.

assignee of the covenantee to show that he had the same legal estate as the original covenantee[5]. Equity, both with the benefit and the burden, developed a different concept of a covenant running with the land, and avoided the requirement that the assignee of the covenantee or covenantor should hold the same estate as his assignor[6].

These factors have to be considered when the question is whether or not an assignee of the covenantee can sue. He may be able to do so under the common law rules alone, as where there is no servient land[7]; or he may have to rely on the further developments in equity and under statute[8].

As indicated, the rules relating to the running of the burden of a covenant between freeholders are almost exclusively equitable. The origin of the rule is the equitable principle that a person cannot come to property with knowledge that a contract affecting the property is in existence and then ignore it. But there has been much development from the general principle in the case of restrictive covenants affecting land[9]. It is not in the general interest to allow burdens to be attached to land unless there is some corresponding benefit to be protected. And a covenant enforceable between adjoining freeholders is now looked upon as an interest which imposes a burden on one piece of land and confers a benefit on another; as something in the nature of an equitable negative easement[10].

This branch of equity grew with the great era of suburban development in the 19th century; control was in the hands of individual landowners. But, since the 1930s, this type of control has been largely superseded by public control in the hands of planning authorities exercised in the public interest[11]. The development or change of user of land may now only be carried out after planning permission has been obtained. Public planning control has thus overtaken the earlier method, both in influence and complexity. But the law relating to covenants between freeholders is still operative. The two methods of control are sometimes complementary, sometimes contrary. They are cumulative, and a purchaser must satisfy himself in respect of both forms of restriction[12].

It has always been clear that no covenant will run with the land unless it "touches and concerns" the land. This requirement exists also in connection with covenants between landlord and tenant, and has been discussed in that

---

[5] But see p. 769, post; *Smith and Snipes Hall Farm Ltd v River Douglas Catchment Board* [1949] 2 KB 500, [1949] 2 All ER 179; LPA 1925, s. 78 (1).

[6] See p. 765, post; *Tichborne v Weir* (1892) 67 LT 735; *Re Nisbet and Potts' Contract* [1906] 1 Ch 386.

[7] *The Prior's Case* (1368) YB 42 Edw 3, fo 3A, pl. 14, discussed under *Spencer's Case* (1583) 5 Co Rep 16a; Smith's *Leading Cases* (13th edn. 1929), vol. I, pp. 51, 65, 73; *Smith and Snipes Hall Farm Ltd v River Douglas Catchment Board*, supra, per TUCKER LJ at 506, at 183.

[8] LPA 1925, s. 78 (1); *Federated Homes Ltd v Mill Lodge Properties Ltd* [1980] 1 WLR 594, [1980] 1 All ER 371, p. 777, post; *Roake v Chadha* [1984] 1 WLR 40, [1983] 3 All ER 503, p. 782, post.

[9] For the operation of this principle in the case of chattels, see Cheshire and Fifoot, *Law of Contract* (10th edn. 1981) pp. 414–419; Treitel, *Law of Contract* (6th edn. 1983, pp. 473–477).

[10] *London and South Western Rly Co v Gomm* (1882) 20 ChD 562, p. 765, post; *LCC v Allen* [1914] 3 KB 642, p. 762, post; *Formby v Barker* [1903] 2 Ch 539, p. 764, post; *Re Nisbet and Potts' Contract* [1906] 1 Ch 386, p. 766, post.

[11] Town and Country Planning Act 1971; Land Compensation Acts 1961, 1973; C & B, pp. 877–918; M & W, pp. 1059–1084; MM, pp. 553–566; pp. 831–834, post.

[12] (1964) 28 Conv (NS) 190 (A. R. Mellows).

connection[13]. An additional point of importance here is the view current before 1926 that Real Property Act 1845 section 5 (under which the benefit of a covenant in an indenture may be given to a person who was not a party to the indenture) applied only to cases of covenants which ran with the land[14]. This section is now repealed and replaced by Law of Property Act 1925, section 56, which has been said to be free from such restriction. The question whether a particular covenant "touches and concerns" the land is, therefore, not material in deciding whether the benefit of it can be given to a person not a party to it; it is material in deciding whether the benefit of the covenant so given will run with the land of the person to whom it was given.

This branch of the law is particularly concerned with covenants between freeholders. Covenants between landlord and tenant have already been discussed, and are governed by rules of their own. Where, however, a covenant between landlord and tenant is not enforceable under those special rules, it may, nevertheless, be enforceable under the rules discussed in this section where they are applicable[15].

Finally, it will be seen that the law relating to the passing of the benefit of restrictive covenants has become difficult and technical. But there is a tendency now to escape from many of the technicalities. This is shown by recent decisions in the context of annexation of the benefit of a covenant to the land of the covenantee[16], and also in connection with schemes of development[17]. "The tendency is . . . to assimilate the law of covenants to the law of easements, where no formalities are required for establishing the right as appurtenant to the dominant tenement"[18]. This policy, as will be seen, is a feature of the Law Commission Report in 1984 on the Law of Positive and Restrictive Covenants[19].

II.   The Burden[20]

A.   Common Law

i.   THE GENERAL RULE
The general rule is that the burden of a covenant affecting land does not run with the land at common law. This is a basic principle, the existence of which has necessitated the development in equity of the doctrine of restrictive

---

[13] See p. 459, ante. The position in connection with covenants between freeholders is not exactly the same, for in this situation there are two pieces of land involved. Preston and Newsom, pp. 30–33; *Rogers v Hosegood* [1900] 2 Ch 388, p. 775, post; *Formby v Barker* [1903] 2 Ch 539 at 554; *Dyson v Forster* [1909] AC 98; *Smith and Snipes Hall Farm Ltd v River Douglas Catchment Board* [1949] 2 KB 500 at 506, [1949] 2 All ER 179 at 183, p. 769, post; *Newton Abbot Co-operative Society Ltd v Williamson and Treadgold Ltd* [1952] Ch 286, [1952] 1 All ER 279, p. 790, post; *Federated Homes Ltd v Mill Lodge Properties Ltd* [1980] 1 WLR 594, [1980] 1 All ER 371, p. 777, post. The distinction is not kept clear by LINDLEY LJ in *Austerberry v Oldham Corporation* (1885) 29 ChD 750 at 781.

[14] *Kelsey v Dodd* (1881) 52 LJ Ch 34 at 39; *Forster v Elvet Colliery Co Ltd* [1908] 1 KB 629, affd. sub nom. *Dyson v Forster* [1909] AC 98; *Westhoughton UDC v Wigan Coal and Iron Co Ltd* [1919] 1 Ch 159; *Re Ecclesiastical Commissioners for England's Conveyance* [1936] Ch 430, p. 811, post.

[15] *Hall v Ewin* (1887) 37 ChD 74, p. 759, n. 12, post; *Patman v Harland* (1881) 17 ChD 353, p. 458, ante.

[16] *Federated Homes Ltd v Mill Lodge Properties Ltd*, supra; *Roake v Chadha* supra.

[17] *Re Dolphin's Conveyance* [1970] Ch 654, [1970] 2 All ER 664, p. 802, post.

[18] (1972 B) 31 CLJ 157 at 163 (H. W. R. Wade).

[19] Law Com No. 127, HC 201, p. 834, post.

[20] C & B, pp. 573–583; M & W, pp. 767–780; MM, pp. 441–446.

covenants. The rule is one of the many results of the wider principle of privity of contract, that a person may neither sue upon nor be made liable upon a contract unless he is a party to it. If, for instance, A sold Whiteacre, part of his land, to B who covenanted with A to lay out pleasure gardens on Whiteacre, A could sue B at law for damages if B refused to perform the covenant; but if B sold or gave the land to C, C could not be made liable on the covenant, because he was not a party to it. This is a matter of the greatest importance because, apart from cases in which specific performance will be decreed, equity only interferes, as will be seen, where the covenant is "restrictive". Positive covenants are therefore not enforceable by an action for damages against an assignee of the covenantor.

It is questionable whether the policy behind such a rule is satisfactory, for it often has the effect of leaving a covenantee without a remedy. The matter was considered in 1965 by the Wilberforce Committee which recommended that, subject to certain conditions, the burden of positive covenants should run, and again in 1984 by the Law Commission on the wider topic of both Positive and Negative Covenants[1]. The rule does not exist in such absolute form in most of the United States[2]. It is, however, possible in England to effect the observance of a positive covenant in other ways[3].

AUSTERBERRY *v* CORPORATION OF OLDHAM
(1885) 29 ChD 750 (CA, COTTON, FRY, LINDLEY LJJ)

In 1837 a company was formed for the purpose of acquiring land and building thereon a road, for the use of the public, on payment of a toll. The road was to pass over the land of John Elliott, who conveyed it to the trustees for the company who covenanted with him, his heirs and assigns to make up the road at their expense, and keep it at all times in repair. The trustees maintained the road until it was taken over by Oldham Corporation in 1880 under statutory powers. In 1868 the plaintiff purchased the land owned by John Elliott adjoining the road. The present dispute arose in connection with the payment of the expenses of 'making up' the street, liability for which is imposed upon the frontagers by the Public Health Act 1875. The plaintiffs argued, inter alia, that the Corporation had taken the land from the trustees with notice of the covenant to maintain, and were bound by that covenant to meet the expenses themselves.

Held. The covenant was not enforceable.

LINDLEY LJ (after dealing with a question arising under section 150 of the Public Health Act 1875):

---

[1] Report of the Committee on Positive Covenants Affecting Land (1965) Cmnd 2719; Law Commission Report on Restrictive Covenants 1967 (Law Com No. 11); Law Commission Report on Positive and Restrictive Covenants 1984 (Law Com No. 127, HC 201). See also (1972 B) 31 CLJ 157 (H. W. R. Wade).

[2] Clark, *Real Covenants* (2nd edn. 1947), pp. 231–232; (1943) 52 Yale LJ 699; (1945) 30 Cornell LQ 378; American Restatement (1944) Property: vol. 5, Servitudes, ch 45.

[3] *Brewster v Kitchell* (1697) 12 Mod Rep 166 at 169; *Morland v Cook* (1868) LR 6 Eq 252; *Aspden v Seddon* (1876) 1 Ex D 496; *Austerberry v Oldham Corpn* (1885) 29 ChD 750 per LINDLEY LJ at 781; *South Eastern Rly Co v Associated Portland Cement Manufacturers (1900) Ltd* [1910] 1 Ch 12; *Westhoughton UDC v Wigan Coal and Iron Co Ltd* [1919] 1 Ch 159; *Halsall v Brizell* [1957] Ch 169, [1957] 1 All ER 371, p. 757, n. 9, post; (1954) 18 Conv (NS) 558–564 (E. H. Scamell); Preston and Newsom, pp. 72–75.

But then arises another and a totally different point. The Plaintiff says:—"You, the corporation, have bought or acquired this road under an Act of Parliament which places you in the position of, and in no better position than, those from whom you got it; you acquired it from certain trustees, and those trustees covenanted with my predecessors in title to keep this road open for the public, and to repair it: You are bound by that covenant to repair, and I am in a position to enforce against you that covenant." . . . That gives rise to one or two questions of law.

The first question which I will consider is whether that covenant runs with the land, as it is called — whether the benefit of it runs with the land held by the Plaintiff, and whether the burden of it runs with the land held by the Defendants; because, if the covenant does run at law, then the Plaintiff, so far as I can see, would be right as to this portion of his claim. Now, as regards the benefit running with the Plaintiff's land, the covenant is, so far as the road goes, a covenant to repair the road; what I mean by that is, there is nothing in the deed which points particularly to that portion of the road which abuts upon or fronts the Plaintiff's land — it is a covenant to repair the whole of the road, no distinction being made between the portion of that road which joins or abuts upon his land and the rest of the road; in other words, it is a covenant simply to make and maintain this road as a public highway; there is no covenant to do anything whatever on the Plaintiff's land, and there is nothing pointing to the Plaintiff's land in particular. Now it appears to me to be going a long way to say that the benefit of that covenant runs with the Plaintiff's land. I do not overlook the fact that the Plaintiff as a frontager has certain rights of getting on to the road; and if this covenant had been so worded as to shew that there had been an intention to grant him some particular benefit in respect of that particular part of his land, possibly we might have said that the benefit of the covenant did run with this land; but when you look at the covenant it is a mere covenant with him, as with all adjoining owners, to make this road, a small portion of which only abuts on his land, and there is nothing specially relating to his land at all. I cannot see myself how any benefit of this covenant runs with his land.

But it strikes me, I confess, that there is a still more formidable objection as regards the burden. Does the burden of this covenant run with the land so as to bind the Defendants? The Defendants have acquired the road under the trustees, and they are bound by such covenant as runs with the land. Now we come to face the difficulty; does a covenant to repair all this road run with the land — that is, does the burden of it descend upon those to whom the road may be assigned in future? We are not dealing here with a case of landlord and tenant. The authorities which refer to that class of cases have little, if any, bearing upon the case which we have to consider, and I am not prepared to say that any covenant which imposes a burden upon land does run with the land, unless the covenant does, upon the true construction of the deed, containing the covenant, amount to either a grant of an easement, or a rent-charge, or some estate or interest in the land. A mere covenant, to repair or to do something of that kind, does not seem to me, I confess, to run with the land in such a way as to bind those who may acquire it.

It is remarkable that the authorities upon this point, when they are examined, are very few, and it is also remarkable that in no case that I know of, except one which I shall refer to presently, is there anything like authority to say that a burden of this kind will run with the land. That point has often been discussed, and I rather think the conclusion at which the editors of the last edition of *Smith's* Leading Cases have come to is right, that no case has been decided which does establish that such a burden can run with the land in the sense in which I am now using that expression. [His Lordship referred to *Holmes v Buckley* (1691) 1 Eq Cas Abr 27; *Morland v Cook* (1868) LR 6 Eq 252; *Cooke v Chilcott* (1876) 3 ChD 694; *Western v MacDermott* (1866) LR 1 Eq 499; affd. 2 Ch App 72, and continued:] I am not aware of any other case which either shews, or appears to shew, that a burden such as this can be annexed to land by a mere covenant, such as we have got here; and in the absence of authority it appears to me that we shall be perfectly warranted in saying that the burden of this covenant does not run with the land. After all it is a mere personal covenant. If the parties had intended to charge this land for ever, into whosesoever hands it came, with the burden of repairing the road, there are ways and means known to conveyancers by which it could be done with comparative ease; all that would have been necessary would have been to create a rent-charge and charge it on the tolls, and the thing would have been done. They have not done anything of the sort, and, therefore, it seems to me to shew that they did not intend to have a covenant which should run with the land. That disposes of the part of the case which is perhaps the most difficult.

The last point was this — that even if it did not run with the land at law, still, upon the authority of *Tulk v Moxhay* (1848) 2 Ph 774, the Defendants, having bought the land with notice of this covenant, take the land subject to it. Mr *Collins* very properly did not press that upon us, because after the two recent decisions in the Court of Appeal in *Haywood v Brunswick Permanent Benefit Building Society* (1881) 8 QBD 403 (see p. 761, post) and *London and South Western Rly Co v Gomm* (1882) 20 ChD 562, that argument is untenable. *Tulk v Moxhay* cannot be extended to covenants of this description. It appears to me, therefore, that upon all points the plaintiff has failed, and that the appeal ought to be dismissed with costs[4].

ii.   METHODS OF CIRCUMVENTION

"A number of current techniques and devices by which lawyers attempt to surmount or circumvent the difficulties of enforcing positive covenants" are listed in the Report of the Committee on Positive Covenants Affecting Land[5]. They are:

(i) To lease land instead of selling it and to rely upon the enforceability of covenants between landlord and tenant[6].

(ii) Chains of Indemnity Covenants. A covenant could be taken by each successive purchaser and liability on the covenant will exist down the line of purchasers[7]. "But in practice this device sooner or

---

[4] The burden of a positive covenant was held by MACNAGHTEN J (following the dicta in *Austerberry v Oldham Corporation*) not to run at law with the land of the covenantor in *E and G C Ltd v Bate* (1935) 79 LJo 203.

[5] (1965) Cmd 2719. The quotations in (ii) and (iv) are from para. 8 of the Report. See also Law Commission Report on Positive and Restrictive Covenants 1984 (Law Com No. 127, HC 201), paras. 3.19–3.42. Farrand (2nd edn.), pp. 422–427; George and George, *The Sale of Flats* (5th edn. 1984), pp. 76–89; (1973) 37 Conv (NS) 194 (A. M. Prichard); *Precedents for the Conveyancer*, 5–22, 19–11; McAuslan, *Land, Law and Planning* (1975), pp. 292–302.

[6] See p. 459, ante.

[7] See Law Society's General Conditions of Sale (1980 revision), Condition 17 (4); National Conditions of Sale (20th edn. 1981), Condition 19 (5), (6).

later becomes ineffective, either in consequence of the death or disappearance of the original covenantor, or because a break occurs in the chain of indemnities."

(iii) Covenants against sale of registered land without the developer's consent[8].

(iv) The doctrine of *Halsall v Brizell*. "In some cases a positive covenant can be enforced in practice by the operation of the maxim '*qui sentit commodum sentire debet et onus*'. This obliges a person who wishes to take advantage of a service or facility (e.g. a road or drains) to comply with any corresponding obligation to contribute to the cost of providing or maintaining it (*Halsall v Brizell* [1957] Ch 169, [1957] 1 All ER 371). The maxim cannot, however, be invoked where the burdened owner does not enjoy any service or facility to which his obligations attach or has no sufficient interest in the continuance of these benefits[9]".

(v) Easement of fencing[10].

(vi) On some occasions on which a long leasehold is converted into a freehold. Two statutes give such a right to a tenant:

(a) The Law of Property Act 1925, section 153, which provides for certain long leases[11] to be enlarged into freeholds, and for the freehold to be subject "to all the same covenants . . . as the term would have been subject to if it had not been so enlarged".

(b) The Leasehold Reform Act 1967 permits the tenant of a leasehold house[12] held on a long tenancy[13] at a low rent[14], which he has occupied as his residence for three years[15], to acquire the freehold[16] on fair terms and free from incumbrances[17], but "Burdens . . . in respect of the upkeep or regulation for the benefit of any locality of any land, building, structure, works,

---

[8] LRA 1925, s. 58, p. 138, ante.

[9] (1957) 73 LQR 154 (R. E. M.); [1957] CLJ 35 (H. W. R. Wade); (1957) 21 Conv (NS) 160 (F. R. Crane); *E R Ives Investment Ltd v High* [1967] 2 QB 379, [1967] 1 All ER 504, p. 542, ante; *Montague v Long* (1972) 24 P & CR 240. For a detailed discussion of the doctrine, see *Tito v Waddell (No 2)* [1977] Ch 106 at 289–311, [1977] 3 All ER 129 at 280–298, where MEGARRY V-C held at 303, at 292 that it covered not merely successors in title but also "anybody whose connection with the transaction creating the benefit and burden is sufficient to show that he has some claim to the benefit whether or not he has a valid title to it". See also (1977) 41 Conv (NS) 432–435 (F. R. Crane); [1985] Conv 12 (E. P. Aughterson).

[10] *Jones v Price* [1965] 2 QB 618, [1965] 2 All ER 625: *Crow v Wood* [1971] 1 QB 77, [1970] 3 All ER 425, p. 576, ante.

[11] Restricted to those: (i) which were originally created for at least 300 years of which not less than 200 years is unexpired; (ii) in which no rent or money value is payable; (iii) which are not liable to be determined by re-entry for condition broken; (1958) 22 Conv (NS) 101 (T. P. D. Taylor).

[12] Not a flat nor a maisonette: s. 2.

[13] I.e., an original term of more than 21 years: s. 3.

[14] I.e., not more than two-thirds of the 1965 rateable value. The Act applies only to properties below certain rateable values. The provisions are complex. Put simply, the Act applies to "older" leases (i.e. granted on or before 18 February 1966) where rateable value does not exceed £1,500 in Greater London or £750 elsewhere. With "newer" leases the limits are £1,000 and £500 respectively: Housing Act 1974, s. 118.

[15] Or for 3 years within the last 10 years: s. 1 as amended by Housing Act 1980, s. 141, Sch. 21.

[16] Or an extended lease for 50 years: ss. 1, 14.

[17] Section 8 (1). For restrictive covenants, see s. 10 (4) (a).

ways or watercourse[18] shall not be treated as incumbrances for purposes of this Part of this Act, but any conveyance executed to give effect to this section shall be made subject thereto . . .'"[19].

(vii) Certain statutory powers which entitle Local Authorities to impose positive obligations on land and to enforce them upon successive owners[20].

There are other possibilities.

(viii) Rentcharge. The creation of a rentcharge to secure the payment of money or contribution to the maintenance of property[1]. This method of enforcing a positive covenant was preserved by the Rentcharges Act 1977[2].

(ix) Right of re-entry. A right of re-entry may be reserved exercisable on events which amount to the breach of a positive covenant[3]. This right of re-entry runs with the land, but is subject to the rule against perpetuities[4].

(x) Law of Property Act 1925, section 79[5]. If this section is given a wide construction similar to that given to s. 78 in *Smith and Snipes Hall Farm Ltd v River Douglas Catchment Board* [1949] 2 KB 500, [1949] 2 All ER 179, p. 769, post, and in *Federated Homes Ltd v Mill Lodge Properties Ltd* [1980] 1 WLR 594, [1980] 1 All ER 371, p. 777, post, the burden of a positive covenant would be able to run with the land.

B. Equity

It was held in the leading case of *Tulk v Moxhay* in 1848[6] that the purchaser of land with notice of a restrictive covenant affecting it would be restrained from using the land in a way inconsistent with that covenant. The vendor, who takes from a purchaser a covenant which restricts the way in which the land can be used, is entitled in appropriate circumstances to an injunction restraining improper use of the land, not only against the original covenantor, but also against other parties coming to the land[7]. This right to an injunction is of course an equitable right, and is never enforceable against

---

[18] This clearly includes provisions of the type found in *Halsall v Brizell* [1957] Ch 169, [1957] 1 All ER 371.

[19] Section 8 (3). There is an exception in the case of rentcharges: s. 11.

[20] TCPA 1971, ss. 29, 30 and 52; Highways Act 1980, s. 35; Local Government (Miscellaneous Provisions) Act 1982, s. 33, and various Private Acts.

[1] *Morland v Cook* (1868) LR 6 Eq 252; *Austerberry v Oldham Corporation* (1885) 29 ChD 750 at 782, p. 756, ante.

[2] Ss. 2 (3) (*c*), (4), (5) (creation of "estate rentcharges"). See C & B, pp. 605–607; M & W, pp. 767–768; MM, p. 392; George and George, pp. 82–89.

[3] *Shiloh Spinners Ltd v Harding* [1973] AC 691, [1973] 1 All ER 90, p. 34, ante. The possibility of relief against forfeiture reduces its effectiveness as a device.

[4] (1950) 14 Conv (NS) 350 at pp. 354–357 (S. M. Tolson).

[5] See p. 461, ante; p. 767, post.

[6] (1848) 2 Ph 774; following Lord COTTENHAM's earlier decision in *Mann v Stephens* (1846) 15 Sim 377.

[7] The court has power to grant damages in lieu of an injunction under Supreme Court Act 1981, s. 50 (formerly Chancery Amendment Act 1858, s. 2). See *Sefton v Tophams Ltd* [1965] Ch 1140, [1965] 3 All ER 1; *Baxter v Four Oaks Properties Ltd* [1965] Ch 816, [1965] 1 All ER 906; Preston and Newsom, pp. 168–174.

bona fide purchasers of the legal estate in the land for value without notice of the covenant[8], but it can be enforced against all other persons. The burden of such a covenant is then said to run with the land in equity.

The conditions on which the burden of a covenant will so run are established in the cases leading from *Tulk v Moxhay*, and these cases show that the basic principle on which such covenants are enforced has changed since 1848. *Tulk v Moxhay* was decided on the general equitable ground that it was contrary to conscience that a person should come to land with notice of a covenant affecting it, and act in a way inconsistent with the covenant. And this principle was applied in a number of subsequent cases[9]. It soon became clear, however, that such a policy would result in the imposition of burdens on land without there being any corresponding interest in the plaintiff which required protection. The end of the 19th century saw the change of emphasis[10]. There must be an intent that the burden of the covenant should run with the land[11]. There must also be land benefited by the covenant, and the plaintiff must show that he has an interest in that land[12]. On the question of benefit, the court does not apply its own standard, but takes a decision on expert evidence presented to it[13]. The onus is on the defendant to show that a covenant does not benefit the land[14], either originally, or at the date of the action. "This means that if there were possible opinions either way, the defendant will still fail unless he can show that the opinions that the covenant benefits the land could not reasonably be held[15]." The benefit of

---

[8] *Pilcher v Rawlins* (1872) 7 Ch App 259, p. 26, ante.

[9] *Luker v Dennis* (1877) 7 ChD 227; *Catt v Tourle* (1869) 4 Ch App 654; *Millbourn v Lyons* [1914] 2 Ch 231; *Clegg v Hands* (1890) 44 ChD 503; *De Mattos v Gibson* (1858) 4 De G & J 276; *Western v MacDermott* (1866) 2 Ch App 72; *Lord Strathcona SS Co Ltd v Dominion Coal Co Ltd* [1926] AC 108.

[10] *London and South Western Rly Co v Gomm* (1882) 20 Ch D 562.

[11] This intent may be clear from the nature of the covenant or by virtue of LPA 1925, s. 79, which will apply unless a contrary intention is shown: *Re Royal Victoria Pavilion (Ramsgate)* [1961] Ch 581, [1961] 3 All ER 83; *Tophams Ltd v Earl of Sefton* [1967] 1 AC 50 at 73, 81, [1966] 1 All ER 1039, at 1048, 1053, pp. 767–768, post.

[12] *Formby v Barker* [1903] 2 Ch 539, p. 764, post; *LCC v Allen* [1914] 3 KB 642, p. 762, post; *Millbourn v Lyons* [1914] 2 Ch 231; *Kelly v Barrett* [1924] 2 Ch 379; *Re Ballard's Conveyance* [1937] Ch 473, [1937] 2 All ER 691; *Tophams Ltd v Earl of Sefton* [1967] 1 AC 50 at 81, [1966] 1 All ER 1039 at 1053, per Lord WILBERFORCE ("under what I am content for present purposes to take as accepted doctrine"). There are exceptions to this rule in Housing Act 1985, s. 609; National Trust Act 1937, s. 8; *Gee v The National Trust* [1966] 1 WLR 170 at 174, [1966] 1 All ER 954 at 957; Green Belt (London and Home Counties) Act 1938, s. 22; Water Act 1945, s. 15; National Park and Access to Countryside Act 1949, s. 16 (4); Forestry Act 1967, s. 5 (2); Town and Country Planning Act 1971, s. 52; Endowments and Glebe Measure 1976 s. 22; Ancient Monuments and Archaeological Act 1979, s. 17 (5); Wildlife and Countryside Act 1981, s. 39 (3); Local Government (Miscellaneous Provisions) Act 1982, s. 33; and a number of local authorities have power under local Acts. There are further exceptions in the cases of (i) schemes of development, p. 800, post; (ii) the landlord's reversion on a tenancy: *Hall v Ewin* (1887) 37 ChD 74; *Teape v Douse* (1905) 92 LT 319; (iii) the mortgagee's interest in the land: *Regent Oil Co Ltd v J. A. Gregory (Hatch End) Ltd* [1966] Ch 402, [1965] 3 All ER 673; following *John Bros Abergarw Brewery Co v Holmes* [1900] 1 Ch 188. On the question whether a covenant to restrain the pursuance of a non-noxious trade so as to avoid competition with the plaintiff can benefit the plaintiff's land, see *Wilkes v Spooner* [1911] 2 KB 473 at 485; *Newton Abbot Co-operative Society Ltd v Williamson and Treadgold Ltd* [1952] Ch 286, [1952] 1 All ER 279, p. 790, post; *Re Royal Victoria Pavilion (Ramsgate)* [1961] Ch 581, [1961] 3 All ER 83.

[13] *Marten v Flight Refuelling Ltd* [1962] Ch 115 at 137, [1961] 2 All ER 696 at 706; *Earl of Leicester v Wells-next-the-Sea UDC* [1973] Ch 110, [1972] 3 All ER 77; *Wrotham Park Estate Co Ltd v Parkside Homes Ltd* [1974] 1 WLR 798, [1974] 2 All ER 321.

[14] *Wrotham Park Estate Co Ltd v Parkside Homes Ltd*, supra, at 808, at 335.

[15] (1974) JPL at p. 133 (G. H. Newsom).

such a covenant then becomes associated with a piece of land in the way that an easement is appurtenant to the dominant tenement; and the phraseology of the law of easements is introduced into the law of restrictive covenants[16].

The doctrine of *Tulk v Moxhay* is applicable only to restrictive covenants; covenants, that is, which are negative in substance, even though positive in form: indeed, the covenant in *Tulk v Moxhay* itself was positive in form. But the boundary between those that are, and those that are not, negative in substance is not always easy to draw[17]; for almost every positive covenant can, in some sense, be regarded negatively. Moreover, it is difficult to see any inherent distinction between negative and positive covenants so far as enforceability is concerned. Positive and negative undertakings may be contained in a single covenant, but "there cannot be any doctrine of contagious proximity whereby the presence of the positive inhibits the enforcement of the neighbouring negative[18]." The Report on Positive Covenants Affecting Land emphasises the inconvenience of the present law (under which the burden of positive covenants does not run) to adjoining owners of land and especially to owners of divided buildings and blocks of flats[19]. In some situations, such as a covenant to supply water to land in a waterless area, the economic and moral reasons for enforcing positive covenants are just as strong as in the case of negative covenants. The jurisdiction, however, is exclusively equitable, and is limited to the situations which are susceptible to equitable remedies.

The positive remedy of specific performance and the doctrine of estate contracts are not indeed aspects of the doctrine of *Tulk v Moxhay*, but they provide an interesting analogy. An option in a lease to purchase the freehold has been held to be one which does not touch and concern the land and therefore does not run with the estate upon assignment by the tenant[20]. But the option to purchase, if specifically enforceable, creates a proprietary interest in the grantee which is good against everyone coming to the land other than a bona fide purchaser of the legal estate for value without notice[1]: registration constituting notice since 1925. An assignee of the covenantor will therefore take subject to the option[2].

However, the burden of a positive covenant does not run in equity any more than it ran at law. Such covenants may, as we have seen[3], be enforced on other grounds, and will, if the Law Commission Report on Positive and

---

[16] Per Jessel MR in *London and South Western Rly Co v Gomm*, quoted at p. 765, post.

[17] *Bridges v Harrow London Borough Council* (1981) 260 EG 284 at 288 (covenant to retain trees in hedgerow held to be probably negative in substance).

[18] *Shepherd Homes Ltd v Sandham (No. 2)* [1971] 1 WLR 1062 at 1067, [1971] 2 All ER 1267 at 1272, per Megarry J; Preston and Newsom, pp. 76–79.

[19] See p. 756, ante; Law Commission Report on Restrictive Covenants 1961 (Law Com No. 11); Law Commission Report on Positive and Restrictive Covenants 1984 (Law Com No. 127, HC 201), paras. 4.3–4.6.

[20] *Woodall v Clifton* [1905] 2 Ch 257, p. 354, ante; *Worthing Corpn v Heather* [1906] 2 Ch 532.

[1] See p. 24, ante.

[2] LCA 1972, s. 2 (4) Class C (iv); *London and South Western Rly Co v Gomm* (1882) 20 ChD 562; *Hutton v Watling* [1948] Ch 26, [1947] 2 All ER 641. The option, unless it be an option for a lessee or his successors in title to acquire an interest reversionary on the term of a lease and which ceases to be exercisable at or before the expiration of one year from the determination of the lease, must comply with the perpetuity rule, and the period, whether the issue is between the original contracting parties or not, is 21 years: Perpetuities and Accumulations Act 1964, ss. 9, 10, p. 355, ante.

[3] See p. 756, ante.

Restrictive Covenants is adopted, be enforceable subject to certain conditions. In the early days of the *Tulk v Moxhay* doctrine, equity made gallant attempts to enforce some positive covenants by issuing an injunction restraining the defendant from omitting to perform the undertaking[4]. This development, not surprisingly, was brought to an abrupt halt five years later in *Haywood v Brunswick Permanent Benefit Building Society* (1881) 8 QBD 403. It is, however, of interest in demonstrating the crucial importance of the scope of equitable remedies in the development of the doctrine of *Tulk v Moxhay*[5].

The burden of a covenant enforceable in equity under this doctrine is, unlike covenants between landlord and tenant, a burden on the land, and not on the estate held by the defendant[6]. Thus it is not necessary to show that the defendant holds the estate which the covenantor held; for the defendant is bound merely by coming to the land, whether as squatter, tenant at will, underlessee — as anyone indeed, other than bona fide purchaser of the legal estate for value without notice[7].

Provision is made in section 2 (5) of the Land Charges Act 1972 for the registration, as a land charge Class D (ii), of a restrictive covenant made after 1925 otherwise than between lessor and lessee[8]; and such registration, in accordance with the usual rules, is notice to all the world[9].

i. THE DOCTRINE OF *TULK V MOXHAY*

TULK *v* MOXHAY
(1848) 2 Ph 774 (Lord COTTENHAM LC)

In 1808, the plaintiff sold a vacant piece of land in Leicester Square to Elms, who covenanted for himself his heirs and assigns with the plaintiff his heirs and assigns that the purchaser would "at all times thereafter at his . . . own costs . . . keep and maintain the said piece of ground . . . in an open state, uncovered with any buildings, in neat and ornamental order . . ." The piece of land passed by "divers mesne conveyances into the hands of the defendant" whose conveyance did not contain any such covenant, but who admitted that he had notice of the covenant in the deed of 1808. The defendant threatened to build on the land in contravention of the covenant. An injunction was granted by Lord Langdale, the Master of the Rolls. On a motion to discharge that order.

Held. The plaintiff was entitled to an injunction to restrain a breach of the covenant by the defendant.

---

[4] *Morland v Cook* (1868) LR 6 Eq 252; *Cooke v Chilcott* (1876) 3 ChD 694, which was expressly disapproved in *Haywood v Brunswick Permanent Benefit Building Society* (1881) 8 QBD 403; *Hall v Ewin* (1887) 37 ChD 74. In *Andrew v Aitken* (1882) 22 ChD 218 at 220 FRY J suggested that, in the case of a covenant to build, the covenantor and his assigns might be called upon to allow the covenantee to enter and carry out the work.

[5] [1981] Conv 55 (C. D. Bell); [1983] Conv 29 (R. Griffith); 327 (C. D. Bell).

[6] *Tichborne v Weir* (1892) 67 LT 735; *Re Nisbet and Potts' Contract* [1905] 1 Ch 391; affd. [1906] 1 Ch 386, p. 766, post; *Mander v Falcke* [1891] 2 Ch 554.

[7] *Pilcher v Rawlins* (1872) 7 Ch App 259; *Wilkes v Spooner* [1911] 2 KB 473.

[8] *Newman v Real Estate Debenture Corpn Ltd and Flower Decorations Ltd* [1940] 1 All ER 131 at 149–150; *Dartstone Ltd v Cleveland Petroleum Co Ltd* [1969] 1 WLR 1807, [1969] 3 All ER 668; (1956) 20 Conv (NS) 370 (R. G. Rowley).

[9] LPA 1925, s. 198 (1), p. 29, ante; positive and negative covenants entered into with a local authority, a Minister of the Crown or Government Department (otherwise than as between landlord and tenant) are registrable as local land charges: LLCA 1975, ss. 1, 2, p. 52, ante.

LORD COTTENHAM: That this Court has jurisdiction to enforce a contract between the owner of land and his neighbour purchasing a part of it, that the latter shall either use or abstain from using the land purchased in a particular way, is what I never knew disputed. Here there is no question about the contract: the owner of certain houses in the Square sells the land adjoining, with a covenant from the purchaser not to use it for any other purpose than as a Square Garden. And it is now contended, not that the vendee could violate that contract, but that he might sell the piece of land, and that the purchaser from him may violate it without this Court having any power to interfere. If that were so, it would be impossible for an owner of land to sell part of it without incurring the risk of rendering what he retains worthless. It is said that, the covenant being one which does not run with the land, this Court cannot enforce it; but the question is, not whether the covenant runs with the land, but whether a party shall be permitted to use the land in a manner inconsistent with the contract entered into by his vendor, and with notice of which he purchased. Of course, the price would be affected by the covenant, and nothing could be more inequitable than that the original purchaser should be able to sell the property the next day for a greater price, in consideration of the assignee being allowed to escape from the liability which he had himself undertaken.

That the question does not depend upon whether the covenant runs with the land is evident from this, that if there was a mere agreement and no covenant, this Court would enforce it against a party purchasing with notice of it; for if an equity is attached to the property by the owner, no one purchasing with notice of that equity can stand in a different situation from the party from whom he purchased. . . .

I think the cases cited before the Vice-Chancellor and this decision of the Master of the Rolls perfectly right, and, therefore, that this injunction[10] must be refused with costs.

ii.   THE NECESSITY FOR BENEFITED LAND

LONDON COUNTY COUNCIL *v* ALLEN
[1914] 3 KB 642 (CA, BUCKLEY and KENNEDY LJJ and SCRUTTON J)

In 1906, the defendant, M. J. Allen, a builder, applied to the L.C.C. for their permission to lay out certain land of which Allen was in possession under an option to purchase. He was treated in the Court of Appeal as if he were the owner. The L.C.C. gave permission subject to a condition that Allen would enter into a covenant not to build upon part of the land which was needed for the continuation of certain proposed streets. By a deed of 1907, Allen covenanted "for himself, his heirs and assigns, and other the persons claiming under him, and so far as practicable to bind the land and hereditaments herein mentioned into whosesoever hands the same may come" that he would not place any erection on the land, and that he would give notice of this covenant in every document dealing with the land.

The land was conveyed to Allen in 1908; and part mortgaged to Willcocks who, in 1911, conveyed it on redemption, with M. J. Allen's concurrence, to

---

[10] Presumably 'motion' was intended here, and not 'injunction'. It is correct in (1848) 1 H & Tw 105 at 117.

Emily Allen, M. J. Allen's wife. Emily Allen built three houses on the plot, and mortgaged it to Norris.

The question was whether the covenant was binding on Emily Allen and Norris.

Held. Not binding, because the plaintiffs held no land for the benefit of which the covenant was taken.

SCRUTTON J: The question then is whether it is essential to the doctrine of *Tulk v Moxhay* that the covenantee should have at the time of the creation of the covenant, and afterwards, land for the benefit of which the covenant is created, in order that the burden of the covenant may bind assigns of the land to which it relates.

[His Lordship then reviewed the authorities, and referred to *Haywood v Brunswick Permanent Benefit Building Society* (1881) 8 QBD 403, *De Mattos v Gibson* (1858) 4 De G & J 276, *Luker v Dennis* (1877) 7 ChD 227, *London and South Western Rly Co v Gomm* (1882) 20 ChD 562, *Clegg v Hands* (1890) 44 ChD 503, and *Catt v Tourle* (1869) 4 Ch App 654, and continued:]

I think the result of this long chain of authorities is that, whereas in my view, at the time of *Tulk v Moxhay* and for at least twenty years afterwards, the plaintiffs in this case would have succeeded against an assign on the ground that the assign had notice of the covenant, since *Formby v Barker* [1903] 2 Ch 539; *Re Nisbet and Potts' Contract* [1905] 1 Ch 391; *affd.* [1906] 1 Ch 386 and *Millbourn v Lyons* [1914] 1 Ch 34; *affd.* [1914] 2 Ch 231, three decisions of the Court of Appeal, the plaintiffs must fail on the ground that they have never had any land for the benefit of which this "equitable interest analogous to a negative easement" could be created, and therefore cannot sue a person who bought the land with knowledge that there was a restrictive covenant as to its use, which he proceeds to disregard, because he is not privy to the contract. I think the learned editors of Dart on Vendors and Purchasers (7th edn.), vol. ii, p. 769, are justified by the present state of the authorities in saying that "the question of notice to the purchaser has nothing whatever to do with the question whether the covenant binds him, except in so far as the absence of notice may enable him to raise the plea of purchaser for valuable consideration without notice". If the covenant does not run with the land in law, its benefit can only be asserted against an assign of the land burdened, if the covenant was made for the benefit of certain land, all or some of which remains in the possession of the covenantee or his assign, suing to enforce the covenant. . . . I regard it as very regrettable that a public body should be prevented from enforcing a restriction on the use of property imposed for the public benefit against persons who bought the property knowing of the restriction, by the apparently immaterial circumstance that the public body does not own any land in the immediate neighbourhood. But, after a careful consideration of the authorities, I am forced to the view that the later decisions of this court compel me so to hold[11].

In my opinion, therefore, the demurrer of Mr Norris and of Mrs Allen succeeds. This action against Mr Norris must be dismissed with costs. I regret that I do not see my way to depriving Mrs Allen of her costs, as, whatever may be her equitable rights, I am not at all favourably impressed with her conduct as a good citizen.

---

[11] For exceptions to this rule, see p. 759, n. 13, ante, especially the statutory exceptions in favour of local authorities.

FORMBY *v* BARKER

[1903] 2 Ch 539 (CA, VAUGHAN WILLIAMS, ROMER and
STIRLING LJJ)

In 1868, R. H. Formby sold all the land owned by him in Formby,
Lancashire, to the Mutual Land Company Ltd, subject to various covenants
restricting the user of the land. The defendant was an assignee of the
company of part of the land, and took with notice of the covenants. R. H.
Formby died in 1884, and letters of administration with the will annexed
were granted to his widow, the plaintiff, to whom he had given all his
property by his will. In 1902, the defendant began to erect certain shops
which were alleged to be in breach of the covenant.

Held (affirming HALL V-C of the County Palatine of Lancaster).

(i) The building of the shops was not a breach of the covenant.

(ii) Even if it were, the plaintiff, having no land capable of benefiting, was
unable to maintain the action.

VAUGHAN WILLIAMS LJ: The plaintiff sues in her individual capacity and
also as administratix with the will annexed of R. H. Formby deceased.

[His Lordship held that, on its proper construction, the covenant had not
been broken by the defendant, and continued:]

This view really puts an end to the plaintiff's case. But, as another defence
was raised and was discussed by the learned Vice-Chancellor, I think it right
to deal with that point also.

The learned Vice-Chancellor expressed an opinion that, even if the
plaintiff's construction of the covenant was right, and there had been a
breach of the covenant, nevertheless the plaintiff was not entitled to sue —
that is, was not entitled to sue either as personal representative of R. H.
Formby or as residuary devisee under his will. . . .

Before dealing with the question of the plaintiff's right to sue, I wish to
point out that that which R. H. Formby conveyed was his whole estate, and
that he had no contiguous estate which would be benefited by the covenant
in question. Moreover, there is in the deed no re-entry clause under which
the vendor could go in as of his old estate, or, indeed, as of any estate. . . .

It becomes necessary, therefore, to ascertain whether the principle of *Tulk
v Moxhay* applies to a case in which the vendor sells his whole estate. I have
not been able to find any case in which, after the sale of the whole of an estate
in land, the benefit of a restrictive covenant has been enforced by injunction
against an assignee of the purchaser at the instance of a plaintiff having no
land retained by the vendor, although there are cases in which restrictive
covenants seem to have been enforced at the instance of plaintiffs, other than
the vendor, for the benefit of whose land it appears from the terms of the
covenant, or can be inferred from surrounding circumstances, that the
covenant was intended to operate. In all other cases the restrictive covenant
would seem to be a mere personal covenant collateral to the conveyance. It is
a covenant which cannot run with the land, either at law or in equity, and
therefore the burden of the covenant cannot be enforced against an assignee
of the purchaser.

———————

In *Re Gadd's Land Transfer* [1966] Ch 56, [1965] 2 All ER 800, BUCKLEY J
held that the retention only of a road to the land burdened by the covenant
was sufficient to enable the covenantee to enforce a restrictive covenant.

BUCKLEY J said at 67, at 809: "The question must, I think, be what is the impact of the covenants on the owner of Bridle Lane in respect of its occupation or enjoyment of that property. . . .

If the use of the pink land is to be changed from agricultural use to use as a building estate of that kind, there will be a great increase in the traffic over the right-of-way. Now the increase in the traffic over the right-of-way must inevitably mean that the maintenance of the roadway will become a more burdensome expense than otherwise it would be. . . .

If the cost of maintaining Bridle Lane became very much heavier than at present because of a great increase in the traffic over the road, it seems to me that there would be a risk that cannot be regarded as non-existent that the frontagers may not all be able to honour their obligations to contribute towards the cost of maintenance. I cannot suppose that that risk is negligible. . . .

Moreover, I think there is substance in the suggestion that if the lane is not kept in a proper state of repair there will be a risk that the road will be taken over by the local authority and the defendant company would thereby be deprived of some element of its ownership in the road.

Now it may be that this road is not a readily saleable asset, but it is not, I think, inconceivable that the residents in the road under certain circumstances would want themselves to acquire the road from the defendant company with a view to preserving it as their private road. If the burden of maintaining the road were to be made substantially more onerous than it is at present owing to an increase of traffic, the likelihood of the defendant company being able to dispose of this asset in any such way as that would, I think, decrease. These may not be very substantial interests or benefits which result to the defendant company from possible enforcement of the restrictive covenants, but nevertheless I do not think they are wholly negligible; I do not think they are matters that the court ought to disregard and I think they are matters of sufficient significance to justify the view that the capacity to enforce the covenants is a matter which does affect the defendant company in its position as owner of Bridle Lane."

iii. THE NATURE OF A RESTRICTIVE COVENANT

In 1882, Sir George JESSEL MR described the doctrine of *Tulk v Moxhay* as follows: "The doctrine of that case, rightly considered, appears to me to be either an extension in equity of the doctrine of *Spencer's Case* to another line of cases, or else an extension in equity of the doctrine of negative easements; such, for instance, as a right to the access of light, which prevents the owner of the servient tenement from building so as to obstruct the light. The covenant in *Tulk v Moxhay* was affirmative in its terms, but was held by the Court to imply a negative. Where there is a negative covenant expressed or implied, as, for instance, not to build so as to obstruct a view, or not to use a piece of land otherwise than as a garden, the Court interferes on one or other of the above grounds. This is an equitable doctrine, establishing an exception to the rules of Common Law which did not treat such a covenant as running with the land, and it does not matter whether it proceeds on analogy to a covenant running with the land or on analogy to an easement[12]." In other

---

[12] *London and South Western Rly Co v Gomm* (1882) 20 ChD at 583; (1971) 87 LQR 539 (D. J. Hayton). See *Spencer's Case* (1583) 5 Co Rep 16a, p. 459, ante.

words, the doctrine of *Spencer's Case* was to apply so as to impose liability between parties, between whom there was no privity of estate; or the concept of a negative easement was to be extended in equity to cover the burden imposed, not by grant but by covenant, upon one piece of land for the benefit of another piece of land.

The latter is the better analogy; for, under *Spencer's Case*, as with all covenants running with land at common law, the covenant ran with the estate and not with the land. A restrictive covenant under the doctrine of *Tulk v Moxhay*, like an easement, runs with the land, and not with the estate.

TICHBORNE *v* WEIR
(1892) 67 LT 735 (CA, Lord Esher MR, Bowen and Kay LJJ)

The plaintiff's predecessor in title was seised of a house in fee simple. In 1802 she leased it to Baxter for eighty-nine years. The lease contained a covenant to repair. Baxter made an equitable mortgage of the premises to Giraud, and Giraud entered on the premises in 1836. In 1836 Baxter disappeared, and Giraud remained in occupation of the premises till 1876. During that period he paid the rent reserved in Baxter's lease to the lessor. In 1876 Giraud purported to assign the lease to the defendant. The defendant entered and paid the rent till the term ended in 1891. He then delivered up possession to the plaintiff. The plaintiff sought to make him liable on the covenant to repair, but the Court of Appeal held that he was not liable.

The Real Property Limitation Act 1833 had barred the action and extinguished the right of Baxter; but it had not vested Baxter's lease in Giraud. The covenant to repair would run with the lease on an assignment; but neither Giraud nor the defendant had taken Baxter's lease and the defendant was not bound by the covenant to repair[13].

To the argument that he was estopped by the payment of rent from denying that he had taken Baxter's estate, it was said that such payment estopped him from disputing the title of the plaintiff, but it did not estop him from denying that he was bound by the terms of the lease. It estopped him from denying that he was a lessee: it did not estop him from denying that he was the holder of Baxter's lease[14].

RE NISBET AND POTTS' CONTRACT
[1905] 1 Ch 391 (Ch D, Farwell J); [1906] 1 Ch 386 (CA, Sir Richard Henn Collins MR, Romer and Cozens-Hardy LJJ)

A summons was taken out by Potts asking for a declaration that Nisbet, the vendor under a contract of sale, failed to produce a good title.

Nisbet had purchased in 1901 from X and Y who had themselves purchased in 1890 from Headde, whose title was based upon occupation since 1878. Nisbet agreed to accept a title commencing at that date. Restrictive covenants had been imposed on the land in 1867 and 1872; Nisbet knew nothing of these but would have discovered them if he had insisted on a forty years' title[15].

---

[13] See especially Kay LJ at 737, p. 191, ante.
[14] Much of this account of *Tichborne v Weir* is taken from Holdsworth, *Historical Introduction to the Land Law* (1927), pp. 286–287.
[15] The period of commencement of title which a purchaser could then require; see LPA 1925, s. 44 (1), and LPA 1969, s. 23, p. 77, ante.

On Potts' complaint that Nisbet was unable to produce a good title because of the restrictive covenants, Nisbet replied:
- (i) that he had purchased without notice; and
- (ii) that, in any case, covenants would not be binding upon a title acquired by adverse possession.

FARWELL J, affirmed by the Court of Appeal, held that a party had constructive notice of all that he would have ascertained if he had made proper enquiries and searched back for forty years; and also that the restrictive covenants were an equitable burden on the land, and were not terminated by the adverse possession. He said at 396:

"But if the covenant be negative, so as to restrict the mode of use and enjoyment of the land, then there is called into existence an equity attached to the property of such a nature that it is annexed to and runs with it in equity . . . This equity, although created by covenant or contract, cannot be sued on as such, but stands on the same footing with, and is completely analogous to, an equitable charge on real estate created by some predecessor in title of the present owner of the land charged."

QUESTION

K Ltd., a garage company, owning the site of a garage, mortgaged it to E, and entered into a "solus" agreement, under which they undertook to sell E's petrol only; and to extract similar undertakings from any person to whom they might sell the garage.

I H purchased all the shares in K Ltd., and took a conveyance of the site of the garage, with the intention of breaking the provision relating to the sale of the petrol. They did so. E owned no land capable of benefiting. E sues for an injunction, joining K Ltd and I H as defendants. What result?

Esso Petroleum Co Ltd v Kingswood Motors (Addlestone) Ltd [1974] QB 142, [1973] 3 All ER 1057.

C. Law of Property Act 1925, Section 79[16]

In *Tophams Ltd v Earl of Sefton* [1967] 1 AC 50, [1966] 1 All ER 1039, Lord UPJOHN said at 72 at 1047: "If this matter was a live issue before your Lordships I conceive that it might indeed be difficult of solution, for I can see arguments both for and against the proposition that the covenant was intended to bind assigns of Tophams. . . . I will only add that upon this aspect of the matter I think too much significance was placed in the courts below upon the impact of section 79 (1) of the Law of Property Act 1925. During the course of the hearing before your Lordships it became common ground that, so far as relevant to any question that your Lordships have to decide, it does no more than render it unnecessary in the description of the parties to the conveyance to add after the respondent's name: 'his executors, administrators and assigns', and after Tophams' name: 'and their successors in title'. This can really have little or no weight in considering the liability of Tophams' assigns in relation to a restrictive covenant affecting land."

---

[16] Page 461, ante; M & W, pp. 742–743. See also *Federated Homes Ltd v Mill Lodge Properties Ltd* [1980] 1 WLR 594 at 606, [1980] 1 All ER 371 at 380, p. 777, post.

Unlike section 78[17], section 79 contains the words "unless a contrary intention is expressed". In *Re Royal Victoria Pavilion, Ramsgate* [1961] Ch 581, [1961] 3 All ER 83, PENNYCUICK J considered a covenant which began "The vendors hereby covenant with the purchasers that they the vendors will . . .". He said at 589, at 87:

"Here it is contended that no contrary intention is expressed in the conveyance, . . . and that, therefore, the covenant in clause 5 must be deemed to be made by Thanet Theatrical on behalf of itself and its successors in title. If the words 'unless the contrary intention is expressed' in section 79 mean: unless the instrument contains express provision to the contrary, this contention would, I think, be unanswerable. But it seems to me the words 'unless a contrary intention is expressed' mean rather: unless an indication to the contrary is to be found in the instrument, and that such an indication may be sufficiently contained in the wording and context of the instrument even though the instrument contains no provision expressly excluding successors in title from its operation. It can hardly be the intention of the section that a covenant which, on its natural construction, is manifestly intended to be personal only, must be construed as running with the land merely because the contrary is not expressly provided. . . .

So here, although the covenant contains no express provision to the effect that it is not made on behalf of successors in title, it does, as it seems to me, contain sufficient indication to this effect."

III.   The Benefit[18]

A.   Common Law

It has long been held that the benefit of a covenant will run with the land at law in certain circumstances[19]. The rule is thought to have its origin in the old warranties for title which were enforceable not only by the covenantee, but also by his heirs, and, later, by assigns; if the warranty were broken, the warrantor would be liable in some cases to provide lands of equal value, in other cases to pay damages[20]. The conditions which are necessary for the benefit of a covenant to run with the land at law are a matter of some doubt, owing to the paucity of modern authority; it is clear however that the covenant will run if the following conditions are complied with[1]:

   (i) The covenant must 'touch and concern' the land[2]. It may do this
        even though the covenantor is a stranger to the land, and there is
        no servient tenement to be bound by the covenant[3].

---

[17] P. 461, ante; pp. 777–785, post. See however, *Roake v Chadha* [1984] 1 WLR 40, [1983] 3 All ER 503, p. 782, post.

[18] C & B, pp. 572–573, 583–594; M & W. pp. 764–767, 780–793; MM, pp. 440–441, 446–456; [1938] CLJ 339 (S. J. Bailey); (1971) 82 LQR 539 (D. J. Hayton); (1982) 2 Legal Studies 53 (D. J. Hurst); (1982) 98 LQR 279 (S. Gardner).

[19] *The Prior's Case* (1368) YB 42 Edw 3, fo 3A pl 14; Smith's *Leading Cases* (13th edn. 1929), vol. i, pp. 51, 65, 73.

[20] Simpson, *Introduction to the History of the Land Law*, pp. 131–132.

[1] Much of this section is based on (1954) 18 Conv (NS) 546 (E. H. Scamell).

[2] See p. 753, n. 13, ante.

[3] *The Prior's Case*, see p. 752, n. 7, ante; *Smith and Snipes Hall Farm Ltd v River Douglas Catchment Board* [1949] 2 KB 500, [1949] 2 All ER 179; and for cases where there is a servient tenement which would not be bound by the covenant, see *Sharp v Waterhouse* (1857) 7 E & B 816; *Shayler v Woolf* [1946] Ch 320, [1946] 2 All ER 54.

(ii) The land to be benefited must be expressly identified by the deed containing the covenant. There appears to be no authority for this; if it is a requirement, it is weakened by the operation of the maxim '*id certum est quod certum reddi potest*'[4].

(iii) There must be an intention that the benefit should run with the land owned by the covenantee at the date of the covenant[5].

(iv) The covenant must have been entered into with the owner of the legal estate in the land to be benefited[6].

(v) Before 1926, it was necessary for a person seeking to enforce the covenant to have the same legal estate in the land as the original covenantee[7]. It has been held that section 78 (1) of the Law of Property Act 1925 excludes this last requirement[8]. It may be that the wide interpretation given to that section in *Federated Homes Ltd v Mill Lodge Properties Ltd*[9] will have the effect of excluding some of the others as well. This was a case dealing with the running of the benefit in equity, which is the context in which the question usually arises; because the burdened land will commonly have also been assigned.

The common law rules continue to apply in cases not covered by equity, as, for example, where there is no land upon which the burden of the covenant is imposed[10].

It should also be noted that, independently of the above rules, the benefit of a covenant can be assigned as a chose in action, under section 136 of the Law of Property Act 1925. To be effective at law, the assignment must be in writing, and express notice in writing given to the covenantor[11].

SMITH AND SNIPES HALL FARM LTD *v* RIVER DOUGLAS CATCHMENT BOARD[12]
[1949] 2 KB 500, [1949] 2 All ER 179 (CA, Tucker, Somervell and Denning LJJ)

The defendant Board was the Drainage Authority for a part of Lancashire. In 1938, the Board covenanted under seal with the freehold owners of land within that area that in consideration of the Board's widening, deepening and making good the banks of the Eller Brook, taking control thereof and maintaining for all time the work when it was completed, the landowners would contribute to the cost.

In 1940, Mrs Ellen Smith, one of the owners, sold her land, expressly with the benefit of the covenant, to the first plaintiff, John Bruce Smith, who

---

[4] *Smith and Snipes Hall Farm Ltd v River Douglas Catchment Board* [1949] 2 KB 500, [1949] 2 All ER 179, at 508, 517, at 184, 189, infra.

[5] *Rogers v Hosegood* [1900] 2 Ch 388 at 396; *Shayler v Woolf* [1946] Ch 320, [1946] 2 All ER 54; *Smith and Snipes Hall Farm Ltd v River Douglas Catchment Board*, supra at 506, at 183.

[6] Co Litt 385a; *Webb v Russell* (1789) 3 Term Rep 393; cf. *Rogers v Hosegood* [1900] 2 Ch 388.

[7] *Westhoughton UDC v Wigan Coal and Iron Co Ltd* [1919] 1 Ch 159; *Smith and Snipes Hall Farm Ltd v River Douglas Catchment Board*, supra.

[8] *Smith and Snipes Hall Farm Ltd v River Douglas Catchment Board*, supra.

[9] [1980] 1 WLR 594, [1980] 1 All ER 371, where the plaintiff took an assignment of part only of the land from the original covenantee; see pp. 777, 787, post.

[10] See p. 752, n. 7, ante.

[11] Cheshire and Fifoot, *Law of Contract* (10th edn. 1981), pp. 455 et seq.

[12] See (1981) 97 LQR 32 at pp. 43–47 (G. H. Newsom).

leased it to the second plaintiff under a yearly tenancy. Owing to the faulty work of the defendants, the brook broke its banks, and flooded the land of the plaintiffs. They brought this action in tort and for breach of contract.

Held (reversing MORRIS J [1948] WN 414). Both plaintiffs could succeed under the contract.

The action in tort did not therefore arise for decision and no decision was reached on that point. The plaintiffs would have found it necessary to distinguish the House of Lords case of *East Suffolk Rivers Catchment Board v Kent* [1941] AC 74, [1940] 4 All ER 527.

TUCKER LJ [having held that the defendants were in breach of the contract and that such breach caused the damage]: . . . It remains to consider whether, in these circumstances, the plaintiffs, or either of them, can sue in respect of this breach. It is said for the defendants that the benefit of the covenant does not run with the land so as to bind a stranger who has not and never had an interest in the land to be benefited and there being no servient tenement to bear the burden. Further, it is contended that such a covenant must by the terms of the deed in which it is contained relate to some specific parcel of land, the precise extent and situation of which can be identified by reference to the deed alone. It is first necessary to ascertain from the deed that the covenant is one which "touches or concerns" the land, that is, it must either affect the land as regards mode of occupation, or it must be such as per se, and not merely from collateral circumstances, affects the value of the land, and it must then be shewn that it was the intention of the parties that the benefit thereof should run with the land. In this case the deed shews that its object was to improve the drainage of land liable to flooding and prevent future flooding. The location of the land is described as situate between the Leeds and Liverpool Canal and the River Douglas and adjoining the Eller Brook. In return for lump sum payments the board covenants to do certain work to the banks of the Eller Brook, one of such banks being in fact situate upon and forming part of the plaintiff's lands, and to maintain for all time the work when completed. In my view the language of the deed satisfies both tests. It affects the value of the land per se and converts it from flooded meadows to land suitable for agriculture, and shows an intention that the benefit of the obligation to maintain shall attach thereto into whosesoever hands the lands shall come.

With regard to the covenantor being a stranger, the case of *The Prior* is referred to in *Spencer's* case, in these words: "In the case of a grandfather, father and two sons, the grandfather being seised of the manor of D, whereof a chapel was parcel: a prior, with the assent of his convent, by deed covenanted for him and his successors, with the grandfather and his heirs that he and his convent would sing all the week in his chapel, parcel of the said manor, for the lord of the said manor and his servants, etc.; the grandfather did enfeoff one of the manor in fee, who gave it to the younger son and his wife in tail; and it was adjudged that the tenants in tail, as terre-tenants (for the elder brother was heir), should have an action of covenant against the prior, for the covenant is to do a thing which is annexed to the chapel, which is within the manor, and so annexed to the manor, as it is there said." . . .

In Rogers v Hosegood [1900] 2 Ch at 395, Farwell J, in a passage where he refers, amongst others, to *The Prior's* case — and I quote from Farwell J's judgment because, although this case went to the Court of Appeal, his judgment was approved, and the Court of Appeal had to deal with a rather different point — after stating what are the requirements in order that the covenant may run with the land, proceeds: "It is not contended that the covenants in question in this case have not the first characteristic, but it is said that they fail in the second. I am of opinion that they possess both. Adopting the definition of Bayley J in *Congleton Corpn v Pattison* (1808) 10 East at 135, the covenant must either affect the land as regards mode of occupation, or it must be such as per se, and not merely from collateral circumstances, affects the value of the land. It is to my mind obvious that the value of Sir J Millais's land is directly increased by the covenants in question. If authority is needed, I would refer to *Mann v Stephens* (1846) 15 Sim 377, a case very similar to the present; *Vyvyan v Arthur* (1823) 1 B & C 410, *The Prior's* case, *Fleetwood v Hull* (1889) 23 QBD 35, *White v Southend Hotel Co* [1897] 1 Ch 767. I see no difficulty in holding that the benefit of a covenant runs with the land of the covenantee, while the burden of the same covenant does not run with the land of the covenantor."

In this state of the authorities it seems clear, despite some dicta tending to the contrary view, that such a covenant if it runs with the land is binding on the covenantor though a mere stranger, and that this point will not avail the defendant board. As to the requirement that the deed containing the covenant must expressly identify the particular land to be benefited, no authority was cited to us and in the absence of such authority I can see no valid reason why the maxim "Id certum est quod certum reddi potest" should not apply, so as to make admissible extrinsic evidence to prove the extent and situation of the lands of the respective land owners adjoining the Eller Brook situate between the Leeds and Liverpool Canal and the River Douglas.

. . . I have accordingly arrived at the conclusion that the covenant by the board in the agreement of 25 April 1938 is one which runs with the land referred to therein, which land is capable of identification, and that it is binding on the defendant board; and, further, that by virtue of section 78 of the Law of Property Act 1925, it can be enforced at the suit of the covenantee and her successors in title and the persons deriving title under her or them, so that both the plaintiff Smith and the plaintiff company can sue in respect of the damage resulting to their respective interests therein by reason of the defendants' breach of covenant.

DENNING LJ: The law on this subject was fully expounded by Mr Smith in his note to *Spencer's* case which has always been regarded as authoritative. Such covenants [relating to land] are clearly intended, and usually expressed, to be for the benefit of whomsoever should be the owner of the land for the time being; and at common law each successive owner has a sufficient interest to sue because he holds the same estate as the original owner. The reason which Lord Coke gave for this rule is the reason which underlies the whole of the principle now under consideration. He said in his work upon Littleton that it was "to give damages to the party grieved". If a successor in title were not allowed to sue it would mean that the covenantor could break his contract with impunity, for it is clear that the original owner, after he has parted with the land, could recover no more than nominal damages for any breach that occurred thereafter. It was always held, however, at common law that, in order that a successor in title should be entitled to sue, he must be of the same estate as the original owner. That alone was a sufficient interest to entitle him to enforce the contract. The covenant was supposed to be made for the benefit of the owner and his successors in title, and not for the benefit of anyone else. This limitation, however, was, as is pointed out in *Smith's* Leading Cases, capable of being "productive of very serious and disagreeable consequences", and it has been removed by section 78 of the Law of Property Act 1925, which provides that a covenant relating to any land of the covenantee shall be deemed to be made with the covenantee and his successors in title, "and the persons deriving title under him or them" and shall have effect as if such successors "and other persons" were expressed.

The covenant of the catchment board in this case clearly relates to the land of the covenantees. It was a covenant to do work on the land for the benefit of the land. By the statute, therefore, it is to be deemed to be made, not only with the original owner, but also with the purchasers of the land and their tenants as if they were expressed. Now if they were expressed, it would be clear that the covenant was made for their benefit; and they clearly have sufficient interest to entitle them to enforce it because they have suffered the damage. The result is that the plaintiffs come within the principle whereby a person interested can sue on a contract expressly made for his benefit.

In *Williams v Unit Construction Co Ltd*[13] the question again arose whether section 78 of the Law of Property Act 1925[14] allowed the benefit of a restrictive covenant to pass at law in favour of persons who did not hold the same legal estate as the original covenantee. Counsel argued that a decision to that effect could only be taken by a court which was prepared also to hold that section 79 would have the same effect upon the burden; in other words, to hold that, since 1925, "successors in title and persons deriving title under him or them" would be bound by the burden of the covenant. The Court of Appeal declined to express a view on the effect of section 79[15] upon the burden — the point not being before the court — and followed *Smith and Snipes Hall Farm Ltd v River Douglas Catchment Board*.

Similarly, in *Federated Homes Ltd v Mill Lodge Properties Ltd* [1980] 1 WLR 594, [1980] 1 All ER 371, BRIGHTMAN LJ said at 606, at 380: "We were referred to observations in the speeches of Lord Upjohn and Lord Wilberforce in *Tophams Ltd v Earl of Sefton* [1967] 1 AC 50 at 73 and 81, [1967] 1 All ER 1039 at 1048, 1053, to the effect that section 79 . . . achieved no more than the introduction of statutory shorthand into the drafting of covenants. Section 79, in my view, involves quite different considerations and I do not think that it provides a helpful analogy[16]."

B.   Equity

Where a person other than the original covenantee desires to enforce a covenant, he must show that he is the person entitled to the benefit of the

---

[13] Unreported, but discussed in (1955) 19 Conv (NS) 262 (W. L. Blease); p. 781, post.

[14] See p. 461, ante.

[15] On the application of s. 79, see p. 767, ante, p. 777, post.

[16] The case held that s. 78 effected an annexation of the benefit of the covenant in equity; p. 777 post. See also M & W, p. 766; W & C vol. i, 162–163; see also (1956) 20 Conv (NS) 43, 52 (D. W. Elliott); [1972 B] CLJ 157 at pp. 171–175 (H. W. R. Wade), *Emmet on Title* pp. 534–536.

covenant. He may do this by showing either that the benefit of the covenant has passed to him, or that he was made an original covenantee by section 56 of the Law of Property Act 1925. As has been seen, the benefit of a covenant would run at law in certain circumstances. But there are some situations outside the limits of the common law where the benefit would run in equity. Generally, equity follows the law, and this development is probably an elucidation of the rules of common law, rather than a separate contribution of equity[17].

The situations in which the equitable rules must be observed are these:

(i) where the plaintiff or the covenantee was an equitable owner[18];

(ii) (subject to section 78 of the Law of Property Act 1925) where the plaintiff does not have the same legal estate as the covenantee[19];

(iii) where the servient land has been assigned, and enforcement depends on the doctrine of *Tulk v Moxhay*[20];

(iv) where the plaintiff relies upon an express assignment of the benefit of the covenant without compliance with section 136 of the Law of Property Act 1925[1];

(v) where the plaintiff takes an assignment of part of the land only, for "at law, the benefit could not be assigned in pieces. It would have to be assigned as a whole or not at all"[2];

(vi) where the plaintiff relies upon his land being part of a scheme of development.

A purchaser of land may show that the benefit of a restrictive covenant has passed to him in one of three ways.

In *Re Pinewood Estate* [1958] Ch 280[3], [1957] 2 All ER 517, WYNN-PARRY J, said at 284, at 519: "I propose first to consider whether there is in existence what is known as a building scheme affecting this area of land which is clearly ascertained; because, if there is an existing building scheme, fulfilling the conditions laid down by Parker J in *Elliston v Reacher* [1908] 2 Ch 374; *affd.* [1908] 2 Ch 665, p. 801, post, then the respondent and the other persons interested will have the benefit of the covenants in the deed. . . It is admitted by Mr Newsom that she could claim the benefit of the restrictive covenants if it could be shown either that the benefit had been annexed by proper words of annexation, or that there was a complete chain of assignments of the benefit of the covenants; but it is conceded on behalf of the respondent that there are no words of annexation, and it is conceded that the chain is not complete. In those circumstances, what the respondent says is that she is

---

[17] (1938) 6 CLJ 339 (S. J. Bailey).

[18] *Fairclough v Marshall* (1878) 4 Ex D 37; *Rogers v Hosegood* [1900] 2 Ch 388 (a mortgagor before 1926), p. 775, post.

[19] *Taite v Gosling* (1879) 11 ChD 273; see also *Westhoughton UDC v Wigan Coal and Iron Co Ltd* [1919] 1 Ch 159; *Smith and Snipes Hall Farm Ltd v River Douglas Catchment Board* [1949] 2 KB 500, [1949] 2 All ER 179, p. 769, ante.

[20] *Renals v Cowlishaw* (1878) 9 ChD 125, p. 777, post; *Re Union of London and Smith's Bank Ltd's Conveyance, Miles v Easter* [1933] Ch 611, per ROMER J at 630, p. 789, post; *Marten v Flight Refuelling Ltd* [1962] Ch 115, [1961] 2 All ER 696, p. 794, post.

[1] See p. 788, post; *Re Union of London and Smith's Bank Ltd's Conveyance, Miles v Easter* supra; *Newton Abbot Co-operative Society Ltd v Williamson and Treadgold Ltd* [1952] Ch 286, [1952] 1 All ER 279, p. 790, post; *Stilwell v Blackman* [1968] Ch 508, [1967] 3 All ER 514.

[2] *Re Union of London and Smith's Bank Ltd's Conveyance*, supra, at 630 per ROMER LJ; *Federated Homes Ltd v Mill Lodge Properties Ltd* [1980] 1 WLR 594, [1980] 1 All ER 371, p. 777, post.

[3] [1957] CLJ 146 (H. W. R. Wade). See p. 797, ante.

entitled to the benefit of the restrictive provisions because it is a deed which shows clearly by its language an intention that the parties should be mutually bound by the restrictions, and that that element of mutuality is enough to carry the benefit of the restrictive stipulations. That means that they are endeavouring to set up a further method by which the benefit of restrictive stipulations can be transferred. . . .

The real question is: Is there a fourth class at all? The first class is the *Elliston v Reacher* type of case; the second consists of cases where there are proper words of annexation; the third consists of cases where there is a continuous chain of express assignments. But is there a fourth class? . . .

But I can find no authority, certainly none was cited to me, which establishes the fourth class suggested. In my opinion, therefore, it is not open either to the respondent or to anybody else upon this line of reasoning to rely on these restrictive covenants."

i.   BY EXPRESS ANNEXATION

Whether or not the benefit of a restrictive covenant has been annexed to the land of the covenantee depends upon the intention of the parties, as construed from the language of the conveyance. If such an intention were manifested, the benefit of the covenant is notionally annexed to the land to be benefited; and the benefit of the covenant then passed automatically on an assignment of the covenantee's land.

This situation was contrasted with a covenant whose terms failed to manifest such an intention. The benefit of such a covenant was available, by the contract, to the covenantee; but was only available to successors in title of the covenantee if the benefit of the covenant was expressly assigned at the time of the conveyance; and, in the case of a series of assignments of the land, it was necessary to show that there was a similar "chain of assignments" of the benefit of the covenant.

The leading cases illustrating these rules were *Rogers v Hosegood* [1900] 2 Ch 388, where annexation was achieved; and *Renals v Cowlishaw* [1878] 9 ChD 125, where it failed. Describing the methods of annexation, Greene LJ said in *Drake v Gray* [1936] Ch 451 at 466:

"There are two familiar methods of indicating in a covenant of this kind the land in respect of which the benefit is to enure. One is to describe the character in which the covenantee receives the covenant. That is the form which is adopted here, a covenant with so and so, owners or owner for the time being of whatever the land may be. Another method is to state by means of an appropriate declaration that the convenant is taken 'for the benefit of' whatever the lands may be."

The language which succeeded in effecting an annexation in *Rogers v Hosegood* was in this form: "with intent that the covenants . . . might enure for the benefit of the [vendors] . . . their heirs and assigns and others claiming under them to all or any of their lands adjoining or near to the said premises." It has never been suggested that that form of words was necessary; what was needed was a manifestation of an intention to annex. Would annexation be effected if the covenant were made in the following form? "With the covenantee and his successors in title (including the owners and occupiers for the time being of the land of the covenantee intended to be benefited) and the persons deriving title under him or them." If such a covenant would be effective to annex the benefit of the covenant, annexation would appear to be effected in every case; for, by section 78 of the Law of Property Act 1925, every covenant "relating to the land of the covenantee" shall be deemed to be made in that form. And the problem of determining whether the language of the conveyance is sufficient to manifest an intention to annex would disappear. That is the decision in *Federated Homes Ltd v Mill Lodge Properties Ltd* [1980] 1 WLR 594, [1980] 1 All ER 371, p. 777, post.

(a) Construction of the Instrument

ROGERS *v* HOSEGOOD
[1900] 2 Ch 388 (Ch D, FARWELL J; affd, CA, Lord ALVERSTONE MR, RIGBY and COLLINS LJJ)

Four partners, carrying on business as builders, were the owners in fee simple, subject to a mortgage, of land at Palace Gate, Kensington. One plot was sold in 1869 to the Duke of Bedford who entered into a covenant "with intent that the covenants . . . might so far as possible bind the premises thereby conveyed and every part thereof and might enure to the benefit of [the vendors] . . . their heirs and assigns and others claiming under them to all or any of their lands adjoining or near to the said premises" . . . that "no more than one messuage or dwelling house . . . should at any one time be erected or be standing on the . . . plot . . .". In 1872, a nearby plot was sold, and in 1873 conveyed to Sir John Millais, who had no knowledge of the covenant given by the Duke. Successors in title of the Duke by purchase proposed, in breach of the restrictive covenant, to erect, on this and adjoining plots, a large building which was to be occupied as residential flats. Among various actions, the trustees of the will of Sir John Millais claimed an injunction to restrain the defendants from erecting the block of flats.

Held. The plaintiffs were entitled to enforce the covenant.

COLLINS LJ (reading the judgment of the court): This case raises questions of some difficulty, but we are of opinion that the decision of Farwell J is right, and ought to be affirmed. . . . The real and only difficulty arises on the question — whether the benefit of the covenants has passed to the assigns of Sir John Millais as owners of the plot purchased by him on 25 March 1873, there being no evidence that he knew of these covenants when he bought. Here, again, the difficulty is narrowed, because by express declaration on the face of the conveyances of 1869 the benefit of the two covenants in question was intended for all or any of the vendor's lands near to or adjoining the plot sold, and therefore for (among others) the plot of land acquired by Sir John Millais, and that they "touched and concerned" that land within the meaning of those words so as to run with the land at law we do not doubt. Therefore, but for a technical difficulty which was not raised before Farwell J, we should agree with him that the benefit of the covenants in question was annexed to and passed to Sir John Millais by the conveyance of the land which he bought in 1873. A difficulty, however, in giving effect to this view arises from the fact that the covenants in question in the deeds of May and July 1869 were made with the mortgagors only, and therefore in contemplation of law were made with strangers to the land: *Webb v Russell* (1789) 3 Term Rep 393, to which, therefore, the benefit did not become annexed. That a court of equity, however, would not regard such an objection as defeating the intention of the parties to the covenant is clear; and, therefore, when the covenant was clearly made for the benefit of certain land with a person who, in the contemplation of such a court was the true owner of it, it would be regarded as annexed to and running with that land, just as it would have been at law but for the technical difficulty. . . .

These observations [referring to observations of Jessel MR in *London and South Western Rly Co v Gomm* (1882) 20 ChD at p. 583] which are just as applicable to the benefit reserved as to the burden imposed, shew that in equity, just as at law, the first point to be determined is whether the covenant or contract in its inception binds the land. If it does, it is then capable of passing with the land to subsequent assignees . . . of the land. The benefit may be annexed to one plot and the burden to another, and when this has been once clearly done, the benefit and the burden pass to the respective assignees, subject, in the case of the burden, to proof that the legal estate, if acquired, has been acquired with notice of the covenant. . . .

[His Lordship then referred to *Renals v Cowlishaw* (1878) 9 ChD 125, infra and *Child v Douglas* (1854) Kay 560.]

These authorities establish the proposition that, when the benefit has been once clearly annexed to one piece of land, it passes by assignment of that land, and may be said to run with it, in contemplation as well of equity as of law, without proof of special bargain or representation on the assignment. In such a case it runs, not because the conscience of either party is affected, but because the purchaser has bought something which inhered in or was annexed to the land bought. This is the reason why, in dealing with the burden, the purchaser's conscience is not affected by notice of covenants which were part of the original bargain or on the first sale, but were merely personal and collateral, while it is affected by notice of those which touch and concern the land. The covenant must be one that is capable of running with the land before the question of the purchaser's conscience and the equity affecting it can come into discussion. When, as in *Renals v Cowlishaw*, there is no indication in the original conveyance, or in the circumstances attending it, that the burden of the restrictive covenant is imposed for the benefit of the land reserved, or any particular part of it, then it becomes necessary to examine the circumstances under which any part of the land reserved is sold, in order to see whether a benefit, not originally annexed to it, has become annexed to it on the sale, so that the purchaser is deemed to have bought it with the land, and this can hardly be the case when the purchaser did not know of the existence of the restrictive covenant. But when, as here, it has been once annexed to the land reserved, then it is not necessary to spell an intention out of surrounding facts, such as the existence of a building scheme, statements at auctions, and such like circumstances, and the presumption must be that it passes on a sale of that land, unless there is something to rebut it, and the purchaser's ignorance of the existence of the covenant does not defeat the presumption. We can find nothing in the conveyance to Sir John Millais in any degree inconsistent with the intention to pass to him the benefit already annexed to the land sold to him. We are of opinion, therefore, that Sir John Millais's assigns are entitled to enforce the restrictive covenant against the defendant, and that his appeal must be dismissed.

Rogers v Hosegood is to be contrasted with *Renals v Cowlishaw* (1878) 9 ChD 125, the difference turning on the language of the covenant. In *Renals v Cowlishaw* trustees sold lands to a purchaser who covenanted "for himself, his heirs, executors and administrators" with the trustees "their heirs, executors, administrators and assigns" that he would not use the lands in certain ways. The lands purchased were later sold to other purchasers who took with notice of the covenant. And the trustees later sold their retained land to the plaintiffs, no mention being made of the covenant in this conveyance.

The question was whether the benefit of the covenant had passed to the plaintiffs. HALL V-C (affirmed by the Court of Appeal (1879) 11 ChD 866) held that it had not. There was no building scheme, no express assignment of the benefit of the covenant; and the language of the covenant was inadequate to annex the benefit of the covenant to the plaintiffs' land.

The modern practice is to draft the covenant so as to mainfest an intention to annex the benefit of the covenant to the land retained by the vendor; unless the vendor wishes to retain the power to choose which of his later purchasers shall be given the benefit (by expressly assigning it[4]). Correct drafting may no longer be important, because it has been held that section 78 of the Law of Property Act 1925 supplies the words necessary to effect annexation[5].

(b) Law of Property Act 1925, Section 78

LAW OF PROPERTY ACT 1925

78. Benefit of covenants relating to land. — p. 461, ante.

FEDERATED HOMES LTD *v* MILL LODGE PROPERTIES LTD
[1980] 1 WLR 594, [1980] 1 All ER 371 (CA, MEGAW, BROWNE and BRIGHTMAN LJJ)

Mackenzie Hill Ltd owned land which was to be the subject of a large development in Newport Pagnell in Buckinghamshire. Planning permission was obtained in 1970, and was valid for 3 years. The building programme was phased, and was subject to restrictions upon the overall density of the number of houses to be built on the area. The present litigation arises out of sales by Mackenzie Hill Ltd of three parts of the land; the blue, the red and the green.

The blue land was sold to Mill Lodge Properties Ltd, the defendant company, subject to various conditions, the one relevant for present purposes being the following covenant:

"The Purchaser hereby covenants with the Vendor that . . . (iv) in carrying out the development of the 'blue' land the Purchaser shall not build at a greater density than a total of 300 dwellings so as not to reduce the number of units which the Vendor might eventually erect on the retained land under the existing Planning Consent."

---

[4] *Marquess of Zetland v Driver* [1937] Ch 651; [1939] Ch 1; *Federated Homes Ltd v Mill Lodge Properties Ltd* [1980] 1 WLR 594 at 606, [1980] 1 All ER 371 at 380, per BRIGHTMAN LJ.
[5] *Federated Homes Ltd v Mill Lodge Properties Ltd*, supra; [1980] JPL 371; (1981) 97 LQR 32; JPL 149; (1982) 98 LQR 202 (G. H. Newsom); (1980) 43 MLR 445 (D. J. Hayton); 130 NLJ 531 (T. Bailey); (1982) 2 Legal Studies (D. J. Hurst); C & B, p. 585–586, esp. n. 3; M & W, p. 785–787.

The red and green lands were also sold, and the plaintiff company eventually became the owner of each. It will be seen that the terms of the covenant were not such as, from the express language of the covenant, to annex the benefit of the covenant to the land of the covenantee under the rule in *Rogers v Hosegood*. There was, however, a complete chain of assignments of the benefit of the covenant, through the various purchasers to the plaintiff, in the case of the *green* land. But not in the case of the red.

The question was whether the plaintiffs could sue to restrain the breach of the defendants' covenant relating to building density.

Held. The plaintiff company was entitled to the benefit of the covenant in respect of the *green* land by reason of the completed chain of assignments; in respect of the *red* land, because section 78 (1) had the effect of annexing the benefit of the covenant to all or any part of the land of the covenantee.

BRIGHTMAN LJ: In September 1978, after much prevarication on the part of Mill Lodge, the plaintiff issued a writ to restrain Mill Lodge from building on the blue land at a greater density than a total of 300 dwellings in breach, it was alleged, of clause 5 (iv) of the Mill Lodge conveyance. The defences raised by Mill Lodge so far as relied upon in this appeal were as follows: (1) the covenant in clause 5 (iv) was said to be personal to Mackenzie Hill so that the benefit thereof was incapable of assignment to the plaintiff; (2) alternatively, it was said that the covenant became spent when the 1970 planning permission became void at the end of the three-year period; and (3) it was said that, if the covenant was assignable and was not spent, then the benefit had not become vested in the plaintiff by assignment or otherwise.

That, in broad effect, was how the defence was pleaded so far as relevant for present purposes. In a reserved judgment Mr Mills held that the covenant was not personal to Mackenzie Hill and was not spent when the original planning permission lapsed. As regards the transmission of the benefit of the covenant, he held that the benefit was not annexed to the red and the green land, so that it did not automatically pass upon conveyances of the red and the green land. However, he found, as was clearly the fact, that there was an unbroken chain of assignments between transferor and transferee of the green land, so that the benefit of the covenant was now vested, by reason of such assignments, in the plaintiff as the present owner of the green land. There was no such unbroken chain of assignments in the case of the red land; but the judge considered that section 62 of the Law of Property Act 1925, which implies general words into a conveyance of land, was apt to carry the benefit of the covenant from U.D.T. Properties Ltd., the previous assignee of such benefit, to the plaintiff when the registered transfer in its favour was made[6]. The defence, therefore, failed. The judge rejected a submission that damages would be the proper remedy. He granted an injunction against building in excess of the permitted density and gave liberty to apply for a mandatory injunction.

I deal first with the question of construction, upon which two issues arise: whether the covenant was personal to Mackenzie Hill, and whether it is spent.

[His Lordship decided that the covenant was not personal to Mackenzie Hill; nor was the covenant "spent" by the lapse of the planning permission in 1973].

---

[6] See *Roake v Chadha* [1984] 1 WLR 40 at 47, [1983] 3 All ER 503 at 509, p. 799, post.

Having reached the conclusion that the restrictive covenant was capable of assignment and is not spent, I turn to the question whether the benefit has safely reached the hands of the plaintiff. The green land has no problem, owing to the unbroken chain of assignments. I am disposed to think that is sufficient to entitle the plaintiff to relief, and that the plaintiff's right to relief would be no greater at the present time if it were held that it also had the benefit of the covenant in its capacity as owner of the red land. However, the judge dealt with both areas of land and I propose to do the same.

An express assignment of the benefit of a covenant is not necessary if the benefit of the covenant is annexed to the land. In that event, the benefit will pass automatically on a conveyance of the land, without express mention, because it is annexed to the land and runs with it. So the issue of annexation is logically the next to be considered. . . .

In my judgment the benefit of this covenant was annexed to the retained land, and I think that this is a consequence of section 78 of the Act of 1925. . . .

[His Lordship read this section and continued:]

Mr Price submitted that there were three possible views about section 78. One view, which he described as "the orthodox view" hitherto held, is that it is merely a statutory shorthand for reducing the length of legal documents. A second view, which was the one that Mr Price was inclined to place in the forefront of his argument, is that the section only applies, or at any rate only achieves annexation, when the land intended to be benefited is signified in the document by express words or necessary implication as the intended beneficiary of the covenant[7]. A third view is that the section applies if the covenant in fact touches and concerns the land of the covenantee, whether that be gleaned from the document itself or from evidence outside the document.

For myself, I reject the narrowest interpretation of section 78, the supposed orthodox view, which seems to me to fly in the face of the wording of the section. Before I express my reasons I will say that I do not find it necessary to choose between the second and third views because, in my opinion, this covenant relates to land of the covenantee on either interpretation of section 78. Clause 5 (iv) shows clearly that the covenant is for the protection of the retained land and that land is described in clause 2 as "any adjoining or adjacent property retained by the vendor." This formulation is sufficient for annexation purposes: see *Rogers v Hosegood* [1900] 2 Ch 388, p. 775, ante.

There is in my judgment no doubt that this covenant "related to the land of the covenantee," or, to use the old-fashioned expression, that it touched and concerned the land, even if Mr Price is correct in his submission that the document must show an intention to benefit identified land. The result of such application is that one must read clause 5 (iv) as if it were written: "The purchaser hereby covenants with the vendor and its successors in title and the persons deriving title under it or them, including the owners and occupiers for the time being of the retained land, that in carrying out the development of the blue land the purchaser shall not build at a greater

---

[7] See *Bridges v Harrow London Borough Council* (1981) 260 EG 284, where STUART-SMITH J held that, even if this second and stricter view were preferable, the plaintiff failed as there was no such signification in the document; [1982] Conv 313 (F. Webb).

density than a total 300 dwellings so as not to reduce, etc." I leave out of consideration section 79 as unnecessary to be considered in this context, since Mill Lodge is the original covenantor.

The first point to notice about section 78 (1) is that the wording is significantly different from the wording of its predecessor section 58 (1) of the Conveyancing Act 1881. The distinction is underlined by section 78 (2), which applies section 78 (1) only to covenants made after the commencement of the Act. Section 58 (1) of the Act of 1881 did not include the covenantee's successors in title or persons deriving title under him or them, or the owner or occupiers for the time being of the land of the covenantee intended to be benefited. The section was confined, in relation to realty, to the covenantee, his heirs and assigns, words which suggest a more limited scope of operation than is found in section 78.

If, as the language of section 78 implies, a covenant relating to land which is restrictive of the user thereof is enforceable at the suit of (1) a successor in title of the covenantee, (2) a person deriving title under the covenantee or under his successors in title, and (3) the owner or occupier of the land intended to be benefited by the covenant, it must, in my view, follow that the covenant runs with the land, because ex hypothesi every successor in title to the land, every derivative proprietor of the land and every other owner and occupier has a right by statute to the covenant. In other words, if the condition precedent of section 78 is satisfied — that is to say, there exists a covenant which touches and concerns the land of the covenantee — that covenant runs with the land for the benefit of his successors in title, persons deriving title under him or them and other owners and occupiers.

This approach to section 78 has been advocated by distinguished textbook writers; see Dr Radcliffe's article "Some Problems of the Law Relating to Restrictive Covenants" (1941) 57 LQR 203, Professor Wade's article, "Covenants — A Broad and Reasonable View" and the apt cross-heading "What is wrong with section 78?" [1972B] CLJ 151, 171, and *Megarry and Wade, The Law of Real Property*, 4th edn. (1975), p. 764. Counsel pointed out to us that the fourth edition of *Megarry and Wade* indicates a change of mind on this topic since the third edition.

Although the section does not seem to have been extensively used in the course of argument in this type of case, the construction of section 78 which appeals to me appears to be consistent with at least two cases decided in this court. The first is *Smith and Snipes Hall Farm Ltd v River Douglas Catchment Board* [1949] 2 KB 500, [1949] 2 All ER 179, p. 769, ante. In that case an agreement was made in April 1938 between certain landowners and the catchment board under which the catchment board undertook to make good the banks of a certain brook and to maintain the same, and the landowners undertook to contribute towards the cost. In 1940 the first plaintiff took a conveyance from one of the landowners of a part of the land together with an express assignment of the benefit of the agreement. In 1944 the second plaintiff took a tenancy of that land without any express assignment of the benefit of the agreement. In 1946 the brook burst its banks and the land owned by the first plaintiff and tenanted by the second plaintiff was inundated. The two important points are that the agreement was not expressed to be for the benefit of the landowner's successors in title; and there was no assignment of the benefit of the agreement in favour of the second plaintiff, the tenant. In reliance, as I understand the case, upon section 78 of the Act of 1925, it was held that the second plaintiff was entitled to sue the catchment board for damages for breach of the agreement. It seems to me that that conclusion can only have been reached on the basis that section 78 had the effect of causing the benefit of the agreement to run with the land so as to be capable of being sued upon by the tenant.

The other case, *Williams v Unit Construction Co Ltd* (unreported in the usual series of law reports but fully set out in 19 Conveyancer 262, p. 772, ante), was decided by this court in 1951. There a company had acquired a building estate and had underleased four plots to Cubbin for 999 years. The underlessors arranged for the defendant company to build houses on the four plots. The defendant covenanted with Cubbin to keep the adjacent road in repair until adopted. Cubbin granted a weekly tenancy of one house to the plaintiff without any express assignment of the benefit of the covenant. The plaintiff was injured owing to the disrepair of the road. She was held entitled to recover damages from the defendant for breach of the covenant.

We were referred to observations in the speeches of Lord Upjohn and Lord Wilberforce in *Tophams Ltd v Earl of Sefton*[1967] 1 AC 50 at 73 and 81, [1966] 1 All ER 1039 at 1048 and 1053, to the effect that section 79 of the Act of 1925, relating to the burden of covenants, achieved no more than the introduction of statutory shorthand into the drafting of covenants. Section 79, in my view, involves quite different considerations and I do not think that it provides a helpful analogy.

It was suggested by Mr Price that, if this covenant ought to be read as enuring for the benefit of the retained land, it should be read as enuring only for the benefit of the retained land as a whole and not for the benefit of every part of it; with the apparent result that there is no annexation of the benefit to a part of the retained land when any severance takes place. He referred us to a passage in *Re Union of London and Smith's Bank Ltd's Conveyance* [1933] Ch 611 at 628, p. 789, post, which I do not think it is necessary for me to read". . . .

I find the idea of the annexation of a covenant to the whole of the land but not to a part of it a difficult conception fully to grasp. . . . [The discussion of this question is postponed to section (*d*) below].

In the end, I come to the conclusion that section 78 of the Law of Property Act 1925 caused the benefit of the restrictive covenant in question·to run with the red land and therefore to be annexed to it, with the result that the plaintiff is able to enforce the covenant against Mill Lodge, not only in its capacity as owner of the green land, but also in its capacity as owner of the red land.

For these reasons I think that the judge reached the correct view on the right of the plaintiff to enforce the covenant, although in part he arrived there by a different route[8].

---

[8] See also *Shropshire County Council v Edwards* (1982) 46 P & CR 270, where Judge Rubin held that, on the construction of a covenant made in 1908, the benefit had been annexed to the land; he left undecided the point whether the Conveyancing Act 1881 s. 58 (1) should be given a wider construction than that of a "word-saving-provision" based on cases decided under its successor, LPA 1925, s. 78.

In *Roake v Chadha* [1984] 1 WLR 40, [1983] 3 All ER 503[9], a part of the Sudbury Court Estate in North Wembley was sold and conveyed to Wembley (C and W) Land Co Ltd, who then proceeded to lay out the land in lots and sell them off, using a standard form of transfer. In April 1934 William Lambert purchased one plot, No 4, Audrey Gardens, and covenanted not to erect any building on the plot apart from one private dwelling-house. The covenant contained the words "so as to bind (so far as practicable) the land hereby transferred into whosesoever hands the same may come . . . but so that this covenant shall not enure for the benefit of any owner or subsequent purchaser of any part of the estate unless the benefit of this covenant shall be expressly assigned."

The defendant was the successor in title to William Lambert, and was proposing to erect an additional house on his plot. The plaintiffs were successors in title to Wembley (C and W) Land Co Ltd; they had subsequently purchased neighbouring plots, but had not had the benefit of the covenant expressly assigned to them.

In holding that the plaintiffs were not entitled to an injunction restraining the defendant from building the additional house, Judge Paul Baker QC said at 43, at 506:

"From these facts, which are not in dispute the plaintiffs contend that the benefit of the covenant of No 4, Audrey Gardens has become annexed to each of the plots respectively owned by them. Alternatively, it is contended that the benefit has passed under the general words of section 62 of the Law of Property Act 1925.

As to annexation, Mr Walter, appearing for the plaintiffs, conceded that the express terms of the covenant appeared to exclude annexation, and there was no suggestion that the case fell within the category known as building schemes. Mr Walter, however, in an interesting argument submitted that annexation had come about through the operation of section 78 of the Law of Property Act, as interpreted in *Federated Homes Ltd v Mill Lodge Properties Ltd* [1980] 1 WLR 594, [1980] 1 All ER 371, p. 777, ante, a Court of Appeal decision. I can summarise his argument by the following four points.

(1) The covenant was a covenant relating to the land of the covenantee.

(2) Section 78 (1) of the Law of Property Act 1925 provides, as regards such covenants relating to land that they are deemed:

'to be made with the covenantee and his successors in title and the persons deriving title under him or them, and shall have effect as if such successors and other persons were expressed. For the purposes of this subsection in connection with covenants restrictive of the user of land 'successors in title' shall be deemed to include the owners and occupiers for the time being of the land of the covenantee intended to be benefited.'

(3) In the *Federated Homes* case it was held that by virtue of section 78 (1) the benefit of a covenant relating to land retained by the covenantee ran with that land and was annexed to it and to every part of it.

(4) The provisions of section 78, unlike those of section 79 relating to the burden of the covenant, cannot be excluded by the expression of a contrary intention. Section 79 reads:

[His Lordship read the section, p. 461, ante, and continued:]

---

[9] [1984] Conv 68 (P. N. Todd); [1983] All ER Rev 231 (P. J. Clarke).

Unlike section 78, which had a counterpart in section 58 of the Conveyancing Act 1881, section 79 was a new section in 1925. The important point to which attention is called is "unless a contrary intention is expressed," in section 79. There is no corresponding expression in section 78. Those are the main points of the argument.

I have no difficulty in accepting that the covenant in the standard form of the 1934 transfer is a covenant relating to the retained land of the covenantee, that is to say, Wembley (C & W) Land Co Ltd, and that therefore section 78 comes into play. It is the third and fourth points which have given rise to the argument in this case.

I must begin, therefore, by examining the *Federated Homes* case. . . . The plaintiff became clearly entitled to the relief sought in right of the green land.

Mr Henty, for the defendant in the present case, has argued that accordingly the Court of Appeal's judgments in relation to the red land were obiter. I am unable to accept this view of the effect of the judgments. As it seems to me, the status of the covenant in relation to both pieces of land — the red and the green — was in issue in the case. If the defendant in subsequent proceedings had sought to challenge the validity of the covenant in relation to the red land, he could, as I would see it, be met by a plea of issue estoppel and consequently the principle underlying the court's conclusion cannot be regarded as obiter. That principle I take from the following passage in the judgment of Brightman LJ, at 605, at 379:

'If, as the language of section 78 implies, a covenant relating to land which is restrictive of the user thereof is enforceable at the suit of (1) a successor in title of the covenantee, (2) a person deriving title under the covenantee or under his successors in title, and (3) the owner or occupier of the land intended to be benefited by the covenant, it must, in my view, follow that the covenant runs with the land, because ex hypothesi every successor in title to the land, every derivative proprietor of the land and every other owner and occupier has a right by statute to the covenant. In other words, if the condition precedent of section 78 is satisfied — that is to say, there exists a covenant which touches and concerns the land of the covenantee — that covenant runs with the land for the benefit of his successors in title, persons deriving title under him or them and other owners and occupiers.'

That seems to be the essential point of the decision. Mr Henty made a frontal attack on this use of section 78, which he reinforced by reference to an article by Mr G. H. Newsom QC in (1981) 97 LQR 32 which is critical of the decision. The main lines of attack are (1) that the conclusion overlooks the legislative history of section 78 which it is said shows that it has a narrower purpose than is claimed and does not in itself bring about annexation; (2) this narrower purpose has been accepted in relation to the corresponding section 79 (relation to burden) by Lord Upjohn and Lord Wilberforce in *Tophams Ltd v Earl of Sefton* [1967] 1 AC 50 at 73, 81, [1966] 1 All ER 1039 at 1048, 1053. Further, it is said by way of argument sub silentio that in a number of cases, notably *Marquess of Zetland v Driver* [1939] Ch 1, [1938] 2 All ER 158 and *Re Jeff's Transfer (No 2)* [1966] 1 WLR 841, [1966] 1 All ER 934, that the argument could have been used to good effect but was not deployed.

Now, all this is very interesting, and the views of Mr Newsom are entitled to very great respect seeing that until his recent retirement he was a practitioner of long experience who had made a special study of this branch of the law. He has written a valuable monograph on it. All the same, despite

Mr Henty's blandishments, I am not going to succumb to the temptation of joining in any such discussion. Sitting here as a judge of the Chancery Division, I do not consider it to be my place either to criticise or to defend the decisions of the Court of Appeal. I conceive it my clear duty to accept the decision of the Court of Appeal as binding on me and apply it as best I can to the facts I find here.

Mr Walter's method of applying it is simplicity itself. The *Federated Homes* case shows that section 78 of the Act of 1925 brings about annexation, and that the operation of the section cannot be excluded by a contrary intention. As I have indicated, he supports this last point by reference to section 79, which is expressed to operate "unless a contrary intention is expressed," a qualification which, as we have already noticed, is absent from section 78. Mr Walter could not suggest any reason of policy why section 78 should be mandatory, unlike, for example, section 146 of the Act of 1925, which deals with restrictions on the right to forfeiture of leases and which, by an express provision "has effect notwithstanding any stipulation to the contrary."

I am thus far from satisfied that section 78 has the mandatory operation which Mr Walter claimed for it. But if one accepts that it is not subject to a contrary intention, I do not consider that it has the effect of annexing the benefit of the covenant in each and every case irrespective of the other express terms of the covenant. I notice that Brightman LJ in the *Federated Homes* case did not go so far as that, for he said, at 606, at 381:

'I find the idea of the annexation of a covenant to the whole of the land but not to a part of it a difficult conception fully to grasp. I can understand that a covenantee may expressly or by necessary implication retain the benefit of a covenant wholly under his own control, so that the benefit will not pass unless the covenantee chooses to assign; but I would have thought, if the benefit of a covenant is, on a proper construction of a document, annexed to the land, prima facie it is annexed to every part thereof, unless the contrary clearly appears.

So at least in some circumstances Brightman LJ is considering that despite section 78 the benefit may be retained and not pass or be annexed to and run with land. In this connection, I was also referred by Mr Henty to *Elphinstone's Covenants Affecting Land* (1946), p. 17, where it is said in a footnote:

'but it is thought that, as a covenant must be construed as a whole, the court would give due effect to words excluding or modifying the operation of the section . . .'

The true position as I see it is that even where a covenant is deemed to be made with successors in title as section 78 requires, one still has to construe the covenant as a whole to see whether the benefit of the covenant is annexed. Where one finds, as in the *Federated Homes* case, the covenant is not qualified in any way, annexation may be readily inferred; but where, as in the present case, it is expressly provided:

'this covenant shall not enure for the benefit of any owner or subsequent purchaser of any part of the vendor's Sudbury Court Estate at Wembley unless the benefit of this covenant shall be expressly assigned . . .'

one cannot just ignore these words. One may not be able to exclude the operation of the section in widening the range of the covenantees, but one has to consider the covenant as a whole to determine its true effect. When one does that, then it seems to me that the answer is plain and in my judgment the benefit was not annexed. That is giving full weight to both the statute in force and also what is already there in the covenant.

[His Honour then considered the alternative claim based on LPA 1925, s. 62; see p. 799, post) and concluded:]

I thus conclude overall that the plaintiffs have failed to show that they are entitled to the benefit of the covenant in relation to their respective properties."

(c) Annexation to the Whole of the Covenantee's Land

The covenantee may enforce the covenant against the covenantor or his assigns, so long as the covenantee has some land capable of benefiting. But, when the question concerns the annexation of the benefit of the covenant to the dominant land, so as to make the benefit run with the land on a conveyance, it has been held that this can only be done at law or in equity, if substantially the whole of the "dominant" land is capable of benefiting; it is not possible for the court to effect a severance and allow the covenant to be annexed to such land as is capable of benefiting[10].

The difficulty, however, disappears if the covenant is correctly drafted, so as to show an intention to annex the benefit to the whole or *any part or parts of* the estate, for the benefit will then be annexed to such parts as are in fact benefited[11]. It has been held that the court will hear evidence as to the capability of the land to be benefited by the covenant[12]; and that the burden of proof is on the defendant to show that it does not do so, either originally, or at the date of the action[13].

(d) Annexation to Part of the Covenantee's Land

Even if the whole of the dominant land is capable of benefiting, and if the benefit of the covenant is annexed to the whole, it has usually been held that the benefit of the covenant will only run in favour of the purchaser of a *part* of the land, if he can show that the benefit was annexed to the part which he purchased, or to each portion of the whole.

"For instance, A, the owner of a large property, sells part of it to Y and takes a covenant that no public house shall be opened on it. This covenant is annexed to A's land. Later A sells part of the dominant land to B. If B seeks to enforce the covenant by virtue of its annexation to A's land, he must prove that its benefit was annexed to each and every part of those lands or to the very part bought by him[14]."

---

[10] *Re Ballard's Conveyance* [1937] Ch 473, [1937] 2 All ER 691; 57 LQR at p. 210 (G. R. Y. Radcliffe); Elphinstone, *Covenants Affecting Land* (1946) p. 60; *Marten v Flight Refuelling Ltd* [1962] Ch 115 at 137, [1961] 2 All ER 696 at 706, p. 794, post.

[11] *Marquess of Zetland v Driver* [1937] Ch 651, [1939] Ch 1; (1941) 57 LQR 203.

[12] *Marten v Flight Refuelling Ltd* supra; *Earl of Leicester v Wells-next-the-Sea UDC* [1973] Ch 110, [1972] 3 All ER 77 (expert evidence admitted to show that a covenant restricting 19 acres afforded "great benefit and much needed protection to the Holkham Estate as a whole" i.e. to 32,000 acres). In *Re Ballard's Conveyance*, supra, no evidence was offered to show benefit to the dominant land as a whole.

[13] *Wrotham Park Estate Co Ltd v Parkside Homes Ltd* [1974] 1 WLR 799, [1974] 2 All ER 321.

[14] C & B, p. 587; Preston & Newsom, pp. 18–23. In *Griffiths v Band* (1974) 29 P & CR 243 at 246, GOULDING J referred to "this somewhat muddy corner of legal history."

In *Drake v Gray* [1936] Ch 451, [1936] 1 All ER 363[15], the Court of Appeal (SLESSER, ROMER and GREENE LJJ) held that a covenant taken with the other parties to the deed . . . "and other the owners or owner for the time being of the remaining hereditaments so agreed to be partitioned" operated to annex the covenant to each portion of the land, so as to allow the benefit of the covenant to run with each portion of the partitioned land.

SLESSER LJ said at 461, at 372: "I recognise, and I accept entirely, what was said by this Court in *Re Union of London and Smith's Bank Ltd's Conveyance, Miles v Easter* [1933] Ch 611, p. 789, post, that it must be shown that the benefit was intended to enure to each portion of the land, and it is true that it has been held that the use of the words 'or any part thereof' may be apt for that purpose; but I cannot read that case as meaning that those words, and those words only, are the sole means by which a conveyance may show that the benefit was intended to enure to each portion. In this case, the intention, as gathered from the documents and the recital of the whole history of the case, is clear that the benefit of the covenant was to enure to the owner of any part of the remaining hereditaments, and as the plaintiff was such an owner, the learned judge was right in the conclusion to which he came."

In *Re Selwyn's Conveyance* [1967] Ch 674, [1967] 1 All ER 339, GOFF J held that a covenant "for the protection of the adjoining or neighbouring land part of or lately part of the Selwyn Estate" was sufficient to annex the benefit to separate parts of the land.

In *Russell v Archdale* [1964] Ch 38, [1962] 2 All ER 305[16], BUCKLEY J held that a restrictive covenant "to benefit and protect the vendor's adjoining and neighbouring land" was annexed to that land as a whole, but that the plaintiff, a subsequent purchaser of only part of that land, was not entitled to rely on the annexation. He said at 45, at 311: "The next question which was debated was whether this annexation was an annexation to the whole of the land referred to by the words 'adjoining and neighbouring land' or to each and every part of it, and in that connection I was referred by Mr Arnold to the decision of the Court of Appeal in *Drake v Gray*. That was relied upon as authority for the proposition that where one finds annexation by general words such as 'for the benefit of the vendor's remaining land' or, such as we have in the present case, 'adjoining and neighbouring land', the proper interpretation is to construe that as a reference to each and every part of the land which falls within the description. . . .

In the course of his judgment, Romer LJ said at 465, at 376: 'Most of the cases that have come before the court have been cases where a covenant has been entered into by a vendor for the benefit of, say, the AB estate for the time being. There, of course, no intention is shown that the benefit should enure for any particular part of the estate; but where one finds not "the land coloured yellow" or "the estate" or "the field named so-and-so" or anything of that kind, but "the lands retained by the vendor", it appears to me that

-----

[15] *Reid v Bickerstaff* [1909] 2 Ch 305.
[16] (1962) 78 LQR 334, 482 (R. E. M.); affd. CA (Lord DENNING MR, dissenting) (1962) Times, 1 December, where only the issue of acquiescence is discussed.

there is a sufficient indication that the benefit of the covenant enures to every one of the lands retained by the vendor, and if a plaintiff in a subsequent action to enforce a covenant can say: "I am the owner of a piece of land that belonged to the vendor at the time of the conveyance", he is entitled to enforce the covenant. . . .'

No doubt every case of this kind, being one of construction, must be determined on the facts and the actual language used, but with the utmost respect to Romer LJ, I cannot see that the mere fact that the land intended to be benefited was described by such an expression as 'the land retained by the vendor' is sufficient to enable the court to come to the conclusion that the covenant is intended to benefit each and every part of that land. This observation of Romer LJ was, I think, clearly obiter dictum, . . . and in my judgment that authority does not assist the plaintiffs to say that the benefit of this covenant is annexed to each and every part of what is described by the conveyance as 'the adjoining and neighbouring land of the vendor'. That being so, I think it must follow that the plaintiffs cannot, merely by reason of annexation of this covenant to the 'adjoining and neighbouring land of the vendor' in the conveyance of 1938 and the fact that they have acquired part only of that land, enforce the covenant[17]."

In *Federated Homes v Mill Lodge Properties Ltd* [1980] 1 WLR 594, [1980] 1 All ER 371 (p. 777, ante), BRIGHTMAN LJ said at 606, at 380:

"It was suggested by Mr Price that, if this covenant ought to be read as enuring for the benefit of the retained land, it should be read as enuring only for the benefit of the retained land as a whole and not for the benefit of every part of it; with the apparent result that there is no annexation of the benefit to a part of the retained land when any severance takes place. He referred us to a passage in *Re Union of London and Smith's Bank Ltd's Conveyance* [1933] Ch 611 at 628, which I do not think it is necessary for me to read.

The problem is alluded to in *Megarry and Wade, The Law of Real Property*, 4th edn., p. 763.

'In drafting restrictive covenants it is therefore desirable to annex them to the covenantee's land 'or any part or parts thereof.' An additional reason for using this form of words is that, if there is no indication to the contrary, the benefit may be held to be annexed only to the whole of the covenantee's land, so that it will not pass with portions of it disposed of separately. But even without such words the court may find that the covenant is intended to benefit any part of the retained land; and small indications may suffice, since the rule that presumes annexation to the whole only is arbitrary and inconvenient. In principle it conflicts with the rule for assignments, which allows a benefit annexed to the whole to be assigned with part, and it also conflicts with the corresponding rule for easements.'

---

[17] Similarly in *Re Jeff's Transfer (No. 2)* [1966] 1 WLR 841, [1966] 1 All ER 937 ("for the benefit of the remainder of the Chorleywood Estate (Loudwater) belonging to the vendor"); *Stilwell v Blackman* [1968] Ch 508, [1967] 3 All ER 514 ("to benefit and protect the adjoining property of the vendor"). The Law Commission Report on Restrictive Covenants (1967 Law Com No. 11), p. 15 recommended that the benefit of a land obligation should be annexed to each and every part unless a contrary intention is expressed. See also Victoria Property Law Act 1958, s. 79A.

I find the idea of the annexation of a covenant to the whole of the land but not to a part of it a difficult conception fully to grasp. I can understand that a covenantee may expressly or by necessary implication retain the benefit of a covenant wholly under his own control, so that the benefit will not pass unless the covenantee chooses to assign; but I would have thought, if the benefit of a covenant is, on a proper construction of a document, annexed to the land, prima facie it is annexed to every part thereof, unless the contrary clearly appears. It is difficult to see how this court can have reached its decision in *Williams v Unit Construction Co Ltd*, 19 Conveyancer 262, unless this is right. The covenant was, by inference, annexed to every part of the land and not merely to the whole, because it will be recalled that the plaintiff was a tenant of only one of the four houses which had the benefit of the covenant.

There is also this observation by Romer LJ in *Drake v Gray* [1936] Ch 451, 465. He was dealing with the enuring of the benefit of a restrictive covenant and he said:

[His Lordship quoted Romer LJ's dictum set out at page 786, ante, and continued]:

In the instant case the judge in the course of his judgment appears to have dismissed the notion that any individual plot-holder would be entitled, even by assignment, to have the benefit of the covenant that I have been considering. I express no view about that. I only say this, that I am not convinced that his conclusion on that point is correct. I say no more about it."

ii.   BY EXPRESS ASSIGNMENT

If the benefit of a restrictive covenant is not annexed to the land of the covenantee, an assignee must show that the benefit passed to him by express assignment of the benefit at the time of the conveyance. Such express assignment will be necessary in fewer cases in the future if, on the authority of *Federated Homes Ltd v Mill Lodge Properties Ltd* [1980] 1 WLR 594, [1980] 1 All ER 371, p. 777, ante, annexation is held to be effected by section 78 of the Law of Property Act 1925. Cases requiring express assignment can, however, still arise; as where there is express provision to the effect that express assignment of the benefit of the covenant shall be required[18]; or where there is no identification in the conveyance of the land to be benefited[19]. Further, it may be possible to argue that the benefit of a covenant passes under the "general words" of section 62 of the Law of Property Act 1925[20].

Preston and Newsom, *Restrictive Covenants Affecting Freehold Land* (7th edn. 1982) p. 40.

"Where the defendant is the original covenantor, he is liable at law. Against him the original covenantee can succeed at common law in an ordinary action on the covenant. Further, a plaintiff who is the express

---

[18] *Marquess of Zetland v Driver* [1937] Ch 651; *Roake v Chadha* [1984] 1 WLR 40, [1983] 3 All ER 503, p. 782, ante.

[19] *Newton Abbot Co-operative Society v Williamson and Treadgold Ltd* [1952] Ch 286, [1952] 1 All ER 279, p. 790, post. But see *Federated Homes Ltd v Mill Lodge Properties Ltd*, supra, at 604, at 379 per BRIGHTMAN LJ.

[20] P. 586, ante; p. 799, post; *Federated Homes Ltd v Mill Lodge Properties Ltd*, supra, at 601, at 376.

assignee of the benefit of the covenant can succeed against the original covenantor in an action at law governed by the ordinary rules as to the assignment of a chose in action. But 'at law the benefit could not be assigned in pieces. It would have to be assigned as a whole or not at all[1].' The plaintiff must therefore rely upon an equitable title even as against the original covenantor if the benefit of the covenant has been assigned "in pieces." And, more importantly, he must always rely on an equitable title against a defendant who is not the original covenantor (or his personal representative). For the burden of a covenant never runs at law and a successor of the covenantor is liable in equity, under the rule in *Tulk v Moxhay*. Requiring the assistance of equity, against a defendant who is liable in equity only or because his own title depends upon equity, a plaintiff must therefore show that he is within the special rules laid down by equity for establishing whether a title by express assignment can be relied upon."

(a) Contemporaneous with Conveyance

It has long been clear that it was possible in equity to assign expressly the benefit of a restrictive covenant on the sale of the land of the covenantee[2]. Such assignment must be contemporaneous with the conveyance; if once the covenant becomes separated from the land to be benefited, it ceases to be operative[3]. It was not, however, until 1952 that it was authoritatively held that the benefit would pass in this way[4]. And this decision has been criticised[5].

In *Re Union of London and Smith's Bank Ltd's Conveyance, Miles v Easter* [1933] Ch 611[6], ROMER LJ referred to *Renals v Cowlishaw* (1878) 9 ChD 125 and *Rogers v Hosegood* [1900] 2 Ch 388 p. 775, ante and said at 629: "In neither of these cases, therefore, did it become necessary for the court to inquire into the circumstances in which an express assignee of the benefit of a covenant that does not run with the land is entitled to enforce it. In the present case, however, it is necessary to do so, inasmuch as the defendants claim to be the express assignees of the benefit of the restrictive covenants contained in the deeds of 23 October 1908 and 11 May 1909.

Now it may be conceded that the benefit of a covenant entered into with the covenantee or his assigns is assignable. The use of the word 'assigns' indicates this: see Williams on Personal Property, 18th edn. p. 33. But it by no means follows that the assignee of a restrictive covenant affecting land of the covenantor is entitled to enforce it against an assign of that land. For the

---

[1] *Miles v Easter* [1933] Ch 611 at 630, per ROMER LJ.
[2] *Renals v Cowlishaw* (1878) 9 ChD 125; *Ives v Brown* [1919] 2 Ch 314; *Lord Northbourne v Johnston & Son* [1922] 2 Ch 309; *Chambers v Randall* [1923] 1 Ch 149; *Re Union of London and Smith's Bank Ltd's Conveyance, Miles v Easter* [1933] Ch 611; *Re Rutherford's Conveyance* [1938] Ch 396, [1938] 1 All ER 495; (1948) 6 CLJ 339 (S. J. Bailey); (1952) 68 LQR 353 (Sir Lancelot Elphinstone). The assignment may be to a lessee; *South Eastern Rly Co v Associated Portland Cement Manufacturers (1900) Ltd* [1910] 1 Ch 12.
[3] *Chambers v Randall*, supra; *Re Union of London and Smith's Bank Ltd's Conveyance, Miles v Easter* supra; cf. *Lord Northbourne v Johnston*, supra; *Newton Abbot Co-operative Society Ltd v Williamson and Treadgold Ltd* [1952] Ch 286, [1952] 1 All ER 279, p. 790, post.
[4] *Newton Abbot Co-operative Society Ltd v Williamson and Treadgold Ltd*, supra.
[5] (1952) 68 LQR 353 (Sir Lancelot Elphinstone).
[6] (1933) 49 LQR 483 (H. A. Hollond).

burden of the covenant did not run with the land at law, and is only enforceable against a purchaser with notice by reason of the equitable doctrine that is usually referred to as the rule in *Tulk v Moxhay*. It was open, therefore, to the Courts of Equity to prescribe the particular class of assignees of the covenant to whom they should concede the benefit of the rule. This they have done, and in doing so have included within the class persons to whom the benefit of the covenant could not have been assigned at law. For at law the benefit could not be assigned in pieces. It would have to be assigned as a whole or not at all. And yet in equity the right to enforce the covenant can in certain circumstances be assigned by the covenantee from time to time to one person after another. Who then are the assignees of the covenant that are entitled to enforce it? The answer to this question is to be found in several authorities which it now becomes necessary to consider.

[His Lordship referred to *Formby v Barker* [1903] 2 Ch 539, p. 764, ante and *LCC v Allen* [1914] 3 KB 642, p. 762, ante, and continued:]

It is plain, however, from these and other cases, and notably that of *Renals v Cowlishaw*, that if the restrictive covenant be taken not merely for some personal purpose or object of the vendor, but for the benefit of some other land of his in the sense that it would enable him to dispose of that land to greater advantage, the covenant, though not annexed to such land so as to run with any part of it, may be enforced against an assignee of the covenantor taking with notice, both by the covenantee and by persons to whom the benefit of such covenant has been assigned, subject however to certain conditions. In the first place, the 'other land' must be land that is capable of being benefited by the covenant — otherwise it would be impossible to infer that the object of the covenant was to enable the vendor to dispose of his land to greater advantage. In the next place, this land must be 'ascertainable' or 'certain', to use the words of Romer and Scrutton LJJ, respectively. For, although the Court will readily infer the intention to benefit the other land of the vendor where the existence and situation of such land are indicated in the conveyance or have been otherwise shown with reasonable certainty, it is impossible to do so from vague references in the conveyance or in other documents laid before the Court as to the existence of other lands of the vendor, the extent and situation of which are undefined. In the third place, the covenant cannot be enforced by the covenantee against an assign of the purchaser after the covenantee has parted with the whole of his land. . . ."

NEWTON ABBOT CO-OPERATIVE SOCIETY LTD *v* WILLIAMSON AND TREADGOLD LTD
[1952] Ch 286, [1952] 1 All ER 279[7] (ChD, Upjohn J)

In 1923, Mrs Mardon, who was owner of premises known as Devonia, in Fore St., Bovey Tracey, on which she carried on business as an ironmonger, conveyed property on the other side of the street to a purchaser who covenanted not to use it for the business of an ironmonger. There was no indication in the conveyance of the land to be benefited, but Mrs Mardon's address was given as Devonia.

---

[7] (1952) 68 LQR 353 (Sir Lancelot Elphinstone).

In 1941, Mrs Mardon died, having left Devonia in her will to her son Leonard Soper Mardon.

In 1947, the purchasers of the property opposite Devonia sold it to the defendants.

In 1948, Leonard Soper Mardon assigned the ironmongery business to Bovey Tracey Co-operative Society (which later amalgamated with the plaintiffs) together with the benefit of the restrictive covenant, and granted them a lease of Devonia for 21 years.

In 1950, the defendants began to expose articles of ironmongery for sale in breach of the restrictive covenant.

Held. The plaintiffs were entitled to an injunction. The covenant touched and concerned the land and had been validly assigned.

UPJOHN J: The sole issue before me is whether the plaintiffs are entitled to the benefit of the restrictive covenant, and, if so, whether they are entitled to enforce it against the defendants.

I will deal with the first point first. Mr Binney on behalf of the plaintiffs submitted first that the benefit of the restrictive covenant was annexed to Devonia so as to pass with the assignment of Devonia in equity without any express mention in that subsequent assignment; in other words, that the covenant runs with the land. Alternatively, he said that the plaintiffs are the express assigns of the benefit of the covenant, and as such are entitled to enforce it. In this difficult branch of the law one thing in my judgment is clear, namely, that in order to annex the benefit of a restrictive covenant to land, so that it runs with the land without express assignment on a subsequent assignment of the land, the land for the benefit of which it is taken must be clearly identified in the conveyance creating the covenant.

[His Lordship referred on this point to *Renals v Cowlishaw* (1878) 9 ChD 125, p. 777, ante, *Re Union of London and Smith's Bank Ltd's Conveyance, Miles v Easter* (1933) Ch 611, p. 789, ante, and came to the conclusion that the land for the benefit of which the covenant was taken was not sufficiently identified by the conveyance to annex the benefit of it to the land.]

I turn then to his second submission, namely, that the plaintiffs are express assigns of the benefit of the restrictive covenant. Mr Bowles, on behalf of the defendants, contends that, even if it be assumed that his submission (with which I shall deal later) that the covenant was not taken for the benefit of Devonia, but of the business carried on thereat, is wrong, and the covenant was taken by Mrs Mardon for the benefit of Devonia to enable her to dispose of it to better advantage, yet there is no complete chain of assignments vesting the benefit in the plaintiffs. He says that there was never any assignment of the benefit of the covenant by the executors of Mrs Mardon to Leonard Soper Mardon and therefore he was not in a position to assign the benefit of the covenant to the plaintiffs' predecessors in title. He relied on *Ives v Brown* [1919] 2 Ch 314 and *Lord Northbourne v Johnston & Son* [1922] 2 Ch 309.

In my judgment those authorities do not support his contention. The position as I see it was this: On the footing that the restrictive covenant was not annexed to the land so as to run with it, the benefit of the covenant is capable of passing by operation of law as well as by express assignment and formed part of Mrs Mardon's personal estate on her death: see *Ives v Brown*.

It was not suggested that there was any implied assent to the assignment of the benefit of the covenant to the residuary legatee, but in my judgment, when her estate was duly wound up and administered, and this case has been argued before me on the footing that that happened many years ago, the benefit of the covenant was held by the executors as bare trustees for the residuary legatee, Leonard Soper Mardon, who was himself one of the executors. He therefore became entitled to the benefit of this restrictive covenant in equity and, in my judgment, he was entitled to assign the benefit in equity on an assignment of Devonia. No doubt had the covenant been assigned to him by the executors, he could also have assigned it at law. That this is the position is, in my judgment, made clear by the . . . judgment of Sargant J in *Lord Northbourne v Johnston & Son*[8]. . . .

The second main question was whether the defendants are liable to have the covenant enforced against them. This was Mr Bowles' main defence in this action and he says that the restrictive covenant was not taken for the benefit of Devonia, and he puts his case in this way: First, he says that in any event this was not taken for the benefit of any land, but was a covenant with Mrs Mardon personally, solely for the benefit of her business. Secondly, he says that in order that an express assign of the benefit may sue an assignee of the burden of the covenant there must be some reference in the conveyance creating that covenant to the land for the benefit of which it was taken. . . .

[His Lordship came to the conclusion that the covenant was taken for the benefit of Devonia, and continued:]

Mr Bowles' second point was that, in order that the benefit of the covenant may be assignable, the land for which the benefit of the covenant is taken must in some way be referred to in the conveyance creating the covenant, and I was naturally pressed with the headnote in *Re Union of London and Smith's Bank Ltd's Conveyance, Miles v Easter* [1933] Ch 611, which reads as follows: "Where on a sale otherwise than under a building scheme a restrictive covenant is taken, the benefit of which is not on the sale annexed to the land retained by the covenantee so as to run with it, an assign of the covenantee's retained land cannot enforce the covenant against an assign (taking with notice) of the covenantor unless he can show (i) that the covenant was taken for the benefit of ascertainable land of the covenantee capable of being benefited by the covenant, and (ii) that he (the covenantee's assign) is an express assign of the benefit of the covenant", and with the following passage in the judgment of Bennett J at 625: "In my judgment, in order that an express assignee of a covenant restricting the user of land may be able to enforce that covenant against the owner of the land burdened with the covenant, he must be able to satisfy the court of two things. The first is that it was a covenant entered into for the benefit or protection of land owned by the covenantee at the date of the covenant. Otherwise it is a covenant in gross, and unenforceable except as between the parties to the covenant; see *Formby v Barker* [1903] 2 Ch 539, p. 764, ante. Secondly, the assignee must be able to satisfy the court that the deed containing the covenant defines or contains something to define the property for the benefit of which the covenant was entered into: see James LJ in *Renals v Cowlishaw* (1879) 11 ChD at 866."

---

[8] See *Marten v Flight Refuelling Ltd* [1962] Ch 115 at 140, [1961] 2 All ER 696 at 708, where WILBERFORCE J relied upon SARGANT J's reasoning; *Earl of Leicester v Wells-next-the-Sea UDC* [1973] Ch 110, [1972] 3 All ER 77 (special executors of settled land held to be bare trustees of benefit of restrictive covenant for beneficiary under SLA 1925, s. 7 (1)), p. 302, ante.

With all respect to the statement of the judge, I am unable to agree that where a person is suing as an assign of the benefit of the covenant there must necessarily be something in the deed containing the covenant to define the land for the benefit of which the covenant was entered into. In the first place, the passage in the judgment of James LJ in *Renals v Cowlishaw*, which I have already read, on which the judge relied, does not in my judgment support the statement of the law for which it was cited. In *Renals v Cowlishaw* there was no express assignment of the benefit of the restrictive covenant (see the statement of fact in the report in the court below); and when James LJ says that to enable an assign to take the benefit of restrictive covenants there must be something in the deed to define the property for the benefit of which they were entered into, he is, I think, dealing with the case where it is contended that the benefit of the covenant has been annexed to the land so as to run with the land. When he uses the word 'assign' he is using the word as meaning an assign of the land and not an assign of the benefit of the covenant. Secondly, the views expressed by Bennett J appear to me to be inconsistent with the views expressed in some of the earlier decisions. I do not propose to cite them, but I refer to the following observations on the law on this point, namely, the observations of Collins LJ, delivering the judgment of the Court of Appeal in *Rogers v Hosegood* [1900] 2 Ch at 407, those of Vaughan Williams LJ in *Formby v Barker* [1903] 2 Ch at 551; and to the observations of Cozens-Hardy MR in *Reid v Bickerstaff* [1909] 2 Ch at 319, 325; and to the words of Buckley LJ in the same case. Finally, in *Re Union of London and Smith's Bank Ltd's Conveyance, Miles v Easter* [1933] Ch at 628, 631, Romer LJ, reading the judgment of the Court of Appeal, having considered the cases where the benefit of the covenant is annexed to land so as to run without express mention, says: "In all other cases the purchaser will not acquire the benefit of the covenant unless that benefit be expressly assigned to him — or to use the words of the Vice-Chancellor, 'it must appear that the benefit of the covenant was part of the subject-matter of the purchase'."

[His Lordship then cited the paragraph from Romer LJ's judgment set out on p. 790, ante, and continued:]

In my judgment, therefore, the problem which I have to consider is this: First, when Mrs Mardon took the covenant in 1923, did she retain other lands capable of being benefited by the covenant? The answer is plainly yes. Secondly, was such land "ascertainable" or "certain" in this sense that the existence and situation of the land must be indicated in the conveyance or otherwise shown with reasonable certainty?

Apart from the fact that Mrs Mardon is described as of Devonia, there is nothing in the conveyance of 1923 to define the land for the benefit of which the restrictive covenant was taken, and I do not think that carries one very far; but, for the reasons I have given, I am, in my judgment, entitled to look at the attendant circumstances to see if the land to be benefited is shown "otherwise" with reasonable certainty. That is a question of fact and, on the admitted facts, bearing in mind the close juxtaposition of Devonia and the defendants' premises, in my view the only reasonable inference to draw from the circumstances at the time of the conveyance of 1923 was that Mrs Mardon took the covenant restrictive of the user of the defendants' premises for the benefit of her own business of ironmonger and of her property Devonia where at all material times she was carrying on that business, which last-mentioned fact must have been apparent to the purchasers in 1923.

I should perhaps mention that at the date of her death, Mrs Mardon owned other property in Fore Steet, but counsel on neither side founded any argument on that circumstance.

It follows, therefore, in my judgment, that Mrs Mardon could on any subsequent sale of her land Devonia, if she chose, as part of the transaction of sale, assign the benefit of the covenant so as to enable the purchaser from her and his assignees of the land and covenant to enforce it against an owner of the defendants' premises taking with notice, and her legatee, Leonard Soper Mardon, was in no worse position. I do not regard the fact that he assigned the covenant in the deed containing the assignment of the business as affecting the matter. I say nothing as to the position when the plaintiffs' lease expires so that their estate in Devonia comes to an end, nor whether Leonard Soper Mardon, having apparently assigned away the entire benefit of the covenant, will then be in any position further to enforce it.

Mr Bowles took one further point. He submitted that a covenant restrictive of business could not be annexed to land, unless it was a covenant not to carry on a business so as to be a nuisance or annoyance to an adjoining occupier, but he cited no authority for that proposition and, in my judgment, it cannot be maintained: see *Nicoll v Fenning* (1881) 19 ChD 258.

Accordingly, in my judgment, the plaintiffs are entitled to succeed in this action and to an injunction.

Marten v Flight Refuelling Ltd [1962] Ch 115, [1961] 2 All ER 696[9], raised again, inter alia, the questions (*a*) of the enforceability of the benefit of a covenant when the identity of the land to be benefited could be shown by the use of extrinsic evidence but was not defined in the conveyance itself; and (*b*) of the devolution of the benefit of a covenant through personal representatives.

In 1943 Mrs Marten, the first plaintiff, was an infant tenant in tail of the Crichel estate, a large agricultural estate in Dorset of about 7,500 acres. In that year, the second plaintiffs, who were then holding the estate in trust for Mrs Marten as special executors under the Settled Land Act 1925, conveyed to Harding in fee simple Crook Farm of some 562 acres of which 200 acres had been requisitioned by the Air Ministry for the establishment of an aerodrome. Harding covenanted with the vendors and their successors in title that no part of the land conveyed nor any building thereon should thereafter be used for any purposes other than agricultural purposes. This covenant was registered in 1943 under Land Charges Act 1925, section 10 (1)[10], as a land charge Class D (ii).

In 1947 the Air Ministry permitted the first defendants, Flight Refuelling Ltd, to occupy the aerodrome. In 1950 Mrs Marten attained her majority and disentailed; the second plaintiffs assented to the vesting in her of the fee simple, but the assent did not mention the covenant. In 1958 the Air Ministry compulsorily purchased most of the land still occupied by Flight Refuelling Ltd from Harding's executors. The plaintiffs claimed a declaration that they were entitled to the benefit of the covenant and an injunction to restrain Flight Refuelling Ltd from using the land for industrial purposes.

---

[9] This is not a case involving annexation or express assignment: (1972) 36 Conv (NS) 20 (E. C. Ryder).
[10] Now LCA 1972, s. 2 (5).

WILBERFORCE J held, inter alia, that the plaintiffs were entitled to the benefit of the covenant and to an injunction to restrain the company from undertaking industrial activities beyond those necessary for Air Ministry purposes.

He said at 129, at 701: "First, are the plaintiffs, or is one of them, entitled to the benefit of the restrictive covenant? This involves several subsidiary questions, namely (a) whether the covenant was entered into for the benefit of any land of the covenantee; (b) whether that land is sufficiently defined or ascertainable by permissible inference or evidence; (c) whether that land is, or was, capable of being benefited by the covenant; (d) whether, since the first plaintiff is not the express assignee of the covenant, the action can be brought by the second plaintiff or by the two plaintiffs jointly.

(a) and (b) . . . An elaborate argument was addressed to me by the defendants to support a contention that the benefit of the covenant was not available to the plaintiffs. The conveyance, it was said, does not 'annex' the benefit of the covenant to any land so that it would pass automatically on a conveyance of the land to a purchaser. Further, it does not indicate that it was made for the benefit of any land, and even supposing that it was so made, it does not identify or provide any material upon which to identify what that land is.

It is, however, well established by the authorities that the benefit of restrictive covenants can pass to persons other than the original covenantee, even in the absence of annexation, provided that certain conditions are fulfilled. There is, however, dispute as to the nature of these conditions.

The defendants' contentions are, first, that there must appear from the terms of the deed itself an intention to benefit some land, and, secondly, that the precise land to be benefited must also be stated in the deed, or at least must be capable of ascertainment from the terms of the deed by evidence which is admissible in accordance with the normal rules of interpretation of documents. They rely principally on *Re Union of London and Smith's Bank Ltd's Conveyance, Miles v Easter* [1933] Ch 611, and submit that the decision of Upjohn J in *Newton Abbot Co-operative Society Ltd v Williamson and Treadgold Ltd* [1952] Ch 286, [1952] 1 All ER 279, p. 790, ante, which appears to admit parol evidence for the purpose of identifying the land to be benefited, goes too far.

[His Lordship then referred to *Re Union of London and Smith's Bank Ltd's Conveyance, Miles v Easter; Formby v Barker* [1903] 2 Ch 539, p. 764, ante; *Lord Northbourne v Johnston & Son* [1922] 2 Ch 309, and *Newton Abbot Co-operative Society Ltd v Williamson and Treadgold Ltd*, and, referring to the last, continued:]

This decision was attacked by the Attorney-General in a lively argument, and I was invited not to follow it. Of course, it relates to its own special facts, and no doubt I could leave it on one side. But I see nothing in it contrary to the principles which appear to be securely laid down. Here were two shops in common ownership facing each other in the same street, one of them, Devonia, an ironmonger's shop. The shops opposite are sold with a covenant against carrying on an ironmonger's business. What could be more obvious than that the covenant was intended for the protection or benefit of the vendor's property Devonia? To have rejected such a conclusion would, I venture to think, have involved not only an injustice, but a departure from common sense. So far from declining the authority of this case, I welcome it as a useful guide. But it is only a guide, and I must ultimately reach my conclusion on the facts of the present case. . . .

On these facts I consider that I should come to the conclusion that the covenant was taken for the benefit of land of the vendors, that land being the Crichel estate. In doing so I do not, so it seems to me, go outside such surrounding or attendant circumstances as, in accordance with the authorities, it is legitimate for the court to take into account. A decision based on the mere wording of cl. 2 of the conveyance would, in my judgment be unduly narrow and indeed technical, and would go far to undermine the usefulness of the rule which equity courts have evolved that the benefit of restrictive covenants may be capable of passing to assigns of the 'dominant' land or of the covenant in cases other than those of annexation. I would add two observations: first, the rules in *Miles v Easter* properly relate to cases where the covenant is sought to be enforced by an assign from the original covenantee. In this case, however, the second plaintiff is the original covenantee and the first plaintiff is the person for whose benefit in equity the covenant was taken. To that important extent the plaintiffs' case is stronger than that of the defendant in *Miles v Easter*. Secondly, in holding that the covenant was for the benefit of the Crichel estate, I mean the Crichel estate as a whole, as a single agricultural estate which it was and is, and I express no opinion whether it enures for the benefit of each and every part, for example, if parts are separately sold off. That is not a question which arises in this case.

There remain certain specific arguments which were put forward, and I must shortly deal with them. . . .

It was said that unless the identity of the land to be benefited was clearly stated in, or directly ascertainable from, the conveyance, a purchaser would be placed in an impossible position: he would never know by whom the covenant could be enforced, or whether it was enforceable at all[11]. I am not impressed by this objection: the original covenantee is ascertainable from the document — and moreover appears on or can be ascertained from the land charges register[12]. In a case where the covenant is sought to be enforced by an assign from him, such assign must always prove his right to sue, whether by virtue of annexation, by devolution, by assignment of the benefit of the covenant. The plaintiff may also (as in *Tulk v Moxhay*) have to show that he retains property for whose benefit the covenant was imposed. These are matters which arise in all cases where restrictive covenants are sought to be enforced otherwise than as between the original parties, and I see no greater difficulty in dealing with them in cases such as the present. . . .

Question (c): Was the land capable of being benefited by the covenant? On this point, as on those last dealt with, the answer would appear to be simple. If an owner of land, on selling part of it, thinks fit to impose a restriction on

---

[11] (1952) 68 LQR 353, 361.

[12] The position is rather more complex. Land charges are registered against the name of the estate owner whose estate is to be affected: that is against the name of the covenantor. A search will not reveal the name of the covenantee, nor a description of the land. The name and address of the original covenantee will be known to the Land Registry, for they would have been stated on the original application to register, and they may be ascertained by an application for an office copy of an entry in the register on Form K19, Land Charges Rules 1974. That will in most cases be sufficient to identify the benefited land; but often only with the assistance of extrinsic evidence.

user, and the restriction was imposed for the purpose of benefiting the land
retained, the court would normally assume that it is capable of doing so.
There might, of course, be exceptional cases where the covenant was on the
face of it taken capriciously or not bona fide, but a covenant taken by the
owner of an agricultural estate not to use a sold-off portion for other than
agricultural purposes could hardly fall within either of these categories. As
Sargant J said in *Lord Northbourne v Johnston & Son* [1922] 2 Ch at 319: 'Benefit
or detriment is often a question of opinion on which there may be the greatest
divergence of view, and the greatest difficulty in arriving at a clear
conclusion.' Why, indeed, should the court seek to substitute its own
standard for those of the parties — and on what basis can it do so? However,
much argument was devoted to this point, and evidence was called as to it.
These I must consider.

First it was said that a mere examination of the figures showed that the
covenant could not benefit the estate: the Crichel estate extends to some
7,500 acres, and it was asked how such a covenant could benefit the estate as
a whole. In my view, there is no such manifest impossibility about this. I
have already referred to the character of the estate, and I can well imagine
that, for the owner of it, whether he wished to retain it in his family or to sell
it as a whole, it might be of very real benefit to be able to preserve a former
outlying portion from development. This seems to me to be a question of fact
to be determined on the evidence: and I note that when a similar argument
was placed before the court in *Re Ballard's Conveyance* [1937] Ch 473, [1937] 2
All ER 691, Clauson J, while accepting it in the absence of evidence, showed
it to be his opinion that evidence could have been called. . . .

Question (*d*): Can the action be brought by the first plaintiffs or by the two
plaintiffs jointly? I can deal with this point quite shortly. The second plaintiff
is the original covenantee, and the first plaintiff is the person for whose
benefit in equity the covenant was made. Taken together, the plaintiffs
represent the whole legal and equitable interest in the covenant. The matter
appears, therefore, to be completely covered by the judgment of Sargant J in
Lord Northbourne v Johnston & Son the reasoning of which I adopt. So much was
not really contested by the Attorney-General, who, however, reserved the
right to challenge that judgment should this case go to a higher court."

(1968) 84 LQR at p. 29 (P. V. Baker)
"From the principles outlined above, and especially from the analogy of
easements, we should expect the right to go along automatically with the
benefited or dominant land, and, indeed, this happens where the benefit has
been annexed by the original covenant[13]. There is, however, a complicating
factor as not every restrictive covenant is initially annexed, and in these cases
the covenantee has the option of annexing it to the land or allowing it to
lapse. As it cannot exist as a separate piece of property like a profit in gross,
there seems to be no justification in principle for requiring it to be passed by
a succession of assignments parallel with the assignment of the benefited
land, for this is still treating it as either a covenant which is only enforceable
as such against the covenantor, or as existing in gross. If the original

---

[13] *Rogers v Hosegood* [1900] 2 Ch 388; and see *Lawrence v South County Freeholds Ltd* [1939] Ch 656 at
680, [1939] 2 All ER 503 at 523 ("a hidden treasure").

covenantor is still the owner of the burdened land, the benefit of the covenant could be assigned separately and then ultimately annexed, but if the burdened land has passed it is annexation or nothing, for it is a piece of property which is an adjunct of the benefited land. In other words, express assignment is delayed annexation. One puts together the deed containing the original covenant and the subsequent conveyance of the benefited land. The original covenant in these cases does not have to indicate the benefited land[14], but that deficiency is naturally supplied by the subsequent conveyance of it. Building schemes go still further since the annexation is effected by facts which are not necessarily or wholly indicated in the conveyance. . . .

The proposition that an express assignment of the benefit of covenant annexes it to the land so that it will thereafter pass to future owners without express assignment is supported by dicta in older cases[15] and by some writers[16]. It is, however, repudiated by others, expressly[17] or by implication[18], and in one recent case it was assumed, though not decided, that a chain of assignments was necessary[19]. Until *Stilwell v Blackman*[20] there was no decision which was inconsistent with the proposition, but it must follow that if express assignment operates as a mode of annexation, it is necessarily excluded where annexation has already occurred. Nevertheless, as we have seen, it was decided that annexation did not preclude the passing of the benefit by express assignment.

To the learned judge it was 'a question of construction whether or not express assignment is excluded by annexation'. There was, he said, nothing to interfere with the ordinary principles of contract so that, for example, the covenant could in express terms provide that either annexation or express assignment should be the only method of passing the benefit, or 'since they do not operate against each other, and if there were any advantage in so doing, by both methods simultaneously'[1]. Reference was then made to the dicta in *Renals v Cowlishaw*[2] which supported the proposition that on express assignment the benefit became automatically annexed, but it was thought that these words were not directed to the question of the simultaneous application of both methods of passing the benefit, 'or, indeed, even to the recognition that this question arose'. Nor was it clear 'whether, if there were such automatic annexation, it is suggested that the annexation would be merely to the whole, or also to each and every part of the land passing to the-

---

[14] *Newton Abbot Co-operative Society Ltd v Williamson and Treadgold Ltd* [1952] Ch 286, [1952] 1 All ER 279.

[15] *Renals v Cowlishaw* (1878) 9 ChD 125 at 130, 131; affd. (1879) 11 ChD 866; *Rogers v Hosegood* [1900] 2 Ch 388 at 408; *Reid v Bickerstaff* [1909] 2 Ch 305 at 320.

[16] M & W (3rd edn. 1966), p. 771; M. Bowles [1962] JPL 234; S. J. Bailey (1938) 6 CLJ 339 at 360, 361.

[17] Preston and Newsom, p. 35, n. 28, relying on a dictum of ROMER LJ in *Re Union of London and Smiths' Bank Ltd's Conveyance* [1933] Ch 611 at 631.

[18] Cheshire (10th edn. 1967) p. 546, relying on another dictum of ROMER LJ at 630 of the case last cited, but this was dealing with concurrent assignments of different parts of the benefited land by the original covenantee.

[19] *Re Pinewood Estate, Farnborough* [1958] Ch 280, [1957] 2 All ER 517, criticised H. W. R. Wade [1957] CLJ 146. [See also *Federated Homes Ltd v Mill Lodge Properties Ltd* [1980] 1 WLR 594 at 603, [1980] 1 All ER 371 at 378, where John Mills QC said: "I am not satisfied or prepared to hold that there is any such thing as 'delayed annexation by assignment' to which the covenantor is not party or privy."]

[20] [1968] Ch 508, [1967] 3 All ER 514.

[1] Ibid. at 525, at 520.

[2] See n. 15, supra.

express assignee of the covenant'. Ungoed-Thomas J expressed his final conclusion that 'there is no reason either in contract or in the relevant principles of equity why an express assignment of the benefit of a covenant with the passing of land should automatically operate exclusively, as an annexation of the covenant to the land (whether to the whole or to any part of it)'[3].

The reason, it is respectfully suggested, for such automatic annexation, is that when the burdened land passes from the covenantor, one leaves the realm of contract and enters that of property. The question then ceases to be exclusively a matter of what the original parties may or may not have agreed, but what incidents the law will allow. When one finds that the benefit of the covenant cannot exist by itself but only alongside the ownership of the benefited land, convenience suggests that it should be annexed to that land and not require a chain of assignments parallel with the conveyances of the land. Further, if the arguments in the earlier part of this article are accepted, the assignment of the benefit of the covenant by the covenantee would prima facie annex that benefit to each and every part of the land comprised in that benefit."

(*b*) *Law of Property Act 1925, Section 62*
In *Roake v Chadha* [1984] 1 WLR 40, [1983] 3 All ER 503, p. 782, ante, Judge Paul Baker QC said at 46, at 508:

"I must not turn to the alternative argument of the plaintiffs based on section 62 of the Law of Property Act 1925. This argument is directed to the conveyances or transfers conveying the alleged benefited land to the predecessors of the plaintiffs, and ultimately to the respective plaintiffs themselves. In each of these transfers, so I am prepared to assume, there is to be implied the general words of section 62 of the Act of 1925:

[His Honour read sub-s. (1), p. 586, ante, and continued:]

I do not think I need read subsection (2) which deals with the conveyance of land having houses and buildings and various corresponding rights in relation to buildings.

The argument is that the benefit of the covenant contained in the original transfer to the predecessor of the defendants, William Lambert, was carried by the words 'rights and advantages whatsoever appertaining or reputed to appertain to the land, or any part thereof.' It seems an argument on these lines was accepted by Mr John Mills QC, the deputy judge who gave the decision at first instance in the *Federated Homes* case [1980] 1 WLR 594, [1980] 1 All ER 371, p. 777, ante, but I have not seen it, and so cannot comment on it. The proposition now contended for is not a new one. In *Rogers v Hosegood* [1900] 2 Ch 388, it was similarly put forward as an alternative argument to an argument based on annexation. In that case however it was decided that the benefit of the covenant was annexed so that the point on section 6 of the Conveyancing Act 1881, the forerunner of section 62 of the Law of Property Act 1925, did not have to be decided. Nevertheless, Farwell J, sitting in the Chancery Division, said, at 398:

'It is not necessary for me to determine whether the benefit of the covenants would pass under the general words to which I have referred above, if such covenants did not run with the land. If they are not in fact

---
[3] At 526, at 520.

annexed to the land, it may well be that the right to sue thereon cannot be said to belong, or be reputed to belong, thereto; but I express no final opinion on this point.'

In the Court of Appeal the point was canvassed in argument but not referred to in the judgment of the court, which was given by Collins LJ.

In the present case, the covenant in terms precludes the benefit passing unless it is expressly assigned. That being so, as it seems to me, it is not a right 'appertaining or reputed to appertain' to land within the meaning of section 62 of the Law of Property Act 1925. As to whether the benefit of a covenant not annexed can ever pass under section 62, I share the doubts of Farwell J. Mr Henty suggested — and there may well be something in this — that the rights referred to in section 62 are confined to legal rights rather than equitable rights which the benefit of restrictive covenants is. But again I place it on construction. It cannot be described as a right appertaining or reputed to appertain to land when the terms of the covenant itself would seem to indicate, or indicates, to be the opposite.

I thus conclude overall that the plaintiffs have failed to show that they are entitled to the benefit of the covenant in relation to their respective properties[4]."

iii.   SCHEME OF DEVELOPMENT[5]

The necessity to show either express annexation or express assignment of the benefit of a restrictive covenant is avoided if the circumstances surrounding a series of sales indicate an intention that all the purchasers should be bound by restrictive covenants, and that each should be able to enforce them against the others. In such circumstances there is a scheme of development. There is created a sort of "local law"[6] among the purchasers, disregarding the ordinary rules of contract and covenants and permitting mutual enforcement. "The major theoretical difficulties", says MEGARRY J,[7] "based on the law of covenant seem to me to disappear when instead there is an equity created by circumstances which is independent of contractual obligation".

When does such a situation arise? It is difficult to answer with confidence. In the past 20 years, the emphasis has changed from a position in which

---

[4] See also (1971) 87 LQR 539 at p. 570 (D. J. Hayton); *Shropshire County Council v Edwards* (1982) 46 P & CR 270 at 279, where Judge Rubin "decided to remain silent on this highly debatable point under section 62, since a determination was not necessary."

[5] For the history of the development of the present doctrine, see *Whatman v Gibson* (1838) 9 Sim 196; *Coles v Sims* (1854) 5 De GM & G 1; *Sidney v Clarkson* (1865) 35 Beav 118; *Western v MacDermott* (1866) 2 Ch App 72; *Renals v Cowlishaw* (1878) 9 ChD 125; *Gaskin v Balls* (1879) 13 ChD 324; *Nottingham Patent Brick and Tile Co v Butler* (1885) 15 QBD 261; on appeal (1886) 16 QBD 778; *Collins v Castle* (1887) 36 ChD 243; *Spicer v Martin* (1888) 14 App Cas 12; *Mackenzie v Childers* (1889) 43 ChD 265; *White v Bijou Mansions Ltd* [1938] Ch 351, [1938] 1 All ER 546. For recent successful schemes, see *Baxter v Four Oaks Properties Ltd* [1965] Ch 816, [1965] 1 All ER 906, p. 802, post; *Re Dolphin's Conveyance* [1970] Ch 654, [1970] 2 All ER 664, p. 802, post; *Eagling v Gardner* [1970] 2 All ER 838; *Brunner v Greenslade* [1971] Ch 993, [1970] 3 All ER 833; *Texaco Antilles Ltd v Kernochan* [1973] AC 609, [1973] 2 All ER 118; *Re 6, 8, 10 and 12 Elm Avenue, New Milton* [1984] 1 WLR 1398, [1984] 3 All ER 632; cf. *Lund v Taylor* (1975) 31 P & CR 167, p. 805, post, especially STAMP LJ at 176; *Kingsbury v LW Anderson Ltd* (1979) 40 P & CR 136, p. 806, n. 14, post. This is in marked contrast to the usual fate of schemes during the previous four decades; Preston and Newsom, pp. 48–68.

[6] *Reid v Bickerstaff* [1909] 2 Ch 305 at 319; *Re Dolphin's Conveyance* [1970] Ch 654 at 663, [1970] 2 All ER 664 at 670, per STAMP J.

[7] *Brunner v Greenslade* [1971] Ch 993 at 1005, [1970] 3 All ER 833 at 842.

specific requirements need to be observed to one in which there must be a defined area and "the existence of the common interest and the common intention actually expressed in the conveyances themselves"[8].

In *Elliston v Reacher* [1908] 2 Ch 374 PARKER J said at 384:

"I pass, therefore, to the consideration of the question whether the plaintiffs can enforce these restrictive covenants. In my judgment, in order to bring the principles of *Renals v Cowlishaw* (1878) 9 ChD 125 and *Spicer v Martin* (1888) 14 App Cas 12 into operation it must be proved (1) that both the plaintiffs and defendants derive title under a common vendor: (2) that previously to selling the lands to which the plaintiffs and defendants are respectively entitled, the vendor laid out his estate, or a defined portion thereof (including the lands purchased by the plaintiffs and defendants respectively), for sale in lots subject to restrictions intended to be imposed on all the lots, and which, though varying in details as to particular lots, are consistent and consistent only with some general scheme of development[9]; (3) that these restrictions were intended by the common vendor to be and were for the benefit of all the lots intended to be sold, whether or not they were also intended to be and were for the benefit of other land retained by the vendor[10]; and (4) that both the plaintiffs and the defendants, or their predecessors in title, purchased their lots from the common vendor upon the footing that the restrictions subject to which the purchases were made were to enure for the benefit of the other lots included in the general scheme whether or not they were also to enure for the benefit of other lands retained by the vendors. If these four points be established, I think that the plaintiffs would in equity be entitled to enforce the restrictive covenants entered into by the defendants or their predecessors with the common vendor irrespective of the dates of the respective purchases. I may observe, with reference to the third point, that the vendor's object in imposing the restrictions must in general be gathered from all the circumstances of the case, including in particular the nature of the restrictions. If a general observance of the restrictions is in fact calculated to enhance the values of the several lots offered for sale, it is an easy inference that the vendor intended the restrictions to be for the benefit of all the lots, even though he might retain other land the value of which might be similarly enhanced, for a vendor may naturally be expected to aim at obtaining the highest possible price for his land. Further, if the first three points be established, the fourth point may readily be inferred, provided the purchasers have notice of the facts involved in the three first points, but if the purchaser purchases in ignorance of any material part of those facts, it would be difficult, if not impossible, to establish the fourth point. . . .

It is, I think, enough to say, using Lord Macnaghten's words in *Spicer v Martin* (1888) 14 App Cas 12, that where the four points I have mentioned

---

[8] *Re Dolphin's Conveyance*, supra at 664, at 671; *Lund v Taylor* (1975) 31 P & CR 167 at 178.

[9] See *Jackson v Bishop* (1979) 48 P & CR 57 (developer held liable for breach of covenant of title and negligence where there was a double conveyance due to inaccurate plans of neighbouring plots).

[10] The reservation to the vendor of the right to sell land free from the restriction is of little force either for or against the existence of a building scheme: *Re Wembley Park Estate Co Ltd's Transfer* [1968] Ch 491 at 498, [1968] 1 All ER 457 at 460; *Eagling v Gardner* [1970] 2 All ER 838.

are established, the community of interest imports in equity the reciprocity of obligation which is in fact contemplated by each at the time of his own purchase.''

A further requirement was added in *Reid v Bickerstaff* [1909] 2 Ch 305, where Cozens–Hardy MR said at 319:

''In my opinion there must be a defined area within which the scheme is operative. Reciprocity is the foundation of the idea of a scheme. A purchaser of one parcel cannot be subject to an implied obligation to purchasers of an undefined and unknown area. He must know both the extent of his burden and the extent of his benefit. Not only must the area be defined, but the obligations to be imposed within that area must be defined. Those obligations need not be identical. For example, there may be houses of a certain value in one part and houses of a different value in another part. A building scheme is not created by the mere fact that the owner of an estate sells it in lots and takes varying covenants from various purchasers. There must be notice to the various purchasers of what I may venture to call the local law imposed by the vendors upon a definite area[11].''

In *Baxter v Four Oaks Properties Ltd* [1965] Ch 816, [1965] 1 All ER 906 there was no evidence that the common vendor ''laid out the part of his estate . . . in plots before beginning to sell it off. He appeared to have sold plots, of the size which purchasers wished to take, to purchasers as they came along''. Cross J held that there was a scheme, having found sufficient evidence of an intention to create mutually binding covenants, although Parker J's second requirement was not observed.

RE DOLPHIN'S CONVEYANCE
[1970] Ch 654, [1970] 2 All ER 664 (ChD, Stamp J)[12]

The Selly Hill Estate, of some 30 acres near Birmingham, became vested in fee simple in Ann and Mary Dolphin as tenants in common. In 1871 they sold off four parcels, and each purchaser entered into a restrictive covenant with them that only detached dwelling houses, each of at least one-quarter acre, should be built on the land. The vendors covenanted to procure similar covenants from subsequent purchasers of any other part of the estate. Ann Dolphin died in 1873, leaving by will her interest in the unsold part of the estate to her nephew, John Watts. In 1876 John became owner in fee simple in possession when Mary Dolphin made a deed of gift to him of her share. He then sold off the remainder of the estate in six parcels, in each case taking a restrictive covenant, and, except for the last parcel, giving a covenant to procure similar covenants from subsequent purchasers.

---

[11] See also Buckley LJ at 323; *Torbay Hotel Ltd v Jenkins* [1927] 2 Ch 225 at 240, per Clauson J.
[12] (1970) 86 LQR 445 (P.V.B.); 117 SJ 798 (G. H. Newsom). For the modification of these covenants under LPA 1925, s. 84, see *Re Farmiloe's Application* (1983) 48 P & CR 317, p. 821, post.

In 1969 part of the estate was purchased by Birmingham Corporation, whose predecessor in title had purchased part in 1871 from Ann and Mary, and part in 1877 from John. The Corporation wished to build in breach of the covenants, of which it had notice. It sought a declaration that the land was no longer subject to them, and argued that there was no building scheme, since there was no common vendor, and no lotted plan prior to the sales.

Held. There was a scheme, and the covenants were binding.

STAMP J: As Cross J pointed out in the course of the judgment in *Baxter v Four Oaks Properties Ltd* [1965] Ch 816, [1965] 1 All ER 906, . . . the intention that the several purchasers from a common vendor shall have the benefit of the restrictive covenants imposed on each of them, may be evidenced by the existence of a deed of mutual covenant to which all the several purchasers are to be parties. That common intention may also be evidenced by, or inferred from, the circumstances attending the sales: the existence of what has often been referred to in the authorities as a building scheme. I have been referred to a considerable number of authorities where the court has had to consider whether there were, or were not, present in the particular case those facts from which a building scheme — and, therefore, the common intention to lay down a local law involving reciprocal rights and obligations between the several purchasers — could properly be inferred. In *Elliston v Reacher* [1908] 2 Ch 374, 384, Parker J laid down the necessary concomitants of such a scheme.

What has been argued before me is that here there is neither a deed of mutual covenant nor a building scheme. In the latter connection, it is pointed out that there was not a common vendor, for the parcels were sold off, first by the Dolphins and then by Watts. Nor, prior to the sales, had the vendors laid out the estate, or a defined portion of it, for sale in lots. Therefore, so it is urged, there were not present the factors which, on the authority of *Elliston v Reacher* [1908] 2 Ch 374, p. 801, ante, are necessary before one can find the existence of a building scheme.

In my judgment, these submissions are not well-founded. To hold that only where you find the necessary concomitants of a building scheme or a deed of mutual covenant can you give effect to the common intention found in the conveyances themselves, would, in my judgment, be to ignore the wider principle on which the building scheme cases are founded and to fly in the face of other authority of which the clearest and most recent is *Baxter v Four Oaks Properties Ltd* [1965] Ch 816, [1965] 1 All ER 906. The building scheme cases stem, as I understand the law, from the wider rule that if there be found the common intention and the common interest referred to by Cross J at 825, at 913 in *Baxter v Four Oaks Properties Ltd* the court will give effect to it, and are but an extension and example of that rule. Hall V-C remarked in his judgment in *Renals v Cowlishaw* (1878) 9 ChD 125 at 129:

"This right exists not only where the several parties execute a mutual deed of covenant, but wherever a mutual contract can be sufficiently established. A purchaser may also be entitled to the benefit of a restrictive covenant entered into with his vendor by another or others where his vendor has contracted with him that he shall be the assign of it, that is, have the benefit of the covenant. And such contract need not be express, but may be collected from the transaction of sale and purchase."

That passage was quoted, with approval, by Lord Macnaghten in *Spicer v Martin* (1889) 14 App Cas 12, 24. (I ought perhaps to mention that the word "contract" in the last sentence I have quoted was substituted for the word "covenant" in the errata in the volume of the reports in which *Renals v Cowlishaw* is reported.) Moreover, where deeds of mutual covenant have fallen to be considered, effect has been given not to the deed of mutual covenant itself as such but to the intention evidenced by its existence. *Baxter v Four Oaks Properties Ltd* is such a case. As Parker J in *Elliston v Reacher* [1908] 2 Ch 374 at 384 pointed out in a passage quoted by Cross J in *Baxter v Four Oaks Properties Ltd* the equity arising out of the establishment of the four points which he mentioned as the necessary concomitants of a building scheme has been sometimes explained by the implication of mutual contracts between the various purchasers and sometimes by the implication of a contract between each purchaser and the common vendor, that each purchaser is to have the benefit of all the covenants by the other purchasers, so that each purchaser is in equity an assign of the benefit of those covenants; but the implication of mutual contracts is not always a satisfactory explanation. Parker J in *Elliston v Reacher* . . . points out that a prior purchaser may be dead or incapable of contracting at the time of a subsequent purchase, and that in any event it is unlikely that the prior and subsequent purchasers are ever brought into personal relationship, and yet the equity may exist between them.

There is not, therefore, in my judgment, a dichotomy between the cases where effect has been given to the common intention inferred from the existence of the concomitants of a building scheme and those where effect has been given to the intention evidenced by the existence of a deed of covenant. Each class of case, in my judgment, depends upon a wider principle. Here the equity, in my judgment, arises not by the effect of an implication derived from the existence of the four points specified by Parker J in *Elliston v Reacher*, or by the implication derived from the existence of a deed of mutual covenant, but by the existence of the common interest and the common intention actually expressed in the conveyances themselves.

In *Nottingham Patent Brick and Tile Co v Butler* (1885) 15 QBD 261 at 268, Wills J, in a passage which I find illuminating and which was referred to with approval in the Court of Appeal (1886) 16 QBD 778, put the matter thus: "The principle which appears to me to be deducible from the cases is that where the same vendor selling to several persons plots of land, parts of a larger property, exacts from each of them covenants imposing restrictions on the use of the plots sold without putting himself under any corresponding obligation, it is a question of fact whether the restrictions are merely matters of agreement between the vendor himself and his vendees, imposed for his own benefit and protection, or are meant by him and understood by the buyers to be for the common advantage of the several purchasers. If the restrictive covenants are simply for the benefit of the vendor, purchasers of other plots of land from the vendor cannot claim to take advantage of them. If they are meant for the common advantage of a set of purchasers, such purchasers and their assigns may enforce them inter se for their own benefit. Where, for instance, the purchasers from the common vendor have not known of the existence of the covenants, that is a strong, if not a conclusive, circumstance to shew that there was no intention that they should enure to their benefit. Such was the case in *Keates v Lyon* (1869) 4 Ch App 218; *Master v*

Hansard (1876) 4 ChD 718; and *Renals v Cowlishaw* (1879) 11 ChD 886. But it is in all cases a question of intention at the time when the partition of the land took place, to be gathered, as every other question of fact, from any circumstances which can throw light upon what the intention was: *Renals v Cowlishaw*. One circumstance which has always been held to be cogent evidence of an intention that the covenants shall be for the common benefit of the purchasers is that the several lots have been laid out for sale as building lots, as in *Mann v Stephens* (1846) 15 Sim 377; *Western v MacDermott* (1866) 2 Ch App 72; *Coles v Sims* (1853) Kay 56, 5 De GM & G 1; or, as it has been sometimes said, that there has been 'a building scheme': *Renals v Cowlishaw* (1879) 11 ChD 866 at 867."

I can approach the matter in another way. The conveyances of the several parts of the estate taking the form they do, and evidencing the same intention as is found in a deed of mutual covenant, I equate those conveyances with the deed of mutual covenant considered by Cross J in *Baxter v Four Oaks Properties Ltd* [1965] Ch 816, [1965] 1 All ER 906 — the deed which he did not treat for the purposes of his judgment as itself bringing all the successive purchasers and persons claiming through them into contractual relations one with the other, but as showing the common intention. So equating them, I follow what I conceive to be the ratio decidendi of *Baxter v Four Oaks Properties Ltd* and give effect to that intention by holding that the restrictive covenants are enforceable by the successors in title of each of the original covenantors against any of them who purchased with notice of those restrictions.

In *Lund v Taylor* (1975) 31 P & CR 167[13], the Court of Appeal (RUSSELL and STAMP LJJ and Sir John PENNYCUICK) held that no scheme of development could be inferred. STAMP LJ (delivering the judgment of the Court) said at 176:

"Because there was no extrinsic evidence, nor anything in his own conveyance to show a purchaser that there was a scheme relating to a defined area or that Tellings [the vendors], if they did, intended that stipulations should be imposed in respect of each part of that area, he could not on the authority of *Reid v Bickerstaff* [1909] 2 Ch 305 be subject to an implied obligation to the other purchasers. On this ground alone the action must in our opinion fail. Whatever scheme involving reciprocal rights and obligations Tellings may have sought to establish, the necessary evidence that the several purchasers intended to be bound by a scheme or local law under which they were to have reciprocal rights and obligations is lacking. The difficulties of the plaintiffs in this regard are perhaps emphasised when one observes that whatever inference you may draw from the conveyances there is nothing in them from which a purchaser could draw the inference that Tellings intended to confer on a purchaser a right to prevent Tellings from dealing as they thought fit — e.g. by the erection of a block of flats — with the unplotted part of the estate. . . .

Because it was submitted that in recent times the courts, in determining whether the necessary ingredients of a building scheme or local law are shown to have existed, have adopted what was called a more liberal approach than was formerly the case it is right that we should refer to the two

---

[13] *Harlow v Hartog* (1977) 245 EG 140 (no scheme of development due to no estate plan).

cases relied upon in support of that submission. They are *Baxter v Four Oaks Properties Ltd* [1965] Ch 816, [1965] 1 All ER 906 and *Re Dolphin's Conveyance* [1970] Ch 654, [1970] 2 All ER 664. In both those cases it had been submitted that in order to establish a building scheme the requirements laid down by Parker J in *Elliston v Reacher* [1908] 2 Ch 374 must be satisfied. One of those requirements was, and we quote Parker J's judgment, that 'in order to bring the principles of *Renals v Cowlishaw* and *Spicer v Martin* into operation it must be proved . . . (2) that previously to selling the lands to which the plaintiffs and defendants are respectively entitled the vendor laid out his estate or a defined portion thereof (including the land purchased by the plaintiffs and defendants respectively) for sale in lots subject to restrictions intended to be imposed on all the lots. . . .'

In his judgment in *Baxter v Four Oaks Properties Ltd* Cross J rejected the condition that the defined estate should have been laid out for sale in lots. He pointed out that *Elliston v Reacher* was not a case in which there was direct evidence afforded by the execution of a deed of mutual covenant that the parties intended a building scheme but *whether one could properly infer that intention in all the circumstances.* Cross J took the view, also adopted in *Re Dolphin's Conveyance*, that Mr Justice Parker was not intending to lay down that the fact that the common vendor did not bind himself to sell off the defined area to which the local law was to apply in lots of any particular size but proposed to sell off parcels of various sizes according to the requirements of the various purchasers must, as a matter of law, preclude the court from giving effect to a clearly proved intention that the purchasers were to have rights *inter se* to enforce the provisions of the local law over the area.

In *Re Dolphin's Conveyance*, in which the *Baxter v Four Oaks* case was followed, the area over which the scheme or local law was to extend was specified and the intention that the purchasers were to have rights *inter se* to enforce the stipulations of the local law was, so the judge thought, expressed clearly in every conveyance. The stipulations which each purchaser covenanted to observe in the several conveyances were identical[14] and the first and every subsequent conveyance by the vendor contained a covenant by him, in effect, to obtain a covenant from every other purchaser to observe them; a useless series of covenants except upon the basis that all could enforce them. It would, no doubt, have been better if the draftsman of the conveyances in that case had added the words 'to the intent that the covenants by the purchasers shall be mutually enforceable' and if a plan had been attached showing the area affected by the scheme; but the judge found a sufficient indication of that intention and a sufficient identification of that area.

No doubt the last mentioned two cases are authorities for the proposition that Mr Justice Parker, in the well known passage of his judgment in *Ellison v Reacher*, did not intend to lay down that the fact that the common vendor did not bind himself to sell off the defined area to which the local law was to apply in lots of any particular size was fatal to the creation of a local law over that area, but rather that if the vendor has done so you have one of the necessary ingredients from which the creation of the local law may be

---

[14] In *Kingsbury v LW Anderson Ltd* (1979) 40 P & CR 136, the scheme failed where covenants imposed on some plots were expressed to be by way of indemnity only, and on others by way of absolute covenant.

inferred. And where you find that all those concerned — the vendor and the several purchasers — have by the effect of the documents they have executed evidenced the intention to create such a local law over a defined area those cases are authority for saying that the court may give effect to that intention. But we find nothing in those cases indicating that the conditions from which a "building scheme" may be inferred from the facts are any different than was formerly the case.

In the instant case the creation of a building scheme cannot for the reasons we have given be inferred; and there is absent from the deeds themselves that clear evidence of intention to create reciprocal rights and obligations over a defined area which was found in *Baxter v Four Oaks Properties Ltd* and in the *Dolphin's Conveyance* cases.

We allow the appeal."

Preston and Newsom: *Restrictive Contracts Affecting Freehold Land* (7th edn. 1982), pp. 61–64.

"If the scheme of local law is modern, the common vendor may be called to give evidence of his own intention[15]. Or evidence may be given by someone who was closely involved with the transactions of the common vendor[16]. In the Lands Tribunal a common vendor has given evidence himself on at least one occasion[17]. Where a scheme is old, there may well be no documents at all except the formal conveyancing instruments, and often only a few of them. The proportion of conveyancing documents that survive varies enormously. In *Dolphin's* case [1970] Ch 654, [1970] 2 All ER 664, almost all of them had been found, though nothing else survived. In the *Wembley Park* case [1968] Ch 491, [1968] 1 All ER 457, a great many conveyancing instruments were in evidence. In the *Texaco* case [1973] AC 609, [1973] All ER 118, where the estate was of some 500 lots, only four conveyances were put in and one of them was of about 300 lots expressed to be subject to no restrictions at all. Nevertheless the scheme was upheld. On the other hand in *White v Bijou Mansions Ltd* [1938] Ch 351, [1938] 1 All ER 546, Lord Greene MR commented adversely on the fact that only two conveyances were available, and the scheme was not upheld. In *Baxter's* case [1965] Ch 816, [1965] 1 All ER 906, the intention of mutuality was evidenced by a deed of mutual covenant.

In regard to the extrinsic evidence, where it survives, a lotted plan is one of the ingredients from which the creation of a local law may be inferred[18]. The same would no doubt be true of a set of particulars and conditions of sale showing that all the lots were to be taken subject to the relevant paragraphs of a set of standard stipulations. A print of a common form of contract or of conveyance would point in the same direction, though the mere fact that the conveyances are broadly in a common form is not by itself enough[19]. The actual evidence in *Elliston v Reacher* itself is always worth study if one has to

---

[15] *Kelly v Battershell* [1949] 2 All ER 830, per COHEN LJ at 839.
[16] *Page v Kings Parade Properties Ltd* [1967] 20 P & CR 710; evidence was given by the conveyancing managing clerk of the solicitors for the alleged common vendor.
[17] *Re Emery's Application* (1956) 8 P & CR 113; this evidence was accepted as a substitute for a lotted plan.
[18] *Lund v Taylor* (1975) 31 P & CR 167, p. 805, ante.
[19] *Re Wembley Park Estate Co Ltd's Transfer* [1968] Ch 491, [1968] 1 All ER 457.

consider a case in which extrinsic evidence is going to be important. In *White v Bijou Mansions Ltd*, Lord Greene MR said that 'an auction sale with provisions for each purchaser to give the same covenants is strong evidence of the intention.'

To conclude this review of the principles underlying the doctrine of schemes, two requirements are essential and are universally insisted upon, *viz.* (i) that the area shall be defined; (ii) that the purchasers from the person who creates the scheme shall purchase on the footing that all purchasers shall be mutually bound by, and mutually entitled to enforce, a defined set of restrictions (varying no doubt to some extent as between lots). A common vendor is usual, but there may be cases in which the purpose of this requirement can be met by some other state of the title. A covenant is probably necessary and a lotted map probably is a great help; but again the purposes which these requirements serve can perhaps be fulfilled in other ways. None of these elements is necessarily decisive in itself or even in combination if the scheme fails for want of either of the two essentials. . . .

Elliston v Reacher appeared to have put the doctrine into something like a final shape, and during the next 60 years schemes were always discussed in terms of the judgment of Parker J in that case. But in retrospect it now seems clear that that judgment was treated too narrowly as defining what came to be known as the rule in *Elliston v Reacher*. This rule was applied with great precision. Thus in *Lawrence v South County Freeholds Ltd* [1939] Ch 656, [1939] 2 All ER 503, Simonds J at 674, at 519 described the doctrine as 'this very artificial branch of the law,' and alleged schemes were held to fail in a remarkable number of cases[20]. Some of these decisions were indeed highly artificial and at least two of the cases (*Re Pinewood Estate, Farnborough* and *Page v Kings Parade Properties Ltd*) might very well be decided otherwise today. Between *Elliston v Reacher* in 1908 and *Baxter v Four Oaks Properties Ltd* in 1965 there appear to be only two reported cases in which schemes were upheld. One of them was *Bell v Norman C Ashton Ltd* (1956) 7 P & CR 359 in 1956, a freehold case noticed above, and the other was a leasehold scheme in *Newman v Real Estate Debenture Corpn* [1940] 1 All ER 131. Of this last case Cohen LJ said in *Kelly v Battershell* [1949] 2 All ER 830 at 842 that it is 'the high water mark of cases where a scheme can be inferred.' Since *Baxter's* case, the courts have been prepared to approach the question of a scheme more broadly[1] appealing to *Renals v Cowlishaw* and *Spicer v Martin* rather than to *Elliston v Reacher*. Although the alleged schemes failed to be upheld in the *Wembley Park* case[2], and in *Lund v Taylor* (1975) 31 P & CR 167 these decisions were based

---

[20] See *Reid v Bickerstaff* [1909] 2 Ch 305; *Willé v St. John* [1910] 1 Ch 84, 325; *Browne v Flower* [1911] 1 Ch 219; *Torbay Hotel Ltd v Jenkins* [1927] 2 Ch 225; *Ridley v Lee* [1935] Ch 591; *White v Bijou Mansions Ltd* [1938] Ch 351, [1938] 1 All ER 546; *Lawrence v South County Freeholds Ltd* [1939] Ch 656, [1939] 2 All ER 503; *Re Pinewood Estate, Farnborough* [1958] Ch 280, [1957] 2 All ER 517; *Page v Kings Parade Properties Ltd* (1967) 20 P & CR 710; *Re Wembley Park Estate Co Ltd's Transfer* [1968] Ch 491, [1968] 1 All ER 475.

[1] But, curiously, in *Eagling v Gardner* (1970) 21 P & CR 723, decided six weeks after *Dolphin's* case, neither that case nor *Baxter's* case seems to have been cited, and the decision of the learned judge was founded entirely upon *Elliston v Reacher*.

[2] If *Federated Homes Ltd v Mill Lodge Properties Ltd* [1980] 1 WLR 594, [1980] 1 All ER 371, was correctly decided the *Wembley Park* case must have been decided wrongly. For, though there was no scheme, the covenants must have been annexed to the land which the common vendor retained at the date of his conveyance to the applicants' predecessor in title. Thus an order under LPA 1925, s. 84 (2) declaring the covenants unenforceable cannot have been right.

on the fundamental ground that there was no defined area[3]. In *Baxter's* case itself and also in *Dolphin's* case schemes were upheld notwithstanding the absence of lotting, and in the *Texaco* case notwithstanding a considerable scarcity of evidence. The doctrine of schemes, which had become very fragile through excessive reliance on *Elliston v Reacher*, has been given new vitality by the appeal to the principles of the earlier decisions. Nevertheless the limits to what can be enforced as a scheme are set by the two fundamental requirements upon which the court always insists."

QUESTIONS

1. Why have the strict technicalities which grew up in relation to restrictive covenants been relaxed in favour of a general rule based on the intention of the parties? *Re Dolphin's Conveyance* [1970] Ch 654, [1970] 2 All ER 664, p. 802, ante; *Brunner v Greenslade* [1971] Ch 993, [1970] 3 All ER 833; *Lund v Taylor* (1975) 31 P & CR 167, p. 805, ante; [1972 B] CLJ 157 (H. W. R. Wade).
2. Are restrictive covenants in schemes of development registrable? (1928) 78 LJ 39 (J.M.L.); (1933) 77 SJ 550: (1950) 20 Conv (NS) 370 (R. G. Rowley); *Emmet on Title* (18th edn. 1983), pp. 552–553; Farrand, *Contract and Conveyance* (2nd edn.), pp. 420–421; Barnsley, *Conveyancing Law and Practice* (2nd edn. 1982), p. 348; Preston & Newsom, pp. 66–68; *Freer v Unwins Ltd* [1976] Ch 288, [1976] 1 All ER 634, p. 831, n. 20, post.
3. Which of the three views of the construction of LPA 1925, s. 78, as set out in the *Federated Homes* case [1980] 1 WLR 594 at 604, [1980] 1 All ER 371 at 378 (p. 779, ante) do you prefer? See the articles at p. 777, n. 5, and [1972 B] CLJ 151 (H.W.R. Wade).

C. Third Party as Covenantee

LAW OF PROPERTY ACT 1925

56. Persons taking who are not parties and as to indentures. — (1) A person may take an immediate or other interest in land or other property, or the benefit of any condition, right of entry, covenant or agreement over or respecting land or other property, although he may not be named as a party to the conveyance or other instrument.

The effect of this section, when it applies, is to make into a covenantee a person claiming the benefit of the covenant, even though he was not a party to the instrument in which the covenant was contained. The situation here is therefore different from those discussed under the previous heading. They dealt with situations in which the benefit of a covenant could pass on a conveyance to a purchaser of the land. Once, however, the benefit of a covenant is given to a person by section 56 (1), the benefit can then pass to his successors in title by annexation or assignment under the rules described above.

---

[3] In the latter case an indication against a scheme was found in the fact that these were provisions requiring the common vendor's consent for such things as lopping trees after the estate was fully developed.

In *Beswick v Beswick* [1968] AC 58, [1967] 2 All ER 1197, Lord UPJOHN said at 102, at 1221: "Section 56 of the Law of Property Act 1925, has a long history behind it. Section 56 replaced section 5 of the Real Property Act 1845, which amended some very ancient law relating to indentures inter partes, so I shall start by stating the common law on the subject.

The rule was that a grantee or covenantee, though named as such in an indenture under seal expressed to be made inter partes, could not take an *immediate* interest as grantee nor the benefit of a covenant as covenantee unless named as a party to the indenture. This rule, as the authorities I shall quote show, applied not only to real estate but to personal grants and covenants.

But how narrow this rule was, but equally, how well understood, will also be shown by those authorities.

[His Lordship referred to *Scudamore v Vandenstene* (1587) 2 Co Inst 673; *Cooker v Child* (1673) 2 Lev 74; *Berkeley v Hardy* (1826) 5 B & C 355 and continued:]

In *Forster v Elvet Colliery Co Ltd* [1908] 1 KB 629 at 639 Farwell LJ pointed out that the old rule of law still holds good that no one can sue on a covenant in an indenture who is not mentioned as a party to it, except so far as it had been altered by the Real Property Act 1845. Substituting a reference to section 56 for the Act of 1845 that statement, I suppose, is still true.

In 1844 Parliament abrogated this rule by section 11 of the Transfer of Property Act 1844, which enacted:

'That it shall not be necessary in any case to have a deed indented; and that any person, not being a party to any deed, may take an immediate benefit under it in the same manner as he might under a deed poll.'

For whatever reason, this short workmanlike section, which plainly applied to all covenants whether relating to realty or personal grants or covenants, never had any operation, for it was repealed by the Real Property Act 1845, and replaced by section 5 of that Act in these terms:

'That, under an indenture, executed after 1 October 1845, an immediate estate or interest, in any tenements or hereditaments, and the benefit of a condition or covenant, respecting any tenements or hereditaments, may be taken, although the taker thereof be not named a party to the same indenture; . . .'

No one has ever suggested that that section was intended to do more than supplant the old common law rule relating to indentures inter partes in relation to realty.

Then came the great changes in the law of real property; the Law of Property Act 1922, and the Law of Property (Amendment) Act 1924. The researches of counsel have not revealed any amendment in those Acts to section 5 of the Act of 1845. The Law of Property Act 1925 was a consolidation Act consolidating those and many earlier Acts. It repealed section 5 of the Act of 1845 and replaced it by section 56 (1)."

Since a person who takes advantage of section 56 is treated as an original covenantee, it is essential that he should be in existence and identifiable at the time when the covenant was made; the section cannot be used to give the benefit of a covenant to future purchasers, for they could not be made covenantees[4]. Indeed, no enactment is needed to guard the interests of future purchasers, for they can obtain the benefit of existing covenants by virtue of the rules of annexation, or express assignment of the benefit of the covenant. The person who would suffer, apart from section 56 or the existence of a scheme of development, is the owner of adjoining land which needs protection from the covenant and which may have been sold to an earlier purchaser of the land sold off in plots by a common vendor.

Assume that X owns a piece of land, Blackacre, which he is selling off in plots, in circumstances which do not give rise to the existence of a scheme of development. Plot 1 is bought by A, who covenants, in terms appropriate to annex the benefit of the covenant to each and every part of the land retained by X, not to use the premises as a fish shop; plot 2 is bought by B who gives a similar covenant, and similarly plot 3 by C. B opens a fish shop. X of course can sue as covenantee; C will be able to sue as being the purchaser of land to which the benefit of the covenant is annexed; but A will not, for the benefit of B's covenant, being given later, was not annexed to the piece of land which he bought. Later purchasers, in other words, can sue earlier purchasers; earlier purchasers cannot sue later. Earlier purchasers can be given the right to sue by section 56. The safe way to do so is to draft the later covenants in such a way as to purport expressly to covenant with "A, his heirs and assigns, successors in title, owners for the time being of (plot 1) land adjoining the premises now sold." Some cases require that the benefit could only be taken by a person "to whom that . . . instrument purports to grant something or with which (*sic*) some agreement or covenant is purported to be made[5]". It appears, however, that the rule is wider than this, and that a person can take the benefit if he is an existing person who, from the circumstances of the case, was clearly intended by the parties to be benefited or, in the case of a covenant which runs with the land, is an assignee of such a person. This will not, however, cover the ordinary case of the prior purchaser, unless there is an indication of an intention to benefit him. The application of section 56 to cases concerning "other property" is a matter beyond the scope of this work[6].

RE ECCLESIASTICAL COMMISSIONERS FOR ENGLAND'S CONVEYANCE
[1936] Ch 430 (ChD, Luxmoore J)

An originating summons was brought under section 84 (2) Law of Property Act 1925[7], to decide whether West Heath House, in the ownership of the

---

[4] *Smith and Snipes Hall Farm Ltd v River Douglas Catchment Board* [1949] 2 KB 500, [1949] 2 All ER 179. See also *Pinemain Ltd v Welbeck International Ltd* (1984) 272 EG 1166 (benefit of covenant to sue surety on contract of guarantee not within s. 56, since plaintiffs were not identifiable when covenant was made); cf. *Wiles v Banks* (1983) 50 P & CR 80 (plaintiff identifiable).

[5] *White v Bijou Mansions Ltd* [1937] Ch 610 at 625, [1937] 3 All ER 269 at 277; affd. [1938] Ch 351, [1938] 1 All ER 546, p. 813, post; *Re Ecclesiastical Commissioners for England's Conveyance* [1936] Ch 430, infra.

[6] Cheshire and Fifoot, *Law of Contract* (10th edn.), pp. 411–414; Treitel, *Law of Contract* (6th edn.), pp. 488–490; *Beswick v Beswick* [1968] AC 58, [1967] 2 All ER 1197, esp. Lord Pearce at 93–94, at 1215–1216, and Lord Upjohn at 102–107, at 1221–1224; (1967) 30 MLR 687 (G. H. Treitel).

[7] See p. 823, post.

applicants, was bound by any, and if so, what, restrictive covenants. The applicants were successors in title of one Gotto who purchased in 1887 from the Ecclesiastical Commissioners giving the following covenant:

"The said Henry Gainsford Gotto doth hereby . . . covenant with the said Ecclesiastical Commissioners and their successors" (in such a way as to annex the benefit of the covenant to the land retained by the vendor) "and also as a separate covenant with their assigns owners for the time being of land adjoining or adjacent to the said land hereby conveyed in manner following, that is to say:" A number of covenants followed.

Some of the defendants were successors in title to land adjoining or adjacent to the applicants' house and which had been bought from the Ecclesiastical Commissioners before the conveyance of 1887. It was as to the position of these defendants that the main issue in the case arose.

Held. The owners of adjacent and adjoining lands and their successors in title were able to enforce the covenants although they or their predecessors in title were not parties to the conveyance of 1887.

Luxmoore J: The questions to be determined are: (1) were any restrictions imposed on West Heath House before or by the conveyance of 21 April 1887; (2) were such restrictions imposed for the benefit of any, and what other hereditaments; and (3) who are the persons, if any, now entitled to the benefit of such restrictive covenants? It is not contended by any of the parties that West Heath House forms part of a larger estate which has been subjected to what is usually referred to as a building scheme, and it is quite plain that there is not sufficient evidence on which it could be argued with any hope of success that such a scheme existed. . . .

Having ascertained that restrictive covenants were imposed in respect of the West Heath House property and that the form of the covenants is such as to make the burden of them run with the land, it is necessary to consider whether they were imposed for the benefit of any and what other hereditaments. For it is well settled that, apart from any building scheme, restrictive covenants may be enforced if they are expressed in the original deed to be for the benefit of a particular parcel or particular parcels of land, either expressly mentioned or clearly identified in the deed containing the original covenants. It was argued on behalf of the applicants that the right to enforce such covenants is limited to the original covenantees and their successors in title — the right in the case of the successors in title being limited to those whose land was the property of the original covenantees at the date when the covenants were imposed. It was also argued that the right to enforce the covenants did not extend to any owners of land who were neither express assignees of the benefit of the covenants, nor successors in title of the original covenantees in respect of land acquired by such successors from the Ecclesiastical Commissioners subsequent to the date of the deed by which the covenants were imposed. I think these arguments failed to give due consideration to the provisions of section 5 of the Real Property Act, 1845, as repealed and re-enacted by section 56 of the Law of Property Act, 1925. Section 5 of the Act of 1845 provides that under an indenture, executed after 1 October 1845, the benefit of a condition or covenant respecting any tenements or hereditaments may be taken, although the taker thereof be not named as a party to the indenture. In the case of *Forster v Elvet Colliery Co Ltd* [1908] 1 KB 629, it was held that the condition or covenant referred to in the section must, in order to be enforceable by a person not a party to the deed, be one the benefit of which runs with the land of the person seeking to enforce it. The actual decision was upheld in the House of Lords under the name *Dyson v Forster* [1909] AC 98, but Lord Macnaghten expressed doubt whether the section ought to be so restricted. He refrained however from resolving the doubt, because he agreed with the view that the covenants in the particular case ran with the land and it was therefore unnecessary to do so.

The alteration which has been made in the verbiage of section 5 of the 1845 Act by section 56 of the 1925 Act, has not in my opinion affected the position so as to limit the right of a person not a party to the deed to enforce covenants affecting land to those which run with the land. The material words are as follows: "A person may take . . . the benefit of any condition . . . covenant or agreement . . . respecting land or other property, although he may not be named as a party to the conveyance or other instrument." It seems to me that the effect of these words is to enlarge the scope of the earlier words, for it extends the rights of a person not a party to a deed to covenants affecting every kind of property personal as well as real. So far as every species of personal property other than leasehold is concerned it is obvious that the covenants to be enforced cannot be restricted to those running with the property, for there are no such covenants. What it is necessary to consider is the true construction of the conveyance of 21 April 1887, in order to ascertain whether any persons, not parties thereto, are described therein as the covenantees, and whether such covenants are expressed to affect any and what hereditaments. To determine what is the true construction of that document it is necessary to consider the surrounding circumstances as they existed at the date when it was executed.

[His Lordship then examined the circumstances existing at the date of execution of the deed and concluded that the covenants were enforceable by the original covenantees, and persons deriving title under them; that the original covenantees need not have been parties to the conveyance of 1887; but that such persons could only enforce the covenant if they held land adjoining or adjacent to the applicants' house.]

WHITE *v* BIJOU MANSIONS LTD
[1937] Ch 610, [1937] 3 All ER 269, *affirmed* [1938] Ch 351,
[1938] 1 All ER 546 (Simonds J, ChD) (CA, Sir Wilfrid Greene MR,
Luxmoore and Farwell JJ)

The owners of the Shaftesbury House Estate conveyed part of it in 1887 to James Israel Fellows. Fellows covenanted that he would build a dwelling house for a certain sum and would use it only as a private dwelling house or as a residence and place of practice of a medical man. The vendors covenanted that every building lease or future sale should include covenants from the lessee or purchaser with the builders imposing similar restrictions on the use of the land, though certain parts were to be permitted to be used as shops. The plaintiff was the successor in title to Fellows.

In 1890, a nearby plot was conveyed to Nicholson, who covenanted for himself, his heirs, executors, administrators and assigns with the intent to bind himself and his successors in title and the owner for the time being of the property thereby conveyed with the vendors, their heirs and assigns, that the piece of land thereby conveyed should be used for the purpose of a private dwelling house only. This plot was later conveyed to Miss Plumbly who, in

1935, leased it to two ladies for a term of 28 years; the lease contained a covenant that no part of the demised premises would be used for any purpose other than a private dwelling house or for private suites or flats. The lease was in due course assigned to the defendants who used the house for flatlets. The action was for an injunction to restrain a breach of covenant.

Held (by SIMONDS J and the Court of Appeal). The plaintiff was not entitled to the benefit of the covenant given by Nicholson in the conveyance of 1890.

SIMONDS J (in the court of first instance): . . . Then the question arises: Can the plaintiff here enforce that covenant? I turn to look at it once more. There are covenants entered into in the year 1890, the first with the Davidsons, the second with the Daws, and they are covenants which are not annexed to any particular parcel of land. They are covenants entered into four years after the plaintiff acquired the title to his land. They are covenants the benefit of which has not expressly or by implication, or in any manner whatsoever, been assigned to the plaintiff, and it appears to me to be quite impossible, apart from any building scheme or from the special statutory provision to which I shall presently refer, that the plaintiff can avail himself of this covenant and enforce it. There is here no question of a building scheme. . . .

It remains to consider the only other ground on which, as it appears to me, Mr Grant can possibly rest his case. He claims that he is entitled to enforce this covenant, entered into on 2 May 1890, on the ground that either under section 5 of the Real Property Act 1845, or under section 56 of the Law of Property Act 1925, that right is conferred on him. In the view which I take of both these sections it is unnecessary for me to consider whether he is in any way entitled to call in aid section 56 of the Act of 1925, with regard to covenants or agreements contained in a deed executed in 1890. It is necessary for me to say something about the earlier section before I come to consider the later section.

Section 5 of the Real Property Act 1845, which was, as its title suggests, an Act to amend the law of real property, was aimed at remedying certain mischiefs in the state of the common law as it then was. There was a highly technical and artifical rule that by an indenture, as distinguished from a deed poll, an immediate interest in land could not be granted in favour of a grantee unless that grantee was a party to the deed. That mischief this section was designed to remedy. Further, there was the defect, as it was supposed, in the common law, that a person could not take advantage of a covenant in a deed unless he was a party to the deed. Be it observed that the Act of 1845 dealt with real property. This section was confined to the case of an indenture, and of an immediate interest created by that indenture, for it was never the law that an estate in remainder could not be validly granted in favour of a grantee if he were not a party. Indeed the common form of settlement then for centuries in vogue had limited estates in remainder not only to persons not parties to the deed but to persons not yet in existence.

[His Lordship read section 5 and continued:] I think the important aspect of that section for my present purpose is this. It appears to me to be quite plain that the section has a limited operation. It is intended to confer a benefit only on those persons to whom the deed purports to grant an estate or interest or those persons with whom there purports to be a covenant or agreement. It is impossible, in my view, to regard this section as creating a benefit in favour of any persons who may like to avail themselves of it and say: "It we can take advantage of this it will be for our benefit." It seems to me clear that this section was intended merely to provide that A.B., the grantee under a deed, might take an immediate interest although he was not a party, and similarly that A.B., with whom the covenant was purported to be made by the deed, should be able to avail himself of it although he was not a party to the deed, and in the few cases which have arisen under this section since 1845 — and there appear to be very few — it will be found in every case where it has been applied that it has been in favour of a person who although not a party to the deed was a person to or with whom a grant or covenant purported to be made. That was the position under the Act of 1845.

I now turn to consider section 56 of the Act of 1925, which, it is said, however inaptly, takes the place of the earlier section. [His Lordship read subsection 1 and continued:] I think many difficulties may well arise on that section which do not fall to me to-day to solve. It appears to one at once that, so far as any other than an immediate interest in land is concerned the section is superfluous, because a person always could take another interest in land though not a party. It is at least a question how far such a provision is necessary at all in the case of personalty. Without deciding it, I should be disposed to think that equitable estates even in land were not subject to the old artificial rule and it is very doubtful if an interest in personalty was ever so subject. However that may be, for the purposes of the present case I think I am only concerned with one aspect of this question. Just as under section 5 of the Act of 1845 only that person could call it in aid who, although not a party, yet was a grantee or covenantee, so under section 56 of this Act only that person can call it in aid who, although not named as a party to the conveyance or other instrument, is yet a person to whom that conveyance or other instrument purports to grant some thing or with which [*sic*] some agreement or covenant is purported to be made. To give it any other meaning appears to me to open the door to claims or assertion of rights which cannot have been contemplated by the Legislature, for if that be not the limitation which must be imposed on this section, it appears to me that there is no limit and it will be open to anybody to come into court and say: "Here is a covenant which if enforced will redound to my advantage, therefore I claim the benefit of the section. I claim that this covenant or condition is one which should be enforced in my favour because it is for my benefit, whether intended for my benefit or not intended for my benefit would not appear to matter." I cannot give to the section any such meaning as that. I interpret it as a section which can be called in aid only by a person in whose favour the grant purports to be made or with whom the covenant or agreement purports to be made[8]. If that is so, whether the plaintiff's claim arises under the earlier or the later Act, he cannot sue on it in this Court because he is not a person who, under the deed of 1890, can point to any grant or any covenant purported to be made to or with him. That is the construction which I place on section 56, with the result that the plaintiff's claim must fail.

In the Court of Appeal, where SIMONDS J's decision was upheld, Sir Wilfrid GREENE MR said at 365, at 554: "Whatever else section 56 may mean, it is, I

---

[8] Similarly per CROSSMAN J in *Re Foster* [1938] 3 All ER 357 at 365; per DILLON J in *Lyus v Prowsa Developments Ltd* [1982] 1 WLR 1044 at 1049, [1982] 2 All ER 953 at 958.

think, confined to cases where the person seeking to take advantage of it is a person within the benefit of the covenant in question, if I may use that phrase. The mere fact that somebody comes along and says: 'It would be useful to me if I could enforce that covenant' does not make him a person entitled to enforce it under section 56. Before he can enforce it he must be a person who falls within the scope and benefit of the covenant according to the true construction of the document in question.''

In *Stromdale and Ball Ltd v Burden* [1952] Ch 223, [1952] 1 All ER 59, the defendant, Mrs Burden, was under-lessee of a house of three storeys at 40 Romford Road, Stratford for an unexpired term of 45 years, the bottom floor of which was used as a café. In 1946, she sold the goodwill of the café business to two persons and granted to them a sub-lease of the ground floor. In 1948, the tenants arranged to sell their business to the plaintiff company. They obtained the consent of the defendant to the assignment of their lease in a deed dated March 1948 to which the defendant, the tenants, and Charles William Stromdale and Stanley Ball (directors of the plaintiff company) were parties. The company was not a party. The deed provided inter alia that the company should have an option to purchase the unexpired term of years in the premises held by the defendant.

In June 1948, the tenants assigned the residue of their lease to the plaintiff company, but the assignment contained no reference to the option.

In August 1948, the plaintiff company gave notice of intention to exercise the option, and in December 1949, brought this action for specific performance.

DANCKWERTS J held that the plaintiff company, although not a party to the instrument granting the option, could enforce it under section 56 (1) Law of Property Act 1925, and said at 233, at 64: "Mr Brightman argues . . . that section 56 of the Law of Property Act, 1925, enables the plaintiff company to take such an interest in land as is created by an option to purchase though not a party to the document conferring the option. In support of this argument, he referred me to certain decisions in which the provisions of the section were considered. In *White v Bijou Mansions Ltd* [1937] Ch 610, [1937] 3 All ER 269, p. 813, ante, a case concerned with covenants restricting the use of land, Simonds J, referring to section 5 of the Real Property Act 1845, after saying that the section had a limited operation, said: 'It is intended to confer a benefit only on those persons to whom the deed purports to grant an estate or interest or those persons with whom there purports to be a covenant or agreement', and he went on to say that the section did not create a benefit in favour of any persons who might like to avail themselves of it. With regard to section 56 of the Law of Property Act 1925, Simonds J said: [His Lordship quoted the four sentences set out on p. 815, ante from 'It appears to one at once that . . .' to '. . . is purported to be made'; and continued:]

In the same case, in the Court of Appeal, Sir Wilfrid Greene MR said: 'Whatever else section 56 may mean, it is, I think, confined to cases where the person seeking to take advantage of it is a person within the benefit of the covenant in question, if I may use that phrase.'

It seems to me that those statements of the limited effect of section 56 of the Law of Property Act 1925 do none the less exactly cover the situation of the plaintiff company in the present case. I have not overlooked the decision of

Crossman J in *Re Foster* [1938] 3 All ER 357 expressly declining to treat section 56 as creating such an enormous change in the law as to enable an agreement by A with B to pay money to C to be enforced by C. But it seems to me that in the present case the intention of clause 4 of the deed of licence is to enable the person therein named, the plaintiff company, and no one else, to obtain the leasehold interest of the defendant in No. 40 Romford Road. In the language of Simonds J, the plaintiff company is a person to whom the instrument purports to grant some thing or with which some agreement or covenant is purported to be made. Section 56 provides that a person may take an immediate or other interest in land or the benefit of any covenant or agreement over or respecting land, although he may not be named as a party to the instrument. It is difficult to see what the intention of clause 4 of the deed of licence was if it was not to confer on the plaintiff company an interest in No. 40 Romford Road and to give to the plaintiff company the benefit of the covenant or agreement conferring an option to acquire the defendant's leasehold interest. The question decided in *Woodall v Clifton* [1905] 2 Ch 257, namely, whether an option to acquire the reversion in fee simple on a leasehold term ran with the leasehold term in the hands of an assignee of the reversion or of the term, seems to me to be a different matter. In the present case, for the purposes of section 56, the 'land' is No. 40 Romford Road, and an option to purchase a leasehold interest in this land seems to me to create an interest in that land and to be an agreement respecting that land, and so to be within the precise words of the section. I do not understand why the words 'agreement respecting land' should not be given their plain meaning. An option to purchase land is an agreement respecting land. Accordingly, I reach the conclusion that the provisions of section 56 of the Law of Property Act 1925 enable the plaintiff company to enforce the option in the present case."

In *Drive Yourself Hire Co (London) Ltd v Strutt* [1954] 1 QB 250, [1953] 2 All ER 1475, DENNING LJ, said obiter at 271, at 1481: "Mr Montague Waters argued, however, that section 56 must be limited to persons 'with whom some agreement or covenant is purported to be made', relying on the observations of Simonds J in *White v Bijou Mansions Ltd* [1937] Ch 610, [1937] 3 All ER 269, p. 813, ante. If the covenant had been formally expressed to be 'with' the superior landlord, it would, he said, have been enforceable by the superior landlord, although he was not a party: but as it was not so expressed, it was not enforceable. But, as Somervell LJ pointed out in the course of the argument, that may be too narrow an interpretation to place on the words used by Simonds J. Enforceability does not depend on the form of the obligation, but on the substance of it. A covenant is, for this purpose, sufficiently made 'with' a person if it is, on the face of it, made directly for his benefit in such circumstances that it was intended to be enforceable by him. In support of this view, I would refer to the recent case of *Stromdale and Ball v Burden*, where Danckwerts J, as one ground of his judgment, held that an option to purchase was enforceable by a company as an 'agreement respecting land', although the company was not a party to the instrument and the agreement was not expressed in terms to be 'with' the company[9]."

---

[9] See also *Re Nesawood Properties' Ltd and Boltmore Properties' Ltd Application* [1975] JPL 733.

The question arises again here, whether a covenant, the benefit of which is given to the plaintiff under section 56, is annexed to the plaintiff's land. It is annexed if the covenantor purports to covenant separately with the plaintiff using language appropriate for annexation, as in *Re Ecclesiastical Commissioners for England's Conveyance* [1936] Ch 430, p. 811, ante; or if section 78 of the Law of Property Act 1925 is held to apply[10]. Where there is no "separate covenant", there appears to be no authority. The section allows the plaintiff to take the benefit of the covenant between other parties, and presumably the question of annexation to the plaintiff's land will turn upon the same factors as that of annexation to the land of the covenantee.

IV.   Declaration, Discharge and Modification[11]

A.   The Position Apart from Statute

i.   CHANGE IN CHARACTER OF NEIGHBOURHOOD. NON-ENFORCEMENT

CHATSWORTH ESTATES CO *v* FEWELL[12]
[1931] 1 Ch 224 (ChD, FARWELL J)

The predecessors in title of the plaintiffs, owners of Compton Place, Eastbourne, had sold land to the predecessors in title of the defendant subject to various covenants, of which the defendant had notice when he purchased, one of which was that he would not use the land "otherwise than as a private dwelling house". The land was on the sea front at Eastbourne, and various owners of adjoining land, which had also been purchased subject to the same covenant from the predecessors in title of the plaintiffs, had, with their consent, used the land for a school, for flats, and in three cases where the circumstances were exceptional for boarding houses. The defendant opened a guest house called Bella Vista; his attention was drawn to the covenant, and he was given an opportunity to apply under section 84 of the Law of Property Act 1925 for the modification of the covenant. He did nothing and this action was for an injunction and damages. The defendant admitted the breach and contended that the covenants were not enforceable for two reasons:

(i)   by reason of the change in the general character of the neighbourhood, whereby the object of those covenants had completely disappeared.

(ii)   by reason of the fact that this change had been brought about by the acts and omissions of the plaintiffs and their predecessors in title.

Held. The plaintiffs were entitled to an injunction.

FARWELL J: Nothing can be said against the defendant's conduct of his establishment except that it is a breach of covenant. That being so ought I to refuse the plaintiffs relief?

---

[10] *Federated Homes Ltd v Mill Lodge Properties Ltd* [1980] 1 WLR 594, [1980] 1 All ER 371, p. 777, ante.

[11] C & B, pp. 594–600; M & W, pp. 793–796; MM, pp. 456–458; Preston and Newsom, pp. 188 et seq.

[12] (1948) 92 SJ 570.

The defendant's first ground of defence is that there has been such a complete change in the character of the neighbourhood, apart 'from the plaintiffs' acts or omissions, that the covenants are now unenforceable. But to succeed on that ground the defendant must show that there has been so complete a change in the character of the neighbourhood that there is no longer any value left in the covenants at all. A man who has covenants for the protection of his property cannot be deprived of his rights thereunder merely by the acts or omissions of other persons unless those acts or omissions bring about such a state of affairs as to render the covenants valueless, so that an action to enforce them would be unmeritorious, not bona fide at all, and merely brought for some ulterior purposes. It is quite impossible here to say that there has been so complete a change in the character of this neighbourhood as to render the covenants valueless to the plaintiffs. Whether right or wrong the plaintiffs are bringing this action bona fide to protect their property, and it is hopeless to say that the change in the character of the neighbourhood is so complete that it would be useless for me to give them any relief.

The defendant really relied on the acts and omissions of the plaintiffs and their predecessors as a bar to equitable relief. Now the plaintiffs are not unduly insistent on the observance of these covenants in this sense, that they do not conduct inquisitorial examinations into their neighbours' lives, and do not make it their business to find out very carefully exactly what is being done, unless the matter is brought to their notice, either by complaints of other inhabitants, or by seeing some board or advertisement. I cannot think ˈ that plaintiffs lose their rights merely because they treat their neighbours with consideration. They are doing what they think sufficient to preserve the character of the neighbourhood. Whether they do enough is another matter, but I am quite satisfied that they are not intending, by their acts or omissions, to permit this area to be turned into anything other than a mainly residential area. There is no doubt however that they have permitted breaches of covenant in several cases where houses have been turned into flats, they have permitted at least four houses to be carried on as boarding-houses or hotels, and they have not prevented — in some cases because they did not know of them — some half a dozen other houses being used as boarding houses or guest houses.

There are still however a very large number of private dwelling houses in the area, and I am satisfied that while the use of Bella Vista as a guest house or boarding house may not at the moment cause any actual damage to Compton Place or its owners, there is a prospect of damage in the future if the defendant is allowed to continue to use Bella Vista in that way, because it might well lead to many other houses being so used which would undoubtedly damnify the owners of Compton Place, especially if they develop the park and grounds as intended. In that way it will certainly be detrimental to the plaintiffs to permit Bella Vista to be used as a guest house. But whether they are entitled to relief depends on the exact effect of their past acts and omissions.

Now, as stated in many authorities, the principle upon which this equitable doctrine rests is that the plaintiffs are not entitled to relief if it would be inequitable to the defendant to grant it. In some of the cases it is said that the plaintiffs by their acts and omissions have impliedly waived performance of the covenants. In other cases it is said that the plaintiffs, having acquiesced in past breaches, cannot now enforce the covenants. It is in all cases a question of degree. It is in many ways analogous to the doctrine of estoppel, and I think it is a fair test to treat it in that way and ask, "Have the plaintiffs by their acts and omissions represented to the defendant that the covenants are no longer enforceable and that he is therefore entitled to use his house as a guest house?[13]"

ii.   UNITY OF SEISIN

In *Texaco Antilles Ltd v Kernochan* [1973] AC 609, [1973] 2 All ER 118, Lord CROSS OF CHELSEA said at 624, at 125:

"Their Lordships now turn to the 'unity of seisin' point which was the main ground upon which the appellants founded their contention that the restrictions were not binding on them. As stated above from 12 January 1942 until 12 November 1951, Chapmans Ltd owned both the lots now owned by the respondents and also the lots now owned by the appellants. As soon as the two sets of lots came into the same hands it became impossible for any action to enforce the covenants to be brought by the owner of one set against the owner of the other since he was the same person and that fact, so the argument runs, put an end to the restrictions so far as concerned the relations of the two sets of lots inter se. . . .

The point of law which arises for consideration is therefore whether in a case where there is nothing in the conveyance putting an end to the unity of seisin or in the surrounding circumstances to indicate that the restrictions in the scheme are no longer to apply as between the owners of the lots previously in common ownership the fact that they have been in common ownership puts an end to the restrictions so far as concerns the relations of subsequent owners for the time being of that part of the estate inter se so that if the common owner of those lots wished them to apply after the severance he would have to reimpose them as fresh restrictions under a sub-scheme relating to them. It would their Lordships think be somewhat unfortunate if this was the law. . . . It is no doubt true that if the restrictions in question exist simply for the mutual benefit of two adjoining properties and both those properties are bought by one man the restrictions will automatically come to an end[14] and will not revive on a subsequent severance unless the common owner then recreates them. But their Lordships cannot see that it follows from this that if a number of people agree that the area covered by all their properties shall be subject to a 'local law' the provisions of which shall be enforceable by any owner for the time being of any part against any other owner and the whole area has never at any time come into common ownership an action by one owner of a part against another owner of a part must fail if it can be shown that both parts were either at the inception of the scheme or at any time subsequently in common ownership. The view which

---

[13] See also *Westripp v Baldock* [1939] 1 All ER 279; *Shaw v Applegate* [1977] 1 WLR 970, [1978] 1 All ER 123, where an injunction was refused against the original covenantor on grounds of acquiescence, but damages were awarded. BUCKLEY LJ said at 978, at 131: "The real test, I think, must be whether upon the facts of the particular case, the situation has become such that it would be dishonest or unconscionable for the plaintiff, or the person having the right sought to be enforced, to continue to seek to enforce it."

[14] *Re Tiltwood, Sussex* [1978] Ch 269, [1978] 2 All ER 1091; (1980) 54 ALJ 156 (G. M. Bates); (1982) 56 ALJ 587 (A. A. Preece); *Re Victoria Recreation Ground, Portslade's Application* (1979) 41 P & CR 119.

their Lordships favour is supported by dicta of Sir H. H. Cozens-Hardy MR in *Elliston v Reacher* [1908] 2 Ch 665 at 673 and of Simonds J in *Lawrence v South County Freeholds Ltd* [1939] Ch 656 at 677, 683, [1939] 2 All ER 503, at 520, 524, but at the time when this case was heard by the Court of Appeal there was no decision on the point. Subsequently, however, in *Brunner v Greenslade* [1971] Ch 993, [1970] 3 All ER 833 which raised the point, Megarry J followed those dicta. The appellants submitted that his decision was wrong but in their Lordships' view it was right."

B. Law of Property Act 1925, Section 84[15]

Under section 84 (2) the court may be asked to declare whether land is affected by a restrictive covenant, and, under section 84 (1) the Lands Tribunal[16] has power in its discretion to modify or discharge such a covenant. Section 84 was substantially amended by Law of Property Act 1969, section 28, extending the powers of the Lands Tribunal to cover a situation where a restrictive covenant which prevents some reasonable use of land confers no substantial benefit on anyone or is contrary to the public interest. Compensation may be ordered in some cases. The section is printed as amended, and the alterations shown in italic.

LAW OF PROPERTY ACT 1925

84. Power to discharge or modify restrictive covenants affecting land. — (1) The *Lands Tribunal* shall (without prejudice to any concurrent jurisdiction of the court) have power from time to time, on the application of any person interested in any freehold land affected by any restriction arising under covenant[17] or otherwise as to the user thereof or the building thereon, by order wholly or partially to discharge or modify any such restriction on being satisfied —

> (*a*) that by reason of changes in the character of the property or the neighbourhood[18] or other circumstances of the case[19] which the *Lands Tribunal* may deem material, the restriction ought to be deemed obsolete; or
>
> (*aa*) that (*in a case falling within subsection (1A) below*) the continued existence thereof would impede *some* reasonable user of the land for

---

[15] See also Housing Act 1985, s. 610 (1), (2); *Josephine Trust Ltd v Champagne* [1963] 2 QB 160, [1962] 3 All ER 136; TCPA 1971, s. 127; Local Government Act 1972, ss. 120 (3), 124 (2). Applications made under the section are noted in Current Law under the heading "Real Property and Conveyancing", and in the Journal of Planning and Environment Law. Some are reported in P & CR and the Estates Gazette. Condensed reports of all applications from 1974–1979 appeared in *Lands Tribunal Cases*. For a detailed commentary, see Preston and Newsom, chap. 7; [1974] JPL 72, 130; [1975] JPL 644; [1976] JPL 407; [1979] JPL 64; [1981] JPL 551, 656; [1982] JPL 552 (G. H. Newsom).

[16] On the Lands Tribunal generally, see *Jones, The Lands Tribunal* (1982); its address is 48/49 Chancery Lane, London WC2.

[17] The covenant may be personal only: *Shepherd Homes Ltd v Sandham (No 2)* [1971] 1 WLR 1062, [1971] 2 All ER 1267; *Gilbert v Spoor* [1983] Ch 27, [1982] 2 All ER 576.

[18] *Keith v Texaco Ltd* (1977) 34 P & CR 249 (coming of oil industry to Aberdeenshire).

[19] *Re Cox's Application* [1985] JPL 564 (covenant requiring occupiers of extension of house in East Sussex to be domestic staff employed for service in the house held absolute).

.   public or private purposes or, as the case may be, would unless
modified so impede such user; or

(*b*)   that the persons of full age and capacity for the time being or from
time to time entitled to the benefit of the restriction, whether in
respect of estates in fee simple or any lesser estates or interests in the
property to which the benefit of the restriction is annexed, have
agreed, either expressly or by implication[20], by their acts or omissions, to the same being discharged or modified; or

(*c*)   that the proposed discharge or modification will not injure the
persons entitled to the benefit of the restriction[1];

*and an order discharging or modifying a restriction under this subsection may direct the
applicant to pay to any person entitled to the benefit of the restriction such sum by way of
consideration[2] as the Tribunal may think it just to award under one, but not both, of the
following heads, that is to say, either —*

(i)   *a sum to make up for any loss or disadvantage suffered by that person in
consequence of the discharge or modification; or*

(ii)   *a sum to make up for any effect which the restriction had, at the time when it
was imposed, in reducing the consideration then received for the land affected by
it.*

(1A)   *Subsection (1) (aa) above authorises the discharge or modification of a
restriction by reference to its impeding some reasonable user of land in any case in which
the Lands Tribunal is satisfied that the restriction, in impeding that user, either —*

(*a*)   *does not secure to persons entitled to the benefit of it any practical benefits of
substantial value or advantage to them; or*

(*b*)   *is contrary to the public interest;*

*and that money will be an adequate compensation for the loss or disadvantage (if any)
which any such person will suffer from the discharge or modification.*

(1B)   *In determining whether a case is one falling within subsection (1A) above, and
in determining whether (in any such case or otherwise) a restriction ought to be discharged
or modified, the Lands Tribunal shall take into account the development plan and any
declared or ascertainable pattern for the grant or refusal of planning permissions in the
relevant areas, as well as the period at which and context in which the restriction was
created or imposed and any other material circumstances.*

(1C)   *It is hereby declared that the power conferred by this section to modify a
restriction includes power to add such further provisions restricting the user of or the
building on the land affected as appear to the Lands Tribunal to be reasonable in view of
the relaxation of the existing provisions, and as may be accepted by the applicant; and the
Lands Tribunal may accordingly refuse to modify a restriction without some such
addition[3].*

---

[20] See *Re Memvale Securities Ltd's Application* (1975) 223 EG 689; *Re Fettishaw's Application (No. 2)*
(1973) 27 P & CR 292.

[1] *Re Forestmere Properties Ltd's Application* (1980) 41 P & CR 390 ("replacement of one eyesore
(Odeon cinema) by another could hardly be said to be an improvement"); *Re Bailey's
Application* (1981) 42 P & CR 108 ("quaint rural backwater" not to be changed into riding
school with attendant manure and noise including sound of human voice); *Re Livingstones'
Application* (1982) 47 P & CR 462 ("eyesore" carport).

[2] In *SJC Construction Co Ltd v Sutton London Borough Council* (1975) 29 P & CR 322, STEPHENSON LJ
said, arguendo, that "consideration" was probably a mis-print for "compensation": Preston
and Newsom, p. 222.

[3] *Re Patten Ltd's Application* (1975) 31 P & CR 180; *Re Dransfield's Application* (1975) 31 P & CR
192; *Re Kershaw's Application* (1975) 31 P & CR 187; *Re Banks Application* (1976) 33 P & CR 138;
Re Forestmere Properties Ltd's Application (1980) 41 P & CR 390; *Re Austin's Application* (1980) 42
P & CR 102.

(2) The court shall have power on the application of any person interested —

    (*a*) to declare whether or not in any particular case any freehold land is, *or would in any given event be*, affected by a restriction imposed by any instrument; or

    (*c*) to declare what, upon the true construction of any instrument purporting to impose a restriction, is the nature and extent of the restriction thereby imposed and whether the same is, *or would in any given event be*, enforceable and if so by whom.

(3) The *Lands Tribunal* shall, before making any order under this section, direct such enquiries, if any, to be made of any *government department or* local authority, and such notices, if any, whether by way of advertisement or otherwise, to be given to such of the persons who appear to be entitled to the benefit of the restriction intended to be discharged, modified, or dealt with as, having regard to any enquiries, notices, or other proceedings previously made, given or taken, the *Lands Tribunal* .may think fit.

(3A) *On an application to the Lands Tribunal under this section the Lands Tribunal shall give any necessary directions as to the persons who are or are not to be admitted (as appearing to be entitled to the benefit of the restriction) to oppose the application, and no appeal shall lie against any such direction; but rules under the Lands Tribunal Act 1949 shall make provision[4] whereby, in cases in which there arises on such an application (whether or not in connection with the admission of persons to oppose) any such question as is referred to in subsection (2) (a) or (b) of this section, the proceedings on the application can and, if the rules so provide, shall be suspended to enable the decision of the court to be obtained on that question by an application under that subsection, or by means of a case stated by the Lands Tribunal, or otherwise, as may be provided by those rules or by rules of court.*

(5) Any order made under this section shall be binding on all persons, whether ascertained or of full age or capacity or not, then entitled or thereafter capable of becoming entitled to the benefit of any restriction, which is thereby discharged, modified or dealt with, and whether such persons are parties to the proceedings or have been served with notice or not.

(8) This section applies whether the land affected by the restrictions is registered or not, but, in the case of registered land, the Land Registrar shall give effect on the register to any order under this section *in accordance with the Land Registration Act 1925*.

(9) Where any proceedings by action or otherwise are taken to enforce a restrictive covenant, any person against whom the proceedings are taken, may in such proceedings apply to the court for an order giving leave to apply to the *Lands Tribunal* under this section, and staying the proceedings in the meantime.

(12) Where a term of more than forty years is created in land (whether before or after the commencement of this Act) this section shall, after the expiration of twenty-five years of the term, apply to restrictions affecting such leasehold land in like manner as it would have applied had the land been freehold:

Provided that this subsection shall not apply to mining leases.

---

[4] Lands Tribunal Rules 1975 (SI 1975, No. 299); Lands Tribunal (Amendment) Rules 1977 (SI 1977 No. 1820); 1981 (SI 1981 No. 105); (Amendment No. 2) Rules 1981 (SI 1981 No. 600); Lands Tribunal (Amendment) Rules 1984 (SI 1984 No. 793).

In *Ridley v Taylor* [1965] 1 WLR 611, [1965] 2 All ER 51, HARMAN LJ said at 617, at 55:

"Section 84 (1) of the Law of Property Act, 1925, primarily applies to restrictions on freehold land, but by subsection (12), as amended by the Landlord and Tenant Act, 1954, is made applicable to restrictions affecting leasehold land where a term of more than 40 years is created by the lease of which more than 25 years have expired. It seems to me that it should be more difficult to persuade the court to exercise its discretion in leasehold than in freehold cases[5]. In the latter the court is relaxing in favour of a freeholder's own land restrictions entered into for the benefit of persons owning other land. In the former the land in question is the property of the covenantee who is prima facie entitled to preserve the character of his reversion. Section 84 cases usually arise between the assigns of both the benefit and the burden of the covenant, and one may suppose that the section was designed with a view to cases within the doctrine of *Tulk v Moxhay*, but there is nothing in the language of the section to limit the power of the court to a case where the lessee is not himself bound by contract, and I do not feel able to say that such a covenant cannot be modified under the section, although it seems to me that the court should be slow to relieve an applicant of covenants which he himself has entered into. Were it otherwise, it would be easy to avoid the effect of the section by an assignment. It is to be observed that what is to be discharged or modified is not the covenant, but any restriction under the covenant, and it was suggested that this would leave direct contractual liability untouched. This would produce an extraordinary result in a case where the restriction was modified in favour of an assign if the covenantee could still sue the original covenantor in damages on his contractual liability although he had parted with all interest in the property. I cannot but think that the covenant must, where an order is made, be treated in all respects as modified or discharged."

(1979) 129 NLJ 523 (H. W. Wilkinson)

"In *Re Bass Ltd's Application* (1973) 26 P & CR 156, the Tribunal (J. S. Daniel QC) accepted the submission of counsel, Graham Eyre QC, that the questions which properly arose [under subsection (1) (*aa*)] were:

1. Is the proposed user reasonable?
2. Do the covenants impede that user?
3. Does impeding the proposed user secure practical benefits to the objectors?
4. If yes, are those benefits of substantial value or advantage?
5. Is impeding the proposed user contrary to the public interest?
6. If no, would money be an adequate compensation?
7. If yes, would money be an adequate compensation?

In considering questions 3 to 7 inclusive, regard must be had to the planning context, by subsection (1B).

The questions will be discussed in the order of formulation.

---

[5] "Since 1950, something over a dozen of cases under s. 84 (12) have appeared in P & CR and in about two-thirds of them the lessee has succeeded": Preston & Newsom, p. 263. See, e.g., *Re Briarwoods Estates Ltd* (1979) 39 P & CR 419; *Re EMI (Social Centres) Ltd's Application* (1979) 39 P & CR 421; *Re Forestmere Properties Ltd's Application* (1980) 41 P & CR 390.

1. *Is the proposed user reasonable?*

In the *Bass* case (1973) the applicants sought the modification of a covenant in order to allow them to use some of their land for the loading and unloading of 228 articulated lorries daily — a 'trunker park'. There had been objections from over 200 nearby house owners. The Tribunal considered that the purpose of the restriction was to make a '*cordon sanitaire* of residential buildings masking any new industrial development'. The applicants already had planning permission for the development and the Tribunal said that 'planning permissions are very persuasive in this connection' though it must not be thought that the question of reasonable user 'could always be concluded in the affirmative by the production of a planning permission'. Partly because of the need for businesses in the area to be provided with communications it was held that the proposed user was reasonable.

The first hurdle is not usually difficult for an applicant to surmount. It is not easy for an objector to establish that there is anything unreasonable about a wish to build houses or flats or to extend a legitimate business enterprise. The requirement of reasonableness was satisfied in all the following cases (though not all the applications eventually succeeded):

Re John Twiname Ltd's Application (1972) 23 P & CR 413; covenant imposed in 1924 not to build within 200 feet of a mansion house, The Towers, which was now four habitations and had two pairs of semi-detached houses in its grounds. A proposal to build three pairs of semis and three detached houses within 200 feet of the house was held to be reasonable.

Re Beardsley's Application (1972) 25 P & CR 233; covenant imposed in 1922 forbade the building of more than two private residences on the site. A proposed development of 12 flats, each with a garage, was held to be reasonable.

Re Carter's Application (1973) 25 P & CR 542; infilling with a second house of conventional design in keeping with the other houses on the site held to be reasonable although there was a covenant against putting more than one dwelling house on the plot.

Re Osborn's and Easton's Application (1978) 38 P & CR 251; restrictions were imposed on two sites in 1913 to ensure that not more than one house was put on to each plot. A proposal to erect two blocks of flats to make 20 flats on one and 12 on the other was held reasonable[6].

2. *Do the covenants impede that user?*

If the applicant did not consider that the covenant impeded or was likely to impede his proposed development he would not make the application under section 84 (1) and if the objector did not feel that the covenant impeded the user he would not object. An affirmative answer to question 2 will almost invariably follow an affirmative answer to question 1. If there is doubt about whether any land is affected by a restriction, or about the nature and extent of the restriction the appropriate procedure is to apply for construction of the restriction, under section 84 (2).

3. *Does impeding the proposed user secure practical benefits to the objectors?*

The following decisions may help to give meaning to the phrase 'practical benefits'. The statute is silent on the matter.

---

[6] See also *Re Manxguard Ltd's Application* [1982] JPL 521 (restriction imposed in 1862 on use of building in Saltburn-by-the-Sea as a public house modified to convert it into Victorian style inn).

(a) Loss of privacy and view

A proposed block of flats would have had a 'devastating effect' on the amenities and value of a house as the house's principal rooms would face it and be overlooked by it, *Re Mercian Housing Society's Application* (1971) 23 P & CR 116.

Gardens of existing houses would be overlooked by two proposed houses. One garden could be screened to some extent by a hawthorn hedge but as the Tribunal said, a hawthorn is a poor substitute for a covenant, *Re Gossip's Application* (1925) 25 P & CR 215[7].

(b) Increase in density

Covenants allowed one house per acre, the proposal was to put 32 houses onto four acres. It was held that this would be alien to the character of the area, 'it is not merely the arithmetic of the density which matters, but the general effect on the amenity of the area', *Re Collins' Application* (1974) 30 P & CR 527.

A proposal to build ten houses on backland where covenants would allow none was refused. It would otherwise result in objectors finding 'dumped virtually on their back doors a group of houses with no apparent visual relationship with their own properties', *Re Patten Ltd's Application* (1975) 31 P & CR 180.

(c) Other loss of amenity

A proposed block of 12 flats would deprive the objectors of space, quiet, light and some sunlight, *Re Ward's Construction (Medway) Ltd's Application* (1973) 25 P & CR 223; another proposal would deprive objectors of 'peace and quiet and the feeling of openness which the restriction gave them', *Re Davies' Application* (1971) 25 P & CR 115. Both applications failed[8].

A local authority which had granted planning permission for six flats in a two-storey block objected validly that the block would injure the view from an old people's dwelling which they proposed to erect on the dominant land, *Re SJC Construction Co Ltd's Application* (1974) 28 P & CR 200.

Increased traffic, noise, fumes, vibration, dirt and the risk of accidents were important factors against the applicants in *Re Bass* (1973)[9].

(d) Loss of value

Loss of amenity will often cause loss of value but the fact that it does not is not a reason for holding that the covenant does not secure a practical advantage. In *Re Collins* (1974) it was not disputed that the proposed development would not reduce the market value of existing houses. Nevertheless it was accepted as important that the objectors regarded the restrictions as having substantial advantage, some having bought their houses in reliance on them. Indeed in *Re Munday's Application* (1954) 7 P & CR

---

[7] See also *Re Banks Application* (1976) 33 P & CR 138 ("direct view of the sea is of immense value"); *Re Bovis Homes Southern Ltd's Application* [1982] JPL 368 (beauty and aesthetic and historic interest of National Trust house and its setting); *Gilbert v Spoor* [1983] Ch 27, [1982] 2 All ER 576 (resplendent view over Tyne Valley from road *adjacent* to objector's land); [1984] Conv 429 (P. Polden).

[8] *Re Ballamy's Application* [1977] JPL 456 ("enjoyment of evening sunshine in the sun-lounge").

[9] See also *Re Crest Homes plc's Application* (1983) 48 P & CR 309 (proposal to build twelve houses to replace neglected Edgware Lawn Tennis Club would cause undesirable increase in housing density and change area from semi-rural to urban); *Re Lake's Application* [1984] JPL 887 (proposal to erect split-level house in Lyme Regis would be design out of character with surroundings).

130 (a claim to declare a covenant obsolete) it was likely that a successful application would increase the value of the objectors' property by giving it a potential commercial user. The claim failed however as it was clear that the personal tastes of the objectors would be adversely affected if the covenant was lifted.

(e) "Thin end of the wedge" argument

It can be a relevant consideration that the proposal, though not particularly harmful in itself, must be rejected in case it gives rise to similar proposals which would succeed because the first had done so, and which would cumulatively be disadvantageous. In *Re Gossip* (1972) the applicant had converted two houses into flats in breach of covenant and now wished to build two further houses in their gardens. He argued that there had already been some breaches of covenant by other house-owners by conversions of single houses into flats but the Tribunal considered that these breaches had been minimal whereas a modification might be the "thin end of the wedge" for a considerable change in the amenities and character of the neighbourhood. The recent case of *Re Osborn* (1979) illustrates this consideration along with several others. The applicants wished to erect two three-storey blocks of flats on a large estate of eight-bedroomed houses. Sixty-three owners of such houses objected. It was held that if the applications were granted it would set an undesirable precedent for other developments on the estate, particularly as there was much profit in such developments. Other important considerations were that the building would be out of place in a high value, low density, single house estate; that the flats would be visually injurious there; and that the traffic noise generated by the greater numbers of people would be injurious.

The validity of the "thin end of the wedge" argument is not universally accepted. In *Re Forgacs' Application* (1976) 32 P & CR 464, Mr J. H. Emlyn-Jones FRICS in his judgment quoted what he said in *Re Gaffney's Application* (1974) 35 P & CR 440 to the effect that if a modification is in itself unlikely to cause injury it should not be refused on the ground that later applications might do so. They should each be looked at on the merits when they arise and should then be rejected if need be[10].

4.   *Are the benefits secured by the restrictions of substantial value or advantage to the objectors?*

The use of the words 'value or advantage' in harness was said by the Tribunal in *Re Bass* (1973) to indicate that pecuniary values are not the only things to be considered in this context and *Re Collins* (1974) and *Re Munday* (1954) support this[11]. However, the benefits secured must be substantial. In *Re Dransfield's Application* (1975) 31 P & CR 192 the objector, in seeking to uphold a covenant made by the applicant himself only 20 years earlier, claimed that the proposed house would obstruct the view from the rear windows of his house and from the first floor terrace where he frequently entertained guests. It was held that the restriction which prevented building

---

[10] See also *Re Chapman's Application* (1980) 42 P & CR 114; *Re Farmiloe's Application* (1983) 48 P & CR 317.

[11] *Re Matcham's Application* [1981] JPL 431 (house built on tranquil site because of wife's severe migraine).

did not secure a substantial benefit to him and that £1,000 was adequate compensation in money terms[12].

5. *Is it contrary to the public interest to impede the proposed user?*

In *Re Collins* (1974) the Tribunal said that for an application to succeed on the ground of public interest 'it must be shown that that interest is so important and immediate as to justify the serious interference with private rights and the sanctity of contract.' Applications based on this ground seem to have a high rate of failure. We will examine three of the lines of approach which have been used.

(a) Shortage of accommodation

In *Re New Ideal Homes Ltd's Application* [1978] JPL 632 a covenant linked with planning permission allowed 79 houses to be built on a plot of land. The applicants asked for the covenant to be modified only four years after they had entered into it, to permit 150 houses to be built there. They claimed that the 1973/4 property collapse has made it uneconomic to build at such a low density and that the covenant was against the public interest in preventing them from satisfying the great need for housing locally. The Tribunal held that the restriction was not against the public interest merely because there was a housing need but modified it, on payment of compensation, because it did not secure practical benefits of substantial value to the objecting local authority.

Similarly in *Re Osborn* (1979) the Tribunal held that although it was government policy to encourage high density development, that did not mean that all low density development was against the public interest and that it ought to be replaced by high density development. In *Re Beardsley* (1972) an acute shortage of building land in a given area was held not of itself to prove that a restriction was contrary to the public interest; the question was to be considered in a wider context, having regard especially to the planning considerations mentioned in section 84 (1B).

(b) Existence of planning permission

It has been argued in several cases that where the local planning authority has granted planning permission a restriction which prevents the development from proceeding must be contrary to the public interest. That argument was firmly dealt with in *Re Bass* (1973) where the Tribunal said, 'a planning permission only says, in effect, that a proposal will be allowed; it implies perhaps that such a proposal will not be a bad thing but it does not necessarily imply tht it will be positively a good thing and in the public interest, and that failure of the proposal to materialise would be positively bad. Many planning permissions have got through by the skin of their teeth'.

The Tribunal will resist attempts to turn the proceedings into a planning enquiry, by the introduction of miscellaneous documents concerning the planning of the vicinity or of wider areas. In *Re Collins* (1974) it refused to consider any documents save those which had been published, subjected to public enquiry and approved by the Minister, such as the approved town map or development plan[13].

---

[12] On the meaning of "substantial" see *Re Gaffney's Application* (1974) 35 P & CR 440.

[13] See also *Re Beecham Group Ltd's Application* (1980) 41 P & CR 369 (refusal to differ from "very carefully reasoned decision" of Secretary of State granting planning permission on appeal from inspector); *Gilbert v Spoor* [1983] Ch 27, [1982] 2 All ER 576 ("The subsection does not make planning decisions decisive", per EVELEIGH LJ at 34, at 581).

(c) Economic advantages

In *Re Bass* (1973) it was said that the company had a need to expand its trunker park because mergers and rationalisations within the company required it to reorganise its distribution system. The Tribunal said that this was not an irrelevant factor but that it must be set against other questions, such as amenity; 'the proposition that this operation is in the public interest is strange indeed unless the public interest is to be equated to the economic benefits to this particular part of the beer trade'.

A case where the public interest argument succeeded was *Re SJC Construction Co Ltd* (1975). Here £47,000 worth of building work on flats had been done with planning permission from the local authority when the same authority issued a writ to enforce restrictive covenants which would have prevented the building of the flats. Modifications of the covenant to permit them to be built was allowed because: planning permission existed, the adverse effect on the dominant land would not be serious, there was a scarcity of building land in the area, the work already done would otherwise have been wasted, the applicants had gone ahead in good faith, and substantial compensation would be paid by them.

6 and 7.   *Would money be an adequate compensation to the objector?*

It was emphasised by Lord Evershed MR in *Ghey and Galton's Application* [1957] 2 QB 650 that section 84 does not enable the court to expropriate objectors merely because an applicant may have put forward a worthy enterprise (in that case a proposal to turn a large house into a convalescent home). When modification is allowed money, in some cases coupled with a restriction on the development, must be capable of being an adequate compensation.

In *Re Carter* (1973) views of the sea from four dominant houses would have been impaired by a proposed bungalow. Sums of £200, £200 and £100 were awarded to three owners but nothing to the fourth as his loss was too small to be compensated. In addition an offer by the applicant to excavate so as to make the bungalow roof 2½ feet lower than originally intended was accepted and was made a condition of the modification order. *Re Banks Application* (1976) 33 P & CR 138 is a similar case but there compensation of £2,000 was ordered to be paid to each objector before the development was begun. In *Re Patten Ltd's Application* (1975) 31 P & CR 180 a proposed development of ten houses which would have caused overcrowding was allowed on payment of up to £750 compensation to objectors and the reduction of the number of houses to seven[14].

It might be thought that all compensation payments must in the nature of things be modest because large awards would indicate that the application should have been refused. This is not necessarily so. In *Re New Ideal Homes* (1978) an agreed sum of £51,000 was awarded, representing the reduction in purchase money which had been allowed because of the covenant when it was imposed. By section 84 (1) the Tribunal can award compensation either

---

[14] See also *Re Edwards' Application* (1983) 47 P & CR 458 (restriction modified to enable house in Mold, North Wales, to be used as a general village store, for "groceries, sweets, tobacco, cigarettes, cigars, soft drinks, ice cream, newspapers, trinkets, haberdashery, gardening utensils and supplies, tools, nuts and bolts", subject to payment of £500 as compensation to objector for loss of amenity).

(*a*) for the loss or disadvantage suffered from the discharge or modification or (*b*) for making up for any effect the restriction had when it was imposed in reducing the consideration then received for the burdened land. In the *SJC Construction* case (1975) compensation was awarded so as to share the development value of the burdened land equally between the applicant and the objector. This decision purported to follow in principle *Wrotham Park Estate Co v Parkside Homes Ltd* (1973) 27 P & CR 296 where the compensation was calculated by taking 5 per cent of the profit made by the developer who had broken a layout covenant. The basis of the award in the *SJC* case was upheld on appeal at (1975) 29 P & CR 322."[14a]

V.   Registered Land[15]

A restrictive covenant is a minor interest; and if it is to be enforceable against a purchaser of the burdened land, it needs to be protected as such[16]. Even if noted on the register, it will of course bind land only if it is of a character which would enable it to do so apart from the notice; noting does not add to its efficacy[17], but only prevents a diminution of its efficacy in relation to purchasers. The noting of the benefit of a covenant involves the further difficulty that it is often difficult to determine the extent to which the covenant runs with the land. The Registrar regards the determination of such issues as not within his task.

"A note is made in the proprietorship register of the existence of positive covenants, when they are created after the date of first registration. This procedure has been adopted, not because of any legal obligation, but because the Chief Land Registrar appreciates that when positive covenants are contained in a transfer which is filed in the registry, they tend to be overlooked, or their exact nature forgotten, so that a vendor's solicitor might omit to take an indemnity covenant from the purchaser on a transfer of the land[18]."

LAND REGISTRATION ACT 1925

40.   Creation and discharge of restrictive covenants. — (3) Entries shall be made on the register in the prescribed manner of all obligations and reservations imposed by the proprietor, of the release or waiver of any obligation or reservation, and of all obligations and reservations acquired by him for the benefit of the registered estate.

[14a] *Re the London Borough of Islington's Application* [1986] JPL 214 (covenant forbidding use of land in Islington "except for open space", purchased from Greater London Council who remitted . half of the purchase price, discharged on repayment of that half with adjustments for inflation.
[15] C & B, pp. 600–602; M & W, p. 348; MM, pp. 458–459; Barnsley, *Conveyancing Law and Practice* (2nd edn.), pp. 476–478; Farrand (2nd edn.), pp. 374–375, 427–429; Ruoff and Roper, pp. 715–720; Registered Land Practice Notes (1982–1983 edn.), pp. 32–36.
[16] See p. 135, ante. It cannot be an overriding interest: *Hodges v Jones* [1935] Ch 657 at 671, per LUXMOORE J.
[17] *Cator v Newton and Bates* [1940] 1 KB 415.
[18] Ruoff and West, *Concise Land Registration Practice* (3rd edn. 1982), p. 111.

LAND REGISTRATION RULES 1925

78. Power for Registrar to decline to enter improper forms. — If it appears to the Registrar that any instrument or entry proposed to be entered or made in the register . . ., being a condition, does not run with the land, or is not capable of being legally annexed thereto, or of affecting assigns by registration of a notice or other entry, . . . he may decline to enter the same in the register, either absolutely or subject only to such modifications therein as he shall approve . . .

LAND REGISTRATION ACT 1925

50. Notices of restrictive covenants. — (1) Any person entitled to the benefit of a restrictive covenant or agreement (not being a covenant or agreement made between a lessor and lessee)[19] with respect to the building on or other user of registered land may apply to the registrar to enter notice thereof on the register, . . .; and where any such covenant or agreement appears to exist at the time of first registration, notice thereof shall be entered on the register. In the case of registered land the notice aforesaid shall take the place of registration as a land charge[20].

(2) When such a notice is entered the proprietor of the land and the persons deriving title under him (except incumbrancers or other persons who at the time when the notice is entered may not be bound by the covenant or agreement) shall be deemed to be affected with notice of the covenant or agreement as being an incumbrance on the land[1].

LAND REGISTRATION RULES 1925

212. Entry and discharge of restrictive covenants. — Restrictive covenants created under section 40, or noted against a title under section 50 of the Act, shall be entered in the Charges Register, in the method directed by section 50, and any release, waiver, discharge, or modification shall be noted on the register in such manner as the Registrar may direct.

VI. Public Planning Control[2]

Tulk v Moxhay was decided in 1848 and the doctrine to which it gave rise was one of the bases for control of land use by private landowners during the

---

[19] *Newman v Real Estate Debenture Corpn Ltd and Flower Decorations Ltd* [1940] 1 All ER 131.
[20] But, if the restrictive covenant was protected under LCA 1972 before first registration, it will become unenforceable if no notice is entered on first registration: *Freer v Unwins Ltd* [1976] Ch 288, [1976] 1 All ER 634; (1976) 40 Conv (NS) 304 (F. R. Crane); (1977) 41 Conv (NS) 1; (1976) 35 CLJ 211 (D. Hayton); (1976) 92 LQR 338 (R. J. Smith); (1976) 126 NLJ 523 (S. M. Cretney). See (1984) 81 LSG 1723, where Chief Land Registrar states that on first registration he does not normally inquire whether a covenant has become void for non-registration under LCA 1925.
[1] *White v Bijou Mansions Ltd* [1937] Ch 610, [1937] 3 All ER 269 (lessee deemed to have notice of restrictive covenants entered on lessor's freehold registered title, even though he had no right to see it). For unregistered land, see p. 457, ante.
[2] C & B, pp. 877–918; M & W, pp. 796–797, 1058–1084; MM, pp. 553–561.

suburban expansion of the 19th century. Together with leasehold and reciprocal positive freehold covenants (and, to a lesser extent, easements), it is fundamental to all private planning. Such private control can however only have a limited effect. It can only be effective where a landowner is in control of a considerable area of undeveloped land, and has the foresight to devise a suitable system of obligations at a time when a demand for the development of that land is beginning to be felt — when that land is "ripe for development". It also requires constant vigilance and determination to enforce the covenants over an indefinite period of time at the discretion of a succession of private owners who are not in any way responsible to the public, legally or politically, for ensuring that the policy is carried out or even that the controls actually imposed are desirable. And so, in spite of the many excellent schemes of residential development carried out under freehold and leasehold covenants in the more spacious suburbs of many large and small towns, including seaside resorts, spas and "garden cities"[3], a system of public control of the use and development of land had to be introduced.

The principal planning statute, which consolidates the previous statutes from the Town and Country Planning Acts of 1947 onwards, is the Town and Country Planning Act 1971. Under it planning control is administered by a system of central and local authorities. The central authority is now the Department of the Environment. The Secretary of State for the Environment does not usually administer planning control directly; but appeals are made to him from decisions of local planning authorities and he has the power to "call in" applications from them for decision at first instance. Detailed administration is in the hands of the local planning authorities, which are county and district councils. The former are "county planning authorities", concerned chiefly with strategic matters; the latter are "district planning authorities", concerned normally with the routine business of planning control.

Private planning thus co-exists side by side with the public control of the use and development of land. A purchaser of land must not only satisfy himself about the existence of private covenants that may bind the land which he is buying, but he must also investigate its planning aspect.

In 1979 the Royal Commission on Legal Services put forward the idea that all, or nearly all, existing and future restrictive covenants should become totally unenforceable except as between the original parties. In 1984 the Law Commission rejected this view.

Law Commission Report on The Law of Positive and Restrictive Covenants 1984 (Law Com No 127, HC 201), paras. 2.5–2.7.

"2.5   Planning law may overlap to some extent with restrictive covenants, but we do not believe that it has removed the need for them. Perhaps especially in residential property developments, restrictive covenants commonly regulate many things for which planning law would not cater — and do so for the mutual benefit of the residents and with the aim of preserving the character and standard of the development as a whole. Nor does it seem to us that these things are confined, as the Royal Commission suggested they might be, to matters affecting privacy. Powerful support for this view is to be

---

[3] See Burke, *Towns in the Making* (1971).

found in this extract from the preface to the sixth edition of *Preston &
Newsom's Restrictive Covenants Affecting Freehold Land:*

'One thing that is abundantly plain is that there is no prospect whatever
that restrictive covenants will become unnecessary and that their place will
be taken by the planning laws. For planning standards are still too often
below the standards imposed by restrictive covenants. Thus in *Re Bass Ltd's
Application*[4] the Lands Tribunal held that the suggested modification would
inflict upon the persons entitled to the benefit of the restriction noise, fumes,
vibrations, dirt and the risk of accidents: these proposals had received
planning permission. Again, in the *Wrotham Park* case [1974] 1 WLR 798,
[1974] 2 All ER 321 it was the local authority itself which, having bought the
land for a very small sum, put it up for sale and received £90,000 on the basis
that it was to be built upon, thereby destroying an open space which the
owners of surrounding houses valued and which had been deliberately
created by the original covenantee.'

It is also true that certain changes of use and building operations to which
an adjoining resident might reasonably and justifiably object do not require
planning permission at all.

2.6   It might perhaps be argued that the answer lies not in preserving the
power to impose private restrictions but in extending the ambit of planning
law. We think it unrealistic, however, to expect planning authorities to
concern themselves with all the detailed matters for which restrictive
covenants now commonly make provision. Indeed a Past President of the
Royal Town Planning Institute[5] has expressed the view that: "It puts
planning authorities under unreasonable pressure if they are expected to
safeguard the interests of adjoining owners." It must also be remembered
that restrictive covenants may be used to serve purposes which are private
and individual and for which planning law would not cater however far it
were extended.

2.7   It must also be remembered that planning restrictions, even if they
are wholly adequate to the needs of adjoining owners, are enforceable only by
the planning authorities. Most owners would wish to have the power of
enforcement in their own hands."

The statutes on Town and Country Planning[6] and Compulsory Purchase
and Compensation of Land[7] and books dealing with them must be consulted

---

[4] (1973) 26 P & CR 156. There have been other cases in which the Lands Tribunal has refused to
modify covenants so as to allow development for which planning permission has already been
obtained — e.g., *Re M Howard (Mitcham) Ltd's Application* (1956) 7 P & CR 219; *Re Sloggetts
(Properties) Ltd's Application* (1952) 7 P & CR 78.

[5] Sir John Boynton, in an address in 1978 to a joint conference of The Law Society, the Bar
Council and the Royal Institution of Chartered Surveyors.

[6] Town and Country Planning Act 1971, as amended by Town and Country Planning
(Amendment) Act 1972; Town and Country Amenities Act 1974; Town and Country
Planning (Amendment) Act 1977; Local Government, Planning and Land Act 1980; Local
Government and Planning (Amendment) Act 1981; Town and Country Planning Act 1984;
Town and Country Planning (Amendment) Act 1985: *Encyclopedia of Planning Law and Practice*;
Heap, *An Outline of Planning Law* (8th edn. 1982); McAuslan, *Land, Law and Planning* (1975);
Telling, *Planning Law and Procedure* (6th edn. 1982).

[7] Compulsory Purchase Act 1965; Acquisition of Land Act 1981; Compulsory Purchase
(Vesting Declaration) Act 1980; Land Compensation Acts 1961 and 1973. Development Land
Tax Act 1976 was repealed by FA 1985, s. 93, Sch. 25, Part I, Sch 27, Part X, where a disposal
takes place on or after 19 March 1985. *Encyclopedia of Compulsory Purchase and Compensation*;
Davies, *Law of Compulsory Purchase and Compensation* (4th edn. 1984).

before a working knowledge of the law of control of land can be obtained; but lack of space forbids their treatment here[8].

VII.   Law Commission Report on Positive and Restrictive Covenants 1984 (Law Com No 127)

(1984) 270 EG, pp. 1154–1156 (H. W. Wilkinson[9]):

"The Law Commission, in a report which many knowledgeable readers will recognise as a *tour de force*, considers that the time has come for a fresh start. After a long period of thorough consideration, in which the reports of the Wilberforce Committee on Positive Covenants (1965), the Law Commission on Restrictive Covenants (1967) and its working paper on Rights Appurtenant to Land (1971) and the Benson Committee on Legal Services (1979)[10] played their part, it has reached the conclusion that there would be no value in proposing reform of the law of restrictive covenants on its own. The law of positive covenants is equally unsatisfactory.

The commission therefore suggests comprehensive reform of the law relating to covenants affecting freehold land 'according to the easement analogy'. It gives a new term, 'land obligation' to both positive and negative covenants and explains:

'The comprehensive reform which we envisage thus involves the creation of a new interest in land, whereby in appropriate circumstances obligations (whether positive or negative) may be imposed on one piece of land for the benefit of other land, and be enforceable by or on behalf of the owners for the time being of the one piece of land against the owners for the time being of the other.'

It is not proposed that the existing law relating to positive and negative covenants should be changed and a knowledge of this law will still be required for a good many years to come. But it will gradually assume only historical importance as more and more covenants, or land obligations as they must be called, are created.

The land obligation

In the draft Land Obligations Bill which is appended to the report the land obligation is defined as an interest in land which 'imposes a burden on one piece of land (in this Act referred to as "the servient land") either —

　　(a) for the benefit of another piece of land; or

---

[8] For a detailed presentation of statutes, cases and materials, see the 4th edn. of this book.

[9] See also [1984] JPL 222, 317, 401, 485 (S. B. Edell); 134 NLJ 459, 481 (H. W. Wilkinson); (1984) 47 MLR 566 (P. Polden); and the statement of the Lord Chancellor in (1984) 81 LSG 2666 that "it would not be sensible to proceed with the Law Commission's proposals without giving consideration to the work and conclusions of the Nugee Committee on the management of blocks of flats, and the recommendations of the Building Societies Association Report 'Leaseholds — Time for a Change', particularly those concerning a strata title scheme for freehold flats". In its report the Nugee Committee 'strongly supported the Law Commission's proposals which, if enacted, should provide a basis for the creation of freehold flats' (para. 7.9.11). See also [1985] Conv 305 on Condo-Conundrums, and 337 on freehold flats in French Law (J. Hill).

[10] 1965 (Cmnd 2719); 1967 Law Com No 11; 1971 Law Com Working Paper No 36; 1979 Cmnd 7648 respectively. See also Second Report of the Conveyancing Committee: Conveyancing Simplifications (1985), paras. 4.52–4.57, 7.21–7.22.

(*b*) in pursuance of a development scheme within the meaning of section 2 below.'

Here the easement model can be clearly seen. The burden of the covenant lies on the servient land and the plot which enjoys the benefit is the dominant land. In the case of a building development, many adjoining plots may be servient to one plot and many others dominant to that plot. There will thus be a complex web of mutual rights, which the proposals carefully provide for.

The land obligation is to be of two types. The first is intended for use where the obligation is imposed on one plot for the benefit of another plot. It is recommended that only the following obligations shall be capable of existing as 'neighbour obligations'. They are, in summary:

(*a*) the equivalent of the present restrictive covenant,

(*b*) the equivalent of the present positive covenant,

(*c*) an obligation requiring the provision of services for the dominant land, such as central heating or gardening,

(*d*) an obligation requiring the making of payments for expenditure incurred by a person who carries out a positive covenant, such as paying half the cost when the neighbour is under a covenant to repair the boundary fence, a 'reciprocal payment obligation'.

The second type of obligation is to be employed where an area of land is to be divided into separately owned but inter-dependent units, such as a block of flats or a housing development. The 'development obligation' so created is to be of necessarily wider scope than the neighbour obligation and it is to be capable of enforcement not only by owners of land on the development but also by a 'manager' acting on their behalf. Four of these obligations are similar to the neighbour obligations, but an additional two are:

(*a*) an obligation requiring the servient land to be used in a way which benefits the whole or part of the development, such as to provide shopping facilities there, and

(*b*) an obligation to pay or reimburse the manager for expenditure incurred in performing his functions under the management scheme.

Additional optional obligations are suggested, such as a right to inspect the servient land to check on compliance with obligations, the right of self-help to ensure compliance with duties and the establishment of a fund for payment for works to be undertaken by the manager.

Creation of land obligations

The Law Commission suggests that the land obligation should always be made in writing and that if it is intended to create a land obligation at law it must be by deed; a writing under hand only would create an equitable land obligation.

A legal land obligation must be made for a term equivalent to a fee simple absolute in possession or for a term of years absolute; one made for any other interest such as for a life interest would necessarily be equitable even if made by deed. It would in addition be necessary to label the obligation as a land obligation so as to distinguish it from an easement or similar right and the servient and dominant land should be identified. The rule against perpetuities would not apply to land obligations.

Protection of the obligation

If a person is under an obligation to repair a fence, an inspection of the land will not make this obvious to a prospective purchaser. It is therefore proposed that land obligations must in all cases be registered as a new type of Class C under the Land Charges Act 1972 or noted on the dominant and servient titles in the case of registered land; in the latter case they would not be overriding interests under section 70 of the Land Registration Act 1925. Even legal land obligations would need registration, which would introduce an unusual feature into the Land Charges Act where legal interests are not usually registrable. In the case of a development scheme it will be impossible to register the rights of each house against the owner of every other house and to register their rights in turn against him, but since it will be obvious from his title documents that he is under a scheme and there will be a copy of the scheme with those documents, there will be no danger of anyone overlooking his rights and duties.

The passing of benefit and burden

The Law Commission makes a radical proposal that the person who enters into the land obligation shall cease to be subject to it when he has disposed of the land. His liability under privity of contract to the person with whom he covenanted will end and thus there will be no value in the long chains of indemnity covenants from owner to owner which are at present utilised with more or less success. The person who owns the dominant land will sue the person who owns the servient land at the time and if that person should prove unable to satisfy an award of damages the claimant may be able to make use of one or other of the additional remedies which the commission has suggested (to be mentioned later).

The commission points out that there are some obligations which should not lie upon every person who has an interest in the burdened land. A weekly tenant, for example, cannot be expected to rebuild the boundary wall, but he can be required not to block the access to the dominant land and not to use the property in breach of covenant. Restrictive and access obligations are to rest upon everyone who is the owner of any estate or interest in the servient land but other obligations should only be on those who have a more substantial interest in it, such as freeholders, leaseholders for a term exceeding 21 years and mortgagees. The benefit of the obligation needs to be subject to no such qualification and to pass to anyone who claims under or through, or is a successor in title of, the person primarily entitled to enforce the obligation. In the case of development obligations, the obligation may be enforced by the manager of the development as well as by an owner of it.

Development schemes and managers

The proposals for development schemes will no doubt be of particular interest to estate builders, land agents and institutional lenders some of whom submitted views to the Law Commission. It is proposed that a development scheme will be set up by a deed executed by the developers and will have the effect of creating a 'local law' for the development.

The scheme may provide for there to be a manager, who could be an estate agent, a management company or a residents' association. He would be able to enforce development obligations even though he has no land which can be his dominant tenement. His management functions could include providing central heating, tending communal gardens and holding the management fund.

In a very useful late section the commission considers whether existing freehold flat schemes might be 'rescued' and brought under the control of a development scheme. There would be no difficulty if all the owners of the properties agreed to set up a development scheme, but if some did not agree they could frustrate the wishes of the majority. The suggestion is therefore made that the willing parties should be able to make a scheme and the court should order that the consent of the rest was not needed. The scheme would then be effective for all the units. The court would need to be satisfied as to several matters, two of which are that any prejudice caused to the non-joiners by a scheme does not substantially outweigh the benefits which they will derive from it and that the main object is to remove something which tends to prejudice good repair or amenities of the whole or part of the building or the disposability of at least one unit.

Remedies

Two remedies are suggested which are not now readily available. The first is a self-help remedy where there has been a failure to carry out works on the servient land, provided that a right to enter on the land has been expressly reserved. This would be useful not only for emergencies such as an overflowing gutter but also for things such as a decaying fence. The costs incurred would need to be recovered from the party at fault and if he were in a weak financial position (such as a pensioner who owns his house but has little cash) the prospect of recovery would seem slim. The second remedy might then be useful; it is a charge facility for 'essential land obligations the performance of which may be vital to the continued existence or viability of property'. It would be like a mortgage on the servient land but would of course take effect subject to prior mortgages and would only be of value if there was then sufficient equity in the property.

If the dominant and servient land comes into one set of hands the obligations will be extinguished, as they will if the dominant and servient owners agree to their extinction and release them by deed. If some plots in a development scheme come into one hand the obligations will not be extinguished, for they exist for the mutual benefit of all the plots or units.

The commission proposes that section 84 of the Law of Property Act 1925 should be enlarged so as to enable the Lands Tribunal to extinguish or modify any land obligation or development scheme on stated grounds. Some of them are: obsolescence, consent of persons of full age and capacity and the benefiting of the development as a whole by the removal of a prejudicial factor.

Other matters discussed

No recommendations were made on other matters, but there is valuable discussion of possible condominium legislation, the control of variable service charges on freehold flats, a statutory regime for development scheme managers, and the redevelopment of uninhabitable flats by compulsion.

This report, as long as a textbook, will be a mine of instruction about the present and future of covenants for many years. The Law Commission has carefully sounded the views of all those in the property field, lawyers, landowners, land developers, surveyors, government, industry, institutional lenders and reformers, and has produced something which should be a potent instrument of change."

Index

Acceleration of Future Interests, 354

Accumulations
abolition, 368–372
commercial arrangements, 365
corporation as settlor, 365
excessive, 366–367
insurance contracts, 365
land, for purchase of, 361–362
maintenance of property, 365
minorities, during, 358–364
permitted periods
Law of Property Act 1925, 358, 361–363
which applicable, 366
Perpetuities and Accumulations Act 1964, 358, 363–364
Trustee Act 1925, 363
perpetuity rule, breaching, 359
rule against, 358–368
abolition, 368–372
exceptions to, 364–365
origin of, 358
reform, 368–372
termination of, 364
trust, termination of, 364

Acknowledgment
agent, by, 185
right of action, of, 184–186

Action
ejectment, of, 376, 430–431
foreclosure, 685, 689n, 717–720
land, for recovery of, 4, 166, 173–174, 181–182, 376, 428
limitation of. *See* Limitation
real, 4, 376
specific performance, for, 80, 84–85, 326–327, 465–468, 581, 760

Actual Occupation. *See* Overriding Interest

Ad Hoc
settlement, 285–286
trust corporation, 206
trust for sale, 206

Administrator. *See* Executor, Personal Representative

Adoption
perpetuities and, 330–331

Advancement
power of, 349n.

Adverse Possession, Adverse Possessor.
See also Limitation
estate created by, 163–164

Adverse Possession, Adverse Possessor—*contd.*
licences, 165
limited owner, against, 173–174
necessity for, 162, 165–166, 177
tenant, by, 163–164
time, running of, 164
what constitutes, 166ff, 177

Advowsons, 181n.

Age
majority, of, 288n., 361n.
reduction of, for perpetuity purposes, 337–339

Agent
acknowledgment by, 185
negotiation by, 29
notice to, 45
signature of, 63, 79

Administrative Powers
trustees, 351

Agreement. *See* Contract

Agreement for Lease. *See* Contract, Lease

Agricultural Charges, 57–58

Agricultural Land
fixtures, 89, 93
statutory code, 377n.

Air
easement, 564–565

Alienation
condition against, 9–12
fee simple, 9–12
strict settlement, under, 215, 284
trust for sale, under, 214–217

Ameliorating Waste, 21–22

Andrews v Partington, **Rule in,** 339–340, 344–346

Annexation
fixtures, of, 90–92
restrictive covenant, of, 774–788, 798–799

Annuity
land charge, as, 31, 32, 33
overreaching of, 207, 284, 286
register of, 30

Appointment
power of
general, 334, 336, 347, 350